Landmark Decisions of the United States Supreme Court

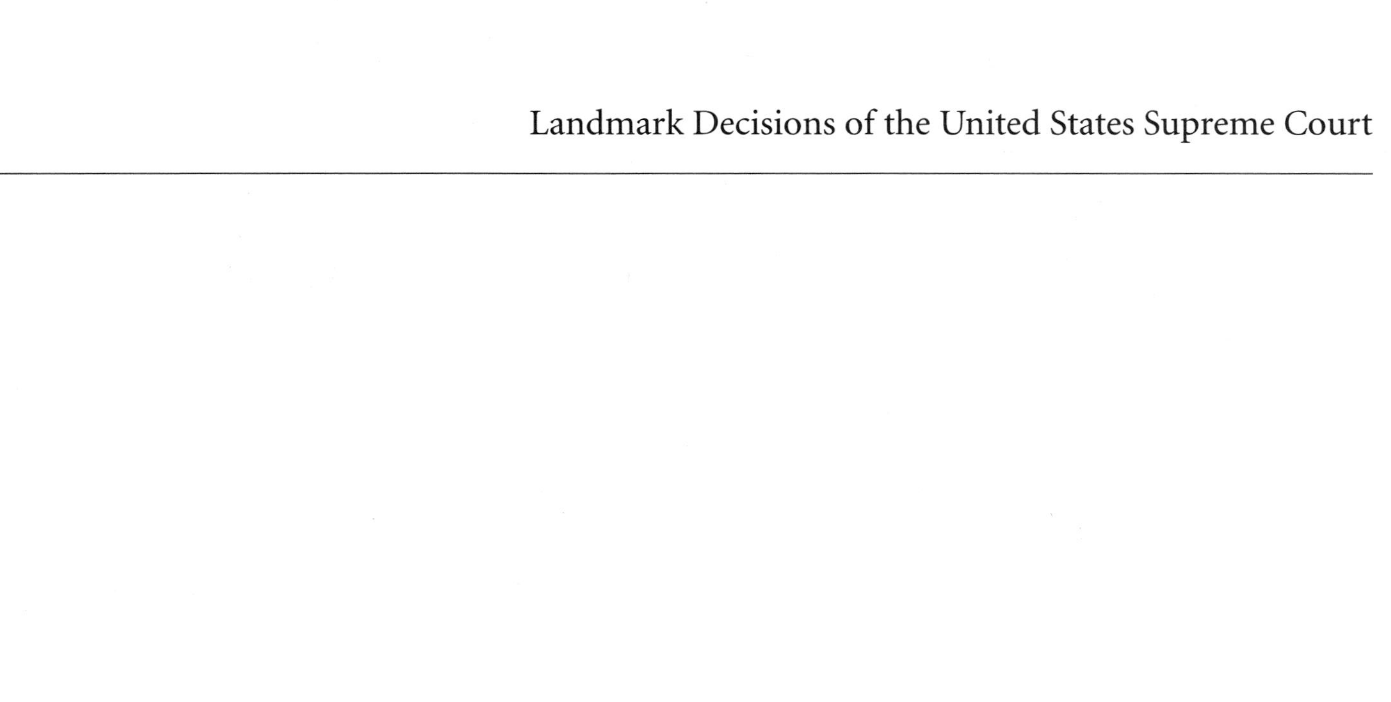

Landmark Decisions of the UNITED STATES SUPREME COURT

Paul Finkelman

University of Tulsa College of Law

Melvin I. Urofsky

Virginia Commonwealth University

A Division of Congressional Quarterly Inc.

Washington, D.C.

CQ Press
1255 22nd Street, N.W., Suite 400
Washington, D.C. 20037

202-729-1900; toll-free: 1-866-4CQ-PRESS (1-866-427-7737)

www.cqpress.com

Printed and bound in the United States of America

06 05 04 03 02 5 4 3 2 1

COVER DESIGN: *Kachergis Book Design, Pittsboro, North Carolina*

About the back cover: The descriptions of the bronze doors of the Supreme Court building are from a Web site maintained by the Office of the Curator, Supreme Court of the United States. See "The Bronze Doors," http://www.supremecourtus.gov/about/bronzedoors.pdf, accessed October 30, 2002.

♾ The paper used in this publication meets the minimum requirements of the American National Standard for Information Sciences—Permanence of Paper for Printed Library Materials, ANSI Z39.48-1992.

LIBRARY OF CONGRESS CATALOGING-IN-PUBLICATION DATA

Finkelman, Paul
Landmark decisions of the United States Supreme Court / Paul Finkelman, Melvin I. Urofsky.
p. cm.
Includes bibliographical references and index.
ISBN 1-56802-720-6 (cloth : alk. paper)
1. Constitutional law—United States—Cases. I. Urofsky, Melvin I. II. United States. Supreme Court. III. Title.
KF4549 .F56 2003
347.73'26—dc21

2002153035

We happily dedicate this book to William M. Wiecek,
a gentleman, a dear friend, and a scholar's scholar.

Contents

Preface

When the men who gathered at the Philadelphia Convention in the summer of 1787 debated the form of the new government they wanted to create, they chose to separate the powers of the sovereign into three clearly defined areas—legislative, executive, and judicial—and to entrust each of these sets of powers to a different branch of government. Although they clearly intended the powers of Congress—the legislative branch—to be broad in scope, they did not intend the executive or judicial branches to be inferior. The government of the United States would be a tripod, and, in order for it to stand, all three branches had to be powerful in their own spheres.

Those who attend to the news media at the beginning of the twenty-first century hear a great deal about what the president proposes or what Congress does, and libraries are full of books on the executive and legislative branches. The public tends to know less about the judiciary, in part because judges operate under different ground rules. Although no one would be naïve enough to argue that politics never influences judicial decisions, the Constitution, the laws passed by the legislature, and the force of prior judicial decisions all serve to constrain the leeway that judges can exercise.

Still, the judicial branch, and especially the Supreme Court of the United States, makes decisions that affect each and every one of us every day of our lives. The Supreme Court is not only the highest court in the land—the court of last resort—but also the most powerful constitutional court in the world. Few courts in any country come near to enjoying the broad range of powers granted to the Supreme Court under Article III of the Constitution.

In this book we explore how the Court influences us through its decisions. Does the government have a right to draft men into the armed forces? May one burn an American flag as a mode of political protest? May a state impose restrictions on a woman's right to have an abortion? Must the state provide a lawyer for a person accused of a crime? May individual states regulate the sale of insurance policies? Is local zoning for the purpose of conservation an infringement of property rights?

These and hundreds of other questions eventually find their way to the courts, for, as French aristocrat Alexis de Tocqueville noted nearly two centuries ago, in the United States every matter of public interest eventually becomes a judicial matter. Americans go to court to resolve their differences, and as a result we have a remarkably varied and interesting judicial history.

We have chosen for inclusion in this volume more than one thousand of what we consider the Supreme Court's most important decisions since its establishment. Some of the cases in this book will be familiar to most readers; after all, what history course in high school or college has not dealt with *Dred Scott v. Sandford* or *Brown v. Board of Education?* But this book offers many other cases the reader may not recognize, even though they have influenced our nation's constitutional and judicial history.

In assembling our list of cases we used a number of methods and criteria. Both of us have worked in this area for many years, and in the end our judgment—aided in part by a commissioned survey of constitutional scholars—determined whether a case should be included and, if so, how thoroughly it should be discussed. We also consulted other important documentary sources, such as casebooks, textbooks, and the like to see what our peers considered important. Not everyone will agree with our final list, but although some might quibble over the inclusion of one case or the exclusion of another, we feel confident that most scholars would validate our choices.

The cases are presented chronologically, and we chose this arrangement for several reasons. First, it seems most logical because it enables the reader who is looking up a particular case to see what other decisions the Court was making around the same time. Although many scholars choose to group cases by subject, the problem with that arrangement is keeping the subject clear because many cases involve more than one issue. Arrangement by subject in a reference book of this type is therefore impractical. We concluded that another approach, an alphabetical presentation by case name, deprives readers of the historical context in which these cases were decided. This reference is not just an explanation of important Supreme Court decisions, but to a very real extent it is also a political history of the United States.

An additional advantage of the chronological arrangement is that readers can get a sense of what occupied the Court's attention at a given time. In the early years, the Marshall Court dealt with how the Constitution distributed powers among the states and the federal government and how far each of these powers extended. Later on, the Taney Court had to contend with the problems of sectionalism and states' rights. After the Civil War, issues spawned by industrialization, such as property rights and freedom of contract, crowded the Court's docket. Since World War II, due process, equal rights, and federalism have been at the top of the nation's and the Court's agenda.

Once we decided on our list, we grouped cases into three broad categories. In what we might call the A list are those decisions generally recognized as the most important handed down by the Court. These include *Marbury v. Madison, McCulloch v. Maryland, Dred Scott v. Sandford, Lochner v. New York,* and so on down to the modern-era decisions that also include *New York Times v. Sullivan, Roe v. Wade,* and the desegregation cases. We have explicated these as fully as possible, given the constraints of space.

The second category, the B-list cases, is clearly significant but may not have as great an impact as the first group has. The third category contains cases that are not as weighty as the others, primarily because their influence has been limited to specific areas or because the issues they dealt with, although important in the late eighteenth or nineteenth century, may not have much effect on our times.

We wanted this book to be useful to a wide audience—high school, college, and university students, historians, political scientists, and law teachers—and so we have tried to provide information these readers need. We discuss not only the basic statutory or constitutional holding of each case but also its impact and, when appropriate, the strength of the dissenting opinion. We list how each justice voted so that political scientists and others searching for voting patterns will have that information close at hand. (CQ's Supreme Court Collection is a useful Web-based research and reference tool that provides this kind of data, along with institutional and biographical information.) And for those for whom these entries are but the first step to wider research, we suggest additional readings and provide cross-references to related cases. To underscore the historical dimension of this resource, many case summaries reference, with full citations, antecedent or subsequent cases. If these cases are included in this volume, they are presented in bold-face type the first time they appear in the case summaries. When appropriate, we call attention to the influence of particular justices in shaping the jurisprudence of certain issues.

In addition to the case and subject indexes, we have also included, in the appendixes, the Constitution of the United States, in keeping with the spirit of the words of the great chief justice John Marshall, who wrote in *McCulloch v. Maryland* (1819), "We must never forget, that it is a constitution we are expounding."

Other useful appendix materials include the table "Confirmed Supreme Court Nominations, by Nominating President," which lists the birth, appointment, confirmation, resignation, and death dates of each confirmed member of the Supreme Court. It also includes the state residence and political party affiliation of each justice. Another table, "Membership Changes in the U.S. Supreme Court, by Chief Justice," provides a precise record of membership of the Court. The "Seat Chart of the Supreme Court Justices" is a graphic representation of Court membership, a snapshot of who was serving on the Court in any given year.

A compendium of this scope could not be brought to fruition without the assistance of many people. Emily Domalski, Tyneka Duncan, and Robert W. Gillikan, students at the University of Richmond Law School, and Tracey Roesle, Christopher King, Sarah Teal, and Melanie Nelson, students at the University of Tulsa Law School, assisted in the research and drafted many of the case entries. The following librarians at the University of Tulsa Law Library were wonderfully supportive throughout this project: Kathy Kane, Carol Arnold, Melanie Nelson, Dan Bell, David Gay, Faye Hadley, and Lou Lindsey. Rita Langford at the University of Tulsa initially put together the database for this project and was invaluable throughout its progress.

Kenneth Jost, a Supreme Court reporter and staff writer for *The CQ Researcher,* stepped in to help with some of the recent cases. At CQ Press, Christopher Anzalone provided not only constant support but also a critical voice in asking questions throughout the process. He and Carolyn Goldinger, who edited the manuscript with intelligence and thoroughness, are relentless and tough editors who always make a project turn out better. We owe a great deal to Chris Karlsten, Gwenda Larsen, Ann O'Malley, Paul Pressau, and Liza Sanchez for handling the final stages of editing and production. We assume responsibility for any defects or errors that might remain.

Landmark Decisions of the United States Supreme Court

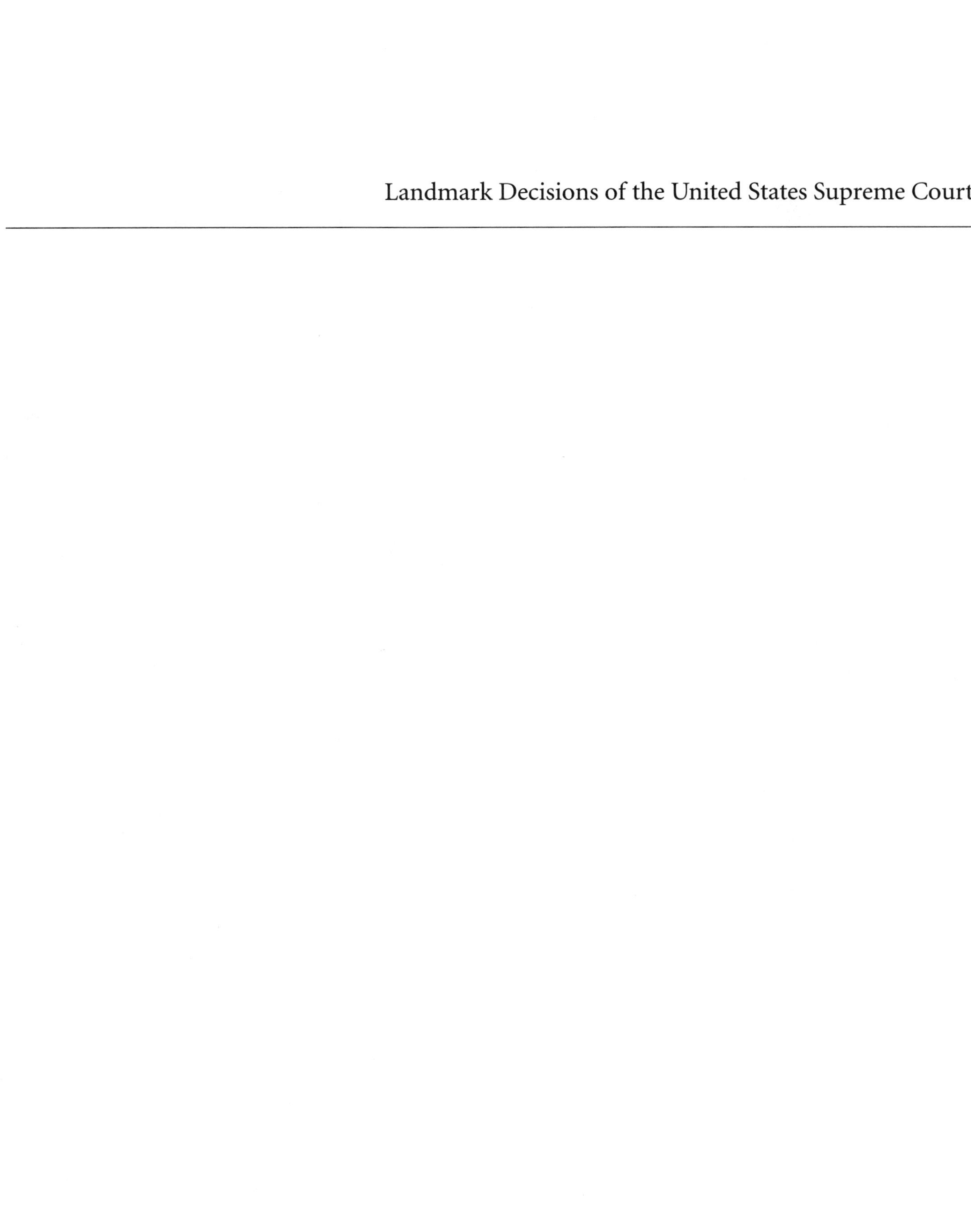

1790–1799

West v. Barnes

2 U.S. 401 (2 Dall. 401) (1791)
Decided: August 3, 1791
Vote: 5 (Jay, Cushing, Wilson, Blair, Iredell)
0
Opinion: *Per curiam*

West v. Barnes was the first case decided by the Supreme Court. David Leonard Barnes, a citizen of Massachusetts, sued to gain possession of land that William West had pledged as security in a business deal that began in 1763. West was never able to pay on his notes, and in April 1791 Barnes sued West in federal court for the land. The U.S. Circuit Court in Rhode Island, with Chief Justice Jay presiding, ruled in favor of Barnes. West secured a writ of error from the circuit court to bring the case to the Supreme Court. Barnes, who later became a federal judge, argued his own case before the Court.

The Court agreed that a writ of error had to be issued from the clerk of the Supreme Court to the lower court. This decision was based on the Court's understanding of its place in the nation's new judicial structure, as well as on its reading of the Judiciary Act of 1789. In 1792, at the prodding of some justices, Congress changed the procedure to allow circuit courts to issues writs of error.

West ultimately sold his interest in the land to his sons-in-law and used the money to pay Barnes, who also received some compensation for his court costs. Barnes became the U.S. district judge in Rhode Island, and West died in poverty.

See Maeva Marcus, ed., *The Documentary History of the Supreme Court of the United States, 1789–1800, Vol. 6: Cases: 1790–1795* (New York: Columbia University Press, 1998).

Oswald v. New York

2 U.S. 401 (2 Dall. 401) (1792)
Decided: February 1792 Term
Vote: Not known
Opinion: *Per curiam*
See page 2.

Georgia v. Brailsford

2 U.S. 402 (2 Dall. 402) (1792)
Decided: August 11, 1792
Vote: 3 (Jay, Blair, Iredell)
2 (Cushing, T. Johnson)
Seriatim opinion: Jay
Seriatim opinion: Cushing
Seriatim opinion: Blair
Seriatim opinion: T. Johnson
Seriatim opinion: Iredell
See page 3.

Hayburn's Case

2 U.S. 409 (2 Dall. 409) (1792)
Decided: August 1792 Term
Vote: Equally divided
Opinion of the Court: None

In an act of March 23, 1792, Congress required that the circuit courts of the United States hear pension claims made by disabled veterans of the Revolution and that the circuit courts should hold extra sessions to accommodate claimants. Under the statute the circuit court was to determine the nature of the veteran's wound and disability and report this information to the secretary of war. The secretary of war could then accept or reject the findings of the circuit court. At the time, the circuit courts consisted of the district judges in each state sitting with members of the U.S. Supreme Court who were assigned to the circuit. The law was passed when the Court was in recess and the justices were out on the circuits, hearing cases.

Almost immediately, the justices protested this addition to their responsibilities. Pension applications would have taken so much time that the justices could not have heard other cases. More important, by requiring the courts to act as an agent of the executive branch, the statute violated the notion of separation of powers. Chief Justice Jay and Justice Cushing, then sitting in the New York circuit, wrote to President George Washington, complaining of the new law. Similarly, Justices Wilson and Blair, sitting in Pennsylvania, and Justice Iredell, holding court in North Carolina, objected to the law.

Hayburn's Case arose when the U.S. Circuit Court in Pennsylvania refused to hear the petition for a pension by

William Hayburn. Attorney General Edmund Randolph then brought a writ of mandamus, asking the Court to order the circuit court to hear the case. Randolph acted *ex officio*, in his capacity as attorney general, and apparently not at the request of Hayburn or any other veteran.

The Court refused to hear Randolph's argument, essentially asserting that he had no standing to bring the case and that there was no "case" or "controversy" as required by Article III, Section 2, of the U.S. Constitution. Randolph then "changed the ground of his interposition," according to the official report of the case, and argued that he was before the Court "on behalf of Hayburn, a party interested." This switch created a case, but the justices declared they would "hold the motion under advisement, until the next term" of the Court. By the time of the next term of the Court, however, Congress was in the process of passing a new statute, which, as Court reporter Alexander J. Dallas noted in his account of the case, "provided, in another way, for the relief of the pensioners."

Hayburn's Case is often cited as the first example of federal judges asserting the power to overturn an act of Congress. Five of the six justices refused to serve as Congress required and declared that the Invalid Pension Act violated the separation of powers created in the Constitution by requiring the justices to perform nonjudicial acts and by allowing the secretary of war to overrule their decisions if they performed these acts. The justices did not, however, issue an official opinion declaring the act unconstitutional; rather, they wrote directly to the president. Congress responded to these arguments by adopting new legislation, the Invalid Pensions Act on February 28, 1793, which relieved the circuit courts of the duties in hearing pension claims. Under the new law, however, the Court was authorized to hear appeals in pension cases brought by the secretary of war. This provision was consistent with the justices' views on their proper constitutional role.

See Max Farrand, "The First Hayburn Case, 1792," *American Historical Review* 13 (1908): 281; Julius Goebel Jr., *History of the Supreme Court of the United States, Vol. I: Antecedents and Beginnings to 1801* (New York: Macmillan, 1971); Maeva Marcus, ed., *The Documentary History of the Supreme Court of the United States, 1789–1800, Vol. 6: Cases: 1790–1795* (New York: Columbia University Press, 1998); and Maeva Marcus and R. Tier, "Hayburn's Case," *Wisconsin Law Review* (1988): 527.

Oswald v. New York

2 U.S. 415 (2 Dall. 415) (1793)
Decided: February 1793 Term
Vote: Not known
Opinion: *Per curiam*

In 1777 John Holt signed a contract with New York State to print various statutes and public documents. He never received his salary, and after his death his wife was able to get only one year's salary from the legislature. In February 1791 the administrator of his estate, Eleazer Oswald, a resident of Pennsylvania, sued the state of New York, serving Gov. George Clinton and Attorney General Aaron Burr, as defendants. The New York leaders refused to acknowledge this process. On February 14, 1792, Oswald withdrew his suit and instituted a new one, based on diversity of citizenship between a resident of Pennsylvania and New York State. The Supreme Court then issued a second summons, returnable on August 6, 1792.

In August 1792 the U.S. marshal returned the writ, saying he had not delivered it because he had received it from the court after the August 6 due date. Jared Ingersoll, the attorney general of Pennsylvania, retained by Oswald, asked for a new summons, to be answered by February 4, 1793. The marshal delivered this summons in a timely manner and Governor Clinton sent it to the state legislature, which ignored it.

On February 20, 1793, Oswald's new attorney, John D. Coxe, persuaded the Supreme Court to grant his client a default judgment if New York did not appear at the next session of the Court. The Court issued a one sentence per curium statement, declaring, "Unless the State appears on the first day of the next Term to the above suit, or shew cause to the contrary, judgment will be entered by default against the said state." This is the whole report of the Court in this case. But, the case did not end here.

In August 1793 Ingersoll, now representing New York State, asserted that as a "free, sovereign, and independent State," New York could not be "drawn or compelled" to submit to the Court's jurisdiction. The case was then continued, until February 1795, when the matter was brought before a jury in a court presided over by four justices of the Supreme Court: Wilson, Blair, Iredell, and Paterson. The jury brought in a verdict of over $5,000 for Oswald. On April 9, 1795, the New York legislature authorized payment, and the case ended.

The case had little precedential value and would have been impossible to pursue after the adoption of the Eleventh Amendment. What the case shows is that in this period, despite strong notions of state sovereignty, New York was at least willing to accept an adverse ruling by the Court and pay a judgment.

See Maeva Marcus, ed., *The Documentary History of the Supreme Court of the United States, 1789–1800, Vol. 5: Suits Against States* (New York: Columbia University Press, 1994).

Georgia v. Brailsford

2 U.S. 415 (2 Dall. 415) (1793)
Decided: February 20, 1793
Vote: 4 (Jay, Cushing, Wilson, T. Johnson)
2 (Blair, Iredell)
Opinion: Jay for the Court
Dissenting opinion: Blair
Dissenting opinion: Iredell
See page 3.

Chisholm v. Georgia

2 U.S. 419 (2 Dall. 419) (1793)
Decided: February 18, 1793
Vote: 4 (Jay, Cushing, Wilson, Blair)
1 (Iredell)
Seriatim opinion: Jay
Seriatim opinion: Cushing
Seriatim opinion: Blair
Seriatim opinion: Wilson
Seriatim opinion: Iredell

This case led to the first great decision by the Court. It also led to the first massive rejection of a decision of the Court. Georgia politicians denounced the result, as did leaders in other states, and the nation effectively nullified *Chisholm* by ratifying the Eleventh Amendment, which prevented citizens of one state from suing another state.

During the Revolutionary War, Robert Farquhar, a citizen of South Carolina, sold clothing and other goods to the state of Georgia. In 1791 Farquhar's executor, Alexander Chisholm, also a South Carolinian, sued Georgia for the value of the goods plus interest. Georgia refused to send counsel to argue the case, but instead responded with an official protest against the Supreme Court's taking jurisdiction in the case. The Court, however, asserted its jurisdiction under Article III, Section 2, of the Constitution, which provided that "the judicial Power shall extend to all Cases . . . between a State and Citizens of another state." U.S. Attorney General Edmund Randolph, who also maintained a private law practice (something common and acceptable at the time) represented Chisholm. Randolph asked for a default judgment.

Following contemporary practice, the justices delivered their opinions seriatim, apparently without any prior conference or discussion. Justice Iredell offered a twenty-one page opinion, unusually long for this period, in which he denied the Court's jurisdiction, arguing that such jurisdiction could be accomplished only by an act of Congress. He furthermore asserted his doubts that such a law could be constitutional, because only "express words" or "an insurmountable implication" could convince him that the Constitution empowered Congress to allow for a private individual to bring "a compulsive suit against a state of the recovery of money."

All the other justices supported the jurisdiction of the Court. Chief Justice Jay and Justice Wilson did so emphatically, while rejecting Georgia's states' rights claims. Wilson noted that this was "a case of uncommon magnitude," in which a state denied the right of the Court's authority. Wilson said that in reality the case raised the question, "Do the people of the United States form a nation?" Emphatically answering in the affirmative, he asserted, "As to the purposes of the union, Georgia is not a sovereign state." Jay offered a ringing endorsement of the idea that the Constitution and the Court guaranteed substantive justice to all Americans, noting that the Constitution "recognizes and rests upon this great moral truth, that justice is the same whether due from one man to a million, or from a million to one man." The Court entered a default judgment in Chisholm's favor, but a trial on the actual damages was never held, and Chisholm did not recover damages. Gov. Edward Telfair declared Georgia would never submit to the result, and the state never did.

Within two days of the decision in *Chisholm,* the Senate received a proposed constitutional amendment to prevent individuals from suing states in federal courts. In early 1794 the House and Senate passed such an amendment, which was ratified by three-fourths of the states by February 7, 1795. The amendment did not become officially part of the Constitution until January 8, 1798, when President Adams announced its ratification in his annual message to Congress.

See Julius Goebel Jr., *History of the Supreme Court of the United States, Vol. I: Antecedents and Beginnings to 1801* (New York: Macmillan, 1971); Maeva Marcus, ed., *The Documentary History of the Supreme Court of the United States, 1789–1800, Vol. 5: Suits Against States* (New York: Columbia University Press, 1994); and John V. Orth, *The Judicial Power of the United States: The Eleventh Amendment in American History* (New York: Oxford University Press, 1987).

Georgia v. Brailsford

3 U.S. 1 (3 Dall. 1) (1794)
Decided: February 7, 1794
Vote: 6 (Jay, Cushing, Wilson, Blair, Iredell, Paterson)
0
Opinion of the Court: Jay

This case began in the U.S. Circuit Court for Georgia when Samuel Brailsford and two others sued James Spalding and his associates for debts based on a commercial transaction that predated the Revolution. Brailsford was in England when the war began and was stuck there for the duration. Although he supported the patriot cause and claimed to be an American, throughout this litigation he was treated as a British subject.

During the war Georgia enacted a law freezing all assets of British subjects and giving the state the right to recover any debts owed to British subjects. In August 1792, after Brailsford won a judgment against Spalding, the state of Georgia sought an injunction from the Supreme Court to prevent any transfer of assets to Brailsford. Justices Johnson and Cushing opposed the injunction, but Chief Justice Jay and Justices Iredell, Blair, and Wilson voted to grant it.

This 4–2 vote did not decide the case, but only allowed it to move forward. Over the objections of Iredell and Blair, Jay noted that the majority of the Court believed that "if the state of Georgia has a right to the debt, due originally from Spalding to Brailsford, it is a right to be pursued at common law." To allow that to happen, however, the Court continued the injunction "till the next term" with the admonition that "if Georgia has not instituted her action at common law, it [the injunction] will be dissolved."

In February 1793 the Court heard four days of oral arguments before deciding to continue the injunction until there could be a trial to determine whether the money should go to Brailsford or to the state of Georgia. In February 1794, with a jury present, the Court heard four days of arguments from five of the leading attorneys in Philadelphia. Alexander Dallas and Jared Ingersoll represented Georgia. Brailsford was represented by William Lewis, Edward Tilghman, and Attorney General William Bradford Jr., who, as was the custom, carried on a private practice. Jay instructed the jury that the Georgia act had not in fact confiscated the debt and the Treaty of Peace did not affect Brailsford's claim.

The jury held for Brailsford, who spent at least six years trying to recover the money. The records indicate that he was only partially successful. In 1798 he attempted to sue the state of Georgia to recover all that he was owed, but the Court vacated the suit after the ratification of the Eleventh Amendment.

See Maeva Marcus, ed., *The Documentary History of the Supreme Court of the United States, 1789–1800, Vol. 6: Cases: 1790–1795* (New York: Columbia University Press, 1998).

Glass v. The Sloop, Betsey

3 U.S. 6 (3 Dall. 6) (1794)
Decided: February 18, 1794
Vote: 6 (Jay, Cushing, Wilson, Blair, Iredell, Paterson)
0
Opinion of the Court: Jay

In June 1793, with war raging in Europe, a French privateer under the command of Capt. Pierre Arcade Johannene, seized *The Betsey* and brought her to Baltimore, where the French consul awarded her to the captain as a prize of war. At the time *The Betsey* was flying the Swedish flag, and the Swedish consul in Philadelphia immediately protested to the French minister, Edmond Charles Genêt, better known as Citizen Genêt. With no help forthcoming, the owners of the vessel, Lucas Gibbes and Alexander S. Glass, filed a libel against the ship in the U.S. District Court in Maryland. (In maritime law, the owner was obliged to sue his ship, if it was in another's custody, to regain possession.) Gibbes, who claimed to be a Swede, asserted that the ship had been illegally seized in American waters. Johannene replied that *The Betsey* was really a British ship and that his ship had seized it in international waters.

The district court refused to take jurisdiction in the case, arguing that under international law and the rules of war only a French admiralty court could determine the validity of the seizure. In reaching this conclusion, Judge William Paca refused to examine the two central claims of the libelants: that *The Betsey* was Swedish, not British, and that it had been taken in American, not international, waters. Glass then appealed to the U.S. circuit court, but in November he lost there as well. He then took the case to the U.S. Supreme Court.

The Court grappled with complex issues of international law and treaties with France. The conclusion, however, was a powerful statement of national sovereignty. Chief Justice Jay held that the district courts of the United States had full admiralty jurisdiction to examine all facts in the case, render a judgment on the ownership of the vessel, and require restitution to the owners of an illegally captured ship. The Court also declared that no foreign nation could set up an admiralty court, or "any court of judicature of any kind, within the jurisdiction of the United States." This decision was a boon to the Washington administration's attempts to avoid being dragged into the European war.

See Maeva Marcus, ed., *The Documentary History of the Supreme Court of the United States, 1789–1800, Vol. 6: Cases: 1790–1795* (New York: Columbia University Press, 1998).

United States v. Peters

3 U.S. 121 (3 Dall. 121) (1795)
Decided: August 24, 1795
Vote: Equally divided
Opinion: *Per curiam*

This case was another of the many stemming from the wars in Europe and the common practice of privateering. In 1795 a French privateer, *Le Cassius,* under the command of an American named Samuel Davis, seized *The William Lindsey,* which was in the waters near present-day Haiti and trading with the Spanish and Danish colonies in the Caribbean. In August 1795 *Le Cassius* was docked in Philadelphia, where James Yard, a merchant and the owner of *The William Lindsey,* sued out a libel against the French ship and Davis. Yard charged that Davis and *Le Cassius* had unlawfully seized *The William Lindsey* while his ship was engaged in lawful commerce, that it was illegal for the French to seize an American ship, and that Davis, an American, did not have a commission from the French to act as a privateer. Because *The William Lindsey* was not physically within the jurisdiction of the United States, Yard went after the privateer that had captured his schooner. U.S. District Court judge Richard Peters ordered Davis arrested and the ship attached.

The French government provided bail for Davis and hired attorney Peter S. Du Ponceau to represent him. In addition, the French government and the French minister, Pierre Adet, complained bitterly to Secretary of State Edmund Randolph that the seizure of the *Le Cassius* violated the Franco-American treaty of 1778. William Rawle, a U.S. district attorney, appeared in district court to argue on behalf of the national government that *Le Cassius,* as the property of the French government, was immune from such an action in U.S. courts. Randolph based this position on international law and the treaty with France.

While argument proceeded before Judge Peters, lawyers for Davis also went to the U.S. Supreme Court to seek a writ of prohibition to prevent Peters from continuing to hear the case. The arguments here were based on international law, treaties, Davis's status as an officer of the French Navy, and the rule that the status of prizes taken on the seas could be adjudicated only in the courts of the nation seizing the ship. A few days later a divided court (there is no record of how the individual justices voted) issued a writ that "prohibited" Judge Peters from taking any further action in the case and ordered that Captain Davis and *Le Cassius* be immediately released. The writ accused James Yard of "contriving and intending to disturb the peace and harmony subsisting between the United States and the French Republic." This result was consistent with international law and the treaty with France and prevented a deterioration of Franco-American relations in a time of great international tensions.

See Maeva Marcus, ed., *The Documentary History of the Supreme Court of the United States, 1789–1800, Vol. 6: Cases: 1790–1795* (New York: Columbia University Press, 1998).

Hylton v. United States

3 U.S. 171 (3 Dall. 171) (1796)
Decided: March 8, 1796
Vote: 4 (Wilson, Iredell, Paterson, S. Chase)
0
Seriatim opinion: Wilson
Seriatim opinion: Iredell
Seriatim opinion: Paterson
Seriatim opinion: S. Chase
Did not participate: Ellsworth, Cushing

This case was the first in which the Court considered the constitutionality of a federal statute. In 1794 Congress imposed a tax on all horse-drawn carriages in the United States. Congress passed this tax to raise money during the crisis with Britain, which many feared would lead to war. The tax ranged from $2 for the smallest carriages to $10 for the largest, called chariots. Southerners considered the tax unfair to them because carriages were more common in that part of the country. Daniel Hylton refused to pay the tax and, when fined, sued to recover his fine. The case seems to have been contrived, with Hylton asserting he owned "125 chariots for the conveyance of persons . . . that the chariots were for the defendant's own private use and not to let out to hire." The tax on this many chariots, combined with the fine for not paying the tax amounted to $2,000, which was the jurisdictional amount necessary to bring the case to the Supreme Court on appeal. In fact, Hylton owned one chariot-sized carriage, and the tax plus penalty amounted to a mere $16. The parties stipulated that Hylton owed $2,000, but that this could "be discharged by the payment of 16 dollars." Hylton argued that the tax was unconstitutional, because it had not been apportioned among the states based on their population, as called for in Article I, Section 2, Clause 3, of the Constitution, dealing with direct taxes. That clause states, "Representatives and direct Taxes shall be apportioned among the several States which may be included within this Union, according to their respective Numbers, which shall be determined by adding to the whole Number of free Persons, including those bound to Service for a Term of Years, and excluding Indians not taxed, three fifths of all other Persons."

The circuit court was divided on the issue, with Justice Wilson upholding the law and Judge Cyrus Griffin voting to declare the act unconstitutional. Hylton's original attorneys apparently decided to appeal the case to the Supreme Court, but the U.S. government then hired counsel for Hylton. The attorney general of the United States, Charles Lee, and former secretary of the Treasury Alexander Hamilton argued the case for the government.

The case is significant for two reasons. First, the justices acknowledged that if the tax violated the "direct taxes" provision of Article I, the law would be unconstitutional and void. Thus, seven years before ***Marbury v. Madison,*** 5 U.S. 137 (1803), the Court asserted its right to strike down acts of Congress. In this case the Court did not exercise this right because the justices believed the act to be constitutional. Second, the case seriously undermined the "direct taxes" provision of the Constitution, thereby allowing the possibility that Congress would be able to impose many taxes in the future. All four opinions concluded that the tax was an indirect tax, similar to an excise tax or an import duty. The justices also agreed it was imperative to read the Constitution in this way. As Justice Chase noted, "The great object of the constitution was, to give congress a power to lay taxes, adequate to the exigencies of government," and he read the "direct taxes" clauses as narrowly applying only to a head tax or a tax on land.

See William R. Casto, *The Supreme Court in the Early Republic: The Chief Justiceships of John Jay and Oliver Ellsworth* (Columbia: University of South Carolina Press, 1995).

Ware v. Hylton

3 U.S. 199 (3 Dall. 199) (1796)
Decided: March 7, 1796
Vote: 4 (Cushing, Wilson, Paterson, S. Chase)
0
Seriatim opinion: Cushing
Seriatim opinion: Wilson
Seriatim opinion: Paterson
Seriatim opinion: S. Chase

In 1783 the Peace of Paris, ending the Revolutionary War against Great Britain, promised that British creditors would be able to sue American debtors and that the creditors could demand payment in hard currency. During the war, however, Virginia, had confiscated debts owed to British citizens and provided the debt could be discharged by payment of the amount owed to the state treasury. The debts could be paid in Virginia currency, which was worth far less than pound sterling.

The case began in the U.S. Circuit Court for Virginia in November 1790, when William Jones, a British citizen, sued Daniel Hylton and other Virginians, to recover prewar debts totaling just under three thousand pounds sterling. The case was set for reargument in 1791, but was held over because only one of the two circuit justices was present. When Jones died, his administrator, Ware, continued the suit, as *Ware v. Hylton.* In 1793 Justice Iredell, riding circuit, upheld the Virginia law and discharged the debts. The case reached the Supreme Court in February 1796. John Marshall argued (and lost) his only case in the Supreme Court. Representing Hylton, Marshall argued that the state law took precedence over the treaty. Public interest ran high, particularly in Virginia, where the debts amounted to more than $2 million. Although Marshall later became known for his belief in a strong central government, in this case the future chief justice argued that treaty provisions did not bind state governments. He referred to his opponents as "those who wish to impair the sovereignty of Virginia." Once on the bench, he consistently opposed such notions of state sovereignty.

The Court held that treaties made by the United States took precedence over state laws. Justice Chase offered the most elaborate opinion in the case. He acknowledged the unique sovereignty of each state and the right of a state to confiscate or sequester enemy assets during wartime, but noted that the states in joining the Union had ceded some of their authority to the federal government. Article VI of the Constitution made it explicit that treaties made by the United States were the supreme law of the land, and this clause worked to "prostrate" state laws such as Virginia's. In meticulous detail, Chase demolished the argument that the states could overrule a national treaty and emphatically concluded that the British creditors had the right to recover debts and could not be barred by state laws. Iredell, who had decided the case on circuit, did not participate in the Court deliberations, but later filed an opinion arguing in favor of the Virginia law.

In addition to affirming the Supremacy Clause, this case also affirmed the power of the Court to strike down state laws that violated the Constitution. Under the Jay Treaty, ratified in 1794, the U.S. government had agreed to pay off controversial debts owed British citizens.

See David P. Currie, *The Constitution in the Supreme Court: The First Hundred Years, 1789–1888* (Chicago: University of Chicago Press, 1985).

United States v. La Vengeance

3 U.S. 297 (3 Dall. 297) (1796)
Decided: August 11, 1796
Vote: No recorded vote
Opinion of the Court: Ellsworth

In 1795 a French privateer, *La Vengeance,* captured a Spanish ship and brought it into New York Harbor. The Spanish owner sought to recover his ship on the grounds that *La Vengeance* had been illegally outfitted in the United States. The U.S. government sought the forfeiture of *La Vengeance* because it had violated the embargo act by exporting arms and munitions. The U.S. District Court in New York concluded that the French ship had not been outfitted in the United States and rejected the Spanish claims. The district court also ruled that *La Vengeance* had violated the embargo act. On appeal, Justice Chase, riding circuit, upheld the prize award to *La Vengeance,* but reversed the forfeiture of *La Vengeance* itself, holding that it had not violated the embargo act.

When the case was appealed to the Supreme Court, Attorney General Charles Lee argued that it should be returned to the district court for a jury trial, based on Section 9 of the Judiciary Act of 1789, which required a jury trial on all factual matters. Even before Lee could make these arguments, however, Chief Justice Ellsworth informed counsel that the case was properly before the Court on admiralty jurisdiction, and, as an admiralty case, no jury was necessary. After hearing Lee's arguments on the merits, Ellsworth called a halt to the proceedings, declaring that "the court did not feel any reason to change the opinion, which they had formed upon opening the case." The next day Ellsworth delivered his first opinion as chief justice. He affirmed Chase's circuit court decision and declared that the case was properly heard without a jury as an admiralty case, that the Spanish ship was properly awarded as a prize and that the French ship had not violated the embargo act.

In the circuit court, Chase apparently had not considered the jury trial issue. From contemporary evidence, it appears that Chase thought the issue should have been decided by a jury, but the official record does not indicate Chase dissenting.

See William R. Casto, *The Supreme Court in the Early Republic: The Chief Justiceships of John Jay and Oliver Ellsworth* (Columbia: University of South Carolina Press, 1995).

Hollingsworth v. Virginia

3 U.S. 378 (3 Dall. 378) (1798)
Decided: February 14, 1798
Vote: 6 (Ellsworth, Cushing, Wilson, Iredell, Paterson, S. Chase)
0
Opinion: *Per curiam*

This case began in 1792 as a suit against the state of Virginia by the Indiana Land Company for compensation for land the company claimed in what is now West Virginia. The dispute had been festering since 1765, when the land company was formed. The company owners were merchants from Pennsylvania and New Jersey who received land from Indians in the region as compensation for goods lost in Pontiac's War (1763). During the American Revolution, Virginia passed legislation that voided titles to western lands by numerous claimants, including Indiana Land Company. The company petitioned the Virginia legislature and Congress under the Articles of Confederation, but got no relief. In 1787 and 1788 some Virginia antifederalists predicted that the land company would sue Virginia in federal court if the Constitution were ratified. In 1792 the company initiated such a suit. Virginia first ignored it and then refused to make appearances before the Court, delaying the case as long as possible. The ratification of the Eleventh Amendment, which President Adams announced on January 8, 1798, ultimately justified this strategy.

The Court declined jurisdiction in the case, declaring that the Eleventh Amendment, "being constitutionally adopted, there could not be any jurisdiction, in any case, past or future, in which a state was sued by the citizens of another state, or by citizens of subjects of any foreign state." In 1803 the land company initiated a suit against the then-current holders of the lands, but this suit was ultimately dismissed.

See Maeva Marcus, ed., *The Documentary History of the Supreme Court of the United States, 1789–1800, Vol. 5: Suits Against States* (New York: Columbia University Press, 1994); and John V. Orth, *The Judicial Power of the United States: The Eleventh Amendment in American History* (New York: Oxford University Press, 1987).

Calder v. Bull

3 U.S. 386 (3 Dall. 386) (1798)
Decided: August 8, 1798
Vote: 4 (Cushing, Iredell, Paterson, S. Chase)
0
Seriatim opinion: Cushing
Seriatim opinion: Iredell
Seriatim opinion: Paterson
Seriatim opinion: S. Chase
Did not participate: Ellsworth, Wilson

The Connecticut legislature, which also served as the state's highest appellate court, set aside a probate court decision that "disapproved" of a will bequeathing property to Caleb Bull and his wife. The legislature then ordered a new trial on the matter, despite the fact that the Bulls had not appealed the probate court decision in a timely matter. The new trial upheld the will and awarded the property in question to the Bulls. The Calders, who had initially been awarded the property, challenged the action of the legislature under the U.S. Constitution's ban on *ex post facto* laws (Article I, Section 9, Clause 3).

The Court held that an *ex post facto* law could apply only to laws that retroactively criminalized previously legal behavior, not to civil matter or a case involving property. In reaching this conclusion, Justices Chase and Paterson argued that the Framers intended to use the *ex post facto* ban as it was used before the American Revolution. These opinions also created the basis for arguing that "vested rights" could exist in property matters.

Justices Chase and Iredell set out quite different views of the role of the judiciary and foreshadowed future debates on the nature of judicial review. In a long, confusing passage, Chase argued that legislative acts were limited by "the first great principles of the social compact," and that an act that violated these principles "cannot be considered a rightful exercise of legislative authority." Chase implied that courts might overturn legislative decisions that violated "the very nature of our free Republican governments." The Court, could, for example, overturn a state law "that takes property from A and gives it to B" as well *ex post facto* laws leading to prosecution for acts that were legal at the time they were committed. Having set out these examples, Chase found that this act of the state legislature did not in fact violate these principles.

Iredell, on the other hand, argued that the courts could not declare a statute "void, merely because it is . . . contrary to the principles of natural justice." Rather, he argued for a strict textual reading of the Constitution, which would not allow judges to determine, for themselves, what might constitute a denial of fundamental rights or an abridgement of natural law.

See William R. Casto, *The Supreme Court in the Early Republic: The Chief Justiceships of John Jay and Oliver Ellsworth* (Columbia: University of South Carolina Press, 1995); and William M. Wiecek, *The Sources of Antislavery Constitutionalism in America, 1760–1848* (Ithaca: Cornell University Press, 1977).

1800–1809

Talbot v. Seeman

5 U.S. 1 (1 Cr. 1) (1801)
Decided: August 11, 1801
Vote: 6 (J. Marshall, Cushing, Paterson, S. Chase, Washington, Moore)
0
Opinion of the Court: J. Marshall

This case was initially argued August 11–13, 1800, and postponed on August 18. This phase of the case was reported as *Talbot v. The Ship Amelia, Seeman,* 4 U.S. 34 (1801). It involved a famous American warship, *The Constitution* and forced the Supreme Court to resolve some of the issues surrounding the "quasi-war" with France. The first argument before the trial court also involved two important figures of the American founding, Alexander Hamilton, who initially represented Silas Talbot, and Brockholst Livingston, a future Supreme Court justice, who represented the company claiming to own *The Amelia.*

The Amelia, owned by Hans Frederic Seeman and Chapeau Rouge, was based in the German city-state of Hamburg. She was therefore a neutral vessel in the on-going war between France and England. Nevertheless, on September 6, 1799, a French naval ship seized *The Amelia* on the high seas and assigned some of its crew to sail her to St. Domingo (Haiti) as a prize of war. On September 15 *The Constitution* intercepted *The Amelia,* claiming it under American law as a lawful capture.

The claimants (Seeman and Company) argued that *The Amelia* could not legally be seized by France and that when the ship was brought to St. Domingo, international law would have required that the ship be released to its owners. Seeman therefore argued that the ship should not be sold for salvage, with half the sale price going to Talbot, the captain of *The Constitution,* and the ship's crew. Talbot argued that under a decree of January 18, 1798, France had declared it would no longer respect the rights of neutral ships.

By the time the Court heard this case, Napoleon Bonaparte had revoked the decree. Ironically, this act supported Talbot's claims, because it proved that before the revocation, *The Amelia* would probably have been awarded as a prize to the French ship. Chief Justice Marshall therefore upheld Talbot's claim, but reduced the salvage award from one-half of the value of the ship to only one-sixth. In reaching this result, Marshall in effect let the facts decide the law. When captured, *The Amelia* was manned by a French crew, was armed, and flying the French flag. Moreover, France had declared it would ignore international law with regard to neutral rights. Marshall concluded that "the recapture was lawful" and Talbot entitled to salvage rights.

See George Lee Haskins and Herbert A. Johnson, *History of the Supreme Court of the United States, Vol. II: Foundations of Power: John Marshall, 1801–1815* (New York: Macmillan, 1981).

Marbury v. Madison

5 U.S. 137 (1 Cr. 137) (1803)
Decided: February 24, 1803
Vote: 5 (J. Marshall, Paterson, S. Chase, Washington, Moore)
0
Opinion of the Court: J. Marshall
Did not participate: Cushing

This case was the first in which the Court used the power of judicial review to overturn an act of Congress. The case stemmed from the presidential election of 1800 and the change, not merely in administrations, but in political parties, that took place with inauguration of Thomas Jefferson as the third president on March 4, 1801.

In the last two weeks of John Adams's administration, and well after he had become a lame-duck president, the Federalist-dominated Congress passed the Judiciary Act of 1801 and the Organic Act for the District of Columbia, which set the stage for *Marbury.* The 1801 act created a new system of federal circuit court judges, and Adams promptly filled each new seat with members of his own party. This law also created two terms for the Supreme Court to hear cases—a June term and a December term. The Organic Act created a government for the newly established national capital, the District of Columbia, and empowered the president to appoint a number of justices of the peace for the city. Among the forty-two Adams nominated was William Marbury, a Maryland banker and longtime public servant. After the Senate confirmed his nominees, Adams signed the official commissions, and the secretary of state (who at the time was John Marshall) affixed the great seal of the United States to them. In the rush at the end of the administration, however, many of the commissions were never delivered. On March 4 Marshall left the office of secretary of state to assume his new position as chief justice, to which Adams had previously appointed him.

When he became president, Jefferson ordered that all the undelivered commissions be withheld. Ultimately, he limited the number of justices to thirty and renominated at least twelve of Adams's nominees, but Marbury was not one of them. Marbury then turned to the Supreme Court, asking the justices to issue a writ of mandamus ordering the new secretary of state, James Madison, to turn over the commission to Marbury. A writ of mandamus is an order, issued by a court, directing that a public official perform his or her public duties.

The case came before the Court in December 1801, and Marshall set it down for argument in the June 1802. In March 1802 Congress passed the Judiciary Act of 1802, which was mainly aimed at abolishing all of the new circuit courts, thereby removing the new circuit judges from their positions. Moreover, to prevent the Court from quickly hearing an appeal on the validity of this law, Congress changed the term of the Court to a single term to begin in February. Because this law was passed in March 1802, the Court did not meet at all in 1802, and Marbury's case did not reach the Court until February 1803.

Marbury's request for the writ was made under Section 13 of the Judiciary Act of 1789, which authorized the Court "to issue writs of mandamus, in cases warranted by the principles and usages of law, to any court appointed, or persons holding office, under the authority of the United States."

Marshall faced a serious political quandary. He believed that as a matter of justice and law Marbury had a right to his commission. But, if he ordered Madison to give Marbury the commission, he was certain that Jefferson would block delivery, which would embarrass the Court and undermine its power. He found a way around this dilemma by concluding that the statute under which Marbury sought the writ of mandamus was unconstitutional.

Most of Marshall's opinion castigates the Jefferson administration for not giving Marbury his commission, to which, Marshall argued, he was entitled as a matter of right and law. In the end, however, Marshall concluded that Marbury sought a remedy in the wrong court. Marshall wrote, "In the distribution of this power it is declared that 'the Supreme Court shall have original jurisdiction in all cases affecting ambassadors, other public ministers and consuls, and those in which a state shall be a party. In all other cases, the Supreme Court shall have appellate jurisdiction.' " Marshall read this clause strictly, noting that Marbury sought the mandamus under the Court's original jurisdiction, but that the Judiciary Act of 1789 could not expand that jurisdiction. Marshall concluded that "the authority, therefore, given to the supreme court" in the Act of 1789 "appears not to be warranted by the constitution."

This led Marshall to assert categorically the power of the Court to review and, if necessary, to strike down legislation passed by Congress. "It is emphatically the province of the judicial department to say what the law is," he wrote. He asserted that it was the "very essence of judicial duty" to refuse to enforce a law that was "in opposition to the constitution." He ended his opinion by noting that "in declaring what shall be the *supreme law* of the land, the *constitution* itself is first mentioned; and not the law of the United States generally, but those only which shall be made in *pursuance* of the constitution, have that rank." Section 13 had, in Marshall's mind, not been made in pursuance to the Constitution and was therefore void. The Supreme Court had no power to issue the writ, and Marbury left the court empty-handed. He would never serve as a justice of the peace.

Modern scholars point out that Marshall could have concluded the statute was constitutional, based on the phrase in Article III noting that the Supreme Court "shall have appellate Jurisdiction, both as to Law and Fact, with such Exceptions, and under such Regulations as the Congress shall make." Others argue that he could have simply told Marbury to seek the mandamus from a lower court, interpreting the statute to mean that the Court could grant a writ of mandamus on appeal. Marshall chose a route that would enhance the power of the Court, in the face of Jeffersonian opposition. Madison—and by extension Jefferson—won the case, and Marbury did not get his commission, but, in the meantime, Marshall shrewdly established that "The judicial power of the United States is extended to all cases arising under the Constitution," and that such power included the authority to strike down laws repugnant to the Constitution.

See Robert Lowry Clinton, *Marbury v. Madison and Judicial Review* (Lawrence: University Press of Kansas, 1989); David Forte, "Marbury's Travail: Federalist Politics and William Marbury's Appointment as Justice of the Peace," *Catholic University Law Review* 45 (1996): 349; Mark A. Graber and Michael Perhoc, *Marbury v. Madison: Documents and Commentary* (Washington, D.C.: CQ Press, 2002); and George L. Haskins and Herbert A. Johnson, *Oliver Wendell Holmes Devise History of the Supreme Court of the United States, Vol. 2, Foundations of Power: John Marshall, 1801–15.* (New York: Macmillan, 1981).

Stuart v. Laird

5 U.S. 299 (1 Cr. 299) (1803)
Decided: May 2, 1803
Vote: 4 (Paterson, S. Chase, Washington, Moore)
0
Opinion of the Court: Paterson
Did not participate: J. Marshall, Cushing

In the waning days of the Adams administration, Congress passed the Judiciary Act of 1801, which reorganized the federal court system and established two terms for the Supreme Court, one in December and one in June. Most important, the new law eliminated the duty of the Supreme Court justices to hear cases on circuit, creating instead sixteen new circuit courts with new judges to preside over them. President John Adams immediately appointed these new judges, whom the lame-duck Senate confirmed, shortly before Thomas Jefferson took office. To the incoming Jefferson administration, the Judiciary Act of 1801 was in part an attempt to pack the judiciary with Federalists in the wake of losing control of the presidency and Congress. In March 1802 Congress passed the Judiciary Act of 1802, which effectively repealed the 1801 act. This law abolished the new circuit courts, eliminated the sixteen new judgeships, and required that the justices resume their pre-1801 duties of riding circuit. The act also reduced the Court's term to one, which was to begin in February. Because the act was passed in March 1802, the next term for the Court would start in February 1803. This change was calculated to prevent the Court from considering the constitutionality of abolishing the judgeships until the new law had been in effect for nearly a year. Jefferson's strategy paid off; before anyone could challenge the law, the new judges had been removed from their offices. *Stuart v. Laird* brought the constitutionality of the repeal of the 1801 act before the Court.

The case was a minor civil suit of little consequence. Laird successfully sued Stuart in the circuit court established by the Judiciary Act of 1801. By the time Laird was able to have the judgment enforced, however, the circuit court had been abolished by the 1802 act, and the judgment was reaffirmed by the newly recreated circuit court, presided over by Supreme Court justices. Stuart appealed to the Supreme Court, claiming that the repeal was unconstitutional and therefore the recreated circuit courts could not enforce the judgment that Laird had obtained under the 1801 law. Stuart's lawyers further argued that the 1802 act unconstitutionally gave Supreme Court justices the power to hear cases in the circuit courts. Justice Paterson upheld the power of Congress "to establish from time to time such inferior tribunals as they may think proper." Without directly saying so, Paterson and the Court upheld the 1802 act. Chief Justice Marshall, who had heard the case while attending his circuit duties, did not participate.

This case was decided six days after the monumental decision in ***Marbury v. Madison,*** 5 U.S. 137 (1803), in which Marshall had asserted the power of the Court to strike down acts of Congress. In *Marbury* Marshall had voided an act of Congress, but did not have to directly confront the Jeffersonians. Here, Marshall privately asserted that the 1802 repeal was unconstitutional, but the Court wisely avoided a direct confrontation with Jefferson on this issue.

See George Lee Haskins and Herbert A. Johnson, *History of the Supreme Court of the United States, Vol. II: Foundations of Power: John Marshall, 1801–1815* (New York: Macmillan, 1981).

Adams v. Woods

6 U.S. 336 (2 Cr. 336) (1805)
Decided: February 18, 1805
Vote: 6 (J. Marshall, Cushing, Paterson, S. Chase, Washington, W. Johnson)
0
Opinion of the Court: J. Marshall

Adams sued to gain a statutory penalty, to be paid by Woods, for informing authorities about Woods's violation of a 1794 federal law that prohibited American ships from participating in the African slave trade. Woods defended the case on the grounds that it had not been filed within two years of the initiation of the prosecution for the illegal voyage, as required by another federal law.

U.S. Attorney General Levi Lincoln represented Adams. Lincoln appeared in his private capacity, as was common at the time, but his position suggested that the government supported Adams's claim. Lincoln argued that the statute of limitations applied only to criminal actions, while this suit was a civil action for debt. Ambiguity in the wording of the statute made such an interpretation plausible, and Lincoln's references to Blackstone, Mansfield, and other English authorities provided strong legal arguments for the distinction between "civil and criminal law" in this matter. So too did public policy because, as Lincoln noted, "No vessel engaged in the slave trade can ever be subjected to condemnation; for the voyage is always circuitous, and generally takes up more than two years to perform it."

The case was argued in February 1804, but no decision came until the following year. Then, in a short opinion, Chief Justice Marshall sided with the defendant. Significantly, Marshall completely ignored the context of the case, and in fact only mentioned the term "slave trade" when he gave the title of the statute.

This decision inhibited suppression of the illegal trade by making it far more difficult for informants to recover a penalty for taking the risk of helping the government suppress a commerce that was considered piracy.

Hepburn and Dundas v. Elizey

6 U.S. 446 (2 Cr. 446) (1804)
Decided: February 1804 Term
Vote: 5 (J. Marshall, Cushing, Paterson, S. Chase, Washington)
0
Opinion of the Court: J. Marshall

Article III, Section 2, of the U.S. Constitution provides that the federal courts have jurisdiction over controversies "between Citizens of different States." This is known as diversity jurisdiction. The Constitution also provides that Congress could create a federal district to serve as the national capital, but does not determine the status of people living in that federal district.

Hepburn and Dundas v. Elizey brought this issue to the Supreme Court just four years after the District of Columbia was established. The case involved a civil suit between residents of the District of Columbia and Virginia. Chief Justice Marshall avoided a final constitutional determination on this issue by noting that, in creating the federal courts, Congress had provided for diversity jurisdiction only for cases between citizens of different states. Marshall agreed that the District of Columbia was a distinct political entity but also noted that it was not represented in the House of Representatives or the Senate and that its residents could not vote in presidential elections. Marshall expressed the view that this problem could be dealt with by Congress, which could easily give the federal courts diversity jurisdiction in cases involving residents of the District of Columbia. Until Congress acted, however, the federal courts had no jurisdiction over such cases.

Strawbridge v. Curtiss

7 U.S. 267 (3 Cr. 267) (1806)
Decided: February 13, 1806
Vote: 6 (J. Marshall, Cushing, Paterson, S. Chase, Washington, W. Johnson)
0
Opinion of the Court: J. Marshall

In this case, the Court settled the important question of who may sue in federal court under diversity jurisdiction. The Constitution provides that federal jurisdiction extends "to controversies" and cases "between citizens of different states." Strawbridge and his co-plaintiffs were citizens of Massachusetts. They sued a group of defendants who were from Massachusetts, except for Curtiss, who was a citizen of Vermont. The U.S. Circuit Court in Massachusetts dismissed the suit on jurisdictional grounds, asserting that there was no diversity of citizenship among the parties.

Chief Justice Marshall held that where an interest was "joint," as it was in the case of the defendants here, the diversity of parties had to be complete. If one of the parties, on one side of the suit, had the same state citizenship as one of the parties on the other side, diversity did not exist. Marshall did not base this ruling on the Constitution, but rather on the language of the Judiciary Act of 1789. After quoting that act he declared: "The court understands these expressions to mean, that each distinct interest should be represented by persons, all of whom are entitled to sue, or may be sued, in the federal courts." This precedent, based on statutory interpretation, has remained in force since the case was decided in 1806, and is still known as the "Strawbridge rule."

Scott v. Negro London

7 U.S. 324 (3 Cr. 324) (1806)
Decided: February 19, 1806
Vote: 6 (J. Marshall, Cushing, Paterson, S. Chase, Washington, W. Johnson)
0
Opinion of the Court: J. Marshall

This case was one of a number involving the municipal law of slavery that reached the U.S. Supreme Court because they originated in the District of Columbia. London sued for his freedom under a Virginia act of 1792 that regulated the importation of slaves into that state. Anyone bringing a slave into Virginia was required to take an oath within sixty days of the slave's arrival, attesting that the slave imported was for personal use, not for resale, and that the owner was a bona fide migrant moving into the state. The law was applied to Alexandria County, which was originally part of the District of Columbia. Scott's father brought London into Alexandria in July 1802 and hired him out for a period of time. The senior Scott later migrated to Alexandria, but failed to take the proper oath. When Scott moved to Alexandria, he also failed to take the oath, but did so in July 1803. The district court declared London free, and Scott appealed to the Supreme Court.

Chief Justice Marshall reversed London's victory. The Virginia law was clearly designed to discourage both the importation of slaves and the casual hiring of slaves within Virginia by people from other states. Marshall might easily have stood on the side of freedom in this case, as the trial court had. Instead, he offered a strained interpretation of the Virginia law, asserting that the importation of the slave and the migration of the master had to be simultaneous. Because that had not happened, Marshall overturned the jury verdict, sending London back to slavery.

See Paul Finkelman, *An Imperfect Union: Slavery, Federalism, and Comity* (Chapel Hill: University of North Carolina Press, 1981).

Ex parte Bollman

8 U.S. 75 (4 Cr. 75) (1807)
Decided: February 21, 1807
Vote: 3 (J. Marshall, S. Chase, Washington)
1 (W. Johnson)
Opinion of the Court: J. Marshall
Dissenting opinion: W. Johnson
Did not participate: Cushing, Livingston

After leaving the vice presidency in 1805, Aaron Burr traveled west, where he apparently planned to engage in land speculation while also organizing frontiersmen and others in preparation for an invasion of Mexico in the event of a war with Spain. Jefferson, who by this time despised his former running mate, believed Burr was involved in a treasonous plot. On November 27, 1806, Jefferson issued a proclamation warning of "sundry persons" engaged in "criminal enterprises" to invade "the dominions of Spain." On January 22, 1807, Jefferson told Congress that Burr was the "prime mover" in this conspiracy and his "guilt is placed beyond question." By this time, Gen. James Wilkinson, the military commander in New Orleans (who was secretly working for Spain and conspiring to accomplish exactly what he claimed Dr. Justus Erick Bollman and Burr were planning), arrested some of Burr's associates, including Bollman and Samuel Swartwout. Wilkinson refused to respond to a writ of habeas corpus on Bollman's behalf on grounds that he was charged with treason.

Bollman and Swartwout were sent to Washington and imprisoned by the military. The U.S. attorney moved to hold them on a charge of treason, which the Circuit Court for the District of Columbia approved, 2–1, over the objections of Chief Judge Cranch. Meanwhile, Jefferson's chief spokesman in the U.S. Senate, William B. Giles, pushed through a bill to suspend the writ of habeas corpus, even though the conditions for suspension required by the Constitution—rebellion or actual invasion during wartime—did not exist. Despite its Jeffersonian majority, the House rejected this bill, 113–19.

It was under these circumstances that *Ex parte Bollman* and *Ex parte Swartwout* reached the Supreme Court. The Court issued two rulings. On February 13, 1807, Chief Justice Marshall ruled on the jurisdiction of the Court to grant a writ of habeas corpus. Marshall acknowledged that as a matter of original jurisdiction the Court could not grant the writ. Marshall, however, considered this case to be an appeal from the ruling of the circuit court ordering the prisoners' commitment, bringing the case under the Court's appellate jurisdiction. "It is the revision of a decision of an inferior court," Marshall declared. Significantly, however, Marshall indicated that the power of the Court (or any federal court) to issue a writ of habeas corpus was based on a federal statute, which Congress could repeal. This issue would arise during Reconstruction, in ***Ex parte McCardle,*** 74 U.S. 506 (1869). Justice Johnson, a recent Jefferson appointee, dissented, asserting that the Court had no jurisdiction to issue the writ. Justice Livingston, another Jefferson appointee, was ill at the time and did not formally participate in the decision, but Johnson indicated that Livingston would also have dissented.

The Court issued the writ of habeas corpus, and three days later heard arguments on whether Bollman and Swartwout were properly incarcerated. Charles Lee and Francis Scott Key, who represented the prisoners, made strong arguments that no probable cause existed for holding them. They pointed out that neither man had committed any "overt acts" against the United States, as the Constitution required for a charge of treason, and Key urged the Court to "look behind the order for commitment, and examine the ground upon which it is made." They pointed out that the arrests were based on unauthenticated affidavits signed by Wilkinson, but that even these affidavits did not prove any attack on the government or any conspiracy. The U.S. government offered a weak response.

Marshall asserted that the charge of treason required evidence that a "war" was "actually levied against the United States." To "complete the crime of levying war against the United States, there must be an actual assemblage of men for the purpose of executing a treasonable design." Marshall concluded, "There is no evidence to support a charge of treason." The two might have committed other crimes, such as conspiracy to commit treason or conspiracy to make war against Mexico, but Marshall further noted that whatever crime they had committed, "no part of this crime was committed in the District of Columbia." Therefore, the Court held unanimously that the prisoners had to be released, noting, however, that "the discharge does not acquit them" from any crimes they might have committed.

In reaching this decision Marshall defined treason narrowly, set a high standard for interpreting the Constitution's phrase "levying war," and thus prevented its misuse or abuse by willful politicians such as Jefferson in this case and in the subsequent trial of Aaron Burr.

See George Lee Haskins and Herbert A. Johnson, *History of the Supreme Court of the United States, Vol. II: Foundations of Power: John Marshall, 1801–1815* (New York: Macmillan, 1981), and Leonard W. Levy, *Jefferson and Civil Liberties: The Darker Side* (Cambridge: Harvard University Press, 1963).

McIlvaine v. Coxe's Lessee

8 U.S. 209 (4 Cr. 209) (1808)
Decided: February 23, 1808
Vote: 5 (J. Marshall, Cushing, S. Chase, Washington, Livingston)
0
Opinion of the Court: Cushing
Did not participate: W. Johnson, Todd

The Court heard full arguments in this case at its February 1804 term and reported these extensive arguments as *McIlvaine v. Coxe's Lessee,* 6 U.S. 280 (1804). The Court gave no opinion at that time but indicated that the "court would advise in the future." The case seems to have then disappeared, but it reemerged in February 1808, when the Court again heard arguments and decided the case later that month. The case was one of many that involved the status of Americans who sided with the British and the ownership of property bequeathed to them.

Rebecca Coxe died in 1802 and under New Jersey law Daniel Coxe was her heir-at-law and would inherit land worth about $5,000, if it was determined that he could legally inherit property in New Jersey. Daniel Coxe was born in New Jersey before the Revolution and served as a member of the King's Council in the New Jersey Colony. He moved to Philadelphia in 1777, when the British occupied that city, and never returned to live in New Jersey. After the war, he moved to England, where he conducted himself as British merchant and received a pension from the king. Attorneys for Coxe argued that he had become a citizen of New Jersey on July 4, 1776, and he had never renounced that citizenship. In the words of one of his lawyers, "Coxe could not, by his own act, get rid of the allegiance he owed to New Jersey." As his counsel noted, during the Revolution New Jersey had passed an attainder against him and confiscated his property for "disloyalty." This proved, his counsel argued, that he was still a citizen of the state, for otherwise he could not be considered disloyal.

Justice Cushing noted that Coxe was living in New Jersey in October 1776, when, under a state law, "he became a member of the new society, entitled to the protection of its government." In other words, because New Jersey had always considered Coxe a citizen and punished him accordingly during the Revolution, Coxe must still be a citizen, and the Court found he could inherit property in the state.

See James Kettner, *The Development of American Citizenship, 1608–1870* (Chapel Hill: University of North Carolina Press, 1978).

Dawson's Lessee v. Godfrey

8 U.S. 321 (4 Cr. 321) (1808)
Decided: March 17, 1808
Vote: 4 (S. Chase, W. Johnson, Livingston, Todd)
0
Opinion of the Court: W. Johnson
Did not participate: J. Marshall, Cushing, Washington

This case determined the inheritance rights of British subjects who had never resided in the colonies or the United States and whose claims emerged after the Revolutionary period. Maryland law prohibited aliens from inheriting property in that state, and this law also applied to that part of the District of Columbia that had once belonged to Maryland. In 1793 Russell Lee, a U.S. citizen, died without a will. Under Maryland law, his heir was a Mrs. Dawson, a British subject who had never lived in the United States or any of the prerevolutionary colonies. The lower court denied her the right to inherit, and the Supreme Court affirmed this result.

Justice Johnson concluded that the doctrine of *antenati* did not apply to American law. This meant, in effect, that British subjects born before the American Revolution could not claim any rights in the United States if they had never lived in the United States or the colonies. Under *antenati* a British subject born before 1776 could claim rights in the United States under the theory that all British subjects, as of 1776, had rights in the colonies that continued after the Revolution. Johnson rejected this concept, thus leaving the states free to prohibit aliens with no connection to the United States from inheriting property in the United States.

See George Lee Haskins and Herbert A. Johnson, *History of the Supreme Court of the United States, Vol. II: Foundations of Power: John Marshall, 1801–1815* (New York: Macmillan, 1981).

Bank of the United States v. Deveaux

9 U.S. 61 (5 Cr. 61) (1809)
Decided: March 15, 1809
Vote: 6 (J. Marshall, Cushing, S. Chase, Washington, W. Johnson, Todd)
0
Opinion of the Court: J. Marshall
Did not participate: Livingston

Like ***Strawbridge v. Curtiss,*** 7 U.S. 267 (1806), this case involved the interpretation of the "diversity" clause of the Constitution, which provides that federal jurisdiction extends "to controversies" and cases "between citizens of different states." Here, the president and directors of the First Bank of the United States, incorporated by Congress in 1791, sued two Georgia tax collectors, Peter Deveaux and Thomas Robertson, who had seized property valued at more than $4,000 after the bank refused to pay a state tax. The lower court dismissed the case for lack of jurisdiction, on the grounds that the bank was not a citizen for purposes of diversity jurisdiction.

Deveaux argued that a corporation had no standing to sue in federal court and that only the individual stockholders might sue. Because some of these stockholders were citizens of Georgia, the defendants asserted there was no diversity of citizenship. Deveaux said the case should be brought in state court, where the bank was sure to lose.

Horace Binney, representing the bank, argued that as a federally chartered corporation, it had a special right to sue in federal court and that all cases in which the bank was a party "involve questions arising under the laws of the United States" and were subject to federal jurisdiction. In addition, Binney argued that the citizenship of its stockholders disappeared into the corporate entity and, therefore, the directors and president of the bank, living in Pennsylvania, had a right to sue in federal court on behalf of the bank.

Chief Justice Marshall agreed with Deveaux. He was quite clear on this point, stating, "No right is conferred on the bank by the act of incorporation to sue in the Federal courts." He also declared that a corporation could not sue in the federal courts. He found that "the invisible, intangible, and artificial being, that mere legal entity, a corporation aggregate, is certainly not a citizen" and therefore could not be party to a diversity suit. At the same time, however, he seemed unsure of this conclusion, later noting that "corporations composed of citizens are considered by the legislature as citizens" for some purposes. Technically, this issue was not actually before the Court, because the Bank of the United States had a federal charter and could not be considered a citizen of any *state* for purposes of jurisdiction.

In the end, however, Marshall sided with the plaintiffs by holding that the bank president and directors could sue in their own names, as individuals with an interest in the corporation. He remanded the case to the lower court for a trial on the merits.

Justice Story, who was not on the Court at this time, later asserted that Marshall had "repeatedly expressed regret" over his conclusion in *Deveaux* that a corporation was not a citizen for purposes of diversity jurisdiction, but there is no independent evidence to support this conclusion. In any event, in *Louisville, Cincinnati & Charleston R. R. v. Letson,* 43 U.S. 497 (1844), the Court reversed course, holding that a corporation could sue in diversity.

See David P. Currie, *The Constitution in the Supreme Court: The First Hundred Years, 1789–1888* (Chicago: University of Chicago Press, 1987).

United States v. Peters

9 U.S. 115 (5 Cr. 115) (1809)
Decided: February 20, 1809
Vote: 7 (J. Marshall, Cushing, S. Chase, Washington, W. Johnson, Livingston, Todd)
0
Opinion of the Court: J. Marshall

In 1778 Gideon Olmstead of Connecticut was captured by the British and impressed into service against the American Revolution. Later that year, he led group of impressed American sailors who seized the British ship, *The Active,* which Olmstead then steered to the New Jersey shore. Before he reached the shore, *The Convention,* a ship owned by the Commonwealth of Pennsylvania, seized *The Active* and brought it into the port of Philadelphia, where the crew of *The Convention* claimed it as a prize of war. Olmstead also claimed the ship. A Pennsylvania court awarded Olmstead one-fourth of the value of *The Active* and the remainder to *The Convention* and another Pennsylvania ship. Olmstead appealed to the Appeals Commission of the Continental Congress, which ruled that Olmstead and his colleagues were entitled to the entire value of the ship. In 1779 the state of Pennsylvania resisted this order. In early January 1803, in *Olmstead v. The Active,* 18 F. Cas. 680 (DC Pa. 1803), federal district judge Richard Peters reaffirmed the commission's decision in favor of Olmstead and ordered Pennsylvania to pay Olmstead accordingly. As it had in 1779, Pennsylvania refused to comply with the ruling of a national authority.

The federal court declared that David Rittenhouse, who had been treasurer of Pennsylvania, was required to pay Olmstead in his personal capacity as state treasurer. This ruling avoided any Eleventh Amendment issues. As Chief Justice Marshall later noted in his opinion, after Rittenhouse's death, this debt "passed, like other property, to his representatives."

Two weeks after Peters issued his opinion, Gov. Thomas McKean of Pennsylvania, a staunch Jeffersonian, denounced Peters and the federal courts. Peters, a strong Federalist, was a target of Jefferson's attempts to purge the courts of his political opponents. Whether fearful of impeachment or hoping to avoid a conflict with the state, Peters did not attempt to enforce his decree. In April the Pennsylvania legislature reaffirmed the earlier state court ruling and declared Peters's ruling "null and void." In 1808 a petition for mandamus reached the Supreme Court to compel Peters to execute his decision. The case now raised ominous questions for federal authority. If a state could successfully refuse to implement the order of a federal court or flagrantly ignore a federal law, the New England states, which bitterly opposed the embargo on international trade, would be able to nullify national policy.

In a powerful opinion, Marshall upheld the nation's authority to enforce its laws. "If the legislatures of the several states may, at will, annul the judgments of the courts of the United States and destroy the rights acquired under those judgments, the constitution itself becomes a solemn mockery; and the nation is deprived of the means of enforcing its laws by the instrumentality of its own tribunals," he wrote. The state was not even a party to the suit, and therefore, "Pennsylvania can possess no constitutional right to resist the legal process which may be directed in this cause."

Although Pennsylvania had no constitutional right to resist, the state had already passed a statute authorizing its governor to do just that. The legislature continued to assert that the federal courts had no jurisdiction in this matter. The legislature also petitioned President James Madison for redress, and, when he refused, Gov. Simon Snyder called out the militia to prevent execution of the decree. Gen. Michael Bright arrived in Philadelphia with his troops and surrounded Peters's courthouse to block access to the federal marshals. The move lacked popular support, however, and many of the recently naturalized militiamen, appalled at bearing arms against their newly adopted country, went home. A federal grand jury indicted Bright for resisting the laws of the United States and ordered his arrest. So unpopular were the actions of the state government and General Bright that the Philadelphia *Aurora,* a strong Jeffersonian paper that had been a vociferous critic of the federal judiciary, now supported Judge Peters, warning that only an independent judiciary could ensure the survival of the Constitution. Madison firmly upheld the power of the courts, and within a few weeks the so-called Pennsylvania Rebellion collapsed.

Meanwhile, a federal marshal quietly served papers on the Rittenhouse executors, as required by the initial decision, and, after some maneuvering, the legislature appropriated money to pay Olmstead and his co-plaintiffs. A federal court convicted Bright and his officers of treason. President Madison pardoned them after they paid fines and served a short time in prison.

See Melvin I. Urofsky and Paul Finkelman, *A March of Liberty: A Constitutional History of the United States* (New York: Oxford University Press, 2002).

1810–1819

Scott v. Negro Ben

10 U.S. 1 (6 Cr. 1) (1810)
Decided: February 7, 1810
Vote: 7 (The vote is unknown.)
0
Opinion of the Court: J. Marshall

Ben, a slave in the District of Columbia, sued for freedom on the ground that he had been imported into Maryland in violation of a 1783 act "to prohibit the bringing of slaves into this state." Ben's owner had subsequently moved to Washington, D.C., where Ben sued for his freedom in the Circuit Court for the District of Columbia. Thus, what would have otherwise been a matter of state law came before the Supreme Court on appeal.

The Maryland law banned the importation into the state of any slaves, except those owned by masters who were migrating there "to reside." Migrating owners had to prove "to the satisfaction of the naval officer or collector of the tax" that any slaves brought into the state had lived in another state of the United States for at least three years.

When Sabrett Scott moved to Maryland, he never took Ben before any official to prove his status, and, on this basis, Ben sued for his freedom in the circuit court. One of his lawyers was Francis Scott Key. The court refused to allow Scott to offer evidence that Ben had lived in Virginia for three years before he was moved to Maryland. Instead, the court ruled that Scott had to prove that he provided such evidence at the time of the move. The Supreme Court rejected this interpretation of the Maryland law.

This rather mundane case illustrates the way slavery affected the early Court and reveals how the Marshall Court protected this institution. The Court might easily have concluded, as the circuit court had, that the statute should be strictly construed to favor liberty. Chief Justice Marshall admitted that "the act" was "ambiguous, and the one construction or the other may be admitted, without great violence to the words which are employed." Marshall passed on this opportunity to strike a small blow for freedom, declaring instead, "The property of the master is not lost by omitting to make the proof which was directed" by the statute "before the naval officer or collector of the tax." Marshall spoke for "a majority of the court," but there is no indication which of the justices would have interpreted the law in a way that leaned toward freedom instead of slavery.

See Paul Finkelman, ed., *Articles on American Slavery, Vol. 11, Law, the Constitution, and Slavery* (New York: Garland, 1989).

Fletcher v. Peck

10 U.S. 87 (6 Cr. 87) (1810)
Decided: March 16, 1810
Vote: 5 (J. Marshall, Washington, W. Johnson, Livingston, Todd)
0
Opinion of the Court: J. Marshall
Concurring opinion: W. Johnson
Did not participate: Cushing, S. Chase

This case grew out of the sale of about 35 million acres of land along the Yazoo River in western Georgia, Alabama, and Mississippi. In what became known as the Yazoo land fraud, in 1795 the Georgia legislature granted this land to four companies for the ridiculously low price of one and a half cents per acre. Every member of the legislature but one had taken bribes from the land speculators. Stockowners in the corrupt companies included members of the U.S. House and Senate, former state governors, and a former Supreme Court justice (Wilson). In the next election virtually all of the bribed legislators lost their seats, and in February 1796 the new legislature declared the first act "null and void" and all grants of land under the act "annulled, rendered void, and of no effect." All deeds granted under the 1795 act were then expunged from the state records, but the state did not return the half million dollar purchase price.

By this time, much of the land had changed hands. The newer purchasers—holders in due course—were now uncertain of the validity of their land titles. The parcel in this particular case, for example, had been sold twice before the state legislature rescinded the original land grant and at least twice since then. The logical course would have been for the landowners to sue the state of Georgia to secure their titles, but the recently adopted Eleventh Amendment prevented a citizen of one state from suing another state without that state's permission. To get around this, Robert Fletcher, who had purchased land from John Peck, sued Peck, claiming that because of the rescinded sale, Peck could not give him good title to his land. Fletcher bought the land from Peck in 1803, well after the Georgia legislature had rescinded the sale. Strong evidence indicates that the sale and the subsequent case were collusive, designed to test the Georgia act. Justice Johnson said as much in his concurring opinion, but the rest of the Court ignored that issue.

Chief Justice Marshall reached three conclusions. First, he held that the land sale was a contract, and, under the Contract Clause of Article X of the Constitution, Georgia could not rescind the land sale, even if the sale resulted from acts by a bribed legislature. The Court, somewhat crassly, asserted that any recourse for such political malfeasance had to come from the political process. In reaching this conclusion, Marshall ignored the fact that the recourse—rescinding the sale—*had* come from the political process, when the new (and unbribed) legislature took over. Marshall also ignored the fact that this ruling enriched those who corrupted the legislature in the first place and that, even if they were convicted of bribery, they would in effect be able to retain the fruits of their illegal action.

Marshall's second conclusion, which comported with traditional English land law, was that the "holder in due course" of land was entitled to his purchase, even if the previous owner had obtained the land under doubtful circumstances. In this case the original seller had legally acquired the land from the state of Georgia, and all subsequent purchasers were innocent of any wrongdoing. The later purchasers, which included both Peck and Fletcher, therefore could not be harmed by Georgia's subsequent decision to rescind the contract. Purchasers had acquired the land in good faith, and as the holders in due course, were entitled to clear titles.

Finally, Marshall discussed the rights of the original landowners, the Cherokee Indians. Here, Marshall developed an entirely new concept of law, which he called "Indian title." He asserted such a title should be "respected by all courts, until it be legitimately extinguished," which would occur through purchase, barter, treaty, or conquest. Marshall made clear that the Indians had no title to the land that the state needed to recognize; instead, their use of the land was "a temporary arrangement, suspending for a time, the settlement of the country."

Justice Johnson dissented from some of Marshall's reasoning, but agreed that "a state does not possess the power of revoking its own grants."

See Peter C. Magrath, *Yazoo: Law and Politics in the New Republic: The Case of Fletcher v. Peck* (Providence: Brown University Press, 1966).

United States v. Hudson and Goodwin

11 U.S. 32 (7 Cr. 32) (1812)
Decided: March 14, 1812
Vote: No recorded vote
Opinion of the Court: W. Johnson
Did not participate: Washington

In 1806 the U.S. district judge for Connecticut, the recently appointed Pierpont Edwards, working with a handpicked grand jury of staunch Jeffersonians secured indictments against Barzillai Hudson and George Goodwin for the common law seditious libel of President Jefferson. Both men had alleged, in articles in the staunchly Federalist *Connecticut Currant,* that Jefferson had conspired to secretly give Napoleon Bonaparte $2 million to secure a treaty with Spain. The same grand jury also brought indictments against Judge Tapping Reeve and three others for articles or sermons attacking Jefferson. All of the defendants were well-known Federalists. These prosecutions were ironic because Jefferson and his followers had denounced on constitutional and states' rights grounds the federal prosecutions under the Sedition Act of 1798. In addition, most Jeffersonians, including the president, had long opposed the idea that the federal government could use common law for criminal prosecutions. Jefferson claimed he knew nothing about these cases until after the indictments were announced. Although he said he opposed them, he did not use his power to have the U.S. attorney stop them.

Judge Edwards pushed for a quick trial, with a jury handpicked by the U.S. marshal, a Jefferson appointee. Edwards refused defense motions that the trials be postponed until Justice Paterson could attend as the circuit justice. Paterson, a Federalist, would have added political balance as well as learning and experience to the proceedings. Edwards also summarily rejected the claim of the defendants that the federal government was bringing a common law prosecution, but that all prosecutions in federal courts had to be under statutes.

When the first case came to trial, faults in the indictments forced a postponement until September 1807. By this time, the Jefferson administration was aware of the political danger of these trials. For example, one of the defendants, Rev. Azel Backus, had been indicted for a sermon in which he accused Jefferson of attempting to seduce Betsey Walker, the wife of his friend and neighbor, John Walker. This was in fact true, and a trial would have reopened the scandal. In part to avoid this trial, the U.S. government stopped the prosecutions of all but Hudson and Goodwin and then arranged to bring directly to the Supreme Court the central legal question in the cases: the legality of a federal common law prosecution. Judge Edwards complied and, joined by the newly appointed Justice Livingston, certified this question to the Court.

For reasons that are unclear, this case did not reach the Court until 1812. Both Attorney General William Pinkney and defense counsel, Rep. Samuel W. Dana, Federalist from Connecticut, "declined arguing the case" before the Court.

Instead, both sides simply submitted briefs. On the last day of the 1812 term, the Court held that the federal courts could not "exercise a common law jurisdiction in criminal cases." Justice Johnson asserted that this position had "been long since settled in public opinion" and that most politicians probably agreed. He also asserted that this position had the "general acquiescence of legal men," which is clearly more problematic. On this point Johnson ignored nearly a dozen lower court decisions in which members of the Supreme Court, while riding circuit, had upheld common law prosecutions. No dissents were issued, but, according to their biographers, Justices Story and Washington, and probably Chief Justice Marshall, disagreed with the decision. Ironically, the Federalists on the bench would have upheld the right of the government to prosecute their political allies in Connecticut, while the Jeffersonians, led by Johnson, opposed the prosecutions brought by one of their own. Despite Johnson's short and somewhat disingenuous opinion, the precedent has never been challenged and remains good law to this day.

See Leonard W. Levy, *Jefferson and Civil Liberties: The Darker Side* (Cambridge: Harvard University Press, 1963); and Charles Warren, *The Supreme Court in the History of the United States* (Boston: Little, Brown, 1922).

New Jersey v. Wilson

11 U.S. 164 (7 Cr. 164) (1812)
Decided: March 3, 1812
Vote: 7 (J. Marshall, Washington, W. Johnson, Livingston, Todd, Duvall, Story)
0
Opinion of the Court: J. Marshall

In 1758 the government of the New Jersey colony signed an agreement with the Delaware Indians providing them with a reservation where the land would be perpetually free of taxation. In response to an 1801 petition from the Delawares, the legislature allowed the Indians to sell the reservation. In August 1803 George Painter and others bought the land, and the New Jersey Delawares then left the state, "joining their brethren at Stockbridge, in the state of New York." At this point Wilson, the assessor of Washington County, levied a tax on the land. In September 1804 the New Jersey Supreme Court quashed the assessment, asserting that the tax exemption ran with the land, but a few months later the New Jersey legislature repealed the tax exemption, and Wilson once again levied an assessment. In 1807 the New Jersey Supreme Court upheld the repeal of the tax exemption (*The State v. Wilson, Assessor of Washington Township,* 2 N.J.L. 282 (1807)). New Jersey, acting on behalf of purchasers of the land, then appealed to the U.S. Supreme Court, arguing that the repeal violated the Contract Clause of the Constitution.

Chief Justice Marshall found that a contract existed between the colony of New Jersey and the Delaware Indians. Citing his own decision in ***Fletcher v. Peck,*** 10 U.S. 87 (1810), Marshall held that the tax exemption ran with the land, not with the Indians. Thus, when the land was sold, the tax exemption went with it. Marshall noted that the state "might have insisted on a surrender of this privilege as the sole condition on which a sale of the property should be allowed." The state had failed to include such a provision in the act allowing the Indians to sell their land, and therefore the tax exemption remained in place. Significantly, Marshall made no distinction between a grant from the New Jersey colony and one from the state of New Jersey. The state, in other words, was bound by the contracts of the colony, the Revolution notwithstanding.

Mima Queen and Child v. Hepburn

11 U.S. 290 (7 Cr. 290) (1813)
Decided: February 13, 1813
Vote: 6 (J. Marshall, Washington, W. Johnson, Livingston, Todd, Story)
1 (Duvall)
Opinion of the Court: J. Marshall
Dissenting opinion: Duvall

Mima Queen and her children were held as slaves in the District of Columbia but claimed to be free because their female ancestor, Mary, was brought to America as a free black, indentured for seven years. As a person held in slavery, Mima Queen had no written documentation of her claim. Her suit was based on hearsay evidence and common knowledge in the community. A number of people testified that they had heard from their parents or others that Mima Queen's family had been free, and therefore she was illegally enslaved. She was represented by Francis Scott Key, author of the national anthem, who later became the district attorney in Washington, D.C.

The trial court rejected Mima Queen's use of hearsay evidence, and she appealed to the Supreme Court. Chief Justice Marshall applied a rigid, narrow analysis of hearsay rules to reject Mima Queen's evidence, which meant that Mima Queen and her children remained slaves.

Justice Duvall, in dissent, argued that Maryland had long allowed the use of hearsay evidence in freedom suits, especially those that turned on remote ancestry. He noted that hearsay is allowed "to prove a custom, pedigree, and the boundaries of law; because from the antiquity of the transactions to which these subjects may have reference, it is impossible to produce living testimony." Duvall argued that "the reason for admitting hearsay evidence upon a question of freedom is much stronger than in cases of pedigree or in controversies relative to the boundaries of land." Displaying a sense of racial justice that few others on the Court had in that period, Duvall noted that "people of color from their helpless condition are under the uncontrolled authority of a master" and were thus "entitled to all reasonable protection." He argued that Marshall's decision against allowing hearsay in freedom suits "cuts up by the root all claims of the kind, and puts a final end to them." Had the hearsay been allowed, the case still would have had to go to a jury, which would have weighed the evidence, thus giving Mima Queen a chance to gain her freedom, but not guaranteeing it.

Brig Caroline v. United States

11 U.S. 496 (7 Cr. 496) (1813)
Decided: February 1813 Term
Vote: 7 (J. Marshall, Washington, W. Johnson, Livingston, Todd, Duvall, Story)
0
Opinion: *Per curiam*

The federal prosecutor in Charleston, South Carolina, brought a libel, a suit to recover the value of a ship or to physically take possession of a ship, against *The Caroline* for violating a 1794 federal act prohibiting American ships from participating in the African slave trade and an 1807 act banning the importation of slaves to the United States. After entering the port of Charleston, *The Caroline* received "fitments" and took on "articles calculated for the slave trade only." Before this slave-trading equipment could be fully attached to the ship, her owners were discovered. They removed the slave-trade fitments, sailed the ship to Havana, and sold it to Spanish subjects "who fitted her out for the African slave trade." The defense argued that the ship had not violated the law because it was in the process of being fitted for the African trade and never actually was fitted for the trade in the United States. The prosecution argued that it was "not necessary that everything necessary to the voyage should be on board before the forfeiture accrues."

The Court declared that the libel was "too imperfectly drawn" to uphold a condemnation of the ship. This decision undermined the ability of the U.S government to suppress the African trade, which was carried out in secret. No one on the Court in 1813 favored the slave trade, but neither did the justices seem to be interested in supporting efforts to suppress it.

Fairfax's Devisee v. Hunter's Lessee

11 U.S. 603 (7 Cr. 603) (1813)
Decided: March 15, 1813
Vote: 3 (Livingston, Duvall, Story)
1 (W. Johnson)
Opinion of the Court: Story
Dissenting opinion: W. Johnson
Did not participate: J. Marshall, Washington, Todd

This case grew out of litigation surrounding the vast estates—approximately 300,000 acres of land—granted to Thomas, Lord Fairfax, a Virginia loyalist, who fled to England during the Revolution. Fairfax died in 1781, bequeathing the property to his nephew, Denny Martin, a British subject who had never lived in Virginia. To fulfill a condition of the will, Martin changed his name to Fairfax. In 1782 a Virginia act voided the original land grant to Lord Fairfax, and thus the transfer of the property to Denny Fairfax, contending that aliens could not inherit real property in the state. Virginia also passed, but never implemented, various other confiscation measures that purported to transfer the property from Lord Fairfax to the state. By the time this case reached the Supreme Court, Denny Fairfax was also dead, and the land was claimed by his brother, General Philip Martin. The main issue for the Court was whether the Treaty of Paris, ending the Revolution, and Jay's Treaty of 1794 overrode the Virginia laws and confirmed title in the lands to Denny Fairfax.

Meanwhile, in 1789 Virginia had confiscated some of the Fairfax lands and sold them to among others, David Hunter, who then brought an ejectment, a common law action to force a tenant to leave land he occupies, against Denny Fairfax, to gain full possession of the land. The district court in Virginia found for Fairfax. Litigation ceased after 1796, when the Virginia legislature passed an act to settle the matter. This compromise, worked out mostly by John Marshall, did not apparently satisfy all claimants. In 1810 Virginia's highest court reversed the decision in a complicated pair of opinions. Judge Spencer Roane ruled that the Fairfax land had been properly confiscated by Virginia during the war and that the Treaties of 1783 and 1794 could not overrule Virginia law. This ruling was a direct confrontation with the Supremacy Clause of the Constitution (Article VI). Roane also wrote that under the compromise legislation of 1796, Denny Fairfax had lost any interest in the lands now claimed by David Hunter. Judge William Fleming categorically rejected Roane's position on the treaties. However, he agreed that under the 1796 law the Fairfax-Martin interest had agreed to give up any rights they might have had to the land claimed by Hunter. Philip Martin appealed to the Supreme Court under Section 25 of the Judiciary Act of 1789, claiming that the Virginia court had misinterpreted the two treaties with England.

The Court heard arguments in February 1812 but held over the decision more than a year. In March 1813 Justice Story, acting under Section 25, reversed this decision and remanded the case to the Virginia courts to settle the matter in accordance with his ruling. Story based his decision entirely on the Supremacy Clause, which obligated the states to respect federal treaties. In retrospect, it is not clear this issue was even before the Supreme Court, because the Virginia court had been divided on the treaty issue. It might be reasonable to argue, however, that Denny Fairfax had been forced to agree to the Compromise of 1796 because Virginia had refused to honor the two treaties and thus the issue of federal supremacy should still be on the table.

In 1815 Virginia's highest court, through Judge Roane, denied the authority of the Supreme Court to review state cases and in effect declared Section 25 of the Judiciary Act to be unconstitutional. This issue would return to the Court as ***Martin v. Hunter's Lessee,*** 14 U.S. 304 (1816).

Chief Justice Marshall had helped defend the Fairfax claims in the earliest litigation over this land and, along with his brother and some other investors, had purchased about 160,000 acres of Fairfax lands. He therefore recused himself from the case.

See George Lee Haskins and Herbert A. Johnson, *History of the Supreme Court of the United States, Vol. II: Foundations of Power: John Marshall, 1801–1815* (New York: Macmillan, 1981).

Terrett v. Taylor

13 U.S. 43 (9 Cr. 43) (1815)
Decided: February 17, 1815
Vote: 5 (Marshall, Washington, Livingston, Duvall, Story)
0
Opinion of the Court: Story
Did not participate: W. Johnson, Todd

Forging new ground in the area of church and state, Justice Story determined that the state of Virginia had no authority to seize lands belonging to the Protestant Episcopal Church for itself and to determine the use of those lands. This early decision helped develop the law of church and state in the United States.

The Anglican Church, or Church of England, was the official, established church in Virginia before the American Revolution. When the Revolution began the church changed its name to the Protestant Episcopal Church. In 1776 the Virginia legislature passed an act confirming the church's title to its property. An act of 1784 incorporated the church with its new name, explicitly stated that the church's property still belonged to it, and authorized the parish to appoint trustees to manage the lands. Two years later the state passed a new law that disestablished the Episcopal Church, revoked its incorporation, and gave the vestrymen of each church the power to control church lands and property, although final disestablishment of the church did not come until 1798, when the state repealed all these laws as "inconsistent with the principles of the constitution and of religious freedom." In 1801 the Virginia legislature claimed title to all the church property, except what was actually used for religious purposes, and proposed selling the land and using the proceeds to aid the parish poor. Shortly after this law was passed, Virginia ceded Alexandria to the national government as part of the District of Columbia. The question remained what would happen to the property of the Protestant Episcopal Church of Alexandria.

As warden of the church and a trustee of the disputed property, Taylor brought an action against Terrett, the overseer of the poor, who also claimed title to it. Story held that the land belonged to the church. He reasoned that the 1801 act bore no authority on the church because Alexandria was part of the District of Columbia and under the authority of Congress before the Virginia legislature passed the act. Prior to the 1801 act, none of the legislation affected the church's title to the disputed property.

The decision is an example of restraint of legislative authority. Story believed that the Constitution would prohibit the state taking of church land. He held that the church was a private corporation and as such had special treatment. This decision anticipated his concurring opinion in ***Dartmouth College v. Woodward,*** 17 U.S. 518 (1819).

See Thomas E. Buckley, S.J., "Evangelicals Triumphant: The Baptists' Assault on the Virginia Glebes, 1786–1801" *William and Mary Quarterly,* 3d Series 45 (1988): 33–69.

Martin v. Hunter's Lessee

14 U.S. 304 (1 Wheat. 304) (1816)
Decided: March 20, 1816
Vote: 6 (Washington, W. Johnson, Livingston, Todd, Duvall, Story)
0
Opinion of the Court: Story
Concurring opinion: W. Johnson
Did not participate: J. Marshall

This case was the culmination of more than twenty years of litigation involving the status of vast lands in Virginia owned by Thomas, Lord Fairfax, who fled to England during the Revolution. Fairfax died in 1781, bequeathing the property to his nephew, Denny Martin, a British subject, on condition that Martin change his name to Fairfax. In 1782, however, Virginia passed an act voiding the original grant, contending that aliens could not inherit real property in the state. Virginia also passed, but never implemented, various other confiscation measures that purported to transfer the property from Lord Fairfax to the state. David Hunter later obtained nearly eight hundred acres of the Fairfax land, and brought an action of ejectment against the Fairfax interests. Virginia's highest court decided for Hunter, but by then Jay's Treaty had reaffirmed title to the original holders of land confiscated by the states during the Revolution. The case dragged on in various Virginia courts and in 1813 reached the Supreme Court on a writ of error, under the title of ***Fairfax's Devisee v. Hunter's Lessee,*** 11 U.S. 603.

In that case Justice Story, acting under Section 25 of the Judiciary Act of 1789, reversed an earlier Virginia decision in favor of Hunter and remanded the case to the Virginia courts to settle the matter. Instead, Virginia's highest court, through Judge Spencer Roane, denied the authority of the Supreme Court to review state cases and in effect declared part of the Judiciary Act unconstitutional. By this time Denny Fairfax was long dead, and his brother and heir, General Philip Martin, now began a new lawsuit which reached the Court in 1816 as *Martin v. Hunter's Lessee.*

Chief Justice Marshall recused himself throughout this litigation because he had invested heavily in the Fairfax lands, which Hunter claimed. Story once again reversed the Virginia court, this time on the issue of judicial review.

Story castigated Virginia for pursuing the states' rights doctrines that resembled those the New England Federalists had invoked to oppose the embargo that President Jefferson and Congress had imposed in the years before the War of 1812, as well as the arguments that these Federalists used to oppose the war itself. He categorically rejected the idea of equal sovereignty between the states and the federal government. The Constitution, he reminded Virginia, had not been formed by the states, but by "the people of the United States." As such, the people had the right and the power to cede to the national government "all the powers which they might deem proper and necessary." Story asserted that the people had lodged the judicial power of the nation in the federal courts, especially the Supreme Court. Conceding that the Constitution did not explicitly grant appellate jurisdiction over state courts, Story argued "this instrument, like every other grant, is to have a reasonable construction, according to the import of its terms; and where a power is expressly given in general terms, it is not to be restrained to particular cases, unless that construction grows out of the context expressly, or by necessary implication."

Citing *Federalist* No. 18, Story asserted that the national judicial power had to be coextensive with the legislative, so that it could decide every question that grew out of the Constitution and laws. Story also found such authority in Article III of the Constitution, which declares that the "judicial Power shall extend to all Cases" arising under the "Constitution, the Laws of the United States, and Treaties." Furthermore, the Constitution granted the Supreme Court original jurisdiction in a handful of circumstances, and that "in all other Cases" the Court "shall have appellate Jurisdiction, both as to Law and Fact." The *case,* Story concluded, not the *court,* determines jurisdiction, and, if a proper case originating in a state court involves the Constitution, laws, or treaties of the federal government, then the Supreme Court had the necessary jurisdiction. Story noted that judges in different states might interpret federal law or the Constitution in a different way:

> If there were no revising authority to control these jarring and discordant judgments, and harmonize them into uniformity, the laws, the treaties, and the constitution of the United States would be different in different states, and might, perhaps, never have precisely the same construction, obligation, or efficacy, in any two states. The public mischiefs that would attend such a state of things would be truly deplorable.

Thus, the very nature of the American system required that "the absolute right of decision, in the last resort, must rest somewhere," and following Marshall's reasoning in ***Marbury v. Madison,*** 5 U.S. 137 (1803), Story found that "somewhere" could only be the Supreme Court.

Martin was among Story's most important opinions in his thirty-four years on the bench. It affirmed, in unusually powerful and sweeping language, the Court's power to override state courts. Story's was also the first Court opinion to deal with implied powers. Chief Justice Marshall perfected this concept a few years later in ***McCulloch v. Maryland,*** 17 U.S. 316 (1819). Of equal importance was the denial of the compact theory of government and the espousal of the doctrine that the Union derived its authority directly from the people. The compact theory did not die easily; in fact, it took a civil war to confirm Story's view. Finally, Story, although a Jeffersonian member of Congress and a Madison appointee, departed radically from the Jeffersonian view that the national government was one of limited powers. But Marshall never went as far as Story in asserting almost unlimited power for the national government and vast power for the Court.

See R. Kent Newmyer, *Supreme Court Justice Joseph Story: Statesman of the Old Republic* (Chapel Hill: University of North Carolina Press, 1985); G. Edward White, *History of the Supreme Court of the United States: The Marshall Court and Cultural Change, 1815–1835* (New York: Macmillan, 1988).

Laidlaw v. Organ

15 U.S. 178 (2 Wheat. 178) (1817)
Decided: March 15, 1817
Vote: 7 (Marshall, Washington, W. Johnson, Livingston, Todd, Duvall, Story)
0
Opinion of the Court: Marshall

Laidlaw grew out of the disruption in commerce during the War of 1812. British naval blockades of U.S. ports led to a decline in market prices across the southern United States, especially for tobacco. Plaintiff in the original suit, Organ, sought to purchase tobacco from an agent of the defendant, Laidlaw. Laidlaw and Company, a tobacco broker in New Orleans, was to furnish 111 hogsheads of tobacco to the plaintiff at a reduced rate because of the war and the blockades. Prior to their negotiation, Organ heard that the Treaty of Ghent had been signed. Peace would end the blockades, and Organ correctly assumed that the market price of tobacco would soar. Organ met with Laidlaw's agent several hours after the first negotiation and signed the contract for the earlier agreed-to price. Later, after hearing the news, Laidlaw refused delivery of the tobacco as stipulated under the contract.

Organ sought to enforce his contract with Laidlaw. The district court of Louisiana held that Organ was entitled to the tobacco and instructed the jury to find for him. On appeal, Chief Justice Marshall found that there was no duty to disclose "intelligence of extrinsic circumstances, which might influence the price of the commodity." But, he rather cryptically declared that "each party must take care not to say or do anything tending to impose upon the other."

Citing no precedent in his one-paragraph opinion, Marshall reversed the trial court's decision. He determined the trial court's "absolute instruction" to the jury to find for the plaintiff was erroneous. He then ordered a new trial.

See Christopher T. Wonnell, "The Structure of a General Theory of Nondisclosure," *Case Western University Law Review* 41 (1991): 351–353.

United States v. Bevans

16 U.S. 336 (3 Wheat. 336) (1818)
Decided: February 21, 1818
Vote: 7 (J. Marshall, Washington, W. Johnson, Livingston, Todd, Duvall, Story)
0
Opinion of the Court: J. Marshall

In the nineteenth century the Supreme Court rarely heard cases involving murder or the death penalty because the federal courts had limited jurisdiction over such matters. *Bevans* was one of these rare cases. William Bevans, a U.S. Marine serving as a sentry aboard *U.S.S. Independence*, killed a sailor on the ship. At the time *Independence* was anchored in a channel leading to Boston Harbor and was no more than a half mile from land. The United States claimed jurisdiction over Bevans, and he was convicted in the circuit court, with Justice Story presiding. Daniel Webster represented Bevans on appeal, arguing that the United States had no jurisdiction over the case, because the ship was neither on the high seas nor outside the jurisdiction of any state. Furthermore, Webster noted that Massachusetts had always asserted jurisdiction over events on this body of water. Henry Wheaton, the official reporter for the Supreme Court and an expert in admiralty law, argued the case for the United States. He claimed that the matter was clearly within the admiralty jurisdiction of the national government.

In overturning the conviction, Chief Justice Marshall noted that no statute governed this crime. He acknowledged that Congress clearly had the power to punish crimes committed on naval vessels, but, in fact, no such law had been passed, which meant that the prosecution was in effect a common law prosecution. But under ***United States v. Hudson and Goodwin,*** 11 U.S. 32 (1812), the Marshall Court had made clear that there could be no federal common law of crimes. Marshall noted that a federal law gave federal courts jurisdiction over crimes committed "in any other place or district of [the] country under the sole and exclusive jurisdiction of the United States." But, following Webster's arguments, Marshall concluded that this language could not refer to a ship in a harbor. Rather, it must refer to physical places, such as military forts or the District of Columbia. Marshall concluded that the crime was within the jurisdiction of Massachusetts and overturned Bevans's conviction.

Sturges v. Crowninshield

17 U.S. 122 (4 Wheat. 122) (1819)
Decided: February 17, 1819
Vote: 6 (J. Marshall, Washington, W. Johnson, Livingston, Duvall, Story)
0
Opinion of the Court: J. Marshall
Did not participate: Todd

Richard Crowninshield, a boyhood friend of Justice Story, was a flamboyant entrepreneur who moved to New York and in 1811 declared bankruptcy under a state law of April 3 of that year. Over the protests of Josiah Sturges, the law discharged Crowninshield of his debts and allocated his assets to his creditors. Crowninshield returned his native Salem, Massachusetts, where he amassed another fortune in the emerging textile industry. In 1816 Sturges, who had lent Crowninshield more than $1,400 on March 22, 1811, challenged the original bankruptcy decree.

Sturges made two points. First, he said the New York law was unconstitutional because the Constitution gave Congress the power "to establish . . . uniform Laws on the subject of Bankruptcies." Chief Justice Marshall concluded that the bankruptcy power was concurrent with the states, unless and until Congress passed a law that provided for bankruptcy, at which time the concurrent power of the states would be suspended. Probably a majority of the Court, including Marshall, wanted to strike down all state bankruptcy laws, but to do so would have been politically imprudent and created chaos in the business community, especially until Congress responded with a national bankruptcy law.

Sturges also argued that the bankruptcy law, when applied to debts made prior to its passage, unconstitutionally impaired the obligation of contracts, which Article I, Section 10, of the Constitution prohibited. Marshall clearly found that this part of the law violated the Contract Clause, and therefore Crowninshield would have to repay his debt to Sturges. Marshall explicitly noted that state laws could not affect "contracts already in existence" at the time the statutes were passed. He also implied that a bankruptcy law could not alter the terms of any contract, even those signed after the bankruptcy law was passed, but this issue was not directly before the Court, and Marshall's dicta (statements in the opinion that are not necessary to the holding) on this is confusing and somewhat contradictory. At the end of his opinion, Marshall emphatically asserted that the opinion applied only to the case at hand—where the contract preceded the bankruptcy law, and that in such cases the New York law was unconstitutional.

Marshall's opinion led many observers to believe that he had made bankruptcy laws impractical by preventing them from discharging debts. Justice Story hoped the ambiguity would speed passage of a federal statute then being debated in Congress, and he lobbied legislators to pass it, but to no effect. Others interpreted the chief justice's opinion to mean that state laws remained valid until or if Congress acted, which seems to be what he intended. As Marshall noted in his opinion, "much inconvenience" results from prohibiting the states to pass bankruptcy laws in the absence of a federal statute. The Court resolved all of these doubts a few years later, in ***Ogden v. Saunders,*** 25 U.S. 213 (1827).

See Edward Balleisen, *Navigating Failure: Bankruptcy and Commercial Society in Antebellum America* (Chapel Hill: University of North Carolina Press, 2001); David Skeel, *Debt's Dominion: A History of Bankruptcy Law in America* (Princeton: Princeton University Press, 2001); and G. Edward White, *History of the Supreme Court of the United States, Vols. III-IV: The Marshall Court and Cultural Change, 1815–1835* (New York: Macmillan, 1988).

McCulloch v. Maryland

17 U.S. 316 (4 Wheat. 316) (1819)
Decided: March 6, 1819
Vote: 6 (J. Marshall, Washington, W. Johnson, Livingston, Duvall, Story)
0
Opinion of the Court: J. Marshall
Did not participate: Todd

In perhaps his greatest opinion and one of the most important "state papers" of American constitutional law, Chief Justice Marshall upheld the constitutionality of the Second Bank of the United States. In upholding the power of Congress to charter the bank, Marshall set out a broad view of the Necessary and Proper Clause while emphatically asserting the supremacy of the national Constitution over the states.

In 1791 Congress chartered the Bank of the United States, with the strong endorsement of Secretary of the Treasury Alexander Hamilton. President Washington signed the bill over the protests of Rep. James Madison, Attorney General Edmund Randolph, and Secretary of State Thomas Jefferson that Congress lacked the power to charter a corporation. In 1811, with Madison president, the twenty-year charter expired. After the War of 1812, however, Madison and his political allies concluded that the bank was a necessary evil. Madison told Congress that "the question of the Constitutional authority of the Legislature to establish an incorporated bank" was "precluded . . . by repeated recognitions under varied circumstances of the validity of such an institution in acts of the legislative, executive, and judicial branches of the Government, accompanied by indications, in different modes, of a concurrence of the general will of the nation." In 1816 Congress chartered the Second Bank of the United States, which was authorized to open branches throughout the nation.

Hostility toward the new bank grew as the postwar economic crisis led to the Panic of 1819, and local banking interests, jealous of its power, attacked it. A Maryland act of 1818 taxed all bank notes issued by banks "not chartered by the legislature." This law applied only to the Baltimore branch of the Bank of the United States. James William McCulloch, the chief operating officer of that bank, refused to pay the tax and was subsequently sued by the state. The state court upheld the tax, and McCulloch appealed on a writ of error to the Supreme Court.

The case brought two major questions before the Court. First, did Congress have the power to create a national bank? In other words, was the bank constitutional? Second, if Congress had the power to create a national bank, could the states tax the bank?

Arguments before the Court lasted nine days in a packed courtroom. Daniel Webster, the great orator and politician from Massachusetts; William Wirt, the attorney general of the United States; and William Pinkney, generally considered the most skillful attorney in the nation, represented the bank. Leading Maryland's legal team was Luther Martin, who had been a delegate to the Constitutional Convention in 1787.

Marshall relied on the Necessary and Proper Clause of Article I of the Constitution to find that it was both necessary and proper for Congress to charter a bank. Without the bank, no system of national currency could exist, and local banks would issue paper money. Marshall readily understood that a system of national currency and a stable banking system were vital for the collection of taxes, the disbursement of federal funds, and the development of national commerce. Asserting a sweeping sense of national power, Marshall declared, "Let the end be legitimate, let it be within the scope of the constitution, and all means which are appropriate, which are plainly adapted to that end, which are not prohibited, but consist with the letter and spirit of the constitution, are constitutional."

In reaching this conclusion, Marshall rejected the argument that Congress could not pass legislation beyond the specific powers enumerated in the Constitution. He noted that even the Tenth Amendment did not limit congressional powers to those "expressly" mentioned in the Constitution. He said that a constitution that listed all the powers of Congress would "partake of the prolixity of a legal code," and such a document "could scarcely be embraced by the human mind." "We must never forget," he told that American people, "that it is a *constitution* we are expounding." Moreover, it was "a constitution intended to endure for ages to come, and, consequently, to be adapted to the various crises of human affairs." Such endurance required a flexible approach to constitutional interpretation.

Marshall also rejected the state's claim of a power to tax the bank. He argued that under the Constitution "the government of the Union, though limited in its powers," was "supreme within it sphere of action." The "great principle" of American government, he declared, was "that the constitution and the laws made in pursuance thereof are supreme; that they control the constitution and laws of the respective States, and cannot be controlled by them." He then asserted "the power to tax involved the power to destroy." Because the bank was constitutional, the states could not destroy it through taxation. Marshall noted that if:

> the States may tax one instrument, employed by the government in the execution of its powers, they may tax every other instrument. They may tax the mail; they may tax the mint; they may tax patent rights; they may tax the papers of the custom-house; they may tax judicial process; they may tax all the means employed by the government, to an excess which would defeat all the end of government. This was not intended by the American people.

Thus, neither Maryland, nor any state, could tax the bank or any other institution created by the national government.

Marshall's opinion deeply angered opponents of a strong national government. Virginians Judge Spencer Roane and former senator John Taylor of Caroline, as he was known, wrote lengthy attacks on Marshall's opinion, which former presidents Thomas Jefferson and James Madison endorsed. Madison supported the bank but, like the other critics, opposed the threat to states' rights posed by Marshall's sweeping opinion. Jefferson said Marshall was like a miner, "constantly working underground to undermine the foundations of our confederated fabric." Madison complained that the opinion would "convert a limited into an unlimited Government." Marshall responded with essays of his own, signed "A Friend of the Constitution," which appeared in the *Alexandria Gazette,* a Virginia newspaper.

With the end of the economic crisis, hostility toward the bank declined. Presidents James Monroe and John Quincy Adams supported it, which helped create national prosperity, but Andrew Jackson and his supporters remained hostile to the idea of a national bank. In 1832 Jackson vetoed a bill to recharter the Bank of the United States, and the government began to withdraw its funds from it. This policy led to not only the destruction of the bank but also to a major depression, the Panic of 1837. Although the bank did not survive after 1836, Marshall's opinion in *McCulloch* remains one of the most important and often cited Supreme Court opinions for the concepts of national supremacy and an expansive interpretation of the Constitution.

See Gerald Gunther, ed. *John Marshall's Defense of McCulloch v. Maryland* (Stanford, Calif.: Stanford University Press, 1969); and G. Edward White, *History of the Supreme Court of the United States, Vols. III–IV: The Marshall Court and Cultural Change* (New York: Macmillan, 1988).

Dartmouth College v. Woodward

17 U.S. 518 (4 Wheat. 518) (1819)
Decided: February 2, 1819
Vote: 5 (J. Marshall, Washington, W. Johnson, Livingston, Story)
1 (Duvall)
Opinion of the Court: J. Marshall
Concurring opinion: Washington
Concurring opinion: Story
Dissenting without opinion: Duvall
Did not participate: Todd

In 1754 Rev. Eleazer Wheelock founded a school to train missionaries and provide education for American Indians. English benefactors—including Lord Dartmouth—became trustees of the institution, and in 1769 Wheelock received a royal charter incorporating Dartmouth College. Under the charter, Wheelock became president for life, with the right to name his successor, but the trustees retained the power to remove the president and to fill subsequent openings on the board. In 1779 Wheelock's son, John, succeeded him, running the school until 1816, when the trustees fired him for his increasingly autocratic behavior. By this time the controversy had become highly politicized, with Republicans backing Wheelock and Federalists arrayed behind the trustees.

In 1816 the Republican-dominated New Hampshire legislature amended the royal charter, reorganized the board of trustees, and created Dartmouth University, with Wheelock as president. In 1817 the old trustees were running Dartmouth College, with ninety-five students, while the new trustees operated Dartmouth University, with only fourteen students. The old trustees hired its most famous alumnus, Daniel Webster, to challenge the new law. The trustees sued William Woodward, the college's secretary and treasurer, who had gone over to the new university, to recover the college's seal, charter, and record books, which Woodward had taken with him. The state superior court found for Woodward, holding that the college was a public corporation and therefore subject to state regulation. The state court rejected the college's arguments that the legislature had violated vested rights, the New Hampshire Constitution, and the Contract Clause of the federal Constitution.

In upholding the claims of the original trustees, Chief Justice Marshall offered one his most audacious, and at the same time one of his least well reasoned, opinions. Relying heavily on Justice Story's distinction in ***Terrett v. Taylor,*** 13 U.S. 43 (1815), between public and private corporations, Marshall asserted that the Contract Clause prevented the state's actions.

Marshall ignored the strong argument of counsel for the new trustees, who said that gratuitous charters lacked consideration, a universally recognized element of any contract; Marshall assumed, without proof of any sort, that all the necessary conditions for a contract existed. He asserted that Dartmouth College, as a "private eleemosynary institution," constituted a private corporation and that its charter was a contract within the protection of Article I, Section 10. New Hampshire could, therefore, neither amend, repeal, nor in any way abridge the rights conferred by that charter.

Marshall's sweeping language would ultimately be used to bring all private corporations within the protection of the Contract Clause, but its manifest weaknesses led Story to take the unusual step of writing a concurring opinion. Taken together, the two opinions effected their joint purpose—to erect legal barriers against arbitrary state interference with rights granted by charter to private corporations.

Marshall's bold and assertive opinion glossed over technical problems. In his statement of constitutional principles, while forceful and broadly construed, he could not cite a single precedent to justify his equation of a corporate charter with a private contract. Story's calm and detached concurrence helped rescue Marshall's position, as he covered the weaknesses in Marshall's exposition of contract with copious detail and voluminous citations to English commentators and English and American precedents. His opinion began with a masterful summary of the nature of corporate charters and the rules governing corporations.

Once a king had created a private eleemosynary corporation, Story asserted, the Crown had no more control over it except for what had been expressly or implicitly reserved in the charter. This important point provided the escape clause that made *Dartmouth College* palatable to the state legislatures. Marshall's opinion implied that once a state granted a charter, it could never exercise any influence or control over corporate activity, a condition that might well have led states to refuse to issue new charters, which would impair economic growth. As part of his overall explanation of the rights of existing corporations, Story told the states that if they wanted to retain some authority over their corporate creations, all they need do was pay attention to basic common law principles and include the powers they wished to reserve as explicit terms of the charter itself. In the future, state legislatures would reserve power to amend or abolish charters, thus retaining the ability to respond to economic changes with flexibility.

Justice Washington endorsed the result, relying almost entirely on Story's earlier opinion in *Terrett,* although that opinion had not dealt with the Contract Clause.

Dartmouth provided a guarantee that corporations could count on the Court to protect their charter rights in the face of changes in state politics. Marshall's opinion implied that, once granted, a corporate charter could never be altered. But for Story's opinion, this ruling might have led to a hostile reaction from the states, fearful of the Court usurping their powers. Story suggested that states could alter corporate charters by reserving the right to do so, and he gave the case enormous utility by assuring that states and emerging corporations could have the security of knowing the limits of their respective rights, and knowing the Court would enforce those rights.

See Francis N. Stites, *Private Interest and Public Gain: The Dartmouth College Case, 1819* (Amherst: University of Massachusetts Press, 1972).

1820–1829

Anderson v. Dunn

19 U.S. 204 (6 Wheat. 204) (1821)
Decided: March 2, 1821
Vote: 6 (J. Marshall, W. Johnson, Livingston, Todd, Duvall, Story)
0
Opinion of the Court: W. Johnson
Did not participate: Washington

The House of Representatives charged John Anderson with contempt for insulting the House. Anderson had asked Rep. Louis Williams of North Carolina to help him recover property in Michigan lost during the War of 1812. On January 6, 1818, as a token of appreciation for his help, Anderson offered to pay Williams $500. Whether this offer was a bribe or merely a clumsy attempt to thank Williams is not known, but Williams clearly believed it was a bribe. The fact that Anderson requested that the offer be kept secret suggests that he understood it was inappropriate. Williams brought the matter to the House on January 7, and the House immediately resolved by unanimous vote: "that Mr. Speaker do issue his warrant, directed to the sergeant-at-arms attending this House, commanding him to take into custody, whenever to be found, the body of John Anderson, and the same in his custody to keep, subject to the further order and direction of this House."

The sergeant-at-arms for the House, Thomas Dunn, arrested Anderson on Speaker Henry Clay's warrant, and Anderson subsequently sued Dunn for false imprisonment and battery. Pleadings and arguments dealt with a wide range of issues, including the contempt powers of Parliament. Justice Johnson, however, found that the issues were relatively narrow, and he focused on the "simple inquiry, whether the House of Representatives can take cognizance of contempts committed against themselves, under any circumstances." Johnson noted that Anderson was arrested to compel his appearance before the bar of the House, and that the arrest and detainment—which was the basis of his suit—was not a punishment *per se,* but merely an incident to compelling him to appear before the House. Johnson asserted that if the House had no power to punish a contempt, then it had no power to compel someone to attend the hearings. Johnson assumed that the House did not have the same powers as Parliament, but that it did have the power to arrest someone for contempt and hold that person until he could be brought before the bar of the House, which had been done in Anderson's case. The Court rejected his lawsuit.

At the beginning of the twenty-first century this case remained good law. Johnson's opinion narrowed the scope of congressional contempt power, denying that it could touch "the liberty of speech and of the press." He noted that the power of Congress was limited to imprisonment and only for the time that Congress was in session. But, speaking for a unanimous Court, he affirmed the power of Congress to protect itself from bribery and other forms of corruption—precisely the issue in *Anderson v. Dunn.*

See Ernest J. Eberling, *Congressional Investigations: A Study of the Origin and Development of the Power of Congress to Investigate and Punish Contempt* (New York: Columbia University Press, 1928); Ronald Goldfarb, *The Contempt Power* (New York: Columbia University Press, 1963); and *Congressional Quarterly's Guide to Congress,* 5th ed., vol. 1 (Washington, D.C.: CQ Press, 2000), 251–254.

Cohens v. Virginia

19 U.S. 264 (6 Wheat. 264) (1821)
Decided: March 3 and March 5, 1821
Vote: 6 (J. Marshall, W. Johnson, Livingston, Todd, Duvall, Story)
0
Opinion of the Court: J. Marshall
Did not participate: Washington

Operating out of their offices at Norfolk's wharf, Philip and Mendes Cohen sold tickets for a District of Columbia lottery. These sales violated Virginia's ban on the sale of foreign, or out-of-state, lottery tickets. The prosecutor and the Cohen brothers agreed to a special verdict, with a $100 fine, if the verdict was upheld. Some scholars believe that this case was contrived for the purpose of testing the authority of the Supreme Court to hear appeals from state courts. The Cohens argued that because the Washington, D.C., lottery was authorized by Congress, Virginia could not prevent them from selling tickets, and they brought the case to the Court under Section 25 of the Judiciary Act of 1789. Virginia argued that the Court had no jurisdiction to hear this case because (1) the state was a defendant and could not be sued under the Eleventh Amendment; (2) the Court could not issue a writ of error to a state court; and (3) the Court had no jurisdiction because the state prosecution violated neither the Constitution of the United States nor a federal statute. Coming on the heels of ***McCulloch v. Maryland,*** 17 U.S. 316 (1819), *Cohens v. Virginia* can be seen as an attempt by Virginia to challenge the Court's jurisdiction and to rein in Chief Justice Marshall's judicial federalism.

Marshall noted that if Virginia's jurisdictional arguments were upheld, the powers of the national government would be virtually destroyed. Virginia's arguments, Marshall said, would support the position that "the nation does not possess a department capable of restraining peaceably, and by authority of law, any attempts which may be made, by a part, against the legitimate powers of the whole; and that the government is reduced to the alternative of submitting to such attempts, or of resisting them by force." Marshall further noted that Virginia's position was that "the constitution of the United States has provided no tribunal for the final construction of itself, or of the laws or treaties of the nation; but that this power may be exercised in the last resort by the Courts of every State in the Union. That the constitution, laws, and treaties, may receive as many constructions as there are States; and that this is not a mischief, or, if a mischief, is irremediable."

Marshall flatly rejected these arguments, asserting that:

> The American States, as well as the American people, have believed a close and firm Union to be essential to their liberty and to their happiness. They have been taught by experience, that this Union cannot exist without a government for the whole; and they have been taught by the same experience that this government would be a mere shadow, that must disappoint all their hopes, unless invested with large portions of that sovereignty which belongs to independent States. Under the influence of this opinion, and thus instructed by experience, the American people, in the conventions of their respective States, adopted the present constitution.

The proof of this argument was, according to Marshall, found in the Article VI Supremacy Clause, which declares, "This Constitution, and the Laws of the United States, which shall be made in Pursuance thereof, and all Treaties made, or which shall be made, under the Authority of the United States, shall be the supreme Law of the Land; and the Judges in every State shall be bound thereby; any Thing in the Constitution or Laws of any State to the Contrary notwithstanding." Marshall asserted that Virginia's position was "mischievous" and "would prostrate" the national "government and its laws at the feet of every State in the Union."

Marshall similarly dismissed Virginia's Eleventh Amendment claims on the grounds that the suit was not brought against the state. The writ of error ordering Virginia to submit the record of the case to the Supreme Court did not violate the Eleventh Amendment because the case had been appealed from the state courts. Such an appeal to raise a federal question was not prohibited by the Eleventh Amendment.

On March 3, 1821, Marshall emphatically rejected Virginia's jurisdictional arguments, and in the process wrote an elaborate affirmation of the power of the Supreme Court to hear appeals from the state courts.

Having rejected Virginia's claims that the Court could not hear this case, Marshall ordered arguments on the merits of the case. Two days later, he issued a second opinion, in which he sided with Virginia on the merits, concluding that the statute creating the lottery in the District of Columbia did not require that the states allow the sale of the lottery tickets. This outcome avoided a conflict with Virginia, but the opinion nevertheless infuriated states' rights advocates because Marshall asserted the supremacy of the Court and the federal Constitution over the states in such a way that Virginia was forced to accept the outcome. This case can also be seen as perhaps the earliest example of the Court limiting the reach of the Commerce Clause, by in effect saying that states could ban the sale of certain products from interstate commerce—such as lottery tickets—which were inherently noxious.

Marshall's opinion on the jurisdictional issues aroused immense hostility in Virginia. Spencer Roane published a series of articles attacking the opinion, and John Taylor of Caroline attacked it in a 1822 book. Privately, Thomas Jefferson endorsed these attacks, calling the Court an "irresponsible body." Despite the contemporary attacks on the decision, it was an important step in the development of a national legal culture and a coherent federal system.

See G. Edward White, *The Marshall Court and Cultural Change, 1815–1835* (New York: Macmillan, 1988); and W. Ray Luce, *Cohens v. Virginia (1821): The Supreme Court and State Rights: A Reevaluation of Influences and Impacts* (New York: Garland, 1990).

Green v. Biddle

21 U.S. 1 (8 Wheat. 1) (1823)
Decided: February 27, 1823
Vote: 4 (Washington, W. Johnson, Duvall, Story)
0
Opinion of the Court: Washington
Concurring opinion: W. Johnson
Did not participate: J. Marshall, Todd, Livingston

Green and other plaintiffs claimed land under a grant from Virginia. Richard Biddle claimed and occupied the same land, which he had settled and improved. At issue was the status of the land and the constitutionality of two Kentucky statutes dealing with Virginia land grants for property located in Kentucky.

In 1789 representatives of Kentucky accepted, as a condition of statehood, an agreement with Virginia "that all private rights, and interests of lands within" Kentucky "derived from the laws of Virginia prior to such separation, shall remain valid and secure under the laws of the proposed State, and shall be determined by the laws now existing in this State." Kentucky's constitutional convention ratified this agreement and incorporated it into the state's first constitution when statehood was achieved in 1791. This agreement to respect land grants previously given to Virginia citizens led to tremendous conflicts between Virginia claimants, such as Green, and actual residents of

Kentucky, such as Biddle, who had occupied the land as squatters and improved it. Through acts of 1797 and 1812 Kentucky attempted to modify this agreement by forcing the Virginia claimants to pay for all squatters' improvements to the land or to relinquish title if the improvements exceeded the value of the land.

The legal issues here seemed straightforward. In 1791 Kentucky had agreed to respect the land claims of Virginians and now violated that agreement in what appeared to be a direct violation of the Contract Clause of the Constitution (Article I, Section 10). The social consequences were more complex. Pioneers crossing the Appalachians had no reason to believe that the unoccupied land they found belonged to anyone. Furthermore, Kentucky had few lawyers, and land ownership developed haphazardly. Some farmers purchased what they believed to be valid titles, settled on the land, and improved it, only to discover they owned neither the property nor the improvements. Other settlers, believing the untouched wilderness to be free, took up land without benefit of deed, assuming that their success in taming the forests provided sufficient evidence of their ownership. The Kentucky legislature, not surprisingly, moved to protect the interests of its citizens at the expense of the Virginia claimants.

In this case, the heirs of John Green sued to obtain land occupied by Richard Biddle. The case was initially argued in February 1821, but no counsel appeared for Biddle. Justice Story noted that the Court would "have been glad in the consideration" of the case "to have had the benefit of an argument on behalf of the tenant." On March 5, 1821, Story, speaking for a unanimous Court, found for Green. A week later, however, Sen. Henry Clay of Kentucky appeared before the Court, asking for a reconsideration, noting that "the rights of numerous occupants of land in Kentucky . . . would be irrevocably determined by this decision." The Court, sensitive to the political issues involved, especially in light of its recent decision in ***Cohens v. Virginia,*** 19 U.S. 264 (1821), granted Clay's motion.

The Court withdrew Story's "unanimous" opinion, and in 1823 Justice Washington wrote an opinion for the Court. Once again the Court upheld the right of the Virginia landowners and struck down the Kentucky statutes. Washington did suggest a way out of the problem: Kentucky could take the land by eminent domain, pay the Virginia landowners, and then sell it to Kentucky residents—a cumbersome and enormously expensive solution.

The constitutionality of these laws had been argued several times and became a focal point for states' rights sentiment as well as for anti-Court feelings in the South and West. Although sensitive to the frontier opposition, the Court nevertheless believed the constitutional issue clear and, following the economic and legal arguments of its earlier decisions, invalidated the Kentucky laws in *Green.* Kentucky had undoubtedly broken its word to Virginia, but the records of the Constitutional Convention of 1787 were silent on whether the Contract Clause extended to agreements between sovereign states. Nor did anyone, with the exception of the Virginia landowners, question the irrationality and unfairness of that state's convoluted property laws.

Kentucky in fact refused to abide by *Green* and adopted new laws to protect squatters' rights. Other frontier states followed suit because failure to protect the interests of their inhabitants against the claims of eastern titleholders would have seriously impaired western expansion. *Green* was consistent with the Court's insistence in other cases that a state's pledged word could not be broken without risking the health of national commerce.

See G. Edward White, *The Marshall Court and Cultural Change, 1815–1835* (New York: Macmillan, 1988); and Maurice Baxter, *Henry Clay the Lawyer* (Lexington: University of Kentucky Press, 2000).

Johnson and Graham's Lessee v. McIntosh

21 U.S. 543 (8 Wheat. 543) (1823)
Decided: March 10, 1823
Vote: 5 (J. Marshall, Washington, W. Johnson, Duvall, Story)
0
Opinion of the Court: J. Marshall
Did not participate: Todd, Livingston

This case was the Court's first significant attempt to define the relationship between the United States and Native Americans. In 1775 the Piankeshaw Indians sold land in present-day Illinois to a group of speculators that included a land speculator named Thomas Johnson. At the time, Virginia claimed ownership of this part of North America. In 1783 Virginia ceded to the national government its claims to the old Northwest. In 1818 William McIntosh bought more than eleven thousand acres of this land from the U.S. government. These lands were also claimed by Johnson's heirs, Joshua Johnson and Thomas J. Graham.

The ownership dispute reached the Court in 1823, after Johnson and Graham had lost in the lower courts. The Marshall Court had a long record of supporting vested rights of property owners, as the decisions in ***Martin v. Hunter's Lessee,*** 14 U.S. 304 (1816), ***Dartmouth College v. Woodward,*** 17 U.S. 518 (1819), and ***Fletcher v. Peck,*** 10 U.S. 87 (1810), indicate. Here, however, Chief Justice Marshall rejected Johnson and Graham's arguments, even though their claims predated those of McIntosh by nearly half a century. Marshall took this position because he rejected the idea that Indians could have any claims to land and therefore have the right to sell land.

Marshall argued that when Europeans arrived in the New World they gained title of all lands they occupied through a right of "discovery." This discovery gave the British and Americans "an exclusive right to extinguish the Indian title of occupancy, either by purchase or by conquest; and gave also a right to such a degree of sovereignty as the circumstances of the people would allow them to exercise." After the British arrived, there was an "absolute title of the crown" in the lands, "subject only to the Indian right of occupancy" with the understanding of "the absolute title of the crown to extinguish that right." Marshall asserted that "the tribes of Indians inhabiting this country were fierce savages, whose occupation was war, and whose subsistence was drawn chiefly from the forest." According to Marshall, "The Indian inhabitants are to be considered merely as occupants, to be protected, indeed, while in peace, in the possession of the lands, but to be deemed incapable of transferring the absolute title to others." In other words, the Piankeshaw Indians had no ownership rights in the lands they occupied and could not sell them to anyone. McIntosh therefore remained the owner of his land. More important, no Native Americans could lay claim to any lands they occupied.

Later, in ***Cherokee Nation v. Georgia,*** 30 U.S. 1 (1831), and ***Worcester v. Georgia,*** 31 U.S. 515 (1832), Marshall attempted to protect Native Americans from whites who wanted their lands. Ironically, his decision in this case created the legal arguments for the destruction of the Cherokee and all other tribes that tried to maintain occupancy, and ownership, of their lands.

See Felix S. Cohen, *Handbook of Federal Indian Law* (Charlottesville, Va.: Michie Bobbs-Merrill, 1982).

Gibbons v. Ogden

22 U.S. 1 (9 Wheat. 1) (1824)
Decided: March 2, 1824
Vote: 6 (J. Marshall, Washington, W. Johnson, Todd, Duvall, Story)
0
Opinion of the Court: J. Marshall
Concurring opinion: W. Johnson
Did not participate: Thompson

In 1808 the New York legislature granted Robert R. Livingston and Robert Fulton a thirty-year monopoly over steamboat transportation on all state waters and all steamboat transportation entering the state from adjacent coastal waters or the Hudson River, which separated New York and New Jersey. By 1815 part of this franchise had passed into the hands of Aaron Ogden, who operated a steamboat running from New York City to Elizabethtown, New Jersey. In 1819, after Thomas Gibbons began operating a competing ferry, Ogden won an injunction from Chancellor James Kent, which New York's highest court affirmed. Gibbons appealed to the Supreme Court, arguing this monopoly violated the Commerce Clause of the Constitution. Gibbons also argued that he had a right to operate his boat anywhere in the nation because he had a federal coasting license. By the time the Court heard arguments in the case in 1824, both New Jersey and Connecticut had passed retaliatory legislation against New York. Such legislation threatened to disrupt all interstate commerce.

In what proved to be his most popular major opinion, Chief Justice Marshall emphatically struck down the New York law giving Ogden a monopoly for steamboat service into and out of New York. Although the Court had not previously decided any important Commerce Clause cases, Marshall grandly declared it was a "well-settled rule" that the enumerated powers had to be construed both by the language of the Constitution and in light of the purpose for which they had been conferred. The Article I powers had been granted to further the "general advantage" of the whole American people. Although not infinite in its reach, in delegated areas the "the sovereignty of Congress, though limited to specified objects, is plenary as to those objects."

Commerce, a vital aspect of national life, included not just the exchange of goods, but "every species of commercial intercourse" among the states. The word "among" meant not only between but also intermingled with. "Commerce among the States, cannot stop at the external boundary line of each State, but may be introduced into the interior." The congressional power to regulate this commerce meant it could reach all aspects of trade; "complete in itself, [it] may be exercised to its utmost extent, and acknowledges no limitations other than are prescribed in the Constitution."

Marshall acknowledged that the states could control commerce that was wholly internal, which was most likely aimed at assuring the slave states that they could regulate free blacks and slaves within their jurisdictions. Marshall was reacting to a recent controversy in South Carolina, which had incarcerated a free black sailor when his ship docked in Charleston. Justice Johnson had written a bitter circuit court opinion in *Elkison v. Deliesseline,* 8 F. Cas. 493 (1823), denouncing South Carolina's position. Thus, in *Gibbons* Johnson took a stronger position than Marshall on the supremacy of federal power.

Although Marshall acknowledged some state power over commerce, he determined that the 1793 Coastal Licensing Act prevented state interference with interstate commerce. Marshall found that New York's law violated the federal act and, on Supremacy Clause grounds, struck down the state law.

Gibbons broke up what had become an unpopular monopoly, treated the nation as a single commercial entity, and prevented states from fragmenting the national economy. Marshall's powerful opinion and broad interpretation of what constituted interstate commerce permitted the government to adapt its policies to new technologies in transportation and communications, and, except for a relatively brief period in the early twentieth century, allowed the continuous expansion of federal regulation over the nation's commerce, banking, industry, and labor. Beyond that, the analysis applied to the commerce power could be used to expand the scope of the other enumerated powers as well.

See Maurice G. Baxter, *The Steamboat Monopoly: Gibbons v. Ogden, 1824* (New York: Knopf, 1972).

The Emily and The Caroline

22 U.S. 381 (9 Wheat. 381) (1824)
Decided: February 1824 Term
Vote: 7 (J. Marshall, Washington, W. Johnson, Todd, Duvall, Story, Thompson)
0
Opinion of the Court: Thompson

In ***Brig Caroline v. United States,*** 11 U.S. 496 (1813), the Supreme Court rejected a prosecution of *The Caroline* for slave trading on the grounds that the indictment had been imperfectly drawn. The decision seemed to support the defense arguments that a ship could not be considered to have violated slave trade bans until it left the port fully equipped for a slaving voyage. Here, the Court rejected this theory of the law. The cases began in the heated atmosphere of Charleston, South Carolina, following the discovery of the Denmark Vesey conspiracy in 1822. Vesey, a free black, had organized as many as eight thousand slaves and free blacks in what would have been the biggest slave rebellion in American history. Shortly before Vesey planned to launch the rebellion, authorities discovered the plot and arrested him along with hundreds of other blacks. Although no insurrection took place, whites in Charleston and the rest of South Carolina remained fearful that a slave rebellion could soon take place.

Authorities seized *The Caroline* and *The Emily* in the port of Charleston before they reached open water. The defense claimed that to be in violation of the law "the vessel must be completely fitted and ready for sea; that no state of preparation, short of this, will satisfy the terms of the law, or furnish any certain rule by which to determine when the offense has been committed, and the penalty incurred." Such an inference was reasonable, given the Court's 1813 decision, but the Court rejected this analysis. Justice Thompson asserted that it was necessary to "look to the object in view" when interpreting the statute. He found that the object, in this case, was the "preparation of vessels in our own ports, which were intended for the slave trade." To sustain a claim against the ships, the prosecution had therefore only to prove the preparation and intent, rather than the completed act. The preparation and intent included "building, fitting, equipping, or loading" of a ship for the trade. Altering the standard in a way that would help suppress the growing illegal trade, Thompson asserted, "As soon, therefore, as the preparations have progressed so far as clearly and satisfactorily to show the purpose for which they are made, the right of seizure attaches." The seizures were affirmed, and the standard of proof brought in line with the reality of the illegal trade.

See W. E. B. Du Bois, *The Suppression of the African Slave Trade to the United States of America, 1638–1870* (Cambridge: Harvard University Press, 1896).

The Merino, The Constitution, and The Louisa

22 U.S. 391 (9 Wheat. 391) (1824)
Decided: February 1824 Term
Vote: 7 (J. Marshall, Washington, W. Johnson, Todd, Duvall, Story, Thompson)
0
Opinion of the Court: Washington

In this case, decided immediately after the ***The Emily and The Caroline,*** 22 U.S. 381 (1824), the Court allowed broad jurisdictional powers for American admiralty courts hearing cases on the illegal African slave trade. The ships in question had been seized in foreign waters for violations of various laws banning the slave trade. The ships were taken to the port of Mobile, Alabama, and condemned by the federal district court there. The shipowners argued that the Alabama court had no jurisdiction over the vessels because the ships had not been on the open seas nor in the waters of any U.S. jurisdiction. The shipowners further argued that they had not violated the federal laws because the ships were bringing slaves from Cuba, not Africa, to Florida and Louisiana.

Justice Washington rejected all of these claims, asserting that foreign waters should be treated like the high seas in admiralty libels, thus giving jurisdiction to the court where the ships landed—in this case, Mobile. The Court also found no merit in the claim that the laws suppressing the slave trade applied only to the African trade. On the contrary, the goal of the laws was to prevent American ships from trading in slaves in any foreign country and to prevent the further importation of slaves into the United States from any other country.

See W. E. B. Du Bois, *The Suppression of the African Slave Trade to the United States of America, 1638–1870* (Cambridge: Harvard University Press, 1896).

The St. Jago de Cuba

22 U.S. 409 (9 Wheat. 409) (1824)
Decided: February 1824 Term
Vote: 7 (J. Marshall, Washington, W. Johnson, Todd, Duvall, Story, Thompson)
0
Opinion of the Court: W. Johnson

This case was the third in a series that included ***The Emily and The Caroline,*** 22 U.S. 381 (1824), and ***The Merino,*** 22 U.S. 391 (1824), and dealt with the illegal African slave trade. Here, an American shipbuilder, Gunn, short of cash, purported to sell a ship to Maher, but in fact this sale was "intended to serve only as the means for enabling Maher to expedite the vessel on a voyage to Cuba, there to be sold, and to account with Gunn for the proceeds, as well as of freight as of sale." Maher and Gunn were then partners in what Gunn believed was a legal voyage and a simple attempt to take the ship to Cuba, where it could be sold. Maher, however, quickly abandoned this legal plan and, instead, working with a man named Strike brought the ship to Cuba where it was "colorably conveyed to Vinente, but still under the absolute control of Strike." The ship was then "completely equipped, colorably a Spaniard, but really an American, for the African slave trade." This case, replete with complicated and fraudulent sales, illustrates the complexity of the African trade and the way some American shipbuilders, investors, and sea captains tried to take part. The ship was damaged on the voyage to Africa, and Strike brought it back to Baltimore for repairs. There Gunn discovered it and tried to recover it as the "original and equitable owner." He had by now lost control of his ship, which was seized under the laws banning the slave trade. Gunn could gain satisfaction only by testifying against Maher in court.

The circuit court upheld the condemnation of the ship, but not all the cargo on board when it reached Maryland. The U.S. government successfully appealed this part of the case. For technical reasons involving traditional admiralty law, as well as to comply with the laws banning the African trade, the Court declared that the entire ship, as well as its cargo, was properly condemned. Combined with the two previous slave-trade cases, this decision gave federal prosecutors one more weapon in their war against the illegal slave trade.

See W. E. B. Du Bois, *The Suppression of the African Slave Trade to the United States of America, 1638–1870* (Cambridge: Harvard University Press, 1896).

United States v. Perez

22 U.S. 579 (9 Wheat. 579) (1824)
Decided: March 17, 1824
Vote: 7 (J. Marshall, Washington, W. Johnson, Todd, Duvall, Story, Thompson)
0
Opinion of the Court: Story

Whether *United States v. Perez* concerns double jeopardy or a hung jury is in dispute. The essence of *Perez* is that in a case in which a hung jury results, the defendant may be retried.

Josef Perez was tried for a capital offense in the federal court in New York City. When the jury was unable to reach a verdict, the court discharged it, without the consent of either Perez or the U.S. attorney. Perez then claimed that he should be released from custody, as he had been tried but not convicted. The issue before the Supreme Court was whether the discharge of the jury was a bar to any future trial for the same offense. If the answer was yes, Perez was entitled to his liberty. If the answer was no, the United States was free to retry him.

Justice Story determined that the discharge of the jury was not a "legal bar to future trial." Because the prisoner had been neither acquitted nor convicted of the crime, he would have to defend himself again. The Court certified that Perez should remain in custody and might be tried again.

Story laid the groundwork regarding hung juries and possibly for interpreting the Double Jeopardy Clause of the Fifth Amendment. In what is commonly referred to as the "manifest necessity" test, Story wrote that the law empowers courts of justice authority to discharge the jury whenever "there is a manifest necessity for the act, or the ends of public justice would otherwise be defeated." The judges discharging the jury under one or the other element must exercise sound discretion; discharging a jury in a case of capital offense, such as *Perez,* is appropriate because a life is at stake.

See Janet E. Findlater, "Retrial After a Hung Jury: The Double Jeopardy Problem," *University of Pennsylvania Law Review* 129 (1981): 701–712.

Osborn v. Bank of the United States

22 U.S. 738 (9 Wheat. 738) (1824)
Decided: March 19, 1824
Vote: 6 (J. Marshall, Washington, Todd, Duvall, Story, Thompson)
1 (W. Johnson)
Opinion of the Court: J. Marshall
Dissenting opinion: W. Johnson

This case, like ***McCulloch v. Maryland,*** 17 U.S. 316 (1819), challenged the constitutionality of the Bank of the United States. In 1819 Ohio levied a tax of $50,000 on each office of the Bank of the United States in Ohio. The bank obtained an injunction from the U.S. district court to prevent Ralph Osborn, the auditor of the state, from collecting the tax. Meanwhile, state officials, in violation of the injunction, entered the bank's offices in Chillicothe, Ohio, and seized $100,000 in specie and currency from the bank's vaults. The bank then sued Osborn and others to recover the money. The state officials claimed that under the Eleventh Amendment they could not be sued, but the circuit court rejected this argument and ordered the defendants to repay the bank $100,000 plus interest on the $19,830 in specie the state had seized. Osborn then appealed to the Supreme Court, again raising the Eleventh Amendment argument. He also argued that there was no federal jurisdiction in this case, because there was in effect no federal question.

In a sweeping opinion, Chief Justice Marshall reaffirmed his holding in *McCulloch* that the Bank of the United States was constitutional and that any litigation concerning the bank came under the jurisdiction of the federal courts because the bank was created by a federal statute. Marshall's opinion greatly expanded federal jurisdiction by broadly reading and applying the language of Article III and giving the courts jurisdiction over all cases "arising under this Constitution, the Law of the United States, and the Treaties made." Marshall also held that state officials could be sued for their actions and that the Eleventh Amendment only prevented a state from being sued. This opinion anticipated the Court's ruling in ***Ex parte Young*** 209 U.S. 123 (1908), that state officials could be sued in their private capacity for enforcing state laws that violated the Constitution.

In dissent, Justice Johnson complained that this decision all but eviscerated the Eleventh Amendment. More important, perhaps, *Osborn*, along with *McCulloch*, heightened hostility to both the Bank of the United States and the Marshall Court. In 1831 President Andrew Jackson rejected Marshall's analysis, asserting that the bank was in fact unconstitutional, as he vetoed a recharter bill. In the short run, the bank lost its war with the states' rights Jacksonians of the 1820s and 1830s; however, Marshall's opinions on the scope of federal power in *McCulloch* and *Osborn* remained a powerful force and important precedents in American constitutional law.

See Gerald Gunther, ed. *John Marshall's Defense of McCulloch v. Maryland* (Stanford, Calif.: Stanford University Press, 1969); and R. Kent Newmyer, *John Marshall and the Heroic Age of the Supreme Court* (Baton Rouge: Louisiana State University Press, 2001).

The Antelope

23 U.S. 66 (10 Wheat. 66) (1825)
Decided: March 16, 1825
Vote: 6 (J. Marshall, Washington, W. Johnson, Duvall, Story, Thompson)
0
Opinion of the Court: J. Marshall
Did not participate: Todd

The Antelope was a Spanish vessel seized on the high seas by pirates. On June 29, 1820, an American revenue cutter seized *The Antelope* (which was flying the revolutionary flag of José Artigas), placed her American captain under arrest for violating the 1807 and 1819 laws banning the slave trade, and towed the ship and its 258 African slaves to Savannah. The slaves on board had been taken from numerous ships owned by citizens of various countries including Spain and the United States. The Court, upholding in part the circuit court ruling of Justice Johnson, ultimately decided that some of the slaves found on this ship were to be returned to the Spanish government because they were lawfully owned by Spanish subjects at the time the ship was captured in American waters. The remaining Africans, those claimed by Americans and others, were turned over to the U.S. government as the fruit of the illegal trade, which Congress had banned in 1808.

Chief Justice Marshall noted that in this case the "sacred rights of liberty and property come in conflict with each other." In the end, the four slaveowners on the Court—Chief Justice Marshall and Justices Washington, Duvall, and Johnson—firmly supported the sacredness of property over liberty. Marshall admitted that the African slave trade was "contrary to the law of nature" but concluded that it was "consistent with the law of nations" and "cannot in itself be piracy." This analysis led to the Court to recognize the right of foreigners to engage in the slave trade, if their own nations allowed them to do so. Marshall wrote, "It if be neither repugnant to the law of nations, nor piracy, it is almost superfluous to say in this Court, that the right of bringing in for adjudication in time of peace, even where the vessel belongs to a nation which has prohibited the trade, cannot exist." This analysis allowed the Court to uphold prosecutions against American traders because they violated the U.S. prohibition on the African trade, while also protecting the property rights in enslaved Africans owned by nationals where the trade was legal.

See John T. Noonan Jr., *The Antelope: The Ordeal of the Recaptured Africans in the Administrations of James Monroe and John Quincy Adams* (Berkeley: University of California Press, 1977); Paul Finkelman, ed. *Articles on American Slavery* vol. 2 *The Slave Trade and Migration* (New York: Garland Publishing, 1989).

The Steamboat Thomas Jefferson

23 U.S. 428 (10 Wheat. 428) (1825)
Decided: March 18, 1825
Vote: 6 (J. Marshall, Washington, W. Johnson, Duvall, Story, Thompson)
0
Opinion of the Court: Story
Did not participate: Todd

Residents of Kentucky brought an action in federal court under its admiralty jurisdiction against the owner of *The Thomas Jefferson* for failing to pay their wages on the steamboat's voyage up the Missouri River. Traditional English admiralty jurisdiction was limited to cases involving the ocean. The usual test was whether an event took place on water that was affected by the rise and fall of the tides.

Justice Story followed this old rule, asserting that if "the service was to be substantially performed on the sea, or on the tide water," admiralty jurisdiction would prevail, even if "the commencement or termination of the voyage may happen at some place beyond the reach of the tide. The material consideration is, whether the service is essentially a maritime service." In this case the service, that is, the work performed by the Kentucky residents who initiated the suit, was not on water affected by the tide, and the Court therefore dismissed the case for want of jurisdiction. Story suggested that Congress might have Commerce Clause jurisdiction over the matter, but that would require a statute, which Congress had not passed.

This case illustrated the failure of law, at least on this subject, to reflect the realities of American geography or the nature of changing technology. Unlike England, the United States has a large system of inland waterways, capable of supporting ocean-going vessels. It was logical to see admiralty jurisdiction as reflecting, not the saline content of the water, but the use of the waterways in commerce. In addition, the Great Lakes and the St. Lawrence formed an international boundary and facilitated international trade even though they were bodies of fresh water and not affected by the tides. Furthermore, this case ignored the reality that steam technology had connected inland waterways to the oceans in ways previously unimaginable. This decision served as an important precedent for nearly three decades, until overturned by *The Propeller Genesee Chief v. Fitzhugh*, 53 U.S. 443 (1852).

See Carl B. Swisher, *The Taney Period: 1836–64* (New York: Macmillan, 1974); and R. Kent Newmyer, *Supreme Court Justice Joseph Story: Statesman of the Old Republic* (Chapel Hill: University of North Carolina Press, 1985).

Martin v. Mott

25 U.S. 19 (12 Wheat. 19) (1827)
Decided: February 2, 1827
Vote: 7 (J. Marshall, Washington, W. Johnson, Duvall, Story, Thompson, Trimble)
0
Opinion of the Court: Story

During the War of 1812 President James Madison called on Gov. Daniel D. Tompkins of New York to mobilize the state militia for national service. Jacob E. Mott, a private in a New York militia company, refused to comply with an order to report for duty. Mott was subsequently court-martialed, fined $96, and then sentenced to twelve months' imprisonment for failure to pay the fine. Instead of sending Mott to jail, however, Martin, the deputy U.S. marshal in New York, seized Mott's property. Mott then sued in the state courts for replevin, the recovery of his property. New York's highest court found for Mott, and Martin appealed to the Supreme Court, which reversed the New York court.

In his opinion for the Court, Justice Story acknowledged that the power to call out the militia was of a "very high and delicate nature" and that the American people were "naturally jealous of the exercise of military power." The power resided with the president, however, and when the nation was invaded, as it had been during the War of 1812, the president clearly had the constitutional power to call forth the militia, and the citizens soldiers were duty-bound to answer the call.

This case helped to define and shape the nature of executive power and set a precedent still in force—that the states cannot prevent the president from calling out the militia under circumstances set out by the Constitution. Lincoln relied on this case at the beginning of the Civil War, and it continues to be a viable precedent for the power of the president and the concept that state courts cannot generally interfere with military justice.

See William Lawrence Shaw, "Conscription by the State Through the Time of the Civil War," *The Judge Advocate Journal* 33 (1962): 1–40.

Ogden v. Saunders

25 U.S. 213 (12 Wheat. 213) (1827)
Decided: February 18, 1827
Vote: 4 (Washington, W. Johnson, Thompson, Trimble)
3 (J. Marshall, Duvall, Story)
Judgment of the Court: W. Johnson
Seriatim opinion: Washington
Seriatim opinion: W. Johnson
Seriatim opinion: Thompson
Seriatim opinion: Trimble
Dissenting opinion: J. Marshall (Duvall, Story)

Ogden v. Saunders was the only constitutional law case of Chief Justice Marshall's career in which he dissented. Oddly, his dissent left the Court without any leadership, and each of the four majority justices wrote an opinion explaining his position. Justice Washington, as the most senior justice in the majority, wrote the first opinion, which set the standard for the other majority opinions. The case was first heard in 1824, but the Court was evenly divided at that time, and it was not reargued until 1827. The case was decided in the wake of the failure of Congress to pass a national bankruptcy law, which left the issue to the states. Article I, Section 8, grants Congress the power to establish uniform bankruptcy laws for the nation. The states also had the power to pass bankruptcy laws, but were limited by the Contract Clause of the Constitution which prohibited the states from "impairing the Obligation of Contracts." This limitation did not apply to the national government, but any bankruptcy laws the states might pass had to avoid impairing the obligations of contract.

At issue here was bankruptcy and the discharge of debts in the absence of a national bankruptcy law. In ***Sturges v. Crowninshield,*** 17 U.S. 122 (1819), the Court had held that a state bankruptcy law could not discharge debts incurred *before* the bankruptcy law was passed. Marshall explicitly noted that state laws could not affect "contracts already in existence" at the time the statutes were passed. Whether a state could discharge obligations of contract made after the law was passed remained open. *Ogden* involved a contract signed after a state bankruptcy law was on the books. It also involved a contract signed in a state that had a bankruptcy law. The majority found no problem in upholding this law, arguing in essence, that the Constitution's Contract Clause was designed to avoid retroactive laws that would release people from their contractual obligations. In this case, however, nothing could be considered retroactive. The parties knew of the New York law when they entered into their agreement. Justice Washington asserted that the existing bankruptcy law was, in effect, part of the contract itself.

Marshall dissented from this position, arguing that a state could never discharge someone from a contractual obligation. While upholding the New York bankruptcy law, the fragile majority switched on how to actually decide the case. Justice Johnson believed New York had the power to discharge debts for contracts, but only for its own citizens. Saunders was a citizen of Kentucky when he signed the contract, and Johnson, joined by Marshall, Story, and Duvall believed that New York's bankruptcy law could not relieve Ogden from a debt owed to a person outside the state. Thus, in the end, Johnson announced the result of the case, in which the three dissenting justices joined him. The case left the states with the power to pass bankruptcy laws that would apply only to their own citizens and, in general, left the issue of bankruptcy confused and uncertain. A federal law was needed to provide a national system for the discharge of debts, but that did not happen until 1898.

See Edward Balleisen, *Navigating Failure: Bankruptcy and Commercial Society in Antebellum America* (Chapel Hill: University of North Carolina Press, 2001); David Skeel, *Debt's Dominion: A History of Bankruptcy Law in America* (Princeton: Princeton University Press, 2001); and Charles Warren, *Bankruptcy in United States History* (Cambridge: Harvard University Press, 1935).

Brown v. Maryland

25 U.S. 419 (12 Wheat. 419) (1827)
Decided: March 12, 1827
Vote: 6 (J. Marshall, Washington, W. Johnson, Duvall, Story, Trimble)
1 (Thompson)
Opinion of the Court: J. Marshall
Dissenting opinion: Thompson

Brown v. Maryland developed what is known as the "original package" rule in interstate commerce and state taxation. An 1821 Maryland law required "all importers of foreign articles, or commodities" and "other persons selling the same by wholesale" to take out a license and pay fifty dollars. Brown and other importers refused to purchase the license and appealed their fine, which was $100 plus the original $50 license fee. Roger B. Taney, a future chief justice, argued this case for Maryland. Although he lost the case, he later supported the outcome.

In striking down Maryland's law, Chief Justice Marshall emphasized the national character of commerce, as he had a few years earlier in ***Gibbons v. Ogden,*** 22 U.S. 1 (1824). The case forced the Court to balance two issues: the right of the states to levy taxes, which was a right concurrent with Congress, and the right of Congress to regulate and tax foreign commerce. Although the Court did not use the phrase *dormant commerce clause,* this case can also be seen as an early example of the use of the concept. Under dormant commerce clause analysis, the Court has decided that state laws regulating commerce can be found unconstitutional, even if Congress has never passed legislation on the issue. The theory is that Congress has plenary power over all interstate commerce, and, even if Congress has chosen not to legislate on a particular matter, states may not do so. The Court has held that the act of *not acting* on an issue means that Congress has chosen to leave the matter alone. A state law on the subject would be seen as impinging on the powers of Congress. The dormant commerce clause did not apply to *Gibbons v. Ogden,* because Congress in fact had regulated coasting vessels, but Congress had never legislated on the subject at issue in *Brown v. Maryland.*

In reaching his decision, Marshall relied on two separate clauses of the Constitution. The first was the Commerce Clause (Article I, Section 8), which Marshall had explained in *Gibbons,* should be interpreted to give Congress broad powers. The second, and more directly pertinent, clause was in Article I, Section 10, where the Constitution says, "No State shall, without the Consent of the Congress, lay any Imposts or Duties on Imports or Exports, except what may be absolutely necessary for executing it's [*sic*] inspection Laws."

Marshall interpreted the license as a tax on imported goods, rather than mere regulation of those in business, which is how Justice Thompson, in dissent, saw the law. Marshall made clear that if the states could tax imported goods, simply as imports, they could destroy all international commerce. He noted that "it is obvious that the same power which imposes a light duty can impose a very heavy one, one which amounts to a prohibition." This argument resembles his assertion in ***McCulloch v. Maryland,*** 17 U.S. 316 (1819), that the power to tax implies the power to destroy. Clearly, Marshall believed that the states could not have the power to destroy international commerce through a licensing system. For this reason, according to Marshall, Article I, Section 10, prohibits the states from levying import taxes.

Marshall also understood that his theory, taken to its natural limits, would prevent the states from taxing any goods made in other states or other countries, which would infringe on the rights of states. Marshall therefore distinguished between the taxation of goods as they were imported into the state or sold to retail merchants and a tax on goods generally sold in the state. The question was, as Marshall put it, when "the power of the state to tax commences." His answer was when the "importer has so acted upon the thing imported that is has become incorporated and mixed up with the mass of property in the country, it has, perhaps, lost its distinctive character as an import, and has become subject to the taxing power of the state; but while remaining the property of the importer, in his warehouse, in the original form or package in which it was imported, a tax upon it is too plainly a duty on imports to escape the prohibition in the constitution." Marshall's definition became the "original package" rule: so long as goods crossing state lines remained in their original packages, they could not be taxed or otherwise regulated by the states. This doctrine remained in effect for over a century and to this day is still applicable in some circumstances.

See R. Kent Newmyer, *John Marshall and the Heroic Age of the Supreme Court* (Baton Rouge: Louisiana State University Press, 2001).

United States v. Gooding

25 U.S. 460 (12 Wheat. 460) (1827)
Decided: February 1827 Term
Vote: 7 (J. Marshall, Washington, W. Johnson, Duvall, Story, Thompson, Trimble)
0
Opinion of the Court: Story

The United States prosecuted John Gooding for violating the act of 1818 banning the African slave trade. Gooding had outfitted *The General Winder* in Baltimore for a voyage to Africa to purchase slaves and bring them to Cuba. His conviction rested in part on the testimony of a sailor, who had been approached by Capt. John Hill, master of *The General Winder,* while the ship was in port on the island of St. Thomas and asked to join the voyage to Africa. Gooding argued that testimony about what Hill said could not link him (Gooding) to the slave-trading voyage, even if it linked the ship to such an illegal voyage.

Justice Story found Hill's testimony acceptable, in light of other evidence that Gooding owned the ship and had been involved with having it prepared for the voyage. Gooding argued that he had not personally prepared the ship, but Story said this was irrelevant, noting the act of Congress "does not require that the fitting out should be by the owner personally, without the assistance of agency of others. The act itself is of a nature which forbids such a supposition." Obviously, Story noted, no single individual prepared a ship for sea, but on the contrary, "the fitment of a vessel is ordinarily, and, indeed, must be done through the instrumentality of others. It is not a single act, but a series of subordinate operations, requiring the co-operation of persons in various trades and arts, all conducing to the same end." Clearly, the owner of the ship would be ultimately responsible for the fitting of his ship. Having decided these questions in favor of the government, Story acknowledged flaws in the indictment and allowed these to be considered by the jury on remand to the U.S. circuit court for Maryland.

This case was significant for Story's practical approach to the federal statute and the slave trade. The trade was illegal, and Story understood that those who indulged in it would do so in roundabout ways. The investor in the trade and the owners of the ships would try to insulate themselves from the illegal activity and then claim, as Gooding did, that they did not actually do anything to further it. The Court rejected these arguments, and, although he affirmed that the burden of proof rested with the prosecutors, Story would not allow investors in the illegal trade to hide behind their agents.

See W. E. B. Du Bois, *The Suppression of the African Slave Trade to the United States of America, 1638–1870* (Cambridge: Harvard University Press, 1896).

American Insurance Company v. Canter

26 U.S. 511 (1 Pet. 511) (1828)
Decided: March 15, 1828
Vote: 7 (J. Marshall, Washington, W. Johnson, Duvall, Story, Thompson, Trimble)
0
Opinion of the Court: J. Marshall

In 1825 a French ship carrying 891 bales of cotton sank off of Key West, Florida, while en route from New Orleans to Harve de Grace, France. A local court created by the territorial government in Florida awarded salvage rights, and at a court-ordered auction David Canter purchased the cotton, which he then took to Charleston, South Carolina, for resale. The local court awarded the salvors, who were local men from Key West, 76 percent of the sale. The U.S. district court in Charleston declared that the sale in Key West was null and void because only federal courts had the power to award salvage rights. The district court ordered that some of the cotton in Canter's possession be awarded to the companies that had insured the voyage and awarded the salvors only 50 percent of the proceeds of the sale. Both sides appealed to the circuit court, where Justice Johnson ruled entirely for Canter, holding that the Florida territorial court was legally constituted and empowered to decide the case.

When the case came to the Supreme Court, Chief Justice Marshall upheld Johnson's order reinstating the original salvage order of the Florida court. To reach this result, Marshall considered the power of Congress to acquire new territories and to govern them. Marshall wrote, "The Constitution confers absolutely on the government of the Union, the powers of making war, and of making treaties; consequently, that government possesses the power of acquiring territory, either by conquest or by treaty." This affirmed practices that had led to the acquisition of both Florida and the Louisiana Territory. It gave a green light for Congress to continue to acquire new territories throughout the rest of the century.

Marshall noted that the people of acquired territories had all of the constitutional rights of American citizens, except political rights. Instead, they were to be "governed by virtue of that clause in the Constitution, which empowers Congress 'to make all needful rules and regulations, respecting the territory, or other property belonging to the United States.' " Indeed, Marshall emphatically asserted that the power of Congress to govern the territories "is unquestioned." From this major premise Marshall concluded that the Florida territorial government had the power to create a court with jurisdiction over maritime salvage.

The significance of *Canter* was Marshall's broad ruling on the power of Congress to govern the territories. In ***Dred Scott v. Sandford,*** 60 U.S. 393 (1857), Chief Justice Taney, over the dissents of Justices Curtis and McLean, would completely ignore this decision, when ruling that Congress had no power to prohibit slavery in the territories.

See Don E. Fehrenbacher, *The Dred Scott Case: Its Significance in American Law and Politics* (New York: Oxford University Press, 1978).

Van Ness v. Pacard

27 U.S. 137 (1829)
Decided: January 1829 Term
Vote: 6 (J. Marshall, Washington, W. Johnson, Duvall, Story, Thompson)
0
Opinion of the Court: Story

This minor real estate case reached the Supreme Court only because the property in question was in Washington, D.C., making the Court, acting as a state supreme court might have done, the final authority. The decision, however, led to a break with British precedent and a fundamental change in American property law. This outcome illustrates how the Court of the early nineteenth century reshaped the common law to create doctrine that served the needs and circumstances of the United States.

Perez Pacard, a carpenter, leased land in Washington for seven years from John P. Van Ness and his wife, Marcia. During the term of the lease, Pacard "erected a building, two stories high in front, with a cellar of stone or brick, and a shed of one story; and . . . the principal building, which had a brick chimney, rested upon this stone or brick foundation." Shortly before the lease expired, Pacard "took down and removed the said house from off the premises." Under traditional English land law, buildings added to rented property became part of the property and had to be left when the tenant vacated, and Van Ness sued for the value of the buildings. Pacard offered evidence that in Washington it was common practice for tenants to remove structures when they vacated rented land. The trial court refused to give instructions that would have aided Van Ness, and the jury returned a verdict for Pacard. Van Ness appealed to the Supreme Court, where his lawyer noted that "no case can be found, in which a building fixed to the freehold was allowed to be taken away."

Justice Story acknowledged that "the general rule of the common law certainly is, that whatever is once annexed to the freehold becomes part of it, and cannot afterwards be removed," but he added that this rule was not "inflexible and without exceptions." He noted the rule was generally construed more strictly when the transaction involved an executor who had use of the land and an heir who would eventually take possession of it. In that sense, the rule was designed to protect the interest of the heir, who could well be a minor when the tenancy or occupancy began. Story also noted the rule was construed "with much greater latitude between landlord and tenant in favor of the tenant." Furthermore, Story said that businesses were allowed to remove fixtures and structures connected to the business. Most important, Story argued that "the common law of England is not to be taken in all respects to be that of America." America was a "wilderness" when first settled by the English, and public policy and common sense worked "to encourage the tenant to devote himself to agriculture and to favor any erection which should aid this result; yet in the comparative poverty of the country, what tenant could afford to erect fixtures of much expense or value, if he was to lose his whole interest therein by the very act of erection?" Public policy therefore dictated a change in the common law.

Having set out these issues, Story returned to the English common law argument that a business could remove its structures from rented land. He concluded that Pacard's buildings, however elaborate, were for his business, despite the fact that his family also lived in them. He asserted that the residential aspects of the buildings were incidental—"merely and accessory"—to the business use of the buildings. Story created, in effect, a new common law for America. It fit with the fast-moving population that settled land and then pushed on. In rural or urban America, any building might be used for business—every farmhouse was part of a working farm. Thus, the Court favored a policy that would encourage tenants to improve land and add to the wealth and commerce of the nation. This policy would not harm landowners, although it would deprive them of the windfall that might come from a tenant erecting a house or shed on land and then having to turn that building over to the landlord at the end of the lease.

Willson v. Black Bird Creek Marsh Co.

27 U.S. 245 (1829)
Decided: March 20, 1829
Vote: 6 (J. Marshall, Washington, W. Johnson, Duvall, Story, Thompson)
0
Opinion of the Court: J. Marshall

In 1822 Delaware authorized Black Bird Creek Marsh Company to construct a dam across Black Bird Creek, which obstructed navigation there. Thompson Willson, who held a federal license to carry on a coasting trade, used his sloop to break through the dam. In response to a suit for the damage, Willson argued that the dam was illegal because it interfered with interstate commerce. Representing the company, the owner of the dam, attorney William Wirt argued that the power of Congress to regulate commerce could not "interfere with the rights of the States over the property within their boundaries." He argued that Black Bird Creek and surrounding marsh were unhealthy and the dam and subsequent draining of the marsh would "draw off the pestilence, and give to those who have before suffered from disease, health and vigor."

Chief Justice Marshall conceded that Black Bird Creek was in fact a navigable waterway and that Congress might, if it so chose, prohibit the damming of the waters. If this had happened, Marshall was fully prepared to strike the law down and uphold Willson's right to ram the illegal dam. Marshall also noted the relative insignificance of the creek, saying that such "small navigable creeks" were common "throughout the lower country of the Middle and Southern States" and that Congress had never regulated them.

The question for the Court was whether, in the absence of congressional regulation, a state might regulate a minor waterway. Marshall concluded it could. This case is often seen as a precursor of the "dormant commerce clause," because the chief justice wrote: "We do not think that the Act empowering the Black Bird Creek Marsh Company to place a dam across the creek, can, under all the circumstances of the case, be considered as repugnant to the power to regulate commerce in its dormant state, or as being in conflict with any law passed on the subject." Here, however, Marshall did not apply the dormant commerce clause, but instead argued that, in the absence of congressional power, the state was free to act. His opinion is also sometimes seen as indication of Marshall pulling back from the nationalist jurisprudence he asserted in ***Gibbons v. Ogden,*** 22 U.S. 1 (1824). Such a view might well overstate the narrow basis for the holding. An alternative analysis is that Marshall correctly saw Black Bird Creek as an insignificant stream that was simply too small for Congress to worry about. Moreover, he noted that the dam "probably improved . . . the health of the inhabitants," and this Marshall believed, was a power reserved to the states. His decision is clearly tied to the facts of the case, which included the general unimportance of the creek and Congress's utter lack of concern with it.

See Martin H. Redish and Shane V. Nugent, "The Dormant Commerce Clause and the Constitutional Balance of Federalism," *Duke Law Journal* (1987): 569; and R. Kent Newmyer, *Supreme Court Justice Joseph Story: Statesman of the Old Republic* (Chapel Hill: University of North Carolina Press, 1985).

Foster and Elam v. Neilson

27 U.S. 253 (1829)
Decided: January 1829 Term
Vote: 7 (J. Marshall, Washington, W. Johnson, Duvall, Story, Thompson, Trimble)
0
Opinion of the Court: J. Marshall

The expansion of the United States into lands once owned by Spain and France created a seemingly endless series of lawsuits over ownership. The cases reflect the complexity of merging two or even three systems of land law, combined with the often extraordinarily dynamic nature of the real estate market in the newly acquired territories.

In January 1804 Jayme Joydra purchased a large tract of land from the Spanish government about thirty miles east of the Mississippi River, in what was believed to be the Spanish colony known as West Florida. In May 1805 he sold a portion of this land to Joseph Marie de la Barba, who in turn, on the same day, sold half to Françoise Poinet. In June 1811 Poinet sold the land to James Foster and Pleasants Elam. In 1819 Spain ceded all of the Floridas to the United States. Meanwhile, David Neilson, a citizen of Louisiana, had taken up residence on this land, claiming that it had been part of the Louisiana territory, not part of West Florida. It was therefore land ceded to France and then sold to the United States in 1803 as part of the Louisiana Purchase. In other words, Neilson argued that the King of Spain did not own the land when he sold it to Joydra in 1804.

In his opinion Chief Justice Marshall noted that this case presented a "very intricate, and at the same time very interesting question: To whom did the country between the Iberville [River] and the Perdido [River] rightfully belong, when the title now asserted by the Plaintiffs was acquired?" The U.S. government claimed that this area, which is today in eastern Louisiana, was ceded by Spain to France in 1800 in the Treaty of St. Ildefonso and subsequently purchased by the United States in 1803. Spain, on the other hand, asserted that when she ceded Louisiana back to France in the Treaty of St. Ildefonso, this area remained Spanish and was considered part of West Florida. At issue then, was the meaning of the secret treaty of 1800 between Spain and France.

After reviewing numerous statements by the United States, Spain, and France, and a good deal of diplomatic material, Marshall concluded that the evidence could sustain either side in the case. "We shall say only, that the language of the article" in the treaty at issue "may admit of either construction, and it is scarcely possible to consider the arguments on either side without believing that they proceed from a conviction of their truth." Marshall, who had been a skilled diplomat before coming to the Court, pointed out that it would have been a simple matter for the treaty between Spain and France to have set out clear boundaries. He noted, with some irony, that "it is difficult to resist the persuasion that the ambiguity was intentional."

Courts, however, must ultimately resolve disputes, even when the evidence is unclear or subject to more than one valid interpretation. Marshall had no problem reaching a decision. He pointed out that the American construction of the treaty between France and Spain was "supported by argument of great strength which cannot be easily confuted." Nor did Marshall think it proper to try to confute them. In the end, he let nationalism decide the issue. Marshall wrote, "In a controversy between two nations concerning national boundary, it is scarcely possible that the courts of either should refuse to abide by the measures adopted by its own government. There being no common tribunal to decide between them, each determines for itself on its own rights."

On its face, Marshall's argument was absurd. He surely did not mean that in litigation over the meaning of a treaty the Supreme Court must always decide for the United States. Indeed, a little more than a decade later the Court emphatically rejected the government's interpretation of a treaty with Spain in ***United States v. Libellants and Claimants of the Schooner Amistad,*** 40 U.S. 518 (1841). In this case, Marshall used nationalism as the tie-breaker between two equally plausible interpretations of a treaty in which the United States was not a party.

Marshall held that the area in dispute had been ceded to France in 1800 and bought by the United States in 1803. Thus, in 1804 Spain had sold land it did not own, and, when Foster and Elam purchased the land, they in turn received it from someone who had no valid title to it.

1830–1839

LaGrange v. Chouteau

29 U.S. 287 (4 Pet. 287) (1830)
Decided: January 1830 Term
Vote: 7 (J. Marshall, W. Johnson, Duvall, Story, Thompson, McLean, Baldwin)
0
Opinion of the Court: J. Marshall

This case had the potential to raise issues about the meaning of the Northwest Ordinance, the nature of freedom in the United States, and interstate conflicts of laws. The decision could have nationalized the concept of freedom and localized slavery, but Chief Justice Marshall did not take that route.

Pascal Carré of St. Louis, Missouri, owned a slave named Francis LaGrange. Carré wanted to sell LaGrange and have him removed from St. Louis. Pierre Chouteau, a leading landowner and businessman in St. Louis, offered to buy LaGrange, but Carré refused to sell him to Chouteau, because Chouteau would keep LaGrange in St. Louis. As a favor to Chouteau, Pierre Menard, who lived in Kaskaskia, Illinois, bought LaGrange and sent him to work first in St. Genevieve, Missouri, and then on a riverboat. On at least two separate occasions, the boat docked in Kaskaskia, where LaGrange worked for a few days each time. Menard testified that he had no intention of making LaGrange a permanent resident of Illinois because he had purchased LaGrange only as a favor to Chouteau. He subsequently sold LaGrange to Chouteau for what he had paid for him.

LaGrange sued for his freedom in the Missouri courts, claiming that his residence in the free state of Illinois had made him free. This argument was consistent with the 1772 English case of *Somerset v. Stewart,* as well as some cases from Missouri, Kentucky, Louisiana, and Mississippi. The Missouri courts rejected LaGrange's arguments, essentially concluding that his casual residence and employment in Illinois did not constitute a sufficient connection with a free jurisdiction to change his status.

After hearing the case, the Supreme Court dismissed the suit, asserting that no act of Congress had been misconstrued. The Court might have considered Section VI of the Northwest Ordinance, which prohibited slavery in what had been the Northwest Territory. The Court ignored this issue. It arose later in ***Strader v. Graham,*** 51 U.S. 82 (1851), and more significantly in ***Dred Scott v. Sandford,*** 60 U.S. 393 (1857).

See Paul Finkelman, *An Imperfect Union: Slavery, Federalism, and Comity* (Chapel Hill: University of North Carolina Press, 1981).

Craig v. Missouri

29 U.S. 410 (4 Pet 410) (1830)
Decided: March 12, 1830
Vote: 4 (J. Marshall, Duvall, Story, Baldwin)
3 (W. Johnson, Thompson, McLean)
Opinion of the Court: J. Marshall
Dissenting opinion: W. Johnson
Dissenting opinion: Thompson
Dissenting opinion: McLean

Article I, Section 10, of the Constitution prohibits states from issuing "bills of credit," coining money, and making "any Thing but gold and silver Coin a Tender in Payment of Debts." The chronic shortage of gold and silver coins, especially in the West, as well as the cumbersome nature of metal coins, led the states to seek ways of circumventing this clause. Missouri issued "certificates" that it exchanged for promissory notes, which were to be paid back to the state, with interest. Under Missouri law these "certificates" could be used to pay taxes and other debts to the state. Hiram Craig received certificates from Missouri for $199.99 and, in exchange, gave a promissory note, agreeing to pay 2 percent interest on the debt. When the note came due, however, he refused to pay, arguing that the entire scheme violated the Constitution.

The Missouri Supreme Court upheld the scheme, and Craig appealed to the U.S. Supreme Court under Section 25 of the Judiciary Act of 1789. Just as Virginia had argued against the constitutionality of this law in ***Martin v. Hunter's Lessee,*** 14 U.S. 304 (1816), and ***Cohens v. Virginia,*** 19 U.S. 264 (1821), Missouri attacked the clause. Representing the state was its respected U.S. senator, Thomas Hart Benton, who complained that Missouri had been "summoned," "commanded," and "enjoined" to appear before the Court. He argued that these "terms" were not "fitting" for a state, even if, as he conceded, they were terms of art. Just as it had done in the earlier cases, the Court rejected the arguments that it did not have jurisdiction in the case. Even the dissenters sided, more or less, with Chief

Justice Marshall on this issue. Justice Thompson suggested that if the jurisdicational issue were one of first impression—that is, if this was the first time the Court had ever considered the question, he might not find Section 25 applicable in this case, but given existing precedent, Thompson was not ready to question the right of the Court to hear it. On the constitutionality of the Missouri law, however, there was little agreement.

Missouri had surely come close to creating its own system of currency. Indeed, in his dissenting opinion arguing that this scheme was constitutional, Justice Johnson conceded that Missouri came "as near to a violation of the constitution as it can well go, without violating its provision." A bare majority of the Court concluded that Missouri had stepped over the constitutional line, arguing that these "certificates" were really a form of paper money, which the Constitution forbade the states from issuing. Marshall reminded Missouri, and the nation, of the horrors of state paper currency during the period before the adoption of the Constitution. Marshall found them to be "bills of credit," and thus unconstitutionally created. The dissenters disagreed among themselves, but all believed the Missouri scheme did not violate the Constitution. Their view prevailed a few years later in ***Briscoe v. Bank of Kentucky,*** 36 U.S. 257 (1837), in which the Court, led by Chief Justice Taney, upheld a Kentucky law that allowed state banks to issue bank notes, which circulated as currency.

See Bray Hammond, *Banks and Politics in America from the Revolution to the Civil War* (Princeton: Princeton University Press, 1957); and Herman E. Krooss, *Documentary History of Banking and Currency in the United States* (New York: Chelsea House, 1977).

Providence Bank v. Billings

29 U.S. 514 (4 Pet. 514) (1830)
Decided: March 22, 1830
Vote: 7 (J. Marshall, W. Johnson, Duvall, Story, Thompson, McLean, Baldwin)
0
Opinion of the Court: J. Marshall

This case illustrates the changing and flexible nature of the Marshall Court in the last years of the chief justice's tenure. In 1791 Rhode Island gave a charter to Providence Bank. The Court had held in earlier cases, most notably, ***Dartmouth College v. Woodward,*** 17 U.S. 518 (1819), that a charter was a contract and a state could not abrogate charter rights without violating the Contract Clause of the Constitution. In 1822 Rhode Island passed a new statute, taxing all corporations in the state, including all state-chartered banks. Providence Bank refused to pay the tax, arguing that it was in effect an amendment to its 1791 charter and, as such, was unconstitutional.

At one time, Marshall and the other members of the Court might have accepted the bank's argument, but after 1830 it was no longer politic to do so. States' rights arguments, hostility to the Court, and growing sectional tendencies made the justices more circumspect in their approach to vested or charter rights. Moreover, the Court had come to understand that an overly rigid reading of the Contract Clause was inconsistent with the dynamic nature of the American economy. Marshall concluded that taxing an existing corporation did not in fact undermine its charter. In this decision, Marshall neither retreated from the support he had previously provided to chartered corporations nor rolled back any law protecting charters. Rather, Marshall simply pointed out that the 1792 charter did not promise the bank that it would be exempt from taxation. The charter, he said, "contains no stipulation promising exemption from taxation. The state, then, has made no express contract which has been impaired by the act of which the plaintiffs complain." Marshall noted that the bank had argued that the power to tax the bank was a power to destroy it—precisely the argument he had offered in defense of the Bank of the United States in ***McCulloch v. Maryland,*** 17 U.S. 316 (1819). Marshall conceded the strength of this argument, but said that the "power of taxing moneyed corporations has been frequently exercised, and has never before, so far as is known, been resisted." He noted that the taxing power is of such "vital importance" to a state that "the relinquishment of such a power is never to be assumed." That a tax might in theory destroy the bank was, in the end, not as important to Marshall as the notion that the states retained the power to tax the entities they created. Marshall rejected the analogy to the Bank of the United States, stating that in *McCulloch* and ***Osborn v. Bank of the United States,*** 22 U.S. 738 (1824), the Court had specifically limited its holding to the Bank of the United States because it was chartered by the national government.

In affirming the ruling of the Rhode Island Supreme Court, and in upholding the contract, Marshall did not attack the notion of vested rights. He merely pointed out that certain powers of the state, such as the right to tax, could not be read out of a charter by implication. Rather, the state retained the right to tax the bank unless it explicitly gave up that right in the charter. This case can be seen as a precursor to ***Charles River Bridge v. Warren Bridge,*** 36 U.S. 420 (1837). As in that case, here the Court read a charter strictly, but narrowly, and did not read into it an implication that the state had given up rights.

See Bray Hammond, *Banks and Politics in America from the Revolution to the Civil War* (Princeton: Princeton University Press, 1957); and Herman E. Krooss, *Documentary History of Banking and Currency in the United States* (New York: Chelsea House, 1977).

Cherokee Nation v. Georgia

30 U.S. 1 (5 Pet. 1) (1831)
Decided: March 18, 1831
Vote: 4 (J. Marshall, W. Johnson, McLean, Baldwin)
2 (Story, Thompson)
Opinion of the Court: J. Marshall for the Court
Concurring opinion: W. Johnson
Concurring opinion: Baldwin
Dissenting opinion: Thompson (Story)
Did not participate: Duvall

Cherokee Nation v. Georgia marked the beginning of a tragedy of national scale, leading to the forced removal of hundreds of thousands of Native Americans from the eastern portion of the United States. It also led to a diminished authority for the Supreme Court and lent encouragement to the states' rights/state sovereignty forces of the American South. All of these trends were furthered by the failure of President Andrew Jackson to support "the law of the land" in the case that followed this one, ***Worcester v. Georgia,*** 31 U.S. 515 (1832).

In 1828 and in 1829 Georgia passed laws claiming jurisdiction over lands ceded to the Cherokee under the Treaty of Hopewell (1785) and the Treaty of Holston (1791). The Cherokee took the issue to Supreme Court under its original jurisdiction because the suit was between a "foreign nation"—the Cherokee—and a state. The Cherokee sought an injunction to prevent the state from exercising jurisdiction over their lands. White Georgians, intent on forcing the Cherokee off their land and out of the state, had no intention of listening to the Supreme Court. Georgia had long had its eye on the Cherokee land, where the discovery of small amounts of gold only hastened the state's all-out assault on the Indians. Chief Justice Marshall undoubtedly hoped that the executive branch would accept its obligations to support and enforce the treaty rights of the Indians, but this outcome was unlikely, given President Jackson's hostility to Indians. Indeed, by the time of the decision, Jackson was already on record favoring the removal of all the eastern Indians.

The legal issues in this case seemed to be entirely with the Cherokee. They had a claim to their lands based on treaties with the national government. Under the Supremacy Clause of the Constitution, Georgia was obligated to accept these treaties as the law of the land. The political momentum, however, was entirely with Georgia. In December 1830 Georgia defied a writ of habeas corpus signed by Marshall on behalf of a Cherokee named Corn Tassel, who had been tried under Georgia law for a crime committed on Cherokee land. Rather than bringing Corn Tassel before a federal court, Georgia authorities executed him. Clearly, Georgia was unlikely to respect any decision Marshall rendered, and, just as clearly, President Jackson was unlikely to back Marshall.

In *Cherokee Nation* Marshall avoided a confrontation by finding that the Court lacked jurisdiction in the case. Marshall showed great sympathy for the Cherokee, a "people once numerous, powerful, and truly independent . . . gradually sinking beneath our superior policy, our arts, and our arms." He noted that the case was brought "to preserve this remnant" of a once great people. But, to help the Cherokee, the Court had to have jurisdiction to hear their case. Such jurisdiction came from the constitutional provision allowing the Court to hear cases between states and "foreign states." Marshall asked, "Is the Cherokee Nation a sovereign state in the sense in which that term is used in the Constitution?" At first glance, the answer would seem to be yes, because the Cherokee had signed treaties with the United States, but Marshall determined that "those tribes which reside within the acknowledged boundaries of the United States" could not "with strict accuracy, be denominated foreign nations." Rather, in language that still haunts American jurisprudence, Marshall declared that Indian tribes were "domestic dependent nations" that occupied land at the sufferance of the national government; they were in fact "in a state of pupilage." He found that their "relation to the United States resembles that of a ward to his guardian." Marshall therefore ruled that the Court lacked jurisdiction. He ended his opinion by saying that if the Cherokee had rights "this is not the tribunal in which those rights are to be asserted." In reaching this conclusion, Marshall helped seal the fate of the Cherokee, abdicating any judicial responsibility for the enforcement of treaty rights or for the protection of Indian lands and peoples. It is unlikely a different result would have led Jackson to do his duty to protect the Indians or enforce the treaties, but it would have helped the Court avoid the dishonor of its complicity in the assault on Indian rights and lands.

In dissent, Justice Thompson, with Story concurring, argued that the Court had jurisdiction over this case because it involved a treaty of the United States and that it was a suit between a foreign nation and state and, as such, was not barred by the Eleventh Amendment. Thompson offered a detailed and convincing analysis showing that in the light of congressional actions, treaties, and the common use of language, Indian tribes were "nations" within the meaning of Article III of the Constitution and that this case was properly within the original jurisdiction of the Supreme Court. Thompson then argued that on the merits of the case the Cherokees were entitled to relief. This issue seemed obvious: under various treaties the Cherokees had claims to certain lands, and Georgia had violated those rights.

Thompson's analysis was more logical and persuasive than Marshall's. It was humane and reasonable and, therefore, politically unacceptable to the majority. More important, it was unacceptable to President Jackson and the political leaders of Georgia. Although Marshall may have been in sympathy with Thompson, as his later opinion in *Worcester v. Georgia* showed,

Marshall was not prepared, at least at this time, to challenge political powers that he could not hope to defeat.

See Tim Alan Garrison, *The Legal Ideology of Removal: The Southern Judiciary and the Sovereignty of Native American Nations* (Athens: University of Georgia Press, 2002); Michael D. Green, *The Politics of Indian Removal* (Lincoln: University of Nebraska Press, 1982); R. Kent Newmyer, *Supreme Court Justice Joseph Story: Statesman of the Old Republic* (Chapel Hill: University of North Carolina Press, 1985); Jill Norgren, *The Cherokee Cases: The Confrontation of Law and Politics* (New York: McGraw Hill, 1995); and Theda Perdue and Michael D. Green, *The Cherokee Removal: A Brief History with Documents* (Boston: Bedford/St. Martins, 1995).

Worcester v. Georgia

31 U.S. 515 (6 Pet. 525) (1832)
Decided: March 3, 1832
Vote 5 (J. Marshall, Duvall, Story, Thompson, McLean)
1 (Baldwin)
Opinion of the Court: J. Marshall
Concurring opinion: McLean
Dissenting opinion: Baldwin
Did not participate: Johnson

In 1831 Georgia authorities arrested Samuel A. Worcester, a Congregational minister, for preaching on Cherokee lands without first obtaining a state license to reside on those lands as required by a Georgia act of 1830. State authorities offered to drop charges if he took a loyalty oath and left Cherokee lands. Worcester refused this offer and was convicted and sentenced to four years at hard labor. The Georgia law was an attempt by the state to assert authority over the Cherokee, in spite of federal treaties and the constitutional provision giving Congress plenary power over relations with the Indians. This law was in fact a first step in a process by which Georgia hoped to force all of the Cherokee out of the state.

This case came to the Court in the wake of ***Cherokee Nation v. Georgia,*** 30 U.S. 1 (1831), and clearly indicated that Georgia refused to accept the Marshall Court's interpretation in that case. Marshall's opinion implied that justice and the Constitution were with the Cherokee, even if the Court believed it lacked jurisdiction to give the tribe the injunction it sought. In *Cherokee Nation* Marshall signaled that he might find for the Cherokee if he had jurisdiction, although it seems equally clear he was trying to avoid a confrontation. In *Worcester v. Georgia* Chief Justice Marshall avoided the ambiguity present in *Cherokee Nation.* Although he did not specifically reject his earlier reference to Indian tribes as "domestic" or "dependent" nations, Marshall emphasized the autonomy of Indians and reaffirmed that only the national government could interfere with this autonomy. The chief justice rejected the idea that Georgia could assert any jurisdiction over the Cherokee.

Marshall found that the Cherokee, and by extension all Indian tribes, constituted a separate political entity with full control over their territory. Indian nations were "distinct, independent political communities, retaining their original natural rights." Marshall therefore declared that "the laws of Georgia can have no force" on Cherokee land, and that the "citizens of Georgia have no right to enter [Cherokee land] but with the assent of the Cherokees themselves."

Georgia officials were openly contemptuous of Marshall and his Court. They sent no counsel to argue the case and took no steps to implement Marshall's decision. In his opinion, the chief justice implied that the president had a duty to enforce the Court's decree just as he was obligated to enforce federal laws and treaties. President Andrew Jackson wanted no part of this duty. He allegedly responded to the opinion by declaring, "John Marshall has made his decision, now let him enforce it." In fact, Jackson had nothing to enforce, at least until Georgia formally refused to release Worcester from jail. Seeking to avoid a crisis, Marshall adjourned the Court shortly after announcing the decision, thereby putting off until the following year a confrontation between the state authorities and the Court.

Jackson's refusal to enforce the treaties with the Cherokee, combined with the enormous pressure from Georgia and other southern states to open Indian lands to white settlement, did not bode well for Worcester or Marshall's opinion. Jackson soon moved to a new policy that would placate the Georgia government: Indian removal. In 1835 the Cherokee, under great coercion, agreed to vacate their land in Georgia and move to the newly created Indian Territory in present-day Oklahoma. Their journey west, which took place over the rest of the decade, is remembered as the "trail of tears," as thousands died on the trek. Other eastern Indians soon followed the Cherokee to Oklahoma.

The response to *Worcester* illustrates the institutional weakness of the Supreme Court in this period, as well as the relentless determination of whites and the federal and state governments to take over Indian lands. Georgia's response also set the stage for states' rights arguments that would lead to secession three decades later. The nullification crisis with South Carolina later that year forced Jackson to confront that state's blatant defiance of federal law. South Carolina had threatened to use force to prevent the enforcement of a federal tariff, while declaring the tariff null within its boarders. Jackson responded with threats of military force, and South Carolina backed down. Georgia and most of the other slave states sided with Jackson in the nullification crisis. Once the crisis passed, Jackson persuaded the governor of Georgia to commute Worcester's sentence to avoid any further confrontations arising from this case. With Jackson's support, Georgia was winning its battle against Marshall and the Cherokee. Once the Cherokee were on their way out of Georgia, the governor could release Worcester from prison without any great consequence. In January 1833 the governor agreed to let Worcester go in exchange for his promise to leave the state. In 1835 Worcester joined the Cherokee on their march to Oklahoma, where he died in 1859. In 1992 Gov. Zell Miller of Georgia posthumously pardoned him.

See Tim Alan Garrison, *The Legal Ideology of Removal: The Southern Judiciary and the Sovereignty of Native American Nations* (Athens: University of Georgia Press, 2002); Michael D. Green, *The Politics of Indian Removal* (Lincoln: University of Nebraska Press, 1982); R. Kent Newmyer, *Supreme Court Justice Joseph Story: Statesman of the Old Republic* (Chapel Hill: University of North Carolina Press, 1985); Jill Norgren, *The Cherokee Cases: The Confrontation of Law and Politics* (New York: McGraw Hill, 1995); and Theda Perdue and Michael D. Green, *The Cherokee Removal: A Brief History with Documents* (Boston: Bedford/St. Martins, 1995).

Barron v. Baltimore

32 U.S. 243 (7 Pet. 243) (1833)
Decided: February 16, 1833
Vote: 7 (J. Marshall, W. Johnson, Duvall, Story, Thompson, McLean, Baldwin)
0
Opinion of the Court: J. Marshall

John Barron owned a wharf in Baltimore. The wharf became virtually worthless after city construction projects made the water surrounding it too shallow for most ships. Barron claimed that the city projects had in effect taken his property for public use without just compensation. At the time Maryland's constitution did not have a "takings" clause, so Barron sued the city under the Fifth Amendment of the U.S. Constitution. The state court dismissed the suit, asserting that the Fifth Amendment did not apply to the states.

Chief Justice Marshall held that the Fifth Amendment did not apply to the states; indeed, none of the provisions of the first eight amendments to the Constitution applied to the states. He asserted that the Constitution was adopted "by the people of the United States . . . for their own national government, and not for the government of the individual states." This simple, straightforward reading was consistent with the history of the drafting of the Bill of Rights. When James Madison introduced the Bill of Rights in Congress, he included specific limitations on state action, but Congress removed them from the proposed amendments.

In the 1850s many Republicans argued that *Barron* was wrongly decided and that the states could not suppress freedom of speech, press, and assembly, as the southern states did in trying to silence abolitionists. Among those taking this position was Rep. John A. Bingham, R-Ohio, who later became the primary author of the Fourteenth Amendment. When he drafted the Privileges and Immunities Clause of that amendment, Bingham believed it could be used to overturn *Barron.* But, in the ***Slaughterhouse Cases,*** 83 U.S. 36 (1873), the Court rejected this theory. *Barron* remained good law until the decision in ***Gitlow v. New York,*** 268 U.S. 652 (1925), in which the Court began to use the Due Process Clause of the Fourteenth Amendment to apply the Bill of Rights to the states.

See Michael Kent Curtis, *No State Shall Abridge: The Fourteenth Amendment and the Bill of Rights* (Durham: Duke University Press, 1986).

Wheaton v. Peters

33 U.S. 591 (8 Pet. 591) (1834)
Decided: March 18, 1834
Vote: 4 (J. Marshall, Story, Duvall, McLean)
2 (Thompson, Baldwin)
Opinion of the Court: McLean
Dissenting opinion: Thompson
Dissenting opinion: Baldwin
Did not participate: Johnson

In 1828 Richard Peters replaced Henry Wheaton as the official reporter for the Supreme Court. Wheaton was tired of the job and happily accepted when President John Quincy Adams appointed him ambassador to Denmark. At the time the Court reporter operated as a semi-independent contractor. After supplying the number of copies of the Court's opinions as required under his contract, the reporter was free to sell others at a profit. To increase his income, Peters embarked on a plan to sell a condensed version of all Supreme Court reports, including those done by his predecessors. The condensed versions would omit all head notes and lawyers' argument and reduce concurrences and dissents to an "abbreviated form."

William Cranch, Court reporter from 1801 to 1815, and Wheaton (1816–1827) objected to this proposed publication as violating their copyright interests. Peters responded privately that he was not republishing their notes or any of their contributions to the reports, but only the facts of the cases and the opinions of the justices, some of which he would edit. Nevertheless, in May 1831 Wheaton and his New York publisher, Robert Donaldson, filed a suit to prevent Peters from publishing the third volume of their reports. In 1833 the circuit court for Pennsylvania dissolved the injunction, asserting that Wheaton had never perfected his copyright under the federal law. In fact, Wheaton had failed to follow the rules for copyright set out in the Copyright Acts of 1790 and 1802. He nevertheless argued for a common law right of copyright, based on the fact that he had edited and published the volumes.

The real problem for Wheaton, however, was the larger question: Could *anyone* copyright the opinions of Supreme Court justices? On this point the Court was clear and in total agreement. Justice McLean's opinion ends with the statement: "It may be proper to remark that the court are unanimously of opinion that no reporter has or can have any copyright in the written opinions delivered by this court; and that the judges thereof cannot confer on any reporter such a right." The Court was divided on any common law or statutory rights that Wheaton might have had in the notes and other materials he published in his reports. In fact, the justices were completely confused and in disagreement and could not muster a clear majority on any of the issues. The Court remanded the case to the circuit court for a trial on what claims Wheaton might have against Peters, and eventually their estates settled out of court.

The major issue in the case, and its importance for American law, was the conclusion that the opinions of justices and by extension other documents written by public officials acting in their official capacity belonged to the public. Such documents were forever in the public domain and immune from copyright.

See G. Edward White, *The Marshall Court and Cultural Change, 1815–1835* (New York: Macmillan, 1988).

New York v. Miln

36 U.S. 102 (11 Pet. 102) (1837)
Decided: February 16, 1837
Vote: 6 (Taney, Thompson, McLean, Baldwin, Wayne, Barbour)
1 (Story)
Opinion of the Court: Barbour
Concurring opinion: Thompson
Concurring opinion: Baldwin
Dissenting opinion: Story

A New York State statute of 1824 required ships' masters to report the names and ages, as well as other information, of all passengers brought into the state. George Miln was the consignee of *The Emily,* whose master failed to comply with the law. Miln argued the law was an unconstitutional interference with interstate and international commerce. New York argued the statute was necessary to control the immigration of poor people who might become a burden on the state. New York sued Miln to recover $15,000 in penalties, when he failed to follow the requirements of the statute. The law was consistent with English statutes that had allowed towns to prevent the settlement of paupers, but the New York law also seemed to be an attempt to regulate international commerce, which states could not do.

Miln was the first major Commerce Clause case to come to the Court under Chief Justice Taney. If the Court had followed the precedent of ***Gibbons v. Ogden,*** 22 U.S. 1 (1824), the decision would have been relatively simple. In *Gibbons,* one of Chief Justice Marshall's most popular decisions, the Court held that the transportation of people was a form of commerce that came under the jurisdiction of Congress. The New York statute seemed to clearly burden interstate commerce.

For the Taney Court, however, the case was far more complicated. By 1837 most of the slave states had prohibited the migration of free blacks. Starting in 1822, South Carolina and other southern coastal states had adopted laws requiring the incarceration of free black sailors who entered their ports as crewmembers from visiting ships. In *Elkison v. Deliesseline,* 8 F. Cas. 493 (1823), Justice Johnson, while riding circuit, had declared in dicta—the parts of an opinion that are not essential to the decision—that such laws were unconstitutional. But he had also asserted that he lacked jurisdiction in the case and had not intervened in South Carolina's enforcement of the laws. If the Court found that the statute in *Miln* violated the Commerce Clause, the Court would soon face the issue of free blacks entering the slave states.

The Court avoided these difficult issues by upholding New York's law as a "regulation . . . of police," rather than a regulation of commerce and by declaring that the exercise of this power "rightfully belonged to the States." The Court asserted that "a state has" an "undeniable and unlimited jurisdiction over all persons and things within its territorial limits" and may regulate its own population "to advance the safety, happiness and prosperity of its people." The Court let the nation know that the states were free to pass "inspection laws, quarantine laws, health laws of every description, as well as laws for regulating the internal commerce of the State."

This decision allowed the slave states, and some of the free states as well, to limit the in-migration of free blacks. It also permitted slave states and free states to ban the importation of slaves. Perhaps more critical, it allowed states to regulate immigration at a time when the national government did not do so. After the Civil War the Court began to interpret the Fourteenth Amendment as preventing states from interfering with the internal migration of Americans, and eventually the national government also assumed the regulation of foreign immigration. The police powers doctrine articulated in *Miln,* however, remains an integral part of American constitutional law and an important component of federalism. In dissent, Justice Story argued that the New York law was a violation of the Commerce Clause.

See R. Kent Newmyer, *Supreme Court Justice Joseph Story: Statesman of the Old Republic* (Chapel Hill: University of North Carolina Press, 1985); Carl B. Swisher, *The Taney Period, 1836–1864* (New York: Macmillan, 1974); and Melvin I. Urofsky and Paul Finkelman, *A March of Liberty: A Constitutional History of the United States,* 2 vols. (New York: Oxford University Press, 2002).

Briscoe v. Bank of the Commonwealth of Kentucky

36 U.S. 257 (11 Pet. 257) (1837)
Decided: February 11, 1837
Vote: 6 (Taney, Thompson, McLean, Baldwin, Wayne, Barbour)
1 (Story)
Opinion of the Court: McLean
Concurring opinion: Thompson
Concurring opinion: Baldwin
Dissenting opinion: Story

This case is one in a series decided in 1837 that marked Roger Taney's first full term as chief justice and signaled his Court's break with the traditions and jurisprudence of the Marshall Court. The decision reflected not only Taney's more flexible constitutional jurisprudence but also the Jacksonian policy of deference to states and hostility to a national banking system. Although it did not overturn any Marshall Court decisions, the case undermined Marshall's jurisprudence on banking and currency.

Article I, Section 10, of the Constitution prohibits states from issuing "bills of credit," coining money, or making "any Thing but gold and silver Coin a Tender in Payment of Debts." The chronic shortage of gold and silver coins, especially in the West, as well as the cumbersome nature of metal coins, led the states to seek ways of circumventing this clause. In ***Craig v. Missouri,*** 29 U.S. 410 (1830), the Court struck down Missouri's system of issuing certificates that could be used to pay state taxes and other debts to the state and therefore function as currency.

Kentucky responded to the chronic shortage of specie, and to the dominance of the Bank of the United States, by chartering the Bank of the Commonwealth of Kentucky. This bank was not private: the Kentucky General Assembly chose the bank's president and directors, the state owned all of the bank's stock, and all taxes and other monies collected by the state were to be deposited in the bank. The bank issued its own notes, which it loaned to borrowers, in the same way a bank might loan specie then or currency today. These notes could be used to pay taxes to the state. Dividends earned by the bank were to be paid into the state treasury.

In 1830 John Briscoe borrowed from the bank and instead of specie (gold or silver) received bank-issued notes. When the debt was due, Briscoe refused to pay, arguing that he had received nothing of value from the bank because the bank notes were illegal and issued in violation of the Constitution's ban on states emitting bills of credit. He argued that the bank, as a state agency, was equivalent to the state itself. The bank won in the state courts, and Briscoe appealed to the Supreme Court, citing *Craig* as the controlling precedent. Sen. Henry Clay of Kentucky represented the bank. Clay, the leader of the Whig Party, was a rival of Andrew Jackson and an opponent in many ways of Taney.

By the time the Court heard this case, the Bank of the United States had ceased to exist as a national institution, the nation was in a depression, and money was in short supply. Justice McLean asserted that no case previously heard by the Court "exceeded," and few had "equalled, the importance of that which arises in this case." The question for the Court was whether the bank notes constituted "bills of credit" or, in more modern terms, currency issued by the state. After a detailed analysis of the bank, McLean concluded that the notes were not bills of credit because they were not backed by the full faith and credit of the state. Rather, they were bank notes, issued by a private corporation, which happened to be owned by the state. At the time, it was common for private banks to issue notes, which circulated as currency, and no one questioned the constitutionality of this practice. McLean concluded that for purposes of issuing notes, the Bank of the Commonwealth of Kentucky should be seen as a private bank.

In dissent, Justice Story argued that such reasoning was fundamentally flawed. For Story, the bank was a creature of the state, and therefore its notes constituted state currency. Story ended an extraordinarily long dissent by saying, "Mr. Chief Justice Marshall is not here to speak for himself," but if he were, he would also find the Kentucky scheme unconstitutional.

At issue for McLean and Story, was the future of banking and currency policy in the United States. The Jacksonians, led in part by Taney, had destroyed the Bank of the United States and with it the nation's currency system. State banks, such as the one in Kentucky, offered a local, state-centered solution to the nation's need for currency. If Story's argument had prevailed, the state banks would have been removed from the equation, and, like it or not, the Jacksonians might have been forced to support a national bank. With a Jacksonian majority on the Court, however, the state banks prevailed.

See Bray Hammond, *Banks and Politics in America from the Revolution to the Civil War* (Princeton: Princeton University Press, 1957); Herman E. Krooss, *Documentary History of Banking and Currency in the United States* (New York: Chelsea House, 1977); and Melvin I. Urofsky and Paul Finkelman, *A March of Liberty: A Constitutional History of the United States,* 2 vols. (New York: Oxford University Press, 2002).

Charles River Bridge v. Warren Bridge

36 U.S. 420 (11 Pet. 420) (1837)
Decided: February 12, 1837
Vote: 4 (Taney, Baldwin, Wayne, Barbour)
3 (McLean, Story, Thompson)
Opinion of the Court: Taney
Concurring opinion: Baldwin
Dissenting opinion: McLean
Dissenting opinion: Story
Dissenting opinion: Thompson

One of the classic cases of the Taney Court, *Charles River Bridge v. Warren Bridge* helped settle the boundaries between vested rights based on charters and contracts and the states' need to respond to changing technologies and economic realities in the early nineteenth century.

In 1785 the new state of Massachusetts issued a charter to the Charles River Bridge Company to build a bridge over the Charles River, to link Boston to Charlestown. The company was granted a forty-year charter, but in 1792 the charter was extended to seventy years, as compensation for allowing another bridge over the river. By 1805 the Charles River Bridge was collecting about $20,000 a year in tolls, and it became even more profitable as the populations of Boston and Charlestown grew. In 1828 the state authorized the construction of another bridge located about 260 feet from the older bridge on the Charlestown side and about 900 feet from the terminus of the older bridge the Boston side. The Warren Bridge opened six months later. It charged the same toll as the Charles River Bridge, but the new structure was to be turned over to the state as a free bridge after the company had recovered its costs plus interest on the investment. Consumers therefore had an incentive to use the new bridge, and revenues quickly declined for the Charles River Bridge.

The proprietors of the Charles River Bridge asserted that the state had violated the Contract Clause of the Constitution by chartering the new bridge. Charles River Bridge claimed that its charter was implicitly a monopoly. The basis of this claim was two-fold. First, the bridge company was the legal successor to a ferry operation owned by Harvard University. In 1650 the Massachusetts colony had granted Harvard a monopoly to operate the ferry, and the Charles River Bridge proprietors claimed that the monopoly had passed to the bridge company in 1785. Their second argument was one of economic logic: no company would invest the large sums of money necessary to build a bridge unless it was given a monopoly. The bridge owners argued that new emerging railroad industry would be harmed if investors could not rely on the state to give railroads a monopoly over their routes.

Chief Justice Taney, in his first major opinion, asserted that the charter had to be read strictly and "interpreted by its own terms." The charter for the Charles River Bridge did not give the bridge owners a monopoly, nor could a monopoly be read into the charter. Taney argued that the "interests" of society outweighed the implied rights of investors. He said that an alternative reading of the bridge charter would be a disaster for newer technologies. He predicted that the older private road and turnpike companies, many of which were no longer economically important, would be "awakening from their sleep" to demand compensation for the railroad tracks that were paralleling their routes.

Taney enunciated a strong assertion of state power that in some ways mirrored the earlier language of Chief Justice Marshall. Taney declared: "The object and end of all government is to promote the happiness and prosperity of the community by which it is established; and it can never be assumed that the government intended to diminish its power of accomplishing the end for which it was created." He noted that in the United States "new channels of communication are daily found necessary, for both travel and trade, and are essential to the comfort, convenience and prosperity of the people." Government charters and grants had to be construed strictly. "A state ought never be presumed to surrender this power" because "the whole community" had "an interest in" the state's "undiminished" power to create and help new technologies and businesses.

Justice Story, in dissent, agreed with Taney that the state had to retain its power to stimulate change and growth, but, he argued, there was "no surer plan to arrest all public improvements, founded on private capital and enterprise, than to make the outlay of that capital uncertain and questionable." Taney's decision, in Story's mind, would scare off investors "in bridges, or turnpikes, or canals, or railroads."

After this decision, most states and most investors avoided the problems that Story predicted by following the strict notions of vested rights Taney had set out. Investors seeking charters for railroads, bridges, and other enterprises, made sure that their rights, including their monopoly or exclusive rights to certain routes or markets, were explicitly protected in their charters.

See Stanley I. Kutler, *Privilege and Creative Destruction: The Charles River Bridge Case* (Philadelphia: Lippincott, 1971); and R. Kent Newmyer, "Justice Joseph Story, the Charles River Bridge Case and the Crisis of Republicanism," *American Journal of Legal History* 17 (July 1973) 232–245.

Kendall v. United States ex rel. Stokes

37 U.S. 524 (12 Pet. 524) (1838)
Decided: March 12, 1838
Vote: 6 (Story, Thompson, McLean, Baldwin, Wayne, McKinley)
3 (Taney, Barbour, Catron)
Opinion of the Court: Thompson
Dissenting opinion: Taney (Catron)
Dissenting opinion: Barbour (Catron)

President Andrew Jackson's first postmaster general, John McLean of Ohio, brought honesty and efficiency to a department that was unwieldy and often corrupt. When Jackson appointed McLean to the Supreme Court, the new postmaster general, William Barry, proved to be incompetent. Under Barry, corruption in the post office was widespread, with various contractors being overpaid. In 1835 Jackson replaced Barry with Amos Kendall, who vowed to clean up the corruption. In carrying out his promise, Kendall refused to honor claims of the Stokes and Stockton firm. The aggrieved contractors appealed to Congress, which passed a special act directing the solicitor of the Treasury Department to investigate the matter. The postmaster general was ordered to credit the account of Stokes and Stockton with the amount the Treasury Department determined was owed. The solicitor investigated and awarded Stokes and Stockton the entire amount they claimed plus an additional amount of about $40,000. The outraged Kendall credited the account for the original amount claimed, but not the additional money. The Senate then passed a resolution directing Kendall to pay the extra money. When Kendall refused, Stokes and Stockton sought a writ of mandamus to force Kendall to pay.

The Court held that a writ of mandamus could properly be directed at the postmaster general, compelling him to do what was in effect a ministerial duty of crediting the account of a contractor. The Court rejected Kendall's claim that as an officer of the executive branch, he could take orders only from the president and that Congress could not require him to perform a specific action of any kind. The Court found that the act of Congress authorizing that the account be credited left "no room for the exercise of any discretion, official or otherwise; all that is shut out by the direct and positive command of the law, and the act required to be done is, in every just sense, a mere ministerial act."

This case was complicated by politics and the taint of corruption. The claims of Stokes and Stockton were almost certainly inflated, and the contract itself was probably a result of political connections and favoritism. The solicitor of the Treasury, who sided with Stokes and Stockton, was a close friend of the claimants. Even so, the ruling of the Court was solid. It reflected a jurisprudential notion going back at least to ***Fletcher v. Peck,*** 10 U.S. 87 (1810), that the Court could not look behind the politics of a contract or a law, but only at the contract or law before it. If corruption was involved, that was a political matter, beyond the reach of the Court. The case before the Court was simple: an act of Congress had directed an executive branch officer to spend money in a certain way, and, once that law was in place, no discretion was available to the executive branch.

See R. Kent Newmyer, *Supreme Court Justice Joseph Story: Statesman of the Old Republic* (Chapel Hill: University of North Carolina Press, 1985); and Carl B. Swisher, *The Taney Period, 1836–1864* (New York: Macmillan, 1974).

Bank of Augusta v. Earle

38 U.S. 519 (13 Pet. 519) (1839)
Decided: March 9, 1839
Vote: 8 (Taney, Story, Thompson, McLean, Baldwin, Wayne, Barbour, Catron)
1 (McKinley)
Opinion of the Court: Taney
Concurring without opinion: Baldwin
Dissenting opinion: McKinley

This case arose when two Alabamans, Joseph B. Earle and William D. Primrose, refused to make payments on bills of exchange drawn on out-of-state corporations. They claimed that the corporations could not legally do business or sue in Alabama and therefore the bills were void. The plaintiffs were the Bank of Augusta, the Bank of the United States (which by this time was a Pennsylvania corporation), and the New Orleans and Carrollton Railroad. Earle owed the Bank of Augusta and the railroad more than $11,000, and Primrose owed the Bank of United States more than $5,000. In the circuit court, Justice McKinley, who was from Alabama, ruled for the defendants. On appeal, the eight other members of the Taney Court overruled McKinley.

The case raised the question whether a state could exclude a foreign (out-of-state) corporation from operating within its boundaries under its general police powers. Most commentators, and a majority of the Court, agreed that by statute a state might exclude foreign corporations from operating within its jurisdiction. In this case, however, no specific statutes banned the foreign corporations—two banks and a railroad—from dealing in bills of exchange in Alabama.

Early in his opinion, Chief Justice Taney noted that this case was "of a very grave character," involving "a multitude of corporations" and "contracts to a very great amount." Indeed, at issue was the entire structure of American business. If corporations could not safely do business in different states, the capital markets would collapse, as would a great deal of trade and commerce.

Taney agreed that a corporation could have "no legal existence out of the boundaries of the sovereignty by which it is created." He also said that a corporation did not have all the rights of a natural person; rather, its legal existence and rights were defined by the chartering state. Although a corporation could not "live" in another state, or "migrate" to another state, Taney found no reason why it could not do business in another state and no reason why its "existence . . . will not be recognized in other places." Taney acknowledged that the states had to consent to an out-of-state, or foreign, corporation doing business in its jurisdiction, but he did not believe this consent needed to be explicit; if a state did not expressly prohibit a particular out-of-state corporation or an entire class of corporations from doing business, its silence implied consent. According to Taney, under theories of comity and international law, foreign corporations should be allowed to do business in other states, unless explicitly prohibited from doing so. States were free to pass reasonable regulations of foreign corporations or even ban them altogether from conducting business within their boundaries, but no implied theory of limitations on corporations existed. Alabama had not prohibited out-of-state banks or railroads from dealing in bills of exchange, and therefore the bills were valid, and the corporations had the right to vindicate their rights and interests in the courts.

This decision was seen as a great victory for the business interests of the nation. Politically, it was a victory of sorts for the Whigs, such as Daniel Webster, who argued the case for the Bank of the United States. In reality, it showed that the Taney Court, dominated by Jacksonian Democrats, understood that a national economy could not be subservient to the states' rights claims of the more populist and narrowly focused elements of the Democratic Party. In the wake of Jackson's assaults on the Bank of the United States, in which Taney had been intimately involved, this decision sent a strong message that the Court and the chief justice were not ideological purists or opponents of economic growth.

The decision left states free to regulate business within their borders, and many states did pass statutes controlling out-of-state corporations. In the absence of federal regulation of interstate companies, these regulations probably had an overall beneficial influence, although they frequently proved confusing. Eventually, however, after the adoption of the Fourteenth Amendment in 1868, the Court began to treat corporations as having the same rights as natural persons, thus expanding the thrust of *Bank of Augusta* and in the process removing from states the power, in most cases, to limit foreign corporations. However, various federal laws would still allow states to regulate—and exclude—foreign banks and insurance companies.

See Carl B. Swisher, *The Taney Period, 1836–1864* (New York: Macmillan, 1974).

1840–1849

Holmes v. Jennison

39 U.S. 540 (14 Pet. 540) (1840)
Decided: March 4, 1840
Vote: 4 (Taney, Story, McLean, Wayne)
4 (Thompson, Baldwin, Barbour, Catron)
Seriatim opinion: Taney (Story, McLean, Wayne)
Seriatim opinion: Thompson
Seriatim opinion: Baldwin
Seriatim opinion: Barbour
Seriatim opinion: Catron
Did not participate: McKinley

George Holmes was indicted for murder in Lower Canada (Quebec). He fled to Vermont, where Gov. Silas H. Jenison, acting on a request from the governor of Lower Canada, ordered that Holmes be arrested and held for extradition. Holmes appealed to the Supreme Court of Vermont for a writ of habeas corpus, arguing that Canada and the United States had no agreement or treaty that would allow for his extradition. The Vermont court denied the writ, and Holmes appealed directly to the Supreme Court.

The case brought two quite different questions to the Court. First, could the Supreme Court review the denial of a writ of habeas corpus by a state court? Second, could a state official authorize a foreign extradition or was international extradition solely a matter for the national government? With Justice McKinley absent for the entire term, the Court voted four to four, leaving intact the Vermont decision denying the writ of habeas corpus.

Chief Justice Taney wrote a strongly nationalistic opinion, in which he supported federal power and rejected states' rights arguments. He said that international extradition was entirely a matter for the executive branch of the federal government. The issue did not, in Taney's mind, affect the police powers of Vermont or any other state; rather, it was "part of the foreign intercourse of this country" and the power to regulate that had "undoubtedly been conferred on the federal government." Taney asserted that the Constitution's clause declaring that "no state shall enter into any treaty, alliance, or confederation" should be construed broadly as prohibiting the states from entering into any "agreement" or "compact" with a foreign nation. Because of this, Taney and the three justices sided with him—as members of a federal court—were prepared to grant the writ of habeas corpus on the theory that Vermont lacked the power to comply with the extradition requisition of a foreign power.

The other four justices, each writing separately, did not believe that the Supreme Court could review a habeas corpus case from a state court, a classic example of states' rights theory at the time. Although Taney often supported states' rights, in this case he offered a strong theory of federal supremacy and constitutional nationalism. His opinion may be a reflection of his experience as an executive branch officer in the Jackson administration. Justice McLean, who had also been in Jackson's cabinet, agreed with this position. Although Justice Thompson did not think the Court had jurisdiction in the case, he also believed that Vermont could not constitutionally extradite Holmes to a foreign country. Because he denied jurisdiction, his views on this matter could not affect the outcome of the case, but they did influence the Vermont Supreme Court, which reconsidered its position, noted that five of the eight justices did not believe Vermont had the power to extradite a person to a foreign country, and voted to release Holmes. In 1842 the Webster-Ashburton Treaty provided for extradition between the United States and Canada.

See Howard Jones, *To the Webster-Ashburton Treaty: A Study in Anglo-American Relations, 1783–1843* (Chapel Hill: University of North Carolina Press, 1977).

Groves v. Slaughter

40 U.S. 449 (15 Pet. 449) (1841)
Decided: March 10,1841
Vote: 5 (Taney, Thompson, McLean, Baldwin, Wayne)
2 (Story, McKinley)
Opinion of the Court: Thompson
Concurring opinion: Taney
Concurring opinion: McLean
Concurring opinion: Baldwin
Dissenting without opinion: Story, McKinley
Did not participate: Catron

The Mississippi Constitution of 1832 prohibited the importation of slaves into the state "as merchandise, or for sale." The provision was not an attempt to limit slavery in Mississippi; rather, it was an attempt to prevent an outflow of capital from

Mississippi to other states. Migrants to the state were free to bring slaves with them, and, by implication, settlers or residents in the state could probably also bring newly purchased slaves into the state. But slaves could not be brought into the state as merchandise and then sold. In 1836 Moses Groves, a Mississippi planter, purchased slaves from Robert Slaughter of Louisiana, giving him note for $7,000. When the note came due, Groves refused to honor it, claiming that the sale of slaves in Mississippi violated the state constitution. Significantly, Groves did not offer to return the slaves. Slaughter successfully sued Groves in Louisiana federal court, and Groves appealed to the Supreme Court. Groves was represented by Robert Walker, one of Mississippi's U.S. senators. Slaughter retained the services of Henry Clay and Daniel Webster. Beyond the immediate parties, more than $3 million was at stake because of the numerous slaves sold to planters in Mississippi.

In a straightforward opinion, Justice Thompson ruled that the Mississippi constitutional provision was not in force until 1837, when Mississippi passed enabling legislation. The contract for sale of slaves from 1836 was therefore valid, and Groves was obligated to pay Slaughter. In reaching this conclusion, Thompson avoided the central constitutional question: Did Mississippi's ban on slaves as merchandise violate the Commerce Clause of the U.S. Constitution?

Thompson avoided the issue, but the three concurring justices did not. They supported the result—that Groves would be paid what was owed him—on the theory that the constitutional provision was not self-executing, but they insisted on preserving the right of the states to limit slavery.

Justice McLean, who was from Ohio, endorsed the idea that Congress could regulate all interstate commerce, noting that the "necessity of a uniform commercial regulation, more than any other consideration, led to the adoption of the federal Constitution." Having taken this strong position, McLean asserted that slaves were not "merchandise" under the Commerce Clause, but "persons," and as such, the states were free to prohibit the introduction of slaves into their domains. McLean asserted that Ohio could not ban the importation "of the cotton of the south, or the manufactured articles of the north," but he defended the right of his home state to ban slaves. He asserted that "the power over slavery belongs to the states respectively. It is local in its character, and in its effects; and the transfer or sale of slaves cannot be separated from this power. It is, indeed, an essential part of it." Here McLean's antislavery stance dovetailed with proslavery arguments that the national government could not touch slavery in the states where it existed. This dovetailing was mere coincidence. McLean took this position to protect the North's right to exclude slaves. He wrote: "The right to exercise this power [to exclude slaves], by a state is higher and deeper than the Constitution." He declared slavery "evil" and insisted that his state could have nothing to do with it. Implicit in McLean's arguments, however, was the notion that Congress might have the power to regulate or even ban the interstate slave trade.

Chief Justice Taney rejected the idea that Congress could ever regulate the slave trade. He was adamant that the "power over this subject is exclusively with the several states; and each of them has a right to decide for itself whether it will or will not allow persons of this description to be brought within its limits, from another states, either for sale, or for any other purpose."

Justice Baldwin agreed with the result, but rejected McLean's claims that the states were free to exclude slavery. Baldwin, a doughface Democrat (a northerner with southern principles) from Pennsylvania, asserted that the free states could not exclude owners traveling with their slaves. In essence, Baldwin suggested that Congress might be able to regulate the movement of slaves, but only to protect slavery.

All of the justices seemed agreed that the Commerce Clause of the U.S. Constitution "did not interfere with the provision of the constitution of the State of Mississippi, which relates to the introduction of slaves as merchandise, or for sale." Justices Story and McKinley dissented from the majority, holding, "both these justices considering the note sued upon void."

This case did not settle any great constitutional issues. Instead, it was a preview of the debates over slavery that would confound the Court and Congress for the next two decades.

See Paul Finkelman, *An Imperfect Union: Slavery, Federalism, and Comity (Chapel Hill: University of North Carolina Press, 1981);* Paul Finkelman, *Slavery in the Courtroom* (Washington, D.C.: Library of Congress, 1985); Felix Frankfurter, *The Commerce Clause Under Marshall, Taney and Waite* (Chapel Hill: University of North Carolina Press, 1937); and Harold M. Hyman and William M. Wiecek, *Equal Justice Under Law: Constitutional Development, 1835–1875* (New York: W. W. Norton, 1982).

United States v. Libellants and Claimants of the Schooner Amistad

Also known as The Amistad
40 U.S. 518 (15 Pet. 518) (1841)
Decided: March 9, 1841
Vote: 7 (Taney, Story, Thompson, McLean, Wayne, Catron, McKinley)
1 (Baldwin)
Opinion of the Court: Story
Dissenting without opinion: Baldwin

With the exception of ***Dred Scott v. Sandford,*** 60 U.S. 393 (1857), *The Amistad* is probably the best known slavery case in American jurisprudence. Yet, it is a case steeped in irony, and its meaning, both for constitutional law and the antislavery movement, is murky. It was famous for its moral issues and because of the huge propaganda effort put forth on behalf of the Africans involved, but it had little impact on American jurisprudence and almost no precedential value. Although sometimes hailed as a great antislavery victory, the case in fact turned on an interpretation of a treaty and was not a defeat for the supporters of slavery in the United States. Moreover, even though the abolitionists who sponsored the litigation won, and the Africans involved gained their freedom, this case freed no American slaves and had no direct impact on the development of American slave law.

The case began in Cuba in 1839, when Pedro Montez and José Ruiz purchased fifty-three native-born Africans who had been taken to Cuba in violation of Spanish law. Ruiz and Montez obtained fraudulent papers to show the blacks had been born in Cuba. This point later became central to the case, which turned on whether the Africans were legally held as slaves in Cuba or whether they had been illegally imported from Africa. The fact that most were adults, but none could speak a word of Spanish, and none responded to the Spanish names on identification papers, helped expose the fraud. Montez and Ruiz left Havana with the Africans on the schooner *L'Amistad* (which, ironically, means "friendship"). On the third or fourth night at sea, the Africans revolted, took over the ship and killed the captain, a mulatto cook, and two sailors. The Africans, led by men later known as Cinque and Grabeau, spared Montez and Ruiz because they believed the two men could navigate the ship back to Africa. They also spared the cabin boy, a Cuban-born slave. Two other crew members jumped overboard. The Africans forced Ruiz and Montez to steer the ship east, toward Africa. Ruiz and Montez followed this course during the day, but at night, they steered north and west, hoping eventually to reach one of the American slave states. Instead, after about two months at sea, they ended up in Long Island Sound. By this time, only thirty-nine of the Africans were still alive.

On August 26 Thomas R. Gedney, a lieutenant of the U.S. Coast Guard, boarded *The Amistad* and towed it to New London, Connecticut, where he entered a claim for salvage with the U.S. district court. Although they were in the service, Gedney and his crew were entitled to salvage rights. Montez and Ruiz also filed a claim with the court. Meanwhile, U.S. District Attorney William Holabird filed a claim to the ship on behalf of the federal government so the Africans could be sent home. On instructions from the Van Buren administration, Holabird later demanded that the court return the Africans to Montez and Ruiz, as required by the 1795 Pinckney Treaty between the United States and Spain. At the same time, Holabird asked that the adult slaves be held for prosecution for murder on the high seas.

While the court tried to sort out these competing claims and assertions, abolitionists, led by Lewis Tappan of New York, began to organize a defense for the "Amistads." The main burden of their legal defense fell to Roger Sherman Baldwin, a Connecticut lawyer; Seth P. Staples and Theodore Sedgwick, antislavery lawyers from New York; and Ellis Gray Loring, the leading antislavery lawyer in Boston. With the help of a Yale linguist and two British sailors who were natives of West Africa, the abolitionists were able to prove conclusively that the Amistads were natives of West Africa and that they spoke only Mende. This testimony also proved that they were not, as Ruiz and Montez claimed, Cuban-born slaves and that they were never legally slaves in Cuba.

In September 1839 Justice Thompson, while riding circuit, ruled that whatever crime may have taken place on the high seas on the Spanish ship, the U.S. courts had no jurisdiction over the matter. This ruling ended the attempt to prosecute the Amistads for murder. The case next went to the U.S. district court in Connecticut, where Judge Andrew T. Judson ruled that because there was no slavery in Connecticut, Gedney could claim no salvage rights in the Africans, but only in the ship and its other cargo. The sole question for Judson was the status of the Amistads. If African-born and illegally taken to Cuba, then they would be set free. If they were legally slaves in Cuba, then he was prepared to turn them over to Ruiz and Montez.

In January 1840 Judson ruled in favor of the Amistads and ordered the U.S. government to return them to Africa. "Cinque and Grabeau shall not sigh for Africa in vain," he declared. "Bloody as may be their hands, they shall yet embrace their kindred." This decision came as a great shock to the Van Buren administration, which, in anticipation of a decision against the blacks, had sent a ship to Connecticut to take the Amistads to Cuba, before any appeal could be lodged. Instead, the government brought an appeal to the Supreme Court.

The government argued that the Amistads should be returned to their Spanish owners, under the treaties of 1795 and 1821. Baldwin once again argued the case, joined by former president John Quincy Adams. Adams argued at great length about the nature of international law and the treaty obligations of the United States. Although the Court's opinion in this case is a mere 10 pages, Adams's argument, printed as a pamphlet, runs to 135 pages of small type. Adams's verbosity clearly annoyed the Court, but it also drove home the point that law and justice required that the Amistads be returned to Africa.

Speaking for the Court, Justice Story upheld the main thrust of Judson's opinion. Story acknowledged that if the Amistads were Cuban and legally enslaved there, they would "justly be deemed within the intent of the treaty" and be returned to Cuba. But Story found "it is beyond controversy, if we examine the evidence, that these negroes never were the lawful slaves of Ruiz and Montez, or of any other Spanish subjects. They are natives of Africa, and were kidnapped there, and were unlawfully transported to Cuba, in violation of the laws and treaties of Spain, and the most solemn edicts and declarations of that government." Story concluded that "these negroes are not slaves" but had been "kidnapped" and were "entitled to their freedom." After upholding Judson's ruling on the freedom of Africans, the Court reversed his order that the Amistads be returned to Africa at government expense. Instead, he ordered them released from confinement in Connecticut. Abolitionists not only raised money to send them back to West Africa but also sent them to school before they left in January 1842.

The Amistad, although legally insignificant, served as a powerful example of the horrors of slavery. It also revealed the extent of proslavery complicity on the part of the national government. As such, it helped educate many northerners about the evils of slavery and the threat it posed to the legitimate administration of justice in the United States. The case is also one of the few to come to the Court that had a happy ending for opponents of slavery, as well as for the thirty-nine captives. The case lingered in the diplomatic world for nearly two decades, with Spain persistently, and unsuccessfully, demanding compensation for the loss of the slaves.

See Paul Finkelman, *Slavery in the Courtroom* (Washington, D.C.: Library of Congress, 1985); and Howard Jones, *Mutiny on the Amistad: The Saga of a Slave Revolt and Its Impact on American Abolition, Law, and Diplomacy* (New York: Oxford University Press, 1987).

Swift v. Tyson

41 U.S. 1 (16 Pet. 1) (1842)
Decided: January 25, 1842
Vote: 9 (Taney, Story, Thompson, McLean, Baldwin, Wayne, Catron, McKinley, Daniel)
0
Opinion of the Court: Story
Concurring opinion: Catron

In *Swift v. Tyson* Justice Story clarified the use of state precedents in commercial litigation in federal courts. Story's opinion was the governing rule until overturned by ***Erie Railroad v. Tompkins,*** 304 U.S. 64 (1938). Section 34 of the Judiciary Act of 1789 declared that when federal courts heard diversity cases, "the laws of the several states . . . shall be regarded as rules of decision." This language was vague and subject to multiple interpretations. Here, Story resolved these ambiguities. The case involved complex financial transactions over timberland in Maine and was brought in the U.S. Circuit Court for New York as a diversity action by John Swift, a resident of Maine, against George W. Tyson, a New Yorker.

The facts of the case illustrate the vibrant nature of the American economy, the difficulties of interstate transactions, and the ever-present possibility of fraud, especially in land transactions. Tyson bought timberlands from two residents of Maine, Nathaniel Norton and Jairus S. Keith. He gave a bill of exchange for the land, payable in six months, but Norton and Keith intentionally defrauded Tyson by selling him land they did not own. Because the bill of exchange lacked consideration—namely, good title to the land—Tyson would not have been obliged to honor it when Norton and Keith presented it to him. Before Tyson learned of the fraud, however, Norton and Keith gave the bill of exchange to Swift, also a resident of Maine. Swift accepted the bill of exchange as payment for a debt Norton and Keith owed him.

When Swift tried to collect on the bill of exchange, Tyson refused to honor it, citing the fraudulent basis of the first transaction. Swift sued Tyson in federal court in New York to obtain payment, asserting that, as a bona fide holder in due course, he could collect from Tyson, even if the original holders of the bill, Norton and Keith, could not. Tyson's response was that Swift was not a bona fide holder in due course because he had received the bill of exchange as payment for a debt, rather than purchasing the bill on the open market. Moreover, because of his prior relationship with Norton and Keith (loaning them money), Swift would have known that the original land transaction was fraudulent. Tyson's argument implied that Swift might even had been involved in the fraud from the beginning.

Tyson correctly argued that his position—that Swift was not a bona fide holder in due course—was consistent with New York common law and that under New York law he was not obligated to honor the original note. Tyson further argued that because the case was brought as a diversity suit before the circuit court, the federal courts were bound to follow New York law.

Story disagreed. For most of his judicial career Story tried to create a federal common law. He failed to do so in criminal law, when the Court ruled in ***United States v. Hudson and Goodwin,*** 11 U.S. 32 (1812), that no federal common law of crimes existed. Here, however, Story was able to accomplish his goal for commercial law. Story interpreted the language of the statute—"the laws of the several states . . . shall be regarded as rules of decision"—to be limited to state statutes. And, as in this case, where no state statute governed the legal question, the federal trial courts could take the general laws of all the states and fashion a national rule. In the same term, Story expanded *Swift* into insurance law. He used the same concept—a national legal system—to nationalize the law of slavery and completely federalize the return of fugitive slaves in ***Prigg v. Pennsylvania,*** 41 U.S. 539 (1842). Even in this case, Story went beyond the facts to suggest new areas where a federal common law might be appropriate, which led Justice Catron to concur in the result but distance himself from Story's expansionist notions of federal law.

Story's position made a great deal of sense for the time because most participants in the national economy found it impossible to grasp the common law rules of each state. Story offered a set of national rules that would be accessible to anyone doing business in the United States. After this case, Story and the rest of the Court expanded the notion of a federal common law for almost all areas of commercial and other business transactions, everything from insurance law to the writing of wills. In the late nineteenth and early twentieth centuries, large corporations depended on the legacy of *Swift* to move simple damage and tort cases into federal court, where they could avoid the state common law rules that were more favorable for plaintiffs. Such abuses, the greater accessibility of state law, and a sense that the Court had gone too far in its nationalization of commercial common law led the Court to overturn *Swift* in *Erie Railroad.*

See Tony Freyer, *Harmony and Dissonance: The Swift and Erie Cases in American Federalism* (New York: New York University Press, 1981).

Dobbins v. Erie County

41 U.S. 435 (16 Pet. 435) (1842)
Decided: March 4, 1842
Vote: 9 (Taney, Story, Thompson, McLean, Baldwin, Wayne, Catron, McKinley, Daniel)
0
Opinion of the Court: Wayne

Acting under Pennsylvania law, Erie County assessed a tax on professionals and all "offices and posts of profit, professions, trades, and occupations." Among those taxed was Daniel Dobbins, a captain on a U.S. revenue cutter stationed on Lake Erie. The Pennsylvania Supreme Court upheld the tax, but the U.S. Supreme Court found it an unconstitutional infringement on the powers of Congress.

Reflecting Chief Justice Marshall's views in ***McCulloch v. Maryland,*** 17 U.S. 316 (1819), that the power to tax implies a power to destroy, the Court ruled that a state cannot tax a federal agency or installation. In modern language, this doctrine is known as intergovernmental tax immunity. The Court essentially held that federal officials were immune from state taxation, even if, as in Dobbins' case, they lived in and derived benefit from the community.

The doctrine no longer applies to income derived from the federal government, but it is still viable for federal buildings and lands, which remain immune from state taxation.

Prigg v. Pennsylvania

41 U.S. 539 (16 Pet. 539) (1842)
Decided: March 1, 1842
Vote: 8 (Taney, Story, Thompson, Baldwin, Wayne, Catron, McKinley, Daniel)
1 (McLean)
Opinion of the Court: Story
Concurring opinion: Taney
Concurring opinion: Thompson
Concurring opinion: Baldwin
Concurring opinion: Wayne
Concurring opinion: Daniel
Dissenting opinion: McLean

In 1837 Edward Prigg and three other men seized as fugitive slaves Margaret Morgan and her children, who were living in Pennsylvania. Prigg and the others brought the blacks back to Maryland without first obtaining a certificate of removal from a state judge, as required by Pennsylvania's 1826 personal liberty law. Prigg was subsequently convicted of kidnapping.

The U.S. Supreme Court overturned his conviction in its first opinion based on the Fugitive Slave Clause of the Constitution (Article IV, Section 2, clause 3) and the federal law of 1793 adopted to implement that clause. (This clause was superseded by the Thirteenth Amendment outlawing slavery in 1865.) Justice Story (1) held that the federal fugitive slave law of 1793 was constitutional; (2) struck down Pennsylvania's 1826 Personal Liberty Law and, by extension, all state personal liberty laws if they added additional requirements that could impede the return of fugitive slaves; (3) ruled that the Constitution provided a common law right of recaption—a right of self-help—which allowed a slaveowner (or an owner's agent) to seize any fugitive slave anywhere and return the slave to the owner's home state without complying with the provisions of the federal fugitive slave law; (4) held that state officials ought to, but could not be required to, enforce the federal law of 1793; and (5) ruled that no fugitive slave was entitled to any due process hearing or trial beyond a summary proceeding to determine if the person seized was the person described in the affidavit or other papers provided by the claimant. What Story's holding meant was complicated by Chief Justice Taney's concurrence, which inaccurately claimed that Story's opinion prevented state officials from voluntarily aiding in the return of fugitive slaves.

This case was one of the earliest examples of the Court's use of the preemption doctrine, as Story declared that the federal law preempted all state laws enforcing the constitutional clause. His assertion that state officials could not be required to enforce the law because Congress did not pay their salaries may be the first example of a court developing the concept of "unfunded mandates." Story said that if Congress repealed the 1793 law, or had never passed it, the states could still not adopt fugitive slave laws. Here, Story was offering one of the earliest examples of the Court proclaiming the dormant powers of Congress.

Justice McLean, in dissent, argued that states had a right and duty to protect their free black citizens from kidnapping. Indeed, he said the opinion threatened the liberty of all free blacks in the United States. McLean also noted that if two different people claimed an alleged fugitive slave, under Story's opinion no mechanism was in place to sort out the claims. Taney concurred in the result, but objected to Story's assertion that the northern states could withdraw their support for the law and leave its enforcement entirely to the federal government. Taney mischaracterized Story's opinion, leading many to believe that Story was hostile to enforcement of the law, when in fact he was not. Many northern states accepted the logic of Story's opinion and passed new personal liberty laws that specifically prohibited their officials from participating in the return of fugitive slaves. These laws led to southern demands for a new law, which resulted in the adoption of the punitive and draconian Fugitive Slave Law of 1850.

Prigg was one of the most important Supreme Court cases dealing with slavery until ***Dred Scott v. Sandford,*** 60 U.S. 393 (1857). The Court cited *Prigg* on numerous occasions well after the Civil War. During Reconstruction, Republicans cited it for the idea that the national government had the power to protect the rights of the freedmen, just as before the war the Court asserted the power of the national government to protect slavery.

See Paul Finkelman, "Story Telling on the Supreme Court: *Prigg v. Pennsylvania* and Justice Joseph Story's Judicial Nationalism," *Supreme Court Review,* 1994 (1995): 247–294; and Paul Finkelman, "Sorting Out *Prigg v. Pennsylvania,*" *Rutgers Law Journal* 24 (1993): 605–665.

Louisville, Cincinnati, and Charleston Railroad v. Letson

43 U.S. 497 (2 How. 497) (1844)
Decided: March 7, 1844
Vote: 5 (Story, McLean, Baldwin, Wayne, Catron)
0
Opinion of the Court: Wayne
Did not participate: Taney, McKinley, Daniel

Thomas W. Letson, a resident of New York, sued the Louisville, Cincinnati, and Charleston Railroad for breach of contract "relating to the construction of the road." Letson brought his suit in federal court under diversity jurisdiction. Because stockholders of the railroad lived in both North Carolina and South Carolina, the railroad said that diversity jurisdiction did not apply because such jurisdiction was confined to a suit "between a citizen of the State where the suit is brought and a citizen of another state." The railroad based its position on *Bank of the United States v. Deveaux,* 9 U.S. 61 (1809), in which the Court held that a corporation could not be sued as a legal entity, but only the members or stockholders could be sued. The railroad tied this case to ***Strawbridge v. Curtiss,*** 7 U.S. 267 (1806), in which the Court held that a diversity suit required full diversity of all the parties and that if even one of the plaintiffs and one of the defendants was from the state, diversity did not exist. Finally, the railroad argued that because the state of South Carolina was also a stockholder, the Eleventh Amendment barred the suit.

The Court rejected all these contentions. The last was perhaps the easiest. When a state purchased stock and acted as an economic entity, it could not hide behind the notion of sovereign immunity or the Eleventh Amendment. As the Court had said in *Bank of United States v. Planters' Bank of Georgia,* 22 U.S. 904 (1824), "When a government becomes a partner in a trading concern, it divests itself, so far as it concerns the transactions of that company, of its sovereign character, and takes that of a private citizen." The Court also rejected the contention that all the defendants in a diversity suit had to be from the same state. The Court said that this point had never been decided and in fact never come before it. In this case, however, the Court created an entirely new rule, declaring that for purposes of diversity jurisdiction a corporation would be considered a citizen of the state in which it was chartered. Therefore, it did not matter where its stockholders lived. This solution was a reasonable and logical response to the huge growth of corporations in the United States and the creation of a national market for stock in these corporations. As it had in other cases, here the Taney Court created a logical and flexible doctrine to deal with the changing nature of the American economy. In 1958 Congress altered these rules slightly by holding that a corporation could be considered as a citizen of the state in which it was chartered (incorporated) and at the same time a citizen in the state where its principal place of business was located.

See Carl B. Swisher, *The Taney Period* (New York: Macmillan, 1974).

Permoli v. First Municipality of New Orleans

44 U.S. 589 (3 How. 598) (1845)
Decided: January 1845 Term
Vote: 8 (Taney, Story, McLean, Wayne, Catron, McKinley, Daniel, Nelson)
0
Opinion of the Court: Catron

This case was the first concerning the free exercise of religion to come to the Supreme Court, but it can also be viewed as an Establishment Clause case. In November 1842 authorities arrested Rev. Bernard Permoli for performing a funeral service at the Church of St. Augustin in the French Quarter of New Orleans. This service violated a new city ordinance requiring that priests of the "Catholic churches of this municipality" conduct funerals only in specific chapels near the edge of the city. This ordinance was ostensibly a health regulation, but in fact it was passed by supporters of a local Catholic elite that was feuding with Bishop Antonie Blanc and the national Catholic hierarchy. Permoli, who supported Blanc, conducted the service to challenge the law and to show his fealty to the bishop.

Permoli (and the bishop) wanted the Court to protect their religious liberty against a municipal government that had "established" the local dissidents in the Catholic Church over the bishop and at the same time prohibited the bishop and his priests from performing burial services in the most of the churches in the city. The Court dismissed the case, saying, "The Constitution makes no provision for protecting the citizens of the respective states in their religious liberties; that is left to the state constitution and laws: nor is there any inhibition imposed by the Constitution of the United States in this respect on the states." This opinion followed the ruling in ***Barron v. Baltimore,*** 32 U.S. 243 (1833), even though Permoli had argued that, because of the terms of the Louisiana Purchase, the Bill of Rights ought to apply to Louisiana, even if it did not apply to any of the original states.

Permoli paid his fine, the law was eventually repealed, and Bishop Blanc ultimately gained full control of his archdiocese.

See Paul Finkelman, ed., *Religion and American Law: An Encyclopedia* (New York: Garland, 2000); and Michael W. McConnell, "The Supreme Court's Earliest Church-State Cases: Windows on Religious-Cultural-Political Conflict in the Early Republic," *Tulsa Law Review* 37 (2001): 7.

Jones v. Van Zandt

46 U.S. 215 (5 How. 215) (1847)
Decided: March 5, 1847
Vote: 9 (Taney, McLean, Wayne, Catron, McKinley, Daniel, Nelson, Woodbury, Grier)
0
Opinion of the Court: Woodbury

John Van Zandt, a Quaker farmer in Ohio, had ties to the antislavery movement. In April 1842 he sold his farm produce in Cincinnati and on his way home offered a ride to nine blacks walking along the road about twelve miles north of the Ohio River. Whether this was a prearranged meeting connected to the underground railroad or a chance encounter is not clear. The blacks were fugitive slaves, but Van Zandt may not have known their status when he offered them the ride. The fact that they were walking in daylight along a main road may have led him to believe they were not fugitives. Other facts surrounding the case are also in dispute. Van Zandt's attorney claimed that he made no attempt to conceal the blacks or to take back roads and that he moved at a leisurely pace, covering only fifteen miles in four hours. Another witness, however, claimed the wagon was traveling at a great speed and all but one of the blacks were hidden in the wagon. Van Zandt's lawyer and the witness for Wharton Jones, who owned the slaves, agreed that the events took place in the early morning, after daylight, but Justice Woodbury, in justifying his opinion, asserted, contrary to these facts, that Van Zandt was driving in the dark.

After Van Zandt had traveled about fifteen miles, two men rode up to him and, without identifying themselves or announcing their intentions, stopped the wagon and seized seven of the blacks. The eighth was captured later, and the ninth, Andrew, escaped. The blacks had run away from Jones, and, although Jones had not authorized the slave catchers to go after them, under Kentucky law he was obligated to pay for their services. Jones sued Van Zandt for his costs, the value of Andrew, and the $500 penalty allowed under the Fugitive Slave Law of 1793. A jury awarded Jones $1,200. Justice McLean and District Judge H. H. Leavitt, sitting together as the circuit court, recorded a pro forma disagreement on the legal issues to ensure that the case would come to the Supreme Court. In ***Prigg v. Pennsylvania,*** 41 U.S. 539 (1842), the Court had upheld the constitutionality of the Fugitive Slave Law, but that case had not raised a challenge to its enforcement, as this case did. Sen. William H. Seward of New York argued Van Zandt's case before the Supreme Court, and Salmon P. Chase, a future chief justice, wrote the main brief.

Justice Woodbury rejected Chase's arguments that the Fugitive Slave Law violated the Bill of Rights by denying alleged fugitives due process rights and a jury trial. He similarly rejected the claim that Article IV of the Constitution did not give Congress power to pass this law. Woodbury upheld McLean's circuit court opinion that "notice" under the 1793 law did not have to be formal, written, or even oral. Rather, "notice" would exist "if it only bring home clearly to the defendant knowledge that the person he concealed was 'a fugitive from labor.' " Van Zandt had argued that there was a presumption of freedom in Ohio and therefore he had the legal right to offer a ride to anyone he found in the state, until he had some form or written notice that the blacks in his wagon were fugitive slaves. In sum, the Court upheld the constitutionality of the 1793 law and provided an interpretation that favored the South on every point. Woodbury rejected any consideration of the morality or justice of owning slaves. Instead, he argued that the justices had to "stand by the Constitution and the laws with fidelity to their oaths. Their path is a straight and narrow one, to go where that Constitution and the laws lead, and not to break both, by traveling without or beyond them." Since the mid-1830s, the most radical opponents of slavery, the Garrisonian abolitionists, had been arguing that the Constitution was proslavery. In this case, a Supreme Court justice from New Hampshire lent support to their position.

Jones spent a number of years trying to recover his judgment. Van Zandt died during this period, and eventually Jones obtained a judgment against his estate. Harriet Beecher Stowe is said to have used Van Zandt as a model for a Quaker participant in the underground railroad in her novel *Uncle Tom's Cabin.*

See Paul Finkelman, *An Imperfect Union: Slavery, Federalism, and Comity* (Chapel Hill: University of North Carolina Press, 1981); and Paul Finkelman, *Slavery in the Courtroom* (Washington, D.C.: Library of Congress, 1985).

Thurlow v. Massachusetts

Also known as The License Cases
46 U.S. 504 (5 How. 504) (1847)
Decided: March 6, 1847
Vote: 9 (Taney, McLean, Wayne, Catron, McKinley, Daniel, Nelson, Woodbury, Grier)
0
Seriatim opinion: Taney (Nelson)
Seriatim opinion: McLean
Seriatim opinion: Catron (Nelson)
Seriatim opinion: Daniel
Seriatim opinion: Woodbury
Seriatim opinion: Grier

These three cases raised the same question: Do the states have the power to prohibit the retail sale of liquor? The cases involved state statutes requiring the venders of liquor to obtain a license from the state or county, but granting that license was discretionary. The liquor interests in Massachusetts, Rhode Island, and New Hampshire challenged the laws as interfering with interstate and international commerce in violation of the Commerce Clause of the Constitution. All three state supreme courts upheld the laws, arguing that they were a legitimate application of state police power. With no opinion of the Court, the case offered neither a clear precedent nor guidelines to future lawmakers, judges, or attorneys, but it did set out broad outlines of what might be constitutional.

All of the justices agreed that the states were free to limit, constrict, or even prohibit the sale of liquor within their boundaries. Two of the cases dealt with the sale of liquor by the glass, and Chief Justice Taney noted that such sales did not affect interstate commerce. Under the "original package rule" set out in ***Brown v. Maryland,*** 25 U.S. 419 (1827), which Taney had argued as counsel for Maryland, he easily determined that states could regulate the sale of liquor at the retail level. The New Hampshire case involved an entire cask of gin, which was brought into the state and sold there in its original package. Here, Taney reverted to the state police powers, arguing that New Hampshire had an inherent right to prevent the sale of liquor, even in the original package, which limited the wholesale transit and sale of liquor in the original packages. Taney conceded that Congress could, under the its Commerce Clause, pass laws prohibiting New Hampshire from banning the sale of goods in the original package, but as Congress had not acted on this subject, the states were free to act as they wished. The other justices more or less followed Taney's lead, except Justice Daniel, who took a states' rights position and argued that the states were essentially free to regulate liquor and that Congress could never interfere in this area.

Although they dealt with liquor, the License Cases were decided with slavery in mind. In his concurring opinion Justice Woodbury cited ***Prigg v. Pennsylvania,*** 41 U.S. 539 (1842), for the proposition that states could ban paupers, vagabonds, and runaway slaves. Taney also hinted that states were free to ban undesirable products and people. Much of this discussion centered on the controversy over the rights of free black sailors serving on ships that docked in southern ports. For more than two decades, the northern states, especially Massachusetts, complained that South Carolina and other southern states abused free black sailors who arrived in their ports. Under South Carolina's "black seamen's law," these sailors were incarcerated in the city jail while their ships were in port and were released only when the ship was ready to sail and the captain had paid the sheriff for the cost of feeding and housing the seaman in the jail. South Carolina and other slave states justified this obvious interference with interstate commerce as a necessary application of their local police powers. Although Justice Johnson had attacked these laws while riding circuit, in *Elkison v. Deliesseline,* 8 F. Cas. 493 (1823), the Court had so far avoided this potentially explosive issue. In the License Cases the Court supported New England laws with arguments that could also be used to uphold South Carolina's black seamen's act. Massachusetts could prohibit liquor; New York, under ***New York v. Miln,*** 36 U.S. 102 (1837), could regulate immigrants; and South Carolina and the other slave states were free to ban the entry of free blacks.

See Felix Frankfurter, *The Commerce Clause Under Marshall, Taney and Waite* (Chapel Hill: University of North Carolina Press, 1937); and Carl B. Swisher, *The Taney Period* (New York: Macmillan, 1974).

West River Bridge Co. v. Dix

47 U.S. 507 (6 How. 507) (1848)
Decided: January 31, 1848
Vote: 7 (Taney, McLean, Catron, Daniel, Nelson, Woodbury, Grier)
1 (Wayne)
Opinion of the Court: Daniel
Concurring opinion: McLean
Concurring opinion: Woodbury
Dissenting without opinion: Wayne
Did not participate: McKinley

In 1795 Vermont granted a one-hundred-year franchise to the West River Bridge Company to operate a toll bridge over the West River. In 1839 the legislature passed an act to allow for the taking of the bridge through eminent domain, and four years later Windham County sought to acquire the bridge and surrounding land for $4,000, which was fair market value. The company sued to prevent the sale, arguing that the taking violated the Contract Clause of the Constitution.

After losing in state court, the bridge company appealed to the Supreme Court, retaining Daniel Webster to argue its case. Webster asserted that if the state could abrogate the charter through an eminent domain proceeding, it would "destroy public faith" in charters granted by states and discourage investment and economic development. He concluded by predicting that if the state could destroy charters and take property at will, then "the most levelling ultraisms of Antirentism or Agrarianism or Abolitionism may be successfully advanced."

Webster's somewhat hysterical argument had little effect on the Court. Speaking for the majority, Justice Daniel, who surely feared Webster's list of "ultraisms" even more than Webster, nevertheless found no problem with what the state had done. Daniel asserted that "the right of eminent domain in government in no wise interferes with the inviolability of contracts." He declared that a franchise was no different from any other form of property, and the state might take any property for public use, provided it offered compensation. Vermont's move was not like the act of Georgia at issue in ***Fletcher v. Peck,*** 10 U.S. 87 (1810), in which the state had tried to retake property previously sold, without offering compensation. Nor was it like ***Dartmouth College v. Woodward,*** 17 U.S. 518 (1819), in which the state in effect seized the property of the trustees.

Justice McLean noted in his concurrence, "The power in a State to take private property for public use is undoubted. It is an incident to sovereignty, and its existence is often essential to advance the public interests." He further pointed out that the act of the state was not against the contract or charter, but against the property itself. He agreed that the state could not take the charter, or revise it, without violating the Contract Clause of the Constitution, but, it could take the land and property owned by the company through eminent domain.

West River Bridge gave important support to the states, as the American economy modernized in the mid-nineteenth century. Investors were reassured that their property would not be taken from them without compensation—as long as a state constitution required compensation—and the public understood that vested interests could not stand in the way of economic and technological progress.

See Carl B. Swisher, *The Taney Period* (New York: Macmillan, 1974); and Benjamin F. Wright, *The Contract Clause of the Constitution* (Cambridge: Harvard University Press, 1938).

Luther v. Borden

48 U.S. 1 (7 How. 1) (1849)
Decided: January 3, 1849
Vote: 5 (Taney, McLean, Wayne, Nelson, Grier)
1 (Woodbury)
Opinion of the Court: Taney
Dissenting opinion: Woodbury
Did not participate: Catron, McKinley, Daniel

After the Revolutionary War all of the states but Connecticut and Rhode Island wrote new constitutions. By 1818 Connecticut had a new charter, but Rhode Island continued to operate under a charter granted by King Charles II. By the end of the 1830s most of the states had eliminated the barriers to suffrage for white adult males. Rhode Island was the exception; about 90 percent of the adult males were not eligible to vote, and most of the political power was in the hands of a small number of rural farmers. In 1841 Thomas W. Dorr helped organize a convention that wrote a new, more inclusive constitution, known as the People's Constitution. Meanwhile, the existing government also wrote a constitution, known as the Freeholders' or Landholders' Constitution, which expanded the franchise, but not nearly to the degree that Dorr's proposed constitution did. Both groups submitted their constitutions to the people. A majority of adult males voted to ratify the People's Constitution, but the voters enfranchised under the Landholder's Constitution defeated that proposed system of government. Clearly, the majority of adult males in the state wanted political reform and a new, democratic constitution. The existing government, however, refused to recognize the validity of Dorr's constitution.

In 1842 supporters of the People's Constitution organized a new government and held an election in which Dorr was elected governor. In May Dorr attempted to seize the state arsenal, but his followers were repulsed by the state militia, which was encouraged by promises of help from President John Tyler. The next month Dorr's forces were once again dispersed by the militia, and most of the Dorrites fled the state. Dorr was arrested, convicted of treason against the state, and sentenced to life in prison. In *Ex parte Dorr,* 44 U.S. 103 (1845), the Court refused to hear his case, but he was later pardoned. In 1842 the official government in Rhode Island wrote a third constitution, which enfranchised virtually all adult males, without regard to property ownership or race. This constitution went into effect the following year.

The Dorrites, dissatisfied with the new constitution, contrived *Luther v. Borden* to test the validity of the original People's Constitution. Martin Luther, a Dorrite, sued various members of the Rhode Island militia, including Luther M. Borden, for breaking into his house while suppressing the Dorr Rebellion. He claimed that the Dorr Constitution was in effect at the time, and thus the militia acted without authority. The Dorrites argued that under Article IV of the U.S. Constitution the national government was bound to protect the right of the people to have a "Republican Form of Government," which implied legitimate representative democracy.

Speaking for a nearly unanimous Court, Chief Justice Taney rejected Luther's arguments. Taney asserted that the issue of which government was legitimate "belonged to the political power and not to the judicial; that it rested with the political power to decide whether the charter government had been displaced or not." Taney concluded that Luther's arguments "turned on political rights and political questions" that the Court would not consider. Taney said, "The sovereignty in every State resides in the people of the State, and that they may alter and change their form of government at their own pleasure. But whether they have changed it or not by abolishing an old government, and establishing a new one in its place, is a question to be settled by the political power." The Court would not even consider the issue.

With this argument, Taney created the political question doctrine, which the Court used over the years to avoid taking politically sensitive and difficult cases. This doctrine served the Court well in many instances, but it also meant that, in some instances, change, even vitally necessary change, was impossible because the political structure precluded it. The logic of Taney's argument is clear, and his return to first principles of democratic government—that the people "may alter and change their form of government at their own pleasure"—makes theoretical sense, but does not solve the problem of how to change government in a democracy when the existing system does not allow for a fair political process. In Rhode Island the 90 percent of the adult males who were disfranchised could hardly have used the political process to gain the vote. Not until the reapportionment case of ***Baker v. Carr,*** 369 U.S. 186 (1962), did the Court finally resolve this dilemma.

See Harold M. Hyman and William M. Wiecek, *Equal Justice Under Law: Constitutional Development, 1835–1875* (New York: W. W. Norton, 1978); and William M. Wiecek, *The Guarantee Clause of the Constitution* (Ithaca: Cornell University Press, 1972).

Smith v. Turner; Norris v. City of Boston

Also known as The Passenger Cases
48 U.S. 283 (7 How. 283) (1849)
Decided: February 7, 1849
Vote: 5 (McLean, Wayne, Catron, McKinley, Grier)
4 (Taney, Daniel, Nelson, Woodbury)
Seriatim opinion: McLean
Seriatim opinion: Wayne
Seriatim opinion: Catron (Grier)
Seriatim opinion: McKinley (Catron, in part)
Seriatim opinion: Grier (Catron)
Dissenting opinion: Taney
Dissenting opinion: Daniel
Dissenting opinion: Nelson
Dissenting opinion: Woodbury

The report of the case, including arguments of counsel, runs 290 pages in *United States Reports.* Each of the nine justices entered an opinion—the first time this had happened in a nine-justice Court—but there was no official opinion of the Court. The issue was a state tax that New York and Massachusetts imposed on passengers, including immigrants, entering their ports. New York used the tax money to support public hospitals for ships' passengers, which mostly served indigent immigrants. Massachusetts used its money to support "foreign paupers." George Smith was convicted of violating the law in New York, and James Norris in Massachusetts. Both appealed to the Supreme Court. The cases were argued separately—*Smith v. Turner* in 1845 and 1847, and *Norris v. Boston* in 1846 and 1847. In 1848 the cases were combined and reargued. Counsel included Daniel Webster, who represented Smith and Norris; Rufus Choate, who represented Norris; and John Van Buren, the son of former president Martin Van Buren, who represented Turner, the health commissioner of New York.

Despite the huge amount of space devoted to the case, the number of arguments, the impressive counsel, and the close vote on the Court, the issues raised were relatively simple. Did these tax laws violate the Commerce Clause of the Constitution by interfering with interstate and international commerce, or were the tax laws like the registration provisions upheld by the Court in ***New York v. Miln,*** 36 U.S. 102 (1837)? By a one-vote margin the Court found the laws unconstitutional. Because of the multiplicity of opinions, no clear doctrine emerged from the case, which does, however, provide a good example of the application of the theory of a dormant commerce clause. Congress had never passed legislation on taxing migrants, immigrants, and passengers in interstate commerce. Nevertheless, the Court majority made clear that the states could not do so either.

One reason the Court was so deeply fractured was that, as with other Commerce Clause cases at this time, this case had important implications for slavery. The states' rights contingent on the Court—Chief Justice Taney and Justices Daniel, Nelson, and Woodbury—supported the legislation. These four were also the Court's most consistent defenders of slavery and the South. Two moderate, commercially oriented southerners, Justices Wayne and Catron, voted to strike down the laws, perhaps because they did not see the power to tax as necessary to protect slavery.

The oddest vote in this case was Justice McKinley's. He was a states' rights, proslavery Alabamian of little distinction, who logically would have been expected to support the right of states to tax immigrants, as did Daniel, the most fanatical states' rights, proslavery justice on the Court. Daniel supported New York's right to tax immigrants, noting that the southern states had a concurrent right to exclude free blacks. He believed the majority position would threaten the rights of the southern states to "repulse" or "tax the nuisance" of free blacks from "Jamaica, Hayti, or Africa." McKinley, however, concluded that the "migration and importation" clause of Article I, Section 9, of the Constitution precluded the states from taxing migrants after 1808. McKinley argued that the states could not prohibit migrants and immigrants and may have had in mind the idea that southerners ought to be allowed to travel into the North with their slaves. At the time, the right of transit with slaves was emerging as a far more important issue to the South than the right to exclude free blacks, which the southern states had successfully been doing for nearly three decades.

The underlying issues of slavery and states rights made it impossible for the Court to present a unified position in this case, or even to have majority opinion. Thus, all nine justices said something in this case, and no clear doctrine emerged.

See Paul Finkelman, *An Imperfect Union: Slavery, Federalism and Comity* (Chapel Hill: University of North Carolina Press, 1981); Felix Frankfurter, *The Commerce Clause Under Marshall, Taney and Waite* (Chapel Hill: University of North Carolina Press, 1937); and R. Kent Newmyer, *The Supreme Court Under Marshall and Taney* (New York: Crowell, 1968).

1850–1859

Strader v. Graham

51 U.S. 82 (10 How. 82) (1851)
Decided: January 6, 1851
Vote: 9 (Taney, McLean, Wayne, Catron, McKinley, Daniel, Nelson, Woodbury, Grier)
0
Opinion of the Court: Taney
Concurring opinion: McLean
Concurring opinion: Catron

Christopher Graham of Kentucky was the owner of three slaves who performed, for a fee, as musicians. At various times the slaves performed in Indiana and Ohio, as well is in Kentucky. Sometimes they traveled with Graham, and sometimes alone. In 1841 they boarded Jacob Strader's steamboat for Ohio, but instead of performing there, they continued on to Canada. Graham sued Strader and won under a Kentucky statute that made steamboat operators liable for the value of any slaves escaping on their vessels. After losing in the Kentucky Supreme Court, which upheld the verdict for Graham, Strader appealed to the U.S. Supreme Court. He based his appeal on two points. First, he argued that because Graham had allowed the slaves to travel and work in free states they had become free. Strader argued that this was a conflict-of-laws case between Kentucky and the free states of Indiana and Ohio. He urged the Court to choose the laws of the free states over those of the slave states. Second, he asserted that under the Northwest Ordinance, any slaves brought into the region north of the Ohio River were free. Strader argued that the Supremacy Clause of the U.S. Constitution obliged Kentucky to respect the Northwest Ordinance because it was a federal law. This argument did not rest on a conflict between the laws of two equal entities—two states—but on the idea that the federal law was superior to the state law.

Chief Justice Taney easily dealt with the first issue, noting that "every State has an undoubted right to determine the *status* or domestic condition of the persons domiciled within its territory." Kentucky could therefore determine whether Graham's slaves became free when they visited and worked in Ohio and Indiana. The Kentucky court determined that these trips had not emancipated the slaves, and the Supreme Court had no jurisdiction to question that conclusion. The Court would have had jurisdiction over the interpretation of the Northwest Ordinance, *if* that law were still in force, but Taney ruled that it ceased to have any force when Indiana and Ohio became states. In his concurring opinion, Justice McLean agreed that the Court had no jurisdiction to hear the case, but he objected to Taney's sweeping assertion that the Northwest Ordinance was no longer in force, noting that Taney's comments on the ordinance were "extrajudicial." Justice Catron similarly argued that other parts of the ordinance might be in force, even if the state constitutions superseded the antislavery provision.

Strader essentially held that the states had the right to determine for themselves the status of people within their jurisdictions and that the states could not be compelled to give comity to the common law of other states. Initially, the Court planned to use *Strader* to dispose of ***Dred Scott v. Sandford,*** 60 U.S. 393 (1857), when that case came before the Court in 1856. A proposed "opinion of the Court" by Justice Nelson in *Dred Scott* would have relied on *Strader* to hold that the Court had no jurisdiction to hear Scott's freedom suit. Ultimately, the southern majority on the Court pushed Taney to write his more comprehensive, and more proslavery, opinion.

See Paul Finkelman, *An Imperfect Union: Slavery, Federalism, and Comity* (Chapel Hill: University of North Carolina Press, 1981).

Cooley v. Board of Port Wardens of Philadelphia

53 U.S. 299 (12 How. 299) (1852)
Decided: March 2, 1852
Vote: 6 (Taney, Catron, Daniel, Nelson, Grier, Curtis)
2 (McLean, Wayne)
Opinion of the Court: Curtis
Concurring in judgment: Daniel
Dissenting opinion: McLean
Did not participate: McKinley

In this case the Court significantly shaped the doctrine of police powers as it affected interstate commerce. Unlike the fractured Court in ***The License Cases,*** 46 U.S. 504 (1847), and ***The Passenger Cases,*** 48 U.S. 283 (1849), here the Court was able to create a meaningful doctrine with a majority opinion that had substantial support. Although slavery issues remained in the background and continued to plague Commerce Clause jurisprudence, the facts of this case enabled the Court to provide a coherent majority opinion without the explosive issue of slavery undermining its words.

Pennsylvania statutes of 1803 and 1832 required that every ship entering or leaving the port of Philadelphia take on a local pilot to guide the ship to the dock. On one hand, these laws made sense because harbors can be treacherous and difficult to navigate, and only a local pilot might know how to avoid sand bars and currents that could not only harm a ship but also create havoc in the port. On the other hand, such a law could also be seen as local self-dealing. The law could have been nothing more than a boondoggle that forced out-of-state and foreign ships to hire local people to do what any good ship captain could accomplish on his own with the help of accurate maps and charts. Congress had never legislated on this subject, but it might have done so if the need for local pilots was clear.

Aaron Cooley refused to hire a local pilot to guide two of his ships out of Philadelphia and was subsequently sued by the port wardens for half the pilot's fee as a penalty. Cooley lost in the state courts and appealed to the Supreme Court, arguing that the law violated the Commerce Clause. Justice Curtis rejected his argument, noting that commerce was such a broad field that the power to regulate it must be flexible. Curtis wrote, "The power to regulate commerce, embraces a vast field, containing not only many, but exceedingly various subjects, quite unlike in their nature; some imperatively demanding a single uniform rule, operating equally on the commerce of the United States in every port; and some, like the subject now in question, as imperatively demanding that diversity, which alone can meet the local necessities of navigation." Where the "nature of the power" required that "it should be exercised exclusively by Congress," the Court would support that exclusivity. Curtis thought this support would apply when commercial issues "in their nature national, or admit only of one uniform system, or plan of regulation, may justly be said to be of such a nature as to require exclusive legislation by Congress." In this case, however, the piloting of a vessel in a port "not only does not require such exclusive legislation, but may be best provided for by many different systems enacted by the states, in conformity with the circumstances of the ports within their limits." The Court upheld the right of the states to regulate local pilots and other issues of a purely local matter. Congress would have the power to regulate pilots if it wished, but until Congress acted the states were free to act on their own.

Justices McLean and Wayne dissented. McLean rejected the majority's argument, seeing the pilot law as a local attempt to usurp the power of Congress to regulate commerce. Daniel, an extremist on states' rights, concurred in the result, but denied that Congress could ever take power away from the states on such issues. Despite the dissents and Daniel's states' rights arguments, *Cooley* offered a workable compromise between the needs of the states to regulate at the local level and the need of Congress to provide a uniform system of commerce. If the states overstepped the bounds of reasonableness, Congress could always step in to regulate even local commerce. Similarly, as the distinction between local and national issues faded in the modern era, Congress could assert its authority to regulate large areas of commerce, even at the local level.

See Felix Frankfurter, *The Commerce Clause Under Marshall, Taney and Waite* (Chapel Hill: University of North Carolina Press, 1937); Harold M. Hyman and William M. Wiecek, *Equal Justice Under Law: Constitutional Development, 1835–1875* (New York: W. W. Norton, 1982); and R. Kent Newmyer, *The Supreme Court Under Marshall and Taney* (New York: Crowell, 1968).

Propeller Genesee Chief v. Fitzhugh

53 U.S. 443 (12 How. 443) (1852)
Decided: February 20, 1852
Vote: 8 (Taney, McLean, Wayne, Catron, McKinley, Nelson, Grier, Curtis)
1 (Daniel)
Opinion of the Court: Taney
Dissenting opinion: Daniel

In ***The Steamboat Thomas Jefferson,*** 23 U.S. 428 (1825), the Court ruled that admiralty jurisdiction did not apply to the nation's inland waterways. Relying on traditional English law, the Court held that admiralty jurisdiction applied only to shipping on water affected by the rise and fall of the tide. The ruling was a proper application of English law, but it ignored the vast river and lake traffic of the United States and the reality that, because of steamboat technology, ocean-going vessels could travel as far inland as St. Louis or Cincinnati. It also ignored the international commerce that took place on the Great Lakes and the St. Lawrence River. In 1845 Congress extended admiralty jurisdiction to the Great Lakes.

In May 1847, while sailing on Lake Ontario, the *Genesee Chief* collided with and sank *The Cuba,* owned by Henry Fitzhugh and others. As the owners of both vessels lived in New York State, diversity of citizenship was not an issue. Fitzhugh sued a libel for money damages against the *Genesee Chief* in the U.S. District Court in New York under the newly extended admiralty jurisdiction. The district judge issued a decree in favor of Fitzhugh, and the owners of the *Genesee Chief* appealed to the Supreme Court, challenging the law's constitutionality.

Chief Justice Taney noted that earlier Court decisions "seemed to imply that under the Constitution of the United States" admiralty "jurisdiction was confined to tidal waters." In a classic example of interpreting a "living Constitution," Taney said "The conviction that this definition of admiralty powers was narrower than the Constitution contemplated, has been growing stronger every day with the growing commerce on the lakes and navigable rivers of the western States."

Taney might have avoided the constitutional question by determining that the new law passed muster under Congress's power to regulate commerce, but he observed that Congress had not done this, and he agreed it was not proper to take this position. As Taney noted, the law expanded the jurisdiction of the courts and did not regulate commerce *per se.* The question, therefore, was: Did admiralty jurisdiction under the

Constitution extend to inland waterways? Taney said that the Great Lakes were "in truth inland seas," with different states on one side and "a foreign nation on the other" and that shipping on them was "subject to all incidents and hazards that attend commerce on the ocean." In wartime they had been the venue for "hostile fleets," and "prizes" had "been made" on them. In other words, if the Great Lakes look like an ocean and function like an ocean, so at law they should be treated like an ocean. Taney also noted that it would be unfair to provide the seaboard states with federal admiralty jurisdiction, but not give the same legal protection for the inland states. Pointing out that England lacked great navigable rivers and lakes, Taney in essence declared that American admiralty law must be developed to respond to American needs.

In dissent, Justice Daniel reiterated the classic definitions of admiralty, citing Chief Justice Marshall, Justice Story, and Chancellor James Kent of New York, the author of *Commentaries on American Law* to support his position.

This decision was crucial to the development of a truly national commerce. It reflected the realities of American life and the flexibility of the Taney Court in dealing with the dynamic economy of the mid-nineteenth century. Although neither dramatic nor controversial, the opinion is one of Taney's best and helped modernize American law.

See Felix Frankfurter, *The Commerce Clause Under Marshall, Taney and Waite* (Chapel Hill: University of North Carolina Press, 1937); and Harold M. Hyman and William M. Wiecek, *Equal Justice Under Law : Constitutional Development, 1835–1875* (New York: W. W. Norton, 1982).

Pennsylvania v. Wheeling and Belmont Bridge Company (I)

54 U.S. 518 (13 How. 518) (1852)
Decided: February 2, 1852
Vote: 7 (McLean, Wayne, Catron, McKinley, Nelson, Grier, Curtis)
2 (Taney, Daniel)
Opinion of the Court: McLean
Dissenting opinion: Taney
Dissenting opinion: Daniel (Taney)

Wheeling Bridge represented a battle between those favoring the railroad as the future means of transportation and those who supported technological advancement in water transportation. In the first of two decisions, the Court found for the state of Pennsylvania, thereby supporting water transportation. But, after winning the initial battle, in the second round, *Wheeling Bridge II,* 59 U.S. 421 (1856), Pennsylvania and the supporters of water transportation lost the war.

Prior to the suit, Pennsylvania and Virginia competed for ownership of a highway that ran in both states. The erection of a bridge over the Ohio River would decide which state truly possessed the highway. Virginia acted first; in 1847 the Virginia legislature chartered Wheeling and Belmont Bridge Company to construct a bridge. In addition to the highway, a bridge at Wheeling (now in West Virginia) would foster the growth of the railroad and capitalize on the already existing Baltimore and Ohio Railroad. Pennsylvania reacted by seeking an injunction to prevent Wheeling and Belmont Bridge Company from proceeding, but, by the time the case came to trial, the bridge across the Ohio River was completed.

Pennsylvania sought relief from the Court for the damages it said were caused by the bridge. Pennsylvania claimed the bridge was a public nuisance because it impeded the movement of larger steamboats on the Ohio River and violated interstate compacts between Virginia and Kentucky.

Justice McLean determined that the Supreme Court had original jurisdiction in the matter. Pennsylvania had standing because of the financial losses it incurred to state-owned improvement projects by the construction of the bridge. Pennsylvania in this case was analogous to an individual; it came before the Court not on behalf of the rights of its citizens, but to defend its rights as an entity. Although a claim at law did not exist, the Court held that the matter had standing as an equitable claim.

In determining whether the bridge constituted a public nuisance, the Court appointed a special commission to report on the matter. Based on this report and other evidence, the Court decided the bridge was a public nuisance. It obstructed navigation on the river and thus interfered with interstate commerce, over which Congress had plenary power. McLean held that because the bridge was nuisance, it must either be torn down or elevated so as not to interfere with navigation. Although McLean and the majority appeared to favor water transportation, the Court was reluctant to abandon all the projects already constructed at much expense for the birth of the railroad.

Chief Justice Taney and Justice Daniel dissented, arguing that the Court lacked jurisdiction in the matter. They held that unless a federal statute declared an obstruction of the Ohio River as a public nuisance, the Court could not make such a determination and order the bridge altered or removed. The bridge, according to Taney, had to violate some law, but neither a height restriction law nor an obstruction law existed. As Taney put it, he did not understand by "what law, or under what authority, this court can adjudge it to be a public nuisance and proceed to abate it." This issue returned to the Court in 1856, in a case with the same name, reported at 59 U.S. 421. See page 65.

See Elizabeth Brand Monroe, *The Wheeling Bridge Case: Its Significance in American Law and Technology* (Boston: Northeastern University Press, 1992); and Melvin I. Urofsky and Paul Finkelman *A March of Liberty: A Constitutional History of the United States,* vol. 1 (New York: Oxford University Press, 2002).

Moore v. Illinois

55 U.S. 13 (14 How. 13) (1852)
Decided: December 21, 1852
Vote: 7 (Taney, Wayne, Catron, Daniel, Nelson, Grier, Curtis)
1 (McLean)
Opinion of the Court: Grier
Dissenting opinion: McLean

In ***Prigg v. Pennsylvania,*** 41 U.S. 539 (1842), the Court struck down Pennsylvania's personal liberty law, which provided that no one could remove an alleged fugitive slave from the state without first obtaining a certificate of removal from a state judge or magistrate. In his opinion for the Court, Justice Story asserted that any state law that interfered with the return of fugitive slaves, or in any way hindered the return of slaves, was unconstitutional. In a concurrence, Chief Justice Taney complained that the decision prohibited the states from helping to return fugitive slaves, which in fact it did not do. *Moore v. Illinois* clarified this issue.

In 1843 the Illinois Supreme Court upheld the conviction of Dr. Richard Eels for "harboring and secreting a negro slave" in violation of an Illinois statute. In his appeal Eels argued that the state law was unconstitutional under *Prigg.* He asserted that Illinois could not punish him for harboring a fugitive slave, because only the federal government could do that. Eels also argued that the slave he helped had been brought to Illinois by the voluntary act of his master and was therefore not a slave at all. The Illinois Supreme Court rejected both arguments. The state court asserted that Illinois had the right to keep out an "unacceptable population." Moore, the executor of Eels's estate, appealed to the Supreme Court, asserting that under *Prigg* Illinois could not prosecute Eels. Moore was represented by Sen. Salmon P. Chase of Ohio, who later became chief justice of the United States.

After a cursory examination of the Illinois statute, Justice Grier asserted it did not conflict with the Constitution because it did not interfere with the right of the master to recover a runaway slave. The law only prohibited someone in Illinois from harboring a runaway. Grier went on to note that states were in fact free to aid in the return of fugitive slaves, as long as such laws did "not directly or indirectly delay, impede or frustrate the reclamation of a fugitive, or interfere with the claimant in the prosecution of his other remedies."

In dissent, Justice McLean argued that by this ruling a person could be punished twice for the same offense, once in state court and once in a federal court. This result, he asserted, was "contrary to the nature and genius of our government," even though it was not, in fact, contrary to the concept of law in the American system of federalism.

The decision left the states free to aid in the return of fugitive slaves and to punish people who aided fugitive slaves, even though they might also be punished in the federal courts. The case did not, however, as McLean wished, allow the states to intercede to protect free blacks from kidnapping or to ensure that alleged fugitive slaves received any due process before being turned over to slave catchers.

See Paul Finkelman, *An Imperfect Union: Slavery, Federalism, and Comity* (Chapel Hill: University of North Carolina Press, 1981); and Thomas D. Morris, *Free Men All: The Personal Liberty Laws of the North, 1780–1861* (Baltimore: Johns Hopkins University Press, 1974).

Smith v. Swormstedt

57 U.S. 288 (16 How. 288) (1854)
Decided: April 25, 1854
Vote: 9 (Taney, McLean, Wayne, Catron, Daniel, Nelson, Grier, Curtis, Campbell)
0
Opinion of the Court: Nelson

Prior to 1844 the Methodist Episcopal Church operated as a single association. The government of the church vested authority in one body called the General Conference and subordinate bodies called annual conferences. In 1844 the General Conference proposed a separation between northern and southern churches because of tensions among members over slavery. According to the proposal, if the annual conferences of the slaveholding states deemed it necessary to form a distinct ecclesiastical union, the southern states would unite under the care of a southern church. Likewise, the northern states would join together under the pastoral care of a northern church. The plan of separation contained several resolutions and included a *pro rata* division of the Book Concern, based on the total number of traveling preachers at the time of the separation. The Book Concern, a fund established by the traveling preachers, allowed the church to print books and papers for preachers to disseminate. By order of the 1796 General Conference the proceeds of this fund were to be used to support aged preachers and the wives, widows, children, and orphans of traveling preachers.

The annual conferences of the slaveholding states passed the resolution and created a distinct and independent society called the Methodist Episcopal Church South. William A. Smith, representing the 1,500 traveling preachers associated with the Methodist Episcopal Church South, brought suit against Leroy Swormstedt to recover their *pro rata* share of the fund.

The defendants, representatives of the 3,800 northern society preachers and members of the Methodist Episcopal Church in control of the Book Concern, denied the proceeds of the business to the beneficiaries of the southern church on the grounds that they were no longer connected with the Methodist Episcopal Church. Swormstedt maintained that the General Conference lacked the power to approve the division and contended that the petitioners were no longer members of the church but a different organization.

The Court upheld Smith's claim for the southern church's share of the fund. Justice Nelson determined that the General Conference had the power to authorize the separation of the church into two divisions. The separation occurred under the proper authority, and "it carried with it, as a matter of law, a division of the common property." The Court remanded the decision to the lower court to determine the proportion of the fund owed to the Methodist Episcopal Church South.

See James Haskins, *The Methodists* (New York: Hippocrene Books, 1992); and John N. Norwood, *The Schism in the Methodist Church, 1844: A Study of Slavery and Ecclesiastical Politics* (Alfred, N.Y.: Alfred University Press, 1923).

Murray's Lessee v. Hoboken Land and Improvement Company

59 U.S. 272 (18 How. 272) (1856)
Decided: February 19, 1856
Vote: 9 (Taney, McLean, Wayne, Catron, Grier, Daniel, Nelson, Curtis, Campbell)
0
Opinion of the Court: Curtis

Murray's Lessee marks the Supreme Court's first analysis of the Due Process Clause. Justice Curtis held that the Fifth Amendment's Due Process Clause applied not only to the judiciary and the executive but also to the legislature.

Murray's Lessee centered on the actions of Samuel Swartwout, a customs collector for the Port of New York. Swartwout embezzled more than $1.5 million from customs receipts and purchased land with the money. He later sold the land to James B. Murray and others, the plaintiffs in this case.

The Treasury Department ordered an audit of Swartwout's accounts and discovered that he owed a substantial sum of money to the government. To remedy the situation, the solicitor of the Treasury issued a distress warrant on the property for the balance due to the government. The distress warrant voided the sale of the disputed property to Murray and the others, and a U.S. marshal in New Jersey sold the property to the Hoboken Land and Improvement Company, which became the defendant.

Murray and the other plaintiffs brought an action of ejectment against the Hoboken Land Company to gain clear title to the property and to force the land company to vacate it. The plaintiffs claimed that the distress warrant, which caused them to forfeit their title to the property, was a violation of the Due Process Clause of the Constitution and that the action by the Treasury Department violated the Due Process Clause because only the judiciary could deprive a person of property. The Treasury, therefore, had overstepped its power in issuing the distress warrant. Because the distress warrant was unconstitutional, the sale of the property by the marshal to the defendant was void. The plaintiffs also claimed that the auditing by the Treasury amounted to a judicial proceeding, which violated Article III of the Constitution, because the Treasury officials were not judges and were not appointed for life as is required of judges under Article III.

The Court, in finding for the defendant, upheld the constitutionality of the Treasury's issuance of the distress warrant as being necessary and proper to collect revenues owed to the government. The Court also found that it was necessary for the collectors to use this process—which was judicial in nature—to achieve its legitimate goal of recovering money stolen from the government. Curtis stated that the act of issuing the distress warrant encompassed both legislative and judicial power, but that it was not simply a judicial act. He pointed out that the plaintiffs assumed incorrectly that the action had to be either judicial or legislative, when clearly the issuance of the warrant was a mixture.

Murray's Lessee declared that due process was not violated when a branch of government other than the judiciary acted in a way to deprive a person of property. Usually, the judiciary alone could deprive a person of property, but the legislature and the executive had the power to take action of a judicial nature that furthered the means to their end. This case is generally seen as a precursor to the substantive due process jurisprudence of the late nineteenth and early twentieth centuries. Significantly, only a year later, in ***Dred Scott v. Sandford,*** 60 U.S. 393 (1857), Chief Justice Taney used a substantive due process analysis to overturn the ban on slavery in the western territories, but in doing so he ignored this opinion.

See Herbert Hovenkamp, "The Political Economy of Substantive Due Process," *Stanford Law Review* 40 (1988): 379–447.

Pennsylvania v. Wheeling and Belmont Bridge Company

59 U.S. 421 (18 How. 421) (1856)
Decided: April 21, 1856
Vote: 6 (Taney, Catron, Daniel, Nelson, Curtis, Campbell)
3 (McLean, Wayne, Grier)
Opinion of the Court: Nelson
Concurring opinion: Daniel
Dissenting opinion: McLean
Dissenting opinion: Wayne
Dissenting opinion: Grier

The 1852 decision in ***Pennsylvania v. Wheeling and Belmont Bridge Company,*** 54 U.S. 518, was short-lived. Under pressure from railroad proponents, Congress added a rider to an August 31, 1852, post office appropriations bill that declared the Wheeling Bridge a "lawful structure," and an official "post road." Congress justified its action under its constitutional power to regulate commerce and to create post roads. Once Congress declared the bridge to be a post road, it came under congressional control. This act of Congress made the Supreme Court decision irrelevant because Congress had plenary power to regulate interstate commerce, and, by endorsing the bridge, Congress in effect sanctioned it, even though the bridge still might obstruct river traffic.

In May 1854 strong winds destroyed much of the Wheeling Bridge. When the bridge company began to reconstruct it, Pennsylvania asked for an injunction to prevent the company from proceeding. Justice Robert Grier issued the injunction while the Court was not in session. The company ignored the injunction and began rebuilding the bridge. At the December 1855 term of the Court, Pennsylvania asked the Court to find the company in contempt for ignoring the injunction.

In April 1856 the Court vacated the injunction. The Court upheld the power of Congress to determine the legality of the bridge under the Commerce Clause. First, Justice Nelson found that the Commerce Clause gave Congress the power to regulate navigation on the Ohio River. Second, although Congress cannot enact legislation to reverse a Court decision on constitutional interpretation, Nelson noted that this was not the issue for this case. The legislation was appropriate because of its concern with free navigation and the post office, all activities within the control of Congress.

Justices McLean, Wayne, and Grier dissented. All three justices had participated in the earlier case and followed McLean's majority opinion, asserting that the bridge was an infringement on interstate commerce. Adopting a narrow interpretation of the Commerce Clause, McLean believed Congress could only remove obstructions to navigation and interstate commerce. Furthermore, Congress lacked the power to alter its own role relating to interstate commerce. These three justices would have upheld a contempt order against the builders of the new bridge. Justice Daniel concurred in the result, but disagreed with the majority and continued to maintain that the Court had no jurisdiction to hear the case at any time.

See Elizabeth Brand Monroe, *The Wheeling Bridge Case: Its Significance in American Law and Technology* (Boston: Northeastern University Press, 1992); and Melvin I. Urofsky and Paul Finkelman, *A March of Liberty: A Constitutional History of the United States,* vol. 1 (New York: Oxford University Press, 2002).

Dred Scott v. Sandford

60 U.S. 393 (19 How. 393) (1857)
Decided: March 6, 1857
Vote: 7 (Taney, Wayne, Catron, Daniel, Nelson, Grier, Campbell)
2 (McLean, Curtis)
Opinion of the Court: Taney
Concurring opinion: Wayne
Concurring opinion: Nelson (Grier)
Concurring opinion: Grier
Concurring opinion: Daniel
Concurring opinion: Campbell
Concurring opinion: Catron
Dissenting opinion: McLean
Dissenting opinion: Curtis

Dred Scott was the second case in Supreme Court history in which all nine justices delivered an opinion. The case involved a suit for freedom by a slave named Dred Scott based on his residence in free jurisdictions. His late owner, Dr. John Emerson, an army surgeon, had previously taken Scott to the free state of Illinois and to Fort Snelling in the Wisconsin Territory (present-day Minnesota), where Congress had prohibited slavery under the Missouri Compromise of 1820.

In 1850 a Missouri court freed Scott on the theory that he had become free while living in Illinois and at Fort Snelling and, once free, he was always free. This decision was consistent with a long line of Missouri cases dating from 1824. In 1852 the Missouri Supreme Court overturned Scott's victory, declaring that because of northern hostility to slavery, Missouri would no longer respect the law of the free states, which ended bondage for slaves brought into their jurisdiction.

In 1854 Scott sued his new owner, John F. A. Sanford (whose name is misspelled in the official report), in federal court under the clause in Article III of the Constitution that allows a citizen of one state to sue a citizen of another state in federal court. Scott argued that he was a citizen of Missouri and could therefore sue Sanford, a citizen of New York, in federal court. In response, Sanford argued that Scott could not sue in a federal court because "Dred Scott, is not a citizen of the State of Missouri, as alleged in his declaration, because he is a negro of African descent; his ancestors were of pure African blood, and were brought into this country and sold as negro slaves." In essence, Sanford argued that blacks, because of their race, could never be citizens of the United States.

Judge Robert W. Wells of the U.S. district court rejected this argument, concluding that *if* Scott were free, he could sue in federal court as a citizen of Missouri. After hearing all the evidence, however, Wells rejected Scott's claim to freedom, basing his charge to the jury on the earlier Missouri decision that Scott was still a slave. Wells did not consider whether the Missouri court had incorrectly applied the Missouri Compromise of 1820, which was a federal law.

Scott then took his case to the U.S. Supreme Court. The Court ruled that the Missouri Compromise, under which Scott claimed to be free, was unconstitutional because it deprived southerners of their property in slaves without due process of law or just compensation, in violation of the Fifth Amendment. In reaching this conclusion, Chief Justice Taney determined that slavery had special constitutional protection because of the special needs of that property and its owners. This decision shocked northerners, who had long seen the Missouri Compromise as a central piece of legislation for organizing the settlement of the West and for accommodating differing sectional interests.

In an aggressively proslavery opinion, Taney also denied that blacks could ever be citizens of the United States. He wrote:

> The question is simply this: Can a negro, whose ancestors were imported into this country, and sold as slaves, become a member of the political community formed and brought into existence by the Constitution of the United States, and as such become entitled to all the rights, and privileges, and immunities, guarantied by that instrument

to the citizen? One of which rights is the privilege of suing in a court of the United States in the cases specified in the Constitution.

Ignoring the fact that free black men in most of the northern states, as well as North Carolina, could vote at the time of the ratification of the Constitution, Taney declared that blacks

are not included, and were not intended to be included, under the word "citizens" in the Constitution, and can therefore claim none of the rights and privileges which the instrument provides and secures to citizens of the United States. On the contrary, they were at that time [1787–1788] considered as a subordinate and inferior class of beings who had been subjugated by the dominant race, and, whether emancipated or not, yet remained subject to their authority, and had no rights or privileges but such as those who held the power and Government might choose to grant them.

According to Taney, blacks were "so far inferior, that they had no rights which the white man was bound to respect."

Each of the other eight justices wrote an opinion. Justice Nelson, a New Yorker, would have avoided the issues of black citizenship and slavery in the territories by simply affirming that the state had the right to decide the status of people within their jurisdiction. Missouri had decided Scott was a slave, which should end the issue. Such a decision would have affirmed the precedent in ***Strader v. Graham,*** 51 U.S. 82 (1851). Justice Catron agreed with this theory and specifically rejected overturning federal laws regulating the territories.

Justices McLean and Curtis wrote devastating critiques of the decision, pointing out that it violated history and precedent. Taney's opinion outraged many northerners, especially members of the new Republican Party. Abraham Lincoln attacked the decision throughout his debates with Stephen A. Douglas in 1858 and again during the presidential campaign of 1860. The decision forced Republicans to take a firm stand in favor of black citizenship and fundamental rights for blacks. Some Republicans went further, arguing for black equality and suffrage.

Although the *Dred Scott* decision denied civil rights to blacks, the Lincoln administration and the Civil War Congress ignored it. During the war Congress banned slavery in all the western territories, despite Taney's assertion that such an act was unconstitutional. In 1866 Congress sent the Fourteenth Amendment to the states. The amendment declared that all persons born in the nation were citizens of the United States and of the state in which they lived. Two years later the ratification of this amendment made the civil rights aspects of *Dred Scott* a dead letter. The decision nevertheless remains a potent symbol of the denial of civil rights, as well as the constitutionalization of racism, under the Constitution of 1787. It is often seen as an example of judicial activism at its worst and has generally been considered a "self-inflicted wound" that the Court could easily have avoided by affirming Scott's slave status and *Strader.*

See Don E. Fehrenbacher, *The Dred Scott Case: Its Significance in American Law and Politics* (New York: Oxford University Press, 1978); and Paul Finkelman, *Dred Scott v. Sandford: A Brief History With Documents* (Boston: Bedford Books, 1997).

Ableman v. Booth

62 U.S. 506 (21 How. 506) (1859)
Decided: March 7, 1859
Vote: 9 (Taney, McLean, Wayne, Catron, Daniel, Nelson, Grier, Campbell, Clifford)
0
Opinion of the Court: Taney

In this case, the Court, for the first time, articulated that state courts could not issue writs of habeas corpus against federal officers. The Court later reaffirmed this position in ***United States v. Tarble,*** 80 U.S. 397 (1872). Because *Ableman* was tied to slavery, the Court ignored it in the short term. During the civil rights struggles of the mid–twentieth century, however, the Court returned to Chief Justice Taney's powerful assertion of national authority that would be available to the Court and the national government in the future. During the civil rights movement, the Court revisited *Ableman,* using Taney's argument against the states' rights arguments of southern politicians fighting integration.

In 1854 a U.S. deputy marshal, acting on behalf of Missouri slaveowner Benjamin S. Garland, seized Joshua Glover, a fugitive slave, who was living in Racine, Wisconsin, and brought him to Milwaukee. The mayor of Racine later issued an arrest warrant for Garland for "kidnapping" Glover. Abolitionists in Racine quickly obtained a writ of habeas corpus from a county judge ordering U.S. Marshal Stephen V. Ableman to bring Glover before him. Before either the warrant or writ could be served, Sherman Booth, an abolitionist activist and newspaper publisher, led a mob to rescue Glover, who soon disappeared, presumably in Canada.

Shortly after Glover's rescue, Ableman arrested Booth and John Rycraft for violating the Fugitive Slave Law of 1850. Ableman acted without an arrest warrant, and in *In re Booth,* 3 Wis. 1 (1854), the Wisconsin Supreme Court released the men from Ableman's custody (and over his protests) under a writ of habeas corpus. Ableman then rearrested both men, who were subsequently convicted in federal court. In *In re Booth and Rycraft,* 3 Wis. 157 (1855), the Wisconsin Supreme Court once again issued a writ of habeas corpus, forcing Ableman to release Booth and Rycraft.

Ableman obtained a writ of error from the U.S. Supreme Court, but the Wisconsin Supreme Court ignored the writ and refused to forward the record of the case to Washington, D.C. The case remained suspended until the Wisconsin Supreme Court published its opinions. The U.S. Supreme Court then used these opinions as the basis for overturning the state supreme court in *Ableman.*

In a powerful opinion Taney condemned the actions of the Wisconsin courts, emphatically denying that state courts could interfere with the acts of the federal courts. With some irony, Taney declared that the states' rights position of the Wisconsin court was "preposterous" and "new in the jurisprudence of the United States, as well as the States."

Wisconsin's states' rights position forced Taney to articulate an emphatic assertion of national power and state subordination to the Constitution and the Supreme Court. Taney asserted that the purpose of the Constitution was to create a government that was "supreme, and strong enough to execute its laws by its own tribunals, without interruption from a State or from State authorities." He asserted that "the language of the Constitution, by which power is granted, is too plain to admit of doubt or to need comment," for "the supremacy thus conferred on this Government could not peacefully be maintained, unless it was clothed with judicial power, equally paramount in authority to carry it into execution," and that each state is obligated "*to support this Constitution.* And no power is more clearly conferred than the power of this court to decide ultimately and finally, all cases arising under such Constitution and laws."

After the decision, Ableman once again arrested Booth, who was rescued from custody. He remained at large for about two months, giving speeches in Wisconsin and challenging Ableman to arrest him. Ableman eventually caught up with him, and Booth remained in jail for another six months, until President James Buchanan pardoned him in March 1861.

See Paul Finkelman, *An Imperfect Union: Slavery, Federalism, and Comity* (Chapel Hill: University of North Carolina Press, 1981); Harold M. Hyman and William M. Wiecek, *Equal Justice Under Law: Constitutional Development, 1835–1875* (New York: Harper and Row, 1982); and Thomas D. Morris, *Free Men All: The Personal Liberty Laws of the North, 1780–1861* (Baltimore: Johns Hopkins University Press, 1974).

1860–1869

Kentucky v. Dennison

65 U.S. 66 (24 How. 66) (1861)
Decided: March 14, 1861
Vote: 8 (Taney, McLean, Wayne, Catron, Nelson, Grier, Campbell, Clifford)
0
Opinion of the Court: Taney

In 1859 Kentucky indicted Willis Lago, a free black from Ohio, for theft. Lago's "crime" was that he had helped a slave named Charlotte escape from Kentucky to Cincinnati. Gov. Salmon P. Chase of Ohio, a committed abolitionist and future chief justice of the United States, refused to extradite Lago on the grounds that he had not committed a crime recognized by Ohio. Gov. Beriah Magoffin of Kentucky waited until Chase left office and in 1860 sought extradition from the new governor, William Dennison, but he too refused to send Lago to Kentucky. Magoffin then sought a writ of mandamus from the Supreme Court to force Dennison to deliver Lago for prosecution, as provided for in Article IV, Section 2, of the Constitution.

Ohio denied that the Supreme Court had jurisdiction over the matter, arguing that the Court had no power to intervene in a dispute over the return of fugitives from justice. Ohio asserted that the Constitution left this matter entirely up to the states and further argued that the Court could not issue a writ of mandamus against a state official. Chief Justice Taney rejected Ohio's jurisdictional pleading. He pointed out, correctly, that seeking a mandamus against a state governor was the equivalent of suing a state, but that this dispute was in fact a suit between two states and therefore came under the Court's original jurisdiction. Taney also rejected Ohio's contention that it could decide for itself what crimes it would recognize. He noted that the "necessity" of allowing extradition "without any exception as to the character and nature of the crime," was a "policy of mutual support" that dated from the colonial period. He further argued that the word "demand" in the constitutional provision "implies that it is an absolute right; and it follows that there must be a correlative obligation to deliver, without any reference to the character of the crime charged, or to the policy or laws of the State to which the fugitive has fled."

Throughout his opinion, Taney asserted that a state governor had a constitutional and statutory obligation to comply with an extradition requisition. But, if a governor refused to act, Taney admitted "there is no power delegated to the General Government, either through the Judicial Department or any other department, to use any coercive means to compel him." For this reason, the Court refused to issue the mandamus.

This case, decided less than two weeks before Abraham Lincoln took office, must be seen in the context of the secession crisis. Although the result favored the free-state position of the Ohio governors, the precedent was designed to head off any notion that the national government could coerce any governor into acting. With seven states already declaring they were no longer in the Union, this decision was more prosecession than antislavery.

Dennison remained good law until the Court overturned it in ***Puerto Rico v. Branstad,*** 483 U.S. 219 (1987). Until then, numerous state governors had used the precedent to protect fugitives from segregationist justice in the Deep South and fugitives who claimed they could not get a fair trial where they were wanted for crimes because of racism or political prejudice.

See Paul Finkelman, *An Imperfect Union: Slavery, Federalism, and Comity* (Chapel Hill: University of North Carolina Press, 1981).

Ex parte Gordon

66 U.S. 503 (1 Black 503) (1862)
Decided: February 17, 1862
Vote: 7 (Taney, Wayne, Catron, Nelson, Grier, Clifford, Swayne)
0
Opinion of the Court: Taney

A federal act of May 15, 1820, made it a crime to forcibly detain or contain Negroes and mulattos, not already bound to service in the United States, aboard a vessel with the intent to enslave them. Under this law, crews aboard an American vessel, either wholly or partially owned by Americans, or American citizens aboard a foreign vessel, caught in the slave trade could be convicted of piracy and sentenced to death. Nathaniel Gordon, found aboard *The Erie*, was indicted for piracy in the Circuit Court for the Southern District of New York.

At trial, Gordon argued that since its sale in Havana in March of 1860, *The Erie* was no longer an American vessel. Gordon also argued that he was not an American citizen, because he had been born outside the United States. Witnesses, however, told the court that Gordon's parents were Americans residing in Portland, Maine, before and after their marriage. The witnesses also testified to knowing Gordon when he was a small boy. Justice Nelson, hearing the case on circuit, stated that the burden would be on Gordon to prove that he was not a U.S. citizen. Nelson said it was "settled law, that, although he was born in a foreign country," both his father and mother were American citizens and because of his father's occupation as a sea captain, his foreign birth did not mean that Gordon was not an American citizen.

Evidence showed *The Erie* had been built in the United States and was wholly owned by Americans. Nothing presented showed that foreigners had purchased it. Nelson pointed out that regardless of whether the ship was foreign owned, according to the law, if either of Gordon's contentions were deemed false, he could be convicted of piracy.

Satisfied with the proof, the jury found Gordon guilty of violating the slave trade act, and he was sentenced to death for piracy. Gordon moved for an arrest of judgment and a new trial. He contended that the language of the act provided that the detained Negroes only had to be held in service prior to boarding the vessel, not that the Negroes had to be enslaved in the United States. Justice Shipman, writing for the circuit court on these motions in *United States v. Gordon,* 25 Fed. Cas. 1364, 1367 (S.D.N.Y. 1861), said that the prisoner's claims were not well founded because they showed only that the act "is more comprehensive than was necessary." The other objection concerned Gordon's contention that *The Erie* was a foreign vessel. Gordon maintained that there was no proof that Americans owned the ship after its sale in Havana. Shipman maintained it was the defendant's burden to prove otherwise.

Attempting to avoid execution, Gordon asked the Supreme Court for a writ of prohibition directed to the judges and officers of the circuit court and to the marshal. He also asked for a writ of certiorari to bring the case before the Supreme Court. The Court rejected both of Gordon's motions. Chief Justice Taney said that because the circuit court had competent jurisdiction in the matter, the judgment could not be appealed, by law, to the U.S. Supreme Court. Further, the Court had no ability to prohibit an execution already in the hands of the marshal. Taney explained that no precedent existed in which the Court could prevent the marshal from performing a duty that a circuit court has the lawful right to command. Gordon was subsequently hanged.

See W. E. B. Du Bois, *The Suppression of the African Slave Trade* (New York: Longmans, Green, 1896); Warren Howard, *American Slavers and the Federal Law* (Berkeley, University of California Press, 1963); and Hugh Thomas, *The Slave Trade: The Story of the Atlantic Slave Trade, 1440–1870* (Simon and Schuster, New York, 1997).

The Prize Cases

67 U.S 635 (2 Black 635) (1863)
Decided: March 10, 1863
Vote: 5 (Wayne, Grier, Swayne, Miller, Davis)
4 (Taney, Catron, Nelson, Clifford)
Opinion of the Court: Grier
Dissenting opinion: Nelson (Taney, Catron, Clifford)

These cases, involving four ships, brought the constitutionality of the Lincoln administration's prosecution of the Civil War before the Supreme Court. On April 19, 1861, immediately after the attack on Fort Sumter, President Abraham Lincoln ordered a blockade of all Confederate ports. On April 27, following secession by Virginia and North Carolina, he extended the blockade to include ports in those states. Congress enacted a formal declaration of hostilities on July 13, and an act Lincoln signed retroactively into law on August 6 confirmed the president's blockade. The four ships in this litigation were seized after Lincoln's proclamation of April 19, but before Congress acted on July 13. Two were owned by Confederates, one was British, and one was Mexican.

The British ship, *The Hiawatha,* was docked at Richmond when Virginia seceded. The captain had fifteen days to leave the port, but he missed that deadline because he was unable to secure a tow out to sea. When the ship finally left Richmond and reached open waters, the U.S. Navy intercepted it. *The Brilliante,* the Mexican ship, ran the blockade at New Orleans, but was captured after attempting to return to Mexico. *The Amy Warwick* and *The Crenshaw* were both owned by Virginians. The first was seized on her way to Richmond with coffee from Brazil, and the second was caught attempting to bring Virginia tobacco to Great Britain.

At issue in all these cases was the legality of the blockade. Arguing for the claimants, James M. Carlisle claimed that Lincoln had no power or authority to issue an order blockading ports. This power, if it existed at all, belonged only to Congress. He further argued that because secession was not an act of war, but a mere rebellion, Congress had no power to interfere with shipping to and from American ports. Justice Nelson, a proslavery northern Democrat, supported this position in his dissent. Nelson asserted that until Congress declared a war, none could legally exist. Nelson denied that the blockade was legal, as defined by international law, because the United States and the Confederate States of America were not at war. Rather, he argued, that until Congress "recognized a state of civil war between" the Confederacy and the United States, this was merely a "personal war" between the insurrectionists in the South and the president of the United States. Nelson claimed Lincoln had no power to issue any orders blockading ports, but could issue orders only to suppress those individuals in rebellion. Justice Clifford, also a doughface Democrat (a term of derision defined at the time as "a northern man with southern principles") and two southern Democrats, Justices Catron and Taney, joined Nelson's dissent.

The Court rejected these arguments by a 5–4 vote. Grier, a northern Democrat, sided with the administration, writing an opinion acknowledging that "a blockade *de facto* existed" when Lincoln, acting in his capacity as commander in chief, issued his proclamation of April 19. Grier asserted that a civil war could exist even if one side did not recognize the sovereignty of the other. Indeed, he noted that a "civil war is never publicly proclaimed," but "its actual existence is a fact in our domestic history which the court is bound to notice and to know."

Thus, by a one-vote margin, the Court supported Lincoln's view of the war. To do otherwise might have been a catastrophic mistake for the Court. Many in the administration considered Taney to be a closet Confederate and perhaps even a traitor. It is unlikely that an adverse decision would have affected the prosecution of the war, but it might have led to impeachments of the justices or perhaps a court-packing plan. The Court's prestige and power would doubtless have been severely undermined by a decision stating, as James Carlisle did, that Congress had no power to impose a blockade. Doubtless, Grier understood this in voting with the majority to uphold the administration. The theory of the war, accepted by the Court in this case, had implications far beyond these cases. In effect, the Court concluded that the president had vast powers to issue proclamations and other executive orders in his capacity as commander in chief. Most important, this decision implicitly endorsed Lincoln's power to issue the Emancipation Proclamation as a war measure, as well as his actions suspending habeas corpus when necessary. In addition, the decision put the international community on notice that for purposes of international law, a blockade of the South was in place and any ships caught would be seized. The narrow victory caused some worry for the administration, but in the end the five-vote majority remained strong enough until Taney died and Lincoln replaced him with an abolitionist, Salmon P. Chase.

See Harold M. Hyman and William M. Wiecek, *Equal Justice Under Law: Constitutional Development, 1835–1875* (New York: W. W. Norton, 1982); Stanley I. Kutler, *Judicial Power and Reconstruction Politics* (Chicago: University of Chicago Press, 1968); and Melvin Urofsky and Paul Finkelman, *A March of Liberty: A Constitutional History of the United States* (New York: Oxford, 2002).

Gelpcke v. City of Dubuque

68 U.S. 175 (1 Wall. 175) (1864)
Decided: January 11, 1864
Vote: 8 (Wayne, Catron, Nelson, Grier, Clifford, Swayne, Davis, Field)
1 (Miller)
Opinion of the Court: Swayne
Dissenting opinion: Miller
Did not participate: Taney

In 1857 the city of Dubuque, Iowa, issued bonds in the sum of $250,000 to aid in the construction of railroads by the Dubuque Western and the Dubuque, St. Peter's and St. Paul Railroad Companies. Gelpcke and others came into possession of these bonds, and, when the city failed to pay the interest on them, they sued in the U.S. district court in Iowa.

The city argued that the act that authorized the bonds violated several articles of the Iowa Constitution. In part, the city claimed that the amount of the bonds exceeded the state constitution's limitations on municipal debt. The city cited as authority the Iowa Supreme Court's decision in *State of Iowa ex rel. v. County of Wapello,* 13 Iowa 388 (1862), which held that the act authorizing the sale of the railroad bonds issued by municipalities was unconstitutional under the Iowa Constitution, and therefore invalid.

Based on *Wapello,* which involved similar facts, the district court found for the city. The bondholders contended that Iowa precedent prior to the decision in *Wapello* and decisions from a majority of other states favored the validity of municipality bonds. The U.S. Supreme Court determined that the city did have the power to issue such bonds, despite the recent decision by the state supreme court.

The Court determined that, if the act was valid, the city had the authority to issue the bonds. Justice Swayne held that the municipality, like a corporation, could expect that the bondholders would rely on the good faith of the municipality or corporation. All of the constitutional objections raised by the city had already been answered by the Supreme Court of Iowa. Decisions from 1853 to 1859 found similar acts did not violate articles of Iowa's constitution. Whether *Wapello* had overruled these prior decisions became a question for the Court. Swayne discussed whether the Supreme Court is bound to follow the latest rules of a state's highest court in forming decisions. He believed that sometimes decisions are not in line and that when this case was reheard in the state, the court should rule accordingly.

Justice Miller, who was from Iowa, dissented, arguing that in this opinion the Court was abandoning the principle of *stare decisis.* by departing from its own precedents. He believed that the Court should not infringe on the right of the state to interpret its constitution.

This case strengthened the position of investors and entrepreneurs, who could now rely on the federal courts to protect them from the whims of state politics. Opponents saw the decision as an assault on the rights of the states to interpret their own constitutions. In retrospect, this case can also be seen as a step toward the substantive due process jurisprudence later characterized by ***Lochner v. New York,*** 198 U.S. 45 (1905).

Gelpcke v. City of Dubuque was decided during the brief period from May 1863 to May 1865 when the Court had ten justices.

See Charles A. Heckman, "Establishing the Basis for Local Financing of American Railroad Construction in the Nineteenth Century: From City of Bridgeport v. The Housatonic Railroad Company to Gelpcke v. City of Dubuque," *American Journal of Legal History* 32 (1988): 236.

Ex parte Vallandigham

68 U.S. 243 (1 Wall. 243) (1864)
Decided: February 15, 1864
Vote: 9 (Taney, Wayne, Catron, Nelson, Grier, Clifford, Swayne, Davis, Field)
0
Opinion of the Court: Wayne
Concurring in judgment without opinion: Nelson, Grier, Field
Did not participate: Miller

Clement Vallandigham was a racist, proslavery Ohio politician before the Civil War and a Confederate sympathizer after the war began. He was also popular, effective, and shrewd. He attacked emancipation, the use of black troops, conscription, and all of Lincoln's other policies. He was careful, however; his tirades against the draft always had the caveat that people should not directly break the law. His strategy was certainly clever. He could attack the war effort, try to persuade all who would listen to resist the administration, but get himself off the hook by making sure that his speeches never directly urged illegal activity.

The administration did not fall for this ruse, and in 1863 military authorities in Ohio arrested and tried Vallandigham for publicly declaring that the Civil War "was a wicked, cruel, and unnecessary war, one not waged for the preservation of the Union, but for the purpose of crushing out liberty and to erect a despotism; a war for the freedom of the blacks, and the enslavements of the whites, and that if the administration had not wished otherwise, that the war could have been honorably terminated long ago." Vallandigham further accused President Abraham Lincoln of trying to set up a monarchy and destroy the liberty of the American people. At his trial Vallandigham refused to enter a plea. He asked for counsel, but the three lawyers he chose refused to enter the courtroom to represent him. He called only one witness in his defense. Vallandigham ended his defense by reading a long statement to the military tribunal, challenging its authority to try him. The court found him guilty and sentenced him to be confined in a military prison. In a brilliant move, Lincoln commuted his sentence to exile, and he was sent to the Confederacy. Vallandigham's goals were clear: to stop conscription, stop the war effort, and prevent emancipation. While carefully avoiding a technical violation of the law, he was urging others to do so. Lincoln understood his motives and asked, "Must I shoot the simple-minded soldier boy who deserts, while I must not touch the hair of a wily agitator who induces him to desert?" Lincoln saw that the agitator had to be suppressed, not only to save the Union, but to save the "simple-minded soldier boy."

Before his exile to the Confederacy, Vallandigham petitioned the Supreme Court for a writ of certiorari. The Court granted the writ, but concluded that it had no jurisdiction to review the proceedings of a military tribunal, noting that the actions of the military tribunal were not "judicial," and that a writ of certiorari could not be directed at the military court. The Supreme Court's jurisdiction was, for most cases, appellate, meaning that the Court could hear appeals from a lower court. The military tribunal was not a "lower court," and so no appeal could be heard. Moreover, because the military tribunal was not a court, there was no court to which a writ of certiorari could be directed. Finally, Justice Wayne noted that the Court had no power of original jurisdiction to issue a writ of habeas corpus on behalf of Vallandigham, and it was denied.

The Court in 1864 was not inclined to challenge presidential authority on the matter of suppressing Vallandigham and other pro-Confederate agitators. The procedural posture of the suit—whether the writ of certiorari was the proper method of bringing the case to the Court—also worked against Vallandigham. After the war the Court did in fact vacate the military prosecution of a civilian in ***Ex parte Milligan,*** 71 U.S. 2 (1866), but that case reached the Court on appeal from a lower federal court, which had denied Milligan a writ of habeas corpus.

Ex parte Vallandigham was decided during the brief period from May 1863 to May 1865 when the Court had ten justices.

See Michael Kent Curtis, *Free Speech, "The People's Darling Privilege": Struggles for Freedom of Expression in American History* (Durham: Duke University Press, 2001); Paul Finkelman, "Speech, Press and Democracy," *William and Mary Bill of Rights Journal* 10 (2002): 813–826; Harold M. Hyman and William M. Wiecek, *Equal Justice Under Law: Constitutional Development, 1835–1875* (New York: W. W. Norton, 1982); and Mark E. Neely Jr., *The Fate of Liberty: Abraham Lincoln and Civil Liberties* (New York: Oxford University Press, 1991).

Roosevelt v. Meyer

68 U.S. 512 (1 Wall. 512) (1863)
Decided: December 21, 1863
Vote: 9 (Taney, Wayne, Catron, Grier, Clifford, Swayne, Miller, Davis, Field)
1 (Nelson)
Opinion of the Court: Wayne
Dissenting without opinion: Nelson

Roosevelt and Meyer entered into a contract for a loan of $8,170. An 1862 federal act issuing U.S. bank notes declared these notes to be legal tender in payment of "all debts, public and private." Meyer attempted to pay Roosevelt $8,170 in U.S. notes, but Roosevelt refused to accept these notes as legal tender.

Roosevelt claimed that the notes were not as valuable as had been represented and, if forced to accept this form of tender, he would be deprived of property and his due process rights. The trial court determined the notes were not legal tender and awarded Roosevelt the $326 difference plus interest. This politically charged, and politically motivated, decision threatened the ability of the United States government to finance the Civil War and was seen as a victory for opponents of the Lincoln administration, the war effort, and emancipation. The New York Court of Appeals, however, declared the notes were legal tender and reversed the lower court decision.

Roosevelt appealed that decision to the U.S. Supreme Court, asserting that the Judiciary Act of 1789 gave the Court judicial power over "all cases in law and equity arising under this Constitution." Justice Wayne dealt with the case in a one-sentence opinion, dismissing the case for lack of jurisdiction.

The Court's conclusion may not have been correct, but it allowed the justices to quickly eliminate a difficult issue and avoid facing the constitutionality of the Legal Tender Act until after the Civil War. The fact that the Court decided the case the same day it was argued suggests the justices' eagerness to dispose of the issue as quickly as possible.

This case was decided during the brief period from May 1863 to May 1865 when the Court had ten justices.

See Carl B. Swisher, *History of the Supreme Court of the United States, Vol. 5, The Taney Period, 1836–1864* (New York: Macmillan, 1974).

The Slavers (The Kate; The Sarah; Weathergage; Reindeer)

69 U.S. 350 (2 Wall. 350) (1865)
Decided: March 8 and March 10, 1865
Vote: 10 (S. P. Chase, Wayne, Catron, Nelson, Grier, Clifford, Swayne, Miller, Davis, Field)
0
Opinion of the Court: S. P. (The Kate)
Opinion of the Court: Clifford (The Sarah; Weathergage; Reindeer)

These four separate cases were argued in January and February 1865 and reported consecutively on pages 350 to 403 of Wallace's Reports. Prosecutors had charged four American vessels, *The Kate, The Sarah, The Weathergage,* and *The Reindeer,* with violating federal acts prohibiting "equipping, fitting, preparations & c." vessels "for the purpose of carrying on a trade in slaves." The respective lower courts found the defendants guilty. The Supreme Court reviewed all four cases at the virtually the same time because each involved similar charges and facts. Although the decision in *The Kate* was announced two days before the other decisions, they were reported consecutively and have traditionally been discussed as a single case, known as *The Slavers.*

The defendants faced a Court led by a new chief justice well known for his abolitionist politics. The cases rested on whether circumstantial evidence, absent positive proof, could sustain a conviction for slave trading. Each of the seized vessels maintained it was conducting legitimate business; no evidence proved otherwise. Appearances, however, were not favorable to the defendants, who had no alibis or explanations for the nature of their ships and cargoes. Most of the ships were characterized by a cargo just below the allowable limit, a change of ownership just before departure, inaccurate crew records, a larger crew than needed, and destinations to known slave ports. Furthermore, the ships carried excessive amounts of water or water drums, extra spars, and abundant amounts of wood. The extra wood and spars could create a temporary deck, and the extra drums were suitable for holding water. Each fact by itself proved nothing but, when combined, appeared suspicious.

The most significant evidence against the defendants was the connection of each vessel with known slave traders. A revenue cutter seized *The Kate* after the marshal saw a tugboat approach her outside the port. On the tugboat, presumably carrying individuals planning to board the ship, the marshal recognized a known slaver wanted in connection with another case. The evidence in the other cases was similar.

Unsympathetic to the accused, the Court affirmed the lower court rulings holding the defendants guilty in all four cases. Pertaining to *The Kate,* Chase said that a trader engaging in business in a suspicious place under suspicious circumstances must "keep his operations so clear and so distinct in their character, as to repel the imputation of prohibited purpose." As the defendants could not sufficiently show their intentions to be pure, the Court assumed their guilt based on the circumstances surrounding the seizures.

This case was decided during the brief period from May 1863 to May 1865 when the Court had ten justices.

See W. E. B. Du Bois, *The Suppression of the African Slave Trade* (New York: Longmans, Green, 1896); Warren Howard, *American Slavers and the Federal Law* (Berkeley: University of California Press, 1963); and Hugh Thomas, *The Slave Trade: The Story of the Atlantic Slave Trade, 1440–1870* (Simon and Schuster, New York, 1997).

Ex parte Milligan

71 U.S. 2 (4 Wall. 2) (1866)
Decided: April 3, 1866
Vote: 9 (S. P. Chase, Wayne, Nelson, Grier, Clifford, Swayne, Miller, Davis, Field)
0
Opinion of the Court: Davis
Concurring opinion: S. P. Chase (Wayne, Swayne, Miller)

Lambdin P. Milligan was a prominent Confederate sympathizer in Indiana during the Civil War. Although he was probably not involved in any illegal conspiracies against the United States, he worked closely with a number of men who were Confederate agents organizing to resist the U.S. government and to aid the Confederacy. One of Milligan's associates, Harrison Horton Dodd, created the Sons of Liberty, a secret society with the aim of opposing the Lincoln administration by force if necessary. Dodd made Milligan a "major general" in the society, although Milligan later swore he knew nothing about the organization. Dodd received at least $10,000 from Confederate agents in Canada to organize a northwestern confederacy to aid the rebellion. In 1864 authorities tried Milligan and three other conspirators before a military commission. In December 1864, after a trial that lacked many safeguards of due process, the military court found all the defendants guilty and sentenced three, including Milligan, to death. Doubts about the guilt of the defendants soon surfaced, and Indiana governor Oliver P. Morton, who had strongly pushed for the trials, urged President Lincoln to pardon the men. Lincoln promised to issue the pardons when the war ended, but he was assassinated before he could carry out his pledge. President Andrew Johnson commuted the prisoners' death sentences, but left them in jail. Meanwhile, Milligan petitioned the U.S. circuit court for a writ of habeas corpus under the Judiciary Act of 1789. When that court denied him relief, he appealed to the Supreme Court. This procedural attack on the military conviction had been suggested by the Court in ***Ex parte Vallandigham,*** 68 U.S. 243 (1864), when it rejected Vallandigham's petition for a writ of certiorari. The Court heard arguments on Milligan's petition in March 1866. He had an impressive legal team: Jeremiah S. Black, a former attorney general; David Dudley Field, an eminent lawyer; and James A. Garfield, a war hero, Republican member of Congress, and future president.

All nine justices agreed that the military court had no jurisdiction to try Milligan. At the time of the trials, Indiana was not a war zone, and the civilians courts were open and operating. It would have been a simple matter for the government to indict Milligan in a federal grand jury and bring him before a federal district court for trial.

Justice Davis was emphatic that "where the courts are all open, and in proper exercise of their jurisdiction," a civilian "cannot, even when the privilege of habeas corpus is suspended, be tried, convicted, or sentenced otherwise than by the ordinary courts of law." Davis then asserted, in language that has since often been quoted,

> The Constitution of the United States is a law for rulers and people, equally in war and peace, and covers with the shield of its protection all classes of men, at all times, and under all circumstances. No doctrine, involving more pernicious consequences, was ever invented by the wit of man than that any of its provisions can be suspended during any of the great exigencies of government. Such a doctrine leads directly to anarchy or despotism, but the theory of necessity on which it is based is false; for the government, within the Constitution, has all the powers granted to it, which are necessary to preserve its existence; as has been happily proved by the result of the great effort to throw off its just authority.

Chief Justice Chase believed that Congress had the power to impose military tribunals on civilians under its war powers, but since this had not been done, the justices agreed that Milligan's conviction was unconstitutional. After eighteen months in jail, Milligan was released.

Milligan has had a mixed history. At the time it was roundly condemned because it undermined the power of the national government to suppress resistance to Reconstruction in the South. These fears were confirmed when President Johnson, who was hostile to black rights, used *Milligan* as an excuse to cut back on the use of the military to implement Reconstruction measures, control violence by southern whites, and protect the rights of former slaves. In the twentieth century it was hailed as a major step in protecting individual liberties, especially during wartime. In World War I, however, the national government found ways to deprive war protestors of their rights to speak freely, and in World War II the government interned more than 100,000 Japanese Americans whose only "crime" was their ethnicity. In ***Korematsu v. United States,*** 323 U.S. 214 (1944), the Court failed to implement either the spirit or the doctrine of *Milligan* to protect Japanese Americans from the internment. After the war the Court struck down, on statutory grounds, the use of martial law in Hawaii in ***Duncan v. Kahanamoku,*** 327 U.S. 304 (1946). The lesson of *Milligan* may be that it is useful for protecting civilians, but that this protection is more likely to occur after hostilities are over, just as it did in Milligan's case.

See Frank L. Klement, "The Indianapolis Treason Trials and *Ex parte Milligan,*" in *American Political Trials,* rev. ed., ed. Michal R. Belknap (Westport, Conn.: Greenwood Press, 1994), 97–118; Mark E. Neely Jr., *The Fate of Liberty: Abraham Lincoln and Civil Liberties* (New York: Oxford University Press, 1991); and Kenneth Stampp, "The Milligan Case and the Election of 1864 in Indiana," *Mississippi Valley Historical Review* (now *Journal of American History*) 31 (1944): 41–59.

Cummings v. Missouri

71 U.S. 277 (4 Wall. 277) (1867)
Decided: January 14, 1867
Vote: 5 (Wayne, Nelson, Grier, Clifford, Field)
4 (S. P. Chase, Swayne, Miller, Davis)
Opinion of the Court: Field
Dissenting without opinion: S. P. Chase, Swayne, Miller, Davis

The Civil War in Missouri was particularly brutal because it was a civil war within a civil war. Missouri was officially loyal, and more of its men fought on the Union side than for the Confederacy, but Missouri was also a slave state with many Confederate sympathizers. Much of the bloodshed was caused by guerrillas, marauders, and criminals posing as Confederate soldiers. Civilians, noncombatants, and injured Union soldiers in hospitals were killed—murdered, many would have said—by these pro-Confederate irregular troops. After the war the Jesse James and Younger gangs emerged from such groups.

In response to these experiences, Missouri revised its constitution in 1865 to require that all persons holding any office in the state and all officers of corporations, lawyers, teachers, professors, and members of the clergy swear an oath that they had always been loyal to the state and the United States. The oath required that the person swear to loyalty not only for acts but also for sympathies and words. A person who sympathized with the Confederacy and perhaps expressed those sympathies, but never took up arms against the United States or broke any laws would be unable to pass this test and take the oath. John Cummings, a Catholic priest, refused to take the oath and after conviction for acting as a priest without first taking the oath, was fined $500. When the case reached the Supreme Court, Cummings assembled a powerful group of lawyer/politicians: Sen. Reverdy Johnson of Maryland, Montgomery Blair, and David Dudley Field.

Justice Field held that "the disabilities created by the Constitution of Missouri must be regarded as penalties—they constitute punishment." Because these punishments were inflicted for acts, or even thoughts, that were not criminal at the time, Field held that the provisions constituted an *ex post facto* law in violation of the U.S. Constitution. Furthermore, because the provisions in effect punished people without trial, they constituted a bill of attainder, which also violated the Constitution.

Chief Justice Chase and Justices Miller, Swayne, and Davis dissented without opinion in this case, but Miller wrote an elaborate dissent in the companion case, ***Ex parte Garland,*** 71 U.S. 333 (1867).

See Paul Finkelman, ed., *Religion and American Law: An Encyclopedia* (New York: Garland, 2000); Harold M. Hyman, *Era of the Oath: Northern Loyalty Tests During the Civil War and Reconstruction* (Philadelphia: University of Pennsylvania Press, 1954); and Harold M. Hyman, *To Try Men's Souls: Loyalty Tests in American History* (Berkeley: University of California Press, 1959).

Ex parte Garland

71 U.S. 333 (4 Wall. 333) (1867)
Decided: January 14, 1867
Vote: 5 (Wayne, Nelson, Grier, Clifford, Field)
4 (S. P. Chase, Swayne, Miller, Davis)
Opinion of the Court: Field
Dissenting opinion: Miller (S. P. Chase, Swayne, Davis)

Decided the same day as ***Cummings v. Missouri,*** 71 U.S. 277 (1867), this case overturned a "test oath" that Congress established during the Civil War. Unlike the provisions in the Missouri constitution, this law was narrowly drawn and limited. A statute of 1862 required that each federal officeholder swear that he had "never voluntarily borne arms against the United States" since becoming a citizen, and had never "voluntarily given . . . aid, countenance, counsel or encouragement" to persons engaged in war with the United States, or supported any government hostile to the United States. In January 1865 this law was extended to lawyers practicing before federal courts. The laws were clearly designed to prevent Confederate operatives and sympathizers from working for the national government or practicing in the federal courts. Augustus H. Garland, an attorney who had practiced before the Supreme Court prior to the war and then served in the Confederate Congress, challenged the law. As in *Cummings,* Justice Field found the statute an *ex post facto* law and a bill of attainder.

In dissent, Justice Miller argued that the national government had the power to exclude from certain offices those who had made war on the United States. He explained that the provisions of the Missouri Constitution at issue in *Cummings* should also have been upheld, but he directed most of his arguments at the federal law. Miller asserted that because the Constitution gave Congress plenary power to establish and regulate the courts, Congress was free to set the standards for practice in those courts. He said that the practice of law was a privilege, not a right, and that this privilege could be suspended or denied to people whose moral character was in question. Garland had been admitted to the Supreme Court bar in 1860. He then left the United States, joined the rebellion, and made war on the United States. Miller argued that Garland's actions constituted a sufficient stain on his character that they were "evidence of bad moral character" to prevent him from practicing law in the federal courts. This law was not a bill of attainder, because it was not inflicting punishment on Garland for criminal behavior. Rather, the law was denying him a privilege because of his past behavior. Miller noted that at no time before these cases had the Court ever defined a bill of attainder, but that in England it had been a process that affected inheritance and the status of the children of offenders. This was surely not the case here, where only those who voluntarily joined the rebellion, and not their children, were barred from the practice of law in the federal courts. Similarly, Miller denied that the law was an *ex post facto* law because it was not a criminal statute; it neither condemned anyone to prison or execution nor created the possibility of a trial for an act that was not criminal at the time. The law created no punishment.

Modern commentators have hailed this decision, as well as *Cummings,* as protective of civil liberties and due process. In doing so, however, they have often failed to understand, as the dissenters did here, that men like Garland had in fact made war against the United States. They might have been tried, convicted, and executed for treason. Instead, Congress wanted only to bar them from holding public office and practicing law in the federal courts. In this sense, the federal law was not different from a modern law, which might prevent someone from practicing law for immoral, but not illegal, behavior.

See Charles Fairman, *History of the Supreme Court of the United States, Vol. 6, Reconstruction and Reunion, 1864–1888,* Part One (New York: Macmillan, 1971); Harold M. Hyman, *Era of the Oath: Northern Loyalty Tests During the Civil War and Reconstruction* (Philadelphia: University of Pennsylvania Press, 1954); and Harold M. Hyman, *To Try Men's Souls: Loyalty Tests in American History* (Berkeley: University of California Press, 1959).

Mississippi v. Johnson

71 U.S. 475 (4 Wall. 475) (1867)
Decided: April 15, 1867
Vote: 9 (S. P. Chase, Wayne, Nelson, Grier, Clifford, Swayne, Miller, Davis, Field)
0
Opinion of the Court: S. P. Chase

Congress passed the First Reconstruction Act on March 2, 1867. It required the president to appoint military commanders to supervise the creation of new governments in ten former Confederate states (Tennessee was excluded). The law also allowed the military to try civilians in these areas because there was no civilian government. Under the law no state could be readmitted to the Union until it ratified the Fourteenth

Amendment and enfranchised all adult males, except certain former Confederate leaders. The civilian governments in these states were deemed "provisional" until new constitutions were written, and Congress reserved the power to "abolish, modify, control or supersede" these provisional governments at any time. The Second Reconstruction Act, passed on March 23, refined the provisions and goals of the first act.

The existing all-white government in Mississippi challenged the constitutionality of the law and asked for an injunction to prevent President Andrew Johnson from enforcing it. Johnson did not like either law, which had been passed over his vetoes, but he viewed Mississippi's suit as a threat to presidential power, which he jealously guarded. The president therefore ordered Attorney General Henry Stanberry to defend the suit.

The Court refused to let the case go forward. Chief Justice Chase asserted that the Court lacked the power to enjoin the president from acting. Chase noted that the president was required to see that the laws were faithfully executed and he would be violating his oath of office by not enforcing them. Chase also said that if the Court issued the injunction, the Court would have no power to enforce it against the president. The separation of powers inherent in the constitutional system prevented the judiciary from enjoining either the executive branch or the legislative branch. Chase added that, once the president acted, it would be possible for the courts to take "cognizance" of his actions. If those actions, under the statute, violated the Constitution, the Court might then intervene on behalf of injured parties. But, until the president executed the laws, there was no case for the Court to hear.

See Harold M. Hyman and William M. Wiecek, *Equal Justice Under Law: Constitutional Development, 1835–1875* (New York: W. W. Norton, 1982); and Melvin Urofsky and Paul Finkelman, *A March of Liberty: A Constitutional History of the United States* (New York: Oxford, 2002).

Crandall v. Nevada

73 U.S. 35 (1868)
Decided: March 16, 1868
Vote: 8 (S. P. Chase, Nelson, Grier, Clifford, Swayne, Miller, Davis, Field)
0
Opinion of the Court: Miller
Opinion concurring in the judgment: Clifford (S. P. Chase)

A Nevada statute levied a dollar head tax on every person carried out of the state by railroads or stagecoach companies. Crandall refused to pay the tax, arguing it violated the Constitution. When the state court upheld the law, he appealed to the U.S. Supreme Court. Nevada claimed it was not taxing passengers or commerce, but was taxing the businesses operating in the state. The tax was similar to that struck down in ***The Passenger Cases,*** 48 U.S. 283 (1849), but the language of the Nevada act made it a personal tax on the individual traveler, rather than a tax on a conveyance, as in the *Passenger Cases.* The Nevada tax also affected people leaving the state, rather than those entering it. In addition, the Nevada tax was not imposed only on immigrants, but on everyone leaving the state. In essence, it was a tax on citizens who traveled from state to state, rather than on immigrants, who were, like "cargo," filling ships.

The Court rejected a straight Commerce Clause analysis. Instead, Justice Miller asserted that the right to travel was a fundamental right of citizenship. Similarly, the right of the national government to call on its citizens to serve in the military or in other national service was a fundamental aspect of nationhood. Citizens had a right to visit the national capital as well as to do business in other states. But, citing ***McCulloch v. Maryland,*** 17 U.S. 316 (1819), Miller noted that if the states could tax these rights, it could destroy them. Reminding Nevada of the recent civil war, Miller pointed out that if Tennessee had imposed such a tax, the federal government would not have had sufficient funds to pay the taxes on the U.S. troops that went in and out of that state. On these rather vague grounds, the Court struck down the Nevada tax.

The Court struck down the Nevada law on the general grounds that citizens have a right to move from place to place, and that the national government might need them to do so. Justice Clifford, joined by Chief Justice Chase, thought the law was unconstitutional as a violation of Congress's plenary power to regulate interstate commerce. Clifford concurred in the result, but "dissented" from the use of the new amendment in this way.

Less than four months after this case, the Fourteenth Amendment was ratified, providing a more secure constitutional basis for a right to travel. Nevertheless, even without that amendment, Miller's opinion offered an important statement on the fundamental relationship of the states to the national government in the wake of the Civil War. Miller reminded Americans that "the people of these United States constitute one nation."

See Charles Fairman, *History of the Supreme Court of the United States, Vol. 6, Reconstruction and Reunion, 1864–1888,* Part One (New York: Macmillan, 1971); and Paul Finkelman, *An Imperfect Union: Slavery, Federalism, and Comity* (Chapel Hill: University of North Carolina Press, 1981).

Georgia v. Stanton, Mississippi v. Stanton

73 U.S. 50 (6 Wall. 50) (1867)
Decided: May 13, 1867 and May 16, 1867
Vote: 9 (S. P. Chase, Wayne, Nelson, Grier, Clifford, Swayne, Miller, Davis, Field)
0
Opinion of the Court: Nelson
Opinion concurring in judgment: S. P. Chase

In ***Mississippi v. Johnson,*** 71 U.S. 475 (1867), the Court refused to enjoin President Andrew Johnson from enforcing the First and Second Reconstruction Acts. The same day the Court, however, allowed Georgia to bring a new suit, directed against

Secretary of War Edwin M. Stanton, Gen. Ulysses S. Grant, and Gen. John Pope. On April 18 the Court granted permission to Mississippi to bring a similar suit against Stanton, Grant, and Gen. E. O. C. Ord, which was called *Mississippi v. Stanton.* The substance of both suits was the same: to prevent the enforcement of the Reconstruction Acts, which abolished the existing state governments and created new governments run by the military under the authority of Stanton, Grant, and specific generals assigned to each military district in the former Confederacy. One of the main complaints of both states was that the military would create new governments in which blacks would be allowed to vote and hold office. Once again, the Court rebuffed the pleas of the former confederates, who still held political power in the South.

Justice Nelson acknowledged that the laws would in fact abolish the existing state governments, but he said this was a purely political issue and that the "prayers for relief, call for the judgment of the court upon political questions, and, upon rights, not of persons, or property, but of a political character." But, as Nelson also noted in the opinion, "the distinction between judicial and political power" was "generally acknowledged in the jurisprudence both of England" and of the United States. With some irony, Nelson relied heavily on Chief Justice Marshall's opinion in ***Cherokee Nation v. Georgia,*** 30 U.S. 1 (1831). In that case, the Cherokee Nation claimed it faced the annihilation of its existing political structure at the hands of the Georgia legislature and begged the Court to prevent the state from accomplishing this. The Court found the case to be a political question, which was beyond its power to solve. Just as in *Cherokee Nation,* in 1867 the Court still had no power to resolve political questions. Moreover, here the political question involved the political judgment of Congress, which had authorized Stanton to act, just as it had authorized President Jackson to act three decades earlier. And just as the Court had refused to enjoin Johnson, so it refused to enjoin Stanton. If the Court stopped the executive branch from following the laws of Congress, then the executive branch officers would be placed in the impossible position of having to choose which branch of the government to obey. Saying it had "no jurisdiction over the subject-matter presented," the Court dismissed the Georgia and Mississippi suits. Congress proceeded to abolish the governments in the former Confederate states and reconstruct them into modern entities, where slavery no longer existed and citizenship was not limited by race.

Ex parte McCardle

74 U.S. 506 (7 Wall. 506) (1869)
Decided: April 12, 1869
Vote: 8 (S. P. Chase, Nelson, Grier, Clifford, Swayne, Miller, Davis, Field)
0
Opinion of the Court: S. P. Chase

In 1867 military authorities in Vicksburg, Mississippi, arrested newspaper editor William McCardle and charged him with libel and inciting violence against the United States. McCardle was a particularly vicious, venomous, and racist opponent of Reconstruction and black freedom. The military prepared to try McCardle under powers granted it by the First and Second Reconstruction Acts of 1867. McCardle sought a writ of habeas corpus under the federal Habeas Corpus Act of 1867 and asked the U.S. circuit court to remove him from military custody. Citing the recent decision in ***Ex parte Milligan,*** 71 U.S. 2 (1866), McCardle argued that the military could not try him because he was a civilian and nonmilitary courts were available and open. When the circuit court denied him relief, McCardle took his case to the Supreme Court, as provided in the Habeas Corpus Act.

Leaders in Congress feared the Court would strike down the Reconstruction Acts and, in doing so, derail the whole process of reconstructing the South and protecting black freedom. Shortly after the Court heard the case, but before it could reach a decision, Congress amended the Habeas Corpus Act to remove a right of appeal to the Supreme Court. When the Court decided the case, in April 1869, Chief Justice Chase dismissed McCardle's appeal for lack of jurisdiction. Chase did point out that the Court might still have jurisdiction to hear a habeas appeal under the Judiciary Act of 1789, but that was not before the Court in this instance.

McCardle remains a viable precedent for the notion that Congress can limit the Supreme Court's appellate jurisdiction. In the modern era politicians have suggested limiting this jurisdiction in cases involving school busing, school prayer, and abortion rights. It is not clear, however, whether Congress would have the power to limit jurisdiction on basic constitutional issues or to prevent the Court from hearing constitutional challenges to acts of Congress or the states. In *McCardle* Congress simply repealed a jurisdiction it had recently created—a far cry from preventing the Court from hearing cases on a particular subject or on a particular constitutional issue or principle.

See Charles Fairman, *History of the Supreme Court of the United States, Vol. 6, Reconstruction and Reunion, 1864–1888,* Part One (New York: Macmillan, 1971); Harold M. Hyman, *A More Perfect Union: The Impact of the Civil War and Reconstruction on the Constitution* (New York: Alfred A. Knopf, 1973); Stanley I. Kutler, "Ex parte McCardle: Judicial Impotency? The Supreme Court and Reconstruction Reconsidered," *American Historical Review* 72 (1967): 835–851; Stanley I. Kutler, *Judicial Power and Reconstruction Politics* (Chicago: University of Chicago Press, 1968); Christopher Waldrep, *Roots of Disorder: Race and Criminal Justice in the American South, 1817–1880* (Urbana: University of Illinois Press, 1998); and William Wiecek, "The Great Writ and Reconstruction: The Habeas Corpus Act of 1867," *Journal of Southern History* 36 (1970): 530.

Texas v. White

74 U.S. 700 (7 Wall. 700) (1869)
Decided: April 12, 1869
Vote: 5 (S. P. Chase, Nelson, Clifford, Davis, Field)
3 (Grier, Swayne, Miller)
Opinion of the Court: S. P. Chase
Dissenting opinion: Grier
Dissenting opinion: Swayne (Miller)

As part of the Compromise of 1850, Texas received indemnity bonds from the U.S. government. In 1865 officials of the Confederate government in Texas sold these bonds to raise money to support the war. When the war was over, the government of Texas sought to recover the bonds. Texas brought suit under the Supreme Court's original jurisdiction. Underlying this case was the power of Congress to govern the former Confederate states, to reconstruct them, and to bring them back into the Union.

Texas argued that the bonds had been illegally sold by a usurper government that had not owned them and had no power to sell them. An attorney for one of the bondholders argued that they had purchased the bonds from the lawful government of Texas and that the contract for sale was legitimate and binding. The attorney for George White, the lead defendant, argued that when the case was brought before the Court, Texas had no government and, therefore, the Court had no jurisdiction to hear it. He pointed out that Texas had no representation in Congress, was not allowed to appoint presidential electors, and its previous state government had been declared illegal by Congress. When the case came to the Court, Texas was governed by a U.S. Army general under the authority of various Reconstruction acts. In other words, counsel for White asserted that Texas did not exist as a state and could not sue in federal court. White argued that he had purchased the bonds from the de facto government of Texas, which was in authority and running the state at the time, and therefore had the power to sell the bonds. White's attorney pointed out that a government had operated in Texas from 1861 until 1865, when that government was deposed by the U.S. Army. Since then Texas had been without a government, and thus had in effect, ceased to exist as a state.

Chief Justice Chase relied on the arguments of the lawyer representing Texas, G. W. Paschal, a prominent constitutional theorist. Chase asserted that Texas did exist as a state because it had a provisional governor, a governor who had appointed Paschal to represent the state. More important, Chase articulated the theory of secession held by the Lincoln administration, namely, that the Constitution "looks to an indestructible Union composed of indestructible states." Therefore, Texas existed as a state and had always existed as a state, even if, in 1869, its government no longer functioned as it had before the Civil War. Chase found support for this idea in the Guarantee Clause of Article IV, Section 4, of the Constitution, which declares, "The United States shall guarantee to every State in this Union a Republican Form of Government." Chase argued that the language here proved that there was "a plain distinction" found in the Constitution "between a State and the government of a State." Secession was illegal because when "Texas became one of the United States, she entered into an indissoluble relation." According to Chase, Texas had never actually left the Union, but remained a state in the Union. The Court could hear the suit under its original jurisdiction, because the moving party was a state.

Just because Texas had always existed as a state did not, however, mean that its government had always existed. In Chase's mind the illegal actions of the secessionists had created an illegitimate government in Texas, which had no power. The Ordinance of Secession and all other acts leading to secession "were absolutely null. They were utterly without operation in law." The illegal regime could not transact business, could not make contracts, and could not sell the bonds owned by the state of Texas. While this illegal government was in power, and was making war on the United States, the rights of the citizens of Texas "were suspended." "The government and citizens of the State, refusing to recognize their constitutional obligations, assumed the character of enemies, and incurred the consequences of rebellion," which naturally created what Chase called "new relations" and "imposed new duties upon the United States" to recreate a legitimate government in Texas. At the end of the war Texas had no government, and therefore the United States had the duty to guarantee a "republican form of government" for Texas, which included enfranchising former slaves.

Chase's opinion was masterful. He managed to provide a constitutional theory that upheld Lincoln's position that the Union was indestructible, legitimated the actions of the United States during the Civil War, supported congressional Reconstruction, and provided for the creation of new governments in the former Confederate states based on enfranchising former slaves. As for the bonds, Chase concluded that the Confederate government had been illegal, and so was the sale. Texas, now under control of Congress and the military, was on its way to a reconstructed republican form of government and entitled to get its bonds back.

In dissent, Justice Grier argued that Texas had ceased to exist as a state in 1861 and could not sue for the recovery of the bonds. Justices Swayne and Miller agreed with this position, but also agreed with Chase that *if* Texas could sue, then on the merits it would win. Significantly, the theory of both the majority and the dissent supported the notion that Congress had the power and the duty to reconstruct the government of Texas.

See Harold M. Hyman, *The Reconstruction Justice of Salmon P. Chase: In Re Turner and Texas v. White* (Lawrence: University Press of Kansas, 1997); Stanley I. Kutler, *Judicial Power and Reconstruction Politics* (Chicago: University of Chicago Press, 1968); and Phillip S. Paludan, *A Covenant With Death: The Constitution, Law, and Equality in the Civil War Era* (Urbana: University of Illinois Press, 1975).

Ex parte Yerger

75 U.S. 85 (8 Wall. 85) (1869)
Decided: October 25, 1869
Vote: 7 (S. P. Chase, Nelson, Grier, Clifford, Swayne, Davis, Field)
1 (Miller)
Opinion of the Court: S. P. Chase
Dissenting without opinion: Miller

In 1869 Edward M. Yerger stabbed to death Maj. Joseph G. Crane, who was the acting mayor of Jackson, Mississippi. Military authorities arrested Yerger and put him on trial by a military commission. During the trial Yerger sought a writ of habeas corpus from the circuit court under the Judiciary Act of 1789, and, when the court denied him relief, he appealed to the Supreme Court. The circuit court upheld the military's jurisdiction under the First Reconstruction Act of 1867.

Chief Justice Chase noted that in 1868 Congress had taken away one route to a habeas corpus hearing before the Court, which led to the decision in ***Ex parte McCardle,*** 74 U.S. 506 (1869). In that case, however, the Court had noted that it could still hear cases of a similar nature under its appellate jurisdiction provided by the Judiciary Act of 1789. Chase concluded that the Court had jurisdiction to hear the case and the power to direct its writ at a military officer. At this point the attorney general and Yerger's counsel worked out a compromise in which the prisoner was turned over to civilian authorities for prosecution in Mississippi. The Court was not actually forced to confront Congress on issues involving Reconstruction, and Congress in turn abandoned plans to completely abolish the Court's appellate jurisdiction in habeas corpus cases.

Yerger was placed in a Mississippi jail, but released on bail and quickly moved to Baltimore, where he died in 1875, never having been tried for murder.

See Charles Fairman, *History of the Supreme Court of the United States, Vol. 6, Reconstruction and Reunion, 1864–1888,* Part One (New York: Macmillan, 1971).

Woodruff v. Parnham

75 U.S. 123 (8 Wall. 123) (1869)
Decided: November 8, 1869
Vote: 7 (S. P. Chase, Grier, Clifford, Swayne, Miller, Davis, Field)
1 (Nelson)
Opinion of the Court: Miller
Dissenting opinion: Nelson

In ***Brown v. Maryland,*** 25 U.S. 419 (1827), the Court held that a state could not tax goods imported from other states or countries if they remained in their original packages after entering the states. *Woodruff* refined this doctrine.

Woodruff and his partners were Alabama auctioneers who challenged a tax on goods from other states that they auctioned off. Woodruff asserted that because the goods remained in their original packages, they could not be taxed, but the Court distinguished this tax from the one at issue in *Brown.* The Maryland tax "was limited by its own terms to importers of foreign articles or commodities," which led the Court to strike it down as a burden on interstate and international commerce. Mobile, Alabama, however, imposed a uniform tax on *all* goods sold at auction within the city, and did not discriminate against foreign or out-of-state goods. This tax was permissible, but the Court reaffirmed that the discriminatory tax was impermissible. The logic of this result was obvious. If the tax was on the sale of goods, at auction or at retail, then the tax had to be uniform for all goods. Otherwise, the tax system would favor the imports—which were not taxed while in the original package—at the expense of locally created goods, which could be taxed.

See Charles Fairman, *History of the Supreme Court of the United States, Vol. 6, Reconstruction and Reunion, 1864–1888,* Part One (New York: Macmillan, 1971).

Paul v. Virginia

75 U.S. 168 (8 Wall. 168) (1869)
Decided: November 1, 1869
Vote: 8 (S. P. Chase, Nelson, Grier, Clifford, Swayne, Miller, Davis, Field)
0
Opinion of the Court: Field

A Virginia act of 1866 required that all out-of-state insurance companies obtain a special license before they could do business in the state. The license process also required depositing with the state a bond of between $30,000 and $50,000. To test the constitutionality of this law, Samuel B. Paul, an agent for various fire insurance companies in New York, applied for the license but refused to post the required bond. His license was denied because of the failure to post the bond, and Paul sold insurance policies in Virginia without a license. He was prosecuted, convicted, and fined $50. The National Board of Fire Underwriters financed his case and his appeal to the Supreme Court. Paul argued that as corporations they were "citizens" of other states and that Virginia unconstitutionally violated the Privilege and Immunities Clause of Article IV of the Constitution by discriminating against them in favor of Virginia corporations.

Following existing precedent, the Court held that corporations were not citizens within the meaning of the Privileges and Immunities Clause. Paul also argued that the Commerce Clause precluded the states from regulating out-of-state insurance companies. Had the insurance industry been successful on this issue, all state regulation of out-of-state insurance companies might have been prohibited. Citing antebellum cases such as ***Bank of Augusta v. Earle,*** 38 U.S. 519 (1839), the Court reaffirmed that foreign—that is, out-of-state—corporations were subject to state regulation. The Court also rejected the notion that the sale of insurance was part of interstate commerce. As Justice Field noted, "If foreign bills of exchange may thus be the subject of state regulation, much more so may contracts of insurance against loss by fire." His words set the standard for the law for nearly eighty years.

In ***United States v. South-Eastern Underwriters Association,*** 322 U.S. 533 (1944), the Court held that insurance companies were engaged in interstate commerce and were therefore subject to regulation under antitrust laws. Congress immediately responded with the McCarran-Ferguson Act of 1945, explicitly authorizing the states to regulate insurance companies and denying that insurance regulation was a matter for federal regulation, unless some future statute provided for it.

See Charles Fairman, *History of the Supreme Court of the United States, Vol. 6, Reconstruction and Reunion, 1864–1888,* Part One (New York: Macmillan, 1971); and Morton Keller, *Affairs of State: Public Life in Late Nineteenth Century America* (1977, reprint, Union, N.J.: Lawbook Exchange, 2000).

Veazie Bank v. Fenno

75 U.S. 533 (8 Wall. 533) (1869)
Decided: December 13, 1869
Vote: 6 (S. P. Chase, Grier, Clifford, Swayne, Miller, Field)
2 (Nelson, Davis)
Opinion of the Court: S. P. Chase
Dissenting opinion: Nelson (Davis)

In 1866 Congress imposed a 10 percent tax on all currency issued by state banks. The Veazie Bank in Maine refused to pay the tax, which led to litigation with Fenno, the collector of revenue. The U.S. Circuit Court for the District of Maine was divided on the constitutionality of the law, which was often a pro forma mechanism for getting an important constitutional issue to the Supreme Court.

The bank claimed that the currency tax was a direct tax, which, according to the Constitution, had to be apportioned among the states according to their population. The bank also said the tax impaired the power of the state to grant a franchise because the bank had a state charter. If the federal government could tax a bank created by a state charter it could destroy the bank altogether. Finally, the bank argued that the tax was so excessive as to be unreasonable.

Relying on its decision in ***Hylton v. United States,*** 3 U.S. 171 (1796), the Court determined that the tax was not a direct tax. In *Hylton* a tax on carriages was determined to be constitutional and not a direct tax. The justices were of the opinion that only poll taxes and land taxes were direct taxes. Turning to the issue of whether Congress has the authority to tax a state franchise, the Court found that franchises were not tax exempt. Categorizing franchises as property, the Court inferred that because property was taxable, so were the franchises.

Chief Justice Chase also argued that if the tax seemed excessive, the remedy lay with the political process, not with the courts. He emphasized that Congress had the power to regulate the national currency in this manner and noted, "To the same end, Congress may restrain, by suitable enactments, the circulation as money of any notes not issued under its own authority." Here Chase also recognized the limitations of the power of the courts, noting that "the Judicial cannot prescribe to the Legislative Department of the Government limitations upon the exercise of its acknowledged powers."

Justice Nelson dissented on the grounds that the majority's decision to validate the tax endangered rights reserved to the states. Nelson wrote that their "powers and prerogative should be exempt from Federal taxation, and how fatal to their existence, if permitted."

See Morton Keller, *Affairs of State: Public Life in Late Nineteenth Century America* (1977, reprint, Union, N.J.: Lawbook Exchange, 2000).

1870–1879

Hepburn v. Griswold

Also known as the First Legal Tender Case
75 U.S. 603 (8 Wall. 603) (1870)
Decided: February 7, 1870
Vote: 4 (S. P. Chase, Nelson, Clifford, Field)
3 (Swayne, Miller, Davis)
Opinion of the Court: S. P. Chase
Dissenting opinion: Miller (Swayne, Davis)

In 1862 and 1863 Congress passed three separate legal tender acts, authorizing the U.S. Treasury, for the first time under the Constitution, to issue paper currency, popularly known as greenbacks.

Since the Revolution most Americans had viewed paper money as dangerous, inflationary, and inherently at odds with principles of good government. The memory of the indiscriminate use of paper money during and after the War for Independence remained a powerful image in American public culture. Nevertheless, Salmon P. Chase, who was then the secretary of the Treasury, urged that Congress pass the law because money was needed to finance the Civil War and to pay soldiers and suppliers. During the war Congress also levied a 10 percent tax on state bank notes, which effectively eliminated them from circulation. Chase saw these as necessary war measures.

The Supreme Court initially dodged the constitutionality of the legal tender acts by denying jurisdiction in ***Roosevelt v. Meyer,*** 68 U.S. 512 (1863). In that case New York's highest court had upheld the act, and the Court decided that it had no power to review the decision, although that decision seems erroneous in light of this case. In 1865, however, Kentucky's highest court struck down the legal tender acts, and the Court had to take the case.

The Court heard arguments twice in 1868 and again in December 1869 and decided the case the following February. At issue was whether a creditor was required to accept greenbacks for payment of debts that were incurred before the legal tender acts were passed. Chief Justice Chase agreed with the creditor. Chase said, "Contracts for the payment of money, made before the Act of 1862, had reference to coined money, and could not be discharged, unless by consent, otherwise than by tender of the sum due in coin." He claimed that forcing creditors to accept greenbacks diminished the value of their contract, because the greenbacks were worth less than the equivalent amount of money in gold or silver. Congress could not, Chase concluded, require that greenbacks be accepted for prior debts without in effect destroying the value of previous business arrangements. Such a policy would be a taking under the Fifth Amendment and violate the spirit of the Constitution.

In dissent, Justice Miller argued that this position led to absurd conclusions. Miller argued that under Chase's theory "a declaration of war against a maritime power would be unconstitutional, because the value of every ship abroad is lessened twenty-five or thirty per cent, and those at home almost as much." In addition, according to Miller, "the abolition of the tariff on iron or sugar would in a like manner destroy the furnaces, and sink the capital employed to manufacture those articles."

In his opinion, Chase cited Justice Story for the notion that Congress should not diminish the value of debts. He also cited Chief Justice Marshall's decision in ***McCulloch v. Maryland,*** 17 U.S. 316 (1819), arguing that the Necessary and Proper Clause of the Constitution was also a *limitation* on congressional action, if the ends are not justified and the means not allowed by the Constitution.

Yet, in the end Chase adopted Marshall's view of the Constitution, that it had to be read expansively and flexibly, to meet the exigencies of the age. He quoted the same passages, and others, from *McCulloch v. Maryland* to argue for the idea that paper currency was not explicitly prohibited by the Constitution, and therefore Congress had the right and power to order its use.

Chase insisted that his opinion applied only to retroactive payments, but he left open the question of whether the Legal Tender Acts were constitutional. Although the narrow issue in this case was the claim that Hepburn should be paid in specie under a preexisting contract, the implication of Chase's opinion was that Congress had no power to issue greenbacks at all, because the law was passed with an unconstitutional objective and through an unconstitutional method. Ironically, as secretary of the Treasury, Chase had been responsible for proposing the Legal Tender Acts in the first place. The First Legal Tender Case was reversed a year later in ***Knox v. Lee*** and ***Parker*** *v. Davis,* 79 U.S. 457 (1871), known as the Second Legal Tender Case.

See David P. Currie, "The Constitution in the Supreme Court: Civil War and Reconstruction, 1865–1873, *University of Chicago Law Review* 51 (1984): 31–86; and J. Willard Hurst, *A Legal History of Money in the United States, 1774–1973* (Lincoln: University of Nebraska Press, 1973).

Virginia v. West Virginia

78 U.S. 39 (11 Wall. 39) (1871)
Decided: March 6, 1871
Vote: 4 (Swayne, Miller, Strong, Bradley)
3 (Clifford, Davis, Field)
Opinion of the Court: Miller
Dissenting opinion: Davis (Clifford, Field)
Did not participate: S. P. Chase, Nelson

This case arose out of the splitting of Virginia into two states and the creation of West Virginia during the Civil War. Article IV, Section 3, of the Constitution says, "No new State shall be formed or erected within the Jurisdiction of any other State; nor any State be formed by the Junction of two or more States, or Parts of States, without the Consent of the Legislatures of the States concerned as well as of the Congress." In addition, Article I, Section 10, Clause 3, says, "No State shall, without the Consent of Congress . . . enter into any Agreement or Compact with another State." The creation of the state of West Virginia during the Civil War tested both of these constitutional provisions.

The overwhelming majority of the residents of the western part of Virginia did not own slaves and opposed secession. When the U.S. military forced Confederate troops out of the region, plans were quickly made to bring it into the Union as a new state. In 1861 the Lincoln administration recognized the existence of a loyal state legislature in Virginia, which was essentially a government in exile, meeting in Wheeling. The United States also recognized Francis Harrison Pierpoint as the governor of this loyal Virginia government. In November 1861 residents of the western part of the state held a constitutional convention to create the independent state of West Virginia. In May 1862 the Virginia legislature of the Pierpoint government gave its consent to all the people in the western counties to form a new state—West Virginia. The Virginia statute provided that certain counties, including Berkeley and Jefferson, be considered part of West Virginia, if the voters approved. In December 1862 Congress voted to admit West Virginia into the Union. Meanwhile, in early 1863 Pierpoint certified that elections had taken place in all the relevant counties, including Berkeley and Jefferson, and by the end of the year West Virginia was admitted to the Union. In December 1865 the state government in Richmond, now dominated by former Confederates, repealed the enabling legislation allowing the separation, but in early 1866 Congress, by joint resolution, reaffirmed that West Virginia was an independent state.

Virginia now turned to the Supreme Court for relief, alleging that Berkeley and Jefferson Counties had not agreed to their transfer to West Virginia and that Virginia was withdrawing its offer to allow West Virginia to annex them. Over West Virginia's objections, the Court ruled that this was not a "political question" beyond the reach of the Court, but a legitimate question of state boundaries that the Court could resolve. The issue was whether the two disputed counties had held elections. The Court easily resolved the question: Governor Pierpoint had certified the elections, and at the time no one had challenged the certification. The Virginia statute creating West Virginia had placed the entire matter of certification in the hands of Virginia's governor, and it was now too late to challenge his decision. Virginia could "have no right, years after all this has been settled, to come into a court of chancery to charge . . . that her own subordinate agents have misled her Governor, and that her solemn act transferring these counties should be set aside."

The dissenters could only argue that Congress had never approved the transfer of these counties to West Virginia. But, to raise that point would have indeed made the case into a "political question" in which the Court was asked to second-guess the political act of Congress in admitting the state with these counties and later, by a joint resolution, confirming this act.

All of the justices evaded the real issue in the case, which was the power of Congress to remake the states during and after the Civil War. In his argument for Virginia, former Supreme Court justice Benjamin R. Curtis, who was by this time a conservative opponent of the Republicans, tried to raise the issue of Reconstruction and the war powers of Congress. The Court, for the most part, ignored him. Virginia's suit was really designed to undo, by litigation, at least one result of the Civil War. It is not surprising Virginia failed to accomplish this.

See Charles Fairman, *Reconstruction and Reunion, 1864–88, Vol. VI, Part I, History of the Supreme Court of the United States* (New York: Macmillan, 1971).

Collector v. Day

78 U.S. 113 (11 Wall. 113) (1871)
Decided: April 3, 1871
Vote: 8 (S. P. Chase, Nelson, Clifford, Swayne, Miller, Davis, Field, Strong)
1 (Bradley)
Opinion of the Court: Nelson
Dissenting opinion: Bradley

Joseph M. Day, a county judge in Massachusetts, sued James Buffington, a federal tax collector, to recover $61.51, plus interest, for income taxes on his salary in 1866 and 1867. This case was the mirror image of ***Dobbins v. Erie County,*** 41 U.S. 435 (1842). In *Dobbins* the Court held "that it was not competent for the legislature of a state to levy a tax upon the salary or emoluments of an officer of the United States." The basis of the decision was that an officer of the federal government "could not be interfered with by taxation or otherwise by the states." This argument resembled the assertion in ***McCulloch v. Maryland,*** 17 U.S. 316 (1819), that the states could not tax federal institutions. Day made the same argument about the taxation of state employees. If the federal government could tax state officials, then it could undermine the states. Justice Nelson quoted *McCulloch,* saying the "the power to tax involves the power to destroy." Relying on this analysis, plus the Tenth Amendment, the Court provided a mutual, reciprocal tax immunity between the states and the national government.

This immunity still exists for real property, so that the states cannot tax federal lands, and the federal government cannot tax state lands. But, in ***Graves v. New York ex. rel. O'Keefe,*** 306 U.S. 466 (1939), the Court held that the national income tax could reach state employees. This was a position sketched out by Justice Bradley in his dissent in *Collector v. Day.* Bradley argued that "the general government has the same power of taxing the income of officers of the state governments as it has of taxing that of its own officers. It is the common government of all alike; and every citizen is presumed to trust his own government in the matter of taxation."

Cherokee Tobacco Case

78 U.S. 616 (11 Wall. 616) (1871)
Decided: May 1, 1871
Vote: 4 (Clifford, Swayne, Miller, Strong)
2 (Davis, Bradley)
Opinion of the Court: Swayne
Dissenting opinion: Bradley (Davis)
Did not participate: S. P. Chase, Nelson, Field

The Internal Revenue Act of July 20, 1868, imposed a tax on "distilled spirits, fermented liquors, tobacco, snuff and cigars, [to] be construed to extend to such articles produced anywhere within the exterior boundaries of the United States, whether the same shall be within a collection district or not." At issue in this case, officially known as *Two Hundred and Seven Half Pound Papers of Smoking Tobacco, etc. Elias C. Boudinot et al., Claimants v. United States,* was whether the statute applied to such goods on Indian lands. The District Court for the Western District of Arkansas concluded that the tax applied to goods in the Cherokee Nation territory.

Represented by Benjamin F. Butler, a Civil War general and Republican politician, the Cherokee owners of the tobacco, Elias C. Boudinot and Stand Wattie, appealed the district court decision. They contended that the court erred by not permitting a jury instruction that a 1866 treaty barred the 1868 tax on products produced within the territory. The 1866 treaty between the United States and the Cherokee Nation protected all products produced within the territory from present and future taxes imposed by the United States.

Boudinot and Wattie claimed that compliance with the tax was not possible. Butler noted that the stamps required by the act, showing an individual had paid the tax, were not available to individuals residing within the Cherokee Nation territory and the Cherokee Nation was not included within a collection district. He asserted that this lack of availability indicated Congress's intent not to tax the Cherokee Nation under the 1868 Internal Revenue Act.

Justice Swayne concluded that the Cherokee Nation territory was included within the United States and therefore the tax was applicable to the territory. Citing Chief Justice Marshall's opinion in ***Cherokee Nation v. Georgia,*** 30 U.S. 1 (1831), Swayne noted, "The Indian territory is admitted to compose a part of the United States. In all our geographical treatises, histories, and laws it is so considered."

Examining the Constitution, Swayne determined that the "act of Congress must prevail as if the treaty were not an element to be considered." He also evoked a policy concern that if the tax were not imposed, the chance of fraud would be high. Swayne qualified his decision by acknowledging the Cherokee's right to redress is with Congress, not the judiciary.

In a strong dissent, Justice Bradley maintained "it was not the intention of Congress to extend the internal revenue law to the Indian territory. That territory is an exempt jurisdiction." His argument stemmed from treaties between the United States and the Cherokee, in which the government treats the Cherokee as autonomous, making and executing laws by their own government. If Congress intended for the tax to apply to the Cherokee Nation territory, Bradley held, the act would have expressly declared it so.

See Melvin I. Urofsky and Paul Finkelman, *A March of Liberty: A Constitutional History of the United States,* vol. 1 (New York: Oxford University Press, 2002); and David E. Wilkins, *The United States Supreme Court and American Indian Tribal Sovereignty: The Masking of Justice* (Austin: University of Texas Press, 1998) .

Knox v. Lee, Parker v. Davis

Also known as the Second Legal Tender Case
79 U.S. 457 (12 Wall. 457) (1871)
Decided: May 1, 1871
Vote: 5 (Swayne, Miller, Davis, Strong, Bradley)
4 (S. P. Chase, Nelson, Clifford, Field)
Opinion of the Court: Strong
Concurring opinion: Bradley
Dissenting opinion: S. P. Chase (Nelson, Clifford, Field)
Dissenting opinion: Clifford
Dissenting opinion: Field

This case allowed the Court to reconsider its decision in ***Hepburn v. Griswold,*** 75 U.S. 603 (1870). It also provided an opportunity to address the question left unanswered in that case, namely, whether the legal tender acts were unconstitutional. The Court membership had changed since the decision in *Hepburn,* and the addition of Justices Bradley and Strong provided solid support for Republican policies, including the legal tender acts.

Strong began his opinion for the Court by asserting that "it would be difficult to overestimate the consequences which must follow our decision." He said the decision would

> affect the entire business of the country, and take hold of the possible continued existence of the government. If it be held by this court that Congress has no constitutional power, under any circumstances, or in any emergency, to make treasury notes a legal tender for the payment of all debts (a power confessedly possessed by every independent sovereignty other than the United States), the government is without those means of self-preservation which, all must admit, may, in certain contingencies, become indispensable, even if they were not when the acts of Congress now called in question were enacted. It is also clear that if we hold the acts invalid as applicable to debts incurred, or transactions which have taken place since their enactment, our decision must cause, throughout the country, great business derangement, widespread distress, and the rankest injustice.

Returning at length to ***McCulloch v. Maryland,*** 17 U.S. 316 (1819), as Justice Miller had in his dissent in *Hepburn,* Strong found that the Necessary and Proper Clause of the Constitution gave Congress sufficient power to issue paper money, and to make it legal tender for all transactions, including those that had taken place before the law was passed. Strong noted that in the past Congress had changed the amount of gold or silver in a dollar, and in other ways altered the nation's money. Such actions neither violated contracts made beforehand nor did they take property from people who had negotiated contracts. Clearly, a plenary aspect of sovereignty was the power of Congress to fix the value of money. In explicitly overruling *Hepburn,* Strong chastised the Court (he was really attacking Chief Justice Chase) for pushing for a decision by an understaffed and almost equally divided Court in a case involving "constitutional questions of the most vital importance to the government and to the public at large."

Beyond settling the issue of the greenbacks, this case settled, forever, the power of the national government to regulate money. The Court relied on it in *Juilliard v. Greenman,* 110 U.S. 421 (1884), with only Justice Field dissenting, to uphold the power of Congress to issue paper money when there was no wartime emergency. During the Great Depression the Court would once again rely on the *Second Legal Tender Case* to uphold the power of Congress to take the nation off of the gold standard. The ***Gold Clause Cases*** (1935) (see page 196) proved to be one of the few important victories for the Roosevelt administration before the judicial revolution of 1937.

See David P. Currie, "The Constitution in the Supreme Court: Civil War and Reconstruction, 1865–1873," *University of Chicago Law Review* 51 (1984): 131–186; Charles Fairman, *Reconstruction and Reunion, 1864–88, Vol. VI, Part I, History of the Supreme Court of the United States* (New York: Macmillan, 1971); and James Willard Hurst, *A Legal History of Money in the United States, 1774–1973* (Lincoln: University of Nebraska Press, 1973).

United States v. Tarble

80 U.S. 397 (13 Wall. 397) (1872)
Decided: March 4, 1872
Vote: 8 (Nelson, Clifford, Swayne, Miller, Davis, Field, Strong, Bradley)
1 (S. P. Chase)
Opinion of the Court: Field
Dissenting opinion: S. P. Chase

May a state court direct a writ of habeas corpus at a federal officer? This issue first arose in the case of Sherman Booth, which involved the Fugitive Slave Law of 1850. The Wisconsin Supreme Court directed a writ at U.S. Marshal Stephen Ableman, directing him to bring Booth before the court, which ultimately released him. The U.S. Supreme Court overturned this result in ***Ableman v. Booth,*** 62 U.S. 506 (1859), but the legal principle was not clear.

In 1869 Abijah Tarble secured a writ of habeas corpus from a Wisconsin county court to release his underage son from the custody of the U.S. Army. Edward Tarble had enlisted under the name Frank Brown, declaring that he was over age twenty-one, when he was actually under eighteen. In April 1870 the Wisconsin Supreme Court affirmed this result and ordered the Army to release Tarble from military service. The United States government then appealed to the U.S. Supreme Court.

Justice Field framed the legal issue broadly. He asked "whether any judicial officer of a state has jurisdiction to issue a writ of habeas corpus, or to continue proceedings under the writ when issued, for the discharge of a person held under the authority, or claim and color of the authority of the United States, by an officer of that government." Field then discussed the nature of federalism and the "distinct and independent character of the two governments" and concluded that "within their separate spheres of action, it follows that neither can intrude with its judicial process into the domain of the other, except so far as such intrusion may be necessary on the part of the national government to preserve its rightful supremacy in cases of conflict of authority." Field noted that "the experience of the late Rebellion" illustrated the danger of allowing state courts to direct writs of habeas corpus at military authorities, and he warned that such a power could be used "to the great detriment of the public service." Field believed that this rule could not threaten the rights and liberties of citizens, because the national government was "as much interested in protecting the citizen from illegal restraint under" its authority "as the several states are to protect him from the more likely restraint under their authority, and no more likely to tolerate any oppression." Indeed, Field might have noted, but did not, that in the South, where resistance to Reconstruction and black freedom was on-going, state courts might have used the writ of habeas corpus to gain the release, from federal custody, of members of the Ku Klux Klan and other terrorist organizations.

In a brief dissent, Chief Justice Chase argued that the states should have the right to initiate the inquiry, through habeas corpus, especially when the situation involved people held in custody "without the sentence of any court whatever, by an officer of the United States." Chase argued that the federal courts could review and reverse such state action.

United States v. Tarble remains a solid precedent for the principle that state courts cannot direct their writs of habeas corpus at the federal government. The second prong of this decision, however, that the federal courts cannot direct writs of habeas corpus at the state governments, is no longer true, as the expansion of rights under the Fourteenth Amendment have led to habeas review by the Court of convictions in state courts.

See William F. Duker, *A Constitutional History of Habeas Corpus* (Westport, Conn.: Greenwood Press, 1980); and Eric Freedman, *Habeas Corpus: Rethinking the Great Writ* (New York: New York University Press, 2001).

Blyew v. United States

80 U.S. 581 (13 Wall. 581) (1871)
Decided: April 1, 1872
Vote: 6 (Nelson, Clifford, Miller, Davis, Field, Strong)
2 (Swayne, Bradley)
Opinion of the Court: Strong
Dissenting opinion: Bradley (Swayne)
Did not participate: S. P. Chase

John Blyew and George Kennard were indicted on October 7, 1868, in the Circuit Court for the District of Kentucky, for murdering a black woman named Lucy Armstrong. The murder and the indictment took place after the ratification of the Fourteenth Amendment in July 1868. Witnesses testified that on August 29, 1868, the defendants entered a cabin of a black family at night, and a short time later the witnesses discovered the bodies of Armstrong and three other victims. Under Kentucky law, the testimony of blacks could not be used in the prosecution of whites, and in this case all of the witnesses were black.

Although Kentucky officials arrested Blyew and Kennard, the U.S. attorney removed the case to federal court, because he believed the prohibition on black testimony, as well as the general hostility towards blacks in Kentucky, would not serve the interests of justice. Indeed, with no white witness to the crime and no black witnesses able to testify, an acquittal seemed a foregone conclusion. The U.S. attorney acted under the Civil Rights Act of 1866, which said, "The District Courts shall, concurrently with the Circuit Courts, have cognizance of all causes, civil and criminal, affecting persons who are denied or cannot enforce in the courts or judicial tribunals of the State or locality where they may be, any of the rights secured to them by the first section of this act." Before Judge Bland Ballard, the defendants were convicted of murder and sentenced to death. The defendants argued that the federal courts lacked jurisdiction to hear this case, that there was no federal crime of murder, and that the state courts were the proper forum for this prosecution. Ballard rejected these arguments, asserting that under the Thirteenth Amendment and the Civil Rights Act of 1866, the federal courts had the power to enforce state laws—including laws against murder—if the state laws were applied discriminatorily.

The Supreme Court overturned the conviction. Justice Strong concluded that only the litigants—the two white defendants and the state of Kentucky—could take their "cause" to a federal court, but the cause did not include the black victims or the black witnesses, who were prohibited, under Kentucky law, from testifying against whites. Taking a narrow view of who might be affected by the law's enforcement, Strong declared:

> We need hardly add that the jurisdiction of the Circuit Court is not sustained by the fact averred in the indictment that Lucy Armstrong, the person murdered, was a citizen of the African race, and for that reason denied the right to testify in the Kentucky courts. In no sense can she be said to be affected by the cause. Manifestly the act refers to persons in existence. She was the victim of the frightful outrage which gave rise to the cause, but she is beyond being affected by the cause itself.

In dissent, Justice Bradley argued that the position of the Court was "too narrow, too technical, and too forgetful of the liberal objects" of the 1866 act. Bradley stated that the act was a "legitimate consequence" of the Thirteenth Amendment. He wrote, "Merely striking off the fetters of the slave, without removing the incidents and consequences of slavery, would hardly have been a boon to the colored race. Hence, also, the amendment abolishing slavery was supplemented by a clause giving Congress power to enforce it by appropriate legislation." He argued that Section 2 of the amendment, the enforcement section, includes the power to protect the lives and safety of former slaves and the "power to do away with the incidents and consequences of slavery, and to instate the freedmen in the full enjoyment of that civil liberty and equality which the abolition of slavery meant."

Robert J. Kaczorowski, *The Politics of Judicial Interpretation: The Federal Courts, Department of Justice and Civil Rights, 1866–1876* (New York: Oceana, 1985).

Watson v. Jones

80 U.S. 679 (13 Wall. 679) (1872)
Decided: April 15, 1872
Vote: 6 (Nelson, Swayne, Miller, Field, Strong, Bradley)
2 (Clifford, Davis)
Opinion of the Court: Miller
Dissenting opinion: Clifford (Davis)
Did not participate: S. P. Chase

In this case the Court, for the first time, dealt with the thorny question of internal religious disputes and church property. *Watson v. Jones* grew out of disputes within the Presbyterian Church over slavery and the Civil War. During the war the national church endorsed emancipation and supported the federal government. The church declared that all members who supported slavery or "had been guilty of voluntarily aiding the

War of the Rebellion" should "be required to repent and forsake these sins before they could be received" within the church. In Louisville, a group led by John Watson tried to take over the Walnut Street Presbyterian Church. Ultimately, this move led to a deep schism within the Presbyterian Church in Kentucky between those who supported the national church's opposition to slavery and those, led by Watson, who disagreed with that position.

The General Assembly of the Presbyterian Church ultimately ruled against Watson and declared that the Walnut Street church belonged to those who supported the national organization. Kentucky's highest court then awarded the church building to Watson, on the grounds that the majority of the congregation favored his faction. William Jones and others from the national organization sued in federal court to regain their building, winning in the circuit court, and Watson appealed to the U.S. Supreme Court.

The Court said that in a church with a congregational polity, the majority of the members might be able to take over the church and its building. The Presbyterian Church, however, was hierarchical, and the Walnut Street building belonged to the General Assembly of the Presbyterian Church, not to the individuals who worshiped there. The ownership of the building, like the doctrine of the church itself, had to be settled internally. According to the Supreme Court, the Kentucky courts could not decide in favor of Watson, but had to defer to the national organization. The Court noted that if a donation was made for a specific doctrinal purpose, and the church departed from that purpose, the court might be able to return the property to the donor. For example, if someone had donated the land for the Walnut Street church with the condition that the Presbyterian Church always support slavery, then it might have been possible to return the land to the donor when the church took a strong stand against slavery. In this case, however, there were no such doctrinally connected donations, and so the building belonged to the national church.

See Paul Finkelman, ed., *Religion and American Law: An Encyclopedia* (New York: Garland, 2000).

The Slaughterhouse Cases

83 U.S. 36 (16 Wall. 36) (1873)
Decided: April 14, 1873
Vote: 5 (Clifford, Miller, Davis, Strong, Hunt)
4 (S. P. Chase, Swayne, Field, Bradley)
Opinion of the Court: Miller
Dissenting opinion: Field (S. P. Chase, Swayne, Bradley)
Dissenting opinion: Swayne
Dissenting opinion: Bradley

This complex case gave the Court its first major opportunity to interpret the Fourteenth Amendment, which had been ratified in 1868. The Court consolidated three cases brought by New Orleans butchers who objected to a Louisiana law requiring that all slaughtering of animals in the city take place at Crescent City Live-Stock Landing and Slaughtering Company. Centralizing the slaughtering and butchering of animals made sense from a public health perspective, and many other cities had adopted similar policies. The law also provided a valuable monopoly to the entrepreneurs who came by it through their political connections to the Republican-dominated Reconstruction legislature. The butchers were mostly Democrats.

Ironically, the butchers, many of whom were Confederate veterans, asked the Court to apply the recently adopted Thirteenth and Fourteenth Amendments to protect them from the legislature. This irony was compounded by the butchers' choice of counsel—John A. Campbell, who had resigned from the Court at the beginning of the Civil War to serve the Confederacy. Using the Thirteenth Amendment, Campbell argued that the monopoly in effect "enslaved" the butchers, preventing them from freely practicing their trade. Campbell also claimed that the monopoly violated the Privileges and Immunities Clause of the newly adopted Fourteenth Amendment, which prevented any state from making or enforcing "any law which shall abridge the privileges and immunities of citizens of the United States."

Justice Miller dismissed both claims, stressing that the Civil War Amendments had been adopted "for one pervading purpose," to ensure "the freedom of the slave race, the security and firm establishment of freedom, and the protection of the newly-made freeman and citizen from the oppressions of those who had formerly exercised unlimited dominion over him." Miller did not deny that the new amendments could protect other Americans, but he had little sympathy for the notion that a limitation on where butchering could take place could be equated with slavery or the denial of civil rights that blacks had faced after the war.

The new amendments had in fact been passed to give the national government the power to protect former slaves, southern Unionists, and northerners living in the South from white terrorist violence from the Ku Klux Klan and similar organizations, and from repressive legislation passed by postwar southern state governments dominated by former Confederates. While acknowledging the great social revolution brought by the Civil War, emancipation, and the new amendments, Miller offered an extremely narrow view of the fundamental constitutional change brought about by the Civil War. Noting that before the war the states were responsible for the protection of the rights of their citizens, Miller rhetorically asked, "Was it the purpose of the fourteenth amendment . . . to transfer the security and protection of all the civil rights which we have mentioned from the States to the Federal government?" "Was it intended to bring within the power of Congress the entire domain of civil rights heretofore belonging exclusively to the States?" In answering these questions, Miller rejected the idea that the Civil War had fundamentally altered the nature of American government.

Miller asserted that the Privilege and Immunities Clause of the amendment did not protect the basic civil rights of all Americans, but only prevented the states from abridging a limited, narrow set of "federal" rights, which Miller refused to define. He also left the freedom and liberty of the recently emancipated slaves and their children in the hands of southern state governments, which were being taken over by former Confederates, former slaveowners, and their heirs. For Miller, this view was the only option; otherwise, he believed, the Court would become "a perpetual censor upon all legislation of the states, on the civil rights of their own citizens."

The dissenters did not fear this outcome. They argued that the new amendment protected the basic rights of all Americans, not just blacks, and the butchers could not be denied their economic rights without due process of law. As Justice Field noted, the issue was "nothing less than the question whether the recent amendments to the Federal Constitution protect the citizens of the United States against the deprivation of their common rights by States legislation." Field and the other three dissenters believed "the fourteenth amendment does afford such protection." Field asserted that "the privilege and immunities designated" in the amendment, "are those *which of right belong to the citizens of all free governments*" and among them was the right "first to pursue a lawful employment in a lawful manner, without other restraint that such as equally affects all persons." Field asserted that the amendment required that all state legislation protect liberty and equal rights for all citizens, and that all laws had to be "just, equal, and impartial," and under the Supremacy Clause of the Constitution the Court had the power through the new amendments, to strike down offending state legislation that did not comply with this standard.

Most commentators agree with the dissenters that the Fourteenth Amendment was designed to apply most of the Bill of Rights to the states and in the process provide a common standard for civil rights and civil liberties throughout the nation. Ultimately, the Court accepted this theory, but piecemeal, by incorporation—the application of the Bill of Rights to the states through the Due Process Clause of the Fourteenth Amendment, starting with ***Gitlow v. New York,*** 268 U.S. 652 (1925).

See Loren Beth, "The Slaughter-House Cases—Revisited," *Louisiana Law Review* 23 (1963): 487–505; Robert J. Kaczorowski, *The Politics of Judicial Interpretation: The Federal Courts, Department of Justice and Civil Rights, 1866–1876* (Dobbs Ferry, N.Y.: Oceana Publications, 1985); and William E. Nelson, *The Fourteenth Amendment: From Political Principle to Judicial Doctrine* (Cambridge: Harvard University Press. 1988).

Bradwell v. Illinois

83 U.S. 130 (16 Wall. 130) (1873)
Decided: April 15, 1873
Vote: 8 (Clifford, Swayne, Miller, Davis, Field, Strong, Bradley, Hunt)
1 (S. P. Chase)
Opinion of the Court: Miller
Concurring opinion: Bradley (Swayne, Field)
Dissenting without opinion: S. P. Chase

Myra Bradwell studied law with her husband, James B. Bradwell, who was an attorney and the publisher of the *Chicago Legal News,* one of the most important legal publications in the Midwest. At the time, most lawyers prepared for the bar by studying with an established lawyer, and Illinois law required that an attorney be a "person" of good character who had sufficiently studied law. The circuit court in Illinois attested to Myra Bradwell's education and character, and everyone involved in the case conceded, as her attorney, Matthew H. Carpenter, noted, that she was "duly qualified in respect to character and attainments" to be admitted to the bar. The Illinois Supreme Court denied her admission solely because she was a woman.

Bradwell claimed her right to practice law as a citizen of the United States and Illinois and as a "person" under Illinois law and the Fourteenth Amendment of the Constitution. Her main argument rested on the clause of the Fourteenth Amendment that declares, "No State shall make or enforce any law which shall abridge the privileges and immunities of citizens of the United States." The U.S. Supreme Court rejected her claim, asserting that the "right to admission to practice in the courts of a state" is not a privilege or immunity of a citizen of the United States. The Court noted that noncitizens had been allowed to practice law in state and federal courts, and therefore the right to practice law had nothing to do with citizenship. Citing its recent decision in ***The Slaughterhouse Cases,*** 83 U.S. 36 (1873), the Court reaffirmed its constricted view of the Fourteenth Amendment. In a concurring opinion, Justice Bradley offered an argument based on the proper roles of the sexes. He asserted that "nature herself, has always recognized a wide difference in the respective spheres and destinies of man and woman. Man is, or should be, woman's protector and defender. The natural and proper timidity and delicacy which belongs to the female sex evidently unfits it for many of the occupations of a civil life." He asserted that "the paramount destiny and mission of woman are to fulfill the noble and benign offices of wife and mother. This is the law of the Creator. And the rules of civil society must be adapted to the general constitution of things, and cannot be based on exceptional cases."

No matter how exceptional Bradwell was, the Court saw no reason why the Constitution gave her a right to practice law in Illinois or anywhere else. Significantly, Bradwell did not argue that the Equal Protection Clause of the Fourteenth Amendment protected her right to practice law, or that the Due Process Clause gave her a right to the economic value of her legal training. Nor did she argue that the Due Process Clause, combined with the Illinois law, which referred to the qualification of a "person" and not a "man" to practice law, meant that she had been denied due process by Illinois.

Although most states soon allowed women to practice law, the theory of *Bradwell* remained good law until ***Reed v. Reed,*** 404 U.S. 71 (1971), when the Court began to use the Fourteenth Amendment to strike at sex discrimination.

See Nancy T. Gillman, "A Professional Pioneer: Myra Bradwell's Fight to Practice Law," *Law and History Review* 5 (1987): 105–133; Joan Hoff, *Law, Gender, and Injustice: A Legal History of U.S. Women* (New York: New York University Press, 1991); Linda Kerber, *No Constitutional Right to Be Ladies: Women and the Obligations of Citizenship* (New York: Hill and Wang, 1998); and Sandra F. VanBurkleo, *"Belonging to the World": Women's Rights and American Constitutional Culture* (New York: Oxford University Press, 2001).

In re Confiscation Cases

87 U.S. 92 (20 Wall. 92) (1874)
Decided: May 4, 1874
Vote: 5 (Waite, Swayne, Miller, Strong, Hunt)
3 (Clifford, Davis, Field)
Opinion of the Court: Strong
Dissenting opinion: Clifford
Dissenting opinion: Field
Dissenting without opinion: Davis
Did not participate: Bradley

Acting under the Confiscation Act of 1862, U.S. authorities in Louisiana condemned property owned by John Slidell, who was at the time was serving as the Confederate envoy to France. In March 1865 the U.S. district court in Louisiana "decreed a condemnation and forfeiture of the property to the United States." Some of the property was subsequently sold. In March 1870 the circuit court reversed the decree, but confirmed the sales. The circuit court believed that the information against Slidell was insufficient. That information, in part, charged that Slidell was "an officer, or as a foreign minister, or as a commissioner, or as a counsel of the so-called Confederate States of America" who "did give aid and comfort to the rebellion against the United States, and did assist such rebellion."

The Supreme Court reversed the holding of the circuit court, noting that the condemnation and forfeiture proceedings were not criminal in nature, but were "proceedings *in rem*" (against property, not a person) and "in no sense criminal proceedings, and they are not governed by the rules that prevail in respect to indictments or criminal information."

Before the Civil War, Slidell had been a U.S. representative, a U.S. senator, and a diplomat. He then became a high Confederate official. He was precisely the sort of individual that Congress had in mind when it passed the Confiscation Acts. The Court also rejected the idea that President Andrew Johnson's amnesty proclamation of 1868 could affect Slidell's property, because "no power was ever vested in the President to repeal an act of Congress." Furthermore, Slidell's property had "become vested in the United States in 1865, by the judgment of forfeiture," and no "subsequent proclamation of amnesty could have the effect of divesting vested rights."

The Court, in essence, reaffirmed the war powers of Congress and the constitutionality of suppressing the rebellion. In this sense, the opinion reflected the Court's decision in ***Virginia v. West Virginia,*** 78 U.S. 39 (1871), in that it would not allow the former Confederate states or individual Confederates, such as Slidell, who had lost the war on the battlefields, to litigate it in courts.

See Charles Fairman, *Reconstruction and Reunion, 1864–88, Vol. VI, Part I, History of the Supreme Court of the United States* (New York: Macmillan, 1971).

Murdock v. Memphis

87 U.S. 590 (20 Wall. 590) (1875)
Decided: January 11, 1875
Vote: 5 (Miller, Davis, Field, Strong, Hunt)
3 (Clifford, Swayne, Bradley)
Opinion of the Court: Miller
Dissenting opinion: Clifford (Swayne)
Dissenting opinion: Bradley
Did not participate: Waite

Sometime before the Civil War Murdock deeded land, in trust, to the city of Memphis for the express purpose of having the city "convey the same as a donation to the United States Government for a naval yard." The United States accepted the land, but found it impossible to use it for a naval yard, and instead used it for the production of rope for the Navy. In 1854 the United States "abandoned the entire project" and, by an act of Congress, returned the land to Memphis. Thomas Murdock and others then sued in state court to recover the land. After losing there, they appealed to the U.S. Supreme Court. The question for the Court was one of jurisdiction: Did it have power to hear the case?

In 1867 Congress reenacted Section 25 of the Judiciary Act of 1789, with some changes. The 1789 act gave the Supreme Court the authority to hear cases on appeal from state courts that raised federal issues, but not to review questions of state law that did not raise federal questions. In 1867 the Congress omitted this exclusion, presumably giving the Court power to review the interpretations given by state supreme courts of their state and constitutions.

The Supreme Court, however, refused to accept this new, enlarged jurisdiction. Justice Miller noted that it was impossible to know why Congress had altered the original language of the 1789 act or what Congress intended, and the Court was not going to guess. But the Court was also not willing to accept this expanded jurisdiction without proof that Congress intended it. Miller declared, "If Congress, or the framers of the bill, had a clear purpose to enact affirmatively that the court should consider the class of errors," which the 1789 law had not allowed them to consider, "nothing hindered that they [members of

Congress] should say so in positive terms; and in reversing the policy of the Government from its foundation in one of the most important subjects on which that body could act, it is reasonable to be expected that Congress would use plain, unmistakable language giving expression to such intention." Miller saw "no sufficient reason" to believe that Congress, "by repealing or omitting this restrictive clause, intended to enact affirmatively" the right of the Court to review state laws that did not raise, what Miller called "federal questions."

This decision preserved modern federalism and secured the notion of "federal question" jurisdiction for the Supreme Court. It also allowed state courts to interpret their own laws and constitutions on what is known as "adequate and independent state grounds." For example, in issues of fundamental liberties, state courts are able to give greater protections than the federal courts, if the state courts ground their reasoning in state law, state constitutional provisions, and state jurisprudence.

Loan Association v. Topeka

87 U.S. 655 (20 Wall. 655) (1875)
Decided: February 1, 1875
Vote: 8 (Waite, Swayne, Miller, Davis, Field, Strong, Bradley, Hunt)
1 (Clifford)
Opinion of the Court: Miller
Dissenting opinion: Clifford

The City of Topeka, Kansas, with the approval of the state legislature, issued $100,000 in bonds for the benefit of King Wrought Iron Bridge Manufacturing and Iron Works, so that the company would locate factories in Topeka. Interest and principal on the bonds were to be paid out of tax revenues. Citizens' Savings and Loan Association of Cleveland, Ohio, purchased these bonds. When the city refused to pay the interest, Citizens' Savings and Loan sued. Topeka argued that the law was unconstitutional because neither the city nor the state had the power to issue bonds for a private company and then pay off those bonds with tax revenues. Citizens' argued that there was nothing in the Kansas constitution to prevent this and that the bonds were issued for a lawful purpose. For many years states had issued bonds to build railroads, and Citizens' argued that a factory was a similar enterprise.

The Supreme Court, however, disagreed. Unlike a railroad, the iron works was not a public utility, and neither the state nor the city had any control over its operations. Justice Miller could see no "public purpose" in aiding a private iron works, unlike public aid to a railroad. Try as he might, Miller could find no provision—either in the federal or state constitution—that specifically prohibited the issuing of such bonds, but the Court was determined to find a way to undermine the bond issue. Miller examined the history and purpose of taxation and concluded that "there can be no lawful tax which is not laid for a public purpose." Because he found no public purpose in the bonds and the iron works, there could be no lawful tax to support the bonds. He considered the bond issue to be an act "perverting the right of taxation" by taking public money to "aid . . . individual interests and personal purposes of profit and gain." He compared the act of the legislature to a "despotism" because it was an abuse of power and threatened "the social compact." He concluded that "to lay, with one hand, the power of the government on the property of the citizen, and with the other to bestow it upon favored individuals to aid private enterprises and build up private fortunes, is not the less a robbery because it is done under the forms of law and is called taxation."

In dissent, Justice Clifford said, "Courts cannot nullify an act of the State legislature on the vague ground that they think it opposed to a general latent spirit supposed to pervade or underlie the Constitution, where neither the terms nor the implications of the instrument disclose any such restriction."

The case illustrates, in many ways, the emerging interests and fears of the post–Reconstruction-era Court. One can imagine the Marshall Court upholding the law creating the bonds under the Contract Clause, noting, as the Court did in ***Fletcher v. Peck,*** 10 U.S. 87 (1810), that any complaints about the acts of the legislature should be dealt with by the political process, or the Taney Court upholding the bonds as an example of creative funding to support emerging industries. The Waite Court, however, was becoming obsessed with taxation. This case can be also seen as a precursor of the substantive due process jurisprudence that dominated the Court during the two decades that followed.

See Morton Keller, *Affairs of State: Public Life in Late Nineteenth Century America* (1977, reprint, Union, N.J.: Lawbook Exchange, 2000).

Minor v. Happersett

88 U.S. 162 (21 Wall. 162) (1875)
Decided: March 9, 1875
Vote: 9 (Waite, Clifford, Swayne, Miller, Davis, Field, Strong, Bradley, Hunt)
0
Opinion of the Court: Waite

Virginia L. Minor, an adult citizen of Missouri and of the United States, sued Reese Happersett, the registrar of voters in St. Louis County, Missouri, when he refused to allow her to register to vote. Minor claimed that the Fourteenth Amendment prevented Missouri from denying her the right to vote because, under the amendment, "No State shall make or enforce any law which shall abridge the privileges or immunities of citizens of the United States." Coming on the heels of ***The Slaughterhouse Cases,*** 83 U.S. 36 (1873), and ***Bradwell v. Illinois,*** 83 U.S. 130 (1873), the Court's rejection of Minor's arguments were predictable on three counts. First, as *Bradwell* made clear—especially Bradley's concurring opinion—the Court was in no mood to expand the rights of women under the Constitution. Second, even if the Court had been sympathetic to these claims, its constricted view of the Privileges and Immunities Clause of the Fourteenth Amendment would have made this case an unlikely vehicle for the Court to use to expand rights. The right to vote had never been seen as a federal right; indeed, in the unamended Constitution, the right to vote was left entirely to the states to bestow. The Court was on strong historical ground in noting, as it did here, that "The United States has no voters in the States of its own creation." In asserting that the Fourteenth Amendment "did not add to the privileges and immunities of citizens," the Court easily concluded that voting was not included in that clause. Third, the text of the Fourteenth Amendment suggested that it did not aim to expand suffrage at the state level. Section 2 provided a method of reducing the representation in Congress of states that failed to extend the franchise to "any of the male inhabitants of such States, being twenty-one years of age, and citizens of the United States." Although it aimed at convincing the southern states to enfranchise black males, the clause did not require enfranchisement—it only provided a penalty for states that did not enfranchise black males. Furthermore, it specifically limited its reach to males, thus implying that the amendment had nothing whatsoever to do with women's suffrage.

Given this text, as well as the history of the Fourteenth Amendment and of voting rights, it is hardy surprising the Court concluded unanimously that "the Constitution of the United States does not confer the right of suffrage upon anyone, and that the Constitutions and laws of the several States which commit that important trust to men alone are not necessarily void."

See Joan Hoff, *Law, Gender, and Injustice: A Legal History of U.S. Women* (New York: New York University Press,1991); Linda Kerber, *No Constitutional Right to Be Ladies: Women and the Obligations of Citizenship* (New York: Hill and Wang, 1998); and Sandra F. VanBurkleo, *"Belonging to the World": Women's Rights and American Constitutional Culture* (New York: Oxford University Press, 2001).

United States v. Reese

92 U.S. 214 (2 Otto 214) (1876)
Decided: March 27, 1876
Vote: 8 (Waite, Clifford, Swayne, Miller, Davis, Field, Strong, Bradley)
1 (Hunt)
Opinion of the Court: Waite
Concurring opinion: Clifford
Dissenting opinion: Hunt

Hiram Reese and Matthew Foushee, Kentucky election officials, refused to receive and count the ballot of William Garner, an African American, in a local election. Federal officials prosecuted Reese and Foushee under the Enforcement Act of 1870, designed to implement the Fifteenth Amendment. Garner had offered to pay his poll tax to an election official who had refused to accept the payment on the grounds that Garner was black. With the tax unpaid, Reese refused to let Garner vote.

The Court majority offered a narrow technical analysis of the enforcement law, saying it was unconstitutional because one section banned discrimination based on race, and another section did not. Chief Justice Waite struck down the entire statute because two of its sections did not "confine their operation to unlawful discriminations on account of race." The narrow reading of the statute, and the broad stroke of negating the entire statute, signaled that the Court had no interest in protecting the rights of blacks to vote in the South.

In dissent, Justice Hunt cited two major fugitive slave cases, ***Prigg v. Pennsylvania,*** 41 U.S. 539 (1842), and ***Ableman v. Booth,*** 62 U.S. 506 (1859), to argue that in the past the Court had given great latitude to Congress to enforce the Constitution to protect slavery. Hunt now wanted to see the same powers used to support the rights of former slaves.

See Robert Kaczorowski, *The Politics of Judicial Interpretation: The Federal Courts, Department of Justice and Civil Rights, 1866–1876* (New York: Oceana, 1985); Xi Wang, *The Trial of Democracy: Black Suffrage and Northern Republicans, 1860–1910* (Athens: University of Georgia Press, 1997); and Lou Falkner Williams, *The Great South Carolina Ku Klux Klan Trials, 1871–1872* (Athens: University of Georgia Press, 1996).

United States v. Cruikshank

92 U.S. 542 (2 Otto 542) (1876)
Decided: March 27, 1876
Vote: 9 (Waite, Clifford, Swayne, Miller, Davis, Field, Strong, Bradley, Hunt)
0
Opinion of the Court: Waite
Concurring opinion: Clifford

In 1873 hundreds of armed whites attacked blacks holding a meeting in Grant Parish, Louisiana. Known as the Colfax Massacre, it resulted in the death of about one hundred blacks. Federal prosecutors tried William H. Cruikshank and other white terrorists for this crime under the Enforcement Act of 1870, which had been passed to suppress the Ku Klux Klan.

The Court ignored the statute, the nature of the crime, the violence in the South, and the large number of people murdered by Cruikshank and his cohorts. Instead, it focused on technical irregularities in the indictment, despite an 1872 statute clearly stating that such technicalities should be ignored if they did not prejudice the defendants. The Court went through each count of the indictment, searching out whatever technical or linguistic problems it could find. The Court asserted that the crimes committed in Louisiana were violations of state laws and should be tried by the states.

In essence, the Court rejected the idea that the Civil War Amendments provided substantive protection for former slaves and that the enforcement clause in each of the amendments allowed the national government to protect the civil rights of individuals. The Court denied that the victims in this case had any federal right to assemble. The Court did not believe that the mob had denied any constitutional rights of the blacks who were killed, wounded, or intimidated. Building on ***The Slaughterhouse Cases,*** 83 U.S. 36 (1873), the Court once again read the Civil War Amendments as narrowly as possible, which prevented the national government from protecting the rights and liberties of former slaves.

See James M. McPherson, *The Struggle for Equality: Abolitionists and the Negro in the Civil War and Reconstruction* (Princeton: Princeton University Press, 1964); George C. Rable, *But There Was no Peace: The Role of Violence in the Politics of Reconstruction* (Athens: University of Georgia Press, 1964); Xi Wang, *The Trial of Democracy: Black Suffrage and Northern Republicans, 1860–1910* (Athens: University of Georgia Press, 1997); and Lou Falkner Williams, *The Great South Carolina Ku Klux Klan Trials, 1871–1872* (Athens: University of Georgia Press, 1996).

Munn v. Illinois

Also known as the Granger Cases
94 U.S. 113 (4 Otto 113) (1877)
Decided: March 1, 1877
Vote: 7 (Waite, Clifford, Swayne, Miller, Davis, Bradley, Hunt)
2 (Field, Strong)
Opinion of the Court: Waite
Dissenting opinion: Field (Strong)

Munn v. Illinois was decided on the same day as five other cases, and, collectively, they are known as the Granger Cases. All were decided by the same vote. Chief Justice Waite wrote the opinion of the Court in each case, and Justice Field, joined by Justice Strong, dissented in each. They are all based on the same principle and similar state acts, but the Illinois case came first and received the most attention.

In 1875 the Illinois legislature set maximum rates that grain elevator operators could charge grain producers. The statute was limited to elevators in Chicago, where farmers complained they were forced to pay exorbitant prices to store their grain. The farmers also complained of price fixing among elevator operators. The companion cases involved similar state laws regulating how much railroads could charge to move goods and people. Waite argued that these regulations fell into the category of traditional police powers of the states and were designed to protect the people from monopolies. Waite also rejected an argument that these regulations interfered with interstate commerce, because it was plain to all that the laws operated only within the states and were reasonable regulations of internal businesses. Furthermore, Waite noted, the businesses involved clearly affected the public interest. The state laws stemmed from the historic government regulation of the rates charged by common carriers, such as railroads, and other public utilities, such as grain elevators. In his opinion Waite cited traditional English cases for the proposition that public utilities, common carriers, and similar enterprises were subject to regulation. As he observed, "When private property is devoted to a public use, it is subject to public regulation."

In a somewhat hysterical dissent, Field argued that these laws undermined private property and due process of law. He declared that "all property and all business in the states are held at the mercy of the legislature" by such laws. In fact, nothing of the kind developed from these or similar laws.

The other cases decided with *Munn* were *Chicago, Burlington & Quincy Railroad v. Iowa,* 94 U.S. 155; *Peik v. Chicago & Northwestern Railway Co.,* 94 U.S. 164; *Chicago, Milwaukee & St. Paul Railroad Co. v. Ackley,* 94 U.S. 179; *Winona and St. Peter Railroad Co. v. Blake,* 94 U.S. 180; and *Stone v. Wisconsin,* 94 U.S. 181.

See Morton Keller, *Affairs of State: Public Life in Late Nineteenth Century America* (1977, reprint, Union, N.J.: Lawbook Exchange, 2000); and Charles Fairman, *Reconstruction and Reunion, 1864–88, Vol. VI, Part I, History of the Supreme Court of the United States* (New York: Macmillan, 1971).

Hall v. DeCuir

95 U.S. 485 (5 Otto 485) (1878)
Decided: January 14, 1878
Vote: 9 (Waite, Clifford, Swayne, Miller, Field, Strong, Bradley, Hunt, Harlan I)
0
Opinion of the Court: Waite
Opinion concurring in judgment: Clifford

The Reconstruction constitution of Louisiana prohibited common carriers in the state—steamboats, stage coaches, and railroads—from segregating blacks and whites. The law simply stated, "All persons shall enjoy equal rights and privileges upon any conveyance of any public character." In 1869 the legislature gave teeth to this provision, providing a private right to sue for damages. John G. Benson, the master of *The Governor Allen* refused to allow Josephine DeCuir, described as "a person of color," from occupying a cabin on his boat on a voyage from New Orleans to Hermitage, Louisiana. DeCuir won a judgment of $1,000 at trial for this indignity, and, when Benson died, the administrator of his estate, Eliza Jane Hall, appealed to the U.S. Supreme Court.

The Louisiana law applied only to public conveyances within the state, and DeCuir had attempted to travel only within the state. Nevertheless, the Court held that this law imposed a burden on interstate commerce and was an unconstitutional violation of congressional jurisdiction. Congress had in fact passed no legislation on this issue, and here the Court applied the dormant commerce power. The Court argued that because steamboats on the Mississippi passed from state-to-state, this law placed an undue burden on such shipping.

Only twelve years earlier, Congress had passed, and sent to the states for ratification, the Fourteenth Amendment, which prohibits the states from denying any person the equal protection of the laws. The Court might easily have concluded that the 1869 statute was nothing more than an implementation of the new amendment. The Court might also have noted that because laws prohibiting integration or requiring segregation would violate the new amendment, the Louisiana law could not actually burden interstate commerce. The Court rejected such an egalitarian analysis in favor of one that struck down the law requiring integration.

Had the Court strictly followed *DeCuir,* it would have subsequently struck down state laws requiring segregation, leaving it entirely up to the private carriers how they would handle the issue. In subsequent cases, however, the Court upheld state laws requiring segregation on common carriers in ***Louisville, New Orleans, and Texas Pacific Railroad v. Mississippi,*** 133 U.S. 587 (1890), and in ***Plessy v. Ferguson,*** 163 U.S. 537 (1896), the Court upheld a Louisiana statute requiring segregation on common carriers that had the same implications for interstate commerce as *DeCuir,* although with a different goal.

Hall v. DeCuir remained good law until effectively overturned by ***Morgan v. Virginia,*** 328 U.S. 373 (1946), which struck down laws requiring segregation in interstate common carriers.

See Richard Kluger, *Simple Justice* (New York: Knopf, 1975).

Pennoyer v. Neff

95 U.S. 714 (5 Otto 714) (1878)
Decided: January 21, 1878
Vote: 8 (Waite, Clifford, Swayne, Miller, Field, Strong, Bradley, Harlan I)
1 (Hunt)
Opinion of the Court: Field
Dissenting opinion: Hunt

Marcus Neff was the owner of land in Oregon that he acquired under the Oregon Donation law of 1850. In 1866 a state court awarded a judgment to J. H. Mitchell, an attorney, in a suit against Neff, for failing to pay Mitchell about $300 in fees. Operating under existing Oregon law, Mitchell brought an action against Neff's land and published in various newspapers his intention to sue Neff. Under Oregon law, Mitchell had gained "constructive service of summons by publication," but Mitchell never personally served Neff, who was not living in the state at the time of action against him. Neff's property, which was worth about $15,000, was then sold at a sheriff's auction to Sylvester Pennoyer. Neff subsequently brought suit in federal court, under diversity jurisdiction, to recover the property. Although it did not strike down the Oregon law, the District Court ruled for Neff on a technicality, and Pennoyer then appealed to the U.S. Supreme Court.

The Supreme Court ruled that the Oregon procedure, which gave Neff neither notice nor personal service, violated the due process protections of the Fourteenth Amendment. Justice Field held that "every State possesses exclusive jurisdiction and sovereignty over persons and property within its territory," but that "no State can exercise direct jurisdiction and authority over persons and property" when the person had never been in within "its territory." This ruling would not have applied to property that was itself at issue. For example, a bank could have foreclosed on a mortgage against Neff and taken the land in question. But, here the land was irrelevant to the action for breach of contract. This decision indicated the post-Reconstruction Court's unwillingness to have the law grow to meet the exigencies of the age. At a time when personal travel was common, but contact was sometimes difficult to establish, the Oregon rule made sense. The Court, however, fiercely protecting property rights, rejected this concept.

The Court modified *Pennoyer* in ***International Shoe Co. v. Washington,*** 326 U.S. 310 (1945). The Court accepted the realities of a complex economy where business was often done from afar, but where there was no personal contact between parties, or where one of the parties had never been in the forum state (the state where the trial was taking place).

See Charles W. McCurdy Jr., "Justice Field and the Jurisprudence of Government-Business Relations: Some Parameters of Laissez-Faire Constitutionalism, 1863–1897," *Journal of American History* 61 (1975): 970–1005; and Wendy Collins Perdue, "Sin, Scandal, and Substantive Due Process: Personal Jurisdiction and Pennoyer Reconsidered," *Washington Law Review* 62 (1987): 479.

Davidson v. New Orleans

96 U.S. 97 (6 Otto 97) (1878)
Decided: January 7, 1878
Vote: 8 (Waite, Clifford, Swayne, Miller, Field, Strong, Bradley, Hunt)
0
Opinion of the Court: Miller
Concurring opinion: Bradley

The City of New Orleans brought a petition against John Davidson asking for an assessment for the draining of swamplands on his property. The district court denied the assessment, and the city appealed. The state supreme court consented to the assessment, and Davison appealed the decision to the Supreme Court by writ of error.

Davidson maintained that the assessment was exorbitant, was made prior to the project being started, and made no improvement to his property. He also contended that New Orleans lacked the power necessary to create a private corporation with fixed wages for clearing swamplands. The plaintiff's main contention, which afforded him jurisdiction, was that the assessment violated the Due Process Clause of the Fourteenth Amendment.

The Supreme Court upheld the decision of the Supreme Court of Louisiana in affirming the assessment on the plaintiff's property. Justice Miller found the assessment did not violate due process. He attempted to answer all of the plaintiff's concerns but focused his efforts on the issue of due process.

The Court looked to the historical development of the Due Process Clauses contained in the Fifth Amendment and the Fourteenth Amendment. Miller noted with interest that there were not many Fifth Amendment cases, but that the

Fourteenth Amendment had been invoked a number of times since its ratification in 1868. Miller attributed this to the lack of a precise definition of due process under the Fourteenth Amendment, and he attempted to formulate such a definition for its intent and application. He held:

> That whenever by the laws of a State, or by State authority, a tax, assessment, servitude, or other burden is imposed upon property for the public use, whether it be used for the whole State or of some more limited portion of the community, and those laws provide for a mode of confirming or contesting the charge thus imposed, in the ordinary courts of justice, with such notice, to the person, or such proceeding in regard to the property as is appropriate to the nature of the case, the judgment in such proceedings cannot be said to deprive the owner of this property without due process of law, however obnoxious it may be to the other objections.

Applying this rule to the assessment for the draining of the swampland, Miller's opinion showed the assessment was within the definition of due process under the Fourteenth Amendment. Miller also noted that the assessment was not forbidden from being applied more than once to the property.

In his concurrence, Justice Bradley contended that the definition formulated by the majority was too narrow in scope. He said there were other takings of property besides taking by non-judicial means or direct enactment that could violate due process. He cited ***Murray's Lessee v. Hoboken Land and Improvement Company,*** 59 U.S. 272 (1856), to defend his position. He extracted from *Murray's Lessee* that it should not be left to the legislature to pass any law or procedure and declare it constituted due process. Bradley's strong addition to the majority's opinion is the phrase that if the process of law is "found to be arbitrary, oppressive, and unjust, it may be declared to be not due process of law." These words moved the Court toward the substantive due process jurisprudence of the late nineteenth and early twentieth centuries.

See John Harrison, "Substantive Due Process and the Constitutional Text," *Virginia Law Review* 83 (1997): 493.

Ex parte Jackson

96 U.S. 727 (6 Otto 727) (1878)
Decided: May 13, 1878
Vote: 9 (Waite, Clifford, Swayne, Miller, Field, Strong, Bradley, Hunt, Harlan I)
0
Opinion of the Court: Field

Federal authorities prosecuted A. Orlando Jackson for mailing a circular about lottery tickets in violation of a statute prohibiting the use of the mails to send such information. The provision involving lotteries was an amendment to an 1873 law, commonly known as the Comstock Act, which banned the mailing of obscene matter. Although used to suppress explicit sexual materials, the Comstock Act was also used to prevent information about birth control, abortion, and sex education in general from being sent through the mails. It was also used to prosecute many serious authors whose work offended the special post office inspector, Anthony Comstock, the chief lobbyist for the law. Jackson's attorneys objected to the statute, suggesting it violated fundamental rights of freedom of speech, even though the printed summary of their arguments contains no direct reference to the First Amendment. They also argued the law violated fundamental rights of communication between husbands and wives, clients and attorneys, and physicians and patients. Although these arguments have a modern ring of a right to privacy, the attorneys did not specifically assert such a right. Finally, Jackson's attorneys argued that the states, not the federal government, had the authority to ban lotteries and regulate morals. They said, "If the People had conferred upon Congress authority to regulate public morals, the statute before us would not be open to judicial criticism." But, they asserted, "The People never conferred and Congress cannot exercise any such right."

The Court rejected these arguments. Justice Field concluded that Congress had the right to regulate the mails and prohibit the mailing of objectionable material. The right stemmed from Congress's power to "establish Post Offices and post Roads" (Article I, Section 8, Clause 7). Field explicitly denied that excluding objectionable material from the mail "interfere[s] with the freedom of the press, or with any other rights of the people."

This case confirmed the right of Congress to regulate the mails and to use the post office as a mechanism for enforcing Congress's notion of morality. The case became a precedent for suppression of the mailing of birth control information from the 1870s to the 1920s, as well as suppressing antiwar literature during World War I. It remains a precedent for the federal suppression of obscene materials.

See Paul Finkelman, "Cultural Speech and Political Speech in Historical Perspective," *Boston University Law Review,* (1999): 717–743; Gaines M. Foster, *Moral Reconstruction: Christian Lobbyists and the Federal Legislation of Morality, 1865–1920* (Chapel Hill: University of North Carolina Press, 2002); and David Rabban, *Free Speech in Its Forgotten Years* (New York: Cambridge University Press, 1997).

Reynolds v. United States

98 U.S. 145 (8 Otto 145) (1879)
Decided: May 5, 1879
Vote: 9 (Waite, Clifford, Swayne, Miller, Field, Strong, Bradley, Hunt, Harlan I)
0
Opinion of the Court: Waite
Concurring opinion: Field

This case was the first in which the Supreme Court seriously considered, interpreted, and applied the Free Exercise Clause of the First Amendment. Here, the Court made a crucial distinction between a right of belief and of practice. The Court held that the government could prohibit religious practice, but not belief. In a subsequent case, ***Davis v. Beason,*** 133 U.S. 333 (1890), the Court upheld a prosecution for "belief" as well as practice. Both *Reynolds* and *Beason* were part of what has been described as the "war on Mormon religion."

The Morrill Anti-Bigamy Act of 1862 made it a federal crime for anyone living in a federal territory to marry a second time if already married. This law was directed at members of the Church of Jesus Christ of Latter-day Saints (LDS), popularly known as Mormons, who at that time practiced polygamy. In 1874 Congress passed another antipolygamy act, and the Grant administration made suppression of polygamy a priority, which led to the arrests of hundreds of Mormon men in the Utah Territory. LDS leaders chose George Reynolds, Brigham Young's secretary, to test the constitutionality of the law. After his conviction, he appealed to the Supreme Court with the help of the church.

Chief Justice Waite initially declared that Congress had no power to pass any law "which shall prohibit the free exercise of religion," but then he asked if the law in question "comes within this prohibition." In his analysis he first sought to determine what the word "religion" meant, and for this he turned to its meaning to the Framers at the Founding. The precise question was "What is the religious freedom which has been guaranteed?" He then briefly examined some of the writings of the Founders, including Jefferson, and essentially concluded that the "religious freedom" in the First Amendment meant "Congress was deprived of all legislative power over mere opinion, but was left free to reach actions which were in violation of social duties or subversive to social order."

His conclusion led to an attack on polygamy as "odious among the Northern and Western Nations of Europe" and, until the advent of the Mormon Church, "almost exclusively a feature of the life of Asiatic and African people." The late nineteenth century was an age of social Darwinism, when the rights of blacks were under constant assault and a powerful movement to ban Chinese immigration was building in the nation. By tying polygamy to Asian and African peoples, Waite set the stage to denounce Mormons as essentially "un-American" and foreign, even though the faith was entirely the product of native-born citizens of Anglo-Saxon origins. He then compared polygamy to human sacrifice and to the Hindu practice of widows throwing themselves on the funeral pyres of their dead husbands.

The Court was developing a doctrine of religious freedom based on ethnic prejudices, a narrow view of the intentions of the Framers, and a deep hostility to the defendants in a criminal case. Convinced that polygamy led to "evil consequences," the Court developed a doctrine to uphold the suppression of the Mormons because their religious practices, involving consenting adults, offended a majority of the Court and of the nation. Here, the "tyranny of the majority," to use Alexis de Tocqueville's apt phrase, overrode the protections written into the Constitution to protect the practices of religious minorities.

By 1900 the war against Mormon religion was over, and the Court never allowed prosecutions for religious belief, as it had in *Beason,* but it continued to use the belief/practice distinction as recently as ***Employment Division, Department of Human Resources of Oregon v. Smith,*** 494 U.S. 872 (1990).

See Edwin B. Firmage and Richard C. Mangrum, *Zion in the Courts: A Legal History of the Church of Jesus Christ of Latter-Day Saints, 1830–1900* (Urbana: University of Illinois Press, 1988); Sarah Barringer Gordon, *The Mormon Question: Polygamy and Constitutional Conflict in Nineteenth-Century America* (Chapel Hill: University of North Carolina Press, 2002); and Carol Weisbrod and Pamela Sheingorn, "*Reynolds v. United States:* Nineteenth Century Forms of Marriage and the Status of Women," *Connecticut Law Review* 10 (1978): 828–858.

1880–1889

Tennessee v. Davis

100 U.S. 257 (10 Otto 257) (1880)
Decided: March 1, 1880
Vote: 7 (Waite, Swayne, Miller, Strong, Bradley, Hunt, Harlan I)
2 (Clifford, Field)
Opinion of the Court: Strong
Dissenting opinion: Clifford

James M. Davis was a tax collector for the Internal Revenue Service. His duties included investigating the production or sale of moonshine, whiskey on which no tax was paid. He was looking for moonshiners when he was attacked and shot at. In defending himself, Davis killed one of his attackers. Tennessee authorities indicted Davis for murder, and he appealed to the U.S. Circuit Court for the Middle District of Tennessee to have his trial removed to a federal court. The circuit court was divided on whether it had jurisdiction to order the removal of a criminal case of this nature.

Speaking for the Supreme Court, Justice Strong said federal courts had the power to try federal officials for alleged crimes committed in the line of duty. Section 643 of the United States Revised Statutes provided for removal to federal court "When any civil suit or criminal prosecution is commenced in any court of a State against any officer appointed under or acting by authority of any revenue law of the United States . . on account of any act done under the color of his office." Strong dismissed arguments that the Tennessee prosecution was not an attempt to undermine the laws of Congress, but rather to punish an act against the "peace and dignity of the State alone." Such an argument would open the door for state prosecutions of federal officials for offenses against the state, both real and imagined, and lead to precisely what Congress wanted to prevent: state authorities using the courts to frustrate the enforcement of federal law. Quoting ***Martin v. Hunter's Lessee,*** 14 U.S. 304 (1816), Strong wrote, "The General Government must cease to exist whenever it loses the power of protecting itself in the exercise of its constitutional powers." Strong reminded Tennessee that the removal act had initially been signed into law by President Andrew Jackson, who was, ironically, from Tennessee, in response to South Carolina's attempt to nullify the federal tariff. The removal act was renewed after the Civil War to keep the former rebellious states from hindering the operations of federal officials. It was central to creating a national system of law and protecting the officers of the United States.

Strauder v. West Virginia

100 U.S. 303 (10 Otto 303) (1880)
Decided: March 1, 1880
Vote: 7 (Waite, Swayne, Miller, Strong, Bradley, Hunt, Harlan I)
2 (Clifford, Field)
Opinion of the Court: Strong
Dissenting opinion: Field (Clifford). Dissent found in *Ex parte Virginia and J. D. Coles*

Taylor Strauder, a former slave, was convicted of murder. He sought removal of his trial to a federal court on the grounds that he could not receive a fair trail in West Virginia where blacks were not allowed to serve on juries. The relevant state law provided said, "All white male persons who are twenty-one years of age and who are citizens of this State shall be liable to serve as jurors," except for exempted state officials.

The Court noted that this case was "important" because the issues "demand a construction of the recent amendments of the Constitution." Justice Strong concluded that the Civil War Amendments had "a common purpose, namely: securing to a race recently emancipated, a race that through many generations had been held in slavery, all the civil rights that the superior race enjoy." Because in the South "discriminations against them [blacks] had been habitual," Strong concluded that Congress adopted the new amendments, especially the Fourteenth, to protect them "against unfriendly action in the States where they were resident." Strong emphatically asserted that the amendment was "designed to assure to the colored race the enjoyment of all the civil rights that under the law are enjoyed by white persons, and to give to that race the protection of the General Government in that enjoyment, whenever it should be denied by the States."

For the Court, *Strauder* was clearly among the easiest race discrimination cases it had to decide. The statute was unambiguous in its discrimination; and the nature of discrimination went to the heart of the political and legal rights that the Civil War Amendments secured for all Americans. After a brief discussion of the importance of a jury trial and of an impartial jury and a similar discussion of the intentions of the framers of the Fourteenth Amendment, Strong observed that it was "hard to see why the Statute of West Virginia should not be regarded as discriminating against a colored man when he is put upon trial for an alleged criminal offense against the State." Although the Court had no difficulty overturning the West Virginia law, the result was not a victory for racial equality. Strong's opinion sent a clear message to the South that what could not be accomplished directly could be accomplished indirectly. He noted that the decision did not prohibit the states from "prescrib[ing] the qualifications of its jurors, and in so doing make discrimination." He suggested that jury service could be limited "to males, to freeholders, to citizens, to persons within certain ages, or to persons having educational qualifications." Strauder's conviction was reversed, but the case, combined with ***Virginia v. Rives,*** 100 U.S. 313 (1880), decided the same day, provided the framework for a gradual removal of blacks from southern juries.

Justices Clifford and Field dissented and referred to Field's dissent in ***Ex parte Virginia,*** 100 U.S. 339 (1880). They consistently opposed decisions that interfered with the rights of states to conduct trials as they wished, and both justices were generally opposed to black rights. The law here seemed so obviously in violation of the Constitution that they perhaps thought it best not to make an argument, even though they did not support the notion that blacks might have a constitutional right not to be discriminated against in jury service.

See Stephen Cresswell, "The Case of Taylor Strauder," *West Virginia History* 4 (1983): 193–211; Donald G. Nieman, *Promises to Keep: African-Americans and the Constitutional Order, 1776 to the Present* (New York: Oxford University Press, 1991); and Benno C. Schmidt Jr., "Juries, Jurisdiction, and Race Discrimination: The Lost Promise of *Strauder v. West Virginia,*" *Texas Law Review* 61 (1983): 1401–99.

Virginia v. Rives

Also known as Ex parte Virginia
100 U.S. 313 (10 Otto 313) (1880)
Decided: March 1, 1880
Vote: 9 (Waite, Clifford, Swayne, Miller, Field, Strong, Bradley, Hunt, Harlan I)
0
Opinion of the Court: Strong
Concurring opinion: Field (Clifford)

This case was one of a series decided in 1880 involving the conflicts between the southern states and the federal government over the treatment of blacks in state courts. The other cases were protective of black rights, but this one was not.

Burwell Reynolds and Lee Reynolds, black teenagers, were charged with murdering a white man. No blacks served on either the grand jury that indicted them or the petit jury that convicted them. The defendants petitioned the trial court to ensure that blacks would be in the jury, arguing that "a strong prejudice existed in the community of the county against them, independent of the merits of the case, and based solely upon the fact that they are negroes, and that the man they were accused of having murdered was a white man." They believed that these facts—their race and the race of the victim—would prevent them from getting a fair trial. They also claimed that no blacks had "been allowed the right to serve as jurors, either in civil or criminal cases" in the county. They asked that their case be removed to federal court, but the state court refused. They were convicted at one trial, but the verdict was set aside. They were then granted separate trials, leading to conviction for one and a hung jury for the other. At this point, Judge Alexander Rives of the U.S. district court issued a writ of habeas corpus and took custody of the two defendants. The commonwealth of Virginia then took the case directly to the Supreme Court, asking for a writ of mandamus to direct Rives to return the prisoners to the custody of the state.

Federal law allowed for the removal to federal court in state cases in which the defendant "is denied or cannot enforce in the judicial tribunals of the State . . . any right secured to him by any law providing for the equal civil rights of citizens of the United States." In a tortured reading of the facts of the case and the federal law, Justice Strong found that the case before him did not come under the federal law. He noted that Virginia law did not prohibit blacks from serving on juries, and therefore no state law denied the defendants their constitutional rights. Strong conceded that the county official may have purposely refused to call blacks for jury service, as lawyers for the young black men argued before the Court. The official's refusal, however, did not indicate that the state was acting in an unconstitutional manner, only that the official was involved in a "criminal misuse of the state law" and was subject to punishment under both state and federal laws. Strong's decision left the defendants with no remedy for what may have been an unfair conviction, even if it raised the possibility of punishment for the person responsible for it.

The legal theory of this case was that no person was entitled to a jury of any particular race. The defendants had argued that blacks should be proportionately represented on the jury. That no blacks were on a particular jury did not create a constitutional problem, according to the Court. In reality, the decision was a huge blow to judicial fairness at the end of the Reconstruction period. The Court essentially held that, short of a statutory discrimination in jury selection, blacks in the South would be left to the tender mercies of the white officials who ran the court system. The case contrasts with ***Strauder v. West Virginia,*** 100 U.S. 303 (1880), decided the same day, in which the Court overturned a conviction because the state law prohibited blacks from serving on juries.

See Benno C. Schmidt Jr., "Juries, Jurisdiction, and Race Discrimination: The Lost Promise of *Strauder v. West Virginia,*" *Texas Law Review* 61 (1983): 1401–99; and Donald G. Nieman, *Promises to Keep: African-Americans and the Constitutional Order, 1776 to the Present* (New York: Oxford University Press, 1991).

Ex parte Virginia and J. D. Coles

100 U.S. 339 (10 Otto 339) (1880)
Decided: March 1, 1880
Vote: 7 (Waite, Swayne, Miller, Strong, Bradley, Hunt, Harlan I)
2 (Clifford, Field)
Opinion of the Court: Strong
Dissenting opinion: Field (Clifford)

Ex parte Virginia and J. D. Coles was the third case dealing with the rights of African Americans to serve on juries decided on March 1, 1880. (The others were ***Strauder v. West Virginia,*** 100 U.S. 303, and ***Virginia v. Rives,*** 100 U.S. 313.) In this case, J. D. Coles, a county judge in Virginia, was indicated by a federal grand jury, and subsequently arrested, for excluding blacks from the grand and petit juries in his courts. His arrest was based on a federal law of 1875, which provided a fine or imprisonment for anyone who excluded otherwise qualified jurors because of race or previous condition of servitude. Coles sought a writ of habeas corpus to free himself from federal custody. The Supreme Court rejected his petition.

Justice Strong upheld the federal law as a legitimate act for the enforcement of the Fourteenth Amendment. Strong noted that the "great purpose" of the amendment "was to raise the colored race from the condition of inferiority and servitude in which most of them had previously stood into perfect equality of civil rights with all other persons within the jurisdiction of the States." Citing *Strauder,* Strong reiterated that "an equal right to an impartial jury trial, and such an immunity from unfriendly discrimination are placed by the Amendment under the protection of the General Government and guaranteed by it."

Strong noted that the Fourteenth Amendment limited only state action, but he refused to let Coles hide behind this limitation. As a county judge, Coles was acting in his capacity as a state official. Strong wrote, "A State acts by its legislative, its executive, or its judicial authorities. It can act in no other way." Therefore, the laws passed to implement the amendment could reach state officials acting in their official capacities to deny rights to African Americans. Strong denied that the federal government had no power to punish a state judge for his official acts. Rather, he asserted that the 1875 act could reach any public official—"court-criers, tipstaves, sheriffs" and in this case a judge who prevented blacks from serving on juries.

This was a remarkable decision, and, had it been applied rigorously across the South by federal prosecutors and judges, the subsequent history of criminal justice in the South might have been different. It was not, however, and within two decades blacks were uniformly absent from jury service throughout the South.

See Benno C. Schmidt Jr., "Juries, Jurisdiction, and Race Discrimination: The Lost Promise of *Strauder v. West Virginia,*" *Texas Law Review* 61 (1983): 1401–99; and Donald G. Nieman, *Promises to Keep: African-Americans and the Constitutional Order, 1776 to the Present* (New York: Oxford University Press, 1991).

Ex parte Siebold

100 U.S. 371 (10 Otto 371) (1880)
Decided: March 8, 1880
Vote: 7 (Waite, Swayne, Miller, Strong, Bradley, Hunt, Harlan I)
2 (Clifford, Field)
Opinion of the Court: Bradley
Dissent: Field (Clifford)

Field's dissent may be found in *Ex parte Clarke,* 100 U.S. 399 (10 Otto 399) (1880).

Albert Siebold, Walter Tucker, Martin C. Burns, Lewis Coleman, and Henry Bowers, election judges in Baltimore, Maryland, were convicted in federal court for stuffing ballot boxes during the congressional election of 1878. The charges and convictions were brought under the Enforcement Acts of 1870–1871. The cases were tied to the politics of the era. Democrats despised the enforcement laws, which had led to black suffrage throughout the South. The enforcement laws also challenged traditional notions of federalism and states' rights by imposing national standards on elections.

Article I, Section 4, of the Constitution gives the states the primary responsibility for setting rules for the election of members of Congress, but also says, "Congress may at any time by Law make or alter such Regulations." Justice Bradley relied on this clause to uphold the enforcement laws and reject the plea for habeas corpus relief. The opinion gave significant support to the national government to protect voting rights in the still volatile post–Civil War South.

The case also acknowledged that the Civil War had in fact altered the politics of federalism and states' rights. Siebold argued that Congress had no power to infringe on the right of the states to regulate elections, short of taking over all aspects of them. His argument was a shrewd strategy because there was no chance of Congress doing any such thing; even in 1870 Congress would not have wanted to federalize all elections in the South. By 1879, when the case was argued, Democrats were in control in Congress, and passage of any new legislation on this issue was unlikely. Siebold therefore tried to convince the Court that Congress either had to take over the entire election process or not interfere at all. The Court emphatically rejected this argument.

Justice Field's dissent, joined by Justice Clifford, may be found in the companion case, *Ex parte Clarke,* 100 U.S. 399 (1880), in which the Court upheld a similar conviction of a corrupt election judge in Cincinnati, Ohio. In *Clarke,* Field argued that Congress could not impose duties on state officials. In *Siebold,* however, the statute did not impose duties *per se,* but merely required that state election judges follow certain guidelines and standards.

Reformers throughout the nation, as well as advocates of civil rights, hailed the decision as a step toward honest elections, but the Democrats in Congress succeeded in undermining the decision and the law by refusing to appropriate money for its enforcement. *Siebold* was a futile attempt to protect voting rights and maintain honest elections at a time of increasing pressure from southern whites to eliminate black voters and widespread corruption in urban elections in the North.

See Xi Wang, *The Trial of Democracy: Black Suffrage and Northern Republicans, 1860–1910* (Athens: University of Georgia Press, 1997).

Kilbourn v. Thompson

103 U.S. 168 (1881)
Decided: January 24, 1881
Vote: 9 (Waite, Clifford, Swayne, Miller, Field, Bradley, Hunt, Harlan I, Woods)
0
Opinion of the Court: Miller

In January 1877 the House of Representatives began an investigation of one of the great financial scandals in an age of great financial scandals, the collapse and bankruptcy of Jay Cooke and Company. Secretary of the Navy George Maxwell Robeson had deposited money in the London branch of Cooke's bank, and, when the entire Cooke operation collapsed, the United States sought to recover its deposits. Cooke and his company had a large interest in a "real estate pool," and the House sought to determine who actually controlled that pool and to discover the properties it owned, as a first step to recovering the government's money. As part of its investigation, the House called Hallett Kilbourn to testify. Kilbourn refused to name the five members of the real estate pool or say where they lived. He refused to bring to the House "certain records, papers and maps relating to the inquiry." The House then issued a subpoena, which he also ignored. The House declared Kilbourn in contempt and issued a warrant for his arrest. John G. Thompson, the sergeant at arms for the House, arranged for Kilbourn's arrest and incarceration. Kilbourn argued that Congress had no lawful authority to arrest him. He lost his initial case before the U.S. District Court of the District of Columbia.

The Supreme Court found the contempt citation invalid because the investigation itself was beyond the power of Congress. In a very narrow reading of congressional power, the Court held that the ownership and holdings of the real estate pool was a matter for the courts, not the legislature. The hearings were not directed at legislation *per se,* and therefore the investigation went beyond the powers of Congress. Because Congress had no power to investigate, it likewise had no power to force Kilbourn to testify. The Court ordered Kilbourn released and remanded the case to the district court for further proceedings.

The Court did not completely rule out the possibility of contempt proceedings by Congress, but it considerably narrowed congressional power. In doing so, the Court distinguished between the broad contempt and arrest powers of the British Parliament and the more narrow powers of the U.S. Congress. In subsequent years, Congress learned to tie its investigations to legislative proposals and avoid claims that the investigations were unconstitutional. For example, the famous Watergate investigations conducted by Sen. Sam Ervin were based on planned campaign finance laws. In *McGrain v. Daugherty,* 273 U.S. 135 (1927), and *Sinclair v. United States,* 279 U.S. 749 (1929), the Court expanded the right of Congress to arrest on contempt charges those who ignored congressional subpoenas.

See Edward Balleisen, *Navigating Failure: Bankruptcy and Commercial Society in Antebellum America* (Chapel Hill: University of North Carolina Press, 2001); Charles Fairman, *Reconstruction and Reunion, 1864–88, Vol. VII, Part II, History of the Supreme Court of the United States* (New York: Macmillan, 1971); and David Skeel, *Debt's Dominion: A History of Bankruptcy Law in America* (Princeton: Princeton University Press, 2001).

Miles v. United States

103 U.S. 304 (1881)
Decided: April 4, 1881
Vote: 8 (Waite, Clifford, Miller, Field, Bradley, Hunt, Harlan I, Woods)
0
Opinion of the Court: Woods

John Miles, a practicing Mormon, was indicted and convicted in Utah for bigamy. In his appeal to the Supreme Court, Miles claimed that the lower courts had violated his constitutional right to a jury of his peers by excluding potential jurors based on their religious beliefs. He also claimed that the trial court had erred by allowing his own admissions concerning his marital status as evidence. Miles also contended that the court had erred in allowing his second wife to provide evidence against him concerning his first marriage; Utah laws held that "a husband shall not be a witness for or against his wife, nor a wife a witness for or against her husband."

Justice Woods, speaking for the Court, upheld the lower court's decision to dismiss jurors based on a discovered bias. Woods stated that a bias clearly existed and the fact that it was based on religious belief was entirely immaterial. The Court also upheld the district court's decision to allow the admissions and declarations of the plaintiff into evidence.

On the issue of his second wife's testimony, however, the Court reversed the Utah Supreme Court. The Court ruled that statements of the second wife could not be admitted to prove the fact that the first marriage existed, and the jury should have been instructed of that fact.

Despite the Court's well-known aversion to bigamy, demonstrated in ***Reynolds v. United States,*** 98 U.S. 145 (1879), for example, it allowed a state law prohibiting spousal testimony to stand, even though the wife in question was the second wife, and under the territorial laws of the United States, an illegal spouse. The Court's admission of Miles's own statements is one of the tribunal's first efforts at interpreting the Self-Incrimination Clause of the Fifth Amendment.

See Edwin B. Firmage, "Free Exercise of Religion in Nineteenth Century America: The Mormon Cases," *Journal of Law and Religion* 7 (1989): 281.

Neal v. Delaware

103 U.S. 370 (13 Otto 370) (1881)
Decided: May 2, 1881
Vote: 6 (Clifford, Miller, Bradley, Hunt, Harlan I, Woods)
2 (Waite, Field)
Opinion of the Court: Harlan I
Dissenting opinion: Waite
Dissenting opinion: Field

The state of Delaware prosecuted William Neal, an African American, for the rape of Margaret E. Gosser, a white woman. No blacks served on either the grand jury that indicted him or the petit jury that tried him. Although no statute barred blacks from juries, Justice Harlan noted in his opinion that "in fact, persons of that race, though otherwise qualified, have always, in that County and State, been excluded, because of their color; from service on juries." The Delaware Constitution of 1831 restricted voting to "free white male citizens," and a statute limited jury service to those who qualified to vote. Neal argued that although blacks could vote in Delaware under the Fifteenth Amendment to the Constitution, the Delaware authorities apparently still applied their state constitution's voter qualifications to jury service. The state denied this charge, asserting that the Fourteenth and Fifteenth Amendments had made the discriminatory clause in the state constitution inoperable.

Reversing Neal's conviction, Harlan accepted the state's claim that it no longer enforced the outdated constitutional provisions, but he found the factual record compelling because it showed that no blacks had ever served on any juries in the state. The Court reaffirmed the holding in ***Strauder v. West Virginia*** 100 U.S. 303 (1880), and ***Virginia v. Rives,*** 100 U.S. 313 (1880), that a black "cannot claim, as a matter of right, that his race shall have a representation on a jury in a particular case," but it also held that the wholesale exclusion of blacks from juries violated the Constitution.

Chief Justice Waite dissented, arguing that the absence of blacks from the juries was not proof of discrimination. Justice Field took the same position, noting that the fact that no blacks had ever been selected as jurors "may be attributable to other causes than those of race."

Neal did not change much in the South, which was moving rapidly to eliminate blacks from jury pools. In the next half-century blacks were almost entirely absent from southern juries. The Court reaffirmed *Neal* in ***Norris v. Alabama,*** 294 U.S. 587 (1935), but blacks did not begin to appear on southern juries in any significant numbers until the civil rights revolution of the 1960s and 1970s.

See Charles Fairman, *Reconstruction and Reunion, 1864–88, Vol. VII, Part II, History of the Supreme Court of the United States* (New York: Macmillan, 1971); and Douglas Colbert, "Challenging the Challenge: Thirteenth Amendment as a Prohibition Against the Racial Use of Preemptory Challenges," *Cornell Law Review,* 76 (1990): 1.

Pace v. Alabama

106 U.S. 583 (1883)
Decided: January 29, 1883
Vote: 9 (Waite, Miller, Field, Bradley, Harlan I, Woods, Matthews, Gray, Blatchford)
0
Opinion of the Court: Field

Tony Pace, an African American man, lived with Mary Cox, a white woman, in violation of Alabama law, specifically, Section 4189: "Any white person and any Negro, or descendant of any Negro to the third generation, which intermarry or live in adultery or fornication can be imprisoned. On the first conviction each of them must be imprisoned in the penitentiary for not less than two years and not more than seven years." Such provisions were typical of the antimiscegenation laws passed by most southern states. Pace and Cox were convicted and sentenced to two years in the state penitentiary.

On appeal, Pace insisted that the law used to convict him was in conflict with the Equal Protection Clause of the Fourteenth Amendment because a same-race couple living in adultery or fornication would not be sentenced to imprisonment until the third offense. Justice Field, speaking for the Court, upheld the conviction and cited language from the Civil Rights Act of 1870 that provided that "all persons within the jurisdiction of the United States shall have the same right, in every state and territory." He found no discrimination against race in either section of the Alabama Code. The same punishment applied for all offenders, both white and black. Whatever discrimination existed in the difference in punishments was directed against the offence and not against the person based on color or race.

This decision is an early example of the Court's growing acceptance of the South's determination to keep former slaves in an inferior position, a policy that evolved, through Jim Crow laws, into a full-blown state-sanctioned segregation. It took more than eighty years for the Court to reverse the *Pace* ruling in ***Loving v. Virginia,*** 388 U.S. 1 (1967).

See R. Carter Pittman, "The Fourteenth Amendment: Its Intended Effect on Anti-Miscegenation Laws," *North Carolina Law Review* 43 (1964): 92; Peter Wallenstein, "Race, Marriage, and the Law of Freedom: Alabama and Virginia, 1860s–1960s," *Chicago-Kent Law Review* 70 (1994): 371; and Peter Wallenstein, *Tell the Court I Love My Wife: Race, Marriage and Law—An American History* (N.Y.: Palgrave Macmillan, 2002).

United States v. Harris

106 U.S. 629 (1883)
Decided: January 22, 1883
Vote: 8 (Waite, Miller, Field, Bradley, Woods, Matthews, Gray, Blatchford)
1 (Harlan I)
Opinion of the Court: Woods

Four black men were in jail when Harris and nineteen other white men forced their way into the sheriff's office, attacked the prisoners, and left three badly beaten and the fourth dead. Harris and the others were indicted under Section 5519 of the federal code on four counts of "depriving (either directly or indirectly) any person or class of people of equal protection, privileges or immunities under the laws . . . or to prevent or hinder the constituted authorities from securing such protection."

Harris and the other defendants claimed that, under the Tenth Amendment, Section 5519 was an infringement of the rights of Tennessee and of its people. On appeal, U.S circuit court judges divided in their opinion concerning the law's constitutionality. Unable to resolve their differences, the judges certified the question to the Supreme Court. (At this time, lower courts, if they could not agree in a case, could "certify" the question, and the Supreme Court, under its then existing jurisdictional rules, would have to accept the case for resolution.)

Woods, speaking for the Court, stated that the lower court had acted correctly in its certificate of division. It also found that the Enforcement Clause of the Fourteenth Amendment (Section 5), under which Congress had passed the law, did not allow for such exercise of federal authority. The decision is a precursor of the ***Civil Rights Cases,*** 109 U.S. 3 (1883), decided later in the year, in which the Court emasculated the Fourteenth and Fifteenth Amendments and interpreted them to prevent Congress from protecting the civil rights and liberties of the former slaves. Here, as in the later case, Harlan objected on grounds that the Court misunderstood the intention of those amendments, namely, to protect the rights of the newly freed slaves.

Civil Rights Cases

109 U.S. 3 (1883)
Decided: October 15, 1883
Vote: 8 (Waite, Miller, Field, Bradley, Woods, Matthews, Gray, Blatchford)
1 (Harlan I)
Opinion of the Court: Bradley
Dissenting opinion: Harlan I

In the last of the great Reconstruction statutes, the Civil Rights Act of 1875, the Republican majority in Congress tried to secure by law some semblance of racial equality that could be protected by the government and the courts. It is doubtful that the country as a whole endorsed this idea. Most white Americans, northern and southern, believed in white supremacy. Few expected that civil rights legislation would change white attitudes or compensate for what many saw as the natural inferiority of blacks; rather, the law aimed to protect the freedmen from deprivation of the minimal rights of citizenship.

A crucial feature of the law was a prohibition of racial discrimination in public places, what would later be called "public accommodations," which rested on Section 5 of the Fourteenth Amendment. Five cases testing the application of this section arose in both the North and the South, and the Court combined them for a single hearing in 1883. The government argued that the Thirteenth Amendment not only abolished slavery but also conferred all the rights of free citizens on former slaves, and that the Fourteenth Amendment gave Congress the power to legislate to protect those rights.

In his opinion for the Court, Bradley denied both contentions and, in doing so, robbed the amendments of much of their meaning. Bradley's premise was based on the argument that not every example of discrimination against Negroes could be interpreted as a renewal of slavery. Therefore, the Thirteenth Amendment could not be invoked as a ban on all forms of racial prejudice.

Although the Fourteenth Amendment had been drafted specifically to ensure freedmen's rights, Bradley rejected the notion that Congress had affirmative powers under the amendment. According to him, Congress could act only in a remedial manner. In other words, if a state enacted a law that restricted the rights of black citizens, Congress could then act to correct the injustice. Absent the prior restrictive state action, Congress was powerless to legislate in this area. Bradley also indicated that the federal government was powerless to legislate against acts of private discrimination—such as race-based exclusion from hotels, restaurants, and clubs. With this decision, the Court severely restricted congressional power under the Fourteenth Amendment to protect the freedmen, leaving their fate to the states and the courts.

The lone dissenter pointed out that the Court had stripped the Fourteenth Amendment of most of its intent. Although he wrote in dissent, Harlan sketched out a theory of "state action" that would become the basis of civil rights jurisprudence six decades later. He used the idea of enterprises "affected with a public interest" that had been expressed" in ***Munn v. Illinois,*** 94 U.S. 113 (1877). Harlan argued that facilities such as railroads, hotels, restaurants, and theaters filled a public function that justified their long history of regulation. If such already regulated businesses discriminated, then they did so with the consent of the state. This constituted state action, and could be reached under the Fourteenth Amendment, even using Bradley's limited view of Section 5 power.

See J. David Hoeveler Jr., "Reconstruction and the Federal Courts: The Civil Rights Act of 1875," *History* 31 (1969): 604; and John A. Scott, "Justice Bradley's Evolving Concept of the Fourteenth Amendment from the Slaughterhouse Cases to the Civil Rights Cases," *Rutgers Law Review* 25 (1971): 552.

Ex parte Crow Dog

109 U.S. 557 (1883)
Decided: December 17, 1883
Vote: 9 (Waite, Miller, Field, Bradley, Harlan I, Woods, Matthews, Gray, Blatchford)
0
Opinion of the Court: Matthews

Crow Dog, a member of the Brule Sioux, was convicted in a Dakota territorial court for the murder of Spotted Tail, another member of the tribe. Sentenced to die, Crow Dog sought release through a writ of habeas corpus, arguing that he should have been tried under tribal law rather than federal law because federal courts did not have jurisdiction over crimes committed by one Indian against another. (Under tribal law, if convicted, Crow Dog would have been required to support Spotted Tail's family, but he would not have been executed.) Crow Dog argued that as an Indian he was not subject to the criminal laws of either the United States or the Dakota territory. The government claimed that under an 1868 treaty with the Sioux, federal authority, including criminal law, had been extended over the tribe.

The Court ruled against the government, holding that the federal courts in the Dakota territory had no jurisdiction over Indian affairs on a reservation. Writing for the Court, Justice Matthews said that the tribe had exclusive jurisdiction over its members living on the reservation and this jurisdiction derived from the surviving aspects of tribal sovereignty recognized by the Constitution, despite treaty language that seemed to make the Sioux subject to federal law.

The decision did not deny to the federal government the power to legislate on Indian affairs or to determine the scope of tribal self-government. Rather, the Court found that Congress had not acted to these ends in any clear fashion, and, until it did so, the tribes could govern themselves under their traditional customs. For the most part, reservation life is still governed by tribal courts applying traditional law.

The fact that Crow Dog would "get away" with murder led to great indignation, especially among those who wanted to assimilate Indians into mainstream culture. In 1885 Congress passed a law—the Major Crimes Act—specifying seven crimes, including murder, which, if committed by an Indian, would fall under the jurisdiction of federal courts. Today, the amended Major Crimes Act includes fourteen such crimes.

Crow Dog remains a major constitutional precedent as it establishes a balanced approach to evaluate legal relations between Indian tribes and the federal government. Absent clear statutory language or treaty provisions to the contrary *Crow Dog* mandates that Indian custom and tribal law is the guiding principle in interpreting treaty language.

See Frederick E. Hoxie, *A Final Promise: The Campaign to Assimilate the Indians, 1880–1920* (Lincoln: University of Nebraska Press, 1984); and David E. Wilkins, *American Indian Sovereignty and the U.S. Supreme Court* (Austin: University of Texas Press,1997).

Hurtado v. California

110 U.S. 516 (1884)
Decided: March 3, 1884
Vote: 7 (Waite, Miller, Bradley, Woods, Matthews, Gray, Blatchford)
1 (Harlan I)
Opinion of the Court: Matthews
Dissenting opinion: Harlan I
Did not participate: Field

Joseph Hurtado was prosecuted for murder in California. He was not indicted by a grand jury; instead, the state used a provision in its constitution that authorized prosecutions based on a bill of information after examination by a magistrate. Hurtado was found guilty and sentence to death. He appealed to the Supreme Court, stating that he had not been legally indicted because the grand jury had not heard his case. He also argued that the California law, the verdict, and the judgment were all in conflict with and prohibited by the Fifth and Fourteenth Amendments to the U.S. Constitution.

The Court rejected the argument, holding that the Due Process Clause of the Fourteenth Amendment could not reasonably encompass the specific procedural guarantees of the Fifth Amendment. The Court held that procedures may be consonant with due process, and it adopted a test that any legal proceeding, whether sanctioned by age or newly devised, that preserved the fundamental principles of liberty and justice at the base of American political institutions, must be deemed to constitute due process. The California procedure, in the Court's opinion, did not violate these principles.

Hurtado is one of the first cases to hold that fundamental fairness in the overall proceedings, rather than specific procedures, constituted the due process required by the Fifth and Fourteenth Amendments. It is also an early rejection by the Court of the idea of incorporation, that is, that the Due Process Clause of the Fourteenth Amendment applies the specific guarantees of the Bill of Rights to the states.

Ex parte Yarbrough

Also known as the Ku Klux cases.
110 U.S. 651 (1884)
Decided: March 3, 1884
Vote: 9 (Waite, Miller, Field, Bradley, Harlan I, Woods, Matthews, Gray, Blatchford)
0
Opinion of the Court: Miller

Although the Fifteenth Amendment explicitly granted citizens, regardless of race, color, or prior conditions of servitude, the right to vote, Congress passed a number of laws implementing that right. The federal courts, however, showed little interest in promoting suffrage for former slaves. This case is the only one during Reconstruction in which the Court upheld federal power to punish a private obstruction of the right to vote.

Jasper Yarbrough and a group of fellow Ku Klux Klansmen were convicted of beating and wounding a former Georgia slave named Berry Saunders to prevent him from voting in a federal congressional election. Yarbrough claimed that no constitutional provision authorized the statute and its provisions that forbade conspiring to injure or intimidate any citizen in the exercise of a federal right. The Court rejected this argument and upheld the conviction.

Justice Miller found several clauses within the Constitution and, most important, in the Fifteenth Amendment conferring the right to vote on the Negro, and thus by its own terms demanded that this federal right be protected. Otherwise, Miller noted, the country would be "at the mercy of the combinations of those who respect no right but brute force."

The Court, however, abandoned this interpretation in *James v. Bowman,* 190 U.S. 127 (1903). It reversed itself, declaring the enforcement statute unconstitutional. The Court would not concern itself with black voting rights again until the 1940s.

Elk v. Wilkins

112 U.S. 94 (1884)
Decided: November 3, 1884
Vote: 7 (Waite, Miller, Field, Bradley, Matthews, Gray, Blatchford)
2 (Harlan I, Woods)
Opinion of the Court: Gray
Dissenting opinion: Harlan I (Woods)

To vote in the United States, a person must be a citizen. John Elk, a Native American, went to the local registrar in Omaha, Nebraska, to register to vote. The registrar, Charles Wilkins, refused to register Elk as a voter because he was a Native American. Elk claimed that Wilkins's refusal to register him violated the Fourteenth Amendment's provision that all persons born or naturalized in the United States are citizens. The issue raised in this case was whether a Native American was legally a citizen of the United States.

The Court ruled that a Native American is not a U.S. citizen and therefore is not allowed to vote. Justice Gray held that even though Elk was born in the United States and had broken away from his Indian tribe, he was not a citizen. The only way a Native American could become a citizen was by treaty, statute, or if the government naturalized him, that is, by the consent and sufferance of the government. The government had not given its consent, and Elk therefore was not a citizen, was not allowed to vote, and there had been no violation of the Fourteenth Amendment. The case was part of a pattern in which all branches of the federal government treated Native Americans as noncitizens with few if any rights.

See Stephen D. Bodayla, " 'Can an Indian Vote?' *Elk v. Wilkins,* A Setback for Indian Citizenship," *Nebraska History* 67 (winter 1986): 372–380.

Chew Heong v. United States

Also known as the Chinese Exclusion Cases.
112 U.S. 536 (1884)
Decided: December 8, 1884
Vote: 7 (Waite, Miller, Harlan I, Woods, Matthews, Gray, Blatchford)
2 (Field, Bradley)
Opinion of the Court: Harlan I
Dissenting opinion: Field

Chew Heong, a Chinese laborer, resided in the United States in 1880 and returned to China in 1881. He was prevented from re-entering the country in 1884. The rationale was that the Chinese Exclusion Act of 1882 prohibited Chinese laborers and miners entry to the United States. An amendment to the act in 1884 required all Chinese laborers who had lived in the United States before 1882 and who left the country with plans to return to obtain a re-entry certificate. Chew Heong, who had left before this provision was enacted, did not have the certificate. The government of China, Chinese aliens living in the United States, and Chinese Americans challenged the constitutionality of the anti-Chinese laws.

Justice Harlan, speaking for the Court, stated that Chew Heong was in a statutory limbo because he had left before the 1882 act and returned after the 1884 amendment, and as such he deserved relief.

Field's dissent charged the majority with ignoring the law as written and interpreting it to suit their inclinations. While Chew Heong received his relief, Field's dissent ultimately became precedent. In the future the Court adhered to a strict interpretation of immigration statutes, even when this meant hardship for particular individuals, and left it to Congress to legislate exceptions to its immigration restrictions.

See Lucy E. Salyer, *Laws Harsh as Tigers: Chinese Immigrants and the Shaping of Modern Immigration Law* (Chapel Hill: University of North Carolina Press, 1995).

Edye v. Robertson

Also known as the Head Money Cases.
112 U.S. 580 (1884)
Decided: December 8, 1884
Vote: 9 (Waite, Miller, Field, Bradley, Harlan I, Woods, Matthews, Gray, Blatchford)
0
Opinion of the Court: Miller

In 1882 Congress passed a law that made ships pay a duty of fifty cents for every immigrant on a ship coming from a foreign port. Ship companies sued the port of New York to recover repayment of what they declared was an unconstitutional tax.

The Court said that the case involved two questions. First, was the duty made for the common defense and general welfare of the United States, and if so, was it uniform throughout all ports in the United States? Second, did the law imposing the duty violate treaties the United States had signed with several European nations?

On the first issue, the Court ruled that the law imposed a duty, not a tax. This duty was humane and benefited poor and helpless immigrants. The duty was also held to be uniform throughout all U.S. ports because no preference was given to any port.

On the second issue, the Court ruled that it did not matter if the law violated any treaties. A treaty has the same effect as a law passed by Congress. Therefore, if Congress passes a law that goes against a treaty, the new law is superior. In other words, when a treaty comes head-to-head with a newer law, the newer law wins.

The latter holding was repudiated in ***Missouri v. Holland,*** 252 U.S. 416 (1920), in which the Court ruled that the power to make treaties antedated the Constitution and was part of the inherent authority of sovereigns. In a conflict between a law and treaty, the treaty always took precedence, regardless of the date of the law.

Union Pacific Railway Co. v. Myers

Also known as the Pacific Railroad Removal Cases.
115 U.S. 1 (1885)
Decided: May 4, 1885
Vote: 7 (Field, Bradley, Harlan I, Woods, Matthews, Gray, Blatchford)
2 (Waite, Miller)
Opinion of the Court: Bradley
Dissenting opinion: Waite (Miller)

The Pacific Railrway Company and six other railroads were sued in state courts in Kansas, Missouri, and Texas. The railroad companies wanted to move the lawsuits from state court to federal court, where they believed the judges would be more sympathetic to business interests. They claimed the right to do so under the Removal Act of 1875, a law originally passed to guard the rights of the freed slaves. The railroads claimed that as corporations they had the same rights as individuals and could sue in federal court.

The Supreme Court held that railroads had such a right, providing that some issue of federal law was involved. Because a corporation is created and organized under the laws of the United States, federal courts have jurisdiction over cases involving them.

This case was one of the first that eventually led the Court to accept that the definition of "persons" in the Fourteenth Amendment also included corporations. This concept made it difficult for states to sue or prosecute corporations in state courts because the companies could almost always come up with some issue of federal law that would justify removal to the friendlier environs of federal court.

Presser v. Illinois

116 U.S. 252 (1886)
Decided: January 4, 1886
Vote: 9 (Waite, Miller, Field, Bradley, Harlan I, Woods, Matthews, Gray, Blatchford)
0
Opinion of the Court: Woods

Herman Presser was convicted for parading with a group of men bearing arms in the state of Illinois, in violation of a statute that prohibited such activity other than by the organized militia. Article XI of the Illinois Military Code read, "It shall not be lawful for any body of men whatever, other than the regular organized volunteer militia of this State, and the troops of the United States, to associate themselves together as a military company or organization, or to drill or parade with arms in any city, or town, of this State, without the license of the Governor thereof, which license may at any time be revoked." Violation of this provision carried a fine of not more than $10 and/or not more than six months in jail.

The Court rejected Presser's claims that the Second Amendment guarantee of the right to keep and bear arms applied not only to the federal government but to the states as well. Justice Woods noted that the Illinois statute did not interfere with the right to keep and bear arms. Moreover, it would be impractical for state governments to disarm their populations because that would interfere with the federal government's ability to raise a militia from the population at large. All Illinois had done was to regulate how people could behave with their weapons.

Although this case is often discussed in the context of the Second Amendment, it is probably better seen as an example of the Court's initial tendency to reject the view that the Fourteenth Amendment applied the Bill of Rights to the states.

See Stuart R. Hays, "The Right to Bear Arms: A Study in Judicial Misrepresentation," *William and Mary Law Review* 2 (1960): 381.

Boyd v. United States

116 U.S. 616 (1886)
Decided: February 1, 1886
Vote: 9 (Waite, Miller, Field, Bradley, Harlan I, Woods, Matthews, Gray, Blatchford)
0
Opinion of the Court: Bradley
Concurring opinion: Miller (Waite)

E. A. Boyd & Sons allegedly entered into an arrangement with Union Plate Glass Company to import plate glass with the intention of avoiding the payment of duties as mandated under the 1874 Customs Act. The U.S. attorney directed the Boyds to produce their invoices for the glass. The Boyds challenged the constitutional validity of the order, arguing that it would violate their rights under the Fourth Amendment, which prohibits unreasonable searches and seizures. They also invoked the Fifth Amendment, which offered protection from compulsory self-incrimination. The Boyds eventually produced the documents as ordered, and these were used against them to secure a conviction. The Boyds appealed, claiming that the compulsory production of the records violated their rights under the Fourth and Fifth Amendments.

Justice Bradley, speaking for the Court, stated that the Fourth and Fifth Amendments protect the privacy of individuals from government intrusion and did not apply only in criminal cases or where there had been a physical invasion of property. The Court found the provision in the Customs Act authorizing such compulsory production unconstitutional, and therefore the admission of the invoices into evidence was unconstitutional.

The decision, although on a relatively minor point, is considered a precursor of the right to privacy. More important, it is one of the Court's earliest interpretations of the Fourth and Fifth Amendments in relation to what the government may do in its investigation of suspected law-breakers.

See Anthony Amsterdam, "Perspectives on the Fourth Amendment," *Minnesota Law Review* 58 (1974): 349.

Yick Wo v. Hopkins

118 U.S. 356 (1886)
Decided: May 10, 1886
Vote: 9 (Waite, Miller, Field, Bradley, Harlan I, Woods, Matthews, Gray, Blatchford)
0
Opinion of the Court: Matthews

A San Francisco ordinance required a permit to operate a laundry in a wooden building. On its face the ordinance seemed like a legitimate fire protection measure. In practice, however, it proved quite discriminatory. The city granted permits to all but one of the non-Chinese applicants and denied licenses to all two hundred Chinese who applied, even though some of them had been operating laundries for more than twenty years. The ordinance and its implementation need to be seen as part of a broader pattern of anti-Chinese legislation at both the state and federal levels that had culminated in the Chinese Exclusion Act of 1882.

Yick Wo had lived in California since 1861 and had been in the laundry business for twenty-two years. In 1884 his laundry was inspected and found safe, but the following year the Board of Supervisors denied him a license to operate. Yick Wo continued to operate his laundry without a license. He was arrested and convicted for violating the ordinance and fined ten dollars. After losing an appeal in state court, he petitioned the U.S. Supreme Court for review.

Yick Wo argued that the ordinance abridged his Fourteenth Amendment rights because of the blatantly discriminatory results of its implementation, and a unanimous bench agreed. Anticipating the equal protection argument used by the Warren Court eight decades later, the Court concluded that the implementation of the city ordinance discriminated against a particular group. The Chinese were not outsiders, Matthews declared. "The Fourteenth Amendment . . . is not confined to the protection of citizens," but applies "to all persons within the territorial jurisdiction."

The effect of the decision proved minimal because the personnel of the Court changed soon afterwards and subsequent Courts did not follow the precedent. This decision, which had the potential for enlarging individual rights, faded into obscurity until the civil rights movement of the 1950s and 1960s.

See Hyung-Chan Kim, *A Legal History of Asian Americans, 1790–1990* (Westport, Conn.: Greenwood Press, 1994); and Stuart Creighton Miller, *The Unwelcome Immigrant: The American Image of the Chinese, 1785–1882* (Berkeley: University of California Press, 1969).

United States v. Kagama

118 U.S. 375 (1886)
Decided: May 10, 1886
Vote: 9 (Waite, Miller, Field, Bradley, Harlan I, Woods, Matthews, Gray, Blatchford)
0
Opinion of the Court: Miller

Kagama murdered Iyouse on the Indian reservation where they both lived and was indicted by the state of California for murder. The case came to the Supreme Court because of a division of opinion between the circuit court and the district judge over the question of whether the indictment was valid, given that states had no jurisdiction over reservations. The indictment, however, came after passage by Congress of the Major Crimes Act of 1885, which extended the jurisdiction of the federal courts onto reservations for seven specific crimes: murder, manslaughter, rape, assault with the intent to kill, arson, burglary, and larceny.

Justice Miller pointed out that the protection of Indians constituted a national obligation and sustained the power of Congress to legislate for Indians on reservations. He asserted that the state courts lacked jurisdiction over crimes committed by Indians on reservations because federal power preempted state authority. He also highlighted the fact that states had historically been the Indians' "deadliest enemies."

The Court relied heavily on the decision in the ***Worcester v. Georgia,*** 31 U.S. 515 (1832), in which Chief Justice Marshall held that a federal criminal statute specifically applicable to Indians was constitutional. The Court upheld the 1885 statute and its application on that basis.

This case reinforced the federal government's power over the Indian tribes, and took another step in blocking the application of state laws to the reservations.

See David E. Wilkins, *American Indian Sovereignty and the U.S. Supreme Court: The Masking of Justice* (Austin: University of Texas Press, 1997).

Santa Clara County v. Southern Pacific Railroad Co.

118 U.S. 394 (1886)
Decided: May 10, 1886
Vote: 9 (Waite, Miller, Field, Bradley, Harlan I, Woods, Matthews, Gray, Blatchford)
0
Opinion of the Court: Harlan I

The California Constitution authorized the legislature to tax railroad property. California assessed Southern Pacific Railroad Company's property, including the value of their railroads, roadways, roadbeds, rails, rolling stocks, franchises, and fences between the roadways and neighboring properties. The assessments were sent to the counties where the properties were located to raise the taxes on the railroad company. When Southern Pacific refused to pay the taxes, Santa Clara County sued to collect.

Southern Pacific raised several defenses, the most important of which was that a corporation should be treated as a legal person and be protected by the Due Process Clause of the Fourteenth Amendment. The main issue before the Court was whether a corporation is legally the same as a person.

The Court agreed with the railroad that a private corporation is entitled to the same constitutional rights as a person, the doctrine of corporate personhood. The Court then ruled that the assessments were void because the fences should not have been taxed. Fences, it said, were improvements, not taxable property.

See Morton J. Horwitz, "*Santa Clara* Revisited: The Development of Corporate Theory," *West Virginia Law Review* 88 (1985): 173.

Wabash, St. Louis & Pacific Railway Co. v. Illinois

118 U.S. 557 (1886)
Decided: October 25, 1886
Vote: 6 (Miller, Field, Harlan I, Woods, Matthews, Blatchford)
3 (Waite, Bradley, Gray)
Opinion of the Court: Miller
Dissenting opinion: Bradley (Waite, Gray)

The Wabash, St. Louis & Pacific Railway Company was charged with violating an Illinois statute prohibiting discrimination in the rates charged for transportation of freight. The trial court found for the railroad, but the Illinois Supreme Court overturned the ruling. The railroad then appealed to the U.S. Supreme Court, claiming that state regulation of interstate commerce violated the Constitution. At the time the prevailing legal doctrine had been expressed in ***Cooley v. Board of Wardens,*** 53 U.S. (12 How.) 299 (1852), which held that even though Congress had plenary power over interstate commerce, in those areas in which it chose not to act the states were free to do so.

Justice Miller now overruled *Cooley,* finding that states had no power to regulate railroad rates for interstate shipments. Miller introduced the "direct" and "indirect" test to determine the domain and extent of the federal versus the state powers, reserving partial power to the state. What this test meant in practice depended on the predilections of the judges, with conservative jurists more willing to find state action violating the dormant Commerce Clause, and more progressive judges finding the actions indirect and therefore constitutional. Most courts, for example, found that a state could set safety regulations on interstate trains, because these are indirect burdens on commerce. Beyond that, however, states found they could do little to regulate trains engaged in interstate commerce.

With the states now prevented from regulating rates on interstate trains, public opinion demanded that Congress act, which it did reluctantly with the creation of the first federal regulatory agency, the Interstate Commerce Commission, in 1887.

See George H. Miller, *Railroads and the Granger Laws* (Madison: University of Wisconsin Press, 1973).

Mugler v. Kansas

123 U.S. 623 (1887)
Decided: December 5, 1887
Vote: 7 (Waite, Miller, Bradley, Harlan I, Matthews, Gray, Blatchford)
1 (Field)
Opinion of the Court: Harlan I
Opinion concurring in part and dissenting in part: Field

Kansas adopted a provision in its state constitution of 1880 that said, "The manufacture and sale of intoxicating liquors shall be forever prohibited in this State, except for medical, scientific, and mechanical purposes." Peter Mugler continued manufacturing beer after the Kansas legislature forbade such manufacture or sale without a license. The state fined and imprisoned Mugler and seized his brewery and inventory.

On appeal to the Supreme Court, Mugler denied that the police power of the state, that is, the power of the state to legislate for the health, safety, and morality of the people, was so broad as to prohibit the manufacture of beer for Mugler's private consumption or for sale outside of Kansas. The state law, he claimed, deprived him of property without due process. Kansas defended its action as a valid exercise of the police power to regulate health and morals.

Although the Court upheld the prohibition statute under the state's police power, Justice Harlan noted that courts might scrutinize the purpose behind state regulations to determine whether the regulation had any real relationship to health, safety, or morals under the police power. Although innocuous in this case, the notion that courts could scrutinize laws on their own to determine their validity as exercises of the police power later led more conservative Courts to essentially veto the legislative prerogative when judges disagreed with the legislative purpose, as in ***Lochner v. New York,*** 198 U.S. 45 (1905).

Justice Field agreed that the state could prohibit liquor, but he dissented on the ground that the seizure of the property and prohibition of beer manufactured for export were violations of the Due Process Clause.

This case brought the Court a step closer to acceptance of economic due process under the Fourteenth Amendment. The opinion by Harlan, together with the dissent by Field, helped lay the foundation for the Court's acceptance of Field's broader property rights theory after 1890.

See Jack S. Blocker, *Retreat from Reform: The Prohibition Movement in the United States, 1890–1913* (Westport, Conn.: Greenwood Press, 1976).

Chae Chan Ping v. United States

Also known as the Chinese Exclusion Cases.
130 U.S. 581 (1889)
Decided: May 13, 1889
Vote: 8 (Fuller, Miller, Field, Bradley, Harlan I, Gray, Blatchford, L. Lamar)
0
Opinion of the Court: Field

Chae Chan Ping, a Chinese laborer living in San Francisco, was denied reentry into the United States after he made a visit to China. While he was overseas, Congress passed an amendment to the Chinese Exclusion Act of 1882, which prohibited Chinese laborers and miners from entering the United States. The 1884 amendment required all Chinese laborers who lived in the United States before 1882 to have a reentry certificate when they left the United States and expected to return. The Scott Act of 1888, however, went further. It prohibited Chinese laborers abroad or those currently residing in the United States and planning future travels abroad from returning to the United States. The law allowed exceptions for merchants and teachers to return providing they had proper papers.

The Scott Act became law on October 1, 1888, and Chae Chan Ping arrived at the port of San Francisco on October 8 with a certificate of reentry that had been issued at the time of his departure. Immigration officials ruled the certificate void and denied him reentry. Chae Chan Ping, backed by the Chinese government, challenged both the Exclusion Act and the Scott Act. He appealed to the Supreme Court for a ruling on the constitutionality of the Scott Act, claiming it violated previous treaties entered into by the two countries to establish friendly relations.

The Court held that although the United States and China had entered into treaties, Congress had the power to pass laws that restricted immigration to protect the interests of U.S. citizens. The Court found the Scott Act constitutional and denied reentry to Chae Chan Ping. In this, as in nearly all cases challenging immigration law at this time, the Court read the Constitution to give Congress plenary power over immigration, a power unlimited by any section of the Constitution or by treaties.

See Lucy E. Salyer, *Laws Harsh as Tigers: Chinese Immigration and the Shaping of Modern Immigration Law* (Chapel Hill: University of North Carolina Press, 1995).

1890–1899

Davis v. Beason

133 U.S. 333 (1890)
Decided: February 3, 1890
Vote: 9 (Fuller, Miller, Field, Bradley, Harlan I, Gray, Blatchford, L. Lamar, Brewer)
0
Opinion of the Court: Field

Idaho territorial law denied the right to vote to any person who advocated or practiced polygamy or who belonged to an organization that did so, a clear attack on the Mormon church and its adherents. Samuel Davis, a Mormon, and other polygamists attempted to vote in the 1888 election and, when turned away, sued authorities on the grounds that the disenfranchisement violated their rights to free exercise of religion guaranteed by the First Amendment. Although the Bill of Rights at that time did not apply to the states, it did apply to territories such as Idaho, which were still under the control of the federal government. The territorial court dismissed the suit, stating that establishing qualifications for suffrage was a "political question" entrusted to the legislative branch and not reviewable by the courts.

On appeal, the Supreme Court affirmed the statute as within the powers of the territorial legislature to determine voter qualifications. Although *belief* in polygamy as a religious matter was protected by the First Amendment, the *practice* was not. The Court had enunciated this distinction in ***Reynolds v. United States,*** 98 U.S. 145 (1879). The Court viewed polygamy as conduct and therefore subject to legislative restrictions and penalties. Moreover, according to *Davis v. Beason,* polygamy was such uncivilized conduct that even belief in it could be punished, a clear contradiction of the *Reynolds* holding. Field, who spoke for the Court, took advantage of the situation to launch into a diatribe against Mormonism and polygamy. The crime, he concluded, "is not the less odious because sanctioned by what any particular sect may designate as religion." A monogamous family system was more important to the preservation of American society than religious liberty for advocates of multiple marriage.

The opinion took a narrow view of religious liberty and its constitutional protection and indicated that those groups whose beliefs varied too far from the norm could expect scant protection from the courts. This view did not begin to change until the Jehovah's Witness cases in the 1940s, such as ***Cantwell v. Connecticut,*** 310 U.S. 296 (1940).

See Joseph H. Groberg, "The Mormon Disenfranchisements of 1882–1892," *Brigham Young University Studies* 16 (1976): 389.

Louisville, New Orleans & Texas Railway Co. v. Mississippi

133 U.S. 587 (1890)
Decided: March 3, 1890
Vote: 7 (Fuller, Miller, Field, Gray, Blatchford, L. Lamar, Brewer)
2 (Bradley, Harlan I)
Opinion of the Court: Brewer
Dissenting opinion: Harlan I

Mississippi required railroads to provide "equal, but separate, accommodations for the white and colored races." The railroad challenged the law on the grounds that it would have a substantial impact on interstate commerce and therefore trespassed on powers that the Constitution reserved to Congress.

The Mississippi law, insofar as it had any effect on interstate commerce, seemed identical in nature and impact to a Louisiana statute the Court had struck down in ***Hall v. DeCuir,*** 95 U.S. 485 (1878). Both laws used race as a criterion for determining where passengers would be seated. In the earlier case, involving a steamship, the Louisiana law had allowed all passengers full use of the ship but required separate sleeping rooms. That case had been decided, not on the question of how individuals had been treated, but simply as a state invasion of interstate commerce. Here, the Mississippi statute required full separation of passengers: neither race could use the facilities reserved for the other.

Although the two laws resembled each other, in this instance the Court upheld the law. The inconsistent rulings may be explained as part of the Court's ongoing efforts after Reconstruction to redefine the federal nature of the Union. The Court had already, through the ***Civil Rights Cases,*** 109 U.S. 3 (1883), and other decisions, narrowed the scope of the Civil War Amendments to preclude the federal government from actively protecting the rights of individuals. By refusing to link civil rights with the national commerce power, the Court in this case closed another door to congressional action to protect former slaves.

Justice Brewer, speaking for the majority, accepted Mississippi's contention that the law applied only to intrastate commerce, that is, trains traveling wholly within the borders of the state. The only burden, which Brewer conceded as a minor one, was that trains entering the state would have to add additional cars to allow for the segregation of passengers. Justice Harlan disagreed. In his dissent he argued that such a burden on interstate commerce was just what the Constitution had been designed to prevent, namely, one state establishing rules dissimilar to those of other states.

Neither the majority or dissenting opinions, nor the railroad, raised the question of the Fourteenth Amendment and whether the state-mandated segregation violated the Equal Protection Clause insofar as the segregation disadvantaged individual blacks. The Court would deal with that issue in ***Plessy v. Ferguson,*** 163 U.S. 537 (1896). *Louisville, New Orleans* was overturned more than a half century later in ***Morgan v. Virginia,*** 328 U.S. 373 (1946), in which the Court reaffirmed the doctrine of *Hall v. DeCuir.*

See C. Vann Woodward, *The Strange Career of Jim Crow,* 3d rev. ed. (New York: Oxford University Press, 1989); and Pauli Murray, ed. and comp., *State Laws on Race and Color* (Cincinnati: Women's Division of Christian Service, 1952; reprint, 1997, by the University of Georgia Press).

Hans v. State of Louisiana

134 U.S. 1 (1890)
Decided: March 3, 1890
Vote: 9 (Fuller, Miller, Field, Bradley, Harlan I, Gray, Blatchford, L. Lamar, Brewer)
0
Opinion of the Court: Bradley
Concurring opinion: Harlan I

In 1874 the Reconstruction government of Louisiana issued bonds and then secured a state constitutional amendment that authorized a special tax to pay for the bonds. In 1879, following the end of Reconstruction, a new Louisiana constitution scrapped the tax plan, and the state refused to pay either principal or interest on the bonds.

Hans, a citizen of Louisiana, had bought some of the bonds and sued the state in federal court to recover the interest he had earned. He argued that the new state constitution violated the U.S. Constitution by eliminating its bond promises. Louisiana countered that the federal courts did not have jurisdiction in this case because the Eleventh Amendment prevents citizens of one state from suing another state in federal court and that prohibition should apply to citizens of their own state as well.

The Supreme Court agreed with Louisiana and ruled that the Eleventh Amendment implies that citizens of a state cannot not sue their state in federal court. Although the amendment refers only to citizens of another state, the Court held that Congress would never have approved the amendment if it meant that citizens could sue their state without the state's permission.

This case is one of the few concerning the Eleventh Amendment in the post–Civil War era. The Court's ruling reinforced the notion of state sovereignty by practically immunizing states from suits in federal court by private citizens.

See Carol F. Lee, "Sovereign Immunity and the Eleventh Amendment: The Uses of History," *Urban Lawyer* 18 (1986): 519.

Chicago, Milwaukee & St. Paul Railway Co. v. Minnesota ex rel. Railroad and Warehouse Commission

134 U.S. 418 (1890)
Decided: March 24, 1890
Vote: 6 (Fuller, Miller, Field, Harlan I, Blatchford, Brewer)
3 (Bradley, Gray, L. Lamar)
Opinion of the Court: Blatchford
Concurring opinion: Miller
Dissenting opinion: Bradley (Gray, L. Lamar)

In ***Munn v. Illinois,*** 94 U.S. 113 (1876) the Court upheld the states' legislative power to set rates for business affected with a public interest. Moreover, these rates would not be subject to judicial review. Subsequent to *Munn,* Minnesota created the Railroad and Warehouse Commission to examine and set rates for the state's railroads. The decisions of the commission were nonreviewable by the state's courts. The legislature assumed that if rates it set were nonreviewable, then so should be rates set by a commission created by the legislature.

The Supreme Court disagreed and voided the rates set by the commission. Aside from the fact that a regulatory commission was not in the same category as a legislature, the Court here began to explore the constitutional dimensions and requirements of a modern regulatory state. Although the Court had been somewhat sympathetic to the early—and few—state regulatory agencies, the creation of the federal Interstate Commerce Commission in 1887 had led the Court to take a more skeptical approach to the new administrative agencies that combined legislative, executive, and judicial functions in one body.

The Court set down one of the basic tenets that would guide the new regulatory state, namely, that due process requires judicial review of administrative procedures and decisions to ensure that they conform to basic constitutional requirements. The Court also reserved to the judiciary the right to determine the reasonableness of the rates. See ***Smyth v. Ames,*** 169 U.S. 466 (1898). For the next thirty years courts attempted not only to address questions about the power of administrative agencies but also to evaluate the wisdom of actual administrative decisions.

See Jordan Jay Hillman, *Competition and Railroad Price Discrimination: Legal Precedent and Economic Policy* (Evanston, Ill: Transportation Center at Northwestern University, 1968); and Gabriel Kolko, *Railroads and Regulation, 1877–1916* (Princeton: Princeton University Press, 1965).

In re Neagle

135 U.S. 1 (1890)
Decided: April 14, 1890
Vote: 6 (Miller, Bradley, Harlan I, Gray, Blatchford, Brewer)
2 (Fuller, L. Lamar)
Opinion of the Court: Miller
Dissenting opinion: L. Lamar (Fuller)
Did not participate: Field

David Neagle was a deputy U.S. marshal assigned to protect Supreme Court justice Stephen J. Field, who had received a death threat. The incident leading to *In re Neagle* took place when Field was traveling to California to hear a case in federal court. He had earlier sentenced David Terry, at the time the chief justice of the California Supreme Court and a former colleague of Field on that bench, to prison for contempt of court. Field had also invalidated the previous marriage of Terry's wife, effectively ending any claim she had to her former husband's estate. Terry threatened to kill Field, and Neagle's job was to escort and protect him.

As Field's train neared Sacramento, Terry boarded it and spotted Field. When the passengers disembarked for a meal, Terry attacked Field in the station dining room. Neagle, in defending the justice, shot and killed Terry and was arrested by California officials for murder. A federal court stepped in and released Neagle on a writ of habeas corpus on the grounds that he was performing his duty. The authority under which Neagle had acted, however, was not a statute, but an executive order of President Benjamin Harrison. The question before the Supreme Court was whether, under these circumstances, a federal court had the power to step into what appeared to be a California state case.

The Supreme Court ruled that a deputy U.S. marshal cannot be sued in a state court when acting according to his federal duties. The Court thus strengthened the doctrine of federal supremacy over the states. Federal courts could intervene in what appeared to be solely state matters if a federal constitutional issue was involved.

See Paul Kens, *Justice Stephen Field* (Lawrence: University Press of Kansas, 1997), 276–283.

Leisy v. Hardin

135 U.S. 100 (1890)
Decided: April 28, 1890
Vote: 6 (Fuller, Miller, Field, Bradley, Blatchford, L. Lamar)
3 (Harlan I, Gray, Brewer)
Opinion of the Court: Fuller
Dissenting opinion: Gray (Harlan I, Brewer)

An Iowa law prohibited the sale of alcoholic beverages in the state. The Leisy family owned a brewery in Illinois, and, when some Leisy beer was shipped from Illinois into Iowa, the state of Iowa seized it. Leisy sued Iowa to recover the beer, claiming that the state had no authority to regulate interstate commerce, a power reserved solely to the federal government.

The Supreme Court ruled that under the Commerce Clause, only Congress may regulate interstate commerce. Although Congress was silent on the issue of alcohol flowing in interstate commerce, the Court held that Iowa had been wrong to prohibit alcohol from coming into the state for sale.

The case departed from the earlier doctrine of ***Cooley v. Board of Wardens,*** 53 U.S. 299 (1852), in which the Court allowed states to regulate interstate commerce in the absence of congressional intent. In 1913 Congress passed the Webb-Kenyon Act, which gave dry states the power to prevent importation of alcohol, and the Court upheld that delegation of authority in ***Clark Distilling Co. v. Western Maryland R. Co.,*** 242 U.S. 311 (1917).

Late Corporation of the Church of Jesus Christ of Latter-Day Saints v. United States

136 U.S. 1 (1890)
Decided: May 19, 1890
Vote: 6 (Miller, Bradley, Harlan I, Gray, Blatchford, Brewer)
3 (Fuller, Field, L. Lamar)
Opinion of the Court: Bradley
Dissenting opinion: Fuller (Field, L. Lamar)

In its effort to eradicate polygamy in the Utah territory, Congress in 1887 abrogated the charter of the Mormon church and directed the Justice Department to initiate legal proceedings to seize the church's property. Although the forfeiture went beyond the attack on polygamy, the Court sustained the act. The Court, through Justice Bradley, likened polygamy to barbarism and summarily dismissed Mormon claims to religious freedom. Bradley described the plenary powers of Congress to legislate for the territories in sweeping terms.

In dissent, Chief Justice Fuller agreed that Congress could punish acts of polygamy through criminal sanctions, but argued that it had no authority to confiscate the property of either persons or corporations that might have been guilty of criminal practices. "I regard it of vital consequence," he wrote, "that absolute power should never be conceded as belonging under our system of government to any one of its departments." Fuller's powerful dissent soon found vindication. In 1893 Congress, by joint resolution, restored most of the confiscated property to the Mormons.

See Edwin B. Firmage and Richard C. Mangrum, *Zion in the Courts: A Legal History of the Church of Jesus Christ of Latter-Day Saints* (Urbana: University of Illinois Press, 1988).

In re Kemmler

136 U.S. 436 (1890)
Decided: May 23, 1890
Vote: 9 (Fuller, Miller, Field, Bradley, Harlan I, Gray, Blatchford, L. Lamar, Brewer)
0
Opinion of the Court: Fuller

New York stopped executing criminals by hanging and obtained an electric chair, which it considered a more humane form of execution, even though at the time, no one in the United States had ever been put to death by electrocution. William Kemmler was convicted of murder and sentenced to death by electric chair. He filed a writ of habeas corpus and argued that use of the electric chair violated the Eighth Amendment, in that it was cruel and unusual punishment.

The Supreme Court ruled otherwise. It held that punishments are cruel only when they involve torture or a drawn-out death. Execution in itself was not cruel. For an execution to be cruel and unusual it had to involve something heinous and barbarous. Because death by electrocution was quick and supposedly painless, it could not be considered cruel or unusual.

In 1890 Kemmler became the first person in the United States to be executed in the electric chair.

See Craig Brandon, *The Electric Chair: An Unnatural American History* (Jefferson, N.C.: McFarland, 1999).

Counselman v. Hitchcock

142 U.S. 547 (1892)
Decided: January 11, 1892
Vote: 9 (Fuller, Field, Bradley, Harlan I, Gray, Blatchford, L. Lamar, Brewer, Brown)
0
Opinion of the Court: Blatchford

Under federal law, an individual could be granted immunity from criminal prosecution based on evidence given as a witness in a judicial proceeding, such as a grand jury investigation. Charles Counselman refused to testify in a grand jury investigation into alleged violations of the Interstate Commerce Act, basing his refusal on the Fifth Amendment claim against self-incrimination. He was found in contempt and taken into custody. Counselman sought and was granted an order of a writ of habeas corpus from the Supreme Court.

Justice Blatchford held that the purpose of the Fifth Amendment was "to insure that a person should not be compelled, when acting as a witness in any investigation, to give testimony which might show that he himself had committed a crime." Blatchford found little reassurance in the immunity statute because it afforded no protection from the use of compelled testimony to find other evidence of a crime.

In this unanimous decision, the Court expanded the reach of the Fifth Amendment's protection to include not only persons actually accused of a crime but also witnesses in any investigation, including investigation by a grand jury.

See Leonard W. Levy, *Origins of the Fifth Amendment* (New York: Oxford University Press, 1968).

Church of the Holy Trinity v. United States

143 U.S. 457 (1892)
Decided: February 29, 1892
Vote: 8 (Fuller, Field, Harlan I, Gray, Blatchford, L. Lamar, Brewer, Brown)
0
Opinion of the Court: Brewer

The Church of the Holy Trinity, a religious society incorporated under the laws of New York, had contracted with E. Walpole Warren, a citizen of England, to move to New York and become its rector. The government argued that such a contract was forbidden by federal law, which made it "unlawful for any person, or corporation to prepay the transportation, assist, and encourage the importation or migration of aliens into the United States under contract to perform labor or service of any kind."

In its opinion the Court placed great emphasis on the title of the law, an act "to prohibit the importation of foreigners and aliens under contract to perform labor," as well as the law's intent. According to Justice Brewer, the evil the statute had been designed to remedy was the influx of unskilled labor; that is, it was intended to reduce the competition between American citizens and aliens imported to perform unskilled labor at low cost. The justices found that the common understanding of the term "labor" did not include preaching and preachers and concluded that it had not been the intention of Congress to interfere with church activities, and therefore the statute did not apply in such cases. This case was one of the first in which the Court used the legislative history of a statute to determine congressional intent.

This was a simple case for the Court to decide, but Brewer took the occasion to launch into an impassioned digression on the proposition that the United States is a religious nation, more specifically a Christian nation, a view shared by the great majority of American Protestants at the end of the nineteenth century.

See Philip Kurland, *Religion and the Law: Of Church and State and the Supreme Court* (Chicago: Aldine, 1962).

Budd v. New York

143 U.S. 517 (1892)
Decided: February 29, 1892
Vote: 5 (Fuller, Harlan I, Gray, Blatchford, L. Lamar)
3 (Brewer, Field, Brown)
Opinion of the Court: Blatchford
Dissenting opinion: Brewer (Field, Brown)

J. Talman Budd was indicted and found guilty of violating a New York State law that established an approved rate for the unloading of grain by floating or stationary elevators and warehouses. On appeal, Budd insisted that the statute conflicted with the constitutions of the United States and of New York State.

The Court ruled in favor of the state and reaffirmed the position it had taken in ***Munn v. Illinois,*** 94 U.S. 113 (1876). Justice Blatchford noted that the *Munn* case had held it legitimate to regulate grain elevators because they were businesses affected with a public interest. In *Budd* the majority also found that rate regulation of grain elevators did not deny the owners' due process of law in violation of the Fourteenth Amendment. In addition, the Court found no violation of the Commerce Clause because the regulation was confined to the territorial jurisdiction of New York.

Justice Brewer filed an impassioned dissent that denounced the basic doctrine of *Munn* as "radically unsound" and trumpeted his call of lenient constitutionalism. In a now-famous phrase, he wrote, "The paternal theory of government is to me odious."

Although the decision appears to expand state authority and has never been explicitly overruled, it has suffered a major erosion of authority through the expansion of federal powers, especially since the 1930s.

See Owen M. Fiss, *Troubled Beginnings of the Modern State, 1888–1910* (New York: Macmillan, 1993).

Fong Yue Ting v. United States

149 U.S. 698 (1893)
Decided: May 15, 1893
Vote: 6 (Harlan I, Gray, Blatchford, Brown, Shiras, H. Jackson)
3 (Fuller, Field, Brewer)
Opinion of the Court: Gray
Dissenting opinion: Fuller
Dissenting opinion: Brewer
Dissenting opinion: Field

An 1892 law required all Chinese workers, who were both legally in the United States and allowed to stay, to obtain a residence permit. The Chinese workers had one year to get the residence permit. If a Chinese person failed to do so, he would become an illegal alien and be deported back to China or the country from which he had emigrated. Congress had the power to control immigration, but the question before the Supreme Court was: Did Congress also have the power to deport aliens?

The Court ruled that a nation has an absolute right to expel any and all aliens. The power of international relations is in the hands of the federal government, not the states. The only government that foreign nations recognize is the federal government, not state governments. Therefore, aliens who do not become citizens are at the mercy of Congress, which may order them deported.

See Lucy E. Salyer, *Laws Harsh as Tigers: Chinese Immigrants and the Shaping of Modern Immigration Law* (Chapel Hill: University of North Carolina Press, 1995).

United States v. E. C. Knight Co.

156 U.S. 1 (1895)
Decided: January 22, 1895
Vote: 8 (Fuller, Field, Gray, Brewer, Brown, Shiras, H. Jackson, E. White)
1 (Harlan I)
Opinion of the Court: Fuller
Dissenting opinion: Harlan I

The Sherman Antitrust Act of 1890, which remains the basis for nearly all federal antitrust prosecutions to this day, outlawed every "contract, combination in the form of trust or otherwise, or conspiracy in restraint of trade or commerce." The act failed to define these terms. Enforcement, like that of other federal laws, would be the responsibility of the executive, in this case the Justice Department, and interpretation would be left to the courts.

In constitutional terms, questions arose about the extent of congressional power to regulate manufacturing. Congress certainly had authority over commerce, and the Court's decisions starting with ***Gibbons v. Ogden,*** 22 U.S. 1 (1824), supported a broad interpretation of what commerce included. But a more recent line of decisions had differentiated between manufacturing and commerce. In the congressional debate over the Sherman bill, several senators claimed that Congress could not regulate manufacturing, which was perceived as essentially a local enterprise.

American Sugar Refining Company, owned by four Philadelphia refineries, controlled more than 90 percent of the nation's sugar-refining capacity. The Justice Department, in seeking the dissolution of the company, argued that the agreements used to create this monopoly substantially restrained trade, resulting in higher sugar prices. The Court, led by Chief Justice Fuller, affirmed the lower court decision against the government and drew a bright line between commerce and manufacturing. "Commerce succeeds to manufacturing," he declared, "and is not a part of it." In other words, the Court failed to see the connection—one that had been established years earlier by Chief Justice John Marshall—that manufacturing was an integral part of commerce. Instead, the Court divided manufacturing from commerce, considered manufacturing an antecedent, and then declared it a local activity beyond the reach of Congress's commerce power. The Sherman Act thus applied only to firms in interstate commerce, and, although the defendants had conspired to monopolize the production (manufacture) of sugar, under the terms of the law that by itself could not be held illegal. Fuller argued that Congress might be able to reach manufacturing if it had a *direct* impact on interstate commerce, but such an impact had not been demonstrated by the government in this case. Fuller denied that federal power could be invoked to control indirect effects, for then "comparatively little of business operations would be left for state control."

The *Knight* decision has been criticized for the Court's apparent blindness to the realities of modern industrial economics, for turning its back on Marshall's broad interpretation of commerce as an organic whole, and for its nit-picking reading of the Sherman Act and of the government's brief. Yet there is a more positive way to interpret Fuller's opinion. He sought not to weaken the federal commerce power—in fact, he hinted that if the government had focused on the company's restraint of trade rather than on the manufacturing monopoly, the decision might have gone in the government's favor—but to strengthen the states and encourage them to carry out their responsibilities. States, not the federal government, issued corporate charters, and states therefore had the authority to revoke these charters if the companies acted beyond the powers granted to them. Fuller believed in the federal system and wanted the states to regulate the firms they chartered; if they did not, as he warned, the federal government would fill the void.

Justice Harlan, in dissent, believed the Sherman Act could reach combinations like the Knight Company. He argued that such firms had the aim and the ability to control not only manufacturing but also the price at which its goods could be sold in interstate commerce, and therefore they could be regulated under the federal government's commerce power.

Because *Knight* made neither legal nor economic sense, the Court could not sustain its logic. In the early 1900s, in cases beginning with ***Northern Securities Co. v. United States,*** 193 U.S. 197 (1904), the Court began to backtrack, although the *Knight* doctrine survived, in part, until the mid-1930s.

See Charles W. McCurdy, "The *Knight* Sugar Decision of 1895 and the Modernization of American Corporation Law, 1869–1903," *Business History Review* 53 (1979): 304; Hans Thorelli, *The Federal Anti-Trust Policy: Origination of an American Tradition* (Baltimore: Johns Hopkins University Press, 1955); and William Letwin, *Law and Economic Policy in America: The Evolution of the Sherman Antitrust Act* (New York: Random House, 1965).

Pollock v. Farmers' Loan & Trust Co. I

Also known as the Income Tax Cases
157 U.S. 429 (1895)
Decided: April 8, 1895
Vote: 6 (Fuller, Field, Gray, Brewer, Brown, Shiras)
2 (Harlan I, E. White)
Opinion of the Court: Fuller
Concurring opinion: Field
Dissenting opinion: E. White (Harlan I)
Dissenting opinion: Harlan I
See page 113

In re Debs

158 U.S. 564 (1895)
Decided: May 27, 1895
Vote: 9 (Fuller, Field, Harlan I, Gray, Brewer, Brown, Shiras, H. Jackson, E. White)
0
Opinion of the Court: Brewer

One week after disposing of the second hearing of ***Pollock v. Farmers' Loan & Trust Co.,*** 158 U.S. 601 (1895), the justices delayed their summer recess to hear the third great case of the 1894 term, *In re Debs.* Late in June 1894, members of the American Railway Union, protesting an arbitrary 20 percent wage cut ordered by the Pullman Palace Car Company, refused to handle Pullman cars. The strike paralyzed rail transportation east and west of Chicago. Attorney General Richard Olney directed the local U.S. attorney to seek an injunction against the union leaders for obstructing passage of the mails, which were sent by rail. The district court issued a broad order against the strikers, which union president Eugene Debs and three other union leaders refused to obey. President Grover Cleveland, over the objections of Illinois Governor John Peter Altgeld, ordered federal troops to break the strike. Following this action the government sought contempt convictions against the strike leaders. When their attorneys claimed that the original injunction had exceeded judicial authority, the trial court judge declared that the defendants had engaged in a combination in restraint of trade, in violation of the Sherman Antitrust law. He imposed a six-month contempt sentence on Debs and three-month sentences on each of the codefendants. Represented by attorneys Clarence Darrow and former senator Lyman Trumbull of Illinois, Debs appealed to the Supreme Court for a writ of habeas corpus.

Two years earlier, in *Pettibone v. United States,* 148 U.S. 197 (1893), the Court had unanimously reversed a federal conviction for conspiracy to obstruct justice in a labor dispute, ruling that federal courts did not have jurisdiction, directly or indirectly, over a state's criminal law process. Because Debs had been imprisoned by a federal court for an offense committed solely within Illinois, the *Pettibone* decision should have led to his release. But Justice Brewer, who had dissented in *Pettibone,* ignored the precedent, as did all of the justices who had been in the majority in that case. Instead, Brewer developed the idea that the injunction was a special form of relief that could be used to prevent irreparable damage to property that could not be adequately compensated in later actions at law. This use of the injunction had long been available through equity to private parties, but Brewer expanded its use to protect public rights and punish public wrongs. In doing so, he significantly enlarged the federal courts' equity jurisdiction and gave the federal and state governments a powerful tool to use against labor.

In stark contrast to the decisions in ***United States v. E. C. Knight,*** 156 U.S. 1 (1895), and ***Pollock v. Farmers' Loan & Trust Co.,*** 157 U.S. 601 (1895), *Debs* proclaimed a broad interpretation of national sovereignty and the supremacy of the federal government over the states. President Cleveland praised the Court for establishing "in an absolutely authoritative manner and for all time, the power of the national government to protect itself in the exercise of its functions." Although the strike had little public support, the specter of "government by injunction," however, caused serious concern among legal scholars as well as great resentment by labor. In 1931 Congress severely curtailed the power of the federal courts to issue injunctions against labor unions by passing the Norris-LaGuardia Act.

See Christopher L. Tomlins, *The State and the Unions: Labor Relations, Law, and the Organized Labor Movement in America, 1880–1960* (New York: Cambridge University Press, 1985); and William E. Forbath, *Law and the Shaping of the American Labor Movement* (Cambridge: Harvard University Press, 1991).

Pollock v. Farmers' Loan & Trust Co. II

Also known as the Income Tax Cases
158 U.S. 601 (1895)
Decided: May 20, 1895
Vote: 5 (Fuller, Field, Gray, Brewer, Shiras)
4 (Harlan I, Brown, H. Jackson, E. White)
Opinion of the Court: Fuller
Dissenting opinion: Harlan I
Dissenting opinion: Brown
Dissenting opinion: H. Jackson
Dissenting opinion: E. White

The demand from reformers, especially the Populists, for a tax on incomes had become an important part of labor and agrarian programs in the late nineteenth century. The depression of 1893 and the accompanying decline in tariff receipts, which had been the chief source of federal revenues, led to a series of government deficits. Congress felt compelled to find additional streams of revenue for government expenditures. Although some decried the income tax as "socialism, communism and devilism," farm and labor interests prevailed. The Wilson-Gorman Tariff of 1894 provided for a 2 percent tax on all corporate and individual incomes, with a $4,000 exemption for the latter.

Charles Pollock, a stockholder of the Farmers' Loan & Trust Company, brought suit against the tariff act. The income tax was challenged on three major points. First, it violated the constitutional ban on direct taxes because a tax on income from property was the same thing as taxing the property itself. Second, the $4,000 exemption violated Article I, Section 8, which required that all taxes be uniform. Finally, Pollock claimed the law violated states' rights by taxing the income from state and municipal bonds.

Judicial precedent, however, sided with proponents of the tax. All previous cases dealing with the question of direct taxes indicated that only capitation (poll) taxes and specific duties on land met the constitutional definition of a direct tax. ***Hylton v. United States,*** 3 U.S. 171 (1796), had sustained a 1794 tax on carriages, and Justice Paterson, who had been at the Philadelphia constitutional convention, noted that the Framers had intended a narrow definition of direct taxes. In the most important precedent, *Springer v. United States,* 102 U.S. 586 (1881), the Court had sustained the constitutionality of the 1864 Civil War income tax; direct taxes, it ruled, consisted only of capitation and real estate taxes.

The precedents, however, proved unpersuasive to the Court. Chief Justice Fuller dismissed them as "a century of error." The Court invalidated the main tax as a direct but unapportioned tax on land. An income tax on land, Fuller declared, was the same as taxing the land itself. The Court also invalidated the income tax of state and municipal bonds as usurping the power of a state to borrow money.

The Court divided 4–4 on three other questions: whether a tax on income from personal property constituted a direct tax; whether the invalidity of the section on income from property voided all of the tax provisions; and whether, if any part of the tax could be considered indirect, it still failed for want of uniformity. Normally, when the Court splits evenly, it leaves the lower court decision in place, but these questions had to be fully resolved because of the great public interest in the issue, so the Court quickly granted Pollock's application for a rehearing. Justice Jackson, who had been ill during the first case (he died a few months later), returned to participate in the second *Pollock* case and voted to sustain the tax. But one of the earlier dissenting justices (it is not known which one) now joined with Fuller and the antitax group to invalidate the entire plan as violating the constitutional ban on direct taxes. Fuller's opinion again distorted history and precedent. The rights of property, and not a strict construction of the Constitution, obviously informed both the majority and minority opinions.

All four members of the minority issued dissenting opinions. Justice Brown—who could hardly be considered a radical—openly expressed the political rather than the judicial concerns that had motivated the Court. "The decision involves nothing less than a surrender of the taxing power to the moneyed class," he asserted. "Even the spectre of socialism is conjured up to frighten Congress from laying taxes upon the people in proportion to their ability to pay them."

The Court had obviously overreached itself, and the extent of its action astonished even conservative opinion. Before the end of 1895 a constitutional amendment to overturn *Pollock* and legitimize income taxes had been introduced into Congress. Moreover, between 1895 and 1912 every session of Congress saw proposals designed to reduce the power of the courts, limit the terms of judges, and give Congress the power to override Court decisions. Congress passed the income tax amendment, with conservatives confident it would not be ratified. They badly misjudged the temper of the country, and by early 1913, forty-two states had ratified the Sixteenth Amendment, six more than the required two-thirds of the states. (Some have argued that it was not ratified because many states had altered it and thus did not agree to exactly the same amendment.) The

Wilson administration quickly took advantage of the new power and wrote an income tax into the Underwood Tariff. The administration then relied heavily on the new tax to finance World War I.

See Robert Stanley, *Dimensions of Law in the Service of Order: Origins of the Federal Income Tax, 1861–1913* (New York: Oxford University Press, 1993); Jerold L. Waltman, *Political Origins of the U.S. Income Tax* (Jackson: University Press of Mississippi, 1985); Gerald E. Eggert, "Richard Olney and the Income Tax Cases," *Mississippi Valley Historical Review* 48 (1961): 24; and David G. Farrelly, "Justice Harlan's Dissent in the Pollock Case," *Southern California Law Review* 24 (1951): 175.

Wong Wing v. United States

163 U.S. 228 (1896)
Decided: May 18, 1896
Vote: 8 (Fuller, Field, Harlan I, Gray, Brown, Shiras, E. White, Peckham)
0
Opinion of the Court: Shiras
Opinion concurring in part, dissenting in part: Field
Did not participate: Brewer

In 1892 Wong Wing and three other Chinese people were arrested as illegal aliens. A federal judge in Michigan sentenced them to sixty days of hard labor in prison, after which they were to be deported to China. Wong Wing argued that although he was an alien, he should receive constitutional protection because he was inside the United States. Aliens located in the United States, he claimed, are due the same constitutional rights as citizens.

The Supreme Court ruled that the federal government may detain or temporarily hold aliens in the course of deporting them. Detention is part of an arrest, but it is different from imprisonment. Congress also has the power to make a law allowing for fines or imprisonment of illegal aliens. Congress, however, may not subject aliens to hard labor or confiscate their possessions without a trial by jury because to do so is a violation of due process. The Court made a sweeping ruling that all persons who are within the jurisdiction of the United States must receive the full protections and rights under the Constitution because of the Due Process Clause of the Fourteenth Amendment.

Plessy v. Ferguson

163 U.S. 537 (1896)
Decided: May 18, 1896
Vote: 7 (Fuller, Field, Gray, Brown, Shiras, E. White, Peckham)
1 (Harlan I)
Opinion of the Court: Brown
Dissenting opinion: Harlan I
Did not participate: Brewer

Louisiana enacted a statute in 1890 that required railroads to provide "equal but separate accommodations for the white and colored races" and barred individuals from occupying rail cars other than those assigned to their race. The only exception was for Negro nurses taking care of white children. In June 1892 Homer Adolph Plessy, who was one-eighth black, boarded an East Louisiana Railway train and took a seat designated for whites. When asked by the conductor to move to the "colored car," Plessy refused, and the conductor had him arrested. The act of defiance had been prearranged by a New Orleans group of Creoles and blacks who organized as the Citizens Committee to Test the Constitutionality of the Separate Car Law.

At the criminal trial, Judge John Ferguson found Plessy guilty of violating the statute. With his conviction, Plessy and the Citizens Committee had the opportunity they wanted—to challenge in the Supreme Court not only the Louisiana statute but also all Jim Crow laws. Their challenge garnered some support from the railroads, who objected to the additional costs of providing separate cars. But the tide of equal rights, which seemingly had been so strong during the Civil War and Reconstruction period, had run out; not just in the South, but throughout the nation, and there was little interest in protecting former slaves from the oppressive regime now commonplace in the South. Moreover, the Supreme Court had already indicated in the ***Civil Rights Cases,*** 109 U.S. 3 (1883), that it saw little in the Reconstruction amendments to protect people of color from such discrimination.

Brown, for the Court, noted that although the Fourteenth Amendment had been intended to establish an absolute equality of the races before the law, "in the nature of things it could not have been intended to abolish distinctions based upon color, or to enforce social, as distinguished from political, equality, or a commingling of the two races unsatisfactory to either." Nowhere in the opinion can the phrase "separate but equal" be found, but the Court's ruling approved legally enforced segregation so long as the law did not make facilities for blacks "inferior" to those for whites.

In one of the best known dissents in the history of the Court, Justice Harlan warned that states could now impose criminal penalties on a citizen simply because he or she wished to use public highways and common carriers. Such legislation, Harlan argued was "inconsistent not only with equality of rights which pertains to citizenship, National and State, but with the personal liberty enjoyed by everyone within the United States." As for the majority's disingenuous contention that segregation did not in itself constitute discrimination, Harlan, a southern-born justice, condemned segregation statutes as "conceived in hostility to, and enacted for the purpose of humiliating citizens of the United States of a particular race." Such laws defeated the purpose of the Civil War Amendments and made any real peace between the races impossible. "The destinies of the two races . . . are indissolubly linked together, and the interests of both require that the common government of all shall not permit the seeds of race hate to be planted under the sanction of law." Harlan's plea that the "Constitution is color-blind" fell on deaf ears, not only within the Court, but in the country as well. The surest sign of the changing temper of the nation was that where there had been a vociferous protest in the North over the *Civil Rights Cases* thirteen years earlier, the *Plessy* decision caused hardly a ripple.

See Charles A. Lofgren, *The Plessy Case: A Legal-Historical Interpretation* (New York: Oxford University Press, 1987); C. Vann Woodward, *The Strange Career of Jim Crow,* 3d rev. ed. (New York: Oxford University Press, 1989); and Pauli Murray, ed. and comp., *State Laws on Race and Color* (Cincinnati: Women's Division of Christian Service, 1952; reprint, 1997, by the University of Georgia Press).

Allgeyer v. Louisiana

165 U.S. 578 (1897)
Decided: March 1, 1897
Vote: 9 (Fuller, Field, Harlan I, Gray, Brewer, Brown, Shiras, E. White, Peckham)
0
Opinion of the Court: Peckham

Louisiana, like many other states, prohibited foreign businesses from operating within its jurisdiction unless they met specified conditions. In an effort to enforce this policy, the state made it illegal for Louisianans to enter into certain insurance contracts by mail with companies operating outside the state. Allgeyer and Company entered into an insurance contract with a New York underwriter and was prosecuted for that action.

Justice Peckham recognized that the Court had earlier held that insurance was not interstate commerce and it could not rule the Louisiana law unconstitutional for invading national jurisdiction. Instead, he pointed out that the contract was effected in New York and lawful in New York. The Court therefore held that the Due Process Clause of the Fourteenth Amendment guaranteed the right to enter into lawful contracts.

Allgeyer was pivotal in the establishment of the doctrine of "liberty of contract." It was the first time the Supreme Court ruled a state law unconstitutional for depriving a person of the right to make a contract.

See Nathan Greene, "The Allgeyer Case as a Constitutional Embrasure of Territoriality," *St. John's Law Review* 2 (1927): 22.

Chicago, Burlington & Quincy Railroad Company v. Chicago

166 U.S. 226 (1897)
Decided: March 1, 1897
Vote: 7 (Field, Harlan I, Gray, Brown, Shiras, E. White, Peckham)
1 (Brewer)
Opinion of the Court: Harlan I
Dissenting opinion: Brewer
Did not participate: Fuller

The city of Chicago, through a jury award of one dollar, took railroad property for the purpose of providing a street. An Illinois Supreme Court upheld the jury award and allowed the street to be opened for public use.

The Court held that the Fourteenth Amendment's Due Process Clause compelled the states to award just compensation when it took private property for public use. The Court in this instance applied the due process concept to protect substantive property rights and to develop limits on state control of economic liberties.

In his dissent, Justice Brewer stated that although he agreed that the Due Process Clause requires states to pay compensation when private property is taken, he thought that the jury verdict called for only nominal, rather than just, compensation to the railroad.

This case was an early example of how the Fourteenth Amendment's Due Process Clause incorporated specific constitutional protections to the states.

United States v. Trans-Missouri Freight Ass'n

166 U.S. 290 (1897)
Decided: March 22, 1897
Vote: 5 (Fuller, Harlan I, Brown, Brewer, Peckham)
4 (Field, Gray, Shiras, E. White)
Opinion of the Court: Peckham
Dissenting opinion: E. White (Field, Gray, Shiras)

The Sherman Antitrust Act of 1890 outlawed unfair competition practices, such as contracts or conspiracies that restrained free trade and interstate commerce. Price-fixing was one of the practices outlawed, but the language of the statute seemed to cover only trust agreements.

Eighteen railroad companies entered into agreements fixing prices for their freight rates. They argued that because the Sherman Act covered only trust agreements, contracts to fix prices entered into by other entities were legal. The government argued that the law covered all forms of agreements that affected interstate commerce. The Court now had to decide just how far the Sherman Antitrust Act reached.

In a 5–4 decision, the Court ruled that the statute covered all agreements that placed restraints on free trade or interstate commerce. Therefore, even agreements by common carriers such as railroads were covered. Price-fixing by any entities restrained trade and commerce. In addition, the Court ruled that the effect of an agreement is what matters, not the parties' intent in making it.

See William Letwin, *Law and Economic Policy in America: The Evolution of the Sherman Antitrust Act* (New York: Random House, 1965).

Holden v. Hardy

169 U.S. 366 (1898)
Decided: February 28, 1898
Vote: 7 (Fuller, Harlan I, Gray, Brown, Shiras, E. White, McKenna)
2 (Brewer, Peckham)
Opinion of the Court: Brown
Dissenting without opinion: Brewer, Peckham

John Anderson worked as an underground miner for Albert Holden in Utah. Holden required his miners to work for ten hours each day, in violation of a state law stating that "the period of employment of workingmen in all underground mines or workings shall be eight hours per day, except in cases of emergency where life or property is in imminent danger." Upon his arrest, Holden contended that the statute deprived him of the freedom to contract with employees and violated three provisions of the Fourteenth Amendment: privileges and immunities, due process, and equal protection.

Justice Brown held that the right to contract was subject to limitation by the state's police power to protect the health, safety, or morals of its citizens. Brown said there was a reasonable basis in fact to support the legislature's judgment about the danger of mining, and he held that the Fourteenth Amendment was not intended to inhibit the states' exercise of powers to protect their citizens. In addition, Brown noted that the traditional notion of contract, a bargain reached between two equals, did not hold true, because mine owners and their employees "do not stand upon an equality, and . . . their interests are, to a certain extent, conflicting."

Although courts in general tended to distrust so-called protective legislation affecting the labor contract, for the most part they did approve them under the rubric of the state's police power to protect the health and safety of its citizens. For conservatives like Brewer and Peckham, however, any regulation of contract violated the Fourteenth Amendment.

See Charles W. McCurdy, "The Roots of 'Liberty of Contract' Reconsidered," *Yearbook of the Supreme Court Historical Society* 20 (1984).

Smyth v. Ames

169 U.S. 466 (1898)
Decided: March 7, 1898
Vote: 9 (Fuller, Harlan I, Gray, Brewer, Brown, Shiras, E. White, Peckham, McKenna)
0
Opinion of the Court: Harlan I

In 1893 the Nebraska legislature, dominated by newly elected Populists, enacted a maximum rate schedule for railroads operating within the state. The new schedule compelled an immediate 30 percent reduction in intrastate freight charges. Stockholders of the Union Pacific Railway Company challenged the law on the grounds that it deprived them of property without due process of law.

The Court unanimously agreed and held that although the state could regulate certain industries, such as common carriers, the businesses were constitutionally entitled to earn a "fair return" on the "fair value" of their investment. Justice Harlan then set out what became known as the fair value rule, listing factors such as cost of equipment, depreciation, and so on, but giving no indication as to how these factors should be used or their relative weight in the equation. Most important, the Court held that to ensure that the rates were fair, courts had the power to review state legislative and regulatory commission rates.

As a result, for the next half-century courts found themselves in an awkward position; judges were asked to review the complex issue of rate-setting without any expertise on their part or a professional staff to evaluate the data. Moreover, if railroads and other utilities did not like the rates set by states, they could then appeal to the courts and introduce "new" evidence in their claim that the rates set did not provide a fair return on their investment.

The Great Depression and the resultant failure of numerous railroads put an effective end to court review of rates, although the doctrine of *Smyth* itself was not finally buried until 1944 with the decision in *Federal Power Commission v. Hope Natural Gas Company*, 320 U.S. 591.

See Mary Cornelia Porter, "That Commerce Shall Be Free: A New Look at the Old Laissez-Faire Court," *Supreme Court Review* (1976): 151.

United States v. Wong Kim Ark

169 U.S. 649 (1898)
Decided: March 28, 1898
Vote: 6 (Gray, Brewer, Brown, Shiras, E. White, Peckham)
2 (Fuller, Harlan I)
Opinion of the Court: Gray
Dissenting opinion: Fuller (Harlan I)
Did not participate: McKenna

Wong Kim Ark was born in the United States to Chinese parents in 1873. After traveling to China for a visit, he was denied readmission to the United States. At issue was the citizenship status of persons of Chinese descent born in the United States. Immigrants from China had been denied the privilege of becoming naturalized citizens under an 1882 act, and exclusionists urged that persons of Chinese descent should be denied birthright citizenship as well. They wanted a definition of citizenship based upon the nationality of the parents rather than upon the place of birth.

Wong Kim Ark's case hinged upon the Court's interpretation of the first clause of the Fourteenth Amendment, which provided that "all persons born or naturalized in the United States, and subject to the jurisdiction thereof, are citizens of the United States." The government argued that Wong Kim Ark was not a citizen because his Chinese parentage made him subject to the emperor of China.

A majority of the Court disagreed, holding that the common law and the Fourteenth Amendment guaranteed citizenship to all persons born in the United States, regardless of their ethnic heritage. This case proved to be an important legal victory for Chinese Americans as well as other persons of Asian descent during a period of intense anti-Asian sentiment.

See Lucy E. Salyer, *Laws Harsh as Tigers: Chinese Immigrants and the Shaping of Modern Immigration Law* (Chapel Hill: University of North Carolina Press, 1995).

Williams v. Mississippi

170 U.S. 213 (1898)
Decided: April 25, 1898
Vote: 9 (Fuller, Harlan I, Gray, Brewer, Brown, Shiras, E. White, Peckham, McKenna)
0
Opinion of the Court: McKenna

The Mississippi constitutional convention in 1890 adopted literacy and poll-tax qualifications that effectively denied the vote to its black citizens. Because only registered voters could serve on juries, blacks were also eliminated from jury rolls after 1892. Henry Williams, a black man, was indicted by an all-white grand jury for murder and convicted and sentenced to hang by an all-white petit jury. He appealed the indictment and trial for violating the Equal Protection Clause of the Fourteenth Amendment in that blacks had been excluded from jury service.

The Court unanimously rejected Williams's contention. Justice McKenna distinguished the facts in this case from the principle of ***Yick Wo v. Hopkins,*** 118 U.S. 356 (1886), that a law fair on its face would be voided if public authorities administered it in an unequal manner. Williams had not shown, to the satisfaction of the Court, that the actual administration of the Mississippi suffrage provisions was discriminatory.

As a result of this case, other southern states quickly followed Mississippi's lead, and the new laws, together with white primary elections, effectively disfranchised southern blacks until the 1940s. For practical purposes, *Williams* was not superseded until the Civil Rights Act of 1964 and the Voting Rights Act of 1965 overturned southern obstacles to black registration and voting.

See Alfred Avins, "The Fourteenth Amendment and Jury Discrimination: The Original Understanding," *Federal Bar Journal* 27 (1967): 257.

Stephens v. Cherokee Nation

174 U.S. 445 (1899)
Decided: May 15, 1899
Vote: 7 (Fuller, Harlan I, Gray, Brewer, Brown, Shiras, Peckham)
2 (E. White, McKenna)
Opinion of the Court: Fuller
Dissenting without opinion: E. White, McKenna

In 1898 Congress passed the Curtis Act, which stripped the Cherokee Indians of their lands. Congress took the land, gave a portion of it to Cherokee who were U.S. citizens, and sold the rest to non-Cherokee U.S. citizens. The act applied to what were then known as the Five Civilized Tribes.

The Cherokee argued that they had a fee simple over their lands; that is, they had complete ownership because Congress had given them a patent to those lands. Did Congress now have the power to take away lands that it had already given full ownership of to the Native American tribes?

The Supreme Court ruled that Congress could reserve lands for the Native American tribes, give them full ownership rights, and then strip it all away under its guardianship interests over the tribes. Therefore, even though Congress had given the land, it was still subject to congressional legislation for the purposes of the government's guardianship interests.

See David E. Wilkins, *American Indian Sovereignty and the U.S. Supreme Court* (Austin: University of Texas Press, 1997).

Addystone Pipe & Steel Co. v. United States

175 U.S. 211 (1899)
Decided: December 4, 1899
Vote: 9 (Fuller, Harlan I, Gray, Brewer, Brown, Shiras, E. White, Peckham, McKenna)
0
Opinion of the Court: Peckham

Six companies entered into a compact to divide up the cast-iron pipe market. They agreed not to compete with each other in the designated territories and, in some cases, entire states. The agreement concerned the manufacturing, transporting, and selling of cast-iron pipe.

The companies argued that the Sherman Antitrust Act did not cover them because, under liberty of contract, they had an absolute right to make such agreements. Congress, they claimed, had no authority to regulate contracts or agreements, even if they directly affected interstate commerce.

The Supreme Court ruled that the Constitution gives Congress authority under the Commerce Clause to regulate interstate commerce and that the power extends to regulating contracts and agreements that directly affect interstate commerce. Manufacturing alone did not directly affect interstate commerce, but the conspiracy in this case also involved the selling and transporting of goods across state lines and therefore did affect interstate commerce. Congress may make laws, such as the Sherman Antitrust Act, regulating commerce, but only if it "directly" affected "interstate" commerce. This wording allowed the Court to hamstring the Sherman Act for several more years, and it did not fully eliminate distinctions between "direct" and "indirect" effect until 1942 in ***Wickard v. Filburn,*** 317 U.S. 111.

See William Letwin, *Law and Economic Policy in America: The Evolution of the Sherman Antitrust Act* (New York: Random House, 1965).

Bradfield v. Roberts

175 U.S. 291 (1899)
Decided: December 4, 1899
Vote: 9 (Fuller, Harlan I, Gray, Brewer, Brown, Shiras, E. White, Peckham, McKenna)
0
Opinion of the Court: Peckham

Designating himself a citizen and a taxpayer, Joseph Bradfield sued the federal government to prevent an agreement that Congress had made with a Catholic hospital in Washington, D.C., to provide care for the indigent. Under the agreement, the federal government was to finance the construction of a building at the hospital and to pay a fee for each indigent patient city officials sent to the hospital.

Bradfield argued that this arrangement violated the religious Establishment Clause of the First Amendment. He did not claim that Congress could not make such an agreement with a hospital; rather, he argued that Congress could not do so with a *religious* hospital. He believed Congress had violated the constitutionally mandated separation of church and state.

The Supreme Court unanimously disagreed. If a hospital is owned by a religious organization, Congress may not help finance its projects, but here the Court found that the hospital was actually owned by a private secular corporation. This corporation was, in fact, made up entirely of Catholic nuns belonging to the Sisters of Charity, which the justices deliberately ignored in finding that the hospital corporation was not a religious corporation.

Peckham dismissed the First Amendment argument out of hand and noted that the hospital had no religious test for the admission of patients. Although later courts would reach similar conclusions in allowing the government to contract with religious bodies for social services, few would say that the ownership and operation of the hospital by a Catholic order was "wholly immaterial." The case is remembered primarily for establishing that more was required to prove a First Amendment violation than a simple contract with a church-owned corporation.

See Carl H. Esbeck, "Government Regulation of Religiously Based Social Services: The First Amendment Considerations," *Hastings Constitutional Law Quarterly* 19 (1992): 343.

Cumming v. Richmond County Board of Education

175 U.S. 528 (1899)
Decided: December 18, 1899
Vote: 9 (Fuller, Harlan I, Gray, Brewer, Brown, Shiras, E. White, Peckham, McKenna)
0
Opinion of the Court: Harlan I

In 1879 officials in Augusta, Georgia, established Ware High School, the first high school for African Americans, and it flourished until 1897. Then, purportedly at the request of a black private school principal, the school board closed Ware, claiming that it had to use the money for black elementary school education. At the same time, however, the school board was subsidizing tuition for white students at private high schools. Black teenagers and their parents sued to enjoin the school board from subsidizing white tuition on the basis that the board's policy violated the Equal Protection Clause.

The Supreme Court rejected the parents' claim. Although he was the author of the powerful dissent in ***Plessy v. Ferguson,*** 163 U.S. 537 (1896), Justice Harlan, speaking for the unanimous Court, accepted the school board's claim of fiscal necessity at face value. The ruling ran contrary to the principles laid down thirteen years earlier in ***Yick Wo v. Hopkins,*** 118 U.S. 356 (1886). Beyond that, Harlan stressed that public education was a matter for state and local jurisdiction and federal courts should not intervene without clear evidence of a constitutional violation.

The decision cleared the way for southern states to divert the majority of their public school resources to all-white schools, leading to an ever-growing disparity in facilities and quality between all-black and all-white schools, a disparity that the Supreme Court would ignore until the 1930s. Where *Plessy* had required separate but equal facilities, the *Cumming* decision facilitated the evolution toward separate and unequal. See ***Missouri ex rel. Gaines v. Canada,*** 305 U.S. 339 (1938).

See J. Morgan Kousser, "Separate but *Not* Equal: The Supreme Court's First Decision on Racial Discrimination in Schools," *Journal of Southern History* 46 (1980): 17; and C. Ellen Connally, "Justice Harlan's 'Great Betrayal'? A Reconsideration of *Cumming v. Richmond County Board of Education,*" *Journal of Supreme Court History* 25 (2000): 72.

1900–1909

Maxwell v. Dow

176 U.S. 581 (1900)
Decided: February 26, 1900
Vote: 8 (Fuller, Gray, Brewer, Brown, Shiras, E. White, Peckham, McKenna)
1 (Harlan I)
Opinion of the Court: Peckham
Dissenting opinion: Harlan I

Charles L. "Gunplay" Maxwell was charged and prosecuted for the crime of robbery on a bill of information rather than by a grand jury indictment. A petit jury of eight members instead of twelve tried and convicted him. According to Maxwell, both actions violated his privileges and immunities as protected by the Fifth and Fourteenth Amendments. Moreover, being convicted by an eight-member jury violated the due process guaranteed by the Fourteenth Amendment.

The Court dismissed Maxwell's arguments and upheld the conviction. Justice Peckham pointed out that this issue had been resolved in prior decisions, such as ***Hurtado v. California,*** 110 U.S. 516 (1884). With this decision the Court continued to minimize the scope of the Privileges and Immunities Clause, which had begun in the ***Slaughterhouse Cases,*** 83 U.S. 36 (1873). Justice Peckham reasoned that to take any other approach would "fetter and degrade the state governments by subjecting them to the control of Congress" as to violate "the structure and spirit of our institutions." The Court at this time still viewed the states as the primary protectors of most rights.

Justice Harlan wrote a strong dissent defending the twelve-member jury. He argued that at a minimum the Bill of Rights identified the privileges and immunities that the Fourteenth Amendment protected. Harlan concluded that the states could not avoid the Sixth Amendment's guarantee of a trial by a jury of twelve members.

The case continued the Court's pattern of deferring to state criminal law and refusing to use the Fourteenth Amendment to expand the reach of the Bill of Rights guarantees to the states.

Neely v. Henkel

180 U.S. 109 (1901)
Decided: January 14, 1901
Vote: 9 (Fuller, Harlan I, Gray, Brewer, Brown, Shiras, E. White, Peckham, McKenna)
0
Opinion of the Court: Harlan I
See *Insular Cases,* page 131.

DeLima v. Bidwell

182 U.S. 1 (1901)
Decided: May 27, 1901
Vote: 5 (Fuller, Harlan I, Brewer, Brown, Peckham)
4 (Gray, Shiras, E. White, McKenna)
Opinion of the Court: Brown
Dissenting opinion: McKenna (Shiras, E. White)
Dissenting opinion: Gray
See *Insular Cases,* page 131.

Downes v. Bidwell

182 U.S. 244 (1901)
Decided: May 27, 1901
Vote: 5 (Gray, Brown, Shiras, E. White, McKenna)
4 (Fuller, Harlan I, Brewer, Peckham)
Opinion of the Court: Brown
Concurring opinion: E. White (Shiras, McKenna)
Concurring opinion: Gray
Dissenting opinion: Fuller (Harlan I, Brewer, Peckham)
Dissenting opinion: Harlan I
See *Insular Cases,* page 131.

Knoxville Iron Co. v. Harbison

183 U.S. 13 (1901)
Decided: October 21, 1901
Vote: 7 (Fuller, Harlan I, Gray, Brown, Shiras, E. White, McKenna)
2 (Brewer, Peckham)
Opinion of the Court: Shiras
Dissenting without opinion: Brewer, Peckham

Samuel Harbison was an employee of Knoxville Iron Company in Tennessee. The employees had the choice of being paid in cash or in coal in the form of a store order. Harbison accepted coal and then attempted to redeem his coal for cash, but the company refused his request. Harbison sued, arguing that by accepting the coal he was a bona fide holder of the coal, which would allow him to redeem it for cash. Knoxville Iron argued that he was not a bona fide holder and that because he accepted coal as payment he could not redeem it for cash.

Tennessee, however, had a statute providing that if a company paid its employees with store orders, the employees could redeem them for cash on any regular payday or within thirty days after they were issued. The company argued that the statute unconstitutionally interfered with its liberty to contract with its employees.

The Supreme Court held that the statute was constitutional and that the company was obliged to redeem Harbison's coal for cash. The right to contract is not absolute in all matters, Justice Shiras noted, and it must be balanced against the state's interest in protecting the safety and welfare of its citizens.

Dooley v. United States

183 U.S. 151 (1901)
Decided: December 2, 1901
Vote: 5 (Gray, Brown, Shiras, E. White, McKenna)
4 (Fuller, Harlan I, Brewer, Peckham)
Opinion of the Court: Brown
Concurring opinion: E. White
Dissenting opinion: Fuller (Harlan I, Brewer, Peckham)

In the Spanish-American War of 1898, the United States acquired several territories previously owned by Spain, including Puerto Rico. In 1900 Congress passed the Foraker Act, which required all goods going into Puerto Rico from the United States to pay a 15 percent duty. Dooley, Smith and Company paid the tax under protest and then went to court to get the money back, arguing that the law violated Article I, Section 9, of the Constitution, which states, "No tax or duty shall be laid on articles exported from any State." The question was whether Puerto Rico had ceased to be a foreign country when the United States acquired it.

The Supreme Court, in a 5–4 decision, ruled that Puerto Rico was to be considered part of the United States. Because the act required the payment of a duty on goods entering Puerto Rico, it was unconstitutional. The case was argued along with *DeLima v. Bidwell,* 182 U.S. 1 (1901), and is best understood as one of the *Insular Cases.* (See page 131.)

Cherokee Nation v. Hitchcock

187 U.S. 294 (1902)
Decided: December 1, 1902
Vote: 8 (Fuller, Harlan I, Brewer, Brown, Shiras, E. White, Peckham, McKenna)
0
Opinion of the Court: E. White

Congress passed a law known as the Indian Appropriation Act (IAA). It gave the secretary of the interior the power to lease lands in the territorial lands set aside for Native Americans. The secretary could lease the lands for oil, coal, and asphalt production without the permission or consent of the tribes that nominally owned them. The Cherokee Nation sued the Interior Department and Secretary Ethan A. Hitchcock, arguing that the IAA was an unconstitutional grant of authority by Congress. The Cherokee claimed that because the lands had been set aside for them, they had full title, possession, and control of them, and that the federal government had exceeded its powers in the appropriation act.

The Supreme Court ruled that Congress had the authority to pass the law. The United States, although providing territory for Native Americans, still retained an interest in the lands, and could therefore exercise authority over them so long as it was in a political and administrative manner. Allowing the Interior Department to lease the lands for economic development was determined to be an administrative decision and therefore constitutional. Neither the Cherokee Nation nor any other tribe could prevent the federal government from leasing their lands for economic development.

See David E. Wilkins, *American Indian Sovereignty and the U.S. Supreme Court* (Austin: University of Texas Press, 1997).

Lone Wolf v. Hitchcock

187 U.S. 553 (1903)
Decided: January 5, 1903
Vote: 9 (Fuller, Harlan I, Brewer, Brown, Shiras, E. White, Peckham, McKenna, Holmes)
0
Opinion of the Court: E. White
Concurring without opinion: Harlan I

Lone Wolf sought to block congressional ratification of an agreement allotting tribal lands to non-Indians on the grounds that this transfer violated the 1867 Treaty of Medicine Lodge. He argued that the agreement had failed to get the required approval of three-fourths of the adult male tribal members before the land cessions.

The Court rejected the argument and denied that the agreement violated the property rights of tribal members or deprived them of due process of law. The Court recognized an almost absolute congressional power over Indian affairs that was virtually exempt from judicial oversight. Justice White held that Congress had plenary power over Indian property "by reason of its exercise of guardianship over their interest." The power, he stated, was political and not subject to judicial review, and under it the United States could unilaterally abrogate provisions of treaties made with Indians nations, subject only to the requirement that actions of the United States toward its "wards" be "guided by perfect good faith." The Court totally ignored the fact that the land transfer had been surrounded by fraud and that the government had failed to comply with the requirements of a treaty it had signed.

The basic holding of *Lone Wolf,* that Congress had plenary powers over tribal affairs, survived through 1996, when the Court in ***Seminole Tribe of Florida v. Florida,*** 517 U.S. 44, struck down as a violation of the Eleventh Amendment a complex statutory scheme enacted by Congress as part of the Indian Gaming Regulatory Act.

See Blue Clark, *Lone Wolf v. Hitchcock: Treaty Rights and Indian Law at the End of the Nineteenth Century* (Lincoln: University of Nebraska Press, 1994).

Champion v. Ames

188 U.S. 321 (1903)
Decided: February 23, 1903
Vote: 5 (Harlan I, Brown, E. White, McKenna, Holmes)
4 (Fuller, Brewer, Shiras, Peckham)
Opinion of the Court: Harlan I
Dissenting opinion: Fuller (Brewer, Shiras, Peckham)

Despite their opposition to many state measures regulating business, the justices, with a few significant exceptions, proved remarkably receptive to reading broad authority into the Commerce Clause (and to a lesser degree, into the taxing power) to create a federal police power in the late nineteenth and early twentieth centuries.

Charles Champion and Charles Park had hired Wells Fargo Company to transport Paraguayan lottery tickets from Texas to California. They were convicted of conspiring to defraud the United States, namely that they violated an 1895 federal statute prohibiting the interstate traffic in lottery tickets. They appealed the denial of writ of habeas corpus, arguing that the *transporting* of lottery tickets across state lines did not constitute interstate commerce. The government's response made three points: first, that express companies such as Wells Fargo were instruments of commerce; second, that Congress could regulate the carrying of any article from one state to another; and finally, that such regulations could take the form of absolute prohibition or even criminal sanctions. The case involved new and difficult questions for the justices, and had to be argued three times before they upheld the conviction.

Justice Harlan, speaking for the Court, termed the federal commerce power near absolute. He defined commerce as embracing "navigation, intercourse, communication, traffic, the transit of persons and the transmission of messages by telegraph." If the legislature viewed an article as evil, it could ban the entry of that article into the stream of commerce. Harlan recognized that such an interpretation would permit Congress to prohibit whatever it chose, and he warned that the legislative power had limits. Although "the possible abuse of power is not an argument against its existence," further adjudication would determine the extent of congressional power.

For the minority, led by Chief Justice Fuller, Congress had already gone too far. Prohibiting the interstate movement of lottery tickets was, according to the dissent, a means to get to the real target of the legislation—the lottery itself, even though gambling had always been a subject for local control.

Fuller objected to the idea of a federal police power as a violation of the Tenth Amendment. He predicted that federal police powers would undermine state powers. Addressing Harlan's argument that only the federal power could suppress evils in interstate commerce, Fuller noted that under the Constitution there might be areas beyond the reach of *either* the state or federal governments. Regrettable as this might be, the Court had to uphold the larger objective of maintaining a federal system under constitutional restraints.

In the end, Harlan's broad reading of the Commerce Clause would prevail, although it suffered several setbacks until finally embraced by the New Deal Court. ***United States v. Darby Lumber Co.,*** 312 U.S. 100 (1941), and ***Wickard v. Filburn,*** 317 U.S. 111 (1942), are good examples.

See John E. Semonche, *Charting the Future: The Supreme Court Responds to a Changing Society, 1890–1920* (Westport, Conn.: Greenwood Press, 1978); and Alexander M. Bickel and Benno C. Schmidt Jr., *The Judiciary and Responsible Government, 1910–1921* (New York: Collier Macmillan, 1984).

Hawaii v. Mankichi

190 U.S. 197 (1903)
Decided: June 1, 1903
Vote: 5 (Brown, E. White, McKenna, Holmes, Day)
4 (Fuller, Harlan I, Brewer, Peckham)
Opinion of the Court: Brown
Concurring opinion: E. White (McKenna)
Dissenting opinion: Fuller (Harlan I, Brewer, Peckham)
Dissenting opinion: Harlan I

Osaki Mankichi was convicted for manslaughter. He then filed a writ of habeas corpus because he had not been indicted by a grand jury, had been brought to trial on the basis of a bill of information, and convicted by a jury vote of 9 to 3. The U.S. district court in Hawaii granted habeas corpus, and Hawaii's attorney general appealed the decision.

At the time, Hawaii was a territory, not a state. Congress had passed the Newland Resolution, which stated that municipal regulations, not contrary to the Constitution, should remain in effect until Congress legislated otherwise. Therefore, the issue in this case was whether citizens in territories such as Hawaii had a Sixth Amendment right to a grand jury indictment.

The Supreme Court ruled, 5–4, that the Sixth Amendment right to a grand jury did not necessarily apply in territories. The Court reasoned that the citizens of these territories were unfamiliar with American constitutional protections. Moreover, the Sixth Amendment right to a grand jury was merely a procedural right, not a substantive right. The Court said that Hawaii's existing procedures should be respected because the Newland Resolution was still in effect. Therefore, the territory's prior rules of criminal procedure, and not those of the Constitution, governed until Congress decided otherwise.

This case should be seen as part and parcel of the debate central to the *Insular Cases* over whether the Constitution and its rights followed the flag. (See page 131.)

Northern Securities Co. v. United States

193 U.S. 197 (1904)
Decided: March 14, 1904
Vote: 5 (Harlan I, Brewer, Brown, McKenna, Day)
4 (Fuller, E. White, Peckham, Holmes)
Opinion of the Court: Harlan I
Concurring opinion: Brewer
Dissenting opinion: Holmes (Fuller, E. White, Peckham)
Dissenting opinion: E. White (Fuller, Peckham, Holmes)

The James J. Hill-J. P. Morgan group owned the Northern Pacific and Great Northern lines and had just bought the Burlington line to secure a terminal in Chicago. The E. H. Harriman group, which controlled the Union Pacific Railroad, had been rebuffed in its efforts to join in the Burlington line. Harriman then tried to buy a controlling interest in the Northern Pacific. This action sent the railroad securities market into a panic. To stabilize the situation, the principal figures agreed to establish the Northern Securities Company, capitalized at $400 million, to hold Great Northern, Northern Pacific, and Burlington stock and to operate the three lines as an integrated system, with both Hill and Harriman interests represented on the board of directors.

When Theodore Roosevelt assumed the presidency after the assassination of William McKinley in September 1901, he and Attorney General Philander Knox decided that, despite the decision in ***E. C. Knight v. United States,*** 156 U.S. 1 (1895), the Sherman Antitrust Act still retained vitality. Looking for a test case, Roosevelt and Knox challenged the formation of the Northern Securities Company, and the Justice Department successfully sued in circuit court to dissolve it. The circuit court decision was appealed to the Supreme Court, which ruled that Northern Securities constituted an unlawful combination under the terms of the Sherman Act.

Northern Securities, relying on *Knight,* claimed first that the merger represented nothing more than a stock transfer, which did not constitute commerce. Second, the corporation had done nothing illegal under the terms of its New Jersey charter and, because state law controlled the incorporation of businesses, application of the Sherman Act would violate the Tenth Amendment by unconstitutionally intruding federal power into a domain reserved to the states.

Justice Harlan rejected both propositions. Whatever the technical aspects of the stock arrangement, the purpose had been to restrain competition in the railroad industry. The Sherman Act outlawed all contracts, combinations, or conspiracies that directly or indirectly affected commerce. As for the states' rights argument, Harlan dismissed it as a false assertion that a state could grant immunity from federal law. The idea that a state could prevent the national government from exercising its constitutional powers could not "be entertained for a moment."

Although the government won the case, the narrowness of the vote indicated that the Court had not yet found a comfortable means of evaluating the Sherman Act. Holmes's dissent questioned the intent of Congress in passing the law. Congress wanted to protect competition from overweening power, but it also wanted to preserve the benefits of consolidation. Although the statute said "every" combination, Holmes argued that it was unlikely that Congress could possibly have meant that, since such an absolute prohibition would "disintegrate society so far as it could into individual atoms." All business, he noted, to some extent "monopolizes whatever business it does," whether within one state or between states. In attempting to discern congressional intent, Holmes hinted that perhaps the law should apply only to those contracts, combinations, or conspiracies that *unreasonably* restrained trade, and not to those where restraint proved ancillary to the major purpose of securing greater efficiency.

The Court adopted the Holmes's "rule of reason" seven years later in ***Standard Oil Co. v. United States,*** 221 U.S. 1 (1911).

See Hans Thorelli, *The Federal Anti-Trust Policy: Origination of an American Tradition* (Baltimore: Johns Hopkins University Press, 1954); Robert H. Bork, *The Antitrust Paradox: A Policy at War with Itself* (New York: Basic Books, 1978); William Letwin, *Law and Economic Policy in America: The Evolution of the Sherman Antitrust Act* (New York: Random House, 1965); and James May, "Antitrust in the Formative Era: Political and Economic Theory in Constitutional and Antitrust Analysis, 1880–1918," *Ohio State Law Journal* 50 (1989): 257.

United States v. Sing Tuck

194 U.S. 161 (1904)
Decided: April 25, 1904
Vote: 7 (Fuller, Harlan I, Brown, E. White, McKenna, Holmes, Day)
2 (Brewer, Peckham)
Opinion of the Court: Holmes
Dissenting opinion: Brewer (Peckham)

Sing Tuck and thirty others were seeking admission into the United States. When an immigration inspector questioned them, five gave their names, stated that they had been born in the United States, and answered no further questions. The rest gave their names and then stood mute, not even alleging citizenship. The inspector decided against admitting them, detained them, but informed them of their right to appeal to the secretary of commerce and labor. A lawyer, purporting to act for them, alleged that they were all citizens of the United States and filed a petition with the circuit court in their behalf. The circuit court, however, determined the statutory provisions governing detention of aliens was lawful, that it did not allow appeal to federal courts, and dismissed the case without a trial.

The Supreme Court agreed, and held that the statutory means for appeal were adequate and that would-be immigrants had no right to circumvent this statutory procedure by direct appeal to the federal courts. Justice Holmes stated, "We are of the opinion that the attempt to disregard and override the provisions or the statutes and the rules of the department and to swamp the courts by a resort to them in the first instance must fail." He added that even if it were beyond the power of Congress to make the decision of the department final upon the question of citizenship, the Court nevertheless agreed with the circuit court that a petition ought not to be entertained unless the petitioner could make out at least a prima facie case for citizenship. A mere allegation of citizenship was not enough.

Justice Brewer's dissent noted that the courts of the Republic were not so burdened with controversies about property that they did not have the time to determine the rights of personal liberty by one claiming to be a citizen.

See Lucy E. Salyer, *Laws Harsh as Tigers: Chinese Immigrants and the Shaping of Modern Immigration Law* (Chapel Hill: University of North Carolina Press, 1995).

McCray v. United States

195 U.S. 27 (1904)
Decided: May 31, 1904
Vote: 6 (Harlan I, Brewer, E. White, McKenna, Holmes, Day)
3 (Fuller, Brown, Peckham)
Opinion of the Court: E. White
Dissenting without opinion: Fuller, Brown, Peckham

The Oleomargarine Act of 1886 taxed uncolored oleo at a rate of .25 of a cent per pound, while imposing a 10 cents per pound levy on oleo artificially colored to make it look more like butter. The law had been passed at the behest of the dairy industry, which feared cheap colored oleomargarine as a threat to butter sales.

The United States sued McCray, a margarine dealer, for the $50 statutory penalty, claiming that he purchased a fifty-pound package of colored oleomargarine for resale without paying the required tax. McCray challenged the constitutionality of the law, stating that Congress had inappropriately used its taxing power for regulation rather than for revenue. As a result, the law violated the Due Process and Taking Clauses of the Fifth Amendment and infringed on the rights of states to regulate business under the Tenth Amendment.

A majority of the Court refused to interfere with Congress's taxing powers. Justice White declared that "the taxing power conferred by the Constitution knows no limits except those expressly stated in that instrument." Due process was not violated when Congress categorized and taxed products at different rates, and therefore the tax was not unconstitutional because of its potential negative impact on production of oleomargarine. The Court ignored the plain fact that this tax was not designed to raise revenue, but to protect the dairy industry against competition by cheaper butter alternatives. Because the taxing power was not restricted to interstate commerce, the *McCray* decision seemed to open the door for Congress to regulate indirectly through taxation all aspects of the economy.

This case established the taxing power as an element of a federal police power. Although constricted in the 1920s, as in ***Bailey v. Drexel Furniture Co.,*** 259 U.S. 20 (1922), the taxing power was reclaimed by the New Deal as a basis for general welfare legislation.

Dorr v. United States

195 U.S. 138 (1904)
Decided: May 31, 1904
Vote: 8 (Fuller, Brewer, Brown, E. White, Peckham, McKenna, Holmes, Day)
1 (Harlan I)
Opinion of the Court: Day
Concurring opinion: Peckham (Fuller, Brewer)
Dissenting opinion: Harlan I
See *Insular Cases,* page 131.

Swift & Co. v. United States

196 U.S. 375 (1905)
Decided: January 30, 1905
Vote: 9 (Fuller, Harlan I, Brewer, Brown, E. White, Peckham, McKenna, Holmes, Day)
0
Opinion of the Court: Holmes

In deciding the initial cases arising from the Sherman Antitrust Act of 1890, the Court divorced manufacturing from commerce. As a result, the decisions made little economic or jurisprudential sense. For example, ***Addystone Pipe & Steel Co.***

v. United States, 175 U.S. 211 (1899), concerned a group of manufacturers who had formed the Southern Associated Pipe Works and agreed to divide the market into territories, fix the price of pipes, and to assess and share a bonus of $2 per ton. Judge William Howard Taft of the circuit court ruled that the group controlled its market. He also found that the Sherman Act applied to "every combination," whether national and local, that restrained trade. The Supreme Court affirmed the decision.

The government embraced this approach a few years later in *Swift.* The government sought to halt collusive practices by the large meatpackers with respect to the buying and selling of meat. In his opinion for the Court, Holmes evaded the manufacturing/commerce distinction by inventing the "stream of commerce" theory to demonstrate the effect of monopolies on interstate commerce. The stockyard constituted a "throat" through which commerce passed, and therefore it came within the reach of Congress. Acknowledging that a majority of the Court still differentiated between "manufacturing" and "commerce," Holmes explained that if one looked at commerce as the distribution of goods, then conditions affecting that distribution came under the commerce power. The interstate distribution of cattle and then dressed meat passed through the stockyards, and therefore they could be regulated. The refusal of the Court to abandon Fuller's dichotomy between commerce and manufacturing led to the awkward reasoning that, although a stockyard was part of commerce, the slaughterhouse to which it sent the livestock remained manufacturing and therefore outside commerce. *Swift* represented an expansive view of commerce and one which, as Holmes declared, must be looked at "not as a technical legal conception but a practical one, drawn from the course of business." Several members of the Court remained ambivalent, aware of the realities of the market, yet unwilling to admit the necessity for the exercise of federal power.

Swift is often seen as evidence that the Fuller Court was not hostile to antitrust enforcement and that it supported enforcement of the Sherman Act in most of the cases it heard, but clung to the notion that commerce did not include manufacturing or production. It took creative craftsmanship such as Holmes displayed in *Swift* to sidestep that issue.

See David Gordon, "*Swift & Co. v. United States:* The Beef Trust and the Stream of Commerce Doctrine," *American Journal of Legal History* 28 (1984): 244; and Barry Cushman, "A Stream of Legal Consciousness: The Current of Commerce Doctrine from *Swift* to *Jones & Laughlin,*" *Fordham Law Review* 61 (1992): 105.

Jacobson v. Massachusetts

197 U.S. 11 (1905)
Decided: February 20, 1905
Vote: 7 (Fuller, Harlan I, Brown, E. White, McKenna, Holmes, Day)
2 (Brewer, Peckham)
Opinion of the Court: Harlan I
Dissenting without opinion: Brewer, Peckham

Massachusetts had passed a statewide compulsory vaccination statute in an effort to eradicate smallpox in the commonwealth. Anyone over twenty-one years old who refused or failed to comply with the law faced a fine of five dollars. Henning Jacobson refused to be vaccinated, and at his trial offered a variety of defenses, including constitutional guarantees of personal liberty.

Justice Harlan made short work of the personal liberty defense. Until this case, the Court had never tried to define the limits of the state police power. Harlan "recognized the authority of a state to enact quarantine laws and 'health laws of every description.' " Moreover, he recognized all laws that relate to matters completely within the boundaries of the state, as long as they do not, by their necessary operation, affect the people of other states.

See Ernst Freund, *The Police Power: Public Policy and Constitutional Rights* (Chicago: Callaghan, 1904).

Lochner v. New York

198 U.S. 45 (1905)
Decided: April 17, 1905
Vote: 5 (Fuller, Brewer, Brown, Peckham, McKenna)
4 (Harlan I, E. White, Holmes, Day)
Opinion of the Court: Peckham
Dissenting opinion: Harlan I (E. White, Day)
Dissenting opinion: Holmes

New York State passed a law limiting the number of hours a week bakery employees could work. The state reasoned that excessively long hours led to illness, which posed a danger to the public because these employees could not afford to take a day off when they were sick. Other considerations may have been behind the legislation, including the desire of unionized bakeries to force non-union shops into working shorter hours and the desire of housing reformers to eliminate bakeries from operating in tenement basements. In *Lochner* the freedom to enter into contracts ran head-on into a claimed exercise of the police power, and a bare majority of the bench came down in favor of contract rights.

Justice Peckham ignored any claims regarding health and safety and condemned the New York law as nothing more than an effort "to regulate the hours of labor between the master and his employees (all being men, *sui juris*), in a private business, not dangerous in any degree to morals, or in any real and substantive degree to the health of the employees." Peckham agreed that a state could enact legislation to protect the health of bakers, but no evidence had been presented to show that the baking trade posed any health problem to workers, nor had the state put forth any rationale tying the number of hours worked to health.

Peckham, undoubtedly the most conservative member of the Court and a disciple of Justice Field, posed the issue in terms of due process: "Is this a fair, reasonable and appropriate exercise of the police power of the State, or is it an unreasonable, unnecessary and arbitrary interference with the rights of the individual?" The phrasing of the question left no doubt that Peckham believed that courts should examine not only the limits of the police power, but also the policy decisions behind state laws, and he said so bluntly: "The Court looks beyond the mere letter of the law in such cases" to determine the *purpose* of the statute. Here the purpose had been labor regulation, which Peckham viewed as beyond the reach of the state. *Lochner* thus became the classic statement of substantive due process.

Justices Harlan and Holmes vigorously dissented. Apparently, the justices had first decided to sustain the law by a five-to-four vote, and Harlan's opinion had been written as the decision of the Court. Then one justice had changed his mind, and Harlan's opinion became a dissent. In many ways his opinion differs little from that of Peckham in accepting the basic premises of freedom of contract and substantive due process. But Harlan denied that the Court had any business inquiring into the legislative motive. "I find it impossible," he wrote, "in view of common experience, to say that there is here no real or substantial relation between the means employed by the State and the end sought by its legislation." He found in the briefs submitted by New York the evidence that Peckham had denied existed—a link between shorter hours and the health of the bakery workers. The Court might not like the policy, but that was not its business; he cited several other cases, including ***Atkin v. Kansas,*** 191 U.S. 207 (1903) (which Harlan had written) to show that the Court had sustained broad legislative discretion in a state's use of the police power.

Holmes dissented alone in a brief statement that soon achieved classic status, to be quoted time and again by those attacking the judiciary for exceeding its authority. "This case," he declared, "is decided upon an economic theory which a large part of the country does not entertain." The Constitution exists "for people of fundamentally differing views, and the accident of our finding certain opinions natural and familiar, or novel, and even shocking, ought not to conclude our judgment upon the question of whether statutes embodying them conflict with the Constitution of the United States." Holmes had little personal sympathy with these laws, yet he believed firmly in judicial restraint. The determination of policy had been delegated to the elected political branches, not to appointed judges, and he struck a popular chord in his deference to democratic rule. By his detached tone, he showed up Peckham and the majority for doing just what they claimed not to be doing—writing their personal preferences into law.

There has been an odium about the case and its alleged abuse of judicial power ever since. Liberals still present *Lochner* as the leading example of improper judicial activism, in particular, a reflection of the justices' anti-labor biases. More than three decades went by before the Court finally buried the concept of substantive due process in economic legislation, and the entire period of conservative domination of the Court known as "the *Lochner* era" passed into history.

See Sidney G. Tarrow, "Lochner Versus New York: A Political Analysis, Labor History" 5 (1964): 277; Bernard H. Siegan, "Rehabilitating *Lochner,*" *San Diego Law Review* 22 (1985): 453; Paul Kens, *Judicial Power and Reform Politics: The Anatomy of Lochner v. New York* (Lawrence: University Press of Kansas, 1990); and Howard Gillman, *The Constitution Besieged: The Rise and Demise of Lochner Era Police Powers Jurisprudence* (Durham: Duke University Press, 1993).

United States v. Ju Toy

198 U.S. 253 (1905)
Decided: May 8, 1905
Vote: 6 (Fuller, Harlan I, Brown, E. White, McKenna, Holmes)
3 (Brewer, Peckham, Day)
Opinion of the Court: Holmes
Dissenting opinion: Brewer (Peckham)
Dissenting without opinion: Day

Returning from China to San Francisco, Ju Toy alleged that he was a native-born citizen of the United States. Port officials in that city refused to let him land, detained him, and the Commerce Department decided to deport him to China without a trial. Ju Toy filed a writ of habeas corpus for his release. The district court granted it and ruled that Ju Toy was a native-born citizen of the United States and that the Commerce Department had abused its discretion. The government appealed the decision, arguing that it had not abused its discretion and that it should be able to send Ju Toy back to China.

The Supreme Court held that the petition for habeas corpus was lacking because Ju Toy had only alleged citizenship but had not provided any evidence; moreover, he had not proven any abuse of discretion. The government, therefore, could deport him to China. In a strange twist of logic, the Court ruled that it did not matter whether Ju Toy was a U.S. citizen. He had not been able to prove it. Congress, in its plenary power over immigration, had the right to discriminate against individuals of any nationality it wished to, deport them, and even deny them the right to a jury trial. The burden is on each person to prove his or her citizenship.

This case is one of a long line of cases discriminating against Chinese immigrants and their native-born children and is of a piece with ***United States v. Sing Tuck,*** 194 U.S. 161 (1904).

See Lucy Salyer, *Laws Harsh as Tigers: Chinese Immigrants and the Shaping of Modern Immigration Law* (Chapel Hill: University of North Carolina Press, 1995).

Patterson v. Colorado

205 U.S. 454 (1907)
Decided: April 15, 1907
Vote: 7 (Fuller, E. White, Peckham, McKenna, Holmes, Day, Moody)
2 (Harlan I, Brewer)
Opinion of the Court: Holmes
Dissenting opinion: Harlan I
Dissenting opinion: Brewer

Thomas Patterson was a Democratic U.S. senator from Colorado and a newspaper publisher. He ran a series of editorials, stories, and cartoons in his papers ridiculing the Republican-dominated Colorado Supreme Court. He was especially incensed that the court had invalidated a referendum granting home rule to Denver. The state's attorney general successfully brought contempt proceedings against Patterson on behalf of the court. Under state law, Patterson could not even offer the truth of his charges as a defense, because his statements, involving cases then pending before the supreme court, tended to obstruct the administration of justice.

In his appeal to the U.S. Supreme Court, Patterson claimed that the state supreme court had violated his federal and state constitutional rights by precluding him from demonstrating the truth of his accusations. He based his claim primarily on the Colorado constitution, which guaranteed free speech to all its citizens, and did not try to link his defense to the First Amendment.

Holmes, speaking for a seven-man majority, upheld the conviction, relying primarily on Blackstone's view that truth or falsity had nothing to do with criminal libel; "the provocation, and not the falsity, is the thing to be punished criminally." Holmes broke no new ground; he merely reiterated that states had the power to punish so-called "bad tendencies" in speech. Because this did not violate any federal rules, he dismissed the case.

Harlan wrote an impassioned dissent that contained a vigorous but undeveloped view of free speech under the First Amendment and called for a rejection of the Blackstone view. Brewer's dissent rested solely on jurisdictional grounds—not addressing the speech issues.

See David M. Rabban, *Free Speech in Its Forgotten Years* (New York: Cambridge University Press, 1997).

Howard v. Illinois Central Railroad Company and the Yazoo and Mississippi Valley Railroad Company; Brooks v. Southern Pacific Company

Also known as First Employers' Liability Cases
207 U.S. 463 (1908)
Decided: January 6, 1908
Vote: 5 (Fuller, Brewer, E. White, Peckham, Day)
4 (Harlan I, McKenna, Holmes, Moody)
Opinion of the Court: White
Concurring opinion: Peckham (Fuller, Brewer)
Concurring without opinion: Day
Dissenting opinion: Harlan I (McKenna)
Dissenting opinion: Holmes
Dissenting opinion: Moody

Will Howard was a fireman for Illinois Central Railroad Company, and Morris Brooks was a fireman for Southern Pacific Company. Each worked on trains engaged in interstate commerce, and each was killed while on the job. Their surviving spouses sued the railroad companies under a federal law allowing for damages against common carriers in interstate commerce for the death or injury of an employee. The railroad companies argued that the law was unconstitutional because Congress lacked the authority to pass such legislation under the Commerce Clause.

Supreme Court agreed, 5–4, that the law was unconstitutional. The Court ruled that the statute was overbroad because it referred to all common carriers engaged in interstate commerce. Not all employee deaths or injuries occur while engaged in interstate commerce. Congressional power was limited to interstate commerce and could not reach beyond that to what the Court considered purely local matters.

See James Weinstein, "Big Business and the Origins of Workmen's Compensation," *Labor History* 8 (1967): 156.

Adair v. United States

208 U.S. 161 (1908)
Decided: January 27, 1908
Vote: 6 (Fuller, Harlan I, Brewer, E. White, Peckham, Day)
2 (McKenna, Holmes)
Opinion of the Court: Harlan I
Dissenting opinion: McKenna
Dissenting opinion: Holmes
Did not participate: Moody

William Adair was a railroad agent for Louisville and Nashville Railroad, and O. B. Coppage was a fireman for the railroad. When Coppage joined the Order of Locomotive Firemen, Adair dismissed him for joining a union.

In the Erdman Act of 1898, however, Congress prohibited employers from making so-called "yellow dog" contracts, agreements by job applicants that they did not belong to a union and that while employed they would not join one. Under federal law, therefore, it was illegal to fire Coppage simply because he had joined a union. The railroad challenged the law, saying that it exceeded congressional power under the Commerce Clause.

The Supreme Court held the statute unconstitutional. In ***Lochner v. New York,*** 198 U.S. 45 (1905), the Court had created the "liberty of contract" doctrine, which could be read to mean that the Fourteenth Amendment protected all contracts from interference by state governments. In *Adair* the Court extended this doctrine to the Fifth Amendment's Due Process Clause, ruling that the "liberty" protection of the Fifth Amendment includes the "liberty to contract." Just as the Fourteenth Amendment restricted states, so the Fifth restricted the federal government and prevented it from interfering with the labor contract. In addition, Congress could not rely on its Commerce Clause powers because labor was a local matter and therefore not part of interstate commerce.

Justice Holmes dissented, repeating much of what he had said in his *Lochner* dissent, namely that the freedom to contract is not absolute and that government can intervene to protect workers. Labor, he added, clearly had a substantial connection to commerce and, if Congress believed that helping labor unions would facilitate interstate commerce, then it also had the power to do so, and the courts had no business second-guessing the wisdom of the measure.

See Christopher L. Tomlins, *The State and the Unions: Labor Relations, Law, and the Organized Labor Movement in America, 1880–1960* (New York: Cambridge University Press, 1985).

Loewe v. Lawlor

Also known as the Danbury Hatters' Case
208 U.S. 274 (1908)
Decided: February 3, 1908
Vote: 9 (Fuller, Harlan I, Brewer, E. White, Peckham, McKenna, Holmes, Day, Moody)
0
Opinion of the Court: Fuller

This case grew out of a strike by the United Hatters of North America against D. E. Loewe Company. The American Federation of Labor, which had no direct interest in the dispute, organized a secondary boycott, one in which people who were not parties to the labor dispute refused to purchase Loewe hats. The company then brought a treble-damage suit under the Sherman Antitrust Act against individual members of the United Hatters, including Martin Lawlor, the resident union agent. The union denied that it was a combination as defined by the Sherman Act.

Even though it had ignored actual monopolistic policies among manufacturers, the Supreme Court insisted that every combination in restraint of trade was illegal. Chief Justice Fuller stated that the Sherman Act required the Court to consider the union's action as a whole, regardless of the intrastate character of particular actions. Fuller denied that Congress had intended to exempt unions from coverage and maintained, therefore, that individual union members could be held liable for damages under Section 7 of the act. After this decision, Loewe won a large monetary recovery at trial, and that judgment was unanimously upheld in *Lawlor v. Loewe,* 235 U.S. 522 (1915).

Loewe v. Lawlor was the most threatening of the Court's labor decisions of the late nineteenth and early twentieth centuries, raising the specter of dissolution and damage suits against unions. The unions therefore moved into the political sphere, seeking statutory exemption from Congress. The Clayton Act of 1914 failed to provide explicit exemption, but relief ultimately came within the changed labor-management context in the late 1930s.

See Daniel R. Ernst, "The Labor Exemption, 1908–1914," *Iowa Law Review* 74 (1989): 1151.

Muller v. Oregon

208 U.S. 412 (1908)
Decided: February 24, 1908
Vote: 9 (Fuller, Harlan I, Brewer, E. White, Peckham, McKenna, Holmes, Day, Moody)
0
Opinion of the Court: Brewer

An Oregon law limited women working in factories and laundries to no more than ten hours a day. Curt Muller, convicted of violating the law, appealed. He believed that the Supreme Court's decision in ***Lochner v. New York,*** 198 U.S. 45 (1905), which had struck down a state law limiting hours for bakery workers, would lead the justices to overturn the Oregon statute.

The National Consumers' League arranged for Louis Brandeis of Boston, the "people's attorney," to represent Oregon. Brandeis defended the law by showing how the legislature could have determined that health and safety required a limitation of hours. In the famed "Brandeis brief," he devoted only a few pages to legal precedent and more than one hundred to facts gleaned from both U.S. and foreign sources detailing the impact of long hours on women's physical and mental well-being. The brief became the model of how lawyers could effectively introduce sociological and economic evidence into a case, and ever since the legal arguments on major social issues, such as civil rights, have elicited extensive "Brandeis briefs" in support of the cause.

The Supreme Court upheld the Oregon law, but did not overrule *Lochner.* Justice Brewer's "discovery" of women's unique physical structure and maternal functions struck many as disingenuous, but his opinion left no doubt that when the state could provide a reasonable justification for its policy, the police powers had extensive reach. Following *Muller,* state courts consistently upheld similar legislation whenever challenged.

For years, the *Muller* decision, and especially the Brandeis brief, enjoyed enormous popularity in the academy and among reformers, for whom it became a model of securing change through law. With the rise of the new feminist movement in the 1960s, however, *Muller*'s reputation began to falter. Some critics charged that the decision embedded the notion of female difference in constitutional law and, thereby, legitimized treating women differently from men. For some feminist critics, *Muller* was not a high point of progressive reform and sociological jurisprudence, but an enormous error that in the long run harmed women far more than it helped them and retarded the arrival of a true sexual equality in American law.

One cannot deny that the arguments put forward by Brandeis and his sister-in-law Josephine Goldmark, a consumer advocate, as well as the Court's opinion, viewed women as different from men, and in some respects inferior to them. But to claim that this case embedded sexual discrimination in constitutional law for three generations is to misread both history and the law and to demonstrate that the marriage of politics and scholarship is not always fruitful.

Discrimination based on gender had been firmly grounded in Anglo-American law long before *Muller*. Married women had been forbidden to own or convey property, to sit on juries, or to vote. Liberty of contract, that core ingredient of classical legal thought, belonged solely to adult males. The idea that women, especially married women, needed special protection had long been a staple of common law. As for viewing women as inferior, the law had frequently classified women along with children and mental incompetents as "persons under a disability" and unable to care for themselves legally.

Finally, the feminist argument not only reads the mentality of the 1960s backward to the Progressive era, but also assumes that women opposed protective legislation. Although some of the early feminists may have thought through the whole issue of women's inequality with men, the women's movement of the Progressive era focused on securing the suffrage. Even on this issue, women were not united; just as some women proved to be among the bitterest foes of the Equal Rights Amendment in the 1970s, so too many women opposed universal suffrage prior to World War I. Nor can protective legislation be characterized as a male device because the Oregon law and others similar to it had been championed by two of the premier women's organizations of the time, the National Consumers' League and the Women's Trade Union League. Most women—including most female social activists—wanted the special protection offered by the law.

See Josephine Goldmark, *Impatient Crusader: Florence Kelley's Life Story* (Champaign: University of Illinois Press, 1953); Judith A. Baer, *The Chains of Protection: The Judicial Response to Women's Labor Legislation* (Westport, Conn.: Greenwood Press, 1978); and Nancy Woloch, *Muller v. Oregon: A Brief History with Documents* (Boston: Bedford Books, 1996).

Ex parte Young

209 U.S. 123 (1908)
Decided: March 23, 1908
Vote: 8 (Fuller, Brewer, E. White, Peckham, McKenna, Holmes, Day, Moody)
1 (Harlan I)
Opinion of the Court: Peckham
Dissenting opinion: Harlan I

A 1907 Minnesota law not only reduced railroad rates but also imposed severe penalties on violators. The large fines and criminal sanctions were clearly intended to intimidate the railroads and keep them from challenging the rates in court. Railroad shareholders immediately brought a derivative suit in federal court seeking to enjoin their companies from complying with the statute and to stop state officials from enforcing it. They claimed that the reduced rates were actually confiscatory in nature and thus deprived the railroads of their property in violation of the Fourteenth Amendment's Due Process Clause. In addition, the penalties imposed on the railroads and their officers were so harsh that the companies could not afford to follow the normal route of violating the law to test its constitutionality. The lower court issued the requested injunction, but Edward Young, the Minnesota attorney general, disregarded it and attempted to enforce the statute. Jailed for contempt, he appealed to the Supreme Court for a writ of habeas corpus.

Justice Peckham declared the statute's penalty provisions unconstitutional on their face because they effectively denied the railroads resort to the courts. He also rejected Young's argument that the Eleventh Amendment immunity of states against suits could be used to give any official of the state immunity from the authority of the United States as exercised through its courts. The Court's distinction between suits against states and suits against state officials acting unconstitutionally provided a legal fiction to circumvent the Eleventh Amendment. Justice Harlan, normally a strong nationalist, objected to this effort to nullify the Eleventh Amendment, and warned that it would work "a radical change in our governmental system" by placing the states in an inferior position.

This case was an important step in the Fuller Court's enlargement of the judicial power, and in essence it provided a jurisdictional equivalent to the Court's oversight of economic legislation. The conservative majority, ever distrustful of economic regulation, had reluctantly acceded to the need and legitimacy of state and federal regulatory commissions and the power of the states to regulate rates. In this decision it did not negate the power of the states to regulate, but it did prevent them from closing the door to the courts, where railroads and other industries could delay and even defeat state efforts at regulation.

See Richard C. Cortner, *The Iron Horse and the Constitution* (Westport, Conn.: Greenwood Press, 1993); and William F. Duker, "Mr. Justice Rufus W. Peckham and the Case of *Ex parte Young:* Lochnerizing *Munn v. Illinois,*" *Brigham Young Law Review* (1980): 539.

Reuben Quick Bear v. Leupp

210 U.S. 50 (1908)
Decided: May 18, 1908
Vote: 9 (Fuller, Harlan I, Brewer, E. White, Peckham, McKenna, Holmes, Day, Moody)
0
Opinion of the Court: Fuller

The Indian Appropriation Act (IAA) created an Indian trust fund and a treaty fund under the supervision of the secretary of the interior, who used some of the money to help start schools for Native Americans. Specifically, he directed the money to an Indian mission that intended to establish Catholic schools. The Sioux Indians sued the secretary for misappropriating the funds, and for violating the religious Establishment Clause of the First Amendment.

The Supreme Court ruled that Congress could appropriate money to religious organizations because Congress had the duty to provide schools for Native Americans under the IAA and was simply using a Catholic organization to satisfy that obligation. The Court practically ignored the First Amendment issues, which in this case were far more important than in ***Bradfield v. Roberts,*** 175 U.S. 291 (1899). The Catholic hospital in *Bradfield* had treated every patient without any religious test; in this case, the church schools clearly aimed at proselytizing the Indians. Although unmentioned in the opinion, the Court may also have been aware that the federal government had been subsidizing Catholic and other religious schools among the Indians for most of the nineteenth century. To declare the practice unconstitutional after all these years would have been embarrassing to the government and to the Court.

Municipality of Ponce v. Roman Catholic Apostolic Church

210 U.S. 296 (1908)
Decided: June 1, 1908
Vote: 9 (Fuller, Harlan I, Brewer, E. White, Peckham, McKenna, Holmes, Day, Moody)
0
Opinion of the Court: Fuller

The Roman Catholic Church had been in possession of two churches in the town of Ponce, Puerto Rico, since their construction with municipal funds in the early 1800s, when Puerto Rico was a Spanish possession. After Spain ceded the island to the United States following the Spanish-American War of 1898, Ponce claimed title to the buildings. The municipality argued that the Roman Catholic Church lacked a juridical personality because it had never been incorporated under the laws of Puerto Rico and therefore it could not possess or retain property it had received from the Spanish government.

The Supreme Court rejected this contention. Justice Fuller noted that under Spanish law the Catholic Church had a corporate existence and that the treaty passing possession of the island from Spain to the United States, as well as international law, recognized this legal status.

Ponce had two important consequences. First, it hastened settlement of a number of pending lawsuits challenging the ability of the Catholic Church to hold property it had acquired during Spanish tenure. Among the cases were several involving the U.S. government, which now compensated the church for property taken for military use. Second, relying on *Ponce,* the Catholic Church in Puerto Rico has never incorporated, as have other religious organizations.

See Anibal Colón-Rosado, "Relations between Church and State in Puerto Rico," *Revista del Colegio de Abogados de Puerto Rico* 46 (1985): 51.

Berea College v. Kentucky

211 U.S. 45 (1908)
Decided: November 9, 1908
Vote: 7 (Fuller, Brewer, E. White, Peckham, McKenna, Holmes, Moody)
2 (Harlan I, Day)
Opinion of the Court: Brewer
Concurring without opinion: (Holmes, Moody)
Dissenting opinion: Harlan I
Dissenting without opinion: Day

Berea College, a private college in Kentucky, had been established in 1859 to promote Christian values. Sometime after the Civil War it began admitting black students. In 1904 the state legislature passed a law forbidding any person or corporation to operate a school in which children of different races were taught together. Relying on ***Lochner v. New York,*** 198 U.S. 45 (1905), the trustees of the college argued that the legislation interfered with their constitutionally protected right to pursue a lawful occupation.

The same Court that had decided *Lochner* would not accept this argument. Justice Brewer and his colleagues, who had often found that corporations did indeed have rights when faced with regulatory legislation, now declared that Berea College, "as a corporation created by this state, has no natural right to teach at all. Its right to teach is such as the state sees fit to give to it. The state may withhold it altogether, or qualify it."

Justice Harlan's dissent invoked the notion of substantive due process and denounced the legislation as "an arbitrary invasion of the rights of liberty and property guaranteed by the Fourteenth Amendment against state action."

It seems clear that, like most northerners, the justices had no more interest in protecting southern blacks, and, as a long line of cases going back for decades showed, they were more than willing to allow the southern states great latitude in race relations. One sign of the changing times was that although the decision in ***Plessy v. Ferguson,*** 163 U.S. 537 (1896) had stirred up a general outcry in the northern press, the decision in *Berea College* occasioned little comment and no protest.

See David E. Bernstein, "*Plessy* versus *Lochner*: The *Berea College* Case," *Journal of Supreme Court History* 25 (2000): 93.

Twining v. New Jersey

211 U.S. 78 (1908)
Decided: November 9, 1908
Vote: 8 (Fuller, Brewer, E. White, Peckham, McKenna, Holmes, Day, Moody)
1 (Harlan I)
Opinion of the Court: Moody
Dissenting opinion: Harlan I

Albert Twining and David Cornell, directors of Monmouth Trust and Safe Deposit Company, were indicted and convicted in New Jersey for deliberately misrepresenting the financial condition of their company. At their trial they refused to testify in their own behalf, and the judge instructed the jury that the defendants' refusal to speak up could be taken into account in determining their guilt or innocence. They were found guilty and in their appeal claimed that the judge's charge to the jury violated the Fifth Amendment's privilege against self-incrimination. That protection, they claimed, bound the states as well under the Fourteenth Amendment's Due Process Clause.

The Court rejected the incorporation argument—that is, that the Fourteenth Amendment incorporated the protections of the Bill of Rights and applied them to the states as well as to the federal government—and declined to consider the specific dimensions of Twining's complaint. Justice Moody acknowledged that, for purposes of discussion, the trial court's comment on the defendants' refusal to take the stand in their own defense constituted an "infringement of the privilege against self-incrimination." He also emphasized that the New Jersey courts did not violate their own interpretation of that privilege and, consequently, the "exemption from compulsory self-incrimination in the courts of the States is not secured by any part of the Federal Constitution."

In dissent, Justice Harlan argued that the Court should first have considered whether the trial court's action constituted a violation of the privilege against self-incrimination. If it did, then the Court had to consider the applicability of federal constitutional provisions to the states. Harlan concluded that the trial court had indeed violated the privilege against self-incrimination and that the privilege applied to all citizens as guaranteed by the Fourteenth Amendment.

This case is one of the first to raise the issue of whether the Fourteenth Amendment incorporated the provisions of the first eight amendments and applied them to the states. The Court began to accept this argument in the 1920s, and *Twining* was reversed in ***Malloy v. Hogan,*** 378 U.S. 1 (1964).

See Leonard W. Levy, "The Right Against Self-Incrimination: History and Judicial History," *Political Science Quarterly* 84 (1969): 1.

Santos v. Holy Roman Catholic Apostolic Church

212 U.S. 463 (1909)
Decided: February 23, 1909
Vote: 9 (Fuller, Harlan I, Brewer, E. White, Peckham, McKenna, Holmes, Day, Moody)
0
Opinion of the Court: Holmes

In 1898 the United States acquired the Philippine Islands at the conclusion of the Spanish-American War, and U.S. courts for the next two decades faced the problem of squaring old Spanish law with the newly imposed American law. Many of these cases dealt with church property and what juridical personality the Roman Catholic Church assumed in American courts.

In 1902 an Aglipayan community took possession of a chapel that had been previously owned by the Roman Catholic Church. The chapel had originally been a gift to the church for the exclusive benefit of those who professed the Roman Catholic faith. The church sought return of possession and won in the lower courts; the Aglipayans then appealed to the Supreme Court.

The Court had heard a similar case from Puerto Rico the previous year, ***Municipality of Ponce v. Roman Catholic Apostolic Church,*** 210 U.S. 296 (1908), and in that case had affirmed that the church held a juridical personality and therefore could continue to hold property it had been given under Spanish law. Justice Holmes for the Court ruled that the Aglipayan community was not a juridical entity and therefore not entitled to possession of property. The Court affirmed the lower court ruling that the Roman Catholic Church was entitled to the property.

This case should be seen as part of the *Insular Cases* in that all dealt with a similar theme, namely, the extent to which American law would replace Spanish law in the territories acquired from Spain in 1898. Unlike the debate in the *Insular Cases,* however, over whether the rights protected in the Constitution followed the flag, the Court for the most part held that property lawfully acquired during the Spanish regime would remain the legal property of the holder under American law as well. See page 131.

See Paul G. Kauper and Stephen C. Ellis, "Religious Corporations and the Law," *Michigan Law Review* 71 (1973): 1499.

Insular Cases, 1901–1920

In the early twentieth century the Supreme Court heard a number of cases, commonly called the Insular Cases, that dealt with the reach of constitutional protection to the native inhabitants of America's newly acquired overseas territories—those gained in the settlement following the Spanish-American War of 1898.

Unlike earlier acquisitions of territory, these new possessions did not strike contemporaries as likely to become future states. The march across the continent following the Revolution had never been imperialistic, even during the fever pitch of Manifest Destiny; Americans had sought new territory to permit growth, not to acquire subordinate colonies. But Puerto Rico, Guam, the Philippines, and Hawaii were already populated—and not by white races with developed cultures. If the United States retained them, it appeared that they would be nothing more than colonies.

No one questioned the right of the nation to acquire new lands under its sovereign powers; that issue had been resolved years earlier in ***American Insurance Co. v. Canter,*** 26 U.S. 511 (1828). But if the new lands were to be colonies, then did the Constitution follow the flag, providing the residents of the new territories with the full range of constitutionally guaranteed rights? The imperialists claimed that the Constitution did not follow the flag and that Congress could govern colonies as it saw fit, its inhabitants enjoying only those rights that Congress specifically extended to them. The anti-imperialists argued that all persons under American jurisdiction had to be treated alike, which was the traditional policy of the Union toward residents of the continental territories.

The political branch resolved the question of whether the United States would keep these new possessions when the Senate ratified the Treaty of Paris with Spain in April 1899 and secured American possession of the former Spanish holdings. Defining the legal status of the new territories proved to be the chief business of the Supreme Court during the 1900–1901 term.

In the first of the Insular Cases, ***Neely v. Henkel,*** 180 U.S. 109 (1901), the justices had little trouble agreeing that Cuba, although occupied by American forces, remained a foreign country, because at the outset of the Spanish-American War Congress had passed a resolution that Cuba could not be annexed to the United States. But the treaty also conveyed Puerto Rico and the Philippines as direct possessions, and their status had to be determined. In cases triggered by the tariff laws, a badly divided Court gradually worked out a doctrine to govern the future status of the new colonies.

In ***DeLima v. Bidwell,*** 182 U.S. 1 (1901), the Court had to decide whether, after Puerto Rico was ceded to the United States but before any specific congressional action, customs duties could be collected on goods imported from Puerto Rico. The collector of the Port of New York had imposed duties on sugar as if that product still came from a foreign country, and the purchaser then sued to recover the payments, claiming that the Constitution prohibited taxes on goods exported from one part of the country to another. The Court held that as a consequence of the Treaty of Paris, Puerto Rico did not constitute a foreign country and that the tariffs had therefore been unlawfully collected. Justice McKenna's dissent claimed that Puerto Rico "occupied a relation to the United States between that of being a foreign country absolutely and of being domestic territory absolutely, and because of that relation its products were subject to the duties imposed by the Dingley Act." The majority claimed that this vague halfway status could not exist. Justice Brown, who delivered the majority opinion, argued that the island had to be one thing or the other and to hold otherwise would place Puerto Rico in a disastrous position of "practical isolation."

The most important of the Insular Cases, ***Downes v. Bidwell,*** 182 U.S. 244 (1901), tested the constitutionality of the Foraker Act of 1900, which established a civil government for Puerto Rico and a schedule of import duties from the island. Challengers claimed that the tariff provisions violated the constitutional requirement that duties be "uniform throughout the United States." A majority sustained the statute, but they could not agree on a common rationale. Justice Brown, speaking for the majority, reflected the imperialistic spirit of the day, and spoke of "alien races" and "Anglo-Saxon principles." While acknowledging that constitutional protections of rights applied to some extent in the territories, he stopped just short of granting Congress unfettered power over the nation's new possessions.

Justice White's concurring opinion in *Downes* proved to be the key in the Court's development of a viable constitutional doctrine, which he termed "incorporation." White emphasized the power of Congress to provide for new territories and its discretion in defining their status. As for the application of the Constitution to these new lands, because mere acquisition did not bring them into the Union, neither did it entitle them to any of the rights and privileges guaranteed by the Constitution. As long as they remained in a subordinate condition, these territories would enjoy only those rights specifically granted by Congress; the full benefits of the Constitution would apply when and if Congress acted to incorporate the territory into the Union. In this case, the Constitution did not follow the flag.

White's theory did not immediately gain adherence from a majority of his brethren. Harlan especially objected to the racist implications of White's argument, and he noted that the natives of these new lands enjoyed no rights but depended on the whims of the legislature, without any judicial review to protect them. In his *Downes* dissent, Harlan claimed that Congress could only act under the Constitution, and "the idea that this country may acquire territories anywhere upon the earth, by conquest or treaty, and hold them as mere colonies or provinces—the people inhabiting them to enjoy only such rights as Congress chooses to accord to them—is wholly inconsistent with the spirit and genius as well as with the words of the Constitution."

Over the next few years, White's incorporation theory moved from dicta in a concurrence to full acceptance as doctrine in ***Dorr v. United States,*** 195 U.S. 138 (1904). Fred Dorr was convicted for libel under an act passed, not by Congress, but by the Philippine Commission, and tried without a jury in Manila. Justice Day, who joined the Court in 1903, delivered the majority opinion. "Until Congress shall see fit to incorporate territory," he wrote, that territory "is to be governed under the power existing in Congress." In a patronizing dictum that fully reflected the racist views of the time, he denied that the Constitution followed the flag, since the natives of the new territories might be totally unfit to enjoy the advanced rights of Western civilization.

Finally, in ***Dowdell v. United States,*** 221 U.S. 325 (1911), the entire Court except Harlan, who consistently opposed the theory, joined in Day's opinion that because the Philippines had never been incorporated into the Union, criminal trials there did not require a twelve-person jury. Justice White's longevity on the bench assured him of success. By 1920 none of the original dissenters remained when he ruled in ***Board of Public Utility Commissioners v. Ynchausti & Co.,*** 251 U.S. 401 (1920), that, again, because the Philippines had never been incorporated, constitutional limitations did not restrain Congress in its governance of the islands.

The Court, however, never imposed an absolute application of the doctrine that the Constitution did not follow the flag, which literally would have denied any rights, except those granted by Congress, to natives of U.S. possessions. The early commercial cases had not involved personal rights, but the later criminal cases provided the basic requirements for a fair trial, although the procedures followed departed in some respects from U.S. standards. But if local law imposed unacceptable results, the Court could find a way around it. In ***Weems v. United States,*** 217 U.S. 349 (1910), for example, a Coast Guard officer had been convicted under an old Spanish law still in effect in the Philippines. He had falsified public documents, and for this he had been sentenced to fifteen years in prison at hard labor in chains and the perpetual loss of his civil liberties. Justice McKenna wrote that "such penalties for such offenses amaze those who have formed their concepts of [justice] . . . from the practice of the American commonwealths, and believe it is a precept of justice that punishment for crime should be graduated and proportioned to the offense." Even though the question had not been raised in the lower court, McKenna cited the Eighth Amendment's ban on cruel and unusual punishment, of which a variant could be found in the Philippine law, and set aside both the conviction and sentence—the first time the Eighth Amendment had been invoked by the Supreme Court on behalf of a convicted defendant.

See James Edward Kerr, *The Insular Cases: The Role of the Judiciary in American Expansionism* (Port Washington, N.Y.: Kennikat Press, 1982); and Robert B. Highsaw, *Edward Douglass White: Defender of the Conservative Faith* (Baton Rouge: Louisiana State University, 1981).

1910–1919

Weems v. United States

217 U.S. 349 (1910)
Decided: May 2, 1910
Vote: 5 (Fuller, Harlan I, McKenna, Day, Moody)
2 (E. White, Holmes)
Opinion of the Court: McKenna
Dissenting opinion: E. White (Holmes)
Did not participate: Lurton
See *Insular Cases,* page 131.

Bailey v. Alabama

219 U.S. 219 (1911)
Decided: January 3, 1911
Vote: 7 (E. White, Harlan I, McKenna, Day, Hughes, Moody, Van Devanter)
2 (Holmes, Lurton)
Opinion of the Court: Hughes
Dissenting opinion: Holmes (Lurton)

Passage of forced labor statutes in all southern states in the post-Reconstruction period permitted arrests for vagrancy, breach of labor contract, and other crimes. Once convicted, the defendant could be bound to a term of labor on a chain gang to work off fines and court costs. Although some whites, especially new immigrants, became ensnared in the peonage system, for the most part it was used as a means to control blacks. Reformers, including white southerners, attacked peonage as a violation of the Thirteenth Amendment's ban on involuntary servitude.

Bailey v. Alabama involved a state statute that made breach of a labor contract by an employee evidence of intent to injure or defraud the employer. In 1908 civil rights leader Booker T. Washington wrote that these so-called contract violations were "simply means that any white man, who cares to charge that a Colored man has promised to work for him and has not done so, or who has gotten money from him and not paid it back, can have the Colored man sent to the chain gang." Washington found a test case, one Alonzo Bailey, who had left his job without repaying a wage advance.

Bailey was convicted in state court, ordered to pay his employer $15, and assessed a fine of $30 plus court costs. Because he had no money, the court sentenced him to four and a half months at hard labor. He appealed the conviction on the grounds that the forced labor contract was a violation of the Thirteenth Amendment ban against involuntary servitude as well as the Fourteenth Amendment's guarantee of due process of law.

Justice Hughes, writing for the majority, attacked the statute as a restriction of personal rights. He noted that the Alabama Supreme Court had previously struck down legislation abridging employees' contractual rights as a violation of the Fourteenth Amendment. The state was now trying to accomplish a similarly impermissible objective by criminal sanctions and in doing so violated the Thirteenth Amendment. Hughes relied on relatively narrow grounds, and the Court chose not to invalidate all forced labor statutes, just those dealing with peonage imposed by the state.

In *United States v. Reynolds,* 235 U.S. 133 (1914), the Court struck down another Alabama forced labor statute, which assigned a person's labor to private parties. The Court rejected the entire peonage scheme in *Pollock v. Williams,* 322 U.S. 4 (1944).

See William Cohen, "Negro Involuntary Servitude in the South, 1865–1940: A Preliminary Inventory," *Journal of Southern History* 42 (1976): 31; and Pete Daniel, *The Shadow of Slavery: Peonage in the South, 1901–1969* (Urbana: University of Illinois Press, 1972).

Muskrat v. United States

219 U.S. 346 (1911)
Decided: January 23, 1911
Vote: 7 (E. White, Harlan I, McKenna, Holmes, Day, Lurton, Hughes)
0
Opinion of the Court: Day
Did not participate: Van Devanter, J. Lamar

To facilitate the resolution of outstanding issues between the Cherokee Nation and the United States, Congress in 1907 enacted legislation to make it easier for Cherokee to bring suit in federal courts. It also directed the attorney general to represent the United States in the litigation and provided that the lawyers for the Cherokee should be paid by the U.S. Treasury. As a result of this law, David Muskrat, a Cherokee, brought suit against the United States in the Court of Claims, with an appeal to the Supreme Court. Muskrat challenged the constitutionality of previous acts of Congress regulating the lands possessed by the Cherokee Nation.

The Court ruled that under Article III of the Constitution the judicial power of the U.S. courts, including that of the Supreme Court, could be exercised only in the decision of actual cases and controversies brought to the courts for resolution. Justice Day noted that the 1907 act of Congress had created a friendly suit, lacking any adverse clash of legal interests between two parties, which a real case or controversy required. Muskrat's case was not within the Court's legitimate jurisdiction under Article III and therefore was dismissed.

Muskrat remains an often-cited precedent for the limitations imposed by the cases and controversies requirement upon the exercise of federal judicial power.

See David E. Wilkins, *American Indian Sovereignty and the U.S. Supreme Court: The Masking of Justice* (Austin: University of Texas Press, 1997).

Hipolite Egg Company v. United States

220 U.S. 45 (1911)
Decided: March 13, 1911
Vote: 9 (E. White, Harlan I, McKenna, Holmes, Day, Lurton, Hughes, Van Devanter, J. Lamar)
0
Opinion of the Court: McKenna

In 1906 Congress passed the Pure Food and Drug Act, the first time the federal government had intervened in the market to assure the quality of particular items. Hipolite Egg Company of St. Louis prepared fifty cans of preserved whole eggs, kept them in storage for five months, and then shipped them to Thomas & Clark in Peoria, Illinois. The eggs were intended for use in baking, not for resale to the public. Nevertheless, when an inspection revealed that one of the cans contained the preservative boric acid, the government seized all fifty cans on the grounds that they were adulterated.

The government relied on Section 10 of the law to justify its action, asserting that it could seize any adulterated goods shipped in interstate commerce providing it followed the procedures laid out in the act. Hipolite did not challenge the procedures or the fact that the eggs contained boric acid. Rather, it claimed the law did not cover goods used as raw materials rather than for resale. Hipolite also pointed out that the cans were no longer in interstate commerce, having been delivered to Peoria at the time of inspection.

The Court dismissed Hipolite's arguments. For the Court, Justice McKenna wrote in broad terms of the power of the government to preserve the purity of food, and he emphasized the company's admission that the eggs had in fact been adulterated. Hipolite had a stronger argument in its contention that, once the eggs had been delivered and came to rest, they were no longer in interstate commerce and therefore beyond the reach of the Food and Drug Administration. To get around this problem, McKenna declared that the government was dealing with "illicit articles," and there "is here no conflict of national and state jurisdiction over property legally articles of trade. The question here is whether articles which are outlaws of commerce may be seized wherever found."

The decision not only gave legitimacy to the newly created Food and Drug Administration but also greatly expanded the police power of the federal government, a power that until then had lain dormant and untested.

See Peter Temin, *Taking Your Medicine: Drug Regulation in the United States* (Cambridge: Harvard University Press, 1980).

Dr. Miles Medical Company v. John D. Parks & Sons Company

220 U.S. 373 (1911)
Decided: April 3, 1911
Vote: 7 (E. White, Harlan I, McKenna, Day, Hughes, Van Devanter, J. Lamar)
1 (Holmes)
Opinion of the Court: Hughes
Dissenting opinion: Holmes
Did not participate: Lurton

Dr. Miles Medical Company manufactured proprietary medicines prepared in accordance with secret formulas. It attempted to fix the retail prices at which its products could be sold through two forms of restrictive pricing agreements, wholesale consignment contracts and retail agency contracts. The company claimed that the restrictions were valid because they related to proprietary medicines manufactured under a secret process and, apart from that, a manufacturer was entitled to control the prices on all sales of his products.

The Court rejected both arguments. With respect to the manufacturer owning a secret, Justice Hughes stated that the manufacturer had no statutory grant, especially as in this case no patents had been granted to the remedies in question. Because the company had not seen fit to secure the secret formula through a patent, the Court found that it stood on a footing no different from any other manufacturer.

More important, the Court denied that a manufacturer was entitled to control retail prices. Because the manufacturer is not legally bound to make or sell a product, it cannot impose restrictions upon retailers or purchasers. The rule that price maintenance is illegal per se survives to this day, although it has been modified in various forms both by acts of Congress and decisions of the Court.

Standard Oil Co. v. United States

221 U.S. 1 (1911)
Decided: May 15, 1911
Vote: 8 (E. White, McKenna, Holmes, Day, Moody, Lurton, Hughes, Van Devanter)
1 (Harlan I)
Opinion of the Court: E. White
Concurring in part, dissenting in part opinion: Harlan I

The Sherman Antitrust Act created a number of problems for the Court, not the least of which was discerning congressional intent. In ***United States v. E. C. Knight Co.,*** 156 U.S. 1 (1895), the Court took a restrictive view of the definition of commerce that in effect excluded all of the large manufacturing corporations from the reach of the act. Eight years later, in ***Northern Securities Co. v. United States,*** 193 U.S. 197 (1903), the Court took a literalist view of the act's language regarding "any combination, conspiracy or contract" in restraint of trade.

With Justice Holmes's dissent in *Northern Securities,* the Court had a more reasoned approach to interpreting the Sherman Act. The so-called "rule of reason" was unanimously embraced in *Standard Oil.* The justices needed some decisional rule that would avoid the limitations of the *Knight* decision and the absolutist approach in *Northern Securities.* Certainly the interpretation meshed well with President Theodore Roosevelt's distinction between good trusts and bad trusts, and it satisfied large segments of both the business community and reform groups.

Chief Justice White ruled that Standard Oil had violated the Sherman Act and should be dissolved. White used most of his opinion to explain the Court's intention behind the rule of reason. The Sherman Act would now be interpreted to mean that only unreasonable restraint of trade would be outlawed. The words used by Congress in the statute were far from clear, thus requiring the courts to perform one of their traditional roles—interpreting the law's meaning. Although the Court had no intention of rewriting the statute, the rule of reason would allow the judiciary to carry out legislative intent without falling into the trap of literalism that Holmes had warned against in his *Northern Securities* dissent.

See William Letwin, *Law and Economic Policy in America: The Evolution of the Sherman Antitrust Act* (New York: Random House, 1965); and James May, "Antitrust in the Formative Era: Political and Economic Theory in Constitutional and Antitrust Analysis, 1880–1918," *Ohio State Law Journal* 50 (1989): 257.

Dowdell v. United States

221 U.S. 325 (1911)
Decided: May 15, 1911
Vote: 8 (E. White, McKenna, Holmes, Day, Moody, Lurton, Hughes, Van Devanter)
1 (Harlan I)
Opinion of the Court: Day
Dissenting without opinion: Harlan I
See *Insular Cases,* page 131.

Gompers v. Buck's Stove & Range Company

221 U.S. 418 (1911)
Decided: May 15, 1911
Vote: 9 (E. White, Harlan I, McKenna, Holmes, Day, Lurton, Hughes, Van Devanter, J. Lamar)
0
Opinion of the Court: J. Lamar

When employees began a strike at Buck's Stove Company, the American Federation of Labor organized a boycott of the company's products. The stove manufacturer secured an injunction against the labor federation, from which the union planned an appeal. But before it could do so, the company also sought a criminal contempt citation against Samuel Gompers and two other union leaders, claiming they had violated the injunction by publishing the company name in the *American Federationist* on its "Unfair" and "We don't patronize" lists. Gompers appealed the citation, claiming what had been printed in the paper was protected speech under the First Amendment.

The Court ignored the First Amendment argument and reversed the criminal contempt citation on a technicality. Justice Lamar made it clear that the Court sided with employers in their battles against labor and cited approvingly one case after another to demonstrate that the courts frowned on any action, including speech, that injured property rights.

The case is an example of how, despite their willingness to allow protective legislation, the courts drew the line when it came to labor unions. The Supreme Court's anti-union bias continued into the 1930s.

See Gary Minda, "The Law and Metaphor of Boycott," *Buffalo Law Review* 41 (1993): 807.

Coyle v. Smith

221 U.S. 559 (1911)
Decided: May 29, 1911
Vote: 7 (E. White, Harlan I, Day, Lurton, Hughes, Van Devanter, J. Lamar)
2 (McKenna, Holmes)
Opinion of the Court: Lurton
Dissenting without opinion: McKenna, Holmes

In the enabling legislation providing for the admission of Oklahoma into the Union, Congress stipulated that Guthrie would be the temporary capital until 1913. Oklahoma accepted the provision and became a state in 1907. Three years later, the Oklahoma legislature declared Oklahoma City the state capital. Residents of Guthrie challenged the action, but the Oklahoma courts upheld the state legislature.

The Court described the question before it as whether Congress, in its acknowledged discretion to admit new states, could impose conditions that would bind the state after its admission. Drawing upon a tradition that stretched back to the Northwest Ordinance of 1787, the majority found the restrictions that Congress placed on Oklahoma invalid and upheld the state's right to locate its capital where it chose. Justice Lurton noted that although congressional discretion to admit a state was not subject to judicial review, once the national legislature had acted, the new states were entitled to all the government powers that any other state enjoyed.

The majority justices could find no constitutional language imposing such a check on congressional power, but they did not hesitate to read the unwritten tradition of state equality into the Constitution itself.

Mondou v. New York, New Hampshire, and Hartford Railroad Co.

Also known as the Second Employers' Liability Cases
223 U.S. 1 (1912)
Decided: January 15, 1912
Vote: 8 (E. White, McKenna, Holmes, Day, Lurton, Hughes, Van Devanter, J. Lamar)
0
Opinion of the Court: Van Devanter

In ***Howard v. Illinois Central Railroad Co.,*** 207 U.S. 463 (1908) and a related case, also known as the First Employers' Liability Cases, the Supreme Court ruled that the federal Employer's Liability Act of 1906 was unconstitutional. The statute had allowed employees of common carriers that engaged in interstate commerce to sue their employers for deaths or injuries caused by their employers' negligence. The Court ruled that the act was overbroad because it included injuries occurring at any time, whether in interstate commerce or in intrastate commerce.

Congress then passed the Employer's Liability Act of 1908, which differed from the 1906 version in that it imputed liability to employers *only* if the injuries or deaths occurred while the railroad was actually engaged in interstate commerce. When railroad employees in Connecticut, Minnesota, and Massachusetts sued their employers under the new act, the railroad companies argued that the new law was also unconstitutional. They argued that Congress had no power to regulate the employer-employee relationship of businesses, even those carrying on interstate commerce.

The Supreme Court held the act constitutional and ruled that under the Commerce Clause Congress may regulate commercial relationships while they are engaged in interstate commerce. Congress therefore may also regulate an employment relationship while it is engaging in interstate commerce.

See James Weinstein, "Big Business and the Origins of Workmen's Compensation," *Labor History* 8 (1967): 146.

Hoke v. United States

227 U.S. 308 (1913)
Decided: February 24, 1913
Vote: 9 (E. White, McKenna, Holmes, Day, Lurton, Hughes, Van Devanter, J. Lamar, Pitney)
0
Opinion of the Court: McKenna

The Mann Act of 1910, commonly known as the White Slave Act, outlawed the transportation of women across state lines "for the purpose of prostitution or debauchery, or for any other immoral purpose." Effie Hoke persuaded Annette Hays, a prostitute, to travel with him from New Orleans to Texas. Arrested and convicted, Hoke challenged the constitutionality of the act. He argued that Congress did not have the power to prohibit prostitution because it was an issue for the states to handle. Congress, he asserted, had no power to prohibit prostitution in interstate commerce.

The Supreme Court held the Mann Act constitutional, ruling that Congress's power to regulate interstate commerce under the Commerce Clause included the transportation of persons and property. Congress may therefore prohibit prostitution if it occurs in interstate commerce. But in reasoning similar to that of ***Mondou v. New York, New Hampshire, and Hartford Railroad Co.,*** 223 U.S. 1 (1912) (the Second Employers' Liability Cases), the regulated action must be done while actually in interstate commerce. Because Hoke was traveling from Louisiana to Texas, he was guilty under the law.

See David J. Langum, *Crossing Over the Line: Legislating Morality and the Mann Act* (Chicago: University of Chicago Press, 1994).

Sturges & Burns Mfg. Co. v. Beauchamp

231 U.S. 320 (1913)
Decided: December 1, 1913
Vote: 9 (E. White, McKenna, Holmes, Day, Lurton, Hughes, Van Devanter, J. Lamar, Pitney)
0
Opinion of the Court: Hughes

Sturges & Burns manufactured tinware and other metal products. Arthur Beauchamp, an employee who was under sixteen years of age, operated a punch press used in stamping sheet metal. He was injured on the job and sued his employer under an Illinois child labor law that prohibited children under sixteen from working under hazardous conditions. The employer argued that the child labor law was an unconstitutional infringement on the liberty of contract.

The Supreme Court held the Illinois child labor law constitutional. The Court ruled that states may reasonably protect their children from working in hazardous conditions. Although the Fourteenth Amendment implicitly creates a substantive due process right of liberty of contract, the right is not absolute. The state's interest in the protection of its children is reasonable and does not violate the Due Process Clause or the Equal Protection Clause.

This challenge to state child labor laws was the only such case to reach the Supreme Court, and in its decision the Court made clear that the state had extensive authority to protect children under its police powers. The Court took a far different view of *federal* child labor laws, however, in ***Hammer v. Dagenhart,*** 247 U.S. 251 (1918), and ***Bailey v. Drexel Furniture Co.,*** 259 U.S. 20 (1922).

See Walter I. Trattner, *Crusade for the Children: A History of the National Child Labor Committee and Child Labor Reform in America* (Chicago: Quadrangle Books, 1970).

Weeks v. United States

232 U.S. 383 (1914)
Decided: February 24, 1914
Vote: 9 (E. White, McKenna, Holmes, Day, Lurton, Hughes, Van Devanter, J. Lamar, Pitney)
0
Opinion of the Court: Day

Freemont Weeks, an employee of an express company at the Union Station in Kansas City, Missouri, was searched and arrested by state officers and a federal marshal without a warrant. He was convicted on charges of using the mails to transport lottery tickets. His pretrial petition for return of his effects and subsequent objection to their introduction at trial laid the grounds for challenges in the Supreme Court based on the Fourth and Fifth Amendments.

The Court narrowed the issue by emphasizing the obligation of federal courts and officers to make real the guarantees of the Fourth Amendment against warrantless search and seizure. Drawing upon ***Boyd v. United States,*** 116 U.S. 616 (1886), Justice Day suggested that the essential violation was the invasion of Weeks's right of personal security, personal liberty, and private property. The original warrantless search by the federal marshal and the trial court's subsequent refusal to return the materials violated Weeks's constitutional rights. Day relied exclusively on Fourth Amendment grounds to order the judgment reversed and ignored Weeks's claim that his Fifth Amendment right against self-incrimination had been violated as well.

The *Weeks* opinion attracted little attention until the enforcement of Prohibition in the 1920s compounded issues of search and seizure. The opinion, however, created the exclusionary rule, by which evidence seized in violation of Fourth Amendment protections could not be used as evidence at a trial, and eventually this rule became the foremost judicial safeguard against warrantless searches.

See Clyde W. Woody and Marian S. Rosen, "Fourth Amendment Viewed and Reviewed," *South Texas Law Journal* 11 (1969): 315.

Shreveport Rate Cases

Also known as *Houston, East & West Texas Railway Co. v. United States; Texas & Pacific Railway Co. v. United States*
234 U.S. 342 (1914)
Decided: June 8, 1914
Vote: 7 (E. White, McKenna, Holmes, Day, Hughes, Van Devanter, J. Lamar)
2 (Lurton, Pitney)
Opinion of the Court: Hughes
Dissenting without opinion: Lurton, Pitney

The Supreme Court originally opposed the new Interstate Commerce Commission (ICC). In the early cases dealing with the ICC, the Court practically crippled the agency, stripping it of most of its investigative and regulatory powers and leaving it little more than a fact-finding body. Then in a series of cases beginning in 1907, the Court did a complete turnabout in its treatment of the ICC. In *Illinois Central Railroad Co. v. Interstate Commerce Commission,* 206 U.S. 441 (1907), the Court acquiesced to the intent of the original 1887 law by declaring that it would not reinvestigate all the facts of a case on appeal. Three years later, in *Interstate Commerce Commission v. Illinois Central Railroad Co.,* 215 U.S. 452 (1910), the Court fully confirmed the basic ideas of administrative regulation. When reviewing regulatory orders, the Court, as announced by Chief Justice White, would examine three issues: first, whether the agency had the necessary constitutional authority; second, whether Congress had delegated the appropriate powers; and, third, whether the action constituted a reasonable exercise of its power. The decision not to evaluate or second-guess policy decisions removed the constant threat of appeals. With these decisions the commission could effectively carry out its mandate of regulation.

The final triumph of the ICC came in the *Shreveport Rate Cases,* in which the Court validated the agency's power to regulate intrastate rates when they directly affected interstate commerce. By posting intrastate rates significantly lower than interstate rates, Texas railroads had imposed rates that discriminated against out-of-state shippers who were located the same distance from Texas markets as shippers within the state. As a result, rates from Shreveport, Louisiana, to points in east Texas, for example, were much higher than rates from Dallas or Houston to the same points, even though the distances were relatively equal. The ICC found the lower intrastate rates injurious to interstate commerce and ordered that the railroads charge the same rates to both intra- and interstate shippers. The railroads appealed. Much to the railroads' surprise, the Supreme Court ruled in favor of the ICC.

The importance of the case is that the Court accepted the legitimacy of regulatory commissions and their decisions. Although the courts continued to meddle in commission rate-making for another decade, the justices were beginning to understand that they lacked the technical expertise to review complicated rate-making decisions. The Constitution clearly gave control over interstate commerce to Congress, and Congress had established policies and delegated the implementation of those policies to an administrative agency. After this case, the number of state and federal regulatory commissions grew slowly but steadily to cover a number of economic areas.

See Ari and Olive Hoogenboom, *A History of the Interstate Commerce Commission: From Panacea to Palliative* (New York: Norton, 1976); and Richard C. Cortner, *The Iron Horse and the Constitution: The Railroads and the Transformation of the Fourteenth Amendment* (Westport, Conn.: Greenwood Press, 1993).

Coppage v. Kansas

236 U.S. 1 (1915)
Decided: January 25, 1915
Vote: 6 (E. White, McKenna, Van Devanter, J. Lamar, Pitney, McReynolds)
3 (Holmes, Day, Hughes)
Opinion of the Court: Pitney
Dissenting opinion: Holmes
Dissenting opinion: Day (Hughes)

A Kansas statute of 1903 prohibited the use of "yellow-dog" contracts. Such a contract demanded that, as a condition of employment, workers sign a statement that they did not belong to and would not join a labor union. T. B. Coppage, the superintendent of a railway company, asked an employee named Hedges to sign the agreement, which he presented to him in writing, at the same time informing Hedges that if he did not sign it he could no longer work for the railroad. Hedges refused to sign and Coppage fired him. Coppage was prosecuted under the state law, and his conviction and fine were upheld by the Kansas Supreme Court.

The Supreme Court relied upon ***Adair v. United States,*** 208 U.S. 161 (1908), in which it had voided a federal law prohibiting yellow-dog contracts. Just as the act of Congress violated the Fifth Amendment's Due Process Clause, so the Kansas act violated the Fourteenth Amendment's Due Process Clause. Justice Pitney, however, used the case to flay all efforts to regulate the labor contract, and he intimated that socialism was the moving force behind such legislation. No coercion of an employee could be allowed, and here Pitney found none; the worker was free to choose whether to work for a particular employer and whether to accept the conditions of employment the employer proposed.

Justice Holmes, who had dissented in *Adair,* argued that there was no free will here because of the overbearing power of the employer, and he urged that *Adair* be overruled. Justice Day wrote that although the federal government had no authority in this area, the state governments did, and he believed that the state police powers could control labor relations.

The case illustrates the Court's continued anti-union animus throughout the Progressive Era.

See Barry Cushman, "Doctrinal Synergies and Liberal Dilemmas: The Case of the Yellow-Dog Contract," *Supreme Court Review* (1992): 235.

Frank v. Mangum

237 U.S. 309 (1915)
Decided: April 19, 1915
Vote: 8 (E. White, McKenna, Day, Hughes, Van Devanter, J. Lamar, Pitney, McReynolds)
1 (Holmes)
Opinion of the Court: Pitney
Dissenting opinion: Holmes

Leo Frank, one of the owners of National Pencil Factory in Atlanta, had been accused, convicted, and sentenced to death for the murder of Mary Fagan, a thirteen-year-old employee. The judge in the criminal trial asked that Frank and his counsel not return to the courtroom for the verdict because the environment around the courtroom was potentially violent. As the jurors were being polled, the cheers of the crowd outside drowned their voices out.

Frank filed numerous motions and appeals in Georgia state courts, all of which failed. Finally, his lawyers sought a writ of habeas corpus in the federal district court, and its denial brought the case to the Supreme Court. Frank argued that mob intimidation had deprived him of due process of law.

Although the Court during this time liberally used the Due Process Clause of the Fourteenth Amendment to supervise state action concerning property, it hesitated to find a similar federal supervisory power over state criminal proceedings. Justice Pitney, speaking for the majority, saw any and all trial impropriety as cleansed by the Georgia appellate process.

Justice Holmes, in a strong dissent, condemned the trial and the intimidation of the jury, declaring that due process of law cannot take place in a hostile environment. As the Court became more attuned to the inequities in many state criminal justice systems, it was more willing to review such decisions. It reversed its holding in *Frank* in ***Moore v. Dempsey,*** 261 U.S. 86 (1923), but this move came too late to save Leo Frank, who was lynched after Georgia's courageous governor commuted his sentence to life imprisonment.

See Leonard Dinnerstein, *The Leo Frank Case* (New York: Columbia University Press, 1968).

Guinn v. United States

238 U.S. 347 (1915)
Decided: June 21, 1915
Vote: 8 (E. White, McKenna, Holmes, Day, Hughes, Van Devanter, J. Lamar, Pitney)
0
Opinion of the Court: E. White
Did not participate: McReynolds

As a means to deter former slaves from voting, southern states in the late nineteenth century imposed a variety of obstacles, including property and literacy requirements. Because these barriers would have disenfranchised many whites as well, political leaders won their support by creating escape clauses. One of the most common was the so-called "grandfather clause," which allowed any man to register to vote if he would have been eligible to do so in 1867, before the ratification of the Fifteenth Amendment, or if he were the legal descendant of an eligible voter. In September 1910 Oklahoma passed a literacy test with a permanent grandfather clause. The Oklahoma Republican Party, which relied heavily on black support, challenged the law in a suit against two election officials. The law aimed primarily at the masked night-riders, but also had provisions protecting the right of the former slaves to vote. The state's Democratic Party provided counsel to defend the law. Only after President William Howard Taft realized he needed the votes of African American delegates to win renomination in 1912 did he instruct the Justice Department to support the suit.

In two earlier cases, the Court had evaded the issue. In ***Williams v. Mississippi,*** 170 U.S. 213 (1898), the Court refused to invalidate Mississippi's blatantly discriminatory voting restrictions because counsel had offered proof only of the intent to discriminate, not proof of actual effect. In *Giles v. Harris,* 189 U.S. 475 (1903), the Court avoided the issue by declaring it a "political question." In *Guinn* and two companion cases, however, Chief Justice White declared the Oklahoma statute a direct violation of the Fifteenth Amendment.

Commentators have suggested that the Court acted as it did because the decision had little practical effect. In the former Confederate states the laws establishing grandfather clauses not only had lapsed, but also many southerners viewed them as an embarrassment. By 1915 southern states had found more subtle but no less effective means of denying blacks the suffrage, and in fact Oklahoma continued to discriminate against blacks despite the decision.

See Ward E. Y. Elliott, *The Rise of Guardian Democracy: The Supreme Court's Role in Voting Rights Disputes, 1848–1969* (Cambridge: Harvard University Press, 1974).

Truax v. Raich

239 U.S. 33 (1915)
Decided: November 1, 1915
Vote: 8 (E. White, McKenna, Holmes, Day, Hughes, Van Devanter, J. Lamar, Pitney)
1 (McReynolds)
Opinion of the Court: Hughes
Dissenting opinion: McReynolds

A 1915 Arizona law stated that if a business employed more than five people, at least 80 percent of the employees had to be native-born U.S. citizens. William Truax Sr. owned a restaurant where Michael Raich, an Austrian, was a cook. Truax was afraid that he might be fined or shut down by the state because of the new law, and he fired Raich. Raich sued Truax, arguing that the law was unconstitutional and that Truax should not have fired him. Raich asserted that even though he was an alien, he should be protected by the Equal Protection Clause of the Fourteenth Amendment.

The Supreme Court ruled the law unconstitutional. Any person in the United States had the right to earn a living, a right protected by the Equal Protection Clause. Any regulation of this right was subject to the Due Process Clause of the Fourteenth Amendment. Therefore, both native-born U.S. citizens and aliens within the country were protected by the Fourteenth Amendment.

Clark Distilling Co. v. Western Maryland Railway Co.

242 U.S. 311 (1917)
Decided: January 8, 1917
Vote: 7 (E. White, McKenna, Day, Pitney, McReynolds, Brandeis, Clark)
2 (Holmes, Van Devanter)
Opinion of the Court: E. White
Concurring without opinion: McReynolds
Dissenting without opinion: Holmes, Van Devanter

Crusaders against alcohol won their first victory in Congress with the passage of the Webb-Kenyon Act in 1913. That measure reinforced state prohibition laws by closing off the channels of interstate commerce to liquor destined for a state where its use or sale had been prohibited. The law did not stop all shipments, however, and, if a state allowed importation for personal use, such shipments remained legal. The law lacked provisions for federal enforcement because the prohibitionists always intended that states should enforce dry laws. The Webb-Kenyon Act embodied the prohibitionist idea of the concurrent exercise of state and national power against liquor. President Taft had vetoed the measure as unconstitutional on the basis of Supreme Court rulings that required common carriers to accept interstate shipments of liquor as not subject to state law until after receipt by the consignee. Soon after Congress overrode the veto, West Virginia, a dry state, obtained injunctions against the

Western Maryland Railway as well as the Adams Express Company to prevent them from carrying liquor into the state. The Clark Distilling Company then sued the carrier to force it to deliver its goods.

The case was first argued in May 1915, ordered for reargument in November, and then reargued November 8 and 9, 1916. Wayne Wheeler, the Anti-Saloon League's general counsel, defended the law before the Court because the Justice Department refused to do so. The Court upheld the law. Chief Justice White ruled that although Congress had unquestioned authority to regulate the interstate shipment of alcohol, the legislature did not have to exercise that power fully or even uniformly and so could use its interstate power to enforce state laws on liquor consumption.

Because many states refused to adopt prohibition, reformers saw the Webb-Kenyon Act not only as a blueprint but also a milestone in the drive toward their ultimate goal, a constitutional amendment to secure the desired national dryness. The world war gave them a great boost. In the spring of 1917, Congress forbade the sale of liquor to servicemen. The Lever Act, under the mandate of preserving scarce food resources, authorized the president to limit or forbid the use of foodstuffs for the production of alcoholic beverages. In December Congress passed a constitutional amendment and sent it on to the states for ratification. President Wilson issued a series of war proclamations from December 1917 through September 1918 that in effect established near total prohibition.

See Richard F. Hamm, *Shaping the Eighteenth Amendment: Temperance Reform, Legal Culture, and the Polity, 1880–1920* (Chapel Hill: University of North Carolina Press, 1995).

Caminetti v. United States

242 U.S. 470 (1917)
Decided: January 15, 1917
Vote: 5 (Holmes, Day, Van Devanter, Pitney, Brandeis)
3 (E. White, McKenna, Clarke)
Opinion of the Court: Day
Dissenting opinion: McKenna (E. White, Clark)
Did not participate: McReynolds

In 1910 Congress passed the Mann Act, also called the White Slave Act, which prohibited transportation of women across state lines for the purpose of prostitution or debauchery. In 1913 F. Drew Caminetti, and Maury I. Diggs took women with whom they were having extramarital affairs from California to Nevada, and L. T. Hays took some girls from Oklahoma to Kansas for a wild joyride of drunkenness and sex. The three men were charged with violating the Mann Act. They argued that because the women had not been paid for sex, it was not prostitution and therefore not covered by the act. They claimed that Congress could not prohibit sex and drunkenness in interstate commerce.

The Supreme Court disagreed, holding that Congress could indeed prohibit these activities in interstate commerce. The Court reasoned that Congress had the power under the Commerce Clause to keep the channels of interstate commerce free from "immoral" usage. The Court also ruled that the Mann Act, although passed to prohibit prostitution in interstate commerce, also covered any "immoral" or "indecent" acts in interstate commerce.

See David J. Langum, *Crossing Over the Line: Legislating Morality and the Mann Act* (Chicago: University of Chicago Press, 1994).

New York Central Railroad Co. v. White

243 U.S. 188 (1917)
Decided: March 6, 1917
Vote: 9 (E. White, McKenna, Holmes, Day, Van Devanter, Pitney, McReynolds, Brandeis, Clarke)
0
Opinion of the Court: Pitney

New York passed a state constitutional amendment providing for workmen's compensation for workers killed or injured on the job while engaged in hazardous activity. Jacob White, an employee for New York Central Railroad Company, was killed on the job, and his family sought workmen's compensation from his employer. The railroad company refused to pay, arguing that the new law was overbroad because it covered any injury on the job, not just injuries caused by an employer's negligence. The question before the Supreme Court was whether a workmen's compensation law, covering only hazardous jobs, yet providing for compensation for all on-the-job injuries or death, violated the Due Process Clause of the Fourteenth Amendment.

The Court ruled that the workmen's compensation amendment was constitutional. States have the power to regulate contract rights among their citizens and have a strong interest and duty to protect the common welfare of their citizens. Mandating compensation for loss of life or limb for employees in hazardous jobs helps to protect the common welfare. The amendment only mandated compensation in such circumstances and did not affect freedom to contract, and, therefore, the Fourteenth Amendment was not violated.

Bunting v. Oregon

243 U.S. 426 (1917)
Decided: April 9, 1917
Vote: 5 (McKenna, Holmes, Day, Pitney, Clarke)
3 (E. White, Van Devanter, McReynolds)
Opinion of the Court: McKenna
Dissenting without opinion: E. White, Van Devanter, McReynolds
Did not participate: Brandeis

A 1913 Oregon law limited the number of hours a factory worker may work in a day. An employee at a mill, factory, or manufacturing business could not work for more than ten hours a day unless there was an emergency or other necessary exceptions. However, if an employee had to work more than ten hours, the law imposed a limit of thirteen hours a day and required the employer to pay an overtime rate of 1.5 times the hourly wage for the extra hours.

F. O. Bunting operated Lakeview Flouring Mills and employed a man named Hammersley, who worked for thirteen hours one day. Bunting refused to pay him overtime, arguing that the law was unconstitutional because it violated the freedom of contract between employer and employee guaranteed under the Fourteenth Amendment.

The Supreme Court held the law constitutional and not in violation of the Fourteenth Amendment. The Court ruled that a state had a strong interest in protecting the welfare and health of its citizens and agreed with Oregon that work in these sorts of jobs for more than ten hours a day could be hazardous. A state had the power to regulate these employment relationships, including the setting of overtime pay. If a state had a strong enough interest in regulating commerce within the state, it may override the liberty of contract protection of the Fourteenth Amendment.

Justice Brandeis recused himself from this case because he had been an attorney for the state of Oregon when President Wilson named him to the Supreme Court in 1916.

Stettler v. O'Hara

243 U.S. 629 (1917)
Decided: April 9, 1917
Vote: 4
4
Opinion of the Court: *Per curium*
Did not participate: Brandeis

Oregon passed a law setting minimum wages for both sexes. It was challenged in state courts, where it was upheld, and came on appeal to the U.S. Supreme Court in late 1914. After two days of oral argument in December the justices were unable to reach agreement. In June 1916 the Court set it down for another hearing, and the case was reargued on January 18 and 19, 1917.

Had the full Court voted, the results would have been a 5–4 affirmation of the law. But Brandeis, who had been counsel for Oregon and had argued the case in 1914, did not participate. The other eight justices split 4–4 (there is no indication of how they voted), and issued a one-sentence per curiam opinion leaving the state court decision in place.

The Court did not take up the issue again until ***Adkins v. Children's Hospital,*** 261 U.S. 525 (1923), in which it held minimum wage laws unconstitutional. Had the Court been able to hand down a definitive decision upholding the constitutionality of minimum wage law—as it would have done had Brandeis voted—it would not have revisited the issue in the 1920s and 1930s, when, with different personnel, it struck down minimum wage laws, specifically noting that no decision had previously been reached on their constitutionality.

Buchanan v. Warley

245 U.S. 60 (1917)
Decided: November 5, 1917
Vote: 9 (E. White, McKenna, Holmes, Day, Van Devanter, Pitney, McReynolds, Brandeis, Clarke)
0
Opinion of the Court: Day

The National Association for the Advancement of Colored People (NAACP) devised a case to test residential segregation ordinances in Louisville, Kentucky. The law, like many throughout the country, prohibited blacks and whites from living in houses where the majority of homes were occupied by persons of the other race. William Warley, a black man, arranged to buy a lot from Charles Buchanan, a white property owner friendly to the NAACP. The contract was drafted to invite litigation. Warley refused to pay for the land, on grounds that because he was black, residential segregation laws prevented him from building a house there, which the sales contract specifically identified as his reason for buying the property. Buchanan sued for payment, but the local court upheld the ordinance and declared it a full defense for Warley. Buchanan then appealed to the Supreme Court. Other southern cities considering similar ordinances awaited the Court's decision. Moorfield Storey, representing Warley and the NAACP, sought to distinguish residential segregation from other Jim Crow laws because it demeaned property rights, one of the basic tenets of free government. Louisville's attorneys responded with the full rhetoric of racism: law and divine writ demanded the separation of the races.

Justice Day's opinion for a unanimous Court masked internal disagreement over how far the Court should go in such essentially local matters. The Fourteenth Amendment protected property, Day noted, but the state could certainly exercise some controls under its police powers to maintain health and safety. But could it regulate property solely on the basis of the skin color of the owner or would-be buyer? After an impassioned review of how the Civil War had been fought to protect civil rights, Day dismissed ***Plessy v. Ferguson,*** 163 U.S. 537 (1896), as controlling: in that case there had been no effort to deprive blacks of the ability to travel, whereas in this case Louisville would neither allow blacks to buy certain property nor permit whites to sell it to them. He then held residential segregation laws unconstitutional—the first time the Supreme Court had so severely restricted the reach of Jim Crow.

See Clement E. Vose, *Caucasians Only: The Supreme Court, the NAACP, and the Restrictive Covenant Cases* (Berkeley: University of California Press, 1959).

Hitchman Coal & Coke Co. v. Mitchell

245 U.S. 229 (1917)
Decided: December 10, 1917
Vote: 6 (E. White, McKenna, Day, Van Devanter, Pitney, McReynolds)
3 (Holmes, Brandeis, Clarke)
Opinion of the Court: Pitney
Dissenting opinion: Brandeis (Clarke)

In 1907 in West Virginia, Hitchman Coal employed between two hundred to three hundred men in a non-union coal mine. The United Mine Workers Association (UMWA) tried to unionize the coal mine and, as a result, many of the miners went out on strike to force the owner to accept union membership among the workers. Hitchman Coal sued the UMWA and its president, John Mitchell, arguing that the union could not interfere with the business in order to unionize the mine.

The Supreme Court agreed with the company and ruled that a strike to force unionization upon an owner is illegal. The Court held that unions may not interfere with the contractual relations between non-union employees and their employers. To do so would be unlawful coercion.

See William E. Forbath, *Law and the Shaping of the American Labor Movement* (Cambridge: Harvard University Press, 1991).

Arver v. United States

Also known as the Selective Draft Law Cases
245 U.S. 366 (1918)
Decided: January 7, 1918
Vote: 9 (E. White, McKenna, Holmes, Day, Van Devanter, Pitney, McReynolds, Brandeis, Clarke)
0
Opinion of the Court: E. White

On May 17, 1917, Congress enacted President Wilson's draft law, which drew an immediate challenge from opponents of World War I. Lower courts expedited the various draft cases; men could not be allowed to die should the law be unconstitutional, nor could the government's mobilization be derailed if it were valid. Six separate suits were consolidated and referred to as the *Selective Draft Law Cases.* All involved convictions for obstructing or resisting conscription.

Harris Taylor, the chief counsel for the defendants, berated Congress for expanding the executive power. Wilson had already become a political dictator, Taylor charged, and his decision to commit American troops abroad, a power nowhere found in the Constitution, had plunged the country into a military dictatorship as well. Taylor claimed that the Militia Clause (Article I, Section 8) limited the military's use "to execute the Laws of the Union, suppress Insurrections and repel Invasions." In other words, Taylor argued that the militia troops could not be used to prosecute foreign conflicts.

The Court handed down its decision in almost summary fashion: it unanimously dismissed all the arguments raised against the law. Chief Justice White noted Congress's explicit powers in Article I to "provide for the common Defence," "to raise and support Armies," "to provide and maintain a Navy," and "to declare War." "As the mind cannot conceive an army without the men to compose it," White asserted, "on the face of the Constitution the objection that it does not give power to provide for such men would seem too frivolous for further notice." The Court also made short shrift of the argument that the Constitution allowed only a volunteer army and did not authorize conscription. White noted that just as the government owed certain obligations to its citizens, so the people had reciprocal duties to the state, including rendering military service, which the government could compel. Beyond that, Congress could deploy the army anywhere it deemed necessary, even overseas.

Most Americans had expected the Court to sustain the draft law. It would have been difficult, declared one journalist, "to conceive how any other view could ever have been seriously argued by anyone familiar with constitutional law or the Anglo-Saxon principles of free institutions." Yet even if the antidraft arguments failed to persuade a single member of the Court, they did raise at least two issues that eventually received attention.

First, the act allowed the president to delegate nearly all the tasks involved in selecting and processing the conscripts to local draft boards. The Court had held laws involving delegation of powers constitutional ever since the question first came before it in *Field v. Clark,* 143 U.S. 649 (1892), but none of the previous statutes had been as vague in prescribing guidance or oversight.

The second issue involved the generous exemption from the draft for ordained ministers, theology students, and members of some sects that opposed war on religious grounds. The Court shrugged off a challenge that this provision violated the First Amendment because it amounted to an establishment of religion. White casually derided the unsoundness of the claim as well as a collateral argument that the limited exemptions violated the Free Exercise Clause. In the future, however, the Court would wrestle with the problem of conscientious objectors in a number of cases.

See John Whiteclay Chambers II, *To Raise an Army: The Draft Comes to Modern America* (New York: Free Press, 1987).

Ruthenberg v. United States

245 U.S. 480 (1918)
Decided: January 14, 1918
Vote: 9 (E. White, McKenna, Holmes, Day, Van Devanter, Pitney, McReynolds, Brandeis, Clarke)
0
Opinion of the Court: E. White

In 1917 Congress passed the Selective Draft Law, which drafted men into the military to fight in World War I. Charles E. Ruthenberg and two other men, all of whom were Socialist Party leaders, persuaded a man named Schue not to register for the draft. All four were arrested; Schue pled guilty, and the other three were tried and convicted under provisions of the draft law prohibiting interference with the raising of an army. The jury that convicted Ruthenberg was, however, not drawn from the entire voting district; rather, the members came from only a particular division of the district, which was politically inclined against Ruthenberg. He argued that under the Sixth Amendment, the jury pool should have been selected from the entire district.

The Supreme Court held that a jury pool does not have to cover the entirety of a jurisdiction. The plain language of the right to a jury in the Sixth Amendment is satisfied even if a jury is made up of a small geographic subdivision of a district.

Hammer v. Dagenhart

247 U.S. 251 (1918)
Decided: June 3, 1918
Vote: 5 (E. White, Day, Van Devanter, Pitney, McReynolds)
4 (McKenna, Holmes, Brandeis, Clarke)
Opinion of the Court: Day
Dissenting opinion: Holmes (McKenna, Brandeis, Clarke)

The Child Labor Act of 1916 was the response to reformers calling for a federal statute to ensure minimal child labor standards nationwide. Congress relied on its interstate commerce power, which the Supreme Court had given fairly broad meaning in efforts to police lottery tickets, impure food and drugs, and even sexual immorality. The Child Labor Act prohibited the transportation and sale in interstate commerce of goods from factories where children under sixteen worked more than eight hours a day or six days a week.

So widespread was support for banning child labor that it came as a shock to the country when the Court struck down the act. Justice Day, speaking for the majority, based his decision on the old distinction between commerce and manufacturing. He conceded that Congress, by its control over commerce, could reach manufacturing on those occasions when commerce furthered harmful results. For example, Congress could use the commerce power to prevent the manufacturing of impure food and drugs, but here the products themselves were not intrinsically harmful. Congress had intended to regulate child labor, which Day categorized as totally local in nature and therefore beyond the reach of the Commerce Clause. As to the government's argument that Congress wanted to close interstate commerce to prevent unfair competition from states having less protective legislation, Day denied that the Constitution gave the federal government the power to coerce the states in the exercise of their police powers over local trade and manufacture. Such power had always been reserved to the states by the Tenth Amendment, which the conservative majority now erected as a substantive barrier to federal control over commerce.

Justice Holmes, in dissent, agreed that Congress could not directly regulate factories, but he argued that because the Constitution granted Congress the power over interstate commerce, its use of that power could not be fettered by any indirect effects it had on production. Precedent, he claimed, clearly supported a broad reading of the Commerce Clause. As for Day's contention that the goods produced by child labor were not intrinsically harmful, Holmes noted that all civilized countries agreed that "premature and excessive child labor" constituted an evil. The majority's reasoning struck him as saying that prohibition "is permissible as against strong drink but not as against the product of ruined lives." Holmes also denied Day's contention that only the states could exercise police power over manufacturing, asserting that "the national welfare as understood by Congress may require a different attitude within its sphere from that of some self-seeking State. It seems to me entirely constitutional for Congress to enforce its understanding by all the means at its command."

Reaction to the decision was so overwhelmingly unfavorable that Congress responded with a second Child Labor Act less than nine months later. This time the legislature relied on the taxing power and imposed heavy duties on goods introduced into interstate commerce by firms employing children. Congress felt itself on sure constitutional footing because the Court had consistently held that the broad reach of the taxing power precluded the judiciary from looking behind the tax to evaluate the motive. When the Court decided ***Bailey v. Drexel Furniture Co.,*** 259 U.S. 20 (1922), Congress learned that it had been mistaken.

See Walter I. Trattner, *Crusade for the Children: A History of the National Child Labor Committee and Child Labor Reform in America* (Chicago: Quadrangle Books, 1970); and Stephen B. Wood, *Constitutional Politics in the Progressive Era: Child Labor and the Law* (Chicago: University of Chicago Press, 1958).

Schenck v. United States

249 U.S. 47 (1919)
Decided: March 3, 1919
Vote: 9 (E. White, McKenna, Holmes, Day, Van Devanter, Pitney, McReynolds, Brandeis, Clarke)
0
Opinion of the Court: Holmes

Ironically, the war to make the world safe for democracy triggered the worst invasion of civil liberties at home in the nation's history up to that point. The government obviously had to protect itself from subversion, but many of the laws it passed after America's entry into the world war were aimed as much at suppressing radical criticism of administration policy as at ferreting out spies. In the Selective Service Act of 1917 Congress authorized the jailing of people who obstructed the draft. The Espionage Act of 1917, aimed primarily against treason, also punished anyone making or conveying false reports for the benefit of the enemy, seeking to cause disobedience in the armed services, or obstructing recruitment or enlistment in the armed forces. The 1918 Sedition Act identified a variety of "undesirable" activities and forbade "uttering, printing, writing, or publishing any disloyal, profane, scurrilous, or abusive language." The federal laws and similar state statutes caught radicals, pacifists, and other dissenters in an extensive web. Indictments ran into the thousands. The U.S. attorney general reported 877 convictions of the 1,956 cases commenced in 1919 and 1920.

Although challenges to the laws arose early, the government had no desire to push for a quick decision on their constitutionality. As a result, some half dozen cases did not reach the Supreme Court until the spring of 1919, after the end of hostilities. These cases marked the beginning of a civil liberties tradition in American constitutional law.

In the first case, Charles Schenck, the general secretary of the Philadelphia Socialist Party, had been indicted for urging resistance to the draft. He had sent out circulars condemning conscription as despotic and unconstitutional and calling on draftees to assert their rights and refuse induction. Under the terms of the Espionage Act, Schenck had urged unlawful behavior. The Court would decide whether the Constitution's guarantee of free speech protected him. Justice Holmes, writing for the Court, attempted to develop a standard based on the common law rule of proximate causation, and he took a fairly traditional view of speech as a limited right. One could not, he pointed out, "falsely shout fire in a theater." In a famous passage, Holmes attempted to define the limits of speech:

> The question in every case is whether the words used are used in such circumstances and are of such a nature to create a clear and present danger that they will bring about the substantive evils that Congress has a right to prevent. It is a question of proximity and degree. When a nation is at war, many things that might be said in time of peace are such a hindrance to its effort that their utterance will not be endured so long as men fight and no Court could regard them as protected by any constitutional right.

The "clear and present danger" test became the starting point for all subsequent free speech cases, and within a week the Court sustained two other convictions under this rule. In ***Frohwerk v. United States,*** 249 U.S. 204 (1919), a German-language newspaper had run articles attacking the draft and challenging the constitutionality of the war, and in ***Debs v. United States,*** 249 U.S. 211 (1919), Holmes accepted a jury finding that in a militant antiwar speech, Eugene V. Debs, the head of the American Socialist Party, had intended to interfere with mobilization.

The three decisions, as well as the clear and present danger test, upset defenders of free speech, especially because they came from a justice they believed to be an ardent libertarian. Legal scholars such as Zechariah Chafee Jr., Ernst Freund, and others attacked Holmes for his insensitivity to the larger implications of free speech. "Tolerance of adverse opinion is not a matter of generosity," Freund declared, "but of political prudence." In an influential article, "Free Speech in the United States," which was later expanded into a book, Chafee insisted that the Framers of the First Amendment had more in mind than simple censorship. Rather, the Framers intended to do away with the common law of sedition and make it impossible to prosecute criticism of the government in the absence of any incitement to law-breaking. In none of these three cases could one argue that the defendants had been attempting to incite active law-breaking. That issue would be in the forefront of ***Abrams v. United States,*** 250 U.S. 616 (1919).

See William Preston Jr., *Aliens and Dissenters: Federal Suppression of Radicals, 1903–1933* (Cambridge: Harvard University Press, 1963); Paul L. Murphy, *World War I and the Origin of Civil Liberties in the United States* (New York: Norton, 1979); and Zechariah Chafee Jr., *Free Speech in the United States* (Cambridge: Harvard University Press, 1920, rev. ed., 1941).

United States v. Doremus

249 U.S. 86 (1919)
Decided: March 3, 1919
Vote: 5 (Holmes, Day, Pitney, Brandeis, Clarke)
4 (E. White, McKenna, Van Devanter, McReynolds)
Opinion of the Court: Day
Dissenting opinion: E. White (McKenna, Van Devanter, McReynolds)

In 1916 Congress passed the Harrison Narcotic Drug Act. This law placed an excise tax on drugs that were not sold to patients, but not on drugs sold to patients. C. T. Doremus, a physician in Texas, sold five hundred 1/6 grain heroin pills to a friend, Alexander Ameris, a drug addict. Doremus attempted to evade the taxes by not reporting the sale to the government. He was arrested and charged with evading the taxes by illegally selling the heroin without permission. He challenged the constitutionality of the law, claiming that purpose of the law was not to generate tax revenue for the government, but to regulate heroin sales and was therefore an unconstitutional invasion of state police power.

In a 5–4 decision the Supreme Court held that the purpose of the act was to generate tax revenues for the federal government. Congress has the power to levy excise taxes, and, if Congress wishes to do so, it has the power to tax narcotics not sold to patients. Even if Congress had an ulterior motive to control addiction by taxing the drugs, the Court had no business looking into it. All that mattered was that Congress has the power to levy excise taxes and make laws reasonably related to that power.

Frohwerk v. United States

249 U.S. 204 (1919)
Decided: March 10, 1919
Vote: 9 (E. White, McKenna, Holmes, Day, Van Devanter, Pitney, McReynolds, Brandeis, Clarke)
0
Opinion of the Court: Holmes

Jacob Frohwerk was the publisher of a small pro-German newspaper in Missouri. After the United States entered World War I, Frohwerk printed pro-German articles opposing

America's involvement in the war. He was arrested and charged with violating the Espionage Act of 1917. The act prohibited any speech intending to interfere with America's military or promoting America's enemies. Violators could be sent to prison for twenty years.

Earlier in 1919 in ***Schenck v. United States,*** 249 U.S. 47, the Supreme Court had laid out its clear and present danger test for speech. Justice Holmes's opinion for the Court had held that speech that is used to create a clear and present danger to society was not entitled to First Amendment protection. In this case Frohwerk had printed his argument in a newspaper, and claimed that he was protected by the First Amendment's freedom of the press clause.

The Supreme Court held that Frohwerk's editorial speech was not protected. The circumstances of the speech had to be examined. His articles appeared in a pro-German newspaper, albeit a paper with a small circulation, and the Court ruled that even the slightest breath of pro-German antiwar sentiment could spark a flame against U.S. involvement in World War I.

First Amendment speech protection tends to weaken during times of national crisis, such as a war. Frohwerk's speech was a clear and present danger and therefore not protected.

See William Preston Jr., *Aliens and Dissenters: Federal Suppression of Radicals, 1903–1933* (Cambridge: Harvard University Press, 1963).

Debs v. United States

249 U.S. 211 (1919)
Decided: March 10, 1919
Vote: 9 (E. White, McKenna, Holmes, Day, Van Devanter, Pitney, McReynolds, Brandeis, Clarke)
0
Opinion of the Court: Holmes

On June 16, 1918, Eugene V. Debs, the head of the American Socialist Party and a fervent pacifist, gave a speech at the party convention in Canton, Ohio. He condemned war and capitalism but was careful not to advocate any illegal activity. While government agents took notes, Debs declared that he abhorred war, saying, "I would oppose war if I stood alone." He went on to state that the courts, the press, and indeed the entire political system were controlled by the rich. He also made it clear that he recognized that the Wilson administration had placed severe limits on free speech, so "I must be exceedingly careful, prudent, as to what I say, and even more careful and prudent as to how I say it." He concluded by urging the delegates to keep up their political and organizing activities. "Vote as you strike and strike as you vote."

For this abstract discussion of socialist theory and opposition to war in general, the government arrested and charged Debs with violating the Sedition Act and urging resistance to the war. After his conviction, Debs appealed to the Supreme Court, which unanimously upheld the verdict. To many civil libertarians *Debs* was a horrifying example of how elastic the clear and present danger test could be. In ***Schenck v. United States,*** 249 U.S. 47 (1919), decided earlier that year, the defendant had urged resistance to the draft; Debs's talk was purely theoretical.

Advocates of free expression now worried that any speech critical of the government in any way could be punished, and not just speech that was clearly seditious in intent. In many ways *Debs* marks the low-water mark of the Court's interpretation of the protection afforded by the First Amendment.

See Nick Salvatore, *Eugene V. Debs: Citizen and Socialist* (Urbana: University of Illinois Press, 1982); and Harry Kalven, "Professor Ernst Freund and *Debs v. United States,*" *Chicago Law Review* 40 (1973): 235.

Abrams v. United States

250 U.S. 616 (1919)
Decided: November 10, 1919
Vote: 7 (E. White, McKenna, Day, Van Devanter, Pitney, McReynolds, Clarke)
2 (Holmes, Brandeis)
Opinion of the Court: Clarke
Dissenting opinion: Holmes (Brandeis)

The defendants in this case had distributed pamphlets in Yiddish and English criticizing the Wilson administration for sending U.S. troops to Russia in the summer of 1918. The government argued that these acts were a violation of the sedition act, although it failed to prove the leaflets actually hindered the war with Germany. The trial court judge found that they *might* have caused revolts and strikes and thereby diminished the number of troops available to fight the Germans. The defendants appealed their convictions. The Supreme Court, led by Justice Clarke, agreed that the government had provided sufficient proof to support this charge and that the conviction could be sustained under the clear and present danger test enunciated by Holmes in ***Schenck v. United States,*** 249 U.S. 47 (1919).

In dissent, Justice Holmes articulated one of the great defenses of free speech. The "silly leaflets" hardly posed a danger to society, he said, and the fact that the ideas expressed were unpopular or even considered dangerous made no difference:

> . . . the ultimate good desired is better reached by free trade in ideas—that the best test of truth is the power of the thought to get itself accepted in the competition of the market and that truth is the only ground upon which their wishes safely can be carried out. That at any rate is the theory of our Constitution. It is an experiment, as all life is an experiment.

Why did Holmes change his mind after the *Schenck* case? The criticism of men he respected, such as Zechariah Chafee Jr. and Ernst Freund, upset him greatly. Chafee met with Holmes and convinced him that the Framers intended the First Amendment to be speech protective and that in a democratic society all viewpoints, even if unpopular, needed to be heard. Although the "clear and present danger" test may have had roots in Blackstone's jurisprudence, it was not speech protective; in fact, it provided an excuse for government to restrict speech.

Because Holmes could not simply abandon the test he had so recently devised, he followed Chafee's advice and converted it from a means for government suppression of speech to a bar against that very repression. Holmes's dissent in *Abrams* is often seen as the beginning of the Court's concern with free speech as a cornerstone of a democratic society. It put forward the notion of democracy resting upon a free marketplace of ideas. Some ideas might be unpopular, some might be unsettling, and some might be false. But in a democracy one had to give all ideas an equal chance to be heard, in the belief that the false, the ignoble, and the useless would be crowded out by the right ideas, those that would facilitate progress in a democratic manner. Only if society took the guarantee of the First Amendment seriously could that happen.

Although Holmes came to believe passionately in free speech, it was an abstract consideration. The marketplace of ideas analogy appealed to the skeptic in him, but it did not fully address the issues he raised, namely, why did a democratic society need free speech as a positive good. Justice Brandeis later provided the answer in ***Whitney v. California,*** 274 U.S. 357 (1927).

See Paul L. Murphy, *World War I and the Origin of Civil Liberties in the United States* (New York: Norton, 1979); Richard Polenberg, *Fighting Faiths: The Abrams Case, the Supreme Court, and Free Speech* (New York: Viking, 1987); and Fred D. Ragan, "Justice Oliver Wendell Holmes, Jr., Zechariah Chafee, Jr., and the Clear and Present Danger Test for Free Speech: The First Year, 1919," *Journal of American History* 58 (1971): 24.

Hamilton v. Kentucky Distilleries & Warehouse Co.

Also known as the Wartime Prohibition Cases
251 U.S. 146 (1919)
Decided: December 15, 1919
Vote: 9 (E. White, McKenna, Holmes, Day, Van Devanter, Pitney, McReynolds, Brandeis, Clarke)
0
Opinion of the Court: Brandeis

One week after World War I ended, President Wilson signed the War-Time Prohibition Act, which made it illegal to sell alcoholic beverages in the domestic market. The alleged purpose of the act was to conserve manpower and to concentrate on efficiently mobilizing America for more war production.

The law prevented Kentucky Distilleries & Warehouse Company from selling its whiskey. The company argued that the act was unconstitutional because the war was over, and Congress could no longer exercise its wartime powers. The law, therefore, was an unconstitutional use of federal police power because only the states had this power under the Tenth Amendment.

The Supreme Court held the act constitutional. Although the Tenth Amendment normally conveyed such power only to the states, Congress had an interest in maintaining wartime mobilization even though the war was over. Just because hostilities had ceased did not mean that fighting could not erupt again. Congress had an interest in ensuring that the country was mobilized to fight again if necessary.

See Richard F. Hamm, *Shaping the Eighteenth Amendment: Temperance Reform, Legal Culture, and the Polity, 1880–1920* (Chapel Hill: University of North Carolina Press, 1995).

1920–1929

Jacob Ruppert v. Caffey

251 U.S. 264 (1920)
Decided: January 5, 1920
Vote: 5 (E. White, McKenna, Holmes, Pitney, Brandeis)
4 (Day, Van Devanter, McReynolds, Clarke)
Opinion of the Court: Brandeis
Dissenting opinion: McReynolds (Day, Van Devanter)
Dissenting without opinion: Clarke

In 1918, after the hostilities of World War I had ended, Congress prohibited the making of alcoholic beverages. The government's purpose was to preserve an adequate food supply for postwar needs and to remain mobilized should fighting break out again. In the ***Wartime Prohibition Cases,*** 251 U.S. 146 (1919), a unanimous Court upheld the prohibition law as a legitimate exercise of the government's war powers, even though hostilities had ceased. In this case, Jacob Ruppert Company, which distilled liquor and other alcoholic beverages, argued that the statute was an unconstitutional use of federal police power. Ruppert argued that with hostilities at an end, Congress could not act as if the country was still at war. War powers are available to the government only during wartime, and not in peacetime, he argued, and because this law could be in effect indefinitely, it was not a wartime measure but an invasion of states' rights.

A majority of the Court ignored this argument and ruled that Congress may prohibit the producing of alcoholic beverages during the winding-down period after a war in order to preserve food supplies and remain ready for the possibility that fighting could break out again. Congress could not simply ban the making of alcohol at any time, but in the circumstances of a postwar climate, it could do so for specified and limited purposes. Four members of the Court, however, showed themselves more sympathetic to the states rights arguments and dissented.

See Richard F. Hamm, *Shaping the Eighteenth Amendment: Temperance Reform, Legal Culture, and the Polity, 1880–1920* (Chapel Hill: University of North Carolina Press, 1995).

Silverthorne Lumber Co., Inc. v. United States

251 U.S. 385 (1920)
Decided: January 26, 1920
Vote: 7 (McKenna, Holmes, Day, Van Devanter, McReynolds, Brandeis, Clarke)
2 (E. White, Pitney)
Opinion of the Court: Holmes
Dissenting without opinion: E. White, Pitney

In 1919 Frederick W. Silverthorne and his father were arrested in their home. Later, without a warrant, federal marshals raided the Silverthornes' lumber company and seized their books, papers, and records. The documents and even some of the employees were taken to the district attorney's office. Once the papers had been examined, the government brought additional charges against the Silverthornes. The accused argued that the illegally confiscated papers could not be used against them because their seizure without a warrant violated the Fourth Amendment. Charges based on the seized papers, therefore, should be dismissed.

In ***Weeks v. United States,*** 232 U.S. 383 (1914), the Court had set forth the exclusionary rule, holding that evidence obtained illegally in violation of the Fourth Amendment was inadmissible. In this case, however, the illegal search and seizure involved a corporation, not a human being, and the government argued that the exclusionary rule did not apply to illegal searches and seizures of corporations.

The Court ruled that the exclusionary rule did apply to corporations, which like human citizens, were protected by the Fourth Amendment's prohibition of illegal searches and seizures.

See David J. Bodenhamer, *Fair Trial: Rights of the Accused in American History* (New York: Oxford University Press, 1992).

Board of Public Utility Commissioners v. Ynchausti & Co.

251 U.S. 401 (1920)
Decided: March 1, 1920
Vote: 9 (E. White, McKenna, Holmes, Day, Van Devanter, Pitney, McReynolds, Brandeis, Clarke)
0
Opinion of the Court: E. White
See *Insular Cases,* page 131.

United States v. U.S. Steel Corp.

251 U.S. 417 (1920)
Decided: March 1, 1920
Vote: 4 (E. White, McKenna, Holmes, Van Devanter)
3 (Day, Pitney, Clarke)
Opinion of the Court: McKenna
Dissenting opinion: Day (Pitney, Clarke)
Did not participate: McReynolds, Brandeis

The Sherman Antitrust Act was enacted to prevent monopolies from forming and to break up companies that monopolized their markets. The U.S. Steel Corporation had grown so large that it had virtual control over the iron and steel industries in the United States. The Taft administration brought suit to break up the monopoly under the Sherman act. The case lingered in federal courts for several years and had been accepted for argument by the Supreme Court just before the United States entered into World War I. At the request of the Wilson administration, which wanted to avoid any actions that would adversely affect the steel industry during wartime, the Court put off consideration of the case until after the war.

When it finally heard the case, the Court held that the U.S. Steel Corporation was not a monopoly. The Court ruled that the mere size and control that a business has over an industry does not prove that the business is monopolistic. The Court stated that the evidence must show intent and overt acts to monopolize. In addition, customer complaints about its products and services must be in evidence to prove a monopoly. Although U.S. Steel was incredibly large, it was not overtly restraining other companies from competing. Any difficulties in competing were the natural consequences of the marketplace. The Court, therefore, would take into account factors such as intent, overt acts to monopolize or to destroy competition, and customer complaints in determining whether a company monopolized a market.

Schaefer v. United States

251 U.S. 466 (1920)
Decided: March 1, 1920
Vote: 6 (E. White, McKenna, Day, Van Devanter, Pitney, McReynolds)
3 (Holmes, Brandeis, Clarke)
Opinion of the Court: McKenna
Dissenting opinion: Brandeis (Holmes)
Dissenting opinion: Clarke

Peter Schaefer owned and published a German-language newspaper in Philadelphia. He allegedly printed pro-German articles and false news reports about World War I. The federal government agued that Schaefer's actions violated the Espionage Act of 1917 and indicted and convicted him and other officers of the paper under this law. The government claimed that the articles constituted a clear and present danger.

The Court held that the First Amendment does not protect any speech during wartime that tends to weaken patriotism, raise skepticism, support the enemy, or in some way deflate the fervor to fight. Virtually any such speech creates a clear and present danger of unlawful activity by citizens against America's involvement in the war.

Justice Brandeis continued the campaign he and Justice Holmes had started in ***Abrams v. United States,*** 250 U.S. 616 (1919), to redefine First Amendment values and make it more difficult for the government to suppress unpopular speech. Here, he urged the Court and the public to apply the clear and present danger test as it would be invoked in the calmer days of peacetime, not in the fervor of war. The puny efforts toward subversion in the paper did not create a clear and present danger. Just because such speech may influence others to also speak out against the war does not make it a clear and present danger. The test is one of proximity and degree. The voicing of an opinion must be weighed to determine if it rises to the level of a substantive evil that Congress has the right to prevent. Otherwise, the decision in this case could allow for a the majority view in society to silence minority views.

See Frank E. Strong, "Fifty Years of Clear and Present Danger: From Schenck to Brandenberg—and Beyond," *Supreme Court Review, 1969,* 41.

Pierce v. United States

252 U.S. 239 (1920)
Decided: March 8, 1920
Vote: 7 (E. White, McKenna, Day, Van Devanter, Pitney, McReynolds, Clarke)
2 (Holmes, Brandeis)
Opinion of the Court: Pitney
Dissenting opinion: Brandeis (Holmes)

A clergyman was arrested and convicted for violating the Espionage Act of 1917. The clergyman, a Socialist, distributed a four-page pamphlet that spoke out against U.S. involvement in

World War I, which the government claimed constituted a clear and present danger, the standard set forth in ***Schenck v. United States,*** 249 U.S. 47 (1919). The defendant claimed that the First Amendment protected the distribution of antiwar literature during the conflict.

The Court held that antiwar speech was not protected because it may tend to influence others to speak out against the war, to protest the war, or even refuse to enlist in the draft. Such speech, the Court reasoned, is against the interests of America, particularly during wartime. The logical result of the majority's reasoning was that if the United States were at war, someone who disagreed with the war and its aims could not speak out because it could create a clear and present danger of dissension in society.

As he had in several similar cases, Justice Brandeis attempted to create a more speech-friendly interpretation of the First Amendment. One of the foundations of American society is the desire to improve our lives through new legislation and new ideas. This ideal would be substantially damaged by not letting socialists, pacifists, and others oppose the nation's involvement in war. It takes more than mere disagreement, Brandeis declared, for speech to be illegal.

See Frank E. Strong, "Fifty Years of Clear and Present Danger: From Schenck to Brandenberg—and Beyond," *Supreme Court Review, 1969,* 41.

Missouri v. Holland

252 U.S. 416 (1920)
Decided: April 19, 1920
Vote: 7 (E. White, McKenna, Holmes, Day, McReynolds, Brandeis, Clarke)
2 (Van Devanter, Pitney)
Opinion of the Court: Holmes
Dissenting without opinion: Van Devanter, Pitney

A 1916 treaty between Great Britain and the United States for the protection of migratory birds called for closed hunting seasons on several species. Congress enacted these provisions into law in the Migratory Bird Act of 1918. The state of Missouri attacked both the law and the treaty, claiming that the subject matter—local hunting—lay beyond the powers of Congress because of the Tenth Amendment. A treaty, the state claimed, could not convey to the federal government powers that were not provided in the Constitution.

Justice Holmes, speaking for the majority, rejected Missouri's argument and advanced a broad interpretation of the treaty power. Unlike acts of Congress, which relied on the Constitution for their authority, the treaty-making power was derived from the basic sovereignty of the nation. The power antedated the Constitution and was independent of it. As a result, virtually everything that the government conceived to be in the national interest could be the subject of a treaty; and under the Supremacy Clause, treaties took precedence over any state powers. Although Holmes conceded that there might be some limits to this power, such parameters would not be determined by the same criteria used to judge acts of Congress.

The opinion, with its expansive view of the treaty power, is largely irrelevant today because of the national government's great scope of power over matters both domestic and foreign. It nevertheless stands as a prime example of the "living Constitution" approach to constitutional interpretation, in which historic practices as well as contemporary conditions are given greater emphasis than the intent of the Framers. Although the case centered on the scope of the treaty power, rather than the supremacy of a treaty under Article VI, it lent support to future decisions such as ***United States v. Belmont,*** 301 U.S. 324 (1937), which upheld the supremacy of executive agreements over state law. Finally, *Missouri v. Holland* was instrumental in establishing the federal common law principle that considerations of foreign affairs took precedence over state law when the two conflicted.

See Charles A. Lofgren, "*Missouri v. Holland* in Historical Perspective," *Supreme Court Review, 1975* (1976): 77; and Louis Henkin, *Foreign Affairs and the Constitution* (Mineola, N.Y.: Foundation Press, 1972).

National Prohibition Cases

Also known as *Rhode Island v. Palmer*
253 U.S. 350 (1920)
Decided: June 7, 1920
Vote: 7 (E. White, Holmes, Day, Van Devanter, Pitney, McReynolds, Brandeis)
2 (McKenna, Clarke)
Opinion of the Court: Van Devanter
Concurring opinion: E. White
Concurring opinion: McReynolds
Dissenting opinion: McKenna
Dissenting opinion: Clarke

Seven different cases all raised the same issue—the constitutionality of the Volstead Act. In 1919 the Eighteenth Amendment had been ratified, banning the production of all alcoholic beverages in the United States. After the amendment went into effect, Congress passed the Volstead Act, which gave the federal government power to enforce Prohibition.

The defendants in the seven cases challenged the constitutionality of the Volstead Act. Section 2 of the Eighteenth Amendment declared that the states and Congress had "concurrent" powers to enforce Prohibition, which they claimed meant Congress could not pass enforcing legislation on its own.

The Court held the Volstead Act constitutional. The Eighteenth Amendment had been properly proposed and ratified under the terms of Article V of the Constitution. Section 2 of the Eighteenth Amendment allowed for "concurrent" enforcement power for Congress and the states, meaning that Congress and the states could pass laws to enforce the amendment, and they did not have to act together.

See Richard F. Hamm, *Shaping the Eighteenth Amendment: Temperance Reform, Legal Culture, and the Polity, 1880–1920* (Chapel Hill: University of North Carolina Press, 1995).

Federal Trade Commission v. Gratz

253 U.S. 421 (1920)
Decided: June 7, 1920
Vote: 7 (E. White, McKenna, Holmes, Day, Van Devanter, Pitney, McReynolds)
2 (Brandeis, Clarke)
Opinion of the Court: McReynolds
Concurring without opinion: Pitney
Dissenting opinion: Brandeis (Clarke)

The Federal Trade Commission Act of 1914 forbade unfair competitive practices. Andrew and Benjamin Gratz, doing business as Warren, Jones & Gratz, sold steel ties that were used for binding cotton bales. Gratz's company, however, would not sell the steel ties unless the customer also bought the jute bagging used to wrap the bales. This practice is known as a "tying arrangement," in which a seller refuses to sell one item unless a buyer also purchases another. The Federal Trade Commission (FTC) ordered an immediate halt to this practice. Gratz argued that tying arrangements did not constitute an unfair competitive practice and therefore the FTC could not outlaw them.

The Court agreed, holding that the FTC could not regulate tying arrangements. The FTC Act, Justice McReynolds argued, did not define what constituted an unfair competitive practice. Therefore, the courts would decide what was a competitive practice and what was not, and tying arrangements were not unfair business practices.

McReynolds knew full well that the act was more specific because Congress had intended the FTC to have flexibility in determining competitive unfairness, and he knew this because he and Justice Brandeis had written the law in 1914, when McReynolds was attorney general. Brandeis in his dissent did not mention McReynolds by name, but he pointed out that context often determined competition and only the flexibility that Congress had provided would make sense.

The effect of this decision was to hamstring the FTC for the remainder of the decade because companies whom the FTC targeted for unfair practices could tie up the agency in the courts for years disputing the ruling.

See G. Cullom Davis, "The Transformation of the Federal Trade Commission, 1914–1929," *Mississippi Valley Historical Review* 49 (1962): 437.

Gilbert v. Minnesota

254 U.S. 325 (1920)
Decided: December 13, 1920
Vote: 7 (McKenna, Holmes, Day, Van Devanter, Pitney, McReynolds, Clarke)
2 (E. White, Brandeis)
Opinion of the Court: McKenna
Concurring without opinion: Holmes
Dissenting opinion: E. White
Dissenting opinion: Brandeis

A Minnesota statute made it a crime to urge people not to enlist in the military. The law prohibited pacifist speech both in wartime and in peacetime. Joseph Gilbert was a pacifist who spoke out against the war and the draft, saying that the United States was fighting to save Great Britain. He also said that in a democracy the citizens should be allowed to vote on whether there should be a draft. Gilbert was arrested and convicted under the state statute for his speech. In his appeal he argued that a state cannot abridge the First Amendment protection of speech.

Ruling that the Minnesota law was constitutional, the Court held that states may override First Amendment free speech rights. The Court said that although the First Amendment protects speech, free speech is not an absolute right. Furthermore, the First Amendment does not apply to the states via the Fourteenth Amendment. Therefore, states may pass laws restricting the freedom of speech. The Fourteenth Amendment's liberty protection protects only the ability to acquire and enjoy property.

Justice Brandeis dissented and in a careful analysis pointed out all of the weaknesses of the statute. It applied in peacetime as well as wartime and thus violated the right of parents to instill ideals in their children. If the Minnesota law applied only in wartime, it might be constitutional, but its true purpose was to chill all pacifist speech at all times. Moreover, a state law cannot supersede the First Amendment. The fundamental protections of speech should apply to all persons, regardless of what state officials believe to be acceptable.

Perhaps the most important line in the dissent read: "I cannot believe that the liberty guaranteed by the Fourteenth Amendment includes only liberty to acquire and to enjoy property." Within a short time, that comment would begin the process of incorporation that applied not only the First Amendment but also most of the Bill of Rights to the states. See ***Gitlow v. New York,*** 268 U.S. 652 (1925).

Duplex Printing Press Co. v. Deering

254 U.S. 443 (1921)
Decided: January 3, 1921
Vote: 6 (E. White, McKenna, Day, Van Devanter, Pitney, McReynolds)
3 (Holmes, Brandeis, Clarke)
Opinion of the Court: Pitney
Dissenting opinion: Brandeis (Holmes, Clarke)

Section 6 of the Clayton Act of 1914 declared that labor did not constitute a commodity or an article of commerce. Antitrust laws, therefore, should not be interpreted to forbid unions from seeking their legitimate objectives. Section 20 prohibited federal courts from issuing injunctions or restraining orders in labor disputes "unless necessary to prevent irreparable injury to property, or to a property right." The same section also forbade injunctions against peaceful picketing or primary boycotts.

The Supreme Court did not rule on these sections of the act until 1921. *Duplex Printing Press Company v. Deering* arose when unions boycotted a manufacturer's products in New York to enforce a strike in Michigan. Justice Pitney ruled that the Clayton Act did not legitimize such secondary boycotts, nor had Section 6 provided a blanket exemption from the antitrust laws. The law, according to a majority of the justices, only protected unions lawfully carrying out their legitimate objectives. Because secondary boycotts were unlawful, neither Section 6 nor Section 20 applied. Moreover, Pitney interpreted Section 20 to mean that injunctions could be issued not only against the immediate parties—the employer and his striking workers—but also to restrain other unions from supporting the strikers.

Justice Brandeis, in dissent, saw the anti-injunction statute as a positive good. He explained how Congress had determined that abuses of the injunction had gone too far in limiting labor's legitimate activities. In response, Congress, through the Clayton Act, had established a standard that it considered fair to both parties. Brandeis felt that judges did not have the prerogative to undo congressional policy because they disagreed with it or because their own economic and social views ran counter to those of the legislative branch.

The *Duplex* decision came down during the same term as ***Truax v. Corrigan,*** 257 U.S. 312 (1921), in which the Court struck down a state anti-injunction statute. With these conflicting decisions, the Court established a no-man's-land in which neither the federal government nor the state governments could act. The gray area was typical of dual federalism arguments and precluded both state and federal restrictions on the injunction. Whenever unions threatened to strike, employers could go into either federal or state court and get an injunction, a court order barring workers from going out on strike. As a result, the rest of the decade saw injunctions against strikes issued as extensively as before the Clayton Act, which had intended to put an end to such practices. Not until the Great Depression undermined the dominance of business interests did reformers finally get the Norris-LaGuardia Anti-injunction Act through Congress in March 1932; a number of states then followed with similar measures of their own.

See Stanley I. Kutler, "Labor, the Clayton Act, and the Supreme Court," *Labor History* 3 (1962): 19; and Christopher L. Tomlins, *The State and the Unions: Labor Relations, Law and the Organized Labor Movement in America, 1880–1960* (New York: Cambridge University Press, 1985).

United States v. L. Cohen Grocery Co.

255 U.S. 81 (1921)
Decided: February 28, 1921
Vote: 8 (E. White, McKenna, Holmes, Van Devanter, Pitney, McReynolds, Brandeis, Clarke)
0
Opinion of the Court: E. White
Concurring opinion: Pitney (Brandeis)
Did not participate: Day

L. Cohen Grocery Company was charging $10.07 for fifty pounds of sugar and $19.50 for one hundred pounds of sugar, prices that were outrageously high even during the inflation that followed World War I.

In 1919 Congress amended Section 4 of the wartime Lever Food Control Act, which criminalized the making of "any unjust or unreasonable rate." The law was intended to prevent usurious rates of interest—that is, rates so high as to be completely unfair and unethical. It also made it illegal to charge unreasonably high prices for necessities. Congress, however, failed to define what constituted either a usurious rate of interest or an unreasonable price and instead delegated that task to the courts.

Under the nondelegation doctrine, Congress cannot assign its legislative powers to another branch of the government. Cohen challenged the food control law, arguing that Congress had acted unconstitutionally in delegating legislative authority to the courts. Cohen also argued that even if the delegation was proper, the law was overbroad and vague.

The Supreme Court agreed with Cohen and struck down the law as overbroad and vague. To declare something illegal, Congress had to do more than merely define it as "unreasonable," which is too sweeping and general; the law needed to be more specific. Because the Court voided the law on vagueness grounds, it did not have to examine whether Congress had unconstitutionally delegated its powers. The Court, however, did not deny the federal government's power to fix food prices during wartime.

United States ex rel. Milwaukee Socialist Democratic Pub. Co. v. Burleson

255 U.S. 407 (1921)
Decided: March 7, 1921
Vote: 7 (E. White, McKenna, Day, Van Devanter, Pitney, McReynolds, Clarke)
2 (Holmes, Brandeis)
Opinion of the Court: Clarke
Dissenting opinion: Holmes
Dissenting opinion: Brandeis

The postmaster general of the United States, Albert S. Burleson, denied second-class mailing privileges to the *Milwaukee Leader* because the paper printed anti–World War I articles. Burleson then warned that future articles might violate the Espionage Act of 1917, that the paper would be denied the right to cheap postage, and that its subversive speech would be considered "non-mailable." The *Milwaukee Leader* could not survive without using second-class postage because first-class postage was too expensive.

The Espionage Act did not address whether future issues of a paper that had printed allegedly subversive materials could have its postage rights stripped away, all on the basis of hypothetic future illegal speech. The Court held that the government may place such a prior restraint upon future speech, based on past record, a decision that gave the Post Office enormous censorship powers over papers that printed anything with which government officials disagreed.

Justice Brandeis dissented, adding one more brick to the structure that would be unveiled in ***Whitney v. California,*** 274 U.S. 357 (1927). The postmaster general had no business stripping postal service rights from people just because he feared what they might say in the future. It should be unconstitutional to place prior restraints on speech, especially speech that has not yet been uttered.

See William Preston, *Aliens and Dissenters: Federal Suppression of Radicals, 1903–1933,* 2d ed. (Urbana: University of Illinois Press, 1963).

Block v. Hirsh

256 U.S. 135 (1921)
Decided: April 18, 1921
Vote: 5 (Holmes, Day, Pitney, Brandeis, Clarke)
4 (E. White, McKenna, Van Devanter, McReynolds)
Opinion of the Court: Holmes
Dissenting opinion: McKenna (E. White, Van Devanter, McReynolds)

During World War I, a local Washington, D.C., statute allowed tenants to stay in their rented property past the day their leases expired. In fact, as long as the tenant paid the rent, he could stay in the property indefinitely. Block, a landlord, argued that the statute was unconstitutional and violated the Fifth Amendment's prohibition against taking property without just compensation.

The Court upheld the statute. Under normal conditions the law would be a violation of the Fifth Amendment's Takings Clause, but the circumstances were not normal. The law had been passed during World War I to address a severe housing shortage in the nation's capital, caused by the influx of people needed to staff new and expanded federal agencies. It was well within the war powers of the government. Furthermore, the landlord was justly compensated for his property because he continued to receive rent payments.

New York Trust Company v. Eisner

256 U.S. 345 (1921)
Decided: May 16, 1921
Vote: 9 (E. White, McKenna, Holmes, Day, Van Devanter, Pitney, McReynolds, Brandeis, Clarke)
0
Opinion of the Court: Holmes

Under Article I, Section 2, of the Constitution, Congress does not have the power to levy direct taxes. The Sixteenth Amendment (ratified in 1913), however, gave Congress the power to impose federal income taxes. In 1916 Congress passed an estate tax, also known as a "death tax." When a person dies, his or her estate passes to other people, most often to children or other relatives. The new law levied a tax on the value of the estate of the deceased, which the heirs had to pay.

In 1917 Purdy died and left his estate to his brother's children, with the New York Trust Company as executor. In an effort to avoid the estate tax, the family and the trustee argued that although the Sixteenth Amendment had permitted a tax on incomes, it did not authorize an estate tax. They claimed that the estate tax violated the constitutional ban on direct taxes.

The Court unanimously held that Congress had the constitutional power to levy an estate tax and ruled that it was an indirect, rather than a direct tax. It was an indirect tax because it taxed the transfer of property, not the ownership of property itself.

See R. Alton Lee, *A History of Regulatory Taxation* (Lexington: University Press of Kentucky, 1973).

Dillon v. Gloss

256 U.S. 368 (1921)
Decided: May 16, 1921
Vote: 9 (E. White, McKenna, Holmes, Day, Van Devanter, Pitney, McReynolds, Brandeis, Clarke)
0
Opinion of the Court: Van Devanter

Convicted for transporting liquor in violation of the Volstead Act, Dillon raised two challenges to Prohibition. The first challenge was to the time limit of seven years for ratification of the Eighteenth Amendment. Dillon argued that Congress could not set a time limit for ratification and that the amendment, therefore, was invalid, even though it had been ratified well before the deadline. The second challenge was that the amendment was not in effect when he was arrested. The amendment was scheduled to go into effect one year after ratification. It was ratified on January 16, 1919, and Dillon was arrested on January 17, 1920. The secretary of state, however, did not proclaim Prohibition as law until January 29, 1919. Therefore, Dillon argued, the amendment should have gone into effect on January 29, 1920, and that the Volstead Act could not become effective until that date either.

The Court held that Congress may set a reasonable time limit for the ratification of an amendment, and the seven-year limit was reasonable. More important, an amendment is considered ratified the day the state that yields a three-fourths majority approves it. This had occurred on January 16, 1919, so the amendment was indeed in effect on January 16, 1920, the day before Dillon was arrested. He was therefore in violation of the law.

Truax v. Corrigan

257 U.S. 312 (1921)
Decided: December 19, 1921
Vote: 5 (Taft, McKenna, Day, Van Devanter, McReynolds)
4 (Holmes, Pitney, Brandeis, Clarke)
Opinion of the Court: Taft
Dissenting opinion: Holmes
Dissenting opinion: Pitney (Clarke)
Dissenting opinion: Brandeis

Truax owned a restaurant in Arizona, the English Kitchen, where the working conditions were allegedly so awful that the cooks and waiters, who were union members, went on strike. They picketed in front of the restaurant, threatened customers, and advertised the strike. Truax saw his business decline by more than 50 percent as a result of the picketing. He sought an injunction to prevent the strike, but Arizona law forbade such injunctions. Truax claimed that as a result of this law he had suffered property loss and been denied equal protection under the Fourteenth Amendment.

The Court declared the Arizona law unconstitutional and held that allowing the strike deprived Truax of equal protection. The strike, according to the new chief justice, William Howard Taft, sought to destroy the restaurant, not to seek sympathy and better working conditions. The anti-injunction law violated the Due Process Clause of the Fourteenth Amendment by depriving the restaurant owner of his property and ran afoul of the Equal Protection Clause by singling out disputes between employers and employees for special treatment.

The three dissents clearly exposed the pro-business, anti-labor bias of the majority. Justice Holmes decried the use of the Fourteenth Amendment to cut off state experimentation. Justice Pitney challenged each of Taft's conclusions and claimed they had no sound basis in law, and Justice Brandeis provided an extensive historical and legal justification for the statute.

The case was ultimately overturned in ***Senn v. Tile Layers Protective Union,*** 301 U.S. 468 (1937).

See Christopher L. Tomlins, *The State and the Unions* (New York: Cambridge University Press, 1985).

Bailey v. Drexel Furniture Co.

259 U.S. 20 (1922)
Decided: May 15, 1922
Vote: 8 (Taft, McKenna, Holmes, Day, Van Devanter, Pitney, McReynolds, Brandeis)
1 (Clarke)
Opinion of the Court: Taft
Dissenting without opinion: Clarke

In 1918 a closely divided Court struck down the Child Labor Act of 1916 in ***Hammer v. Dagenhart,*** 247 U.S. 251 (1918), declaring that Congress did not have power under the Commerce Clause to keep goods made by child labor out of the stream of commerce. Public reaction to the decision proved so overwhelmingly unfavorable that Congress responded with a second Child Labor Act less than nine months later. This time the legislature relied on the taxing power and imposed a 10 percent tax on net profits on goods introduced into interstate commerce by firms employing children under fourteen years of age. Congress felt itself on sure constitutional footing because the Court had consistently held, in cases such as ***Veazie Bank v. Fenno,*** 75 U.S. 533 (1869), and later in ***McCray v. United States,*** 195 U.S. 27 (1904), that the broad reach of the taxing power precluded the judiciary from looking behind the tax to evaluate the motive.

Nevertheless, in *Bailey,* the Court struck down the statute as an invasion of an exclusive state function. Chief Justice Taft denied that the Court had gone behind the tax to judge intent; the justices had found the law unconstitutional because Congress had tried to use the tax not as a revenue measure but as a criminal penalty, a power beyond its authority. Extolling the dual nature of the federal system, Taft's opinion repeated and enlarged on the traditional arguments of laissez faire, declaring that if the Court permitted the law to stand, it would break down the traditional limits on congressional authority imposed by the Tenth Amendment. Even Justices Holmes and Brandeis joined the majority, not out of sympathy for Taft's conservatism, but because they too believed that Congress had abused its taxing power. Not until 1941 did the Court grant Congress the power to control labor conditions when it overruled *Hammer* in **United States v. Darby Lumber Co.,** 312 U.S. 100, and adopted a broad reading of the Commerce Clause. But even as the Court nullified federal child labor laws, at no time did it deny to the *states* the authority to control child labor under their police powers. See ***Sturges & Burns Manufacturing Co. v. Beauchamp,*** 231 U.S. 320 (1913).

See Stephen B. Wood, *Constitutional Politics in the Progressive Era: Child Labor and the Law* (Chicago: University of Chicago Press, 1958); and Lee R. Altman, *A History of Regulatory Taxation* (Lexington: University Press of Kentucky, 1973).

Ng Fung Ho v. White

259 U.S. 276 (1922)
Decided: May 29, 1922
Vote: 9 (Taft, McKenna, Holmes, Day, Van Devanter, Pitney, McReynolds, Brandeis, Clarke)
0
Opinion of the Court: Brandeis

In 1917 Congress passed an expanded Chinese Exclusion Act, giving administrative officials the power to determine whether to deport a Chinese person to China. Five Chinese were detained in San Francisco and ordered deported to China. Of the five only Ng Fung Ho claimed that he was an American citizen, and he filed for a writ of habeas corpus so that a court could decide the issue. The district court denied the writ, and he appealed, arguing that under the Due Process Clause of the Fifth Amendment, a person claiming American citizenship is entitled to a judicial decision about deportation, rather than an administrative decision.

The Court agreed and held that a person claiming to be an American citizen cannot be denied habeas corpus when threatened with deportation. Due process dictates that he should be able to plead his case in court rather than before an administrative official making the final decision. As the other four Chinese persons had not claimed citizenship, they could be immediately deported.

See Lucy E. Salyer, *Laws Harsh as Tigers: Chinese Immigrants and the Shaping of Modern Immigration Law* (Chapel Hill: University of North Carolina Press, 1995).

Prudential Insurance Co. v. Cheek

259 U.S. 530 (1922)
Decided: June 5, 1922
Vote: 6 (McKenna, Holmes, Day, Pitney, Brandeis, Clarke)
3 (Taft, Van Devanter, McReynolds)
Opinion of the Court: Pitney
Dissenting without opinion: Taft, Van Devanter, McReynolds

Robert T. Cheek was an employee of Prudential Insurance Company in Missouri. After he left his job, he asked Prudential for a letter explaining his employment history at the company. The company refused, although a Missouri law required production of such a letter if an employee or former employee asked for it. Prudential argued that the law violated due process, because it interfered with its liberty to contract.

The Court upheld the law, ruling that the law did not come remotely close to interfering with the freedom to contract. Freedom to contract involved the making and breaking of private agreements. The Missouri law simply required a brief statement of an employee's record at work, a requirement that hardly constituted an unreasonable interference with a corporation's liberty to contract.

Ozawa v. United States

260 U.S. 178 (1922)
Decided: November 13, 1922
Vote: 9 (Taft, McKenna, Holmes, Day, Van Devanter, Pitney, McReynolds, Brandeis, Sutherland)
0
Opinion of the Court: Sutherland

Takao Ozawa was born in Japan, but grew up in Hawaii. He attended the University of California, educated his children in American schools, and "that he was well qualified by character and education for citizenship is conceded." In the 1906 Naturalization Act, however, Congress had reserved naturalization for white persons and those from Africa.

For the Court the question was relatively easy. Despite Ozawa's sterling personal attributes, the Constitution had granted power over immigration and naturalization to Congress, and it appeared clear that Congress did not intend for Japanese aliens to secure U.S. citizenship through naturalization. Although Congress could not discriminate among its citizens, it had the power to determine which persons, if any, it would allow to enter the country and become citizens.

The law was not changed until after World War II.

See Milton R. Konvitz, *The Alien and the Asiatic in American Law* (Ithaca, N.Y.: Cornell University Press, 1946).

Pennsylvania Coal Co. v. Mahon

260 U.S. 393 (1922)
Decided: December 11, 1922
Vote: 7 (Taft, McKenna, Holmes, Van Devanter, Pitney, McReynolds, Sutherland)
1 (Brandeis)
Opinion of the Court: Holmes
Dissenting opinion: Brandeis

A Pennsylvania law precluded the underground mining of coal in areas of severe ground subsidence. In other words, digging for coal could not take place in areas where the ground above the mines had a good chance of collapsing. The law was aimed specifically at areas where houses had been built above coal seams because of the danger not only to miners but also to families living above the mine.

Pennsylvania Coal Company owned mineral rights to lands where houses had been built and wanted to dig new mines. One of these mines was to be under Mahon's house, but he refused to let the company proceed. As a result of the law and Mahon's refusal, the coal under Mahon's house became worthless. The coal company went to court and argued that the law was unconstitutional because it deprived the company of its property in violation of the Fifth Amendment's Takings Clause.

The Court agreed and struck down the law. The Court ruled that under the Takings Clause no government can deprive a person of his property without just compensation. A state may regulate property, but if the regulation goes "too far" it becomes a taking. Because the law deprived the coal company of its mine without a fair compensation, the law did in fact violate the Fifth Amendment.

Although there was a risk of death to the families in the coal mining region, it was their responsibility to find out whether anyone owned underground property rights before they bought or built a house. The Pennsylvania Coal Company could continue mining under Mahon's house.

Federal Trade Commission v. Curtis Publishing Co.

260 U.S. 568 (1923)
Decided: January 8, 1923
Vote: 7 (Taft, McKenna, Holmes, Van Devanter, McReynolds, Brandeis, Sutherland)
0
Opinion of the Court: McReynolds
Concurring opinion: Taft (Brandeis)

Curtis Publishing Company sold its products to retailers through an exclusive assortment arrangement, whereby a retailer purchased magazines and other publications for resale from only one distributor. The Federal Trade Commission (FTC) declared that such exclusive dealing arrangements violated the Clayton Act, which forbade practices that decreased the amount of competition in the marketplace.

The Court struck down the FTC's decision and held that the exclusive arrangements did not constitute unfair competitive practices. The FTC did not have the power to determine what is an unfair competitive practice; rather, that was a question for the courts to decide. Administrative agencies make findings of fact; courts make findings of law. Once a court has declared what is an unfair competitive practice, then an administrative agency may apply that law.

See G. Cullom Davis, "The Transformation of the Federal Trade Commission, 1914–1929," *Mississippi Valley Historical Review* 49 (1962): 437.

Moore v. Dempsey

261 U.S. 86 (1923)
Decided: February 19, 1923
Vote: 6 (Taft, McKenna, Holmes, Van Devanter, Brandeis, Butler)
2 (McReynolds, Sutherland)
Opinion of the Court: Holmes
Dissenting opinion: McReynolds (Sutherland)

A white man was killed during a 1919 Arkansas race riot. At trial an all-white jury sentenced six blacks to death and a large number of others to long prison terms. Black witnesses at the trial were whipped until they agreed to say that the black people were guilty. A mob outside the courtroom threatened violence and death if the jury did not convict all of the black defendants. The court had appointed a lawyer to represent the defendants, but the defense attorney did not ask the judge for a change of venue to move the trial to a safer location. In addition, he called no witnesses. The trial lasted forty-five minutes, and the jury took only five minutes to return guilty verdicts for all of the defendants.

The National Association for the Advancement of Colored People (NAACP) then entered the picture and filed writs of habeas corpus for each of the convicted blacks, claiming that the trial violated due process. Habeas corpus was denied for all of the defendants, and the NAACP appealed, claiming that the Due Process Clause of the Fourteenth Amendment required far more than a perfunctory trial.

The Supreme Court granted the writs of habeas corpus, reversed the convictions, and ordered new trials. Justice Holmes noted that the threat of mob violence had dominated the proceedings. Such an atmosphere, he held, amounted to little more than judicially sanctioned lynching, and when state courts could not provide minimal procedural fairness, then the federal courts had a clear duty to "secure to the petitioners their constitutional rights."

The case marked a departure for the Court; hitherto it had avoided taking on an oversight role over state criminal courts. But the mob rule that marked this case and the indifference of local courts to minimum procedural fairness could not be ignored. The decision also vindicated Holmes' dissent in a similar case, ***Frank v. Mangum,*** 237 U.S. 309 (1915).

See Loren Miller, *The Petitioners* (New York: Pantheon, 1966).

Akron, Canton & Youngstown Railway Co. v. United States

Also known as the New England Divisions Case
261 U.S. 184 (1923)
Decided: February 19, 1923
Vote: 8 (Taft, McKenna, Holmes, Van Devanter, McReynolds, Brandeis, Sutherland, Butler)
0
Opinion of the Court: Brandeis

The Transportation Act of 1920 authorized the Interstate Commerce Commission to set division rates, both for passengers and freight, for railroad carriers. The commission was to take into consideration the importance of the public traveling by railroad. The purpose was to set the rates in a way that helped railroad companies that had in effect been nationalized and run under government control during the war and were struggling following the conversion from wartime to a peacetime footing.

Several railroad companies in New England were given larger division rates than railroads in other parts of the country. Some of the disfavored railroads objected. They argued that the act was an unconstitutional violation of the Due Process Clause of the Fifth Amendment because Congress was deciding which railroad companies would succeed and which would fail.

The Court upheld the act. Congress wanted to help the railroad industry grow to meet the transportation and commercial needs of a quickly expanding America. Congress had the power under the Commerce Clause to help out certain firms in an industry as long as it is in interstate commerce. Railroad companies receiving the lower rates had not been deprived of property without due process just because the government gave greater help to other companies. Nothing had been taken away from the railroads who were complaining about the act, and there had been no Fifth Amendment violation.

United States v. Bhagat Singh Thind

261 U.S. 204 (1923)
Decided: February 19, 1923
Vote: 8 (Taft, McKenna, Holmes, Van Devanter, McReynolds, Brandeis, Sutherland, Butler)
0
Opinion of the Court: Sutherland

The Immigration and Naturalization Act of 1870 formally limited naturalization to "free white people." In ***Ozawa v. United States,*** 260 U.S. 178 (1922), decided earlier in the term, the Court unanimously interpreted the act as excluding Japanese immigrants from becoming United States citizens. Bhagat Singh Thind was from India, and he argued that the term "white people" meant "Caucasian." He claimed that he should be allowed to become a citizen because Indians are of the Caucasian race.

The Court ruled that Indians were not white people and therefore could not become U.S. citizens. Justice Sutherland, who also wrote the opinion in *Ozawa,* reasoned that "white people" did not mean "Caucasian," but should be interpreted as to what it would mean to an everyday common man. The common man would not think of an Indian as "white."

Adkins v. Children's Hospital

261 U.S. 525 (1923)
Decided: April 9, 1923
Vote: 5 (McKenna, Van Devanter, McReynolds, Sutherland, Butler)
3 (Taft, Holmes, Sanford)
Opinion of the Court: Sutherland
Dissenting opinion: Taft (Sanford)
Dissenting opinion: Holmes
Did not participate: Brandeis

Progressive legislation fell on judicial hard times in the 1920s, but even some conservatives protested when the majority resurrected the substantive due process doctrine of ***Lochner v. New York,*** 198 U.S. 45 (1905), in *Adkins.* In striking down a federal statute establishing minimum wages for women in the District of Columbia, Justice Sutherland reaffirmed the paramount position of freedom of contract in economic affairs. Freedom, he declared, "is the general rule and restraint the exception; and the exercise of legislative authority to abridge it can be justified only by the existence of exceptional circumstances." Emancipated by the Nineteenth Amendment, women no longer had need for protective laws, but could work for whatever amount they freely chose to contract for, just like men.

The decision shocked the nation for the holding as well as for the reasoning behind it. After ***Muller v. Oregon,*** 208 U.S. 412 (1908), and ***Bunting v. Oregon,*** 243 U.S. 426 (1917), most people assumed that the Court accepted the need to protect certain classes of society through the state's police power. Sutherland ignored a decade of cases and went back to *Lochner;* even in the conservative 1920s, his opinion seemed overly reactionary. He vigorously attacked minimum wage legislation of any sort. Wages constituted the "heart of the contract," and could never be fixed by legislative fiat. Human necessities could never take precedence over economic rights, for "the good of society as a whole cannot be better served than by the preservation of the liberties of its constituent members." In his denunciation of wage legislation, Sutherland went far beyond constitutional arguments and launched into an attack better suited for a legislative assembly than for a judicial chamber, as he denied that such laws helped anyone or that more highly paid women "safeguard their morals more carefully than those who are poorly paid."

Even Chief Justice Taft, who could hardly be described as liberal, could not swallow this, and he registered one of the twenty dissents he filed during his decade on the Court. He conceded that people differed over the efficacy of minimum wage legislation, but in as strong a statement of judicial restraint as Holmes or Brandeis ever delivered, Taft argued that "it is not the function of the Court to hold congressional acts invalid simply because they are passed to carry out economic views which the Court believes to be unwise or unsound." Holmes agreed with Taft and added a few pithy comments in a dissent of his own. He deplored the fact that liberty of contract, which had started out as an "innocuous generality," had now become dogma. As for Sutherland's claim that women's suffrage had ended the need for special legislation, Holmes observed that "it will need more than the Nineteenth Amendment to convince me that there is no difference between women and men." Brandeis took no part in the 5–3 decision because his daughter Elizabeth served on the District of Columbia Minimum Wage Board.

See Joel F. Paschal, *Mr. Justice Sutherland: A Man Against the State* (Princeton: Princeton University Press, 1951); and Robert C. Post, "Defending the Lifeworld: Substantive Due Process in the Taft Court Era," *Boston University Law Review* 76 (1998): 1489.

Southwestern Bell Telephone Co. v. Public Services Commission of Missouri

262 U.S. 276 (1922)
Decided: May 21, 1923
Vote: 7 (Taft, McKenna, Van Devanter, McReynolds, Sutherland, Butler, Sanford)
2 (Holmes, Brandeis)
Opinion of the Court: McReynolds
Dissenting opinion: Brandeis (Holmes)

When the Court upheld public regulation of utilities during the first decade of the twentieth century, it also decreed that a company had a constitutionally protected right to a fair return on its property. Although few economists agreed on what constituted the best way to determine the value of property, the Court insisted that the rate-making commissions use a formula based on current or replacement value of the property. Current value, however, often proved difficult to determine as compared to original costs, which could be accurately ascertained. In *Southwestern Bell,* Justice McReynolds charged that the Public Services Commission had not allowed for a fair return on invested capital because it had been negligent in assessing the current value of the property. The case demonstrated how a determined company could eviscerate state rate-making agencies by constant appeals to sympathetic courts, claiming that valuations had been incorrectly determined.

Although he agreed that in this case the rates had been too low, Justice Brandeis entered a separate opinion that attacked current valuation as the criterion for return. He noted that prices fluctuated from year to year, making it impossible to establish any fixed amount on which to base a reliable rate schedule. As soon as a commission had completed the lengthy process of determining replacement costs, the companies could appeal on grounds that prices had changed. The current value system might make some sense legally, but it made no sense economically.

Brandeis did not simply attack the current system, but proposed an alternative, the so-called "prudent investment principle," which defined a fair return as equivalent to the rate that a prudent investor could earn on conservative investments. Although the system had its own initial complexities, its benefit was that once value had been ascertained and the methods and standards approved, the courts could withdraw from the regulatory procedure, leaving the administrative agencies free to do their work. In the 1920s Brandeis's proposal received little interest from his fellow justices or from businesses owners who believed that courts would give them a more sympathetic hearing than regulatory agencies. Eventually, however, Brandeis's arguments against courts regulating public utilities bore fruit, and in the 1930s the judiciary withdrew from the rate-making business, although not every state and court adopted the prudent investment scheme.

See Lawrence P. Simpson, "Development of Public Utility Rate Valuation," *Alabama Law Journal* 5 (1930): 195.

Meyer v. Nebraska

262 U.S. 390 (1923)
Decided: June 4, 1923
Vote: 7 (Taft, McKenna, Van Devanter, McReynolds, Brandeis, Butler, Sanford)
2 (Holmes, Sutherland). The dissent is found in the companion case, *Bartels v. State of Iowa,* 262 U.S. 404 (1923).
Opinion of the Court: McReynolds
Dissenting without opinion: Holmes, Sutherland

In his dissent in ***Gilbert v. Minnesota,*** 254 U.S. 325 (1920), Justice Brandeis argued that the liberty guaranteed by the Fourteenth Amendment went beyond property rights to include personal freedoms. The first fruits of that dissent appeared when the Court struck down a state statute, passed during the anti-alien hysteria of 1919, that forbade the teaching of modern languages other than English to children who had not passed the eighth grade. Meyer taught in a parochial school and used a German bible history as a text for teaching. In *Meyer,* Justice McReynolds applied the doctrine of ***Lochner v. New York,*** 198 U.S. 45 (1905), declaring that liberty denotes:

> not merely freedom from bodily restraint but also the right of the individual to contract, to engage in any of the common occupations of life, to acquire useful knowledge, to marry, to establish a home and bring up children, to worship God according to the dictates of his own conscience, and generally to enjoy those privileges long recognized at common law as essential to the orderly pursuit of happiness by free men.

To be sure, McReynolds found property rights involved in the case because the Nebraska law "materially" interfered "with the calling of modern language teachers." But he also found the measure a violation of free speech. The goal of the legislature to foster "a homogeneous people with American ideals" was understandable in light of the recent war, but now "peace and domestic tranquility" reigned, and McReynolds could find no adequate justification for the restraints on liberty. Without using the exact words, McReynolds in effect applied the clear and present danger test and found the statute lacking.

In a companion case, *Bartels v. State of Iowa,* 262 U.S. 404 (1923), Justice Holmes entered a dissent based on judicial restraint. He saw nothing wrong with the ideal that all citizens of the United States should speak a common tongue, and therefore the Nebraska experiment was reasonable and not an infringement on Fourteenth Amendment rights.

Meyer remained a relatively unknown case for forty years until it resurfaced in the 1960s as a doctrinal precedent for a constitutional right of privacy.

See Orville H. Zabel, *God and Caesar in Nebraska: A Study of the Legal Relationship of Church and State, 1854–1954* (Lincoln, Neb.: The University, 1955); and William G. Ross, *Forging New Freedoms: Nativism, Education and the Constitution, 1917–1927* (Lincoln: University of Nebraska Press, 1994).

Massachusetts v. Mellon

262 U.S. 447 (1923)
Decided: June 4, 1923
Vote: 9 (Taft, McKenna, Holmes, Van Devanter, McReynolds, Brandeis, Sutherland, Butler, Sanford)
0
Opinion of the Court: Sutherland

In 1921 Congress passed the Sheppard-Towner Maternity Act, which provided federal funds to states to reduce infant mortality rates by providing health care to pregnant women and infants. The conditions of the law applied only to states that chose to accept the grants.

Massachusetts argued that the act was unconstitutional because by its terms the federal government usurped local maternity laws and involved itself in an area that had traditionally been state responsibility. It asked the Court to enjoin the enforcement of the act and to protect its citizens from an unconstitutional enactment.

Massachusetts v. Mellon was argued and decided with *Frothingham v. Mellon.* Harriet Frothingham, a taxpayer, argued that the act was unconstitutional because it spent her tax dollars on programs she did not like. Tax dollars spent in such a way, she claimed, deprived her of her property in violation the Due Process Clause of the Fifth Amendment.

The Court denied both suits. The federal government had not encroached on states' rights, but through a matching funds program had given states an opportunity to join in the program. If Massachusetts did not wish to join, nothing in the law required it to do so.

As for Frothingham, the Court held that a taxpayer did not have standing to sue the government over its spending decisions. Of all the tax revenue the government receives, the percentage of that amount that is paid by a single taxpayer is so incredibly small that it would be impossible to determine damages. As such, the damages to the taxpayer are so minuscule that she did not have standing to sue.

Although the rule—that a taxpayer cannot challenge government spending decisions—still stands, the Court has from time to time ignored it when it wanted to hear certain issues, as in ***United States v. Butler,*** 297 U.S. 1 (1936).

Wolff Packing Co. v. Court of Industrial Relations

262 U.S. 522 (1923)
Decided: June 11, 1923
Vote: 9 (Taft, McKenna, Holmes, Van Devanter, McReynolds, Brandeis, Sutherland, Butler, Sanford)
0
Opinion of the Court: Taft

In ***Adkins v. Children's Hospital,*** 261 U.S. 525 (1923), Justice Sutherland conceded four types of laws under which courts would accept restraints on contractual freedom: (1) statutes relating to contracts for work on public projects; (2) statutes prescribing the character, time, and method of wage payments; (3) statutes relating to fixing the hours of labor; and (4) statutes relating to rates charged by businesses affected with the public interest. Reformers saw very little flexibility in the first three categories, but hoped that an expansive view of the fourth would permit some experimentation by the states. They soon learned differently.

After World War I Kansas embarked on a major experiment in molding law to meet current needs. In 1920 it passed the Industrial Relations Act requiring arbitration of all disputes in crucial industries such as food, clothing, and shelter, and it created a special industrial court to handle the arbitration. The act also gave the court powers to enforce its decisions, including the authority to set wages and control working conditions. In the *Wolff* case, Chief Justice Taft destroyed the industrial court by ruling the act unconstitutional and putting forward a narrow view of business affected with a public interest. A mere declaration by a state that a business is affected with a public interest did not make it so, and the state could not use that rationalization to interfere with property rights.

Taft listed the only businesses that could be so characterized: public utilities, which were carried on by a public license; traditional businesses long recognized as subject to regulation, such as inns and gristmills; businesses where natural economic laws did not operate, such as monopolies; and businesses whose nature had changed so much as to warrant some government regulation. For all practical purposes, Taft apparently negated a half-century of legal development since ***Munn v. Illinois,*** 94 U.S. 113 (1877), and put nearly all businesses outside the reach of state regulation. The distinction between public and private, an important element of classic thought, might have faded in stream of commerce cases, but Taft and the conservatives here reminded the nation that they intended to view that as an exception rather than as the rule.

See Barry Cushman, *Rethinking the New Deal Court: The Structure of a Constitutional Revolution* (New York: Oxford University Press, 1998).

United States ex. rel. Bilokumsky v. Tod

263 U.S. 149 (1923)
Decided: November 12, 1923
Vote: 9 (Taft, McKenna, Holmes, Van Devanter, McReynolds, Brandeis, Sutherland, Butler, Sanford)
0
Opinion of the Court: Brandeis

Bilokumsky was arrested for possession and distributing papers urging the overthrow of the U.S. government by force or violence. After his arrest, federal officials discovered that he was not a citizen and decided to deport him. Bilokumsky filed for a writ of habeas corpus, which was denied, and he then appealed to the Supreme Court. He argued that the government could not deport him because there was no evidence that he was an alien, although he never claimed to be or provided proof that he was an American citizen. He also argued that the way his papers had been seized was illegal and that evidence gathered in violation of the Fourth Amendment should not be admitted at his trial.

The Court held that the evidence proving Bilokumsky was an alien was sufficient and therefore he could be deported. Because he never claimed that he was an American citizen, had never produced any evidence proving his citizenship, and had remained silent when questioned about his citizenship, it could properly be inferred that he was not an American citizen, but an alien.

Dayton-Goose Creek Railway Co. v. United States

263 U.S. 456 (1924)
Decided: January 7, 1924
Vote: 9 (Taft, McKenna, Holmes, Van Devanter, McReynolds, Brandeis, Sutherland, Butler, Sanford)
0
Opinion of the Court: Taft

During World War I the nation's railroads had been taken over by the government and run as a single unified system. The Transportation Act of 1920 restored the nation's railroads to private control and expanded the authority of the Interstate Commerce Commission. In the law was a recapture provision that required setting aside a reserve fund from railroad earnings over and above a fair return. These recaptured funds were distributed to keep less-productive lines in business. The measure in effect treated all the lines as the unified system they had been during the war. Although some sectors were more profitable than others, the public interest required that the less-profitable roads be kept in operation. Dayton-Goose Creek Railway Company argued that the recapture provision was unconstitutional and that Congress lacked the authority under the Commerce Clause to impose such a plan.

Chief Justice Taft denied that a public service industry had any constitutional right to more than a fair return on its property. To the argument that the recaptured profits constituted a taking without due process, Taft replied that because the roads had never been entitled to income above the fair return, they had never owned that revenue, and therefore it had not been taken from them.

Radice v. New York

264 U.S. 292 (1924)
Decided: March 10, 1924
Vote: 9 (Taft, McKenna, Holmes, Van Devanter, McReynolds, Brandeis, Sutherland, Butler, Sanford)
0
Opinion of the Court: Sutherland

New York State had a law that prohibited restaurants in certain cities from having women work between 10:00 p.m. and 6:00 a.m. Radice, the owner of a restaurant in Buffalo, was charged with violating this law. He argued that the law was unconstitutional on two grounds: it violated the Due Process Clause of the Fourteenth Amendment by depriving him and his employees of the liberty to contract and it violated the Equal Protection Clause by arbitrarily classifying women as people who cannot work night shifts.

The Court upheld the law. First, it ruled that there was no due process violation of the liberty to contract because women are "more delicate" creatures than men. Women do not have the strength to work these hours, particularly in cities where the nightlife is more rowdy than in other areas. Second, the Court ruled there was no equal protection violation because classifying women as a group is not an arbitrary classification. Moreover, if there is a reasonable purpose behind classifying women, such as for protection, then it is constitutional. The Court here continued its practice of classifying women as persons under a disability (being the weaker sex) and therefore subject to the police power protection of the state.

See Judith Baer, *The Chains of Protection* (Westport, Conn.: Greenwood Press, 1978).

Jay Burns Baking Co. v. Bryan

264 U.S. 504 (1924)
Decided: April 14, 1924
Vote: 7 (Taft, McKenna, Van Devanter, McReynolds, Sutherland, Butler, Sanford)
2 (Holmes, Brandeis)
Opinion of the Court: Butler
Dissenting opinion: Brandeis (Holmes)

A 1921 Nebraska law regulated the weight of loaves of bread sold at retail. The state's purposes were to make it easier for customers to understand the sizes and prices of bread they were buying, to prevent "short weights" (bread sold as a loaf that was lighter in weight because of air), and to protect honest bakers from unfair competition. Jay Burns Baking Company argued that the law was arbitrary and was not needed to protect consumers from bakers, and that it violated their property rights under the Due Process Clause.

The Court held that there was no reason for Nebraska to pass such a law. Regulating weights and measures of bread was unreasonable and arbitrary because customers did not need this kind of protection.

Justice Brandeis entered a lengthy dissent, full of facts and figures on the baking industry, in an effort to show that the law was neither unreasonable nor arbitrary.

The case is part of a string of decisions during the 1920s in which a conservative court continued to oppose reform measures that regulated business.

Carroll v. United States

267 U.S. 132 (1925)
Decided: March 2, 1925
Vote: 7 (Taft, McKenna, Holmes, Van Devanter, Brandeis, Butler, Sanford)
2 (McReynolds, Sutherland)
Opinion of the Court: Taft
Concurring without opinion: McKenna
Dissenting opinion: McReynolds (Sutherland)

During Prohibition, bootleggers applied the latest technology to their efforts to give a thirsty citizenry what it wanted. They used a relatively new invention, the automobile, to run illegal liquor into the United States from Canada or from rural stills into the cities. In December 1921 federal agents stopped a car outside Detroit, which because of its proximity to Ontario, Canada, had become a major entrepot for imported liquor. The agents searched the car without a warrant and found sixty-eight quarts of whiskey and gin behind the upholstery. After conviction for violation of the Volstead Act, the defendants appealed to the Supreme Court, claiming that their Fourth Amendment rights had been violated.

The Court upheld the conviction. Chief Justice Taft found the search reasonable because the agents had probable cause: the defendants, all suspected of previous bootlegging operations, had been traveling on a road frequently used by smugglers. Because of time constraints, the officers had been unable to get a warrant; had they applied for one, the car would have been gone by the time it arrived. With this case, the Court carved the automobile exception out of the Fourth Amendment's requirement that no search or seizure take place without a warrant. Where a warrant could be reasonably secured, Taft urged that it should be; otherwise, police did not need warrants to stop and search automobiles. The decision generated a strong albeit confusing dissent from Justice McReynolds, as well as much criticism from legal scholars. The car exception and variants upon it would come back before the Court for further exposition over the next half-century, but the *Carroll* doctrine is still the law.

See Forrest R. Black, "A Critique of the Carroll Case," *Columbia Law Review* 29 (1929): 1068.

Coronado Coal Co. v. United Mine Workers

268 U.S. 295 (1925)
Decided: May 25, 1925
Vote: 9 (Taft, Holmes, Van Devanter, McReynolds, Brandeis, Sutherland, Butler, Sanford, Stone)
0
Opinion of the Court: Taft

Coronado Coal Company sued the International Union of United Mine Workers of America (UMWA) for damages after a local union chapter purposely destroyed mining equipment and other company property. The workers intended to inhibit Coronado's ability to engage in trading coal in interstate commerce, and they armed themselves with guns and used dynamite to blow up shipments of coal, attacked security guards, and assaulted nonunion employees. Antitrust law clearly prohibits such actions, but could the UMWA be held responsible for the actions of a local chapter?

The Court held that the UMWA was not liable for the actions of its local chapter. A corporation is liable for the actions of its employees if they are acting in the normal course of business, and the same rule of agency also applies to unions. In this case, however, it was highly doubtful that the activities of the local chapter in arming themselves, attacking people, and blowing things up was part of the work of the UMWA as a whole. The parent union could not be held liable, but the local chapter and those individuals involved would be.

Toyota v. United States

268 U.S. 402 (1925)
Decided: May 25, 1925
Vote: 8 (Holmes, Van Devanter, McReynolds, Brandeis, Sutherland, Butler, Sanford, Stone)
1 (Taft)
Opinion of the Court: Butler
Dissenting without opinion: Taft

Hidemitsu Toyota was born in Japan, came to the United States in 1913, and served in the Coast Guard and the Navy during World War I. In 1921 he tried to become a naturalized U.S. citizen, but federal naturalization law permitted only "free white persons" to be eligible to apply for citizenship.

This issue had been before the Court before in ***Ozawa v. United States,*** 260 U.S. 178 (1922), and the Court here reaffirmed its earlier ruling that under existing law a native-born Japanese person could not become a naturalized citizen. No native-born Asian, Butler explained, could become a citizen, except for Filipinos because the United States owned the Philippines.

Frick v. Pennsylvania

268 U.S. 473 (1925)
Decided: June 1, 1925
Vote: 9 (Taft, Holmes, Van Devanter, McReynolds, Brandeis, Sutherland, Butler, Sanford, Stone)
0
Opinion of the Court: Van Devanter

Henry Clay Frick died in 1919 and by the terms of his will gave his estate, worth well over $100 million, to charities and to his family. He had property in Pennsylvania as well as in New York and Massachusetts. Pennsylvania charged a 2 percent estate tax on the transfer of property at the time of death and included the transfer of any property in other states into the taxable amount. In this case Frick's property in New York and Massachusetts would be included to compute the tax. Frick's widow argued that for a state to impose an estate tax on property outside of its jurisdiction was a violation of due process.

The Court agreed with her argument. It held that a state has the power to impose an estate tax on anything within its own jurisdiction, even property that is owned by someone not from that state, but the reach of its tax power goes only to its own borders.

Pierce v. Society of Sisters

268 U.S. 510 (1925)
Decided: June 1, 1925
Vote: 9 (Taft, Holmes, Van Devanter, McReynolds, Brandeis, Sutherland, Butler, Sanford, Stone)
0
Opinion of the Court: McReynolds

In 1922 Oregon voters approved an initiative requiring parents to send all children between the ages of eight and sixteen to public schools. The initiative developed from the world war and postwar prejudice against aliens as well as from a strong vein of anti-Catholicism. The drive had been organized by the Ku Klux Klan and the Scottish Rite Masons, and its aim was to close down the state's Catholic schools.

A federal district court ruled that the Oregon initiative violated the Fourteenth Amendment's Due Process Clause and issued an injunction preventing the state from enforcing the law. On appeal, the Supreme Court affirmed. Justice McReynolds used the same principles he had earlier enunciated in ***Meyer v. Nebraska,*** 262 U.S. 390 (1923).The statute, he held, interfered with the liberty of parents and guardians to control the education of their children, and it also interfered with the property interests vested in the private schools. The state had the power to require that children attend school and to regulate public and private schools to ensure that subjects necessary to good citizenship be taught, but it could not arbitrarily put one set of schools off limit. Parents, according to McReynolds, had a constitutional right to choose between public and private schools.

Some subsequent courts have tried to read a free exercise basis into the McReynolds decision. It is not there. Instead, what is there is the doctrine of substantive due process protecting the property rights of the school owners and the rights of parents to control their children's education. Even though the notion of substantive due process was repudiated after the constitutional crisis of 1937, when Franklin Roosevelt attempted to pack the Supreme Court, *Pierce* has never been overruled, and it is generally considered one of the major cases in the Court's initial efforts to expand the rights protected by the Fourteenth Amendment.

See William G. Ross, *Forging New Freedoms: Nativism, Education and the Constitution, 1917–1927* (Lincoln: University of Nebraska Press, 1994); and David B. Tyack, "The Perils of Pluralism: The Background of the Pierce Case," *American Historical Review* 74 (1968): 74.

Gitlow v. New York

268 U.S. 652 (1925)
Decided: June 8, 1925
Vote: 7 (Taft, Van Devanter, McReynolds, Sutherland, Butler, Sanford, Stone)
2 (Holmes, Brandeis)
Opinion of the Court: Sanford
Dissenting opinion: Holmes (Brandeis)

Gitlow posed a challenge to New York's 1902 Criminal Anarchy Act. Benjamin Gitlow, a leading figure in the American Communist Party, was convicted for publishing a radical newspaper, the "Left-Wing Manifesto," and other allegedly subversive materials. If Fourteenth Amendment liberty reached as far as Justice McReynolds had suggested in ***Meyer v. Nebraska,*** 262 U.S. 390 (1923), and ***Pierce v. Society of Sisters,*** 268 U.S. 510 (1925), then surely it would include the protection of the press and speech. Although the Court affirmed the conviction, Justice Sanford agreed with this argument. "For present purposes we may and do assume that freedom of speech and of the press—which are protected by the First Amendment from abridgement by Congress—are among the fundamental personal rights protected by the due process clause of the Fourteenth Amendment from impairment by the States." With this statement, the Supreme Court for the first time put forward what came to be known as the doctrine of incorporation, by which the Fourteenth Amendment "incorporated" the liberties protected in the Bill of Rights and applied them to the states.

Debate has continued ever since over whether the writers of the Fourteenth Amendment intended to extend the Bill of Rights to the states, with historical evidence marshaled on both sides of the argument. The weight of the evidence supports the claim that the drafters wanted to extend and protect the rights of the new freedmen and to apply the Bill of Rights to the states. The "original intent" argument, however, is somewhat sterile, given the subsequent perversion of the Civil War Amendments in the retreat from Reconstruction. Justice Brandeis was certainly correct in his claim that due process had to include more than just protection of property, and he could refer to the older English idea of the "law of the land," which went way beyond the rights of property. That notion, which derives from a phrase in the Magna Carta, refers to the legal customs of the people, which subsume accepted rights as well as procedures spelled out either by statute or common law.

Sanford did not explore the full extent of this theoretical argument in his *Gitlow* opinion; in fact, he concluded that the state could limit Gitlow's speech in this instance. The New York statute was a legitimate response to a perceived threat, and although he accepted the clear and present danger test, Sanford interpreted it as more restrictive of speech rather than less. As Justice Holmes had refined the test in ***Abrams v. United States,*** 250 U.S. 616 (1919), the rule applied to speech that directly caused bad acts; the New York law, however, aimed not at the deed but at the evil words themselves, which might, or might not, incite action. Sanford's ruling meant that words could now be punished for their bad nature regardless of whether they caused particular acts. The legislature could brand certain ideas and sentiments dangerous to society and outlaw their dissemination.

Holmes entered a brief opinion agreeing with the Court's application of the First Amendment to the states, but dissenting from the majority's ruling that words separated from action could be punished. "It is said," he wrote, "that this manifesto was more than a theory, that it was an incitement. Every idea is an incitement. . . . Eloquence may set fire to reason. But . . . the only meaning of free speech is that [beliefs] should be given their chance and have their way." Holmes implied that a mere statement of an idea, no matter how objectionable the sentiment, should never be punished, but he did not directly confront the question of whether a legislature could judge some ideas so dangerous as to warrant criminal sanctions for their mere utterance, a position that his advocacy of deference to legislative discretion might have commanded.

See Charles Warren, "The New 'Liberty' Under the Fourteenth Amendment," *Harvard Law Review* 39 (1926): 431; and Richard C. Cortner, *The Supreme Court and the Second Bill of Rights: The Fourteenth Amendment and the Nationalization of Civil Liberties* (Madison: University of Wisconsin Press, 1981).

Corrigan v. Buckley

271 U.S. 323 (1926)
Decided: May 24, 1926
Vote: 9 (Taft, Holmes, Van Devanter, McReynolds, Brandeis, Sutherland, Butler, Sanford, Stone)
0
Opinion of the Court: Sanford

Irene Corrigan and thirty other white people owned some parcels of land in Washington, D.C. They made a covenant that no black people should live on the land for at least twenty-one years. Corrigan, however, later sold a parcel of the land to Helen Curtis, a black woman. John J. Buckley went to court to enforce the covenant, but Curtis argued that the covenant was unconstitutional because it violated the Fifth, Thirteenth, and Fourteenth Amendments. She claimed that the private covenant deprived her of property without due process of law, that refusing to sell property to black people was indicia of slavery, and that it violated equal protection of the laws guaranteed under the Fourteenth Amendment.

The Court unanimously upheld the covenant. It reasoned that the Fifth, Thirteenth, and Fourteenth Amendments applied only to government actions, not to private contracts. The covenant was a private agreement and, as such, could discriminate against persons based upon race.

The decision stood until 1948 when the Court in ***Shelley v. Kraemer,*** 334 U.S. 1, found that court enforcement of racially discriminatory private agreements, such as property covenants, constituted state action. Thus, one might have a discriminatory covenant, but it could no longer be enforced by the state.

See Clement E. Vose, *Caucasians Only: The Supreme Court, the NAACP, and the Restrictive Covenant Cases* (Berkeley: University of California Press, 1959).

Myers v. United States

272 U.S. 52 (1926)
Decided: October 25, 1926
Vote: 6 (Taft, Van Devanter, Sutherland, Butler, Sanford, Stone)
3 (Holmes, McReynolds, Brandeis)
Opinion of the Court: Taft
Dissenting opinion: Holmes
Dissenting opinion: McReynolds
Dissenting opinion: Brandeis

In order to prevent President Johnson from removing any government officials appointed by President Lincoln from office, Congress in 1876 passed the Tenure in Office Act. This law required the president to get the Senate's approval to fire certain appointed officials, including postmasters.

In 1920 President Wilson removed Frank S. Myers, the postmaster of Oregon, without the consent of the Senate. Myers died a little while later, and his estate then sued for damages and lost wages, claiming that under the Reconstruction-Era law, Wilson had to get the Senate's approval before dismissing him. Myers's appeal gave the Court its first opportunity to review the validity of a fifty-year-old law and determine whether Congress could limit the president's power to remove appointed officials.

The Court held that Congress cannot limit this power. Chief Justice Taft, himself a former president, wrote an opinion giving the chief executive broad powers, especially in the removal of appointed officials from office, a power that was not limited by the need for Senate approval.

The case was reversed nine years later in ***Humphrey's Executor v. United States,*** 295 U.S. 602 (1935).

Village of Euclid, Ohio v. Ambler Realty Co.

272 U.S. 365 (1926)
Decided: November 22, 1926
Vote: 6 (Taft, Holmes, Brandeis, Sutherland, Sanford, Stone)
3 (Van Devanter, McReynolds, Butler)
Opinion of the Court: Sutherland
Dissenting without opinion: Van Devanter, McReynolds, Butler

No case better illustrates the conflicted rulings of the Taft Court than one involving zoning for land use. Among conservatives, property enjoyed a near sacred status, and the core of substantive due process was the almost unlimited right of an owner to use and dispose of property. In 1917 the Court in ***Buchanan v. Warley,*** 245 U.S. 60, struck down a local ordinance prohibiting blacks from living in certain areas but had done so, not on equal protection grounds, but because the rule deprived people of their right to buy and sell property.

During the first quarter of the twentieth century many municipalities enacted comprehensive land use or zoning plans in an effort to manage growth and preserve the aesthetic nature of the community. The codes varied, but nearly all of them included some limits on land use in certain areas and placed limits on the type and size of buildings that could be erected. A commercial establishment, for example, could not be built in an area designated for residential use. Land owners and developers challenged these codes on a variety of constitutional grounds, but state courts disagreed on their legitimacy. In 1926 the challenge to the Village of Euclid's zoning ordinance reached the Supreme Court.

Ambler Realty owned a parcel of 68 acres in Euclid, a suburb of Cleveland, and intended to develop it for industrial purposes. Most of the land had a U-6 designation, which allowed for commercial development, but some parts had different ratings that restricted use and thus made the property less valuable for Ambler's purposes. Ambler sued in district court on due process, equal protection, and taking grounds and won. The village appealed to the Supreme Court, which by a 6–3 vote reversed and held the zoning ordinance constitutional.

Justice Sutherland, who had written the highly conservative decision in ***Adkins v. Children's Hospital,*** 261 U.S. 525 (1923), wrote the majority opinion in *Village of Euclid.* Sutherland had been absent during oral argument and apparently doubted the ordinance's constitutionality. Justice Stone convinced him to rethink the case. The Court ordered the case re-argued. This time Sutherland was present, and he abandoned the conservative block to uphold the law. Sutherland's opinion describes the zoning act not as a deprivation of property but as an enhancement. Common law had long allowed for the abatement of nuisances even if doing so restricted property rights because all adjoining property would increase in value. The fact that Euclid was undergoing rapid expansion could not be denied, and overcrowding as well as chaotic development would be harmful to all property owners. Sutherland also may have been influenced by the fact that when Ambler bought the property the zoning ordinance was already in effect, and this undermined the company's claim that its property had been taken without due process; he might have thought differently had the ordinance been passed *after* Ambler had purchased the land.

The opinion cleared the way for more extensive zoning rules throughout the nation. In the 1990s the Supreme Court returned to reexamine the limits, if any, on the police power as expressed in land regulation.

See Michael Allan Wolf, " 'Compelled by Conscientious Duty': *Village of Euclid v. Ambler Realty Co.* as Romance," *Journal of Supreme Court History* (1977): 88.

Virginia Railway Co. v. United States

272 U.S. 658 (1926)
Decided: December 13, 1926
Vote: 9 (Taft, Holmes, Van Devanter, McReynolds, Brandeis, Sutherland, Butler, Sanford, Stone)
0
Opinion of the Court: Brandeis

A particular coal-mining area of West Virginia was served by three railroad companies. Limited to these roads, the mines in this region could ship their coal only to certain locations. The mine operators wanted to ship to western markets, but the railroads did not go there. The mines complained to the Interstate Commerce Commission (ICC) that the rates they were being charged were outrageous and unfair and that they were discriminated against because there were no competing carriers that could take their coal to other markets. Other coal mines in neighboring areas, which were served by other rail lines, could ship their coal west, and at a lower cost. The ICC investigated and found the complaints valid; it then made the three railroad companies lower their rates. The railroads went to court, claiming that the ICC lacked the power to require them to lower their rates.

The Court upheld the commission's decision, ruling that the ICC could make such a decision concerning carriers in interstate commerce if substantial evidence supported the decision. In this case, the evidence showed that the three railroads discriminated against the West Virginia coal mines and charged them unfair rates. Given this proof, the ICC had the authority to force lower rates.

Tyson & Brother v. Banton

273 U.S. 418 (1927)
Decided: February 28, 1927
Vote: 5 (Taft, Van Devanter, McReynolds, Sutherland, Butler)
4 (Holmes, Brandeis, Stone, Sanford)
Opinion of the Court: Sutherland
Dissenting opinion: Holmes (Brandeis)
Dissenting opinion: Stone (Holmes, Brandeis)
Dissenting opinion: Sanford

The Tyson brothers were licensed ticket brokers doing business as United Theatre Ticket Offices, which resold tickets for entertainment venues at fifty cents above the retail price. New York had a law that fixed commissions on resold tickets and attempted to revoke the Tysons' license. In defending the law, New York invoked a public policy argument that theaters are of public interest and that prices and commissions could be regulated. See ***Munn v. Illinois,*** 94 U.S. 113 (1877). The Tysons in turn argued that the law violated the liberty to contract protected by the Due Process Clause of the Fourteenth Amendment.

The Court found that theaters had no public interest that could justify the state imposing price controls on either the tickets or on commissions for resale. The law violated the Fourteenth Amendment in that it interfered with the liberty to contract between resellers and customers. For a state to regulate the freedom to contract, there must be an important public policy interest, and keeping a limit on resold ticket prices was not important enough to qualify.

See Walton H. Hamilton, "Affectation with a Public Interest," *Yale Law Review* 39 (1930): 1089.

Nixon v. Herndon

273 U.S. 536 (1927)
Decided: March 7, 1927
Vote: 9 (Taft, Holmes, Van Devanter, McReynolds, Brandeis, Sutherland, Butler, Sanford, Stone)
0
Opinion of the Court: Holmes

Following the collapse of Reconstruction and Republican rule in the South, one-party government dominated all of the former confederate states. As a result, whoever won the Democratic primary in effect won the office. As part of the drive to keep blacks from voting, state legislatures enacted laws to prevent blacks from voting in the Democratic primary, the one election that counted. Dr. Lawrence Nixon, a black man from El Paso, challenged the Texas white primary law as a violation of the Fourteenth and Fifteenth Amendments.

Although both sides focused their arguments on Fifteenth Amendment issues, the Court found it unnecessary to discuss it. The Court held that the Texas law violated the Equal Protection Clause of the Fourteenth Amendment. Holmes's brief opinion assumed that the writers of the Fourteenth Amendment had intended it to apply to voting, but the historical record does not justify such an assumption. In fact, in a prior decision, ***Minor v. Happersett,*** 88 U.S. 162 (1875), the Court held that the Equal Protection Clause did not apply to voting.

Nixon v. Herndon was not the last word on white primaries in the South. After this decision, southern states declared the Democratic Party to be a private organization and therefore immune from constitutional limitations on whom it would allow to vote. Finally, in ***Smith v. Allwright,*** 321 U.S. 649 (1944), the Court, relying on the Fifteenth Amendment, outlawed white primaries altogether.

See Darlene Clark Hine, *Black Victory: The Rise and Fall of the White Primary in Texas* (Millwood, N.Y.: KTO, 1979).

Bedford Cut Stone Co. v. Journeymen Stone Cutters Association

274 U.S. 37 (1927)
Decided: April 11, 1927
Vote: 7 (Taft, Van Devanter, McReynolds, Sutherland, Butler, Sanford, Stone)
2 (Holmes, Brandeis)
Opinion of the Court: Sutherland
Concurring opinion: Sanford
Concurring opinion: Stone
Dissenting opinion: Brandeis (Holmes)

Labor's supposed protection under the Clayton Act suffered serious erosion in the 1920s. In ***Coronado Coal Co. v. United Mine Workers,*** 268 U.S. 295 (1925), Chief Justice Taft ruled that coal mining itself did not constitute interstate commerce. A strike, as the simple withholding of labor, could therefore not be enjoined under the Clayton Act. But a strike that aimed at stopping the interstate shipment of nonunion coal certainly fell within the proscriptions of the Sherman Act. Therefore, any labor activity that had the intent, and not just an incidental result, of interfering with interstate commerce violated the antitrust laws. Two years later, in *Bedford Cut Stone,* the Court again showed how it would manipulate definitions to restrict labor.

In conformity with their union's constitution, a handful of stonecutters refused to work on limestone cut by nonunion workers in the unorganized Bedford Cut Stone Company. The company sought an injunction, but to enjoin the strikers, the lower court had to rely on the Sherman Act's restriction on secondary boycotts. The Supreme Court agreed with this approach and then justified it by turning a local and limited strike into a burden on the stream of interstate commerce. The difference between the Court's decision in the child labor cases—***Hammer v. Dagenhart,*** 247 U.S. 251 (1918), and ***Bailey v. Drexel Furniture Co.,*** 259 U.S. 20 (1922), where it had taken a narrow view of commerce, and *Bedford,* where it all but obliterated any distinction between local and national commerce, could hardly be missed. Reasonable restrictions on trade caused by industry would be tolerated by the Court under the rule of reason; but the bench would disregard its own rule when asked to apply it to the clearly reasonable activities of a labor union. What is noteworthy here is not necessarily the Court's logic. In the 1940s the Court took a similar view of commerce to *justify* state intervention. But the later Court was at least consistent, applying the same definition of commerce to industry, agriculture, and labor.

Until the Supreme Court handed down these decisions, lower federal courts had shown a marked diversity in how they interpreted the labor provisions of the Clayton Act and the validity of injunctions in labor disputes. The Taft Court rulings in effect told federal judges to issue as many injunctions as they wanted, that for all practical purposes the Clayton Act labor exemptions meant nothing. Moreover, even when antilabor judges went too far, the Supreme Court could offer organized labor little relief. By the time the Court heard an appeal against an overly broad injunction, so much time had passed that the restraining order had already served its purpose. In one instance, four years passed between the time a federal judge issued an injunction and the Court overturned it. The case was *United Leather Workers v. Herkert & Meisal et al.,* 265 U.S. 457 (1924).

See Daniel R. Ernst, *Lawyers Against Labor: From Individual Rights to Corporate Liberalism* (Urbana: University of Illinois Press, 1995); and Christopher L. Tomlins, *The State and the Unions: Labor Relations, Law and the Organized Labor Movement in America, 1880–1960* (New York: Cambridge University Press,1985).

Buck v. Bell

274 U.S. 200 (1927)
Decided: May 2, 1927
Vote: 8 (Taft, Holmes, Van Devanter, McReynolds, Brandeis, Sutherland, Sanford, Stone)
1 (Butler)
Opinion of the Court: Holmes
Dissenting without opinion: Butler

One case from the 1920s that shocks the modern conscience, and displays in full the Taft Court's indifference to individual liberties, dealt not with people of color, aliens, or pacifists, but with a white southern girl, Carrie Buck. The eugenics movement that spread across the United States in the early twentieth century led a number of states to enact involuntary sterilization laws in efforts to "improve" the race. Virginia enacted such a law, but it remained unclear whether it would pass constitutional muster. Albert Priddy, the superintendent of the State Colony for Epileptics and Feeble-Minded at Lynchburg, decided to test the validity of the law, and the person he chose for his test case was eighteen-year-old Carrie Buck.

A victim of rape, Buck was pregnant, and the family with whom she was living committed her to the Lynchburg institution, where a relatively primitive I.Q. test showed her to have the intelligence of a nine-year-old. Buck's mother, Emma, also confined to the colony, tested out at eight years. After Buck gave birth to her daughter, Vivien, Priddy recommended that she be sterilized, began the administrative process, and hired lawyers to test the law in the courts. At the trial the state presented witnesses to prove Buck's feeblemindedness, and one described the Buck family as part of the "shiftless, ignorant, and worthless class of anti-social whites." Young Vivien was described as "not quite normal."

Buck's attorney, paid for by the institution, put on a weak defense. He admitted that he agreed with the sterilization policy. Nevertheless, he carried an appeal to the Supreme Court, offering an equal protection argument. The law, he claimed, discriminated against people confined to institutions and denied them their "full bodily integrity." Justice Holmes, speaking for the Court, dismissed all of these arguments in a short, five-paragraph opinion, three paragraphs of which described the facts of the case. He dismissed the equal protection claim as "the usual last resort of constitutional arguments." He cited only one case in support of the judgment, ***Jacobson v. Massachusetts,*** 197 U.S. 11 (1905), a ruling that upheld compulsory vaccination in Massachusetts. Paying his usual deference to the legislature, Holmes affirmed the judgment and stated his agreement with its policy. "It is better for all the world," he wrote, "if instead of waiting to execute degenerate offspring for crime, or to let them starve for their imbecility, society can prevent those who are manifestly unfit from continuing their kind. . . . Three generations of imbeciles are enough." Only Justice Butler dissented without opinion.

Although Holmes became the darling of the eugenics movement, that movement faded with the rise of Nazism in the 1930s, and the *Buck* case has had a bad odor about it ever since. The worst aspect of it is that years later it turned out that Carrie Buck was not mentally retarded. She had advanced with her class grade by grade in public school until taken out to work in her foster home. Her final report card rated her as "very good—deportment and lessons." In her later years she was active in reading groups and dramatics, and, despite her hard life, a social worker described her as an "alert and pleasant lady." There were no imbeciles at all among the three generations of Buck women.

See William E. Leuchtenburg, "Mr. Justice Holmes and Three Generations of Imbeciles," in *The Supreme Court Reborn: The Constitutional Revolution in the Age of Roosevelt* (New York: Oxford University Press, 1995); and Paul A. Lombardo, "Three Generations: No Imbeciles: New Light on *Buck v. Bell,*" *New York Law Review* 60 (1985): 30.

Whitney v. California

274 U.S. 357 (1927)
Decided: May 26, 1927
Vote: 9 (Taft, Holmes, Van Devanter, McReynolds, Brandeis, Sutherland, Butler, Sanford, Stone)
0
Opinion of the Court: Sanford
Concurring opinion: Brandeis (Holmes)

Charlotte Anita Whitney, a niece of Justice Stephen J. Field and "a woman nearing sixty, a Wellesley graduate long distinguished in philanthropic work," was convicted under the California Criminal Syndicalism Act of 1919 for helping to organize the Communist Labor Party there. Originally aimed at the Industrial Workers of the World, the law made it a felony to organize or knowingly become a member of an organization founded to advocate the commission of crimes, sabotage, or acts of violence as a means of bringing about political or industrial change. Whitney denied that the Communist Labor Party ever intended to become an instrument of crime or violence; nor was there any proof that it had ever engaged in violent acts. Nevertheless, the conservative majority, led by Justice Sanford, upheld the act as a legitimate decision by the California legislature to prevent the violent overthrow of society. The Due Process Clause did not protect one's liberty to destroy the social and political order.

Because of technical issues, Justice Brandeis chose not to dissent, but his concurring opinion provided an eloquent defense of intellectual freedom unmatched in the annals of the Court for its powerful reasoning. The justices in the majority, Justice Brandeis claimed, not only here but also in other speech cases, were operating on a totally inappropriate set of assumptions. They had measured the limits of free speech against potential danger to property, thus ignoring the benefits that free exchange of ideas bestowed on society as a whole. He agreed that under certain circumstances a legislature could limit speech, but the proper test for exercising that power would be if the words posed a clear and imminent danger to *society,* not just to property interests. Suppression of ideas worked a great hardship on society, and before that could be allowed, the Court had the responsibility of developing objective standards, which it had not yet done. Brandeis made it clear that, like Justice Holmes, he did not fear ideas, and Americans need not do so either. In addition, Brandeis set out what would become the basis for First Amendment jurisprudence.

Unlike Holmes, who rested his First Amendment views on the marketplace of ideas, Brandeis saw free speech as an essential aspect of citizenship. Men and women had the duty in a democracy to be good citizens, which meant being informed on the issues confronting them. How could they make intelligent decisions about these matters unless they could hear all sides and join in the debate? The fact that some viewpoints ran against the grain or disturbed popular sensibilities made no difference; history was replete with examples of unpopular ideas that had eventually gained public acceptance. Brandeis here provided a positive justification for the protection of speech—the necessity for the citizenry to be fully informed about issues and to be aware of all viewpoints. But Brandeis would not limit First Amendment protection to political speech alone; his opinion in *Whitney* clearly portrays speech as a cultural, social, and educational value as well as a political value in a free society.

See Vincent Blasi, "The First Amendment and the Ideal of Civil Courage: The Brandeis Opinion in *Whitney v. California,*" *William & Mary Law Review* 29 (1988): 653; and Pnina Lahav, "Holmes and Brandeis: Libertarian and Republican Justifications for Free Speech," *Journal of Law & Politics* 4 (1987): 451.

Fiske v. Kansas

274 U.S. 380 (1927)
Decided: May 16, 1927
Vote: 9 (Taft, Holmes, Van Devanter, McReynolds, Brandeis, Sutherland, Butler, Sanford, Stone)
0
Opinion of the Court: Sanford

Harold Fiske was an organizer for the International Workers of the World (IWW) in Kansas. The Wobblies, as they were called, wanted to end what they deemed to be the present oppressive system of capitalism and usher in a world of equality, free of wages and industrialization. When Fiske was arrested for violating a Kansas criminal syndicalism statute, he claimed that the law infringed on liberties protected by the Due Process Clause of the Fourteenth Amendment.

The Court, which only a few years earlier had ruled that similar activities posed a clear and present danger to social order, held that Fiske had not violated the statute. The state had presented no evidence that Fiske or others advocated criminal activity or violence to achieve their goals, but had merely campaigned for abstract goals. They did not go out and revolt or commit unlawful activity. Applying the statute to Fiske therefore violated due process of law under the Fourteenth Amendment.

Today this case would be decided under the First Amendment protection of speech, a position the 1920s Court did not reach for several years. Although Justice Sanford made clear that the criminal syndicalism law was constitutional, his decision showed a significant retreat from the position taken by the majority less than a decade earlier in the postwar speech cases. In those cases it had not mattered whether the accused actually advocated violence or criminal activity; the mere fact of belonging to a socialist organization was enough to support the charge of clear and present danger.

See Richard C. Cortner, "The Wobblies and *Fiske v. Kansas:* Victory Amid Disintegration," *Kansas History* 4 (spring 1981): 30.

Gong Lum v. Rice

275 U.S. 78 (1927)
Decided: November 21, 1927
Vote: 9 (Taft, Holmes, Van Devanter, McReynolds, Brandeis, Sutherland, Butler, Sanford, Stone)
0
Opinion of the Court: Taft

Chinese had lived in the Mississippi Delta since at least the 1870s, and in many areas they had distinguished themselves by hard work and economic success. Even as Jim Crow laws gradually forced the segregation of blacks into separate and inferior schools, Chinese were often able to stay in white schools. In many small towns and cities, local white elites thought well enough of the Chinese communities to see them, if not as white, then certainly not as black.

In Bolivar, Mississippi, a local judge ruled that despite the state's new Jim Crow laws, Chinese children could continue to attend the all-white schools. Some locals objected, however, and got the state to appeal the ruling. Gong Lum lost the battle at the state level to keep his daughter Martha, who had been born in the United States, in the white school, and he appealed to the Supreme Court.

Chief Justice Taft, speaking for the Court, declared that "were this a new question, it would call for very full argument and consideration, but we think that it is the same question which has been many times decided." Questions of racial classification for the purposes of school attendance were matters of state and local law, and the Court would not intervene.

The Delta Chinese, however, would not accept the ruling and refused to send their children to the all-black schools. They placed their children in local religious schools or sent them out of the region. In cities with a large enough Chinese population, they built their own schools. Following World War II, in which the Chinese had been America's allies, Mississippi Delta schools all opened their doors to Chinese American students, a full decade before ***Brown v. Board of Education,*** 347 U.S. 483 (1954), sounded the death knell for Jim Crow laws.

See Jeannie Rhee, "In Black and White: Chinese in the Mississippi Delta," *Journal of Supreme Court History, 1994,* 117; and James Loewen, *Mississippi Chinese: Between Black and White* (Cambridge: Harvard University Press, 1971).

Gambino v. United States

275 U.S. 310 (1927)
Decided: December 12, 1927
Vote: 9 (Taft, Holmes, Van Devanter, McReynolds, Brandeis, Sutherland, Butler, Sanford, Stone)
0
Opinion of the Court: Brandeis

Rosario Gambino and Joseph Lima were driving down a New York road when police pulled them over. Without probable cause and without a warrant, the police searched the vehicle, found alcohol, and arrested the two men for violating Prohibition. At trial, the evidence of alcohol was introduced, and they were found guilty. On appeal, Gambino argued that because the evidence was obtained by an illegal search and seizure, it should be inadmissible at trial.

The Court agreed, ruling that the way the evidence was obtained violated the Fourth Amendment ban on illegal search and seizure. Under the exclusionary rule, evidence illegally seized cannot be admitted as evidence into a criminal trial. Although the Court had earlier held in ***Carroll v. United States,*** 267 U.S. 132 (1925), that normal warrant requirements did not apply to automobiles, it now modified that rule to declare that police, even without a warrant, had to at least have probable cause to stop and search a vehicle. With probable cause the exclusionary rule would not apply; without probable cause seized evidence would be excluded.

Black & White Taxicab Co. v. Brown & Yellow Taxicab Co.

276 U.S. 518 (1928)
Decided: April 9, 1928
Vote: 6 (Taft, Van Devanter, McReynolds, Sutherland, Butler, Sanford)
3 (Holmes, Brandeis, Stone)
Opinion of the Court: Butler
Dissenting opinion: Holmes (Brandeis, Stone)

The Judiciary Act of 1789 ordered federal courts to follow the decisional rules of the states in which they were located. Justice Story, however, believed that the country needed a national commercial law, and in ***Swift v. Tyson,*** 41 U.S. 1 (1842), promulgated the rule that in matters of general law, federal courts could follow principles of general commercial law. As a result, in diversity suits, which involve parties from different states, the plaintiff or the defendant might well go forum shopping, looking for a federal court where the rules would be more favorable. This rule became an issue during the Progressive Era. Large corporations would try to have their cases moved to what they considered the more favorable atmosphere of the conservative federal courts as a way to thwart state laws meant to control corporations.

One of the most blatant examples occurred when a taxicab company, facing an unfavorable Kentucky law in its conflict with a local competitor, assigned all of its assets to a new corporation chartered in Tennessee, even though it continued doing business in Kentucky. The new corporation, now able to assert diversity of citizenship vis-à-vis its Kentucky-chartered rival, sued for an injunction in the Kentucky federal court. Holding that it was not bound by Kentucky common law, the federal court applied what it considered sound commercial law and gave the Tennessee company an injunction voiding the Kentucky law.

A majority of the Supreme Court affirmed, basing its decision on a long line of cases going back to *Swift.* Justice Holmes dissented vigorously, attacking the idea that federal courts could substitute their judgments for state law on a notion he derided as a "transcendental body of law outside any particular State." There is no such body of law, he charged, and concluded that, if he were correct, then there has been "an unconstitutional assumption of powers by the Courts of the United States."

Ten years later Justice Brandeis put an end to such practices with his opinion in ***Erie Railroad Co. v. Tompkins,*** 304 U.S. 64 (1938).

See Edward A. Purcell Jr., *Brandeis and the Progressive Constitution* (New Haven: Yale University Press, 2000).

Ribnik v. McBride

277 U.S. 350 (1928)
Decided: May 28, 1928
Vote: 6 (Taft, Van Devanter, McReynolds, Sutherland, Butler, Sanford)
3 (Holmes, Brandeis, Stone)
Opinion of the Court: Sutherland
Concurring opinion: Sanford
Dissenting opinion: Stone (Holmes, Brandeis)

A New Jersey law required all employment agencies to obtain a license from the state. Failure to comply could result in a fine. Rupert Ribnik's employment agency filed for a license and, although it met all of the requirements, the state denied him a license because officials thought the fees the agency planned to charge were unreasonable. Ribnik argued that New Jersey could not deny him a license because of his rates and that the state was attempting to fix prices, a power it did not have.

The Court struck down New Jersey's decision to deny the license. Justice Sutherland wrote that a state has power to require a license and to regulate the business of an employment agency, but not to fix the fees. The public interest argument was not strong enough to allow such regulation. New Jersey may require a license, but it cannot deny a license to the agency because of what prices it may charge.

In his dissent, Justice Stone argued that states did have the power to regulate businesses affected with a public interest and, if New Jersey believed that finding people jobs was a matter of public interest, then it could regulate the rates.

See Richard Maidment, "Law and Economic Policy in the United States: The Judicial Response to Governmental Regulation of the Economy," *Journal of Legal History* 7 (1986): 196.

Olmstead v. United States

277 U.S. 438 (1928)
Decided: June 4, 1928
Vote: 5 (Taft, Van Devanter, McReynolds, Sutherland, Sanford)
4 (Holmes, Brandeis, Butler, Stone)
Opinion of the Court: Taft
Dissenting opinion: Holmes (Stone)
Dissenting opinion: Brandeis (Stone)
Dissenting opinion: Butler (Stone)
Dissenting opinion: Stone

In the 1920s, technology gave the government new means to prosecute its fight against crime, including the ability to pry into the private affairs of a suspect without actually entering his or her premises. Olmstead was convicted under the National Prohibition Act of unlawfully transporting and selling liquor; and the evidence leading to his conviction had been secured through a warrantless tap on his telephone. By a bare majority, the Court gave its blessing to such wiretapping. Chief Justice Taft took a formalistic view of wiretapping, completely ignoring the Fourth Amendment's intent. There had been no actual entry, he declared, but only the use of an enhanced sense of hearing, and to pay too much attention to "nice ethical conduct by government officials would make society suffer and give criminals greater immunity than has been known heretofore."

The Taft opinion elicited dissents from Justices Butler, Holmes, Brandeis, and Stone. In a well-reasoned historical analysis, the generally conservative Butler repudiated Taft's sterile interpretation of what the Fourth Amendment meant. Holmes, in a comment that soon caught the liberal imagination, condemned wire tapping as "a dirty business." But the most impressive opinion came from Brandeis, who forthrightly declared that he considered it "less evil that some criminals should escape than that the government should play an ignoble part. . . . If government becomes a lawbreaker, it breeds contempt for law."

The most noted and influential part of Brandeis's dissent dealt with the question of privacy. As a practicing attorney, he and his partner, Samuel Warren, had written a pioneering article in 1891, "The Right to Privacy," on the common law right of privacy, an article that Roscoe Pound, the longtime dean of the Harvard Law School and a noted legal theorist, later credited with creating an entire new area of law. The Framers of the Constitution, Brandeis wrote in *Olmstead,* "sought to protect Americans in their beliefs, their thoughts, their emotions and their sensations. They conferred, as against the Government, the right to be let alone—the most comprehensive of rights, and the right most valued by civilized men." That passage was picked up and elaborated on until finally, in ***Griswold v. Connecticut,*** 381 U.S. 479 (1965), the Court recognized privacy as a constitutionally guaranteed liberty.

Wiretapping itself remained legally permissible for many years, although Congress in 1934 prohibited admitting evidence obtained by wiretapping in federal courts. Not until ***Berger v. New York,*** 388 U.S. 41 (1967), did the Court finally bring wiretapping within the reach of the Fourth Amendment; now wiretap evidence may be introduced, but only if it has been secured after the issuance of a proper warrant.

See Walter F. Murphy, *Wiretapping on Trial: A Case Study in the Judicial Process* (New York: Random House, 1965): and R. F. Scoular, "Wiretapping and Eavesdropping: Constitutional Development from *Olmstead* to *Katz,*" *St. Louis Law Journal* 12 (1968): 513.

United States v. Schwimmer

279 U.S. 644 (1929)
Decided: May 27, 1929
Vote: 6 (Taft, Van Devanter, McReynolds, Sutherland, Butler, Stone)
3 (Holmes, Brandeis, Sanford)
Opinion of the Court: Butler
Dissenting opinion: Holmes (Brandeis)
Dissenting opinion: Sanford

Rosika Schwimmer was born in Hungary and came to the United States to teach and lecture. After a while, she decided to apply for citizenship. To become a naturalized citizen, however, one had to promise to take up arms and fight for the United States if necessary. A religious pacifist, Schwimmer opposed war and considered killing a sin. She could not take an oath that would require her to kill people for the United States. As a result, she was denied citizenship, and she appealed her case to the courts.

The Court held that she had properly been denied citizenship. It did not matter what a person's reasons were for not taking the oath of allegiance. Congress had prescribed the oath as a necessary part of the naturalization process, and Congress constitutionally had plenary power over immigration and naturalization. The government has an interest in choosing who may become a naturalized citizen, and it has a legitimate interest in ensuring that those who come to live in the United States be willing to fight in its defense. If a person could not take the oath, then that person could not become a naturalized citizen.

Justice Holmes entered a blistering dissent, stating that he did not see the point in denying citizenship to Schwimmer "in as much as she is a woman over fifty years of age, and would not be allowed to bear arms if she wanted to." He did not believe that because some people took the Sermon on the Mount more seriously than others that they would make bad citizens. Then, in words that have been cited countless times, he declared, "Some of her answers might excite popular prejudice, but if there is any principle of the Constitution that more imperatively calls for attachment than any other it is the principle of free thought—not free thought for those who agree with us but freedom for the thought that we hate."

The Pocket Veto Case

Also known as *Okanogan Indians v. United States*
279 U.S. 655 (1929)
Decided: May 27, 1929
Vote: 9 (Taft, Holmes, Van Devanter, McReynolds, Brandeis, Sutherland, Butler, Sanford, Stone)
0
Opinion of the Court: Sanford

Congress passed a bill requiring certain Indian tribes in Washington State to present any claims against the government to the Court of Claims. Congress sent the bill to President Coolidge to sign. Coolidge, however, neither signed nor vetoed the bill. It was presented to him June 27, 1927, and Congress adjourned on July 3. The president therefore was given only six days to act on the bill.

Later in 1927 the Okanogan Indians filed a claim in the Court of Claims, which dismissed it because, according to the court, the bill had never become law. The Okanogan Indians argued that the bill had become law even though the president had not signed it, and they appealed the decision.

The Court held that the bill had not become law; the failure to sign, under specific circumstances, is tantamount to a veto. Under Article I, Section 7, Clause 2, of the Constitution, if a bill is presented to the president and he does not sign it within ten days, it becomes law. However, if a bill is presented to the president, Congress adjourns within ten days of presentation, and the president does not sign the bill, then it does not become law. This procedure, known as a "pocket veto," prevents Congress from passing last-minute legislation that a president will have no chance to consider. In this case, the president killed the bill by a "pocket veto," and it never became law.

See John W. Dumbrell and John D. Lees, "Presidential Pocket-Veto Power: A Constitutional Anachronism?" *Political Studies* 28 (1980): 109.

Old Colony Trust Co. v. Commissioner

279 U.S. 716 (1929)
Decided: June 3, 1929
Vote: 8 (Taft, Holmes, Van Devanter, Brandeis, Sutherland, Butler, Sanford, Stone)
1 (McReynolds)
Opinion of the Court: Taft
Dissenting opinion: McReynolds

Old Colony Trust Company paid the federal income tax for its executives directly to the Internal Revenue Service (IRS) and claimed that this money should not be considered additional executive income. The IRS said that Old Colony could not do that because the payment of taxes constituted additional income. It was the same as if Old Colony gave its executives extra income, that the executives used to pay their taxes but did not claim as income. Old Colony went to court to determine whether the bank had to pay taxes on what it called "taxable compensation."

The Court held that Old Colony had to pay taxes on everything. It agreed with the IRS that the corporation was not really paying its executives' income taxes. Rather it was paying its executives extra income and not reporting it as income. The Court ruled that if the corporation wanted to pay its executives like that, then it had to pay taxes on the entire amount of income given to the executives, both regular income and the so-called "taxable compensation."

1930–1939

Florida v. United States

282 U.S. 194 (1931)
Decided: January 5, 1931
Vote: 9 (Hughes, Holmes, Van Devanter, McReynolds, Brandeis, Sutherland, Butler, Stone, Roberts)
0
Opinion of the Court: Hughes

The Interstate Commerce Commission (ICC) ordered the state of Florida and its railroad commission to establish fixed rates for railroad transportation within the state. The ICC had set rates for interstate railroad transportation and wanted the same rates to apply to Florida's intrastate transportation because the commission believed the state's intrastate rates were unfair compared with the interstate rates. Florida resisted, claiming that the regulation of intrastate rates exceeded the federal government's power under the Commerce Clause.

The Court agreed and struck down the ICC's order. In general, the Court ruled, the federal government has no authority to regulate matters of intrastate commerce, except when the evidence shows a pattern of unfair discrimination. In this case, however, the ICC had presented no evidence of unfair discrimination. Although Congress can regulate interstate commerce, the ICC could not force Florida to change its intrastate railroad rates.

O'Gorman and Young v. Hartford Fire Insurance Co.

282 U.S. 251 (1931)
Decided: January 5, 1931
Vote: 5 (Hughes, Holmes, Brandeis, Stone, Roberts)
4 (Van Devanter, McReynolds, Sutherland, Butler)
Opinion of the Court: Brandeis
Dissenting opinion: Van Devanter, McReynolds, Sutherland, Butler (signed by all four justices)

A New Jersey statute that regulated fees paid to local agents by insurance companies was challenged as a violation of the Fourteenth Amendment's Due Process Clause. Justice Brandeis wrote a detailed explanation as to why the state legislature had determined it necessary to regulate the fees and declared that the presumption of constitutionality must prevail in the absence of factual material to justify overturning a law. In addition, he said the courts should defer to legislative judgment unless it could be shown that such judgment had been completely arbitrary. No such demonstration had been made of either argument, merely the assertion that the limits violated the freedom of contract. Brandeis also claimed that the business of insurance was so far affected with the public interest that a state could regulate rates and fees under the aegis of its police power.

The four dissenters, on the other hand, strongly supported the notion of freedom of contract, not realizing that this case was the last they would hear involving that claim. And, as conservative jurists had maintained for so long, the courts ought to be the final judge of what was reasonable in economic legislation.

Stromberg v. California

283 U.S. 359 (1931)
Decided: May 18, 1931
Vote: 7 (Hughes, Holmes, Van Devanter, Brandeis, Sutherland, Stone, Roberts)
2 (McReynolds, Butler)
Opinion of the Court: Hughes
Dissenting opinion: McReynolds
Dissenting opinion: Butler

California had a law prohibiting the flying of a red flag in a public place. At the time, the red flags symbolized socialist and communist groups and were often interpreted as a representation of the Soviet Union's flag. Yetta Stromberg, a nineteen-year-old teacher, was arrested for flying a red flag in a public place, and she argued that the law violated the Fourteenth Amendment.

Speaking for the Court, Chief Justice Hughes struck down the law and ruled that it was vague and overbroad. Just because communists flew red flags, he reasoned, did not mean that all people who flew red flags were communists. Flags are symbols that can be used for different purposes. American citizens have the right to express their thoughts, and a ban on red flags violated due process.

Today, the Court would deal with this case as a First Amendment free speech case. In early 1931, however, the Court had not yet completed the incorporation of the First Amendment through the Due Process Clause of the Fourteenth Amendment in order to apply it to the states as well as to the federal government. The decision can be viewed as a step away from the unquestioning acceptance of all antisocialist laws that the Court had demonstrated a decade earlier.

See Paul L. Murphy, *The Meaning of Freedom of Speech: First Amendment Freedoms from Wilson to FDR* (Westport, Conn.: Greenwood Press, 1972).

United States v. Macintosh

283 U.S. 605 (1931)
Decided: May 25, 1931
Vote: 5 (Van Devanter, McReynolds, Sutherland, Butler, Roberts)
4 (Hughes, Holmes, Brandeis, Stone)
Opinion of the Court: Sutherland
Dissenting opinion: Hughes (Holmes, Brandeis, Stone)

Douglas Clyde Macintosh, a Canadian, wanted to become a U.S. citizen. At the time, he was chaplain of the Yale Graduate School and Dwight Professor of Theology in the Divinity School. Macintosh was also a pacifist, and he refused to swear to take up arms in defense of the United States. He said he would fight only if a war were morally justified. He claimed he could give his allegiance to the United States, but not before his responsibilities to God. The government denied his application for citizenship, and he appealed to the courts. The question before the Supreme Court in this case was similar to that in ***United States v. Schwimmer,*** 279 U.S. 644 (1929). May an alien be naturalized as a citizen without pledging to take up arms in defense of the country?

The Court upheld the government's denial of citizenship. Justice Sutherland ruled that Congress had an interest in requiring such oaths because it had the responsibility for raising armies in wartime. If one person were allowed to disregard the oath, a slippery slope might allow others not to take the oath. Therefore, no matter how pure an alien's convictions may be, he or she cannot become a citizen without affirming the willingness to go to war.

See Ronald B. Flowers, "The Naturalization of Douglas Clyde Macintosh, Alien Theologian," *Journal of Supreme Court History* 25 (2000): 243.

Near v. Minnesota

283 U.S. 697 (1931)
Decided: June 1, 1931
Vote: 5 (Hughes, Holmes, Brandeis, Stone, Roberts)
4 (Van Devanter, McReynolds, Sutherland, Butler)
Opinion of the Court: Hughes
Dissenting opinion: Butler (Van Devanter, McReynolds, Sutherland)

An explosion of "yellow" journalism led the Minnesota legislature in 1925 to pass a Public Nuisance Abatement Law, authorizing suppression of any "malicious, scandalous and defamatory newspaper, or other periodical." The law was aimed at silencing the *Saturday Press,* a tabloid that had exposed corruption in the Minneapolis government, but in a lurid and at times irresponsible manner. Jay Near, the publisher was an unsavory character who often published articles attacking Jews, Catholics, blacks, and labor. Civil libertarians opposed the law because it imposed a prior restraint on publishers, a type of censorship that Blackstone had held could not be imposed on the press. The American Civil Liberties Union offered to defend Near, but the organization was quickly forced aside by Robert McCormick, a conservative Chicago publisher, who assigned his large legal staff to handle the appeal to the Supreme Court.

Chief Justice Hughes voided the law as a form of prior restraint, condemning the act as "the essence of censorship." This case marked the beginning of the Court's long and consistent opposition to any form of prior restraint of the press. More important, as Hughes declared, "it is no longer open to doubt that the liberty of the press and of speech is within the liberties safeguarded by the due process clause of the Fourteenth Amendment from invasion by state action." The process of incorporation of the Bill of Rights that had started with speech in the 1920s now included freedom of the press as well.

The four dissenters, through Justice Butler, claimed that the decision gave freedom of the press a meaning and a scope that had never been recognized before and that it imposed on the states "a federal restriction that is without precedent."

Near set forth a general principle that has ever since characterized the Court's interpretation of the First Amendment's press clause—that there can be no prior restraint by the government of the press absent an overwhelming and clearly demonstrated necessity, a standard so high that it has never been met in the Supreme Court.

See Fred W. Friendly, *Minnesota Rag: The Dramatic Story of the Landmark Supreme Court Case That Gave New Meaning to Freedom of the Press* (New York: Random House, 1981).

New State Ice Co. v. Liebmann

285 U.S. 262 (1932)
Decided: March 21, 1932
Vote: 6 (Hughes, Van Devanter, McReynolds, Sutherland, Butler, Roberts)
2 (Brandeis, Stone)
Opinion of the Court: Sutherland
Dissenting opinion: Brandeis (Stone)
Did not participate: Cardozo

One of the earliest Great Depression cases to come before the Court involved an Oklahoma statute that treated the manufacture of ice as a public utility and required a certificate of convenience and necessity for anyone wishing to start such a business. The state justified its law on the grounds that too many competitors would drive the price down, which would cause many companies to go out of business and deprive the public of needed ice. The practical effect of the law was to shut out new enterprises and give existing companies a monopoly.

When Liebmann opened an ice business without a state certificate, New State Ice, which had a certificate, sued to stop him.

Chief Justice Hughes, who had voted earlier in ***O'Gorman and Young v. Hartford Fire Insurance Co.,*** 282 U.S. 251 (1931), to sustain a New Jersey law regulating commission rates for insurance agents, now joined with the conservative block to invalidate the Oklahoma law. Speaking through Justice Sutherland, the majority denied that ice manufacture could be considered affected with the public interest and concluded that it could not be legitimately regulated by the state. Furthermore, the law tended to foster monopoly.

With his well-known antipathy toward monopoly, Justice Brandeis might have been expected to vote against the regulation as well; instead, he entered a powerful dissent. He criticized the majority for failing to take account of the economic conditions that had led the Oklahoma legislature to view ice-making as affected with the public interest. "The true principle," he wrote, "is that the State's power extends to every regulation of any business reasonably required and appropriate for the public protection." In a depression, it might be necessary to limit certain types of business, and the state legislature had decided to try this approach. Whether it would work he did not know; nor did it matter. "It is one of the happy incidents of the federal system that a single courageous State may, if its citizens choose, serve as a laboratory, and try novel social and economic experiments without risk to the rest of the country."

Brandeis ended with an eloquent plea for judicial restraint. The Court, he said, had the power to prevent experiments because the Due Process Clause had been interpreted to include substantive as well as procedural rights. "But in the exercise of this high power," he warned, "we must be ever on our guard, lest we erect our prejudices into legal principles. If we would guide by the light of reason, we must let our minds be bold."

Although the case has never been specifically overruled, it has in effect been abandoned, as subsequent Courts recognized a broad range of legislative discretion. *New State Ice* is still defended by some scholars, however, as an effort to protect consumers from classic special interest legislation.

See Philippa Strum, *Brandeis: Beyond Progressivism* (Lawrence: University Press of Kansas, 1993).

Nixon v. Condon

286 U.S. 73 (1932)
Decided: May 2, 1932
Vote: 5 (Hughes, Brandeis, Stone, Roberts, Cardozo)
4 (Van Devanter, McReynolds, Sutherland, Butler)
Opinion of the Court: Cardozo
Dissenting opinion: McReynolds (Van Devanter, Sutherland, Butler)

Once Reconstruction ended, the Democratic Party quickly gained control of southern politics and government. With the introduction of the primary election, any real contest took place in the Democratic primary because the winner would face only token opposition from the Republicans in the general election. Because victory in the Democratic primary meant election to office, every southern state passed laws designed to keep African Americans from voting in the primary. The National Association for the Advancement of Colored People (NAACP) claimed that such laws, which in effect disenfranchised blacks, violated the Fourteenth and Fifteenth Amendments.

In ***Nixon v. Herndon,*** 273 U.S. 536 (1927), the Court held that a Texas law barring blacks from voting in the primary violated the Equal Protection Clause of the Fourteenth Amendment. Texas responded by shifting responsibility for the primary away from the state to the Democratic Party and allowing the party to set whatever qualifications it wanted for eligibility. The party's executive committee immediately limited participation to whites. When Dr. Lawrence Nixon was denied a ballot, he claimed that because the party was acting under state authority, its refusal to allow him a ballot violated the Fourteenth Amendment. Party officials responded that the Democratic Party was a private group, which could determine its own membership.

In his first opinion for the Court, Justice Cardozo found the Texas arrangement unconstitutional, saying that the state had by statute delegated to the party what it could not do itself. This narrow ruling left Texas the option—which it quickly exercised—of repealing all state statutes regarding primaries, a move that left the primary completely under the control of the party with no state involvement. This method of black disfranchisement continued in southern states until ***Smith v. Allwright,*** 321 U.S. 649 (1944), when the Court ruled that a primary, no matter how sponsored or administered, was an integral part of the election process and therefore state action that was subject to constitutional provisions.

See Conrey Bryson, *Dr. Lawrence A. Nixon and the White Primary* (El Paso: Texas Western Press, 1974); and Darlene Clark Hine, "The Elusive Ballot: The Black Struggle Against the Texas Democratic White Primary, 1932–1945," *Southwestern Historical Quarterly* 81 (1978): 371.

United States v. Swift & Co.

286 U.S. 106 (1932)
Decided: May 2, 1932
Vote: 4 (McReynolds, Brandeis, Roberts, Cardozo)
2 (Van Devanter, Butler)
Opinion of the Court: Cardozo
Dissenting opinion: Butler (Van Devanter)
Did not participate: Hughes, Sutherland, Stone

Meatpackers Swift & Company decided to expand its business by going into the retail grocery trade. The federal government opposed this move, claiming it would violate the antitrust laws. Swift already had facilities that it could use to sell groceries and would therefore have little additional overhead to pay. The government claimed this situation gave the company an unfair advantage over its competitors.

Swift initially agreed to a consent decree barring it from going into retail groceries. The company then decided to appeal, arguing that it did not have a big enough competitive advantage to justify the government keeping it out of retail.

The Court agreed with the government that Swift should be prevented from entering the field. Swift's large size did not by itself indicate a violation of the antitrust laws. Size, however, carried with it the opportunity for abuse. It would be a reasonable assumption that Swift, by taking advantage of its size to enter the grocery business, would force many small retail grocers out of business.

See Timothy Stolzfus Jost, "From *Swift* to *Stotts* and Beyond: Modification of Injunctions in the Federal Courts," *Texas Law Review* 64 (1986): 1101.

Powell v. Alabama

Also known as the Scottsboro Case
287 U.S. 45 (1932)
Decided: November 7, 1932
Vote: 7 (Hughes, Van Devanter, Brandeis, Sutherland, Stone, Roberts, Cardozo)
2 (McReynolds, Butler)
Opinion of the Court: Sutherland
Dissenting opinion: Butler (McReynolds)

In the infamous Scottsboro affair, nine black teenagers were accused of raping two white girls on a freight train in March 1931. The nine were quickly indicted, and Alabama officials raced through the legal motions of their trials. All the trials were held in one day, and eight of the nine were sentenced to die in the electric chair.

As required under Alabama law, the trial court had appointed counsel. To avoid the stigma that he might be associated with the black defendants, the lawyer, who had never met his clients, indicated that, even though he appeared on their behalf, he would not formally represent them. The judge then appointed all the members of the local bar present to represent the defendants, at which point all the lawyers in the courtroom left. Finally, two attorneys appeared on behalf of the black youths. These lawyers had no opportunity to investigate the case and had only thirty minutes just before the trial to consult with their clients. The jury found eight of the defendants guilty, and the court sentenced them to death; the ninth defendant was acquitted.

In his opinion for the Court, Justice Sutherland carefully detailed how unfair the trial had been and concluded that the lack of effective counsel violated the defendants' rights to due process as required in the Fourteenth Amendment and to counsel as guaranteed in the Sixth Amendment. The Court thus overruled its earlier decision in ***Hurtado v. California,*** 110 U.S. 516 (1884), where in sweeping language it had specifically excluded Fifth and Sixth Amendment rights from the due process protected by the Fourteenth. *Powell* represented a significant step in extending the Bill of Rights to the states, and the opinion came from a justice noted for his great concern that the federal government should not trespass on states' rights. Although the decision did not technically incorporate the Sixth Amendment right to counsel and apply it to the states, it did make effective counsel an essential ingredient of due process in state criminal cases. The next step came in formally incorporating the Sixth Amendment, which the Court did in ***Johnson v. Zerbst,*** 304 U.S. 458 (1938).

The Scottsboro youths were retried, convicted, and sentenced to prison terms. Powell, the lead plaintiff, escaped to Michigan, where the governor refused to extradite him; the others were eventually paroled.

See Dan T. Carter, Scottsboro: *A Tragedy of the American South, rev. ed.* (Baton Rouge: Louisiana State University Press, 1979); and David J. Bodenhamer, *Fair Trial: Rights of the Accused in American History* (New York: Oxford University Press, 1992).

Sterling v. Constantin

287 U.S. 378 (1932)
Decided: December 12, 1932
Vote: 9 (Hughes, Van Devanter, McReynolds, Brandeis, Sutherland, Butler, Stone, Roberts, Cardozo)
0
Opinion of the Court: Hughes

Because of low oil prices caused by the Great Depression, Texas ordered certain oil companies to decrease the amount of oil they produced daily. The companies refused. In 1931 Texas governor Ross S. Sterling declared martial law in several counties because of alleged riots and insurrection, and he again ordered the oil companies in those areas to cut back their daily production. The oil companies argued that the Texas law violated the Fifth and Fourteenth Amendments by depriving them of their property without due process of law and the equal protection of the laws.

The Court upheld Sterling's order. Chief Justice Hughes noted that people normally have the right to the use and enjoyment of their property, but property remained subject to reasonable regulation by the state, if the state chose to exercise its police powers to prevent unnecessary loss, destruction, and waste. Such use of the police power complied with due process and equal protection. Because the counties in which the oil companies were located were in a state of riot and insurrection, Texas's order to curtail oil production to reduce possible waste and destruction of the oil was a reasonable regulation.

Nashville, Chattanooga & St. Louis Ry. Co. v. Wallace

288 U.S. 249 (1933)
Decided: February 6, 1933
Vote: 9 (Hughes, Van Devanter, McReynolds, Brandeis, Sutherland, Butler, Stone, Roberts, Cardozo)
0
Opinion of the Court: Stone

The Nashville railroad bought large amounts of gasoline outside of Tennessee for its own use. The railroad transported the gasoline to Tennessee, placed it in company-owned storage tanks, and used it for trains traveling across several states. Tennessee had a law taxing gasoline stored within the state. The Nashville line argued that its gasoline should not be taxed because it was part of interstate commerce and therefore beyond the taxing power of the state.

The Court ruled that Tennessee could tax the fuel. Justice Stone reasoned that once the gasoline had been placed in storage it had left interstate commerce. The gasoline actually in use on trains in interstate commerce could not be taxed, but the gasoline in storage was not in interstate commerce at the given moment and therefore the state could tax it.

Welch v. Helvering

290 U.S. 111 (1933)
Decided: November 6, 1933
Vote: 9 (Hughes, Van Devanter, McReynolds, Brandeis, Sutherland, Butler, Stone, Roberts, Cardozo)
0
Opinion of the Court: Cardozo

Thomas H. Welch was the secretary of the E. L. Welch Company. After he left the corporation, he paid some of its debts out of his own pocket and wrote off the payments as business deductions from his taxable income. The Internal Revenue Service (IRS) claimed that the only way to write off these payments would be if they were done as "ordinary and necessary" payments for the business. The IRS did not see them as ordinary or necessary and charged that Welch was avoiding his income taxes.

The Court agreed with the IRS, and held that Welch had not paid the debts in an ordinary and necessary way, and therefore owed the IRS income taxes on the amounts that he paid to the business. This case and others heard during this period helped to flesh out the relatively sparse terms of the tax code as it existed at the time. The main question, then as now, is what constitutes income, and, until the establishment of the Tax Court to handle IRS appeals, many of these questions of definition came to the Supreme Court.

Home Building and Loan Association v. Blaisdell

290 U.S. 398 (1934)
Decided: January 8, 1934
Vote: 5 (Hughes, Brandeis, Stone, Roberts, Cardozo)
4 (Van Devanter, McReynolds, Sutherland, Butler)
Opinion of the Court: Hughes
Dissenting opinion: Sutherland (Van Devanter, McReynolds, Butler)

In 1933, during the Great Depression, Minnesota farmers, like farmers across the country, were losing their property through foreclosure. The state responded with the enactment of the Mortgage Moratorium Law. The statute, clearly an emergency measure, allowed local courts to extend the period of redemption between foreclosure and sale to give farmers additional time to raise money. The law did not permit an indefinite extension, nor did it cancel the debt; it did no more than adjust the remedy available to the creditor. The Court affirmed the constitutionality of the state law. Although an "emergency does not create power," Chief Justice Hughes noted, it could be the occasion for the exercise of latent powers. He recited a lengthy list of devices that states had previously used to protect the health and safety of their citizens that also affected contracts. Aware that the minority upheld the inviolability of contracts under all circumstances, Hughes reminded them of Chief Justice Marshall's famous dictum in ***McCulloch v. Maryland,*** 17 U.S. 316 (1819): "We must never forget, that it is a *constitution* we are expounding, a constitution intended for ages to come, and, consequently, to be adapted to the various *crises* of human affairs." The Court, therefore, had to look at the Contract Clause anew, in the light of the current emergency and recognize that the states' higher need to protect the welfare of their citizens justified a departure from traditional interpretations.

Joined by his conservative colleagues, Justice Sutherland dissented, making an appeal to keep the Contract Clause inviolate. He refused to acknowledge that emergencies could justify impairment of obligations. In fact, he claimed, the clause had been designed specifically to prevent states from granting relief to debtors in emergencies. While conceding that the Minnesota law made relatively minor changes, he warned that if the Court allowed it to stand, it would be the harbinger of greater invasions of the sanctity of contract—and if contract went, then all constitutional restrictions would inevitably collapse.

The majority had approved the Minnesota law because it had not ruled out foreclosures, had been specific in how it adjusted the remedy, and had put a time limit on the extensions. When states attempted more than this, the Court proved less receptive. The same year as *Blaisdell,* for example, the justices struck down an Arkansas law exempting payments for life insurance policies from garnishment in *W. B. Worthen Co. v. Thomas,* 292 U.S. 426 (1934). As Hughes explained, the relief was "neither temporary nor conditional," and the law contained "no limitations as to time, amount, circumstances, or need." The dissenters in *Blaisdell* concurred in *Worthern,* stating that they saw no difference between the Minnesota law and the Arkansas law.

See William Prosser, "The Minnesota Mortgage Moratorium," *Southern California Law Review* 7 (1934): 353.

Nebbia v. New York

291 U.S. 502 (1934)
Decided: March 5, 1934
Vote: 5 (Hughes, Brandeis, Stone, Roberts, Cardozo)
4 (Van Devanter, McReynolds, Sutherland, Butler)
Opinion of the Court: Roberts
Dissenting opinion: McReynolds (Van Devanter, Sutherland, Butler)

In an effort to ameliorate some of the economic dislocations caused by the Great Depression and in response to the declining prices the state's dairy farmers received for milk, New York created a control board to regulate the milk industry within the state and gave it the power to set minimum wholesale and retail prices. The law paralleled the Roosevelt administration's efforts to stabilize markets and eliminate cutthroat competition, and it elicited the same challenges in court. Leo Nebbia, a grocer from Rochester, was convicted of selling milk below the price set by the board. He appealed on the grounds that the statute violated his Fourteenth Amendment rights. The law unduly restricted the use of his property, he argued; moreover, the milk industry could not be considered as affected with a public interest, so any state control interfered unconstitutionally with the market.

The majority opinion in *Nebbia* came not from one of the liberals, but from Justice Roberts, who apparently adopted *in toto* the argument that the public need overrode traditional property rights. The state had recognized a problem and had taken reasonable steps to mitigate the difficulties. The wisdom of those steps did not concern the Court. Did any constitutional prohibition exist, Roberts asked, to prevent the state from attempting to alleviate problems caused by an aberrant market? In words that surely chilled the conservative members of the Court, Roberts declared, "We think there is no such principle." The relation of any business to the public interest depended on current conditions; therefore, any business might legitimately be deemed affected with the public interest and subject to regulation. Only a showing that the regulations had been unreasonable, arbitrary, or discriminatory would justify judicial intercession.

Justice McReynolds, in his dissent, openly admitted that in his view the Court should look at the prudence of the act as well as its constitutionality. "This Court must have regard to the wisdom of the enactment," he wrote, conceding that he believed the Court should act as a superlegislature. Thus, justices could, through the Due Process Clause, uphold the laws they liked and strike down those they did not.

McReynolds objected to Roberts's definition of the public interest as nearly anything the legislature declared it to be, for it removed one of the Court's main weapons against economic regulation—the ability to declare a business as not affected with a public interest and therefore immune from state control. Following this decision, McReynolds wrote to a friend that the decision marked "the end of the constitution as you and I regarded it. An alien influence has prevailed."

See John A. C. Hetherington, "State Economic Regulation and Substantive Due Process of Law," *Northwestern University Law Review 53* (1958): 13 (pt. 1), 222 (pt. 2); and Barry Cushman, *Rethinking the New Deal Court* (New York: Oxford University Press, 1998).

Panama Refining Co. v. Ryan

293 U.S. 388 (1935)
Decided: January 7, 1935
Vote: 8 (Hughes, Van Devanter, McReynolds, Brandeis, Sutherland, Butler, Stone, Roberts)
1 (Cardozo)
Opinion of the Court: Hughes
Dissenting opinion: Cardozo

The first case involving federal legislation aimed at ameliorating the Great Depression, *Panama Refining Company v. Ryan*, highlighted many of the problems the Roosevelt administration was to face in the courts. Several of the oil-producing states, in an effort to raise oil prices, had imposed maximum production limits on wells within their borders, although they had no power to control excess illegal production, so-called "hot oil," from being sold in interstate commerce. Section g(c) of the 1933 National Industrial Recovery Act (NIRA) gave the president authority to bar interstate shipment of oil produced in excess of state limits, a policy akin to the earlier Webb-Kenyon Act of 1913, in which federal power had been used to enforce state prohibition laws.

An astounded Court heard counsel for the oil producers tell how they had been unable to secure copies of the regulations and of the careless and casual way in which these regulations, which had the force of law, had been promulgated. At one point, Justice Brandeis asked Assistant Attorney General Harold Stephens, "Is there any way by which to find out what is in these executive orders when they are issued?" An embarrassed Stephens confessed it would be difficult, but, he claimed, "it is possible to get certified copies of the executive orders and codes from the National Recovery Administration."

The Court invalidated Section g(c). Chief Justice Hughes noted that, although the Court recognized the legitimacy and utility of delegating power, Congress in Section g(c) had given the president great authority over interstate commerce without any policy or standards to guide him. Although the decision did not touch the rest of the NIRA, the administration realized that the delegation there and in other programs could not measure up any better. The Court did not deny that Congress had the power to regulate hot oil, but it could not overlook the slipshod way it went about the job.

One positive result of *Panama Oil* was that soon after the decision the government began publishing the *Federal Register*, which made government regulations available in an orderly and easily ascertainable manner.

See Louis L. Jaffe, "An Essay on Delegation of Legislative Power," *Columbia Law Review* 47 (1947): 359 (pt. 1), 561 (pt. 2); and Ronen Shamir, *Managing Legal Uncertainty: Elite Lawyers in the New Deal* (Durham: Duke University Press, 1995).

Pennsylvania v. Williams

294 U.S. 176 (1935)
Decided: February 4, 1935
Vote: 9 (Hughes, Van Devanter, McReynolds, Brandeis, Sutherland, Butler, Stone, Roberts, Cardozo)
0
Opinion of the Court: Stone

Edwin B. Elson, a citizen of New York, owned shares in Mortgage Building & Loan Association, a Pennsylvania corporation. When the association became insolvent, Elson sued to recover his investment in federal court in Pennsylvania. Elson claimed that the federal court had jurisdiction because of "diversity of citizenship," a constitutional provision that if the plaintiff and defendant are from two different states, a legal matter may be brought in federal court. The federal court accepted the case and named John G. Williams as a trustee for the bankrupt loan association. Pennsylvania, in a countersuit against Williams, asserted its claim that as a matter of equity—in other words, dealing with stock shares—the case should be tried in a Pennsylvania state court rather than in federal court.

The Court agreed that the Pennsylvania state court had proper jurisdiction of the case. Although federal courts may hear cases of equity, they are primarily supposed to hear cases of law. If a state court is better suited to handle a case of equity, then a federal court should relinquish its own jurisdiction and let the state court handle the matter, even if the parties come from different states.

Norman v. Baltimore & Ohio Railroad Co.; United States v. Bankers' Trust Co.

294 U.S. 240 (1935)
Decided: February 18, 1935
Vote: 5 (Hughes, Brandeis, Stone, Roberts, Cardozo)
4 (McReynolds, Van Devanter, Sutherland, Butler)
Opinion of the Court: Hughes
Dissenting opinion: McReynolds (Van Devanter, Sutherland, Butler)
See *Gold Clause Cases,* page 196.

Nortz v. United States

294 U.S. 317 (1935)
Decided: February 18, 1935
Vote: 5 (Hughes, Brandeis, Stone, Roberts, Cardozo)
4 (McReynolds, Van Devanter, Sutherland, Butler)
Opinion of the Court: Hughes
Dissenting opinion: McReynolds (Van Devanter, Sutherland, Butler). This dissent is found in *Norman v. Baltimore & Ohio Railroad Co., United States v. Bankers' Trust Co.;* 294 U.S. 240 (1935).
See *Gold Clause Cases,* page 196.

Perry v. United States

294 U.S. 330 (1935)
Decided: February 18, 1935
Vote: 5 (Hughes, Brandeis, Stone, Roberts, Cardozo)
4 (McReynolds, Van Devanter, Sutherland, Butler)
Opinion of the Court: Hughes
Concurring Opinion: Stone
Dissenting opinion: McReynolds (Van Devanter, Sutherland, Butler). This dissent is found in *Norman v. Baltimore & Ohio Railroad Co., United States v. Bankers' Trust Co.;* 294 U.S. 240 (1935).
See *Gold Clause Cases,* page 196.

Baldwin v. G. A. F. Seelig, Inc.

294 U.S. 511 (1935)
Decided: March 4, 1935
Vote: 9 (Hughes, Van Devanter, McReynolds, Brandeis, Sutherland, Butler, Stone, Roberts, Cardozo)
0
Opinion of the Court: Cardozo

G. A. F. Seelig, a New York milk dealer, bought milk products from Seelig Creamery, a Vermont corporation. Because of low dairy prices caused by the Great Depression, New York had set minimum prices for dairy products, and these prices were higher than the prevailing market rate in Vermont. New York stopped Seelig from bringing the Vermont milk into New York unless he paid the higher price. Seelig charged the state with exceeding its authority by attempting to regulate interstate commerce.

The Court agreed in a unanimous decision that New York had unreasonably interfered with interstate commerce. The Court ruled that a state cannot impose its laws in another state or place price regulations on goods coming from another state. Doing so exceeds a state's authority and constitutes an interference with interstate commerce. A state could place a barrier on interstate commerce only when justified by a strong public policy concern, such as a realistic fear of disease or fraud.

Norris v. Alabama

294 U.S. 587 (1935)
Decided: April 1, 1935
Vote: 8 (Hughes, Van Devanter, Brandeis, Sutherland, Butler, Stone, Roberts, Cardozo)
0
Opinion of the Court: Hughes
Did not participate: McReynolds

Clarence Norris was one of nine young black men arrested for raping a young white woman in Alabama. The trial was moved to a location in Alabama where no black people would be placed on the jury, and the nine men were tried and convicted by an all-white jury. Norris argued that the trial violated the Equal Protection and Due Process Clauses of the Fourteenth Amendment because the venue change and jury selection was based upon race and color.

In the "Second Scottsboro Case," the Court held that race could not be used in the jury selection process. Refusing to place people on a jury or refusing to call people to jury duty because of the color of their skin was repugnant to the Constitution and violated the due process and equal protection guarantees of the Fourteenth Amendment. See ***Powell v. Alabama,*** 287 U.S. 45 (1932).

See Benno C. Schmidt Jr., "Juries, Jurisdiction, and Race Discrimination: The Lost Promise of *Strauder v. West Virginia,*" *Texas Law Review* 61 (1983): 1401.

Continental Illinois National Bank & Trust Co. v. Chicago, Rock Island & Pacific Ry. Co.

294 U.S. 648 (1935)
Decided: April 1, 1935
Vote: 8 (Hughes, Van Devanter, McReynolds, Sutherland, Butler, Stone, Roberts, Cardozo)
0
Opinion of the Court: Sutherland
Did not participate: Brandeis

Chicago, Rock Island & Pacific Railway Company filed for bankruptcy in 1933. Under Chapter 11 of the bankruptcy law, a corporation is allowed to reorganize itself and find new ways to handle its debts. The Chicago line owed money to Continental Illinois National Bank and other banks in the form of bonds. The banks wanted to sell the bonds, which would have given other creditors a claim against the line. The railroad, for reasons related to the reorganization, did not want the banks to sell the bonds and went back into bankruptcy court, where it asked for and received an injunction to stop the banks. The banks appealed, arguing that the bankruptcy court did not have jurisdiction over their assets and therefore did not have the authority to issue such an injunction.

The Court held that the bankruptcy court did have jurisdiction under the Federal Bankruptcy Act. The bonds were indeed assets of the banks, but they were also liabilities of the railroad and therefore came within the broad discretion given by federal legislation in handling bankruptcy matters.

Grovey v. Townsend

295 U.S. 45 (1935)
Decided: April 1, 1935
Vote: 9 (Hughes, Van Devanter, McReynolds, Brandeis, Sutherland, Butler, Stone, Roberts, Cardozo)
0
Opinion of the Court: Roberts

R. R. Grovey, a black resident of Houston, Texas, wanted to vote in the Democratic Party's primary, but the Democrats, claiming to be a private organization, allowed only white people to be members of the party and to vote in its primaries. Grovey argued that the Democrats, even if they claimed to be a private party, could not deny him membership or the right to vote in the primaries.

The Court unanimously held that a political party was a private organization and that it could discriminate against a person because of his race and keep black people from voting in their primaries. Justice Roberts distinguished the facts of this case from ***Nixon v. Condon,*** 286 U.S. 73 (1932). There, the state had enacted legislation barring blacks from voting in the primaries. Such action by a state violated the Fifteenth Amendment, which held that a state could not deny a person the right to vote on the basis of race. Private organizations, however, may discriminate on the basis of race, and this did not constitute a violation of equal protection under the Fourteenth Amendment.

The Court reversed itself in ***United States v. Classic,*** 313 U.S. 299 (1941).

See Ward Y. Elliott, *The Rise of Guardian Democracy: The Supreme Court's Role in Voting Rights Disputes, 1848–1969* (Cambridge: Harvard University Press, 1974).

Railroad Retirement Board v. Alton Railroad

295 U.S. 330 (1935)
Decided: May 6, 1935
Vote: 5 (Van Devanter, McReynolds, Sutherland, Butler, Roberts)
4 (Hughes, Brandeis, Stone, Cardozo)
Opinion of the Court: Roberts
Dissenting opinion: Hughes (Brandeis, Stone, Cardozo)

Congress passed the Railroad Retirement Act as part of President Roosevelt's New Deal legislation. The act established a mandatory retirement and pension system for all railroad carriers. Its rationale was to promote efficiency and safety by making it possible for aging employees to stop working. Under the law, all railroads had to provide retirement and pension plans for their employees.

Alton Railroad sued, arguing that the act was an unconstitutional interference with its liberty to contract. It argued that

Congress had no power under the Commerce Clause to make employers provide retirement plans for employees. This was legislation designed for social welfare, not to regulate commerce.

The Court ruled that Congress had no such powers and that the act was unconstitutional. Under the Commerce Clause, according to Justice Roberts, Congress may regulate only matters that directly affect interstate commerce. Employee benefits affect interstate commerce only indirectly and were therefore beyond the scope of congressional power. The law also violated the Fifth Amendment, because it deprived corporations of property without due process. Companies could not be made to provide pension plans for their employees, no matter how strong a public interest there might be in such a scheme. The Railroad Retirement Act violated the railroads' property rights, their freedom of contract rights, and their economic rights.

Schechter Poultry Corp. v. United States

295 U.S. 495 (1935)
Decided: May 27, 1935
Vote: 9 (Hughes, Van Devanter, McReynolds, Brandeis, Sutherland, Butler, Stone, Roberts, Cardozo)
0
Opinion of the Court: Hughes
Concurring opinion: Cardozo (Stone)

The centerpiece of the New Deal's economic program, as well as its most controversial measure, was the National Industrial Recovery Act, (NIRA) the constitutionality of which relied on an expansive interpretation of the Commerce Clause.

The bill was a hodgepodge of proposals designed to satisfy a number of interest groups. Various segments of business received permission to draft code agreements intended to govern the conduct of business, labor relations, pricing, and other matters, which, when approved by the members of the industry and by the government, would have the force of law and be exempt from antitrust laws. The planners won their demand for government licensing of business through federal oversight of the codes. In an effort to placate labor, a section was included that guaranteed the right to bargain collectively and required the codes to set minimum wages and maximum hours. The bill established an oversight agency, the National Recovery Administration (NRA), to facilitate code drafting. The theory behind the bill was that if business could agree on what had to be done and on a fair way to cooperate, then the economic recovery would soon follow. If businesses proved obstinate, the NRA had the power, acting for the president, to draft codes and impose them. All codes, once approved by the president, had the force of law.

The Schechter brothers operated a kosher poultry business in Brooklyn. The government charged them with violating the live poultry code provisions on wages, hours, and fair trade requirements, including counts of selling chickens that were unfit for human consumption. The government prepared an elaborate exhibit to show the interstate implications of the Schechter plant, but, as one of the Justice Department officials later conceded, "no amount of economic research to unearth a judicially noticeable matter could . . . show in a convincing manner that these practices in New York substantially affected the interstate poultry market."

Although the Court, as a matter of jurisprudential practice, normally tries to decide cases on the narrowest basis possible, Chief Justice Hughes's opinion posed three major questions: Did the economic crisis create extraordinary government powers? Had Congress lawfully delegated power to the president? Did the act exceed the government's authority under the Commerce Clause? This radical departure from the conservative procedures of the Court convinced many observers that not only Hughes, but also the entire bench, wanted to make sure that after the Court had killed the NIRA, it would stay dead.

In ***Home Building and Loan Association v. Blaisdell,*** 290 U.S. 398 (1934), upholding the Minnesota mortgage moratorium, Hughes stated that emergencies could call forth latent powers, that is, powers not explicitly spelled out in the Constitution but which could be inferred from language in the War Powers and the Necessary and Proper Clauses. In *Schechter,* however, Hughes reversed himself and declared that "extraordinary conditions do not create or enlarge constitutional power." The elaborate rationale in the NIRA's preamble tying the remedy to the depression made not the slightest impression on the Court. As for the delegation of power, Hughes reiterated the Court's objections in ***Panama Refining Co. v. Ryan,*** 292 U.S. 388 (1935). Congress certainly had the power to delegate power to the president, but it had to establish clear guidelines and standards. Here, in "a sweeping delegation of legislative power" it had given the president a blank check to create and enforce codes, or worse yet, to enforce as the law of the land codes that were drafted by private parties. Justice Cardozo, who had entered the lone dissent in *Panama Refining,* added a concurring opinion here in which he described the problem as "delegation running riot."

In answering the third question, Hughes—joined by all his colleagues—took a quite restrictive a view of commerce. He revived the old distinction between the direct and indirect effects of local activity on interstate commerce. He declared that only those intrastate activities that directly affected interstate commerce fell within the reach of the federal government's powers. The Schechter brothers' business had no direct effect—and in fact very little indirect effect—on interstate commerce and therefore could not be regulated by Congress.

Cardozo's concurrence stated that clear principles determined the distinction between direct and indirect effects. He thought it more a matter of degree, but in this case, he too could find no relation between selling sick chickens in Brooklyn and interstate commerce.

President Roosevelt received the news of Black Monday, when three decisions went against the administration, in astonishment; he could hardly believe that even the liberals had gone against him. "Where was Ben Cardozo?" he asked. "And what about old Isaiah [Brandeis]?" To reporters he complained that the *Schechter* decision had relegated the nation "to the horse-and-buggy definition of interstate commerce."

See Ellis Wayne Hawley, *The New Deal and the Problem of Monopoly: A Study in Economic Ambivalence* (Princeton: Princeton University Press, 1966); Robert F. Himmelberg, *The Origins of the National Recovery Act,* 2d ed. (New York: Fordham University Press, 1993); and Bernard Bellush, *The Failure of the NRA* (New York: Norton, 1975).

Louisville Joint Stock Land Bank v. Radford

295 U.S. 555 (1935)
Decided: May 27, 1935
Vote: 9 (Hughes, Van Devanter, McReynolds, Brandeis, Sutherland, Butler, Stone, Roberts, Cardozo)
0
Opinion of the Court: Brandeis

In 1924 Radford mortgaged his farm to the Louisville Joint Stock Land Bank. When, during the Great Depression, Radford could not make his mortgage payments, the bank called in the loan. Unable to pay, Radford lost his farm to the bank.

In 1934 Congress passed the Frazier-Lemke Act, which allowed a farmer to buy back his farm and make deferred payments on the debt. If a bank refused to enter into such an agreement, the farmer could make payments to a court that would then disperse the money to the bank. Radford attempted to make such an arrangement, and, when the bank refused, the two parties went to court, with the bank claiming that the Frazier-Lemke Act was unconstitutional.

The Court agreed with the bank, holding the act unconstitutional. Although Justice Brandeis agreed that the government had the power to change the terms of federal bankruptcy law, it could not transfer property rights to a debtor that now belonged to the creditor. If Congress changed the law, it would apply only to future mortgage arrangements. The Louisville bank had already foreclosed on Radford and owned his farm. It could not be forced by the government to give it back. Such a provision, Brandeis held, violates the Fifth Amendment prohibition against the taking of private property without just compensation.

The decision came as a surprise because a year earlier the Court had upheld a Minnesota state moratorium on farm foreclosures in ***Home Building & Loan Assn. v. Blaisdell,*** 290 U.S. 398 (1934). But, as Brandeis explained, the Minnesota law did not deprive creditors of their property; it merely changed the manner and time in which debtors had to repay their loans. Here, the foreclosure had taken place, the property had transferred, and the debtor no longer had any interest in the farm.

The decision was one of three handed down on so-called "Black Monday," the day the Court also invalidated the National Industrial Recovery Act in ***Schechter Poultry Corp. v. United States,*** 295 U.S. 495 (1935) and decided ***Humphrey's Executor v. United States,*** 295 U.S. 602 (1935).

Humphrey's Executor v. United States

295 U.S. 602 (1935)
Decided: May 27, 1935
Vote: 9 (Hughes, Van Devanter, McReynolds, Brandeis, Sutherland, Butler, Stone, Roberts, Cardozo)
0
Opinion of the Court: Sutherland
Concurring without opinion: McReynolds

In ***Myers v. United States,*** 272 U.S. 52 (1926), the Court ruled that the powers of the president included the authority to remove executive officers without senatorial approval. The Court's broad interpretation of executive power, as written by Chief Justice Taft, drew dissents from Justices Holmes, McReynolds, and Brandeis, the latter noting that separation of powers had been adopted "not to promote efficiency but to preclude the exercise of arbitrary power."

Relying on *Myers,* President Roosevelt forced William Humphrey, a conservative advocate of big business, to resign from the Federal Trade Commission. Humphrey challenged this action in the U.S. Court of Claims. After his death, his estate continued the suit.

The Court now said that, at least regarding the regulatory commissions, it had been the intent of Congress to make them independent of the executive and subject only to the legislature and the judiciary. A president could remove a commissioner only for cause, and an unqualified power of removal violated the separation of powers. Sutherland distinguished this case from *Myers* by asserting that, unlike a postmaster with executive branch functions only, a regulatory agency commissioner is a government official with quasi-judicial, quasi-legislative, and quasi-executive responsibilities and obligations.

The decision was delivered the same day as ***Schechter Poultry Corp. v. United States,*** 295 U.S. 495 (1935), invalidating the National Industrial Recovery Act, and ***Louisville Joint Stock Bank Co. v. Radford,*** 295 U.S. 555 (1935), voiding the Frazier-Lemke Farm Mortgage Act. This day, known as "Black Monday" served as a catalyst to Roosevelt's ill-fated Court-packing plan, when in 1937 he tried to secure legislation to add six new justices to the Court. Unlike other decisions striking down New Deal measures, nearly all of which have been reversed, the basic principle of *Humphrey's Executor* remains intact, and was reaffirmed in 1958 in ***Wiener v. United States,*** 357 U.S. 349.

Although it is still good law, *Humphrey's Executor* has received mixed reviews over the years. On the one hand, it has been praised for assuring the independence of members of federal regulatory commissions from political reprisal by a president who does not agree with a member's policies. On the other hand, a commission member is considered part of the executive branch, and the inability to dismiss an uncooperative member thwarts a president who is trying to develop a consistent and unified policy.

See William E. Leuchtenburg, "The Case of the Contentious Commissioner: *Humphrey's Executor v. United States*," in *Freedom and Reform: Essays in Honor of Henry Steele Commager,* ed. Harold M. Hyman and Leonard W. Levy (New York: Harper and Row, 1967).

Fox Film Corp. v. Muller

296 U.S. 207 (1935)
Decided: December 9, 1935
Vote: 8 (Van Devanter, McReynolds, Brandeis, Sutherland, Butler, Stone, Roberts, Cardozo)
0
Opinion of the Court: Sutherland
Did not participate: Hughes

The Fox company had two motion picture contracts with A. B. Muller, and both included arbitration agreements. Muller wanted to break free of the contracts and went into state court claiming that the arbitration clause was illegal under federal antitrust law. A Minnesota state court ruled that the arbitration agreement was severable from the contract, meaning that the remainder of the contract was still enforceable. Had the case been decided in federal court, it is possible that Muller would have won. He now claimed that the state court lacked jurisdiction to decide the case.

The Supreme Court held that if a case rests upon two different grounds, one federal and one state, and if the state decision is able to support the judgment, then federal courts have no jurisdiction. In other words, if a state court can adequately handle a case under appropriate state law, then it should go to that court, not to the federal courts. The decision in the Minnesota court stood.

United States v. Butler

297 U.S. 1 (1936)
Decided: January 6, 1936
Vote: 6 (Hughes, Van Devanter, McReynolds, Sutherland, Butler, Roberts)
3 (Brandeis, Stone, Cardozo)
Opinion of the Court: Roberts
Dissenting opinion: Stone (Brandeis, Cardozo)

The Agricultural Adjustment Act of 1933 (AAA) was the pivotal measure in the New Deal effort to aid agriculture during the Great Depression. It was based on the notion of "parity," a system to regulate the market so as to assure farmers the same purchasing power for their crops as they had in the base period of 1909 to 1914. If farmers accepted voluntary federal restrictions on acreage, they could then participate in federal government price supports. The scheme would be financed by a federal tax on food processors, such as the millers who converted wheat to flour.

During President Roosevelt's first term, farmers' gross income rose more than 50 percent and rural debts fell sharply—although the drought of 1934–1935 may deserve as much credit as the government for limiting production. But New Dealers worried that the conservative justices' restrictive view of the Commerce Clause would invalidate the AAA, so they relied instead on the taxing power, which until this point the Court had accorded a broad interpretation.

Officials of Hoosac Mills Corporation attacked the levy, which they characterized as an integral part of an unconstitutional plan to control agricultural production. The district court found the taxes valid and ordered that they be paid. The circuit court reversed this order. The government challenged Hoosac's right to sue because several cases, especially ***Frothingham v. Mellon,*** 262 U.S. 447 (1923), held that taxpayers had no standing to question in court how the federal government spent its tax revenues. The conservatives on the bench brushed this defense aside. The plaintiffs had not challenged just the tax and its uses, but the whole plan of which the tax, according to Justice Roberts, "is a mere incident of such regulation."

Roberts's opinion is perhaps the most tortured and confusing of all the Court's New Deal decisions. The tax, Roberts held, could not be considered a true tax, for none of the proceeds went into the general coffers; instead, the tax purchased compliance with a program that went beyond the legitimate bounds of congressional power. Because of its local nature, agriculture could be regulated only by the state, and, even if the sum of many local conditions had created a national problem, Congress was still not permitted to "ignore constitutional limitations" imposed by the Tenth Amendment.

Roberts next turned to the government's reliance on Article I, Section 8, which authorizes Congress to "lay and collect Taxes . . . and provide for the common Defence and general Welfare of the United States." The federal government has the unquestioned right to tax, and Congress has the discretion to determine how those revenues could best be used to provide for the general welfare. Roberts then reviewed the debate between James Madison and Alexander Hamilton on the meaning of this clause. Madison claimed that it served merely as an introduction to the enumerated powers and conferred no additional authority. Hamilton, on the other hand, believed that the words had a separate meaning and allowed Congress a general power to tax and spend for what it believed to be in the best interests of the country. Roberts agreed with Hamilton but then declared that crop payments could not be justified under the General Welfare Clause because the payments were no more than a subterfuge to circumvent the Tenth Amendment.

As for the government's claim that the voluntary nature of the plan distinguished it from an impermissible regulatory scheme, Roberts asserted that the power to confer or withhold government benefits "is the power to coerce or destroy. . . . The asserted power of choice is illusory." Roberts ignored the decision in ***Massachusetts v. Mellon,*** 262 U.S. 447 (1923), in which the Court had upheld a plan whereby states could choose or decline to participate in a federal program, with federal grants reserved for those who joined.

Justice Stone dissented sharply from what he considered Roberts's myopic view of the taxing power. He pointed out that unlike the child labor tax, which had been regulatory, the processing tax did no more than raise revenue; the regulatory part of the farm program came through appropriations. He also attacked Roberts's "tortured construction of the Constitution" and the majority's resort to *argumentum ad horrendum* its claim that if this terrible program were approved, it follows that Congress would attempt to regulate all areas of the nation's economic life.

Congress responded quickly to *Butler* with the passage of the Soil Conservation Act, which contained no tax and tried to avoid any semblance of coercion. It offered farmers rewards for planting grasses and legumes rather than commercial crops, a device that still aimed at limiting crop production.

See Paul L. Murphy, "The New Deal Agricultural Program and the Constitution," *Agricultural History* 29 (1955): 160; Van L. Perkins, *Crisis in Agriculture: The Agricultural Adjustment Administration and the New Deal* (Berkeley: University of California Press, 1969); and Robert H. Jackson, *The Struggle for Judicial Supremacy* (New York: Knopf, 1941).

Grosjean v. American Press Co., Inc.

297 U.S. 233 (1936)
Decided: February 10, 1936
Vote: 9 (Hughes, Van Devanter, McReynolds, Brandeis, Sutherland, Butler, Stone, Roberts, Cardozo)
0
Opinion of the Court: Sutherland

Louisiana taxed publications that carried advertisements, but only large-scale publishers. American Press Company argued that the policy was unconstitutional, that placing special higher taxes on certain newspapers and publications violated the freedom of press guaranteed in the First Amendment.

The Court agreed, holding that taxing only large publishers violated the First Amendment. Although states have the power to tax, they may not do it in a discriminatory manner that infringes upon an individual's free press rights. Because the tax targeted only large-scale press companies, it constituted viewpoint/content-based discrimination. It also violated the Equal Protection and Due Process Clauses of the Fourteenth Amendment. Large newspaper companies cannot be taxed at a higher rate merely because of their size. Such a tax would in effect punish speech for reaching a large audience.

Brown v. Mississippi

297 U.S. 278 (1936)
Decided: February 17, 1936
Vote: 9 (Hughes, Van Devanter, McReynolds, Brandeis, Sutherland, Butler, Stone, Roberts, Cardozo)
0
Opinion of the Court: Hughes

Three black Mississippi tenant farmers were arrested for the murder of a white landowner and tortured into confessing the crime. These confessions were the chief evidence against the defendants, although prosecution witnesses freely noted that the defendants had confessed only after being brutally whipped by the sheriff's officers. Nevertheless, the judge admitted the confessions into evidence, and the three men were found guilty and sentenced to be hanged. On appeal, the state's high court affirmed the convictions.

Earl Leroy Brewer, a former governor of Mississippi, led the defense team that appealed the convictions to the U.S. Supreme Court. Although noting that the Self-Incrimination Clause of the Fifth Amendment did not apply to the states, Chief Justice Hughes condemned the manner in which the so-called confessions had been elicited as a clear violation of the Due Process Clause of the Fourteenth Amendment. Physical torture and brutality violated the very notion of a fair trial and fundamental principles of decency.

This case is one in a string of cases, beginning in the 1920s, in which the Court paid greater notice to the due process elements of state criminal trials. Although *Brown* did not incorporate the Fourteenth Amendment, it established a beachhead that would later be used to guarantee that the Fourth, Fifth, and Sixth Amendments would eventually be applied to the states.

Brown was also first in a line of cases in which the Court looked at how confessions were secured from people accused of crimes, a line that runs to ***Miranda v. Arizona,*** 384 U.S. 436 (1966).

See Richard C. Cortner, *A "Scottsboro" Case in Mississippi: The Supreme Court and Brown v. Mississippi* (Jackson: University of Mississippi, 1986).

Ashwander v. Tennessee Valley Authority

297 U.S. 288 (1936)
Decided: February 17, 1936
Vote: 8 (Hughes, Van Devanter, Brandeis, Sutherland, Butler, Stone, Roberts, Cardozo)
1 (McReynolds)
Opinion of the Court: Hughes
Concurring opinion: Brandeis (Stone, Roberts, Cardozo)
Dissenting opinion: McReynolds

The Tennessee Valley Authority (TVA) was one of the most ambitious and most successful of all the New Deal's experimental programs. Covering a seven-state area with the nominal purpose of erecting dams for flood control on the Tennessee River, it set out to reclaim land, build parks, and raise the standard of living of one of the poorest parts of the country. It also established a yardstick for the costs of producing electricity that regulatory commissions could use to set rates for private utilities.

The TVA sold the electricity it produced to distribution companies—not directly to the public. A group of shareholders in one of the distribution companies brought suit in an effort to annul their company's contract to purchase electricity from the TVA, claiming that the TVA was unconstitutional.

Ignoring all but the very narrow question that he framed, Chief Justice Hughes found the TVA a constitutional exercise of federal power. Congress clearly had the power to build dams for national defense as well as to facilitate interstate commerce; the electricity produced by those dams was a by-product, and Article IV, Section 3, of the Constitution, which gives the government power to sell property that it owns, could justify its sale.

The decision is most notable for Justice Brandeis's concurring opinion. He believed that the constitutional question should never have been addressed because the case was really no more than an internal squabble among shareholders. The Court, he argued, should avoid whenever possible making judgments on the constitutionality of legislation, and he set out guidelines calling for judicial restraint. The "Ashwander Rules" hold that (1) the Court will not determine the constitutionality of legislation in nonadversary proceedings; (2) the Court will not anticipate a constitutional question; (3) in formulating a decision, the Court will not fashion a rule broader than needed for the question before it; (4) it will not rule on the constitutionality of a statute, if there are other grounds available for deciding the case; (5) unless the party attacking a law has been injured by a statute, the Court will not judge its validity; (6) the Court will not invalidate a law at the behest of a person who has benefited from it; and (7) the Court will always seek to find some reasonable interpretation of a statute in order to avoid a constitutional question. Judges still cite this part of the opinion as their guide to constitutional adjudication. It is especially revered by advocates of judicial restraint, who see these tenets as imposing proper restraints on the judicial power.

See Joseph C. Swidler and Robert H. Marquis, "TVA in Court: A Study of TVA's Constitutional Litigation," *Iowa Law Review* 32 (1947): 296; and G. D. Haimbaugh Jr., "The TVA Cases: A Quarter Century Later," *Indiana Law Journal* 41 (1966): 197.

Jones v. Securities and Exchange Commission

298 U.S. 1 (1936)
Decided: April 6, 1936
Vote: 6 (Hughes, Van Devanter, McReynolds, Sutherland, Butler, Roberts)
3 (Brandeis, Stone, Cardozo)
Opinion of the Court: Sutherland
Dissenting opinion: Cardozo (Brandeis, Stone)

J. Edward Jones filed an application statement with the Securities Exchange Commission (SEC) to sell some proposed trust certificates, for which he needed the SEC's permission. The commission discovered that the statement contained false statements and concealed the fact that the trust certificates were phony. The SEC denied permission, which prevented the trust certificates from coming into the market. The SEC also subpoenaed Jones to explain why he had made false statements. Jones clearly did not want to answer any questions, but, when he tried to withdraw the application, the SEC would not let him. Jones sued the commission, claiming that the SEC had no authority to investigate the matter or to refuse to allow him to withdraw the application and walk away.

The Court ruled that the SEC was in the wrong. Justice Sutherland reasoned that anyone filing an application with the SEC should be allowed to withdraw it at any time. He condemned the SEC as arbitrary for not allowing Jones to cancel the application and for continuing to investigate the matter to see if Jones had broken the law. The justices agreed that Jones had the right to take back the application. An application with illegal information need only be denied.

Carter v. Carter Coal Co.

298 U.S. 238 (1936)
Decided: March 18, 1936
Vote: 5 (Van Devanter, McReynolds, Sutherland, Butler, Roberts)
4 (Hughes, Brandeis, Stone, Cardozo)
Opinion of the Court: Sutherland
Opinion concurring in part, dissenting in part: Hughes
Opinion concurring in part, dissenting in part: Cardozo (Brandeis, Stone)

In response to ***Schechter Poultry Corp. v. United States,*** 295 U.S. 495 (1935), Congress tried to salvage part of the National Recovery Administration (NRA) with the Guffy-Snyder Coal Conservation Act of 1935. Coal mining was hard hit by the Great Depression, and the NRA coal code brought a desperately needed stabilization to the industry. The new law established the National Bituminous Coal Commission, with representatives of management, labor, and the public empowered to control production and prices. Mines that produced two-thirds of the nation's tonnage signed agreements with the commission that included provisions for wages, hours, and collective bargaining. To enforce the code, the act imposed a 15 percent tax at the mine head, nearly all of which would be remitted to operators abiding by the agreement. To avoid the problems raised in *Schechter,* Congress declared coal production "affected with a national public interest" and so much a part of interstate commerce as to require federal regulation. Because nearly the entire industry, labor as well as management, supported the act, it seemed unlikely there would be an opportunity for judicial review. But in ***United States v. Butler,*** 297 U.S. 1 (1936), the Court had opened the door to allow stockholders to sue company officials for obeying allegedly unconstitutional federal laws, and such a stockholders' suit brought the Guffy Act to the Court early in 1936.

Justice Sutherland declared the entire bill unconstitutional. He relied on *Schechter* for a highly restrictive view of interstate commerce and bolstered his opinion with citations to nineteenth century cases such as *Kidd v. Pearson,* 128 U.S. 1 (1888), and ***United States v. E. C. Knight,*** 156 U.S. 1 (1895), which many thought had been repudiated years earlier. Sutherland's determination to thwart the Roosevelt program could not be hidden behind neutral-sounding formulas. He ignored more than two decades of congressional studies that supported the argument for treating coal as a national rather than a local energy resource, and he dismissed the *amici* briefs of seven states that claimed that only federal regulation would save the industry. Moreover, despite the clear intention of Congress that the different sections of the act be considered separately, he invalidated the labor provisions, even though they had not been implemented at the time of the case. He declared that all the provisions were intertwined and all were unconstitutional.

Chief Justice Hughes, in a separate opinion, agreed that the labor provisions were invalid, but charged that the majority had no right to ignore the separability clause. In his view, the price control provision met the test of constitutionality and should have been approved.

Justice Cardozo said he could hardly believe that the majority could turn its back on the realities outside the courtroom. If an industry so disrupted as coal was, and so central to the nation's economic well-being, could not be federally regulated, then little hope remained for solving the country's economic woes.

Carter fueled the growing public protest against the Court's war on the administration's recovery program and strengthened President Roosevelt's resolve that something had to be done to save the nation from the Court.

See Eugene V. Rostow, "Bituminous Coal and the Public Interest," *Yale Law Journal* 50 (1941): 543.

Morehead v. New York ex rel. Tipaldo

298 U.S. 587 (1936)
Decided: June 1, 1936
Vote: 5 (Van Devanter, McReynolds, Sutherland, Butler, Roberts)
4 (Hughes, Brandeis, Stone, Cardozo)
Opinion of the Court: Butler
Dissenting opinion: Hughes (Brandeis, Stone, Cardozo)
Dissenting opinion: Stone (Brandeis, Cardozo)

In the early 1930s the Court upheld several state laws designed to regulate their economies to meliorate the effects of the Great Depression. These decisions, especially ***Nebbia v. New York,*** 291 U.S. 502 (1934), in which the Court upheld a price regulation statute, led many to believe that the Court had eliminated the last vestiges of substantive due process and abandoned freedom of contract. In June 1936 they learned they were mistaken.

Three years earlier New York had enacted a minimum wage law for women and children. Joseph Tipaldo, the manager of a laundry, refused to pay the minimum wage and was arrested for violating the law. On appeal, he claimed that the statute was unconstitutional, relying on the Court's opinion in ***Adkins v. Children's Hospital,*** 261 U.S. 525 (1923). Justice Roberts, the author of *Nebbia,* now joined the conservatives to invalidate New York's minimum wage law. Justice Sutherland's majority decision rested entirely on the *Adkins* reasoning, that such laws violated freedom of contract and the Due Process Clause of the Fourteenth Amendment. Even normally conservative newspapers termed the ruling "regrettable," and the Republican candidate for president, Alfred M. Landon, carefully distanced himself from the Court's conservative bloc. The Republican Party platform, in fact, specifically approved state regulation of hours and wages for women and children.

Justice Stone's dissent called for the Court to be consistent; it should follow the ruling in *Nebbia* and leave the wisdom of solving economic problems to the legislative branch. Chief Justice Hughes also found the majority ruling incomprehensible, declaring that he found nothing in the Constitution "which denies to the State the power to protect women from being exploited."

Ten months later, Roberts switched his position again and voted with the liberal bloc to uphold an almost identical law in ***West Coast Hotel v. Parrish,*** 300 U.S. 379 (1937). Subjected to bitter criticism for his change in position from *Nebbia* to *Morehead* and then back again in such a short time, Roberts later explained that he had been willing to overrule *Adkins* from the start, but the counsel for New York in *Morehead* had not asked the Court to do so. Rather, the lawyer had tried to distinguish the New York situation from that in *Adkins;* Roberts had been unable to see any difference and believed *Adkins* had to govern the case. When, in *West Coast Hotel,* the attorney called on the Court to abandon *Adkins,* Roberts willingly did so.

Morehead was the last minimum wage law declared unconstitutional by the Court. This decision, which tarnished the Court, helped trigger the constitutional crisis of 1937 in which President Franklin Roosevelt tried to pack the Court.

See Barry Cushman, *Rethinking the New Deal Court* (New York: Oxford University Press, 1998); and John W. Chambers, "The Big Switch: Justice Roberts and the Minimum Wage Cases," *Labor History* 10 (1969): 44.

United States v. Curtiss-Wright Export Corp.

299 U.S. 304 (1936)
Decided: December 21, 1936
Vote: 7 (Hughes, Van Devanter, Brandeis, Sutherland, Butler, Roberts, Cardozo)
1 (McReynolds)
Opinion of the Court: Sutherland
Dissenting opinion: McReynolds
Did not participate: Stone

In a joint resolution, Congress authorized the president to embargo arms shipments to countries at war in the Chaco region of South America. Using this authority, President Roosevelt issued a proclamation to carry out the congressional mandate. Eighteen months later he revoked the proclamation as no longer relevant. Curtiss-Wright Corporation was indicted for violating the embargo. The company appealed on the grounds that the embargo was unconstitutional because Congress had improperly delegated legislative power to the executive. Congress left what should have been a legislative judgment to the president's "unfettered discretion." The company relied on the Court's denunciation of delegation in the National Industrial Recovery Act that had been struck down in ***Schechter Poultry Corp. v. United States,*** 295 U.S. 495 (1935).

The Court, however, drew a significant distinction between domestic and foreign affairs. Because the Constitution has little to say about foreign affairs, congressional and presidential powers must be derived from inferences and the constitutional structure rather than from specific wording. The Court interpreted the Constitution as granting the presidency a broad sweep of power in foreign affairs, akin to what Justice Holmes had done for the treaty-making power in ***Missouri v. Holland,*** 252 U.S. 416 (1920).

The powers of the sovereign in foreign affairs, Justice Sutherland wrote, did not depend solely on the Constitution, but derived from the very nature of sovereignty. The most controversial part of the decision was Sutherland's grant of extremely broad authority to the presidency in the conduct of foreign affairs, making him the voice of the nation and granting to him plenary powers in this area well beyond those listed in Article II.

Many have argued that the case never should have involved the existence of an independent presidential power because the litigants raised only the question of whether Congress had exceeded its powers. Sutherland's opinion closely tracked an article he had written as a senator in 1910 and published in his 1919 book, *Constitutional Power and World Affairs.* There and in other places Sutherland advocated a vigorous—even belligerent—diplomacy that unceasingly asserted American rights. In *Curtiss-Wright,* Sutherland claimed that only the federal government had any control over foreign affairs and, with the exception of the advice and consent powers of the Senate, all foreign powers resided in the executive branch. Scholars have attacked the history on which Sutherland relied, showing that the states did not give up all of their powers following the Revolution. They also maintain that the Constitution grants Congress a voice in foreign policy, including the power of the purse. The Framers, it is claimed, made no distinction between foreign and domestic affairs, and certainly in modern times the line is often difficult to discern.

See Louis Henkin, ed., *Foreign Affairs and the U.S. Constitution* (Ardsley-on-Hudson, N.Y.: Transnational Publishers, 1990); and Charles Lofgren, "*United States v. Curtiss-Wright Export Corporation:* An Historical Reassessment," *Yale Law Journal* 83 (1973): 1.

DeJonge v. Oregon

299 U.S. 353 (1937)
Decided: January 4, 1937
Vote: 8 (Hughes, Van Devanter, McReynolds, Brandeis, Sutherland, Butler, Roberts, Cardozo)
0
Opinion of the Court: Hughes
Did not participate: Stone

Dirk DeJonge, a communist, was charged with violating Oregon's criminal syndicalism statute, which prohibited any speech advocating illegal activity to achieve political goals. He was arrested for speaking at a Communist Party rally in Portland that was called to protest police shootings of striking longshoremen. Despite the sponsorship of the Communist Party, no more than 15 percent of those present were communists. DeJonge tried to sell some party publications. None of the speakers advocated any criminal activity, and the meeting was peaceful and orderly. The principal evidence against DeJonge was party literature found elsewhere that police and the trial court read to mean that communists advocated criminal syndicalism. On appeal, DeJonge claimed that Oregon's law deprived him of his First Amendment rights of free speech, but the Oregon Supreme Court held that he could be arrested for doing nothing more than participating in a peaceful meeting if that meeting was sponsored by a communist group.

The U.S. Supreme Court reversed, holding that the law as applied to DeJonge deprived him of his right of free speech. The First Amendment right of free speech is applied to individuals via the Due Process Clause of the Fourteenth Amendment. Although DeJonge was a communist, he was still entitled to speak. He could advocate communist principles as long as he did it in a lawful manner and did not incite violence or unlawful activity. As Chief Justice Hughes wrote for the Court, "Peaceable assembly for lawful discussion cannot be made a crime."

The case continued the Court's trend of incorporating the First Amendment through the Due Process Clause of the Fourteenth Amendment and applying it to the states. It also marked another step away from the speech-limiting decisions of 1919 and 1920 and toward a more speech-protective interpretation of the First Amendment.

West Coast Hotel Co. v. Parrish

300 U.S. 379 (1937)
Decided: March 29, 1937
Vote: 5 (Hughes, Brandeis, Stone, Roberts, Cardozo)
4 (Van Devanter, McReynolds, Sutherland, Butler)
Opinion of the Court: Hughes
Dissenting opinion: Sutherland (Van Devanter, McReynolds, Butler)

In the midst of the congressional debate over President Roosevelt's Court-packing plan, in which he tried to secure legislation allowing him to name up to six additional justices to the Supreme Court, the Court apparently reversed course in its efforts to repudiate the New Deal and sustained a Washington State minimum wage law. Justice Roberts, who had written the decision invalidating a similar New York law a year earlier in ***Morehead v. New York ex rel. Tipaldo,*** 298 U.S. 587 (1936), now joined the liberals in Chief Justice Hughes's opinion that overruled ***Adkins v. Children's Hospital,*** 261 U.S. 525 (1923). Hughes dismissed the relevance of *Morehead,* asserting that the Court had not reexamined the constitutionality of minimum wage legislation at that time because it had not been asked to do so.

Justice Sutherland used his dissent to lash out against what he saw as the theory that the Constitution's meaning changed depending on current economic conditions. He agreed that "the Constitution is made up of living words that apply to every new condition which they include." But he cautioned against what he saw as the Court's illegitimate effort to change the nature of the Constitution: ". . . to say . . . that the words of the Constitution mean today what they did not mean when written—that is, that they do not apply to a situation now to which they would have applied then—is to rob that instrument of the essential element which continues it in force as the people have made it until they, and not their official agents, have made it otherwise."

Roberts's change of heart led to much speculation that the Court-packing plan influenced some members of the Court who reversed themselves to avoid drastic reorganization and loss of power. "A switch in time," contemporary wits claimed, "saves nine." It is now fairly certain that Roosevelt's plan had nothing to do with the result in this case. Roberts had been dissatisfied with *Adkins,* but because the state had not been willing to challenge *Adkins,* Roberts believed that he had no choice but to go along.

When *Parrish* was argued, counsel asked for a reversal of *Adkins,* and Roberts informed his colleagues that he would vote to sustain the Washington State statute. But Justice Stone was seriously ill at that time; he had missed both oral argument and had not voted at the conference, thus leaving the justices evenly divided. Had Stone been present, the Court would have issued a decision upholding state minimum wage legislation before Roosevelt delivered his Court-packing speech, and the decision might even have deterred the president from doing so. Roberts's decision can be criticized as resulting from mechanistic decision making (he had not been asked to decide a question, and so had ignored it) or praised as adhering to principle (his views had not changed, but merely needed a proper vehicle for expression), but in neither case can it be seen as a response to political pressure.

West Coast Hotel v. Parrish helped pull the Court back to the path it had followed prior to 1935 in sustaining state economic regulations under the broad rubric of the police power. That same day, the Court approved three federal statutes, each similar to one struck down a few years earlier. One case, *Sonzinsky v. United States,* 300 U.S. 506 (1937), validated the use of the taxing power for regulatory purposes in direct opposition to the Court's decision in ***United States v. Butler,*** 297 U.S. 1 (1936).

See John W. Chambers, "The Big Switch: Justice Roberts and the Minimum Wage Cases," *Labor History* 10 (1969): 44; and Charles A. Leonard, *A Search for a Judicial Philosophy: Mr. Justice Roberts and the Constitutional Revolution of 1937* (Port Washington, N.Y.: Kennikat Press, 1971).

National Labor Relations Board v. Jones & Laughlin Steel Corporation

301 U.S. 1 (1937)
Decided: April 12, 1937
Vote: 5 (Hughes, Brandeis, Stone, Roberts, Cardozo)
4 (Van Devanter, McReynolds, Sutherland, Butler)
Opinion of the Court: Hughes
Dissenting opinion: Sutherland (Van Devanter, McReynolds, Butler). This dissent is found in *National Labor Relations Board v. Friedman-Harry Marks Clothing Co.,* 301 U.S. 58, at 76 (1937).

Through ***Schechter Poultry Corp. v. United States,*** 295 U.S. 495 (1935), the Court invalidated Section 7(a) of the National Industrial Recovery Act, (NIRA), which guaranteed workers the right to organize and to bargain collectively. In 1935 Congress passed the National Labor Relations Act, commonly referred to as the Wagner Act, which reaffirmed labor's right to organize and prohibited employers from firing or otherwise discriminating against union members and organizers. The law also set down a list of unfair practices and established the National Labor Relations Board (NLRB) to enforce these provisions.

Supporters were concerned about how the justices would view the constitutionality of the act in light of a string of Supreme Court decisions hostile to union activities. The notion of a freedom of contract embedded in the Due Process Clause had been interpreted to mean that employers and laborers were free to bargain without government interference, while union activities had often been seen as a conspiracy in violation of the Sherman Act. Moreover, the broad interpretation of the commerce power, which underlay the Wagner Act ran counter to recent Court rulings—especially *Schechter*—that took a narrow view of commerce.

Jones & Laughlin, with its principal office in Pittsburgh, was the fourth largest producer of steel in the United States. It had nineteen subsidiaries, including mines, towboats, steam barges, railroads, and manufacturing plants. The NLRB required the Jones & Laughlin subsidiary in Alquippa, Pennsylvania, to recognize and bargain with a union, and the company went to court to challenge the constitutionality of the order.

Oral argument took place in the Supreme Court less than a week after President Roosevelt sent his Court reform message to Congress, and although there is debate over how much impact this may have had on the justices, it is difficult to believe that they were unaware of it.

Chief Justice Hughes brushed aside the due process and freedom of contract arguments against government protection of workers' rights. He held that the government could legitimately protect the right of labor to organize as a means of preventing strikes that would have a detrimental effect on interstate commerce. Hughes abandoned the distinction between direct and indirect effects on interstate commerce and essentially held that under the Commerce Clause Congress can reach any activity affecting commerce. The decision signaled that the Court would no longer attempt to block congressional efforts to regulate the economy, removing one of the main reasons for the president's Court-packing plan.

See Richard C. Cortner, *The Jones & Laughlin Case* (New York: Knopf, 1970); and Christopher L. Tomlins, *The State and the Unions: Labor Relations, Law, and the Organized Labor Movement in America, 1880–1960* (New York: Cambridge University Press, 1985).

NLRB v. Friedman-Harry Marks Clothing Co.

301 U.S. 58 (1937)
Decided: April 12, 1937
Vote: 5 (Hughes, Brandeis, Stone, Roberts, Cardozo)
4 (Van Devanter, McReynolds, Sutherland, Butler)
Opinion of the Court: Hughes
Dissenting opinion: McReynolds (Van Devanter, Sutherland, Butler)

The National Labor Relations Board (NLRB) ordered Friedman-Harry Marks Clothing Company to stop firing employees because they joined unions or were helping unions. The NLRB also ordered the company to reinstate employees it had dismissed for union membership and to pay them back wages. Friedman-Harry Marks argued that the National Labor Relations Act, which created the NLRB, was unconstitutional. Although the company had some relation to interstate commerce, it carried on much of its business in Virginia. It argued that the act allowed the NLRB to regulate intrastate commerce in addition to interstate commerce and exceeded the limits of federal power granted in the Commerce Clause.

The Court held that the act and the NLRB were constitutional and, over the objections of the four conservatives, announced a new test to determine Congress's powers to regulate commerce. The Court eliminated the interstate/intrastate distinction and instituted the "close and substantial relation test." If a commercial activity is closely and substantially related to interstate commerce, Congress may regulate it under the Commerce Clause. The Court determined that Friedman-Harry Marks was such a commercial activity and therefore subject to NLRB regulation.

See Richard Cortner, *The Wagner Act Cases* (Knoxville: University of Tennessee Press, 1964).

Herndon v. Lowry

301 U.S. 242 (1937)
Decided: April 26, 1937
Vote: 5 (Hughes, Brandeis, Stone, Roberts, Cardozo)
4 (Van Devanter, McReynolds, Sutherland, Butler)
Opinion of the Court: Roberts
Dissenting opinion: Van Devanter

Angelo Herndon was a black Communist Party organizer who traveled around the country holding meetings and rallies and distributing party literature. In Georgia he tried to organize an integrated union of black and white workers and was arrested and convicted for attempting to incite an uprising in violation of Georgia's anti-insurrection statute. Herndon filed for a writ of habeas corpus, claiming that he had not violated the state's anti-insurrection statute but had merely exercised his freedom of speech. The Committee on the Bill of Rights of the American Bar Association provided his legal representation, and in both the trial court and appeals he was represented by lawyers with impeccable conservative Republican credentials and a strong attachment to civil liberties.

The Court held that Herndon's actions did not violate the anti-insurrection statute. The evidence, according to Justice Roberts, showed neither a clear and present danger nor any tendency toward violence. The statute intended to serve as a "dragnet which may enmesh anyone who agitates for a change in government." Herndon had a First Amendment right to speak and to assemble peacefully. He had done no more than offend local officials with his ideas and for that he could not be punished.

United States v. Belmont

301 U.S. 324 (1937)
Decided: May 3, 1937
Vote: 9 (Hughes, Van Devanter, McReynolds, Brandeis, Sutherland, Butler, Stone, Roberts, Cardozo)
0
Opinion of the Court: Sutherland
Concurring opinion: Stone (Brandeis, Cardozo)

When the United States recognized the Union of Soviet Socialist Republics (USSR) in 1933, President Roosevelt signed an executive agreement with Maxim Litvinov of the Soviet government. The Litvinov agreement assigned to the United States government all Soviet claims against Americans who held funds of Russian companies seized after the Russian Revolution. Relying on that agreement, the United States brought suit to recover funds deposited by a Russian corporation with a private New York banker. Lower courts dismissed the federal action on the ground that implementing the USSR's confiscation of private property would violate the public policy of New York.

The Court emphasized that recognition, the establishment of diplomatic relations, and the assignment of claims were all part of one transaction, resulting in "an international compact between the two governments." These negotiations and agreements were well within the competence of the president, and, as Justice Sutherland had written a year earlier in ***United States v. Curtiss-Wright Corp.,*** 299 U.S. 304 (1936), the chief executive had full authority to speak for the country in foreign affairs.

The opinion, like *Curtiss-Wright,* is remarkable for the broad scope of power Sutherland—and all of his colleagues on the Court—recognized in the presidency in foreign affairs. *Belmont* established precedent that executive agreements would have the full force of law, superseding state law, even though, unlike treaties, the Senate need not approve them. The Court reinforced this last point, also in regard to the Litvinov agreement, in ***United States v. Pink,*** 315 U.S. 203 (1942).

See Louis Henkin, ed., *Foreign Affairs and the U.S. Constitution* (Ardsley-on-Hudson, N.Y.: Transnational Publishers, 1990).

Senn v. Tile Layers Protective Union

301 U.S. 468 (1937)
Decided: May 24, 1937
Vote: 5 (Hughes, Brandeis, Stone, Roberts, Cardozo)
4 (Van Devanter, McReynolds, Sutherland, Butler)
Opinion of the Court: Brandeis
Dissenting opinion: Butler (Van Devanter, McReynolds, Sutherland)

A Wisconsin law made peaceful picketing lawful and nonenjoinable; that is, it said courts could not issue injunctions to prevent peaceful picketing. The law also provided for publicity in labor disputes so that the facts could be known to the public. In 1935 the tile layers union picketed Paul Senn's construction business. The union and Senn tried to reach a compromise agreement under which Senn would allow the unionization of his workforce. When the negotiations broke down, the union employees went out on strike and formed picket lines. The picketing and protesting were peaceful and free of unlawful activity. Senn challenged the constitutionality of the law by attempting to get an injunction. He claimed that the law violated his property rights and his right to earn a living.

The Court upheld the law. Justice Brandeis intimated that picketing, aside from its value as a tool in a labor dispute, might also be a form of speech. Union members, he held, did not have to rely upon such a statute to make the facts of a labor dispute public "for freedom of speech is guaranteed by the Federal Constitution." To the contractor who claimed the law interfered with his right to earn a living, Brandeis replied, "One has no constitutional right to a 'remedy' against the lawful conduct of another."

Senn did not determine conclusively whether the First Amendment provided special protection for labor activities, and the Court would later refuse to categorize picketing *per se* as a protected activity.

Steward Machine Co. v. Davis

301 U.S. 548 (1937)
Decided: May 24, 1937
Vote: 5 (Hughes, Brandeis, Stone, Roberts, Cardozo)
4 (Van Devanter, McReynolds, Sutherland, Butler)
Opinion of the Court: Cardozo
Dissenting opinion: McReynolds
Dissenting opinion: Sutherland (Van Devanter)
Dissenting opinion: Butler

Chas. C. Steward Machine Company, an Alabama corporation, paid its taxes as required under the Social Security Act. The act required companies with eight or more employees to pay a tax into the Social Security trust fund, which was to be used to fund both an unemployment insurance partnership between the states and the federal government and a future old age retirement plan. Steward argued that the tax was unconstitutional because Congress had no power to levy a tax that helped out the states.

The Court held that Social Security taxes were constitutional. First, employment relations were a part of business and commerce and, as such, could be taxed under Congress's Commerce Clause powers. Second, the tax did not violate the Tenth Amendment because the states receiving the tax funds from the federal government were voluntarily participating in the unemployment insurance program and thus had not been stripped of any of their powers.

This case was one of the first to follow the battle over President Roosevelt's Court-packing plan. This time the Court upheld New Deal legislation. In earlier cases, the Court had held that employment was only technically and indirectly related to commerce and therefore could neither be regulated nor taxed. Beginning with this case, the Court began to abandon the direct/indirect effects doctrine.

See Thomas R. McCoy and Barry Friedman, "Conditional Spending: Federalism's Trojan Horse," *Supreme Court Review* (1988): 85.

Helvering v. Davis

301 U.S. 619 (1937)
Decided: May 24, 1937
Vote: 7 (Hughes, Van Devanter, Brandeis, Sutherland, Stone, Roberts, Cardozo)
2 (McReynolds, Butler)
Opinion of the Court: Cardozo
Dissenting opinion: McReynolds, Butler

The Social Security Act taxed employers to create a government trust fund that would eventually pay pensions to retired workers. George P. Davis, a shareholder in Edison Illuminating Company, sued to prevent the company from having to pay the tax. He argued that the federal government did not have the power to tax employment because nowhere in the Constitution is Congress given explicit power to levy such a tax. Therefore, he claimed, the tax violated the Tenth Amendment.

The Court held the Social Security Act constitutional. Congress, explained Justice Cardozo, had the power to tax employment as a part of commerce. In addition, Congress may use the taxing power to promote the general welfare. Because elderly Americans were suffering from unemployment caused by the Great Depression, a tax to provide pension funds to aid those citizens clearly promoted the general welfare.

See Thomas R. McCoy and Barry Friedman, "Conditional Spending: Federalism's Trojan Horse," *Supreme Court Review* (1988): 85.

Breedlove v. Suttles

302 U.S. 277 (1937)
Decided: December 6, 1937
Vote: 9 (Hughes, McReynolds, Brandeis, Sutherland, Butler, Stone, Roberts, Cardozo, Black)
0
Opinion of the Court: Butler

Georgia levied a poll tax of one dollar on all its citizens between the ages of twenty-one and sixty, with the exception of the blind and unregistered females. Nolen R. Breedlove, a twenty-eight-year-old white man, did not pay the poll tax and consequently was denied the right to vote. He argued that the poll tax was sexually discriminatory because all men had to pay it. The question in this case, therefore, was whether the poll tax violated the Equal Protection Clause of the Fourteenth Amendment as well as the Nineteenth Amendment.

The Court upheld the tax. The purpose of the Nineteenth Amendment was to give women the right to vote, and the poll tax did not prevent people from voting on the basis of their sex. Men and women who wanted to vote could do so by paying the poll tax. The equal protection argument was dismissed out of hand because the states had flexibility in how they wished to apply a tax so long as no one was denied the vote by the method of inclusion or exclusion. The poll tax was abolished with ratification of the Twenty-fourth Amendment, which dealt with federal elections, and the Court's decision in ***Harper v. Virginia Board of Elections,*** 383 U.S. 663 (1966), dealing with state elections.

Palko v. Connecticut

302 U.S. 319 (1937)
Decided: December 6, 1937
Vote: 8 (Hughes, McReynolds, Brandeis, Sutherland, Stone, Roberts, Cardozo, Black)
1 (Butler)
Opinion of the Court: Cardozo
Dissenting without opinion: Butler

When Justice Cardozo delivered the opinion in *Palko,* one of the crucial cases in civil liberties history, he defined much of the judicial debate on the question of incorporation for the next generation.

Palko v. Connecticut involved a relatively limited question: Did the Fourteenth Amendment incorporate the guarantee against double jeopardy in the Fifth Amendment and apply it to the states?

Frank Palko was indicted and tried for first-degree murder, but convicted of the lesser crime of second-degree murder. He was sentenced to life imprisonment. The state appealed the conviction under a law permitting the prosecution to appeal a verdict in certain criminal cases. The state supreme court allowed a new trial, in which the prosecution won a conviction for first-degree murder, and Palko was sentenced to death. At the time, the Fifth Amendment bar against double jeopardy did not apply to the states.

Palko appealed the first-degree murder conviction, basing his argument on the Due Process Clause of the Fourteenth Amendment and requesting incorporation.

Full incorporation would have applied all of the guarantees in the first eight amendments to state behavior. Before use of the Fourteenth Amendment as an instrument of incorporation, the guarantees of the Bill of Rights applied to the relationship of the individual and the federal government. Because a defendant could not be tried twice for the same crime in federal court, those in favor of incorporation argued that a defendant should not be tried twice in a state court either. Just as the Supreme Court had incorporated other rights, such as press in ***Near v. Minnesota,*** 283 U.S. 697 (1931), speech in ***DeJonge v. Oregon,*** 299 U.S. 353 (1937), and counsel in ***Johnson v. Zerbst,*** 304 U.S. 458 (1938), so now it should incorporate the bar against double jeopardy.

The Court rejected this argument. Cardozo held that the Fourteenth Amendment did not automatically subsume the entire Bill of Rights. This statement implied that it did incorporate some amendments, but which ones? Cardozo included all the protections of the First Amendment because freedom of thought and speech "is the matrix, the indispensable condition, of nearly every other form of [freedom]." But as for the Second through Eighth Amendments, the Court should apply only those that are "of the very essence of a scheme of ordered liberty" and "so rooted in the traditions and conscience of our people as to be ranked as fundamental." The majority did not find the protection against double jeopardy to be one of those fundamental rights.

The doctrine of "selective incorporation" lodged enormous discretionary power in the Court. Nothing in the Constitution provided guidance; rather, the justices "modernized" the Bill of Rights. It would be incumbent on the judiciary to decide which parts of it applied to the states, based on their own views, guided in some small degree by history and precedent, of what constituted a fundamental right. Following World War II, the justices engaged in an extensive debate between Cardozo's idea of selective incorporation, as continued by Justice Frankfurter, and the theory of total incorporation advanced by Justice Black.

See Richard C. Cortner, *The Supreme Court and the Second Bill of Rights: The Fourteenth Amendment and the Nationalization of Civil Liberties* (Madison: University of Wisconsin Press, 1981); Felix Frankfurter, "Memorandum on 'Incorporation' of the Bill of Rights into the Due Process Clause of the Fourteenth Amendment," *Harvard Law Review* 78 (1965): 746; and James F. Simon, *The Antagonists: Hugo Black, Felix Frankfurter and Civil Liberties in Modern America* (New York: Simon and Schuster, 1989).

Nardone v. United States

302 U.S. 379 (1937)
Decided: December 20, 1937
Vote: 7 (Hughes, Brandeis, Butler, Stone, Roberts, Cardozo, Black)
2 (McReynolds, Sutherland)
Opinion of the Court: Roberts
Dissenting opinion: Sutherland (McReynolds)

Frank Carmine Nardone and others were convicted of smuggling alcohol in violation of the Volstead Act. Federal agents wiretapped Nardone's telephone, and his telephone conversations were used against him at trial. Nardone argued that the intercepted telephone conversations should have been excluded from trial because wiretaps violated Section 605 of the Federal Communications Act, which allowed for interception only if authorized by the sender, that is, the speaker. The federal government argued that it could wiretap telephones if the conversations occurred in interstate commerce. The question before the Court was whether the communications act applied to the federal government to forbid wiretapping.

The Court, partially reversing ***Olmstead v. United States,*** 277 U.S. 438 (1928), held that wiretapping in general was unconstitutional and applied the exclusionary rule to evidence obtained by illegal wiretaps. If the federal government used an illegal wiretap to obtain evidence, that evidence would be inadmissible at trial.

Nardone was tried again, and his appeal came to the Court once again in ***Nardone v. United States,*** 308 U.S. 338 (1939).

See Edith J. Lapidus, *Eavesdropping on Trial* (Rochelle Park, N.Y.: Hayden Books, 1973).

South Carolina State Highway Dept. v. Barnwell Bros., Inc.

303 U.S. 177 (1938)
Decided: February 14, 1938
Vote: 7 (Hughes, McReynolds, Brandeis, Butler, Stone, Roberts, Black)
0
Opinion of the Court: Stone
Did not participate: Cardozo, Reed

South Carolina banned from its highways trucks with a gross weight, including their load, of more than twenty thousand pounds and an outside width greater than ninety inches. Barnwell Brothers, a trucking company, argued that the law violated due process under the Fourteenth Amendment and that South Carolina was interfering with interstate commerce.

The Court held that although the regulation of interstate commerce is normally reserved to Congress alone, in some instances states may enact laws controlling interstate commerce. As long as a state law does not discriminate against interstate commerce and Congress has not passed a law contrary to the state law, a state may regulate interstate commerce if it has a justifiable public policy argument. In this case, Congress did not have a law contrary to the South Carolina law, and the weight and size requirements were justified by safety reasons. The Court therefore upheld South Carolina's restrictions.

Electric Bond & Share Co. v. Securities and Exchange Commission

303 U.S. 419 (1938)
Decided: March 28, 1938
Vote: 6 (Hughes, Brandeis, Butler, Stone, Roberts, Black)
1 (McReynolds)
Opinion of the Court: Hughes
Dissenting without opinion: McReynolds
Did not participate: Cardozo, Reed

Through a system of stock control, a small number of holding companies directed the operations of subsidiaries that supplied gas and electricity in many states. Some of the subsidiary companies provided electricity across state lines, while others conducted business within a state. The holding companies provided expert service and contracted construction work for the subsidiaries. Quite often the holding companies were involved with interstate commerce transactions, and they also were responsible for the sale and distribution of securities in interstate commerce.

The Public Utility Act required holding companies to register with the Securities and Exchange Commission (SEC). If they did not, they were denied use of the postal service to solicit for sale of securities across state lines. Electric Bond & Share Company argued that the SEC did not have the power to make them register as a condition of using the postal system.

The Court held that the SEC had the authority to require holding companies to register with it if they wish to enjoy certain interstate commerce privileges, such as the postal service.

Lovell v. City of Griffin

303 U.S. 444 (1938)
Decided: March 28, 1938
Vote: 8 (Hughes, McReynolds, Brandeis, Butler, Stone, Roberts, Black, Reed)
0
Opinion of the Court: Hughes
Did not participate: Cardozo

Griffin, Georgia, prohibited the distribution of pamphlets unless those seeking to hand out the materials obtained a permit from the city. Griffin claimed its ordinance placed a content-neutral time, place, and manner restriction on speech. Alma Lovell, a Jehovah's Witness, was arrested for passing out religious literature without obtaining the permit. She argued that she had both a religious right and a free press right to distribute literature without first obtaining government approval of the content of the literature.

The Court held that the city ordinance was unconstitutional. Chief Justice Hughes condemned the regulation as too broad and sweeping and in violation the First Amendment. It was overbroad because it prohibited legal and illegal speech. Illegal speech, such as obscenity or speech inciting violence may be prohibited, but otherwise protected religious speech cannot be silenced. Time, place, and manner regulations cannot be so sweeping as to eliminate otherwise protected speech.

This case was the first in the Jehovah's Witnesses' legal campaign to gain the freedom to preach and proselytize under the Free Exercise Clause of the First Amendment. In these early cases, the Court concentrated more on the speech aspects of their appeals than on the free exercise claims.

See Shawn Francis Peters, *Judging Jehovah's Witnesses* (Lawrence: University Press of Kansas, 2000).

Erie Railroad Co. v. Tompkins

304 U.S. 64 (1938)
Decided: April 25, 1938
Vote: 6 (Hughes, Brandeis, Stone, Roberts, Black, Reed)
2 (McReynolds, Butler)
Opinion of the Court: Brandeis
Opinion concurring in part: Reed
Dissenting opinion: Butler (McReynolds)
Did not participate: Cardozo

The Judiciary Act of 1789 ordered federal courts to follow the decisional rules of the states in which they were located. In ***Swift v. Tyson,*** 41 U.S. 1 (1842), the Court promulgated the rule that in matters of general law, federal courts could follow principles of general commercial law. As a result, in diversity suits (involving parties from different states), the plaintiff or the defendant might well go forum shopping, looking for a federal court where the rules would be more favorable.

During the Progressive Era, large corporations generally sought to move a case in which they were a defendant to what they considered the more favorable atmosphere of the conservative federal courts. In doing so, corporations managed to thwart state regulations. Justice Brandeis had long opposed the *Swift* rule and finally found a majority willing to overrule it.

Harry Tompkins was walking along the right of way of the Erie Railroad, a New York corporation, in Hughestown, Pennsylvania, late one night. A train with an object protruding from it struck Tompkins, knocking him under the wheels of the train. He was found unconscious, his right arm severed. He recovered and filed suit against the railroad. According to Pennsylvania law, Tompkins would be considered a trespasser, which would weaken or negate his opportunity for a judgment against the railroad. His lawyer, therefore, filed the action in federal court in New York, where state law viewed Tompkins as a "licensee" permitted to walk on the path. Tompkins prevailed, and the railroad appealed. Neither party wanted to overrule *Swift,* and the railroad merely argued that the lower court had misinterpreted the law.

Speaking for the Court, Brandeis ruled for the first and only time in the Court's history that a prior decision was unconstitutional. The *Swift* Court, he explained, had exceeded its authority as granted by the Constitution or Congress. In determining federal court jurisdiction, he argued, Congress, as provided for in the Constitution, had primacy. The judiciary could go as far as Congress could but no further. Because there was no federal common law, he ruled that federal courts had to follow the substantive law of the state as well as the decision rules of the highest court in the state to have spoken on the matter—that is, federal courts had to follow not only state statutory law but also the precedents of the state courts. In *Erie* the accident had taken place in Pennsylvania, and federal courts were bound to follow that state's rules.

Although a technical decision, *Erie* is the starting point for all discussion and determination of federal jurisdiction. The full potential impact of *Erie* was blunted, however, by the adoption of the Federal Rules of Civil Procedure, which set up an independent set of decisional rules for federal courts, although they are still required to follow substantive state law.

See Edward A. Purcell Jr., *Brandeis and the Progressive Constitution: Erie, the Judicial Power, and the Politics of the Federal Courts in Twentieth-Century America* (New Haven: Yale University Press, 2000).

Hindelider v. La Plata River & Cherry Creek Ditch Co.

304 U.S. 92 (1938)
Decided: April 25, 1938
Vote: 8 (Hughes, McReynolds, Brandeis, Butler, Stone, Roberts, Black, Reed)
0
Opinion of the Court: Brandeis
Did not participate: Cardozo

La Plata River & Cherry Creek Ditch Company, a Colorado business, siphoned water from the La Plata River for irrigation. Hindelider, the state engineer for Colorado, stopped the company from drawing water on the grounds that it violated a congressionally approved compact between Colorado and New Mexico over how water from the river would be divided between the two states. The company, relying on the state water law, sued Hindelider, claiming that he had no authority to stop its operations. He in turn relied on the interstate compact to back his actions. The question that came to the Court on appeal was whether state law or federal common law governed the case. The Colorado River ran between the two states and the La Plata River was part of the Colorado system.

The decision in this case was handed down the same day as ***Erie Railroad Co. v. Tompkins,*** 304 U.S. 64 (1938), in which the Court said there is no federal common law. Here, however, Justice Brandeis held that there *is* a federal common law when interstate boundary disputes are involved. Even though states may be parties to a suit, if the case is about a boundary dispute or the distribution of interstate waters, then federal law applies.

In applying federal law, the Court ruled that New Mexico and Colorado had made an agreement allowing for Colorado to use the water in the La Plata River, and therefore upheld the state's claims as against the company.

See Edward A. Purcell Jr., *Brandeis and the Progressive Constitution* (New Haven: Yale University Press, 2000).

United States v. Carolene Products Co.

304 U.S. 144 (1938)
Decided: April 25, 1938
Vote: 6 (Hughes, Brandeis, Butler, Stone, Roberts, Black)
1 (McReynolds)
Opinion of the Court: Stone
Concurring opinion: Butler
Opinion concurring in part, dissenting in part: Black
Dissenting without opinion: McReynolds
Did not participate: Cardozo, Reed

This relatively insignificant case is remembered primarily for a footnote that launched a constitutional revolution. The case concerned a federal law prohibiting the interstate shipment of so-called "filled milk," defined in the statute as skim milk "compounded with . . . any fat or oil other than milk fat." Although the law was clearly special interest legislation favoring particular parts of the dairy industry, Justice Stone put forward a simple test for weighing economic regulation. Legislation "affecting ordinary commercial transactions is not to be pronounced unconstitutional unless in the light of the facts made known or generally assumed it is of such a character as to preclude the assumption that it rests upon some rational basis within the knowledge and experience of the legislators." The "rational basis" test became the least demanding of all constitutional tests, and few laws have ever failed it.

The significance of the decision lay in footnote four, inserted immediately after Stone's statement of the rational basis test. In it he declared:

> There may be narrower scope for operation of the presumption of constitutionality when legislation appears on its face to be within a specific prohibition of the Constitution, such as those of the first ten amendments, which are deemed equally specific when held to be embraced within the Fourteenth.

The footnote goes on to say that such legislation may be subject to a "more exacting judicial scrutiny," as could laws aimed at particular religions, the integrity of the political process, or at "discrete and insular minorities."

Although Stone did not use the term "strict scrutiny," the footnote led to a new jurisprudence that emerged full-blown in the Warren Court era, when the Court applied the minimal "rational basis" test to all economic regulation, but applied a much higher standard to laws affecting First Amendment guarantees—especially speech—and statutes affecting race. As a result of footnote four, lower courts began assuming the role as protector of property rights against unreasonable government intrusion and regulation. They would apply the rational basis test, and the Supreme Court rarely granted review to such cases. But in areas of free speech and other constitutionally protected rights—especially after 1953 in regard to laws classifying people on the basis of race—the Court became the prime guardian of civil liberties and rights.

See Michael Perry, "Mr. Justice Stone and Footnote 4," *George Mason University Civil Rights Law Journal* 6 (1996): 35; and Lewis F. Powell Jr., "Carolene Products Revisited," *Columbia Law Review* 82 (1982): 1087.

Johnson v. Zerbst

304 U.S. 458 (1938)
Decided: May 23, 1938
Vote: 6 (Hughes, Brandeis, Stone, Roberts, Black, Reed)
2 (McReynolds, Butler)
Opinion of the Court: Black
Concurring without opinion: Reed
Dissenting without opinion: McReynolds, Butler
Did not participate: Cardozo

Johnson was convicted of possessing and distributing counterfeit money. At the time of his trial he was indigent and unable to hire counsel. While in prison, he filed for habeas corpus because he had not been represented by a lawyer at trial, which, he argued, violated his Sixth Amendment right to counsel. He claimed that he wanted a lawyer to represent him, but the trial court had denied him counsel because it believed that he had waived his right to counsel. In so doing, Johnson said, the trial court also denied him habeas corpus.

The Court reversed the conviction. In his first opinion as a member of the Court, Justice Black remanded the case for a new trial and stated that the Sixth Amendment required that in criminal trials defendants have the right to counsel. A defendant can waive the right, but evidence must show that he had done so knowingly and voluntarily, and the record in this case failed to prove that he had done so. The ruling extended the Sixth Amendment protection the Court had begun to sketch out six years earlier in ***Powell v. Alabama,*** 287 U.S. 45 (1932).

This case applied only to federal trials, but it marks the beginning of Black's crusade to extend the right of counsel to all defendants, in state as well as federal trials, a drive that ultimately succeeded in ***Gideon v. Wainwright,*** 372 U.S. 335 (1963).

Missouri ex rel. Gaines v. Canada

305 U.S. 337 (1938)
Decided: December 12, 1938
Vote: 6 (Hughes, Brandeis, Stone, Roberts, Black, Reed)
2 (McReynolds, Butler)
Opinion of the Court: Hughes
Dissenting opinion: McReynolds (Butler)

Lloyd Gaines, an African American, wished to become a lawyer. Because there was no law school for blacks in his home state of Missouri, he sought admission to the all-white law school at the University of Missouri. His application was denied on the grounds that the university did not take blacks. His legal challenges in state court failed.

Gaines provided an early test case for the National Association for the Advancement of Colored People (NAACP), which earlier in the decade had decided to mount an all-out legal campaign against the concept of separate but equal facilities in education. First, the NAACP attacked the equal part, forcing southern states to significantly increase appropriations for school buildings, textbooks, and teacher salaries. But the ultimate goal of the NAACP was to prove that separate could never be equal, an argument the Court finally accepted in ***Brown v. Board of Education,*** 347 U.S. 483 (1954).

Chief Justice Hughes, speaking for the Court, ordered Gaines admitted to the law school and dismissed the state's offer to pay Gaines's tuition to an out-of-state institution. As a resident of Missouri, he was entitled to the same educational opportunities as white residents. In essence, Hughes was warning the southern states that if they wanted to maintain segregation, they would have to provide facilities for blacks roughly equal to those available for whites.

The decision gave the NAACP a great boost toward its legal goals, and over the next several years the group filed dozens of suits seeking equality in education and equalization of wages and in facilities. Ironically, Lloyd Gaines never did go to law school. Shortly after the decision, he disappeared and was never heard from again.

See Mark V. Tushnet, *The NAACP's Strategy Against Segregated Education, 1925–1950* (Chapel Hill: University of North Carolina Press, 1987); and Kevin M. Kruse, "Personal Rights, Public Wrongs: The *Gaines* Case and the Beginning of the End of Segregation," *Journal of Supreme Court History* (1997):113.

Currin v. Wallace

306 U.S. 1 (1939)
Decided: January 30, 1939
Vote: 6 (Hughes, Brandeis, Stone, Roberts, Black, Reed)
2 (McReynolds, Butler)
Opinion of the Court: Hughes
Dissenting without opinion: McReynolds, Butler

In 1935 Congress passed the Tobacco Inspection Act, but because the number of federal tobacco inspectors was insufficient, the secretary of agriculture directed that inspections take place only at the tobacco markets where the greatest number of growers would be present. Even though tobacco inspections clearly involved interstate commerce, Congress conditioned the secretary's decision upon the consent of the growers. The law required that two-thirds of the growers had to agree on the location of the inspections for the law to become operable.

Currin, a tobacco warehouseman and auctioneer, argued that the law was discriminatory because it targeted only the larger markets to inspect. He also claimed that Congress had exceeded its authority by delegating legislative decision making—in this case, whether there should be inspections—to tobacco growers.

The Court upheld the act, and Chief Justice Hughes's opinion implies that congressional power to regulate interstate commerce is virtually unlimited. Tobacco inspections were well-established practices; states had been conducting them since colonial days. Because the inspections in this case involved sales in interstate commerce, Congress had the power to order the inspections. In addition, allowing a two-thirds vote of the tobacco growers was well within the power of Congress to decide. Congress had to be allowed flexibility to achieve its goals and objectives. Furthermore, when interstate and intrastate commerce are so related that state and federal rules collide, Congress will have the final word.

Hale v. Bimco Trading Co.

306 U.S. 375 (1939)
Decided: February 27, 1939
Vote: 8 (Hughes, McReynolds, Butler, Stone, Roberts, Black, Reed, Frankfurter)
0
Opinion of the Court: Frankfurter

Florida law required the inspection of cement to ensure that it met certain standards, and to pay for the inspection the state charged a fee. Thirty percent of Florida's cement came from other states or from foreign nations, and the inspection law applied only to that cement and not to the local product. Bimco Trading argued that the law violated the Commerce Clause because the state was regulating interstate commerce. Florida countered that the law was for safety purposes.

The Court struck down the law. In his first opinion on the Court, Justice Frankfurter applied what is known as the "dormant" or "negative commerce clause." Under the Commerce Clause, Congress has the power to regulate interstate commerce. If stated in the negative, the clause means that the states cannot regulate interstate commerce. A state can place a burden on interstate commerce only if it has a legitimate public policy concern. If Florida had been serious about the safety of cement, it would have inspected all cement. By targeting only out-of-state or foreign cement, the state impinged on congressional authority, even though Congress had not spoken to this matter. Congress, through the so-called dormant commerce clause, still had sole power over interstate commerce, and, even if it did not act, the states could act only when given permission by Congress to do so.

Graves v. New York ex rel. O'Keefe

306 U.S. 466 (1939)
Decided: March 27, 1939
Vote: 6 (Hughes, Stone, Roberts, Black, Reed, Frankfurter)
2 (McReynolds, Butler)
Opinion of the Court: Stone
Concurring opinion: Frankfurter
Concurring in judgment without opinion: Hughes
Dissenting opinion: Butler (McReynolds)

James B. O'Keefe was an attorney for Home Owners' Loan Corporation, a federal government corporation. He worked and lived in New York, where he filed his state and federal income taxes. He claimed that New York owed him a tax refund because, as a federal employee, he believed that his salary was exempt from state income taxes. He based his argument on the doctrine that state and federal governments cannot impose their taxes on other sovereign bodies and that as an employee of a sovereign body—the federal government—he could not be taxed by the state.

The Court held that a state could tax the income of a federal employee. Employment with the federal government did not confer immunity from state income taxes. As long as the income tax was nondiscriminatory, a federal employee was subject to state income taxes. New York's state income tax was nondiscriminatory because it applied to all people regardless of their jobs, and therefore O'Keefe had to pay it.

Mulford v. Smith

307 U.S. 38 (1939)
Decided: April 17, 1939
Vote: 7 (Hughes, Stone, Roberts, Black, Reed, Frankfurter, Douglas)
2 (McReynolds, Butler)
Opinion of the Court: Roberts
Dissenting opinion: Butler (McReynolds)

The Agriculture Adjustment Act of 1938, part of President Franklin Roosevelt's New Deal, regulated the marketing of farm products such as cotton, wheat, corn, tobacco, and rice in interstate commerce. The purpose of the law was to control the supply of these goods in order to maintain a decent income for farmers and affordable prices for consumers. To do this, the act established production quotas for different crops and rewarded farmers who agreed to the quotas with a system of price subsidies.

Mulford, a tobacco farmer, argued that the quotas for tobacco were unconstitutional. He claimed that Congress had no authority under the Commerce Clause to impose quotas, which also deprived him of his property without due process of law under the Fifth Amendment.

The Court upheld the act. First, the act regulated tobacco that was intended for interstate commerce. The act did not limit the amount of tobacco grown, only the amount that could be sold. The Court said setting limits was a valid exercise of power by Congress under the Commerce Clause. Second, no violation of the Fifth Amendment's Takings Clause had occurred because the act regulated only the selling of tobacco, not the growing of it. Farmers could keep the excess crops to sell or use at a later date.

Miller v. United States

307 U.S. 174 (1939)
Decided: May 15, 1939
Vote: 8 (Hughes, McReynolds, Butler, Stone, Roberts, Black, Reed, Frankfurter)
0
Opinion of the Court: McReynolds
Did not participate: Douglas

Jack Miller and Frank Layton were arrested for transporting an unregistered double-barreled 12-gauge shotgun, with a barrel of less than eighteen inches, in interstate commerce. They were accused of violating the National Firearms Act, which taxed firearms and required registration of certain weapons if someone wanted to carry them over state lines. Miller argued that the act was an unconstitutional violation of the Second

Amendment, and the lower court agreed with him. The government claimed that the Second Amendment applied only to the right to have a gun for militia purposes and that the federal government, under its commerce power, could require the registration of guns and tax guns that are transported in interstate commerce.

The Court upheld the act, agreeing with the government that the purpose of the Second Amendment was to maintain effective state militias. Miller had no evidence that a double-barreled, sawed-off 12-gauge shotgun was an ordinary weapon used in militias or the military. As Miller was not using the shotgun for a state militia, Congress had the authority to make him register the gun if he was going to carry it across state lines.

Miller is one of just a handful of Second Amendment cases the Court has heard. Justice McReynolds relied heavily on the two earlier cases, ***United States v. Cruikshank,*** 92 U.S. 542 (1876), and ***Presser v. Illinois,*** 116 U.S. 252 (1886), to frame his decision. The holding in *Miller* that the right to bear arms must be read in the light of the militia clause is still the governing law on interpreting the amendment.

See Robert J. Spitzer, *The Right to Bear Arms* (Santa Barbara: ABC-CLIO, 2001).

Coleman v. Miller

307 U.S. 433 (1939)
Decided: June 5, 1939
Vote: 7 (Hughes, Stone, Roberts, Black, Reed, Frankfurter, Douglas)
2 (McReynolds, Butler)
Opinion of the Court: Hughes
Concurring opinion: Black (Roberts, Frankfurter, Douglas)
Concurring opinion: Frankfurter (Roberts, Black, Douglas)
Dissenting opinion: Butler (McReynolds)

In 1924 Congress proposed a new amendment to the Constitution, the so-called Child Labor Amendment, to allow the federal government, under either its taxing or commerce powers, to prohibit the shipment of goods made by children in interstate commerce. The proposed amendment was a direct reaction to the Court's decisions in ***Hammer v. Dagenhart,*** 247 U.S. 251 (1918), and ***Bailey v. Drexel Furniture Co.,*** 259 U.S. 20 (1922), that had nullified two earlier laws aimed at discouraging child labor.

In 1925 the Kansas legislature rejected the amendment. Twelve years later, still within the time limit allowed by Congress for passage, the Kansas legislature voted on it again and this time approved the amendment. Opponents argued that Kansas had no power to take that vote, and the Supreme Court was asked to decide whether a state legislature that once rejected a proposed constitutional amendment could vote on it again.

The Court held that Kansas could vote on the amendment again. The Court ruled that states do not determine the rules for voting on constitutional amendments; rather, ratification of constitutional amendments is a political issue that Congress controls. A state's initial rejection of an amendment did not bar the state from ever voting on it again. Congress had set a time limit for the vote, and because Kansas's second vote fell within the allowed time period, the vote was legitimate.

The amendment, however, never garnered the necessary approval by three-fourths of the states to be ratified.

See David Kyvig, *Explicit and Authentic Acts* (Lawrence: University Press of Kansas, 1996).

Hague v. Committee for Industrial Organization

307 U.S. 496 (1939)
Decided: June 5, 1939
Vote: 5 (Hughes, Stone, Roberts, Black, Reed)
2 (McReynolds, Butler)
Judgment of the Court: Roberts (Black, Hughes)
Judgment of the Court: Stone (Reed, Hughes)
Dissenting opinion: McReynolds
Dissenting opinion: Butler
Did not participate: Frankfurter, Douglas

Jersey City, New Jersey, had a time, place, and manner regulation prohibiting public assemblies unless they received a permit from the city's director of public safety. When the Committee for Industrial Organization (CIO) distributed pamphlets and leaflets encouraging the unionization of the city's workforce, Jersey City applied its assembly regulation to stop the CIO's activities. The CIO argued that the city ordinance violated the First Amendment and the Due Process Clause of the Fourteenth Amendment.

Although five members of the Court sided with the CIO, they disagreed over the rationale. Justice Roberts, arguing on the basis of the Privileges and Immunities Clause of the Fourteenth Amendment, claimed that the National Labor Relations Act granted citizens the right to air labor disputes. New Jersey, therefore, could not restrict the rights granted under the act because doing so would deprive labor speakers of privileges and immunities they enjoyed elsewhere. Justice Stone, however, believed that the ordinance violated the First Amendment because it restricted speech. It is inherent in the First Amendment that U.S. citizens may discuss political topics in public areas, and making people obtain a permit before speaking out on political issues is an infringement of this fundamental freedom. In terms of speech jurisprudence, the Court has not followed Roberts's suggestion that the Privileges and Immunities Clause protects labor rights; rather, it has looked at the larger notion of free speech as a protector of labor speech as well as other forms of discourse.

United States v. Rock Royal Cooperative, Inc.

307 U.S. 533 (1939)
Decided: June 5, 1939
Vote: 5 (Stone, Black, Reed, Frankfurter, Douglas)
4 (Hughes, McReynolds, Butler, Roberts)
Opinion of the Court: Reed
Concurring opinion: Black, Douglas
Dissenting opinion: McReynolds, Butler
Dissenting opinion: Roberts (Hughes, McReynolds, Butler)

Rock Royal Cooperative produced milk in New York, but did not comply with the Agricultural Marketing Agreement Act of 1937, which set standards for the handling of milk and a minimum sale price for milk sold at retail. Rock Royal argued that because it did not have complete freedom to set its price it was being denied the use of its property as protected by the Fifth Amendment. In addition, it entered Tenth and Fourteenth Amendment claims. Under the Tenth Amendment, it argued that selling the milk was a purely intrastate matter and that its regulation was reserved to the states and denied to the federal government. Under the Fourteenth Amendment, it claimed a denial of due process.

The Court upheld the act. Justice Reed ruled that if a product is sold only in intrastate commerce but later taken and used beyond state lines, it involves interstate commerce. Congress has the power under the Commerce Clause to regulate intrastate pricing of products if it can show an incidental effect on interstate commerce, and the act did not violate the Fifth, Tenth, or Fourteenth Amendments.

Schneider v. Town of Irvington

308 U.S. 147 (1939)
Decided: November 22, 1939
Vote: 8 (Hughes, Butler, Stone, Roberts, Black, Reed, Frankfurter, Douglas)
1 (McReynolds)
Opinion of the Court: Roberts
Dissenting without opinion: McReynolds

This case consolidated four similar cases from California, Wisconsin, Massachusetts, and New Jersey. Los Angeles, Milwaukee, Worcester, and Irvington, New Jersey, had time, place, and manner ordinances that prohibited the distribution of literature on public streets and prohibited door-to-door solicitations without a license. The cities argued that they were trying to keep their streets clean and maintain a good appearance.

Clara Schneider, a Jehovah's Witness, was distributing religious literature in the streets and conducting door-to-door solicitations in Irvington. She was convicted for violating the distribution ordinances and in her defense argued that the restrictions interfered with her free exercise of religion.

The Court struck down all four ordinances. Justice Roberts ruled that any litter caused by distributing the literature was an indirect effect, that the distributor was not the one who would be littering. Second, requiring a permit for door-to-door solicitations was unconstitutional because it subjected the literature to possible censorship. The First Amendment freedoms of religion, speech, and press cannot be generally abridged by requiring permits or not allowing such rights to be practiced in public places. The Court did not rely on the Free Exercise Clause but, as in its earlier religion cases, continued to interpret the ordinances and the assailed activities in light of the Speech Clause.

See Shawn Francis Peters, *Judging Jehovah's Witnesses* (Lawrence: University Press of Kansas, 2000).

Nardone v. United States

308 U.S. 338 (1939)
Decided: December 11, 1939
Vote: 7 (Hughes, Butler, Stone, Roberts, Black, Frankfurter, Douglas)
1 (McReynolds)
Opinion of the Court: Frankfurter
Dissenting opinion: McReynolds
Did not participate: Reed

In ***Nardone v. United States,*** 302 U.S. 379 (1937), the Court reversed the conviction of Frank Carmine Nardone and ordered a new trial because federal agents had placed an illegal wiretap on his telephone to gather evidence against him. The Court ruled that the evidence obtained by the wiretap was inadmissible evidence. At the new trial, the prosecution introduced evidence that it obtained as a result of the illegal wiretap. It did not use the actual illegally recorded conversations at trial, but it used evidence that had been discovered solely as a result of the recorded conversations. Nardone was convicted again. On appeal, he argued that the prosecution should have been completely barred from entering any evidence that came about as a direct or indirect result of the illegal wiretap.

The Court held that any and all evidence resulting from an illegal wiretap is inadmissible at trial. This extension of the exclusionary rule is known as the "fruits of the poisonous tree" doctrine. In other words, any evidence that was discovered as a result of the illegal wiretap, in addition to the actual conversations recorded, is inadmissible at trial. The Court reversed the conviction again and ordered yet another trial.

See Edith J. Lapidus, *Eavesdropping on Trial* (Rochelle Park, N.Y.: Hayden Books, 1973).

Gold Clause Cases

As part of its inflation program, the Roosevelt administration ended the country's monetary policy with respect to currency based strictly on gold in the nation's reserves (the gold standard). Congress, by joint resolution, canceled clauses in both private and government bonds that called for repayment in gold. The administration and many economists believed that these measures would halt the severe deflation afflicting the country and trigger the price increases considered necessary for recovery. Even the bankers in the House of Morgan approved of the policy, and its head, Russell Leffingwell, praised Roosevelt for saving the country from "complete collapse."

Not everyone agreed, however. Irate bondholders went to court to force repayment of their securities in gold, challenging the government's action as a breach of the obligation of contract and a deprivation of private property without due process of law.

There were two sets of decisions that responded to these complex—but nonetheless constitutional—issues. The first set dealt with the cancellation of the clause in private obligations. The second set dealt with the same issue for government bonds. First, in *Norman v. Baltimore & Ohio Railroad Company* and *United States v. Bankers' Trust Co.,* the Court sustained the government's power to define the country's money. Chief Justice Hughes explained that the contracts merely defined gold as a method of payment. Relying on the *Second Legal Tender Cases,* 79 U.S. 457 (1871), he affirmed that Congress could declare what would pass as legal tender and that it could, under this broad authority, abrogate private contracts if they ran counter to a legitimate exercise of the national power.

Second, in *Perry v. United States,* the federal government emerged with a technical victory but sustained a moral loss not seen since ***Marbury v. Madison,*** 5 U.S. 137 (1803). Hughes distinguished between private obligations, which always had to bend to the public good, and government bonds, which represented the pledged word of the government of the United States. Congress could not break its promises, even in carrying out legitimate powers. The Court held the joint resolution of June 1933 unconstitutional, insofar as it abrogated the gold clauses in government bonds. Recognizing that enforcement of the decision might wreak havoc with the nation's finances and that the administration might very likely ignore it, Hughes then denied the plaintiff relief. He said in effect that the government had done a terrible thing, but since the plaintiff had suffered no real damages, he had no standing to sue.

Justice McReynolds dissented in such vitriolic terms that parts of his comments did not appear in the decision. At one point he bitterly commented "This is Nero at his worst. The Constitution as we know it is gone!"

See John P. Dawson, "The Gold-Clause Decisions," *Michigan Law Review* 33 (1935): 647.

1940–1949

Chambers v. Florida

309 U.S. 227 (1940)
Decided: February 12, 1940
Vote: 8 (Hughes, McReynolds, Stone, Roberts, Black, Reed, Frankfurter, Douglas)
0
Opinion of the Court: Black
Did not participate: Murphy

Isiah Chambers and three other young black men were found guilty of the murder of a white man in Pompano, Florida, and sentenced to death. On appeal, the Florida Supreme Court affirmed the sentence. When the state supreme court received information that the confessions had not been voluntary, but in fact resulted from round-the-clock questioning and harassment for four days, it sent the case back to the county court, which refused to hear it. The Florida Supreme Court then ordered a new trial and a change in venue. Another all-white jury again found the defendants guilty. The defendants appealed to the U.S. Supreme Court, but Florida objected, claiming that the Supreme Court had no jurisdiction to go behind the final verdicts of a duly constituted court to look at the facts anew.

To this Justice Black replied that the use by a state of an improperly obtained confession constituted a denial of due process of law as guaranteed in the Fourteenth Amendment. The defendants had the right under the federal Constitution to require that the state prove them guilty without relying on illegally obtained confessions. The Court had the authority to determine independently whether petitioners' confessions were in fact obtained by impermissible means.

Black admitted that the so-called "third degree" was standard police practice in many states and condemned it as a violation of due process. Although the Court normally would pay deference to a state's criminal proceedings, once a defendant claimed that a federal right had been transgressed, the Court had the duty under the Constitution to step in. As Black wrote: "Due process of law, preserved for all by our Constitution, commands that no such practice as that disclosed by this record shall send any accused to his death."

See Rocco J. Tresolini, *Justice and the Supreme Court* (Philadelphia: Lippincott, 1963).

Thornhill v. Alabama

310 U.S. 88 (1940)
Decided: April 22, 1940
Vote: 8 (Hughes, Stone, Roberts, Black, Reed, Frankfurter, Douglas, Murphy)
1 (McReynolds)
Opinion of the Court: Murphy
Dissenting without opinion: McReynolds

Byron Thornhill was arrested while picketing Brown Wood Preserving Company and convicted for violating an Alabama statute that prohibited loitering or picketing around places of business. The purpose of the statute, according to the state, was to protect people from violence and breaches of the peace. Thornhill, however, claimed that the statute prohibited certain forms of speech and violated the First Amendment, as applied to the states through the Fourteenth Amendment.

The Court struck down the statute. Justice Murphy, in his first opinion for the Court, developed two themes. First, he built upon the notion in footnote four of ***United States v. Carolene Products Co.,*** 304 U.S. 144 (1938), that restrictions on individual liberties required strict scrutiny by the courts. Second, he adopted Justice Black's notion that the liberties protected by the First Amendment, especially speech, held a "preferred position" in the constitutional firmament. Although Justice Brandeis had earlier suggested in ***Senn v. Tile Layers Protective Union,*** 301 U.S. 468 (1937), that picketing might be a form of protected speech, this notion was not fully explicated until *Thornhill.* Murphy's opinion extended First Amendment protection to peaceful picketing and enlarged upon the *Carolene Products* footnote to justify the Court's invalidation of laws that invaded civil liberties.

The Court held that the First Amendment protected the freedom to publicly discuss all matters of public concern without prior restraints. A labor dispute constituted an important issue of public concern, and people should be able to discuss such issues in public. Free discussion about labor disputes, Murphy wrote, "appears to be indispensable to the effective and intelligent use of the processes of popular government to shape the destiny of modern industrial society."

Furthermore, public streets were a traditional public forum for discourse. State governments cannot prohibit people from speaking out in a public forum just because other places to speak were available or the speech involved a labor dispute. For freedom of discussion to "fulfill its historic function, it must embrace all issues about which information is needed or appropriate."

Thornhill proved to be both influential and enduring; it has been cited in more than three hundred subsequent Supreme Court opinions. In 1969 Justice Clark wrote that the opinion was "the bedrock upon which many of the Court's civil rights pronouncements rest."

See William E. Forbath, *Law and the Shaping of the American Labor Movement* (Cambridge: Harvard University Press, 1991).

Cantwell v. Connecticut

310 U.S. 296 (1940)
Decided: May 30, 1940
Vote: 9 (Hughes, McReynolds, Stone, Roberts, Black, Reed, Frankfurter, Douglas, Murphy)
0
Opinion of the Court: Roberts

Jehovah's Witnesses consider proselytizing to be part of their religious obligations. This practice includes preaching on street corners and selling or otherwise distributing pamphlets describing their religion. Under the old belief/action dichotomy first enunciated in ***Reynolds v. United States,*** 98 U.S. 145 (1879), such activities did not fall under the protection of the First Amendment and therefore could be regulated by the state. In a line of cases beginning in the late 1930s, however, the Court gradually came to understand that the belief/action distinction could not be sustained when certain practices were clearly tied to the faith itself.

For example, in ***Lovell v. City of Griffin,*** 303 U.S. 444 (1938), the Court struck down a municipal ordinance requiring groups to get a permit before distributing circulars. The decision gave the Witnesses a victory based on free speech grounds. In *Cantwell* the Court began to explore the meaning of another part of the First Amendment, the Free Exercise Clause.

Newton Cantwell went door-to-door in overwhelmingly Catholic neighborhoods asking residents if they would hear a recording or accept one of the Witnesses' pamphlets. Both materials included attacks on Catholicism. When locals objected, Cantwell was arrested and convicted of failing to secure from the secretary of public welfare the necessary approval for door-to-door solicitation.

In overturning the conviction, the Court took two significant actions. First, it relied on the Free Exercise Clause. The state had the power to license solicitors, Justice Roberts declared, even for religious causes, but the arbitrary power lodged in the secretary created an impermissible censorship over religion. Even though Roberts reiterated the belief/action doctrine, he noted that the type of action would now have to be examined to see how closely it followed belief and how it affected others, and the courts would determine that balance. Second, Roberts set out what became a universal rule of First Amendment law: a state may regulate the time, place, and manner of soliciting contributions and holding public meetings, but it cannot ban them altogether or discriminate on the basis of the content of that speech.

See Leo Pfeffer, *Church, State and Freedom,* rev. ed. (Boston: Beacon Press, 1967); and Edward F. Waite, "The Debt of Constitutional Law to Jehovah's Witnesses," *Minnesota Law Review* 28 (1944): 209.

Apex Hosiery Co. v. Leader

310 U.S. 469 (1940)
Decided: May 27, 1940
Vote: 6 (Stone, Black, Reed, Frankfurter, Douglas, Murphy)
3 (Hughes, McReynolds, Roberts)
Opinion of the Court: Stone
Dissenting opinion: Hughes (McReynolds, Roberts)

Apex Hosiery Company manufactured hosiery and shipped it in interstate commerce. Apex sued William Leader and the American Federation of Full Fashion Hosiery Workers for striking; the company claimed that the strike was a conspiracy to damage its business, which would constitute a violation of the Sherman Antitrust Act.

The Court held that the Sherman Antitrust Act did not prohibit strikes. Although strikes shut down production in an attempt to force an employer to meet the employees' demands, doing so has only an indirect effect on interstate commerce. The Sherman Act had originally been intended to prohibit only activity that directly affected interstate commerce, and therefore it did not cover strikes.

See Elinor R. Hoffmann, "Labor and Antitrust Policy: Drawing a Line of Demarcation," *Brooklyn Law Review* 50 (fall 1983): 1.

Minersville School District v. Gobitis

310 U.S. 586 (1940)
Decided: June 3, 1940
Vote: 8 (Hughes, McReynolds, Roberts, Black, Reed, Frankfurter, Douglas, Murphy)
1 (Stone)
Opinion of the Court: Frankfurter
Concurring without opinion: McReynolds
Dissenting opinion: Stone

Pennsylvania law required that all public school children begin each day with a salute to the American flag. Any child who refused to participate could be expelled from school. Because of their literal reading of Exodus 20:4–5, Jehovah's Witnesses objected to the salute. They equated saluting the flag with bowing down to graven images. They challenged the law as a violation of their constitutionally protected free exercise of religion.

Whether a state could compel school children to salute the flag was an issue in twenty states between 1935 and 1940, and the question had been litigated in seven states. Prior to *Gobitis* the U.S. Supreme Court had upheld four state court decisions validating compulsory flag salute laws.

Justice Frankfurter, a naturalized American citizen, had little sympathy for those who, in his eyes, refused to meet their civic obligations. He framed what he saw as the "precise" issue in terms of judicial restraint and called upon the Court to defer to the wisdom and prerogatives of local school authorities. Legislative "guardianship of deeply cherished liberties," according to Frankfurter, was not to be taken lightly.

An almost formulaic quality characterizes the opinion. Is the legislative end legitimate? Are the means chosen reasonable? If so, then it is not up the courts to say that a better way exists. Frankfurter was essentially applying a rational basis test, even though the Jehovah's Witnesses had claimed that a fundamental right—religious freedom—was involved.

Justice Stone's dissent began to underscore the scope of his intentions in his famous footnote four in ***United States v. Carolene Products Co.,*** 304 U.S. 144 (1938). The question before the Court was not a matter of economic regulation, Stone reasoned, but of infringement of a claimed right. As such, the law had to be examined, not with a minimal scrutiny, but with a much higher standard. By this standard, the law had to fail, and the government, despite the noble end of fostering patriotism, had to respect and protect the free exercise of religion of even a small group. Stone circulated his dissent late in the term, and three members of the Court—Black, Douglas, and Murphy—indicated that had they seen it earlier they would have joined Stone.

The decision was announced during the Dunkirk evacuation, and no doubt the concern that the United States would soon be drawn into World War II informed Frankfurter's opinion. Should the nation go to war, all citizens would be expected to shoulder their responsibilities, and the schools were the chief instruments for fostering such patriotism. One immediate consequence of the *Gobitis* decision was that so-called patriots launched hundreds of attacks on Witness members and their children, especially in small towns and rural areas. Two years after *Gobitis,* the Court agreed to review the same issue and reversed itself in ***West Virginia Board of Education v. Barnette,*** 319 U.S. 624 (1943).

See Leo Pfeffer, *Church, State and Freedom,* rev. ed. (Boston: Beacon Press, 1967); and David Manwaring, *Render unto Caesar: The Flag Salute Controversy* (Chicago: University of Chicago Press, 1962).

Hansberry v. Lee

311 U.S. 32 (1940)
Decided: November 12, 1940
Vote: 9 (Hughes, McReynolds, Stone, Roberts, Black, Reed, Frankfurter, Douglas, Murphy)
0
Opinion of the Court: Stone
Concurring in judgment without opinion: McReynolds, Roberts, Reed

Anna M. Lee and other owners of a housing development signed an agreement that none of the land should be sold or leased to black people or occupied by any black person. The agreement was to become effective once 95 percent of the landowners signed it. One of the landowners, however, sold his property to a bank that in turn sold it to Carl A. Hansberry, a black man. Lee and others sued to void the sale. They relied on the fact that in an earlier case it had been held that the covenant was in effect because 95 percent of the owners had agreed. If this were the case, the sale would have been voided because at that time restrictive covenants were still legal. Under the doctrine of *res judicata,* once a court has determined a factual or legal question, that holding will be binding on all related cases. Hansberry, however, said that the agreement had never become effective, because only 56 percent of the owners had signed, and the matter had been fraudulently presented in the earlier case. If the agreement had not, in fact, gone into effect, the sale of the property to him was valid.

The Court held that *res judicata* did not apply because the earlier court finding had been based on fraudulent information. To allow such a ruling to stand, wrote Justice Stone, would be a mockery of due process.

See Allen R. Kamp, "The History Behind *Hansberry v. Lee,*" *University of California at Davis Law Review* 20 (1987): 481.

Smith v. Texas

311 U.S. 128 (1940)
Decided: November 25, 1940
Vote: 9 (Hughes, McReynolds, Stone, Roberts, Black, Reed, Frankfurter, Douglas, Murphy)
0
Opinion of the Court: Black

Edgar Smith, an African American man convicted of rape, based his appeal for a new trial on the assertion that blacks were systematically excluded from both grand and petit jury service. This exclusion denied him a trial by a jury of his peers. In a county in which blacks constituted more than 20 percent of the population, nearly 10 percent were poll-tax payers, meaning that their names were on the roles from which jurors were selected. Even though three thousand to six thousand black residents satisfied the statutory qualifications for grand jury service, of the 512 persons summoned for grand jury duty over an eight-year period only 18 were black. Of these eighteen, five had served—one of them three times. By comparison, in the same eight years, 379 of the 494 white men summoned actually served.

Justice Black found that the conviction of a black man upon a grand jury indictment, where blacks were excluded from service, violated the Equal Protection Clause of the Fourteenth Amendment. "The fact that the written words of a state's laws hold out a promise that no such discrimination will be practiced is not enough," he wrote. "The Fourteenth Amendment requires that equal protection to all must be given—not merely promised."

See Hiroshi Fukurai, Edgar W. Butler, and Richard Krooth, *Race and the Jury: Racial Disenfranchisement and the Search for Justice* (New York: Plenum, 1992).

Sibbach v. Wilson & Co., Inc.

312 U.S. 1 (1941)
Decided: January 13, 1941
Vote: 5 (Hughes, McReynolds, Stone, Roberts, Reed)
4 (Black, Frankfurter, Douglas, Murphy)
Opinion of the Court: Roberts
Dissenting opinion: Frankfurter (Black, Douglas, Murphy)

Sibbach sued Wilson and Company, claiming that Wilson inflicted bodily injuries to him in Indiana. Wilson denied the allegations and tried to have Sibbach see a physician, appointed by the court, to determine the extent of the injuries. The trial court ordered the examination under Rule 35 of the Federal Rules of Civil Procedure, which allows for such physical examinations. Sibbach refused to comply, and the trial court found her guilty of contempt. The question before the Supreme Court was whether a plaintiff must comply with a court order to be medically examined.

The Court said no. It held that Rule 35 is a procedural rule, not a substantive rule. In other words, it provides the steps to follow in ordering a physical examination; it does not state when or under what circumstances one may be ordered. Sibbach, therefore, did not have to comply with the order to submit to a physical examination, and the Court reversed the judgment that she was in contempt.

The case is one of the earliest to start interpreting the Federal Rules of Civil Procedure, which the Court had promulgated in 1938. The decisions involved not just a question of interpretation of language, but also a justification of the Court's power to issue these rules under an act of Congress of 1935 authorizing the Court to do so.

Hines v. Davidowitz

312 U.S. 52 (1941)
Decided: January 20, 1941
Vote: 6 (Roberts, Black, Reed, Frankfurter, Douglas, Murphy)
3 (Hughes, McReynolds, Stone)
Opinion of the Court: Black
Dissenting opinion: Stone (Hughes, McReynolds)

The Pennsylvania Alien Registration Act required aliens eighteen years or older to register once each year, provide certain information, pay a $1.00 annual registration fee, receive an alien identification card and carry it at all times, show the card whenever any police officer requested, and show the card to register a car or to get a driver's license. Aliens who violated the act were subject to a fine of no more than $100.00 or imprisonment for not more than sixty days, or both. Failure to carry the identification card or failing to show it when requested meant a fine of not more than $10 or imprisonment for not more than ten days, or both.

The federal Alien Registration Act was far more stringent than Pennsylvania's standards. The lower court struck down Pennsylvania's law, stating that the state did not have the power to enact the law because it was an issue covered by the federal government's act. Federal agencies such as the Federal Bureau of Investigation also did not want states interfering with security measures, especially because it seemed clear that the United States might well be drawn into World War II as a combatant.

The U.S. Supreme Court upheld the lower court decision. The Court ruled that, under the Supremacy Clause of Article VI of the Constitution, when the federal government by treaty or statute establishes rules covering the rights of aliens, that law is the supreme law of the land, and no state can add or subtract from the authority of a federal statute. This principle is known as the "preemption doctrine"; the federal government, when acting in an area in which it has powers delegated to it by the Constitution, automatically preempts any state action in this field. States may act in such areas only when the federal government has chosen not to do so.

United States v. Darby Lumber Co.

312 U.S. 100 (1941)
Decided: February 3, 1941
Vote: 9 (Hughes, McReynolds, Stone, Roberts, Black, Reed, Frankfurter, Douglas, Murphy)
0
Opinion of the Court: Stone

The Fair Labor Standards Act of 1938 was the last major piece of New Deal reform legislation. The law provided federal standards for minimum wages and maximum hours in all businesses engaged in interstate commerce. Congress clearly was relying on the new Court that emerged after the "crisis" of 1937—in which President Roosevelt had unsuccessfully tried to add more justices to the Court in order to get a judiciary more favorable to New Deal legislation—to reverse itself and take a far broader view of what constituted interstate commerce and the federal power under the Commerce Clause than had been shown by conservatives, especially in rulings such as ***Hammer v. Dagenhart,*** 247 U.S. 251 (1918). In that case the Court defined manufacturing as a purely local enterprise and therefore not subject to federal control. In the 1920s the Taft Court negated a number of state measures that attempted to regulate business and, through a doctrine called "dual federalism," created a no-man's land where neither the federal government nor the states could regulate business.

Justice Stone, speaking for the Court in *Darby,* demolished this no-man's land as well as dual federalism. First, he invoked Justice Holmes's dissent in *Dagenhart* to declare that it and other cases relying on it were departures from well-established rules regarding the definition of commerce and were now overruled. Although the decision did not explore all the details and nuances of the law, Stone made it clear that under the Commerce Clause, Congress had the power to reach individual manufacturers, and that henceforth the Court would apply a broad and generous interpretation of what constituted interstate commerce.

Second, Stone applied the rational basis test he had outlined in ***United States v. Carolene Products Co.,*** 304 U.S. 144 (1938), to hold that courts would not question the wisdom of legislative acts so long as the power to act in that area existed. By limiting the power of the courts to review such legislation, Stone and the majority destroyed the argument of substantive due process, which went into a decline. It resurfaced in the 1960s, but this time it was invoked in behalf of individual liberties.

See Edward S. Corwin, "The Passing of Dual Federalism," *Virginia Law Review* 36 (1950): 1.

Milk Wagon Drivers' Union v. Meadowmoor Dairies

312 U.S. 287 (1941)
Decided: February 10, 1941
Vote: 6 (Hughes, McReynolds, Stone, Roberts, Frankfurter, Murphy)
3 (Black, Reed, Douglas)
Opinion of the Court: Frankfurter
Dissenting opinion: Black (Douglas)
Dissenting opinion: Reed

Under a vendor system for distributing milk in Chicago, dairy companies sold milk to vendors operating their own trucks who resold to other vendors. Meadowmoor Dairies disregarded the working standards the Milk Wagon Drivers' Union had set for its dairy employee members, and in response the union began picketing Meadowmoor. Although the picketing itself was peaceful, it occurred at the same time as fifty instances of window smashing, bombings, stench bombings, destruction of trucks, beatings of drivers, arson, and armed violence.

Meadowmoor secured an injunction to stop the picketing, and the union appealed, claiming it was a violation of the their First Amendment right of speech. The Court disagreed and upheld the injunction prohibiting the peaceful picketing because of the violence that accompanied it. The picketing had taken place in a context of repeated violence and destruction of property, and shutting it down was justified as an effort to prevent future coercion and violence. The Court said that past acts of violence that coincide with one's speech may be used as evidence to prevent or chill such speech.

This view has been surpassed. In his dissent, Justice Reed pointed the way by noting that one should not allow the fear of disorder to limit speech; rather, the answer lay in keeping the peace and not penalizing speech.

Railroad Commission of Texas v. Pullman Co.

312 U.S. 496 (1941)
Decided: March 3, 1941
Vote: 8 (Hughes, McReynolds, Stone, Black, Reed, Frankfurter, Douglas, Murphy)
0
Opinion of the Court: Frankfurter
Did not participate: Roberts

The Texas Railroad Commission ordered that no sleeping cars could be operated on any railroad line in Texas unless a conductor was continuously in charge of the cars. At this time, porters were often in charge of sleeping cars on trains. Most of the porters were black, and most of the conductors were white.

Pullman Company and several railroads argued that the law violated equal protection, due process, and was a dormant Commerce Clause violation by Texas. They claimed that the Texas law unconstitutionally discriminated against the black porters, treated the railroads unfairly, and that Texas was intruding into interstate commerce matters that Congress alone could handle.

The Court upheld the Texas law and invoked what is known as the doctrine of abstention. If a state has a legal procedure or remedy that is easy to use to determine whether that state's action was proper, the state's methods should be used. In other words, federal courts should not interfere with cases that can be properly handled by state procedure. In such a decision, the Court does not address the merits of the substantive issues, but defers to established state procedures.

Cox v. New Hampshire

312 U.S. 569 (1941)
Decided: March 31, 1941
Vote: 9 (Hughes, McReynolds, Stone, Roberts, Black, Reed, Frankfurter, Douglas, Murphy)
0
Opinion of the Court: Hughes

An ordinance in Manchester, New Hampshire, required that every parade or procession on public streets be licensed and pay a fee. A large group of Jehovah's Witnesses met at City Hall for what they termed an "information march." They divided into four or five groups and marched through different parts of the city's business district. They then lined up in single file and marched along the sidewalk. Each person carried a sign that with a religious message on it. They also handed out leaflets with similar religious messages. The Jehovah's Witnesses had not obtained a permit.

Several of the marchers were arrested and convicted for conducting a public parade without a permit. The Jehovah's Witnesses argued that what they did was not a parade and that the permit law violated the First Amendment freedoms of religion and assembly.

The Court unanimously upheld the convictions and the New Hampshire law. First, the Court ruled that the Jehovah's Witnesses' actions constituted a parade. Second, the Court ruled that if a state or local government has authority to set time, place, and manner regulations in traditionally open public forums, then the law need only pass a rational basis test. The Court found that the city ordinance was a reasonable police regulation designed to promote the safe and orderly use of its public streets and that it had an interest in knowing about parades ahead of time so that it could arrange proper policing. Thus, the Court allowed states and local governments to create licensing fees and require permits for parades.

See David Goldberger, "A Reconsideration of Cox v. New Hampshire: Can Demonstrators be Required to Pay the Costs of Using America's Public Forums?" *Texas Law Review* 62 (1983): 403.

Mitchell v. United States

313 U.S. 80 (1941)
Decided: April 28, 1941
Vote: 8 (Hughes, Stone, Roberts, Black, Reed, Frankfurter, Douglas, Murphy)
0
Opinion of the Court: Hughes

Arthur W. Mitchell, an African American member of the U.S. House of Representatives from Chicago, had paid a first-class fare for a train ride from Chicago to Arkansas. From Chicago to Memphis he was provided with a sleeper car as part of that first-class fare, but once the train entered Arkansas the conductor, under Arkansas's "separate but equal" law, asked Mitchell to leave the sleeper car and ride in a second-class car for "colored" people, a car significantly substandard in comparison to the sleeping cars for white people.

Mitchell filed a complaint, not in court, but with the Interstate Commerce Commission, arguing that the discrimination to which he had been subjected violated the Interstate Commerce Act. The railroad responded that it was not their rule, but that of the state, which apparently was valid under ***Plessy v. Ferguson,*** 163 U.S. 537 (1896).

The Court held that the Interstate Commerce Act forbade segregation in interstate commerce. Chief Justice Hughes ruled that interstate common carriers, such as trains, cannot segregate passengers based on race. To do so would be to inhibit interstate commerce. The decision may be seen as part of the Supreme Court's shift from the economic issues that had dominated its agenda in the 1920s and 1930s toward a greater concern with civil liberties and civil rights. As the NAACP Legal Defense Fund began filing more suits attacking segregation, it found an increasingly sympathetic judiciary, one that would eventually overturn segregation in the major civil rights cases of the 1950s.

See Catherine A. Barnes, *Journey from Jim Crow: The Desegregation of Southern Transit* (New York: Columbia University Press, 1983).

United States v. Classic

313 U.S. 299 (1941)
Decided: May 26, 1941
Vote: 4 (Stone, Roberts, Reed, Frankfurter)
3 (Black, Douglas, Murphy)
Opinion of the Court: Stone
Dissenting opinion: Douglas (Black, Murphy)
Did not participate: Hughes

Patrick B. Classic, the commissioner of elections in Louisiana, was charged with altering, falsely counting, and falsely certifying the votes cast in a state primary election. When the case went to trial, the court ruled that the right to vote in a state primary election is not protected by the U.S. Constitution, and that was the question the U.S. Supreme Court was asked to decide.

Holding that citizens have a fundamental right to vote in state primary elections, the Court ruled that this right derives from the states' constitutional authority to hold congressional elections. Because the states are obliged to protect voting for congressional seats, they must also protect voting in primary elections for these contests.

The case is a significant step away from the Court's ruling in ***Grovey v. Townsend,*** 295 U.S. 45 (1935), in which the Court had validated black disenfranchisement in primaries. Henceforth, the Court would view primaries as integral parts of the voting process.

See David M. Bixby, "The Roosevelt Court, Democratic Ideology, and Minority Rights: Another Look at *United States v. Classic,*" *Yale Law Review* 90 (1981): 741.

Edwards v. California

314 U.S. 160 (1941)
Decided: November 24, 1941
Vote: 9 (Stone, Roberts, Black, Reed, Frankfurter, Douglas, Murphy, Byrnes, R. Jackson)
0
Opinion of the Court: Byrnes
Concurring opinion: Douglas (Black, Murphy)
Concurring opinion: R. Jackson

Edwards was a U.S. citizen and a resident of California. He left California for Texas to get his brother-in-law, Frank Duncan, a Texas resident, to come to California. Duncan was unemployed, and more important, did not have a job in California.

Because of the Great Depression, which brought a large number of unemployed people into the state, California required anyone crossing its borders to prove that he or she had work in California. Neither Edwards nor Duncan was employed, and the state attempted to stop their entry.

The Court held that the California law violated the Commerce Clause. The Court ruled that the free passage and travel of persons from state to state are protected under interstate commerce because labor is a commercial issue. A state law legislation that prevents U.S. citizens from entering the state for being indigent violates the Commerce Clause.

The majority took the Commerce Clause route at Stone's urging, because he believed it the least controversial means of voiding the California law. Although the three liberals, Justices Douglas, Black, and Murphy, concurred in the result, they based their opinion on the Privileges and Immunities Clause and claimed that the right to travel anywhere in the country was a privilege protected by the Constitution. In the end, it was Douglas's view that informed future cases regarding limits on internal travel.

See Edward W. Adams, "State Control of Interstate Migration of Indigents," *Michigan Law Review* 40 (1942): 711.

Bridges v. California

314 U.S. 252 (1941)
Decided: December 8, 1941
Vote: 5 (Black, Reed, Douglas, Murphy, R. Jackson)
4 (Stone, Roberts, Frankfurter, Byrnes)
Opinion of the Court: Black
Dissenting opinion: Frankfurter (Stone, Roberts, Byrnes)

Bridges v. California, consolidated with *Times-Mirror Co. v. Superior Court of California,* brought together two unlikely allies—radical West Coast labor leader Harry Bridges and the ultraconservative *Los Angeles Times.* California state courts had found both in contempt, the newspaper for its editorial urging a judge, while sentence was pending, to send two convicted members of a labor "goon squad" to prison, and Bridges for sending a telegram threatening a longshoremen's strike if a state court enforced what he labeled an "outrageous" decision in a labor dispute. The two cases presented a direct confrontation between First Amendment rights of free speech and press and Sixth Amendment protection of a fair trial.

The cases had first come up in the 1940 term, when Justice Frankfurter apparently had a 6–3 majority to uphold the state courts. But Justice McReynolds and Chief Justice Hughes retired, and Justice Murphy changed his mind, so the case was scheduled for reargument in fall 1941. Then, by a bare majority, the Court for the first time reversed a state court finding of fact in a case of contempt by publication and extended First Amendment freedom of the press to published comments regarding pending court decisions.

Justice Black's opinion applied the traditional speech test of clear-and-present danger and ruled that the "substantive evil" must have a "degree of imminence extremely high" before courts could punish allegedly contemptuous speech or writings. States would have to show that comments posed a real threat to a fair trial, and neither the *Times* editorial nor the Bridges telegram met that test. Judges might find such criticism disrespectful, but "the assumption that respect for the judiciary can be won by shielding judges from published criticism wrongly appraises the character of American public opinion. For it is a prized American privilege to speak one's mind, although not always with perfect good taste, on all public institutions."

See Anthony Lewis, "Justice Black and the First Amendment," *Alabama Law Review* 38 (1987): 289.

United States v. Wrightwood Dairy Co.

315 U.S. 110 (1942)
Decided: February 2, 1942
Vote: 8 (Stone, Black, Reed, Frankfurter, Douglas, Murphy, Byrnes, R. Jackson)
0
Opinion of the Court: Stone
Did not participate: Roberts

Wrightwood Dairy Company bought its total daily raw milk requirements from producers located within Illinois, processed the milk in its Chicago plant, and sold and distributed the milk within Illinois.

The Agricultural Marketing Agreement Act authorized the secretary of agriculture to regulate milk. One such regulation fixed prices for milk. Wrightwood violated the fixed prices, but argued that it was engaged solely in intrastate commerce, not interstate commerce. The dairy was, however, competing against other dairy companies that were engaged in interstate commerce. Therefore, the question in this case was whether a business that sells only to intrastate customers, processes its product solely intrastate, and buys its materials solely intrastate in engaged in interstate commerce.

The Court held that Wrightwood was engaged in interstate commerce and therefore violated the fixed prices for milk. The Court stated that the Commerce Clause extends to intrastate activities that substantially interfere with or obstruct interstate commerce and that Congress can regulate the price of milk sold in intrastate commerce. In other words, interstate competition can make an otherwise intrastate company be engaged in interstate commerce.

See Ashley Sellers and Jesse E. Baskette Jr., "Agricultural Marketing Agreements and Order Programs, 1933–1943," *Georgetown Law Journal* 33 (1945): 123.

United States v. Pink

315 U.S. 203 (1942)
Decided: February 2, 1942
Vote: 5 (Black, Frankfurter, Douglas, Murphy, Byrnes)
2 (Stone, Roberts)
Opinion of the Court: Douglas
Concurring opinion: Frankfurter
Dissenting opinion: Stone (Roberts)
Did not participate: Reed, R. Jackson

In 1918 and 1919 the communist government of the Soviet Union nationalized the properties of various Russian insurance companies, including properties abroad. First Russian Insurance Company had offices and assets in New York, and that state, acting through the superintendent of insurance, seized the company's assets to pay off its New York policyholders and creditors. In 1931 the New York Court of Appeals directed the superintendent to dispose of the remaining assets to foreign creditors.

In 1933, however, the United States recognized the Soviet Union, and, as part of the Litvinov agreement, the United States agreed to become the assignee of Soviet claims in the United States, which included the remaining assets of the insurance company. The federal government sued the New York superintendent of insurance to recover the balance of the assets. The government lost in state court and appealed the decision.

The Court held that the order recognizing the Soviet Union was a valid exercise of presidential power. As it had done a few years earlier in ***United States v. Curtiss-Wright Export Corp.,*** 299 U.S. 304 (1936), the Court reiterated that the executive branch has far-reaching powers when it comes to foreign affairs. Moreover, it does not always need the consent of Congress to conduct foreign relations. This power is implicit in the nature of sovereignty. An executive order such as the Litvinov agreement carries the same authority as a statute, and under the Supremacy Clause all states must abide by executive orders.

See Philip Jessup, "The Litvinov Assignment and the Pink Case," *American Journal of International Law* 36 (1942): 282.

Chaplinsky v. New Hampshire

315 U.S. 568 (1942)
Decided: March 9, 1942
Vote: 9 (Stone, Roberts, Black, Reed, Frankfurter, Douglas, Murphy, Byrnes, R. Jackson)
0
Opinion of the Court: Murphy

Walter Chaplinsky was a Jehovah's Witness. While preaching, he created a public disturbance, and the police came to escort him away. Chaplinsky protested his removal and called an officer a "goddamn racketeer" and a "damned fascist." He was convicted under a statute that prohibited speech that was likely to cause an average listener to fight. He appealed, claiming that the statute restricted his First Amendment freedom of speech.

The Court upheld the conviction, ruling that the First Amendment does not protect "fighting words." The right of free speech is not absolute at all times. The Court reasoned that "fighting words" by their very nature tend to inflict injury or incite an immediate breach of the peace. The Court also reasoned that such speech is not a part of the marketplace of ideas that the First Amendment protects. The Court went even further to rule that lewd, obscene, profane, and libelous words are not protected.

The ruling that "fighting words" were not protected remained good law for almost a half-century. The Court never overruled *Chaplinsky,* but appeared to bury the fighting words doctrine in ***R. A. V. v. City of St. Paul,*** 505 U.S. 377 (1992).

See Shawn Francis Peters, *Judging Jehovah's Witnesses: Religious Persecution and the Dawn of the Rights Revolution* (Lawrence: University Press of Kansas, 2000).

Carpenters' and Joiners' Union v. Ritter's Cafe

315 U.S. 722 (1942)
Decided: March 30, 1942
Vote: 5 (Stone, Roberts, Frankfurter, Byrnes, R. Jackson)
4 (Black, Reed, Douglas, Murphy)
Opinion of the Court: Frankfurter
Dissenting opinion: Black (Douglas, Murphy)
Dissenting opinion: Reed

Ritter hired a contractor to put up a building in Houston and allowed the contractor to make his own hiring arrangements. The contractor hired nonunion painters and carpenters. Ritter also owned Ritter's Cafe, a restaurant that employed union members. The new building had nothing to do with the restaurant, which was located about a mile and a half away. The union members peacefully picketed in front of the restaurant for the hiring of nonunion subcontractors, which caused the cafe's business to fall by 60 percent. Ritter went to court, invoking a Texas antitrust law that prohibited all picketing, including peaceful picketing.

Although the Court had previously included peaceful picketing as a protected form of speech, in this case a bare majority upheld the Texas antitrust law. Justice Frankfurter ruled that the Due Process Clause does not make peaceful picketing immune from regulation. He propounded a balancing approach, in which courts take into consideration the competing interests among an employer, an employee, and the public in regard to labor disputes. In this case, the construction was separate from the restaurant and therefore was protected by the state antitrust law.

Valentine v. Chrestensen

316 U.S. 52 (1942)
Decided: April 13, 1942
Vote: 9 (Stone, Roberts, Black, Reed, Frankfurter, Douglas, Murphy, Byrnes, R. Jackson)
0
Opinion of the Court: Roberts

Chrestensen, a Florida businessman, owned a former Navy submarine that he brought to New York for display and promotion. He distributed leaflets that had a commercial advertisement for the submarine on one side and on the other side what could be interpreted as a message of political protest. He was arrested for violating a New York law that prohibited distribution of advertising literature on the streets. The Court was asked to decide whether First Amendment protection extended to commercial speech.

The Court, in what Justice Douglas later called a "casual, almost offhand" manner, held that the First Amendment did not protect commercial speech and imposed no "restraint on government as respects purely commercial advertising." As to the political message on the leaflets, Justice Roberts reasoned that the only reason the political message was included was to avoid the anticommercial speech law.

The case remained good law for more than thirty years, until the Court extended First Amendment protection to commercial speech in ***Virginia Pharmacy Board v. Virginia Citizens Consumer Council,*** 425 U.S. 748 (1976).

See Edwin P. Rome and William H. Roberts, *Corporate and Commercial Free Speech* (Westport, Conn.: Quorum Books, 1985).

Betts v. Brady

316 U.S. 455 (1942)
Decided: June 1, 1942
Vote: 6 (Stone, Roberts, Reed, Frankfurter, Byrnes, R. Jackson)
3 (Black, Douglas, Murphy)
Opinion of the Court: Roberts
Dissenting opinion: Black (Murphy, Douglas)

Following his indictment for a robbery, Smith Betts asked the trial court to appoint a lawyer to defend him. The court refused, arguing that counsel for indigents was permitted only for the crimes of rape and murder. Forced to defend himself, Betts was convicted and sentenced to eight years in prison. He filed a petition for habeas corpus, claiming that his Sixth Amendment right to counsel had been violated.

At this time, the Supreme Court was still in the early stages of determining which of the rights enumerated in the first eight amendments applied to the states through incorporation by the Fourteenth Amendment's Due Process Clause. The Court had required states to appoint counsel in capital cases in ***Powell v. Alabama,*** 287 U.S. 45 (1932), but had not extended that holding to trials for lesser crimes. Justice Frankfurter, appointed to the Court in 1938 to replace Justice Cardozo, had taken on Cardozo's view of selective incorporation. He argued that so long as the fundamental fairness of the trial had not been affected, counsel was not a right that needed to be expanded to the states. Justice Black, who disagreed with the Cardozo/Frankfurter position, was well on his way to believing that all of the guarantees in the Bill of Rights should be incorporated. Black was the only member of the Court with extensive criminal trial experience, and he argued that a trial could never be fair without an attorney.

Justice Roberts, writing for the majority, agreed with the stance advanced by Frankfurter. Roberts wrote that most states did not provide counsel to indigents in noncapital cases. He reasoned that the circumstances in the case did not suggest that Betts had received an unfair trial. Moreover, he said that in the event of unusual circumstances—such as the mental retardation or illiteracy of the defendant or the complex nature of the charges—then counsel would be required, but that it would fall to the trial courts on a case-by-case basis to make that determination.

In dissent Black noted that had Betts been charged with a federal crime and tried in a federal court he would have been afforded an attorney by right. These same rights should apply to defendants in state criminal trial proceedings. The right to counsel, he argued, was fundamental to a fair trial, and the Sixth Amendment should be extended to the states.

Over the next twenty years the Court heard a number of claims for counsel and, applying the *Betts* rule, almost always managed to find an "unusual" circumstance requiring the appointment of counsel. Finally, in ***Gideon v. Wainwright,*** 372 U.S. 335 (1963), a unanimous Court adopted Black's dissent in *Betts* and overruled the 1942 case.

See Anthony Lewis, *Gideon's Trumpet* (New York: Random House, 1964); and Yale Kamisar, "*Betts v. Brady* Twenty Years Later: The Right to Counsel and Due Process Values," *Michigan Law Review* 61 (1962): 219.

Skinner v. Oklahoma ex rel. Williamson

316 U.S. 535 (1942)
Decided: June 1, 1942
Vote: 9 (Stone, Roberts, Black, Reed, Frankfurter, Douglas, Murphy, Byrnes, R. Jackson)
0
Opinion of the Court: Douglas
Concurring opinion: Stone
Concurring opinion: R. Jackson

In 1942 many states, relying on the Court's decision in ***Buck v. Bell,*** 274 U.S. 200 (1927), sterilized "feeble-minded" or habitual criminals. Jack T. Skinner, convicted once for stealing chickens and twice for armed robbery, was ordered to submit to a vasectomy under the Oklahoma Criminal Sterilization Act.

Justice Douglas engaged in a fine example of creative jurisprudence and in essence resurrected the Equal Protection Clause, which Justice Holmes had once derided as the last refuge of a constitutional lawyer. Douglas noted that the law did not apply equally to all: a chicken thief could be sterilized, but the same penalty did not apply to persons convicted of white collar crimes such as embezzlement. This discrimination opened the door to an equal protection argument.

He identified the right to procreate as a "fundamental right," saying that any legislation restricting that right would be subject to strict scrutiny by the courts. Because the law did not apply equally to all, it violated the Equal Protection Clause.

The Court had never before identified procreation as a fundamental right—that is, as a basic right essential for individual freedom—and Douglas did not offer a single precedent to buttress his assertion. Beyond that, he connected fundamental rights to a strict scrutiny standard even though the Court had only just begun to identify the criteria for reviewing constitutional claims. More than any other case of the time, *Skinner* animated the new jurisprudence suggested by Stone in ***United States v. Carolene Products Co.,*** 304 U.S. 144 (1938). By pronouncing the "invidious discrimination" in the law's enforcement unconstitutional, Douglas opened a new avenue for courts to review state legislation that treated some people differently from others.

Chief Justice Stone's concurrence simply stated that he would reverse the order on due process grounds. Such a holding, Stone knew, would not require a hearing on whether Skinner's criminal propensities were inheritable. Justice Jackson also concurred, declaring that there are limits to the extent to which the state may conduct biological experiments at the expense of the dignity of a minority, even a criminal minority.

See Melvin I. Urofsky, "William O. Douglas as a Common Law Judge," *Duke Law Journal* 41 (1991): 133.

Jones v. Opelika

316 U.S. 584 (1942)
Decided: June 8, 1942
Vote: 5 (Roberts, Reed, Frankfurter, Byrnes, R. Jackson)
4 (Stone, Black, Douglas, Murphy)
Opinion of the Court: Reed
Dissenting opinion: Stone (Black, Douglas, Murphy)
Dissenting opinion: Murphy (Stone, Black, Douglas)
Dissenting opinion: Black, Douglas, Murphy

The City of Opelika, Alabama, charged Rosco Jones, a Jehovah's Witness, with violating a city ordinance prohibiting the selling of books without a license. Jones, however, did not require people to buy his books. Those who had money paid, and those who did not have money received the literature for free. Under the ordinance, the city had the power to revoke licenses without giving advance notice. Jones, who refused on principle to obtain a license, argued that he should be allowed to distribute his religious message without government regulation and that the city ordinance violated his First Amendment freedoms of press and religion.

By a bare majority, the Court upheld the ordinance, which Justice Reed ruled constitutional because it regulated only commercial literature, not religious literature. Although Jones's rights to religious freedom were inhibited, the Court reasoned that the freedom of religion did not make an otherwise valid act of state authority unconstitutional. Because Jones sold some of the books, he was engaged in a commercial activity and the ordinance applied to him.

The case was a logical extension of the earlier Jehovah's Witness cases such as ***Minersville School District v. Gobitis,*** 310 U.S. 586 (1940), and ***Cox v. New Hampshire,*** 312 U.S. 569 (1941), in which the Court had refused to acknowledge the free exercise rights of the Witnesses. But this time four members of the Court dissented, and, in an unprecedented step, three of them—Black, Douglas and Murphy (without saying which of them wrote it)—appended a statement acknowledging *Opelika* as a logical extension of *Gobitis* and saying they had been wrong in supporting the majority in the earlier case. The majority opinion "put the right freely to exercise religion in a subordinate position in violation of the First Amendment. With the appointment of Justice Rutledge to the Court in late 1942, the dissenters became a majority, and the Witnesses began winning their challenges to local regulations in two cases handed down the same day, ***Murdock v. Pennsylvania,*** 319 U.S. 105 (1943), and ***Martin v. City of Struthers,*** 319 U.S. 141 (1943).

See Shawn Francis Peters, *Judging Jehovah's Witnesses: Religious Persecution and the Dawn of the Rights Revolution* (Lawrence: University Press of Kansas, 2000).

Ex parte Quirin

317 U.S. 1 (1942)
Decided: July 31, 1942
Vote: 8 (Stone, Roberts, Black, Reed, Frankfurter, Douglas, Byrnes, R. Jackson)
0
Opinion of the Court: Stone
Did not participate: Murphy

In June 1942 German submarines landed eight Nazi agents on Long Island and Florida with orders to sabotage bridges, industrial plants, and military installations. The eight and their few American confederates were quickly apprehended, and President Roosevelt ordered them tried by a special military tribunal of seven generals. In the same proclamation, the president ordered the civilian courts closed to all persons charged with committing or attempting sabotage.

The military panel began its operations in secret, but the two officers appointed to defend the Germans filed a writ of habeas corpus seeking a change in the trial venue from the military tribunal to a civilian court. To bolster their argument, they cited the precedent in the Civil War case, ***Ex parte Milligan,*** 71 U.S. 2 (1866). In that case the Court had ruled that if civilian courts remained open in time of war, the government could not bypass them and try persons accused of crimes in military tribunals.

The Court agreed to hear the appeal, and in an extraordinary step the justices convened in a special summer session on July 29, 1942. The Court's decision to hear the case was also highly unusual, because the existing rules of military justice, adopted in the so-called Chamberlain reforms of 1920, did not mention appeal to civilian courts.

Although several of the justices raised questions in oral argument about possible procedural irregularities, in conference the justices agreed that the military tribunal had to be upheld and that the decision of the Court had to be unanimous. To ensure unanimity, Chief Justice Stone narrowed the questions to whether the Court had jurisdiction to hear an appeal for habeas corpus and whether the president had the authority to order the saboteurs tried by a military tribunal. Although all eight justices agreed on the result, they could not agree on a common rationale. So, less than forty-eight hours after hearing the case, the Court issued a brief *per curiam* opinion upholding the power of the military commission and announcing that a formal opinion would be filed later.

By the time the Court convened in October, Stone had crafted an elaborate opinion, relying on thirteen separate constitutional clauses relating to presidential war powers, confirming the authority of the president to establish military commissions to try such crimes. He also noted congressional adoption of the common law of war and declared that Congress need not specifically define all the acts that violated that war. Stone distinguished *Quirin* from *Milligan* on the grounds that Lambdin P. Milligan was not an enemy belligerent, as were the saboteurs in *Quirin.* Therefore, not only was the president's order valid but also the military commission had followed lawful procedure.

See Robert E. Cushman, "The Case of the Nazi Saboteurs," *American Political Science Review* 36 (1942): 1082; and Michal R. Belknap, "The Supreme Court Goes to War: The Meaning and Implications of the Nazi Saboteur Case," *Military Law Review* 89 (1980): 59.

Wickard v. Filburn

317 U.S. 111 (1942)
Decided: November 9, 1942
Vote: 9 (Stone, Roberts, Black, Reed, Frankfurter, Douglas, Murphy, Byrnes, R. Jackson)
0
Opinion of the Court: R. Jackson

No case better exemplified the antagonism of conservatives on the Supreme Court to the New Deal than ***United States v. Butler,*** 297 U.S. 1 (1936), in which the majority struck down the Agricultural Adjustment Act of 1933. The measure, aimed at eliminating the large crop surpluses that depressed farm prices, placed limits on how much individual farmers could grow and rewarded them for participation in the program through subsidies. Financing for the scheme came from a tax on the first processor. Justice Roberts, speaking for the Court, held that Congress had no power in this area because farming was essentially a local activity.

With only two *Butler* Court members, Stone and Roberts, still on the bench, the new Roosevelt Court had little difficulty sustaining New Deal legislation. (FDR had nominated seven of the *Wickard* justices—Black, Reed, Frankfurter, Douglas, Murphy, Byrnes, and Jackson—and elevated Stone to chief justice.) The result was a demonstrable expansion and reach of the federal commerce power. The question remained, however, whether the states retained any control over local commerce.

Roscoe Filburn ran a small chicken farm in Ohio. Each year he planted a few acres of wheat to feed his poultry and livestock. Under the Agricultural Marketing Agreement Act of 1937, Filburn had signed an allotment agreement allowing him to plant 11.1 acres of wheat, but he actually planted 23 acres. The yield was 239 bushels beyond his assigned quota. The Agriculture Department invoked the penalty provisions of the law, and brought suit to collect the fines.

Filburn defended himself on the grounds that the regulations exceeded the federal powers granted by the Commerce Clause because the excess wheat had not gone into interstate commerce; rather, it had been grown for and used by his chickens. This argument caused some doubt among at least five justices—Jackson, Murphy, Roberts, Byrnes, and Frankfurter—who were also dissatisfied with the presentations by the government's and Filburn's attorneys, and the case was set down for reargument.

After rehearing the case that fall, Justice Jackson proceeded to write one of the Court's strongest opinions upholding the federal commerce power. Even though Filburn's wheat had been intended for his own chickens, "such wheat overhangs the market and if induced by rising prices tends to flow into the market and check price increases." Even if it never did enter the market, "it supplies a need of the man who grew it which would otherwise be reflected by purchases in the open market. Home-grown wheat in this sense competes with wheat in commerce."

Jackson, despite his earlier doubts, had precedent on which to rely. Justice Hughes had written in the ***Shreveport Rate Cases,*** 234 U.S. 342 (1914), that Congress could regulate intrastate rates of railroads if these rates had a substantial effect on interstate rates. Later, using a similar argument, Chief Justice Taft—whom no one would accuse of being overly sympathetic to federal regulation—had upheld in *Chicago Board of Trade v. Olsen,* 262 U.S. 1 (1923), congressional control over the Chicago Board of Trade because its activities had an impact on interstate commerce. But Jackson's opinion went further. In the earlier cases Hughes and Taft had required some evidence that the intrastate activities did in fact have an interstate effect, other than that Congress said so. "If we are to be brutally frank," Jackson wrote shortly after the opinion came down, "I suspect what we would say is that in any case where Congress thinks there is an effect on interstate commerce, the Court will accept that judgment."

See Edward S. Corwin, "The Passing of Dual Federalism," *Virginia Law Review* 36 (1950): 1; Paul R. Benson Jr., *The Supreme Court and the Commerce Clause, 1937–70* (New York: Dunellen, 1970); and Ashley Sellers and Jesse E. Baskette Jr., "Agricultural Marketing Agreements and Order Programs, 1933–1943," *Georgetown Law Journal* 33 (1945): 123.

Williams v. North Carolina

317 U.S. 287 (1942)
Decided: December 21, 1942
Vote: 7 (Stone, Roberts, Black, Reed, Frankfurter, Douglas, Byrnes)
2 (Murphy, R. Jackson)
Opinion of the Court: Douglas
Concurring opinion: Frankfurter
Dissenting opinion: Murphy
Dissenting opinion: R. Jackson

Otis Williams and Lillie Hendrix met, fell in love, and wanted to marry. These circumstances were not unusual, except that at the time both happened to be married to other people. So they packed their bags, left North Carolina, and went to Las Vegas. After the requisite six weeks of residence, they secured divorces from a Nevada court. They immediately married and returned to North Carolina, where local authorities arrested, tried, and convicted them for "bigamous cohabitation." The state considered the Nevada divorce decrees invalid because their spouses had not appeared in person in the Nevada courts to contest the decrees, and North Carolina did not recognize divorces based on "substituted service," that is, cases in which notice of the action had been sent to agents of the parties. North Carolina also charged that Williams and Hendrix had not gone to Nevada to establish a legitimate residence, but simply to secure a divorce, and therefore had committed a fraud on that state's courts.

On appeal, the supreme court of North Carolina upheld the conviction based on *Haddock v. Haddock,* 201 U.S. 562 (1906). In that case, the U.S. Supreme Court, over a dissent by Justice Holmes, had ruled that the Constitution's Full Faith and Credit Clause did not require one state to recognize a divorce granted by another state when one of the parties to that divorce was a "nonresident who did not appear and was only . . . served with notice of the pendency of the action." A majority of the Court concluded that *Haddock* had to be overruled. In his opinion for the Court, Justice Douglas held that decrees of the state of one spouse's domicile had to be recognized throughout the nation under the Full Faith and Credit Clause, even if such decrees conflicted with the policy of another state.

But if a majority saw this question simply as a legal issue, Justice Murphy did not. He believed that law embodied morality and that a ruling that went against moral values could not be considered "good law." Although he personally abhorred the Nevada arrangements, he recognized that his dissent would have to be based on legal rather than moral grounds, and he fastened on the same issue that had caused Douglas some doubts—the jurisdictional question arising out of the legitimacy of the Nevada residence. Six weeks in a hotel, he believed, did not constitute a *bona fide* domicile sufficient to meet the requirements of the Full Faith and Credit Clause.

Neither did Justice Jackson. In a witty and brilliant dissent he charged that the Court had repealed the divorce laws of forty-seven states and had substituted "the law of Nevada as to all marriages one of the parties to which can afford a short trip there." Along with Murphy, Jackson stressed the domicile issue, noting that "the only suggestion of a domicile within Nevada was a stay of about six weeks at the Alamo Auto Court, an address hardly suggestive of permanence."

Many people saw the case as more of a moral question than a legal dispute. At that time most states made divorce difficult, often requiring stringent evidentiary rules that one partner had committed adultery. The notion that divorce should be granted because the marriage had not worked out and that one or both partners no longer wanted to stay married did not receive widespread acceptance until the 1960s.

See Glenda Riley, *Divorce: An American Tradition* (New York: Oxford University Press, 1991).

SEC v. Chenery Corp.

318 U.S. 80 (1943)
Decided: February 1, 1943
Vote: 5 (Stone, Roberts, Frankfurter, R. Jackson, W. Rutledge)
3 (Black, Reed, Murphy)
Opinion of the Court: Frankfurter
Dissenting opinion: Black (Reed, Murphy)
Did not participate: Douglas

Chenery Corporation was organized and registered as a holding company under the Public Utility Holding Company Act of 1935. While the plans to reorganize the company were pending, some of the officers, directors, and shareholders bought some of its preferred stock. (Holders of preferred stock receive dividends or profits, but do not have voting rights.) The Securities and Exchange Commission (SEC) refused to distinguish between purchases of preferred and regular stock, and charged that the purchasers had violated federal law by engaging in insider trading. The corporation argued that the SEC was wrong not to make the distinction between common and preferred stock.

The Supreme Court held that courts should not reverse administrative agency decisions unless an abuse of discretion was evident. Courts should defer to agency decisions, such as those by the SEC, unless it could be shown that the agency based its decision on incorrect grounds or gave a wrong reason for why it decided a certain way. The Court ruled that it would defer to the SEC's finding.

McNabb v. United States

318 U.S. 332 (1943)
Decided: March 1, 1943
Vote: 7 (Stone, Roberts, Black, Frankfurter, Douglas, Murphy, R. Jackson)
1 (Reed)
Opinion of the Court: Frankfurter
Dissenting opinion: Reed
Did not participate: W. Rutledge

Government agents, posing as buyers, persuaded several members of the McNabb family to agree to sell to them whiskey on which the McNabbs had not paid federal taxes. Later that night, when the government revealed its sting operation, the McNabb family fled the scene of the crime into a cemetery. One officer was shot and killed. Officers went to the McNabb house and arrested several of them. Instead of being brought before a judge for a preliminary hearing, they were kept in a detention room for fourteen hours without a lawyer. They were questioned, also without a lawyer, nonstop for several days. Eventually, they confessed to the killing and were indicted and convicted on the basis of the confessions. The McNabbs argued that the confessions should be suppressed because they were coerced in violation of the Fifth Amendment.

The Court suppressed the confessions and ruled that a prompt preliminary hearing is required. The officers had blatantly violated proper criminal procedure, and, therefore, the illegally obtained confessions were inadmissible at trial. Justice Frankfurter's opinion for the Court condemned such violations as undermining the integrity of the criminal justice system.

Murdock v. Pennsylvania

319 U.S. 105 (1943)
Decided: May 3, 1943
Vote: 5 (Stone, Black, Douglas, Murphy, W. Rutledge)
4 (Roberts, Reed, Frankfurter, R. Jackson)
Opinion of the Court: Douglas
Dissenting opinion: Reed (Roberts, Frankfurter, R. Jackson)
Dissenting opinion: Frankfurter (R. Jackson)
Dissenting opinion: R. Jackson. This dissent is found in *Douglas v. City of Jeannette,* 319 U.S. 157 (1943).

Robert Murdock, a Jehovah's Witness, distributed religious books and pamphlets as part of the Jehovah's Witness's door-to-door solicitations in Jeanette, Pennsylvania. Murdock asked for contributions and donations from persons accepting the literature. The town, however, had an ordinance requiring solicitors to purchase a license, and it argued that accepting contributions was the same as selling. The town wanted to tax Murdock for his activities, and the question brought to the Supreme Court was whether the distribution of religious literature could be subject to taxation.

The Court struck down the town ordinance. In a major victory for the Witnesses, Justice Douglas ruled that the ordinance was an unconstitutional tax on the right of the Witnesses to exercise their religious freedoms. The Court admitted that drawing the line between what is a commercial and what is a religious activity may at times be difficult. But in contrast to the decision in ***Jones v. Opelika,*** 316 U.S. 584 (1942), the Court in this case ruled that an otherwise valid law is invalid if it infringes on the freedom of religion. As Douglas stated, it is one thing to tax a preacher's income; it is another to tax his sermons. To allow for the taxing of religious speech is to chill religious speech and to silence many forms of religious speech whose adherents cannot afford to pay the taxes.

See Shawn Francis Peters, *Judging Jehovah's Witnesses: Religious Persecution and the Dawn of the Rights Revolution* (Lawrence: University Press of Kansas, 2000).

Martin v. City of Struthers

319 U.S. 141 (1943)
Decided: May 3, 1943
Vote: 5 (Stone, Black, Douglas, Murphy, W. Rutledge)
4 (Roberts, Reed, Frankfurter, R. Jackson)
Opinion of the Court: Black
Concurring opinion: Murphy (Douglas, W. Rutledge)
Dissenting opinion: Frankfurter
Dissenting opinion: Reed (Roberts, R. Jackson)
Dissenting opinion: R. Jackson. This dissent is found in *Douglas v. City of Jeannette,* 319 U.S. 157 (1943).

Martin, a Jehovah's Witness, went door-to-door in a conventional and orderly fashion distributing leaflets advertising a religious meeting. The City of Struthers, Ohio, however, had an ordinance that made it illegal to distribute information door-to-door. Martin argued that the ordinance violated her right to the free exercise of religion under the First Amendment.

The Court struck down the ordinance. The Court ruled that the freedom to distribute information, particularly religious material, must be preserved. The fundamental right to freely express one's religious views is so important that a law can prevent door-to-door distributing of religious information only if the homeowner tells the distributor to leave and the person does not leave.

See Shawn Francis Peters, *Judging Jehovah's Witnesses: Religious Persecution and the Dawn of the Rights Revolution* (Lawrence: University Press of Kansas, 2000).

Douglas v. City of Jeanette

319 U.S. 157 (1943)
Decided: May 3, 1943
Vote: 9 (Stone, Roberts, Black, Reed, Frankfurter, Douglas, Murphy, R. Jackson, W. Rutledge)
0
Opinion of the Court: Stone
Concurring opinion: R. Jackson (Frankfurter)

The city of Jeanette, Pennsylvania, had an ordinance that prohibited soliciting without getting a license from the city and paying a license tax. Robert L. Douglas, a Jehovah's Witness, distributed religious material under the Witness's "Watch Tower" campaign without a license and was threatened with criminal prosecution. Douglas sued in federal district court on behalf of himself and all other Witnesses to enjoin enforcement of the statute, claiming that the ordinance impinged on his First Amendment religious rights and that his prosecution should be stopped. The Supreme Court was asked to decide whether a federal court had jurisdiction to decide a case involving citizens of Pennsylvania against their state, and whether the court, citing the free exercise of religion under the First Amendment, can stop a prosecution from occurring.

The Court held that the federal district court had such jurisdiction because a federal question—the meaning of rights under the Constitution—was involved. But it refused to stop the prosecution. The Court ruled that lower courts should not end ongoing criminal prosecutions, even if they are based on allegedly unconstitutional laws. Procedurally, the criminal case should be decided and then appealed. Only if the government acts in bad faith in prosecuting the case or if the law is unconstitutional in every part—in other words, no provision could withstand constitutional scrutiny—should a court interfere with a criminal prosecution.

NBC, Inc. v. United States

319 U.S. 190 (1943)
Decided: May 10, 1943
Vote: 5 (Stone, Reed, Frankfurter, Douglas, R. Jackson)
2 (Roberts, Murphy)
Opinion of the Court: Frankfurter
Dissenting opinion: Murphy (Roberts)
Did not participate: Black, W. Rutledge

The Federal Communications Act of 1934 authorized the Federal Communications Commission (FCC) to promulgate regulations that encouraged the largest and most effective use of radio in the public interest, convenience, or necessity. The FCC adopted "chain broadcasting regulations," which curbed the power of the existing radio networks and encouraged the development of new networks. The regulations prevented radio stations from having a monopoly on certain kinds of broadcasting. The regulations also allowed for simultaneous broadcasting of identical programs. Two networks, NBC and CBS, attacked the broadcast regulation as violating their First Amendment rights and raised questions about the constitutionality of the FCC regulations in particular and on radio broadcasting in general.

The Court upheld the regulations. It looked at the law to see if the authority to regulate radio broadcasting, an interstate commerce issue, was too broad and expansive. The Court found that the authority granted to the FCC was neither vague nor overbroad. Once the authority was judged valid, the issue became whether the FCC had committed an abuse of discretion. The Court found that there was no abuse of discretion because the purpose of the regulations was to foster new radio stations and commerce and prevent the monopolization of the industry by NBC and CBS. The Court held that the public interest was furthered and the regulations were valid. As for the broader constitutional issues, the Court held then, and would continue to hold, to the notion that broadcast media did not enjoy the same First Amendment rights as did print journalism, and that broadcast media could be regulated by the federal government.

See Lucas A. Powe Jr., *American Broadcasting and the First Amendment* (Berkeley: University of California Press, 1987).

West Virginia State Board of Education v. Barnette

319 U.S. 624 (1943)
Decided: June 14, 1943
Vote: 6 (Stone, Black, Douglas, Murphy, R. Jackson, W. Rutledge)
3 (Roberts, Reed, Frankfurter)
Opinion of the Court: R. Jackson
Concurring opinion: Black (Douglas)
Concurring opinion: Murphy
Dissenting opinion: Frankfurter
Dissenting without opinion: Roberts, Reed

Following the decision in ***Minersville School District v. Gobitis,*** 310 U.S. 586 (1940), in which the Court rejected a claim by Jehovah's Witnesses that compulsory flag salutes in school violated their religious freedom, the Witnesses were subjected to hundreds of attacks, especially in rural areas and small towns. Over the next few years, the Court had a chance to become better acquainted with the notion of what the Free Exercise Clause meant, as Jehovah's Witnesses brought one suit after another challenging laws they saw as restricting their religious freedom. In one such case, ***Jones v. Opelika,*** 316 U.S. 584 (1942), three members of the *Gobitis* majority—Black, Douglas, and Murphy—indicated that the earlier case had been "wrongly decided." Given this, it was inevitable that the Court would take another flag salute case, this time from West Virginia. It dealt with the same question: Could the state force someone to salute the flag if doing so violated the person's religious beliefs? Influential groups such as the American Bar Association Committee on the Bill of Rights and the American Civil Liberties Union urged the Court to overturn *Gobitis.*

Chief Justice Stone's dissent in *Gobitis* had suggested that people with religious objections were entitled to a special exemption from what was otherwise a valid requirement, a view echoed by the three penitents in *Opelika.* But Justice Jackson took a much broader view by declaring that no one could be compelled to salute the flag. Freedom of speech, he declared, includes the freedom not to speak, and no state interest, even that of inculcating patriotism, justified such an infringement on individual autonomy. In one of his most eloquent defenses of liberty, Jackson wrote, "If there is any fixed star in our constitutional constellation, it is that no official, high or petty, can prescribe what shall be orthodox in politics, nationalism, religion or other matters of opinion or force citizens to confess by word or act their faith therein."

"The very purpose of a Bill of Rights," Jackson declared, "was to withdraw certain subjects from the vicissitudes of political controversy, to place them beyond the reach of majorities and officials and to establish them as legal principles to be applied by the courts. One's right to life, liberty, and property, to free speech, a free press, freedom of worship and assembly, and other fundamental rights may not be submitted to vote; they depend on the outcome of no elections."

In addition, Jackson's opinion endorsed Stone's suggestion in ***United States v. Carolene Products Co.,*** 304 U.S. 144 (1938), that measures affecting First Amendment freedoms were subject to a stricter scrutiny than the rational basis test applied to economic regulation. "Freedoms of speech and press, of assembly, and of worship may not be infringed on such slender grounds," he wrote. "They are susceptible of restriction only to prevent grave and immediate danger to interests which the State may lawfully protect."

Justice Frankfurter's impassioned dissent left no doubt that he rejected this distinction completely, giving credence to Justice Douglas's comment that Frankfurter saw no distinction between an economic regulation and one limiting speech. Frankfurter completely rejected the notion that the courts had a special role to play in protecting minorities and civil liberties. The Framers, he claimed, knew that minorities may disrupt society, and he repeated the formula he had used in the earlier flag salute case, that "this Court's only and very narrow function is to determine whether within the broad grant of authority vested in legislatures they have exercised a judgment for which reasonable justification can be offered." Because of Jackson's eloquent defense of religious freedom, Frankfurter could not pass over it as lightly as he had in *Gobitis,* but he took a minimalist approach. The First Amendment did no more than offer freedom from conformity to religious dogma, not exemption from laws of general application.

The judgment of history has validated Jackson's opinion, and ever since the Court has been solicitous of free exercise claims. Frankfurter's argument that the First Amendment does not provide for exemption from general laws was partially resurrected, but to much criticism, in ***Employment Division v. Smith,*** 494 U.S. 872 (1990). Both experience and logic also support Jackson and Stone rather than Frankfurter, and most commentators today accept as a given that the Court, more than any other instrument of government, is charged with the protection of individual rights guaranteed by the Constitution.

See Leo Pfeffer, *Church, State and Freedom,* rev. ed. (Boston: Beacon Press, 1967); and David Manwaring, *Render unto Caesar: The Flag Salute Cases* (Chicago: University of Chicago Press, 1962).

Hirabayashi v. United States

320 U.S. 81 (1943)
Decided: June 21, 1943
Vote: 9 (Stone, Roberts, Black, Reed, Frankfurter, Douglas, Murphy, R. Jackson, W. Rutledge)
0
Opinion of the Court: Stone
Concurring opinion: Douglas
Concurring opinion: Murphy
Concurring opinion: W. Rutledge

The first of the Japanese internment cases, which include ***Korematsu v. United States,*** 323 U.S. 214 (1944), and ***Ex parte Endo,*** 323 U.S. 283 (1944), grew out of Executive Order 9066, issued on February 19, 1942. The order authorized the secretary of war to designate certain parts of the country as military zones, from which any and all persons could be excluded and in which travel restrictions, including daily curfews, could be imposed. In successive steps the army designated the entire Pacific Coast a military area and then imposed nightly curfews for German and Italian nationals and for all persons of Japanese ancestry. It then prohibited Nisei (American-born citizens of Japanese ancestry) and Issei (Japanese nationals) from leaving the coastal areas, and finally it excluded them from the same area. The only way Issei and Nisei could comply with these contradictory orders was to report to designated control locations, from which they would be transported to relocation centers away from the West Coast. The centers were operated by the War Relocation Authority. Executive Order 9066 and the order establishing the Relocation Authority were later confirmed by congressional action. The relocation program proceeded on racist assumptions and violated the Equal Protection and Due Process Clauses of the Constitution.

Gordon Kiyoshi Hirabayashi, a native-born American citizen and a student at the University of Washington, was arrested for failing to report to a control center and for violating the curfew. He was convicted and sentenced to two three-month terms. The lower appeals courts upheld the conviction.

Chief Justice Stone, backed by Justices Black and Frankfurter, was determined to uphold the army's actions with a unanimous decision. Justices Douglas and Murphy, however, condemned the overt racism of the relocation program and had trouble accepting it, even under the mantle of supporting the war effort. Other members of the Court, including Justices Jackson and Rutledge, had strong reservations about the legality of the program.

Stone's views prevailed, but only because he limited the question to whether the president had the power to designate a war zone and impose a curfew there. He began with a broad reading of constitutional war powers. Such authority went far beyond military matters on the battlefield and could be directed at any and all evils that attended the rise and progress of war. At the urging of Black and Frankfurter, Stone also added a section on judicial deference, in which he declared that the power of conducting war resided in the executive and legislative branches and that the judiciary should defer to their judgments. The final opinion evaded all of the constitutional issues raised by the doubters. By focusing solely on the question of the curfew, Stone managed to get all of his colleagues to agree in the result.

But not all the justices agreed with Stone's broad enunciation of the war powers or his cavalier attitude toward labeling all Japanese Americans as potentially disloyal. The Douglas, Murphy, and Rutledge concurring opinions came close to being dissents. All three indicated that they had agreed to what they considered an unconstitutional program because of the allegedly critical military situation. The tone of their opinions indicated that it would be far more difficult to get unanimity if and when another challenge reached the Court.

History has not been kind to the opinion. When the curfew was imposed, military analysts viewed the Pacific as a Japanese lake, and, until the Battle of Midway in June 1942, it appeared that nothing could stop the Imperial Fleet or prevent an invasion of the West Coast. By the time the case reached the Court, however, the military situation had changed dramatically, and government officials knew that a threat to the West Coast no longer existed. There is evidence that Charles Fahy, the U.S. solicitor general, deliberately misled the Court because he knew when *Hirabayashi* was argued that the military necessity had evaporated. In addition, the blatant racism of the opinion—condemning an entire group as unpatriotic because of their racial background—offended many people at the time and has been generally condemned ever since.

In 1980 Congress established the Commission on Wartime Relocation, which detailed and condemned the grave injustices done during the war. In 1988 Congress passed a redress bill providing $20,000 to each internment camp survivor, as well as a national apology. At the same time lawyers for Gordon Hirabayashi, employing the rarely used writ of *coram nobis*, successfully secured the overturn of his conviction.

See Page Smith, *Democracy on Trial: The Japanese-American Evacuation and Relocation in World War II* (New York: Simon and Schuster, 1995); Commission on Wartime Relocation, *Personal Justice Denied: Report of the Commission on Wartime Relocation and Internment of Civilians* (Washington, D.C.: Government Printing Office, 1983); and Peter Irons, *Justice at War* (New York: Oxford University Press, 1983).

Schneiderman v. United States

320 U.S. 118 (1943)
Decided: June 21, 1943
Vote: 5 (Black, Reed, Douglas, Murphy, Rutledge)
3 (Stone, Roberts, Frankfurter)
Opinion of the Court: Murphy
Concurring opinion: Douglas
Concurring opinion: W. Rutledge
Dissenting opinion: Stone (Roberts, Frankfurter)
Did not participate: R. Jackson

William Schneiderman, had been naturalized in 1927 and was by then a member of several communist groups. In 1932 he ran for governor of Minnesota as the Communist Party candidate. In 1939 the government moved to strip Schneiderman of his citizenship on the grounds that his communist activities in the five years prior to his application for citizenship showed that he was not truly "attached" to the principles of the Constitution. Schneiderman argued that he had been a good citizen; he had never been arrested and had used his rights to advocate change and greater social justice. Moreover, the activities in which he had engaged had at the time been legal.

The Court held that the government had not met the burden of proof to show that Schneiderman had not been a good citizen or that he was not attached to American principles. Justice

Murphy stated that nowhere in the world is the right of citizenship worth more than it is in the United States. While a naturalized person's citizenship can be taken away with appropriate proof, there must be an overwhelming reason to do so. Schneiderman had done nothing illegal.

The case aroused great emotion within the Court because the United States was then at war, but its holding is rather simple. Denaturalizing a citizen requires sufficient proof that he had done something illegal either before or after his application for citizenship, and not that he had espoused unpopular views. A naturalized citizen holds all the rights that natural-born citizens enjoy.

See N. S. Timahseff, "The Schneiderman Case: Its Political Aspects," *Fordham Law Review* 12 (1943): 209.

Prince v. Massachusetts

321 U.S. 158 (1944)
Decided: January 31, 1944
Vote: 5 (Stone, Black, Reed, Douglas, W. Rutledge)
4 (Roberts, Frankfurter, Murphy, R. Jackson)
Opinion of the Court: W. Rutledge
Dissenting opinion: R. Jackson (Roberts, Frankfurter)
Dissenting opinion: Murphy

Sarah Prince, a Jehovah's Witness, and the guardian of her nine-year-old niece, Betty Simmons, was convicted for violating the state's child labor laws. She had brought Simmons with her onto the streets to preach, and the little girl distributed religious literature for voluntary contributions. The child labor laws prohibited girls under eighteen from selling literature or other goods on public streets.

Prince was an ordained minister and often took children out to distribute religious literature. She claimed that the Massachusetts child labor laws violated her First Amendment and Fourteenth Amendment rights to freely exercise her religion. She also argued that she was denied equal protection because the children themselves were ministers of their religion. The question in this case was whether a child can be prevented from distributing religious literature.

The Court upheld the Massachusetts law and ruled that states have a strong interest in protecting the welfare of their children. Therefore, even when religious freedoms conflict with such laws, the states' interest outweighs the rights of the children. The Court concluded that children do not have the same First Amendment freedom of religion rights as adults.

See Shawn Francis Peters, *Judging Jehovah's Witnesses: Religious Persecution and the Dawn of the Rights Revolution* (Lawrence: University Press of Kansas, 2000).

Yakus v. United States

321 U.S. 414 (1944)
Decided: March 27, 1944
Vote: 6 (Stone, Black, Reed, Frankfurter, Douglas, R. Jackson)
3 (Roberts, Murphy, W. Rutledge)
Opinion of the Court: Stone
Dissenting opinion: Roberts
Dissenting opinion: W. Rutledge (Murphy)

Under the Emergency Price Control Act of 1942, Congress gave the price administrator, an agent of the executive branch, authority to establish maximum prices that would be fair and equitable. The price administrator set certain maximum prices for meat and other foodstuffs. Albert Yakus, a meat cutter, argued that the act went beyond the government's power to regulate commerce and that it was an improper delegation of power by Congress to the executive branch. Therefore, the questions in this case were how broad is the government's power to regulate commerce and whether Congress had violated the nondelegation doctrine.

The Court upheld the act and its application to the maximum prices it set for meat. Under the nondelegation doctrine, for Congress to delegate authority to the executive branch, the delegating of power must be sufficiently precise. Congress cannot delegate power that is too broad. The Court found that the delegation of power in the Act was sufficiently precise and upheld both the law and the actions of the price administrator.

See Symposium, "Some Aspects of O.P.A. in the Courts," *George Washington Law Review* 12 (1944): 414.

Smith v. Allwright

321 U.S. 649 (1944)
Decided: April 3, 1944
Vote: 8 (Stone, Black, Reed, Frankfurter, Douglas, Murphy, R. Jackson, W. Rutledge)
1 (Roberts)
Opinion of the Court: Reed
Concurring without opinion: Frankfurter
Dissenting opinion: Roberts

The Democratic Party of Texas, claiming to be a voluntary organization, excluded blacks from voting in Democratic Party primaries. Specifically, in this case, S. S. Allwright, a county official, denied Lonnie Smith, a black man, the right to vote in the 1940 Texas Democratic primary.

The Court had wrestled with the question of what part a primary played in the electoral process and whether denial of the right to vote in a primary on the basis of race violated the Fifteenth Amendment. In an earlier case, ***Grovey v. Townsend,*** 295 U.S. 45 (1935), the Court upheld the notion of an all-white primary, ruling that a primary was not part of the regular election process. That reasoning, however, disregarded the fact that in many southern states the winner of the Democratic primary faced no meaningful opposition in the general election.

The Court had taken a step away from that position in ***United States v. Classic,*** 313 U.S. 299 (1941), when it ruled that Congress could regulate a primary where it constituted part of the overall machinery for choosing elected federal officials. That case, however, had been decided on narrow grounds and resulted from claims by white voters in Louisiana that their votes had not been counted. It thus appeared more as a voter fraud case than as a civil rights case.

The National Association for the Advancement of Colored People, however, saw *Classic* as a wedge it could use to attack the all-white primary, and it achieved some success in *Allwright.* In a cautious opinion by Justice Reed, the Court ruled that although the Democratic Party was a voluntary organization, Texas statutes governed the selection of county party leaders, the party conducted the primary under state authority, and state courts had exclusive jurisdiction over contested elections, and these circumstances combined to make the primary an official state activity. Denial of the right to vote in a primary on the basis of race, therefore, violated the Fifteenth Amendment. The case, despite Reed's narrow opinion, proved to be the instrument that toppled the white primary system in the South.

See Robert E. Cushman, "The Texas 'White Primary' Case—*Smith v. Allwright,*" *Cornell Law Quarterly* 30 (1944): 66.

L. P. Steuart & Bro. Inc. v. Bowles

322 U.S. 398 (1944)
Decided: May 22, 1944
Vote: 8 (Stone, Black, Reed, Frankfurter, Douglas, Murphy, R. Jackson, W. Rutledge)
1 (Roberts)
Opinion of the Court: Douglas
Dissenting without opinion: Roberts

During the Second World War Congress established rationing of food, fuel, and other items and delegated to the president power to establish such regulations and enforce them. Under the War Powers Act, the president could withhold additional supplies from any retailer found guilty of violating rationing regulations.

Steuart Company claimed that the president did not have the power to do this on his own and that Congress had unlawfully delegated such powers to him. The Court dismissed both claims in a summary manner and reaffirmed the broad emergency powers of both president and Congress in wartime.

See D. D. Holdoegel, "The War Powers and the Emergency Price Control Act of 1942," *Iowa Law Review* 29 (1944): 454.

United States v. South-Eastern Underwriters Association

322 U.S. 533 (1944)
Decided: June 5, 1944
Vote: 4 (Black, Douglas, Murphy, W. Rutledge)
3 (Stone, Frankfurter, R. Jackson)
Opinion of the Court: Black
Dissenting opinion: Stone (Frankfurter)
Dissenting opinion: Frankfurter
Opinion dissenting in part: R. Jackson
Did not participate: Roberts, Reed

Ever since the decision in ***Paul v. Virginia,*** 75 U.S. 168 (1869), insurance had been considered a matter for state regulation. The Court held that even though the parties might be domiciled in different states, the actual insurance contract constituted a local transaction, and Congress had acquiesced in the decision. As a result, over the next seventy years the insurance industry was governed by a patchwork of state regulations.

In 1942 the Justice Department secured antitrust indictments against the 196 members of the South-Eastern Underwriters Association, charging them with conspiracies to fix rates for fire insurance and to monopolize commerce in violation of the 1890 Sherman Antitrust Act. The federal district court, which heard the initial case, felt bound by precedent and dismissed the indictments.

Three members of the Court—Chief Justice Stone and Justices Frankfurter and Jackson—believed that precedent should govern the case. They also agreed that the lower court decision should be affirmed because Congress had not explicitly brought insurance within the compass of the 1890 Sherman Act. To overrule *Paul* would mean the dismantling of an elaborate array of state regulation, a result that adherents of judicial restraint feared.

The four justices in the majority—Black, Douglas, Murphy, and Rutledge—believed not only that *Paul* had been wrongly decided but also that the complex arrangements that had resulted from it should not be a bar to correcting it. A majority—perhaps all seven of the justices who took part in the decision—agreed that insurance constituted part of interstate commerce. The issue dividing the justices was not whether insurance could be categorized as interstate commerce but who should correct the problems that had resulted from the *Paul* decision—the Court or the elected members of the Congress.

Stone, Frankfurter, and Jackson chose Congress. Black thought the Court should correct its own error and let Congress and the states deal with the problems. In his opinion for the Court, Black reexamined the line of cases extending from *Paul.* He reported that all of them involved the validity of state laws and the extent to which the Commerce Clause deprived states of the power to regulate insurance. In these cases, the Court had consistently upheld state power. Now, for the first time, Black looked at the record in determining *federal* authority. Historically, the Court had upheld the power of Congress to regulate a variety of transactions across states. Whether one held the actual contract to be local in nature or not, there could be no question that insurance involved a chain of transactions that crossed state lines.

Stone's dissent warned against overturning the vast scheme of state regulation that had been promulgated in the seventy-five years since *Paul,* but the turmoil predicted by the dissenters did not materialize. Congress declined the invitation to regulate insurance and allowed the states to continue regulating and taxing the insurance business despite its interstate character. It would be fair to say that the majority opinion caused exactly the results desired by the minority, namely that Congress should make its intentions clear.

See Thomas Reed Powell, "Insurance as Commerce in Constitution and Statute," *Harvard Law Review* 57 (1944): 937; and C. Herman Pritchett, *The Roosevelt Court: A Study in Judicial Politics and Values, 1937–1947* (New York: Macmillan, 1948).

Hartzel v. United States

322 U.S. 680 (1944)
Decided: June 12, 1944
Vote: 5 (Stone, Roberts, Black, Murphy, W. Rutledge)
4 (Reed, Frankfurter, Douglas, R. Jackson)
Opinion of the Court: Murphy
Concurring opinion: Roberts
Dissenting opinion: Reed (Frankfurter, Douglas, R. Jackson)

During World War II, Hartzel and two others were charged with publishing and disseminating three pamphlets to men available and eligible for recruitment and enlistment in the military, as well as to men already in the military. The literature opposed the war and allegedly was done to cause insubordination, disloyalty, and refusal to join the military and to dodge the draft, and Hartzel was convicted of violating the Espionage Act of 1917. Hartzel argued that he did not have the intent to commit espionage. The question before the Court was how the clear and present danger test should be applied.

The Court ruled that an espionage conviction requires both a finding of specific intent to cause harm and evidence of a clear and present danger that the harm would occur. The specific intent finding is a subjective test. The clear and present danger finding is an objective test. In this case, the Court found that although Hartzel's message was antiwar, there was not enough evidence to show that he had the intent to subvert the war effort. The First Amendment right to free speech can be overcome only if such speech carries the intent to cause lawless activity and that the illegal activity would be a clear and present danger to the United States.

Korematsu v. United States

323 U.S. 214 (1944)
Decided: December 18, 1944
Vote: 6 (Stone, Black, Reed, Frankfurter, Douglas, W. Rutledge)
3 (Roberts, Murphy, R. Jackson)
Opinion of the Court: Black
Concurring opinion: Frankfurter
Dissenting opinion: Roberts
Dissenting opinion: Murphy
Dissenting opinion: R. Jackson

In the second of the Japanese internment cases—the first was ***Hirabayashi v. United States,*** 320 U.S. 81 (1943)—the Court was unable to evade the larger constitutional issues, as it had done earlier. Toyosaburo "Fred" Korematsu was charged with failing to report to an assembly center for relocation. He claimed that the exclusion order violated the Constitution by depriving citizens of due process guarantees. Moreover, the mass expulsion of an entire group based solely on a racial classification constituted a cruel and unusual punishment forbidden by the Eighth Amendment.

Chief Justice Stone wanted to limit the discussion to a narrow technical question. Korematsu had been convicted of violating the exclusion order designed to keep Japanese out of certain areas designated as military. The only question the Court had to answer, according to Stone, was the constitutionality of that exclusion order.

Justice Black, in his opinion for the majority, tried, as Stone had done in *Hirabayashi,* to base the rationale on deference to military and congressional judgment. But the situation had changed dramatically since then: the tide in the Pacific war had turned, and Japan was headed for defeat. Moreover, not a single charge of espionage or treason had been brought against any Japanese American. It was clear to many that the internment program had been ill-conceived and based on faulty premises.

Justice Roberts, who had joined the narrow ruling in *Hirabayashi,* refused to go along this time. The combination of exclusion and prohibition orders gave Japanese Americans a cruel choice—defy the order and be imprisoned or report to an assembly point and be relocated to a concentration camp. Roberts, who knew from his work heading the first Pearl Harbor commission that no evidence existed of Japanese sabotage on the West Coast, along with Justices Murphy, who had always been unhappy about the relocation policy, and Jackson, dissented on grounds that the military had overstepped its constitutional bounds of authority. Jackson, normally a supporter of strong government, declared, "I stop at *Hirabayashi.*"

Whatever his personal feelings about the relocation, Jackson took the most lawyerly approach; he was concerned about what the decision would mean if the Court approved a policy based entirely on racial classification. No matter what the military necessity may be, Jackson warned, once the Court approved that action it became a precedent ready to be used—and abused—in the future:

The principle then lies about like a loaded weapon ready for the hand of any authority that can bring forward a plausible claim of an urgent need. . . . All who observe the work of the courts are familiar with what Judge Cardozo described as "the tendency of a principle to expand itself to the limit of its logic." A military commander may overstep the bound of constitutionality, and it is an incident. But if we review and approve, that passing incident has become the doctrine of the Constitution.

Justice Douglas grudgingly joined the majority when Black agreed to add a paragraph noting that the minority viewed the issues of evacuation and detention as inseparable, and therefore raising additional constitutional issues.

The Court's decision was condemned by most legal scholars almost from the time it appeared. Law review articles immediately attacked it as a "disaster" and a travesty of justice. The condemnation has not weakened with the passage of time. If anything, it has intensified with the discovery of evidence proving that the government lied to the Court. U.S. Solicitor General Charles Fahy knew when *Hirabayashi* was argued that the military necessity for relocation had evaporated, and he deliberately misled the Court. In addition, the blatant racism of the opinion offended many people at the time and has been generally condemned ever since.

In 1980 Congress established the Commission on Wartime Relocation, which detailed and condemned the injustices done during the war. In 1988 Congress passed a redress bill providing $20,000 to each internment camp survivor, as well as a national apology. In 1998 President Clinton awarded Fred Korematsu the Presidential Medal of Freedom, the nation's highest civilian award, for his role in resisting racism.

See Page Smith, *Democracy on Trial: The Japanese-American Evacuation and Relocation in World War II* (New York: Simon and Schuster, 1995); Commission on Wartime Relocation, *Personal Justice Denied: Report of the Commission on Wartime Relocation and Internment of Civilians* (Washington, D.C.: Government Printing Office, 1983); and Peter Irons, *Justice at War* (New York: Oxford University Press, 1983).

Ex parte Endo

323 U.S. 283 (1944)
Decided: December 18, 1944
Vote: 9 (Stone, Roberts, Black, Reed, Frankfurter, Douglas, Murphy, R. Jackson, W. Rutledge)
0
Opinion of the Court: Douglas
Concurring opinion: Murphy
Opinion concurring in judgment: Roberts

Mitsuye Endo was American citizen of Japanese ancestry. Earlier in the war she and tens of thousands of other Japanese Americans as well as alien Japanese had been interned in relocation camps, because of fear that in the event of a Japanese invasion they would aid the enemy. Endo had done nothing to betray her country. She argued that the government had no authority to detain a loyal citizen simply because of the person's ethnicity, race, or national origin.

This case was the third involving the detention and internment of Japanese Americans. In the earlier two, ***Hirabayashi v. United States,*** 320 U.S. 81 (1943), and ***Korematsu v. United States,*** 323 U.S. 214 (1944), the Court had upheld the internment plan, but by this time it was clear that the United States would prevail in its war against Japan and that there would be no Japanese invasion.

The Court this time ruled unanimously that the government had no right to detain U.S. citizens indefinitely. The Court ruled that the government had the power to protect the war effort against espionage and sabotage, but this did not allow it to send loyal citizens into internment camps. Justice Douglas's opinion carefully avoided mentioning the reasoning that had led the Court to uphold the plan earlier.

This decision ended the entire Japanese internment program. Within forty-eight hours of the ruling, the government announced that, except for a few suspicious individuals, the Japanese were free to go home.

See Peter Irons, *Justice at War* (New York: Oxford University Press, 1983).

Thomas v. Collins

323 U.S. 516 (1945)
Decided: January 8, 1945
Vote: 5 (Black, Douglas, Murphy, R. Jackson, W. Rutledge)
4 (Stone, Roberts, Reed, Frankfurter)
Opinion of the Court: W. Rutledge
Concurring opinion: Douglas (Black, Murphy)
Concurring opinion: R. Jackson
Dissenting opinion: Roberts (Stone, Reed, Frankfurter)

A Texas law required labor organizers to register with and procure an organizer's card from a designated state official before soliciting memberships in labor unions. While a state court order restraining R. J. Thomas, a Congress of Industrial Organizations (CIO) vice president, from violating the statute was in effect, he made a speech before an assemblage of oil workers. At the end of his speech, he broadly urged his audience to join a union and asked an individual by name to become a member. Thomas was sentenced to a fine and imprisonment for contempt.

Although the Court refused to exempt public meetings from state control, it stood ready to intervene when local laws clearly discriminated against groups such as labor unions. In this case Justice Rutledge voided the Texas statute as an invalid interference with the rights of free speech and assembly, as protected under the First Amendment.

The four dissenters claimed that a state could license public meetings in order to maintain peace and order, provided it administered the rules in a neutral manner. Within a few years this view became dominant until finally buried by the Warren Court in the 1960s.

See Harry Kalven Jr., ed., *A Worthy Tradition: Freedom of Speech in America* (New York: Harper and Row, 1988).

Georgia v. Pennsylvania R.R. Co.

324 U.S. 439 (1945)
Decided: March 26, 1945
Vote: 5 (Black, Reed, Douglas, Murphy, W. Rutledge)
4 (Stone, Roberts, Frankfurter, R. Jackson)
Opinion of the Court: Douglas
Dissenting opinion: Stone (Roberts, Frankfurter, R. Jackson)

The state of Georgia claimed that Pennsylvania Railroad Company and others were involved in a conspiracy to restrain trade and interstate commerce. The state claimed that the lines fixed illegal prices, rates, and charges for transporting freight by railroad to and from Georgia, and, as a result, shippers preferred ports in other states to Georgia's. At issue, however, was not whether the railroads had actually engaged in this behavior, but the state's efforts to invoke the Supreme Court's original jurisdiction—that is, taking the case directly to the Supreme Court and not filing it in a lower federal court. The railroad companies argued that the Court did not have original jurisdiction over the matter.

The Court held that it had original jurisdiction over the case. Article III, Section 2, of the Constitution, confers original jurisdiction on the Court for cases between states or by one state against a citizen of another state. The Court found that Georgia properly stated a claim as *parens patriae* (literally means "the state as parent"). Thus, Georgia brought the case on its own behalf and not on behalf of any particular citizen.

Cramer v. United States

325 U.S. 1 (1945)
Decided: April 23, 1945
Vote: 5 (Roberts, Frankfurter, Murphy, R. Jackson, W. Rutledge)
4 (Stone, Black, Reed, Douglas)
Opinion of the Court: R. Jackson
Dissenting opinion: Douglas (Stone, Black, Reed)

Anthony Cramer, a naturalized American citizen, was convicted of giving aid and comfort to two of the German saboteurs who had landed on U.S. shores from German submarines in 1942 with a mission to disrupt industry in the country. Cramer was convicted of treason based on two witnesses who testified that he gave aid and comfort to the Germans. Cramer appealed, arguing that the evidence was insufficient to convict him of treason.

The Court held that the evidence was insufficient to convict Cramer of treason. Treason against the United States occurs only in waging war against the nation, or in adhering to the enemies, or giving the enemies aid and comfort. Moreover, the Constitution requires that for a treason conviction to be sustained, the defendant either must confess in open court or two witnesses must testify that he committed the acts constituting the treason.

The Court held that the Treason Clause (Article III, Section 3) requires that in addition to all other evidence, every act, movement, deed, and word of a person charged with treason has to be supported by the testimony of two witnesses. In this case, although the weight of all other evidence was damning toward Cramer, the witnesses showed only that he drank with the Germans at local bars and pubs, not enough to show that Cramer had the intent to aid and comfort the German saboteurs.

See J. Willard Hurst, *The Law of Treason in the United States* (Westport, Conn.: Greenwood, 1971).

Screws v. United States

325 U.S. 91 (1945)
Decided: May 7, 1945
Vote: 5 (Stone, Black, Reed, Douglas, W. Rutledge)
4 (Roberts, Frankfurter, Murphy, R. Jackson)
Opinion of the Court: Douglas
Opinion concurring in judgment: W. Rutledge
Dissenting opinion: Murphy
Dissenting opinion: Roberts, Frankfurter, R. Jackson

The Court described this case as "a shocking and revolting episode in law enforcement." The facts support this conclusion. Sheriff Claude Screws of Baker County, Georgia, and two of his deputies arrested Robert Hall, an African American, on the suspicion that he stole a tire. Hall was handcuffed and then beaten into unconsciousness. As a result of the injuries sustained he died soon after.

The U.S. Justice Department's Civil Rights Division could not persuade Georgia officials to prosecute the three men, so the federal government went into court and secured convictions that "under color of law" the sheriff and his deputies had deprived Hall of rights accorded by the Fourteenth Amendment. The circuit court of appeals affirmed the convictions.

The Supreme Court reversed and ordered a new trial for the sheriff. The case caused a deep rift among the justices, not because any of them approved of the sheriff's brutality but because of differing views on the statute involved. After the Civil War a number of laws were passed to protect the freedmen's newly acquired rights, but many of them had been eviscerated in the ***Civil Rights Cases,*** 109 U.S. 3 (1883). In 1940, however, two still remained on the books: one forbidding conspiracies to deny any person the rights ensured by the Constitution and the laws of the United States, and the other making it illegal to subject any person to "different pains or penalties on account of race." The problem was that when they heard *Screws* on appeal, the justices had practically nothing to guide them as to what these laws meant. Did a state official acting in an official capacity, but clearly violating the state's laws, act "under color" of state law?

Justices Roberts, Frankfurter, and Jackson, although shocked at the sheriff's conduct and believing him guilty of murder, nevertheless thought the statute unconstitutional because of vagueness. They feared that if they allowed the convictions to stand, it would open a Pandora's box of federal interference in matters clearly within state purview. Only Murphy thought the statute fully constitutional.

Justice Douglas wrote a careful and restrictive opinion. The law could be upheld as constitutional, but only if applied to state officials acting "under color of law." To save the statute from vagueness grounds, Douglas suggested that the lower court also needed to look at whether Screws had acted "willfully."

Because the Court had not struck down the Reconstruction Era statute, it remained alive for the government to use in later years. Many of its defects were resolved in the Civil Rights Acts of 1964 and 1965.

See Robert K. Carr, "Screws v. United States: The Georgia Brutality Case," *Cornell Law Quarterly* 31 (1945): 48; and Stephen Duke, "Justice Douglas and Criminal Law," in *"He Shall Not Pass This Way Again": The Legacy of Justice William O. Douglas,* ed. Stephen L. Wasby (Pittsburgh: University of Pittsburgh Press for the William O. Douglas Institute, 1990).

Jewell Ridge Coal Corp. v. Local No. 6167, UMWA

325 U.S. 161 (1945)
Decided: May 7, 1945
Vote: 5 (Black, Reed, Douglas, Murphy, W. Rutledge)
4 (Stone, Roberts, Frankfurter, R. Jackson)
Opinion of the Court: Murphy
Dissenting opinion: Jackson (Stone, Roberts, Frankfurter)

After arriving at Jewell Ridge Coal Corporation's mines, workers enter a portal and were transported down to the underground mines, a journey varying in time and distance. The coal company argued that the miners should not be paid for the travel time to get to the working places, the actual coal seams. The United Mine Workers Association (UMWA) argued that the traveling down into the earth and the safety tasks the miners did during that journey should be seen as "work" and therefore payable as part of hourly wages. The Court had to decide whether, under the Fair Labor Standards Act, a coalminer's traveling down underground constituted work for which he should be paid.

The Court held that the miners should be paid "portal to portal," that is, from the time they clocked in at the mine's entrance until they returned to that same spot at the end of the day. The nature of the journey, the Court ruled, was mentally and physically exhausting, was controlled by the employer, and for the benefit of the employer. Therefore, the coalminers must be paid for what they go through just to get to and from their workstations.

Southern Pacific Company v. Arizona ex rel. Sullivan

325 U.S. 761 (1945)
Decided: June 18, 1945
Vote: 7 (Stone, Roberts, Reed, Frankfurter, Murphy, R. Jackson, W. Rutledge)
2 (Black, Douglas)
Opinion of the Court: Stone
Concurring in judgment without opinion: W. Rutledge
Dissenting opinion: Black
Dissenting opinion: Douglas

Southern Pacific Company operated two interstate trains through Arizona. The company ran trains longer than the fourteen–passenger car or seventy–freight car maximum set by a 1912 Arizona law. Arizona argued that the law was for safety for railroad workers and automobile motorists.

The railroad argued that shortening the train length could double the number of trains on the interstate tracks, doubling the potential for accidents. Southern Pacific also argued that the state law affected interstate commerce and exceeded the power of the state.

The Court struck down the state law. Chief Justice Stone ruled that although states may make minor regulations affecting interstate commerce to preserve an overriding state concern, they cannot place a substantial burden upon interstate commerce. States may inhibit interstate commerce for health or safety effects, but not if such effects are merely "slight or problematic." Shortening the length of trains might only slightly help the issue of train accidents, but could also make the problem worse. At the same time, the Arizona law substantially burdened interstate commerce and therefore violated the Commerce Clause.

Guaranty Trust Company v. York

326 U.S. 99 (1945)
Decided: June 18, 1945
Vote: 5 (Stone, Black, Reed, Frankfurter, R. Jackson)
2 (Murphy, W. Rutledge)
Opinion of the Court: Frankfurter
Dissenting opinion: W. Rutledge (Murphy)
Did not participate: Roberts, Douglas

In a complicated financial deal involving banks in several states, the bankruptcy of a large corporation, and the alleged financial mismanagement of Guaranty Trust Company, York sued to recover the value of some $6,000 in notes from the failed company that she had received from Guaranty Trust. Later, York sued the trust company for a breach of its fiduciary duty to her. The details of the complicated transaction were not at issue, however. York brought suit in federal court based only on diversity of citizenship. The trust company moved for summary judgment, arguing that the time limit for suing had expired under New York's statute of limitations. The question for the Court in this case was this: Under what circumstances are federal courts bound by state law in a diversity of citizenship action?

Since ***Erie Railroad Co. v. Tompkins,*** 304 U.S. 64 (1938), the Court had held that federal courts were bound by state law in diversity cases, if it would "significantly affect the result" of the case to not apply the state law. In such cases, therefore, federal courts were acting as just another state court. The difference between "substance" and "procedure" was not the dividing line for when to apply state law. Instead, the issue was if the state law provisions would "substantially affect the result." In this case, the Supreme Court ruled that because New York law barred York's lawsuit, the federal court should also bar the action.

Bridges v. Wixon

326 U.S. 135 (1945)
Decided: June 18, 1945
Vote: 5 (Black, Reed, Douglas, Murphy, W. Rutledge)
3 (Stone, Roberts, Frankfurter)
Opinion of the Court: Douglas
Concurring opinion: Murphy
Dissenting opinion: Stone (Roberts, Frankfurter)
Did not participate: R. Jackson

Harry Bridges was a permanent alien in the United States. A leader of the longshoreman's union, he was also allegedly affiliated with the Communist Party. The government had been trying to deport Bridges for several years, but had been unable to provide sufficient evidence to do so. Under a new statute, however, aliens could be deported if they were affiliated with communists. Bridges appealed, claiming that the law violated his First Amendment rights, and the Court was asked to determine to what extent aliens have free speech rights.

In a 5–3 decision, the justices held that Bridges was not "affiliated" with the Communist Party. The Court found that Bridges' relationship with the Communist Party was only for the purposes of handling the union's activities. He never gave direct support to the party and did not advocate lawless activity. Most important, the Court ruled that permanent alien residents have the same First Amendment's right of free speech that citizens do and cannot be deported for espousing unpopular views.

International Shoe Co. v. Washington

326 U.S. 310 (1945)
Decided: December 3, 1945
Vote: 8 (Stone, Black, Reed, Frankfurter, Douglas, Murphy, W. Rutledge, Burton)
0
Opinion of the Court: Stone
Concurring opinion: Black
Did not participate: R. Jackson

Although the Constitution permits citizens of two states to go into federal courts, many states, when suing citizens of other states, preferred to have the matter tried at home in state court. The Supreme Court early on held that so-called "long arm" statutes, giving states jurisdiction over citizens and corporations that, although domiciled in another state, did business within their states, were constitutional.

In this case, traveling salesmen of International Shoe Company, a Delaware corporation headquartered in St. Louis, Missouri, conducted substantial business in Washington State. Washington sued the company to recover unpaid contributions to the state's unemployment compensation fund. The company filed a motion, asserting that it was exempt from the contributions because it was not a Washington corporation. The motion was denied. The company appealed, citing that the state law violated its Fourteenth Amendment due process rights.

Congress had passed a law, 26 U.S.C. § 1606(a), providing that no person shall be relieved from compliance with a state law requiring payments to an unemployment fund on the ground that he is engaged in interstate commerce. The Court therefore found the company liable for the payments. In addition, it found the state's jurisdictional reach adequate, due to the large amount of business International Shoe did within the state, to bring the company into state court. Finally, the Court found that the tax imposed by the state unemployment compensation statute—as construed by the state court, in its application to the corporation, as a tax on the privilege of employing salesmen within the state—did not violate the Due Process Clause of the Fourteenth Amendment.

Marsh v. Alabama

326 U.S. 501 (1946)
Decided: January 7, 1946
Vote: 5 (Black, Frankfurter, Douglas, Murphy, W. Rutledge)
3 (Stone, Reed, Burton)
Opinion of the Court: Black
Concurring opinion: Frankfurter
Dissenting opinion: Reed (Stone, Burton)
Did not participate: R. Jackson

A member of the Jehovah's Witnesses insisted on distributing religious literature in Chickasaw, Alabama. Although the Witnesses had earlier won a right to such activity, *Marsh* raised a different issue because Chickasaw was a company town, owned completely by Gulf Shipbuilding Company, which claimed that as the town was private property, speakers had no First Amendment rights there.

Grace Marsh distributed the literature outside of the sidewalk next to the post office. She was warned that she was distributing the literature without a permit and, after refusing to stop, was arrested for violating the state law that made it a crime to enter or remain on the premises of another after being warned not to do so. The state court of appeals affirmed her conviction. She appealed on the grounds that the state law violated her First and Fourteenth Amendment right to freedom of press and religion.

The Court reversed the lower court ruling. Even though Chickasaw was privately owned, the town functioned like any other town. People were free to enter the business district, buy goods, eat in restaurants, and the government had erected two post office buildings in the town from which it delivered mail to the occupants.

People living in company-owned towns, Justice Black maintained, are free citizens of their state and country, just as residents of municipalities, and there is no more justification for depriving them of the liberties guaranteed by the First and Fourteenth Amendments than there is for curtailing these freedoms with respect to any other citizen.

The dissenters pointed out that both federal and state law recognized the right of corporate towns and, by definition, private property, to exist. And as such they viewed the Court's opinion as a novel encroachment on the protection of private property.

See Shawn Francis Peters, *Judging Jehovah's Witnesses: Religious Persecution and the Dawn of the Rights Revolution* (Lawrence: University Press of Kansas, 2000).

In re Yamashita

327 U.S. 1 (1946)
Decided: February 4, 1946
Vote: 6 (Stone, Black, Reed, Frankfurter, Douglas, Burton)
2 (Murphy, W. Rutledge)
Opinion of the Court: Stone
Dissenting opinion: Murphy
Dissenting opinion: W. Rutledge (Murphy)
Did not participate: R. Jackson

Gen. Tomoyuki Yamashita was commanding general in the Imperial Japanese Army in charge of Japanese forces in the Philippines. In the last months of World War II, Yamashita was cut off from forces nominally under his command that went on a rampage of murder, looting, and rape in Manila. He was charged with war crimes, specifically for the command responsibility of the rampaging troops. At the military trial, convened under the direction of Gen. Wilhelm Styer, Army prosecutors were unable to prove that Yamashita had either knowledge of or control of the troops, and they built their case on hearsay and other types of evidence that would not be allowed in a civilian court. In his defense, Yamashita produced witnesses who directly testified that they were responsible for the activities and that Yamashita had had no knowledge of them. Nonetheless, the commission found him guilty and sentenced him to death. Yamashita filed a writ of habeas corpus, claiming that the commission had been unlawfully convened, that the charges had failed to specify any violation, and that the commission did not follow proper procedure.

The Court originally did not want to take the case, preferring to leave postwar justice in the hands of the military, but the procedural irregularities so upset Justices Murphy and Rutledge that they were able to get review. The Court heard arguments, and a majority voted to uphold the military. Because the United States was technically still at war with Japan (a peace treaty would not be signed until 1952), Chief Justice Stone ruled that the Articles of War allowed military commissions to operate without regard to the due process requirements of the Constitution.

Justices Murphy and Rutledge filed strong dissents. Murphy argued that the whole notion of "drumhead" justice—a term referring to a hasty battlefield court-martial—embodied in the trial violated basic American values as well as natural law. Rutledge filed a more careful dissent that took apart Stone's opinion and showed that the rules of war contained no such notion as command responsibility for troops violating the law, that if punishment were to be meted out, it should go to the perpetrators of the crimes and those who led them in their actions. Commentators generally agree that as far as legal arguments went, Rutledge's was the stronger, and it is the one that has subsequently been referred to in questions of war crimes.

This case presented a political quandary for the Court. The United States had won the Pacific war, but Americans still felt a great deal of animosity toward the Japanese, not only for their harsh treatment of American prisoners of war but also for their brutal occupation of the Philippines. No city in the war, with the exception of Warsaw, suffered as much as Manila, and tens of thousands of Filipino civilians had been killed. Had the Court voted to nullify the decision, it is likely that either Gen. Douglas MacArthur or President Truman might well have ignored the decision.

See A. Frank Reel, *The Case of General Yamashita* Chicago: University of Chicago Press, 1949); and Richard Lael, *The Yamashita Precedent* (Wilmington, Del.: Scholarly Resources, 1982).

Duncan v. Kahanamoku

327 U.S. 304 (1946)
Decided: February 25, 1946
Vote: 6 (Stone, Black, Reed, Douglas, Murphy, W. Rutledge)
2 (Frankfurter, Burton)
Opinion of the Court: Black
Concurring opinion: Murphy
Opinion concurring in judgment: Stone
Dissenting opinion: Burton (Frankfurter)
Did not participate: R. Jackson

Following the December 7, 1941, attack on Pearl Harbor, the governor of Hawaii placed the territory under martial law, acting under the authority of the territorial Organic Act of 1900. The governor replaced Hawaii's civil and criminal courts with military tribunals, which do not follow standard rules of evidence and forbid trial by jury. The petitioners in this case were sentenced to prison by military tribunals. They filed writs of habeas corpus challenging the power of military tribunals to try and convict them. The district court ruled the trials invalid because there was no military necessity for trying civilians by military tribunals. The circuit court reversed, saying that the

Organic Act's authorization of martial law included the establishment of a total military government.

The Court held that the Organic Act of 1900 did not authorize the replacement of civil courts with military tribunals. Justice Black relied on an overview of the nation's history to interpret the statute. He said that Americans have traditionally feared subordination to military rule, and that Congress therefore would not have written the Organic Act to allow total military occupation of the democratic branches of government. On the contrary, courts and their procedural safeguards remain a necessary part of American government even under martial law.

Because the Court was able to answer petitioners' claims by interpreting the Organic Act, it did not directly address the constitutional validity of the governor's actions.

See Harry N. Scheiber and Jane L. Scheiber, "Constitutional Liberty in World War II: Army Rule and Martial Law in Hawaii, 1941-1946," *Western Legal History* 341 (1990).

Bell v. Hood

327 U.S. 678 (1946)
Decided: April 1, 1946
Vote: 6 (Black, Reed, Frankfurter, Douglas, Murphy, W. Rutledge)
2 (Stone, Burton)
Opinion of the Court: Black
Dissenting opinion: Stone, Burton
Did not participate: R. Jackson

Arthur Bell filed suit against officers of the Federal Bureau of Investigation (FBI) for imprisoning him in violation of his right to due process and for illegally searching and seizing his property in violation of the Fourth and Fifth Amendments. Bell claimed $3,000 worth of resulting damages. The FBI moved to dismiss the complaint for failure to state a claim for which relief could be granted. The FBI said its officers acted within the scope of their authority and all actions were incidental to a lawful arrest. The district judge dismissed the case, saying that a federal court did not have jurisdiction because the issue did not pose a federal question. The federal appellate court affirmed and denied Bell's request to amend his complaint.

The Supreme Court held that where complaints are drawn to seek recovery directly under the Constitution or the laws of the United States, a federal court has jurisdiction over the suit regardless of whether the plaintiff has a claim upon which relief could be granted. Jurisdiction, therefore, was not defeated because Bell might not have a cognizable claim. Should a court decide that Bell's case did not have merit, this would be a legal rather than jurisdictional decision.

The Court did not decide the merits of Bell's case but commented that federal courts should be open to adjusting remedies so that necessary relief may be granted.

Girouard v. United States

328 U.S. 61 (1946)
Decided: April 22, 1946
Vote: 5 (Black, Douglas, Murphy, W. Rutledge, Burton)
3 (Stone, Reed, Frankfurter)
Opinion of the Court: Douglas
Dissenting opinion: Stone (Reed, Frankfurter)
Did not participate: R. Jackson

James Louis Girouard petitioned for U.S. citizenship in a Massachusetts district court. He took the oath of citizenship, but wrote on his application that he would not be willing to take up arms for the defense of the country because he was a Seventh Day Adventist. Girouard explained at his hearing that his religious beliefs prevented him from engaging in combat, but that he could serve in noncombat capacities for the armed forces. The district court approved Girouard's petition for citizenship, but the circuit court reversed, basing its decision on Supreme Court opinions saying that an alien who refuses to bear arms should not be granted citizenship. See ***United States v. Schwimmer,*** 279 U.S. 644 (1929), and ***United States v. Macintosh,*** 283 U.S. 605 (1931).

The Court overturned its rulings in the previous cases to hold that willingness to bear arms is not a valid requirement for citizenship. Justice Douglas explained that bearing arms is not the only way to support and defend the nation, and that noncombatant service is just as valuable. Furthermore, natural born citizens enjoy the religious liberty of refusing to participate in combat, and naturalized citizens should have the same right.

The Court felt justified in overturning its former holdings, even though Congress had never weighed in on this subject. Douglas commented that Congress's silence did not necessarily indicate consent, and that Congress should not always be responsible for reversing an error by the Court.

See Michael S. Satow, "Conscientious Objectors: Their Status, the Law and Its Development," *George Mason Civil Rights Law Journal* 3 (1992): 113.

United States v. Lovett

328 U.S. 303 (1946)
Decided: June 3, 1946
Vote: 8 (Black, Reed, Frankfurter, Douglas, Murphy,
W. Rutledge, Burton)
0
Opinion of the Court: Black
Concurring opinion: Frankfurter (Reed)
Did not participate: R. Jackson

Congress passed a bill saying that Robert Morss Lovett and two other government employees could no longer receive compensation from their federal jobs. The bill was drafted after a House of Representatives subcommittee decided Lovett was guilty of participating in "subversive activity." Lovett continued to work for the government after the bill was passed, but received no payment for his work. He filed a complaint in the Court of Claims, arguing that the statute was a bill of attainder, which the Constitution forbids Congress from passing. (A bill of attainder is a legislative act that inflicts punishment on a citizen without a judicial trial.) The Court of Claims disagreed, holding that the bill was a valid exercise of the House's power over appropriations.

The Supreme Court agreed with Lovett that the bill punished him without a trial and was therefore unconstitutional. The Court refused to conclude that the bill was merely an act of congressional appropriation because it resulted not only in a spending decision but also in the unemployment of Lovett and two other government employees. Justice Black said that the bill "falls precisely within the category of Congressional actions which the Constitution barred by providing that 'No Bill of Attainder . . . shall be passed.' "

Pennekamp v. Florida

328 U.S. 331 (1946)
Decided: June 3, 1946
Vote: 7 (Black, Reed, Frankfurter, Douglas, Murphy, W. Rutledge, Burton)
0
Opinion of the Court: Reed
Concurring opinion: Frankfurter
Concurring opinion: Murphy
Concurring opinion: W. Rutledge
Did not participate: R. Jackson

John D. Pennekamp, associate editor of the *Miami Herald,* published two editorials criticizing Florida's circuit court specifically in regard to cases pending before the court at the time. The court held both Pennekamp and the publisher of the *Miami Herald* in contempt of court, saying that the editorials posed a danger to the administration of justice in the state by inappropriately questioning the integrity of the court. Pennekamp was fined $250, and the publisher was fined $1,000. Both appealed, saying that their words did not pose a "clear and present danger" to the functioning of the court and were therefore protected by the First Amendment.

The Court overturned the charges of contempt against both Pennekamp and the newspaper's publisher, saying that the freedom of public comment granted in the Constitution should weigh more heavily than the possible tendency of open discussion to negatively influence pending cases. Justice Reed said that it was clear that the primary purpose of the editorials was not to influence the Florida court. He also noted that the editorials had very little possibility of swaying the opinions of future juries or individual justices. The editorials posed no clear and present danger to the operations of the Florida judicial system and deserved full First Amendment protection.

Morgan v. Virginia

328 U.S. 373 (1946)
Decided: June 3, 1946
Vote: 6 (Black, Reed, Frankfurter, Douglas, Murphy, W. Rutledge)
1 (Burton)
Opinion of the Court: Reed
Concurring opinion: Black
Concurring opinion: Frankfurter
Concurring in judgment without opinion: W. Rutledge
Dissenting opinion: Burton
Did not participate: R. Jackson

Irene Morgan, an African American woman, boarded a bus in Virginia headed for Baltimore, Maryland. Under Virginia law she was required to sit in the back of the bus, but she refused. She was arrested and convicted of violating the Virginia law requiring bus segregation. The state supreme court affirmed her conviction. An attorney for the National Association for the Advancement of Colored People appealed Morgan's conviction to the Supreme Court, arguing that Virginia's law violated the interstate commerce clause of the U.S. Constitution.

The Court overturned the conviction, ruling that the law violated the Commerce Clause because it burdened interstate travel and did not promote uniformity among states. Because Morgan's bus trip crossed state lines, it was part of interstate commerce. The law burdened interstate commerce because it required African American passengers to sit in the back of the bus while traveling in Virginia even though they might have been sitting in the front of the bus before they entered the state. Justice Reed explained that such inconsistency among states was an inconvenience to bus owners and travelers, and he therefore held that seating arrangements for various races required a single, uniform rule to protect national travel. Although segregated travel arrangements would continue, the Court made it clear that interstate segregation would not be allowed when challenged before a federal court.

See Catherine A. Barnes, *Journey from Jim Crow: The Desegregation of Southern Transit* (New York: Columbia University Press, 1983).

Prudential Insurance Co. v. Benjamin

328 U.S. 408 (1946)
Decided: June 3, 1946
Vote: 7 (Black, Reed, Frankfurter, Douglas, Murphy, W. Rutledge, Burton)
0
Opinion of the Court: W. Rutledge
Concurring in judgment without opinion: Black
Did not participate: R. Jackson

Prudential Insurance Company challenged a South Carolina law imposing a tax on out-of-state insurance companies doing business in the state. Prudential argued that this law discriminated against interstate commerce by favoring local business and that it violated the Constitution's Commerce Clause.

Congress, however, had passed a law that allowed states to impose taxes on out-of-state insurance companies. Prudential claimed that the law was unconstitutional because the dormant commerce clause, which is Congress's plenary power over interstate commerce even when it is unexercised, forbade the discriminatory results of such laws even if approved by Congress.

The Court held that the Commerce Clause gave Congress an affirmative power to make laws about commerce regardless of discriminatory effects. The dormant commerce clause applies only when a state acts in defiance of congressional law, in which case the Court will yield to Congress's authority, even if it has been silent on the matter that the state legislation addresses. Likewise, Justice Rutledge wrote that the Court should grant even more deference to an explicit expression of congressional intent when enacted in a statute.

The Court in this case expressed an unwillingness to regulate when Congress had already spoken and noted that Congress, not the courts, should decide what regulations should apply to interstate commerce.

Colegrove v. Green

328 U.S. 549 (1946)
Decided: June 10, 1946
Vote: 4 (Reed, Frankfurter, W. Rutledge, Burton)
3 (Black, Douglas, Murphy)
Judgment of the Court: Frankfurter
Opinion concurring in judgment: W. Rutledge
Dissenting opinion: Black (Douglas, Murphy)
Did not participate: R. Jackson

Three Illinois voters petitioned an Illinois district court to require the state to change the sizes and shapes of its congressional voting districts. The petitioners claimed that the Illinois law creating these districts violated both the Constitution and the federal Reapportionment Act because the districts did not cover the same amount of territory and did not encompass equal portions of the population.

The Court held that neither the Constitution nor the Reapportionment Act contained requirements about the compactness and population equality of congressional voting districts. The Court relied on the precedent set in *Wood v. Broom,* 287 U.S. 1 (1932). Justice Frankfurter commented that Congress had never protested the decision in *Wood,* which indicated that it agreed with the Court's analysis.

The Court further held that it could not decide the issue anyway because it was of a "peculiarly political nature" and therefore could not be addressed by a court. The Constitution gives the legislature, not the judiciary, authority to decide the "time, place, and manner" of federal elections. Citizens can vote against members of the legislature if they disagree with their decisions, so the remedy ultimately lies with the people rather than the judiciary.

The three dissenters, as well as Justice Rutledge, did believe that the Court could decide the issue and it agreed to do so in ***Baker v. Carr,*** 369 U.S. 186 (1962).

See Lawrence R. Caruso, "The Rocky Road From Colegrove to Wesberry: Or, You Can't Get There From Here," *Tennessee Law Review* 36 (1969): 621.

Ballard v. United States

329 U.S. 187 (1946)
Decided: December 9, 1946
Vote: 5 (Black, Reed, Douglas, Murphy, W. Rutledge)
4 (Vinson, Frankfurter, R. Jackson, Burton)
Opinion of the Court: Douglas
Concurring opinion: R. Jackson
Dissenting opinion: Frankfurter (Vinson, R. Jackson, Burton)
Dissenting opinion: Burton (Vinson, Frankfurter, R. Jackson)

Edna Ballard was convicted of mail fraud, the charges stemming from the "I Am" movement that Ballard headed. Its teachings included that Ballard, her husband, and son were in spiritual touch with Saint Germain and that as a result the Ballards had performed hundreds of miracle cures. In an earlier case, *United States v. Ballard,* 322 U.S. 78 (1944), the Court had remanded the case for a new trial because the jury had been asked to determine the validity and sincerity of the "I Am" movement. Justice Douglas had ruled that the sincerity of a religious belief, no matter how bizarre, could not be used as the basis for determining guilt for another offense. When Ballard was again found guilty, she appealed on the grounds that federal courts in California systematically excluded women from juries.

Federal law at the time required that federal juries have the same qualifications as those in the highest state trial court. California considered women eligible for jury duty, but as a matter of practice California courts did not summon women to serve. Federal courts followed the same practice.

The Court reversed Ballard's conviction on the grounds that federal law on jury selection, taken as a whole, was intended to make juries fair cross-sections of the community and as truly representative of the community as possible. Because California made women eligible, they were therefore part of the community from which jurors should be drawn and which juries should reflect. All-male juries were inconsistent with the congressional mandate.

Although the case relied on statutory interpretation of a federal law, its comments on juries being representative of the community would be recalled in later cases—***Taylor v. Louisiana,*** 419 U.S. 522 (1975), is one example—in which the Court developed the meaning of the Sixth Amendment phrase, "trial by jury."

State of Louisiana ex. rel. Francis v. Resweber

329 U.S. 459 (1947)
Decided: January 13, 1947
Vote: 5 (Vinson, Black, Reed, Frankfurter, R. Jackson)
4 (Douglas, Murphy, W. Rutledge, Burton)
Judgment of the Court: Reed
Opinion concurring in judgment: Frankfurter
Dissenting opinion: Burton (Douglas, Murphy, W. Rutledge)

Petitioner Willie Francis was a convicted murderer sentenced to death by electrocution. Strapped into the electric chair, Francis received an electrical jolt insufficient to kill him due to a malfunction of the machine. The execution was rescheduled for the following week, and Francis immediately filed suit, claiming that his due process rights under the Fourteenth Amendment would be violated by a second attempt to execute him. He also claimed that the second attempt put him in double jeopardy, was cruel and unusual punishment, and violated his right to equal protection. The state supreme court denied all of these claims.

The Court found that a second execution would not violate the Constitution. Regarding double jeopardy, the Court applied an earlier decision saying that if a new trial is required because of errors, this is not the kind of hardship forbidden by the Constitution. Because Louisiana made an error in its original electrocution, no double jeopardy resulted from the correction of error. The Court also found that it was not cruel and unusual punishment for the same reason. The Eighth Amendment protects individuals from methods of punishment that are inherently cruel, not from the necessary suffering involved in an otherwise humane execution. Finally, the Court rejected Francis's equal protection claim. The Court explained that the Equal Protection Clause prevents purposeful attempts to treat people differently and does not apply when mistakes result in different applications of the law.

In his dissent, Justice Burton said that Francis's execution should be compared to a lawful execution, which sets the standard for cruel and unusual punishment. If no state would purposefully allow a convict to endure two execution attempts, Louisiana should not allow it because of a mistake.

See Arthur S. Miller, *Death by Installments: The Ordeal of Willie Francis* (New York: Greenwood Press, 1988).

Hickman v. Taylor

329 U.S. 495 (1947)
Decided: January 13, 1947
Vote: 9 (Vinson, Black, Reed, Frankfurter, Douglas, Murphy, R. Jackson, W. Rutledge, Burton)
0
Opinion of the Court: Murphy
Concurring opinion: R. Jackson (Frankfurter)

Immediately following the sinking of the *J. M. Taylor* and the loss of several lives, the boat's owners, Taylor and Anderson, hired legal counsel to defend against possible wrongful death claims. In anticipation of litigation, attorneys interviewed witnesses and survivors of the accident and took notes. A lawyer representing the widows of two passengers filed interrogatories during the discovery process demanding that the lawyers for Taylor and Anderson provide copies of the notes they had taken at these prelitigation interviews. Taylor's attorneys refused and were held in contempt of court. The circuit court reversed this charge, and Hickman, the administrator for one of the decedent's estate, appealed.

The Court held that the notes and mental impressions of Taylor's attorneys were not discoverable by Hickman and his attorneys and therefore upheld the circuit court's decision in support of the attorneys. The Court agreed that although the documents were not privileged *per se*, they reflected the work product of an attorney, created in anticipation of litigation, and such product was the sole property of that attorney. An attorney can be required to release his work product only if there is a showing of necessity. Hickman's attorney had not proven that he needed the documents, and therefore Taylor's attorneys did not need to release them.

This case reaffirmed the doctrine of attorney work product, which says that an attorneys' thoughts and impressions can be discovered only if opposing counsel can show compelling need.

See Samuel B. Fortenbaugh Jr., "Hickman versus Taylor Revisited," *Defense Law Journal* 13 (1964): 1.

Everson v. Board of Education of Ewing Township

330 U.S. 1 (1947)
Decided: February 10, 1947
Vote: 5 (Vinson, Black, Reed, Douglas, Murphy)
4 (Frankfurter, R. Jackson, W. Rutledge, Burton)
Opinion of the Court: Black
Dissenting opinion: R. Jackson (Frankfurter)
Dissenting opinion: W. Rutledge (Frankfurter, R. Jackson, Burton)

Observers assumed that when the Court incorporated the Free Exercise Clause during World War II, the Establishment Clause would also apply to the states. The first of the modern Establishment Clause cases reached the Court in 1947 and involved a challenge to a New Jersey law allowing townships to reimburse parents for bus fare for their children attending private or parochial schools. A local taxpayer challenged the payments as a form of establishment of religion. The trial court found for the taxpayer, and that decision was reversed by the state court of appeals.

The Supreme Court was asked to decide what constituted an establishment of religion. Writing for the Court, Justice Black not only made incorporation clear but also set down what remains basic jurisprudence for Establishment Clause cases:

> The "establishment of religion" clause of the First Amendment means at least this: Neither a state nor the Federal Government can set up a church. Neither can pass laws which aid one religion, aid all religions, or prefer one religion over another. Neither can force nor influence a

person to go to or to remain away from church against his will or force him to profess a belief or disbelief in any religion. No person can be punished for entertaining or professing religious beliefs, for church attendance or nonattendance. No tax in any amount, large or small, can be levied to support any religious activities or institutions, whatever they may be called, or whatever form they may adopt to teach or practice religion. Neither a state nor the Federal Government can, openly or secretly, participate in the affairs of any religious organizations or groups and vice versa. In the words of Jefferson, the clause against establishment of religion by law was intended to erect a "wall of separation between Church and State."

Black then went on to write a brilliant exposition of the historical forces that led to the adoption of the First Amendment.

Given all that, one would expect Black to find the New Jersey statute unconstitutional. Instead, he upheld the program, leading to one of the great judicial epigrams, Justice Jackson's comment comparing Black's reasoning to Byron's Julia, who "whispering 'I will ne'er consent,'—consented." Justice Rutledge took the logic of Black's historical argument and reached the inevitable conclusion that if "the test remains undiluted as Jefferson and Madison made it, [then] money taken by taxation from one is not to be used or given to support another's religious training or belief, or indeed one's own. The prohibition is absolute."

It is surprising to find Black, famous for his absolutist position, here taking a balancing approach, finding the state's subsidy of bus fare a "reasonable" means of promoting the welfare of the children.

Four justices—Frankfurter, Jackson, Rutledge, and Burton—dissented. The theme of the dissents was that a wall of separation did in fact exist and the New Jersey plan violated it.

Despite the 5–4 split on the case, all nine justices agreed on two basic propositions—that the Establishment Clause of the First Amendment did apply to the states by incorporation through the Fourteenth Amendment and that the Framers had intended the clause to create a wall of separation between church and state. In dozens of cases since 1947, the Court has wrestled with the notion of just how high that wall should, with some justices arguing that the wall was a metaphor and not the intention of the Founders. But whatever their views, Black's *Everson* arguments on this point remain the starting point of the debate.

See Leonard W. Levy, *The Establishment Clause: Religion and the First Amendment* (New York: Macmillan, 1986); Theodore Powell, *The School Bus Law: A Case Study in Education, Religion, and Politics* (Middletown, Conn.: Wesleyan University Press, 1960); and Frank J. Sorauf, *The Wall of Separation: The Constitutional Politics of Church and State* (Princeton: Princeton University Press, 1976).

United Public Workers v. Mitchell

330 U.S. 75 (1947)
Decided: February 10, 1947
Vote: 4 (Vinson, Reed, Frankfurter, Burton)
3 (Black, Douglas, W. Rutledge)
Opinion of the Court: Reed
Concurring opinion: Frankfurter
Dissenting opinion: Black
Dissenting opinion: Douglas
Dissenting opinion: W. Rutledge
Did not participate: Murphy, R. Jackson

Several members of United Public Workers, a labor union of federal government employees, filed suit against members of the U.S. Civil Service Commission to challenge the Hatch Act, which prohibits employees of the federal government from participating in political campaigns. The workers wanted to stop Mitchell and the other Civil Service commissioners from enforcing the Hatch Act because to do so, they claimed, would prohibit federal employees from engaging in activities that are otherwise protected by the Constitution.

The Court noted that although individuals have a fundamental right to express themselves politically, this right was not absolute. Here, the government's interest in maintaining an orderly, nonpartisan employee base was given precedent over the free speech rights of those employees. The Court relied heavily on its decision in *Ex parte Curtis,* 106 U.S. 371 (1882), in which it held that effective administration was threatened by actively partisan government personnel. It also explained that when federal employees were involved in politics, the danger increased of them making politically based decisions or channeling government favors through political connections. Because of these concerns, the Court found the government's interest sufficient to outweigh individual employee interest in political participation. The Court therefore upheld the Hatch Act.

In his partial dissent, Justice Douglas agreed that allowing unlimited employee participation in politics posed some danger, but said that the all-encompassing nature of the Hatch Act was too broad. Douglas urged the Court to narrow the act to the specific conduct deemed offensive. Justice Black went even further in his dissent, finding no justification for depriving government employees of their fundamental right to speak.

United States v. United Mine Workers

330 U.S. 258 (1947)
Decided: March 6, 1947
Vote: 7 (Vinson, Black, Reed, Frankfurter, Douglas, R. Jackson, Burton)
2 (Murphy, W. Rutledge)
Opinion of the Court: Vinson
Concurring opinion: Black, Douglas
Opinion concurring in judgment: Frankfurter
Dissenting opinion: Murphy
Dissenting opinion: W. Rutledge (Murphy)

As a result of wartime strikes by miners, Congress in 1943 passed the Smith-Connally, or War Labor Disputes Act, which empowered the president to take over control of plants or whole industries critical to the war effort. The law also provided criminal penalties for persons who instigated such strikes. Following the end of the war in May 1946, the United Mine Workers (UMW) went out on strike. President Truman, claiming that coal was necessary to the war effort and shortage of coal would constitute a national emergency, seized the mines. The UMW refused to work for the government-held mines, and the government asked the court for an injunction that would force the miners back to work. The injunction was granted, but the UMW continued to refuse to work and was fined $3.5 million for contempt of court. The UMW appealed, claiming that the injunction issued by the district court directly violated the Norris-LaGuardia Act, which provides that "no . . . injunction shall prohibit any person or persons from recommending, advising, or persuading others to strike."

The Court rejected this argument, however, by saying that the statute applied only to controversies between employers and employees, and the United States could not be defined as an "employer" under the terms of this statute. Rather, a statute can apply against the sovereign only if it contains words to that effect. Because the Norris-LaGuardia Act did not claim to allow jurisdiction over the United States, it could not be so applied.

Finding none of the UMW's arguments persuasive, the Court held that the trial court had properly found the workers guilty of criminal and civil contempt because of their willful disobedience to the court's orders. The Court did, however, reduce the fine against the UMW from $3.5 million to $700,000, finding the original amount excessive.

See Melvyn Dubofsky and Warren Van Tine, *John L. Lewis: A Biography,* abr. ed. (Urbana: University of Illinois Press, 1986), 331–336.

Haupt v. United States

330 U.S. 631 (1947)
Decided: March 31, 1947
Vote: 8 (Vinson, Black, Reed, Frankfurter, Douglas, R. Jackson, W. Rutledge, Burton)
1 (Murphy)
Opinion of the Court: R. Jackson
Concurring opinion: Douglas
Dissenting opinion: Murphy

Hans Max Haupt was convicted of treason against the United States. A military tribunal had earlier convicted Haupt's son Herbert of performing sabotage and spy work for the German Reich during World War II, a conviction that was upheld in ***Ex parte Quirin,*** 317 U.S. 1 (1942). While Herbert was engaged in treasonous activities, Haupt had sheltered him, assisted him in obtaining a government job, and acquired an automobile for his use. The district court found this evidence of aid sufficient to convict Haupt as a conspirator in treason.

Article III, Section 3, of the Constitution says that a citizen may be convicted of treason only when two or more witnesses can testify to the commission of an overt act that provided aid and comfort to the enemy. Haupt argued that he was aiding only his son and not the German Reich, but the court held that because he knew his son was involved in treason, the jury had properly inferred that the help he gave to his son also was also intended to aid the Germans. The court also disregarded Haupt's argument that although more than one witness testified regarding each act of treason, the testimony was not valid because the witnesses did not say precisely the same thing. The court held that the clause requiring the testimony of two witnesses did not demand identical stories, but only testimony that added credibility to the same accusation.

The Supreme Court affirmed Haupt's conviction. Justice Jackson said that although the law of treason makes proper conviction difficult, it should not be impossible. In this case Haupt's overt acts, observed by more than one witness, were sufficient to justify conviction.

The decision, the first in which the Court sustained a treason conviction, permitted the government to prosecute other Americans who had aided the enemy during the war, such as Douglas Chandler, who had broadcast English-language programs from Berlin.

United States v. California

332 U.S. 19 (1947)
Decided: June 23, 1947
Vote: 6 (Vinson, Black, Douglas, Murphy, W. Rutledge, Burton)
2 (Reed, Frankfurter)
Opinion of the Court: Black
Dissenting opinion: Reed
Dissenting opinion: Frankfurter
Did not participate: R. Jackson

The United States brought suit against California, claiming that the federal government owned the land under the three miles of ocean bordering the state, and that California therefore did not have the right to sell the oil and minerals under that land. California claimed that the three miles of ocean were part of its original boundaries and that California gained title to that land when it became a state.

The Court held that the United States owned title to the three miles of ocean land off California. The state relied heavily on *Pollard's Lessee v. Hagan,* 44 U.S. 212 (1845), in which the Court held that the original thirteen states owned the navigable tidewaters within each states' boundaries. If the original states owned the water within their state, California reasoned, it owned the water around it as well. The Court distinguished *Pollard,* however, saying that it applied only to bodies of water within the state, not to ocean water on the state borders. In fact, the "three-mile" rule—political entities own the water and ocean land for three miles off their borders—applies specifically to sovereign nations, not states. The purpose of the rule was to allow nations to protect their shores from foreign invasion. Because states do not perform a security role, there is no reason to give them the land off their shores, and the Court found California's claim invalid. The United States gained title to the ocean, the land, and everything underneath it.

Adamson v. California

332 U.S. 46 (1947)
Decided: June 23,1947
Vote: 5 (Vinson, Reed, Frankfurter, R. Jackson, Burton)
4 (Black, Douglas, Murphy, W. Rutledge)
Opinion of the Court: Reed
Concurring opinion: Frankfurter
Dissenting opinion: Black (Douglas)
Dissenting opinion: Murphy (W. Rutledge)

Admiral Dewey Adamson, a poor, illiterate black man, had twice served time for robbery. He had, however, been out of prison for seventeen years when police arrested him for the murder of an elderly white widow. The only evidence connecting Adamson to the crime was six fingerprints on a door leading to the garbage container in the woman's kitchen. Police linked the prints to Adamson.

Adamson, on the advice of his attorney, did not take the stand in his own defense. Under California law, the prosecutor was allowed to point out to the jury Adamson's failure to testify. He reasoned that this surely proved Adamson's guilt. The jury convicted Adamson. He appealed, challenging the state law as violating the Fourteenth Amendment. He argued that allowing the comment on his constitutional rights not to testify was equivalent to forcing a defendant to take the stand, which violated his right not to incriminate himself and due process.

Prior to this case, Justices Frankfurter and Black had for several years carried on a debate on the meaning of the Fourteenth Amendment's Due Process Clause. Both started from the same place—their opposition to the use of substantive due process by earlier courts to strike down reform legislation. For Frankfurter, the answer to this abuse of power lay in judicial restraint and appropriate deference to the policy decisions of the political branches. Black objected to the great discretion the Frankfurter approach vested in the courts, but had been unsure of the proper answer. He found it in *Adamson.*

Justice Reed, in the Court's opinion, conceded that such behavior by the prosecutor in a federal proceeding would be unacceptable and a violation of the Fifth Amendment. But it was "settled law" that the Self-incrimination Clause did not apply to the states. "For a state to require testimony from an accused," Reed concluded, "is not necessarily a breach of a state's obligation to give a fair trial."

Black dissented, setting forth his belief in the "total incorporation" of the first eight amendments by the Fourteenth. Just as the Bill of Rights applied objective standards to the behavior of the federal government, so the application of the first eight amendments to the states would provide equally ascertainable criteria by which to judge state action. In a lengthy appendix he presented the historical evidence he had assembled to support this position, an essay most scholars find less than convincing.

Frankfurter set out his response to Black. In probably no other statement, either for the Court or in dissent, do we get such a clear exposition of Frankfurter's philosophy of judging, which scholars have termed "process jurisprudence." Relying on his own historical research, Frankfurter denied that the framers of the Fourteenth Amendment had intended to subsume all of the Bill of Rights. Frankfurter also responded to what he took as the most serious of Black's charges, that the vague criteria Cardozo had enunciated in ***Palko v. Connecticut,*** 302 U.S. 319 (1937), left judges too much discretion, so that the protection of rights depended on the mercy of individuals. Frankfurter portrayed judging as a process removed from the fray of daily pressures. Protected in their sanctum, justices may engage in that process of discovery that will yield *the* right answer—not an objective, eternally fixed answer, but the right answer for the time.

The great appeal of process jurisprudence is that it attempts to remove idiosyncrasy and individuality from judicial decision making and replace them with objectivity and consistency. Public faith in the judicial process is enhanced if the public believes the judges are acting fairly and adhering to a common set of methods and principles in all cases, regardless of the results in specific instances.

But can judging ever be quite this impersonal? As Black asked, how did one objectively determine the "canons of decency and fairness" that everyone accepted? Moreover, while one might say that due process is meaningful over a whole gamut of cases, individuals are on trial; individuals must cope with the criminal justice system; individuals must pay the penalties if found guilty; individuals suffer if deprived of their rights. For Black, total incorporation provided at least a partial answer because judges would no longer subjectively determine what rights met the "canons of decency and fairness."

Although the *Adamson* Court adopted the Cardozo/Frankfurter approach of selective incorporation, during the 1950s and 1960s nearly all of the first eight amendment guarantees were applied to the states. Black's approach proved too rigid, however, and Frankfurter's notion of due process as fundamental fairness became a useful tool for judges confronting new and unusual situations in the Warren, Burger, and Rehnquist Courts.

See Mark Silverstein, *Constitutional Faiths: Felix Frankfurter, Hugo Black, and the Process of Judicial Decision Making* (Ithaca: Cornell University Press, 1984); James F. Simon, *The Antagonists: Hugo Black, Felix Frankfurter and Civil Liberties in Modern America* (New York: Simon and Schuster, 1989); and Melvin I. Urofsky, *Division and Discord: The Supreme Court Under Stone and Vinson, 1941–1953* (Columbia: University of South Carolina Press, 1997).

Sipuel v. Oklahoma State Board of Regents

332 U.S. 631 (1948)
Decided: January 12, 1948
Opinion: *Per curiam*

Ada Lois Sipuel, a black woman, compiled an excellent record at the State College for Negroes in Langston, Oklahoma. She applied to the University of Oklahoma Law School, the only one in the state. The president of the University of Oklahoma, George Lynn Cross, personally opposed racial segregation, as did a majority of the students. State law, however, prohibited the university from accepting African Americans; in fact, the legislature was so vehement in its opposition to racially integrated education that it enacted statutes calling for fines of $100 to $500 a day against any institution that taught whites and blacks together; any student—white or black—attending such a school could be fined $5 to $20 a day.

Sipuel was denied relief in the state court, and that decision was affirmed by the state supreme court. The National Association for the Advancement of Colored People (NAACP), which supported Sipuel's efforts, appealed to the Supreme Court using the precedent established in ***Missouri ex rel. Gaines v. Canada,*** 305 U.S. 337 (1938).

The Court, in a *per curiam* opinion, ordered Oklahoma to provide Sipuel with a legal education "in conformity with the equal protection clause of the Fourteenth Amendment and provide it as soon as it does for applicants of any other group." It sent the case back to the Oklahoma Supreme Court, which now had no choice but to order the university to admit Sipuel to the existing all-white law school, open a separate one for her, or close the existing law school until such time as there would be one for blacks.

The state board of regents angrily created a law school overnight, roping off a small section of the state capitol in Oklahoma City. Three teachers were assigned to provide instruction to Sipuel and "others similarly situated."

Sipuel would have nothing to do with this farce, and more than a thousand white students on the University of Oklahoma campus held a protest rally against the regents' decision. When the NAACP sought another review by the Supreme Court, a majority of the justices refused to consider whether the state had in fact established an equal facility. Chief Justice Vinson struggled to keep the Court from going beyond what he termed "the only question before us," namely, "whether or not our mandate has been followed." According to Vinson, "it is clear that it has been followed." In *Fisher v. Hurst,* 333 U.S. 147 (1948), another *per curiam* opinion, but with Justices Murphy and Rutledge dissenting, the Court held that the original *Sipuel* case had not presented the issue of whether the Equal Protection Clause prevented a state from establishing a separate law school for blacks.

The NAACP could not claim any real victory in the *Sipuel* case, mainly because the Court refused to consider the central issue of whether separate education could be truly equal under the Constitution. Ada Sipuel Fisher continued to fight her case, however, and eventually graduated from the University of Oklahoma Law School, where she later became a trustee.

See David W. Levy, "Before the *Brown* Decision: The Integration Struggle at the University of Oklahoma," *Extensions* (Fall 1994): 10–14; Ada Lois Sipuel Fisher, *A Matter of Black and White: The Autobiography of Ada Lois Sipuel Fisher* (Norman: University of Oklahoma Press, 1996).

Oyama v. California

332 U.S. 633 (1948)
Decided: January 19, 1948
Vote: 6 (Vinson, Black, Frankfurter, Douglas, Murphy, W. Rutledge)
3 (Reed, R. Jackson, Burton)
Opinion of the Court: Vinson
Concurring opinion: Black (Douglas)
Concurring opinion: Murphy (W. Rutledge)
Dissenting opinion: Reed (Burton)
Dissenting opinion: R. Jackson

The state of California attempted to seize property given to Fred Oyama, a citizen of the United States, by his father, a Japanese citizen living in California. The seizure was based on California's Alien Land Law, which forbade aliens ineligible for American citizenship to own, occupy, or lease property, or to take steps to evade or avoid the law. The state claimed that Fred's father, Kajiro Oyama, gave the land to his son to sidestep the law. The Oyamas said that the application of the law against them violated the Equal Protection Clause of the Fourteenth Amendment.

The Court agreed, finding that the California court's judgment against the Oyamas violated the Equal Protection Clause because the court had applied a heightened standard when defining "gift" to prove that the elder Oyama had attempted to violate the law. California law permits people to give gifts of property to their family members. Kajiro Oyama therefore had made a lawful gift to his son. Chief Justice Vinson ruled that when a state challenges the validity of a gift, courts should presume that the gift was made correctly unless it can be clearly proven otherwise. Here, the California court did not give the Oyamas the benefit of the doubt, but assumed that the gift was invalid because the donor was an alien. He was treated differently under the law because of his national origin.

Given that only the most exceptional circumstances justify discrimination based on citizenship or alienage, and that the cumulative effect of the California court's action in this case resulted in discrimination against the Oyamas, the Court found the decision against them invalid.

Bob-Lo Excursion Co. v. Michigan

333 U.S. 28 (1948)
Decided: February 2, 1948
Vote: 7 (Black, Reed, Frankfurter, Douglas, Murphy, W. Rutledge, Burton)
2 (Vinson, R. Jackson)
Opinion of the Court: W. Rutledge
Concurring opinion: Douglas (Black)
Dissenting opinion: R. Jackson (Vinson)

Bob-Lo owned steamships that carried passengers from Detroit to Bois-Blanc Island, an amusement park in Canada visited mostly by Michigan citizens. Bob-Lo prohibited African Americans from riding the ferry and thus from visiting Bois-Blanc Island. Sarah Elizabeth Ray, a high school student, attempted to ride the ferry with some of her classmates as part of a school trip. She was the only African American student in the class, and when the students boarded the ferry she was asked to leave. Ray filed charges, and a criminal prosecution was brought against Bob-Lo for violating Michigan's civil rights act.

A Michigan court found that Bo-Lo was a public conveyance within the meaning of the civil rights act and could therefore be prosecuted for discrimination. The Supreme Court agreed with this premise, but then had to decide whether the Commerce Clause of the Constitution allowed Michigan to apply this statute against Bob-Lo, which was clearly engaged in interstate commerce when ferrying people between the United States and Canada. Under the Court's previous rulings in ***Hall v. DeCuir,*** 95 U.S. 485 (1878), and ***Morgan v. Virginia,*** 328 U.S. 373 (1946), the Court should have upheld the company's claim that its interstate business was immune from state regulation.

The Court, however, held that Michigan could apply the statute against Bob-Lo without violating the Commerce Clause, saying that when a segment of foreign commerce has a special local interest apart from the necessity of federal regulation, the state may act. Bob-Lo ferried Michigan residents to Bois-Blanc and then back to Michigan. Applying the state's civil rights act violated no law or policy of Canada and did not encroach on a U.S. interest. Because Michigan had a strong interest in preventing discrimination on public conveyances within the state, the Court held that it could enforce the civil rights act against Bob-Lo.

The case is one of several in which the Court in the late 1940s began to take a stronger stance in favor of civil rights, cases that eventually led to the decision in ***Brown v. Board of Education,*** 347 U.S. 483 (1954).

See Herman Pritchett, *Civil Liberties and the Vinson Court* (Chicago: University of Chicago Press, 1954).

Woods v. Cloyd W. Miller Co.

333 U.S. 138 (1948)
Decided: February 16, 1948
Vote: 9 (Vinson, Black, Reed, Frankfurter, Douglas, Murphy, R. Jackson, W. Rutledge, Burton)
0
Opinion of the Court: Douglas
Concurring opinion: Frankfurter
Opinion concurring in judgment: R. Jackson

During World War II Congress passed a number of price control laws, including one that established a maximum rent that landlords could charge and making it a crime to charge more. Cloyd W. Miller Company felt that the law was unconstitutional because Congress's "war power" did not extend to domestic matters occurring after the termination of war, and it purposely raised its rents 40 percent to 60 percent to challenge the law. Tighe Woods, housing expediter for the federal government, immediately began proceedings to enjoin the violation.

The Court held that the war power provision of the Constitution sustained Congress's rent-control legislation. It explained that the war powers include power to remedy evils arising during the war but that they continue after the war is officially terminated. The Court relied on an almost identical precedent, ***Hamilton v. Kentucky Distilleries and Warehouse Co.,*** 251 U.S. 146 (1919), to explain that the war power does not end with the cessation of hostilities, and that Congress's war powers were bolstered by the Necessary and Proper Clause to extend beyond the simple confines of the hostilities themselves.

The Court admitted that such a broad reading of the war powers might encourage abuse by Congress, but said that it trusted Congress to curtail its power when necessary. Furthermore, the present case involved a valid exercise of war power, so the Court only had to address this issue and promised to address abuses if they occurred.

Illinois ex rel. McCollum v. Board of Education

333 U.S. 203 (1948)
Decided: March 8, 1948
Vote: 8 (Vinson, Black, Frankfurter, Douglas, Murphy, R. Jackson, W. Rutledge, Burton)
1 (Reed)
Opinion of the Court: Black
Concurring opinion: Frankfurter (R. Jackson, W. Rutledge, Burton)
Concurring opinion: R. Jackson
Dissenting opinion: Reed

The Champaign, Illinois, public school system had, like many across the country, put aside one hour a week when clergymen from various denominations could come into the schools and provide religious instruction to adherents of their sects. These instructors received no public funds, but were subject to approval by the school superintendent. Students whose parents did not request religious instruction went elsewhere in the building; those enrolled were required to attend the religious classes.

Vashti McCollum, resident and taxpayer of Champaign and parent of a child enrolled in the school system, petitioned to end this practice, arguing that it violated the First and Fourteenth Amendments. The denial of her petition was affirmed by the state supreme court.

Justice Black, by this time, was firmly committed to the absolutist position as outlined in Rutledge's dissent in ***Everson v. Board of Education,*** 330 U.S. 1 (1947). His opinion for the Court stated that the issue could not have been clearer: "Not only are the state's tax-supported public school buildings used for the dissemination of religious doctrines, the State also affords sectarian groups an invaluable aid in that it helps to provide pupils . . . through use of the state's compulsory public school machinery."

Although Black and Justice Frankfurter agreed that the released-time plan violated the First Amendment, Black was unwilling to overturn or abandon *Everson,* the opinion he had written barely a year earlier, while Frankfurter wanted the Court's decision to avoid any reliance on it. Black agreed to omit certain references to *Everson* that offended Justices Burton and Rutledge, and they signed on to his opinion. A furious Frankfurter decided that much as he preferred to remain silent on this issue and let others make his case, he had to write his own concurrence. He concluded his opinion with the forceful and unequivocal "separation means separation, not something less."

An important influence on Frankfurter's decision in *McCollum* was his view of the public school as an Americanizing and unifying force, a place where children from all backgrounds developed a common American outlook. He warned that religious education in the schools would destroy that "most powerful agency for promoting cohesion among a heterogeneous democratic people. The public school must keep scrupulously free from entanglement in the strife of sects."

McCollum stirred up a furor among religious groups, nearly all of whom operated some form of released-time program. Black somewhat laconically commented that "few opinions from this Court in recent years have attracted more attention or stirred wider debate." Enforcement of the opinion varied. In northern states where instruction actually took place in public school classrooms there seems to have been general compliance. But in most southern states and in areas where local school boards could differentiate between the Illinois model and theirs, religious instruction continued.

See Leonard W. Levy, *The Establishment Clause: Religion and the First Amendment* (New York: Macmillan, 1986); and Frank J. Sorauf, *The Wall of Separation: The Constitutional Politics of Church and State* (Princeton: Princeton University Press, 1976).

United States v. United States Gypsum Co.

333 U.S. 364 (1948)
Decided: March 8, 1948
Vote: 8 (Vinson, Black, Reed, Frankfurter, Douglas, Murphy, Rutledge, Burton)
0
Opinion of the Court: Reed
Concurring opinion: Frankfurter
Did not participate: R. Jackson

The United States instituted suit against United States Gypsum Company and five other gypsum companies, claiming that they conspired to violate the Sherman Antitrust Act by creating patents that resulted in price fixing and elimination of competition. A lower court found that if the patents were valid the United States had no claim, so the Justice Department amended its complaint to challenge the validity of the patents. Before trial United States Gypsum Company moved to dismiss the amended complaint, saying that the government had no right to relief under valid patents. The trial court agreed, the case was dismissed, and the United States appealed.

The Court held that the patent arrangement between the gypsum companies violated the Sherman Antitrust Act and that the patents were therefore invalid. The patents sought to eliminate competition by securing the right to all closed-sided gypsum board. This board was superior to open-sided board because it was stronger, cheaper to make, and did not break as easily. By creating agreements under which only United States Gypsum and five other companies could produce this board, these firms froze the market and created a situation in which they could set unfair prices.

The Court held that when otherwise valid patents are created for the purpose of violating antitrust laws, they are invalid because the result—monopoly—is illegal. Here the companies showed clear intent to monopolize and fix prices, and they could not hide behind patents to pursue their illegal purposes.

Shelley v. Kraemer

334 U.S. 1 (1948)
Decided: May 3, 1948
Vote: 6 (Vinson, Black, Frankfurter, Douglas, Murphy, Burton)
0
Opinion of the Court: Vinson
Did not participate: Reed, R. Jackson, W. Rutledge

The Court in ***Buchanan v. Warley,*** 245 U.S. 60 (1917), voided local residence ordinances enforcing racial segregation as a deprivation of property rights in violation of the Fourteenth Amendment. To circumvent this ruling, white property owners turned to restrictive covenants, which, as private agreements between buyers and sellers, presumably did not come within the reach of the Due Process or Equal Protection Clauses.

By the time a case reached the Court, the cold war had erupted, and at an NAACP lawyers conference on January 26, 1947, Francis Dent predicted that, given the current state of international relations, the Court "would be most loath to uphold and enforce restrictive covenants since it would be embarrassing to the American position in foreign policy in which we propose to be the leader of the democratic forces."

The Court determined that because state courts would be called upon to enforce the discriminatory intent of the covenants, the states were sanctioning racial discrimination in violation of the Fourteenth Amendment. The Court did not rule that covenants themselves were illegal because private discrimination remained constitutionally permissible. It did, however, make them unenforceable.

In a companion case, ***Hurd v. Hodge,*** 334 U.S. 24 (1948), the Court also voided enforcement of restrictive covenants in the District of Columbia. Although the Fourteenth Amendment did not apply to the national government, Chief Justice Vinson (for a 6–0 Court, Frankfurter concurring) held that such agreements violated the Civil Rights Act of 1866. Moreover, it was contrary to public policy to allow a federal court to enforce an agreement that was unenforceable in state courts.

The decision has been criticized for its allegedly fuzzy constitutional logic, and questions have been raised about whether the Court took the doctrine of state action further than it should have. Courts normally do not look into the nature of private contracts, and, even though the contracts discriminated against African Americans, the state itself did no more than neutrally enforce private agreements. Nevertheless, by expanding the notion of state action to permit enforcement of a private contract by state courts, the decision significantly expanded the meaning of state action.

Under Chief Justice Warren, the Court used the *Shelley* opinion, with its nexus of state action, to strike down any form of segregation that had even a remote connection to state government. The state action doctrine proved a potent tool against discrimination and put teeth into the Fourteenth Amendment's Equal Protection Clause.

See Mark V. Tushnet, "*Shelley v. Kraemer* and Theories of Equality," *New York Law School Review* 33 (1988): 383; and Clement Vose, *Caucasians Only: The Supreme Court, the NAACP, and the Restrictive Covenant Cases* (Berkeley: University of California Press, 1959).

Hurd v. Hodge

334 U.S. 24 (1948)
Decided: May 3, 1948
Vote: 6 (Vinson, Black, Frankfurter, Douglas, Murphy, Burton)
0
Opinion of the Court: Vinson
Concurring opinion: Frankfurter
Did not participate: Reed, R. Jackson, W. Rutledge

Decided along with ***Shelley v. Kraemer,*** 334 U.S. 1 (1948), which invalidated the enforcement of restrictive covenants in state courts, *Hurd* concerned the District of Columbia. A block of twenty lots in a Washington, D.C., neighborhood carried a restrictive covenant that prohibited their sale to blacks. When Raphael Urciolo sold seven of the lots to blacks, Frederic Hodge, along with other white citizens of the neighborhood, filed suit in D.C. District Court against James Hurd and the other black property owners, asking the court to revoke the purchasers' titles to the property. The district court entered judgment against Hurd and the others, declaring their deeds null and void and enjoining Urciolo from selling property to African Americans. Hurd appealed, claiming that enforcement of the covenant by a court violated the Fifth and Fourteenth Amendments, which prohibit federal and state governments from discriminating against people because of their race.

The Supreme Court acknowledged the validity of Hurd's argument, citing *Shelley,* which had just been announced, to say that judicial enforcement of discriminatory covenants constituted discriminatory government action. However, unlike *Shelley,* which rested on Fourteenth Amendment constitutional grounds and applied to state action, the Court found that it could reach the same result based on the federal Civil Rights Act of 1866. That act required that all citizens of the United States have the same right to inherit, purchase, lease, and hold real and personal property. In order for a black person to have the same rights as a white person, courts cannot enforce discrimination via restrictive covenants.

Under the Civil Rights Act, the Court found the district court decision invalid, and reinstated the title to Hurd's property. Justice Frankfurter argued that sound judicial discretion required the denial of relief in a federal court where the granting of like relief in state courts would violate the Fourteenth Amendment. Using either rationale, however, the Court made restrictive covenants based on race or religion ineffective and continued on its road to roll back the segregation established after the Court's decision in ***Plessy v. Ferguson,*** 163 U.S. 537 (1896).

See Clement Vose, *Caucasians Only: The Supreme Court, the NAACP, and the Restrictive Covenant Cases* (Berkeley: University of California Press, 1959).

Takahashi v. Fish and Game Commission

334 U.S. 410 (1948)
Decided: June 7, 1948
Vote: 7 (Vinson, Black, Frankfurter, Douglas, Murphy, W. Rutledge, Burton)
2 (Reed, R. Jackson)
Opinion of the Court: Black
Concurring opinion: Murphy (W. Rutledge)
Dissenting opinion: Reed (R. Jackson)

During World War II California enacted a law that "persons ineligible for citizenship" in the United States could not obtain commercial fishing licenses in the state. At the time, Japanese aliens, even if admitted to residence in the country, remained ineligible for citizenship. Torao Takahashi, a Japanese alien, had been a commercial fisherman before the war. When he returned to California after his wartime internment, the state refused to renew his fishing license because of the new law. Takahashi filed suit, claiming violation of the Equal Protection Clause.

The Court invalidated the California law because it deprived people who were granted admission to the United States by the federal government a chance to earn a livelihood once here. Although California claimed "special circumstances" to justify this discrimination, the Court found no such circumstances present.

Only the federal government has the power to grant immigrants admission to the United States and to determine their status. At the time, the U.S. government had chosen to admit Japanese immigrants into the country but made them ineligible for citizenship. If California were allowed to exploit that distinction by denying noncitizens an opportunity to work, it would counteract federal immigration policy by discouraging otherwise eligible immigrants from coming to the United States. The Court held that California could not encroach federal power in this manner. Furthermore, the Equal Protection Clause prohibited curtailment of work opportunities for some people and not others absent special circumstances. The Court found that California's desire to ensure fish conservation and adequate fishing opportunities for state citizens were not special circumstances to justify discrimination, and that the law was therefore invalid.

Saia v. New York

334 U.S. 558 (1948)
Decided: June 7, 1948
Vote: 5 (Vinson, Black, Douglas, Murphy, W. Rutledge)
4 (Reed, Frankfurter, R. Jackson, Burton)
Opinion of the Court: Douglas
Dissenting opinion: Frankfurter (Reed, Burton)
Dissenting opinion: R. Jackson

Samuel Saia, a Jehovah's Witness minister, was convicted in police court for violating a Lockport, New York, city ordinance making it a crime to use sound equipment to project a message on city streets without obtaining permission from the police chief. Saia got permission the first time he made his speeches, but when his permit expired the chief of police refused to renew it because residents had complained that the broadcasts were too loud. Saia continued to use his equipment on four occasions and was arrested. At his trial many people testified that the volume of his speaking was annoying, saying nothing about the content of his speech, and he was convicted.

Despite the neutral appearance of the statute, the Court found it unconstitutional on its face because it imposed prior restraint on free speech. The Court noted that the statute did not specify what volume of speech violated the law; rather, it left the restraint of speech to the discretion of the police chief. The Court feared that the police chief could thwart speech he found offensive and still be within the boundaries of the ordinance, thereby using the statute as a "dangerous weapon" against free communication. Because it granted unbridled discretion to enforce prior restraints, the law violated the First Amendment despite its appearance as a neutral time, place, and manner restriction.

See Shawn Francis Peters, *Judging Jehovah's Witnesses* (Lawrence: University Press of Kansas, 2000).

Goesaert v. Cleary

335 U.S. 464 (1948)
Decided: December 20, 1948
Vote: 6 (Vinson, Black, Reed, Frankfurter, R. Jackson, Burton)
3 (Douglas, Murphy, W. Rutledge)
Opinion of the Court: Frankfurter
Dissenting opinion: Rutledge (Douglas, Murphy)

The Goesaerts—a mother who owned a bar and her daughter who worked as a barmaid—challenged a Michigan law that prohibited women from working as barmaids, unless their husbands or fathers owned the bar.

The Court held that, without question, Michigan had the power to exclude all women from tending bars. Although the social position of women had improved since the law was written, Justice Frankfurter could still perceive social and moral problems raised by allowing women to work as bartenders, although he gave no indication of what these problems might be.

The only question, according to Frankfurter, was whether distinguishing between women whose husbands or fathers owned bars, and other women, violated the Equal Protection Clause of the Constitution. The Court held that the line drawn between these two groups was reasonable because the problems posed by women bartenders could be mitigated by allowing them to work only under the watchful eye of a male relative. Because Michigan believed that the presence of a father or husband "minimized the hazards" of allowing women to tend bar, the distinction was justifiable, and the law was upheld as posing no equal protection problem.

Justice Rutledge took the view that the statute arbitrarily discriminated between male and female owners of liquor establishments in that, under its provisions, a male owner might employ his wife or daughter as a barmaid, but a female owner could not employ her daughter nor work as a barmaid herself, issues completely ignored in the majority opinion.

See Carol H. Lefcourt, ed., *Women and the Law* (New York: Boardman, 1984).

Kovacs v. Cooper

336 U.S. 77 (1949)
Decided: January 31, 1949
Vote: 5 (Vinson, Reed, Frankfurter, R. Jackson, Burton)
4 (Black, Douglas, Murphy, W. Rutledge)
Judgment of the Court: Reed
Opinion concurring in judgment: Frankfurter
Opinion concurring in judgment: R. Jackson
Dissenting opinion: Black (Douglas, W. Rutledge)
Dissenting opinion: W. Rutledge
Dissenting without opinion: Murphy

Charles Kovacs was caught using a sound amplifying device mounted on the back of a truck to disseminate a message about labor unions. The statute under which he was convicted made it a crime to use such a device to make a "loud and raucous" noise. Albert Cooper Jr. was the Trenton, New Jersey, police court judge who first convicted Kovacs. Kovacs appealed his conviction to the state supreme court and then to the U.S. Supreme Court, claiming that the ordinance violated the First Amendment of the Constitution by being too vague and by limiting his right to free speech.

Although it would seem that just seven months after the decision in ***Saia v. New York,*** 334 U.S. 558 (1948), the Court would strike down the local ordinance, it did not. Kovacs argued that the statute was so vague that an ordinary person could not know what was forbidden and would have to suppress all speech to comply with the statute. Justice Reed explained that the ordinance gave a "sufficiently accurate concept of what is forbidden," that the forbidden conduct was content neutral, and therefore it was not protected by the First Amendment. The Court also noted that the ordinance applied only to "loud and raucous" noises that unnecessarily interrupted downtown businesses and communities.

Kovacs maintained that he had the right to express himself with the amplifiers despite their disruptive nature, but the Court said that First Amendment rights can be curtailed when municipalities have other interests to protect. Here, it was within the police powers of the city to prevent the disruptive noise prohibited by the statute. Such prohibition does not violate the First Amendment because the well-being and tranquility of the community necessitated such time, place, and manner restrictions.

Justice Black agreed that the government could limit sound volume and impose other time, place, and manner regulations, but could not ban any form of speech altogether. Sound trucks, he noted, were the poor man's press, and barring them gave people with more money and other outlets a greater say in public debates.

Giboney v. Empire Storage and Ice Co.

336 U.S. 490 (1949)
Decided: April 4, 1948
Vote: 9 (Vinson, Black, Reed, Frankfurter, Douglas, Murphy, R. Jackson, W. Rutledge, Burton)
0
Opinion of the Court: Black

Members of the Ice and Coal Drivers and Handlers Local Union began a membership drive to persuade retail ice peddlers to join the union. When many nonunion peddlers refused to join, the union asked all wholesale ice distributors to sell only to union peddlers. Empire Storage and Ice Company refused to limit its sales to union peddlers, and the union put up picket line at Empire in an effort to force its compliance. Union drivers were prohibited from breaking the picket line to obtain ice from Empire, leaving the company with a greatly reduced client base (85 percent of drivers were in the union). Empire sought an injunction to stop the picketing, claiming that the union's activities violated the state's statute prohibiting restraint of trade. The union claimed a right to picket as part of its First Amendment protection, saying any harm inflicted on Empire was an incidental result of the exercise of a protected fundamental right.

The Court held that Missouri's law against restraint of trade was a proper exercise of its police powers and that the First Amendment did not protect union members from prosecution under a valid criminal statute. Missouri had a substantial interest in preventing restraints on trade. Although the union's picketing had a speech element, its main purpose was not to peacefully disseminate information about the dispute, but to prevent Empire from selling ice. The Court held that conduct remained criminal even if a form of speech had been used to promote it. The union's activities violated a valid state law, and could not be protected by the First Amendment.

See Harry A. Millis and Emily Clark Brown, *From the Wagner Act to Taft-Hartley* (Chicago: University of Chicago Press, 1950).

H. P. Hood and Sons v. Du Mond

336 U.S. 525 (1949)
Decided: April 4, 1949
Vote: 5 (Vinson, Reed, Douglas, R. Jackson, Burton)
4 (Black, Frankfurter, Murphy, W. Rutledge)
Opinion of the Court: R. Jackson
Dissenting opinion: Black (Murphy)
Dissenting opinion: Frankfurter (W. Rutledge)

H. P. Hood and Sons operated milk plants in New York State and shipped much of its product to Massachusetts. When it petitioned a New York agency for license to open a fourth milk plant in New York, its application was denied by an administrative agency headed by C. Chester Du Mond. He justified his decision by saying that local economic interests required the prevention of new facilities designed to serve an interstate rather than a local market. H. P. Hood protested the decision, saying that the New York agency violated the Commerce Clause by making regulations that infringed on freedom of interstate commerce.

The Court held that the state could not limit the creation of local facilities serving interstate markets for reasons solely linked to protection of the local economy. Although states have some power to regulate commerce when a unique health or safety interest is at stake, that interest must not be linked to the promotion of economic advantage. The Commerce Clause of the Constitution vested commercial power in the federal Congress to prevent state laws that are "hostile in conception as well as burdensome in result." Under federal law, every farmer and craftsman should have equal access to the national market.

The state contended that its regulations complemented federal regulations related to milk pricing and equalization of market profit, but the Court rejected this argument. Justice Jackson said that the federal act was passed to prevent disruption of the national milk market and that the New York law achieved the opposite goal by making rules that treated New York milk producers differently from other producers. Because the goal of federal control is to unify, individual state laws undermine that purpose.

Terminiello v. Chicago

337 U.S. 1 (1949)
Decided: May 16, 1949
Vote: 5 (Black, Reed, Douglas, Murphy, W. Rutledge)
4 (Vinson, Frankfurter, R. Jackson, Burton)
Opinion of the Court: Douglas
Dissenting opinion: Vinson
Dissenting opinion: Frankfurter (R. Jackson, Burton)
Dissenting opinion: R. Jackson (Burton)

Arthur Terminiello, a defrocked priest, specialized in attacking Jews and the Roosevelt administration, and he went after both before eight hundred sympathizers in a Chicago auditorium in 1946. Outside, more than a thousand protesters rioted, throwing rocks and stink bombs through the windows, and police had all they could do to prevent the mob from storming the hall. After managing to escort Terminiello and his party safely out of the building, the police arrested him on a disorderly conduct charge under an ordinance prohibiting "making any improper noise, riot, disturbance, breach of the peace, or diversion tending to a breach of the peace." The state supreme court affirmed his conviction.

The case seemed custom-made for the Court to reexamine the question of whether "fighting words," those that by their very offensiveness tended to disrupt the social order, qualified for protection under the First Amendment. The Court, however, ducked the constitutional issue and voided the conviction on an allegedly improper charge by the judge, even though Terminiello's attorneys had never raised this issue.

Justice Jackson's dissent described the inflammatory situation and noted that the episode bore a startling resemblance to the prewar struggle between totalitarian groups for what Hitler had called "the conquest of the streets . . . [as the] key to power in the state." The memories of the Nazi atrocities he had prosecuted so recently at Nuremburg still fresh in his mind, Jackson compared the rioting that Terminiello had incited to the street battles between fascists and communists that preceded Hitler's grab for power. Jackson asked whether Terminiello's anti-Semitic diatribe constituted the free discussion, the tool of democracy, that the First Amendment had been designed to protect. He doubted it and believed that Terminiello's speech had created the clear-and-present danger of a riot that the state had the right and the obligation to prevent.

Although Douglas's opinion received wide notice in the press as proof of the high level of tolerance in America, the Court provided no guidelines for itself or for lower courts by which to decide future cases of a similar nature. It remains a classic example of the difficulties involved when courts try to apply the abstract principles of free speech to situations in which a speaker with unpopular views may inflame an unfriendly or even hostile audience.

See C. Herman Pritchett, *Civil Liberties and the Vinson Court* (Chicago: University of Chicago Press, 1954); and Harry Kalven Jr., *A Worthy Tradition: Freedom of Speech in America* (New York: Harper and Row, 1988).

Williams v. New York

337 U.S. 241 (1949)
Decided: June 6, 1949
Vote: 7 (Vinson, Black, Reed, Frankfurter, Douglas, R. Jackson, Burton)
2 (Murphy, W. Rutledge)
Opinion of the Court: Black
Dissenting opinion: Murphy
Dissenting without opinion: W. Rutledge

Samuel Williams was convicted of murder in the first degree by a New York jury. The jury recommended life imprisonment based on the evidence presented at trial. The judge, however, sentenced Williams to death, relying on information from the pretrial record and from Williams's criminal record to conclude that he posed a menace to society and should be executed. Williams appealed, saying that the judge's use of out-of-court evidence violated his right to confront the witnesses against him.

The Court found that allowing a judge to rely on outside information at the sentencing phase of a trial posed no constitutional problems, citing history and legal analysis to support this conclusion. The Court noted that English and American courts traditionally gave sentencing judges wide discretion when deciding what types of evidence to consider at sentencing.

The Court explained that, legally, the use of evidence at the trial and sentencing phases served different purposes. The rules of evidence at trial were necessarily strict to ensure a fair trial that avoided wasting time on irrelevant issues. Once the defendant had been found guilty, however, the judge was not confined to the narrow issue of guilt, but had to consider what sentence best matched the crime and the criminal. This process required a wide range of information, some of which would have been irrelevant at trial. The criminal need not "confront" the evidence on this issue because it is unrelated to guilt.

The Court commended the trend in American law to tailor sentencing to individual crimes. Given this interest, the Court supported the use of nontrial evidence to achieve the goal.

Wolf v. Colorado

338 U.S. 25 (1949)
Decided: June 27, 1949
Vote: 6 (Vinson, Black, Reed, Frankfurter, R. Jackson, Burton)
3 (Douglas, Murphy, W. Rutledge)
Opinion of the Court: Frankfurter
Concurring opinion: Black
Dissenting opinion: Douglas
Dissenting opinion: Murphy (W. Rutledge)
Dissenting opinion: W. Rutledge (Murphy)

The Court had begun to hold federal agents to a strict accountability under the Fourth Amendment when it imposed the exclusionary rule in ***Weeks v. United States,*** 232 U.S. 383 (1914). The exclusionary rule prohibited the use of evidence seized illegally, thus providing a simple preventative standard. As a result, the government, especially the Federal Bureau of Investigation, trained its officers in proper constitutional procedures.

The Fourth Amendment, however, does not mention an exclusionary rule. In fact, it makes no mention of the means by which to enforce its ban against unreasonable searches and seizures. Justice Day, the author of the *Weeks* opinion, explicitly noted that the exclusionary rule applied only to federal agents, not to state or local police. In the thirty years that followed, not only did officials in some states ignore the warrant clause, but also an active collusion developed between state and federal officials under the so-called "silver platter doctrine," by which state officials secured information in ways forbidden to federal agents, but which they could use once they received it.

Dr. Julius Wolf was convicted twice for conspiring to perform abortions. The indictment was based partly on the list of patients contained in his appointment books, which police seized during a warrantless arrest. Justice Frankfurter, implicitly applying the selective incorporation standard, incorporated part of the Fourth Amendment and applied it to the states through the Fourteenth Amendment. Frankfurter declared that unreasonable searches and seizures on the part of state officials ran afoul of the Constitution because such searches violated the test for due process.

But if the core of the Fourth Amendment's search-and-seizure policy now applied to the states, that did not mean that the methods used to enforce that right also applied. The exclusionary rule, effective as it might be, remained judge-made law and not part of the Fourth Amendment. States, therefore, could develop their own minimal standards. They could ignore the Fourth Amendment, even though it now "applied" to them, provided they did not act so unreasonably as to shock the conscience.

Justice Douglas, in his dissent, argued that even without judicial articulation of the exclusionary rule, it existed implicitly in the Fourth Amendment by a simple common sense reading: if the amendment protected against search and seizure without an appropriate warrant, then it could only do so by making any evidence seized—even incontestably reliable evidence—inadmissible.

Justice Murphy, in his dissent, wrote that the "conclusion is inescapable that but one remedy exists to deter violations of the search and seizure clause. That is the rule which excludes illegally obtained evidence." The exclusionary rule served primarily as a prophylactic caution to the police, namely, obey the rules or you cannot use what you find.

The voice of the dissenters eventually prevailed, and the Court explicitly overruled *Wolf* in ***Mapp v. Ohio,*** 367 U.S. 643 (1961).

See Francis A. Allen, "The Wolf Case: Search and Seizure, Federalism, and Civil Liberties," *Illinois Law Review* 45 (1950): 11; and Jacob W. Landynski, *Search and Seizure and the Supreme Court: A Study in Constitutional Interpretation* (Baltimore: Johns Hopkins University Press, 1966).

Brinegar v. United States

338 U.S. 160 (1949)
Decided: June 27, 1949
Vote: 6 (Vinson, Black, Reed, Douglas, W. Rutledge, Burton)
3 (Frankfurter, Murphy, R. Jackson)
Opinion of the Court: W. Rutledge
Concurring opinion: Burton
Dissenting opinion: R. Jackson (Frankfurter, Murphy)

Virgil Brinegar was convicted of importing liquor into Oklahoma in violation of a federal statute that forbade importation of alcoholic beverages into dry states. The prosecution relied on evidence from a search of Brinegar's car that revealed twelve cases of liquor. Brinegar challenged the legality of this search, saying that the police did not have probable cause. The police, however, contended that probable cause stemmed from the facts that Brinegar's car appeared to be "weighted down with something" when the police pulled him over, and that the police knew he had smuggled liquor into Oklahoma before.

In ***Carroll v. United States,*** 267 U.S. 132 (1925), officers searched a car carrying liquor between Detroit and Canada after the driver attempted to sell liquor to undercover police. Here, the Court held that the police did not need a warrant to search the car because they had probable cause to do so. Brinegar challenged the application of *Carroll* in his situation, however, because the police search was based only on circumstantial evidence and on a hearsay comment from another police officer indicating that Brinegar was involved in bootlegging. The Court found this evidence sufficient for a search, explaining that probable cause did not require the same level of proof as the "beyond a reasonable doubt" standard applied to criminal convictions and could therefore be based on evidence inadmissible in court. In this case, the police observed something suspicious about the car, and they had a tip that Brinegar imported liquor. The Court found this sufficient, noting the importance of allowing the police to search suspicious vehicles in order to maintain public safety.

Hirota v. MacArthur

338 U.S. 197 (1948)
Decided: December 20, 1948
Vote: 6 (Vinson, Black, Reed, Frankfurter, Douglas, Burton)
1 (Murphy)
Opinion: *Per curiam*
Opinion concurring in judgment: Douglas
Dissenting without opinion: Murphy
Reserved the right to decide: W. Rutledge
Did not participate: R. Jackson

The Court held that it had no power or authority to review, affirm, set aside, or annul the judgments imposed on Japanese citizens tried by the International Military Tribunal of the Far East. Koki Hirota and other petitioners were high officials of the Japanese government during World War II. They were found guilty of war crimes by the tribunal and confined under the custody of Gen. Douglas MacArthur. They filed for writs of habeas corpus directly with the Court.

The Court held that because the sentencing tribunal was not a court of the United States, but of the allied powers who currently occupied and controlled Japan, the Court had no power of review over the tribunal, and could not entertain writs stemming from its adjudications.

Justice Douglas agreed with the decision but disagreed with the logic behind it. For Douglas the matter turned on whether the tribunal was a judicial court or a political entity set up by the allies to achieve various political goals. He found the tribunal to be a political entity, taking its power not from international law but from the political goals and decisions of the allied powers. As such, the court had no jurisdiction because the tribunal was an exercise in politics, not law.

See Richard H. Minear, *Victor's Justice: The Tokyo War Crimes Trial* (Princeton: Princeton University Press, 1971).

1950–1959

Wong Yang Sung v. McGrath

339 U.S. 33 (1950)
Decided: February 20, 1950
Vote: 6 (Vinson, Black, Frankfurter, R. Jackson, Burton, Minton)
1 (Reed)
Opinion of the Court: R. Jackson
Dissenting opinion: Reed
Did not participate: Douglas, Clark

Wong Yang Sung was arrested by immigration officials for overstaying his shore leave and for being in the United States unlawfully. He was tried before an inspector of the Immigration and Naturalization Services (INS), who recommended deportation. Sung sought release from custody by filing a writ of habeas corpus in which he claimed that the hearing decision was invalid because it had not been conducted according to the rules of the Administrative Procedure Act (APA).

The Court agreed that deportation hearings must be conducted in accordance with the APA and ordered Sung's release from custody. Justice Jackson explained that exempting an agency from the rules of the APA, as the INS had urged, would defeat the statute's purpose of reforming the federal administrative system. One of the primary purposes of the APA was to ensure that all administrative hearings would be conducted in front of a neutral decider who would preserve agency impartiality throughout the hearing. The INS had tried Sung before a hearing officer who also served several prosecutorial functions in the agency and could have brought further charges against Sung while serving as the judge in his case. The APA was passed to avoid such unfair practices, and the Court found the agency's conduct "a perfect exemplification of the practices so unanimously condemned" by the passage of the APA.

The INS also argued that following the APA burdened the agency, but the Court said the need for reform far outweighed any burden. As for the government's argument that the APA applied only when Congress enforced it by statute, the Court held that when hearings are required to meet the due process requirements of the Constitution, they are governed by the APA regardless of statutory language.

United States v. Rabinowitz

339 U.S. 56 (1950)
Decided: February 20, 1950
Vote: 5 (Vinson, Reed, Burton, Clark, Minton)
3 (Black, Frankfurter, R. Jackson)
Opinion of the Court: Minton
Dissenting opinion: Black
Dissenting opinion: Frankfurter (R. Jackson)
Did not participate: Douglas

Government agents obtained a valid arrest warrant for Albert Rabinowitz on charges of selling forged stamps. During the arrest, the agents searched the filing cabinets and drawers of the office where Rabinowitz was taken into custody and found more than five hundred forged stamps. Rabinowitz was also charged with possessing forged stamps with intent to defraud. To defend himself against this additional charge, Rabinowitz moved to suppress the contents of the search because it had been conducted without a valid search warrant. The trial court denied his motion, and he was convicted of both charges. An appeals court, however, overturned his conviction as having been based on evidence obtained without a warrant. The United States appealed.

The Court held that a warrant is not required for searches taking place incident to an arrest and that a search of the office in which Rabinowitz was arrested was valid under the Fourth Amendment. Historically, Justice Minton explained, the American legal system had always allowed police to search a person during arrest. The Court had expanded this rule in other decisions to say that a search of a person included other proofs of guilt within the immediate control of the accused upon his arrest. Here, police searched the office where Rabinowitz was arrested. Such a search was not unreasonable because the police had probable cause to believe that Rabinowitz, who was being arrested for stamp fraud, had other illegal stamps within his immediate vicinity.

Although the officers could have obtained a search warrant in this situation, the Court held that they were not required to do so. The Fourth Amendment protects against unreasonable searches, and, although warranted searches may be preferable, reasonable searches are also permissible even without a warrant under the language of the Constitution.

See Jacob W. Landynski, *Search and Seizure and the Supreme Court* (Baltimore: Johns Hopkins University Press, 1966).

American Communications Association v. Douds

339 U.S. 382 (1950)
Decided: May 8, 1950
Vote: 5 (Vinson, Reed, Frankfurter, R. Jackson, Burton)
1 (Black)
Opinion of the Court: Vinson
Opinion concurring in part: Frankfurter
Opinion concurring in part, dissenting in part: R. Jackson
Dissenting opinion: Black
Did not participate: Douglas, Clark, Minton

The Court's record in reviewing the loyalty cases that came before it during the McCarthy era shows that the judiciary, like the other branches of government, was caught up in the anti-communist fever of the times. In 1950 the Court upheld section 9(h) of the Taft-Hartley Act, denying access to the National Labor Relations Board to unions whose officers had refused to swear they were not communists. Chief Justice Vinson admitted that the statute discouraged the lawful exercise of political freedom by requiring oaths related to individual political beliefs. This abridgement of free speech, however, had to be weighed against the government's power to regulate commerce, and, by using the Commerce Clause, the Court managed to evade the First Amendment issues.

Justices Frankfurter and Jackson concurred in the result but objected to imposing a test on beliefs. Jackson in particular, while laying out the dangers of communism, argued that Congress had no power to proscribe opinions that had not led to overt acts. In words that the majority should have recalled in later Red Scare cases—see especially ***Dennis v. United States,*** 341 U.S. 494 (1951), and ***Adler v. Board of Education,*** 342 U.S. 485 (1952)—Jackson wrote, "Under our system, it is time enough for the law to lay hold of the citizen when he acts illegally, or in some rare circumstances where his thoughts are given illegal utterance. I think we must let his mind alone."

For Justice Black this infringement upon personal beliefs went beyond constitutional bounds, and he would have held section 9(h) void. The Commerce Clause, he concluded, does "not restrict the right to think."

The problem with Vinson's opinion, according to Black, Frankfurter, and Jackson, lay not in his argument that rights could sometimes be abridged in return for government benefits, because he recognized that in some circumstances the condition might be a denial of the right itself. Rather, the problem was that Vinson totally disregarded the First Amendment issues raised by the other members of the Court. The opinion also ignored the overly broad sweep of the Taft-Hartley provision. Section 9(h) could disqualify unions whose officers were Communist Party members regardless of whether they shared all of the party's goals or were merely intellectual adherents of socialism. That Vinson wanted to balance national security interests against free expression is not unusual, but by relying on the commerce power he tipped the scales far more than if he had used a free speech analysis.

Within a short time, the fruits of *Douds* could be seen in a number of cases in which the Court upheld measures designed to keep alleged subversives from engaging in a variety of activities. Examples include *Gerende v. Board of Supervisors,* 341 U.S. 56 (1951), which dealt with running for public office; *Garner v. Board of Public Works,* 341 U.S. 716 (1951), (municipal employment); and *Adler* (teaching in the public schools). In 1952 the Court even held in *Harisiades v. Shaughnessy,* 342 U.S. 580, that a longtime resident alien could be deported for once holding membership in the Communist Party. It looked for a while as if a majority of the Court would validate any measure in the name of national security, but, with the arrival of Chief Justice Warren and Justices Brennan and Harlan in the mid-1950s, the balance on the Court began to swing to a more speech-protective stance. See, for example, ***Yates v. United States,*** 354 U.S. 298 (1957).

See Michal R. Belknap, *Cold War Political Justice* (Westport, Conn.: Greenwood Press, 1977); and David Caute, *The Great Fear: The Anti-Communist Purges under Truman and Eisenhower* (New York: Simon and Schuster, 1978).

Sweatt v. Painter

339 U.S. 629 (1950)
Decided: June 5, 1950
Vote: 9 (Vinson, Black, Reed, Frankfurter, Douglas, R. Jackson, Burton, Clark, Minton)
0
Opinion of the Court: Vinson

Heman Marion Sweatt, a black mailman, sought admission to the University of Texas Law School. He had first applied for admission in 1946, and a trial court in Travis County gave the state six months to establish a law school at the all-black Prairie View University. Prairie View represented all that was wrong with segregated higher education; it had a ramshackle physical plant and gave college credit for broom-making and other vocational skills. If the state did not establish a law school, Sweatt would have to be admitted to the University of Texas in Austin.

Homer Rainey, the president of the University of Texas, believed that segregation should end, and his remarks about providing better educational opportunities for blacks so displeased the trustees that they replaced him with an arch-segregationist, Theophilus Schickel Painter. Texas was fighting integration on many fronts, even to the point of appropriating $3 million to create a new Texas State University for Negroes, of which $100,000 was to be used to establish and maintain a law school. In the meantime, the state abandoned the Prairie View travesty and, as an interim solution, opened a law school in downtown Austin, just blocks away from the state capitol and the

University of Texas. The school consisted of three small rooms in a basement, three part-time faculty members, who were first-year instructors across town at the regular law school, a library of ten thousand volumes and access to the state law library in the capitol. It would open on March 10, 1947, if Sweatt chose to attend. He did not and instead went back to court. In a move no one had anticipated, the Justice Department filed an *amicus* brief that bluntly urged the Court to abandon ***Plessy v. Ferguson,*** 163 U.S. 537 (1896).

Chief Justice Vinson, at Justice Frankfurter's urging, drafted narrow opinions both in this case and in the companion case of ***McLaurin v. Oklahoma State Regents for Higher Education,*** 339 U.S. 637 (1950). Vinson was able to attain unanimity in both cases. The state contended that it had in fact created an equal law school and just because Sweatt chose not to attend did not mean he should be admitted to the University of Texas. But if nothing else, the justices knew what made a good law school, and they rejected the claim that this separate law school was equal to that at Austin. The Court ordered Sweatt admitted to the University of Texas Law School, the first time it ever ordered a black student admitted to a previously all-white institution.

Some southern states responded positively to the *Sweatt* decision. South Carolina, for example, had previously established a black law school at South Carolina State College, but after *Sweatt,* the state closed it down and gradually began to accept blacks into the previously all-white University of South Carolina Law School.

See Mark V. Tushnet, *The NAACP's Strategy Against Segregated Education, 1925–1950* (Chapel Hill: University of North Carolina Press, 1987); and Richard Kluger, *Simple Justice* (New York: Knopf, 1976).

McLaurin v. Oklahoma State Regents for Higher Education

339 U.S. 637 (1950)
Decided: June 5, 1950
Vote: 9 (Vinson, Black, Reed, Frankfurter, Douglas, R. Jackson, Burton, Clark, Minton)
0
Opinion of the Court: Vinson

George W. McLaurin, a sixty-eight-year-old black man, sought admission to Oklahoma State University to pursue a doctoral degree in education. The university denied his application, but a district court forced Oklahoma State to admit him. Complying with the court order, the school noted that McLaurin's admission would be subject to "such rules and regulations as to segregation as the President of the University shall consider to afford McLaurin substantially equal educational opportunities." The president interpreted these conditions to allow the university to subject McLaurin to various forms of discrimination. During class McLaurin was required to sit at designated tables in the anteroom of the classroom. He also had a designated desk at the library and was allowed to use the school cafeteria only when other students were not present. To remove these conditions, McLaurin filed a motion to modify the original court order admitting him to the school.

The Court held that the conditions imposed on McLaurin were unlawful because they made it more difficult for him to pursue his graduate studies. They impaired his ability to work efficiently, to engage in discussions and exchange views with other students, and to learn his profession. The Court noted that a person with a doctorate in education will have an opportunity to affect many people around him, who will in turn be influenced by the education he received. For these reasons, it was imperative that the state allow McLaurin to learn equally with the other members of his class.

The Court acknowledged that in some ways it would appear that McLaurin was allowed to receive the same education as his classmates, just in a different manner. But his admission to a state-supported institution precluded the school from treating him differently. This case, decided the same day as the Texas law school opinion, ***Sweatt v. Painter,*** 339 U.S. 629 (1950), gave the National Association for the Advancement of Colored People (NAACP), which represented McLaurin, its first indication that the Court might now be willing to hear a case attacking head-on the notion of separate but equal.

See Mark V. Tushnet, *The NAACP's Strategy Against Segregated Education, 1925–1950* (Chapel Hill: University of North Carolina Press, 1987).

Henderson v. United States

339 U.S. 816 (1950)
Decided: June 5, 1950
Vote: 8 (Vinson, Black, Reed, Frankfurter, Douglas, R. Jackson, Burton, Minton)
0
Opinion of the Court: Burton
Did not participate: Clark

Elmer Henderson was a passenger on a Southern Railway Company train. The railroad had a policy that African Americans could dine at only one table in the dining car and that a curtain had to be pulled to shield that table from the rest of the room. If white diners were already occupying the table, blacks had to wait, even if there were empty seats at the table. Henderson was refused a seat in the dining car when the table reserved for blacks was given to white people, even though the table still had a place available. A porter told him that he would be informed when the table became available, but he never was, and Henderson had no opportunity to dine. He brought suit under the Interstate Commerce Act, which made it unlawful for a railroad to subject a person to an "unreasonable prejudice or disadvantage."

The issue before the Court was whether Southern Railway's discriminatory policy posed an unreasonable disadvantage to African Americans. The Court held that it did and that

Henderson was entitled to relief. Justice Burton explained the two problems with the Southern Railway policy. First, the curtain used to separate black and white passengers was an artificial classification that served only to draw attention to racial differences. Second, the policy resulted in inability to obtain services. While white passengers could always dine in the car, either at the white seats or at the seats reserved for black passengers, blacks could dine only if the one table was available. This denial of equal opportunity posed an unreasonable disadvantage under the statute, and the Court found it sufficient to sustain a claim against Southern Railway.

See Catherine A. Barnes, *The Desegregation of Southern Transit* (New York: Columbia University Press, 1983).

Niemotko v. Maryland

340 U.S. 268 (1951)
Decided: January 15, 1951
Vote: 9 (Vinson, Black, Reed, Frankfurter, Douglas, R. Burton, Clark, Minton)
0
Opinion of the Court: Vinson
Concurring in judgment without opinion: Black
Opinion concurring in judgment: Frankfurter

A group of Jehovah's Witnesses wanted to give Bible talks in a public park in Maryland. No ordinance regulated the uses of the park, but citizens generally petitioned for permission from the town's park commission before engaging in public demonstrations. The park commission refused the Witnesses' petition. The group appealed to the city council, which also denied the request. On the first Sunday the talks were scheduled, the group did not use the park because an Elks' Flag Day ceremony was taking place at the same time. On subsequent Sundays, however, the group held their meetings without a permit. Daniel Niemotko was arrested as soon as he opened the first meeting. The following week another member of the group, Neil W. Kelley, was arrested. Both were convicted of disorderly conduct. They challenged their convictions and the denial of their permit applications as violations of the First Amendment.

The Court noted the lack of an ordinance or regulation dictating the kind of activity that could take place at the park. Furthermore, the city had presented no evidence of violence, disorder, or potential riots occurring during the meetings. Under these circumstances, it appeared that the park commission and city council denied the Jehovah's Witnesses' permit requests simply because the commission and council disagreed with their views. The only questions asked for the permit application related to the groups' beliefs and interpretation of the Bible. The Court held that the permit process violated the First Amendment's prohibition against prior restraint of speech. The Court therefore held that the convictions against Niemotko and Kelley could not stand.

See Shawn Francis Peters, *Judging Jehovah's Witnesses: Religious Persecution and the Dawn of the Rights Revolution* (Lawrence: University Press of Kansas, 2000).

Feiner v. New York

340 U.S. 315 (1951)
Decided: January 15, 1951
Vote: 6 (Vinson, Reed, Frankfurter, R. Jackson, Burton, Clark)
3 (Black, Douglas, Minton)
Opinion of the Court: Vinson
Concurring in judgment without opinion: Frankfurter
Dissenting opinion: Black
Dissenting opinion: Douglas (Minton)

Irving Feiner delivered a speech from a soapbox on a street corner in New York, gathering a crowd of approximately eighty people, both black and white. He urged his listeners to attend a meeting that night, but he also made derogatory remarks about the president and the mayor throughout his speech. Police came to the area to control the crowd, which became restless after Feiner urged black members of the crowd to "rise up in arms" against white people. An officer approached Feiner and asked him three times to end his speech in order to break up the crowd. When Feiner refused, he was arrested and charged with a breach of the peace.

The Court held that Feiner's arrest was valid. Feiner was not arrested for the content of his speech, nor had the police approached him until his words began to incite riot among his listeners. The Court explained that breach of peace is a valid claim, encompassing a variety of conduct that disturbs public order and tranquility. When either actions or words pose a clear and present danger of encouraging immediate violence, a speaker can be arrested regardless of his message.

In general, Chief Justice Vinson explained, the ordinary objections of a hostile crowd cannot be used to silence a speaker with a valid message. However, when that message "passes the bounds of argument or persuasion and undertakes incitement to riot," the conduct becomes criminal, and a speaker can be arrested.

Justice Black objected to what is now termed a "heckler's veto" and said that the job of the police was to ensure a speaker's freedom to make his statement. If the crowd had grown unruly, then the job of the police was to control the crowd, not silence the speaker.

See C. Herman Pritchett, *Civil Liberties and the Vinson Court* (Chicago: University of Chicago Press, 1954).

Dennis v. United States

341 U.S. 494 (1951)
Decided: June 4, 1951
Vote: 6 (Vinson, Reed, Frankfurter, R. Jackson, Burton, Clark, Minton)
2 (Black, Douglas)
Opinion of the Court: Vinson
Opinion concurring in judgment: Frankfurter
Concurring opinion: R. Jackson
Dissenting opinion: Black
Dissenting opinion: Douglas
Did not participate: Clark

In this case the Court pondered the constitutionality of the Smith Act as applied to eleven leaders of the Communist Party. They were indicted on two counts. The first was conspiring to organize an assembly of persons to teach and advocate the overthrow and destruction of the government of the United States by force and violence. The second was advocating and teaching the duty and necessity of overthrowing the government by force and violence. The government never claimed that any revolutionary acts other than teaching and advocating had taken place. In addition, the Justice Department did not charge the eleven men with conspiring to overthrow the government, although "seditious conspiracy" remained a crime on the statute books. Because the government would have been unable to show that the defendants' speech raised a clear and present danger, it resorted to the conspiracy charge. In essence, the defendants were tried and convicted for a conspiracy to form a political party, which would then be used to teach and advocate the overthrow of the government.

The central issue involved reconciling the constitutional guarantee of free speech with a conviction for doing no more than speaking and teaching. The trial judge, Harold Medina, solved the problem by the bridge of intent. He instructed the jury that it could find the defendants guilty if it believed they intended to overthrow the government as soon as the opportunity arose. In light of the Soviet Union's postwar actions in Europe and Asia, it seemed evident that the USSR was bent on world domination, and the American Communist Party, as a highly disciplined arm of the international movement, stood ready to act at a moment's notice to facilitate this mission. The conspiracy existed, and the government could act to avert the evil. To sustain the conviction, however, the Court would either have to modify or abandon the Holmes-Brandeis test of a clear and present danger in ***Schenck v. United States,*** 249 U.S. 47 (1919).

Although Chief Justice Vinson paid lip service to the test, he pointed out that communism posed a far different and more menacing danger than the anarchism and socialism Justices Holmes and Brandeis had dealt with three decades earlier. The clear and present danger test, therefore, could not possibly mean that before the government could act, it had to wait "until the *putsch* is about to be executed, the plans have been laid and the signal is awaited." By this line of reasoning, the government could not only reach speech directly inciting unlawful action, or conspiring to promote such action, or teaching that such action should occur, but also penalize conspiring to organize a group that would teach that such action ought to occur.

The majority opinion is labored and its logic faulty, first because it recognized that in large measure the Court was dealing not with an issue of law but of politics. Eugene Dennis and his colleagues, leaders of the American Communist Party, had been put on trial for political ideas not actions. Moreover, Vinson struggled to prove something that is impossible to prove, namely, that thinking about ideas, or even thinking about teaching and discussing ideas, without any overt action, constitutes a clear and present danger to the state. To do so, he had to read evil intent into the record, a notion that Holmes and Brandeis had specifically disavowed.

Justices Black and Douglas tried in vain to tone down the Court's opinion, pointing out the fallacies in Vinson's reasoning and the fact that the dreaded conspiracy was, in Black's words, a "ghost conspiracy." To Black, the indictment for conspiracy amounted to a "virulent form of prior censorship of speech and press." Black said he could not believe that the First Amendment "permits us to sustain laws suppressing freedom of speech and press on the basis of Congress' or our own notions of mere 'reasonableness.' " Such a doctrine "waters down the First Amendment to little more than an admonition to Congress." He could only hope that in calmer times "this or some later Court will restore the First Amendment liberties to the high preferred place where they belong in a free society."

Douglas, perhaps more than any other member of the Court, worried constantly about the effects of the latest Red Scare on American society. In *Dennis* he searched the voluminous record to find evidence—any evidence—that the defendants had engaged in actual acts of terror or seditious conduct that fell outside the ambit of First Amendment protection. He found only that they had attempted to teach Marxist-Leninist doctrine, and the First Amendment, he believed, fully protected instruction.

Much as he believed in an absolutist interpretation of the First Amendment, Douglas drew a clear distinction between thought and speech on the one hand and action on the other; the first enjoyed absolute protection, but the second did not. *Dennis* involved only speech, not "speech plus acts of sabotage or unlawful conduct. Not a single seditious act is charged in the indictment." Douglas did not deny that communism posed a threat on the world stage, but the "witch hunt" launched against the Communist Party leaders constituted an even greater threat to American values.

Douglas's opinion, for which he was roundly criticized at the time, later came to be seen as one of the great defenses of free thought during the McCarthy era. Thomas Emerson, a leading First Amendment theorist, noted an essential ingredient in Douglas's thought: a "remarkable ability to grasp the realities of the system of freedom of expression." For Douglas, free speech could be understood only in the larger context of facts. The power of his dissent lies in his reliance on the facts of the case, which show that the government did not prove that Dennis and the other defendants posed the clear and present danger that, at the very least, was required before government could stifle expression.

Ultimately, the majority opinion retained almost no doctrinal significance; a few years later the Court buried *Dennis* with almost indecent haste in ***Yates v. United States,*** 354 U.S. 298 (1957). About the only thing positive that might be said of it is that the clear and present danger test never recovered from the beating it received at the hands of the majority. When the Court next faced the issue of seditious conspiracy, it did not apply the test, but instead formulated a more liberal interpretation of free speech in ***Brandenburg v. Ohio,*** 395 U.S. 444 (1969).

See Thomas Emerson, "Mr. Justice Douglas' Contribution to the Law: The First Amendment," *Columbia Law Review* 74 (1974): 354; Robert Mollan, "Smith Act Prosecutions: The Effect of the Dennis and Yates Decisions," *University of Pittsburgh Law Review* 26 (1965): 710; and Michal R. Belknap, *Cold War Political Justice: The Smith Act, the Communist Party, and American Civil Liberties* (Westport, Conn.: Greenwood Press, 1977).

Rochin v. California

342 U.S. 165 (1952)
Decided: January 2, 1952
Vote: 8 (Vinson, Black, Reed, Frankfurter, Douglas, R. Jackson, Burton, Clark)
0
Opinion of the Court: Frankfurter
Concurring opinion: Black
Concurring opinion: Douglas
Did not participate: Minton

Antonio Rochin was convicted of possessing morphine. To obtain evidence, the police who arrested Rochin had entered his home and forced open his bedroom door. On the nightstand, the police saw three pills of morphine, which Rochin immediately swallowed. The police tried to forcibly remove the morphine pills from Rochin's mouth, and, when that failed, they took him to a hospital, where his stomach was pumped and the two capsules of morphine were recovered. Rochin challenged the legality of the evidence leading to his conviction. Both the trial court and California appeals court affirmed the conviction, saying that if defendants were allowed to go free because of police brutality, the state would be issuing an invitation to commit lawless acts free from penalty.

In a strongly worded opinion the Court overturned the California conviction and held that due process requires that evidence gained as a result of police brutality not be used to convict an accused person. Justice Frankfurter explained that the Due Process Clause of the Fourteenth Amendment requires appellate courts to enforce decency and to ensure that human rights are not lost in the machinery of government. The actions against Rochin, the Court said, "shocked the conscience." They were so far outside the spectrum of human decency that it would violate the Constitution to allow their use, even absent a specific constitutional provision regarding the issue. To Frankfurter, the methods used were "too close to the rack and screw to permit constitutional differentiation."

See Jacob W. Landynski, *Search and Seizure and the Supreme Court* (Baltimore: Johns Hopkins University Press, 1966).

Morissette v. United States

342 U.S. 246 (1952)
Decided: January 7, 1952
Vote: 8 (Vinson, Black, Reed, Frankfurter, Douglas, R. Jackson, Burton, Clark)
0
Opinion of the Court: R. Jackson
Did not participate: Minton

Joseph Morissette, a Michigan farmer, was convicted of stealing government property from a rural forest area where he hunted. The land was used by the United States as a practice bombing range. After an unsuccessful day of hunting, Morissette decided to clear some of the bomb casings and sell them as scrap metal. He was caught and convicted of "stealing and converting" government property. In his defense, Morissette argued that he did not know that the bomb casings were still the property of the government, but assumed they were abandoned. The trial judge refused to hear this argument, saying that the crime required no intent to steal. He said stealing was a crime whether or not the defendant knew he was stealing.

The Court overturned the decision of the trial court, explaining that the crime of larceny must involve an element of criminal intent. The requirement of intent required no statutory affirmation, as it was rooted in the common law. Because Morissette had no intention of stealing, he could not be convicted under the government's larceny statute.

To support his holding Justice Jackson made an interesting distinction between criminal laws and laws that exercised state or federal police powers. On the one hand, criminal laws require the element of intent because they seek to punish only those whose "malicious intent" or guilty mind threatens society. On the other hand, the government makes some rules that do not require intent because their purpose is to achieve social betterment by requiring a degree of diligence from the public. In this case Jackson interpreted the statute as a plain criminal law not designed to elicit diligence, and therefore he said that intent was a required element of the crime.

Adler v. Board of Education of City of New York

342 U.S. 485 (1952)
Decided: March 3, 1952
Vote: 6 (Vinson, Reed, R. Jackson, Burton, Clark, Minton)
3 (Black, Frankfurter, Douglas)
Opinion of the Court: Minton
Dissenting opinion: Black
Dissenting opinion: Frankfurter
Dissenting opinion: Douglas (Black)

Irving Adler and other teachers brought suit against the Board of Education of New York City to stop it from enforcing rules that prevented members of subversive organizations from teaching in New York public schools. The New York legislature authorized the board to make a list of subversive organizations and to deny employment to anyone admitting membership in any of them, following a full hearing on the issue. The teachers challenged the law by saying that it violated their freedom of speech and assembly and that it violated due process by presuming that people who belonged to certain organizations had subversive tendencies.

The Court held that the rules did not violate freedom of speech or assembly and that they did not prevent teachers from receiving due process under the statute. The school board had the right to enforce reasonable terms of employment. The teachers had a choice of whether to accept these terms or seek employment elsewhere. The Court held that membership in subversive organizations was indicative of teaching quality because the schoolroom is a sensitive area and subversive ideas can easily infiltrate teaching, even if unintended.

It did not violate due process for the school board to make a list of subversive organizations and to presume that people who were members of such organizations were unfit teachers. The Court held that whether an organization was subversive was a "legislative fact," which the board could rely on when making decisions, just as it would rely on any other law.

See Stanley I. Kutler, *The American Inquisition: Justice and Injustice in the Cold War* (New York: Hill and Wang, 1982).

Sacher v. United States

343 U.S. 1 (1952)
Decided: March 10, 1952
Vote: 5 (Vinson, Reed, R. Jackson, Burton, Minton)
3 (Black, Frankfurter, Douglas)
Opinion of the Court: R. Jackson
Dissenting opinion: Black
Dissenting opinion: Frankfurter
Dissenting opinion: Douglas
Did not participate: Clark

Following the Court's upholding the conviction of several communist leaders for violations of the Smith Act in ***Dennis v. United States,*** 341 U.S. 494 (1951), the judge in the proceedings, Harold R. Medina, held the attorneys who represented the communists in criminal contempt of court and sentenced them to six months in jail. The judge charged that the attorneys—Harry Sacher, Richard Gladstein, George Crockett, Abraham Isserman, Eugene Dennis (who had represented himself), and Lewis McCabe—had willfully obstructed the proceedings on numerous occasions and had repeatedly resisted his rulings. The attorneys did not deny their bad behavior, but claimed that the judge could not hold them in contempt at the completion of the trial because there was no urgency to his decision. The attorneys maintained that if proceedings were to occur after the trial, a new judge should hear evidence regarding the convictions and make an unbiased decision.

The Supreme Court held that contempt could be charged either during or after a federal trial and that the attorneys were properly charged. Judges often must make immediate contempt charges to ensure that attorney misbehavior does not disrupt the remainder of the trial. Justice Jackson explained, however, that reasons for implementing contempt proceedings do not require that judges charge contempt only during the immediate proceedings. Rather, the judge may choose to postpone contempt proceedings when making such a charge against an attorney might prejudice the defendant or when charges are not necessary for the efficiency of the trial. The Court held that a judge should have both options at his disposal, to exercise as circumstances require. The nature of contempt does not merit allowing a second judge to make the decision, because the first judge best knows what conduct must be punished. The judge in *Dennis,* therefore, acted properly in sentencing the attorneys for contempt after the trial finished, and the convictions were affirmed.

Justice Black dissented, stating that given the behavior of both judge and attorneys, due process entitled the lawyers to a trial before another judge. Justice Frankfurter spelled out what he saw as Medina's sins chapter and verse and, while acknowledging the misbehavior of the attorneys, showed that "the contempt of the lawyers had its reflex in the judge."

See Michal R. Belknap, *Cold War Political Justice: The Smith Act, the Communist Party, and American Civil Liberties* (Westport, Conn.: Greenwood Press, 1977).

Beauharnais v. Illinois

343 U.S. 250 (1952)
Decided: April 28, 1952
Vote: 5 (Vinson, Frankfurter, Burton, Clark, Minton)
4 (Black, Reed, Douglas, R. Jackson)
Opinion of the Court: Frankfurter
Dissenting opinion: Black (Douglas)
Dissenting opinion: Reed (Douglas)
Dissenting opinion: Douglas
Dissenting opinion: R. Jackson

Joseph Beauharnais, head of the White Circle League, was convicted under an Illinois statute making it a crime to publish propaganda depicting depravity or lack of virtue in any class of citizens. Beauharnais distributed leaflets that depicted members of the Negro race engaging in criminal behavior and calling on the mayor and city council of Chicago "to halt the further encroachment, harassment and invasion of white people, their property, neighborhoods and persons, by the Negro." Beauharnais did not challenge the facts of the charge at trial, but contended that under his right to free speech he could be convicted only if his leaflets posed a "clear and present danger." He was convicted and appealed on the basis that the statute violated the First Amendment.

Rather than address the "clear and present danger" argument, the Court held that Beauharnais was rightfully convicted of libel, the crime for which he was charged. The defendant offered truth as his defense, and the jury was instructed to convict only if the leaflets were published untruthfully. Recounting the history of libel convictions in America, Justice Frankfurter pointed out that the First Amendment had never protected libelous speech, and he cited ***Chaplinsky v. New Hampshire,*** 315 U.S. 568 (1942), as precedent. Although Beauharnais had argued that a libel law could not designate groups of persons who could not be libeled, Frankfurter responded that if utterances directed at individuals could be libel, untruthful comments about a group of people could be considered libel as well.

Although the Court categorized the Beauharnais prosecution as an ordinary libel trial, it went on to say that the racial turmoil in Chicago made the statute in question a necessity.

See Loren P. Beth, "Group Libel and Free Speech," *Minnesota Law Review* 39 (1955): 167.

Zorach v. Clauson

343 U.S. 306 (1952)
Decided: April 28, 1952
Vote: 6 (Vinson, Reed, Douglas, Burton, Clark, Minton)
3 (Black, Frankfurter, R. Jackson)
Opinion of the Court: Douglas
Dissenting opinion: Black
Dissenting opinion: Frankfurter
Dissenting opinion: R. Jackson

A New York City program allowed public schools to release students during the school day to receive religious education. A student could be released only on written request of his or her parent, and no student was compelled to participate in the program. Classroom activities were provided for students who did not participate. Religious institutions taking part in the program had some contact with the school and reported attendance to the school each week, but had no access to school facilities or funds. A group of New York City taxpayers, led by Tessim Zorach, joined to challenge the released time program on the grounds that it violated the First Amendment by providing students to religious establishments and their agendas.

Four years earlier in *McCollum v. Board of Education,* 333 U.S. 203 (1948), the Court struck down a released time program that took place on school property, but had intimated that different questions would be involved in a program located off school grounds. The Court here seemed to backtrack from the strict separation stance it had taken in *McCollum* and held that the First Amendment did not require a total separation of church and state, but only a reasonable one. Justice Douglas, in what many have characterized as the first accommodationist decision, declared that the New York law neither violated the free exercise of religion nor established religion within the meaning of the First Amendment. The program was entirely voluntary, contained no element of coercion, and left students to pursue religious devotion only as they desired. Furthermore, the law did not encourage the kind of union or co-dependence between church and state that is forbidden by the Establishment Clause. Rather, it fostered separation without creating hostility between schools and religious institutions.

In upholding New York's law, Douglas noted that "we are a religious people whose institutions presuppose a Supreme Being." While the government may not show partiality to one or more religions, the Court held that it could contribute to an atmosphere in which religion could flourish, as New York had chosen to do here.

Joseph Burstyn Inc. v. Wilson

343 U.S. 495 (1952)
Decided: May 26, 1952
Vote: 9 (Vinson, Black, Reed, Frankfurter, Douglas, R. Jackson, Burton, Clark, Minton)
0
Opinion of the Court: Clark
Opinion concurring in judgment: Reed
Opinion concurring in judgment: Frankfurter (R. Jackson, Burton)

Under New York law, any film shown in the state had to first be approved by the state board of education. The board judged each film to ensure that it was not "indecent, immoral, inhuman, or sacrilegious." Joseph Burstyn obtained a license to show a film, "The Miracle." The board received hundreds of letters and other communications denouncing the film, and it sent a second panel of reviewers to judge the work. This panel decided that the film was "sacrilegious" and ordered the commissioner of education to rescind Burstyn's license.

Burstyn brought several claims, including violations of free speech, the separation of church and state, and the Due Process Clause. The Court chose to look at the free speech issue. It held that motion pictures were expressive forms of communication protected by the First Amendment and that the state could not restrain their dissemination. The Court found the New York law to be an exercise of prior restraint because it allowed a panel of judges to prohibit speech, based on its content, before it was allowed access to the marketplace.

In his opinion, Justice Clark reiterated the First Amendment principle that free speech is not absolute and that states may curtail it when they have compelling reasons for doing so. Here,

New York had suggested no compelling interest. Furthermore, its means of censorship was too broad, vesting all power to restrain in one body, which was free to use its discretion in defining what violated the vague statute. Such prior restraint absent compelling interest violated the First Amendment, and the Court ordered Burstyn's license to exhibit the Italian-made film reinstated.

Youngstown Sheet & Tube Co. v. Sawyer

343 U.S. 579 (1952)
Decided: June 2, 1952
Vote: 6 (Black, Frankfurter, Douglas, R. Jackson, Burton, Clark)
3 (Vinson, Reed, Minton)
Opinion of the Court: Black
Concurring opinion: Frankfurter
Concurring opinion: Douglas
Concurring opinion: R. Jackson
Concurring opinion: Burton
Opinion concurring in judgment: Clark
Dissenting opinion: Vinson (Reed, Minton)

In the spring of 1952 the United Steel Workers threatened to strike after the Wage Stabilization Board failed to negotiate a settlement between the union and the mill owners. President Truman believed that with American troops fighting in Korea he had the same broad authority to mobilize the country that Roosevelt had used between 1941 and 1945. In early April Truman issued Executive Order 10340 directing Secretary of Commerce Charles Sawyer to seize and operate most of the nation's steel mills and to assure continued production of steel for defense needs.

The president had no statutory authority for this action. In fact, the Taft-Hartley Act of 1946 included procedures by which the government could secure an eighty-day "cooling off" period to postpone any strike that might adversely affect the public interest. But Truman had vetoed the measure, which Congress then passed over his veto, and he did not want to make use of a law he had condemned and tried to stop. Instead, he simply seized the steel mills, informed an astonished Congress of what he had done, and invited the members to take legislative action if they thought it necessary.

The steel operators immediately sought to enjoin the government's actions. They conceded that an emergency existed, and that in an emergency the government had the right and the power to take over their businesses. They objected that the *wrong branch* of government had proceeded against them. In essence, they complained that the executive had unconstitutionally infringed upon the powers of the legislative branch. Rarely does a private party sue on behalf of a branch of government, and the courts could have dismissed the suit for lack of standing. But the district court ruled against the government on all points and issued an injunction, which was immediately stayed by the federal court of appeals. Seven steel companies appealed the stay to the U.S. Supreme Court.

The Court handed down its decision three weeks after oral argument. Four members of the majority agreed that the Taft-Hartley act prohibited the seizure. The legislative history showed that Congress had rejected an amendment that would have authorized seizure of plants in national emergencies and passed a provision to enjoin strikes. According to Justice Frankfurter, "The authoritatively expressed purpose of Congress to disallow such power to the President could not be more decisive if it had been written into . . . the Labor Management Relations Act."

Justice Black took a broader approach. Neither statute nor constitutional provision gave the president power to act as he had done; the constitutional provisions of the commander-in-chief, which executives had always used to justify wartime acts, did not extend this far. In essence, Black took a Jeffersonian position: if neither the Constitution nor an act of Congress specifically gave the chief executive the power, then the president did not have it. Power to authorize seizure of the mills did exist, but in the legislative branch, and when the president acted on his own authority in this manner he encroached on congressional responsibility and violated the separation of powers.

For Justice Jackson, the issue was not whether specific statutory authority or implied constitutional powers existed to justify the seizure; rather, in this case, Congress had specifically said that it did not want to delegate such power. Presidential authority, Jackson continued, stood at its height when the chief executive acted at the direct or implied command of Congress, and in such situations the president relied on his own powers as well as those given to him by the legislature. In circumstances in which Congress had not acted, the president might act relying on his own powers, but here a twilight zone existed in which it would not be clear who had the ultimate responsibility. Presidential authority was weakest, Jackson noted, when the executive acted in defiance of either the express or implied legislative intent, and in such circumstances the Court could uphold the president only by ruling that Congress lacked power to legislate on the subject. In this instance, Congress had the power, and it had spoken quite clearly as to its intent.

If in Black's view the president could do only what statute or Constitution authorized, Chief Justice Vinson in dissent took the exact opposite stance. The president could, in response to a national emergency, do everything except that which had been specifically prohibited. Taking an expansive reading of Article II, Vinson read broad authority into the Constitution's delegation of the "executive power" and this power went far beyond the few examples the Framers had enumerated.

In an era when the Court enlarged greatly the powers of the federal government, *Youngstown* remained a salutary reminder that constitutional limits, especially on executive authority, still existed.

See Maeva Marcus, *Truman and the Steel Seizure Case: The Limits of Presidential Power* (New York: Columbia University Press, 1977); and Alan F. Westin, *The Anatomy of a Constitutional Law Case* (New York: Macmillan, 1958).

Kawakita v. United States

343 U.S. 717 (1952)
Decided: June 2, 1952
Vote: 4 (Reed, Douglas, R. Jackson, Minton)
3 (Vinson, Black, Burton)
Opinion of the Court: Douglas
Dissenting opinion: Vinson (Black, Burton)
Did not participate: Frankfurter, Clark

Tomoya Kawakita was born in the United States of Japanese parents and had dual citizenship. During World War II he lived in Japan and worked in a manufacturing plant. The plant used American prisoners of war as laborers, and Kawakita allegedly assaulted and ridiculed several of these prisoners. After the war he returned to the United States and was charged with treason for his treatment of American POWs. Kawakita argued that he could not be charged with treason because he had denounced his American citizenship while living in Japan and therefore had no duty or loyalty to the United States. He argued alternatively that his actions did not "aid or provide comfort" to the enemy and did not meet the constitutional definition of treason.

The Court affirmed Kawakita's conviction, finding sufficient evidence of his citizenship and holding that his treatment of American POWs benefited Japan's war effort. The Court noted that Kawakita had renewed his American passport on many occasions and that even though he had never joined the Japanese army or renounced the United States, neither had he done anything to indicate the rejection of his U.S. citizenship.

The main question before the Court in some ways was whether treason encompassed actions by American citizens only within the territorial boundaries of the United States or whether the actions could take place anywhere. The decision made the status of the actor (American citizenship) and not the location the determining factor in treason.

See J. Willard Hurst, *The Law of Treason in the United States* (Westport, Conn.: Greenwood Press, 1971).

Kedroff v. St. Nicholas Cathedral of Russian Orthodox Churches in North America

344 U.S. 94 (1952)
Decided: November 24, 1952
Vote: 8 (Vinson, Black, Reed, Frankfurter, Douglas, Burton, Clark, Minton)
1 (R. Jackson)
Opinion of the Court: Reed
Concurring opinion: Frankfurter (Black, Douglas)
Dissenting opinion: R. Jackson

In 1925 the New York legislature created a corporation with the purpose of acquiring a cathedral for the Russian Orthodox church in North America. At the time of the proceedings, the cathedral was occupied by the patriarch of Moscow. The corporation filed suit to eject the patriarch from the cathedral so that the North American archbishop could use it for the purposes of the Russian Orthodox church in North America. The trial court refused to eject the patriarch of Moscow, but the New York Court of Appeals (the highest court in New York) held that under the legislation creating the church corporation, the corporation had a right to occupy the church. The patriarch appealed.

The Court held that the patriarch of Moscow had a right to continue occupying the church because the legislation that incorporated the Russian Orthodox church in North America violated the Free Exercise Clause of the First Amendment and was therefore invalid. The state had no right to incorporate a religious group that inhibited the free exercise of another religious group, the Russian Orthodox church headquartered in Moscow. Although the state claimed subversive influences in the Moscow church, no such influences had yet been seen. The state would have a right to quell subversion if it were to occur, but until it did it could not preemptively prevent misconduct by inhibiting the free exercise of a church. Because the New York statute incorporating the petitioner church was invalid, the original Russian Orthodox church had the sole right to use the cathedral.

Wieman v. Updegraff

344 U.S. 183 (1952)
Decided: December 15, 1952
Vote: 8 (Vinson, Black, Reed, Frankfurter, Douglas, Burton, Clark, Minton)
0
Opinion of the Court: Clark
Concurring opinion: Black (Douglas)
Concurring opinion: Frankfurter (Douglas)
Concurring in judgment without opinion: Burton
Did not participate: R. Jackson

An Oklahoma law required all state employees to take a loyalty oath in order to continue their employment. The employees swore that they were not members of any organizations that wanted to overthrow the United States government. Several employees of an Oklahoma state college failed to sign the oath within the thirty-day time limit. When they were allowed to keep their jobs, a citizen of Oklahoma filed suit to prevent the state from paying further compensation to employees who had not signed. The employees intervened, requesting a court order directing the state to continue paying their salaries and saying that the oath violated the Due Process Clause of the Fourteenth Amendment.

Deciding the case on the narrowest possible grounds, the Court held that such a sweeping provision caught up too many people and could implicate people who had joined an organization without knowing it was a subversive group. Justice Clark distinguished this situation from that of earlier cases, such as ***American Communications Association v. Douds,*** 339 U.S. 382 (1950), on the grounds that in *Douds* the law had been interpreted to apply only to people who knowingly participated in subversive organizations or personally sought to destroy the government. Mere membership was not enough to prove that a person was subversive.

Although it would be a few more years before the Court completely negated such cold war loyalty measures, by 1952 it had started to tighten the evidentiary requirement that at the least prevented the laws from ensnaring innocent people.

Brown v. Allen

344 U.S. 443 (1953)
Decided: February 9, 1953
Vote: 6 (Vinson, Reed, R. Jackson, Burton, Clark, Minton)
3 (Black, Frankfurter, Douglas)
Opinion of the Court: Reed
Concurring opinion: R. Jackson
Dissenting opinion: Black (Douglas)
Dissenting opinion: Frankfurter (Black, Douglas)

This case is a compilation of three petitions for writs of habeas corpus from three death row inmates. All lost their appeals in state appellate courts and were denied certiorari by the Court. Each filed a writ of habeas corpus in federal district court, arguing state error. One claimed that he had been denied a fair trial because the jury lists in his state contained more white people than African Americans. Another argued that his confession had been coerced and was therefore invalid. The third said that he had been convicted solely because of race. Federal district courts dismissed each petition, and the petitioners appealed.

The Court held that federal district courts may consider the validity of state procedures and remedies when deciding whether a writ of habeas corpus is necessary. If the state decision provided sufficient remedy on state grounds for deprivations of federal rights, the district court need not grant a habeas petition. Even if there is a conflict about how the federal problem could be remedied, federal courts may accept state court interpretations.

The Court also held that writs of habeas corpus need not be issued when a state court error did not affect the results of the trial. For example, even if the state court erroneously admitted a coerced confession of one of the petitioners, the federal court did not have to grant a writ of habeas corpus if the confession had no effect on the results of the trial. For these reasons, the Court held that lower federal courts had properly dismissed each of these petitions, and the decisions were affirmed.

Terry v. Adams

345 U.S. 461 (1953)
Decided: May 4, 1953
Vote: 8 (Vinson, Black, Reed, Frankfurter, Douglas, R. Jackson, Burton, Clark)
1 (Minton)
Judgment of the Court: Black
Concurring opinion: Frankfurter
Concurring opinion: Clark (Vinson, Reed, R. Jackson)
Dissenting opinion: Minton

For more than fifty years the Jaybird Democratic Association of Fort Bend County, Texas, had been holding a May primary separate from the official primary run by the county the following month. The criteria for voting in the Jaybird election were almost identical to those of the county except that African Americans could not participate, as they could in the county primary, thanks to ***Smith v. Allwright,*** 321 U.S. 649 (1944). In court the Jaybird officials acknowledged that their intent was to exclude blacks. Whoever won the Jaybird primary always won the county primary and the general election. The Jaybirds argued that they were a private club, that their election was a private canvass without money or regulation from the state, and therefore that their exclusion of blacks did not qualify as state action.

The Court, however, saw the Jaybird primary as a subterfuge, one tolerated by Texas to defeat the purpose of the Fifteenth Amendment. As Justice Black explained, "The only election that has counted in this Texas county for more than fifty years has been that held by the Jaybirds. . . . It has become an integral part, indeed the only effective part, of the elective process that determines who shall rule and govern in the county." Only Justice Minton accepted the Jaybird claim of being a private group.

Terry was the final case in which the Court dismantled the notion that party primaries could be closed to blacks; full implementation would not come, however, until the Voting Rights Act of 1965 finally swept away the various stratagems southern states used to prevent black registration.

See Darlene Clark Hine, *Black Victory: The Rise and Fall of the White Primary in Texas* (Millwood, N.Y.: KTO Press, 1979).

Rosenberg v. United States

346 U.S. 273 (1953)
Decided: June 19, 1953
Vote: 6 (Vinson, R. Jackson, Reed, Burton, Clark, Minton)
3 (Black, Frankfurter, Douglas)
Opinion: *Per curiam*
Opinion of the Court: Vinson
Concurring opinion: R. Jackson (Vinson, Reed, Burton, Clark, Minton)
Concurring opinion: Clark (Vinson, Reed, Jackson, Burton, Minton)
Dissenting opinion: Black
Dissenting opinion: Frankfurter
Dissenting opinion: Douglas

Julius and Ethel Rosenberg were sentenced to death after their convictions for conspiracy between 1944 and 1950 to violate the Espionage Act of 1917 by providing atomic secrets to Russia. The Rosenbergs tried several times to get the Supreme Court to review their case, and on June 17, 1953, Justice Douglas issued a stay of execution on grounds that the Atomic Energy Act had repealed that part of the Espionage Act that provided for a death penalty. The stay allowed Justice Frankfurter to get three other members of the Court to join him in voting for review. But a majority of the Court believed the Rosenbergs guilty and found no constitutional defects in their trial. The Court heard oral argument on June 18 and issued its ruling the next day.

Six members of the Court, in a *per curiam* opinion, subsequently supplemented by full opinions by Chief Justice Vinson and Justices Jackson and Clark, vacated the stay granted by Douglas and held that the Atomic Energy Act did not repeal the Espionage Act. The Rosenbergs were executed later the same day.

Justice Black argued there were substantial grounds to believe that the death sentences were imposed in violation of law. Justice Douglas based his dissent on grounds that only a jury and not the judge could impose the death penalty. Frankfurter attacked the Court's rush to judgment and thought that an opportunity should have been afforded for counsel to argue and for the Court to consider a more adequate presentation of the issues involved.

Controversy has arisen ever since over the Rosenbergs' guilt, but in general scholars have condemned the Court for its refusal to hear the issues and for its unseemly haste in deciding the case without full debate and discussion.

See Michael E. Parrish, "Cold War Justice: The Supreme Court and the Rosenbergs," *American Historical Review* 82 (1977): 805.

Irvine v. California

347 U.S. 128 (1954)
Decided: February 8, 1954
Vote: 5 (Warren, Reed, R. Jackson, Clark, Minton)
4 (Black, Frankfurter, Douglas, Burton)
Judgment of the Court: R. Jackson
Concurring opinion: Clark
Dissenting opinion: Black (Douglas)
Dissenting opinion: Frankfurter (Burton)
Dissenting opinion: Douglas

Irvine was convicted by a state court of bookmaking and illegal gambling. Support for his conviction came from searches conducted by state police officers. The police entered Irvine's house when no one was at home and placed a microphone in his hall closet. The microphone, later moved to the master bedroom, revealed conversations about Irvine's gambling activities, which police officers were allowed to testify about in court. Irvine appealed, claiming that use of the overheard evidence violated his federal due process rights.

The Court held that the federal rules excluding evidence gained from an illegal search do not apply in state courts. The Fourth Amendment restricts the federal government from conducting intrusive searches without a warrant, but the Court held that the Fourteenth Amendment does not incorporate this amendment against state action. Although an earlier case, ***Rochin v. United States,*** 342 U.S. 165 (1952), barred states from unreasonable searches of a person, that application applied only when a coercive element was present. (In *Rochin,* police had the defendant's stomach pumped to find drugs, which violated the suspect's Fourteenth Amendment rights.) Furthermore, the search did not violate the Federal Communication Act because it did not involve telephone tapping. Rather, the microphones gathered evidence that an eavesdropper hiding in the hall or the bedroom might have heard.

Although the Court denounced the invasion suffered by Irvine at the hands of the California police, it declined to expand the federal rules against a state court, especially after providing no prior notice to the state. A state might choose to follow the federal standards, but it could not be forced to do so at the hands of the federal government.

United States ex rel. Accardi v. Shaughnessy

347 U.S. 260 (1954)
Decided: March 15, 1954
Vote: 5 (Warren, Black, Frankfurter, Douglas, Clark)
4 (Reed, R. Jackson, Burton, Minton)
Opinion of the Court: Clark
Dissenting opinion: R. Jackson (Reed, Burton, Minton)

Accardi was living in the United States illegally, having entered the country from Italy in 1932 without an immigration visa. Deportation proceedings against him began in 1947. He applied for suspension of deportation under Section 19 (c) of the Immigration Act of 1917, which said that the Board of Immigration Appeals had discretion to suspend deportation in cases with special circumstances or if the alien had been a resident for more than seven years. The board approved deportation. Accardi's wife filed a habeas corpus petition on his behalf, claiming that the board did not use its discretion when making its decision. To the contrary, the board had relied on a list created by the attorney general that listed Accardi, among others, as an "unsavory character . . . whose deportation he [the attorney general] wished." A federal district court dismissed her petition.

The question on which the habeas corpus petition hinged was whether the attorney general's list deprived Accardi of the rights guaranteed to him by the Immigration Act, which seemed to require the board to make a decision about suspension using its own discretion. Here, the board apparently had been precluded from using its own judgment because the attorney general's list had essentially dictated the decision it should make. Because the statute required that both the board and the attorney general exercise separate discretion, the Court held that Accardi's claim should not have been dismissed. If he could prove in the district court that the board was influenced by the attorney general's list, he would be entitled to a new hearing. The Court reversed the dismissal of his case, and remanded it for further action consistent with its opinion.

Hernandez v. Texas

347 U.S. 475 (1954)
Decided: May 3, 1954
Vote: 9 (Warren, Black, Reed, Frankfurter, Douglas, R. Jackson, Burton, Clark, Minton)
0
Opinion of the Court: Warren

Following his conviction for murder, Pete Hernandez challenged the systematic exclusion of Mexican Americans from jury duty in the state of Texas. He did not claim that his rights were violated because no Mexican Americans sat on his particular jury, but because he was tried before a jury from which members of his race were systematically excluded. Systematic exclusion, he contended, violated the Equal Protection Clause of the Fourteenth Amendment by subjecting all members of his race to a discriminatory judicial system.

The Court agreed that excluding jury members solely on the basis of race or color violated the Equal Protection Clause. Furthermore, equal protection is violated when members of a certain race are excluded for reasons other than race or color, when the result is that no members of that race may ever serve on a jury. To show that systematic discrimination resulted in an equal protection violation, Hernandez had the burden of proving two things: first, that Mexican Americans were a unique race of peoples and were perceived as such within the state, and second, that they were in fact excluded.

Hernandez met the Court's burden by showing that in Texas, communities regarded Mexican Americans as a separate class distinct from "whites." Texans considered Mexican Americans as inferior, had until recently maintained segregated schools, and even required Mexican Americans to use separate bathrooms. Hernandez also proved exclusion to the satisfaction of the Court, showing that although Mexican Americans made up 14 percent of the state's population, not one Mexican American had served on a Texas jury in twenty-five years. The Court found this a sufficient prima facie case, to which the state could offer no rebuttal, and therefore found an equal protection violation.

Brown v. Board of Education of Topeka, Kansas

347 U.S. 483 (1954)
Decided: May 17, 1954
Vote: 9 (Warren, Black, Reed, Frankfurter, Douglas, R. Jackson, Burton, Clark, Minton)
0
Opinion of the Court: Warren

In June 1952 the Court announced that it would hear arguments in cases challenging school segregation in laws in Delaware (*Gebhart v. Belton*), Virginia (*Davis v. County School Board of Prince Edward County*), South Carolina (*Briggs v. Elliott*), Kansas (*Brown v. Board of Education, Topeka*), and the District of Columbia (*Bolling v. Sharpe*). The Court had consolidated the cases with the Kansas appeal as the lead case so that, according to Justice Clark, "the whole question would not smack of being a purely Southern one."

After the case was argued, the justices were unable to reach agreement on what constitutional authority it could use to strike down segregation, and the Court requested that counsel reargue the case in December 1953. Specifically, the justices wanted both sides to address whether Congress in proposing, and the states in adopting, the Fourteenth Amendment had intended to ban racial segregation in schools. Further, if the Court ruled against continued segregation, how should the decision be put into effect?

Instead of the usual one to two hours permitted for oral argument, the justices sat through ten hours spread over three days. John W. Davis, a former solicitor general of the United States, represented South Carolina. He defended racial segregation in an emotional coda to a long and distinguished career. For Thurgood Marshall, leader of the NAACP legal team, the moment was equally dramatic. His very presence in the courtroom symbolized what he demanded of the Court and of the nation—equality for all people regardless of the color of their skin.

Considering its epochal significance, the *Brown* decision was deceptively simple, running a mere eleven pages. Chief Justice Warren intended it to be short enough so that newspapers could reprint it in its entirety, and he read the whole opinion from the bench. He began by stating that the history of the Fourteenth Amendment and its relation to education, which the Court had asked both sides to argue, was "inconclusive"—in part because public education in the South in 1868 was almost nonexistent. Most white children were privately educated, and black children were not educated at all. Warren then briefly examined the doctrine enunciated in ***Plessy v. Ferguson,*** 163 U.S. 537 (1896), as well as the extent of segregation in northern and southern states. Times had changed, Warren declared. "In approaching this problem," he said, "we cannot turn the clock back to 1868 when the Amendment was adopted, or even to 1896 when *Plessy* was written. We must consider public education in the light of its full development and its present place in American life throughout the Nation." Education played a crucial role in training people to become productive members of society; even more important, it prepared them to be citizens and to participate in the critical political choices facing the country. When the state undertook to provide education, it had to do so on equal terms to all.

Warren read through two-thirds of the opinion before he reached the crucial question: "Does segregation of children in public schools solely on the basis of race . . . deprive the children of the minority group of equal educational opportunities?" Pausing for a moment, Warren said, "We unanimously believe it does." Reaffirming the eloquent dissent of the first Justice Harlan in *Plessy,* that separate could never be equal, Warren declared that to segregate black schoolchildren

> from others of similar age and qualifications solely because of their race generates a feeling of inferiority as to their status in the community that may affect their hearts and minds in a way unlikely ever to be undone. . . . Segregation with the sanction of law, therefore, has a tendency to retard the educational and mental development of Negro children.

As a result, the Court concluded "that in the field of public education the doctrine of 'separate-but-equal' has no place. Separate educational facilities are inherently unequal." When Warren announced that the decision was unanimous, he later recalled, "a wave of emotion swept the room."

The last paragraph of *Brown* showed Warren's well-known political astuteness. Noting the wide applicability of the decisions and the complexity of devising an appropriate solution, he invited the parties to assist the Court in fashioning a proper remedy and declared that arguments would be heard that fall. The "wide applicability" phrase broadcast the intention of the Court to order desegregation in all school districts, North and South, urban and rural. The reference to the complexity of the problem and the delay in issuing implementing orders signaled to the South that the justices recognized the emotional crisis that the decision would cause and that they would allow time for the states to accustom themselves to the idea. By inviting the different parties to join in fashioning a remedy, the Court hoped that the Jim Crow states would cooperate and thereby avoid the imposition of harsher solutions. Finally, Warren carefully framed the opinion to apply to only one area, the legal segregation of children by race in primary and secondary public schools, the group most likely to win public sympathy as victims of racism. The decision did not strike down all Jim Crow laws, nor did it declare all discriminatory statutes unconstitutional. Critics might predict that such moves would be the logical extension of *Brown,* but for the moment the Court concerned itself only with education.

Within an hour of the opinion, the Voice of America beamed news of the decision around the world in more than thirty languages. Northern newspapers generally hailed the decision as "momentous." What the justices have done, declared the *Cincinnati Enquirer,* "is simply to act as the conscience of the American nation." Within the black community, reaction was mixed, as leaders waited to see how the lofty words would be translated into action.

Initially, the South heard voices of moderation, more so than one might have expected. Gov. Thomas Stanley of Virginia called for "cool heads, calm study, and sound judgment." "Big Jim" Folsom of Alabama declared, "When the Supreme Court speaks, that's the law." The governor of Arkansas, Francis Cherry promised, "Arkansas will obey the law. It always has." The respected *Louisville Courier-Journal* assured its readers that "the end of the world has not come for the South or for the nation. The Supreme Court's ruling is not itself a revolution. It is rather acceptance of a process that has been going on for a long time." The editors urged southerners to follow the Court's example of moderation, advice akin to that of the *Atlanta Constitution,* which called on Georgians "to think clearly."

The Court had expected criticism of the decision not only from the South, which would naturally defend its way of life, but from the scholarly community as well. The chief justice's insistence that the opinion be "short, readable by the lay public, non-rhetorical, unemotional and, above all, non-accusatory," was a brilliant political stroke, papering over theoretical differences among the justices, but it robbed the decision of intellectual force and authority. The Court's dismissal of the background and relevance of the Fourteenth Amendment as "inconclusive," for example, led to charges that the Court had misunderstood history. One group argued that the amendment had been designed to ensure black equality, and therefore that its framers intended it to prevent segregation in the schools and elsewhere. Another faction weighed in with convincing evidence that the "original understanding" of those responsible for the Fourteenth Amendment did not encompass regulation of race relations.

The famous footnote 11 elicited a far more serious and enduring attack. In its brief, the NAACP had cited whatever material it could find to support the claim that segregation hurt black children. Warren, in an effort to buttress his finding that segregation was psychologically harmful to black children, cited a number of works, including Gunnar Myrdal's classic study of racism, *An American Dilemma* (1944), and Kenneth B. Clark's highly controversial studies of negative self-image among black children. Warren later said, "It was only a note," but critics seized on it as proof that the Court had not interpreted law but had applied its own sociological views.

Critics also accused the Court of judicial activism. Whether one agreed or disagreed with *Brown,* the decision was a dramatic departure from earlier rulings in this area. The Court had been chipping away at *Plessy* for some time, but its recent decisions gave little indication that it would so precipitately abandon the fifty-year-old doctrine of separate-but-equal. Unlike most Court opinions, the decision contained few citations to precedents—other than the latest NAACP cases such as ***Sipuel v. Oklahoma,*** 332 U.S. 631 (1948), and ***Sweatt v. Painter,*** 339 U.S. 629 (1950)—because so few existed. Critics charged the Court with engaging in the same type of policy-making activism as in the Progressive and New Deal eras. In *Brown,* however, the Court overturned its own ruling in *Plessy,* a decision that today nearly everyone agrees had been wrongly decided; in the reform cases, the Court interposed its own views over that of the legislature. Granted, the whole edifice of segregation statutes relied on that decision, but if *Plessy* was wrong, then so too were the laws that resulted from it.

Warren also presented two very different and contradictory ideas of constitutional interpretation. When he announced that "separate educational facilities are inherently unequal," he appeared to be saying that racial segregation violated the constitutional mandate at all times and in all places. In essence, he intimated that constitutional meaning is unchanging, and that the Equal Protection Clause had always meant what the Court now said it meant, that racial discrimination had been unconstitutional since 1868, and that cases that declared otherwise, such as *Plessy,* had been wrongly decided.

Warren also implied an opposing view of constitutional interpretation, that constitutional meaning changes with changing times and circumstances. Chief Justice John Marshall had lectured the American people to always remember that the Constitution is intended "to be adopted to the various crises of human affairs." This notion of a "living constitution" could be seen in Warren's dismissal of what the framers of the Fourteenth Amendment had intended in regard to public education in the South in 1868. From this point of view, one could argue that at the time, *Plessy* was correctly decided.

Defenders of the Court conceded most of these points but insisted that the justices had followed the right moral as well as legal course. No one needed fancy studies to see that "racial segregation under government auspices inevitably inflicts humiliation." In response to southern charges that the Court had promulgated a lawless decision, some scholars responded that massive racial discrimination constituted so great a violation of moral law as to make lawful a court ruling against it. As neither Congress nor the states showed any inclination to promote civil rights, the Court's action may have been the only way to get the country moving on the road toward full racial equality. Although following that path has at times been painful and even violent, without *Brown* it is doubtful that legal segregation could have been ended except through massive protest and civil unrest, such as afflicted South Africa in the 1980s.

See Richard Kluger, *Simple Justice* (New York: Knopf, 1975); Mark V. Tushnet, *The NAACP's Legal Strategy Against Segregated Education, 1925–1950* (Chapel Hill: University of North Carolina Press, 1987); Alexander M. Bickel, *The Least Dangerous Branch* (Indianapolis: Bobbs-Merrill, 1962); and Charles L. Black Jr., "The Lawfulness of the Segregation Decisions," *Yale Law Journal* 69 (1960): 421.

Bolling v. Sharpe

347 U.S. 497 (1954)
Decided: May 17, 1954
Vote: 9 (Warren, Black, Reed, Frankfurter, Douglas, R. Jackson, Burton, Clark, Minton)
0
Opinion of the Court: Warren

Argued together and decided with the state school desegregation cases in ***Brown v. Board of Education of Topeka,*** 347 U.S. 483 (1954), this case dealt with segregated schools in the District of Columbia. Having just ruled that the Equal Protection Clause of the Fourteenth Amendment restricted the states and precluded them from segregating schools on the basis of race, Chief Justice Warren held that "to impose a lesser duty" in the District of Columbia would be "unthinkable."

The Court found its justification for striking down segregation in Washington in the Due Process Clause of the Fifth Amendment. Although scholars agreed that the same rules should apply in the District as in the states, they found the Court's reliance on the Fifth Amendment questionable.

See Richard Kluger, *Simple Justice* (New York: Knopf, 1975); Mark V. Tushnet, *The NAACP's Legal Strategy Against Segregated Education, 1925–1950* (Chapel Hill: University of North Carolina Press, 1987); Alexander M. Bickel, *The Least Dangerous Branch* (Indianapolis: Bobbs-Merrill, 1962); and Charles L. Black Jr., "The Lawfulness of the Segregation Decisions," *Yale Law Journal* 69 (1960): 421.

Muir v. Louisville Park Theatrical Ass'n

347 U.S. 971 (1954)
Decided: May 24, 1954
Vote: 9 (Warren, Black, Reed, Frankfurter, Douglas, R. Jackson, Burton, Clark, Minton)
0
Opinion: *Per curiam*

The Court heard this case along with two others, *Florida ex rel. Hawkins v. Board of Control of Florida* and *Tureaud v. Board of Supervisors of Louisiana State University and Agricultural and Mechanical College.* The Court vacated the lower court decisions in all three cases in a brief *per curium* opinion that instructed the lower courts to reconsider the cases in light of ***Brown v. Board of Education,*** 347 U.S. 483, which had been decided eight days earlier on May 17.

The lower court decision in *Muir* involved a black man, P. O. Sweeney, who wanted to play golf on a public golf course limited to use by whites only. Even though Sweeney promised to pay all the uniform charges and fees necessary for use of the course, and to abide by the rules and regulations of the course, his application was denied. Sweeney argued that he must be given access to the golf course because the city of Louisville had no golf course designated for use by African Americans.

The trial court held that the city of Louisville did not discriminate against Sweeney by failing to allow him to play at the golf course designated for white use, but that it did discriminate by providing a golf course for whites without providing one for African Americans. The court based its decision on ***Plessy v. Ferguson,*** 163 U.S. 537 (1896), explaining that while accommodations may be separate, they must be provided equally. The circuit court affirmed the trial court's decision, and the Supreme Court vacated both decisions in light of *Brown.*

Muir and its companion cases began a pattern that the Court would use frequently in the next few years. Although in *Brown* it had said that the decision applied only to public education, in fact the Court applied it to all segregated public facilities without hearing formal arguments in most cases. It merely issued a *per curiam* opinion sending the case back to the lower court with orders to reconsider in light of *Brown.* As a result, within less than a decade it had become a violation of the Equal Protection Clause to segregate any public facilities.

Berman v. Parker

348 U.S. 26 (1954)
Decided: November 22, 1954
Vote: 9 (Warren, Black, Reed, Frankfurter, Douglas, R. Jackson, Burton, Clark, Minton)
0
Opinion of the Court: Douglas

Congress created a redevelopment plan to improve housing standards in the District of Columbia. It determined that Washington needed more low-income housing and that the city would also benefit from general aesthetic improvements within existing low-income communities. A retail store owner protested the demolition of his building as part of the improvements, saying that commercial buildings were outside of the purpose of the project and that it therefore violated Fifth Amendment due process to target them. It was one thing to tear down slum housing, the store owner argued, but quite another to take a man's property merely to develop a more attractive community.

The Court held that it was within Congress's police powers to determine where community improvements were needed and to take whatever steps were necessary to achieve those goals. In fact, deciding where and how to improve property was a uniquely legislative function in which the Court felt it should not interfere. Justice Douglas explained that improving the appearance of low-income housing would aid residents by lifting their spirits and relieving them of the "insufferable burden" of enduring miserable living conditions. If Congress felt that public morale would be improved by making the District of Columbia beautiful as well as sanitary, it could exercise its legislative powers to execute its objectives. This in no way violated the Fifth Amendment, which allows government to take property when it justly compensates property holders and has a legitimate government interest for doing so.

In re Murchison

349 U.S. 133 (1955)
Decided: May 16, 1955
Vote: 6 (Warren, Black, Frankfurter, Douglas, Clark, Harlan II)
3 (Reed, Burton, Minton)
Opinion of the Court: Black
Dissenting opinion: Reed and Minton (Burton)

Michigan law allowed a judge sitting alone to serve as a "one-man grand jury" in certain proceedings. During such proceedings, however, he could not summarily convict a witness for contempt of court. Lee Roy Murchison, a Detroit policeman, was called as a witness before one of these one-man grand juries in which the judge was looking into alleged police corruption. The judge charged him with contempt of court and ordered him to appear in a subsequent proceeding to defend himself against the charge. The same judge oversaw the contempt hearing and convicted Murchison, who appealed, saying that allowing a grand jury judge to oversee a contempt proceeding violated due process.

The Court agreed, holding that allowing the grand jury judge to preside over contempt proceedings violated due process because the judge was deciding a case in which he had an interest. As Justice Black explained, one of the mainstays of due process is that no man can be a judge in his own case, and no one can judge a case where he has an interest in the outcome. This is true even when such an arrangement would not actually result in bias, because "justice must satisfy the appearance of justice."

The judge in Murchison's case could not free himself from the influence of what had happened in the closed grand jury proceedings. He had even written on the record of the contempt hearing that part of the conviction was based on Murchison's insolent attitude, which clearly offended the judge. With his personal interests and feelings at stake, the judge could not offer Murchison a fair trial for contempt, and his conviction was overturned.

Emspak v. United States

349 U.S. 190 (1955)
Decided: May 23, 1955
Vote: 6 (Warren, Black, Frankfurter, Douglas, Burton, Clark)
3 (Reed, Minton, Harlan II)
Opinion of the Court: Warren
Dissenting opinion: Harlan II

Emspak was summoned before the House Un-American Activities Committee (HUAC) to testify about the electrical workers union in which he was secretary/treasurer. He cooperated with most of the interrogation, but refused to testify about his affiliations with various subversive organizations, supporting his refusal with "the first amendment, supplemented by the fifth." He also refused to inform on other members of the union. HUAC took Emspak to court for noncompliance, saying that he had not properly invoked a Fifth Amendment privilege, and that even if he had, he had waived that privilege.

The Court ruled that Emspak's assertion of the Fifth Amendment was sufficient to grant him the privilege against self-incrimination and that he had not waived the privilege at any time. The Fifth Amendment, according to Chief Justice Warren, need not be invoked by a ritualistic formula, and witnesses can gain the privilege by a good-faith attempt at citing it. Furthermore, HUAC had not at any time opposed Emspak's invocation of the Fifth, so if he did it wrong he was given no chance to correct his mistake. Although the government maintained that Emspak waived his right when he replied "no" to a question about whether an answer would subject him to criminal liability, the Court did not find the "no" to be an unequivocal statement of waiver.

Finally, the Court held that a defendant can refuse to answer questions about other people with whom he associates. These people may be "links in a chain" of subversive activity, but a defendant need not reveal the rest of the chain.

See Leonard W. Levy, *Origins of the Fifth Amendment* (New York: Oxford University Press, 1968).

Brown v. Board of Education of Topeka, Kansas (Brown II)

349 U.S. 294 (1955)
Decided: May 31, 1955
Vote: 9 (Warren, Black, Reed, Frankfurter, Douglas, Burton, Clark, Minton, Harlan II)
0
Opinion of the Court: Warren

Chief Justice Warren's strategy in ***Brown I,*** 347 U.S. 483 (1954), assumed that the states would accept the inevitability of school desegregation by the time the Court handed down the implementation decree, and initial signs seemed encouraging. Some southern communities did not wait for the Court to act. They began desegregating schools by the time the 1954 academic year began. Ominous signs soon appeared, however. Gov. Thomas Stanley of Virginia abandoned his earlier moderation and announced that he would do everything he could to continue segregation in his state. In Mississippi, White Citizens Councils began to form in July, pledged to total war in defense of segregation. For the most part, however, a wait-and-see attitude in the South marked the twelve months following *Brown.* After all, no one knew exactly what the Court would order, and until then the schools remained segregated.

The Court heard arguments on proposed remedies that winter and again in April. The subject was controversial enough, but the justices also realized that they had to decide whether to abandon, at least in this area, the Court's traditional policy of ruling only on the case before it. Normally, if someone raises a valid claim that his or her constitutional rights have been violated, the decree is directed only to that petitioner's case; other persons "similarly situated" do not immediately gain the benefit of the decision. Lower federal courts then take notice of the ruling and apply it to future petitioners raising the same issue. In the school cases, however, this would mean that every black child wishing to enroll in a previously all-white school would have to go to court to secure the same rights that Linda Brown now enjoyed in Topeka. Determined states and localities, armed with sufficient resources, could delay desegregation for years by litigating every such claim.

Moreover, the Court usually takes little notice of practical matters of implementation. Once a right has been defined, it has to be available to all citizens, despite any institutional dislocations. But circumstances in public education varied enormously, and the Court understood that in some schools desegregation would mean a few blacks sitting in predominantly white classrooms and in other schools just the opposite—and it made a difference. Finally, how long could the Court give the South? Every day that black children continued to attend segregated schools they suffered a loss of their constitutional rights in violation of the Fourteenth Amendment's assurance of the equal protection of law. But to precipitate an order might lead to widespread obstruction, perhaps even violence.

The NAACP pushed for full integration in the shortest possible time. The group reasoned that blacks had been waiting three and a half centuries to be treated as equals and should not have to wait any longer to claim their constitutional rights.

The South seemed equally intransigent. Virginia urged the Court to face the "reality" of major differences between the two races and offered statistics to prove the inferiority of blacks. Florida had commissioned a poll and briefed the Court that only one in seven police officers would enforce attendance at racially mixed schools. The state also put forward such a complicated plan that, according to author Richard Kluger, "the most ungainly camel in Islam would have had an easier time passing through the eye of a needle than a black child getting into a white school in Florida."

At the request of the Court, the federal government appeared as *amicus.* The government's brief urged a middle position between "integration now" and "segregation forever." The states should submit timetables within ninety days, and implementation should be supervised by the local district courts. The courts would have the discretion to make adjustments in the schedules depending on local conditions. Communities would have a chance to change their attitudes and accept desegregation as necessary for all Americans to enjoy their full constitutional rights. An immediate start would have to be made, however, and the decision would have to be enforced by federal, state, and local officials, all of whom had taken an oath to support the Constitution.

On May 31, 1955, Warren handed down a seven-paragraph implementing decision, commonly known as *Brown II*. It stated that school segregation had to be ended everywhere but that the Court recognized that varying local conditions required different solutions. Local school districts must "make a prompt and reasonable start toward full compliance," and oversight was to be lodged in the federal district courts. The local judges should exercise the "practical flexibility" traditionally associated with equity, but delay and noncompliance should not be contemplated. Desegregation of public schools should proceed "*with all deliberate speed.*"

The Court did not fix a date for the end of segregation, nor did it require that initial plans be filed within ninety days, as the federal government had suggested. In fact, it gave the South far more than the segregationists had expected, raising hopes that the actual implementation of the decree could be delayed indefinitely. Assignment of primary responsibility to the local district courts led some southerners to assume that the decree could be completely ignored.

The implementation plan with its "all deliberate speed" provision, has, in fact, been generally condemned as giving the South far too much time, time it used not to desegregate but to become further entrenched. The Court also failed to give much guidance to the district courts that were charged with implementation. Consequently, timetables and plans varied enormously. If *Brown I* was a triumph of justice, *Brown II* was a failure.

See Richard Kluger, *Simple Justice* (New York: Knopf, 1975); Benjamin Muse, *Ten Years of Prelude: The Story of Integration Since the Supreme Court's 1954 Decision* (New York: Viking Press, 1964); and Jack W. Peltason, *Fifty-Eight Lonely Men* (Urbana: University of Illinois Press, 1961).

Peters v. Hobby

349 U.S. 331 (1955)
Decided: June 6, 1955
Vote: 7 (Warren, Black, Frankfurter, Douglas, Clark, Minton, Harlan II)
2 (Reed, Burton)
Opinion of the Court: Warren
Concurring opinion: Black
Concurring opinion: Douglas
Dissenting opinion: Reed (Burton)

John R. Peters, a professor at Yale University, worked seven to ten days a year assisting the federal Department of Health, Education, and Welfare to determine the validity of research grant proposals. The Loyalty Review Board charged Peters with communist associations and sympathies, and the HEW Agency Board held a hearing to determine whether Peters was disloyal and therefore ineligible for government service. The Agency Board did not find sufficient evidence to convict Peters, but the Loyalty Review Board did a "post-audit" of the hearing and found a "reasonable doubt" as to Peters's loyalty. He was subsequently barred from federal service for three years. Peters appealed on several claims. First, he argued that the Loyalty Review Board did not have authority to review the Agency Board's decision. Second, he argued that his due process rights had been denied by the secret information used against him.

The Court declined to decide the constitutional issues presented. It confined itself to deciding whether the Loyalty Review Board had the authority to review and overturn lower decisions and found that it did not. Congress gave the board authority to review proceedings appealed only by the accused. Here, it reviewed the case on its own authority rather than waiting for an appeal. This act not only violated the statute but also the deeply rooted principle that a positive decision may not be appealed against an accused.

Because the board acted outside of the scope of its authority, Peters's removal was invalid, and the Court issued a declaratory judgment on his behalf. By the time the Court heard this case, the Eisenhower administration had abolished the Loyalty Review Board, leaving decision making in agency hands. That decision, as well as the one in this case, represent a continued withdrawal from the witch-hunting mentality of the postwar Red Scare.

See David Caute, *The Great Fear: The Anti-Communist Purge under Truman and Eisenhower* (New York: Simon and Schuster, 1978).

United States ex rel. Toth v. Quarles

350 U.S. 11 (1955)
Decided: November 7, 1955
Vote: 6 (Warren, Black, Frankfurter, Douglas, Clark, Harlan II)
3 (Reed, Burton, Minton)
Opinion of the Court: Black
Dissenting opinion: Reed (Burton, Minton)
Dissenting opinion: Minton (Burton)

Robert Toth served in the U.S. Air Force in Korea and was honorably discharged. Five months after his service, he was arrested at his home in Pittsburgh and charged with conspiracy to commit murder while serving in Korea. Under authority of a 1950 act of Congress, Toth was taken to Korea to be tried by court-martial. Toth's sister filed a writ of habeas corpus on his behalf, arguing that Congress had no authority to try civilians who had completed their military service.

The Court held that neither Congress nor the president had court-martial authority over a civilian once he was no longer involved in the military. Under Article I of the Constitution, Congress has some authority over military matters, and the Fifth Amendment allows it to subject persons "in the land or naval forces" to trial by court-martial. In his opinion for the Court, however, Justice Black ruled that people "in the land or naval forces" must be limited to those presently serving. To hold otherwise would overly broaden the scope of the constitutional language. Furthermore, both Article III and the Sixth Amendment guarantee jury trials to citizens facing criminal charges, and they trump the narrow Fifth Amendment exception. The Constitution prefers trial by jury over any other method, so jury trials are the rule unless the Constitution dictates otherwise.

In response to another argument posed by the Air Force, the Court held that the president's power as commander in chief did not allow him to assert authority over civilians.

Ullman v. United States

350 U.S. 422 (1956)
Decided: March 26, 1956
Vote: 7 (Warren, Reed, Frankfurter, Burton,
Clark, Minton, Harlan II)
2 (Black, Douglas)
Opinion of the Court: Frankfurter
Dissenting opinion: Douglas (Black)

William Ludwig Ullman was a senior economic analyst at the Treasury Department who was named by an admitted Soviet spy, Elizabeth Bentley, as part of a spy ring. He was summoned before a grand jury investigating attempts to invade national security by espionage and conspiracy. Ullman attempted to plead the Fifth Amendment to several of the questions posed, but a federal district court ordered him to testify under the Immunity Act of 1954. In exchange for his testimony, the Immunity Act would grant Ullman immunity from federal and state prosecution regarding everything he testified about. Ullman, however, still refused to testify, saying that although the Immunity Act granted him freedom from prosecution, it did not protect him from the nonlegal ramifications of his testimony, such as loss of job or reputation. He was held in contempt of court and sentenced to six months in prison. Ullman appealed, arguing that the Fifth Amendment protected testimony with nonlegal as well as criminal consequences.

The Court held that the Fifth Amendment's privilege against self-incrimination applied only to testimony that might result in criminal prosecution and did not extend to testimony that may result in personal harm. Justice Frankfurter explained that the Immunity Act did not violate the Fifth Amendment because it offered Ullman sufficient protection from any criminal penalties resulting from his testimony. With this protection in place, Ullman could be compelled to testify without any Fifth Amendment difficulties. His testimony might harm him in other ways, but the Constitution did not protect him from those results.

Although Frankfurter went out of his way to write like a civil libertarian, Justice Douglas's dissent shredded the opinion. Douglas pointed out the very real problems that forced disclosure would bring down on Ullman, including loss of employment, blacklisting, and for all practical purposes, excommunication from society. In his view, the Fifth Amendment placed "the right of silence beyond the reach of government."

The case illustrates the issues in the debate over the reach of the privilege against self-incrimination, issues that remain unresolved.

See Leonard W. Levy, *Origins of the Fifth Amendment* (New York: Oxford University Press, 1968).

Pennsylvania v. Nelson

350 U.S. 497 (1956)
Decided: April 2, 1956
Vote: 6 (Warren, Black, Frankfurter, Douglas, Clark, Harlan II)
3 (Reed, Burton, Minton)
Opinion of the Court: Warren
Dissenting opinion: Reed (Burton, Minton)

Steve Nelson, a self-acknowledged member of the Communist Party of the United States, was convicted for sedition under a Pennsylvania law, one similar in most features to those that the Court had upheld in the 1920s. In his appeal Nelson argued that the Smith Act, which gave the federal government authority to prosecute sedition against state and local governments as well as the federal government, preempted the state statute, making Pennsylvania's sedition statute invalid.

The Court explained three reasons why the Smith Act superseded state sedition acts, which were no longer necessary with the creation of the Smith Act. First, the Smith Act along with other anticommunist statutes indicated Congress's intent to have sole authority over sedition. The Smith Act covered every area where sedition posed a threat, leaving no room for state supplementation.

Second, there was a dominant federal interest in addressing issues of sedition. The national government was concerned not only with peace within state borders but also with world peace. Congress viewed communism as a world conspiracy and believed it was the duty of the federal government to provide a "common defense" against its threat. Sedition in any form is a crime against the nation and its values.

Third, the Court found that allowing federal and state sedition acts to work together posed a threat of conflict within the administration of federal goals. The Court feared conflicting approaches and decisions that would weaken the federal government's unified stance against communism.

The case, along with ***Slochower v. Board of Higher Education of New York City*** 350 U.S. 551 (1956), came only a few weeks after issuance of the Southern Manifesto, in which 101 members of Congress from the southern states attacked the Court's desegregation decisions as an unlawful usurpation of states' rights. In addition to southerners, those people still obsessed with the Red Scare now had reason to assail the Court as procommunist.

See Michal R. Belknap, *Cold War Political Justice: The Smith Act, the Communist Party, and American Civil Liberties* (Westport: Greenwood Press, 1977).

Slochower v. Board of Higher Education of New York City

350 U.S. 551 (1956)
Decided: April 9, 1956
Vote: 5 (Warren, Black, Frankfurter, Douglas, Clark)
4 (Reed, Burton, Minton, Harlan II)
Opinion of the Court: Clark
Concurring opinion: Black
Concurring opinion: Douglas
Dissenting opinion: Reed (Burton, Minton)
Dissenting opinion: Harlan II

Harry Slochower, a faculty member at Brooklyn College, was called to testify before a congressional committee investigating subversive activity in academia. He testified willingly about his activities and associates in the years following 1941, but claimed Fifth Amendment protection against self-incrimination in response to questions about 1940 and 1941. The committee did not penalize Slochower for invoking the Fifth Amendment. Under New York State law, however, he lost his job as a professor because New York automatically terminated any state employee who refused to answer questions about his or her official activities. Slochower challenged New York's policy as a violation of the Fourteenth Amendment's Due Process Clause.

The Court held that a state could not automatically enforce a penalty against a state employee because he claimed the Fifth Amendment protection in response to congressional questioning. New York had erred, Justice Clark said, in treating Slochower's Fifth Amendment plea as a presumptive admission of guilt. The Fourteenth Amendment guarantees due process before a state may infringe on life, liberty, or property, and penalizing Slochower for exercising his constitutional rights affronted the requirements of due process. A state may not terminate an employee's government job just because he cited the Fifth Amendment without also looking into other evidence regarding his job performance.

Naim v. Naim

350 U.S. 891 (1955)
Decided: November 14, 1955
Vote: 9 (Warren, Black, Reed, Frankfurter, Douglas, Burton, Clark, Minton, Harlan II)
0
Opinion: *Per curiam*

Virginia, like many southern states, had an antimiscegenation law prohibiting marriages between people of different races. North Carolina had a similar law, but one aimed at marriage between whites and Negroes. Han Say Naim, a Chinese man, and Ruby Elaine Naim, a white woman, went to North Carolina to be wed and then returned to live in Virginia. After a while, Mrs. Naim went into court seeking an annulment on grounds that the marriage had never been legal and was therefore not binding. Mr. Naim claimed that the local court was without jurisdiction because the antimiscegenation law was unconstitutional. The Virginia court annulled the marriage, and Mr. Naim appealed.

According to the logic of ***Brown v. Board of Education,*** 347 U.S. 483 (1954), the Virginia law should have been declared unconstitutional. But the Court at this time was attempting to avoid major race cases while it saw how the *Brown* decision played out. It found a technicality, an alleged inadequacy of the record, to send the case back to the state courts and thus evade a decision. The Court eventually confronted the miscegenation issue in ***Loving v. Virginia,*** 388 U.S. 1 (1967), striking down the law down as a violation of the Fourteenth Amendment's Equal Protection Clause.

See Peter Wallenstein, "Race, Marriage, and the Supreme Court: From *Pace v. Alabama* to *Loving v. Virginia,*" *Journal of Supreme Court History* 65 (1998).

Butler v. Michigan

352 U.S. 380 (1957)
Decided: February 25, 1957
Vote: 9 (Warren, Black, Reed, Frankfurter, Douglas, Burton, Clark, Harlan II, Brennan)
0
Opinion of the Court: Frankfurter
Concurring in judgment without opinion: Black

Under Michigan law, anyone who distributed a book containing obscenity or material "tending to incite minors to violent or depraved or immoral acts" was guilty of a misdemeanor. Butler sold a book to a police officer that a trial judge found corruptive to youthful morals. Butler appealed his conviction, saying that the ordinance violated the First Amendment by prohibiting the distribution of books to the general public because of the affect that they might have on children. He also argued that the trial judge failed to look at the book as a whole and had failed to provide a sufficient standard of guilt.

The Court only had to address Butler's first argument to find the Michigan statute offensive to the Constitution. Butler had sold his book to an adult, but was convicted for the effect the book might have on children. Justice Frankfurter held that this approach "burned the house to roast the pig," and condemned the statute as not narrowly tailored to the government's interest in protecting minors. The government could legitimately create laws targeted at youth, but it could not make laws saying that the adult population of Michigan could read material suitable only for children.

See Harry M. Clor, *Obscenity and Public Morality: Censorship in a Liberal Society* (Chicago: University of Chicago Press, 1969).

Gayle v. Browder

352 U.S. 903 (1956)
Decided: November 13, 1956
Vote: 9 (Warren, Black, Reed, Frankfurter, Douglas, Burton, Clark, Harlan II, Brennan)
0
Opinion: *Per curiam*

On December 1, 1955, Rosa Parks, a black seamstress, refused to move to a seat in the back of a Montgomery, Alabama, bus. When the bus driver had her arrested, the black community mounted a boycott against the bus company that soon brought international attention to the civil rights struggle and propelled a new black leader, Martin Luther King Jr., to national prominence.

At the same time that King led the boycott, the National Association for the Advancement of Colored People (NAACP) mounted a legal challenge against segregated busing. Aurelia Browder, Susie McDonald, Claudette Colvin, and others sued W. A. Gayle and other members of the Board of Commissioners of the City of Montgomery, claiming that the bus segregation laws violated the Equal Protection Clause of the Fourteenth Amendment.

The Supreme Court's decision in this case is typical of many others it decided at this time. As the NAACP and others challenged segregation laws, they would often lose in the state courts. They would then appeal to the Court, which would accept the case but not hear oral argument. Instead, it would issue a terse *per curiam* remanding the case back to the lower court in light of the holding in ***Brown v. Board of Education,*** 347 U.S. 483 (1954). Similarly, as in this case, if the plaintiffs won in lower federal court and the state appealed, the Court would not hear oral argument but affirm *per curiam* in light of *Brown.*

See Catherine A. Barnes, *Journey from Jim Crow: The Desegregation of Southern Transit* (New York: Columbia University Press, 1983).

United States v. E. I. Du Pont de Nemours & Co. et al.

353 U.S. 586 (1957)
Decided: June 3, 1957
Vote: 4 (Warren, Black, Douglas, Brennan)
2 (Frankfurter, Burton)
Opinion of the Court: Brennan
Concurring opinion: Burton (Frankfurter)
Did not participate: Clark, Harlan II, Whittaker

In 1917 and 1919 E. I. Du Pont Corporation, a supplier of automotive finishers and fabrics, purchased a 23 percent stock interest in General Motors Corporation. Thereafter, Du Pont became General Motors' primary supplier of automotive finishers and fabrics. The United States brought suit against Du Pont under Section 7 of the Clayton Act, which says that no corporation engaged in commerce may acquire stock in another corporation if the effect of the stock acquisition is to create a monopoly in any "line of commerce." A federal district court dismissed the case because, until this time, the Federal Trade Commission and the business community assumed that Section 7 applied only to horizontal mergers between competitors (for example, two companies making the same product, such as cars), and not vertical holdings (one company making a product used by another). The Justice Department, however, believed that Section 7 should apply in this instance, and appealed.

The Court held that the government had sufficient evidence to prove a violation of Section 7. It explained that the statute enforced sanctions and equitable relief any time an acquisition presented a "reasonable likelihood" of creating monopoly in a line of commerce. The statute did not require intent to create a monopoly, only a possibility that one would emerge. Therefore, Du Pont could be liable under Section 7 even if it intended to buy the stocks only for investment purposes.

Justice Brennan held that the automotive finishes and fabrics sold by Du Pont were a "line of commerce" sufficient to bring the company under the requirements of the statute because the products were distinct from other automobile supplies. The facts also confirmed that a monopoly had been created because, following the acquisition of stock, Du Pont became General Motors' main supplier of these products. The Court found not only a "reasonable likelihood" of a monopoly emerging but also proof of an actual monopoly.

Three justices did not participate: Clark, because he was serving as attorney general when the original suit was filed; Harlan, because in private practice he had been a Du Pont attorney; and Whittaker, because he had not been confirmed at the time of oral argument.

Reid v. Covert

354 U.S. 1 (1957)
Decided: June 10, 1957
Vote: 6 (Warren, Black, Frankfurter, Douglas, Harlan II, Brennan)
2 (Burton, Clark)
Judgment of the Court: Black
Opinion concurring in judgment: Frankfurter
Concurring in judgment without opinion: Harlan II
Dissenting opinion: Clark (Burton)
Did not participate: Whittaker

Clarice Covert killed her husband, a sergeant in the United States Air Force, at an air base in England. She was tried by court-martial under the Uniform Code of Military Justice (UCMJ), which said that all persons serving in, employed by, or accompanying the armed forces could be tried by military tribunal. Following her conviction, Covert filed a writ of habeas corpus, arguing that her conviction was illegal because civilians cannot be tried by military courts. Her petition was heard in conjunction with a similar writ filed by Dorothy Kreuger, who killed her serviceman husband while they were stationed in Japan and was tried by a similar tribunal.

The Court had originally heard this case in 1956 (351 U.S. 487), when it appeared that a majority would confirm the power of the military courts. Instead, the dissenters managed to convince the majority to have the case reargued the following term, and after reargument a different majority emerged.

Four members of the Court held that civilians cannot be tried by military tribunals under any circumstances. According to Justice Black, both Article III and the Sixth Amendment of the Constitution guarantee the provision of a jury in civilian criminal trials. The U.S. government cannot deprive a citizen of his constitutional rights even if he is tried on foreign soil, because the Constitution directs all government action regardless of boundaries. The UCMJ directly conflicted with these mandates and was therefore invalid.

Justices Frankfurter and Harlan joined in the judgment of the Court but argued that only in capital cases would civilians attached to the armed forces have to be tried before a civilian court; for lesser offenses they would have permitted the UCMJ to govern trials.

See Jonathan Lurie, *Military Justice in America: The U.S. Court of Appeals for the Armed Forces, 1775–1980,* rev. ed. (Lawrence: University Press of Kansas, 2001).

Watkins v. United States

354 U.S. 178 (1957)
Decided: June 17, 1957
Vote: 6 (Warren, Black, Frankfurter, Douglas, Harlan II, Brennan)
1 (Clark)
Opinion of the Court: Warren
Concurring opinion: Frankfurter
Dissenting opinion: Clark
Did not participate: Burton, Whittaker

John Watkins, a labor organizer, was summoned to testify before the House Un-American Activities Committee (HUAC). He freely answered questions about himself and his activities, but refused to answer questions about other people. He was charged with and convicted of refusing to answer any question "pertinent to the question under inquiry." Watkins argued that questions about other people were not pertinent to the committee's purpose under the resolution authorizing HUAC's activity, and that if they were, the committee failed to explain the purpose to him.

The Court held Watkins's conviction invalid because he had not been informed of the purpose of the committee's questions and did not therefore know if he was obliged to answer. For a congressional committee to function legitimately, Chief Justice Warren explained, it had to have a clear definition of the scope of its powers. Here, no such definition had been provided, and Watkins had no way of knowing whether the questions asked were pertinent to the unexplained purpose of the committee. Congressional committees admittedly had broad power to investigate, but their powers were not unlimited. Watkins could not be forced to answer questions that Congress was not authorized to ask, just as Congress could not violate his constitutional rights during the course of the investigation.

Scholars have noted that the opinion implicitly criticizes the tone of the anticommunist congressional hearings, their invasions of individual privacy, and their violations of First and Fifth Amendment rights. The Court in this and other cases was trying to rein in the excesses of those hearings, and yet had to do so without impinging on legitimate congressional prerogatives. The stratagem here—of declaring that there had been no definition of the committee's scope—fooled no one, but it did put Congress on notice that it could no longer authorize committees to go fishing without limits in the name of anticommunism.

See David Caute, *The Great Fear: The Anti-Communist Purge under Truman and Eisenhower* (New York: Simon and Schuster, 1978).

Sweezy v. New Hampshire

354 U.S. 234 (1957)
Decided: June 17, 1957
Vote: 6 (Warren, Black, Frankfurter, Douglas, Warren, Harlan II, Brennan)
2 (Burton, Clark)
Judgment of the Court: Warren
Opinion concurring in judgment: Frankfurter (Harlan II)
Dissenting opinion: Clark (Burton)
Did not participate: Whittaker

A 1951 New Hampshire law gave the state attorney general power to investigate "subversive persons." Paul Sweezy, a classical Marxist economist and a state college professor, was called before a committee created by the attorney general. He answered questions about his communist affiliations, but refused to reveal the content of his lectures, information about his political activities, or the names of his associates. A state court held Sweezy in contempt for refusing to answer questions presented. He appealed, claiming that the attorney general's questions were outside the scope of the authority given to him by the legislature. He argued that the questions did not relate to suspected subversive activities and that asking them without legislative authority violated the Fourteenth Amendment's Due Process Clause.

The Court said that all persons, even those suspected of subversive activity, have some right to privacy from legislative scrutiny. Although the New Hampshire legislature had an interest in revealing true subversive activity, it had no business asking questions unrelated to the subject. Chief Justice Warren affirmed Sweezy's right to protest the questions presented to him and commented that his academic growth required freedom from revealing the content of every lecture and information about associates.

In concurrence Justice Frankfurter wrote the most powerful First Amendment defense of academic freedom in the Court's history. In addition, Frankfurter, who believed that even First Amendment rights were not absolute, introduced for the first time the standard by which state infringements upon freedom of speech would be judged: for a state to trench upon a constitutional right, it must be acting because of a compelling state interest.

Yates v. United States

354 U.S. 298 (1957)
Decided: June 17, 1957
Vote: 6 (Warren, Black, Frankfurter, Douglas, Burton, Harlan II)
1 (Clark)
Opinion of the Court: Harlan II
Opinion concurring in judgment: Burton
Opinion concurring in part, dissenting in part: Black (Douglas)
Dissenting opinion: Clark
Did not participate: Brennan, Whittaker

Dennis v. United States, 341 U.S. 494 (1951), marked such a low point in the Court's cold war record and so strongly disdained free speech that even the majority members realized they would have to rethink the issue. The Court, in fact, did show itself more sensitive to free speech and security issues in subsequent Smith Act prosecutions.

In *Yates* the Court set aside the conviction of fourteen mid-level communist leaders. Justice Harlan found two significant differences in the fact situations between this case and *Dennis.* First he read the words "to organize" in the act to mean to organize a new entity, and, because the Communist Party had been in existence when Congress passed the Smith Act, that section did not apply, as "to organize" could not mean to carry on a continuous activity.

Second, Harlan found the instructions to the jury defective. The defendants had been charged, as had those in *Dennis,* with conspiring to advocate and teach the duty and necessity of overthrowing the government of the United States by force and violence. Unlike the majority in *Dennis,* however, the Court now adopted the view that significant difference existed between such advocacy as an abstract doctrine and advocacy of direct action. Unless the government could show the latter, it could not prosecute people for mere abstract discussions. The judge's charge to the jury had failed to specify that this was the burden of proof that the government had to meet for the defendants to be found guilty.

Justice Black would have found the entire Smith Act unconstitutional as a violation of the First Amendment, a step the majority refused to take. But Harlan's gloss on *Dennis* set the evidentiary bar so high that for all practical purposes Smith Act prosecutions stopped.

Commentators have praised Harlan, a conservative Republican, for reinvigorating free speech protection and curtailing prosecutions under the Smith Act, even though the Court held the act constitutional in *Dennis.* By "interpreting" *Dennis* and finding judicially manageable standards, he led the Court in a new direction. It would have been politically troublesome to a Court already charged with being too liberal and "soft on criminals" to have reversed itself on *Dennis;* Harlan's approach avoided that danger while strengthening protection of speech. A similar pattern can be found in the Court's treatment of other anticommunist legislation of the period.

See Stanley I. Kutler, *The American Inquisition: Justice and Injustice in the Cold War* (New York: Hill and Wang, 1982); and Michal R. Belknap, *Cold War Political Justice: The Smith Act, the Communist Party, and American Civil Liberties* (Westport, Conn.: Greenwood Press, 1977).

Alberts v. California

354 U.S. 476 (1957)
Decided: June 24, 1957
Vote: 7 (Warren, Frankfurter, Burton, Clark, Harlan II, Brennan, Whittaker)
2 (Black, Douglas)
Opinion of the Court: Brennan
Opinion concurring in judgment: Warren
Opinion concurring in judgment: Harlan II
Dissenting opinion: Douglas (Black)

Alberts was argued and decided with *Roth v. United States* and carries the same U.S. citation, but the votes in the two cases vary slightly. *Roth* was based on a federal law conviction, but *Alberts* originated as a matter of California state law. Because both dealt with obscenity, the Court held both cases to the same standard and handed down an opinion in *Roth* that also encompassed the facts and decision in *Alberts.*

David S. Alberts conducted a mail-order pornography business. He had been convicted under a California law of keeping for sale obscene and indecent books and of advertising these books. He challenged his convictions, arguing that California's obscenity laws violated the First Amendment.

The Court held that obscenity is not a constitutionally protected form of speech and that California's laws did not violate the First Amendment. As Justice Brennan explained, the First Amendment was not intended to protect every utterance, but only those forms of speech that added to the unfettered interchange of ideas contributing to the political and social good. Obscenity did not achieve a political or social goal; rather, it created a clear and present danger of antisocial conduct. Therefore, it merited no First Amendment protection.

To say that obscene speech merited no First Amendment protection, the Court had to create a clear definition of obscenity. The Court held that the standard for judging obscenity is "whether, to the average person, applying contemporary community standards, the dominant theme of the material, taken as a whole, appeals to the prurient interest." Under this definition the Court found the material Alberts sold was obscene, and the justices therefore upheld his conviction under California law.

Justice Harlan concurred in *Alberts* because, he argued, states could use their police powers to regulate obscenity. He dissented in *Roth* because he believed the censorship of obscenity was beyond the reach of the federal government.

See Harry M. Clor, *Obscenity and Public Morality: Censorship in a Liberal Society* (Chicago: University of Chicago Press, 1969).

Roth v. United States

354 U.S. 476 (1957)
Decided: June 24, 1957
Vote: 6 (Warren, Frankfurter, Burton, Clark, Brennan, Whittaker)
3 (Black, Douglas, Harlan II)
Opinion of the Court: Brennan
Opinion concurring in judgment: Warren
Opinion concurring in part, dissenting in part: Harlan II
Dissenting opinion: Douglas (Black)

Obscenity, like libel, was long considered outside First Amendment protection and subject to state control. The Supreme Court's first encounter with obscenity came in a little noticed but unanimous decision, ***Butler v. Michigan,*** 352 U.S. 380 (1957), in which Justice Frankfurter threw out a state statute as a violation of freedom of the press. The law banned books containing obscene, immoral, or lewd language for their potentially harmful effect on youth. The law "would reduce the adult population of Michigan to reading what is fit for children," Frankfurter said. Although the case put forward no judicial standards by which to judge what was obscene, it made clear that Victorian values could not be sustained in a First Amendment challenge.

The following year the Court tried to establish a new standard in *Roth* and its companion case ***Alberts v. California.*** Samuel Roth was convicted under a federal statute prohibiting the mailing of obscene materials, and *Alberts* involved a state obscenity law.

Justice Brennan noted that "obscenity is [historically] not within the area of constitutionally protected speech or press," but any idea having "the slightest redeeming social importance" could claim First Amendment protection. He drew a distinction between sex and obscenity, defining the latter as material "which deals with sex in a manner appealing to prurient interests." The Court rejected the earlier test for obscenity, developed from the English case, *Regina v. Hicklin,* L.R. 3 Q.B. 360 (1868), which judged the material by the effect of selected passages on particularly susceptible persons. In its place the Court adopted a standard already in use in some American courts: "Whether to the average person, applying contemporary community standards, the dominant theme of the material taken as a whole appeals to prurient interests."

Justices Douglas and Harlan in their separate dissents pinpointed the main problem: How does one identify obscene material? The Brennan test, although more liberal and fairer than the *Hicklin* standard, still required subjective judgment as to whether the allegedly prurient material had any redeeming social value. Many new and shocking works of art were initially attacked as obscene. For example, when James Joyce's *Ulysses* was first published, critics condemned it, and the U.S. government refused to allow its importation into the country. Yet within a few years, writers and scholars were hailing *Ulysses* as a masterpiece, and in the famous case of *United States v. One Book Called "Ulysses,"* 5 F. Supp. 182 (S.D.N.Y. 1933), *aff'd,* 72 F.2d 705 (2d Cir. 1934), Judge John Woolsey of the federal district court in New York relied on expert witnesses to testify on the literary value of Joyce's novel; in doing so, Woolsey anticipated much of the *Roth* test.

The determination of what constituted obscenity troubled the Court for the next two decades. As Harlan noted, in ***Ginsberg v. New York,*** 390 U.S. 629 (1968), the subject had produced a variety of views "unmatched in any other course of constitutional adjudication." Thirteen obscenity cases between 1957 and 1968 produced a total of fifty-five separate opinions. The justices seemed preoccupied with the question of "What is obscenity?" and failed to conduct the type of inquiry normal to First Amendment litigation, "What state interests justify restraint?" Brennan's flat-out "obscenity is not speech" put it into a category apart from the well-defined analyses that the Court had developed for other speech issues. Not until the Burger Court refined the *Roth* test in ***Miller v. California,*** 413 U.S. 15 (1973), did the Court finally confront the question of why the states had an interest in such controls.

See David Lowenthal, *No Liberty for License: The Forgotten Logic of the First Amendment* (Dallas: Spence Publishers, 1997), part II; Harry M. Clor, *Obscenity and Public Morality: Censorship in a Liberal Society* (Chicago: University of Chicago Press, 1969); C. Peter Magrath, "The Obscenity Cases: Grapes of Roth," *Supreme Court Review, 1966* (1967): 7.

McGee v. International Life Insurance Co.

355 U.S. 220 (1957)
Decided: December 16, 1957
Vote: 7 (Black, Frankfurter, Douglas, Burton, Clark, Harlan II, Brennan)
0
Opinion of the Court: Black
Did not participate: Warren

Lowell Franklin, a resident of California, purchased a life insurance contract from an Arizona insurance company in 1944. The Arizona company later sold all of its insurance obligations to International Life Insurance in Texas. International sent a letter to Franklin informing him of the change, and he began paying his premiums directly to the Texas office. In 1950 Franklin died, and International refused to pay the proceeds of his life insurance policy to his mother, Lulu McGee. McGee sued International in a California court, sending service of process to Texas via mail. She obtained a judgment against International, but International appealed, saying that California did not have jurisdiction over it.

The Court held that California could assert jurisdiction over International because International's relationship with Franklin constituted sufficient "minimum contacts." It would violate the Fourteenth Amendment to force a company to be sued in a state where it did no business, and where it did not anticipate being sued. In ***International Shoe Co. v. Washington,*** 326 U.S. 310 (1945), however, the Court held that a state could assert jurisdiction over someone outside of the state if the person had enough contacts with the state to know that he could be sued there. International knew that Franklin lived in California, and they sent him a letter in that location. It would be too difficult for Franklin's heirs to come to Texas to sue International there, so it made sense that International would have to come to California. Because International knew that being sued in California was a possibility, its due process rights were not violated by being made to stand trial there.

Perez v. Brownell

356 U.S. 44 (1958)
Decided: March 31, 1958
Vote: 5 (Frankfurter, Burton, Clark, Harlan II, Brennan)
4 (Warren, Black, Douglas, Whittaker)
Opinion of the Court: Frankfurter
Dissenting opinion: Warren (Black, Douglas)
Dissenting opinion: Douglas (Black)
Dissenting opinion: Whittaker

Clemente Martinez Perez was born in Texas but lived in Mexico as a child. In 1943 he began applying for admission to the United States to work on the railroad, but he did not register for the military draft despite his obligation as an American citizen to do so. When Perez reapplied for admission in 1947 he was refused entry by the Board of Special Inquiry, which contended that Perez had expatriated himself by remaining outside of the United States to avoid the draft and by voting in Mexican elections. The latter specifically violated the Nationality Act of 1940, which made voting in foreign elections grounds for expatriation. Perez filed suit in district court for a judgment declaring him an American citizen, but that court also found that he had expatriated himself.

The main issue confronting the Supreme Court was whether the Nationality Act of 1940 could validly be applied against a U.S. citizen, and, by a slim majority, the Court held that it could. According to Justice Frankfurter, the Nationality Act was a valid exercise of federal power because Congress had sovereign power over issues involving citizenship and relationships with other nations. Congress had been legitimately making expatriation statutes since the 1800s, and its decision to expatriate those who participated in foreign elections was reasonable. Showing allegiance to the political affairs of one nation is inconsistent with continued allegiance to another. Nations often have conflicting interests, Frankfurter said, and it is impossible to support more than one at the same time.

The dissenters believed that citizenship could not be so easily stripped from a native-born American, but the greater implication of the case is that it reflected the near stalemate in the Court at this time. On the one hand, a centrist-conservative bloc led by Justices Frankfurter and Harlan took a limited view of individual rights and was willing to defer to congressional power, even when it infringed on those rights. The liberal bloc of Chief Justice Warren and Justices Black, Douglas, and Brennan could occasionally muster a fifth vote, but were often in the minority. Not until the appointment of Justice Goldberg to replace Frankfurter would the liberals gain a working majority.

Trop v. Dulles

356 U.S. 86 (1958)
Decided: March 31, 1958
Vote: 5 (Warren, Black, Douglas, Brennan, Whittaker)
4 (Frankfurter, Burton, Clark, Harlan II)
Judgment of the Court: Warren
Concurring opinion: Black (Douglas)
Opinion concurring in judgment: Brennan
Dissenting opinion: Frankfurter (Burton, Clark, Harlan II)

Albert L. Trop, while serving as a private in the U.S. Army stationed in French Morocco, caused some discipline problems within his unit and was confined to barracks. He escaped and began walking away from camp. He was found less than twenty-four hours later and willingly returned to his unit. Nevertheless, he was charged and found guilty of desertion, for which the penalty was loss of U.S. citizenship. Trop challenged this penalty, saying that it was not proper punishment for desertion and that it constituted cruel and unusual punishment.

The Court found that loss of citizenship was an excessive punishment for desertion. The Nationality Act of 1940, from which the desertion statute derived, defined several ways for an individual to lose his or her citizenship. Most involved participating in the politics or military of another nation, which the Court agreed merited loss of citizenship because it was impossible to be an active citizen of two states. The desertion statute, however, involved no element of involvement with a foreign state and this, Chief Justice Warren held, was a vital difference. The choice to desert often involved no other loyalties; rather, it reflected fear, laziness, or emotional imbalance, for which loss of citizenship was too severe a punishment.

Furthermore, the Court found that complete loss of citizenship, leaving a person "stateless," was cruel and unusual punishment. It involved the total destruction of an individual's role in society and caused him to lose his "right to have rights." Cruel and unusual punishment, the Court held, includes non–death penalty punishments that subject an individual to "a fate of ever-increasing fear and distress," as a stateless person would experience under this law.

Justice Brennan rested the decision on the ground that expatriation on the ground of wartime desertion had no relevant connection with the war power or any other power of Congress. Justice Frankfurter dissented on grounds similar to that in ***Perez v. Brownell,*** 356 U.S. 44 (1958), namely, that control over citizenship belonged to Congress, which could define the conditions under which U.S. citizens could be stripped of that status.

Kent v. Dulles

357 U.S. 116 (1958)
Decided: June 16, 1958
Vote: 5 (Warren, Black, Frankfurter, Douglas, Brennan)
4 (Clark, Burton, Harlan II, Whittaker)
Opinion of the Court: Douglas
Dissenting opinion: Clark (Burton, Harlan II, Whittaker)

During the cold war era, the government began the practice of refusing passports to known or suspected communists. In this case, Secretary of State John Foster Dulles refused to issue a passport to artist Rockwell Kent because he would not file an affidavit concerning his alleged membership in the Communist Party. The district court and the court of appeals upheld the secretary's decision, and Kent appealed to the Supreme Court.

The Court reversed. Justice Douglas held that the Immigration and Nationality Act of 1952 did not authorize the secretary of state to withhold a passport because an applicant refused to filed an affidavit regarding his political beliefs or actions.

Wiener v. United States

357 U.S. 349 (1958)
Decided: June 30, 1958
Vote: 9 (Warren, Black, Frankfurter, Douglas, Burton, Clark, Harlan II, Brennan, Whittaker)
0
Opinion of the Court: Frankfurter

President Truman appointed Myron Wiener to the War Claims Commission, which Congress created to adjudicate claims from World War II prisoners of war and internees. Commissioners understood that their jobs would expire when their work was complete, but no other terms were placed on their removal. When Dwight Eisenhower became president in 1953, he removed Wiener from the commission, replacing him, as Eisenhower put it, with "personnel of my own selection." Weiner sued for back pay from the time he was laid off until the commission ended a few months later.

The Court held that Wiener was entitled to back pay because Eisenhower had no authority to remove him from office. The president has absolute power of appointment and removal only when Congress grants such power or when the office in question is exclusively part of the executive branch. Here, Congress made no provision for the removal of commission members and intended for them to remain on the commission until the completion of its work. Furthermore, Congress purposely made the commission adjudicatory rather than executive in nature, meaning that it was not an executive department.

Separation of powers requires that the president not be allowed to exercise arbitrary authority over all branches of government. When Congress purposefully does not invest removal power in the executive, and does not place an organization in the executive branch, the president has no removal authority. The Court had reached the same opinion in the historic case of ***Humphrey's Executor v. United States,*** 295 U.S. 602 (1935), and it affirmed the holding here.

NAACP v. Alabama ex rel. Patterson

357 U.S. 449 (1958)
Decided: June 30, 1958
Vote: 9 (Warren, Black, Frankfurter, Douglas, Clark, Harlan II, Brennan, Whittaker, Stewart)
0
Opinion of the Court: Harlan II

Alabama required most out-of-state corporations to file corporate charters with the secretary of state. Fines and criminal prosecution could be imposed on a corporation and its officers for conducting intrastate business before filing the charter. Asserting that the National Association for the Advancement of Colored People (NAACP) had not complied with the law, the state instituted legal proceedings against the group, seeking ultimately to prevent it from conducting business within the state.

The circuit court issued an order restraining the NAACP from engaging in further activities in Alabama. The NAACP challenged the order, arguing that the group's activities did not violate the state law and that by seeking to remove the association from the state, Alabama was violating the NAACP's First and Fourteenth Amendment rights to freedom of speech and assembly.

Over NAACP objections, the court ordered, as requested by the state, the production of a substantial part of the requested records, including the membership lists. The NAACP argued that producing the list would put its members at risk of economic or physical reprisals and other forms of harassment. The trial judge held the NAACP in contempt and fined it $100,000. Under state law the contempt charges ended the organization's right to a hearing. The state supreme court twice affirmed the lower court, and the NAACP turned to the U.S. Supreme Court.

This case is one of a number from the late 1950s and early 1960s that arose from the NAACP's resistance to the efforts of southern states to inhibit its activities by requiring it to disclose membership lists. The Court recognized these laws for what they were—attempts to gut the activities of the nation's leading civil rights organization by forcing it to name its members.

The Court held that the NAACP could assert as a full defense the constitutional rights of its members to freedom of association, rather than having each member come forward to do so, and in the process reveal his or her identity. In addition, Justice Harlan found that the membership list reflected, and was therefore an integral part of, each member's right to pursue lawful interests—namely the ending of desegregation—privately and to associate freely with others of a like mind. Although the First Amendment does not specifically mention the right to associate, the Court found it implied there, enunciated it, and applied it to the states.

Like all First Amendment rights, the state could infringe only if it showed some compelling interest in doing so, and here it had not. The Court overturned both the contempt citation and the fine.

For similar cases, see ***Bates v. Little Rock,*** 361 U.S. 516 (1960), invalidating a requirement that membership lists be disclosed in connection with an occupational license tax, and *Louisiana ex rel. Gremillion v. NAACP,* 366 U.S. 293 (1961), restraining enforcement of a law requiring nonprofit organizations to file membership lists. In these cases associational liberty issues were raised when state governments sought information not only about the organization's members but also about association activities and beliefs. Government requests for such lists are seen as efforts to chill the free exercise of First Amendment rights.

See Harry A. Kalven Jr., *The Negro and the First Amendment* (Chicago: University of Chicago Press, 1965).

Giordenello v. United States

357 U.S. 480 (1958)
Decided: June 30, 1958
Vote: 6 (Warren, Black, Frankfurter, Douglas, Harlan II, Brennan)
3 (Burton, Clark, Whittaker)
Opinion of the Court: Harlan II
Dissenting opinion: Clark (Burton, Whittaker)

Following his conviction for unlawful purchase of narcotics, Veto Giordenello challenged evidence presented at trial by saying that it was obtained via an illegal arrest. Giordenello contended that the arrest warrant used against him was invalid because it was based entirely on hearsay evidence and because it contained only a conclusion of law with no supporting facts. In obtaining the warrant, the investigating officer had filed an affidavit saying only that someone had told him that Giordenello possessed illegal drugs and he concluded that Giordenello had violated the law against purchasing such drugs.

The Court found it unnecessary to address Giordenello's hearsay complaint and left unanswered the question of whether an arrest warrant could be based solely on hearsay evidence. It held that the warrant was not based on sufficient evidence and that it was invalid on those grounds alone. The Federal Rules of Criminal Procedure require that an arrest warrant be issued only upon a showing of "essential facts constituting the offense charged" and a conclusion that those facts provided probable cause for arrest. Here, the officer had provided no facts, supplying only the conclusion that Giordenello possessed illegal drugs. Only the issuing magistrate is supposed to make conclusions of law in a warrant procedure, based on facts provided. Absent proof that a crime has probably occurred, it is improper to issue an arrest warrant.

Because the warrant for Giordenello's arrest was illegal, anything found during an arrest-related search was inadmissible as evidence. The bag of heroin taken from Giordenello at his arrest was not valid evidence and should not have been used in his conviction. The Court therefore reversed judgment against him.

See Fred Graham, *The Due Process Revolution: The Warren Court's Impact on Criminal Law* (New York: Hayden, 1970).

Cooper v. Aaron

358 U.S. 1 (1958)
Decided: September 12, 1958
Vote: *Per curiam* (signed by all nine justices)
Concurring opinion: Frankfurter

The implementation of a Supreme Court decision is not based on the proverbial sword or purse, but rather on the moral authority the Court commands. Naturally, assistance from Congress or the president is welcome. In the years just after the two decisions in ***Brown v. Board of Education,*** 347 U.S. 483 (1954), and 348 U.S. 294 (1955), such assistance failed to materialize. President Eisenhower complained that *Brown* had set back the cause of racial progress in the South by fifteen years.

In the fall of 1957 the Little Rock, Arkansas school board agreed to a court order to admit nine black students to Central High School. Gov. Orville Faubus, once considered a moderate, called out the national guard to prevent the blacks from entering. He withdrew the troops on a court order, but when the black students again tried to attend, a mob attacked the school and drove them off. Eisenhower, who only two months earlier said he could not envision any situation where he would use federal troops to enforce desegregation orders, could no longer passively sit by and watch federal authority flouted. He ordered a thousand paratroopers into Little Rock, and federalized ten thousand Arkansas national guardsmen to protect black students and maintain order in the schools.

In *Cooper v. Aaron,* for the first time in its history the Court issued a unanimous *per curiam* decision signed by all nine justices, a sign, they hoped, that would indicate their unanimity on this issue. (Justice Frankfurter infuriated his colleagues when he insisted on adding a separate concurrence.) *Cooper* not only affirmed *Brown* but also reasserted the Court's authority as the ultimate interpreter of the Constitution. Arkansas claimed that it was not bound by *Brown* because it had not been a party to that suit. The Court could have limited itself to a sharp reminder that state officials, including the governor and the state legislature, have no power to nullify a federal court order. Instead, it reminded Arkansas—and the nation—that since ***Marbury v. Madison,*** 5 U.S. 137 (1803), it is well established constitutional practice that it is "the province and duty of the judicial department to say what the law is." That principle, the Court continued, "has ever since been respected by this Court and the Country as a permanent and indispensable feature of our constitutional system. It follows that the interpretation of the Fourteenth Amendment enunciated by the Court in the *Brown* cases is the supreme law of the land," binding not only the federal government but state officials as well.

Rather than obey the Court, Faubus closed the Little Rock public schools in 1958 and 1959; he reopened them only in response to another court order. In Virginia, three cities and two counties also closed their schools to prevent integration, and the General Assembly provided funds to promote private schools. The pace of desegregation slowed to a crawl: only thirteen additional school districts in 1958, nineteen the following year, and seventeen in 1960 integrated their schools. Congress debated legislation restricting the Court's power or nullifying its decisions, but none was ever signed into law. Six years after the first *Brown* decision, thousands of school districts in the South remained segregated, moderate voices had been muted, and politicians loudly claimed that Supreme Court decisions need not be obeyed as the law of the land.

See Tony Freyer, *The Little Rock Crisis: A Constitutional Interpretation* (Westport, Conn.: Greenwood Press, 1984); and Daniel A. Farber, "The Supreme Court and the Rule of Law in *Cooper v. Aaron* Revisited," *University of Illinois Law Review* (1982): 387.

Lassiter v. Northampton County Board of Elections

360 U.S. 45 (1959)
Decided: June 8, 1959
Vote: 9 (Warren, Black, Frankfurter, Douglas, Clark, Harlan II, Brennan, Whittaker, Stewart)
0
Opinion of the Court: Douglas

North Carolina law required all citizens, regardless of race, to submit to a literacy test prior to registering to vote. Prospective voters would need to demonstrate an ability to read and write any section of the state constitution. Lassiter refused to take the test and was subsequently denied the right to vote.

She appealed to the County Board of Elections and at a *de novo* hearing again refused the literacy test and was again denied registration. She then appealed to the state courts, and every state court that heard the case, including the North Carolina Supreme Court, upheld the test requirement.

The U.S. Supreme Court held that no constitutional defect inhered in the North Carolina statute. A state may properly conclude that only those who are literate should exercise the franchise. The states, Justice Douglas noted in the opinion for the Court, traditionally had broad powers to determine the conditions of suffrage. Lassiter did not claim that the literacy test was applied in a discriminatory manner, and so the Court had to assume that all citizens faced the same threshold qualifications.

Congress dealt with *Lassiter* when it debated and passed the Voting Rights Act of 1965. The act temporarily suspended literacy and other tests used as a prerequisite to voting. But in ***South Carolina v. Katzenbach,*** 383 U.S. 301 (1966), the Court distinguished *Lassiter* by noting that Congress had found that such tests were often used in a discriminatory manner to exclude blacks, and that Congress had sufficient authority under the Enforcement Clause of the Fifteenth Amendment to override the states' traditional discretion in this area. In ***Katzenbach v. Morgan,*** 384 U.S. 641 (1966), the Court went further, striking down English literacy tests to Spanish-speaking citizens who had completed the sixth grade in a non–English-speaking American school.

See Donald S. Strong, *Negroes, Ballots, and Judges* (University: University of Alabama Press, 1968); and Steven F. Lawson, *Black Ballots: Voting Rights in the South, 1944–1969* (New York: Columbia University Press, 1976).

Uphaus v. Wyman

360 U.S. 72 (1959)
Decided: June 8, 1959
Vote: 5 (Frankfurter, Clark, Harlan II, Whittaker, Stewart)
4 (Warren, Black, Douglas, Brennan)
Opinion of the Court: Clark
Dissenting opinion: Brennan (Warren, Black, Douglas)
Dissenting opinion: Black, Douglas

New Hampshire commissioned its attorney general to investigate subversive activities within the state. Attorney General Louis C. Wyman called Willard Uphaus to testify before a legislative committee concerning the summer camp that he ran, which had allegedly hired many procommunist speakers in the summers of 1954 and 1955. Uphaus testified before the committee, but refused to respond to a subpoena demanding that he produce records of his employees, visitors, and speakers for the years in question. The attorney general tried to enforce the subpoena by court order, and when Uphaus refused to comply he was held in contempt of court and imprisoned. He appealed, saying that only the federal government could investigate subversive behavior and that the state attorney general's probe was invalid.

The Court held that a state has the authority to investigate subversive behavior that threatens the welfare of the state and that the subpoena was justified. In an earlier case, ***Pennsylvania v. Nelson,*** 350 U.S. 497 (1956), the Court had said that only the federal government could investigate sedition, but that case referred to sedition against the federal government and was only intended to prevent state and federal attorneys from pursuing the same claims. Here, New Hampshire had a state claim separate from any federal interest. Because states have full police power to deal with internal disturbances, Uphaus could be investigated for subversion within New Hampshire's borders.

According to Justice Clark, for New Hampshire to enforce its subpoena against Uphaus, the state had to prove that its interest in stopping subversion was more critical than Uphaus's privacy interest. The Court found that the state's interest was indeed superior. The state had valid evidence that the speakers hired by Uphaus harbored communist sentiments, and the investigation had been conducted in a nonintrusive way. The Uphaus camp was public, and he was already required by law to keep public records of visitors. Under these circumstances, the interest of the state outweighed Uphaus's privacy concerns.

Justice Brennan dissented. He said that Uphaus's and his guests' constitutionally protected rights of speech and assembly could not be subordinated to New Hampshire's legislative investigation because the legislature had failed to provide a rational connection between its legislative purpose and the activities of the camp.

See Richard Fried, *Nightmare in Red: The McCarthy Era in Perspective* (New York: Oxford University Press, 1990).

Barenblatt v. United States

360 U.S. 109 (1959)
Decided: June 8, 1959
Vote: 5 (Frankfurter, Clark, Harlan II, Whittaker, Stewart)
4 (Warren, Black, Douglas, Brennan)
Opinion of the Court: Harlan II
Dissenting opinion: Black (Warren, Douglas)
Dissenting opinion: Brennan

Lloyd Barenblatt, a former college teacher, was called as a witness before a subcommittee of the House Committee on Un-American Activities (HUAC) looking into alleged communist subversion in education. Barenblatt refused to answer questions as to whether he had been a member of the Communist Party and was subsequently convicted of contempt of Congress as well as of congressional committees. The case had come before the Court in 1957, (354 U.S. 930), and remanded to the court of appeals for further consideration. When the court of appeals reaffirmed the conviction, Barenblatt came back to the Supreme Court, claiming that HUAC had no authority to investigate education and that its directions from Congress lacked required specificity.

The Court disagreed and affirmed the conviction. Justice Harlan held that the subcommittee had the appropriate authority to investigate communist infiltration into education and that this authority was not subject to attack because of vagueness. Barenblatt had been apprised of the relevance of the committee's questions to its inquiry, and the committee's questions did not infringe Barenblatt's First Amendment rights.

Justice Black dissented, saying that the committee's methods violated both First and Fifth Amendment rights. Justice Brennan also dissented on the ground that the committee had no legitimate purpose to investigate Barenblatt, but did so to expose him.

See Stanley I. Kutler, *The American Inquisition: Justice and Injustice in the Cold War* (New York: Hill and Wang, 1982).

Spano v. New York

360 U.S. 315 (1959)
Decided: June 22, 1959
Vote: 9 (Warren, Black, Frankfurter, Douglas, Clark, Harlan II, Brennan, Whittaker, Stewart)
0
Opinion of the Court: Warren
Concurring opinion: Douglas (Black, Brennan)
Concurring opinion: Stewart (Douglas, Brennan)

Joseph Spano, a twenty-five-year-old Italian immigrant with a junior high school education, shot and killed a man after the man severely injured Spano in a barroom brawl. Police had sufficient evidence to arrest Spano, and, following indictment by a grand jury, Spano turned himself over to the police on the advice of his lawyer. Spano's lawyer instructed him to not answer any questions asked by the police upon interrogation. The police began to question Spano, and he refused to talk. Spano repeatedly asked to speak to his attorney, but his request was refused. The police enlisted one of Spano's childhood friends to come to the police office and beg Spano to confess. The friend said that Spano's problems might cause him (the friend) to lose his job and that he would not be able to care for his family. The interrogation went on for eight hours, beginning in the late evening and going into the early morning hours, when Spano confessed. This confession was used against him in court, and he was convicted and sentenced to death.

The Court overturned the conviction because it was obtained through practices that violated the traditional principles of the due process. Involuntary confessions are not only untrustworthy, but also they violate the general principle that police must obey the law while enforcing the law. Spano confessed only after the fatigue of an eight-hour interrogation had sufficiently worn him down. He did not even create his own confession, but responded to leading questions by a relentless prosecutor. Furthermore, the police used the pleas of a childhood friend to successfully break Spano's will.

Justice Douglas added that the justices could have reversed on the denial of counsel to a defendant who had already been indicted. Justice Stewart argued along a similar line—that the absence of counsel when the confession was elicited was alone enough to render it inadmissible under the Fourteenth Amendment.

Spano might well be seen as an early case in which the Court began to explore the interrelationship of the Fifth and Sixth Amendments, ties that it would ultimately bring together in ***Miranda v. Arizona,*** 384 U.S. 436 (1966).

See Fred Graham, *The Due Process Revolution: The Warren Court's Impact on Criminal Law* (New York: Hayden, 1970).

Greene v. McElroy

360 U.S. 474 (1959)
Decided: June 29, 1959
Vote: 8 (Warren, Black, Frankfurter, Douglas, Harlan II, Brennan, Whittaker, Stewart)
1 (Clark)
Opinion of the Court: Warren
Opinion concurring in judgment: Frankfurter
Opinion concurring in judgment: Harlan II
Opinion concurring in judgment: Whittaker
Dissenting opinion: Clark

William L. Greene was an aeronautical engineer working in a private defense corporation. His government security clearance, issued by the secretary of defense, allowed him to work on projects involving military secrets. Secretary of Defense Neil H. McElroy then issued new regulations governing security clearances, and, after a short hearing in which Greene was not given the opportunity to confront witnesses against him, Greene lost his security clearance because of alleged communist sympathies. He subsequently lost his job and was unable to find work as an aeronautical engineer. Greene appealed the revocation, arguing that he was not given sufficient due process under the Fifth Amendment.

To challenge an administrative proceeding on due process grounds, a person has to prove that he or she has a liberty or property interest in the issue and was not given a fair opportunity to be heard before this interest was violated. The Court held that the right to hold private employment free from government interference constituted a liberty interest under the Fifth Amendment.

Chief Justice Warren further held that nothing in U.S. law gave the secretary of defense the ability to infringe the liberty interest of employment without giving accused individuals an opportunity to be heard. The law clearly made it a crime to communicate intelligence secrets to agents of foreign governments or members of communist organizations, but this did not justify a regulatory scheme that arbitrarily lifted security clearances. Greene was entitled to a formal hearing, complete with an opportunity to confront and cross-examine the witnesses against him, before his security clearance could be lifted.

Kingsley International Pictures Corp. v. Regents of the University of the State of New York

360 U.S. 684 (1959)
Decided: June 29, 1959
Vote: 9 (Black, Frankfurter, Douglas, Clark, Warren, Harlan II, Brennan, Whittaker, Stewart)
0
Opinion of the Court: Stewart
Concurring opinion: Black
Concurring opinion: Douglas (Black)
Opinion concurring in judgment: Frankfurter
Opinion concurring in judgment: Clark
Opinion concurring in judgment: Harlan II (Frankfurter, Whittaker)

Kingsley International Pictures Corporation was denied a license in New York to show the movie *Lady Chatterley's Lover* because it presented the idea that adultery is "right and desirable for certain people under certain circumstances." Under New York law, no "immoral" film could receive a license, and positive depictions of adultery were considered immoral under the statute. Even though the movie did not meet the definition of obscenity created by the Court in ***Roth v. United States,*** 354 U.S. 476 (1957), the New York Court of Appeals found that a license was properly denied to Kingsley because of the film's immoral content. Kingsley appealed, challenging the validity of the law.

The Supreme Court held that the New York law violated Kingsley's First Amendment right of speech and expression. It admitted that the movie fit the statutory definition of immorality, but held that it merited a license because the film was not pornographic and posed no threat of inciting "imminent lawless action." The Court noted that the First Amendment is not limited to the protection of ideas that are conventional or shared by the majority. Rather, it protects advocacy of opinion. The opinion that adultery is sometimes proper is no different from the advocacy of a political or religious idea.

The Court found that the New York law "cut so closely to the core of constitutional freedom" that it was unnecessary to address Kingsley's specific violation. The whole law was deemed unconstitutional, and Kingsley's license was granted.

See Harry M. Clor, *Obscenity and Public Morality: Censorship in a Liberal Society* (Chicago: University of Chicago Press, 1969).

1960–1969

Bates v. City of Little Rock

361 U.S. 516 (1960)
Decided: February 23, 1960
Vote 9 (Warren, Black, Frankfurter, Douglas, Reed, Clark, Harlan II, Brennan, Stewart)
0
Opinion of the Court: Stewart
Concurring opinion: Black, Douglas

Little Rock, Arkansas, had an occupation license tax ordinance that required that any organization operating within the city to submit the names of all of its members to the city licensing office. Daisy Bates, the secretary of the NAACP chapter in Little Rock, refused to supply members' names, fearing that if the information became public, NAACP members could suffer economic or physical reprisals. After conviction for refusing to submit the list, Bates appealed to the Supreme Court of Arkansas, claiming that the ordinance violated the constitutional rights of the members. The Arkansas court upheld the law.

The Supreme Court unanimously reversed the Arkansas court. Justice Stewart's opinion held that the ordinance violated the Due Process Clause of the Fourteenth Amendment by infringing on the First Amendment right of free association, which was applied to the states by the Fourteenth Amendment.

Justices Black and Douglas concurred in the judgment, simply noting that they would have found that the Little Rock ordinance violated the right of free speech as well as of association.

United States v. Raines

362 U.S. 17 (1960)
Decided: February 29, 1960
Vote: 9 (Warren, Black, Frankfurter, Douglas, Clark, Harlan II, Brennan, Whittaker, Stewart)
0
Opinion of the Court: Brennan
Concurring opinion: Frankfurter (Harlan II)

The attorney general of the United States brought suit against James Griggs Raines and other members of the Board of Registrars in Terrell County, Georgia, charging that they had used illegal means to prevent African Americans from voting. The complaint sought immediate injunction against the board's activities and based its claim for relief on the Civil Rights Act of 1957, which forbade anyone from engaging in discriminatory voting practices. The district court dismissed the complaint, saying that the Civil Rights Act was unconstitutional because it forbade anyone, including nonstates, from violating the Fifteenth Amendment, which applies only to states. Although the defendant in the case was in fact a state, the district court nevertheless ruled that the statute was unconstitutionally broad on its face and therefore could not be applied to anyone.

The Supreme Court reversed the district court's decision, explaining that a court may apply a law only to the narrow facts before it and may not expand its holding to address questions not in controversy. The district court had power under both the Fifteenth Amendment and the Civil Rights Act to declare state actions that prevented African Americans from voting unconstitutional. Because the case called for a constitutional application of the statute, that should have been the end of the court's inquiry. The district court erred in judging the constitutionality of the rest of the statute, and its decision was therefore reversed.

See Steven F. Lawson, *Black Ballots: Voting Rights in the South, 1944–1969* (New York: Columbia University Press, 1976).

Jones v. United States

362 U.S. 257 (1960)
Decided: March 28, 1960
Vote: 8 (Warren, Black, Frankfurter, Clark, Harlan II, Brennan, Whittaker, Stewart)
1 (Douglas)
Opinion of the Court: Frankfurter
Dissenting opinion: Douglas

Cecil Jones was charged with distributing and hiding illegal drugs. Officers who performed the search found several packages of narcotics hidden in an awning of the apartment where Jones was staying at the time of the search. The dwelling did not belong to Jones but to a friend who was not present at the time. Before trial Jones moved to suppress evidence from the search because, he claimed, the police did not have probable cause for obtaining a warrant. The evidence was however admitted, and Jones was convicted on both counts. He appealed to the Supreme Court.

The government argued that Jones did not have standing to challenge the search, because he was only a guest at the home of his friend, not the owner. The Court found this argument preposterous and cited the Federal Rules of Civil Procedure to say that any "person aggrieved by an unlawful search and seizure" may petition to suppress evidence used against him. Although Jones did not own the house, he had been held criminally liable for the proceeds of the search and therefore had been directly aggrieved. To allow the government to argue otherwise would permit it to argue contrary positions, saying that Jones had no stake in the property because he did not own it, but that he could be prosecuted for it.

As to whether the officers had probable cause for the search, Justice Frankfurter held that hearsay evidence alone was sufficient to merit probable cause. In this case, the officers had obtained a search warrant based on an affidavit of another police officer, who had notified them that an informant had purchased drugs from Jones on several occasions. Although none of the officers had firsthand knowledge of Jones's activities, the Court said that the hearsay testimony of the informant provided sufficient information to support a search warrant.

Justice Douglas concurred with the part of the opinion holding that Jones had standing to challenge the warrant, but dissented with the holding there had been sufficient probable cause for a warrant.

Gomillion v. Lightfoot

364 U.S. 339 (1960)
Decided: November 14, 1960
Vote: 9 (Warren, Black, Frankfurter, Douglas, Clark, Harlan II, Brennan, Whittaker, Stewart)
0
Opinion of the Court: Frankfurter
Concurring opinion: Douglas
Opinion concurring in judgment: Whittaker

Black voters in Tuskegee, Alabama, charged that the state had drawn the city's boundaries so as to exclude all but a handful of African American voters without eliminating a single white voter. The district court dismissed the complaint, and the Court of Appeals for the Fifth Circuit agreed. The U.S. Supreme Court reversed, a move that should have surprised no one, given its other civil rights decisions at this time.

What makes the decision unusual is Justice Frankfurter's opinion: he ruled that Alabama had deprived its citizens of their suffrage solely on the basis of race, in direct violation of the Fifteenth Amendment. The problem for Frankfurter was squaring this decision with the opinion he had written fourteen years earlier in ***Colegrove v. Green,*** 328 U.S. 549 (1946), in which he declared that the Constitution gave no relief for malapportioned districts, and that the courts should stay out of the "political thicket." In the earlier case, he said that the appellants would have to rely on the political process to alter the district lines, but in *Gomillion v. Lightfoot* he found a way for the courts to get involved.

Frankfurter explained that in *Colegrove* the appellants complained only of a dilution of their vote and no remedy for that existed under the Fourteenth Amendment. In *Gomillion,* however, the state was depriving blacks of their votes entirely, and a remedy did exist in the Fifteenth Amendment, because the deprivation was based solely on race.

Justices Douglas and Whittaker pointed out in their concurrences that if black voters could sue for a deprivation of their vote, then white voters could sue for a deprivation of theirs because, no matter how Frankfurter phrased it, a "dilution" of a vote had roughly the same effect as a "deprivation." Douglas and Whittaker said they would have based the decision on the Fourteenth Amendment's Equal Protection Clause. A few days later, the Court noted probable jurisdiction in ***Baker v. Carr,*** 369 U.S. 186 (1962), which directly overruled *Colegrove.*

See See Richard C. Cortner, *The Apportionment Cases* (Knoxville: University of Tennessee Press, 1970).

Shelton v. Tucker

364 U.S. 479 (1960)
Decided: December 12, 1960
Vote: 5 (Warren, Black, Douglas, Brennan, Stewart)
4 (Frankfurter, Clark, Harlan II, Whittaker)
Opinion of the Court: Stewart
Dissenting opinion: Frankfurter (Clark, Harlan II, Whittaker)
Dissenting opinion: Harlan II (Frankfurter, Clark, Whittaker)

Arkansas required every teacher in a state-supported school to file an annual affidavit listing every organization to which he or she had belonged or had regularly contributed money within the preceding five years. The requirement was clearly aimed not at communist subversives, but at the National Association for the Advancement of Colored People (NAACP), in an effort to target and intimidate its members. The local state court, the Supreme Court of Arkansas, and the U.S. District Court for the Eastern District of Arkansas upheld the statute.

The U.S. Supreme Court reversed on grounds that the law was overly broad, that its unlimited and indiscriminate sweep violated the First Amendment. Justice Stewart acknowledged that a state could have a legitimate interest in organizational memberships of its teachers, but here the state had asked for far too much information, because those asked to disclose, especially members of the NAACP, had very real interests at stake. The state had to proceed "more narrowly" and use "less drastic means." Stewart did not, however, indicate what those less drastic means might be.

Justices Frankfurter and Harlan, in their dissents, picked up on what they charged was a lack of direction from the majority. Neither believed that the statute transgressed the constitutional limits of a state's authority to determine the qualifications of its teachers, although Harlan's dissent was far more speech protective than Frankfurter's. Frankfurter indicated that he thought the state had a rational reason for wanting this information, and that was sufficient.

See Harry Kalven, *The Negro and the First Amendment* (Chicago: University of Chicago Press, 1965).

Monroe v. Pape

365 U.S. 167 (1960)
Decided: February 20, 1961
Vote: 8 (Warren, Black, Douglas, Clark, Harlan II, Brennan, Whittaker, Stewart)
1 (Frankfurter)
Opinion of the Court: Douglas
Concurring opinion: Harlan II (Stewart)
Dissenting opinion: Frankfurter

The civil rights movement affected not only school desegregation, public accommodations, and voting rights; it also touched all areas of modern life in which people are discriminated against because of their skin color. Attorneys for civil rights groups developed fresh interpretations of constitutional provisions, and they even dusted off some old Reconstruction Era laws that had never been purged from the statute books. For example, 42 U.S.C. 1983 is derived from the Civil Rights Act of 1871 and reads:

Civil action for deprivation of rights. Every person who, under color of any statute, ordinance, regulation, custom, or usage, of any State or Territory, subjects, or causes to be subjected, any citizen of the United States or other persons within the jurisdiction thereof to the deprivation of any rights, privileges or immunities secured by the Constitution and laws, shall be liable to the person injured in any action of law, suit in equity, or other proper proceedings for redress.

The widespread use of Section 1983 in civil rights litigation relies on *Monroe v. Pape,* which permitted a damage suit against police officers for an unlawful invasion of the petitioner's home and a subsequent illegal search, seizure, and detention. In this case, thirteen Chicago police officers broke into the Monroe family's house in the early morning, got them out of bed, made them stand naked in the living room, and ransacked every room, emptying drawers and ripping mattresses. Monroe was then taken to the police station, detained for ten hours, and questioned about a murder that had taken place two days earlier. He was not allowed to call his family or a lawyer. He was later released. It was alleged that the officers had neither a search warrant nor an arrest warrant and that they acted "under color of the statutes, ordinances, regulations, customs and usages" of Illinois and of the City of Chicago.

Justice Douglas's opinion imposed a strict liability standard "that makes a man responsible for the natural consequences of his actions." Although there are limits to Section 1983 liability, Douglas's interpretation gave civil rights advocates a potent weapon to use against individuals, including some government officials, who could no longer claim immunity because they acted under color of law.

See Richard A. Matasar, "Personal Immunities Under Section 1983: The Limits of the Court's Historical Analysis," *Arkansas Law Review* 40 (1987): 741.

Burton v. Wilmington Parking Authority

365 U.S. 715 (1961)
Decided: April 17, 1961
Vote: 6 (Warren, Black, Douglas, Clark, Brennan, Stewart)
3 (Frankfurter, Harlan II, Whittaker)
Opinion of the Court: Clark
Concurring opinion: Stewart
Dissenting opinion: Frankfurter
Dissenting opinion: Harlan II (Whittaker)

The Eagle Coffee Shop, a privately owned restaurant, leased its space from the Wilmington (Delaware) Parking Authority and was situated in a parking garage owned by the authority. The restaurant refused to serve William H. Burton, an African American, and he claimed a violation of the Equal Protection Clause of the Fourteenth Amendment.

The Court held that Delaware was sufficiently involved in the restaurant to make its activities a state function governed by provisions of the Fourteenth Amendment. Although no precise formula existed for determining what is private action and what is public, the decision in ***Shelley v. Kraemer,*** 334 U.S. 1 (1948), indicated that the Fourteenth Amendment applied to any kind of state action, no matter how tenuous, that supported discriminatory activity. Here, the state owned the property in which the restaurant was located, and it provided money to the restaurant to defray expenses and assure its profitability. The restaurant could be accessed directly from the public parking garage. The Court held that it would be a grave injustice for African Americans to be allowed to use the parking spaces in the public garage, but be treated as second-class citizens without any rights in another area of the same building.

Because the Parking Authority was involved with the restaurant in so many ways, it had a responsibility to ensure that the restaurant did not discriminate. Even absent explicit instructions from the authority to prohibit discrimination, the Court held that when the government leases a property, the lessee is bound by the Fourteenth Amendment as if it were acting as the government itself.

See Thomas P. Lewis, "Burton v. Wilmington Parking Authority—A Case Without Precedent," *Columbia Law Review* 61 (1961): 1458.

Konigsberg v. State Bar of California

366 U.S. 36 (1961)
Decided: April 24, 1961
Vote: 5 (Frankfurter, Clark, Harlan II, Whittaker, Stewart)
4 (Warren, Black, Douglas, Brennan)
Opinion of the Court: Harlan II
Dissenting opinion: Black (Warren, Douglas)
Dissenting opinion: Brennan (Warren)

Raphael Konigsberg applied for membership in the State Bar of California, a requirement for practicing law in the state, and was subjected to standard administrative proceedings to determine his eligibility. Under California law, applicants to the bar were to be of "good moral character" and belong to no organization that advocated the overthrow of government. Applicants had the burden of proving their good character, and the California Committee of Bar Examiners could rebut arguments of good character by asking further questions.

The committee asked Konigsberg if he had ever been a member of the Communist Party. Konigsberg refused to answer, calling the question irrelevant. In his first appeal, *Konigsberg v. State Bar of California,* 353 U.S. 252 (1957), the Supreme Court said that the committee could not use his refusal to answer as substantive evidence of bad character and could not rely on it to ban him from the bar. The committee began a new proceeding, asked the question again, and refused to admit Konigsberg because he would not cooperate with the committee's question and answer procedure.

This time a slim majority of the Court agreed with the committee that, by refusing to answer the question, Konigsberg had obstructed the committee's full investigation into his qualifications. It was this procedural issue, not the substantive evidence that the committee gained from the refusal, that prompted it to refuse membership. Under the established system, the committee was given a full range of investigatory powers. If candidates were allowed to ignore certain questions, the committee would not be able to achieve its goals effectively. The committee explained that an answer to the initial question of communist affiliation was necessary to develop a line of inquiry intent on determining whether Konigsberg was involved in subversive activities. Because this was relevant to his fitness for membership in the bar, his refusal to answer posed a procedural violation that justified the committee's refusal to admit him.

In his dissent Justice Black declared that the questions violated Konigsberg's First Amendment rights and the rule laid down in *Speiser v. Randall,* 357 U.S. 513 (1958). That case held unconstitutional an administrative rule requiring an applicant to bear the burden of proof to show that he had not engaged in subversive activities. Justice Brennan dissented solely on the grounds of *Speiser.*

See Stanley I. Kutler, *The American Inquisition: Justice and Injustice in the Cold War* (New York: Hill and Wang, 1982).

McGowan v. Maryland

366 U.S. 420 (1961)
Decided: May 29, 1961
Vote: 8 (Warren, Black, Frankfurter, Clark, Harlan II, Brennan, Whittaker, Stewart)
1 (Douglas)
Opinion of the Court: Warren
Concurring opinion: Frankfurter (Harlan II)
Dissenting opinion: Douglas

McGowan v. Maryland is the principal case of several testing the validity of laws that required most businesses to close on Sunday. The employees of a large discount department store were convicted in state court of making sales on a Sunday in violation of Maryland law. The trial court rejected their contentions that such laws violated the Equal Protection and Due Process Clauses of the Fourteenth Amendment and the constitutional guarantees of freedom of religion and separation of church and state. The Maryland Court of Appeals affirmed.

The Supreme Court also affirmed. Chief Justice Warren rejected out of hand the equal protection and due process claims, but conceded that the plaintiffs had standing to attack the closing law on the ground that it violated the constitutional provision prohibiting laws "respecting an establishment of religion." Although it was true that at one time the laws had a religious intent, over time the purpose had changed. The states went from believing that church attendance played an important role in keeping the family together to believing that time for rest and recreation made for a more stable family life, and this concept provided an acceptable secular purpose for creating a "family day of rest." The fact that Sunday was primarily a day of rest tied to Christian tradition seemed to matter little, although the law clearly affected Muslims, Jews, atheists, and even devout Christians, who did not view Sunday as a day for recreation.

Justices Stewart and Brennan, who in ***Braunfeld v. Brown,*** 366 U.S. 599 (1961), had dissented from the Court's opinion in the challenge to Sunday blue laws by Orthodox Jews, joined in this opinion. Justice Frankfurter could not accept Warren's facile explanation of Sunday as a day of rest, and he entered an elaborate concurrence, joined by Justice Harlan, to rationalize the blue laws, even with a religious interpretation, as not a violation of the First Amendment.

Justice Douglas was the only dissenter, confronting the majority's rationalizations head on: "No matter how much is written, no matter how much is said, the parentage of the laws is the Fourth Commandment." To be sure, a state could mandate a day of rest, but not Sunday, because that would force minorities to obey the majority's religious teachings.

See Richard E. Morgan, *The Supreme Court and Religion* (New York: Free Press, 1972).

Braunfeld v. Brown

366 U.S. 599 (1961)
Decided: May 29, 1961
Vote: 6 (Warren, Black, Frankfurter, Clark, Harlan II, Whittaker)
3 (Douglas, Brennan, Stewart)
Judgment of the Court: Warren
Concurring opinion: Frankfurter (Harlan II)
Opinion concurring in judgment: Harlan II
Dissenting opinion: Douglas
Dissenting opinion: Brennan
Dissenting opinion: Stewart

Abraham Braunfeld and other Orthodox Jewish merchants filed a challenge to Pennsylvania's Sunday closing laws, claiming that the laws illegally established a religion and violated their free exercise of religion. The laws required all businesses in Pennsylvania to be closed on Sunday. The plaintiffs owned retail stores that they had to close on Sunday because of the law, but they also had to close their stores on Saturday because as Orthodox Jews they could not do business on the Sabbath. They contended that by forcing them to be closed for two days of the week, the state inhibited their exercise of religion by making it economically difficult for them to operate their business.

The Court had just heard the same challenge in *Two Guys from Harrison-Allentown, Inc. v. McGinley,* 366 U.S. 582 (1961), in which it held that Sunday closing laws did not violate the First Amendment. Sunday closing laws were not created to establish religion, but to create a day of rest and tranquility for the community. Because the state had police power to improve the health, safety, and morale of its citizens, the Court found that the Sunday closing law was a valid exercise of state power. Furthermore, the law imposed only an indirect burden on the free exercise of religion. The retailers remained free in the states' eyes to open on Saturday, and it was their religious convictions, not state action, that prevented them from doing so. Although states may not directly force people to do something forbidden by their religion, and cannot force them not to do something required by it, the state need not craft each law to meet the religious needs of every member of the community when the effect is only tenuous.

The decision drew a great deal of criticism, not only from the religious community, but from academics as well, and most scholars praised the dissents, especially Justice Brennan's. He argued that the state ought to, under the First Amendment, make an accommodation for religious observance, a position that within a few years won over a majority of the Court; see ***Sherbert v. Verner,*** 374 U.S. 398 (1963).

See Candida Lund, "Religion and Commerce—The Sunday Closing Cases," in *The Third Branch of Government,* ed. C. Herman Pritchett and Alan F. Westin (New York: Harcourt, Brace, and World, 1963).

Gallagher v. Crown Kosher Supermarket of Massachusetts

366 U.S. 617 (1961)
Decided: May 29, 1961
Vote: 6 (Warren, Black, Frankfurter, Clark, Harlan II, Whittaker)
3 (Douglas, Brennan, Stewart)
Judgment of the Court: Warren
Opinion concurring in judgment: Frankfurter (Harlan II)
Dissenting opinion: Douglas
Dissenting opinion: Brennan
Dissenting opinion: Stewart

This suit was brought by Crown Kosher Supermarkets, three of Crown's Orthodox Jewish customers, and the chief Orthodox rabbi of Springfield, Massachusetts, to challenge the state's Sunday closing laws. Prior to the enactment of the laws, Crown Kosher operated its supermarkets on Sundays but was closed on Saturday to observe the Jewish Sabbath. It did one-third of its business on Sunday. Along with many other exceptions—for example, allowing drug stores, tobacco shops, and places of amusement to open on Sunday—the law allowed kosher grocery stores to sell meat until 10:00 a.m. on Sundays. Crown Kosher said that opening for those short hours was economically unfeasible. It argued that the law violated the Equal Protection Clause of the Fourteenth Amendment and established religion while prohibiting the free exercise thereof in violation of the First Amendment.

The Court decided this case along with ***Braunfeld v. Braun,*** 366 U.S. 599 (1961), and *Two Guys from Harrison-Allentown, Inc. v. McGinley,* 366 U.S. 582 (1961), and affirmed Massachusetts's ability to enforce the Sunday closing law. Although Crown Kosher argued that the many exemptions to the rule made it all the more unfair as applied to grocery stores, the Court found justifications for each of the exemptions, saying that they added to the enjoyment of the special day. Because the exemptions were based in reason, the Court found no equal protection problem.

Scholars and the religious community joined in criticizing this decision and its companion case, ***Braunfeld v. Brown,*** while praising the dissents, especially that of Justice Brennan who argued that the state should accommodate religious observance.

See Candida Lund, "Religion and Commerce—The Sunday Closing Cases," in *The Third Branch of Government,* ed. C. Herman Pritchett and Alan F. Westin (New York: Harcourt, Brace, and World, 1963).

Irvin v. Dowd

366 U.S. 717 (1961)
Decided: June 5, 1961
Vote: 9 (Warren, Black, Frankfurter, Douglas, Clark, Harlan II, Brennan, Whittaker, Stewart)
0
Opinion of the Court: Clark
Concurring opinion: Frankfurter

Leslie Irvin was accused of six murders and was set to be tried in Evansville, Indiana. Before the trial, local newspapers published Irvin's confession, accounts of the evidence against him, and a detailed record of his criminal history. Irvin's attorney moved for a change of venue, and the trial was moved to a neighboring county that also had access to the newspaper stories. The court denied further changes of venue under an Indiana statute that said only one change of venue should be granted per case. Irvin was convicted, and he applied to a federal court for a writ of habeas corpus against his conviction.

The Supreme Court held that Indiana's law against more than one change of venue was unconstitutional because an accused is always entitled to an impartial jury, no matter what procedure must be followed to make that possible. Trial by jury, guaranteed by the Sixth Amendment, is one of the most basic safeguards to individual liberty and dignity. The Fourteenth Amendment guarantees an impartial jury as part of its due process protection. Although it is impossible for a jury to be totally ignorant of the facts surrounding a case, too much knowledge results in bias and an inability to decide issues fairly. Here, the jury had been exposed to news reports, editorials, and cartoons intended to sway members of the public, and eight of the twelve jury members admitted that they believed Irvin was guilty before the trial began. Under these circumstances, the Court ruled, there could not be a fair and impartial trial.

Communist Party of the United States v. Subversive Activities Control Board

367 U.S. 1 (1961)
Decided: June 5, 1961
Vote: 5 (Frankfurter, Clark, Harlan II, Whittaker, Stewart)
4 (Warren, Black, Douglas, Brennan)
Opinion of the Court: Frankfurter
Dissenting opinion: Warren
Dissenting opinion: Black
Dissenting opinion: Douglas
Dissenting opinion: Brennan (Warren)

Congress passed the Subversive Activities Control Act, commonly known as the McCarran Act, in the spring of 1950. The statute required communist organizations to register with the attorney general, and it created the Subversive Activities Control Board (SACB) to administer the registration process. President Truman vetoed the measure, calling it "the greatest danger to freedom of speech, press, and assembly since the Sedition Act of 1798," but Congress, fearful of being considered "soft" on communism in an election year, overrode the veto by large margins in both chambers.

Through a series of highly complex procedures, the SACB tried to force the Communist Party to register as a subversive organization. Had the party agreed to do so, it would have forfeited nearly all the rights that nonviolent political groups enjoy in the United States. After eleven years of litigation, the Supreme Court upheld the *registration* provisions by a 5–4 vote, with Justice Frankfurter denying that the First Amendment prevented Congress from requiring membership lists of organizations "substantially dominated or controlled by that foreign power controlling the world Communist movement." The Court did not rule on the *punitive* provisions because they had never been enforced.

By the time the Court heard cases dealing with the punitive provisions, its personnel had changed. The new majority had little sympathy for Red Scare legislation and proceeded to make the enforcement of both the registration as well as the punishment provisions impossible. In ***Albertson v. SACB,*** 382 U.S. 70 (1965), for example, the Court set aside convictions of communists who refused to register on grounds that the SACB orders were worded so as to constitute a violation of the Fifth Amendment's right against self-incrimination. In ***Aptheker v. Secretary of State,*** 378 U.S. 500 (1964), it also overturned as overly broad and vague provisions denying passports to communists and prohibiting them from working in defense facilities.

See See Stanley I. Kutler, *The American Inquisition: Justice and Injustice in the Cold War* (New York: Hill and Wang, 1982); and Michal R. Belknap, *Cold War Political Justice* (Westport, Conn.: Greenwood Press, 1977).

Scales v. United States

367 U.S. 203 (1961)
Decided: June 5, 1961
Vote: 5 (Frankfurter, Clark, Harlan II, Whittaker, Stewart)
4 (Warren, Black, Douglas, Brennan)
Opinion of the Court: Harlan II
Dissenting opinion: Black
Dissenting opinion: Douglas
Dissenting opinion: Brennan (Warren, Douglas)

Junius Irving Scales, a member of the Communist Party, was convicted of violating the "membership clause" of the Smith Act, which made it a felony to participate actively in an organization that advocated the overthrow of the federal government. On appeal, Scales challenged the statute by saying that it was unconstitutionally broad, violated the Due Process Clause of the Fifth Amendment, and violated freedom of speech and association under the First Amendment.

The Supreme Court upheld Scales's conviction, finding that the statute did not violate the Constitution. Scales argued that the statute was too broad because it did not require a suspect to know that his organization engaged in violent activities. The

Court found that intent was implied. The only people prosecuted under the statute were individuals who actively participated in subversive organizations and knew that the organizations plotted to overthrow the government. Because the statute allowed prosecution only for intentional criminal conduct, the Court found no due process violation. Although the Due Process Clause does not allow conviction for mere association in an organization, it does not bar conviction for participation in criminal conduct, even if the illegal activities occur within the context of an organization. Each member of the group might not actively participate in each criminal activity, but every member had the same intent and contributed in some way to the criminal results. Finally, the Court held that criminal activities are not immune from prosecution because they involve a speech element. Although advocacy is normally considered constitutionally protected speech, when it is coupled with illegal activity, it need not be treated as speech at all.

Torcaso v. Watkins

367 U.S. 488 (1961)
Decided: June 19, 1961
Vote: 9 (Warren, Black, Frankfurter, Douglas, Clark, Harlan II, Brennan, Whittaker, Stewart)
0
Opinion of the Court: Black
Concurring in judgment without opinion: Frankfurter, Harlan II

Roy R. Torcaso was denied a commission as a notary public by Clayton Watkins because he refused to declare his belief in God, as required by the Maryland Constitution.

The Court held that Maryland's requirement violated at least two provisions of the federal Constitution. Article VI says that "no religious test shall ever be required as a qualification to any office or public trust under the United States." The Court construed Maryland's requirement as a religious test because it favored those who believe in God over those who do not. The requirement also violated the Establishment Clause of the First Amendment, as explained in ***Everson v. Board of Education,*** 330 U.S. 1 (1947). There, the Court held that the Establishment Clause was violated any time a state or federal government passed a law that showed preference for one religion over another. Here Maryland showed a preference for religion over lack of religion.

Justice Black used this case to explain the history behind the Article VI provision and the Establishment Clause, saying that many wise men in the early colonies knew of the problems created when the government attempted to dictate religious practice. They sought to prevent such problems by including rules against unfair practices directly in the Constitution. As one member of the North Carolina ratifying convention asked, "How it is possible to exclude any set of men, without taking away that principle of religious freedom which we ourselves so warmly contend for?"

See John T. Noonan Jr., *The Lustre of Our Country: The American Experience of Religious Freedom* (Berkeley: University of California Press, 1998).

Poe v. Ullman

367 U.S. 497 (1961)
Decided: June 19, 1961
Vote: 5 (Warren, Frankfurter, Clark, Brennan, Whittaker)
4 (Black, Douglas, Harlan II, Stewart)
Judgment of the Court: Frankfurter
Opinion concurring in judgment: Brennan
Dissenting opinion: Black
Dissenting opinion: Douglas (Stewart)
Dissenting opinion: Harlan II (Stewart)

Paul and Pauline Poe (pseudonyms for the real litigants), after several failed pregnancies, desired to receive advice about birth control from their physician. Under Connecticut law, a physician could not dispense advice about birth control, even when the life of the mother was in danger. The Poes sought declaratory relief from the Supreme Court, asking it to declare the law unconstitutional. They claimed that the law violated the Fourteenth Amendment's protection of life and liberty without due process of law, and they said that they feared prosecution if they violated the law.

The Connecticut law had been placed on the books in 1879, but the state had never tried to prosecute anyone for its violation. The Court perceived that the state had a policy of not enforcing the statute, which was deeply imbedded in its traditions. As such, the Poes were in no danger of prosecution if they received contraceptive advice from their physician. Justice Frankfurter therefore held that there was no real case or controversy involved, because the state's policy of nonenforcement posed no danger to people seeking birth control information.

Justice Harlan entered a lengthy dissent that proved far more influential in future cases than the majority opinion. He disagreed that there was no case or controversy. Even if the state did not enforce the law, he said, it remained on the books and could be enforced, thereby posing a threat. Beyond that point, Harlan explored the rights of people under the Due Process Clause of the Fourteenth Amendment and how new rights can be discovered through the idea of substantive due process. The Court was reminded of Harlan's opinion only a few years later when, as he had warned, the state did enforce the law. See ***Griswold v. Connecticut,*** 381 U.S. 479 (1965).

See David J. Garrow, *Liberty and Sexuality: The Right to Privacy and the Making of Roe v. Wade* (New York: Macmillan, 1994).

Mapp v. Ohio

367 U.S. 643 (1961)
Decided: June 19, 1961
Vote: 5 (Warren, Black, Douglas, Clark, Brennan)
3 (Frankfurter, Harlan II, Whittaker)
1 (Stewart)
Opinion of the Court: Clark
Concurring opinion: Black
Concurring opinion: Douglas
Memorandum opinion: Stewart
Dissenting opinion: Harlan (Frankfurter, Whittaker)

Mapp v. Ohio initially seemed to be a First Amendment case. Seven police officers attempted to gain entrance to the Cleveland home of Dollree Mapp, claiming they had information that a person wanted in connection with a bombing was hiding there. She refused to let them in without a warrant. Three hours later the police officers forced open a door and waved a piece of paper they claimed was a warrant, which they refused to let her read. She grabbed the paper and "placed it . . . in her bosom," and in the ensuing scuffle the police manhandled and handcuffed her for, as Justice Clark noted in the Court's opinion, resisting the policemen's "official rescue of the 'warrant' from her person." After subduing her, police searched the house, found a cache of pornographic items in a trunk in the basement, and arrested her for possession of obscene materials. She claimed that the trunk did not belong to her but to a former tenant, for whom she was storing it, and that she had no idea of its contents.

The state courts conceded that there had probably never been a warrant, but the prosecution correctly claimed that under existing law, it could use evidence obtained by a warrantless, unreasonable search. The Ohio Supreme Court by a 4–3 vote ruled that the statute was unconstitutional, but to no avail; Ohio's constitution required a 6–1 majority to strike down a state statute.

On appeal, Mapp's attorney briefed and argued the case primarily on the obscenity issue. In an amicus brief, however, the American Civil Liberties Union suggested that the case offered an opportunity to ask whether the Fourteenth Amendment applied the Fourth Amendment to the states. Five justices seized on this idea and, although neither the state nor the appellant briefed or argued the exclusionary rule, the Court in *Mapp* overruled ***Wolf v. Colorado,*** 338 U.S. 25 (1949), and held that the Fourteenth Amendment not only incorporated the Fourth Amendment and applied it to the states, but also that it applied the exclusionary rule remedy. The exclusionary rule was first enunciated by Justice Day in ***Weeks v. United States,*** 232 U.S. 383 (1914). The rule denied federal prosecutors the opportunity to use evidence seized without a valid search warrant. Both the majority and minority in *Mapp* agreed that the police had acted egregiously, but the three dissenters objected to imposing a federal judge-made rule on the states. The majority argued, however, as Day had a half century earlier, that the only remedy to a violation of the Fourth Amendment—the only way to ensure that police did not act as they did in Dollree Mapp's home—was to deprive the government of the fruits of an illegal search.

Most people agree that for the Fourth Amendment to be effective, there has to be some remedy for its violation. This conclusion is clouded, however, by the public's failure to understand why evidence that clearly establishes guilt cannot be used and, as Justice Cardozo once said, "the criminal is to go free because the constable has blundered."

The exclusionary rule rests on several considerations. In *Mapp* the Court spelled out one of them, namely that the only way to deter police from illegal searches is to deprive them of the evidence they obtain. Another was later described by Chief Justice Burger as "the 'sporting contest' thesis that the government must 'play the game fairly' and cannot be allowed to profit from its own illegal acts." Justice Brandeis may have said it best in his dissent in the original wiretapping case:

> Decency, security, and liberty alike demand that government officials shall be subject to the same rules of conduct that are commands to the citizen. Our government is the potent, the omnipresent teacher. For good or ill, it teaches the whole people by its example. If the government becomes a lawbreaker, it breeds contempt for the law; it invites every man to become a law unto himself; it invites anarchy.

The exclusionary rule limits police investigations, and it may make it somewhat more difficult to obtain proof and convict criminals, although evidence on this claim is inconclusive. But as Clark noted, "nothing can destroy a government more quickly than its failure to observe its own laws, or worse, its disregard of the charter of its own existence."

The debate continues over the exclusionary rule, although by this time nearly everyone agrees that, at least in some circumstances, it is necessary. Chief Justice Rehnquist has argued that the rule, while necessary to deter police misconduct, is not an integral part of the Fourth Amendment but derives from it. Justice Thurgood Marshall, on the other hand, believed that the exclusionary rule is an integral component of the Fourth Amendment and that the protections against unreasonable search and seizure require the rule.

See Fred Graham, *The Due Process Revolution: The Warren Court's Impact on Criminal Law* (New York: Hayden, 1970); A. E. Dick Howard, ed., *Criminal Justice in Our Time* (Charlottesville: University Press of Virginia, 1965); and Claude R. Sowle, ed., *Police Power and Individual Freedom: The Quest for Balance* (Chicago: Aldine, 1962).

Hoyt v. Florida

368 U.S. 57 (1961)
Decided: November 20, 1961
Vote: 9 (Warren, Black, Frankfurter, Douglas, Clark, Harlan II, Brennan, Whittaker, Stewart)
0
Opinion of the Court: Harlan II
Concurring opinion: Warren, Black, Douglas

Gwendolyn Hoyt beat her husband, Clarence, to death with a baseball bat and was convicted of second-degree murder. She challenged the validity of her conviction because she had been tried by an all-male jury and because Florida's statutory scheme for jury membership did not require women to serve. Hoyt maintained that she deserved female as well as male jury members to receive a fair trial. She also argued that Florida's law violated the Equal Protection Clause of the Fourteenth Amendment by limiting the number of women who served on juries. The law said that women were eligible for jury selection only if they registered themselves, and few women chose to register.

The Court was not impressed with Hoyt's arguments. Although the Constitution entitles every criminal defendant to a jury of his or her peers, and bars arbitrary exclusion of jury members, it does not entitle the accused to a jury tailored to the particular circumstances of his or her case. As for the Florida law, the Court pointed out that a law does not violate the Equal Protection Clause if it is grounded in a reasonable classification. Here, allowing women to serve on juries only if they chose to register was reasonably based on the unique role of women as the "center of home and family life." The Court agreed with Florida that it was harder for women to get away from the home to serve on juries and that they should be required to do so only if they chose.

Florida had no deliberate intent to exclude women from jury participation, and the law was not invalid because it resulted in only 5 percent female participation in the jury process. Because an all-male jury triggered no constitutional significance for those on trial, the Court found no problem with Florida's system.

The concurring opinion by Chief Justice Warren, joined by Justices Black and Douglas, found that on the record Florida had made no conscious effort to exclude women. Three decades later, the Court held in *J. E. B. v. Alabama ex rel. T. B.,* 511 U.S. 127 (1994), that a deliberate effort to keep women off a jury violated the Constitution.

Garner v. Louisiana

368 U.S. 157 (1961)
Decided: December 11, 1961
Vote: 9 (Warren, Black, Frankfurter, Douglas, Clark, Harlan II, Brennan, Whittaker, Stewart)
0
Opinion of the Court: Warren
Concurring opinion: Douglas
Opinion concurring in judgment: Frankfurter
Opinion concurring in judgment: Harlan II

This case represents the consolidation of three almost identical cases. In each, African American students attempted to eat at the lunch counters of drugstores in Baton Rouge, Louisiana. These drugstores did not refuse to serve African Americans, but served them only in certain areas of the store. At each store, the students sat at the whites-only counters and attempted to order. They were asked to leave but refused, saying nothing. Store managers called the police, who arrested the students and charged them with disturbing the peace. At three trials before the same judge, each group of students was convicted and sentenced to four months in jail.

Louisiana law defined "disturbing the peace" as doing specified violent, boisterous, or disruptive acts that disturb or alarm the public. The Supreme Court found that the students had not engaged in such behavior and that there was no evidence on the record to indicate that they had. The Court found that their convictions violated the Due Process Clause of the Fourteenth Amendment, which requires that a conviction be supported by sufficient evidence. Both the statute and Louisiana decisions about disturbing the peace indicated that more was required for a conviction than merely sitting quietly in a chair, waiting for service. Because the students only sat and did not do anything to upset the public, there was not enough evidence to merit their convictions.

The opinion rendered no judgment about the state of race relations in Louisiana or the validity of separate lunch counters, not only because both were outside of the question presented, but because the Court was deeply divided over the constitutional questions related to the sit-ins. The divisions finally manifested themselves in a variety of opinions in ***Bell v. Maryland,*** 378 U.S. 226 (1964).

Justice Douglas, in his concurrence, pointed the way that Congress took in the 1964 Civil Rights Act. Douglas saw the lunch counters as public accommodations that traditionally were barred from discriminating against customers.

See Kenneth L. Karst, "Foreword: Equal Citizenship Under the Fourteenth Amendment," *Harvard Law Review* 91 (1977): 1.

Baker v. Carr

369 U.S. 186 (1962)
Decided: March 26, 1962
Vote: 6 (Warren, Black, Douglas, Clark, Brennan, Stewart)
2 (Frankfurter, Harlan II)
Opinion of the Court: Brennan
Concurring opinion: Douglas
Concurring opinion: Clark
Concurring opinion: Stewart
Dissenting opinion: Frankfurter (Harlan II)
Dissenting opinion: Harlan II (Frankfurter)
Did not participate: Whittaker

The Constitution is clear that each state is to have two senators and that members of the House of Representatives are to be apportioned according to the state's share of the population as determined by a required census every ten years. The Constitution, however, provides no guidance as to how these representatives are to be assigned within each state. James Madison believed that the arrangement should be equitable, so that one man's vote would have approximately the same weight as his neighbor's in both state and federal elections.

Some states periodically redrew the lines of their congressional districts as well as their state assembly districts to ensure at least a rough equity among voters. In fact, during the 1950s, three-fifths of all the states reapportioned one or both of their legislative chambers. Twelve states, however, had not redrawn their districts for more than three decades, despite major population shifts; Alabama had not reapportioned its legislature since 1901, and Delaware not since 1897. Amazing discrepancies existed in a number of states: in Vermont, for example, the most populous assembly district had 33,000 persons, the least populous 238, yet each district had one representative. The distortions ran even higher in state senate districts, which, like the federal model, often followed geographical lines. In California, the Los Angeles senatorial district included 6 million people; in a more sparsely populated rural section of the state, the senate district had only 14,000 persons. Such distortions grossly undervalued urban and suburban votes and overvalued the ballot in older rural districts. Naturally, the rural minorities who controlled state government had little incentive to reapportion, because to do so would mean giving up their power.

Unable to secure change from the state legislatures themselves, reform groups turned to the courts, invoking the constitutional guarantee of a "Republican Form of Government" (Article IV, Section 4), but the Supreme Court initially refused to get involved. Challengers of an Illinois law prescribing unevenly apportioned congressional districts brought their suit to the Court in ***Colegrove v. Green,*** 328 U.S. 549 (1946). A bare plurality of the seven justices who heard the argument ruled that the issue was a "political question" and therefore outside the jurisdiction of the Court. In a now-famous remark, Justice Frankfurter warned that "courts ought not to enter this political thicket."

In the wake of the great civil rights cases of the 1950s, voters who believed their ballots were diluted or even nullified by malapportionment went back into federal courts seeking relief not only under Article IV but also under the Equal Protection Clause. Following the Court's decision in ***Gomillion v. Lightfoot,*** 364 U.S. 339 (1960), striking down a blatant gerrymandering scheme in Alabama designed to disenfranchise black voters, reformers thought they now had an opening to renew their battle for reapportionment. The Court accepted *Baker v. Carr,* a suit brought by urban voters in Tennessee, where no redistricting had occurred since 1901, even though the state constitution required reapportionment every ten years. The case was argued in April 1961 and reargued in October.

In its March 1962 decision the Court moved away from its traditional policy of avoiding questions of legislative representation. Justice Brennan ruled that such issues *were* justiciable and that citizens who believed their vote had been diluted had standing to sue in federal district court. He did not prescribe any particular remedy. "We have no cause at this stage to doubt the District Court will be able to fashion relief if violations of constitutional rights are found," and the Supreme Court would wait to see what happened. The Court thus assigned the power and responsibility to afford relief from malapportionment to the lower courts, much as they had already been mandated to remedy voting discrimination based on race.

Brennan could not simply ignore the political question doctrine, so he drew a careful distinction between recognized political questions and apportionment. In all other cases, either the Constitution explicitly or implicitly assigned the issue to another branch of government, or the Court had refused jurisdiction because the question lacked "judicially discoverable and manageable standards for resolving it." In *Colegrove,* Brennan correctly noted, a majority of the Court had believed the issue justiciable, and in *Gomillion,* it had specifically asserted judicial power and ability to resolve such problems.

Predictably, the Court's two leading advocates of judicial restraint, Frankfurter and Harlan, entered bitter protests. Justice Frankfurter accused the majority of risking the Court's prestige in an area that should be left to the political process. "In a democratic society like ours," he argued, "relief must come through an aroused popular conscience that sears the conscience of the people's representative." Justice Harlan thought the system could be improved, but he found nothing in the Constitution to prevent a state while "acting not irrationally, from choosing any electoral structure it thinks best suited to the interests, tempers and customs of the people." Both men ignored the heart of the complaint—that a majority of the people could not adopt the system "best suited" to their needs because of an entrenched minority.

Baker v. Carr led many legislatures to redistrict voluntarily; elsewhere reformers launched dozens of suits in state and federal courts to force reapportionment. Half of the states reapportioned at least one house, but there was confusion over what the Court considered proper standards. Did the districts have to be mathematically equal in population, or would the Court permit some variance? Could one house of a bicameral legislature be apportioned on other grounds, such as geography? Could a state recognize certain historic divisions as a factor in drawing lines? If a plan had some questionable features, yet a majority of the electorate approved it in a referendum, would this meet judicial approval? Obviously, the Supreme Court would have to hear more cases to determine what Justice Brennan had implied existed on this issue, "judicially discoverable and manageable standards."

See Richard C. Cortner, *The Apportionment Cases* (Knoxville: University of Tennessee Press, 1970); Robert G. Dixon Jr., *Democratic Representation: Reapportionment in Law and Politics* (New York: Oxford University Press, 1968); Nelson W. Polsby, ed., *Reapportionment in the 1970s* (Berkeley: University of California Press, 1971); and Robert McKay, "Reapportionment: Success Story of the Warren Court," *Michigan Law Review* 67 (1968): 223.

Brown Shoe Co. v. United States

370 U.S. 294 (1962)
Decided: June 25, 1962
Vote: 7 (Warren, Black, Douglas, Clark,
Harlan II, Brennan, Stewart)
0
Opinion of the Court: Warren
Concurring opinion: Clark
Opinion concurring in part and dissenting in part: Harlan II
Did not participate: Frankfurter and B. White

The United States brought an antitrust suit to block the merger of Brown Shoe Company and G. R. Kinney. Given the magnitude of mergers in the 1990s between corporate giants such as Boeing and McDonnell Douglas, it is difficult to understand the fuss. Both companies manufactured shoes and owned retail outlets. Brown was the country's fourth largest manufacturer of shoes, with 4 percent of the nation's production; Kinney was the twelfth largest, with .005 percent of production. Between them they would own about 2.3 percent of the seventy thousand retail outlets in the country and become the second largest retailer.

Chief Justice Warren upheld the government, noting that the merger would "force Brown shoes into Kinney stores," while other manufacturers' brands would be frozen out. Rejecting Brown's arguments that there would be no efficiencies realized in the merger, the Court found that, to the contrary, significant efficiencies would be realized and put independent shoe retailers at a disadvantage. The intent of Congress in the 1890 Sherman Act, according to the majority, had been to protect small, locally owned stores from the competition of larger national corporations, regardless of any price benefits to the consumer.

The decision, one of a relatively few antitrust cases heard by the Warren Court, nevertheless added to its reputation as an antibusiness Court.

Engel v. Vitale

370 U.S. 421 (1962)
Decided: June 25, 1962
Vote: 6 (Warren, Black, Douglas, Clark, Harlan II, Brennan)
1 (Stewart)
Opinion of the Court: Black
Concurring opinion: Douglas
Dissenting opinion: Stewart
Did not participate: Frankfurter, B. White

The New York Board of Regents had prepared for use in public schools a "nondenominational" prayer that read: "Almighty God, we acknowledge our dependence upon Thee, and we beg Thy blessings upon us, our parents, our teachers and our country." Many local school boards required that the prayer be recited daily in each class. A number of parents challenged the prayer as "contrary to the beliefs, religions, or religious practices of both themselves and their children." The state's highest court upheld the rule so long as the schools did not compel students to join in the prayer if their parents objected.

The Supreme Court held the practice "wholly inconsistent with the Establishment Clause." The prayer, according to Justice Black, could not be interpreted as anything but a religious activity, and the Establishment Clause "must at least mean that it is no part of the business of government to compose official prayers for any group of American people to recite as a part of a religious program carried on by government."

Justice Stewart in his dissent considered that the practice did no more than recognize "the deeply entrenched and highly cherished spiritual tradition of our Nation."

Not since ***Brown v. Board of Education,*** 347 U.S. 483 (1954), was the Court subjected to so much public criticism, much of it stemming from a misunderstanding of what the Court had said. Conservative religious leaders attacked the decision for promoting atheism and secularism. Southerners saw *Engel* as proof of judicial radicalism. "They put the Negroes in the schools," Rep. George Andrews, D-Ala., lamented, and "now they have driven God out." Sen. Robert Byrd, D-W. Va., summed up the feelings of many when he complained that "someone is tampering with America's soul."

The Court had its champions as well as critics. Liberal Protestant and Jewish groups interpreted the decision as a significant move to divorce religion from meaningless public ritual and to protect its sincere practice. The National Council of Churches, a coalition of Protestant and Orthodox denominations, praised *Engel* for protecting "the religious rights of minorities," while the Anti-Defamation League, a Jewish organization, applauded the "splendid reaffirmation of a basic American principle." President Kennedy, the target of religious bigotry in the 1960 campaign from many of the sources now attacking the Court, urged support of the decision even if one disagreed with it. As he told a news conference:

> We have, in this case, a very easy remedy. And that is, to pray ourselves. And I would think that it would be a welcome reminder to every American family that we can pray a good deal more at home, we can

attend our churches with a good deal more fidelity, and we can make the true meaning of prayer much more important in the lives of all of our children.

Kennedy's commonsense interpretation of what the *Engel* decision meant captured the Court's intent. The justices did not oppose prayer or religion; the Framers had gone to great lengths to protect individual freedom in this area. But to protect *individual* freedom, the state could not impose any sort of religious requirement, even an allegedly nonsectarian prayer. When the power and prestige of government is placed behind any particular belief, Justice Black argued, "the inherent coercive pressure upon religious minorities to conform to the prevailing officially approved religion is plain." The Framers understood that "governmentally established religion and religious persecutions go hand in hand."

See John T. Noonan Jr., *The Lustre of Our Country* (Berkeley: University of California Press, 1998); John H. Laubach, *School Prayers: Congress, the Court, and the Public* (Washington, D.C.: Public Affairs Press, 1969); and Kenneth M. Dolbeare and Phillip E. Hammond, *The School Prayer Decision: From Court Policy to Local Practice* (Chicago: University of Chicago Press, 1970).

Glidden Co. v. Zdanok

370 U.S. 530 (1962)
Decided: June 25, 1962
Vote: 5 (Warren, Clark, Harlan II, Brennan, Stewart)
2 (Black, Douglas)
Judgment of the Court: Harlan II
Opinion concurring in judgment: Clark (Warren)
Dissenting opinion: Douglas (Black)
Did not participate: Frankfurter, B. White

Glidden Company employees brought suit against it for breaching a collective bargaining agreement. Glidden removed the case to federal court, and that court decided in favor of the employees. Glidden appealed, and the federal court of appeals also found for the employees. On appeal to the Supreme Court, Glidden argued that both the trial court and court of appeals decisions were void because they were presided over by judges from the federal Court of Claims and Court of Customs and Patents, respectively. The legislature created these courts to hear specific types of cases. According to Glidden, allowing the judges from these legislative courts to hear general cases violated the company's right to have a judge with tenure and compensation, as required by Article III.

Article III vests judicial power in "one supreme Court, and in such inferior Courts as the Congress may from time to time ordain and establish." Judges of all courts hold their offices for good behavior and must receive just compensation for their services. The Supreme Court agreed with Glidden that these requirements were not just technical duties, but rather expressed a constitutional desire to maintain proper and fair judicial bodies. The Court also found that the Court of Claims and the Court of Customs and Patents were created under the authority of Article III, and therefore both courts met the requirements of that article.

Legislative history indicated that Congress intended these courts to be Article III courts. Furthermore, it gave each court the same powers as general district courts, albeit in relation to a smaller range of cases. The Supreme Court held that when a court complies with the limitations of Article III, engages in federal judicial business, and makes independent and binding judgments, it is an Article III court. The Court of Claims and the Court of Customs and Patents handled issues that could be addressed by federal district courts, because they had power to hear "cases and controversies" arising under federal law. Because the judges of these courts were subject to the same privileges and restrictions as other federal judges, they could serve interchangeably in any federal court. Therefore, they served properly in Glidden's trial and appeal, and Glidden had no grounds for complaint.

Robinson v. California

370 U.S. 660 (1962)
Decided: June 25, 1962
Vote: 6 (Warren, Black, Douglas, Harlan II, Brennan, Stewart)
2 (Clark, B. White)
Opinion of the Court: Stewart
Concurring opinion: Douglas
Concurring opinion: Harlan II
Dissenting opinion: Clark
Dissenting opinion: B. White
Did not participate: Frankfurter

Lawrence Robinson was arrested for violating a California statute that made it a crime to "be under the influence of, or be addicted to the use of narcotics." At a jury trial in Los Angeles, two police officers testified against Robinson. They said they examined Robinson's arm on the evening of his arrest and observed scar tissue, discoloration, and needle marks. They each agreed that Robinson was not under the influence of drugs at the time of his arrest, but that the marks on his arm indicated prior drug use and addiction. The trial judge instructed the jury that they could convict Robinson if they found that he had the condition or status of being a drug addict, even if he was not involved with drugs at the time of the arrest. The jury found Robinson guilty, and he appealed.

Although state governments have extensive power to regulate drug use within their borders, the Supreme Court held that a state may not punish a status or condition with no further evidence of wrongdoing. It would be ludicrous for a state to punish someone for having a chronic disease or mental illness, and such punishment would be cruel and unusual. Likewise, the state of California may not criminalize the condition of drug addiction. Although the punishment given to Robinson was not severe, it was cruel and unusual because he was convicted without any proof that he had actively committed a crime or that he had committed a crime within the state of

California. The Court overturned the California court's definition of "addiction," as applied to Robinson.

NAACP v. Button

371 U.S. 415 (1963)
Decided: January 14, 1963
Vote: 6 (Warren, Black, Douglas, Brennan, B. White, Goldberg)
3 (Clark, Harlan II, Stewart)
Opinion of the Court: Brennan
Concurring opinion: Douglas
Opinion concurring in part, dissenting in part: B. White
Dissenting opinion: Harlan (Clark, Stewart)

The National Association for the Advancement of Colored People (NAACP) sued in federal court to restrain enforcement of a 1956 Virginia statute against barratry. Under the law, attorneys who represented organizations having no "pecuniary interest" in the litigation were subject to disbarment. The law clearly struck at the NAACP and other civil rights groups that brought suits to block enforcement of racially discriminatory laws. The Virginia Supreme Court of Appeals struck down part of the law, but upheld those sections that expanded the definition of improper solicitation of legal business.

The Supreme Court reversed. The opinion by Justice Brennan upheld the right of the NAACP to defend its members against the claim that they had engaged in illegal solicitation of business. The opinion also said that the group's efforts to provide attorneys in suits challenging racial discrimination were protected by the First and Fourteenth Amendments. Such sponsored litigation, the majority believed, might be the only way some groups, such as the NAACP, could express the grievances of their members and seek redress. *Button* was a landmark decision defending the right of an interest group to include the judicial process as a major component of their activities.

Justice Douglas concurred in the Court's judgment, but emphasized that, in his view, the statute discriminated specifically against the NAACP. Justice White concurred in part and dissented in part. He agreed that the Virginia law was unconstitutional but believed that a narrowly drawn statute would be constitutional if it proscribed only the actual day-to-day management and dictation of the tactics, strategy, and conduct of litigation by a lay entity such as the NAACP. (In fact, even the majority justices agreed that the state was not powerless in this arena, but that in order to regulate litigation the controls would have to be narrowly drawn.)

Justice Harlan dissented, claiming that unlike other group activities such as association, discussion, and advocacy—all of which were clearly protected by the First and Fourteenth Amendments—litigation was conduct, not expression, and could be regulated by the state. Although Harlan favored protection of speech, he believed that it had to be balanced against the interests of the states, with courts giving due deference to legislative judgment.

Wong Sun v. United States

371 U.S. 471 (1963)
Decided: January 14, 1963
Vote: 5 (Warren, Black, Douglas, Brennan, Goldberg)
4 (Clark, Harlan II, Stewart, B. White)
Opinion of the Court: Brennan
Concurring opinion: Douglas
Dissenting opinion: Clark (Harlan II, Stewart, B. White)

Narcotics agents in San Francisco learned from an informant that "Blackie" Toy sold narcotics. On this information alone federal agents went to the home of James Wah Toy and arrested him. He denied selling narcotics, but said that Johnny Yee was doing so. Federal agents went to Yee's house, arrested him, and found several vials of heroin in his bedroom. Yee claimed that a man named "Sea Dog" had brought the drugs to his house. The agents questioned Toy and determined that "Sea Dog" was Wong Sun, who they arrested the next day.

All three men were convicted of fraudulent and knowing transportation of heroin. A federal court of appeals affirmed each conviction despite finding that the arrests were not based on probable cause. The convicted men appealed, claiming that if their arrests were illegal, the evidence used against them was also illegal. The contested evidence included Toy's statements against Yee, the heroin found in Yee's bedroom, and unsigned statements issued by each petitioner.

The Supreme Court held that the statements and drugs found during the arrests of each petitioner were fruits of the illegal arrests and therefore inadmissible. The federal agents erred first by arresting Toy, Yee, and Sun solely because of a tip offered by an unknown informant. Once they conducted the illegal arrests, any evidence gathered in the course of the arrests was also illegal, because the statements would not have been made and the drugs would not have been found absent the arrests. As a result, Toy's conviction was set aside for lack of evidence. Sun's conviction, however, was based not only on the illegal evidence but also on a statement made several days after the arrest. The statement was not sufficiently related to arrest and was therefore admissible and sufficient to uphold his conviction.

Bantam Books Inc. v. Sullivan

372 U.S. 58 (1963)
Decided: February 18, 1963
Vote: 8 (Warren, Black, Douglas, Clark, Brennan, Stewart, B. White, Goldberg)
1 (Harlan II)
Opinion of the Court: Brennan
Concurring opinion: Douglas
Concurring in judgment: Clark
Concurring in judgment without opinion: Black
Dissenting opinion: Harlan II

The Rhode Island legislature created the Commission to Encourage Morality in Youth to educate the public on books, publications, pictures, and other materials that could lead to the corruption of young people. Although it had no prosecutorial powers, the commission could investigate publications and recommend prosecution when appropriate. It sent several letters to Max Silverstein and Sons, a Rhode Island book distributor, reminding Silverstein that the commission had a duty to report book distributors who sold "obscene" books and saying that prosecution was likely for several of the titles Silverstein distributed. The commission provided a list of books it deemed immoral, many of which were published by Bantam Books. Silverstein complied with the letters, refusing to fill pending orders from bookstores and ceasing to buy any more of the listed books from Bantam. The publisher brought suit in a Rhode Island court to have the law creating the commission declared unconstitutional under the First and Fourteenth Amendments, but lost the case.

On appeal to the Supreme Court, Bantam argued that the effect of the Rhode Island law was to curtail the dissemination of books that were not obscene by the constitutional standard of obscenity and therefore should be allowed to circulate freely. The Court agreed, saying that the First Amendment requires states to pursue only those actions that will punish obscenity without also curtailing nonobscene expression. Although the commission had no power to prosecute immoral material, it used threats and coercion to achieve the suppression of publications it found "objectionable," and its methods achieved that goal. Silverstein felt bound by the commission's letters, and that was sufficient to constitute state coercion in violation of the First Amendment.

See Harry M. Clor, *Obscenity and Public Morality: Censorship in a Liberal Society* (Chicago: University of Chicago Press, 1969).

Kennedy v. Mendoza-Martinez

372 U.S. 144 (1963)
Decided: February 18, 1963
Vote: 5 (Warren, Black, Douglas, Brennan, Goldberg)
4 (Clark, Harlan II, Stewart, B. White)
Opinion of the Court: Goldberg
Concurring opinion: Brennan
Dissenting opinion: Harlan II (Clark)
Dissenting opinion: Stewart (B. White)

Mendoza was a U.S. citizen with dual Mexican citizenship. During World War II he resided in Mexico to avoid the draft. In 1947 he was convicted of draft evasion and served a year in jail. In 1953 he was arrested and served with deportation proceedings under Section 401 (j) of the Nationality Act of 1940, which said that avoiding military service during a national emergency could result in loss of citizenship. Mendoza filed a declaratory judgment action to have his citizenship affirmed by a federal district court. The district court denied Mendoza's petition, and he appealed.

In a related case, *Rusk v. Cort,* 369 U.S. 367 (1962), the United States denied passport renewal to an American citizen doing research in Great Britain. The government claimed that Cort refused to report to his local draft board for military service because of his residence in a foreign country. Under Section 401 (j) Cort could lose his citizenship for this violation.

The Supreme Court held that Section 401 (j) violated the basic requirements of the U.S. Constitution. The problem with Section 401 (j) was that it imposed penal rather than regulatory sanctions without affording accused citizens due process of law. Although Congress had extensive power to regulate wartime emergencies, it could not do so without providing procedural safeguards that ensured fair implementation of the statutes. Both Mendoza and Cort were entitled to receive the Fifth Amendment's guarantee against self-incrimination and the Sixth Amendment's assurance of right to counsel.

Edwards v. South Carolina

372 U.S. 229 (1963)
Decided: February 25, 1963
Vote: 8 (Warren, Black, Douglas, Harlan II, Brennan, Stewart, B. White, Goldberg)
1 (Clark)
Opinion of the Court: Stewart
Dissenting opinion: Clark

In protest against what they saw as anti-Negro laws, 187 black high school and college students assembled at the site of the state government—a traditional public forum—and there peacefully expressed their grievances "to the citizens of South Carolina, along with the Legislative Bodies of South Carolina." When told by police officials that they must disperse within fifteen minutes or face arrest, they failed to do so. Instead, they sang patriotic and religious songs after one of their leaders had delivered what a local police official described as a "religious harangue." There was no violence or threat of violence on their part or on the part of any member of the crowd of some two hundred to three hundred curious but not hostile onlookers. The petitioners were arrested and convicted of the common law crime of breach of the peace, which the state supreme court said "is not susceptible of exact definition."

The U.S. Supreme Court reversed. Justice Stewart held that the convictions, under the circumstances disclosed by the record, infringed the defendants' constitutionally protected rights of free speech, free assembly, and freedom to petition the government for redress of their grievances. The importance of the case is that the Court used the Due Process Clause of the Fourteenth Amendment to incorporate the Assembly Clause of the First Amendment and apply it to the states. States could not criminalize the peaceful expression of unpopular views.

Only Justice Clark dissented. He read the record differently from the majority and believed there existed "a much greater danger of riot and disorder" that warranted the state's action.

The case went a long way toward overturning ***Feiner v. New York,*** 340 U.S. 315 (1951), which had given police far greater leeway in silencing unpopular speakers.

See Harry Kalven, *A Worthy Tradition: Freedom of Speech in America* (New York: Harper and Row, 1988).

Townsend v. Sain

372 U.S. 293 (1963)
Decided: March 18, 1963
Vote: 5 (Warren, Black, Douglas, Brennan, Goldberg)
4 (Clark, Harlan II, Stewart, B. White)
Opinion of the Court: Warren
Concurring opinion: Goldberg
Dissenting opinion: Stewart (Clark, Harlan II, B. White)

Charles Townsend was accused of murder and tried in an Illinois state court. At trial his confession was used as evidence against him. Townsend's attorney objected the admission of the confession because it was the product of coercion, but the trial court entered it into evidence, and Townsend was convicted and sentenced to death. The state supreme court affirmed the conviction. Townsend next sought collateral relief (that is, relief in a federal court on federal grounds) from his conviction in Illinois state court, and his complaint was dismissed. Finally, Townsend petitioned for habeas corpus in a federal district court, arguing that the use of his confession violated the Fourteenth Amendment because it was coerced. Townsend explained that he confessed only because police gave him a drug that acted as a "truth serum." The district court dismissed the writ, refusing to hear further evidence on the matter.

The Supreme Court held that Townsend had a valid claim of constitutional deprivation, and was therefore entitled to have his habeas corpus petition heard by a federal court. A petition for habeas corpus is not an appeal of the original conviction. Unlike an appeal, a habeas petition is an original civil proceeding that merits renewed consideration of issues that might have been ignored in state court. The federal court therefore has an obligation to receive evidence and try facts independently when a valid issue is raised in a petition for habeas corpus. Here, because Townsend raised an issue that had not been properly decided in state court, the federal district court erred in dismissing his petition.

Gideon v. Wainwright

372 U.S. 335 (1963)
Decided: March 18, 1963
Vote: 9 (Warren, Black, Douglas, Clark, Harlan II, Brennan, Stewart, B. White, Goldberg)
0
Opinion of the Court: Black
Concurring opinion: Douglas
Concurring opinion: Clark
Concurring opinion: Harlan II

Although the Sixth Amendment right to counsel was not nationalized in ***Powell v. Alabama,*** 287 U.S. 45 (1932), that case made effective counsel an essential ingredient of due process in capital cases. The formal incorporation of the Sixth Amendment came a few years later in ***Johnson v. Zerbst,*** 304 U.S. 458 (1938). It was one of the first guarantees spelled out in the Bill of Rights to be applied to the states. Four years later, however, in ***Betts v. Brady,*** 316 U.S. 455 (1942), the Court backtracked and declared that the Fourteenth Amendment had not incorporated the specific guarantees of the Sixth. A majority held that counsel for an indigent defendant did not constitute a fundamental right essential to a fair trial. In such cases, the justices would make a case-by-case inquiry into the totality of circumstances to see if the lack of counsel had deprived the defendant of a fair trial. Over the next twenty years, the Court heard many special circumstances, and in most of the cases it determined that a lawyer should have been provided to ensure fairness.

This approach proved enormously time-consuming, and, despite hearing dozens of cases, the Court never established clear criteria to guide state judges in determining when counsel had to be provided. Moreover, it found special circumstances present in so many instances that by 1962 it had for all practical purposes abandoned the *Betts* rule. The justices decided to revisit the issue and accepted an appeal filed by Clarence Earl Gideon, an indigent who had requested and been denied counsel in a Florida breaking-and-entering case. The Court named as his attorney an influential Washington lawyer and future member of the Court, Abe Fortas, and specifically requested both sides to argue whether *Betts* should be overruled.

The *Betts* rule had come under increasing criticism over the years, and most states had voluntarily adopted the federal standard of providing counsel to indigents accused in felony trials. In fact, by 1962 only five states—Alabama, Florida, Mississippi, North Carolina, and South Carolina—did not provide counsel for all or nearly all indigent felony defendants. Even in these states some cities and counties assigned attorneys to poor defendants charged with serious crimes.

Writing for the Court, Justice Black, who twenty years earlier had dissented in *Betts,* declared that *Betts* had been wrongly decided. Numerous cases in the intervening years had proven conclusively that no one could have a fair trial without the assistance of counsel and that it was therefore "implicit in the concept of ordered liberty." The Court's decision meant that the Fourteenth Amendment's Due Process Clause incorporated the Sixth Amendment right to counsel and applied it to the states. Moreover, the Court took the unusual step of applying *Gideon* retroactively, so that states that had originally not supplied counsel in felony cases now either had to retry the defendants properly, or, as it often happened, with witnesses dispersed and evidence grown cold, let them go.

Gideon was the Warren Court's most popular criminal justice decision because it rested on an insight most people could understand, namely, that without a lawyer a defendant in a criminal case could not receive justice. *Gideon* also provides a clear example of how the Court controls its image as well as its docket. By the time the Court took the case, at least five of the justices had already joined an opinion in another case that would have effectively overruled *Betts.* In fact, even as the chief justice directed his clerks to look for a good case on which to overturn *Betts,* the Court had decided but not released two decisions regarding indigents' rights to counsel. Willard Carnley was convicted of incest and indecent assault upon a minor in Florida. The state had not provided a lawyer for Carnley, who, like Gideon, filed an *in forma pauperis* petition from state prison. Poor and Illiterate, Carnley would have been an ideal case except for the crime—incest—and the fact that, unlike Gideon, eyewitnesses had testified to Carnley's guilt. So in *Carnley v. Cochran,* 369 U.S. 506 (1962), the justices reversed, but did so on the *Betts* "special circumstances" rule.

Another case, first argued in 1962, involved two men, Bennie Meyes and William Douglas, who were convicted in California for robbery and assault with intent to commit murder. Here, too, the Court decided to reverse, but then ordered the case reargued on the same day as *Gideon* and released the decision the same day it handed down *Gideon.* ***Douglas v. California,*** 372 U.S. 353 (1963), relates the complicated story of the Court's decision.

In fact, *Carnley* and *Douglas* determined what the opinion in *Gideon* would be, but the unsavory nature of the defendants and of their crimes led the Court to wait. In Clarence Earl Gideon, a drifter accused of a nonviolent crime and convicted on primarily circumstantial evidence, the Court had the petitioner it wanted. And when Abe Fortas agreed to represent Gideon, the justices had the stage set for the drama as they wanted it played out.

See Anthony Lewis, *Gideon's Trumpet* (New York: Random House, 1964); John F. Decker and Thomas J. Lonigan, "The Right to Counsel: The Impact of *Gideon v. Wainwright* on the Fifty States," *Creighton Law Review* 3 (1969): 103; and Fred Graham, *The Due Process Revolution: The Warren Court's Impact on Criminal Law* (New York: Hayden, 1970).

Douglas v. California

372 U.S. 353 (1963)
Decided: March 18, 1963
Vote: 6 (Warren, Black, Douglas, Brennan, B. White, Goldberg)
3 (Clark, Harlan II, Stewart)
Opinion of the Court: Douglas
Dissenting opinion: Clark
Dissenting opinion: Harlan II (Stewart)

In ***Betts v. Brady,*** 316 U.S. 455 (1942), a divided Court ruled that counsel for indigents did not constitute a fundamental right "implicit in the concept of ordered liberty," nor was it an essential of a fair trial. The Court endorsed a case-by-case review with an emphasis on the totality of the circumstances. In situations involving illiterate defendants or complex legal questions, due process required an attorney.

This approach proved enormously time-consuming, and even after hearing dozens of such cases over the next two decades, the Court still had not established clear criteria to guide state judges in determining when counsel had to be provided. Moreover, the Court found special circumstances present in so many instances that by 1962 it had for all practical purposes abandoned the *Betts* rule. The decision overturning *Betts* came in ***Gideon v. Wainwright,*** 372 U.S. 335 (1963).

Leading up to *Gideon,* however, is the story of two men, Bennie Meyes and William Douglas, whose case was argued before the Supreme Court a year before *Gideon,* but decided the same day. Meyes and Douglas were convicted in California for robbery and assault with intent to commit murder. They had a lawyer but claimed that the overworked public defender had done an inadequate job of defense. They also claimed that their two cases should have been separated because Meyes was willing to cooperate with the prosecution, and this created an inherent conflict of interest with the same lawyer defending both defendants. Here was an opportunity for the Court to overrule *Betts* outright or reverse on special circumstances. At conference, six of the eight justices voted to reverse but could not agree on a rationale. Then evidence appeared that the wrong man had appealed the conviction, and the justices voted, 6–2, to dismiss the case on the rarely used grounds that certiorari had been improvidently granted.

Normally, such a ruling carries little or no explanation, but in *Douglas v. California,* Justice Douglas, joined by Justice Brennan, dissented and presented such a powerful argument on the rights of the indigent to counsel that on circulation three more members of the Court joined, and Douglas's dissent became the opinion of the Court. In fact, *Douglas* determined what the opinion would be in *Gideon.* The Court, however, was uncomfortable with the idea of overturning *Betts* in this case because, even though the procedure was clearly flawed, there was still sufficient evidence to show that the men were guilty of the crime for which they had been convicted. The Court therefore held the *Douglas* decision until it could find a case in which a potentially innocent man had been convicted because he did not have an attorney. Clarence Gideon was that man, and, because Hugo Black had dissented in the earlier case, Chief Justice Warren now gave him the opportunity to write the opinion that would overturn *Betts.*

See Anthony Lewis, *Gideon's Trumpet* (New York: Random House, 1964); John F. Decker and Thomas J. Lonigan, "The Right to Counsel: The Impact of *Gideon v. Wainwright* on the Fifty States," *Creighton Law Review* 3 (1969): 103; and Fred Graham, *The Due Process Revolution: The Warren Court's Impact on Criminal Law* (New York: Hayden, 1970).

Gray v. Sanders

372 U.S. 368 (1963)
Decided: March 18, 1963
Vote: 8 (Warren, Black, Douglas, Clark, Brennan, Stewart, B. White, Goldberg)
1 (Harlan II)
Opinion of the Court: Douglas
Concurring opinion: Stewart (Clark)
Dissenting opinion: Harlan II

The decision in ***Baker v. Carr,*** 369 U.S. 186 (1962), led many legislatures to redistrict voluntarily; elsewhere, reformers launched dozens of suits in state and federal courts to force reapportionment. Half of the states reapportioned at least one house, but confusion persisted over what the Court considered proper standards. Did the districts have to be mathematically equal in population, or would the Court permit some variance? Could one house of a bicameral legislature be apportioned on other grounds, such as geography? Could a state recognize certain historic divisions as a factor in drawing lines? If a plan had some questionable features, yet a majority of the electorate approved it in a referendum, would this meet judicial approval? It was clear that the Court would need to hear more cases to determine what Justice Brennan had implied existed on this issue—"judicially discoverable and manageable standards."

In fact, the criterion adopted by the Court proved remarkably clear and relatively easy to apply—one person, one vote. In March 1963, with Attorney General Robert Kennedy arguing the case for the federal government as *amicus,* the Court heard a challenge to Georgia's county unit system. Georgia's system assigned each county a number of units, and successful candidates for state offices had to win a majority of units in statewide primaries. Because population was only one factor in the distribution of units, rural counties had more units than the heavily populated urban areas. The district court had ruled the system unconstitutional in 1962 and ordered a redistribution of units so that the disparities would be no greater than those existing between states in the electoral college system. Justice Douglas, speaking for the Court, ruled that the entire county unit system violated the Fourteenth Amendment's Equal Protection Clause, and he also overturned the district court's proposed solution.

Gray technically dealt with voting rights rather than with apportionment, but Douglas—despite the lone dissenter's assertion that a "one man, one vote rule flies in the face of history"—had happily hit on a formula that not only provided judicial guidance, but also caught the popular imagination. All other formulations of the issue appeared to pit one group against another—rural versus urban, old settler against newcomers—but "one person, one vote" (or, in the coinage of the time, "one man, one vote") had a democratic ring to it. Who could object to assuring every person that his or her vote was worth the same as the next person's? Supporting this formula meant upholding democracy and the Constitution; to oppose it seemed mean and petty.

With this formula now in place, the Court could hear the various cases, such as ***Reynolds v. Sims,*** 377 U.S. 533 (1964), dealing with apportionment.

See Richard C. Cortner, *The Apportionment Cases* (Knoxville: University of Tennessee Press, 1970); Robert G. Dixon Jr., *Democratic Representation: Reapportionment in Law and Politics* (New York: Oxford University Press, 1968); Nelson W. Polsby, ed., *Reapportionment in the 1970s* (Berkeley: University of California Press, 1971); and Robert McKay, "Reapportionment: Success Story of the Warren Court," *Michigan Law Review* 67 (1968): 223.

Fay v. Noia

372 U.S. 391 (1963)
Decided: March 18, 1963
Vote: 6 (Warren, Black, Douglas, Brennan, B. White, Goldberg)
3 (Clark, Harlan II, Stewart)
Opinion of the Court: Brennan
Dissenting opinion: Clark
Dissenting opinion: Harlan II (Clark, Stewart)

In 1942 Charles Noia and two codefendants were convicted in New York of murder committed during a robbery, and all three were sentenced to life imprisonment. The sole evidence against each man was his confession. Noia did not appeal, but his codefendants did. Although their appeals were unsuccessful, subsequent proceedings resulted in their release on the ground that their confessions had been coerced and that their convictions violated the Fourteenth Amendment. Noia then applied to the state court for a writ of *coram nobis,* a writ addressed to a court calling attention to errors of fact that would affect a judgment previously determined. The state court denied him a review of his conviction on the grounds that he had not appealed. He then applied to federal court for a writ of habeas corpus, but that too was denied on the ground that his failure to appeal was a failure to exhaust available state remedies, although the court conceded that Noia's confession also had been coerced. The court of appeals reversed the district court, and the state appealed to the Supreme Court.

The Supreme Court affirmed the judgment of the court of appeals. Justice Brennan held that federal courts have power under the federal habeas corpus statute to grant relief, despite the applicant's failure to pursue a state remedy not available to him at the time he applies.

This case is part of the "due process revolution" of the Warren Court. The majority refused to apply the older rule that failure to follow all state procedures constituted an adequate and independent bar to review by the Supreme Court of the original conviction. The basis for this decision was less constitutional than statutory—the Court's broad reading of the federal habeas corpus law. Because of the importance of the writ of habeas corpus in maintaining a fair criminal justice system, Noia's failure to make a timely appeal in state courts did not constitute an intelligent and knowledgeable waiver of his right to seek federal relief.

In addition, the decision reversed a long line of court rulings that had established the proposition that after a state prisoner had been convicted in a state trial court, he had to exhaust all state remedies before applying for federal relief, and this usually meant review by the state's highest court. In doing so, the justices overturned their own ruling in *Darr v. Burford,* 339 U.S. 200 (1950).

Justice Harlan dissented on the ground that the district court had no power, statutory or constitutional, to release the petitioner from state detention. Noia's custody by the state did not violate any federal right because it resulted from a conviction the validity of which rested upon an adequate and independent state ground—his failure to appeal—that the federal courts were required to respect. Justice Clark, in a separate dissenting opinion, elaborated on what he saw as the unfortunate consequences of the Court's holding on state law enforcement. If the federal courts set themselves up as continuous reviewers of state criminal decisions, it would throw the whole criminal justice system—most of which involved state trials for violations of state criminal statutes—into disarray, with every state prisoner appealing for review by the federal courts.

See Fred Graham, *The Due Process Revolution: The Warren Court's Impact on Criminal Law* (New York: Hayden, 1970).

Gibson v. Florida Legislative Investigation Committee

372 U.S. 539 (1963)
Decided: March 25, 1963
Vote: 5 (Warren, Black, Douglas, Brennan, Goldberg)
4 (Clark, Harlan II, Stewart, B. White)
Opinion of the Court: Goldberg
Concurring opinion: Black
Concurring opinion: Douglas
Dissenting opinion: Harlan II (Clark, Stewart, B. White)
Dissenting opinion: B. White

The Florida legislature created a committee to investigate subversive activity. In 1957 the committee sought to investigate the National Association for the Advancement of Colored People (NAACP) for alleged communist membership. The committee asked the president of the Miami NAACP to appear before it with the membership records of the entire Miami chapter. The committee, many people suspected, wanted to get the names of people engaged in civil rights activities and used the search for communists as a cover. Theodore R. Gibson agreed to testify but refused to bring membership records, saying that to do so would violate his group's freedom of association. A Florida court held Gibson in contempt for his refusal.

Prior to this case, the Supreme Court held in ***NAACP v. Alabama,*** 357 U.S. 449 (1958), and ***Bates v. Little Rock,*** 361 U.S. 516 (1960), that the freedom to engage in associations for the advancement of ideas is an aspect of liberty protected by the Due Process Clause of the Fourteenth Amendment and can be violated only if the state has a compelling interest. Florida argued a compelling interest in preventing subversion and cited several cases saying that individuals could be compelled to testify about their communist affiliations. The Court distinguished these cases, however, saying that, although legislatures may ask questions about communist activity, they must prove a nexus between communist activity and the questions asked when the questions are not directly concerned with individual subversion.

Here, Florida's legislature asked questions not about individual membership in subversive organizations, but about an entire group's supposed communist affiliations. Because Florida could prove no connection between asking for NAACP membership and eradicating subversive activity, the Court held that it could not demand NAACP membership records in violation of the group's freedom of association.

See Harvard Sitkoff, *The Struggle for Black Equality* (New York: Hill and Wang, 1981).

Ferguson v. Skrupa

372 U.S. 726 (1963)
Decided: April 22, 1963
Vote: 9 (Warren, Black, Douglas, Clark, Harlan II, Brennan, Stewart, B. White, Goldberg)
0
Opinion of the Court: Black
Opinion concurring in judgment: Harlan II

Frank Skrupa brought suit against William Ferguson, the attorney general of Kansas, to enjoin the enforcement of a state law forbidding anyone but a lawyer to engage in the business of debt adjustment. Skrupa, who was not an attorney, had a successful debt adjustment practice. He sued to prove that his business was "useful and desirable" and that the Kansas legislature could therefore not stop him from practicing. A Kansas court held that the statute could not be applied against Skrupa because it was prohibitory rather than regulatory, and the Kansas legislature could not prohibit lawful business practices without violating the Fourteenth Amendment's guarantee of due process.

The Supreme Court held that it is not the province of any court to draw on its own definition of morality in order to overturn a valid legislative statute, and therefore the Kansas court had no power to enjoin the application of the statute against Skrupa. The Court also held that Kansas's statute did not violate the Fourteenth Amendment's guarantee of equal protection. The statute was based on a reasonable distinction between attorneys and nonattorneys, and the Equal Protection Clause does not prevent a state from making rationally justified classifications.

White v. Maryland

373 U.S. 59 (1963)
Decided: April 29, 1963
Vote: 9 (Warren, Black, Douglas, Clark, Harlan II, Brennan, Stewart, B. White, Goldberg)
0
Opinion of the Court: *Per curiam*

Robert White was arrested for murder, and before he could obtain a lawyer the state forced him to appear in a preliminary hearing where he pled guilty to the charges against him. After obtaining a lawyer, White changed his plea to "not guilty" and "not guilty by reason of insanity." At his trial his original guilty plea was used as evidence against him, and he was convicted of murder.

White argued that his original plea was inadmissible because he did not have an attorney at the time it was entered. In *Hamilton v. Alabama,* 368 U.S. 52 (1961), the Court held that an accused had a right to counsel at his arraignment, when he entered a plea. Maryland argued that *Hamilton* did not apply because the preliminary hearing was not a "critical stage in a criminal proceeding."

The Court quickly disposed of Maryland's argument, saying that a preliminary hearing in Maryland was equivalent to an arraignment in Alabama. White entered a plea in the preliminary hearing, and his plea affected the outcome of his trial. Given this direct effect, White should have been assigned an attorney for his preliminary hearing. Because Maryland violated his right to counsel, White's statements made without an attorney present could not be used against him, and the Court reversed his conviction.

Peterson v. City of Greenville

373 U.S. 244 (1963)
Decided: May 20, 1963
Vote: 9 (Warren, Black, Douglas, Clark, Brennan, Harlan II, Stewart, B. White, Goldberg)
0
Opinion of the Court: Warren
Concurring opinion: Harlan II

James Richard Peterson and nine other black teenagers were eating in a restaurant in Greenville, South Carolina. When the manager of the restaurant saw that there were black people eating there, he called the police, closed the restaurant, and told the black youths to leave. The manager asked them to leave because serving black people at restaurants with white people was contrary to local customs and a violation of a city ordinance requiring separate but equal eating facilities. They remained seated at the lunch counter in protest against the segregation policy. They were subsequently arrested and convicted of violating the local trespass statute. They appealed, claiming that the law violated the Equal Protection Clause.

The Supreme Court struck down the ordinance, ruling that a law that allows for segregation to bring about trespassing violates the Equal Protection Clause of the Fourteenth Amendment. The Court ruled that a law that compels people to discriminate against other people because of race is an absolute violation of the Equal Protection Clause. Justice Harlan concurred, but he believed the proper question should be whether the discriminatory exclusion had in fact been caused by the ordinance, and in this instance he was satisfied that it had been. In future cases such as ***Bell v. Maryland,*** 378 U.S. 226 (1964), however, the Court divided over this issue and whether a private restaurant could discriminate.

See Harvard Sitkoff, *The Struggle for Black Equality, 1954–1980* (New York: Hill and Wang, 1981).

Arizona v. California

373 U.S. 546 (1963)
Decided: June 3, 1963
Vote: 5 (Black, Clark, Brennan, B. White, Goldberg)
3 (Douglas, Harlan II, Stewart)
Opinion of the Court: Black
Dissenting opinion: Douglas
Dissenting opinion: Harlan II (Douglas, Stewart)
Did not participate: Warren

This controversy arose from several agreements about how the water of the Colorado River should be apportioned among seven arid western states. Congress had passed several acts early in the twentieth century to address the Colorado water issue and to ensure that conflicts among equally needy states were addressed conclusively. In cases of shortage, the burden would be borne by all western states in proportion to their original shares. Several years after the agreements were signed, the West experienced a water shortage, and California challenged the amount of water it received. It argued that water should be apportioned from the entire Colorado River system, not just the main stream, and that the shortage should be apportioned equitably rather than by the stringent rules of the agreement.

To look into the matter, the Court appointed a special master, who searched the legislative history of each ordinance to determine that they were intended to address only the main stream of the Colorado River. The river's tributaries were specifically allocated to the states wherein they lay. Arizona insisted on sole use of its tributaries throughout discussions about allocation, and it would be wrong to take them now.

The Court agreed with California on the second issue, the sharing of water during shortages. The water agreements created by Congress did not have specific instructions for allocating water during shortages, but they had been followed in a formulaic way. Although this appeared fair on the surface, it actually resulted in some states experiencing greater shortages than others. The Court left lower federal courts with the duty of determining the amount of water to be rationed to California.

All told, the special master made ten specific recommendations, and the majority of the Court accepted seven of them.

Goss v. Board of Education of the City of Knoxville, Tennessee

373 U.S. 683 (1963)
Decided: June 3, 1963
Vote: 9 (Warren, Black, Douglas, Clark, Harlan II, Brennan, Stewart, B. White, Goldberg)
0
Opinion of the Court: Clark

Josephine and Thomas Goss and other African American schoolchildren brought suit against the Board of Education of Knoxville, Tennessee, to challenge a transfer provision the board had approved. Following ***Brown v. Board of Education,*** 347 U.S. 483 (1954), the Knoxville board created a system of desegregated schools. The desegregation plan included a transfer provision stating that a request for transfer would be honored "when a white student would otherwise be required to attend a school previously serving colored students only," or vice versa. The provision also allowed transfer when a student would otherwise be required to attend a school where the majority of students were of a different race. According to the black plaintiffs, the effect of the provision was to allow students to choose segregation but not desegregation.

The Court held that the transfer provision violated the Equal Protection Clause of the Fourteenth Amendment because it was based solely on race. Racial classifications are both irrelevant and invidious, and should play no role in deciding where students attend school. The board further erred by recognizing race only to allow students to attend schools where their race was the majority, without allowing transfers to schools where a student's race was the minority.

In ***Brown II,*** 349 U.S. 294 (1955), the Court said that jurisdictions should achieve desegregated schools "in good faith" and with "all deliberate speed." Although these words provided leeway to struggling schools in the early years after *Brown,* the Court displayed little tolerance for noncompliance nine years later. Accordingly, it struck down the transfer policy.

See Benjamin Muse, *Ten Years of Prelude: The Story of Integration Since the Supreme Court's 1954 Decision* (New York: Viking Press, 1964).

Rideau v. Louisiana

373 U.S. 723 (1963)
Decided: June 3, 1963
Vote: 7 (Warren, Black, Douglas, Brennan, Stewart, B. White, Goldberg)
2 (Clark, Harlan II)
Opinion of the Court: Stewart
Dissenting opinion: Clark (Harlan II)

Wilbert Rideau robbed a bank in Lake Charles, Louisiana, kidnapped three of the bank's employees, and killed one of them. The next morning he was interrogated by the sheriff and admitted to bank robbery, kidnapping, and murder. The interrogation was videotaped by a film company and broadcast over local television stations. It was so popular that an estimated 106,000 people in Lake Charles saw the interrogation on television. The town had a population of about 150,000 people.

Because most of the people in town had seen his confession on television, Rideau asked for a change of venue. He feared jury prejudice and town pressure to convict him. The change of venue was denied, however; his trial was held in the town, and he was sentenced to death. He appealed, claiming that the televised confession had tainted the town so much that a fair trial could not occur, and that his due process rights had been violated by not having a change of venue.

The Court held that there should have been a change of venue and reversed the conviction. It ruled that the town, made up of the prospective jurors, had been so tainted by the televised confession that a fair and impartial trial could not be had there and should have been held elsewhere.

Ker v. California

374 U.S. 23 (1963)
Decided: June 10, 1963
Vote: 5 (Black, Clark, Harlan II, Stewart, B. White)
4 (Warren, Brennan, Douglas, Goldberg)
Judgment of the Court: Clark
Concurring in judgment: Harlan II
Dissenting opinion: Brennan (Warren, Douglas, Goldberg)

George and Diane Ker were convicted of possession of marijuana under California state law. To establish probable cause for the Kers' arrest, police followed George Ker's car from a known drug distribution site and corroborated their suspicions with information from a reliable informant who said that he had been buying marijuana from a man Ker had previously been seen with. The police obtained a warrant of arrest and went to the Ker home. When they entered, they saw a brick of marijuana next to the kitchen sink. They arrested the Kers and then searched the house. They found more marijuana in a bedroom dresser and in the car. The fruits of all the searches were used at trial, and the Kers were convicted. They appealed, claiming that the California court erred in using the evidence against them because the police did not have a warrant to conduct the search.

The Kers based their appeal on the decision of ***Mapp v. Ohio,*** 367 U.S. 643 (1961), in which the Court held that evidence from an illegal search should be excluded from use in state court as well as federal court. In this case, however, the Court held that the evidence used against the Kers had not been unlawfully obtained because it was seized subsequent to a valid arrest. The police had sufficient reason to arrest the Kers, and the Court did not question the validity of the arrest warrant. Because the arrest was valid, anything obtained by the police in a search subsequent to the arrest was legally obtained.

Justice Clark spoke for all of the Court except Justice Harlan in holding that the same standards for search and seizure that applied to federal law enforcement officials should also apply to state and local police officers. Harlan believed a more flexible standard should be applied to the states. Clark believed that these standards had been met in this case, while Justice Brennan believed they had not. Harlan concurred with the first group in upholding the arrest and conviction.

School District of Abington Township v. Schempp

374 U.S. 203 (1963)
Decided: June 17, 1963
Vote: 8 (Warren, Black, Douglas, Clark, Harlan II, Brennan, B. White, Goldberg)
1 (Stewart)
Opinion of the Court: Clark
Concurring opinion: Douglas
Concurring opinion: Brennan
Concurring opinion: Goldberg (Harlan II)
Dissenting opinion: Stewart

In the school prayer decision, ***Engel v. Vitale,*** 370 U.S. 421 (1962), the Court held that to protect the *individual's* freedom of religion, the state could not impose any sort of religious requirement, even in an allegedly "neutral" prayer. As soon as the power and prestige of the government is placed behind any religious belief or practice, according to Justice Black, "the inherently coercive pressure upon religious minorities to conform to the prevailing officially approved religion is plain." One year after the decision, the Court extended this reasoning in *Schempp* and a companion case from Maryland, *Murray v. Curlett,* 228 Md. 239 (1962), in which the nation's most notorious atheist, Madalyn Murray, was the plaintiff.

Schempp dealt with a Pennsylvania law requiring that:

> At least ten verses from the Holy Bible shall be read, without comment, at the opening of each public school on each school day. Any child shall be excused from such Bible reading, or attending such Bible reading, upon the written request of his parent or guardian.

In addition, the students were to recite the Lord's Prayer in unison.

The Court, through Justice Clark, who was usually considered a conservative, struck down the required Bible reading. Clark built on Black's comments in *Engel* that the neutrality commanded by the Constitution stemmed from the bitter lessons of history, which recognized that a fusion of church and state inevitably led to persecution of all but those who adhered to the official orthodoxy.

Anticipating that the Court might be confronted with additional Establishment Clause cases in the future, Clark attempted to set out rules by which lower courts could determine when a statute breached the constitutional barrier. The test, he said, may be stated as follows:

> What are the purpose and the primary effect of the enactment? If either is the advancement or inhibition of religion then the enactment exceeds the scope of legislative power as circumscribed by the Constitution. That is to say that to withstand the strictures of the Establishment Clause there must be a secular legislative purpose and a primary effect that neither advances nor inhibits religion.

Formal coercion was not an issue in this case, as students could be excused from the exercises, but Clark noted that nonparticipating students inevitably called attention to themselves by their absence and thus invited retribution in the form of peer ostracism. The Court held that the coercion needed to trigger a free exercise claim might be indirect, but it was nevertheless caused by the government's actions.

Only Justice Stewart dissented, and he argued against either the necessity or the desirability of having a single constitutional standard. "Religion and government must interact in countless ways," most of which were harmless and should not be subject to a "doctrinaire reading of the Establishment Clause." He chastised the majority for violating the free exercise claims of those who wanted their children to start the school day with exposure to the Bible. He also objected to the majority's assumption that every involvement by the state necessarily led to coercion. Such an assumption would cast suspicion on every type of activity in which one might find some religious component, and he wanted to shift the burden of proof from a presumption of coercion to an actual showing that it had occurred.

Although the *Schempp* case did not trigger quite the uproar that had followed *Engel*, Stewart's dissent reflected the feeling of many people that *their* rights had been restricted for the sake of a few secular extremists. Moreover, the Court seemed to say (despite Clark's specific assurances to the contrary) that the Bible could no longer be read in the schools. It could be studied as either literature or history, but it could no longer be used in a mandatory religious devotion.

See Kenneth M. Dolbeare and Philip E. Hammond, *The School Prayer Decisions: From Court Policy to Local Practice* (Chicago: University of Chicago Press, 1971); and Thomas Mengler, "Public Relations in the Supreme Court: Justice Tom Clark's Opinion in the School Prayer Case," *Constitutional Commentary* 6 (1989): 331.

Sherbert v. Verner

374 U.S. 398 (1963)
Decided: June 17, 1963
Vote: 7 (Warren, Black, Douglas, Clark, Brennan, Stewart, Goldberg)
2 (Harlan II, B. White)
Opinion of the Court: Brennan
Concurring opinion: Douglas
Opinion concurring in judgment: Stewart
Dissenting opinion: Harlan II (B. White)

Adell Sherbert, a Seventh-day Adventist living in Spartanburg, South Carolina, was discharged from her job in a textile mill because she would not work on Saturday. Her refusal to work on her Sabbath prevented her from accepting other job offers, which resulted in the state denying her unemployment compensation payments. South Carolina law barred benefits to workers who refused, without "good cause," to accept suitable work when it was offered.

In what is now termed the "modern" approach to First Amendment issues, Justice Brennan posed the same question he had in his dissent in ***Braunfeld v. Brown,*** 366 U.S. 599 (1961): Did the state have a compelling interest sufficient to warrant an abridgement of a constitutionally protected right? This is the same question the Court asks in regard to speech restrictions because the analytical process in speech and free exercise claims are similar. Free expression of ideas is involved in religion just as in speech, press, assembly, or petition—namely, the right to say what one believes, whether it involves political, economic, social, or religious ideas. Only the most compelling societal need can warrant any restrictions on these rights.

Brennan found no compelling interest presented by the state, which had done little more than suggest that some applicants might file fraudulent claims alleging that they could not find work for religious reasons. Brennan recognized, however, the difficulties Justice Stewart raised in his dissent—that forcing South Carolina to pay unemployment compensation benefits to Sherbert meant that the state was favoring the adherents of one particular sect. Brennan therefore went out of his way to indicate the limited nature of the decision. The Court, he explained, was not establishing Seventh-Day Adventism as the religion of South Carolina, nor was it establishing a constitutional right "to unemployment benefits on the part of all persons whose religious convictions are the cause of their unemployment."

Stewart's dissent raised a valid question and explicated, more than any other decision of this era, the inherent conflict between the Establishment Clause and the Free Exercise Clause. By allowing for religious accommodation, the Court had in fact granted a preference to a religious group.

The *Sherbert* case and one involving the Amish, ***Wisconsin v. Yoder,*** 406 U.S. 205 (1972), raise the question of whether the Constitution can be read as totally "religion-neutral" or "religion-blind." The argument parallels the suggestion made by the first Justice Harlan that the Constitution is "color-blind," and, like that argument, is manifestly incorrect. Neither the Constitution nor the Court has been color-blind or completely neutral in religious matters. Neutrality in religious matters is more of an ideal than a reality in constitutional adjudication and for the same reason. Religion, like race, is a tangled skein and not amenable to simple solutions.

Sherbert remained the definitive word on the Free Exercise Clause for nearly three decades, until practically reversed in ***Employment Division v. Smith,*** 494 U.S. 872 (1990).

See Marc Galanter, "Religious Freedom in the United States: A Turning Point?" *Wisconsin Law Review* (1966): 217; and Stephen Pepper, "Taking the Free Exercise Clause Seriously," *Brigham Young University Law Review* (1986): 299.

Wesberry v. Sanders

376 U.S. 1 (1964)
Decided: February 17, 1964
Vote: 6 (Warren, Black, Douglas, Brennan, B. White, Goldberg)
3 (Clark, Harlan II, Stewart)
Opinion of the Court: Black
Opinion concurring in part, dissenting in part: Clark
Dissenting opinion: Harlan II (Stewart)
Dissenting opinion: Stewart

After ***Baker v. Carr,*** 369 U.S. 186 (1962), established that the Supreme Court had jurisdiction over issues of congressional and state apportionment, states voluntarily began to reapportion to equalize their legislative districts. Some states did not, however, and beginning in 1963 the Court heard a number of these suits, including a group of cases gathered under ***Reynolds v. Sims,*** 377 U.S. 533 (1964), that would be decided later in the same term.

Georgia's Fifth Congressional District had a population of 823,680, while the average population of the state's ten districts was 394,312. Two voters in the Fifth District brought suit against the state seeking to have the Georgia congressional districting statute declared invalid and enjoining the state from conducting elections under it. The district court dismissed the case for nonjusticiability, despite the Supreme Court's earlier decision in *Baker v. Carr.*

On appeal, the Court reversed, 6–3. Justice Black's opinion said that Georgia's statute was invalid because it abridged Article 1, Section 2, of the Constitution, which states that members of Congress are to be chosen "by the People of the several States," and that requires that as nearly as practicable one man's vote in a congressional election must be worth as much as another's.

Justice Clark concurred in part and dissented in part, agreeing with the majority that the trial court erred in dismissing the case for nonjusticiability and want of equity, but arguing that Article 1, Section 2, does not forbid disproportionate congressional districts. He wanted the case remanded to decide whether the apportionment statute violated the Equal Protection Clause of the Fourteenth Amendment. Justice Harlan dissented on the ground that the Constitution expressly provides that state legislatures and Congress have exclusive jurisdiction over problems of congressional apportionment of the type involved in the case. Although Justice Stewart joined in Harlan's dissent, he believed that the issues involved were in fact justiciable, that is, they could be heard and resolved by the judiciary.

This case is best understood as a precursor to the major apportionment cases decided only a few months later. By this time, eight members of the Court believed that the issues were justiciable, and a clear majority believed that malapportioned state legislatures, as well as congressional districts, violated one or more provisions of the federal Constitution.

See Richard C. Cortner, *The Apportionment Cases* (Knoxville: University of Tennessee Press, 1970); and Robert G. Dixon Jr., *Democratic Representation: Reapportionment in Law and Politics* (New York: Oxford University Press, 1968).

New York Times v. Sullivan

376 U.S. 254 (1964)
Decided: March 9, 1964
Vote: 9 (Warren, Black, Douglas, Clark, Harlan II, Brennan, Stewart, B. White, Goldberg)
0
Opinion of the Court: Brennan
Concurring opinion: Black (Douglas)
Opinion concurring in judgment: Goldberg (Douglas)

As late as 1942, in ***Chaplinsky v. New Hampshire,*** 315 U.S. 568, a unanimous Court had confidently listed "fighting words," obscenity, and libel as examples of expression outside First Amendment protection. The United States had long ago done away with the English common law on libel and defamation of character, in which the mere publication of a defamatory statement—whether true or not—could be punished. American law allowed the defendant to offer evidence of the truth of the statement, which, if accepted by judge or jury, served as a complete defense. All states, however, still permitted civil actions for false or malicious statements, and wide gradations existed among the jurisdictions. Some states differentiated degrees of malice; others distinguished between simple errors and more serious distortions of truth.

The Supreme Court had, with few exceptions, left libel a matter for state law. In 1952 a closely divided Court in ***Beauharnais v. Illinois,*** 343 U.S. 250, upheld a state statute prohibiting the libel of any group. Justice Frankfurter denied that libel came within the constitutional protection of speech; the state legislature had as good reason to try to prevent defamatory attacks on groups as on individuals, and he saw no reason for the courts to interfere. Justices Black, Douglas, Reed, and Jackson wrote dissents, ranging from Black's absolutist view of criminal libel laws as unconstitutional to Jackson's anticipation of the overbreadth doctrine. Despite the closeness of the vote, the Court did not return to the libel issue for a dozen years, and *Beauharnais* itself has never been overruled.

In this context the Court handed down its decision in *New York Times v. Sullivan.* An advertisement in the *Times* signed by dozens of clergy and other civil rights advocates charged the police and city officials of Montgomery, Alabama, with unleashing "an unprecedented wave of terror" against blacks engaged in nonviolent demonstrations against discrimination. L. B. Sullivan, Montgomery's police and fire commissioner, sued the newspaper and several of the black clergy who had signed the ad and won a $500,000 judgment under Alabama law. The ad contained several factual errors, such as the claim that Rev. Martin Luther King Jr. had been arrested seven times, when it was actually four times. Alabama law held publications "libelous per se" if the words tended "to injure a person [in] his reputation" or "to bring [him] into public contempt." The statute retained many elements of the old common law, and, although the defendant could offer truth as a defense, he had a heavy burden to prove.

The nexus between the First Amendment and civil rights could not have been clearer. If Alabama could damage the *Times* financially (and $500,000 was an enormous judgment in the 1960s), the state could insulate itself from public scrutiny of its treatment of blacks. Criticizing the South, or even just reporting events there, could prove too costly for news organizations. One did not even have to have much of a presence in the state to come within its civil jurisdiction; the *Times* distributed only 394 copies of its daily press run of 650,000 in Alabama, and only 35 of them went to Montgomery. The paper had no full-time reporters assigned to the state.

The Court found the statute "constitutionally deficient for failure to provide the safeguards for freedom of speech and of the press that are requirements" of the First Amendment. Justice Brennan's opinion explained that there is always a balancing test between unlimited speech and the legitimate interests of the state; in matters of public interest and concerning public officials, he struck that balance on the side of free speech, with the exception of "recklessly false statements" made with "actual malice." The Court considered the case, Brennan wrote, "against the background of a profound national commitment to the principle that debate on public issues should be uninhibited, robust, and wide-open, and that it may well include vehement, caustic, and sometimes unpleasantly sharp attacks on government and public officials."

Why should libel—a false and defamatory statement—be accorded constitutional protection? According to Brennan, quoting nineteenth century English philosopher John Stuart Mill, "even a false statement may be deemed to make a valuable contribution to public debate," because in the exchange of views this may help bring out the truth. Under the First Amendment, there is no such thing as a false idea, but there are false facts, and no constitutional value attaches to them. But because false statements are inevitable in public debate, if the Court drew the line only at truth, people would say less, there would be less debate, and consequently less exchange of ideas. As Brennan wrote in another libel case, "Speech concerning public affairs is more than self-expression; it is the essence of self-government." In effect, the Court proposed a strategy, which has governed ever since, that extended the line of protection past the constitutional minimum all the way to facts, even false facts, to encourage the debate that we deem valuable.

Within a few years of this case, the law of libel had been effectively nationalized. Although states could still control the procedural aspects of actions for libel, the substantive criteria had to conform to the Court's ruling in *New York Times* and subsequent cases. If speech dealt with public officials and their conduct, it came within constitutional protection.

See William J. Brennan Jr., "The Supreme Court and the Meikeljohn Interpretation of the First Amendment," *Harvard Law Review* 79 (1965): 1; Rodney A. Smolla, *Suing the Press* (New York: Oxford University Press, 1986); and Anthony Lewis, *Make No Law: The Sullivan Case and the First Amendment* (New York: Random House, 1991).

Schneider v. Rusk

377 U.S. 163 (1964)
Decided: May 18, 1964
Vote: 5 (Warren, Black, Douglas, Stewart, Goldberg)
3 (Clark, Harlan II, B. White)
Opinion of the Court: Douglas
Dissenting opinion: Clark (Harlan II, B. White)
Did not participate: Brennan

German-born Angelika Schneider was brought to the United States as a small child and became a naturalized citizen at age sixteen. After attending Smith College, she did postgraduate work in France. She married a German man and lived with him in Germany, returning to the United States only on a few temporary visits. In 1959 Schneider's application for an American passport was denied under a provision of the Immigration and Nationality Act of 1952, which said that a naturalized citizen automatically lost her citizenship if she lived for three years or more in the foreign state of which she was previously a national. Schneider challenged the law as a violation of her Fourteenth Amendment due process rights.

The Court held that Congress did not have the power to regulate the citizenship of naturalized citizens who merely lived in their former homelands for more than three years. The Court distinguished this case from ***Perez v. Brownell,*** 356 U.S. 44 (1958), in which it held that a naturalized citizen could lose his citizenship by voting in a foreign election. Here, the Court said that Schneider's activities did not pose the same risk to foreign relations as Perez's conduct did. According to the Court, naturalized citizens hold all of the same rights as natural-born citizens (except the ability to be president), and Congress cannot take those rights away unless their acts threaten national security or interests.

Massiah v. United States

377 U.S. 201 (1964)
Decided: May 18, 1964
Vote: 6 (Warren, Black, Douglas, Brennan, Stewart, Goldberg)
3 (Clark, Harlan II, B. White)
Opinion of the Court: Stewart
Dissenting opinion: B. White (Clark, Harlan II)

Prior to 1964 the Court had taken a due process, totality of the circumstances approach to confession, ruling that appellate courts would have to determine on a case-by-case basis whether a confession had been given voluntarily and free from police coercion. In 1964 the Court began to emphasize the Sixth Amendment right to counsel and tied the voluntariness of confession to the condition of a lawyer being present. The shift occurred in *Massiah,* a confusing case that some commentators believe to have been wrongly decided.

Winston Massiah, a merchant seaman, had been indicted along with Jesse Colson for attempting to smuggle cocaine into the United States. Massiah retained a lawyer and pleaded not guilty. Colson decided to cooperate with federal agents and agreed to have a radio transmitter placed in his car. He and Massiah subsequently had a long conversation in the car, which an agent monitored. The prosecution later used a number of incriminating statements made in that conversation against Massiah at his trial. Justice Stewart, for the Court, held that use of the defendant's statements, obtained in a surreptitious manner after his indictment and retention of a lawyer, violated his Fifth Amendment rights against self-incrimination. Justice White dissented, saying that the Court had no reason to scrap the voluntary/involuntary test and had not substituted another test for it.

Although nominally a Fifth Amendment case, *Massiah* is the intersection between the Court's development of Fifth and Sixth Amendment doctrines. Just as the various First Amendment guarantees cannot always be neatly differentiated, the bundle of rights granted to accused persons are also closely interwoven. *Massiah* applied to the states as well as to the federal government, but what did it mean other than that the police could not use his statements "after indictment and in the absence of counsel"? Was the timing at all important? Why should it matter if police surveillance secured incriminating statements before or after indictment? The Court did not, in fact, indicate when it considered a defendant formally charged. It answered many of these questions two years later in ***Miranda v. Arizona,*** 384 U.S. 436 (1966).

See Yale Kamisar, *Police Interrogation and Confessions* (Ann Arbor: University of Michigan Press, 1980); and Arnold N. Enken and Sheldon H. Elsen, "Counsel for the Suspect: *Massiah v. United States* and *Escobedo v. Illinois,*" *Minnesota Law Review* 49 (1964): 47.

Griffin v. County School Board of Prince Edward County

377 U.S. 218 (1964)
Decided: May 25, 1964
Vote: 9 (Warren, Black, Douglas, Clark, Harlan II, Brennan, Stewart, B. White, Goldberg)
0
Opinion of the Court: Black
Opinion concurring in part: Clark, Harlan II

To avoid the desegregation ordered by the Supreme Court in ***Brown v. Board of Education,*** 347 U.S. 483 (1954), officials in Prince Edward County, Virginia, closed the county's public schools and voted funds for the support of private segregated white schools, which took the place of the public schools. At the same time, public schools in all other Virginia counties were being maintained, but due to the "massive resistance" of whites, few if any had been desegregated. Because of mixed decisions in state and federal courts, Prince Edward County managed to avoid desegregation for nearly a decade.

By this time the Supreme Court, which with one exception—its decision in ***Cooper v. Aaron,*** 358 U.S. 1 (1958)—had remained silent since its decision in *Brown II,* 349 U.S. 294 (1955), was growing impatient with the South's delays in implementing the decree. Sweeping aside all procedural questions, Justice Black for a unanimous Court announced that "the time for mere 'deliberate speed' has run out." The federal district court had the power to enjoin any further use of public funds for private segregated schools. It could also superintend the school board's taxing and appropriation powers, and could, in fact, order the public schools reopened. On this last point Justices Harlan and Clark disagreed, although they did not spell out their reasons.

This case marked the first time since the 1940s segregation cases that the justices displayed even partial disagreement over this issue. The one thing all nine agreed on, however, was that the delaying tactics adopted by southern states could no longer be tolerated. Henceforth, southern school districts had to maintain desegregated public schools, even in the face of white flight to the suburbs.

See Bob Smith, *They Closed Their Schools: Prince Edward County, Virginia, 1951–1964* (Chapel Hill: University of North Carolina Press, 1965).

Reynolds v. Sims

377 U.S. 533 (1964)
Decided: June 15, 1964
Vote: 8 (Warren, Black, Douglas, Clark, Brennan, Stewart, B. White, Goldberg)
1 (Harlan II)
Opinion of the Court: Warren
Concurring opinion: Clark
Concurring opinion: Stewart
Dissenting opinion: Harlan II

The Court's decision in ***Baker v. Carr,*** 369 U.S. 186 (1962), led many state legislatures to redistrict voluntarily. In other states, however, reformers had to sue in state and federal courts to force reapportionment. Half the states reapportioned at least one house, but confusion existed over what the Court considered proper standards. Did the districts have to be mathematically equal in population, or would the Court permit some variance? Could one house of a bicameral legislature be apportioned on other grounds, such as geography? Could a state recognize certain historic divisions as a factor in drawing lines? If a plan had some questionable features, yet a majority of the electorate approved it in a referendum, would this meet judicial approval? Justice Frankfurter had warned in his dissent in *Baker* that the Court would not be able to fashion judicially manageable standards, but in ***Gray v. Sanders,*** 372 U.S. 368 (1963), Justice Douglas enunciated a "one person, one vote" standard that immediately caught the popular imagination. It proved to be the key to the Court's decisions in the apportionment cases and to popular acceptance of the decisions.

In June 1964 the Court handed down decisions in six cases involving apportionment schemes in Alabama, Colorado, Delaware, Maryland, New York, and Virginia. The Alabama and Colorado decisions are discussed here. Chief Justice Warren delivered the Court's opinion in the lead case of *Reynolds v. Sims,* which invalidated a complex Alabama plan using both population and a "federal" arrangement. The state claimed that because the Constitution permitted disparities between the states, each state should be allowed similar deviations within its borders. Warren dismissed the federal analogy as inapposite and irrelevant and declared that "one man, one vote" would now be the rule for all state legislative bodies, including upper houses. Warren dismissed any and all formulas that attempted to weight certain factors:

> To the extent that a citizen's right to vote is debased, he is that much less a citizen. The weight of a citizen's vote cannot be made to depend on where he lives. . . . A citizen, a qualified voter, is no more nor no less so because he lives in the city or on the farm. This is the clear and strong command of our Constitution's Equal Protection Clause. . . .
>
> . . . Neither history alone, nor economic or other sorts of group interests, are permissible factors in attempting to justify disparities from population-based representation. . . . Citizens, not history or economic interests cast votes. People, not land or trees or pastures vote. As long as ours is a representative form of government, and our legislators are those instruments of government elected directly by and directly representative of the people, the right to elect legislators in a free and unimpaired fashion is a bedrock of our political system.

The Colorado case, ***Lucas v. Forty-Fourth General Assembly of Colorado,*** 377 U.S. 713 (1964), presented a unique problem. The electorate, by a 2–1 vote, had approved a plan that had a fairly clear population ratio for the lower house, but greater variance for the senate, so as to give rural areas some weighted power, although far from a controlling voice. The state made much of the fact that a majority of the voters had agreed to the dilution of their voting power in order to protect the minority. The chief justice dismissed the argument out of hand; the Court was dealing here not with the rights of minorities but with the rights of individuals. "It is a precept of American constitutional law," he declared, "that certain rights exist which a citizen cannot trade, barter, or even give away. . . . A citizen's constitutional right can hardly be infringed simply because a majority of the people choose that it be."

Justice Harlan dissented in all six cases. The chief justice's opinion, he charged, rested on bad history and bad law and undermined the essence of a federal system. In a pluralistic society, Harlan would have allowed apportionment formulas to take into account a number of considerations, including history, economics, geography, adequacy of representation for sparsely settled areas, theories of bicameralism, urban-rural balance, and the preference of a majority of voters for a particular scheme.

On Justice Douglas's urging, the Court decided the six cases at the end of the term rather than holding them over until the fall, so that reapportionment could take place before that year's elections. Despite the sweep of the rulings, the Court indicated that it expected rapid compliance. It eschewed anything resembling an "all deliberate speed" formula, and urged that unless the district courts could be convinced by unusually strong reasons to the contrary, they should allow no more state elections to be held under invalidated plans.

The apportionment decisions fit with the Warren Court's general determination to expand and protect individual rights and to promote equality before the law. Fairness in voting seemed of a piece with fairness in criminal procedures and in the treatment of Americans of different races or religions.

See See Richard C. Cortner, *The Apportionment Cases* (Knoxville: University of Tennessee Press, 1970); Robert G. Dixon Jr., *Democratic Representation: Reapportionment in Law and Politics* (New York: Oxford University Press, 1968); Nelson W. Polsby, ed., *Reapportionment in the 1970s* (Berkeley: University of California Press, 1971); and Robert McKay, "Reapportionment: Success Story of the Warren Court," *Michigan Law Review* 67 (1968): 223.

Lucas v. Forty-Fourth General Assembly of Colorado

377 U.S. 713 (1964)
Decided: June 15, 1964
Vote: 6 (Warren, Black, Douglas, Brennan, B. White, Goldberg)
3 (Clark, Harlan II, Stewart)
Opinion of the Court: Warren
Dissenting opinion: Harlan II. This dissent may be found in *Reynolds v. Sims,* 377 U.S. 533, 589 (1964).
Dissenting opinion: Clark (Stewart)
Dissenting opinion: Stewart (Clark)
See *Reynolds v. Sims,* 377 U.S. 533 (1964), on page 295

Malloy v. Hogan

378 U.S. 1 (1964)
Decided: June 15, 1964
Vote: 5 (Warren, Black, Douglas, Brennan, Goldberg)
4 (Clark, Harlan II, Stewart, B. White)
Opinion of the Court: Brennan
Concurring opinion: Douglas
Dissenting opinion: Harlan II (Clark)
Dissenting opinion: B. White (Stewart)

William Malloy was a witness in a state inquiry into gambling and other crimes. He invoked his privilege against self-incrimination, refusing to answer a number of questions related to events surrounding his previous arrest during a gambling raid and his conviction for selling chances in a sports pool. The Connecticut Superior Court found him in contempt and sent him to prison until he was willing to answer. The same court denied his application for habeas corpus, and the Connecticut Supreme Court of Errors affirmed, holding that the Fifth Amendment's privilege against self-incrimination was not available to a witness in a state proceeding.

The Supreme Court reversed. Justice Brennan's opinion held that the Fourteenth Amendment incorporated the Fifth Amendment privilege against self-incrimination, and made it applicable to the states. Justice Douglas joined the opinion, reiterating his view that the Fourteenth Amendment incorporated *all* of the Bill of Rights. Justices Harlan and White dissented, believing that the Court had no basis for going as far as it did.

As some scholars have noted, *Malloy* is a result looking for a reason. Brennan believed that the law of coerced confessions had developed to the point where it needed a reconsideration of prior cases that had held the Self-Incrimination Clause as not incorporated. He also drew an analogy between the law of search and seizure and that of confessions, and he believed the two issues related. If the Fourth Amendment had been incorporated, then the Fifth should be as well.

See Leonard W. Levy, *Origins of the Fifth Amendment* (New York: Oxford University Press, 1968).

Murphy v. Waterfront Commission of New York Harbor

378 U.S. 52 (1964)
Decided: June 15, 1964
Vote: 9 (Warren, Black, Douglas, Clark, Harlan II, Brennan, Stewart, B. White, Goldberg)
0
Opinion of the Court: Goldberg
Concurring opinion: B. White (Stewart)
Opinion concurring in judgment: Black
Opinion concurring in judgment: Harlan II (Clark)

On the same day the Court decided in ***Malloy v. Hogan,*** 378 U.S. 1 (1964), that the Fifth Amendment privilege against self-incrimination applied to the states via the Fourteenth Amendment, it also decided this case about the extent of that privilege. William Murphy and his colleagues were members of a labor union summoned to testify before the Waterfront Commission of New York Harbor. They invoked the Fifth Amendment to avoid answering incriminating questions and were offered immunity from prosecution in New York and New Jersey in exchange for their testimony. They continued to refuse, however, saying that answering the questions might lead to incrimination under federal law. A New Jersey court held all who refused in contempt of court. They appealed, claiming that the Fifth Amendment protected an individual from testifying about matters that could be incriminating in any U.S. jurisdiction.

The purpose of the Fifth Amendment, the Supreme Court held, was to ensure that no citizen was subjected to the "cruel trilemma" of choosing self-accusation, perjury, or contempt. The problem of choosing among these evils emerged regardless of whether the witness faced incrimination in the same jurisdiction or another. Therefore, Murphy was not obligated to testify against himself in front of the Waterfront Commission. Because states had an obligation to respect the Fifth Amendment, the Waterfront Commission could require Murphy to testify only if it could ensure that the federal government would not use his testimony against him. The commission failed to do this, and the Court reversed Murphy's contempt conviction.

Jacobellis v. Ohio

378 U.S. 184 (1964)
Decided: June 22, 1964
Vote: 7 (Black, Douglas, Clark, Brennan, Stewart, B. White, Goldberg)
2 (Warren, Harlan II)
Opinion of the Court: Brennan
Concurring opinion: Black (Douglas)
Concurring opinion: Stewart
Concurring opinion: Goldberg
Concurring in judgment without opinion: B. White
Dissenting opinion: Warren (Clark)
Dissenting opinion: Harlan II

During the 1960s the Warren Court struggled valiantly to deal with the problem of obscenity. Because obscenity was held to be outside the protection of the First Amendment, the issue became one of definition. The task of finding a workable definition fell to Justice Brennan in *Jacobellis v. Ohio,* in which the Court overturned the conviction of a theater owner for showing the French film, *Les Amants* (The Lovers). Brennan expanded the "contemporary community standards" test enunciated in ***Roth v. United States,*** 354 U.S. 476 (1957), to mean national rather than local standards; otherwise, "the constitutional limits of free expression in the Nation would vary with state lines." Moreover, Brennan made explicit what had been implicit in his *Roth* opinion, that the phrase "utterly without social importance" was part of the constitutional test.

Jacobellis is perhaps best remembered for Justice Stewart's concurring opinion, in which he pointed out that the Court's opinions since 1957 had moved in the direction of a "hard-core only" test for obscene materials. As he noted, however, a definition of hard-core obscenity had evaded the Court, and would probably continue to do so:

> I shall not today attempt to define the kinds of material I understand to be embraced within that short-hand definition; and perhaps I could never succeed in intelligibly doing so. But I know it when I see it and the motion picture involved in this case is not that.

Stewart later complained that people remembered only his "I know it when I see it" test, but, in fact, he had put his finger directly on the central problem of the obscenity issue. He knew what offended him, and this picture did not, even though it obviously had offended others. Obscenity, like beauty, is in the eye of the beholder, and as long as the United States is an open, tolerant, and pluralistic society, one will find an enormous range of opinion on the nature of sexually oriented material.

Even so, the Court continued doggedly to seek a workable definition.

See Harry M. Clor, *Obscenity and Public Morality: Censorship in a Liberal Society* (Chicago: University of Chicago Press, 1969); and Harry Kalven, *A Worthy Tradition: Freedom of Speech in America* (New York: Harper and Row, 1988).

Bell v. Maryland

378 U.S. 226 (1964)
Decided: June 22, 1964
Vote: 6 (Warren, Douglas, Clark, Brennan, Stewart, Goldberg)
3 (Black, Harlan II, B. White)
Opinion of the Court: Brennan
Concurring opinion: Douglas (Goldberg in part)
Concurring opinion: Goldberg (Warren, Douglas in part)
Dissenting opinion: Black (Harlan II, B. White)

In February 1960, four neatly dressed students from the all-black Agricultural and Technical College in Greensboro, North Carolina, asked for coffee at a Woolworth's lunch counter. When they were refused service, they remained in their seats until arrested for trespassing. Within a short time, militant black youths took up the sit-in tactic, and by the end of the year, they had desegregated lunch counters in 126 cities. They soon turned the weapon against other areas of discrimination, with "kneel-ins" at churches and "wade-ins" at public pools. Boycotts supplemented the sit-ins, bringing economic pressure on white merchants to support civil rights demands.

Prior to the Civil Rights Act of 1964, restaurants were considered private and, in the absence of any state law commanding desegregation, retained the right to grant or refuse service to anyone they chose. A protester sitting in at a lunch counter or in a restaurant therefore violated the owner's property rights and could be prosecuted for trespass or disturbing the peace. Although obviously in sympathy with the protesters, the Court failed to develop a rule to cover the situation. Justice Douglas alone appeared willing to eliminate the distinction between state action and private discrimination, but his colleagues believed that some forms of private discrimination were permissible in a free society. People have the right, providing they do not use the power of the state, to associate with whom they please.

Douglas received more support when he suggested that restaurants and hotels should not be seen as totally private, but as a type of public activity and therefore subject to law. Under the old common law, common carriers, for example, had to offer their services without discrimination. A third approach conceded that although restaurants had the right to refuse service, for the state to arrest the protesters involved state action to enforce discrimination. A broad reading of ***Shelley v. Kraemer,*** 334 U.S. 1 (1948), would have prohibited the state's enforcement of trespass laws against persons excluded from private property on racial grounds, and this would have provided a consistent doctrinal approach to sit-in cases.

The Court, however, set aside all the convictions without, in most instances, even citing *Shelley,* perhaps signaling that unconstitutional state action had to involve more than even-handed enforcement of private biases. Most of the time it found some technicality to justify its action and avoided reaching the core constitutional issues. In only one case, *Bell v. Maryland,* did six of the justices reach the broader *Shelley* issue, and they divided 3–3 on whether enforcement of trespass laws against civil rights activists constituted a form of state action that violated the Equal Protection Clause. The case arose from the conviction of twelve sit-in demonstrators under Maryland's criminal trespass law. After their trial, the state enacted a public accommodations law forbidding restaurants and similar facilities from refusing service because of race, so that the offense for which they had been convicted was no longer a crime in Maryland. Justice Brennan's opinion for the Court simply vacated the lower court ruling and remanded the case for further consideration in light of the new state law. For the first time, however, members of the Court actually addressed the substantive issues in the sit-in cases.

Justice Douglas entered a lengthy opinion arguing that restaurants constituted businesses dealing with the public, and therefore came within the *Shelley* doctrine. Justice Black took a far narrower view of both *Shelley* and Section 1 of the Fourteenth Amendment. By itself, he claimed, Section 1 did not forbid owners of property, including restaurants, to ban people from entering or remaining on that property, even if the owners acted out of racial prejudice. Bigots also had the right to call on the state to protect their legitimate property interests.

Shortly afterward, the Court ruled in *Hamm v. Rock Hill,* 379 U.S. 306 (1964), that enactment of the Civil Rights Act abated prosecutions against persons, who, if the act had been in force at the time they had been arrested for sitting in, would have been entitled to service. This did not, however, put an end to the sit-in cases because, despite its broad wording, the 1964 act did not reach all the types of establishments that protesters wanted desegregated.

See Kenneth L. Karst, "Foreword: Equal Citizenship Under the Fourteenth Amendment," *Harvard Law Review* 91 (1977): 1; and Monrad G. Paulson, "The Sit-In Cases of 1964: 'But Answer Came There None,' " *Supreme Court Review* (1964): 137.

Escobedo v. Illinois

378 U.S. 478 (1964)
Decided: June 22, 1964
Vote: 5 (Warren, Black, Douglas, Brennan, Goldberg)
4 (Harlan II, Clark, Stewart, B. White)
Opinion of the Court: Goldberg
Dissenting opinion: Harlan II
Dissenting opinion: Stewart
Dissenting opinion: B. White (Clark, Stewart)

Danny Escobedo was taken into custody and interrogated about the fatal shooting of his brother-in-law. He repeatedly asked to see his attorney, who was in the station house, and the attorney repeatedly asked to see his client. The police refused to allow the two to meet until after Escobedo had made statements incriminating himself in the shooting. The police charged him and only then allowed him access to his attorney.

In ***Massiah v. United States,*** 377 U.S. 201 (1964), the Court had not given a clear indication of when a defendant is considered formally charged and in custody and therefore within the protective reach of the Fifth Amendment. In *Escobedo* the Court rejected the state's claim that a person must be formally charged before he or she can ask to see a lawyer. In this case, Justice Goldberg noted that when Escobedo "requested, and was denied, an opportunity to consult with his lawyer, the investigation had ceased to be a general investigation of an 'unsolved crime.' Petitioner had become the accused." It made no difference that he had not been formally charged; once a suspect is treated as if accused, then he or she must have all the rights afforded to accused persons. Goldberg anticipated much of the criticism that the decision aroused, and his opinion indicates the emphasis the Warren Court placed on protection of rights and fairness in the criminal justice system:

> It is argued that if the right to counsel is afforded prior to indictment, the number of confessions obtained by the police will diminish significantly, because most confessions are obtained during the period between arrest and indictment, [and] "any lawyer worth his salt will tell the suspect in no uncertain terms to make no statement to police under any circumstances."... This argument, of course, cuts two ways. The fact that many confessions are obtained during this period points up its critical nature as a "stage when legal aid and advice" are surely needed. The right to counsel would indeed be hollow if it began at a period when few confessions were obtained. There is necessarily a direct relationship between the importance of a stage to the police in their quest for a confession and the criticalness of that stage to the accused in his need for legal advice. Our Constitution, unlike some others, strikes the balance in favor of the right of the accused to be advised by his lawyer of his privilege against self-incrimination.

Most of this rationale dealt with the right to counsel, a Sixth Amendment right, and only at the end did Goldberg mention the Fifth Amendment right against self-incrimination. The Court had gradually come to see the close connection between the two and realized that accused persons, often confused after police took them into custody, needed legal advice in order to exercise their Fifth Amendment right. Confessions need not be extracted by physical coercion to be involuntary; modern psychological methods could be just as effective in wearing down a suspect's will.

Despite the sweeping language quoted above, the actual holding in *Escobedo* proved fairly narrow: when police took a person into custody for interrogation and the suspect requested counsel, a lawyer had to be provided and given access to the client or the statements made during the interrogation could not be used against the suspect. But what if the suspect were illiterate, or did not know his or her rights, or had become confused by the station house procedures and failed to ask for counsel? These considerations did not appear to bother the dissenters in *Escobedo,* Justices Harlan, Stewart (author of the majority opinion in *Massiah*), Clark, and White. Their emphasis seemed to be that so long as the government did not use physical coercion and in the end allowed people to choose what to do, it could discourage people from exercising their rights. The majority of the Court took a different view, that the government had an obligation to nurture constitutional rights and to encourage its citizens to exercise those rights.

Reactions from the public and law enforcement officials were predictable. Many believed that Goldberg's opinion for the five liberals exhibited disdain not only for confessions but also for how police operated generally. That same term, in ***Malloy v. Hogan,*** 378 U.S. 1 (1964), the Court ruled that the Fifth Amendment right against self-incrimination is applicable to the states through the Fourteenth Amendment. With *Escobedo,* the Court now moved from the due process concept of voluntariness as the standard for confessions to the belief that presence of counsel at the accusatory stage determined whether a confession had been properly obtained. All of these decisions, however, lacked precision; they lacked a bright-line test that would tell police, prosecutors, and trial and appellate judges whether constitutional standards had been violated or observed. The answer to that question came in ***Miranda v. Arizona,*** 384 U.S. 436 (1966).

See Fred Graham, *The Due Process Revolution: The Warren Court's Impact on Criminal Law* (New York: Hayden, 1970); Claude R. Sowle, ed., *Police Power and Individual Freedom: The Quest for Balance* (Chicago: Aldine, 1962); and Arnold N. Enken and Sheldon H. Elsen, "Counsel for the Suspect: *Massiah v. United States* and *Escobedo v. Illinois,*" *Minnesota Law Review* 49 (1964): 47.

Aptheker v. Secretary of State

378 U.S. 500 (1964)
Decided: June 22, 1964
Vote: 6 (Warren, Black, Douglas, Brennan, Stewart, Goldberg)
3 (Clark, Harlan II, B. White)
Opinion of the Court: Goldberg
Concurring opinion: Black
Concurring opinion: Douglas
Dissenting opinion: Clark (Harlan II, B. White)
Dissenting opinion: B. White

During the cold war Congress pressured the State Department to control the movement of suspected subversives in and out of the United States. In ***Kent v. Dulles,*** 357 U.S. 116 (1958), the Court struck down provisions of the Passport Act of 1926, a law that allowed the State Department to refuse passports to American communists or persons whose travels abroad could prejudice American interests. The Court said that the right of American citizens to travel across national frontiers was part of the liberty interest protected by the Fifth Amendment.

The Internal Security Act of 1950 required all communist-action organizations to register with the attorney general and denied passports to members of these organizations. The Court had upheld the registration provisions in ***Communist Party v. Subversive Activities Control Board,*** 367 U.S. 1 (1961), but in this case rejected the State Department's efforts to deny passports.

The chairman of the American Communist Party and the editor of *Political Affairs,* its "theoretical organ," filed suit to have Section 6 of the Subversive Activities Control Act, under the authority of which passports had been denied to them, declared unconstitutional. A three-judge federal district court sustained the constitutionality of the statute, but on direct appeal, the Supreme Court reversed.

In holding Section 6 unconstitutional on its face as too broadly and indiscriminately restricting the right to travel and thereby abridging the liberty guaranteed by the Fifth Amendment, Justice Goldberg in essence reaffirmed the holding in *Kent v. Dulles.* Justice Black concurred and expressed his view that the entire Subversive Activities Control Act was unconstitutional. Justice Douglas, also concurring, added that, absent war, there was no constitutional way to restrict a citizen's right to travel, unless there was sufficient cause to detain him.

Justice Clark, joined by Justice Harlan, dissented, finding no constitutional barrier to Congress or the State Department denying passports to people associated with communist groups, a view echoed by Justice White.

Tancil v. Woolls

379 U.S. 19 (1964)
Decided: October 26, 1964
Vote: 9 (Warren, Black, Douglas, Clark, Harlan II, Brennan, Stewart, B. White, Goldberg)
0
Opinion of the Court: *Per curiam*

This case was appealed along with a similar case, *Virginia Board of Elections v. Hamm,* 230 F. Supp. 156, from the U.S. District Court for the Eastern District of Virginia. Plaintiffs in both cases sued to challenge Virginia laws that required voting, property tax assessment, and divorce records to be kept on the basis of race. The statutes under attack either required that the state keep separate books for white and black citizens or that the records for each race be created on different colored paper. African American citizens of Virginia challenged these requirements as violations of the Fourteenth and Fifteenth Amendments.

The district court held that Virginia could no longer maintain voting and property records on a racially segregated basis. The only purpose of the statutes requiring segregated record keeping was to separate individuals by race, and the court found that this subtle discrimination violated the Equal Protection Clause of the Fourteenth Amendment. The trial court allowed Virginia to continue recording divorces on a racially segregated basis as long as divorces of both races were recorded. It explained that maintaining vital population statistics necessarily required the inclusion of racial classification and that the state had a justifiable interest in knowing the marital status and race of its citizens.

In a one-sentence per curiam opinion, the Supreme Court affirmed the trial court's holdings in both cases.

Garrison v. Louisiana

379 U.S. 64 (1964)
Decided: November 23, 1964
Vote: 9 (Warren, Black, Douglas, Clark, Harlan II, Brennan, Stewart, B. White, Goldberg)
0
Opinion of the Court: Brennan
Concurring opinion: Black (Douglas)
Concurring opinion: Douglas (Black)
Concurring opinion: Goldberg

Jim Garrison, a district attorney in New Orleans, held a press conference at which he issued a statement disparaging eight New Orleans district court judges. He was subsequently convicted of criminal defamation under the Louisiana Criminal Defamation Statute. He appealed, arguing that the statute unconstitutionally abridged his freedom of expression.

The first issue before the Court was whether the defamation standard created by the Court in ***New York Times Co. v. Sullivan,*** 376 U.S. 254 (1964), applied in criminal cases. *Sullivan* had held that in civil cases, a court could punish defamation only if the speaker knew his words were false and spoke them with "actual malice." The Court held that because civil and criminal defamation cases seek the same end—the restoration of the victim by either damages or criminal judgment—the same standard should apply to both. Louisiana could therefore punish defamation only if it was false and malicious.

The Louisiana statute failed the *Sullivan* test. It imposed sanctions on Garrison not because his statements were false, but because he spoke them with ill will and enmity. The state did not prove that Garrison's statements were false. Although false statements lend nothing to public discourse because they are at odds with the creation of an orderly society, true statements must be protected despite their unpopular content in order to keep members of the government in check and ensure that the people maintain a voice in democracy. The Court held that the Louisiana rule violated the First Amendment by punishing true, unpopular speech, and it therefore reversed Garrison's conviction.

See Norman L. Rosenberg, *Protecting the Best Men: An Interpretive History of the Law of Libel* (Chapel Hill: University of North Carolina Press, 1986).

McLaughlin et al. v. Florida

379 U.S. 184 (1964)
Decided: December 7, 1964
Vote: 9 (Warren, Black, Douglas, Clark, Harlan II, Brennan, Stewart, B. White, Goldberg)
0
Opinion of the Court: B. White
Concurring opinion: Harlan II
Concurring opinion: Stewart (Douglas)

Dewy McLaughlin and Connie Hoffman were convicted under a Florida statute that made it a crime for a mixed-race couple to "habitually live in and occupy in the nighttime the same room." The statute was part of a larger section of Florida law addressing issues of adultery and fornication. Although other Florida laws made it a crime for any couple to commit adultery or fornicate, conviction under these statutes required proof of intercourse. The interracial statute did not require proof, but relied solely on the skin color of the cohabitants. Several couples convicted under the statute challenged its validity, claiming a violation of the Equal Protection Clause of the Fourteenth Amendment.

The Supreme Court held that the interracial cohabitation statute violated the Equal Protection Clause, which prohibits arbitrary racial classifications. Any racial classification made by the government is subject to strict scrutiny and will be approved only if it serves a compelling state interest and achieves its goal in the least restrictive way possible. Here, Florida had no compelling interest in preventing interracial cohabitation rather than cohabitation in general.

The case should be seen as a step in the Court's move toward striking down antimiscegenation laws, which it did in ***Loving v. Virginia,*** 388 U.S. 1 (1967).

See Peter Wallenstein, "Race, Marriage and the Supreme Court: From *Pace v. Alabama* (1883) to *Loving v. Virginia* (1967)," *Journal of Supreme Court History* 65 (1998).

Heart of Atlanta Motel v. United States

379 U.S. 241 (1964)
Decided: December 14, 1964
Vote: 9 (Warren, Black, Douglas, Clark, Harlan II, Brennan, Stewart, B. White, Goldberg)
0
Opinion of the Court: Clark
Concurring opinion: Black
Concurring opinion: Douglas
Concurring opinion: Goldberg

The Civil Rights Act of 1964 consisted of eleven titles—or subsections—covering education, public accommodations, expanded powers for the attorney general, and voting rights; it also coordinated different federal agencies to promote desegregation. Under the threat of losing federal aid if they failed to make a "good faith, substantive start," hundreds of southern school districts finally began to desegregate. Using its commerce authority, Congress prohibited racial discrimination in restaurants, hotels and motels, filling stations, and soda fountains and required equal access to parks, pools, and stadiums. The bill also strengthened the earlier voter registration protections and established a sixth-grade education as a presumption of literacy. Congress relied on the commerce power because, despite the Warren Court's civil rights decisions, neither President Lyndon Johnson nor congressional leaders knew whether the Court would feel bound by its decision in the ***Civil Rights Cases,*** 109 U.S. 3 (1883), which had effectively nullified the enforcement provisions of the Fourteenth Amendment.

The members of the Supreme Court paid close attention to the progress of the 1964 Civil Rights Act, recognizing that its passage would mark the alignment of the three branches of the federal government in strong advocacy of civil rights. Within six months of the president's signing the law, the Court heard challenges seeking to prevent enforcement of the public accommodations section of Title II. In *Heart of Atlanta,* in which a motel owner challenged the law's constitutionality, and ***Katzenbach v. McClung,*** 379 U.S. 294 (1964), which concerned a restaurant, a unanimous Court sustained the law.

In *Heart of Atlanta* the Court upheld congressional power not only under the Commerce Clause, but also under the Equal Protection and enforcement clauses of the Fourteenth Amendment. According to Justice Clark, "Congress possessed ample power" to reach such discrimination, and the fact that it used commerce powers to deal with a moral issue made no difference. In legislating under the Commerce Clause, Congress had on numerous occasions chosen to resolve moral questions. If Congress had the power, how it chose to use that power did not concern the Court. Clark rejected out of hand the claim that a motel located in a city did not fall within the meaning of interstate commerce; the record clearly showed that the hotel advertised along interstate highways, that it catered to conventions, and that approximately 75 percent of its registered guests came from out of state. Although Clark contended that such a broad interpretation had been accepted by the Court for 140 years, in fact, the decision marked one of the most expansive views of the Commerce Clause ever offered by a federal court.

In their concurrences, Justices Douglas and Goldberg noted that neither Congress nor the Court had to rely on the commerce power; they believed that the enforcement clause of the Fourteenth Amendment was sufficient to support the act's constitutionality.

See Harry T. Quick, "Public Accommodations: A Justification of Title II of the Civil Rights Act of 1964," *Western Reserve Law Review* 16 (1965): 660; and Richard C. Cortner, *Civil Rights and Public Accommodations: The Heart of Atlanta and McClung Cases* (Lawrence: University Press of Kansas, 2001).

Katzenbach v. McClung

379 U.S. 294 (1964)
Decided: December 14, 1964
Vote: 9 (Warren, Black, Douglas, Clark, Harlan II, Brennan, Stewart, B. White, Goldberg)
0
Opinion of the Court: Clark
Concurring opinion: Black
Concurring opinion: Douglas
Concurring opinion: Goldberg
Black, Douglas, and Goldberg opinions are found in *Heart of Atlanta Motel v. United States,* 379 U.S. 241 (1964).

In the decade following ***Brown v. Board of Education,*** 347 U.S. 483 (1954), the Supreme Court decided many cases dealing with state-sanctioned segregation. As in all other legal areas, all the Court could do was respond to cases brought before it; it could not affirmatively move to protect civil rights. Therefore, the justices watched with great interest as President Kennedy proposed, and then after his death, President Johnson moved the most comprehensive civil rights bill since Reconstruction through Congress.

The eleven titles, or subsections, of the Civil Rights Act of 1964 covered education, public accommodations, expanded powers for the attorney general, and voting rights; it also coordinated different federal agencies to promote desegregation. Hundreds of southern school districts were threatened with the loss of federal aid if they failed to make a "good faith, substantive start" to desegregate, and they began to comply. Using its commerce authority, Congress prohibited racial discrimination in restaurants, hotels and motels, filling stations, and soda fountains, and required equal access to parks, pools, and stadiums. The bill also strengthened the earlier voter registration protections, establishing a sixth-grade education as a presumption of literacy. The 1964 Civil Rights Act marked the alignment of all three branches of the federal government in strong advocacy of civil rights. Within six months of the president's signing the law, the Court heard two challenges seeking to prevent enforcement of the public accommodations section of Title II. In both cases, a unanimous Court sustained the law.

In ***Heart of Atlanta Motel v. United States,*** 379 U.S. 241 (1964), the Court upheld congressional power under the Commerce Clause, the Equal Protection Clause, and Section 5 of the Fourteenth Amendment to forbid hotels to discriminate on the basis of race. In the companion case of *Katzenbach v. McClung,* the Court unanimously sustained the law as it applied to restaurants.

Ollie's Barbecue in Birmingham, Alabama, did not solicit interstate business; it was not located near an interstate road or bus or train connections; and it served primarily local customers. But approximately half of the food it bought each year came from outside the state, and that provided a sufficient nexus to interstate commerce. Congress had conducted extensive hearings into the effect of racial discrimination on interstate commerce and had concluded that such discrimination had a direct and adverse effect on the free flow of such commerce, and the Court saw no reason to challenge that finding.

The Court unanimously upheld the act insofar as it affected restaurants, even those with attenuated links to the direct stream of interstate commerce. Deciding the case on commerce grounds, the Court reasoned that Congress need only demonstrate a rational basis for concluding that local activities, such as the operations of Ollie's Barbecue, taken together with numerous other local activities, aggregated to create a substantial burden on interstate commerce. Congress had rationally assumed that race discrimination by local restaurants could reduce the total amount of food consumed and purchased in interstate commerce. Moreover, local segregation practices could deter individuals and businesses from relocating to areas that practiced such discrimination.

Although one can understand why the Court wanted to grant Congress such broad powers to combat racial discrimination, nothing in the Court's opinion actually limited this broad grant of power to racially related matters. The Court speaks of the commerce power in terms far more expansive than Chief Justice John Marshall did, and a fair reading of the opinion seems to indicate an almost unlimited power in any area that Congress can claim to fall within its commerce authority.

The three justices who concurred did not disagree with the Court's opinion so much as indicate that they, at least, found adequate authority in other parts of the Constitution as well. Justice Black, in his concurrence, stated that the statute as applied was valid under the Commerce Clause and the Necessary and Proper Clause. Justice Douglas joined in the Court's opinion, but added that he preferred to base the constitutionality of the statute on the power conferred on Congress by Section 5 of the Fourteenth Amendment. Justice Goldberg also joined in the Court's opinion but added that Congress had authority both under the Commerce Clause and Section 5 of the Fourteenth Amendment to enact the statute.

See Harry T. Quick, "Public Accommodations: A Justification of Title II of the Civil Rights Act of 1964," *Western Reserve Law Review* 16 (1965): 660; and Harvard Sitkoff, *The Struggle for Black Equality, 1954–1992,* rev. ed. (New York: Hill and Wang, 1993).

Cox v. Louisiana

379 U.S. 536 (1965)
Decided: January 18, 1965
Vote: 7 (Warren, Black, Douglas, Clark, Brennan, Stewart, Goldberg)
2 (Harlan II, B. White)
Opinion of the Court: Goldberg
Concurring opinion: Black
Concurring opinion: Clark
Opinion concurring in part and dissenting in part: B. White (Harlan II)
Black, Clark, and B. White opinions are found in the companion case, *Cox v. Louisiana,* 379 U.S. 559 (1965).

Two thousand black students gathered in Baton Rouge, Louisiana, to protest not only segregation but also the arrest and imprisonment the day before of other black students who had participated in a protest against racial segregation. The group assembled a few blocks from the courthouse, where Rev. B. Elton Cox identified himself to officers as the group's leader and explained the purpose of the demonstration. Cox refused a request to disband and instead led the students in an orderly march toward the courthouse. Near the courthouse, officers stopped them, and the chief of police told the demonstrators that they could hold the meeting as long as they confined it to the west side of the street. Cox obeyed, and the demonstrators, standing across the street from the courthouse and 101 feet from its steps, displayed signs and sang songs that evoked responses from the students inside the courthouse jail. Cox exhorted the students to hold sit-ins at uptown lunch counters, and the sheriff, who considered the remarks "inflammatory," ordered the group to disperse and then directed a tear gas attack against them.

Cox was arrested the next day and convicted of disturbing the peace, obstructing public passages, and courthouse picketing. The Louisiana Supreme Court affirmed the convictions. The two counts of disturbing the peace and obstructing public passages were considered in this case, and the third count, courthouse picketing, was dealt with in the companion case, *Cox v. Louisiana,* 379 U.S. 559 (1965).

Five members of the Court joined Justice Goldberg's opinion that the breach of the peace conviction infringed the protesters' rights of free speech and assembly. Cox did not engage in any conduct that the state had a right to prohibit as a breach of the peace. Moreover, the state courts' definition of breach of the peace—to agitate or to disquiet—was unconstitutionally broad in scope, because it allowed punishment merely for peacefully expressing unpopular views. The conviction for unlawfully obstructing public passages, too, was an unwarranted abridgment of freedom of speech and assembly because the city authorities had complete and uncontrolled discretion to permit or prohibit parades or street meetings.

Justice Black concurred on both grounds, but went further to note that the statute prohibiting the obstruction of public passages specifically permitted picketing by labor union. By allowing it for some causes and not others, the statute constituted both censorship forbidden by the First and Fourteenth Amendments and an invidious discrimination forbidden by the Equal Protection Clause of the Fourteenth Amendment.

Justice Clark did not believe that the breach of the peace statute was unconstitutionally vague, but considered both it and the obstructing public passages statute unconstitutional under the Equal Protection Clause because they expressly excepted labor union activities. Justice White, joined by Justice Harlan, concurred in the reversal of the breach of the peace conviction because it violated the Free Speech Clause, but dissented from the reversal of the conviction of obstructing public passages, stating that the statute had not been applied as an "open-ended licensing statute."

Although the Court did not deal with many straightforward political speech cases in the 1960s, it nevertheless developed a new free speech jurisprudence in the civil rights cases it heard. As a result, by the end of the decade, the Court had completely refashioned its speech jurisprudence into one that was highly speech protective, especially of unpopular views, leading to a new standard articulated in *Brandenberg v. Ohio,* 395 U.S. 444 (1969).

See Harry Kalven, *The Negro and the First Amendment* (Columbus: Ohio State University Press, 1965).

Cox v. Louisiana

379 U.S. 559 (1965)
Decided: January 18, 1965
Vote: 5 (Warren, Douglas, Brennan, Stewart, Goldberg)
4 (Black, Clark, Harlan II, B. White)
Opinion of the Court: Goldberg
Dissenting opinion: Black (B. Harlan, White)
Dissenting opinion: Clark
Dissenting opinion: B. White (Harlan II)

The facts are the same as in the companion case of ***Cox v. Louisiana,*** 379 U.S. 536, decided the same day. This case dealt with the third count, picketing near a courthouse.

The majority opinion by Justice Goldberg held that the statute was constitutional, but, because city officials had told the demonstrators that they could gather on the sidewalk across from the courthouse, the conviction violated due process of law as "an indefensible sort of entrapment."

Justice Black, joined by Justices Harlan and White, dissented on the ground that officials cannot authorize violations of criminal laws. Moreover, testimony in the record denied that the permission had been given, and, even if given, it was quickly revoked. Justice Clark dissented on similar grounds; he believed that no permission had been given for the picketing and, even if given, it was not binding on the state. The dissenters' position regarding the facts of the case seems weak because a videotape of the protest, which the justices looked at as part of the record, clearly showed the chief of police giving the demonstrators permission to gather across from the courthouse.

The opinion is interesting for two reasons. The first is the continued willingness of the majority to expand the First Amendment in support of civil rights demonstrations, an indication that the justices recognized that the Supreme Court had played a major part in triggering the civil rights movement and now had an obligation to protect those involved. The second reason is that all nine justices saw protection of the judiciary as a special case and, therefore, the majority and dissenting opinions said that a law prohibiting picketing of courthouses is constitutional.

See Harry Kalven, *The Negro and the First Amendment* (Columbus: Ohio State University Press, 1965).

Udall v. Tallman

380 U.S. 1 (1965)
Decided: March 1, 1965
Vote: 7 (Warren, Black, Clark, Brennan, Stewart, B. White, Goldberg)
0
Opinion of the Court: Warren
Did not participate: Douglas, Harlan II

James K. Tallman applied for a federal permit to lease land and drill for oil on an Alaskan moose reserve. His permit was denied because another company had already been approved to drill, and the Mineral Leasing Act said that the first qualified applicant for a lease would be entitled to receive it. Tallman contended that when the other company received its lease, the secretary of the interior was not authorized to issue leases for national wildlife preserves. The rule forbidding the secretary from doing so was not overturned until 1958, and Tallman was the first to petition for a lease on the moose preserve after 1958. He argued that he was therefore entitled to receive the lease under the terms of the Mineral Leasing Act.

The Court noted that the secretary, acting on behalf of the Department of the Interior, had always interpreted the rules restricting the use of national wildlife preserves to not bar oil and gas leases. The Court found this to be a reasonable interpretation. Even though there were other ways to interpret the statute, the secretary's decision was permissible within the words and intent of the act. The Court held that the secretary and agency controlled decisions about how to interpret statutes and regulations unless their readings are clearly erroneous. This is especially true when, as here, the agency is responsible for "setting the machinery in motion" for how laws will be applied and for carrying out the statutory scheme on a day-to-day basis.

Freedman v. Maryland

380 U.S. 51 (1965)
Decided: March 1, 1965
Vote: 9 (Warren, Black, Douglas, Clark, Harlan II, Brennan, Stewart, B. White, Goldberg)
0
Opinion of the Court: Brennan
Concurring opinion: Douglas (Black)

Ronald L. Freedman challenged a Maryland statute requiring that all motion pictures shown in the state be approved by the Board of Censors. Freedman showed the film *Revenge at Daybreak* without approval of the board. Although the board conceded that he would have received a license to show the film if he had applied, they fined him for failure to do so. Freedman appealed, saying that the Maryland system unconstitutionally impaired freedom of expression by imposing prior restraint on publication.

Prior to Freedman's case, the Court held in *Times Film Corp. v. City of Chicago,* 365 U.S. 43 (1961), that requiring motion pictures to be screened in advance does not necessarily violate the First Amendment. Freedman sought to distinguish *Times Film* by saying that the Maryland system unnecessarily curtailed expression by not providing direct judicial review and by subjecting questionable films to a lengthy appeals process.

The Court recognized these differences and held that censorship systems that place an undue burden on distributors violate the First Amendment. The Court held that a censorship scheme could pass constitutional muster only if it facilitated quick appeals in which the censor, not the distributor, bore the burden of proof about the film's worthiness. Because Maryland's system did not fill these criteria, the Court reversed Freedman's conviction.

United States v. Seeger

380 U.S. 163 (1965)
Decided: March 8, 1965
Vote: 9 (Warren, Black, Douglas, Clark, Harlan II, Brennan, Stewart, B. White, Goldberg)
0
Opinion of the Court: Clark
Concurring opinion: Douglas

Daniel Andrew Seeger, along with fellow draftees Amo Sascha Jakobson and Forest Britt Peter, filed suit to challenge the conscientious objector exemption in the United States Universal Military and Training and Service Act. The statute exempted from combatant service in the armed forces anyone who opposed participation in war as part of his "religious training and belief." Religious belief was defined as belief in relation to a Supreme Being, and the statute specifically said that a person could not be exempted for political, social, or philosophical views that did not constitute religion. Seeger claimed that he had a religious faith apart from mere philosophical views, but did not relate that faith to a Supreme Being. As a result, he was not exempted under the act. In his suit he claimed that the statute violated the First Amendment by refusing to exempt nonreligious objectors and by discriminating between different types of religion in violation of the Fifth Amendment.

The Court held that the statute did not err in requiring religious belief as a requisite for exemption, but further held that the government could not distinguish between religions that ascribed to a Supreme Being and those that did not. Seeger had a religion that made him believe that "there is a higher loyalty than loyalty to country." Although he did not personify that religion in one "God," Justice Clark explained that was not necessary under the legislative intent of the statute. Congress left out the word "God," leaving room for recognition of a "sincere and meaningful belief which occupies in the life of its possessor a place parallel to that filled by the God of those admittedly qualifying for an exemption." Under this "sincere and meaningful belief" test, Seeger qualified for an exemption.

Pointer v. Texas

380 U.S. 400 (1965)
Decided: April 5, 1965
Vote: 9 (Warren, Black, Douglas, Clark, Harlan II, Brennan, Stewart, B. White, Goldberg)
0
Opinion of the Court: Black
Concurring opinion: Goldberg
Opinion concurring in judgment: Harlan II
Opinion concurring in judgment: Stewart

Bob Granville Pointer was arrested for robbery and brought before a Texas state judge for a preliminary hearing. In Texas, the sole purpose of a preliminary hearing is to see if the state has enough evidence to go before a grand jury. Pointer did not have counsel and did not cross-examine Phillips, the state's main witness against him. Before the trial, Phillips moved to California. In his absence, the state offered his pretrial testimony into evidence. Pointer's attorney objected but was overruled. Pointer was convicted. In his appeal he argued that the introduction of Phillips's testimony transcript violated his right to confront the witnesses against him at trial.

Two years prior to hearing Pointer's case, the Court had held in ***Gideon v. Wainwright,*** 372 U.S. 335 (1963), that the Sixth Amendment right of a defendant to be represented by counsel applied to the states. Here, the Court was asked to decide whether another Sixth Amendment right, the right to confront witnesses against an accused, also applied to the states via the Fourteenth Amendment. Given the crucial role of confrontation in the American justice system, the Court held that the Sixth Amendment right of confrontation should be applied to the states. Pointer should have been given the right to cross-examine Phillips at trial because cross-examination is necessary for bringing out the truth and exposing falsehoods. Pointer did not cross-examine at the pretrial hearing because he did not feel it necessary, but the trial presented much higher stakes, and Pointer deserved full constitutional protection. Because Texas did not give him his full Sixth Amendment protection, the Court reversed the decision against him.

Dombrowski v. Pfister

380 U.S. 479 (1965)
Decided: April 26, 1965
Vote: 5 (Warren, Douglas, Brennan, B. White, Goldberg)
2 (Clark, Harlan II)
Opinion of the Court: Brennan
Dissenting opinion: Harlan II (Clark)
Did not participate: Black, Stewart

James A. Dombrowski, the executive director of the Southern Conference Education Fund, an organization active in fostering civil rights for African Americans in Louisiana, sought declaratory relief and an injunction restraining the state from prosecuting or threatening to prosecute him and other civil rights leaders for alleged violations of the Louisiana Subversive Activities and Communist Control Law and the Louisiana Communist Propaganda Control Law. He alleged that the statutes were invalid on their face and that the threats to enforce them were meant to discourage him and his colleagues from continuing their civil rights activities. A three-judge district court dismissed the complaint, holding among other things, that federal courts should abstain from interpreting state laws until the state's highest court had authoritatively spoken.

On appeal, the Supreme Court reversed, and the majority opinion held that the complaint alleged sufficient injury to warrant equitable relief. The heart of the opinion dealt with the abstention doctrine which is an essential component of federalism. Under this doctrine, federal courts will not review state court decisions until the state's highest court has spoken on the issue, just as the district court in this case had decided. Because these appeals may take months and even years, the damages to the victims will continue without relief. The Court here carved out an exception to the rule, namely, that when state statutes violate federal rights, such as freedom of speech, or tend to discourage protected activities, then federal courts may intervene at any stage in the judicial process. Once having justified federal court intervention, Brennan went on to hold the statute, which made it a felony to create, manage, or support any subversive organization, invalid on grounds of vagueness; similarly, the law requiring registration of members of allegedly communist-front organizations was also ruled unconstitutionally vague.

Justice Harlan, joined by Justice Clark, dissented, arguing that federal courts should not be allowed to circumvent the abstention doctrine simply because a federal right was involved. He said that the state courts, also bound by the Constitution, should be allowed to interpret state law first.

Civil rights lawyers immediately seized upon *Dombrowski* as a loophole in the Court's otherwise strict adherence to the abstention doctrine. They began to file hundreds of lawsuits in federal courts seeking protection against state prosecution of civil rights activists under state laws, on the grounds that enforcement of these laws violated a federal right. The Court closed the loophole, in essence adopting Harlan's view, in ***Younger v. Harris,*** 401 U.S. 37 (1971).

See Harvard Sitkoff, *The Struggle for Black Equality, 1954–1992,* rev. ed. (New York: Hill and Wang, 1993).

Veterans of the Abraham Lincoln Brigade v. Subversive Activities Control Board

380 U.S. 513 (1965)
Decided: April 26, 1965
Vote: 5 (Warren, Clark, Brennan, Stewart, Goldberg)
3 (Black, Douglas, Harlan II)
Opinion of the Court: *Per curiam*
Dissenting opinion: Douglas (Black, Harlan II)
Did not participate: B. White

The Subversive Activities Control Board ordered the Veterans of the Abraham Lincoln Brigade to register as a communist-front organization under Section 7 of the Subversive Activities Control Act. The board based its order entirely on investigations conducted in the 1940s and early 1950s. The hearings on whether the group was a subversive organization took place in 1954, ten years prior to the appeal. A U.S. court of appeals affirmed the order, and the issue was appealed to the Supreme Court.

Rather than deciding the constitutional issues raised by the act, the Court vacated the judgment of the court of appeals and held that the record of the case was too stale to warrant judgment.

Justices Douglas, Black, and Harlan expressed a strong dissent to the Court's *per curiam* opinion. Although the record was old, it offered tremendous detail about the communist affiliations of the organization. Furthermore, evidence showed that the organization had been engaging in the same communist-front activities in the years following the original hearing. The dissenters believed it was not necessary for the parties to present more information or for the Court to ignore the information presented because it was "stale." Given the constitutional questions at stake, the dissent found it "indefensible" to ignore the issues as the majority chose to do.

Griffin v. California

380 U.S. 609 (1965)
Decided: April 28, 1965
Vote: 6 (Black, Douglas, Clark, Harlan II, Brennan, Goldberg)
2 (Stewart, B. White)
Opinion of the Court: Douglas
Concurring opinion: Harlan II
Dissenting opinion: Stewart (B. White)
Did not participate: Warren

Griffin was convicted of murder in a California state court. During his trial he did not testify. In his closing arguments, the prosecutor noted Griffin's failure to testify and his lack of denial and explanation of the charges. In his instructions to the jury, the judge told the panel members that they may take failure to testify into consideration as "tending to indicate the truth of such events." On appeal, Griffin argued that the state violated the Fifth Amendment by using his right of refusal against him.

The Supreme Court held that it was improper to regard a defendant's use of the Fifth Amendment privilege as evidence of guilt. The Court explained that an accused might have many reasons for refusing to testify, including excessive timidity or nervousness. Furthermore, Griffin may have wanted to avoid being impeached on the witness stand with evidence of earlier crimes. In any case, many inferences can be drawn from a refusal to testify, and it is improper for a prosecutor or the court to make one of those inferences for the jury. To do so imposes a penalty on the exercise of a constitutional protection, and the state may never sanction a citizen for invoking a constitutional right. The Court reversed Griffin's conviction.

Zemel v. Rusk

381 U.S. 1 (1965)
Decided: May 3, 1965
Vote: 6 (Warren, Clark, Harlan II, Brennan, Stewart, B. White)
3 (Black, Douglas, Goldberg)
Opinion of the Court: Warren
Dissenting opinion: Black
Dissenting opinion: Douglas (Goldberg)
Dissenting opinion: Goldberg

After the United States broke diplomatic ties with Cuba in 1961, the State Department decided, pursuant to the Passport Act of 1926, that no passport would be approved for travel to Cuba unless specific requirements were met. Louis Zemel wanted to travel to Cuba to "satisfy [his] curiosity" about Cuba and become a "better informed citizen." His request was denied, and he brought suit against the secretary of state and attorney general of the United States. He claimed that he had a constitutional right to travel to Cuba and have his passport validated for that purpose, and that the Passport Act of 1926 violated the due process protection of the Fourteenth Amendment.

The Court held that the Passport Act was a valid use of federal power. Although citizens have a general right to travel freely, they may not do so when compelling government interests preclude that right. Liberty may not be inhibited without due process, but that does not mean that it may not be inhibited in all circumstances.

According to Chief Justice Warren, the State Department had rightly decided that allowing American citizens to travel to Cuba would put the United States in danger of encountering hazardous international incidents. Cuba was the only communist country in the Western Hemisphere, and the United States feared that Cuba would detain U.S. citizens to further its communist agenda if given the opportunity. Furthermore, the Court did not agree with Zemel's argument that he was entitled to become better informed about Cuba through travel, in accordance with his First Amendment right to free speech. Almost any restriction will result in a decreased flow of information, but the Court held that the right to speak does not carry with it the unrestrained right to gather information with which to communicate.

Lamont v. Postmaster General

381 U.S. 301 (1965)
Decided: May 24, 1965
Vote: 8 (Warren, Black, Douglas, Clark, Harlan II, Brennan, Stewart, Goldberg)
0
Opinion of the Court: Douglas
Concurring opinion: Brennan (Goldberg)
Opinion concurring in judgment: Harlan II
Did not participate: B. White

Corliss Lamont and several other recipients of mail containing "communist political propaganda" challenged the federal statute under which the U.S. Post Office was obligated to deliver such mail. According to the statute, the postmaster general had to detain all unsealed foreign mail indicating communist affiliation. The post office would then contact the addressee by letter to ask if the person wanted to receive it. The original statutory scheme allowed recipients to put their names on a list that allowed them to receive all future communist mailings. During the course of litigation, however, the post office changed the rule so that recipients had to respond to a letter and affirmatively request each piece of communist mail they were intended to receive. Petitioners challenged the law, saying that it violated the First Amendment.

The Court held the federal statute unconstitutional because it required an official act—returning the reply letter—which the Court said was a limitation on the unfettered exercise of recipients' First Amendment rights. Just as the government cannot require citizens to obtain a permit before giving a public speech or distributing literature, it cannot restrain free speech by placing limits on its receipt. The affirmative obligation placed on addressees receiving communist political propaganda promised to have a deterrent effect on free expression by making receipt of the mail less likely. Not only would recipients not want the bother of responding to the post office's request, but they might be afraid to admit their desire for communist literature.

Griswold v. Connecticut

381 U.S. 479 (1965)
Decided: June 7, 1965
Vote: 7 (Warren, Douglas, Clark, Harlan II, Brennan, B. White, Goldberg)
2 (Black, Stewart)
Opinion of the Court: Douglas
Concurring opinion: Goldberg (Warren, Brennan)
Opinion concurring in judgment: Harlan II
Opinion concurring in judgment: B. White
Dissenting opinion: Black (Stewart)
Dissenting opinion: Stewart (Black)

In the spring of 1965 the Supreme Court decided one of a handful of cases that can truly be said to have established a new area of constitutional law. In *Griswold v. Connecticut* the Court resurrected substantive due process to establish a constitutionally protected right of privacy.

Various privacy rights existed within the common law, but often they were attached to property, such as in the old adage that "a man's home is his castle." In the United States, the law of privacy remained poorly defined; commentators believed that a right existed, but there was practically no case law on the subject.

The Court had previously indicated the existence of unenumerated rights that were embodied in so-called "personal liberties." Over the years, these had been held to include the right to marry and have children, to educate one's child, to travel, and to associate with others. The most striking statement on privacy was found in Justice Brandeis's stirring dissent in the first wiretap case, ***Olmstead v. United States,*** 277 U.S. 438 (1928), in which he declared that the Framers had "conferred, as against the government, the right to be let alone—the most comprehensive of rights and the right most valued by civilized men."

Griswold involved an 1879 statute prohibiting the use of any drug or device to prevent conception and penalizing any person who advised on or provided contraceptive materials. Civil libertarians had tried twice before without success to get the Supreme Court to review this law, most recently in ***Poe v. Ullman,*** 367 U.S. 497 (1961). In his dissent, Justice Harlan had suggested that a liberty interest (a personal right that came within the protection of the Fourteenth Amendment) existed that deserved protection.

Shortly after *Poe,* New Haven officials prosecuted Estelle Griswold, the executive director of the Connecticut Planned Parenthood League, along with a doctor in the league's clinic who had prescribed contraceptives to a married woman. Justice Douglas delivered one of the most creative and innovative opinions in his thirty-six years on the bench. Most of the references to privacy in earlier cases had relied on a liberty embodied in substantive due process, which in the mid-1960s still suffered from association with earlier cases that put property rights above the rights of workers. Douglas did not want to invoke substantive due process, so he cobbled together justifications from various parts of the Bill of Rights. The amendments, he said, "have penumbras, formed by emanations from those guarantees that help give them life and substance." These emanations together (joined in what one wit described as Amendment 3½) form a constitutionally protected right of privacy, and no privacy could be more sacred or more deserving of protection from intrusion than that of the marital chamber.

Justice Goldberg concurred, relying on the rarely cited Ninth Amendment, which reserves to the people all unenumerated rights. The right to privacy, Goldberg maintained, predated the Constitution, and the Framers intended that all such ancient liberties should also enjoy constitutional protection. Justice White concurred on due process grounds. Justice Stewart dissented, claiming that the Court had exceeded the limits of judicial restraint. Stewart thought the statute "an uncommonly silly law," but he could find nothing in the Bill of Rights forbidding it.

The dissent by Justice Black and the concurrence by Justice Harlan are of special interest because they illustrate two major theories of constitutional interpretation. Although Black advocated total incorporation of the Bill of Rights, he remained in many ways a strict constructionist; he would incorporate only those rights specified in the first eight amendments. He dismissed Goldberg's Ninth Amendment opinion scornfully, declaring, "Every student of history knows that it was intended to limit the federal government to the powers granted expressly or by necessary implication."

Harlan did not fear the idea of substantive due process and based his concurrence on that theme. Due process, he claimed, reflects fundamental principles of liberty and justice, but these change over time as society progresses. The Court has the responsibility of reinterpreting phrases such as "due process" and "equal protection" so that the Constitution grows with the times. Harlan saw Black's view as too rigid; both the states and the federal government needed the flexibility to experiment in means to expand the protection of individual rights.

Douglas's result—the creation of a constitutionally protected right to privacy—and Harlan's substantive due process rationale established the basis for the expansion of autonomy rights in the 1970s. *Griswold* is the forebear of ***Roe v. Wade,*** 410 U.S. 113 (1973), and many other cases enlarging personal freedoms. *Griswold* became the launching pad for the new substantive due process and a progenitor of the fundamental interest interpretation of the Due Process Clause.

Griswold and its progeny triggered one of the most intense debates over constitutional jurisprudence in the late twentieth century and one of the bitterest. Although the Ninth Amendment refers to unenumerated rights, its meaning is vague. Strict constructionists have argued that the amendment is merely a truism and that the only rights that matter are those spelled out in the Constitution. Because there is no explicit mention of a right to privacy, such a right, although it may exist, has no constitutional status. The various interpretations put forth in *Griswold* of how this right is based in the Constitution are also confusing, although Harlan's reliance on substantive due process makes the most conceptual sense.

Had the doctrine of privacy been expounded in regard to nonsexual matters, it might have won greater acceptance from conservatives. But its use as a rationale for abortion in ***Roe v. Wade*** tied it indelibly to that issue, and, as a result, opponents of abortion rights have become vehement critics of a right to privacy as well. On the other hand, critics on the left have attacked the Court for not extending this right to persons who do not fit into the conventional norms of gender and marriage. In particular, they criticize the Court for failing to grant homosexuals a right to privacy in ***Bowers v. Hardwick,*** 478 U.S. 186 (1986).

Griswold may be the archetypical case in the debate over a "living constitution." Critics attack the case as a prime example of liberal judges writing their own biases into the law and therefore amending the Constitution without the people's approval. Supporters argue that the document written at the end of the eighteenth century has to be constantly interpreted and reinterpreted so that the intent of the Framers can be articulated in areas that are unique to the present. According to this view, privacy is inherent in the Constitution and *Griswold* is an effort to animate that view.

See Alan F. Westin, *Privacy and Freedom* (New York: Atheneum, 1967); Robert G. Dixon, "The Griswold Penumbra: Constitutional Charter for an Expanded Law of Privacy?" *Michigan Law Review* 64 (1965): 197; and David J. Garrow, *Liberty and Sexuality* (New York: Macmillan, 1994).

Estes v. Texas

381 U.S. 532 (1965)
Decided: June 7, 1965
Vote: 5 (Warren, Douglas, Clark, Harlan II, Goldberg)
4 (Black, Brennan, Stewart, B. White)
Opinion of the Court: Clark
Concurring opinion: Warren (Douglas, Goldberg)
Concurring opinion: Harlan II
Dissenting opinion: Brennan
Dissenting opinion: Stewart (Black, Brennan, B. White)
Dissenting opinion: B. White (Brennan)

On the day his trial for swindling began, Billy Sol Estes asked the judge to exclude television and radio broadcasters from the courtroom during the trial. The judge denied his motion. Four future members of the jury saw the pretrial proceedings and became aware of the notorious character that the trial would take. After pretrial motions, the judge continued the case for a month, giving the media time to build sound booths and place camera equipment throughout the courtroom. During the trial, the media were allowed to tape opening and closing statements, the jury's verdict of guilty, and its receipt by the judge. These tapes were played on regularly scheduled news programs. On appeal, Estes argued that excessive media presence prevented him from receiving a fair trial under the Due Process Clause of the Fourteenth Amendment.

The Supreme Court held that the purpose of public trials is to ensure that the accused is dealt with fairly. When publication of trial proceedings achieves the opposite goal, due process is violated. The high degree of publicity given to the pretrial hearing influenced future jury members and was therefore unacceptable. Furthermore, the presence of cameras in the courtroom likely continued to influence the jury, impair the testimony of witnesses, and distract the judge.

The press has a right to report on public trials, but it may not use methods that infringe on the right to a fair trial. Intrusive television equipment and widespread dissemination of material about the case prevented Estes from receiving a fair trial. The public would have been equally served by members of the press reporting the trial in print media.

Linkletter v. Walker

381 U.S. 618 (1965)
Decided: June 7, 1965
Vote: 7 (Warren, Clark, Harlan II, Brennan, Stewart, B. White, Goldberg)
2 (Black, Douglas)
Opinion of the Court: Clark
Dissenting opinion: Black (Douglas)

Victor Linkletter was convicted of burglary by a Louisiana state court in 1959. Evidence used against him included items seized during searches of his property conducted without a warrant. Although the state court admitted the searches violated the Fourth Amendment, it allowed the evidence to be introduced at trial. The state supreme court affirmed the use of illegal evidence and the conviction. Two years later the Supreme Court decided in ***Mapp v. Ohio,*** 367 U.S. 643 (1961), that states must exclude illegally seized evidence from court. Linkletter filed a writ of habeas corpus in federal court, arguing that the rule in *Mapp* should be applied retroactively to overturn his conviction.

The Court said it must follow a new law if the original law leading to conviction has been changed while the case is on direct review (pending appeal), but the Court held that it was not bound by new law if a final decision had been reached in a case. Here, the state supreme court had made a final decision in Linkletter's case, and he had not appealed that determination to the Supreme Court. The judgment against him was therefore final, and the Supreme Court could not use a habeas corpus petition to make a different ruling in retrospect.

In addition, the Louisiana courts had correctly relied on existing rules of law when making its decision. Judicial credibility would be undermined if the Supreme Court said that reliance on the first rule was wrong and must be overturned.

Albertson v. Subversive Activities Control Board

382 U.S. 70 (1965)
Decided: November 15, 1965
Vote: 8 (Warren, Black, Douglas, Clark, Harlan II, Brennan, Stewart, Goldberg)
0
Opinion of the Court: Brennan
Concurring opinion: Black
Concurring opinion: Clark
Did not participate: B. White

The Subversive Activities Control Board (SACB) ordered the Communist Party to submit a list of its members, pursuant to Section 7 of the Subversive Activities Control Act of 1950. The attorney general then asked the SACB to order each Communist Party member to submit a registration. William Albertson, Roscoe Quincy Proctor, and other members of the Communist Party filed suit in refusal, arguing that to do so would violate their Fifth Amendment right against self-incrimination.

The SACB argued that the suit was not ripe because no Communist Party member had yet been prosecuted for refusal to register. The Court held, however, that because the communists knew of the penalties they faced, they could challenge them before they occurred. It was clear that the Communist Party would not submit a list and that individuals would have to register themselves. Furthermore, individuals faced accumulating fines for every day they did not register. If the members had to choose between imminent prosecution and giving their names to SACB, the law would do exactly what the Fifth Amendment was intended to prevent—force them to choose between incriminating themselves or the possibility of serious punishment. The Court held that this situation was sufficiently ripe to merit adjudication.

The Court also held that requiring Communist Party members to register with the SACB violated their Fifth Amendment right against self-incrimination by forcing them to provide information that could be used in an investigation or charge against them. Although the SACB promised immunity from prosecution for being a communist, it did not promise the full immunity of not having the communist information used in related investigations.

See Stanley I. Kutler, *The American Inquisition: Justice and Injustice in the Cold War* (New York: Hill and Wang, 1982).

South Carolina v. Katzenbach

383 U.S. 301 (1966)
Decided: March 17, 1966
Vote: 8 (Warren, Douglas, Clark, Harlan II, Brennan, Stewart, B. White, Goldberg)
1 (Black)
Opinion of the Court: Warren
Opinion concurring in part, dissenting in part: Black

The 1965 Voting Rights Act authorized the attorney general to send federal registrars into any county he suspected of practicing racial discrimination, in particular those counties where 50 percent or more of the voting-age population had failed to register and vote in 1964. Local voting regulations and procedures could be suspended, as could literacy tests and any other devices used to preclude otherwise eligible voters from registering. Attorney General Nicholas Katzenbach soon issued a proclamation identifying Alabama, Alaska, Georgia, Louisiana, Mississippi, South Carolina, Virginia, thirty-four counties in North Carolina, and isolated counties in Arizona, Hawaii, and Idaho as meeting the criteria for federal action, and now, for the first time, federal law would protect the integrity of the registration and voting processes in the South.

The southern states quickly challenged the Voting Rights Act, and the Supreme Court agreed to take *South Carolina v. Katzenbach* on original jurisdiction, meaning it was the first court to hear the case. South Carolina objected to the provisions dealing with literacy tests and the powers of federal registrars, as well as the length of time Congress permitted the attorney general to suspend local procedures. Some question existed as to whether South Carolina had proper standing to sue, because in ***Massachusetts v. Mellon,*** 262 U.S. 447 (1923), the Court had held that a state could not bring suit to shield its citizens from the operation of a federal statute. The Court, however, ignored this ruling whenever it considered state interests sufficiently affected. After watching southern states flout desegregation rulings for a decade, no doubt the justices wanted to resolve the constitutionality of the Voting Rights Act as quickly as possible, so that a sympathetic administration could continue to enforce it.

South Carolina's long and involved brief boiled down to three main challenges to the law. First, the state claimed that Section 2 of the Fifteenth Amendment gave Congress power to forbid violations of Section 1 only in general terms; specific remedies had to be left in the hands of the judiciary. Second, the formula for determining which areas fell within coverage violated the constitutional guarantee that all states had to be treated equally. Third, the provision barring court review of administrative findings constituted a bill of attainder and infringed on the separation of powers.

For a nearly unanimous court (Justice Black dissented on only one point), Chief Justice Warren dismissed all the state's challenges and sustained the major provisions of the act. Going back to ***McCulloch v. Maryland,*** 17 U.S. 316 (1819), and ***Gibbons v. Ogden,*** 22 U.S. 1 (1824), he held that Congress had a full range of means to choose from in carrying out any legitimate ends. Congress "may use any rational means to effectuate the constitutional prohibition of racial discrimination in voting." As for the areas to which Congress applied these remedies, the Court noted that Congress had studied the problem at length, had taken note of information provided by the Civil Rights Commission and the Justice Department as to where the greatest impediments existed, and had properly chosen "to limit its attention to the geographic areas where immediate action seemed necessary." Warren also gave short shrift to the equality-of-states argument, which he interpreted to mean only that all states had to be admitted into the Union on an equal basis; afterward, nothing prevented the treatment of localized evils by discrete remedies.

The Court also dismissed the separation of powers claim. Prescribing remedies "which go into effect without any need for prior adjudication is clearly a legitimate response to the problems, for which there is ample precedent under other constitutional provisions." Congress had determined that case-by-case litigation would only delay remedy of the evil and would "shift the advantage of time and inertia from the perpetrators of the evil to its victims." The "specific remedies," the chief justice concluded, are "appropriate means of combating the evil."

More than any other statute, the Voting Rights Act gave blacks real political power. Two months after a federal registrar arrived in Selma, the percentage of voting-age blacks on the rolls rose to sixty from ten; within five years, black registration in the South increased to 65 percent from 36 percent of the black adults in the region. Before long, these figures translated into elected black legislators, sheriffs, and mayors—more than five hundred elected officials in the lower South alone by 1969. The fact that blacks now had a significant voice in the election of sheriffs significantly affected the way law officers behaved toward African Americans, who, if mistreated by these officials, could conceivably vote them out of office at the next election.

See Alexander M. Bickel, "The Voting Rights Cases," *Supreme Court Review* 79 (1966); Ward Y. Elliott, *The Rise of Guardian Democracy: The Supreme Court's Role in Voting Rights Disputes, 1848–1969* (Cambridge: Harvard University Press, 1974); and Steven F. Lawson, *Black Ballots: Voting Rights in the South, 1944–1969* (New York: Columbia University Press, 1976).

A Book Named "John Cleland's Memoirs of a Woman of Pleasure" v. Massachusetts

383 U.S. 413 (1966)
Decided: March 21, 1966
Vote: 6 (Warren, Black, Douglas, Brennan, Stewart, Fortas)
3 (Clark, Harlan II, B. White)
Opinion of the Court: Brennan
Concurring opinion: Black
Concurring opinion: Stewart
Opinion concurring in judgment: Douglas
Dissenting opinion: Clark
Dissenting opinion: Harlan II
Dissenting opinion: B. White

The attorney general of Massachusetts went into state court and persuaded it to rule as obscene a book commonly known as "Fanny Hill," which related the story of a young girl who became a prostitute. The court ruled that because the book was obscene it was not entitled to the protection of the U.S. Constitution's guarantees of freedom of speech and press.

On appeal, the Supreme Court reversed, but the six members of the Court who voted for reversal could not agree on an opinion. Justice Brennan, joined by Warren and Fortas, rested the reversal on the ground that the Massachusetts Supreme Judicial Court erred in holding that a book need not be "unqualifiedly worthless before it can be deemed obscene," thereby misinterpreting the social value criterion of the Court's earlier definition of obscenity in ***Roth v. United States,*** 354 U.S. 476 (1957).

Justice Black concurred on the ground that in his view the Court was without constitutional power to censor speech or press regardless of the particular subject matter. Justice Douglas concurred on the ground that the Constitution leaves no power in government over expression of ideas, while Justice Stewart, who believed states did have the power to ban obscene materials, concurred on the ground that "Fanny Hill" was not "hardcore pornography."

Justice Clark dissented on the ground that in his view the book was obscene, having no conceivable social importance. Justice Harlan believed that, although the federal government had no power to ban pornography, the states did, and the Fourteenth Amendment required a state only to apply obscenity criteria rationally related to the accepted notion of obscenity. The third dissenter, Justice White, wrote that if a state insists on treating "Fanny Hill" as obscene and forbidding its sale, the First Amendment does not prevent it from doing so.

The case demonstrates the Warren Court's inability to develop useful criteria for guiding the states and lower courts in judging obscenity statutes. Although a majority of the Court believed that obscene material did not enjoy First Amendment protection, a majority could never agree on what constituted obscenity. The Warren Court brought ever larger areas of speech and literature under the First Amendment umbrella, but obscenity remained, in Justice Brennan's phrase, "an intractable problem."

See Harry M. Clor, *Obscenity and Public Morality: Censorship in a Liberal Society* (Chicago: University of Chicago Press, 1969); and Harry Kalven, *A Worthy Tradition: Freedom of Speech in America* (New York: Harper and Row, 1988).

Ginzburg v. United States

383 U.S. 463 (1966)
Decided: March 21, 1966
Vote: 5 (Warren, Clark, Brennan, B. White, Fortas)
4 (Black, Douglas, Harlan II, Stewart)
Opinion of the Court: Brennan
Dissenting opinion: Black
Dissenting opinion: Douglas
Dissenting opinion: Harlan II
Dissenting opinion: Stewart

In ***Memoirs v. Massachusetts,*** 383 U.S. 413 (1966), decided the same day as *Ginzburg v. United States,* Justice Brennan elaborated on the obscenity test as first enunciated in ***Roth v. United States,*** 354 U.S. 476 (1957), and now refined by nearly a decade's experience:

> Three elements must coalesce: it must be established that (a) the dominant theme of the material taken as a whole appeals to a prurient interest in sex; (b) the material is patently offensive because it affronts contemporary community standards relating to the description or representation of sexual matters; and (c) the material is utterly without redeeming social value.

The new tripartite test did not command the full allegiance of the justices, who, when they tried to apply it in *Ginzburg v. United States,* only muddied the waters. The case involved a glossy, sophisticated magazine, *Eros,* which featured erotic articles and pictures. Whether it met the tripartite test is unclear because the case centered on the prosecution's claim that the material had been promoted and marketed to appeal to the lascivious. The Court upheld the conviction, thereby adding the offense of "pandering" to the obscenity morass.

The decision is troubling and confusing because there is a strong argument that the defendant was denied due process. As the dissenters pointed out, the Court rewrote the law so that it sustained Ginzburg's conviction on pandering instead of distributing obscene materials, the offense for which he had been convicted. Moreover, "pandering" is perhaps an even more obscure term than "obscene" and calls into question all sorts of subjective judgments. It has been suggested that the Court, concerned at the time by charges that it was "soft" on criminals and was fostering moral permissiveness by its obscenity decisions, wanted to show that convictions could be secured against pornographers.

Ginzburg reflects the ambivalence that marked the Warren Court's efforts to deal with obscenity and to determine how much freedom of expression is protected when it deals primarily with sexually oriented material. As Justice Black noted in dissent in *Ginzburg,* fourteen separate opinions were handed down that day in three obscenity cases—the third was *Mishkin v. New York,* 383 U.S. 502 (1966)—and "no person, not even the most learned judge much less a layman, is capable of knowing in advance of ultimate decision in his particular case by this Court whether certain material comes within the area of 'obscenity.' "

With *Memoirs* and *Ginzburg,* the Court seemed to abandon its effort to articulate a definition of obscenity. Instead, the justices began to look at whether sufficient state interests existed to regulate such material, and if so, under what rationale. The following year the Court in *per curiam* decisions reversed several obscenity convictions, and an accompanying brief opinion noted that the seven justices who constituted the majority for reversal held four different theories to justify their views.

See David Lowenthal, *No Liberty for License: The Forgotten Logic of the First Amendment* (Dallas: Spence Publishers, 1997), part II; and Harry M. Clor, *Obscenity and Public Morality: Censorship in a Liberal Society* (Chicago: University of Chicago Press, 1969).

Harper v. Virginia State Board of Elections

383 U.S. 663 (1966)
Decided: March 24, 1966
Vote: 6 (Warren, Douglas, Clark, Brennan, B. White, Fortas)
3 (Black, Harlan II, Stewart)
Opinion of the Court: Douglas
Dissenting opinion: Black
Dissenting opinion: Harlan II (Stewart)

A few days after the decision in ***South Carolina v. Katzenbach,*** 383 U.S. 301 (1966), the Court in *Harper v. Virginia State Board of Elections* overturned the use of poll taxes in state elections. The Twenty-fourth Amendment, ratified in January 1964, abolished the poll tax in federal elections, and the Court invoked the Equal Protection Clause to inter the state poll tax as well. Justice Douglas's opinion relied on two different equal protection analyses, "fundamental interests" and "suspect classification." The Constitution, he conceded, nowhere specifically mentioned a right to vote in state elections, but voting constituted such a basic right of free citizens that any effort to restrict it ran into a strong presumption of unconstitutionality. To limit it on the basis of wealth created a classification that could not withstand equal protection analysis. "Wealth, like race, creed, or color, is not germane to one's ability to participate intelligently in the electoral process. Lines drawn on the basis of wealth or property, like those of race, are traditionally disfavored." Douglas argued that the meaning of the Equal Protection Clause "is not shackled to the political theory of a particular era.... Notions of what constitutes equal treatment for purposes of the Equal Protection Clause do change."

Douglas's opinion is one of his boldest as well as one of the most activist of the Warren Court era, and it brought forth impassioned dissents from Justices Black and Harlan. Although Black stood willing to expand the reach of the Bill of Rights through the Fourteenth Amendment, both he and Harlan took a fairly conservative approach in requiring some textual basis for establishing a constitutionally protected right. They attacked the majority opinion as akin to earlier Courts' use of due process to strike down economic legislation the justices had not liked, and they also objected to the notion of a "living Constitution," the idea that the meaning of the Constitution changed over time.

"I did not join the opinion of the Court in *Brown* [*v. Board of Education*] on any theory that segregation ... denied equal protection in 1954 but did not similarly deny it in 1896," Black wrote. "I thought when *Brown* was written, and I think now, that Mr. Justice Harlan was correct in 1896 when he dissented from *Plessy v. Ferguson.*" (See 163 U.S. 537.) For Black, the Constitution did not change with the years. But Douglas had also cited the "one person, one vote" decision in the apportionment cases, such as ***Reynolds v. Sims,*** 377 U.S. 533 (1964), for his argument that the meaning of equal protection does change over time. It is difficult to see how Black could have denied Douglas's assertion that the original understanding of the Fourteenth Amendment did not require that both houses of a state legislature be apportioned by population. That conclusion could only have been reached because ideas about equality and democracy had changed over time.

To conservatives, this argument smacked of heresy, for in their eyes it deprived the Constitution of fixed meaning and left it subject to the passing whims of changing judicial personnel. Equal protection, due process, all had to mean something, and that meaning had to be stable so that people could rely on it. But a fixed and rigid interpretation, as Douglas recognized, would be just as bad because it would preclude the Constitution from ever having a contemporary meaning.

See Ward Y. Elliott, *The Rise of Guardian Democracy* (Cambridge: Harvard University Press, 1974); and Steven Lawson, *Black Ballots: Voting Rights in the South, 1944–1969* (New York: Columbia University Press, 1976).

United States v. Guest

383 U.S. 745 (1966)
Decided: March 28, 1966
Vote: 9 (Warren, Black, Douglas, Clark, Harlan II, Brennan, Stewart, B. White, Fortas)
0
Opinion of the Court: Stewart
Concurring opinion: Clark (Black, Fortas)
Opinion concurring in part, dissenting in part: Harlan II
Opinion concurring in part, dissenting in part: Brennan (Warren, Douglas)

This case, along with *United States v. Price,* 383 U.S. 787 (1966), arose from violent incidents related to the civil rights movement. *Guest* resulted from the Klan-style murder of Lemuel Penn, a black teacher. The defendants were indicted in federal court in Georgia for a conspiracy, in violation of 18

U.S.C. 241, to deprive black citizens of the right to use public accommodations such as movie theaters and restaurants, the right to equal use of public facilities operated by state or local government, the right to use the public streets and highways in the state, and the right to travel freely to and from the state. (The defendants were not indicted for murder because, at that time, murder was not a federal offense. Because the state prosecutors would not indict for murder, federal prosecutors had no other option than to try to secure conviction under the civil rights conspiracy laws.) The district court dismissed the indictment following a motion by the defendants. Upon appeal, the Supreme Court reversed, although the Court divided over certain sections of the majority opinion by Justice Stewart.

In Part I of the opinion, the Court held that it had jurisdiction over all but one count of the indictment, and it lacked jurisdiction there because of a technicality—a defect in the pleading. But the Court did have jurisdiction over all of the other counts, and it held that the lower court had misconstrued 18 U.S.C. 241, a remnant of one of the Reconstruction Era civil rights laws that had never been taken off the books.

The Court divided over the extent to which state action (involvement) in alleged violations of civil rights had to be established to trigger the old Reconstruction statute and to what extent Section 5 of the Fourteenth Amendment allowed Congress to regulate state action. But whatever their rationale, all members of the Court believed the statute, despite its age, remained valid. It thus provided the federal government with stronger tools with which to prosecute both state officials as well as private persons for violating the rights of black Americans.

See Harvard Sitkoff, *The Struggle for Black Equality, 1954–1992,* rev. ed. (New York: Hill and Wang, 1993).

Elfbrandt v. Russell

384 U.S. 11 (1966)
Decided: April 18, 1966
Vote: 5 (Warren, Black, Douglas, Brennan, Fortas)
4 (Clark, Harlan II, Stewart, B. White)
Opinion of the Court: Douglas
Dissenting opinion: B. White (Clark, Harlan II, Stewart)

An Arizona law required all state employees to take a loyalty oath as a condition of employment. A statute passed in relation to the loyalty act said that anyone who took the oath and later became a member of the Communist Party or any other "subversive organization" would be subject to prosecution for perjury and discharge from his or her job. Barbara Elfbrandt, a junior high school teacher, refused to take the oath because she said it was too ambiguous, and the Arizona government declined to provide a hearing to explain the precise scope of the oath's requirements.

The Court held that the loyalty oath and its statutory support suffered from the constitutional infirmity of punishing people who had a mere knowledge of their organizations' subversive activities, but did not engage in those activities themselves. The requirements subjected any member of a subversive organization to immediate criminal penalties and discharge, whether he or she was in fact guilty of subversive activity or had the "specific intent" of getting involved in crime. Furthermore, the statutes violated the First Amendment's freedom of association by making no distinction between membership and criminal behavior and by punishing mere membership.

Elfbrand marked a significant departure from the earlier loyalty oath cases, in which the Court gave states the presumption that they had the power to require such oaths, provided that statutory requirements were clear and that administrative review processes were in place. Here, Justice Douglas's opinion placed the liberty interests of the individual above the alleged security requirements of the state, and it was this aspect of the case that evoked a strong dissent from Justice White. The four dissenters believed that Arizona had the right to condition employment on abstention from communist activities.

See Stanley I. Kutler, *The American Inquisition: Justice and Injustice in the Cold War* (New York: Hill and Wang, 1982).

Sheppard v. Maxwell

384 U.S. 333 (1966)
Decided: June 6, 1966
Vote: 8 (Warren, Douglas, Clark, Harlan II, Brennan, Stewart, B. White, Fortas)
1 (Black)
Opinion of the Court: Clark
Dissenting without opinion: Black

In 1954 Sam Sheppard was accused of bludgeoning his pregnant wife to death as she slept in their Cleveland residence. In the three months before the trial, the Cleveland media consistently published virulent, incriminating, and often false information about the crime. Sheppard was even examined by the police in a public gymnasium with full press coverage. The names of potential jury members were published before trial, and they received letters and calls from people interested in the outcome.

When the trial began, the judge and prosecutor were two weeks away from an election to secure their positions for the next term. The judge allowed unlimited press coverage during the trial, and permitted the press to sit anywhere in the courtroom including directly behind the defense counsel's table. The press published all witness testimony, as well as commentaries and stories about things that did not actually happen at trial. Newspapers published more than forty pictures of the jury. The jury admitted being exposed to most of this media coverage despite being instructed to avoid newspapers outside of the courtroom. Sheppard was convicted, and his appeals were denied. He filed a federal writ of habeas corpus, claiming that the judge and the media prevented him from receiving a fair trial consistent with the requirements of due process.

The Supreme Court held that Sheppard had been denied a fair trial. Although trials are public affairs and should be open to some media coverage, the rights of the press must not interfere with the judicial process. The facts of the case should be tried only in the courtroom, not in the media, especially when the jury is exposed to the media's interpretation of the events as well as the courtroom evidence. The Court held that the trial court erred in not taking further steps to control the press. It should have granted a change of venue or insulated the witnesses and the jury from extrajudicial statements that almost certainly had an effect on their testimony and decision-making process.

The Court remanded the case to the trial court for a new trial and ordered that Sheppard, who had already served ten years in jail, be released if he did not receive a fair trial in a reasonable amount of time. At the new trial, a jury acquitted Sheppard, and, many years after his death, DNA tests proved conclusively that he was not the murderer.

See James Neff, *The Wrong Man: The Final Verdict on the Dr. Sam Sheppard Murder Case* (New York: Random House, 2001).

Miranda v. Arizona

384 U.S. 436 (1966)
Decided: June 13, 1966
Vote: 5 (Warren, Black, Douglas, Brennan, Fortas)
4 (Clark, Harlan II, Stewart, B. White)
Opinion of the Court: Warren
Opinion concurring in part, dissenting in part: Clark
Dissenting opinion: Harlan II (Stewart, B. White)
Dissenting opinion: B. White (Harlan II, Stewart)

Ernesto Miranda, an indigent and semiliterate twenty-three-year-old, was arrested at his home and taken to a police station. There, he was identified by the victim of a rape-kidnapping and moved to an interrogation room where police questioned him. At first he maintained his innocence, but after two hours gave the police a signed confession of his guilt. At his trial the confession was an important factor in the jury finding him guilty. Police admitted that neither before nor during the questioning had Miranda been advised of his right to consult an attorney before answering questions.

This case gave the Warren Court the opportunity to answer questions that had been raised in the trio of cases two terms earlier: ***Massiah v. United States,*** 377 U.S. 201 (1964); ***Malloy v. Hogan,*** 378 U.S. 1 (1964); and ***Escobedo v. Illinois,*** 378 U.S. 478 (1964). Although the final holding, expressed in the famous "Miranda warnings," was clear, Chief Justice Warren's majority opinion rambled all over the constitutional landscape, occasionally lapsing into specifics, but for the most part getting lost in generalities. It made an all too easy target for critics, a "self-inflicted wound," in legal reporter Fred Graham's words.

In essence, the *Miranda* majority identified coercion in any form as the chief problem in determining the validity of confessions. Rather than proceed on a case-by-case basis attempting to evaluate the totality of the circumstances, as they had been doing since ***Betts v. Brady,*** 316 U.S. 455 (1942), the justices now handed down definite rules to guide police and lower courts. If the rules were obeyed and the suspect confessed, the confession would be admissible as evidence. If police failed to obey the rules, the confession would be thrown out.

The police had to inform a person in clear and unequivocal terms that he or she had a right to remain silent; that anything said could be used in court; that the accused had a right to a lawyer; and, if he or she had no money, the state would provide a lawyer. If the interrogation continued without the presence of an attorney, "a heavy burden rests on the Government to demonstrate that the defendant knowingly and intelligently waived his privilege against self-incrimination and the right to counsel."

Miranda, despite the objections of the four dissenting members, is a logical culmination of the Warren Court's journey to find a workable method to curtail forced confessions. It started out with the premise of earlier courts, that physical coercion could not be allowed and that an evaluation of the totality of the circumstances would determine whether due process had been violated. At the same time, the Court had been developing a broader interpretation of the Sixth Amendment right to counsel, and these doctrines coalesced in the *Massiah* and *Escobedo* rulings that if suspects asked for but were denied counsel, then confessions under such circumstances had to be considered involuntary because coerced. In *Miranda* these various strands came together in the belief that for rights to be meaningful, a suspect must know about them before interrogation begins, a process in which the physical and psychological advantage resides with the police. As Warren explained, police custody and interrogation contain "inherently compelling pressures which work to undermine the individual's will to resist and to compel him to speak where he would not do so freely."

Because *Miranda* merged self-incrimination law and confession law and tied them to the right to counsel, it departed from the due process analytical framework that had been the norm until the mid-1960s. Many critics, including the dissenters, characterized this as a radical departure from accepted doctrine. But the earlier due process, totality-of-the-circumstances rulings had never been all that clear, and one can certainly chart the seeds of *Miranda* in decisions reaching back nearly eight decades.

In *Miranda* the Court tried to do two separate things. First, it wanted to establish a prophylactic rule to aid judicial review. Although it is still possible to have a tainted confession even if the warning is given, the failure to inform a suspect of his or her rights is a clear indicator that the confession should not be admitted. Some state and local police departments that had never paid scrupulous attention to constitutional protection, ran into methodological problems following the decision. Once they adopted the *Miranda* warning as part of their standard procedures, they discovered that it did not undermine their effectiveness; in many cases, the accused wanted to confess, and could hardly wait for the police to finish reading them their rights.

The second aspect of the decision reflected the Warren majority's view that in a democracy, with rights embedded in a written constitution, everyone should understand their rights so that, if faced with police interrogation, they could make voluntary and intelligent choices. Prior to 1966 few secondary schools taught much in the way of law, and few people were aware of their rights. This situation has changed considerably, and, today, almost every state includes segments on the Constitution and law in their public school social studies curricula.

The chief justice no doubt anticipated that the *Miranda* decision would evoke strong criticism, and he tried to point out that the states remained free to experiment with how they implemented the basic procedural safeguards the Court now required. "Our decision in no way creates a constitutional straightjacket," he declared. "We encourage Congress and the states to continue their laudable search for increasingly effective ways of protecting the rights of the individual while promoting efficient enforcement of our criminal law."

The level of response had been anticipated in Justice White's dissent that the new rule would have the effect of "returning a killer, a rapist, or other criminal to the streets to repeat his crime whenever it pleases him." The uproar over *Miranda* continued for the remainder of Earl Warren's tenure, affected provisions of the 1968 Omnibus Crime Control Act, and played a role in that year's presidential election.

In many ways, however, the public quickly internalized the *Miranda* decision. In 1967 the police show "Dragnet" was brought back to the air, and actor Jack Webb as Sgt. Joe Friday gave the requisite Miranda warning, while making it clear that he considered this a hindrance to good police work. In contrast, in the 1970s the star of "Hawaii Five-O" treated the Miranda warning just as Chief Justice Warren would have wanted, as a means of making the police more professional. Because giving the warning did not seem to interfere with good police work, before long all but the most fanatic conservatives stopped looking at *Miranda* as in any way "handcuffing" the police. Thanks in large measure to the media, one could argue that in this area Warren had been successful in achieving his goal of equalizing knowledge, so that poverty would not be a bar to exercising one's rights.

See Liva Baker, *Miranda: Crime, Law and Politics* (New York: Atheneum, 1983); Gerald Caplan, "Questioning *Miranda*," *Vanderbilt Law Review* 38 (1985): 1417; Yale Kamisar, *Police Interrogation and Confessions: Essays in Law and Policy* (Ann Arbor: University of Michigan Press, 1980); and Stephen Schulhofer, "Reconsidering *Miranda*," *University of Chicago Law Review* 54 (1987): 435.

Katzenbach v. Morgan

384 U.S. 641 (1966)
Decided: June 13, 1966
Vote: 7 (Warren, Black, Douglas, Clark, Brennan, B. White, Goldberg)
2 (Harlan II, Stewart)
Opinion of the Court: Brennan
Concurring opinion: Douglas
Dissenting opinion: Harlan II (Stewart)

Section 4(e) of the Voting Rights Act of 1965 provided that no person who had successfully completed the sixth grade in Puerto Rico in which the language of instruction was other than English could be denied the right to vote in any election because of his or her inability to read or write English. Registered voters in New York City brought suit challenging the constitutionality of Section 4(e) because it conflicted with a New York election law that required the ability to read and write English as a condition of voting. The district court granted the declaratory injunction they sought preventing 4(e) from being enforced.

On direct appeal (allowed under terms of the Voting Rights Act), the Supreme Court reversed. In an opinion by Justice Brennan the majority held that Section 4(e) was a proper exercise of the powers granted to Congress by Section 5 of the Fourteenth Amendment, and that by force of the Supremacy Clause of Article 6 of the Constitution, the New York English-literacy requirement could not be enforced.

To reach this conclusion, the majority had to ignore its holding in ***Lassiter v. Northampton Board of Elections,*** 360 U.S. 45 (1959), that the ability to read English was not an irrational requirement for voting and, therefore, it was not a violation of the Equal Protection Clause to distinguish between those who could read English and those who could not. Absent a showing that a literacy test was used in racial discrimination, it seemed unlikely the Court would uphold it. Brennan did so by shifting the argument away from the rationality of the test to the supremacy of the federal Constitution and the power of the Court as its ultimate interpreter. His opinion made it appear that New York was treating its Spanish-speaking citizens unfairly, an equal protection issue that Congress—and the courts—had the power to address.

Justices Harlan and Stewart dissented, holding that New York's English-literacy requirement did not violate the Equal Protection Clause of the Fourteenth Amendment and that, consequently, Section 4(e) was invalid.

See Lucas A. Powe Jr., *The Warren Court and American Politics* (Cambridge: Harvard University Press, 2000); and Alexander M. Bickel, "The Voting Rights Cases," *Supreme Court Review* (1966): 79.

Johnson v. New Jersey

384 U.S. 719 (1966)
Decided: June 20, 1966
Vote: 7 (Warren, Clark, Harlan II, Brennan, Stewart, B. White, Goldberg)
2 (Black, Douglas)
Opinion of the Court: Warren
Concurring opinion: Clark
Concurring opinion: Harlan II (Stewart, B. White)
Dissenting opinion: Black (Douglas)

Sylvester Johnson and his accomplice, Stanley Cassidy, were arrested for felony murder on January 29, 1958. Police questioned Johnson after giving him a warning approved by the state, and he confessed. Cassidy was questioned for several hours, giving first a partial confession and later including incriminating details. Both men claimed on appeal that they asked to speak to a lawyer but were denied. Their confessions were used against them in court, and they were convicted and sentenced to death. The New Jersey Supreme Court affirmed the convictions, and neither man appealed.

After the convictions were final, the U.S. Supreme Court decided the cases of ***Escobedo v. Illinois,*** 378 U.S. 478 (1964), and ***Miranda v. Arizona,*** 384 U.S. 436 (1966), holding that arrestees were entitled to the presence of counsel and an explanation of their constitutional rights prior to questioning. Johnson and Cassidy petitioned the Court for postconviction relief, saying that the use of their confessions against them violated the Fifth Amendment standards created in *Escobedo* and *Miranda* and that their convictions were therefore invalid.

The Court held that *Escobedo* and *Miranda* did not apply retroactively to finalized cases. Admitting into evidence confessions made without counsel or *Miranda* warnings did not violate "the very integrity of the fact-finding process" in a way that indicated a fundamental violation of rights. On the contrary, applying these cases retroactively would seriously disrupt the administration of the criminal justice system and would punish police for relying on valid laws at the time of the arrest.

But not all cases where confessions had been obtained without *Miranda* warnings were finalized; that is, some cases had not been through the entire route of state appeals. The Court held that *Miranda* applied only to trials commenced after the decision had been announced, which occurred June 13, 1966.

See Liva Baker, *Miranda, Crime, Law and Order* (New York: Atheneum, 1983).

Schmerber v. California

384 U.S. 757 (1966)
Decided: June 20, 1966
Vote: 5 (Clark, Harlan II, Brennan, Stewart, B. White)
4 (Warren, Black, Douglas, Fortas)
Opinion of the Court: Brennan
Concurring opinion: Harlan II (Stewart)
Dissenting opinion: Warren
Dissenting opinion: Black (Douglas)
Dissenting opinion: Douglas
Dissenting opinion: Fortas

Schmerber was involved in a car accident. At the hospital he was confronted by a police officer who had smelled alcohol on his breath and noticed symptoms of drunkenness at the scene of the accident. The officer placed Schmerber under arrest and asked a doctor to take a sample of his blood to be tested for alcohol content. Schmerber refused to give blood upon advice of his attorney, but the officer persisted. The blood showed a high alcohol content, and the test was admitted as evidence in Schmerber's trial for driving while intoxicated, and he was convicted. He appealed, claiming that the blood was inadmissible evidence because its withdrawal violated his Fourteenth Amendment due process rights, his Fifth Amendment privilege against self-incrimination, his Sixth Amendment right to counsel, and his Fourth Amendment right to be free from unreasonable searches and seizures.

The Court held that the withdrawal of Schmerber's blood did not offend the "sense of justice" necessary to claim a due process violation. The Court reaffirmed its ruling in *Breithaupt v. Abram,* 352 U.S. 432 (1957), that a blood sample could be unwillingly taken from a person without violating the privilege against self-incrimination. Justice Brennan's opinion acknowledged the tension between the purposes of the Fifth Amendment and allowing blood to be taken unwillingly, but distinguished between the taking of physical evidence, such as blood or fingerprints, and oral testimony.

The Court conceded that Schmerber had a viable Fourth Amendment claim stemming from his substantial interest in privacy concerning his blood. However, the police did not violate the Fourth Amendment because the blood test was ordered following a valid arrest, and the officer had probable cause to believe alcohol would be found. The officer had no obligation to obtain a warrant because the alcohol was likely to be out of Schmerber's system before a warrant could be secured.

Adderley v. Florida

385 U.S. 39 (1966)
Decided: November 14, 1966
Vote: 5 (Black, Clark, Harlan II, Stewart, B. White)
4 (Warren, Douglas, Brennan, Fortas)
Opinion of the Court: Black
Dissenting opinion: Douglas (Warren, Brennan, Fortas)

A group of about two hundred students demonstrated by singing, clapping, and dancing on a nonpublic jail driveway, which they blocked, and on adjacent county jail premises. They were protesting against their schoolmates' arrest and against segregation in the jail and elsewhere. The sheriff advised them that they were trespassing on county property and would have to leave or be arrested. Of the student demonstrators, 107 refused to depart. They were arrested and convicted under a Florida law against "trespass with a malicious and mischievous intent." The thirty-two students who brought this case contended that their convictions, affirmed by the Florida Circuit Court and the district court of appeal, deprived them of their "rights of free speech, assembly, petition, due process of law and equal protection of the laws" under the Fourteenth Amendment.

Justice Black, who consistently believed that sit-ins and similar protests that violated private property rights did not enjoy constitutional protection (see ***Bell v. Maryland,*** 378 U.S. 226 (1964)), gained the fifth vote he needed when Justice White joined the more conservative block. Black saw the case as nothing more than trespass, and he saw no difference between trespass on public as opposed to private property.

The Supreme Court affirmed the convictions. Black, writing for the five-member majority, rejected all of the students' First Amendment claims. The Florida trespass statute was quite clear in the type of activity it proscribed, and the Civil Rights Act of 1964 did not prevent a state from enforcing trespass laws. Moreover, the evidence showed that the students had indeed trespassed on private property. As a result, Black concluded, there had been no denial of due process, nor did the convictions unconstitutionally deprive the defendants of their rights to freedom of speech, press, assembly, or petition.

Justice Douglas, joined by Chief Justice Warren and Justices Brennan and Fortas, dissented in what some considered Douglas's best opinion in many years. He agreed with the majority that not all demonstrations were constitutionally protected, but this one took place at a jail, a public institution in which classmates of the protesters were being held for attempting to exercise their constitutional rights. "The jailhouse," he wrote, "like an executive mansion . . . or the state house itself . . . is one of the seats of government, whether it be the Tower of London, the Bastille, or a small county jail. And when it houses political prisoners, or those whom many think are unjustly held, it is an obvious center for protest." The appropriateness of the site must be defined by context and not by the wishes of law enforcement officials.

By the time this case was decided, however, initial public sympathy for the sit-in demonstrations had changed to fear of mob action, and the majority opinion clearly caught that shift in the nation's mood.

See Robert Weisbrot, *Freedom Bound: A History of America's Civil Rights Movement* (New York: Norton, 1990); and Harvard Sitkoff, *The Struggle for Black Equality, 1954–1992,* rev. ed. (New York: Hill and Wang, 1993).

Bond v. Floyd

385 U.S. 116 (1966)
Decided: December 5, 1966
Vote: 9 (Warren, Black, Douglas, Clark, Harlan II, Brennan, Stewart, B. White, Fortas)
0
Opinion of the Court: Warren

Julian Bond was elected to the Georgia House of Representatives in June 1965. Several months later, the Student Non-Violent Coordinating Committee, a civil rights organization of which Bond was a staff member, issued a statement opposing U.S. policy in Vietnam and the operation of the Selective Service laws. Bond endorsed the statement in a news interview. He stated, among other things, that as "a second class citizen" he was not required to support the war, as a pacifist he was opposed to all war, and he saw nothing inconsistent with his statement and his taking the oath of office. A number of Georgia house members filed petitions challenging Bond's right to be seated. They charged that his statements aided America's enemies, violated the Selective Service laws, discredited the house, and were inconsistent with a legislator's mandatory oath to support the Constitution.

After the house clerk's refused to seat him, Bond demanded to take the oath and challenged the petitions as depriving him of his First Amendment rights and being racially motivated. At a house committee hearing, Bond amplified his views and denied having urged draft card burning or other law violations. The committee concluded that Bond should not be seated. Bond went into federal district court seeking an injunction to stop the house from barring him, but a three-judge panel ruled that Bond had been accorded procedural due process through the hearing. It also held that the house had a rational basis for concluding that Bond's remarks exceeded criticism of national policy and that he could not in good faith take an oath to support the state and federal constitutions and, therefore, could not meet a qualification for membership that the house had the power to impose.

While Bond's appeal to the Supreme Court was pending, he was again elected as a representative in a special election. When he refused to recant, he was again rejected by the House Rules Committee. Bond was elected yet again in the regular 1966 primary and general elections.

On direct appeal from the district court, the Supreme Court reversed. Chief Justice Warren spoke for a unanimous Court, holding that, because constitutional issues were involved, the Court had jurisdiction to hear a case involving the qualifications of a state legislator, an issue normally beyond its purview. Warren ruled that Bond's disqualification from membership in the Georgia House of Representatives because of his statements violated his right of free expression under the First Amendment.

At the time, everyone understood that Bond's case dealt partly with speech and partly with race. Bond was one of the first six African Americans elected to the Georgia legislature since Reconstruction, and his election was possible because the 1965 Voting Rights Act and the Court's reapportionment decisions had given blacks in Georgia increased power at the polls. As the other five blacks had been seated without objection, it was clear that the only impediment to Bond's taking his seat was his advocacy of an unpopular opinion in Georgia, opposition to the Vietnam War.

As for Georgia's contention that as a legislator Bond had to be held to a higher standard than other citizens, Warren dismissed it with a reminder that "the manifest function of the First Amendment in a representative democracy requires that legislators be given the widest latitude to express their views on issues of policy." He followed that with the famous line from Justice Brennan's majority opinion in ***New York Times v. Sullivan,*** 376 U.S. 254 (1964), that "debate on public issues should be uninhibited, robust, and wide-open."

One might well compare the civics lesson Warren handed down in this case with a similar one he delivered in one of the last cases of the Warren Court, ***Powell v. McCormack,*** 395 U.S. 486 (1969).

See Julian Bond, *A Time to Speak, A Time to Act* (New York: Simon and Schuster, 1972).

Hoffa v. United States

385 U.S. 293 (1966)
Decided: December 12, 1966
Vote: 4 (Black, Harlan II, Brennan, Stewart)
3 (Warren, Douglas, Clark)
Opinion of the Court: Stewart
Dissenting opinion: Warren
Dissenting opinion: Clark (Douglas)
Did not participate: B. White, Fortas

James Hoffa, president of the International Brotherhood of Teamsters, was tried in a federal court in Tennessee for violating the Taft-Hartley Act. During the course of the trial Hoffman was visited several times by Edward Partin, a local Teamsters Union official. The men discussed union business and Hoffa's trial strategy. After Partin heard Hoffa make plans to bribe members of the Tennessee jury, he began to make frequent reports to a federal agent about the jury tampering. When Hoffa's trial resulted in a hung jury, the government brought charges against him for bribery, and he was convicted. Hoffa appealed, claiming that Partin's actions on behalf of the government violated the Fourth, Fifth, and Sixth Amendments.

Regarding the Fourth Amendment, Hoffa argued that the presence of a federal agent in his hotel room during the trial constituted an illegal search and seizure. The Supreme Court held, however, that because Hoffa was not relying on the security of his hotel room to protect him from Partin, but rather spoke to Partin freely, no invasion and no illegal search took place. Hoffa then argued that the government violated the Fifth Amendment by using against him the statements he made to Partin. Justice Stewart explained that the purpose of the Fifth Amendment is to protect citizens from being compelled to testify against themselves. If they choose to voluntarily make comments against their own interests, there is no compulsion and no Fifth Amendment violation. The Court quickly disposed of Hoffa's Sixth Amendment arguments as well, saying that his right to counsel had not been denied because a government agent (Partin) was occasionally present when he spoke with his attorney.

The Court also rejected Hoffa's Fifth Amendment due process argument. It held that Hoffa received a fair trial despite the government's use of an informant against him because he was given a chance to confront and cross-examine the informant and was not deceived by the way the testimony was used against him.

See Arthur A. Sloane, *Hoffa* (Cambridge: MIT Press, 1991).

Time, Inc. v. Hill

385 U.S. 374 (1967)
Decided: January 9, 1967
Vote: 6 (Black, Douglas, Harlan II, Brennan, Stewart, B. White)
3 (Warren. Clark, Fortas)
Opinion of the Court: Brennan
Concurring opinion: Black (Douglas)
Concurring opinion: Douglas
Opinion concurring in part and dissenting in part: Harlan II
Dissenting opinion: Fortas (Warren, Clark)

In 1952, three escaped convicts held the Hill family hostage in their home for nineteen hours. The Hills were released unharmed. They later moved away and discouraged further publicity efforts about the incident, which had earned them extensive notoriety. A novel, *The Desperate Hours,* about a hostage incident that involved considerable violence appeared later and was subsequently made into a play. *Life* magazine's account of the play related it to the Hill incident, described the play as a reenactment, and illustrated the article with photographs of scenes staged in the former Hill home. Because New York law allowed a claim of invasion of privacy only if it could be shown that the statements made were false, James Hill had to allege that the article gave the knowingly false impression that the play depicted the Hill incident. The family sued for damages under a New York statute providing a cause of action to a person whose name or picture is used by another without consent for purposes of trade or advertising. Although the family prevailed at the trial court level, subsequent appeals reversed or limited some of the damage awards, and, by the time the case came to the Supreme Court, it was unclear what law, if any, applied.

Justice Brennan's opinion for the majority built on the decision he had written in ***New York Times v. Sullivan,*** 376 U.S. 254 (1964). That James Hill and his family may have wanted to slide back into obscurity was irrelevant, Brennan explained, because "exposure of the self to others in varying degrees is a concomitant of life in a civilized society." Although the hostage situation and a Broadway play are not the stuff of politics that stood at the heart of *Sullivan,* "the line between the informing and the entertaining is too elusive for the protection" of freedom of the press. *Hill* and subsequent cases increasingly freed the press from fear of libel for reporting on people or events that could be considered newsworthy. The press could not escape liability for reckless negligence regarding the truth, but simple errors of fact by themselves could not be the basis for a libel suit.

Black, joined by Douglas, concurred in the judgment, but expressed the view that the liability test announced in opinion—"knowing and reckless falsity"—was inadequate to protect freedom of the press from destruction in libel cases. Douglas, in a separate concurring opinion, also expressed the view that the constitutional guarantees barred the exceptions for "knowing and reckless falsity."

Justice Harlan concurred in the result, but dissented as to the proper standard of liability to be applied on remand, holding that the federal constitutional requirement would be met if the jury, on retrial, should find negligent, rather than reckless or knowing, falsity in the publication of the article.

Justice Fortas, joined by Warren and Clark, dissented on the ground that there was no reason to order a new trial because the trial court's instructions were acceptable even within the principles announced by the Court.

A minor note of interest is that Richard M. Nixon argued his only Supreme Court case on behalf of Hill.

See Norman L. Rosenberg, *Protecting the Best Men: An Interpretive History of the Law of Libel* (Chapel Hill: University of North Carolina Press, 1986).

Keyishian v. Board of Regents of the University of the State of New York

385 U.S. 589 (1967)
Decided: January 23, 1967
Vote: 5 (Warren, Black, Douglas, Brennan, Fortas)
4 (Clark, Harlan II, Stewart, B. White)
Opinion of the Court: Brennan
Dissenting opinion: Clark (Harlan II, Stewart, B. White)

Samuel Keyishian and others were teachers at the University of Buffalo, a private school that merged with State University of New York, thus becoming a public institution and making its faculty members state employees. Under New York law, all public employees were required to sign a loyalty oath, the purpose of which was to prevent the commission of "treasonable or seditious" acts by New York State employees. Keyishian refused to sign an oath created by the university, saying that he was not a communist and that he had told the president of the university of any former communist affiliations. He challenged the New York regulatory scheme, asserting that the purpose of preventing "treasonable and seditious" activities was overly vague and did not put employees on notice about what kind of activities they could or could not participate in.

The Supreme Court agreed with Keyishian, holding that teachers in New York public universities had no way of knowing the boundaries of seditious utterances and actions forbidden by the statute and therefore could not be forced to sign an oath promising to abstain from such things. Justice Brennan, relying in large part upon ***Elfbrandt v. Russell,*** 384 U.S. 11 (1966), decided earlier that term, ruled that the statutes might have a stifling effect on the "free play of the spirit which all teachers ought especially to cultivate and practice." Forcing teachers to sign loyalty oaths posed the risk of curtailing free speech in the academic arena, where individuals had a special interest in learning things that were not orthodox.

The Court also found the regulations overbroad because they prohibited membership in the Communist Party even if members had no intent to further the unlawful aims of the organization. Only actions should be regulated, the Court said, not mere membership in an organization.

Vaca v. Sipes

386 U.S. 171 (1967)
Decided: February 27, 1967
Vote: 8 (Warren, Douglas, Clark, Harlan II, Brennan, Stewart, B. White, Fortas)
1 (Black)
Opinion of the Court: B. White
Concurring opinion: Fortas (Warren, Harlan II)
Dissenting opinion: Black

Discharged from his job at Swift & Company, Benjamin Owens asked his union, the Kansas City local of the National Brotherhood of Packing House Workers, to take his grievance to binding arbitration, which was available under the union's collective bargaining agreement. When the union refused to assist him, Owens sued Manuel Vaca, the local's president, as well as the union itself. A jury awarded Owens both compensatory and punitive damages, but the trial judge set aside the jury verdict and entered judgment for the union. The judge held that because the suit involved an unfair labor practice, it was within the exclusive jurisdiction of the National Labor Relations Board (NLRB). Owens appealed the decision. He died during the appeals process, and the suit was continued by Niles Sipes, the administrator of his estate. The Missouri Supreme Court reversed, holding that the NLRB did not have exclusive jurisdiction, and that Owens could sue for recovery of damages in state court.

The Supreme Court reversed. In the opinion by Justice White, the Court held that although the state court had jurisdiction to hear the case, its rulings regarding evidence, levels of proof, and damages would have to be governed by federal law. Under those federal standards, Owens had failed to establish that the union had acted arbitrarily or in bad faith so as to have breached its duty of fair representation. Furthermore, the union could not properly be held liable for damages attributable solely to the employer's allegedly wrongful discharge.

This case demonstrates how the Court viewed federal labor law within the context of federalism. Although the National Labor Relations Act governed the situation, the NLRB, the agency created to enforce that law, did not have sole jurisdiction over cases arising from labor disputes or claims of wrongful discharge. Rather, state courts could hear such cases, provided they followed the procedural and evidentiary rules required under federal law.

Klopfer v. North Carolina

386 U.S. 213 (1967)
Decided: March 13, 1967
Vote: 9 (Warren, Black, Douglas, Clark, Harlan II,
Brennan, Stewart, B. White, Fortas)
0
Opinion of the Court: Warren
Concurring in judgment without opinion: Stewart
Opinion concurring in judgment: Harlan II

Peter Klopfer was indicted by a grand jury for a criminal trespass misdemeanor in February 1964. His case went to trial the following month, but a hung jury resulted in the declaration of a mistrial. The case was continued, but was not placed on the 1965 trial calendar. Klopfer filed a motion petitioning the court to "permanently conclude" the activities against him, claiming that the pending charges interfered with his professional activities and ability to travel abroad. In response, the prosecutor requested a *nolle prosequi* against Klopfer. A *nolle prosequi* is a procedural device allowing the prosecutor to drop the charges against a defendant, but remain free to bring the case back to court at any time. The trial court granted the prosecutor's request, and Klopfer appealed, claiming that the *nolle prosequi* violated his right to a speedy trial.

The Supreme Court unanimously agreed that the *nolle prosequi* violated Klopfer's Sixth Amendment right to a speedy trial, even though no trial was pending. Chief Justice Warren explained that the right to a speedy trial was foundational to Anglo-American law, citing the Magna Carta as an early example of society's desire to not "defer to any man either justice or right." Furthermore, forcing Klopfer to remain ready for prosecution placed limitations on his liberty, leaving him open to public scorn, deprivation of employment, and curtailment of his freedom of speech and association. In addition, the indefinite prolonging of his legal ordeal subjected him to ongoing anxiety and concern.

See Warren Freedman, *The Constitutional Right to a Speedy and Fair Trial* (New York: Quorum Books, 1989).

Redrup v. New York

386 U.S. 767 (1967)
Decided: May 8, 1967
Vote: 7 (Warren, Black, Douglas, Brennan,
Stewart, B. White, Fortas)
2 (Clark, Harlan II)
Opinion of the Court: *Per curiam*
Dissenting opinion: Harlan II (Clark)

This consolidated case addressed three convictions under three separate state laws regulating the distribution of objectionable books and magazines. Redrup was a clerk at a New York City book stand. He sold a plainclothes policeman two books, *Lust Pool* and *Shame Agent*, and was charged with violating a state criminal law. In *Austin v. Kentucky* a book store owner in Paducah, Kentucky, sold a woman magazines called *High Heels* and *Spree* and was criminally convicted. In *Gent v. Arkansas* the attorney general of Arkansas brought civil actions in state court to have various pornographic magazines declared obscene. The state supreme court complied with the requests. None of the laws applied in these cases were aimed specifically at protecting juveniles, and none of the convictions involved unique privacy claims.

The Supreme Court did not find that any of the material condemned under these state laws met the constitutional definition of obscenity. The *per curiam* opinion explained that two justices of the Court believed that obscene material could never be regulated under the sweeping power of the First Amendment. Most others believed that obscenity could be regulated by states, but felt that the material in question did not meet the constitutional definition of obscenity. These justices defined obscene material as material that (a) appeals to a prurient interest in sex, (b) is patently offensive by contemporary community standards, and (c) lacks any redeeming social value. Because none of the material in question met these standards, the judgments against their sellers could not stand.

See Harry A. Clor, ed., *Censorship and Freedom of Expression* (Chicago: Rand McNally, 1971).

In re Gault

387 U.S. 1 (1967)
Decided: May 15, 1967
Vote: 8 (Warren, Black, Douglas, Clark, Harlan II, Brennan, B. White, Fortas)
1 (Stewart)
Opinion of the Court: Fortas
Concurring opinion: Black
Concurring opinion: B. White
Opinion concurring in part, dissenting in part: Harlan II
Dissenting opinion: Stewart

An enduring reform of the Progressive Era was the establishment of juvenile courts where minors were tried under rules far different from those of a regular criminal court and judges had great discretion over the type of punishment meted out to offenders. Under the general police power of *parens patriae,* the state could take a protective and paternal interest in the well-being of its minor citizens. As a result, every state had different criminal procedure codes for adults and juveniles. The traditional adversary system predominated in the adult system, while for juveniles, a collaborative system tried to save each child from future difficulties with the law. But if children benefited from the more lenient system of juvenile justice, they also did not have many of the protections of the Fourth, Fifth, and Sixth Amendments in their hearings.

Fifteen-year-old Gerald Gault was sentenced to the Arizona State Industrial School until he turned twenty-one after the juvenile court determined that he was a delinquent for making obscene calls to a neighbor while on probation for another offense. Had he been an adult, Gault's maximum punishment would have been a $50 fine or two months in jail instead of the six-year sentence he received. Moreover, Arizona juvenile law afforded Gault no due process: he was given no official notice of the hearing; he was arrested, tried, and incarcerated within one week of the offense; he had no counsel present, nor notice that he might retain a lawyer; he had no opportunity to confront or cross-examine witnesses against him and no protection against self-incrimination. A system that had started out to protect children had, at least in this case, become a travesty of justice.

In his opinion for the Court, Justice Fortas questioned the whole system of juvenile justice and its reliance on *parens patriae* and then held that many but not all of the protections afforded adults in criminal proceedings had to be provided to minors as well. Fortas claimed that the flexibility that was the hallmark of juvenile justice would not be destroyed, but the system now had to act in a less arbitrary manner and allow minors the minimal due process requirements.

Justices Harlan and Black concurred, and continued their debate over what the Fourteenth Amendment's Due Process Clause meant, a debate that reached back to ***Poe v. Ullman,*** 367 U.S. 497 (1961), and intensified in a later juvenile justice case, ***In re Winship,*** 397 U.S. 358 (1970).

Justice Stewart's dissent raised the issue of whether requiring adult protections for juveniles would destroy the juvenile justice system. The debate on how *Gault* has affected the juvenile justice system continues, and it is still not clear whether the results have been as beneficial as its adherents claim or as destructive as its critics charge.

See John R. Sutton, *Stubborn Children: Controlling Delinquency in the United States, 1640–1981* (Berkeley: University of California Press, 1988); and Stanton Wheeler and Leonard S. Cottrell Jr., *Juvenile Delinquency: Its Prevention and Control* (New York: Russell Sage Foundation, 1966).

Afroyim v. Rusk

387 U.S. 253 (1967)
Decided: May 29, 1967
Vote: 5 (Warren, Black, Douglas, Brennan, Fortas)
4 (Clark, Harlan II, Stewart, B. White)
Opinion of the Court: Black
Dissenting opinion: Harlan II (Clark, Stewart, B. White)

Beys Afroyim was born in Poland and immigrated to the United States in 1912; he became a naturalized citizen in 1926. In 1950 he went to Israel and voted in an Israeli election the following year. In 1960 he applied for a renewal of his United States passport and was refused. Section 401(e) of the Nationality Act of 1940 said that a naturalized citizen could "lose" his citizenship if he chose to vote in a foreign election. The Court had upheld this statute in ***Perez v. Brownell,*** 356 U.S. 44 (1958). Afroyim nonetheless brought a declaratory judgment action against Secretary of State Dean Rusk to challenge the statute, saying that it violated the Due Process Clause of the Fifth Amendment and the citizenship clause of the Fourteenth Amendment.

The Court held that the Constitution did not give Congress the power to strip an individual of his U.S. citizenship. Furthermore, the implied power of the Necessary and Proper Clause did not extend to decisions about citizenship. Justice Black noted that the power of the federal government is limited, and that "in our country the people are sovereign and the government cannot sever its relationship to the people by taking away their citizenship."

The Court further held that the Fourteenth Amendment placed a specific limit on Congress's power in this area by providing that "all persons born or naturalized in the United States . . . are citizens of the United States." This clause completely controls the terms of U.S. citizenship and leaves no room for congressional action. The Court explicitly overruled *Perez,* and reversed the lower court decision.

See Earl M. Maltz, "Citizenship and the Constitution: A History and Critique of the Supreme Court's Alienage Jurisprudence," *Arizona State Law Journal* 28 (1996): 1135.

Warden v. Hayden

387 U.S. 294 (1967)
Decided: May 29, 1967
Vote: 8 (Warren, Black, Clark, Harlan II, Brennan, Stewart, B. White, Fortas)
1 (Douglas)
Opinion of the Court: Brennan
Concurring opinion: Fortas (Warren)
Concurring in judgment without opinion: Black
Dissenting opinion: Douglas

Bennie Joe Hayden was convicted of armed robbery by a Maryland court. Evidence used against him included items of clothing seized during a warrantless search of his house. Hayden did not object to admission of the clothing during trial but later claimed in a federal habeas corpus petition that the items should not have been seized and were therefore inadmissible in court. The items had merely evidentiary value, and were not tools related to the crime. Supreme Court precedent indicated that police could only seize items directly related to the crime.

The Court decided that the Fourth Amendment allowed the seizure of evidence as well as items linked directly to a crime during a search. Here, the police found clothing in Hayden's house that matched a description of the suspect's clothing. Although these items were merely evidence linking Hayden to the crime, and were not the means or fruit of his actions, the Court held that the Constitution made no distinction between what police can and cannot seize during a valid search. The purpose of the Fourth Amendment is to protect individual privacy, and making a distinction between "mere evidence" and "instrumentalities" does not further the goal of privacy. In addition, the words of the Fourth Amendment do not differentiate between types of evidence that can be seized. For these reasons the Court held that seizure of Hayden's property was legal and denied his habeas corpus petition.

Reitman v. Mulkey

387 U.S. 369 (1967)
Decided: May 29, 1967
Vote: 5 (Warren, Douglas, Brennan, B. White, Fortas)
4 (Black, Clark, Harlan II, Stewart)
Opinion of the Court: B. White
Concurring opinion: Douglas
Dissenting opinion: Harlan II (Black, Clark, Stewart)

Lincoln Mulkey and his wife attempted to rent an apartment and were turned down because of their race. They sued the apartment owner, Neil Reitman, and asked the court for an injunction to prevent Reitman from renting the apartment to someone else; they also asked for damages. The owner moved for summary judgment under a California law saying that the state could not deny, limit, or abridge a property owner's right to sell or rent private property only to those he chose. The district court granted summary judgment, and the Mulkeys appealed.

The California Supreme Court held that the apartment owner acted illegally and that the California statute allowing him to do so was unconstitutional. It appeared to the California court that the purpose of the law was to overturn state law that forbade discrimination in private land sales. The state had two laws that made it illegal for private owners to discriminate. The law in question undermined that objective, and the California court said that this "significant state involvement in private discrimination" was unconstitutional.

The Supreme Court agreed with the California court. The Fourteenth Amendment forbids not only blatant discrimination by a state but also state action that makes private discrimination legally possible. The California statute achieved no other purpose than allowing private owners to choose to discriminate. This goal was contrary to other California laws seeking to achieve further equality. Given the purpose and effect of the statute, the Supreme Court found that it violated the Fourteenth Amendment and affirmed the decision of the California court.

Camara v. Municipal Court

387 U.S. 523 (1967)
Decided: June 5, 1967
Vote: 8 (Warren, Black, Douglas, Harlan II, Brennan, Stewart, B. White, Fortas)
1 (Clark)
Opinion of the Court: B. White
Dissenting opinion: Clark

Acting under the San Francisco Housing Code, a Department of Public Health inspector attempted to enter an apartment building to make a routine annual inspection. The building manager, Roland Camara, refused entrance, saying that the inspection violated the Fourth Amendment's prohibition against unreasonable searches and seizures. The inspector did not have a warrant, and Camara claimed that he lacked probable cause to search the building. The Department of Public Health filed a criminal complaint, Camara was arrested, and his demurrer against the charge was denied. He then filed a writ of prohibition against the court that denied his demurrer.

The Supreme Court held that the inspector was not authorized to inspect Camara's property without a warrant. The purpose of the Fourth Amendment is to safeguard the privacy and security of individuals against invasion by the government, and this interest applies to both criminal and administrative investigations. Although the health and safety of urban environments benefit from administrative investigations, a warrant requirement ensures that the system does not abuse individuals.

The Court further held that probable cause for administrative inspections could be granted for an entire area if the government had reasons to believe that the buildings in that area contained structural defects. Local governments have a high interest in ensuring that properties meet minimum standards of safety, and area code-enforcement inspections are a reasonable way to achieve that important goal. The age of buildings in an area, their nature and condition, were all factors that could be looked at to determine whether there was probable cause to grant an area code-enforcement warrant.

Loving v. Virginia

388 U.S. 1 (1967)
Decided: June 12, 1967
Vote: 9 (Warren, Black, Douglas, Clark, Harlan II, Brennan, Stewart, B. White, Fortas)
0
Opinion of the Court: Warren
Opinion concurring in judgment: Stewart

State laws regulating private conduct obviously constituted state action. Nearly all of the southern states had on their books laws prohibiting sexual relations, cohabitation, or marriage between members of different races. In the only previous case on this subject to reach the Supreme Court, ***Pace v. Alabama,*** 106 U.S. 583 (1883), the justices sustained a state law imposing higher penalties on adultery or fornication between a white person and a black person than between members of the same race, but the higher penalty applied equally to both offenders. Because sexual relations between the races was such a sensitive issue in the South and Border States, the Court had avoided taking challenges to the antimiscegenation laws. In ***McLaughlin v. Florida,*** 379 U.S. 184 (1964), however, the Court invalidated a criminal statute prohibiting cohabitation by interracial married couples as a violation of the Equal Protection Clause. Justice White's majority opinion declared any racial classification constitutionally suspect and subject to the strictest scrutiny. Justice Stewart, in his concurrence, said that "it is simply not possible for a state law to be valid under our Constitution which makes the criminality of an act depend upon the race of the actor."

Sixteen states still had laws prohibiting and punishing marriage between the races. Challenges to such laws had twice been carried to the Supreme Court but had been dismissed in 1955 and 1956 as lacking any federal question. After *McLaughlin,* the Court could not help but find that such an issue existed, and it took the next case that came to it.

Richard Loving, a white man, married Mildred Jeter, a black woman, in Washington, D.C., in June 1958, and the couple moved back to rural Caroline County, Virginia. They were arrested and convicted in January 1959 for violating the Virginia antimiscegenation law. They were sentenced to a year in jail, but the sentence was suspended for twenty-five years provided they left the state and did not return at any time during that period. The Lovings moved to Washington, where their three children were born, but they wanted to return to Virginia. They appealed their convictions, and in 1967 the Supreme Court struck down the prohibition against interracial marriage as a violation of the Fourteenth Amendment. "Restricting the freedom to marry solely because of racial classification," declared Chief Justice Warren, "violates the central meaning of the Equal Protection Clause."

In his famous dissent in ***Plessy v. Ferguson,*** 163 U.S. 537 (1896), the first Justice Harlan had declared that "our Constitution is color-blind," and some members of the Warren Court suggested a *per se* rule to invalidate all legislative distinctions requiring racial classification. Although it did not go that far, the Court did place a heavy burden of proof on the states to show that a racial classification fulfilled a compelling government interest. It is a difficult burden to carry, and, in all but a few very narrow situations, states have been unable to do so.

See Harvey M. Applebaum, "Miscegenation Statutes: A Constitutional and Social Problem," *Georgia Law Review* 53 (1964): 49; and Peter Wallenstein, "Race, Marriage, and the Supreme Court: From *Pace v. Alabama* (1883) to *Loving v. Virginia* (1967)," *Journal of Supreme Court History* (1998): 65.

Berger v. New York

388 U.S. 41 (1967)
Decided: June 12, 1967
Vote: 6 (Warren, Douglas, Clark, Brennan, Stewart, Fortas)
3 (Black, Harlan II, B. White)
Opinion of the Court: Clark
Concurring opinion: Douglas
Concurring in judgment: Stewart
Dissenting opinion: Black
Dissenting opinion: Harlan II
Dissenting opinion: B. White

Ralph Berger was convicted of conspiracy to bribe the chairman of the New York State Liquor Authority. His conviction was based on evidence received from a recording device placed in his office. New York law permitted the placement of recording devices in attorneys' offices when any state officer swore an oath that there was reasonable grounds to believe that evidence of a crime might be obtained. The law allowed the devices to remain in place for sixty days and approved a sixty-day renewal, if necessary. Berger challenged his conviction based on the evidence obtained under this statute, claiming that the use of recording devices violate the Fourth Amendment's protection against unreasonable searches and seizures.

The Court held that the New York law was too broad because it permitted intrusions into constitutionally protected areas and therefore sanctioned unreasonable searches and seizures. The Fourth Amendment protects individual privacy and extends to privacy of conversations as well as tangible items. Searches may take place only if they are based on probable cause. Here, searches were taking place without a reasonable belief that they would yield evidence of crime. In addition, Justice Clark explained, they permitted officers to seize all conversations, not just incriminating ones, and to do so for a two-month period of time. The two-month warrants also allowed police to continue monitoring calls even after they had seized sufficient evidence. For these reasons, the Court reversed Berger's conviction.

See Clifford S. Fishman and Anne T. McKenna, *Wiretapping and Eavesdropping,* 2d ed. (Deerfield, Ill.: Clark Boardman Callaghan, 1995).

Curtis Publishing Co. v. Butts

388 U.S. 130 (1967)
Decided: June 12, 1967
Vote: 5 (Warren, Clark, Harlan II, Stewart, Fortas)
4 (Black, Douglas, Brennan, B. White)
Judgment of the Court: Harlan II
Opinion concurring in judgment: Warren
Dissenting opinion: Black (Douglas)
Dissenting opinion: Brennan (B. White)

This case is a compilation of two libel cases the Court addressed together. In the first, Wallace Butts, athletic director of the University of Alabama, sued Curtis Publishing Company for willfully publishing false and uncorroborated information accusing him of fixing a football game. Butts won, and the decision was affirmed on appeal. In the second case, Gen. Edwin Walker, a politically prominent conservative, sued the Associated Press (AP) for falsely reporting that he led a group of students at the University of Mississippi in a protest against desegregation at the school. Walker won a jury verdict despite no showing of malice, but the judge refused to enter an award because he heard no evidence of negligence on AP's part. Both decisions were appealed under ***New York Times Co. v. Sullivan,*** 376 U.S. 254 (1964), which said that a "public official" may not recover damages for defamation unless he could prove actual malice.

The main purpose of *Sullivan* was to protect the media from prosecution for seditious journalism criticizing official conduct. The Court held that *Sullivan* did not apply to public figures when the person claiming libel is not doing so in relation to criticism of government business. When the libel is of a personal nature and does not resemble sedition, a public figure can recover damages by showing highly unreasonable conduct. Proof of malice is not necessary.

In *Butts,* the Court held that the jury was justified in deciding that the magazine's investigation was grossly inadequate and therefore unreasonable. In *Walker,* the Court agreed with the trial court in overturning the jury's decision, because there was absolutely no evidence of negligence presented at trial.

United States v. Wade

388 U.S. 218 (1967)
Decided: June 12, 1967
Vote: 5 (Warren, Douglas, Clark, Brennan, Fortas)
4 (Black, Harlan II, Stewart, B. White)
Opinion of the Court: Brennan
Concurring opinion: Clark
Opinion concurring in part and dissenting in part: Fortas (Warren, Douglas)
Opinion concurring in part and dissenting in part: Black
Opinion concurring in part and dissenting in part: B. White (Harlan II, Stewart)

Billy Joe Wade was accused of robbing a bank and placed in an identification lineup. During the lineup he was required to wear tape on his face like the alleged robber had worn, and to say things that the robber had said. Two bank employees identified Wade as the robber. They testified against him at trial and identified him based on the lineup. Wade objected, claiming that the lineup violated his Fifth Amendment right against self-incrimination. He further argued that the absence of his lawyer at the lineup proceedings violated his Sixth Amendment right to counsel.

The Court held that participating in a lineup does not violate the Fifth Amendment rights of an accused. At the lineup Wade was only required to exhibit his body and his voice. He was not asked to provide any evidence of a testimonial nature. The Fifth Amendment protects an accused only against giving compelled testimony against himself, and appearing in a lineup does not violate that right.

The Court agreed that the accused had a right to have his attorney present at the lineup. The Sixth Amendment guarantees counsel not just at trial but also at any critical confrontations between the accused and the state's prosecutors. A lineup is a critical prosecutorial stage, and the accused must be protected from a false eyewitness or from eyewitnesses seeing him in custody before the proceedings. Here, the bank employees who identified Wade saw him in FBI custody before the lineup. Their identification was therefore inadmissible unless they could prove it was of independent origin or was harmless error.

Gilbert v. California

388 U.S. 263 (1967)
Decided: June 12, 1967
Vote: 6 (Warren, Black, Douglas, Clark, Brennan, Fortas)
3 (Harlan II, Stewart, B. White)
Opinion of the Court: Brennan
Concurring opinion: Douglas
Concurring opinion: Fortas (Warren)
Opinion concurring in judgment: Black
Dissenting opinion: B. White (Harlan II, Stewart)

Jesse James Gilbert was convicted in the Superior Court of California for robbing a bank and murdering a police officer. A jury sentenced him to death. His appeal was based on four pieces of evidence used against him, two of which the Court addressed. He first claimed that a handwriting sample taken from him and matched to a note given to the bank teller violated his Fifth Amendment right against self-incrimination. He also claimed constitutional error in the admission of an in-court identification against him that might have been tainted by an illegal lineup procedure.

The Supreme Court held that use of handwriting samples does not violate the Fifth Amendment because handwriting is not a compulsory communication. The Fifth Amendment applies only to communication, not physical evidence that has value outside of the words used. Furthermore, it was proper for Gilbert to give this handwriting sample without the presence of his attorney because it was not a critical stage in the proceedings.

The Court agreed with Gilbert that allowing an in-court identification, possibly tainted by an illegal lineup, was a constitutional error. It held, however, that the state should be given an opportunity to prove that the identification was proper before overturning the conviction. The conviction could be overturned if the California court found that the testimony given by people involved with the tainted lineup was not "harmless error."

Stovall v. Denno

388 U.S. 293 (1967)
Decided: June 12, 1967
Vote: 6 (Warren, Clark, Harlan II, Brennan, Stewart, B. White)
3 (Black, Douglas, Fortas)
Opinion of the Court: Brennan
Opinion concurring in judgment: B. White (Harlan II, Stewart)
Dissenting opinion: Black
Dissenting opinion: Douglas
Dissenting opinion: Fortas

Theodore Stovall allegedly stabbed Paul Behrendt to death in the kitchen of his home. He also stabbed Behrendt's wife eleven times, critically injuring her. Stovall left behind a shirt and a set of keys in the Behrendts' kitchen, and police arrested him the day after the murder. Before Stovall could retain an attorney, the police arranged for him to go to the hospital to be identified by the surviving Behrendt. Handcuffed to a police officer, Stovall was brought into her hospital room. He was the only black man in the room. She asked him to speak, then identified him as the man who killed her husband. Stovall was convicted by a New York state court and sentenced to death. He filed a federal habeas corpus petition to challenge Behrendt's identification, claiming that attending the confrontation without an attorney violated his Sixth Amendment right to counsel and his Fourteenth Amendment right to due process.

Regarding the Sixth Amendment, the Supreme Court held that, although the right to counsel applied to the confrontation stage of criminal proceedings, the right created by precedent cases could not be applied retroactively in this case. Retroactivity depends on whether the omission of counsel had an unfair effect on the outcome of the case. Right to counsel is important but not necessary for fundamental fairness, so the Court held that it did not apply retroactively.

The Court further held that under the totality of circumstances in this case, Stovall received his due process rights. Allowing a witness to confront a suspect alone, in other words, without counsel was usually frowned upon. Here, however, Behrendt was the only person who could exonerate Stovall. Furthermore, she could not go to the police station for a lineup, and police did not know how long she would survive her injuries.

Walker v. City of Birmingham

388 U.S. 307 (1967)
Decided: June 12, 1967
Vote: 5 (Black, Clark, Harlan II, Stewart, B. White)
4 (Warren, Douglas, Brennan, Fortas)
Opinion of the Court: Stewart
Dissenting opinion: Warren (Brennan, Fortas)
Dissenting opinion: Douglas (Warren, Brennan, Fortas)
Dissenting opinion: Brennan (Warren, Douglas, Fortas)

In response to civil rights demonstrations, officials in Birmingham, Alabama, filed a bill of complaint in state circuit court to obtain an injunction against individuals and organizations involved in the demonstrations. The circuit court granted a temporary injunction, but demonstrators vowed to disobey, characterizing the injunction as "raw tyranny" in violation of the First Amendment. Marches took place on Good Friday and Easter Sunday. Rev. Wyatt Tee Walker, along with eight organizers, including Martin Luther King Jr., Ralph Abernathy, and Fred Shuttlesworth, were arrested and charged with contempt of court. They maintained that the injunction violated their right to free speech, but the circuit judge found them guilty and sentenced them to jail. He explained that because the petitioners did not move to dismiss the injunction or obtain a marching permit in compliance with its requirements, they had no standing to challenge it at the contempt hearing.

On appeal, the issue before the Court was whether the Constitution compelled the demonstrators to violate the injunction without previous effort on their part to have the injunction dissolved or modified, and without effort to obtain a valid permit. The Court held that the demonstrators had a duty to challenge the injunction legally before violating it in protest. The city government had a legitimate interest in maintaining order on its public streets. Although it was likely that the injunction created by the city in response to this problem was overly broad and threatened a violation of the right to free speech, demonstrators erred by not challenging it before they disobeyed it. Furthermore, even if the injunction violated the rights of these particular demonstrators, that did not mean that it was void on its face. They should have sought individual action before claiming that the whole injunction was created in error.

Mempa v. Rhay

389 U.S. 128 (1967)
Decided: November 13, 1967
Vote: 9 (Warren, Black, Douglas, Harlan II, Brennan, Stewart, B. White, Fortas, T. Marshall)
0
Opinion of the Court: T. Marshall

Jerry Mempa was convicted in a Washington State court for the crime of "joyriding." At his trial, he was represented by a court-appointed attorney and pleaded guilty. He received two years' probation, but four months later a Washington prosecutor moved to have Mempa's probation revoked because he allegedly committed robbery. At his probation hearing, Mempa was not given an attorney. The trial court simultaneously revoked Mempa's probation and sentenced him to ten additional years in prison. Mempa filed a writ of habeas corpus in the Washington Supreme Court, claiming that the trial court had denied his Sixth Amendment right to counsel by hearing his probation motion without providing an attorney. The Washington Supreme Court denied his petition.

The Supreme Court held that the right to counsel extends to post-trial proceedings such as Mempa's probation hearing. In ***Gideon v. Wainwright,*** 372 U.S. 335 (1963), the Court acknowledged that all defendants have a right to an attorney. Although *Gideon* applied only to the trial phase of a hearing, its logic extended to post-trial hearings. Here, the judge at the probation hearing had the power to recommend to the probation board the length of time the defendant should serve in jail and to provide information about the circumstances of the crime and the defendant's character. Because the proceedings affected the amount of time a defendant was likely to serve, he required an attorney to point out important facts and introduce evidence about mitigating circumstances in an effort to get the best outcome for the client. Furthermore, an attorney is often necessary to preserve a defendant's right to appeal from post-trial hearings. Because provision of counsel was necessary at both trial and post-trial hearings, the Court reversed the state supreme court's dismissal of Mempa's petition.

United States v. Robel

389 U.S. 258 (1967)
Decided: December 11, 1967
Vote: 6 (Warren, Black, Douglas, Brennan, Stewart, Fortas)
2 (Harlan II, B. White)
Opinion of the Court: Warren
Opinion concurring in judgment: Brennan
Dissenting opinion: B. White (Harlan II)
Did not participate: T. Marshall

Eugene Frank Robel, a member of the Communist Party, was employed as a machinist at Todd Shipyard Corporation. In 1962 the secretary of defense declared Todd Shipyard Corporation to be a "defense facility" subject to the control of the Subversive Activities Control Act of 1950. The act specified in Section 5 (a)(1)(D) that it was against the law for any member of the Communist Party to "engage in any employment in a defense facility." Robel nevertheless stayed on the job, and in 1963 he was charged by a federal prosecutor with "unlawfully and willfully" continuing his employment despite the requirements of Section 5 (a)(1)(D). A district court dismissed Robel's indictment because he was not an active member in the party and never expressed specific intent to engage in subversive activity. The government appealed, claiming that Section 5 (a)(1)(D) should not be given such a narrow interpretation.

The Supreme Court not only affirmed the district court's dismissal of the indictment but also held that Section 5 (a)(1)(D) was an unconstitutional abridgment of the right of association protected by the First Amendment. The limited application of the district court could not save the statute from its overall constitutional infirmities. The statute was not limited on its face, and could be applied indiscriminately to all types of people associated with communist groups, even if they had no intention of subversion. Furthermore, the statute could not be construed as an exercise of Congress's war power, because war power does not extend to the infringement of essential liberties.

Katz v. United States

389 U.S. 347 (1967)
Decided: December 18, 1967
Vote: 7 (Warren, Douglas, Harlan II, Brennan, Stewart, B. White, Fortas)
1 (Black)
Opinion of the Court: Stewart
Concurring opinion: Douglas (Brennan)
Concurring opinion: Harlan II
Concurring opinion: B. White
Dissenting opinion: Black
Did not participate: T. Marshall

The Fourth Amendment expressed the Framers' opposition to the offensive practices of the British prior to the Revolution, and it governs how police may carry out one of their major responsibilities, gathering evidence during the investigation of crimes. The amendment sets limits on what the police may do, but recognizes the legitimacy of reasonable search and seizure and does not erect insurmountable obstacles to that process. To secure a warrant, investigating officers need to show "probable cause" and spell out with some precision the places to be searched and the type of evidence sought.

Technology gave rise to new questions about what constitutes a search. In ***Olmstead v. United States,*** 277 U.S. 438 (1928), the Court held that a wiretap did not constitute a search because no actual entry was made into the house. That decision evoked one of Justice Brandeis's most powerful dissents, in which he set forth the argument for a constitutionally based right to privacy. According to Brandeis, even though no one entered the man's house, his privacy had been invaded, which violated the intent of the Fourth Amendment. The Court reaffirmed the notion of the Fourth Amendment requiring an actual physical intrusion in *Silverman v. United States,* 365 U.S. 505 (1961). In *Katz v. United States* the Supreme Court overruled *Olmstead* and adopted the view of Justice Brandeis.

At Charles Katz's trial for bookmaking, the government introduced wiretap evidence of his part in a number of conversations the police obtained by putting a listening device on a phone booth Katz frequently used. The lower court upheld the use of such evidence, because the walls of the booth had not been physically penetrated. The Supreme Court reversed, and Justice Stewart's opinion stated that the Fourth Amendment protects people, not places. If a person had an expectation of privacy in a particular setting, whether a house or a phone booth, then the style of the intrusion did not matter.

Stewart's opinion sounded the proper tone, but it was Justice Harlan's concurrence that gave lower courts the guidance they needed in implementing *Katz.* "There is a twofold requirement, first that a person has exhibited an actual (subjective) expectation of privacy and, second, that the expectation be one that society is prepared to recognize as 'reasonable,' " Harlan declared.

Wiretaps are still a common method of police investigation, but since *Katz* warrants are required, and police must submit the same type of probable cause evidence in a wiretap application as they would for a regular search warrant.

See Fred Graham, *The Due Process Revolution: The Warren Court's Impact on Criminal Law* (New York: Hayden, 1970); and Alan F. Westin, *Privacy and Freedom* (New York: Atheneum, 1967).

Sims v. Georgia

389 U.S. 404 (1967)
Decided: December 18, 1967
Vote: 9 (Warren, Black, Douglas, Harlan II, Brennan, Stewart, B. White, Fortas, T. Marshall)
0
Opinion: *Per curiam*

This case was making its second appearance before the U.S. Supreme Court and is indicative of the problems the Court had in imposing not only higher constitutional standards for criminal procedure in general but also in getting those standards applied in cases involving black defendants. Sims was indicted for raping a white woman; a jury convicted him based in part on his confession to the crime; and the trial judge sentenced him to death. On appeal Sims claimed that his confession had been physically coerced and that the jury trying him had been discriminatorily selected.

The Supreme Court remanded the first case, *Sims v. Georgia,* 385 U.S. 538 (1966), back to the trial court with specific standards to evaluate whether the confession was voluntary and directing it to show that the jury selection was nondiscriminatory. The Court noted that the state had not produced as witnesses the police officers who were present at the time the defendant claimed he was physically maltreated and therefore the state had failed to rebut his claim of physical abuse. Nor had the state shown that the jury had been fairly selected, since the proportion of blacks on the tax rolls—the source for jury selection—was much higher than the proportion of blacks on the jury lists. The state had produced only a jury commissioner's testimony that he did not discriminate in compiling the lists. Following the Supreme Court's remand, the judge who had presided at Sims's first trial, without hearing any further testimony, decided that the confession was voluntary and that Georgia law governed the matter; he refused to decide other issues and denied Sims a new trial. The Georgia Supreme Court affirmed.

In a unanimous *per curiam* opinion indicating its anger at the lower courts, the Supreme Court reversed and remanded the case to the court below, holding that the trial judge had not determined the voluntariness of the confession under proper standards and that the defendant was indicted and tried by juries from which members of his race had been unconstitutionally excluded. In effect, it ordered a new trial and served notice that southern courts that attempted to continue blatant discrimination against black defendants could assume that these results would be closely scrutinized by federal courts.

See Otis H. Stephens, *The Supreme Court and Confessions of Guilt* (Knoxville: University of Tennessee Press, 1973).

Marchetti v. United States

390 U.S. 39 (1968)
Decided: January 29, 1968
Vote: 7 (Black, Douglas, Harlan II, Brennan, Stewart, B. White, Goldberg)
1 (Warren)
Opinion of the Court: Harlan II
Concurring opinion: Brennan
Concurring opinion: Stewart
Dissenting opinion: Warren
Did not participate: T. Marshall

James "Toto" Marchetti and his associates ran an illegal gambling business. Marchetti was convicted in federal district court of conspiring to evade payment of federal wagering taxes and willfully failing to register his business for tax purposes. He challenged the tax laws under which he was convicted, claiming that their requirements forced him to admit illegal activities in violation of the Fifth Amendment. The statutes required him to pay taxes on all of the illegal bets he took as part of his business and to register his business for tax purposes, alerting state and federal authorities to the illegal activities taking place.

The Court held that federal wagering tax laws violated the Fifth Amendment by forcing taxpayers to incriminate themselves. Connecticut, where Marchetti was convicted, had laws against betting. Law enforcement officials in the state were free to use wagering tax records and registries to enforce penalties against people conducting illegal gambling in the state. In fact, such evidence had been used in Connecticut to convict other gamblers. For these reasons the Court found that the tax requirements posed a "real and appreciable" risk of self-incrimination. In the opinion, the Court overruled two prior cases that had permitted gambling registration, *United States v. Kahriger,* 345 U.S. 22 (1953), and *Lewis v. United States,* 348 U.S. 419 (1955).

The Court did not agree with the federal government that the tax statutes fell under the "required records" exception to the Fifth Amendment privilege. In *Shapiro v. United States,* 335 U.S. 1 (1948), the Court had held that public records required by law could not "self-incriminate" their owner because they did not demand specific admissions of wrongdoing. The wagering tax laws, however, were not customary records, but required Marchetti to keep track of information he might not otherwise record. Furthermore, the records in *Shapiro* had been used for regulatory, noncriminal purposes, whereas these tax statutes targeted illegal activity.

Ginsberg v. New York

390 U.S. 629 (1968)
Decided: April 22, 1968
Vote: 6 (Warren, Harlan II, Brennan, Stewart, White, T. Marshall)
3 (Black, Douglas, Fortas)
Opinion of the Court: Brennan
Concurring opinion: Harlan II
Concurring opinion: Stewart
Dissenting opinion: Douglas (Black)
Dissenting opinion: Fortas
Harlan opinion is found in *Interstate Circuit Inc. v. Dallas,* 390 U.S. 676 (1968).

Sam Ginsberg operated a luncheonette and stationery store. He was convicted of selling "girlie" magazines to minors in violation of a New York law that, on the basis of harm to minors, made it illegal to sell to them any picture depicting nudity or any magazine containing such pictures. His conviction was affirmed by an intermediate appellate court, and his appeal to the state's highest court was denied.

The Warren Court had been wrestling with obscenity cases for more than a decade, but this case proved relatively easy. In the other cases, even when a majority reversed a conviction for selling pornography, the justices had been unable to come up with a consistent rationale to explain their decision. In some of the cases, the Court issued a *per curiam* opinion indicating that a majority favored reversal but could not agree on the reasoning. In *Ginsberg v. New York* the justices had a useful rationale: the law was aimed at protecting juveniles, a responsibility often associated with a state's police powers. The majority, therefore, did not have to deal with whether the work involved was obscene because that question was not even before the Court; Ginsberg had made no challenge to his conviction on that ground. The justices simply needed to decide whether New York's obligation to protect children provided the necessary compelling state interest to justify a regulation of expression.

In his majority opinion, Justice Brennan held that the state traditionally had an obligation to protect the welfare and morals of minors and that this responsibility gave the state greater leeway in intruding into areas that would otherwise be protected by the First Amendment. As for the freedom of expression of the minors themselves (Ginsberg argued that minors had the freedom to read this material), Brennan held that such content fell outside the area of free expression that the Constitution guaranteed to minors. Finally, the Court held that the provisions defining obscenity "harmful to minors" was not unconstitutionally vague.

Justice Douglas, joined by Justice Black, dissented, repeating his belief that even obscene material was protected by the constitutional guarantee of freedom of speech and press. He said a constitutional amendment would be required to achieve the result reached by the Court. Justice Fortas dissented on the ground that the Court should have determined whether the magazines were obscene and that the defendant should not be convicted for selling magazines which are presumably not obscene.

See Harry M. Clor, *Obscenity and Public Morality: Censorship in a Liberal Society* (Chicago: University of Chicago Press, 1969); and Harry Kalven, *A Worthy Tradition: Freedom of Speech in America* (New York: Harper and Row, 1988).

Duncan v. Louisiana

391 U.S. 145 (1968)
Decided: May 20, 1968
Vote: 7 (Warren, Black, Douglas, Brennan, B. White, Fortas, T. Marshall)
2 (Harlan II, Stewart)
Opinion of the Court: B. White
Concurring opinion: Black (Douglas)
Concurring opinion: Fortas
Dissenting opinion: Harlan II (Stewart)
Fortas opinion is found in *Bloom v. Illinois,* 391 U.S. 194 (1968).

Gary Duncan was convicted of simple battery, a misdemeanor that under Louisiana law could be punished by no more than two years' imprisonment and a $300 fine. Duncan was tried without a jury, found guilty, and sentenced to sixty days in prison and a fine of $150. His request for a jury trial had been denied because Louisiana allowed jury trials only in cases in which the judge could impose either the death penalty or imprisonment at hard labor.

The Supreme Court reversed. In an opinion by Justice White, the Court held that trial by jury in criminal cases is fundamental to the American scheme of justice and, therefore, the Fourteenth Amendment guaranteed the right to a jury trial in all criminal cases that—were they to be tried in a federal court—would come within the Sixth Amendment's guarantee of a jury trial. Moreover, a crime punishable by two years in prison constitutes a serious crime, not a petty offense. Petty offenses, the Court held, do not require a trial by jury.

The case marked the "incorporation" of the jury trial provision of the Sixth Amendment so that, under the Due Process Clause of the Fourteenth Amendment, it applied to the states. It was also was one of the final steps in the Warren Court's so-called "due process revolution," in which guarantees of fairness in criminal trials were imposed upon the states.

See Fred Graham, *The Due Process Revolution: The Warren Court's Impact on Criminal Law* (New York: Hayden, 1970).

Amalgamated Food Employees Union Local 590 v. Logan Valley Plaza

391 U.S. 308 (1968)
Decided: May 20, 1968
Vote: 6 (Warren, Douglas, Brennan, Stewart, Fortas, T. Marshall)
3 (Black, Harlan II, B. White)
Opinion of the Court: T. Marshall
Concurring opinion: Douglas
Dissenting opinion: Black
Dissenting opinion: Harlan II
Dissenting opinion: B. White

Weis Markets operated a supermarket, employing nonunion workers, in a large shopping center complex owned by the Logan Valley Plaza. Members of the Amalgamated Food Employees Union picketed Weis's store, confining the picketing almost entirely to a parcel pickup zone and the parking area adjacent to it. The picketing was peaceful, although there was some congestion of the parcel pickup area. The operators of the mall sought an injunction against the picketing, claiming that the mall and the parking areas were private property and that union members had no right to picket there. A Pennsylvania state court agreed and issued an injunction on the grounds that it was necessary both to protect private property rights and because the picketing was unlawfully aimed at coercing Weis to compel its employees to join a union. The Pennsylvania Supreme Court affirmed the injunction on the sole ground that the picketers' conduct constituted a trespass on private property.

Under precedents dating back into the 1920s, the Court had held that public streets and sidewalks were appropriate places for picketing and leafleting. To uphold the Pennsylvania court would, therefore, create a more property-conscious rule for the suburbs than existed in the city, and this the Court refused to do. "Business enterprises located in downtown areas would be subject to on-the-spot public criticism of their practices," Justice Marshall wrote, "but businesses situated in the suburbs could largely immunize themselves from similar criticism by creating a cordon sanitaire of parking lots around their stores." The Court's opinion held that because the shopping center served as a community business block and was freely open and accessible to the public, the state could not delegate power, through the use of its trespass laws, to exclude people wishing to exercise their First Amendment rights in a manner and for a purpose that was normally permitted on public streets. The state's generally valid rules against trespass to private property, therefore, could not be applied here to bar the union from the premises of the shopping center and supermarket.

The decision's significance lies in the Court's expansive view of what constituted a public forum. Until this point most of the cases had resulted from disputes in cities, where public thoroughfares had traditionally been considered public forums. The Court recognized that although suburbs may look different, it was the functional use and not the geographic arrangement that mattered.

United States v. O'Brien

391 U.S. 367 (1968)
Decided: May 27, 1968
Vote: 7 (Warren, Black, Harlan II, Brennan, Stewart, White, Fortas)
1 (Douglas)
Opinion of the Court: Warren
Concurring opinion: Harlan II
Dissenting opinion: Douglas
Did not participate: T. Marshall

As an expression of his strong beliefs against U.S. involvement in Vietnam, David O'Brien burned his draft card before a sizable crowd at an antiwar demonstration. He was indicted, tried, and convicted for violating the section of the Universal Military Training and Service Act, as amended in 1965, that applied to any person "who forges, alters, knowingly destroys, knowingly mutilates, or in any manner changes any such certificate." The district court rejected O'Brien's argument that the amendment was unconstitutional because it was enacted to abridge free speech and served no legitimate legislative purpose. The court of appeals, however, held the amendment unconstitutional under the First Amendment because it singled out for special treatment persons engaged in protests. After all, according to the court of appeals, conduct under the 1965 amendment was already punishable because a Selective Service System regulation required registrants to keep their draft cards in their "personal possession at all times," and willful violation of regulations was made criminal by another section.

The Supreme Court reversed the court of appeals and reinstated the conviction and sentence of the district court. Chief Justice Warren's opinion held that the statute was constitutional both on its face and as applied and could not properly be attacked on the ground that Congress intended it to suppress freedom of speech. Although the Warren Court had significantly expanded the meaning of "speech" to include action in certain circumstances, here it held that the burning of the draft card was primarily action, not speech. Moreover, with the responsibility to raise an army, Congress had a legitimate interest in having every draft-age male carry a card.

Justice Douglas, the only member of the Court who wanted his colleagues to take up the issue of the constitutionality of the Vietnam War, dissented, and urged the Court to restore the case to the calendar for reargument on the question of the constitutionality of a peacetime draft.

Green v. County School Board of New Kent County

391 U.S. 430 (1968)
Decided: May 27, 1968
Vote: 9 (Warren, Black, Douglas, Harlan II, Brennan, Stewart, B. White, Fortas, T. Marshall)
0
Opinion of the Court: Brennan

In 1968 the Court decided its last "easy" school desegregation case, one in which the justices took a significant new step in interpreting the constitutional mandate. *Green v. County School Board* involved a "freedom of choice" plan that supposedly allowed students of either race to attend whatever school they wanted. Local officials in predominantly rural New Kent County, Virginia, adopted the plan after passage of the Civil Rights Act of 1964 threatened the county with the loss of federal monies. They defended the plan as a good faith effort to comply with ***Brown v. Board of Education,*** 337 U.S. 483 (1954), but critics charged that it discouraged blacks from attending white schools and had little overall effect. After three years, not one white child had chosen to attend Watkins High, a formerly all-black school, and only 115 black students attended New Kent High, the formerly all-white school; 85 percent of the black students in the county still went to all-black schools. New Kent County was not an aberration: fourteen years after *Brown,* segregated schools continued to be the rule in most of the country, North and South. To force a true desegregation of the New Kent County schools, Calvin and Mary Green brought suit on behalf of their three school-age children, along with other black parents.

Speaking for the Court, Justice Brennan declared that, henceforth, results, not good intentions, would be the mark of an acceptable plan. In addition, the Court took the unusual step of indicating specific proposals that would be acceptable, such as dividing the county geographically, with all students living in each half attending the schools in that half.

Green was "easy" in the sense that it marked the last case dealing with a school system in which black students had been segregated on the basis of law or of easily perceived racial discrimination. The freedom of choice plan struck down in this case, and which lower courts overturned in similar situations, had been designed specifically to avoid the *Brown* mandate. The case also marked the end of what may be called the first phase of school desegregation, in which the Court, following its initial pronouncements, showed a willingness to allow the states and localities to work things out, to accept tokens of good faith in the hope that a gradualist approach would work in the end.

The case is also important because the opinion redefined the substantive right enshrined in *Brown.* Under a formalistic reading of *Brown,* school systems could meet their constitutional obligations by simply removing legally imposed school assignments based on race, and, for a while, this was actually the plan endorsed by the NAACP. What Brennan recognized in *Green* is that such plans placed a heavy burden on black children; in short, freedom of choice plans could not work. From now on, the Court said, schools had to do their best to make the school population in each school reflect the overall school population. Schools were now obliged to take positive steps to ensure not only the end of segregation but also the beginning of true integration.

See Henry J. Abraham, *Freedom and the Court: Civil Rights and Liberties in the United States,* 6th ed. (New York: Oxford University Press, 1994); Richard Kluger, *Simple Justice* (New York: Knopf, 1976); and Harvard Sitkoff, *The Struggle for Black Equality, 1954–1992,* rev. ed. (New York: Hill and Wang, 1993).

Witherspoon v. Illinois

391 U.S. 510 (1968)
Decided: June 3, 1968
Vote: 6 (Warren, Douglas, Brennan, Stewart, Fortas, T. Marshall)
3 (Black, Harlan II, B. White)
Opinion of the Court: Stewart
Concurring opinion: Douglas
Dissenting opinion: Black (Harlan II, B. White)
Dissenting opinion: B. White

William C. Witherspoon was found guilty of murder, and the jury fixed his penalty at death. An Illinois statute provided for challenges for cause in murder trials "of any juror who shall, on being examined, state that he has conscientious scruples against capital punishment, or that he is opposed to the same." At Witherspoon's trial, the prosecution eliminated forty-seven prospective jurors, nearly half of the venire list, by challenging all who expressed qualms about the death penalty. Most of the veniremen challenged for cause were excluded with no effort to find out whether their scruples would invariably compel them to vote against capital punishment. The Illinois Supreme Court denied postconviction relief, and Witherspoon appealed. The Supreme Court accepted the case to decide whether the Constitution permits a state to carry out a death sentence imposed by a jury made up entirely of people who either approve of capital punishment or do not oppose it.

The Court reversed the penalty, but not Witherspoon's conviction for murder. In an opinion by Justice Stewart, the Court held that a jury from which all veniremen having conscientious scruples against or opposition to capital punishment had been excluded, without their having an opportunity to state whether they would automatically vote against the imposition of the death penalty no matter what the trial revealed, fell short of the impartiality to which petitioner was entitled under the Sixth and Fourteenth Amendments. The state, Stewart implied, had stacked the deck against the defendant. Under these circumstances, the execution of the death sentence would deprive the petitioner of his life without due process of law.

The majority's feelings were so strong on the subject that in an unusual move the Court made the holding fully retroactive in application. Normally, when the Court hands down a constitutional ruling, it applies only to the specific case before it and is to be applied in the future. The Court does not make the ruling retroactive because of the great confusion that might cause, especially in the criminal justice system, where thousands, or perhaps tens of thousands, of new appeals might overwhelm the courts. But a life was at stake here, and the number of prisoners to whom it might apply was, in the Court's opinion, manageable.

Justice Douglas, who by this time had moved away from his earlier support for the death penalty and toward a position of believing it a violation of the Eighth Amendment ban against cruel and unusual punishment, wrote in a separate opinion that he believed no distinction should be made between those veniremen who merely voice scruples against capital punishment and those who are so opposed to the death sentence that they would never inflict it on a defendant. He also thought Witherspoon's guilty verdict should be reversed.

Justice Black, joined by Justices Harlan and White, dissented on the ground that the state should not be forced to accept jurors who are bound to be biased against one of the critical issues in a trial. White, in a separate opinion, expressed the view that the constitutional grounds provided in the opinion were inadequate to support the Court's holding. Both dissents were impassioned; and, if Stewart indicated that the old system stacked the deck against the defendants, they believed the new system crippled the state. As Black wrote, "If this Court is to hold capital punishment unconstitutional, it should do so forthrightly, not by making it impossible for the States to get juries that will enforce the death penalty."

Advocates of a strong law-and-order system reacted to the decision by lumping it with other Warren-era opinions they condemned as favoring the criminal and crippling the police and prosecutors. In fact, the majority opinion did not say that the state had to accept as a juror someone who stated that under no circumstances would he or she vote for the death penalty. Rather, the jury had to reflect the population, in which people may have qualms about the death penalty but who, given particular circumstances, would vote for it.

See Welsh S. White, "Witherspoon Revisited: Exploring the Tension Between Witherspoon and Furman," *University of Cincinnati Law Review* 45 (1976): 19.

Terry v. Ohio

392 U.S. 1 (1968)
Decided: June 10, 1968
Vote: 8 (Warren, Black, Harlan II, Brennan, Stewart, B. White, Fortas, T. Marshall)
1 (Douglas)
Opinion of the Court: Warren
Concurring opinion: Black
Concurring opinion: Harlan II
Concurring opinion: B. White
Dissenting opinion: Douglas

Officer Martin McFadden, dressed in plainclothes, was patrolling a section of downtown Cleveland one afternoon when he noticed two men who, he explained later, "didn't look right to me at the time." The two men, John Terry and Richard Chilton, kept walking up and down past a certain store, and McFadden suspected them of "casing" the store. When a third man joined them, McFadden decided to investigate further; he approached the three men, identified himself as a police officer, and asked their names. Terry "mumbled something" in response, and McFadden grabbed him, spun him around between himself and the other two men, and patted down his outer clothing. He felt a pistol on Terry and then one on Chilton, seized their weapons, and arrested them.

The defendants tried to suppress evidence of the guns, claiming that McFadden had not patted them down in a search incident to an arrest and that he had no probable cause to stop them. The trial court and the Supreme Court upheld McFadden's actions. He had been a policeman for thirty-nine years, a detective for thirty-five, and during that time he had built up instincts and habits based on experience. To deny the public the benefit of that experience would be foolish, declared Chief Justice Warren, and would hamper the police in their work. In addition, police officers had the right to take reasonable measures to ensure their own safety.

The "stop-and-frisk" decision is a good indication of the Warren Court's philosophy. In situations involving private quarters or immobilized vehicles, where the evidence could not "walk away," the Court insisted that the police comply with regular warrant procedures. In on-the-street situations or when the police were in hot pursuit of a suspect, rigid application of constitutional rules could not be expected. In the Terry case the Court adopted what might be called a "rule of reason," which allowed police wide discretion provided they had some reasonable basis to support their action.

See Fred Graham, *The Due Process Revolution: The Warren Court's Impact on Criminal Law* (New York: Hayden, 1970); A. V. Leonard, *The Police, the Judiciary, and the Criminal,* 2d ed. (Springfield, Ill.: Thomas, 1975).

Sibron v. New York

392 U.S. 40 (1968)
Decided: June 10, 1968
Vote: 8 (Warren, Douglas, Harlan II, Brennan, Stewart, B. White, Fortas, T. Marshall)
1 (Black)
Opinion of the Court: Warren
Concurring opinion: B. White
Opinion concurring in judgment: Douglas
Opinion concurring in judgment: B. White
Opinion concurring in judgment: Fortas
Opinion concurring in part and dissenting in part: Black

This case consolidated two appeals from the New York Court of Appeals, companion cases to ***Terry v. Ohio,*** 392 U.S. 1 (1968), decided the same day. In the first case, New York police officers observed Nelson Sibron talking to known drug dealers. Although the police did not hear any discussion of drugs and did not see anything change hands, they ordered Sibron to leave the restaurant he was sitting in. Outside, a police officer put his hand in Sibron's pocket and found a bag of heroin. At trial, Sibron moved to suppress the heroin as the fruit of a warrantless and unjustified search and arrest, but the evidence was admitted and he was convicted. In the second case, a woman heard noise outside her apartment door, saw two strangers through her peephole, and called the police. They arrived and questioned John Francis Peters, who was in the hallway of the apartment building. He offered no explanation for his presence, and the police patted him down for a weapon. They found an object they thought was a knife, but it turned out to be a box of burglar's tools. At trial, the box was admitted as evidence against Peters despite his objection.

Both petitioners appealed, challenging New York's "stop-and-frisk" rule that allowed police officers to stop suspicious-looking individuals on the street and frisk them for weapons. The Court declined to decide the constitutionality of the statute, however, because both cases could be decided based on the Fourth Amendment. The Court reversed Sibron's conviction, saying the evidence used against him was not justified as incident to a lawful arrest because the police had no probable cause to arrest him. The officers also had no reason to believe Sibron was dangerous, so searching his pockets was unjustified. The Court upheld Peters's conviction, finding his arrest justified by his suspicious activity.

Flast v. Cohen

392 U.S. 83 (1968)
Decided: June 10, 1968
Vote: 8 (Warren, Black, Douglas, Brennan, Stewart, B. White, Fortas, T. Marshall)
1 (Harlan II)
Opinion of the Court: Warren
Concurring opinion: Douglas
Concurring opinion: Stewart
Concurring opinion: Fortas
Dissenting opinion: Harlan II

The Elementary and Secondary Education Act of 1965 provided massive amounts of federal aid to public, private, and parochial schools. Florence Flast and other taxpayers filed suit in New York to challenge the law's provisions regarding aid to religious schools. They claimed that the government's expenditures were unconstitutional because the provision of books and resources to church-related schools constituted a law respecting the establishment of religion. The trial court dismissed the complaint on the grounds that the taxpayers lacked standing to bring suit.

In 1923 the Court had held in ***Massachusetts v. Mellon,*** 262 U.S. 447, that taxpayers lacked standing to bring claims against congressional spending that they disapproved.

The Court said that *Massachusetts v. Mellon* was not binding in *Flast,* holding instead that taxpayers could achieve standing to sue in some cases. The Court created a two-prong test to determine when taxpayers could bring suit in federal court. First, the taxpayer must establish a logical link between his or her status and the type of legislative enactment attacked. In other words, the issue had to be related to spending and the use of money contributed by the taxpayer to the federal system. Second, the taxpayer must establish a nexus between his or her taxpayer status and the precise nature of the constitutional infringement alleged. An attack based on Congress's Article I powers was not sufficient. Rather, a specific constitutional infringement had to be proven.

Here, the taxpayers satisfied both prongs. The statute under attack involved congressional spending, and the spending violated not only Congress's general powers but also the Establishment Clause of the First Amendment. The Court therefore held that the taxpayers had standing to sue.

Board of Education of Central School District No. 1 v. Allen

392 U.S. 236 (1968)
Decided: June 10, 1968
Vote: 6 (Warren, Harlan II, Brennan, Stewart, B. White, T. Marshall)
3 (Black, Douglas, Fortas)
Opinion of the Court: B. White
Concurring opinion: Harlan II
Dissenting opinion: Black
Dissenting opinion: Douglas
Dissenting opinion: Fortas

New York required local school boards to lend textbooks to all students in grades seven to twelve, including students in private and parochial schools. In districts that had significant numbers of students attending parochial schools, this requirement placed a heavy financial burden on the public schools. Several local boards of education challenged the law as a violation of the Establishment Clause because public funds were used to benefit religious institutions. A trial court agreed and entered summary judgment for the local boards. On appeal the state's highest court ruled that because the law was designed to benefit all students, whether they attended public, private, or parochial schools, and because only texts approved by the public school authorities could be loaned, the law did not violate either the New York or the U.S. Constitution. The statute, the state court held, was "completely neutral with respect to religion."

The Supreme Court affirmed the judgment of the New York Court of Appeals. In an opinion by Justice White, the majority held that the constitutional provisions concerning the establishment and free exercise of religion were not violated because the statute merely made available to all children the benefits of a general program to lend schoolbooks free of charge. No funds or books were furnished to parochial schools; the books were lent directly to students, and the financial benefit was to the parents and children, not to schools. Only secular books, not religious books, could receive approval for loans, and the statute did not in any way coerce individuals in the practice of their religion. The rationale in many ways derived from the child benefit first articulated by Justice Black in ***Everson v. Board of Education,*** 330 U.S. 1 (1947).

Justices Black, Douglas, and Fortas, each dissenting in a separate opinion, would have held the New York statute unconstitutional as a law respecting the establishment of religion.

King v. Smith

392 U.S. 309 (1968)
Decided: June 17, 1968
Vote: 9 (Warren, Black, Douglas, Harlan II, Brennan, Stewart, B. White, Fortas, T. Marshall)
0
Opinion of the Court: Warren
Concurring opinion: Douglas

Alabama, like every other state and U.S. territory, participated in the federal government's Aid to Families with Dependent Children Program (AFDC). The state's Department of Pensions and Security issued a so-called "substitute father" regulation that denied AFDC payments to children of a mother who "cohabits" in or outside her home with any single or married man. A class action suit in federal court won an injunction against the new regulation, and Alabama appealed the ruling.

The Supreme Court affirmed. In an opinion by Chief Justice Warren, the Court held that the Alabama regulation was invalid because it conflicted with the AFDC provisions of the Social Security Act and other federal policies. Warren ruled that the state's asserted interest in discouraging illicit sexual behavior and illegitimacy did not constitute sufficient grounds to nullify federal policy. Justice Douglas concurred on the ground that the regulation violated the Equal Protection Clause of the Fourteenth Amendment.

Epperson v. Arkansas

393 U.S. 97 (1968)
Decided: November 12, 1968
Vote: 9 (Warren, Black, Douglas, Harlan II, Brennan, Stewart, B. White, Fortas, T. Marshall)
0
Opinion of the Court: Fortas
Concurring opinion: Black
Concurring opinion: Harlan II
Concurring in judgment opinion: Stewart

One of the most famous battlegrounds of the 1920s between the forces of tradition and modernism was the Scopes "Monkey Trial" in Dayton, Tennessee. A young biology teacher, John Scopes, was convicted of violating a state law by teaching Darwin's theory of evolution in his high school biology class. The Tennessee Supreme Court reversed the conviction on a technicality, which forestalled any appeal to the Supreme Court. The law remained on the Tennessee statute books, however, and similar laws could be found in other Bible Belt states. These laws remained unenforced and in many cases nearly forgotten.

In Arkansas, a 1928 statute forbade teachers in state schools from teaching the "theory or doctrine that mankind ascended or descended from a lower order of animals." An Arkansas biology teacher, Susan Epperson, sought a declaratory judgment on the constitutionality of the statute. The Arkansas Supreme Court, aware of anti-evolution sentiment within the state, evaded the constitutional issue entirely, by expressing "no opinion" on "whether the Act prohibits any explanation of the theory of evolution or merely prohibits teaching that the theory is true."

On either ground the law ran afoul of the Constitution. Without a dissenting vote, the Court struck down the Arkansas statute as a violation of the Establishment Clause. Justice Fortas concluded that the Arkansas law "selects from the body of knowledge a particular segment which it proscribes for the sole reason that it is deemed to conflict with a particular religious doctrine, that is, with a particular interpretation of the Book of Genesis by a particular religious group." The Court, having found what it considered a sufficiently narrow ground on which to rule, ignored the larger issues of academic freedom.

Justices Black and Stewart concurred in the result, though they considered the statute void for vagueness. In addition, Black's opinion raised some troubling questions that foreshadowed issues that would later come back to the Court. A state law, for example, that completely forbade all teaching of biology would be constitutionally different from one that compelled a teacher to teach that only a particular theory is true.

Black's most interesting point involved the question of whether the majority opinion actually achieved the constitutional desideratum of "religious neutrality." If the people of Arkansas considered the theory of evolution an attack on religion, did the Constitution nonetheless require the state to permit its teaching? Had the Court infringed "the religious freedom of those who consider evolution anti-religious doctrine?" Could a state law prohibiting the teaching of evolution be considered a neutral statute if it removed a contentious issue from the classroom? He saw no reason "why a State is without power to withdraw from its curriculum any subject deemed too emotional and controversial for its public schools."

Black's reasoning, or rather its obverse, proved the vehicle by which anti-evolutionists in Arkansas and elsewhere sought to bypass the *Epperson* ruling a generation later. Instead of removing biology and the evolutionary theory from the schools, they added so-called "creation science," and required that any school teaching evolution had to give "equal time" in the classroom to "creation science." Their solution was tested in ***Edwards v. Aguillard,*** 482 U.S. 578 (1987).

See Edward J. Larson, *Trial and Error: The American Controversy over Creation and Evolution* (New York: Oxford University Press, 1985); and Garry Wills, *Under God: Religion and American Politics* (New York: Simon and Schuster, 1990).

Presbyterian Church in United States v. Mary Elizabeth Blue Hull Memorial Presbyterian Church

393 U.S. 440 (1969)
Decided: January 27, 1969
Vote: 9 (Warren, Black, Douglas, Harlan II, Brennan, Stewart, B. White, Fortas, T. Marshall)
0
Opinion of the Court: Brennan
Concurring opinion: Harlan II

Two local Presbyterian churches in Savannah, Georgia, voted to withdraw from the Presbyterian Church in the United States because of doctrinal differences with the church at large. The local churches believed that the church at large had abandoned its faith and religious practices.

The dispute involved property rights to the land the two churches occupied. The church at large argued that the land belonged to it, and the local churches argued that they owned the land. Under Georgia law, a jury would have to decide whether there were violations of Presbyterian religious doctrines to determine who owned the property. The church at large argued that this sort of inquiry violated the First Amendment.

The Supreme Court held that no court may examine and rule on religious disputes within a church. As Justice Brennan explained, it is not the role of the government to enter into religious disputes. The Court ruled that the First Amendment prevents government interference with questions of ecclesiastical doctrine, and a court cannot award church property on the basis of interpreting church doctrine.

Tinker v. Des Moines Independent Community School District

393 U.S. 503 (1969)
Decided: February 24, 1969
Vote: 7 (Warren, Douglas, Brennan, Stewart, B. White, Fortas, T. Marshall)
2 (Black, Harlan II)
Opinion of the Court: Fortas
Concurring opinion: Stewart
Concurring opinion: B. White
Dissenting opinion: Black
Dissenting opinion: Harlan II

On December 16, 1965, Mary Beth Tinker, her brother John, and another student, Christopher Eckhardt, were sent home and then suspended from their respective schools in Des Moines, Iowa, for wearing black armbands to protest the U.S. government's policy in Vietnam. They went to court to seek an injunction against a school board regulation that banned the wearing of armbands. The district court dismissed the complaint on the ground that the regulation was within the school board's power, despite the absence of any finding of substantial interference with the conduct of school activities. The court of appeals, sitting *en banc,* affirmed by an equally divided court. With the help of the American Civil Liberties Union, Mary Beth Tinker appealed.

The U.S. Supreme Court reversed. In an opinion by Justice Fortas, the Court held that the wearing of armbands was entirely divorced from actual or potential disruptive conduct by those participating in it, and as such was closely akin to "pure speech," which is entitled to comprehensive protection under the First Amendment. The school regulation prohibiting students from wearing the armbands violated the students' rights of free speech under the First Amendment, and no evidence had been offered to show that the wearing of the armbands would substantially interfere with the work of the school or impinge upon the rights of other students. Rather, it appeared that the authorities' action was based upon nothing more than an urgent wish to avoid controversy that might result from the antiwar expression.

But, even if there had been a possibility of a disturbance, Fortas wrote, "Our history says that it is this sort of hazardous freedom—this kind of openness—that is the basis of our national strength." Students, who are in school to learn about democracy, do not abandon their rights as Americans when they pass through the schoolhouse door.

Justice Black dissented on the grounds that the Court arrogated to itself power that should reside in local school boards, and that it was up to the boards to decide what standards of discipline should prevail within school buildings and classes. Justice Harlan also dissented, saying that he would, in cases such as this, require those complaining to prove that a particular school measure was motivated by other than legitimate school concerns. He could find nothing in the record that impugned the good faith of the school board in promulgating the armband regulation.

The case was a high-water mark of the expansion of juvenile rights, and it followed directly from the concerns Fortas had expressed two years earlier in ***In re Gault,*** 387 U.S. 1 (1967). Although *Tinker* has never been overruled, subsequent decisions have tended to favor local school authorities in determining rules for governing school curriculum and conduct.

See Peter Irons, *The Courage of Their Convictions* (New York: Free Press, 1988), chap. 10; and John W. Johnson, *The Struggle for Student Rights: Tinker v. Des Moines and the 1960s* (Lawrence: University Press of Kansas, 1997).

Allen v. State Board of Elections

393 U.S. 544 (1969)
Decided: March 3, 1969
Vote: 7 (Warren, Douglas, Brennan, Stewart, B. White, Fortas, T. Marshall)
2 (Black, Harlan II)
Opinion of the Court: Warren
Concurring opinion: T. Marshall (Douglas)
Dissenting opinion: Black
Opinion concurring in part and dissenting in part: Harlan II

Mississippi passed three laws that adversely affected the voting rights of African Americans. One law changed district voting to county voting, which in essence was a gerrymandering move. Another law changed the office of county superintendent of education from an elected position to an appointed position. The third law made it more difficult to become a political candidate. In a case joined to this one, Virginia had also passed a law that changed the write-in ballot process, making it more difficult for black people to vote. Each of these laws adversely affected black voters' rights.

Under Section 5 of the Voting Rights Act of 1965, a person cannot be disenfranchised because of race. The issue in these cases was whether diluting the vote of a minority group violated the Voting Rights Act of 1965. The Court held that it did, saying that a state could neither prevent someone for voting because of race nor pass laws to dilute the vote of a group of people because of race.

See Steven F. Lawson, *Black Ballots: Voting Rights in the South, 1944–1969* (New York: Columbia University Press, 1976).

Gregory v. Chicago

394 U.S. 111 (1969)
Decided: March 10, 1969
Vote: 9 (Warren, Black, Douglas, Harlan II, Brennan, Stewart, B. White, Fortas, T. Marshall)
0
Opinion of the Court: Warren
Concurring opinion: Black (Douglas)
Concurring opinion: Douglas
Opinion concurring in judgment: Harlan II
Opinion concurring in judgment: Stewart (B. White)

Comedian and civil rights activist Dick Gregory and other demonstrators marched peacefully through the streets of Chicago protesting the city's refusal to desegregate its schools. The march made many onlookers angry, and they became violent. The police ordered the marchers to stop because of the unruly mobs forming, but the demonstrators refused. The police then arrested the demonstrators for disorderly conduct. After conviction, they appealed, claiming that police had violated their First Amendment right to assemble.

The Supreme Court agreed with the demonstrators that their First Amendment rights had been violated, even while ruling that demonstrators may be arrested for disobeying police orders. The Court found that the facts of this case showed that the demonstrators were actually arrested for protesting the continued segregation of Chicago's public schools and ruled that the First Amendment protects a peaceful march and peaceful demonstration.

Shuttlesworth v. Birmingham

394 U.S. 147 (1969)
Decided: March 10, 1969
Vote: 8 (Warren, Black, Douglas, Harlan II, Brennan, Stewart, B. White, Fortas)
0
Opinion of the Court: Stewart
Concurring opinion: Harlan II
Concurring in judgment without opinion: Black
Did not participate: T. Marshall

On Good Friday 1963, three black ministers, including Rev. Fred Shuttlesworth, led fifty-two African Americans out of a Birmingham church. They walked in orderly fashion, protesting the denial of civil rights to black people in Birmingham, Alabama. They marched on sidewalks and did not interfere with other pedestrians. Traffic was never obstructed. The marchers obeyed all pedestrian and traffic laws. A crowd of spectators began to follow them. The spectators began spilling out into the street, but streets and cars were never obstructed.

After walking four blocks, the marchers were arrested by the Birmingham police for not having a permit to assemble in public. The city was responsible for granting permits and could deny them. The marchers knew that if they had applied for a permit, it would have been denied. Therefore, the question in this case was whether the marchers' First Amendment rights of assembly and speech were violated by the permit requirement.

The Court ruled that the permit process was a prior restraint on speech and assembly in violation of the First Amendment, because the facts showed that it was unlikely that the city of Birmingham would allow African Americans to conduct a civil rights march. The Court also ruled that, to be constitutional, a permit process must be narrowly tailored with a compelling reason.

Kirkpatrick v. Preisler

394 U.S. 526 (1969)
Decided: April 7, 1969
Vote: 6 (Warren, Black, Douglas, Brennan, Fortas, T. Marshall)
3 (Harlan II, Stewart, B. White)
Opinion of the Court: Brennan
Opinion concurring in judgment: Fortas
Dissenting opinion: Harlan (Stewart)
Dissenting opinion: B. White

In 1967 Missouri redrew its voting districts to recognize the changes in its population. Federal law required that districts be drawn in such a way that one person's vote carried the same weight as another's, and Missouri created some districts with 420,000 people and other districts with 450,000 people. When compared with the entire population of Missouri, the discrepancy between districts was only a few percentage points. The Court was asked to determine how finely tuned voting districts had to be to comply with the federal guidelines.

The Court struck down the Missouri redistricting plan. It ruled that small population variances in voting districts are allowed only if they are unavoidable, there is a good faith effort to achieve absolute equality, or if there is a justification for the small amount of inequality. The Court found that Missouri did not satisfy any of these requirements. Although it found that there was no evidence of gerrymandering, Missouri was still required to draw its voting districts in a way that no person's vote was worth more than another's.

See Richard Cortner, *The Apportionment Cases* (Knoxville: University of Tennessee Press, 1970).

Stanley v. Georgia

394 U.S. 557 (1969)
Decided: April 7, 1969
Vote: 9 (Warren, Black, Douglas, Harlan II, Brennan, Stewart, B. White, Fortas, T. Marshall)
0
Opinion of the Court: T. Marshall
Concurring opinion: Black
Concurring opinion: Stewart (Brennan, B. White)

Police officers had a warrant to search Robert Stanley's home for evidence of alleged bookmaking activities. Instead, in his bedroom they found some films, which, after viewing, were deemed to be obscene. Stanley was arrested, indicted, tried, and convicted for "knowingly having possession of . . . obscene matter" in violation of a Georgia law. The Georgia Supreme Court affirmed, holding that it did not matter that Stanley had this material for his private use and did not intend to sell it. He appealed, contending that the Georgia obscenity statute was unconstitutional because it punished the private possession of obscene matter. Georgia, relying on ***Roth v. United States,*** 354 U.S. 476 (1957), responded that its law was valid on the ground that "obscenity is not within the area of constitutionally protected speech or press."

The Supreme Court reversed. Justice Marshall held that the Georgia statute was unconstitutional under the First and Fourteenth Amendments. He ignored the Court's earlier rationales in *Roth* and other cases that obscene material lacked First Amendment protection. Rather, he treated as a regular First Amendment in case in which the state had a heavy burden of justifying its action. "While it may be a noble purpose," Marshall wrote, to protect someone from bad thoughts, "it is wholly inconsistent with the philosophy of the First Amendment."

Justice Stewart, joined by Brennan and White, also concurred in the result, but would have reversed the conviction on the ground, disregarded by the Court, that the films had been seized in violation of the Fourth and Fourteenth Amendments, and hence were inadmissible in evidence at the defendant's trial.

The case is considered one of the important decisions in developing a constitutionally protected right to privacy. "If the First Amendment means anything," Marshall wrote, "it means that a State has no business telling a man, sitting alone in his own house, what books he may read or what films he may watch. Our whole constitutional heritage rebels at the thought of giving government the power to control men's minds."

See David Lowenthal, *No Liberty for License: The Forgotten Logic of the First Amendment* (Dallas: Spence Publishers,1997), part II; and David Richards, "Free Speech and Obscenity Law: Toward a Moral Theory of the First Amendment," *University of Pennsylvania Law Review* 123 (1974): 45.

Street v. New York

394 U.S. 576 (1969)
Decided: April 21, 1969
Vote: 5 (Douglas, Harlan II, Brennan, Stewart, T. Marshall)
4 (Warren, Black, B. White, Fortas)
Opinion of the Court: Harlan II
Dissenting opinion: Warren
Dissenting opinion: Black
Dissenting opinion: B. White
Dissenting opinion: Fortas

After civil rights leader James Meredith was shot by a sniper in Mississippi, Sidney Street took an American flag to a New York street corner and set it on fire in protest. A small crowd gathered on the corner while the flag was burning. When a police officer arrived, Street admitted to burning the flag. Street also yelled out to the police officer, "If they did that to Meredith, we don't need an American flag," and he said to the crowd, "We don't need no damn flag." Street was convicted for violating a New York law outlawing the mutilation of the American flag, either by words or by actions. In his appeal Street argued that the law was a violation of First Amendment rights.

The Court overruled the conviction. Justice Harlan explained that punishing Street for speaking out against the American flag violated his First Amendment free speech rights. The Court found that in Street's protest against alleged government inaction in connection with the assassination attempt against James Meredith, his words were an essential element. If he had not spoken, no one would have known the reason for his protest. Thus, the Court found that Street was really being punished for his speech and message against the American flag, not for merely burning the flag.

The Court did not go so far as to rule that flag burning by itself was protected. That occurred some years later in ***Texas v. Johnson,*** 491 U.S. 397 (1989), and was reaffirmed in ***United States v. Eichman,*** 496 U.S. 310 (1990).

Shapiro v. Thompson

394 U.S. 618 (1969)
Decided: April 21, 1969
Vote: 6 (Douglas, Brennan, Stewart, B. White, Fortas, T. Marshall)
3 (Warren, Black, Harlan II)
Opinion of the Court: Brennan
Concurring opinion: Stewart
Dissenting opinion: Warren (Black)
Dissenting opinion: Harlan II

Many states had mandatory residency periods, usually one year, before people moving into the state could apply for welfare assistance or other forms of state aid. The states believed that such provisions were needed to protect the fiscal integrity of the programs and to prevent them from becoming "dumping grounds" for indigents moving from poor states with minimal welfare benefits to richer states with more generous programs. In addition, the states believed that Congress had approved the imposition of one-year requirements in Section 402(b) of the Social Security Act. These provisions had been challenged by people denied benefits in Connecticut, Pennsylvania, and the District of Columbia, and this case combined appeals from lower court decisions that invalidated the waiting periods on Fourteenth Amendment equal protection grounds (for the states) and the Due Process Clause of the Fifth Amendment for the District of Columbia.

When the case was first argued during the 1967 term, the Court voted 6–3 to uphold the residency requirements, and Chief Justice Warren, a former governor of a state with high welfare benefits, wrote an opinion that followed the rationale that if Congress enacted provisions relating to an appropriations measure, its words were final and presumed constitutional. Although Section 402(b) did not, in fact, require a residency requirement, it forbade the states from imposing a waiting period longer than one year, which seemed to support the position of the states, many of whom filed amici briefs in support of the requirement.

Justice Douglas drafted a dissent that found in the Fourteenth Amendment's Privileges and Immunities Clause a right to travel, which the residency requirement burdened. Then Justice Fortas filed a dissent directly attacking Warren's rationale as "ignoring reality" and shifted his vote. This caused Justice Stewart, a firm believer in the right to travel, to reconsider. Stewart was unwilling to cast the deciding vote, so the case was set for reargument.

After rehearing the case, the Supreme Court affirmed the judgments of the district courts in all three cases. In an opinion by Justice Brennan, the Court held that absent a compelling state interest, the Connecticut and Pennsylvania statutory provisions violated the Equal Protection Clause of the Fourteenth Amendment by imposing a classification on welfare applicants that impinged upon their constitutional right to travel freely from state to state. Similarly, absent a compelling government interest, the District of Columbia statutory provision violated the Due Process Clause of the Fifth Amendment by imposing a discrimination that impinged upon the constitutional right to travel. As to the Social Security Act, the Court held that Section 402(b) did not, and constitutionally could not, authorize the states to impose a one-year waiting period requirement.

The significance of Brennan's opinion is that he shifted the "compelling state interest" from speech and religion cases into equal protection analysis. In many ways Brennan was rejecting the post-1937 nationalism that gave Congress almost unlimited power in commerce and money transactions. Although Douglas had first raised the right to travel argument, he deferred to Brennan and supported his opinion that tied together a number of equal protection arguments that had been developing ever since ***Skinner v. Oklahoma,*** 316 U.S. 535 (1942), where Douglas had first started the resuscitation of the Equal Protection Clause from Justice Holmes's near fatal blow to it in ***Buck v. Bell,*** 274 U.S. 200 (1927). In doing so, he also changed the nature of welfare payments from simple charity doled out at the government's whim to an entitlement that enjoyed constitutional protection and placed strict restraints on the bureaucracy.

Chief Justice Warren, joined by Black, dissented on the grounds that Congress, under the Commerce Clause, had the power to impose minimal nationwide residence requirements or to authorize the states to do so. Justice Harlan objected specifically to Brennan's extension of the "compelling interest" doctrine, and warned against its expansion. The Court, he warned, was picking out certain activities and making them constitutional by declaring them to be "fundamental" rights. This elicited a response from Justice Stewart, who in his concurrence said that the Court had not created a new right but had merely recognized an established constitutional right, the right to travel.

See Lucas A. Powe Jr., *The Warren Court and American Politics* (Cambridge: Belknap Press of Harvard University Press, 2000).

Boykin v. Alabama

395 U.S. 238 (1969)
Decided: June 2, 1969
Vote: 6 (Warren, Douglas, Brennan, Stewart, B. White, T. Marshall)
2 (Black, Harlan II)
Opinion of the Court: Douglas
Dissenting opinion: Harlan II (Black)

In 1966 a series of armed robberies occurred in Mobile, Alabama. In several of the robberies, the bandit fired his gun, and in one of them, a by-stander was shot in the leg. A twenty-seven-year-old black man, Edward Boykin Jr., was arrested for the armed robberies and pled guilty to the charges. Under Alabama law, armed robbery was a capital offense, and Boykin received the death sentence. Boykin had not been advised by a lawyer about the implications of pleading guilty, and the judge did not determine whether the guilty plea was voluntary. In his appeal, Boykin argued that his Fifth and Fourteenth Amendment rights had been violated. The question in this case therefore was whether a guilty plea must be voluntary to be valid.

The Court held that a guilty plea must be voluntary. Justice Douglas explained that a guilty plea is the same as a confession, and, if confessions must be voluntary to be valid, so too must guilty pleas. Under the Fifth Amendment, a person can waive his rights of self-incrimination only if he does so voluntarily. Otherwise, it would be a Fifth Amendment violation and a violation of due process under the Fourteenth Amendment. Because the judge did not determine whether the plea was voluntary, it could not be assumed that in fact it was. The Court reversed the conviction and sentence.

Sniadach v. Family Finance Corp.

395 U.S. 337 (1969)
Decided: June 9, 1969
Vote: 7 (Warren, Douglas, Harlan II, Brennan, Stewart, B. White, T. Marshall)
1 (Black)
Opinion of the Court: Douglas
Concurring opinion: Harlan II
Dissenting opinion: Black

Christine Sniadach owed money to Family Finance, and, when she failed to make her payments, the company instituted an action against her and her employer to garnishee her wages. Sniadach owed $420 and earned about $63 a week. Her employer said it would pay one-half to Sniadach as a subsistence wage and hold the balance pending an order of the court. These procedures were allowed under Wisconsin state law, but Sniadach claimed that she had been denied due process of law because she had been given neither notice of the garnishment nor a chance to respond to the claim before the local court issued the garnishment order.

The Supreme Court agreed with her. Justice Douglas held that the Wisconsin procedure, in which the defendant's wages were frozen at the beginning of the suit and without a final judgment, violated the Due Process Clause of the Fourteenth Amendment. In the event that she might be found to be innocent of the claim, she was being deprived of the use of the withheld wages for what might be a period of weeks or even months.

Red Lion Broadcasting Co. v. Federal Communications Commission

395 U.S. 367 (1969)
Decided: June 9, 1969
Vote: 8 (Warren, Black, Harlan II, Brennan, Stewart, B. White, Fortas, T. Marshall)
0
Opinion of the Court: B. White
Did not participate: Douglas

The Federal Communications Commission (FCC) for many years imposed on broadcasters a "fairness" doctrine, requiring broadcasters to present public issues and give fair coverage to each side. In one of the two cases decided jointly, the FCC declared that Red Lion Broadcasting Company had failed to meet its obligation under the fairness doctrine. The company carried, as part of a "Christian Crusade" series, a fifteen-minute segment in which a third person's honesty and character were attacked. The FCC ordered Red Lion to send a transcript of the broadcast to this person and provide reply time, free of charge, if necessary. The court of appeals upheld the FCC's position.

After the Red Lion litigation was under way, the FCC began a rule-making proceeding to make the personal attack aspect of the fairness doctrine more precise and more readily enforceable and to specify its rules relating to political editorials. The FCC said that if an attack is made upon an individual, the station had to give that person an opportunity to respond. Moreover, if a station editorially endorsed one candidate, equal time had to be given to all other candidates for the office to present their views. The rules, as adopted and amended, were held unconstitutional in the second case by the court of appeals as abridging the freedoms of speech and press.

The Supreme Court unanimously upheld the FCC's equal time provision in the one case, and reversed the court of appeals to sustain the FCC's new rules. Justice White held that the commission's equal-time rules were authorized by Congress and did not abridge the freedoms of speech and press.

The rationale in this case derived from the original Communications Act of 1934, which saw the airwaves as a "scarce" commodity, which therefore had to be owned by the public. Particular frequencies were then licensed to stations who had to operate those stations and control their content in a manner prescribed by the FCC.

Although the case has never been overruled, with the advent of cable and satellite programming, the rationale of scarcity no longer makes sense. Nevertheless, courts still continue to give limited First Amendment protection to the broadcast media and full freedom of the press to the print media. ***Miami Herald Publishing Co. v. Tornillo,*** 418 U.S. 241 (1974) provides an example of the different treatments.

See Lucas A. Powe Jr., *American Broadcasting and the First Amendment* (Berkeley: University of California Press, 1987).

Brandenburg v. Ohio

395 U.S. 444 (1969)
Decided: June 9, 1969
Vote: 9 (Warren, Black, Douglas, Harlan II, Brennan, Stewart, White, T. Marshall)
0
Opinion: Per curiam
Concurring opinion: Black
Concurring opinion: Douglas (Black)

The Supreme Court reached the position it had been searching for regarding "subversive speech" in the final term of the Warren Court. In a *per curiam* decision, it did away with the last vestiges of seditious libel. The issue in *Brandenburg,* as it had been in all the libel cases, is the problem of regulating speech that carries the risk of moving the audience to forbidden action—whether it be directed against one individual (a speaker urging the lynching of a prisoner in a local jail) or against the state (advocacy of rebellion). Justice Holmes had previously noted that all ideas are incitements to action, and no doubt fringe groups as well as mainstream bodies hope that their words will move their listeners to particular actions.

In ***Schenck v. United States,*** 249 U.S. 47 (1919), the Court held that the First Amendment did not protect general advocacy of violence. Starting with their dissent in ***Abrams v. United States,*** 250 U.S. 616, that same year, Holmes and Brandeis set out the argument that radical speech could be curtailed only by showing that it would provoke an imminent danger. During the early 1940s, the clear and present danger test, as articulated by Holmes and Brandeis, seemed to gain ascent, and it was used to protect dissident speech in several cases. Then in ***Dennis v. United States,*** 341 U.S. 494 (1951), the Court reformulated the test to make it an even more stringent limitation on speech, one that penalized thought as well as action. Between *Dennis* and *Brandenburg,* however, the country rid itself of the suspicions of the McCarthy era, and the Court carried out an active examination of what freedom of expression meant. The core of the First Amendment, the Court agreed, was a belief that democracy cannot function without free speech. In *Brandenburg,* the Court articulated what Justice Harlan had intimated in ***Yates v. United States,*** 354 U.S. 298 (1957), that only "incitement to imminent lawless action" can justify restriction of free speech.

This case concerned a rally held by the Ku Klux Klan near Cincinnati. The Klan invited a local television station to cover the event. About a dozen members of the Klan, garbed in white sheets and hoods, with some carrying arms, burned a cross in an open field. Their leader, Clarence Brandenburg, then proceeded to deliver anti-black and anti-Semitic remarks, called for the expulsion of blacks and Jews from the country, and declared that the Klan would resort to violent action if Congress and the Supreme Court did not stop denying true Americans their country. Brandenburg was arrested and convicted under the Ohio Criminal Syndicalism statute, fined $1,000, and sentenced to one to ten years in prison.

The Ohio law dated back to 1919, and in 1927, over a strenuous protest by Brandeis and Holmes, the Court had upheld a similar statute in ***Whitney v. California,*** 274 U.S. 357 (1927). The Court now validated Brandeis's opinion calling for full and unfettered speech. It enunciated the rule that "the constitutional guarantees of free speech and free press do not permit a State to forbid or proscribe advocacy of the use of force or of law violation except where such advocacy is directed to inciting or producing imminent lawless action and is likely to incite or produce such action."

Brandenburg remains the clearest statement of the Warren Court's understanding of the First Amendment's protection of political ideas. It concedes that if speech can incite imminent unlawful action, it may be restricted, but the burden of proof in all speech cases rests on the state to show that action will result, rather than on the defendant to show that it will not. It retains, as do all First Amendment cases, an element of judicial balancing, a fact that upsets those who would prefer a completely objective test. In constitutional law, however, there are few completely objective rules; the judicial process is at heart a balancing of rights and interests, and all of the speech cases from 1919 on involved the same process. There is a clear line from Holmes's classic dissent in *Abrams* through Brandeis's concurrence in *Whitney* to *Brandenburg*. The Court had slowly expanded the meaning of First Amendment rights. Although the extent of First Amendment protection had never before been stated quite so broadly, the Warren Court in fact did no more than develop the precedents it inherited. *Dennis,* although it cast such a huge shadow in the 1950s, may be better understood as an aberration, the last gasp of the older restrictive view of speech set forth in *Schenck* and the majority opinion in *Whitney.* The Warren Court recognized this and moved quickly to disencumber itself of the *Dennis* ruling.

See William J. Brennan Jr., "The Supreme Court and the Meikeljohn Interpretation of the First Amendment," *Harvard Law Review* 79 (1965): 1; Harry Kalven, *A Worthy Tradition: Freedom of Speech in America* (New York: Harper and Row, 1988); and Lillian A. BeVier, "The First Amendment and Political Speech: An Inquiry into the Substance and Limits of Principle," *Stanford Law Review* 30 (1978): 299.

Powell v. McCormack

395 U.S. 486 (1969)
Decided: June 16, 1969
Vote: 8 (Warren, Black, Douglas, Harlan II, Brennan, B. White, Fortas, T. Marshall)
1 (Stewart)
Opinion of the Court: Warren
Concurring opinion: Douglas
Dissenting opinion: Stewart

Adam Clayton Powell Jr., a member of Congress from Harlem, was reelected to the House in 1966. Although he met the age, citizenship, and residency requirements for membership spelled out in Article I, Section 2, of the Constitution, the House refused to seat him. A select committee had reported that Powell had "wrongfully diverted House funds . . . and that he had made false reports on expenditures." Article I, Section 5, states, "Each House [of Congress] shall be the Judge of the . . . Qualifications of its own Members" and may "expel a Member" with the concurrence of a two-thirds majority. The House leadership did not have the necessary votes to *expel* Powell, but, by a vote of 307 to 116, it *excluded* him from membership in the Ninetieth Congress.

This would appear to be a distinction without a difference because it had the effect of keeping Powell out of his seat. Its importance lay in a House technicality: it allowed the leadership to persuade enough members to vote to exclude rather than expel, because to expel Powell would have meant allowing him to first take his seat. Enough members had qualms about doing this, but agreed to what they saw as the less questionable exclusion.

Powell sued the House, seeking his salary for the duration of the Ninetieth Congress and a declaratory judgment that the House had no constitutional power to deny him his seat. In circuit court, Judge Warren Burger (a future chief justice) ruled that Powell had no standing and the court no jurisdiction because the matter constituted a political question. According to Burger, judicial intervention would violate the doctrine of separated powers. Powell's district reelected him in 1968, and the House in the Ninety-first Congress permitted him to take his seat, rendering moot a major part of his suit.

A nearly unanimous Supreme Court—only Justice Stewart thought the case should have been dismissed because it was moot—ruled in Powell's favor. Although a "textually demonstrable constitutional commitment" gave each House the power to judge its members' qualifications in Article I, Section 5, this power, according to Chief Justice Warren, related only to the qualifications listed in Article I, Section 2, namely, age, citizenship, and residency. By this reading, the House had no power to exclude for any reason other than failure to meet the three criteria. "The Constitution leaves the House without authority," Warren wrote, "to *exclude* any person duly elected by his constituents, who meets all the requirements for membership expressly prescribed in the Constitution." Any other rule, he held, would deprive people of the right to elect their own representative.

The political question boundary was considerably narrowed in ***Baker v. Carr,*** 369 U.S. 186 (1962), and some commentators believed that it vanished completely in *Powell.* Warren took the old ***Marbury v. Madison,*** 5 U.S. 137 (1803) syllogism and reasserted the Court's role as the ultimate arbiter of constitutional issues. Is there a constitutional question? If so, then the Court is the appropriate body to make constitutional interpretations, and the Supreme Court decides *all* constitutional questions. Even if another branch has authority under the Constitution to decide the merits of an issue (the "who decides" question), the Court has the power to determine if in fact that other branch does have the authority ("who decides who decides") and the ultimate appellate power to review the decision to see if that other branch got it right.

See Kent M. Weeks, *Adam Clayton Powell and the Supreme Court* (New York: Dunellen, 1971); C. P. Kindregan, "The Cases of Adam Clayton Powell, Jr., and Julian Bond: The Right of Legislative Bodies to Exclude Members-Elect," *Suffolk University Law Review* 2 (1968): 58; and Note, "Legislative Exclusion: Julian Bond and Adam Clayton Powell," *University of Chicago Law Review* 35 (1968): 151.

Kramer v. Union Free School District No. 15

395 U.S. 621 (1969)
Decided: June 16, 1969
Vote: 5 (Warren, Douglas, Brennan, B. White, T. Marshall)
3 (Black, Harlan II, Stewart)
Opinion of the Court: Warren
Dissenting opinion: Stewart (Black, Harlan II)

Morris Kramer was a bachelor who lived with his parents in Long Island, New York. He neither owned nor leased taxable real property in the school district in which he lived. Under state law, the only people who could vote in elections for the school board were those who owned or leased real property in the district or had school-age children attending the local schools. Kramer sued, claiming that the law violated his rights under the Equal Protection Clause. A three-judge federal panel heard his case and ruled against him, reasoning that the state's qualifications limiting voting to people who either paid a tax or had children in the school was a reasonable rule.

The Supreme Court disagreed. According to Chief Justice Warren, if the purpose of the law was to limit voting to people who had a strong and direct interest in the management of the school district, then the law failed, because it allowed people with only an indirect interest—but who met the property requirement—to vote. In essence, the state used what amounted to a property qualification for voting, and this was where the Equal Protection violation could be found.

North Carolina v. Pearce

395 U.S. 711 (1969)
Decided: June 23, 1969
Vote: 6 (Warren, Douglas, Brennan, Stewart, B. White, T. Marshall)
2 (Black, Harlan II)
Opinion of the Court: Stewart
Concurring opinion: Douglas (T. Marshall)
Concurring in judgment: B. White
Dissenting opinion: Black
Dissenting opinion: Harlan II

Clifton Pearce was convicted in a North Carolina court of assault with intent to commit rape and was sentenced to prison for twelve to fifteen years. He appealed, and the process took several years, but then the Supreme Court of North Carolina reversed his conviction on the ground that an involuntary confession had been unconstitutionally admitted in evidence against him. At a new trial, Pearce was again found guilty. This time he was sentenced to an eight-year prison term, which, when added to the time he had already served, amounted to a longer total sentence than that originally imposed. An appellate court upheld this result, and Pearce then filed for habeas corpus proceeding in federal district court. That court held that the longer sentence imposed on retrial was "unconstitutional and void," and, after the state failed to resentence Pearce, the federal court ordered his release. The state appealed the habeas ruling, but the Court of Appeals for the Fourth Circuit upheld the release.

The case was heard along with *Simpson v. Rice,* 396 F. 2d 499, a case from Alabama in which a defendant had his initial conviction overturned, but then in the new trial was found guilty and given a harsher sentence than had been originally applied. That decision was also reversed in federal court.

The Supreme Court affirmed the judgment of the appellate courts in both cases. Justice Stewart held the Fifth Amendment ban against double jeopardy meant that punishment already exacted had to be fully "credited" when imposing sentence upon a new conviction for the same crime. However, the Fourteenth Amendment's Equal Protection Clause did not impose an absolute bar to a more severe sentence upon reconviction, and neither did the Double Jeopardy Clause of the Fifth Amendment. The Court relied primarily on the Due Process Clause of the Fourteenth Amendment, which barred the state or the trial courts from exhibiting vindictiveness against a defendant for having successfully attacked his first conviction. Should a second and more severe penalty be imposed, the trial judge had to state the reasons for doing so, and this rationale, along with any supporting information, had to be part of the record so that appellate courts could review the decision.

Chimel v. California

395 U.S. 752 (1969)
Decided: June 23, 1969
Vote: 6 (Warren, Douglas, Harlan II, Brennan, Stewart, T. Marshall)
2 (Black, B. White)
Opinion of the Court: Stewart
Concurring opinion: Harlan II
Dissenting opinion: B. White (Black)

Police arrested Ted Steven Chimel in his home for the burglary of a coin shop. They then searched his entire house, including the attic, garage, a small workshop, and various drawers. They found some coins that the prosecution, over defense objection that there had been no valid search warrant, introduced as evidence at Chimel's trial. Chimel was found guilty and appealed. The intermediate appellate court and California's Supreme Court held that the police officers did not need a warrant for a search that took place incident to a valid arrest.

The Court overruled the lower courts and reversed two earlier cases, *Harris v. United States,* 331 U.S. 145 (1947), and ***United States v. Rabinowitz,*** 339 U.S. 56 (1950), both of which had been generous in permitting wide-ranging searches incident to arrest. Here, the Court narrowed the permissible search to the person and the immediate surroundings, and it held that in Chimel's case the search of the defendant's home went far beyond the area in which he might be concealing a weapon or critical evidence. If they wanted to search beyond that immediate area, the police would have to get a search warrant in addition to the warrant for arrest.

Benton v. Maryland

395 U.S. 784 (1969)
Decided: June 23, 1969
Vote: 6 (Warren, Black, Douglas, Brennan, B. White, T. Marshall)
2 (Harlan II, Stewart)
Opinion of the Court: T. Marshall
Concurring opinion: B. White
Dissenting opinion: Harlan II (Stewart)

Maryland charged John Dalmer Benton with burglary and larceny, and the trial jury found him not guilty of larceny, but convicted him on the burglary count, for which he was sentenced to ten years in prison. On appeal, it was determined that both the grand and petit juries had been unconstitutionally selected, and the case was remanded. The state offered Benton the option of demanding both reindictment by a grand jury as well as trial by the petit jury, because, if the grand jury failed to indict, he would not have to stand trial at all. Benton took this choice. The grand jury indicted him for larceny and burglary, and this time the petit jury found him guilty on both counts. Benton appealed and claimed that making him stand trial for larceny, of which he had been acquitted at the first trial, amounted to double jeopardy. The appellate courts in Maryland declined to review, because under ***Palko v. Connecticut,*** 302 U.S. 319 (1937), the Double Jeopardy Clause of the Fifth Amendment did not apply to the states.

The Supreme Court overruled *Palko* and held that the Double Jeopardy Clause did apply to the states through the Fourteenth Amendment. Under that standard, Benton's larceny conviction could not stand.

The Double Jeopardy Clause was the last major provision of the Bill of Rights to be made applicable to the states through the process of incorporation, by which the Due Process Clause of the Fourteenth Amendment was interpreted to mean that the guarantees in the Bill of Rights applied to the states as well as to the federal government.

See Richard C. Cortner, *The Supreme Court and the Second Bill of Rights* (Madison: University of Wisconsin Press, 1981).

Alexander v. Holmes County Board of Education

396 U.S. 19 (1969)
Decided: October 29, 1969
Vote: 8 (Burger, Black, Douglas, Harlan II, Brennan, Stewart, B. White, T. Marshall)
0
Opinion of the Court: *Per curiam*

In the summer of 1969 President Richard Nixon attempted to implement his so-called "southern strategy," in which his administration would take a less aggressive role in forcing southern school districts to desegregate. The secretary of Health, Education, and Welfare wrote to the chief judge of the Court of Appeals for the Fifth Circuit asking for a delay in desegregation rulings for thirty Mississippi school districts. On August 18 the circuit court granted a three-month delay. The decision, and the complicity of Nixon-appointed high-level Justice Department officials, sparked a revolt among government attorneys in the Civil Rights Division, and in many cities they refused to defend Nixon's policies and passed information along to the NAACP Legal Defense Fund.

The NAACP appealed, and the Supreme Court reversed the circuit court's decision. The Court stated that continued operation of segregated schools under the standard of "all deliberate speed" for desegregation was no longer constitutionally permissible and that "the obligation of every school district is to terminate dual school systems at once."

The decision had its impact. Over the next ten months, the circuit courts issued 166 desegregation orders in school cases. On the negative side, the decision in this case is often credited with triggering "white flight," a mass exodus of white pupils from public to private schools, and from cities to the predominantly white suburbs. In some Mississippi districts more than 90 percent of the white students left the public schools.

See James T. Patterson, *Brown v. Board of Education: A Civil Rights Milestone and Its Troubled Legacy* (New York: Oxford University Press, 2001).

1970–1979

Evans v. Abney

396 U.S. 435 (1970)
Decided: January 26, 1970
Vote: 5 (Burger, Black, Harlan II, Stewart, B. White)
2 (Douglas, Brennan)
Opinion of the Court: Black
Dissenting opinion: Douglas
Dissenting opinion: Brennan
Did not participate: T. Marshall

In his 1911 will, Sen. Augustus Bacon, D-Ga., left property in trust to Macon, Georgia, to create a park for the exclusive use of white people. Black residents of Macon successfully challenged the continued discriminatory operation of the park in the Supreme Court case *Evans v. Newton,* 382 U.S. 296 (1966). The Georgia Supreme Court then ruled that the trust was void and that the property would revert to Bacon's heirs on the theory that the park could no longer be operated according to Bacon's wishes. Disappointed that their *Newton* victory had not resulted in the integration of the park, the same black plaintiffs sued to enjoin the Georgia Supreme Court from giving the property back to Bacon's heirs and to force Macon to integrate the park by striking the racial language from the trust document under the *cy pres* doctrine. (*Cy pres* is Old French for *as near as.* The doctrine refers to a court's attempt to carry out a testator's intentions, as far as the rules respecting perpetuities permit.) They sued the state on the grounds that the termination of the trust deprived them of due process and equal protection rights under the Fourteenth Amendment.

The U.S. Supreme Court held that the termination of the trust did not violate the black citizens' equal protection or due process rights. The Court in *Newton* had disagreed with the Georgia Supreme Court, which said that Bacon had the right to dispose of his property as he chose, because the public nature of the park he created "require[d] that it be treated as a public institution subject to the command of the Fourteenth Amendment, regardless who now has title under state law." In *Abney,* however, the Court accepted Georgia's claim that the *cy pres* doctrine did not operate to save a will that was impossible to execute because the testator intended only one goal to be furthered by the will and probably would have preferred the will to fail than to be executed without the restriction.

The Court distinguished this decision from ***Shelley v. Kraemer,*** 334 U.S. 1 (1948), in which it held unconstitutional state judicial action enforcing private discrimination. Eliminating the park was not a discriminatory action; rather, it affected white and black citizens of Macon equally. In response to the petitioners' concern that the ruling would open the door to other charitable trusts being terminated, the Court emphasized that states were free to apply their *cy pres* doctrines in cases such as this, but that it was in states' discretion not to apply them.

In dissent, Justice Douglas said that Bacon's will left remainders to Macon, not to his heirs, and that giving the remainder to the heirs rather than the city betrayed his wishes as much as converting an all-white park into an integrated park.

Justice Brennan's dissent emphasized that Macon had invested large sums of money in the park and operated it as a public place for many years. He said that shutting it down was "the closing of a public facility for the sole reason that the authority that owns and maintains it cannot keep it segregated." Under the Equal Protection Clause, argued Brennan, a public facility may not be closed merely to avoid the duty of desegregating it.

Goldberg v. Kelly

397 U.S. 254 (1970)
Decided: March 23, 1970
Vote: 5 (Douglas, Harlan II, Brennan, B. White, T. Marshall)
3 (Burger, Black, Stewart)
Opinion of the Court: Brennan
Dissenting opinion: Burger
Dissenting opinion: Stewart
Dissenting opinion: Black

In New York, state and city officials charged with disbursing funds under the federal Aid to Families with Dependent Children and the state's Home Relief program terminated benefits as soon as they suspected a recipient was not eligible. The government's procedure gave recipients whose benefits were to be cut off written notice and an opportunity to write a letter contesting the proposed termination. It did not allow for in-person hearings, either before or after termination of benefits. Plaintiffs in this case were welfare recipients who sought relief when the government stopped their benefits without a hearing. The plaintiffs alleged that denying them a hearing was a deprivation of their property interest in continued welfare benefits without due process of law under the Fourteenth Amendment.

After the plaintiffs, John R. Kelly and other welfare recipients, brought their suit, the government adopted new procedures that provided for in-person hearings in which the recipients could confront adverse witnesses. Even under the new procedures, however, the in-person hearings did not occur until after benefits were terminated. The plaintiffs challenged the revised procedures as well, arguing that due process required that they have the benefit of an in-person hearing before the termination of benefits. The district court agreed, ruling that "to cut off a welfare recipient in the face of 'brutal need' without a prior hearing of some sort is unconscionable, unless overwhelming considerations justify it." The government argued that protection of tax revenues supplied the necessary "overwhelming" consideration. According to the government, most termination decisions were not contested at all and mandatory pretermination hearings would be an unnecessary drain on tax revenues because most such hearings could be avoided. Furthermore, any payments the government made to an ineligible recipient from the time of ineligibility to the end of a hearing would be unrecoverable, because the recipients usually would have no resources and so be unable to pay. In the language of lawyers, they would be judgment-proof. The district court found the stated interest in preserving tax revenues less than "overwhelming" and ruled that only a pretermination hearing could satisfy due process.

The Supreme Court affirmed. The Court held that procedural due process applies to the statutory right to welfare benefits and that the government could not argue that procedural due process does not apply because the benefits are a "privilege" and not a "right." Denial of welfare benefits is a government action that interferes with a substantial right. The extent of the process due a right-holder affected by government action is proportionate to the extent the right-holder may be "condemned to suffer grievous loss" by the action. The government may terminate some statutory benefits without a preliminary hearing. In the case of the welfare beneficiary, however, such government action may deprive the recipient of the basic requirements of life and cause immediate desperation. This desperation necessitates a search for subsistence that adversely affects the recipients' ability to concentrate on obtaining legal redress and taking steps to improve their condition. The government's interest in providing the poor with basic subsistence so they can take advantage of the opportunities that are available to everyone counterbalances the government's proffered interest in protecting tax revenues.

Although the government had a strong interest in saving the cost of hearings and illegitimate payments to welfare recipients, it is not as strong as avoiding catastrophic consequences to recipients who have no other means of support. The government may mitigate the added expense of mandatory pretermination hearings by holding them promptly and efficiently. Furthermore, the hearings need not have all the formal requirements of a "quasi-judicial trial," because recipients have the benefit of an administrative review. In addition, the due process right to be heard entails the right to be heard by counsel, so recipients must be allowed to be represented by counsel at the hearings if they choose. The factual decision-maker should provide some form of written opinion explaining the factual basis for the decision.

In his dissent, Justice Black criticized the Court for using the Due Process Clause to usurp the legislative function. In his opinion, the Due Process Clause does not invalidate any legislative action that a majority of the Supreme Court finds unfair or unconscionable.

This case has generally been seen as a keystone in the modernization of due process rights and civil procedure and in the "rights" revolution of the last half of the twentieth century. Most legal scholars and commentators agree with Professor Sylvia Law's analysis:

> John Kelly's case was won on the facts. Plaintiffs told of dozens of stories about individuals devastated by erroneous terminations of subsistence aid. Further, experience under the lower court injunction demonstrated that when prior hearings were granted, few poor people challenged terminations and, when they did, they usually prevailed. The case was grounded in the real lives of ordinary poor people and the pervasive meanness and incompetency of an ordinary bureaucracy. The facts sang.

See Sylvia A. Law, "Some Reflections on *Goldberg v. Kelly* at Twenty Years," *Brooklyn Law Review* 56 (1990): 805; Cesar A. Persales, "The Fair Hearings Process: Guardian of the Social Service System," *Brooklyn Law Review* 56 (1990): 882; and Lucie E. White, "*Goldberg v. Kelly* on the Paradox of Lawyering for the Poor," *Brooklyn Law Review* 56 (1990): 861.

In re Winship

397 U.S. 358 (1970)
Decided: March 31, 1970
Vote: 6 (Douglas, Harlan II, Brennan, B. White, T. Marshall, Blackmun)
3 (Burger, Black, Stewart)
Opinion of the Court: Brennan
Concurring opinion: Harlan II
Dissenting opinion: Burger (Stewart)
Dissenting opinion: Black

When a juvenile is legally judged to be a delinquent, the Fourteenth Amendment Due Process Clause requires that he be provided with a hearing. In ***In re Gault,*** 387 U.S. 1 (1967), the Court held that such a hearing need not comport with all the requirements of an adult criminal trial or even an administrative hearing, but it should provide "the essentials of due process and fair treatment." In this case, Samuel Winship, a twelve-year-old boy, was sentenced to six years' confinement for delinquency without a finding of guilt beyond a reasonable doubt. The issue before the Supreme Court was whether the possibility of six years' confinement without proof beyond a reasonable doubt met "the essentials of due process and fair treatment." The Court found that it did not.

Winship was accused of entering a locker and stealing $112 from a woman's purse. The state charged that his act, if done by an adult, would constitute larceny. The trial judge found that the state's evidence against the boy did not meet the "beyond a reasonable doubt" standard that would apply in an adult criminal trial. Under New York law, however, a juvenile could be sentenced if the court found guilt based on a preponderance of the evidence. The judge sentenced the boy to a training school for eighteen months, subject to annual extensions of his commitment until his eighteenth birthday or six years for a crime that the state did not, and perhaps could not, prove beyond a reasonable doubt he had committed.

The New York Court of Appeals (the state's highest court) upheld the finding of guilt and the punishment, arguing that juvenile adjudications do not call for the same protections that would be appropriate in a criminal trial. Unlike criminal trials, juvenile proceedings do not affect future rights such as obtaining a license or holding public office. Furthermore, juvenile proceedings are not made public, so the child is not stigmatized. The Court of Appeals argued that because of these protections, the danger of an erroneous finding of guilt is not as great as in a criminal trial. The reasonable doubt standard is required to protect the heightened liberty threat to the accused in a criminal case, but in a juvenile proceeding the preponderance of evidence standard adequately protects the accused's lesser liberty threat.

The Supreme Court reversed. The Court found that the reasonable doubt standard for criminal convictions is constitutionally required under the Due Process Clause. The same danger of erroneous conviction that necessitates the reasonable doubt standard in criminal cases applies in juvenile cases. The Court of Appeals' reasoning that juvenile cases are not "criminal," but "quasi-civil," was overruled by *Gault.* That case held that regardless of whether it is labeled "civil," a proceeding in which a person is subject to loss of liberty for years requires protections similar to those afforded a criminal accused.

In his dissent, Chief Justice Burger said the juvenile court was intended to intervene in the lives of children who are pursuing destructive paths. The court's remedies are not intended to be punitive, but rehabilitative. The erosion of the distinction between criminal and juvenile proceedings that motivated the majority is the result of ineffective stewardship the juvenile court's rehabilitative mission. The remedy is not to place greater constitutional restrictions on the operation of the juvenile court, because that risks "turning back the clock to the pre-juvenile court era," when young people were exposed to the harshness of criminal conviction.

See John R. Sutton, *Stubborn Children: Controlling Delinquency in the United States, 1640–1981* (Berkeley: University of California Press, 1988).

Dandridge v. Williams

397 U.S. 471 (1970)
Decided: April 6, 1970
Vote: 5 (Burger, Black, Harlan II, Stewart, B. White)
3 (Douglas, Brennan, T. Marshall)
Opinion of the Court: Stewart
Concurring opinion: Black (Burger)
Concurring opinion: Harlan II
Dissenting opinion: Douglas
Dissenting opinion: T. Marshall (Brennan)

The Maryland welfare system's method of computing a family's financial need was based on the number of children in the family. The additional need per child diminished incrementally as the family had more children. The state imposed a maximum benefit amount of $250, regardless of need. Several large families claimed the system discriminated against them in violation of the Fourteenth Amendment's Equal Protection Clause.

Before addressing the Fourteenth Amendment claim, the Court first disposed of a statutory challenge that Maryland's scheme contradicted the federal statute's requirement that all needy children receive aid. The Court held that the act gave states broad latitude in disbursing welfare funds. Because the states have finite resources, they cannot give uniform disbursements to all needy families, or no needy family would receive adequate assistance. Maryland was therefore free to give smaller per capita payments to larger families on the theory that the economies of scale made the increased financial burden of each new child smaller. Furthermore, this system fostered the policy of keeping families together. If large families "farmed out" young children, the families would receive less money because no funds were available to children not living with certain enumerated relatives. As long as some aid was delivered to all families with needy children, the Maryland scheme did not contradict the law.

In dealing with the Fourteenth Amendment equal protection claim, the Court applied the "reasonable basis" standard (although it acknowledged the case involved not just economics or business decisions but the basic needs of the poor). The Court found that Maryland's benefit maximum was reasonably related to encouraging welfare recipients to seek employment to earn the difference between need and the welfare payment (even though only members of large families were given this incentive to work) and therefore upheld the scheme.

Justice Harlan reaffirmed his belief, stated in his dissent in ***Shapiro v. Thompson,*** 394 U.S. 618 (1969), that "rational basis" is the only standard of review for equal protection questions other than questions involving racial classifications.

Justice Douglas dissented because he believed the Maryland scheme violated the federal law. He argued that by imposing a maximum benefit, Maryland was denying benefits to children born into families of six or more children, contrary to the act's imperative that all needy children receive some aid. The majority had disposed of this by saying that it was not the seventh child that received no benefits, but the entire family that had reduced benefits.

Justice Marshall asserted that the Maryland scheme contradicted the federal law and added that the Court should have used a stricter standard of review for equal protection analysis in social welfare cases.

Walz v. Tax Commission of the City of New York

397 U.S. 664 (1970)
Decided: May 4, 1970
Vote: 8 (Burger, Black, Harlan II, Brennan, Stewart, B. White, T. Marshall)
1 (Douglas)
Opinion of the Court: Burger
Concurring opinion: Brennan
Concurring opinion: Harlan II
Dissenting opinion: Douglas

Frederick Walz, an owner of real estate in New York City, sued to enjoin the city's tax commission from granting a tax exemption to religious organizations for property used solely for religious worship. He argued that the exemption created a religious establishment. With some irony, Chief Justice Burger noted, "The Establishment and Free Exercise Clauses of the First Amendment are not the most precisely drawn portions of the Constitution." The Court pointed out that at times they were inherently in conflict with each other, but their purpose was clear: "to insure that no religion be sponsored or favored, none commanded, and none inhibited."

An issue such as tax exemption for property used for religious purposes illustrates the difficulties of balancing the two clauses. Walz argued that the tax exemption established religion because the state was granting a financial benefit to religious organizations at the expense of the citizenry. To deny such an exemption, however, could easily be seen as threatening the free exercise of religion. The notion of the tax assessor placing a value on religious property would raise the danger of religious discrimination. Furthermore, it might be impossible to tax a church building without destroying it. How would one determine the taxable value of a cathedral on prime downtown real estate?

The Court avoided this thicket by noting that New York (like all other jurisdictions) had "not singled out one particular church or religious group or even churches as such" for exemptions. Nor did it limit the exemptions to buildings used for religious purposes. Rather, it "granted exemption to all houses of religious worship within a broad class of property owned by nonprofit, quasi-public corporations which include hospitals, libraries, playgrounds, scientific, professional, historical, and patriotic groups." The Court could uphold tax exemptions for religious buildings on the grounds that they were used by nonprofit groups.

See Brian E. Cumerford, "Tax Law and American Religion," in *Religion and American Law: An Encyclopedia,* ed. Paul Finkelman (New York: Garland, 2000), 499–514; John W. Whitehead, "Tax Exemption and Churches: A Historical and Constitutional Analysis," *Cumberland Law Review* 22 (1992): 521; and John Witte Jr., "Tax Exemption of Church Property: Historical Anomaly or Valid Constitutional Practice?" *Southern California Law Review* 64 (1991): 363.

Welsh v. United States

398 U.S. 333 (1970)
Decided: June 15, 1970
Vote: 5 (Black, Douglas, Harlan II, Brennan, T. Marshall)
3 (Burger, B. White, Stewart)
Judgment of the Court: Black
Opinion concurring in judgment: Harlan II
Dissenting opinion: B. White (Burger, Stewart)
Did not participate: Blackmun

This case interpreted the Establishment Clause of the First Amendment regarding the religious requirement for conscientious objector (c.o.) status. Elliot Ashton Welsh II refused to be inducted into the armed forces, claiming conscientious objector status under Section 6(j) of the Universal Military Training and Service Act. Section 6(j) allows c.o. status to persons who "by reason of religious training and belief . . . [are] conscientiously opposed to participation in war in any form." Such belief cannot be based on "essentially political, sociological, or philosophical views, or a merely personal moral code." Welsh was brought up in a religious household but had not continued his religious affiliation into adulthood and belonged to no organized religious group. The Selective Service System found that although his beliefs were held with the conviction of traditional religious beliefs, Welsh's pacifism was insufficiently religious in origin to qualify for c.o. status.

In ***United States v. Seeger,*** 380 U.S. 163 (1965), the Court determined that belief in a Supreme Being was not necessary to qualify as a religious belief for c.o. purposes. The Court said the "task is to decide whether the beliefs professed by a registrant are sincerely held and whether they are, in his own scheme of things, religious." The question therefore was whether the beliefs played a role equivalent to religion in the person's life. The government sought to distinguish *Welsh* from *Seeger* because Welsh insisted that his beliefs were not religious. Recognizing that draft registrants might not be aware of the broad definition of "religion" applicable under Section 6(j), the Court declined to accept Welsh's characterization of his views as not religious, even though the Court had placed great emphasis on Daniel Seeger's view that his belief was religious. Furthermore, the fact that Welsh was in part motivated by political or sociological views did not disqualify him because his primary motivation was "religious." In effect, the Court extended c.o. status based on "political, sociological, or philosophical views" despite the language of the statute, where those views were "religious" in the broadest sense of the term.

Justice Harlan argued that the statutory construction of Section 6(j) in *Seeger* was a mistake. In that case the Court had eliminated theistic belief from its definition of religion, even though the statute included the words *Supreme Being*. The *Seeger* Court read Supreme Being as a reflection of Congress's struggle to define religion broadly without using the term *God*. In *Welsh* the Court concluded that Congress intended to include all types of religions and had made an understandable mistake in choosing a term that still limited religious belief to theistic belief. With its decision in *Welsh*, the Court eliminated theism from the requirement of the statute. Harlan believed the Court was making a mistake and that Congress said Supreme Being because it intended to limit religion to theistic religion.

In fact, Harlan believed the Court was inappropriately interpreting the statute in order to avoid running afoul of the Constitution. The Court often applies an informal rule of statutory construction—how it reads and interprets a statute—that in effect says that, in deference to Congress, whenever possible the Court should read and interpret a statute in a way that allows the Court to uphold its constitutionality. In this case, Harlan believed that the language of the statute could not be read to save the statute and make it constitutional. Harlan argued that Section 6(j) did not fall into any of the categories, such as constitutional. He would have held the statute unconstitutional for violating the Establishment Clause of the First Amendment.

Justice White in dissent treated "religion" as an essentialistic category that is easily demarcated from history, philosophy, and sociology. Because Welsh claimed to be motivated by readings in those subjects, in White's opinion his beliefs were not religious. The dissenters agreed with Harlan that the statute intended only theistic beliefs to qualify. In their opinion, the statute was either valid (but did not apply to Welsh) or is invalid (and was of no use to Welsh). In either case, they believed Welsh had no excuse to refuse induction.

See Jack Sahl, "Conscientious Objection and the Free Exercise Clause," in *Religion and American Law: An Encyclopedia*, ed. Paul Finkelman (New York: Garland, 2000), 103–105.

Coleman v. Alabama

399 U.S. 1 (1970)
Decided: June 22, 1970
Vote: 6 (Black, Douglas, Harlan II, Brennan, B. White, T. Marshall)
2 (Burger, Stewart)
Judgment of the Court: Brennan
Concurring opinion: Black
Concurring opinion: Douglas
Concurring opinion: B. White
Concurring opinion: Harlan II
Dissenting opinion: Burger
Dissenting opinion: Stewart (Burger)
Did not participate: Blackmun

This case further developed Justice Brennan's jurisprudence on the Sixth Amendment's guarantee of the right to counsel and a fair trial. The petitioners, John Henry Coleman and Otis Stephens, were two suspects identified from a police lineup by a shooting victim. The victim claimed to have seen the faces of his assailants at night in headlights as they were running away. The victim told police before the lineup that they were black, about the same height and age, and one had been wearing a hat. Both petitioners were black, but one was five feet, four inches tall, and the other was six feet, two inches. One was twenty-eight, and the other eighteen. One wore a hat in the lineup (no other suspect in the lineup wore a hat), but the record did not show he was forced to wear the hat. The victim identified the petitioners as his assailants as soon as they walked into the lineup room, before they could assume lineup positions or speak the words the police asked them to say. After the witness had picked them out, the two petitioners were asked to speak the assailants' words, and no others in the lineup were required to say anything. Justices Douglas, White, and Marshall agreed with Brennan that under these circumstances the trial court was correct in finding that the witness's later identification of the plaintiffs in court was not tainted, despite circumstances "so impermissibly suggestive."

The Court then turned to petitioners' Sixth Amendment claim that they should have been provided with counsel before the pretrial hearing. The Court quoted from ***United States v. Wade***, 388 U.S. 218 (1967), that it was "central" to the Sixth Amendment right to counsel that "the accused is guaranteed that he need not stand alone against the State at any stage of the prosecution, formal or informal, in court or out, where counsel's absence might derogate from the accused's right to a fair trial." In any pretrial confrontation with the sovereign that involves potential prejudice to a defendant's rights, the defendant has the right to have counsel present. Although in the Alabama system, a pretrial hearing is not a necessary step in prosecution, is not used to determine guilt or innocence, and the defendant does not waive any defenses by not raising them at a pretrial hearing, a skilled lawyer might discover flaws in the prosecutor's case and persuade the judge to dismiss the action or learn how to develop impeachment strategies for prosecutors' witnesses. Denying counsel at a pretrial hearing therefore violated the petitioners' Sixth Amendment rights. On this issue, Douglas, White, and Marshall again joined Brennan.

The Court found, however, that if the lack of counsel at the preliminary hearing was harmless error, the case could stand. The fact that the trial court did not use the evidence obtained at the hearing did not necessarily mean the lack of counsel at the hearing was harmless error because the record did not show whether counsel, if present at the hearing, could have developed the correct strategies for dealing with witnesses. The Court remanded the case for a finding on the extent of harm caused by the denial of counsel at the hearing. Douglas, White, Marshall, and Black, joined Brennan on this point.

Chief Justice Burger conceded that "as a matter of sound policy counsel should be made available to all persons subjected to a preliminary hearing and that this should be provided either by statute or by the rulemaking process," but he dissented from the notion that the "Constitution commands" this result in a "criminal prosecution." Justice Stewart dissented, asserting that the prosecution had made no use of anything said at the preliminary hearing, where the defendant was not represented by counsel. If the prosecution had used any statement made there, Stewart was prepared to reverse to conviction. But, he did not believe that either the Constitution or ***Miranda v. Arizona,*** 384 U.S. 436 (1966), required that someone arrested had to have a lawyer at this preliminary stage, as long as nothing said in these proceedings was used against him.

See Alfredo Garcia, *The Sixth Amendment in Modern American Jurisprudence: A Critical Perspective* (Westport, Conn.: Greenwood, 1992).

Chambers v. Maroney

399 U.S. 42 (1970)
Decided: June 22, 1970
Vote: 7 (Burger, Black, Douglas, Brennan, Stewart, B. White, T. Marshall)
1 (Harlan II)
Opinion of the Court: B. White
Concurring opinion: Stewart
Dissenting opinion: Harlan II
Did not participate: Blackmun

Chambers sought relief from his two robbery convictions on the theory that the evidence that put him away was the fruit of an illegal search that should have been suppressed under ***Mapp v. Ohio,*** 367 U.S. 643 (1961). He and his partner were arrested after the second robbery because they fit an eyewitness description of a man in a green sweater and a man in a trench coat driving a blue compact station wagon. While the men were in police custody and the car was in the police parking lot, police searched the car without a warrant and found evidence of both robberies, which was used at trial.

The Court found that the arrest was based on probable cause, and, although the search of the car after Chambers and his partner were in custody could not stand as a search incident to arrest, the same facts that gave the police probable cause to arrest the suspects gave them probable cause to search the car. The Court held that automobiles may be searched for contraband, such as the fruits of a crime, without a warrant as long as the searching officer has probable cause to believe the vehicle contains contraband, even though the vehicle is in no danger of disappearing with the evidence. The same circumstances would not justify a warrantless search of a home or office.

Chambers also claimed ineffective assistance of counsel because his Legal Aid attorney at his second trial—the first ended in mistrial—did not consult with him until a few minutes before the trial began. The Court dismissed this claim because it centered around the attorney's allegedly inadequate effort to suppress certain evidence, the admission of which was held to be harmless error.

Justice Stewart stated his dissatisfaction with Fourth Amendment jurisprudence that would have overturned an otherwise valid criminal conviction if evidence found in violation of the Fourth Amendment had been used at trial.

Justice Harlan's dissent criticized the Court's casual treatment of Chambers's claim of ineffective assistance of counsel, pointing to numerous instances on the record that implied the attorney was not familiar enough with the case to have a trial strategy. He also objected to the Court's handling of the search of the automobile, saying that the Court was wrong in suggesting that once the car had been brought to the police station, the bigger invasion of privacy had already occurred, and that obtaining a warrant to take the further step of searching it was therefore unnecessary.

Williams v. Florida

399 U.S. 78 (1970)
Decided: June 22, 1970
Vote: Multiple
Opinion of the Court: B. White
Concurring opinion: Burger
Opinion concurring in judgment: Harlan II
Opinion concurring in judgment: Stewart
Dissenting opinion: Black (Douglas)
Dissenting opinion: T. Marshall
Did not participate: Blackmun

In this case and the companion case, *Baldwin v. New York,* 399 U.S. 66 (1970), the Supreme Court dealt with issues involving the fairness of criminal prosecutions. *Baldwin* concerned the denial of a jury trial for someone charged with a misdemeanor. By a vote of 5–3, Justice White held for the Court that Baldwin was entitled to a jury trial under the Fourteenth Amendment and the Sixth Amendment. Justices Harlan and Stewart dissented in *Baldwin,* but added the dissents to their concurrences in *Williams v. Florida. Williams* focused on two issues: an "alibi notice rule" and the use of a six-person jury. The Court upheld both aspects of Florida criminal law. With Justices Black and Douglas dissenting, the Court upheld the alibi notice rule by a 7–2 vote, and, with only Justice Marshall dissenting, the Court upheld the six-person jury, 8–1.

Florida law required a defendant "to give notice in advance of trial if the defendant intends to claim an alibi, and to furnish the prosecuting attorney with information as to the place where he claims to have been and with the names and addresses of the alibi witnesses he intends to use." At the same time, the prosecution had to give the same notice of any rebuttal witnesses that it would call. Justice White described how this process is supposed to work. "Both sides are under a continuing duty promptly to disclose the names and addresses of additional witnesses bearing on the alibi as they become available. The threatened sanction for failure to comply is the exclusion at trial of the defendant's alibi evidence—except for his own testimony—or, in the case of the State, the exclusion of the State's evidence offered in rebuttal of the alibi."

Williams gave notice of his intent to use an alibi defense, but refused to disclose the required information before trial, on the theory that doing so forced him to be a witness against himself in violation of his Fifth and Fourteenth Amendment rights. He argued that the state was forcing him to show prosecutors how to prepare rebuttal evidence against him at trial. The Court disagreed, saying that the alibi notice requirement involved reciprocal duties of the state to reveal any witnesses it planned to present in rebuttal of the alibi, and that requiring early notice of the alibi was no more a self-incrimination than presenting the alibi witnesses at trial, where the state has an opportunity to cross-examine them. Black and Douglas argued that this was, in fact, a violation of the Fifth Amendment.

The defendant's second motion asked the Florida court to impanel a twelve-person jury instead of the six-person jury required by Florida for all but capital cases. The Court held that, although the Sixth Amendment right to jury trial applied to this case, there was no constitutional requirement that a jury have twelve people. The rationale for juries is that they protect against the sovereign's arbitrary abuse of power by making the outcome of a trial depend on the common sense of the defendant's peers. In an interesting historical digression, the Court reflected on the reason why the common law settled on twelve as the number of jurors, ultimately concluding that it was a historical accident with no theoretical significance. As long as the number of jurors is large enough to reflect a cross-section of the community, the Constitution is satisfied. The Court said six was more than the minimum number, but did not say what the minimum number was.

Marshall vehemently objected to this result, citing a number of recent cases, and also asserting his support for *Thompson v. Utah,* 170 U.S. 343 (1898), in which the Court held "that the jury guaranteed by the Sixth Amendment consists 'of twelve persons, neither more nor less.' " Marshall emphatically argued that under the precedent in ***Duncan v. Louisiana,*** 391 U.S. 145 (1968), all criminal defendants had the right to a jury trial and that, in his view, a state jury should consist of twelve members, just like a federal jury.

See Larry T. Bates, "Trial by Jury After *Williams v. Florida,*" *Hamline Law Review* 10 (1987): 53.

Oregon v. Mitchell

400 U.S. 112 (1970)
Decided: December 21, 1970
Vote: Multiple
Judgment of the Court: Black
Concurring in judgment: Douglas
Concurring in judgment: Brennan (B. White, T. Marshall)
Dissenting opinion: Harlan II
Dissenting opinion: Stewart (Burger, Blackmun)

The 1970 amendments to the Voting Rights Act effectively enfranchised eighteen-year-olds in all state and federal elections, restricted the states for a period of five years from imposing literacy tests as a prerequisite to vote, and abolished state-imposed residency requirements as a prerequisite to vote. Oregon, Texas, and Arizona challenged the constitutionality of the amendments as beyond congressional power. In a splintered decision the Court upheld the amendments, but limited the enfranchising amendment to federal elections. The votes were 5–4 on the lower voting age, with Burger, Stewart, Harlan, and Blackmun dissenting; 8–1 on residency requirements, with Harlan dissenting; and 9–0 on the literacy test ban.

Oregon alleged that the amendments infringed on the right of the state to conduct elections as authorized by the Constitution. Considering this argument, Justice Black examined each of the amendments and found that Congress does have the power to regulate national elections.

Black looked first at the amendment enfranchising eighteen-year-olds. Article I, Section 2, and the Necessary and Proper Clause extend to Congress the power to "make or alter election regulations in national elections." Upholding the amendment's constitutionality, Black determined that it could apply only to national elections. Congress is free to create or alter federal election regulations but does not have this power with respect to state elections.

Turning to the amendment prohibiting states from imposing literacy tests, Black found it "constitutional under the Enforcement Clause of the Fifteenth Amendment." Literacy tests in effect are a denial of equal protection to minorities and the uneducated. Considering the history of discrimination in the United States, Black maintained that Congress's action to eradicate some of that discrimination by enacting this amendment was not only constitutional but also a crucial step towards alleviating "a serious national dilemma that touches every corner of our land."

Finally, Black analyzed the amendment prohibiting states from imposing residency requirements. In an effort to prevent states from denying a citizen the right to vote because he or she has not lived in the state long enough to meet a residency requirement, Congress passed this amendment creating absentee ballots. Black found congressional power to support the amendment.

While concurring in the overall results, Justices Douglas and Brennan dissented in part because they would have extended the amendment enfranchising eighteen-year-olds to all elections, state and federal. Relying on the Fourteenth Amendment's Equal Protection Clause and Immunities Clause, Douglas preferred to uphold the original amendment. Brennan did not support this contention in his opinion, but devoted his attention to the other two amendments. Of significance is his point that the residency amendment is constitutional because of the settled belief that all citizens are entitled "to unhindered interstate travel and settlement."

In their partial dissents, Justices Harlan and Stewart found the enfranchising amendment unconstitutional because in their view Congress lacks the power to interfere with the right of states to regulate elections. Stewart first questioned the whether an act of Congress could give all eighteen-year-olds the vote because it took constitutional amendments to enfranchise African Americans and women. "It is . . . plain to me," Stewart wrote, "that the Constitution . . . completely withholds from Congress the power to alter by legislation qualifications for voters in federal elections, in view of the explicit provisions of Article I, Article II, and the Seventeenth Amendment."

Harlan's opinion went even further, maintaining that the residency amendment was also unconstitutional. In a lengthy history of the Fourteenth Amendment, Harlan maintained that the Fourteenth Amendment does not protect political rights and cannot be the basis for sustaining the constitutionality of the enfranchising amendment or the residency amendment.

See Marsha J. Darling, *Race, Voting, Redistricting and the Constitution* 3 vols. (New York: Routledge, 2001).

Massachusetts v. Laird

400 U.S. 886 (1970)
Decided: November 9, 1970
Vote: 6 (Burger, Black, Brennan, B. White, T. Marshall, Blackmun)
3 (Douglas, Harlan II, Stewart)
Opinion: *Per curiam*
Dissenting opinion: Douglas
Dissenting without opinion: Harlan II, Stewart

Massachusetts sought to have U.S. involvement in Vietnam declared unconstitutional "in that it was not initially authorized or subsequently ratified by Congressional declaration." In addition, the state sought to enjoin Secretary of Defense Melvin R. Laird from increasing troop levels in Vietnam or sending any Massachusetts citizen to fight in Vietnam without congressional authorization. In short, Massachusetts was trying to force the Supreme Court to rule on the legality of the Vietnam War, the longest undeclared war in United States history.

Justice Douglas dissented from the Court's decision not to grant leave to file a complaint because he felt Massachusetts had standing and justiciability and therefore met the two threshold requirements for filing a law suit.

The Court apparently accepted the solicitor general's argument, based on ***Massachusetts v. Mellon,*** 262 U.S. 447 (1923), that Massachusetts did not have standing to sue on behalf of its citizens as *parens patriae* when the federal government acts in conflict with their citizens' federal rights. In reality, however, this case was the sort the Court traditionally ducks. The majority of the justices clearly did not want to allow a state, or anyone else, to litigate America's role in Vietnam. It would have created a situation that was politically impossible for the Court to resolve.

In Douglas's opinion, *Mellon* proved only that states did not have standing when a federal violation of federal rights was caused by federal statutes. For example, in ***Georgia v. Pennsylvania Railroad Co.,*** 324 U.S. 439 (1945), the Court found a state had standing to challenge the federal violation of federal rights occasioned by a federal executive action. Douglas believed that when a state alleges specific harm to its citizens by federal action, rather than generally criticizing the soundness of federal law, the state should have standing to sue despite *Mellon.* Douglas suggested a parallel between the relationship of this case to *Mellon* and the relationship of ***Flast v. Cohen,*** 392 U.S. 83 (1968), to *Frothingham v. Mellon,* 262 U.S. 447 (1923). (*Frothingham v. Mellon* was decided with *Massachusetts v. Mellon,* and both denied standing to states to sue Congress for exceeding powers delegated to it under Article I, Section 8, of the Constitution.) *Flast* held that if a plaintiff could instead prove that Congress violated a specific Section 8 power, the plaintiff would have standing. Furthermore, ***South Carolina v. Katzenbach,*** 383 U.S. 301 (1966), held that South Carolina had standing to challenge the constitutionality of the Voting Rights Act of 1965, when the only interest South Carolina claimed it was asserting was to ensure the effectiveness of its own voting laws—a less significant interest than Massachusetts' interest in protecting the lives of its citizens from being forfeited in an unconstitutional war. (It should be noted that in fact South Carolina was trying to prevent blacks from voting, which is why the Court took that case.) As in *Flast,* Massachusetts pointed to a specific Section 8 violation—of Congress's war power—and, thus, *Mellon* does not apply to deny Massachusetts standing. Because *Mellon* does not apply, and Massachusetts' citizens will suffer clear harm by being drafted, Massachusetts is the proper party to protect them as *parens patriae.*

With regard to justiciability—the matter's appropriateness to be heard by a court—Douglas felt this case was justiciable because it did not involve a political question. In ***Baker v. Carr,*** 369 U.S. 186 (1962), the Court recognized six situations in which a question is deemed political and not justiciable: (1) "a textually demonstrable constitutional commitment of the issue to a coordinate political department," (2) "a lack of judicially discoverable and manageable standards for resolving it," (3) "the impossibility of deciding without an initial policy determination of a kind clearly for nonjudicial discretion," (4) "the impossibility of a court's undertaking independent resolution without expressing lack of the respect due coordinate branches of government," (5) "an unusual need for unquestioning adherence to a political decision already made," or (6) "the potentiality of embarrassment from multifarious pronouncements by various departments on one question."

Douglas felt that none of these tests applied to render the question nonjusticiable, and he addressed them in turn. First, Article I, Section 8, gives Congress the power to declare war—the clear textual commitment of the issue to another political department—and Congress had not declared war. Second, the standards are easy to identify—whether the Gulf of Tonkin Resolution amounted to a congressional declaration of war. Third, the Court would not have to make a policy determination in this case because the issue would not be whether the United States should be involved in the Vietnam War but whether the president has involved the nation in a war without congressional authorization. Fourth, even though the Court must question the legality of power exercised by the president does not mean the question is political and not justiciable because the Court had already done so in ***Youngstown Sheet & Tube v. Sawyer,*** 343 U.S. 579 (1952). Fifth, "This test is essentially a reference to a commitment of a problem," Douglas wrote, "and its solution to a coordinate branch of government—a matter not involved here." Sixth, Douglas did not believe that this test created a "general" principle of nondecision that allowed the Court to ignore the question of whether unconstitutional harms were being committed by another branch.

Justices Harlan and Stewart dissented on similar grounds but did not join in Douglas's opinion.

Younger v. Harris

401 U.S. 37 (1971)
Decided: February 23, 1971
Vote: 8 (Burger, Black, Harlan II, Brennan, Stewart, B. White, T. Marshall, Blackmun)
1 (Douglas)
Opinion of the Court: Black
Concurring opinion: Stewart (Harlan II)
Opinion concurring in judgment: Brennan (B. White, T. Marshall)
Dissenting opinion: Douglas

John Harris Jr. was indicted under the California Criminal Syndicalism Act, which prohibited advocating criminal activity such as "sabotage" or terrorism as a means of bringing about economic change in the United States. The Court had upheld this law in ***Whitney v. California,*** 274 U.S. 357 (1927), but struck down a nearly identical statute in ***Brandenburg v. Ohio,*** 395 U.S. 444 (1969). Harris sought an injunction, on the grounds that the Criminal Syndicalism Act was unconstitutional, to prevent Evelle Younger, the Los Angeles district attorney, from prosecuting him. The district court granted the injunction, and Younger appealed.

The Court reversed, concluding that the injunction was "a violation of the national policy forbidding federal courts to stay or enjoin pending state court proceedings except under special circumstances." The Court found that federal courts had no authority to enjoin California's prosecution of Harris. It observed that federal law embodied a deep belief in preventing federal injunctions of state court proceedings. This policy was partly motivated by the general prohibition on the federal government interfering in state proceedings with an injunction when the plaintiff still had an adequate remedy under state law, which was a trial before a jury. In legal terminology, this meant that the federal courts would not use an "equitable remedy"—an injunction—as long as an adequate remedy—possible acquittal in the state court—existed. This policy represents a traditional federalist concern that the federal government show sensitivity to the legitimate interests of the states. Under ***Ex parte Young,*** 209 U.S. 123 (1908), even when state criminal statutes are unconstitutional on their face, federal courts enjoin their enforcement only under extraordinary circumstances that pose an immediate threat of irreparable harm. Under traditional notions of federalism, once convicted in the state court, the plaintiff in this case might turn to the federal courts if the state had abridged his federal constitutional rights. The Court observed that in earlier First Amendment cases in which a state statute was held unconstitutional for being vague and overbroad, the statutes were vague and overbroad as applied to a particular individual. If a statute was overbroad, but sufficiently narrow in its application, the Court would not interfere.

The district court had assumed jurisdiction of this case because it believed that ***Dombrowski v. Pfister,*** 380 U.S. 479 (1965), had substantially widened the jurisdiction of federal courts to enjoin the enforcement of unconstitutional state statutes. In *Dombrowski,* a Louisiana attorney general had raided the plaintiffs' offices and seized documents under a statute that was ruled unconstitutional, and, despite the ruling, he continued to threaten a repeat of the seizures. Had the attorney general carried out his threat, he would not have been acting in hopes of securing a conviction, but to harass and intimidate the plaintiffs in retaliation for their support for black civil rights in Louisiana. In such a situation, the plaintiffs would be unable to protect their constitutional rights by defending a prosecution in state court. The threat of deprivation of rights they faced was not from conviction, but from continued harassment by a state official.

In reversing the district court's finding of jurisdiction, the Supreme Court distinguished this case from *Dombrowski* because it produced no evidence that the state was using the statute to harass communists. The threat to Harris's liberty was that he would be convicted. He could adequately protect himself from this threat by defending against the prosecution in state court. Furthermore, *Dombrowski* did not hold that a statute's "chilling effect" on the exercise of free speech rights was in itself sufficient for federal courts to enjoin its enforcement, as long as the state courts apply a "narrowing construction" that saves it from overbreadth.

In the end, the case was about federalism and the belief that the federal courts should not routinely preempt state adjudications. Unlike *Dombrowski,* this case showed "no suggestion that this single prosecution against Harris is brought in bad faith or is only one of a series of repeated prosecutions to which he will be subjected." The Court concluded that because the "proceeding was already pending in the state court," Harris had ample "opportunity to raise his constitutional claims," and likewise the California courts had ample opportunity to rule on them. If the California courts upheld the state statute, Harris could still turn to the federal courts for relief.

In dissent, Justice Douglas praised *Dombrowski,* which he would have applied here. Douglas feared that this case would lead to state officials harassing political dissidents with prosecutions under laws that eventually would be struck down.

Harris v. New York

401 U.S. 222 (1971)
Decided: February 24, 1971
Vote: 5 (Burger, Harlan II, Stewart, B. White, Blackmun)
4 (Black, Douglas, Brennan, T. Marshall)
Opinion of the Court: Burger
Dissenting without opinion: Black
Dissenting opinion: Brennan (Douglas, T. Marshall)

This case established the rule that statements made to police by a suspect in custodial interrogation, who was not advised of his rights against self-incrimination and counsel, are admissible for impeaching the suspect's testimony at trial. Although these statements would be inadmissible if offered by the prosecutor to prove his case in chief, they are admissible to impeach the defendant's testimony. In theory, the jury may then consider the statements only with regard to how they reflect on the defendant's credibility, but not as proof of defendant's wrongdoing.

Harris was arrested for selling heroin to undercover agents and made self-incriminating statements. At the time he made these statements, Harris had not asked for an attorney or been offered one. Nevertheless, following the rule in ***Miranda v. Arizona,*** 384 U.S. 436 (1966), at the trial the prosecution did not attempt to introduce what Harris had said. When Harris testified in his own defense, however, and stated that what he sold was baking powder, the prosecution introduced the statements to impeach Harris's testimony. Harris appealed his conviction on the grounds that these statements, made to the police without the benefit of counsel, were inadmissible, even to impeach his own testimony.

New York argued, and the Court agreed, that this case was similar to *Walder v. United States,* 347 U.S. 62 (1954), where the Court allowed physical evidence that had been obtained illegally to be used to contradict a defendant's testimony in a criminal trial, even though that evidence would be inadmissible in the prosecutor's case in chief. This decision was based on ***Weeks v. United States,*** 232 U.S. 383 (1914). In *Walder,* the Court maintained, "It is one thing to say that the Government cannot make an affirmative use of evidence unlawfully obtained. It is quite another to say that the defendant can turn the illegal method by which evidence in the Government's possession was obtained to his own advantage, and provide himself with a shield against contradiction of his untruths." Here the Court applied this rationale to the existing doctrine in *Miranda,* which required that a lawyer be provided to someone arrested and that the person be offered a lawyer. Any confession made before the arrestee had been offered counsel would not be admissible as part of the prosecution's case in chief. As with the use of other tainted evidence, however, the Court allowed the lawyerless confession as evidence to impeach the defendant.

In dissent, Justice Brennan distinguished *Walder* from *Harris* by pointing out that in *Walder* the tainted evidence that was not offered to rebut the defendant's statements about the case before the jury, but about an earlier prosecution. The evidence did not tend to prove the prosecutor's case in the minds of jurors who would be likely to ignore their charge to use the tainted evidence only to determine the defendant's credibility as a witness. Here, the tainted evidence, if believed by the jurors, would completely prove the prosecutor's case. Allowing tainted evidence on the case's central issue is the same as proving the prosecutor's case with tainted evidence. Brennan relied on a long list of cases holding that a defendant's privilege against self-incrimination includes the ability to deny all elements of a state's charge against him and that allowing the state to use tainted evidence against the defendant whenever he exercises his right to deny the charges is an infringement on his constitutional rights. It is equally important to understand that *Walder* was a pre-*Miranda* precedent, and that it was possible to imagine that after *Miranda* the precedent in *Walder* would no longer be valid. As Brennan noted, *Miranda* guaranteed that a defendant's statements made before he could talk to an attorney would not be used against him in court.

See Ira Marcus, "Note: The Injustice of Justice: *Harris v. New York,*" *New England Law Review* 7 (fall 1971).

Boddie v. Connecticut

401 U.S. 371 (1971)
Decided: March 2, 1971
Vote: 8 (Burger, Douglas, Harlan II, Brennan, Stewart, B. White, T. Marshall, Blackmun)
1 (Black)
Opinion of the Court: Harlan II
Concurring opinion: Brennan
Opinion concurring in judgment: Douglas
Dissenting opinion: Black

This case gave due process protection to poor people who needed to have court fees and costs waived in divorce proceedings. Access to courts is not a matter of due process if alternative methods of resolving problems are available, but, with regard to marriage, the state has a "monopoly" on the legal means of ending it—divorce. If some people are excluded from the opportunity of obtaining a divorce because of the fees, the Court said the fees must be waived. "Due process requires, at a minimum, that . . . persons forced to settle their claims of right and duty through the judicial process must be given a meaningful opportunity to be heard." The Court compared the court fees to inadequate notice in that both denied parties the opportunity to be heard.

Justice Douglas felt that the result should be based on the Equal Protection Clause, not the Due Process Clause. He said that having courts open only to those who could afford to pay court fees was discrimination against the indigent. He preferred not to use the Due Process Clause because it reminded him of the era ushered in by ***Lochner v. New York,*** 198 U.S. 45 (1905), when judges used the Due Process Clause to invalidate statutes they considered unwise.

Justice Brennan objected to a suggestion made in the majority opinion that the application of the Due Process Clause to this case turned to some extent on the importance of the marriage relationship in society, that other types of proceedings might not be covered, and that the decision applied only to cases where the state has a monopoly on the resolution. He also felt the majority should have mentioned the Equal Protection Clause in its rationale.

Justice Black's dissent distinguished the due process protections afforded criminal defendants from those afforded civil litigants. The state does not coerce married people to obtain a divorce, but does coerce defendants to defend themselves in court. According to Black, that difference means less due process is required to protect the rights of married people to have access to the courts. In his opinion, a $60 court fee was not high enough to impinge due process in a civil case.

See Mary McCrory Krupnow, "Protecting Familial Bonds and Creating a New Right of Access in the Civil Courts," *North Carolina Law Review* 76 (1998): 621; Christopher E. Austin, "Due Process, Court Access Fees, and the Right to Litigate," *New York University Law Review* 57 (1983): 768; and "Free Access to Divorce Courts for Indigents," *Harvard Law Review* 85 (1971): 104.

Griggs v. Duke Power Co.

401 U.S. 424 (1971)
Decided: March 8, 1971
Vote: 8 (Burger, Black, Douglas, Harlan II, Stewart, B. White, T. Marshall, Blackmun)
0
Opinion of the Court: Burger
Did not participate: Brennan

A group of black workers brought a class action suit against Duke Power Company for employment discrimination. The complaint alleged that Duke required a high school education for promotion or transfer to certain more desirable positions, even though a high school education was not necessary to do the job. This requirement, the employees argued, precluded a disproportionately high number of black workers from promotion or transfer; moreover, the jobs in question had traditionally been reserved for white employees.

Prior to passage of Title VII of the Civil Rights Act of 1964, Duke had openly discriminated on the basis of race in hiring and promotion. After Title VII's enactment, Duke reorganized into seven occupational categories, the lowest-paid of which was "labor." The highest paying labor job paid less than the lowest paying of any job in any of the other categories. Duke had seventeen black employees, and all were assigned to labor. In 1965 the company gave up its policy of restricting black employees to labor, but limited promotion out of labor to those holding high school diplomas. If an employee lacked a high school diploma, he could transfer out of labor by passing two professional aptitude tests: the Wonderlic Personnel Test and the Bennett Mechanical Comprehension Test. Neither test was intended to measure specific skills required by any of the jobs to which the employees sought promotion.

The district court found that Duke's promotion policies were not discriminatory within the meaning of Title VII. Furthermore, the district court held that Title VII did not provide a remedy for prior discrimination. The court of appeals said that in close cases such as this one, the subjective intent of the employer governed the outcome. The court held that "in the absence of a discriminatory purpose, use of such requirements was permitted by the Act." In this holding, the court of appeals rejected the claim that because these two requirements operated to render ineligible a markedly disproportionate number of Negroes, they were unlawful under Title VII unless shown to be job related. The court of appeals found that even if the new job requirements were not job related, the company could legitimately use them as long as there was no "discriminatory purpose." Because the court of appeals found no evidence that the restrictions were meant to be discriminatory against blacks, it concluded that Duke's promotion policies were nondiscriminatory. The court of appeals reversed the district court on one point, finding that Title VII does provide a remedy for prior discrimination.

The Supreme Court reversed on the issue of actual discrimination. The Court found that Title VII does not permit hiring or promotion policies that maintained a pattern of racial inequality, even if those policies are neutral on their face. Duke employed tests designed to measure "general intelligence." Although general intelligence may be a racially neutral criterion, the tests served to exclude black employees from promotion opportunities because the inferior education afforded blacks in North Carolina put them at a disadvantage in taking the tests. The Court compared this situation to the literacy requirement for registering to vote that it had struck down in *Gaston County v. United States,* 395 U.S. 285 (1969). The Court held that although Title VII does not guarantee a job to all seekers merely because of past discrimination, it does require "the removal of artificial, arbitrary, and unnecessary barriers to employment when the barriers operate invidiously to discriminate on the basis of racial or other impermissible classification."

In reaching this result the Court rejected a search for the intent of the defendant. It did not matter whether Duke Power wanted to discriminate or not; what mattered is that its policies denied opportunity to blacks. The goal of Title VII was "to achieve equality of employment opportunities and remove barriers that have operated in the past to favor an identifiable group of white employees over other employees. Under the Act, practices, procedures, or tests neutral on their face, and even neutral in terms of intent, cannot be maintained if they operate to 'freeze' the status quo of prior discriminatory employment practices."

See George W. Dent Jr., "Note: Employment Testing: The Aftermath of *Griggs v. Duke Power Co.*," *Columbia Law Review* 72 (1972): 900.

Gillette v. United States and Negre v. Larsen

401 U.S. 437 (1971)
Decided: March 8, 1971
Vote: 8 (Burger, Black, Harlan II, Brennan, Stewart, B. White, T. Marshall, Blackmun)
1 (Douglas)
Opinion of the Court: T. Marshall
Concurring in judgment without opinion: Black
Dissenting opinion: Douglas

Guy Porter Gillette and Louis A. Negre were draftees who objected to the Vietnam War. Gillette refused to report for induction, and Negre sought a writ of habeas corpus to be released from service after going through basic training. They requested conscientious objector status on the grounds that their religious beliefs prohibited them from participating in an "unjust war," although they said their religious convictions would allow them to participate in a "just war." The sincerity of their religious beliefs was not in question. This case called upon the Court to interpret Section 6(j) of the Military Selective Service Act of 1967, which says, "Nothing in this title. . . shall be construed to require any person to be subject to combatant training and service in the United States who, by reason of religious training and belief, is conscientiously opposed to participation in war in any form." The petitioners in this case were not opposed to all wars, only to the ongoing conflict in Vietnam. The Court was therefore called upon to decide whether they were entitled to the protection of Section 6(j), even though they were not opposed to participation in every war, but only an "unjust war."

Gillette and Negre claimed "participation in war in any form" did not mean that only those whose religious beliefs would never permit them to participate in any war were exempt from military service. They claimed that "in any form" modified "participation," not "war." Furthermore, they pointed to an earlier Supreme Court case, *Sicurella v. United States,* 348 U.S. 385 (1955), which exempted a Jehovah's Witness who objected to all wars except "theocratic wars" commanded by Jehovah, as support for the proposition that the phrase did not exclude those who objected to some, but not all, wars. The Court disagreed.

Justice Marshall held that whether "in any form" modifies "participation" or "war" in Section 6(j) does not matter in determining that war means every war, because even the unmodified word *war* must mean *every war.* Interpreting the phrase as "participation in any form" is nonsensical because one of the remedies offered by the statute is to assign objectors to noncombat forms of participation. In addition, according to Marshall, *Sicurella* was not a true case of someone who objected to only some wars because the "theocratic war" envisioned by Sicurella was not a "real shooting war" that would involve the use of "carnal weapons."

Gillette and Negre claimed that Section 6(j), as thus construed, violated the Establishment Clause by favoring religions that object to all wars over religions that object to only some wars. Furthermore Section 6(j) violated the Free Exercise Clause by compelling religious persons to choose between their religious convictions and secular punishment. The majority rejected the Establishment Clause argument, finding "no claim that exempting conscientious objectors to war amounts to an overreaching of secular purposes and an undue involvement of government in affairs of religion. To the contrary, petitioners ask for greater 'entanglement' by judicial expansion of the exemption to cover objectors to particular wars." Quoting Justice Brennan's concurring opinion in ***Abington School District v. Schempp,*** 374 U.S. 203 (1963), the petitioners asserted, "When government activities touch on the religious sphere, they must be secular in purpose, evenhanded in operation, and neutral in primary impact."

Marshall concluded that this argument was wrong. The statute "simply does not discriminate on the basis of religious affiliation or religious belief, apart of course from beliefs concerning war," Marshall wrote. "The section says that anyone who is conscientiously opposed to all war shall be relieved of military service. The specified objection must have a grounding in 'religious training and belief,' but no particular sectarian affiliation or theological position is required." The Court said that Section 6(j), on its face, did not separate out certain religions for special treatment, and it was therefore not necessary to either nullify the statute or expand it to cover all religions. It also said that the government had substantial nonreligious reasons for the "preference," such as the difficulty of distinguishing in particular cases between an objection to a particular war based on religion and one based on political beliefs. The Court also rejected the Free Exercise Clause argument, saying that the clause had never been interpreted to mean that the dictates of conscience are always sufficient to relieve a person of his duty under law. Finally, the Court disposed of due process objections that the statute discriminated arbitrarily and invidiously "in contravention of the 'equal protection' principles embodied in the Fifth Amendment" on the grounds that this argument was a more general version of the First Amendment objections and therefore the same reasoning applied to it.

See Spencer E. Davis, "Constitutional Right or Legislative Grace? The Status of Conscientious Objection Exemptions," *Florida State University Law Review* 19 (1991): 191–208; and Jack Sahl, "Conscientious Objection and the Free Exercise Clause," in *Religion and American Law: An Encyclopedia,* ed. Paul Finkelman (New York: Garland, 2000), 103–105.

Mackey v. United States

401 U.S. 667 (1971)
Decided: April 5, 1971
Vote: 7 (Burger, Harlan II, Brennan, Stewart, B. White, T. Marshall, Blackmun)
2 (Black, Douglas)
Judgment of the Court: B. White
Opinion concurring in judgment: Harlan II
Opinion concurring in judgment: Brennan (T. Marshall)
Dissenting opinion: Douglas (Black)

This case involved a request for retroactive relief. Fred T. Mackey was convicted in January 1964 of tax evasion after a trial in which the prosecution introduced gambling excise tax statements Mackey had submitted to the government as required by law. In 1968 the Supreme Court in ***Marchetti v. United States,*** 390 U.S. 39, and *Grosso v. United States,* 390 U.S. 62, held that the Fifth Amendment privilege against self-incrimination was a valid objection to submitting the gambling excise taxes required by the statute. Mackey then moved for postconviction relief on the theory that he had been compelled to testify against himself by submitting the excise tax statements.

The Court held that *Marchetti* and *Grosso* did not provide retroactive relief for convictions in cases prior to those decisions. Relying on *Tehan v. United States ex rel. Shott,* 382 U.S. 406 (1966), and ***Johnson v. New Jersey,*** 384 U.S. 719 (1966), the Court concluded that *Marchetti* would be applied retroactively only if Mackey's compelled self-incrimination had affected the reliability of the excise tax statement information used by the prosecutors in Mackey's trial. Determining that it did not, the plurality let Mackey's conviction stand.

Justice Brennan focused on the fact that the excise tax statement statute was never intended to collect incriminating evidence but merely to aid in collecting revenue.

Justice Douglas's dissent was based on his belief that once a constitutional rule was determined that would aid a defendant in a criminal proceeding, it was always retroactive. Otherwise, the case would be decided not on principles of justice, but on the accident of whether the prosecution occurred before or after the rule was announced.

Swann v. Charlotte-Mecklenburg County Board of Education

402 U.S. 1 (1971)
Decided: April 20, 1971
Vote: 9 (Burger, Black, Douglas, Harlan II, Brennan, Stewart, B. White, T. Marshall, Blackmun)
0
Opinion of the Court: Burger

More than a decade after the decision in ***Brown v. Board of Education,*** 347 U.S. 483 (1954), many of the schools in the South remained largely segregated. In ***Green v. County School Board of New Kent County,*** 391 U.S. 430 (1968), the Court held that segregated districts had a duty to do more than end their *de jure* segregation. The Court overturned Virginia's so-called freedom of choice plan and compelled the district to integrate. In *Green,* however, the school district was small, involving two schools that had been legally segregated before *Brown. Swann* applied the logic of *Green* to a large district that included a major city, Charlotte, North Carolina, and the surrounding suburbs. This school system was the forty-third largest in the nation, with more than 100 schools and more than 84,000 pupils, 24,000 of whom (about 29 percent) were black. Most of the black students—21,000—lived in Charlotte, and fifteen years after *Brown* about 14,000 of these students were attending schools that were 99 percent black.

In deciding *Swann,* a unanimous Court firmly declared that its "objective" remained "to eliminate from the public schools all vestiges of state-imposed segregation." This was the mandate of *Brown,* and the Court was prepared to achieve this goal with whatever powers it needed to use. The Court asserted that the "school authorities" had "affirmative obligations" to integrate their schools, and, if they failed, "judicial authority may be invoked. Once a right and a violation have been shown, the scope of a district court's equitable powers to remedy past wrongs is broad, for breadth and flexibility are inherent in equitable remedies." The Court in *Swann* upheld a district court mandate that schools in the county be integrated with schools in the city and that the schools throughout the county have a racial mix of 71 percent white and 29 percent black, numbers that reflected the racial make-up of the entire school system. To achieve the correct ratio, the county would have to adopt a pupil assignment system that was race conscious, crossed city and suburban lines, and bused black and white students. The Court also put the school system on notice, saying that "where the school authority's proposed plan for conversion from a dual to a unitary system contemplates the continued existence of some schools that are all or predominately of one race, they have the burden of showing that such school assignments are genuinely nondiscriminatory." The Court asserted that the district court (and if necessary the Supreme Court) "should scrutinize such schools, and the burden upon the school authorities will be to satisfy the court that their racial composition is not the result of present or past discriminatory action on their part." The Court also endorsed the use of "frank—and sometimes drastic—gerrymandering of school districts and attendance zones" to achieve integration. Where assignment and zoning did not work, the Court was prepared to order other steps. Noting that "bus transportation has been an integral part of the public education system for years" and that in 1969–1970, 18 million public school children, approximately 39 percent, were bused to school in all parts of the country, the Court found that bus transportation was a reasonable method of creating unitary schools.

Swann represented a dramatic change in the way the Court dealt with integration from this point on. No longer could schools claim to be following *Brown* by merely opening all schools to all children or by continuing neighborhood schools that would be integrated if the housing were integrated. Rather, the schools were now on notice that they had "affirmative obligations" to achieve integration.

"All things being equal," Chief Justice Burger wrote, "with no history of discrimination, it might well be desirable to assign pupils to schools nearest their homes." But, where local and state governments had created dual, segregated systems, "all things" were clearly "not equal." Furthermore, Burger said, "Absent a constitutional violation there would be no basis for judicially ordering assignment of students on a racial basis." But, where a school system had "been deliberately constructed and maintained to enforce racial segregation" the Court had to step in. "The remedy for such segregation may be administratively awkward, inconvenient, and even bizarre in some situations and may impose burdens on some; but all awkwardness and inconvenience cannot be avoided in the interim period when remedial adjustments are being made to eliminate the dual school systems." In a note of caution that would later affect other jurisdictions, the Court also declared that once a balance had been achieved and new district lines had been set out, "it would not be necessary to make year-by-year adjustments of the racial composition of student bodies." The Court understood that "in a growing, mobile society," few school districts would "remain demographically stable." Change would take place, and, although the federal courts could "deal with future problems," they would not be called on to do so "in the absence of a showing that either the school authorities or some other agency of the State has deliberately attempted to fix or alter demographic patterns to affect the racial composition of the schools."

In reality, the power of *Swann* proved to be limited to states and school districts, mostly in the South, where *de jure* segregation had been in effect. Moreover, it was something of a one-time fix. In ***Milliken v. Bradley,*** 418 U.S. 717 (1974), which involved Detroit and its suburbs, the Court refused to order city-county busing. When unitary schools were established in other places, the Court was reluctant to "deal with future problems" as segregation reemerged.

See Davison Douglas, *Reading, Writing, and Race: The Desegregation of the Charlotte Schools* (Chapel Hill: University of North Carolina Press, 1995); Davison Douglas, *School Busing: Constitutional and Political Developments* (New York: Garland, 1997); and Bernard Schwartz, *Swann's Way: The School Busing Case and the Supreme Court* (New York: Oxford University Press, 1986).

McGautha v. California

402 U.S. 183 (1971)
Decided: May 3, 1971
Vote: 6 (Burger, Black, Harlan II, Stewart, B. White, Blackmun)
3 (Douglas, Brennan, T. Marshall)
Opinion of the Court: Harlan II
Concurring opinion: Black
Dissenting opinion: Douglas (Brennan, T. Marshall)
Dissenting opinion: Brennan (Douglas, T. Marshall)

This case combined the appeals of two defendants sentenced to death, one in California (McGautha) and the other in Ohio (Crampton). Both defendants were sentenced under a system allowing "absolute" jury discretion to impose a death sentence. In addition, Crampton was sentenced under a system in which guilt and punishment were determined in a unitary trial.

The Court made three findings. First, permitting a jury unlimited discretion to sentence a defendant to death does not violate any constitutional protection. Second, it is not unconstitutional for a state to allow juries to determine guilt and punishment in the same trial. Third, the privilege against self-incrimination is not violated when a defendant is forced to choose between testifying in his own defense at trial, which allows the prosecution to cross-examine him, and not testifying, which would deny the defendant an opportunity to introduce potentially mitigating facts only he would know.

The Court held that absolute jury discretion is not unconstitutional because, given the vast universe of considerations that could inform the jury as to when the death penalty is just and when it is not, it is impossible to establish any clear guidelines to limit the jury's discretion. Noting that some commentators had recommended abolishing the death penalty because of the lack of guidelines, the Court found that jury discretion in itself does not make the death penalty unconstitutional.

Justice Black criticized the majority for implying that due process compliance turns on whether a trial comports with Supreme Court justices' subjective judgment of the fairness of a trial. In his view, the Court is free to overturn a state's imposition of the death sentence only when the state violates a right expressly guaranteed or implied by the Constitution.

In a passionate appeal for reading evolving standards of fairness into due process, Justice Douglas argued that Ohio's unitary trial violated the Fourteenth Amendment by denying the defendant the right to offer personal mitigating evidence by testifying without subjecting himself to cross-examination on a wide variety of subjects.

Justice Brennan's dissent criticized the majority for assuming that it is impossible to have legal standards for determining who should live and who should die and for concluding that in such a case the states should be allowed to impose the death penalty at all. In Brennan's opinion, if the death penalty can be administered in a principled way, the Constitution requires that it be so administered; and if it cannot, the Constitution requires that it be abolished.

Blonder-Tongue Laboratories, Inc. v. University of Illinois Foundation

402 U.S. 313 (1971)
Decided: May 3, 1971
Vote: 9 (Burger, Black, Douglas, Harlan II, Brennan, Stewart, B. White, T. Marshall, Blackmun)
0
Opinion of the Court: B. White

This case put an end to the privilege, previously enjoyed by holders of patents, of relitigating the validity of a patent with each new infringement action, provided it was against a new defendant. This practice was a part of the "mutuality" doctrine of *res judicata,* which held that a plaintiff could litigate again an issue he had previously lost as long as he did so against a new defendant. Because subsequent infringement actions usually were against new defendants, the mutuality doctrine, as embodied in *Triplett v. Lowell,* 297 U.S. 638 (1936), allowed patent holders to relitigate the validity of a patent that had been determined invalid in a previous lawsuit.

In this case, the University of Illinois Foundation held a patent that had been determined invalid in a patent infringement action. In a later patent infringement action, the alleged infringer defended by claiming that the first decision estopped—legally barred because of the earlier decision—the foundation from suing. The foundation replied that the *Triplett* doctrine allowed it to sue a new defendant without being estopped.

The Court rejected the *Triplett* rule, saying it "should be overruled to the extent it forecloses a plea of estoppel by one facing a charge of infringement of a patent that has once been declared invalid." The foundation's defense of the *Triplett* rule—that it protected against judicial error in complex patent cases—was weak because there was no reason to believe the judge in a subsequent case would be less prone to error than the judge in the first. Furthermore, other, less wasteful checks could be placed on judicial error. The decision pointed out the cost of devoting court time to an issue that had already been resolved and the fact that, because of the enormous expense of defending patent infringement actions, patent holders could often bully alleged infringers into paying royalties even though the patent had already been determined invalid.

The Court preserved the *Triplett* rule to this extent: as long as the party claiming a right in the patent has a chance to show that he did not have "a fair opportunity procedurally, substantively and evidentially to pursue his claim the first time," the party will not be estopped from raising the patent in a later suit. The Court included this step to allow a party to relitigate a patent that was erroneously invalidated by an earlier court because of a misunderstanding caused by the technical issues involved.

United States v. Thirty-Seven Photographs

402 U.S. 363 (1971)
Decided: May 3, 1971
Vote: 6 (Burger, Harlan II, Brennan, Stewart, B. White, Blackmun)
3 (Black, Douglas, T. Marshall)
Judgment of the Court: White
Opinion concurring in judgment: Harlan II
Opinion concurring in judgment: Stewart
Dissenting opinion: Black (Douglas)
Dissenting opinion: T. Marshall

Customs agents seized thirty-seven photographs from Milton Luros's luggage upon his reentering the United States from Europe. The photographs were intended to illustrate an edition of the Kama Sutra, an ancient Hindu text. The agents acted under 19 U.S.C. Section 1305(a), which prohibited anyone from importing obscene pictures into the United States. The law also provided that the secretary of the Treasury had the discretion to admit the classics or works of established literary or scientific merit. Luros sued to have Section 1305(a) declared unconstitutional. He argued that it violated procedural due process under ***Freedman v. Maryland,*** 380 U.S. 51 (1965), because it did not provide for prompt judicial review of the customs agents' decision to seize "obscene" items. Moreover, according to Luros, Section 1305(a) could not be applied to the photographs because the standards set out in ***Stanley v. Georgia,*** 394 U.S. 557 (1969), allowed adults to possess obscene material for purely private purposes. Luros argued that he had not sold or attempted to sell these photographs and therefore they should be seen as privately held under the standards of *Stanley.*

The Supreme Court acknowledged that the statute did not contain the time limits for prosecution required by its decision in *Freedman v. Maryland.* Nevertheless, Justice White "read explicit time limits into the section" to save it from being unconstitutional, even though the law set no explicit time limits. Based on the government's past practices, the Court concluded it was reasonable to require proceedings to be instituted within fourteen days and concluded within seventy-four days of seizure, and to assume that the statute included such standards, because clearly Congress would not deliberately write a statute that rejected constitutional standards.

The Court also held that *Stanley* did not prevent the government from seizing obscene items from the channels of foreign and interstate commerce. The Court did not determine in this case whether obscene items intended for home use could be seized from interstate commerce in light of *Stanley,* but it did say that such items could be seized from interstate commerce when they were intended for commercial use.

What is odd about the case is that Luros failed to argue that the statute would not apply to his pictures because they were intended to illustrate the Kama Sutra, which almost anyone would consider a classic. Instead, he attacked the statute as overbroad "because of its apparent prohibition of importation for private use," but, as he was importing for commercial use, Justice Harlan pointed out that he did not have standing to raise that claim.

Justice Stewart wrote to dissociate himself from the majority's implication that the government could prevent the importation of obscene materials intended for household use in light of *Stanley.*

Justice Black's dissent further developed his First Amendment jurisprudence of free speech absolutism that appeared in earlier cases such as *Smith v. California,* 361 U.S. 147 (1959), and ***Ginzburg v. United States,*** 383 U.S. 463 (1966). He criticized the Court for returning to the doctrine announced in ***Roth v. United States,*** 354 U.S. 476 (1957), that "obscenity" is a form of "unprotected" speech. He pointed to the hopelessness of judges deciding what work has "redeeming social value." The majority's emphasis on "redeeming social value" meant, for him, that "for the foreseeable future this Court must sit as a Board of Supreme Censors, sifting through books and magazines and watching movies because some official fears they deal too explicitly with sex." He added that this "absurd spectacle" could be avoided if the Court adhered to the First Amendment, which Black interpreted literally: Congress shall make *no* law abridging the freedom of speech, or of the press. He also attacked the plurality's implication that *Stanley* did not protect the importation of "obscene" material for private use as an evisceration of that decision. Finally, he criticized the plurality's "saving" of the statute by "reading in" specific time limits as an unconstitutional assumption of the legislative power.

Cohen v. California

403 U.S. 15 (1971)
Decided: June 7, 1971
Vote: 5 (Douglas, Harlan II, Brennan, Stewart, T. Marshall)
4 (Burger, Black, B. White, Blackmun)
Opinion of the Court: Harlan II
Dissenting opinion: Blackmun (Burger, Black, B. White)

This case asked whether a state can outlaw an "offensive" word altogether. Paul Robert Cohen was convicted of violating California Penal Code Section 415 for wearing a jacket bearing the words *Fuck the Draft* in the Los Angeles County Courthouse, where, according to the complaint, "there were women and children present." Section 415 prohibited "maliciously and willfully disturb[ing] the peace and quiet of any neighborhood or person ... by ... offensive conduct." The California court interpreted "offensive conduct" to mean conduct that caused a reasonably foreseeable likelihood that others would react violently.

The majority ruled out all the normal exceptions to the First Amendment. First, Cohen's message was not subject to regulation as "conduct" because there was no conduct other than conveying the message. Second, California did not show that Cohen intended to incite disobedience to the draft. Third, the statute was not a "time and place" restriction because it applied equally throughout the whole state. Fourth, Cohen's message was not "obscenity." Fifth, Cohen's message did not amount to "fighting words" because it was not "directed to the person of the hearer." Sixth, because the message was conveyed in a public place, the privacy interest necessary to curtail speech on the theory that it might be "thrust upon" an unwitting hearer in his home was not present. According to the Court, it appeared that none of the typical exceptions to free speech rights was present.

The majority therefore framed the issue as whether California can outlaw the word *fuck* in public. The majority found California's asserted rationale—that the word "is inherently likely to cause violent reaction" or that it was necessary to protect morals—too weak to support a wholesale ban on a particular word. The majority pointed out that "the State has no right to cleanse public debate to the point where it is grammatically palatable to the most squeamish among us." If the legislature were to try to pick and choose which words to outlaw, it would surely cause trouble, for "one man's vulgarity is another's lyric." According to the Court, the "Constitution leaves matters of taste and style ... largely to the individual." Furthermore, verbal discourse is composed not only of cognitive messages but also emotional ones. If the Constitution leaves people free to express content, but sharply circumscribes the manner in which they may do so by forbidding the use of provocative epithets and intensifiers, it would take away what is often the most important part of the message. Therefore, the statute as applied by the California court was unconstitutional.

Justice Black, long a defender of free speech, took a surprising turn in joining Justice Blackmun's dissent. The dissenters would have upheld the constitutionality of Section 415 because Cohen's message *was* conduct, which can be regulated. In addition, the Court based its finding of unconstitutionality on the California Court of Appeals' construction of Section 415, which was no longer controlling; the California Supreme Court had recently interpreted the section in a way that appeared more consistent with the First Amendment.

This opinion is as interesting for what the Court's rhetoric reveals about the social pressures on the justices as the legal rule it established. Although the majority decided in favor of Cohen's First Amendment right, it could not hide its distaste for his behavior. In a patronizing tone, the Court suggests that his message is a crude, semiliterate annoyance to be tolerated by those who are mature enough not to seek attention in such childish ways. The majority opinion opens by saying that the fate of Cohen's freedom of speech is "too inconsequential to find its way into our books" and that Cohen "crudely defaced" his jacket. The dissent calls Cohen's message "an absurd and immature antic." It is not clear why the justices felt compelled to trivialize a political debate that was not trivial to Cohen or his "listeners." At the height of the Vietnam War, the draft was a matter of life or death, and to any casual observer it went to the heart of the First Amendment's protections.

See William S. Cohen, "A Look Back at *Cohen v. California,*" *UCLA Law Review* 34 (1987): 1595; and Ronald J. Krotoszynski Jr., "*Cohen v. California:* 'Inconsequential' Cases and Larger Principles," *Texas Law Review* 74 (1996): 1251.

Bivens v. Six Unknown Named Agents of Federal Bureau of Narcotics

403 U.S. 388 (1971)
Decided: June 21, 1971
Vote: 6 (Douglas, Harlan II, Brennan, Stewart, B. White, T. Marshall)
3 (Burger, Black, Blackmun)
Opinion of the Court: Brennan
Opinion concurring in judgment: Harlan II
Dissenting opinion: Burger
Dissenting opinion: Black
Dissenting opinion: Blackmun

Federal narcotics agents entered Bivens's apartment without a warrant, manacled him in front of his wife and children, threatened to arrest his family, searched the place, and took him to the police station for a strip search. Bivens sued for damages for emotional distress, alleging that the agents carried out the search and arrest without probable cause in violation of the Fourth Amendment. The agents asserted that Bivens's right to privacy, the violation of which he claimed led to his emotional distress, was created by state law, not the Fourth Amendment. They argued that because there was no federal question at issue, the federal court lacked jurisdiction and the case should be dismissed. Should Bivens refile his case in state court, it could be decided under state law. The Fourth Amendment would then be irrelevant to the decision of the case, unless Bivens brought it up to rebut a claim by the agents that their actions were a "valid exercise of federal power." The district court apparently agreed with the agents and dismissed the case for failure to state a federal cause of action, and the court of appeals affirmed.

The Supreme Court reversed, holding that when federal agents, acting under color of their authority, violate the Fourth Amendment, the victim may sue for damages. The Court said that the fact that the agents exceeded the bounds of the Fourth Amendment does not mean the case should be treated the same as a trespassing suit against a private citizen. Justice Brennan's opinion pointed out that the Fourth Amendment does not forbid only such action as would be forbidden to private citizens. For example, officers making an arrest without probable cause violate the Fourth Amendment even if the arrestee has actually committed a felony, but a private person making a "citizen's arrest" is not liable for damages in the same circumstances. Furthermore, if a private citizen is allowed to enter a home after demanding entry, he is not liable for trespass, but if a federal officer without probable cause is allowed to enter because he claims federal authority, he has violated the Fourth Amendment. According to Brennan, "It is . . . well settled that where legal rights have been invaded, and a federal statute provides for a general right to sue for such invasion, federal courts may use any available remedy to make good the wrong done."

Justice Harlan found no reason to treat a constitutional provision any differently from a statutory provision with regard to whether the judiciary can create a remedy to enforce it. He also addressed the policy considerations of allowing an action for damages, saying that the "exclusionary rule," in itself, does not provide a remedy for Bivens—it merely prevents the further harm of his being convicted. Harlan rejected the government's argument that allowing Bivens's suit would set a precedent for frivolous lawsuits wasting judicial resources. "When we automatically close the courthouse door solely on this basis," he wrote, "we implicitly express a value judgment on the comparative importance of classes of legally protected interests," and Fourth Amendment rights should be valued as highly as, "for example, the interests of stockholders defrauded by misleading proxies."

Chief Justice Burger's dissent focused on the exclusionary rule (even though it was not an issue in the case), making a broad appeal for its abandonment. According to Burger, the exclusionary rule should be replaced by an act of Congress that would overcome its shortcomings and provide a remedy to people like Bivens. Burger believed the proper place for such a remedy was the legislature, not the courts. Justice Black dissented because he also felt that the Court was usurping legislative authority and because he was concerned about a flood of Fourth Amendment lawsuits choking the federal courts.

See Susan Bandes, "Reinventing *Bivens:* The Self-Executing Constitution," *Southern California Law Review* 68 (1995): 28; Cornelia T. L. Pillard, "Taking Fiction Seriously: The Strange Results of Public Officials' Individual Liability Under *Bivens,*" *Georgetown Law Journal* 88 (1999): 65; Note, "Damage Remedies Against Municipalities for Constitutions Violations," *Harvard Law Review* 89 (1976) 922; and Mariana Claridad Pastore, "Running From the Law: Federal Contractors Escape *Bivens* Liability," *University of Pennsylvania Journal of Constitutional Law,* 4 (2002): 850.

Coolidge v. New Hampshire

403 U.S. 443 (1971)
Decided: June 21, 1971
Vote: 5 (Douglas, Harlan II, Brennan, Stewart, T. Marshall)
4 (Burger, Black, B. White, Blackmun)
Opinion of the Court: Stewart
Concurring in judgment: Harlan II
Dissenting opinion: Burger
Dissenting opinion: Black (Blackmun)
Dissenting opinion: B. White (Burger)

This case highlighted the Burger Court's lack of consensus regarding Fourth Amendment issues such as the extent of the warrant requirement, the scope of the "plain view" doctrine, and the "neutral and detached magistrate" requirement for search warrants.

In the course of investigating the murder of fourteen-year-old Pamela Mason, police questioned Edward Coolidge, who voluntarily showed them three of his guns and took a lie detector test. "The police later described his attitude on the occasion of this visit as fully 'cooperative.' " While he was taking the test, two police officers went to his house and interviewed his wife. They obtained from her four guns belonging to Coolidge and clothing that she thought Coolidge might have been wearing on the evening the girl disappeared. Police held Coolidge in jail on an unrelated charge for the night and then released him.

During the next two weeks, the state attorney general took charge of the investigation and ultimately concluded he had enough evidence to arrest Coolidge. The chief of police of Manchester, New Hampshire, then sought a warrant to search Coolidge's car. The attorney general, who was running the investigation, was also a justice of the peace under New Hampshire law. Acting in his capacity as justice of the peace, the attorney general granted the police chief's request for a search warrant. Over Coolidge's objections, evidence from the car as well as evidence offered by his wife was used to convict him at trial.

The Supreme Court held that the search warrant for the car violated the Fourth Amendment because it was issued by the district attorney, who was a professional with a stake in the outcome, not a "neutral and detached magistrate." The Court also held that the evidence offered by Coolidge's wife was admissible because the Fourth Amendment is not implicated when evidence is offered by a private citizen who is not an agent of the police.

The government argued that the search of the car was legal under an exception to the warrant requirement, even though the search warrant was invalid. The Court rejected each proposed exception. First, the search was not valid as a "search incident to arrest," because an arrest of a person outside a car does not justify a search of the car. Second, the search was not justified by ***Carroll v. United States,*** 267 U.S. 132 (1925), in which the Court held that police may make a warrantless search of a car as long as they have probable cause, if there is a danger of the car being driven out of the jurisdiction or "cleaned" out by the defendant's associates if the police do not act quickly. In this case, the car was parked in the defendant's driveway, and police could easily have watched it while they obtained a warrant. Because the search was not justified under *Carroll,* it was also not justified under ***Chambers v. Maroney,*** 399 U.S. 42 (1970), which held that police may take a car to the police station to search it, if they are justified in making a warrantless search under *Carroll.* Third, the search could not be justified on the theory that, as an "instrumentality of the crime," the car could be seized because it was in "plain view." The plain view doctrine does not mean that any item that is in plain view may be seized without a warrant. Instead, the doctrine "supplement[s] . . . prior justification" for an intrusion of privacy and limits the seizure of evidence not related to the original justification to contraband in plain view, which prevents searches from becoming "exploratory" searches. The Court also said that "the discovery of evidence in plain view must be inadvertent," meaning that the police could not legitimate a "planned warrantless seizure on plain-view grounds." The police may not "justify a planned warrantless seizure by maneuvering themselves within 'plain view' of the object they want."

Justice Harlan concurred in the result because of the precedent established in ***Mapp v. Ohio,*** 367 U.S. 643 (1961), which created the exclusionary rule, and ***Ker v. California,*** 374 U.S. 23 (1963), which applied federal standards to the states. In his opinion, however, Harlan said he thought those cases should be overruled. Harlan agreed with the Court that the district attorney could not be considered a "neutral and detached magistrate," that the Warrant Clause required the police to obtain a warrant whenever they could feasibly do so—in other words, no exigent circumstances were present—and that the Fourth Amendment was not violated when the police accepted Mrs. Coolidge's uncoerced offer of evidence.

Justice Black's dissent also called for the elimination of the exclusionary rule. He pointed out that the language of the Fourth Amendment did not exclude an attorney general from acting as a magistrate and that, even if it did, the search of the car should have been valid on all three exceptions to the warrant requirement put forth by the government.

Justice White believed that the search of the car should have been valid as a seizure of "evidence of the crime in plain sight."

Chief Justice Burger joined White and concurred with Black's opinion regarding the attorney general being constitutionally capable of signing a search warrant as a magistrate and that the car was searchable under the plain view doctrine.

See Jacob Landynski, "The Supreme Court's Search for Fourth Amendment Standards: The Extraordinary Case of *Coolidge v. New Hampshire,*" *Connecticut Bar Journal* 45 (December 1971).

Lemon v. Kurtzman

403 U.S. 602 (1971)
Decided: June 28, 1971
Vote: Multiple
Opinion of the Court: Burger
Concurring opinion: Douglas (Black, T. Marshall)
Concurring opinion: Brennan
Concurring in judgment (Pennsylvania case): B. White
Dissenting opinion (Rhode Island cases): B. White
Did not participate (Pennsylvania case): T. Marshall

The Court decided three cases—*Lemon v. Kurtzman* from Pennsylvania and *Earley v. DiCenso* and *Robinson v. DiCenso* from Rhode Island and developed a test, known as the *Lemon* test, for determining whether a state statute violates the Establishment Clause of the Constitution by aiding religion. The *Lemon* test consists of three prongs, and a statute that violates any of the prongs would be considered a violation of the Establishment Clause. Chief Justice Burger did not invent these tests, but claimed they could be gleaned from previous cases. He asserted that for a statute involving aid to religion to pass constitutional muster, "First, the statute must have a secular legislative purpose; second, its principal or primary effect must be one that neither advances nor inhibits religion; finally, the statute must not foster 'an excessive government entanglement with religion.' "

The Rhode Island cases involved a program under which the state would pay 15 percent of the salaries of parochial school teachers who taught only secular subjects and who had state teaching certificates. The state passed this law because about 25 percent of Rhode Island students attended Catholic schools, which needed additional funding to hire lay teachers who required competitive salaries. If these schools closed for lack of funds, the state would have to build and staff many new schools, at great expense. After an extensive factual investigation, the district court found

> that the parochial schools constituted "an integral part of the religious mission of the Catholic Church." The various characteristics of the schools make them "a powerful vehicle for transmitting the Catholic faith to the next generation." This process of inculcating religious doctrine is, of course, enhanced by the impressionable age of the pupils, in primary schools particularly. In short, parochial schools involve substantial religious activity and purpose.

The district court concluded that the Rhode Island law violated the Establishment Clause, "holding that it fostered 'excessive entanglement' between government and religion. In addition two judges thought that the Act had the impermissible effect of giving 'significant aid to a religious enterprise.' " Seven justices agreed with the district court, with only Justice White dissenting.

Pennsylvania's program authorized the "state Superintendent of Public Instruction to 'purchase' specified 'secular educational services' from nonpublic schools" at rates negotiated between the schools and the superintendent. Under these " 'contracts' authorized by the statute, the State directly reimburses nonpublic schools solely for their actual expenditures for teachers' salaries, textbooks, and instructional materials." Alton Lemon, an African American parent of a public school student, sued David Kurtzman, the state superintendent of public instruction, on First Amendment grounds and on an Equal Protection claim under the Fourteenth Amendment. The federal court rebuffed, on standing grounds, attempts by the National Association for the Advancement of Colored People (NAACP) to challenge the law on the grounds that it discriminated against minorities who were more likely to be in public school. Lemon, a taxpayer, was able to gain standing, but a three-judge panel dismissed the suit. The majority on the panel found that the statute had a secular purpose of promoting the welfare of the state. The Supreme Court reversed and remanded the case to the district court. The district court then struck down the Pennsylvania law, but allowed the state to reimburse schools for funds they had spent before the law was challenged. A bitterly divided Supreme Court upheld this complicated ruling in *Lemon v. Kurtzman.*

Although the *Lemon* test has been criticized by conservatives as being too hard, and by liberals, for being too vague, it has remained viable. In ***Lamb's Chapel v. Center Moriches Union Free School District,*** 508 U.S. 384 (1993), for example, Justice Scalia complained, "Like some ghoul in a late-night horror movie that repeatedly sits up in its grave and shuffles abroad after being repeatedly killed and buried, *Lemon* stalks our Establishment Clause jurisprudence . . . frightening . . . little children and school attorneys." Others, however, see it as a workable and useful test for mediating the tensions between citizens who want tax dollars to support their parochial schools, and other citizens who believe no one's tax dollars should ever support someone else's religion. Even in the light of recent cases expanding the use of school vouchers, *Lemon* remains alive as a test for determining the extent to which church and state can mix.

See Paul Finkelman, *Religion and American Law: An Encyclopedia* (New York: Garland, 2000); Leonard W. Levy, *The Establishment Clause: Religion and the First Amendment* (New York: Macmillan, 1988); Michael Stokes Paulsen, "*Lemon* Is Dead," *Case Western Reserve Law Review* 43 (1993): 795; and Robert L. Kilroy, "A Lost Opportunity to Sweeten the *Lemon* of Establishment Clause Jurisprudence: An Analysis of *Rosenberger v. Rector & Visitors of the University of Virginia,*" *Cornell Journal of Law and Public Policy* 6 (1997): 701.

Tilton v. Richardson

403 U.S. 672 (1971)
Decided: June 28, 1971
Vote: 5 (Burger, Harlan II, Stewart, B. White, Blackmun)
4 (Black, Douglas, Brennan, T. Marshall)
Judgment of the Court: Burger
Opinion concurring in judgment: B. White
Dissenting opinion: Douglas (Black, T. Marshall)
Dissenting opinion: Brennan

This case was a companion to ***Lemon v. Kurtzman,*** 403 U.S. 602 (1971), which involved various types of state aid to primary parochial education. In *Lemon* the Court struck down the aid schemes on Establishment Clause grounds, but here the Court narrowly upheld some federal aid to religious colleges.

Title I of the Higher Education Facilities Act of 1963 provided "construction grants for buildings and facilities used exclusively for secular educational purposes." The purpose of the act was to provide facilities to meet a dramatic increase in the demand for higher education. No facility built under the act could be used for religious instruction, and this requirement was enforced by on-site inspections. Section 754(b)(2), however, stated that after twenty years the religious colleges could use the government-financed facilities for any purpose, including religious instruction.

In *Tilton v. Richardson* taxpayers sought a declaration that the act exceeded Congress's spending authority by aiding religion in violation of the Establishment Clause of the First Amendment. Specifically, this case involves the severability of the unconstitutional portions of an otherwise constitutional act of Congress. The Court held that Section 754(b)(2) was unconstitutional, but that it could be severed from the rest of the law. The Court found that the act reflected a secular legislative purpose, which was to ensure ample opportunity for the intellectual development of America's youth. The "principal or primary effect" of the act was not to aid religion, and the mere possibility that it might be subverted to that end did not invalidate it. Unlike the statute in *Lemon,* the enforcement of the act would not require "excessive entanglements" with religion. *Lemon* involved state aid for primary parochial schools, and the record in those cases showed that religious indoctrination was a primary task for such schools. The critical and free-thinking nature of collegiate curricula and the substantially diminished impressionability of the college student make religious indoctrination a less feasible goal of higher education than primary education, and the colleges in question did not seem to attempt any indoctrination. Because religion was less likely to permeate the curricula in these schools, less government supervision was necessary, obviating the risk of excessive entanglement. This was especially true because the act called for a one-time grant, instead of ongoing aid as in *Lemon.* Finally, appellants did not attempt to show that the act interfered with their free exercise of religion. The Court found that the act survived First Amendment scrutiny, except for Section 754(b)(2), which unconstitutionally allowed federal money to advance religion.

Justice Douglas dissented on the theory that government money for the construction of buildings was aid to the religious schools, not the students, and did not meet the narrow exception carved out by ***Everson v. Board of Education,*** 330 U.S. 1 (1947), which allowed public-financed transportation to parochial schools. Even if Section 754(b)(2) were severed, the funding of the facilities was unconstitutional because the money would get mixed up with other funds of the school and be diverted to religious uses. Moreover, acceptance of the funds would require the schools to observe public school standards, such as no requirement of prayer, that would be obnoxious to religion and would require an excessive entanglement for the government to enforce.

See J. Wilson Parker, "State Support for Religious Colleges," in *Religion and American Law: An Encyclopedia,* ed. Paul Finkelman (New York: Garland, 2000), 474–477.

New York Times v. United States

403 U.S. 713 (1971)
Decided: June 30, 1971
Vote: 6 (Black, Douglas, Brennan, Stewart, B. White, T. Marshall)
3 (Burger, Harlan II, Blackmun)
Opinion: *Per curiam*
Concurring opinion: Black (Douglas)
Concurring opinion: Douglas (Black)
Concurring opinion: Brennan
Concurring opinion: Stewart (B. White)
Concurring opinion: B. White (Stewart)
Concurring opinion: T. Marshall
Dissenting opinion: Burger
Dissenting opinion: Harlan II (Burger, Blackmun)
Dissenting opinion: Blackmun

The case collectively known as the *Pentagon Papers Case—New York Times Company v. United States* and *United States v. The Washington Post Company*—was profoundly important for the development of freedom of the press in the late twentieth century. The case was tied to the failure of the national administration to either win the Vietnam War or end it and the increasing domestic opposition to that war.

In the mid-1960s the Defense Department initiated an internal study of how the United States became involved in Vietnam. Much of this classified study, formally titled "History of U.S. Decision-Making Process on Viet Nam Policy," was truly embarrassing to the government because it revealed the extent to which the Johnson administration had misled Congress and the American people not only about the causes of the war but also U.S. military and political policies in Vietnam. When President Richard Nixon took office and failed to fulfill his campaign promise to end the war, one of the national security experts who worked on the study, Daniel Ellsberg, leaked it to the *New York Times.* The first installment appeared on June 13, 1971.

The Nixon administration initially ignored the publication because it merely embarrassed Nixon's Democratic predecessor, Lyndon Johnson. Two days later, however, the administration recognized that publication was a threat to its policies and sought an injunction to prevent the *New York Times* from publishing any more of the Pentagon Papers. The district court refused the injunction, but the Second Circuit Court granted it. Immediately, the *Washington Post* received a copy of the documents and began publishing them. The Nixon administration sought an injunction against the *Post* as well, but neither the district court nor the Circuit Court for the District of Columbia would grant it. These courts, along with the District Court for the Southern District of New York, agreed that "any system of prior restraints of expression comes to" the court "bearing a heavy presumption against its constitutional validity" and that the government "carries a heavy burden of showing justification for the imposition of such a restraint." Three of the four lower courts that heard the cases believed the government had not met its burden.

The Supreme Court granted certiorari on June 25 and held oral arguments the next day. Four days later, on June 30, the Court decided the case in a brief *per curiam* decision, followed by nine separate opinions. By the time the case was decided, most of the Pentagon Papers had been published by U.S. newspapers. Moreover, papers in Toronto, Canada, beyond the reach of American injunctions, were also publishing installments of the secret history of the war. The case pitted Solicitor General Erwin Griswold, a former Harvard Law School dean, against Alexander Bickel, Yale Law School's prominent First Amendment specialist.

Griswold argued that the publication of the Pentagon Papers threatened on-going peace negotiations as well as the lives of soldiers in the field and prisoners of war in North Vietnam. The newspapers made it clear that they would not publish anything that touched on diplomatic negotiations and that they were prepared to publish only materials on U.S. internal policy. Griswold later expressed doubts about the government's position in the case, saying that the final decision "came out exactly as it should" have.

The Court divided into three groups. Justices Black, Douglas, and Brennan argued that any form of prior restraint was unconstitutional. As Black put it, "Both the history and language of the First Amendment support the view that the press must be left free to publish news, whatever the source, without censorship, injunctions, or prior restraints." Brennan asserted that "the First Amendment tolerates absolutely no prior judicial restraints of the press predicated upon surmise or conjecture that untoward consequences may result." Citing ***Schenck v. United States,*** 249 U.S. 47 (1919), Brennan conceded that "there is a single, extremely narrow class of cases in which the First Amendment's ban on prior judicial restraint may be overridden." If the nation is at war, as Justice Holmes wrote in *Schenck,* "No one would question but that a government might prevent actual obstruction to its recruiting service or the publication of the sailing dates of transports or the number and location of troops." But, Brennan noted, the nation was not legally at war in 1971, and, even if it were, the Pentagon Papers did not reveal on-going military activities, but discussed only the history of the war.

The second group, Justices Stewart, White, and Marshall, conceded that some form of government control, perhaps greater than Brennan would allow, might be permissible if it could be shown that the censorship was absolutely necessary for the security of the nation. This standard was difficult for the government to meet, and, as Stewart noted with regard to the facts in the material, "I cannot say that disclosure of any of them will surely result in direct, immediate, and irreparable damage to our Nation or its people." The government might be embarrassed, but it was not the role of the courts to save the executive branch from embarrassment. Indeed, in an analysis that in another context might have been about separation of powers, Stewart argued that in keeping national secrets, "The responsibility must be where the power is. If the Constitution gives the Executive a large degree of unshared power in the conduct of foreign affairs and the maintenance of our national defense, then under the Constitution the Executive must have the largely unshared duty to determine and preserve the degree of internal security necessary to exercise that power successfully."

The third group, led by Chief Justice Burger, objected to the speed of the proceedings and would have granted the temporary injunctions to allow more time to evaluate the Pentagon Papers. Burger also stressed that Daniel Ellsberg was subject to criminal prosecution for leaking the papers. On this point, Burger was correct. Ellsberg was ultimately tried for his role in leaking classified material, but all charges were dropped when the courts learned of the illegal activities of the Nixon administration in gathering information against him, including having White House employees burglarize the offices of Ellsberg's therapist.

In the end, the publication of the Pentagon Papers did not undermine national security. Instead, it awoke the American people to the dangers of secrecy in government and the lengths to which several presidential administrations went to mislead the people about U.S. involvement in Southeast Asia. More important, the Court preserved the First Amendment right of publishers to publish and the people to read, without government censorship.

See Daniel Ellsberg, *Secrets: A Memoir of Vietnam and the Pentagon Papers* (New York: Viking Press, 2002); and David Rudenstine, *The Day the Presses Stopped: A History of the Pentagon Papers Case* (Berkeley: University of California Press, 1996).

Reed v. Reed

404 U.S. 71 (1971)
Decided: November 22, 1971
Vote: 7 (Burger, Douglas, Brennan, Stewart, B. White, T. Marshall, Blackmun)
0
Opinion of the Court: Burger

When Richard Lynn Reed, a minor, died without a will, both of his parents petitioned to be appointed the administrator of his estate. At the time Sally Reed and Cecil Reed were legally separated. The child's estate was valued at less than $1,000. In a joint hearing, the probate court appointed the father based on Section 15–314 of the Idaho Code, which gave preference to males if both applicants were from the same entitlement class, meaning they had the same relationship to the deceased. Reversed by the district court, the father appealed. The Idaho Supreme Court reinstated the probate court's order appointing the father.

In appealing the decision, Sally Reed contended that the statute violated the Equal Protection Clause. The district court agreed and reversed the decision of the probate court. This time Cecil Reed appealed. The state supreme court "reinstated the original order naming the father administrator of the estate."

The U.S. Supreme Court found that Idaho's statute violated the Equal Protection Clause of the Fourteenth Amendment. Analyzing the statute, Chief Justice Burger determined that it created a classification scheme. The statute's treatment of an individual was determined by that person's sex, but the Equal Protection Clause guarantees that states give similar treatment to all classes. Sally Reed's lawyers asked the Court to apply a standard of strict scrutiny to the statute. Under strict scrutiny, the statute must bear some rational relationship to its intended objective to survive scrutiny. The state asserted that the statute "reduc[es] the workload on probate courts by eliminating one class of contestants," but the Court found that objective did not justify the discrimination built into the statute.

This very short opinion signaled a significant change in Supreme Court jurisprudence. Before this case, the Court had consistently allowed states to discriminate on the basis of gender. Thus, in ***Bradwell v. Illinois,*** 83 U.S. 130 (1873), the Court allowed a state to prevent women from becoming lawyers; in ***Goesaert v. Cleary,*** 335 U.S. 464 (1948), the Court upheld a law preventing women from tending bar; and in ***Hoyt v. Florida,*** 368 U.S. 57 (1961), the Court allowed a statute that exempted women from jury service. Here, for the first time, the Court rejected this line of cases, holding that statutes that made distinctions based on gender, although not always unconstitutional, were subject to a heightened scrutiny because they were "the very kind of arbitrary legislative choice forbidden by the Equal Protection Clause" of the Fourteenth Amendment. *Reed* eventually became an important precedent for striking down other laws that discriminated on the basis of gender.

See Deborah L. Markowitz, "In Pursuit of Equality: One Women's Work to Change the Law," *Women's Rights Report* 14 (1992): 335.

Dunn v. Blumstein

405 U.S. 330 (1972)
Decided: March 21, 1972
Vote: 6 (Douglas, Brennan, Stewart, B. White, T. Marshall, Blackmun)
1 (Burger)
Opinion of the Court: T. Marshall
Opinion concurring in judgment: Blackmun
Dissenting opinion: Burger
Did not participate: Powell, Rehnquist

Approximately three weeks after moving to Tennessee to become a law professor at Vanderbilt University, James Blumstein attempted to register to vote in the August and November elections. His registration was denied because of a Tennessee constitutional provision and statute requiring residency in the state for at least one year prior to the election date. Tennessee claimed the constitutional provision and statute ensured bona fide residency and an informed voting population. Because the right to vote is a fundamental right, and because the classification of "old" and "new" residents is suspect, the appropriate equal protection test was whether the statute was necessary to meet a compelling state interest.

Several years earlier, the Court had held in ***Kramer v. Union Free School District,*** 395 U.S. 621 (1969), that voting was a fundamental right. That case dealt with a requirement to own property to be eligible to vote on raising property taxes. Discrimination on the basis of recent arrival in the state is suspect because it penalizes citizens for exercising their fundamental right to travel. Furthermore, because the Tennessee residence scheme discriminated against new residents, it was irrelevant whether the denial of voting rights to new residents actually deterred travel. Although the state interests asserted by Tennessee (ensuring bona fide residency and an informed voting public) were compelling, discriminating against new residents was not a necessary means of satisfying that interest. A potential voter's status as a bona fide resident can be determined when he registers to vote.

Justice Blackmun determined that this decision overruled *Pope v. Williams,* 193 U.S. 621 (1904), in which the Court held that states may limit the franchise to residents who declare an intent to vote one year in advance. He called for a reasonable standard, saying that some residency requirement that was less than one year, but more than thirty days, might be constitutional.

Chief Justice Burger claimed that the Tennessee residency requirement was constitutional because it furthered the interest of ensuring an informed, bona fide electorate, even if those interests could have been met by a more narrowly drawn system. He appeared to disapprove of the majority's application of the "compelling interest" test and to advocate for a "rational relationship" test.

Eisenstadt v. Baird

405 U.S. 438 (1972)
Decided: March 22, 1972
Vote: 6 (Douglas, Brennan, Stewart, B. White, T. Marshall, Blackmun)
1 (Burger)
Opinion of the Court: Brennan
Concurring opinion: Douglas
Concurring in judgment: B. White (Blackmun)
Dissenting opinion: Burger
Did not participate: Powell, Rehnquist

William Baird was convicted of giving a contraceptive to an unmarried person in violation of Massachusetts law. Under Section 21 of the statute, contraceptives for the purpose of preventing pregnancy could be distributed only by licensed physicians or pharmacists to married persons. Violators of the statute could be sentenced to up to five years in prison. The Court held that Section 21 violated the Equal Protection Clause because the different treatment it gave to single people and married people was not rationally related to the statute's purpose. (The Court did not have to use the "compelling interest" test because it the statute did not satisfy even the "rational basis" test.)

The state argued that Section 21 had one of three alternative purposes, each of which would have explained the difference in treatment: preventing premarital sex, protecting public health from potentially harmful contraceptives, and protecting public morals. The Court determined that only preventing premarital sex would have justified a different treatment of married and single persons, and that was clearly not Section 21's objective. Single people could obtain contraceptives for purposes other than preventing pregnancy, and the punishment for distributing contraceptives to single people was far out of proportion to the punishment for engaging in premarital sex. On the other hand, if the statute was meant as a ban on contraceptives *per se,* then it must treat single and married people alike to survive equal protection scrutiny.

Baird was not a licensed physician, a pharmacist, or a single person seeking contraceptives for preventing pregnancy. If he did not suffer a direct harm from Section 21, did he have standing to challenge it? The majority reasoned that because Section 21 did not penalize single persons who received contraceptives for preventing pregnancy, such persons would never have an opportunity to defend their interests in court. Because Baird was an advocate of their rights, the Court found that he had standing.

This case was one in a series of decisions that helped develop the constitutional right of privacy and equal protection in areas of sexuality. It followed ***Griswold v. Connecticut,*** 381 U.S. 479 (1965), which struck down a total ban on the use of contraception, and it set the stage for ***Roe v. Wade,*** 410 U.S. 113 (1973), which legalized abortion in the United States.

See David J. Garrow, *Liberty and Sexuality: The Right to Privacy and the Making of* Roe v. Wade (New York: Macmillan, 1994).

Stanley v. Illinois

405 U.S. 645 (1972)
Decided: April 3, 1972
Vote: 5 (Douglas, Brennan, Stewart, B. White, T. Marshall)
2 (Burger, Blackmun)
Opinion of the Court: B. White
Dissenting opinion: Burger (Blackmun)
Did not participate: Powell, Rehnquist

An Illinois statute provided that when an unmarried mother died, the state would assume custody of her children without a hearing on the father's fitness as a parent. For eighteen years Peter Stanley had lived intermittently with Joan Stanley, but they were never legally married. When Joan Stanley died, Illinois declared their three children wards of the state and assigned them to court-appointed guardians. Peter Stanley appealed this decision. He said he had never been shown to be an unfit parent, and, because married fathers and unwed mothers could not be deprived of their children without such a showing, he was being denied the equal protection of the laws in violation of the Fourteenth Amendment. The Supreme Court agreed with Stanley, finding "as a matter of due process of law, Stanley was entitled to a hearing on his fitness as a parent before his children were taken from him."

The state argued that as a matter of administrative convenience, "unwed fathers are presumed unfit to raise their children and that it is unnecessary to hold individualized hearings to determine whether particular fathers are in fact unfit parents before they are separated from their children." When it accepted the case, the Court noted that "Illinois allows married fathers—whether divorced, widowed, or separated—and mothers—even if unwed—the benefit of the presumption that they are fit to raise their children." The Court rejected the state's argument, holding that administrative convenience is an insufficient justification for depriving fathers of such an important interest without first affording them an opportunity to defend their interest in raising their children. Although not directly a sex discrimination case, this decision reflected the new jurisprudence seen in ***Reed v. Reed,*** 404 U.S. 71 (1971), which began to undermine laws that made distinction on the basis of gender.

Sierra Club v. Morton

405 U.S. 727 (1972)
Decided: April 19, 1972
Vote: 4 (Burger, Stewart, B. White, T. Marshall)
3 (Douglas, Brennan, Blackmun)
Opinion of the Court: Stewart
Dissenting opinion: Douglas
Dissenting opinion: Brennan
Dissenting opinion: Blackmun
Did not participate: Powell, Rehnquist

This case involved the standing of an environmental advocacy organization to sue to prevent environmental damage that does not specifically harm any members of the organization. The Court held that the organization did not have standing.

The Sierra Club sued to enjoin the construction of a ski resort in the Sequoia National Forest, not because the development would interfere with the club or its members, but because it would hurt the aesthetics and ecology of the forest. The Administrative Procedure Act (APA) provided that those who were "injured in fact" by an administrative action had standing to challenge the action in court. The Court determined that the "injury" contemplated by the act was economic injury, not injury to the public interest. The Court noted, however, that once a litigant establishes a personal economic injury, he is free to assert any public injury that might bolster his case. The Court stressed that the Sierra Club never alleged that any of its members would be adversely affected by the construction of the ski resort. Had harm been alleged, that person would have standing and the Court would have had jurisdiction to consider whether the government had improperly allowed the Disney Corporation to build the ski resort. Of the goal of keeping the decision to seek judicial review in the hands of a stakeholder, Justice Stewart wrote, "That goal would be undermined were we to construe the APA to authorize judicial review at the behest of organizations or individuals who seek to do no more than vindicate their own value preferences through the judicial process. The principle that the Sierra Club would have us establish in this case would do just that."

In dissent, Justice Douglas wrote, "Contemporary public concern for protecting nature's ecological equilibrium should lead to the conferral of standing upon environmental objects to sue for their own preservation." Citing an article by law professor Christopher Stone, Douglas would have allowed environmental groups to represent the environment in litigation. Significantly, while denying standing here, the Court validated the idea that environmental injury could give a plaintiff standing.

See Laurence H. Tribe, "Ways Not To Think About Plastic Trees: New Foundations for Environmental Law," *Yale Law Journal* 84 (1974): 1315; and Christopher D. Stone, "Should Trees Have Standing?—Toward Legal Rights for Natural Objects," *Southern California Law Review* 45 (1972): 450.

Wisconsin v. Yoder

406 U.S. 205 (1972)
Decided: May 15, 1972
Vote: 6 (Burger, Brennan, Stewart, B. White, T. Marshall, Blackmun)
1 (Douglas)
Opinion of the Court: Burger
Concurring opinion: Stewart (Brennan)
Concurring opinion: B. White (Brennan, Stewart)
Dissenting opinion: Douglas
Did not participate: Powell, Rehnquist

Members of the Amish Mennonite Church, sometimes know as the Old Order Amish, regularly withdrew their children from public school at age fourteen, in violation of state law that required attendance until age sixteen. The Amish believed that attending high school would corrupt their children, make them question their religious values, and lead them away from the church and out of the Amish community. Wisconsin prosecuted the Amish under the state's compulsory school attendance law. The Wisconsin Supreme Court held that the First Amendment to the U.S. Constitution protected the religious rights of the Amish to withdraw their children from school, and the U.S. Supreme Court affirmed.

Chief Justice Burger stressed the quaintness of the Amish, their long history, which predated the Constitution, and their record of being law-abiding, productive citizens. He argued that the parents have a right to remove the children from school to protect their religious faith. Burger tied this argument to older cases involving education and children, including ***Meyer v. Nebraska,*** 262 U.S. 390 (1923), and ***Pierce v. Society of Sisters,*** 268 U.S. 510 (1925).

Justice Douglas in dissent argued that the principal issue in the case was the desire of the children, who at fourteen were capable of deciding for themselves if they wanted to attend school. He noted that by allowing the parents to remove their children from school, the Court was complicit in preventing Amish children from obtaining the education necessary to compete in the larger society.

The decision was marked by tensions between religious traditions and the traditions of civil republicanism, with its emphasis on a well-educated population. Burger tried to limit the decision to the Amish, on the grounds that they form a unique community, but such a result was not possible. *Yoder* led to demands from other religions, primarily fundamentalist Protestants, for the right to remove children from public school because of perceived challenges to specific religious beliefs. One result has been the growth of private schools and home schooling, but, in addition, parents feel free to remove their children from science or literature classes that, they assert, teach material that violates their religious values and beliefs. *Yoder* has not only undermined public education but also led to children not getting the full benefit of education because of the demands of religiously motivated parents. This result mirrors Justice Douglas's partial dissent, which stressed that in deferring to the parents' wishes, the Court was crippling the children who might actually want a better education.

See James D Gordon III, "*Wisconsin v. Yoder* and Religious Liberty," *Texas Law Review* 74 (1996): 1237; Jay S. Bybee, "Substantive Due Process and Free Exercise of Religion: Meyer, Pierce and the Origins of *Wisconsin v. Yoder*," *Capital University Law Review* 25 (1996): 887; Paul Finkelman, *Religion and American Law: An Encyclopedia* (New York: Garland, 2000); Thomas L. Lehamn, "The Plain People: Reluctant Parties in Litigation to Preserve a Life Style," *Journal of Church and State* 16 (1974): 287–300; and Norman Prance, "The Amish and Compulsory School Attendance: Recent Developments," *Wisconsin Law Review* (1971–1972): 832–853.

Johnson v. Louisiana

406 U.S. 356 (1972)
Decided: May 22, 1972
Vote: 5 (Burger, B. White, Blackmun, Powell, Rehnquist)
4 (Douglas, Brennan, Stewart, T. Marshall)
Opinion of the Court: B. White
Concurring opinion: Blackmun
Concurring opinion: Powell
Dissenting opinion: Douglas (Brennan, T. Marshall)
Dissenting opinion: Brennan (T. Marshall)
Dissenting opinion: Stewart (Brennan, T. Marshall)
Dissenting opinion: T. Marshall (Brennan)

Frank Johnson was convicted of armed robbery by a vote of nine jurors to three. Louisiana statutes and its constitution allow nonunanimous convictions for noncapital cases. Johnson argued that the conviction was invalid under the Due Process Clause because it did not satisfy the reasonable doubt standard, and invalid under the Equal Protection Clause because convictions in capital cases and cases involving five-person juries require jury unanimity.

The Court disagreed, holding that the fact that three jurors voted to acquit does not necessarily imply reasonable doubt and that allowing nonunanimous verdicts in noncapital cases is rationally related to the goal of increasing judicial efficiency. The different treatment of capital cases, the Court said, is justified by the greater gravity of potential harm to the defendant.

Johnson's "reasonable doubt" argument actually involved two finely distinguishable threads. The first is that the jurors who voted to convict have disobeyed their duty to cast a "guilty" vote only if guilt was beyond a reasonable doubt. In effect, Johnson said they should have found reasonable doubt because some jurors were not convinced of his guilt. The Court held, however, that reasonable doubt is a question for each juror to answer individually. One juror's doubts about the defendant's guilt does not require another juror to conclude that there is reasonable doubt. The second is that the state cannot claim it has proven a defendant's guilt beyond a reasonable doubt when three jurors are not convinced. Here, the Court said that the mere existence of a dissenting minority does not in itself indicate reasonable doubt.

Justice Stewart's dissent focused on the danger that nonunanimous juries would be divided along class or racial lines, and that the majority would simply ignore the minority. "Only a unanimous jury [selected according to an impartial system] can serve to minimize the potential bigotry of those who might convict on inadequate evidence, or acquit when evidence of guilt was clear."

Justice Blackmun questioned the wisdom of the "split-jury" system, saying he would oppose it if he were a legislator, but he could find no constitutional objection to it.

Justice Powell's concurrence points out that ***Apodaca v. Oregon,*** 406 U.S. 404 (1972), decided on the same day as *Johnson,* had resolved the question left open in ***Duncan v. Louisiana,*** 391 U.S. 145 (1968), of whether the Fourteenth Amendment requires unanimity in state jury trials. In *Duncan* the Court held that the amendment requires states to conduct jury trials for serious crimes. *Apodaca* established that the Fourteenth Amendment does not require jury unanimity in state trials. Although Johnson was convicted before *Duncan* was decided (and therefore Louisiana was not constitutionally required to give Johnson a jury trial at all), Powell found the same considerations that led the Court to reject Apodaca's claim that due process requires unanimity persuasive with regard to Johnson.

See Michael H. Glasser, "Letting the Supermajority Rule: Nonunanimous Jury Verdicts in Criminal Trials," *Florida State University Law Review* 24 (1997): 659.

Apodaca v. Oregon

406 U.S. 404 (1972)
Decided: May 22, 1972
Vote: 5 (Burger, B. White, Blackmun, Powell, Rehnquist)
4 (Douglas, Brennan, Stewart, T. Marshall)
Judgment of the Court: B. White
Concurring opinion: Blackmun
Concurring in judgment: Powell
Dissenting opinion: Douglas (Brennan, T. Marshall)
Dissenting opinion: Brennan (T. Marshall)
Dissenting opinion: Stewart (Brennan, T. Marshall)
Dissenting opinion: T. Marshall (Brennan)

This case and its companion, *Johnson v. Louisiana,* 406 U.S. 356 (1972), confirmed that jury unanimity is not required to convict in a state criminal proceeding under the Fourteenth Amendment. Robert Apodaca was convicted of burglary by a less than unanimous jury verdict, and he argued that such a conviction was unconstitutional under the Sixth Amendment as applied to the states under the Fourteenth Amendment.

Although a plurality of justices, led by Justice White, felt that the Sixth Amendment did not require jury unanimity in state cases, a majority of justices found that unanimity was required in federal criminal proceedings. In his concurring opinion, Justice Powell asserted that the Sixth Amendment requires jury unanimity in federal criminal proceedings, but that the

Fourteenth Amendment does not incorporate that aspect of the right to jury trial to the states. Thus, a majority of justices held that under the Fourteenth Amendment, states may convict in criminal proceedings on nonunanimous verdicts. Powell set out his views on this issue in *Johnson.*

The four dissenters also wrote detailed opinions in *Johnson.* Justice Stewart's reiterated his view that a unanimous jury was central to the meaning of due process. As Stewart bitterly noted, "Until today, it has been universally understood that a unanimous verdict is an essential element of a Sixth Amendment jury trial."

Argersinger v. Hamlin

407 U.S. 25 (1972)
Decided: June 12, 1972
Vote: 9 (Burger, Douglas, Brennan, Stewart, B. White, T. Marshall, Blackmun, Powell, Rehnquist)
0
Opinion of the Court: Douglas
Concurring opinion: Brennan (Douglas, Stewart)
Opinion concurring in judgment: Burger
Opinion concurring in judgment: Powell (Rehnquist)

Argersinger, an indigent, was convicted in a Florida court of carrying a concealed weapon, an offense punishable by a maximum of six months' imprisonment. He could not afford to retain an attorney and was not provided with a state-appointed attorney at his trial. He filed a habeas corpus action, alleging that he had been deprived of liberty without the assistance of counsel in violation of his Sixth Amendment rights. The Florida Supreme Court held that the right to a court-appointed attorney, like the right to a jury trial, extends only to felony trials. The Supreme Court reversed.

The Court observed that, by its own words, the Sixth Amendment applies to all criminal trials. It is true that the right to jury trials, another Sixth Amendment right, does not extend to misdemeanor trials, but the Court noted that none of the other rights guaranteed by the Sixth Amendment, such as the right to a public trial, the right to compulsory process for obtaining favorable witnesses, or the right to be informed of the nature of the accusation, had ever been limited only to felony trials. Indeed, some, such as the right to a public trial or the right to cross-examination, had been expressly applied to misdemeanor trials. The fact that the right to a jury trial did not apply to misdemeanor trials did not mean that the Sixth Amendment as a whole did not apply to misdemeanor trials. Furthermore, the restriction of the right to a jury trial was explainable by that right's etymology, which was different from the right to counsel's. The jury trial right was meant to protect citizens from overzealous prosecution, which was mainly feared when the offense involved a serious loss of liberty, while the right to counsel was essential to the very idea of a fair trial.

According to the Court, the right to be heard was without value if it did not entail the right to counsel. The Court observed that, because of the enormous volume of misdemeanor cases clogging the court system, judges were tempted to engage in "assembly-line justice," and the rush to dispose of cases without sufficient consideration poses a substantial threat of prejudice to defendants in misdemeanor trials. The Court also noted that defendants in misdemeanor trials who were represented by counsel were five times more likely to be acquitted than those without counsel. Here, the Court ruled that the Constitution does not permit courts to impose a prison sentence of any duration on an accused unless the accused was represented by counsel at trial.

Fuentes v. Shevin

407 U.S. 67 (1972)
Decided: June 12, 1972
Vote: 4 (Douglas, Brennan, Stewart, T. Marshall)
3 (Burger, B. White, Blackmun)
Opinion of the Court: Stewart
Dissenting opinion: B. White (Burger, Blackmun)
Did not participate: Powell, Rehnquist

In this case, combined with *Parham v. Cortese,* the petitioners were consumers from Florida and Pennsylvania who contested the constitutionality of prejudgment replevin (repossession) statutes. Under both states' statutes, a seller of goods on an installment contract could repossess the goods without judgment as long as he posted a bond for double the value of the goods involved. Neither statute required that notice be given to the possessor of the property or that he be given an opportunity to challenge the seizure at a hearing before the property was repossessed. The various petitioners were deprived of goods under these statutes when they fell behind on payments and the sellers repossessed with state authority under those statutes.

The arbitrary nature of this process, and the way it impacted on the poorest Americans, was illustrated by the facts of these cases. Margarita Fuentes purchased a stove, a stereo, and a service contract from Firestone for $500, with an additional $100 in financing charges. With about $200 remaining to be paid, Fuentes and Firestone had a dispute over the servicing of the stove. Firestone sued in small claims court for repossession of the stove and the stereo, claiming that Fuentes had refused to pay what was owed. At the same time, and before Fuentes had even received a summons, Firestone obtained a writ of replevin ordering a sheriff to seize the disputed goods. The Court described the case of one of the other parties, Rosa Washington, as "bizarre." Washington was the former wife of a local deputy sheriff and was engaged in a dispute with him over the custody of their son. The deputy sheriff had obtained a writ that ordered the seizure of the boy's clothes, furniture, and toys. In these cases the property was seized after a court clerk stamped a form filled out by the original seller, without any procedures at all.

Petitioners argued that their procedural due process rights had been violated because they were not given an opportunity to show that they had a superior interest in the property to the sellers. The district court rejected this argument because the goods involved were not necessities.

The Supreme Court disagreed, holding that the Due Process Clause requires a hearing before state authority can be used to repossess property, regardless whether the property is a necessity. Furthermore, the fact that the sellers had posted a bond and that the property might be returned to the consumers after a later hearing did not save the statutes from due process failure. The Court found that the conditional sales contracts did not constitute a waiver of constitutional rights by the purchasers and that the contracts themselves, which stated that "upon a default" the seller may repossess merchandise, were "no more than a statement of the seller's right to repossession upon occurrence of certain events." The Court noted that the sales contracts "included nothing about the waiver of a prior hearing. They did not indicate how or through what process—a final judgment, self-help, prejudgment replevin with a prior hearing, or prejudgment replevin without a prior hearing—the seller could take back the goods." The Court struck down the laws allowing for such arbitrary seizures of property.

Moose Lodge v. Irvis

407 U.S. 163 (1972)
Decided: June 12, 1972
Vote: 6 (Burger, Stewart, B. White, Blackmun, Powell, Rehnquist)
3 (Douglas, Brennan, T. Marshall)
Opinion of the Court: Rehnquist
Dissenting opinion: Douglas (T. Marshall)
Dissenting opinion: Brennan (T. Marshall)

Moose Lodge is significant for beginning the curtailment of the state action doctrine the Supreme Court had expanded during the civil rights era of the 1960s. K. Leroy Irvis, a black man, was the guest of a white member of the Moose Lodge located in Harrisburg, Pennsylvania. Following its racially discriminatory policy, the lodge refused to serve Irvis. He sued, arguing that because the lodge was licensed by the state to serve liquor, Pennsylvania was supporting the lodge's racially discriminatory policy and that the license should be suspended until the lodge changed its policy.

The Fourteenth Amendment applies only to state action, not private action. In ***Burton v. Wilmington Parking Authority,*** 365 U.S. 715 (1961), however, the Court found sufficient state involvement in the private action to invoke the Equal Protection Clause. In *Burton* a privately owned restaurant, which refused to serve blacks, was operating on land leased from the government. Justice Rehnquist distinguished *Moose Lodge* from *Burton* as involving only a licensing, not a landlord-tenant relationship. The licensing relationship was less ongoing and mutual and therefore did not create a state action.

In his dissent, Justice Douglas pointed out that the First Amendment indeed allowed all-white private clubs, but where those clubs intersected with the public domain, the Equal Protection Clause prohibited discrimination. In his view, issuing a liquor license was not enough of an intersection. He said, however, that Pennsylvania's practice of issuing a quota of licenses to each county perpetuated a system in which all the available liquor licenses had already been granted, and the state was acting to support discrimination by allowing segregated clubs to hold the scarce licenses. In this way, Pennsylvania engaged in a state action that supported discrimination.

Justice Brennan, joined by Justice Marshall, said that issuing a liquor license to a discriminatory club meant that the state had acted to support discrimination.

United States v. United States District Court

407 U.S. 297 (1972)
Decided: June 19, 1972
Vote: 8 (Burger, Douglas, Brennan, Stewart, B. White, T. Marshall, Blackmun, Powell)
0
Opinion of the Court: Powell
Concurring opinion: Douglas
Concurring in judgment without opinion: Burger
Opinion concurring in judgment: B. White
Did not participate: Rehnquist

This case is rooted in the massive opposition to the war in Vietnam and the cultural conflicts of the 1960s and early 1970s. It involved surveillance, wiretapping, and political dissent and raised First Amendment and Fourth Amendment issues, as well as claims of presidential power and national security. Ironically, the Supreme Court issued its opinion in the case two days after five men working for the Committee to Re-elect the President were arrested for breaking into Democratic National Headquarters in the Watergate and planting illegal bugging devices. These arrests eventually led to a full-blown scandal and President Richard Nixon's resignation. Although the issues in this case were not directly tied to Watergate, they illustrate the policies of the Nixon administration that led to the downfall of the president and the jailing of members of his administration, including former attorney general John Mitchell.

The U.S. government prosecuted Robert "Pun" Plamondon, a radical opponent of the Vietnam War, for bombing a Central Intelligence Agency office in Ann Arbor, Michigan. Before the trial Plamondon moved to compel the United States to disclose information it had gathered about him through electronic surveillance. He also asked for a hearing "to determine whether this information 'tainted' the evidence on which the indictment was based or which the Government intended to offer at trial." The U.S. attorney responded with an affidavit from Attorney General Mitchell, declaring that he had authorized the Plamondon wiretaps "to gather intelligence information deemed necessary to protect the nation from attempts of domestic organizations to attack and subvert the existing structure of the Government." Mitchell admitted that these wiretaps were placed without judicial approval, but argued that the action was permissible as a matter of national security. The district court ordered full disclosure of the wiretap information, an order the court of appeals upheld. The government argued that the president had the authority, under the Omnibus Crime Control and Safe Streets Act of 1968, to conduct "warrantless domestic security surveillance" whenever national security dictated such actions.

After a detailed discussion of the legislative history of this act, the Court concluded that Congress had not granted the president such power. The Court further asserted that this power would violate not only the Fourth Amendment but also the First Amendment because investigations of "national security" were often used to investigate political dissent. As Justice Powell noted,

> History abundantly documents the tendency of Government—however benevolent and benign its motives—to view with suspicion those who most fervently dispute its policies. Fourth Amendment protections become the more necessary when the targets of official surveillance may be those suspected of unorthodoxy in their political beliefs. The danger to political dissent is acute where the Government attempts to act under so vague a concept as the power to protect "domestic security." Given the difficulty of defining the domestic security interest, the danger of abuse in acting to protect that interest becomes apparent.

The Court concluded that the surveillance of Plamondon was illegal and upheld the district court's order the U.S. government turn over all evidence based on the illegal wiretaps.

Barker v. Wingo

407 U.S. 514 (1972)
Decided: June 22, 1972
Vote: 9 (Burger, Douglas, Brennan, Stewart, B. White, T. Marshall, Blackmun, Powell, Rehnquist)
0
Opinion of the Court: Powell
Concurring opinion: B. White (Brennan)

Willie Barker and Silas Manning were arrested for the beating death of an elderly couple. The prosecution postponed Barker's trial until it could get a conviction against Manning, so it could use his trial testimony against Barker. Manning's trial bogged down in a series of hung juries and reversals of convictions, and the prosecution did not succeed in getting a conviction against Manning until its sixth attempt. Because of these delays, the prosecution did not try Barker until five years after his arrest. Barker spent most of that time released on bail, although he was in jail for ten months. At first, Barker did not complain about the delays, but when the prosecution asked for its twelfth continuance in his case (three and a half years after his arrest), he asked for a dismissal of his indictment. The court denied Barker's request for dismissal and granted the prosecution another continuance. Although that was not the last continuance the prosecution asked for, Barker lodged no further objections. He was finally tried and convicted. He then appealed, arguing that his Sixth Amendment right to a speedy trial had been violated. The Supreme Court rejected his argument and affirmed his conviction.

The Court observed that few decisions on the right to speedy trial had been made and that the right had not been clearly defined. The Court noted that the right was designed to protect society from potentially dangerous suspects remaining at large for lengthy periods before a determination of their guilt or innocence. Because the right was so undefined, some amicus curiae (literally, friend of the court) briefs submitted to the Court urged the Court to impose a bright-line time limit similar to the Second Circuit's, which held that the government must be ready to go to trial within six months of an arrest or charges would be dropped. The Court declined to do so, finding that such rulemaking would be legislative in nature. Other friend of the court briefs urged the Court to hold that a defendant waives the right to a speedy trial for any period of time before he demands one. The Court was not willing to do this either because such a solution amounted to denying a defendant a fundamental right (to have a speedy trial) through mere inaction. Furthermore, proponents of the "demand-waiver" doctrine assumed that defendants benefited by delay because the prosecution's witnesses' memories faded and its evidence was lost. The Court observed that a defendant waiting in jail for vindication at trial is obviously not benefiting from the delay. In addition, the Court observed that an ordinary person would not demand a trial until the delay had become unreasonable, so denying that a delay existed prior to his demand was illogical.

In the end, the Court issued no hard guidelines for determining when the right to speedy trial has been violated. The Court announced four factors it considered relevant in an ad-hoc balancing approach: the length of the delay, the reason for the delay, the defendant's assertion of his right, and prejudice to the defendant. The length of the delay would change depending on the nature of the charge: a routine street crime charge would permit less delay than a complex conspiracy case. If the reason for the delay was overcrowded courts, the government would be allowed more time than if the reason were to prejudice the defendant. If a defendant does not assert his right at all, he will probably not be able to claim the defense. Finally, prejudice to the defendant will be found when the interests of the defendant that the rule was designed to protect are impinged. If the defendant is subjected to lengthy pretrial detention, is caused unnecessary anxiety, or suffers loss of exculpatory evidence, he will have been prejudiced.

Under this test, the Court held that the prosecution's delay did not violate Barker's right to a speedy trial. The Court conceded that the delay was excessively long considering that the government could give no better reason for it than obtaining evidence from the accomplice's trial, especially because the government's mismanagement of that trial caused the delay. The Court also conceded that Barker suffered a prolonged indictment and ten months in jail while he waited to be tried, but held that he did not suffer any prejudice. None of his evidence disappeared as a result of the delay. Furthermore, Barker did not appear to want a speedy trial, since he waited three and a half years before challenging a motion for continuance. The Court found the lack of prejudice to Barker and his acceptance of the delays to outweigh the excessively long wait and the government's weak reason for the delay.

See H. Richard Uviller, "*Barker v. Wingo:* Speedy Trial Gets a Fast Shuffle, *Columbia Law Review* 72 (1972): 1376.

Lloyd Corp., Ltd. v. Tanner

407 U.S. 551 (1972)
Decided: June 22, 1972
Vote: 5 (Burger, B. White, Blackmun, Powell, Rehnquist)
4 (Douglas, Brennan, Stewart, T. Marshall)
Opinion of the Court: Powell
Dissenting opinion: T. Marshall (Douglas, Brennan, Stewart)

Donald Tanner and others sought to pass out flyers for a Vietnam War protest meeting inside Lloyd Corporation's privately owned shopping mall, Lloyd Center, which had a strict no-handbill policy. Lloyd's security guards asked them to leave, and Tanner sued to enjoin the enforcement of that policy as a violation of his First Amendment rights. Relying on ***Marsh v. Alabama,*** 326 U.S. 501 (1946), and ***Amalgamated Food Employees Union Local 590 v. Logan Valley Plaza,*** 391 U.S. 308 (1968), the district court found that because the mall was open to the public, it could not interfere with Tanner's exercise of his First Amendment rights.

The Supreme Court disagreed, holding that unless a private building is dedicated to public use, the public is not entitled to use the property as a forum for exercising its First Amendment rights. The Court pointed out that *Marsh* involved a company town and that it was necessary to limit the town owner's Fifth and Fourteenth Amendment property rights by allowing the residents to exercise their First Amendment rights because they had nowhere else to do so. Tanner's case was different because he was free to exercise his rights on the sidewalk outside the mall. In *Logan Valley* the picketing involved a store's policies, and, for the picketing to be effective, it had to occur in close proximity to the store. Here, the content of Tanner's flyers was unrelated to the mall. The Court pointed out that although the mall invited the public onto the private property, it did so for the limited purpose of shopping.

The dissenters focused on the large size and multiple uses of the mall and its similarity to public forums, such as city squares, that traditionally received the most First Amendment protection. According to the dissenters, the need to extend First Amendment protection to privately owned shopping malls has become more compelling in recent years because the traditional public forums in most American cities have fallen into almost complete disuse and malls have taken their place.

Police Department of City of Chicago v. Mosley

408 U.S. 92 (1972)
Decided: June 26, 1972
Vote: 9 (Burger, Douglas, Brennan, Stewart, B. White, T. Marshall, Blackmun, Powell, Rehnquist)
0
Opinion of the Court: T. Marshall
Concurring opinion: Burger
Concurring in judgment without opinion: Blackmun, Rehnquist

A Chicago city ordinance prohibited all picketing within 150 feet of a school that is in session, except peaceful picketing during a labor dispute. For seven months Earl D. Mosley, a postal employee, regularly and peacefully picketed Jones Commercial High School. Mosley walked up and down the public sidewalk next to the school, carrying a sign that read: "Jones High School practices black discrimination. Jones High School has a black quota." In March 1968 the Chicago City Council passed the ordinance at issue in the case. Mosley asked the Chicago police to find out how the law would affect him and was told that if he continued his picketing he would be arrested. The day before the ordinance went into effect, Mosley stopped picketing next to the school. He then sued in the U.S. District Court for the Northern District of Illinois, seeking declaratory and injunctive relief. Mosley alleged a violation of his First Amendment rights because the statute punished a protected activity. Moreover, by allowing only peaceful labor picketing, the statute denied him equal protection of the law in violation of the First and Fourteenth Amendments.

The district court dismissed his suit, but the Seventh Circuit reversed, "holding that because the ordinance prohibited even peaceful picketing next to a school, it was overbroad and therefore 'patently unconstitutional on its face.' " The Supreme Court struck the ordinance down on equal protection grounds, pointing out that it prohibited peaceful as well as disruptive picketing. According to the Court, the ordinance created an invidious discrimination because it permitted labor picketing but not other kinds of picketing. The Court did not have to address the First Amendment validity of the ordinance. As Justice Marshall noted, the "central problem with Chicago's ordinance is that it describes permissible picketing in terms of its subject matter." This amounted to content-based censorship, which the Constitution clearly forbids.

Grayned v. City of Rockford

408 U.S. 104 (1972)
Decided: June 26, 1972
Vote: 8 (Burger, Brennan, Stewart, B. White, T. Marshall, Blackmun, Powell, Rehnquist)
1 (Douglas)
Opinion of the Court: T. Marshall
Opinion concurring in judgment: Blackmun
Dissenting opinion: Douglas

Richard Grayned took part in a demonstration outside a high school protesting its lack of black faculty, black cheerleaders, and courses in black history. He was convicted under two separate statutes: an antinoise law and an antipicketing law that prohibited picketing near a school building when school is in session, except when the school is involved in a labor dispute. He was fined $25 for each offense.

The Court held that the antipicketing statute was identical to the statute that was struck down in a companion case decided that day, ***Police Department of Chicago v. Mosley,*** 408 U.S. 92 (1972), for violating the Equal Protection Clause. The Court reversed his conviction under this statute for the same reasons stated in *Mosley.*

Grayned was also convicted under an antinoise statute that prohibited making or helping to make "any noise or diversion which disturbs or tends to disturb the peace or good order of [a] school" while on ground adjacent to a school. Grayned argued that this provision was unconstitutionally vague because it did not give fair warning to the public of what conduct was prohibited and invited discriminatory enforcement by the police. The Court disagreed, saying that the statute specifically prohibited willful disturbances that were "actual and imminent." Grayned also argued that the statute was overbroad because it prohibited all First Amendment activity that might "disturb" a school. The Court disagreed here as well, reading in a requirement that the disturbance must be "material."

Justice Douglas, the lone dissenter, would have reversed on the antinoise conviction as well. The Court had noted that the record was contradictory on exactly how much noise there had been and who made it, and Douglas found the record favored Grayned. Moreover, unlike the majority opinion, Douglas focused on the racial conflict at the school. He also pointed out that the police, with their bullhorns and loudspeakers, had clearly made the most noise. Douglas said the record showed no evidence that Grayned had been "noisy or boisterous or rowdy." "As I read this record," he wrote, "the disruptive force loosed at this school was an issue dealing with race—an issue that is preeminently one for solution by First Amendment means. That is all that was done here; and the entire picketing, including appellant's part in it, was done in the best First Amendment tradition."

Furman v. Georgia

408 U.S. 238 (1972)
Decided: June 29, 1972
Vote: 5 (Douglas, Brennan, Stewart, B. White, T. Marshall)
4 (Burger, Blackmun, Powell, Rehnquist)
Opinion: *Per curiam*
Opinion concurring in judgment: Douglas
Opinion concurring in judgment: Brennan
Opinion concurring in judgment: Stewart
Opinion concurring in judgment: B. White
Opinion concurring in judgment: T. Marshall
Dissenting opinion: Burger (Blackmun, Powell, Rehnquist)
Dissenting opinion: Blackmun
Dissenting opinion: Powell (Burger, Blackmun, Rehnquist)
Dissenting opinion: Rehnquist (Burger, Blackmun, Powell)

This case involved three appeals from death penalty convictions, one for murder and two for rape. The cases came from Georgia and Texas. The majority held that the death penalty, as implemented by these states, was inherently "cruel and unusual" in violation of the Eighth Amendment.

In his opinion, Justice Douglas pointed out that blacks were more likely to be sentenced to death than whites and, if sentenced, more likely to be executed. Whites sentenced to capital punishment were more likely to have their sentences commuted. Furthermore, Douglas and other majority justices noted that poor defendants were more likely than rich defendants to receive the death penalty. Quoting former attorney general Ramsey Clark, Douglas pointed out, " 'It is the poor, the sick, the ignorant, the powerless and the hated who are executed.' One searches our chronicles in vain for the execution of any member of the affluent strata of this society." Douglas observed that the three defendants in this case were black, and that the two convicted of rape had assaulted white women. Furman had only a sixth grade education, and the Georgia Central State Hospital superintendent "reported that a unanimous staff diagnostic conference had concluded 'that this patient should retain his present diagnosis of Mental Deficiency, Mild to Moderate, with Psychotic Episodes associated with Convulsive Disorder.' The physicians agreed that 'at present the patient is not psychotic, but he is not capable of cooperating with his counsel in the preparation of his defense'; and the staff believed 'that he is in need of further psychiatric hospitalization and treatment.' " The defendant in the Texas case was "found to be a borderline mental deficient and well below the average IQ of Texas prison inmates. He had the equivalent of five and a half years of grade school education. He had a 'dull intelligence' and was in the lowest fourth percentile of his class."

Douglas concluded, as did the rest of the majority, that findings such as these illustrated how the death penalty was imposed in a way that discriminated against minorities, the poor, and the least educated. Douglas declared: "In a Nation committed to equal protection of the laws there is no permissible 'caste' aspect of law enforcement. Yet we know that the discretion of judges and juries in imposing the death penalty enables the penalty to be selectively applied, feeding prejudices against the accused if he is poor and despised, and lacking political clout, or if he is a member of a suspect or unpopular minority, and saving those who by social position may be in a more protected position." The facts of Furman's murder conviction also suggest the inherent prejudice in the prosecution. No one claimed that Furman intentionally killed anyone. In fact, the Georgia court conceded that the death was accidental, caused when Furman tripped leaving the scene of a burglary and the gun went off. As in the two rape cases, Furman's victim was white.

The majority stressed the randomness of the imposition of death penalties, the great discretion granted to the jury, and the lack of specific guidelines and standards for death penalties. The majority also argued that it was clearly "cruel and unusual" to execute someone when the victim was not killed, as in the two rape cases. Race was a critical factor. Between 1930 and 1967, 54 percent of those executed in the United States were black. The cases in this litigation—where blacks were sentenced to death for harms against whites—seemed to illustrate the inherent lack of equal protection in the imposition of the death penalty.

The dissenters argued against the Court second-guessing the legislatures. They said that the death penalty was historically not cruel and unusual, and thus on original intent grounds the Eighth Amendment could not be used to overturn a death penalty. Finally, the dissenters pointed out that the majority of Americans favored the death penalty and therefore courts should not interfere with its imposition.

Furman effectively suspended death penalties in the United States, as state legislatures were forced to draw coherent guidelines for judges and juries in capital cases. In ***Gregg v. Georgia,*** 428 U.S. 153 (1976), the Court, with Douglas gone, upheld the state's new death penalty statute, which gave juries discretion in death penalty cases, but with clear guidelines.

See Harry Henderson, *Capital Punishment* (New York: Facts on File, 1991); Carol S. Steiker and Jordan M. Steiker, "Sober Second Thoughts: Reflections on Two Decades of Constitutional Regulation of Capital Punishment," *Harvard Law Review* 109 (1995): 355; Srikanth Srinivasan, "Capital Sentencing Doctrine and the Weighing-Nonweighing Distinction," *Stanford Law Review* 47 (1995): 1347.

Morrissey v. Brewer

408 U.S. 471 (1972)
Decided: June 29, 1972
Vote: 8 (Burger, Brennan, Stewart, B. White, T. Marshall, Blackmun, Powell, Rehnquist)
1 (Douglas)
Opinion of the Court: Burger
Opinion concurring in judgment: Brennan (T. Marshall)
Dissenting opinion: Douglas

Morrissey was paroled from a prison sentence, but seven months later he was arrested again as a parole violator and sent to the county jail in his hometown. After reviewing the parole officer's report, the state parole board sent Morrissey back to prison, one hundred miles away, without giving him a hearing. The district court and court of appeals upheld this process, but the Supreme Court reversed and remanded.

The Court held that Morrissey was not due the full process afforded a defendant in a criminal prosecution, but, before his parole-status liberty could be taken away, he was entitled to a hearing to determine whether the parole officer's report was accurate. The hearing should be held near the place of the alleged parole violation, and the parolee should be given notice and an opportunity to question adverse witnesses. All the justices agreed on this, but Justices Brennan and Marshall also wanted the Court to require that counsel be given to indigent parolees at such a hearing.

Justice Douglas dissented in part, asking for stricter standards for revocation of parole and a rule that the alleged violator should remain free until after a determination on his status.

Board of Regents of State Colleges v. Roth

408 U.S. 564 (1972)
Decided: June 29, 1972
Vote: 5 (Burger, Stewart, B. White, Blackmun, Rehnquist)
3 (Douglas, Brennan, T. Marshall)
Opinion of the Court: Stewart
Concurring opinion: Burger
Dissenting opinion: Douglas
Dissenting opinion: Brennan (Douglas)
Dissenting opinion: T. Marshall
Did not participate: Powell

A nontenured state university professor does not have a due process right in a hearing before his employment is terminated, unless he can show that his firing has resulted in a loss of liberty or he had a property interest in continued employment. David Roth was fired by a state college, and the college would not explain the reason for his termination. Roth alleged that he was fired because he had criticized the board's policies.

The Court held that because no stigma was attached to Roth's termination that would preclude later employment, he had not been deprived of any liberty interest, and because the terms of his employment contract were "at will," he did not have a property interest in continued employment. He was therefore not entitled to a hearing before the termination.

Justice Douglas, in dissent, argued that this case dealt essentially with free speech, and the failure to renew the contract was in retaliation for statements hostile to the board of trustees.

In his dissent, Justice Marshall said that the failure to renew the contract did indeed stigmatize Roth and that as a public employee he was entitled to due process. Quoting Justice Frankfurter, Marshall reminded the majority that "the history of American freedom is, in no small measure, the history of procedure."

Perry v. Sindermann

408 U.S. 593 (1972)
Decided: June 29, 1972
Vote: 5 (Burger, Stewart, B. White, Blackmun, Rehnquist)
3 (Douglas, Brennan, T. Marshall)
Opinion of the Court: Stewart
Concurring opinion: Burger
Dissenting opinion: Brennan (Douglas)
Dissenting opinion: T. Marshall
Did not participate: Powell

In this companion case to ***Board of Regents of State Colleges v. Roth,*** 408 U.S. 564 (1972), Robert Sindermann, a nontenured professor, challenged his summary dismissal on First Amendment and due process grounds. Sindermann was nontenured because his state college system had no formal tenure system, but the board of regents argued that it consistently observed a de facto tenure system in making employment decisions. Sindermann had been teaching in the Texas college system for ten years, four of them at Odessa Junior College, where he had been appointed co-chairman of the Government and Social Science Department. When he was dismissed without a hearing, he claimed that he had been denied due process. He also claimed that the real reason he was fired was his criticism of the board's policies and that his dismissal therefore violated his First Amendment rights. In fact, in the year before he was fired, Sindermann served as the president of the Texas Junior College Teachers Association. In this capacity, he disagreed publicly with the policies of the college's board of regents, in particular, over the elevation of the college to four-year status, which the regents opposed. "On one occasion, a newspaper advertisement appeared over his name that was highly critical of the Regents." When they fired Sindermann, the regents issued a press release listing "allegations of the respondent's insubordination." This insubordination appeared to be his political stance and nothing to do with his teaching duties.

The Court held that if the reason for his dismissal was in fact his criticism of policy, the board of regents violated his First Amendment rights. The Court also held that the system could not avoid a judicial determination of whether it had denied Sindermann's First Amendment rights by claiming he was not entitled to a hearing because he was not tenured. As the board admitted to operating under a de facto tenure system, the Court said Sindermann he should had the benefit of it and that he is entitled to a hearing.

The dissenters wanted a stronger result. Justice Marshall thought the Court should "direct the district court to enter summary judgment for respondent entitling him to a statement of reasons why his contract was not renewed and a hearing on disputed issues of fact."

Branzburg v. Hayes

408 U.S. 665 (1972)
Decided: June 29, 1972
Vote: 5 (Burger, B. White, Blackmun, Powell, Rehnquist)
4 (Douglas, Brennan, Stewart, T. Marshall)
Opinion of the Court: B. White
Concurring opinion: Powell
Dissenting opinion: Douglas
Dissenting opinion: Stewart (Brennan, T. Marshall)

Branzburg was consolidated with *In re Pappas* and *United States v. Caldwell,* all of which involved news reporters who claimed a First Amendment privilege not to reveal their confidential sources to grand juries. Paul M. Branzburg was a reporter for a Kentucky newspaper. He conducted two interviews with marijuana and hashish users in the state and obtained the interviews by promising to change the names of his sources and not to reveal their true identities. When he was summoned before a grand jury and ordered to reveal his sources, he refused, arguing that freedom of the press entailed the freedom to keep sources confidential. Branzburg told the grand jury that if he were required to reveal the names, he would be unable to gather news in the future. The Kentucky Court of Appeals disagreed, finding that Branzburg's fear was too attenuated from the freedom of the press to receive First Amendment protection, and it denied Branzburg's motion to quash the subpoena. Branzburg appealed this decision to the Supreme Court.

Pappas involved similar facts, except that Paul Pappas was a television news photographer covering an anticipated raid on the Black Panther Party headquarters, which did not take place. Pappas refused to tell a grand jury what he had seen during his time with the Black Panthers, and his assertion of a news reporter's privilege was denied in Massachusetts court.

Earl Caldwell was a *New York Times* reporter covering the Black Panthers in California. In his case, the Ninth Circuit Court of Appeals accepted his assertion of a First Amendment privilege for reporters. The Ninth Circuit held that the negative effect on news gathering that would result from requiring reporters to testify before grand juries was so detrimental to the policy of the First Amendment that reporters must be granted a privilege to refuse to appear.

By a slim margin the Supreme Court held that the First Amendment affords no news reporter privilege. The Court said that the government need not show either a compelling interest for subpoenaing reporters or that it has no other way to obtain the requested information because such subpoenas do not violate a First Amendment right. Simply put, to subpoena a reporter and request the names of his sources is not the same as prohibiting a reporter from consulting the sources or writing about what they tell him. The Court emphasized that the government is not prohibited from enforcing every civil and criminal law against the press that might have an incidental impact on the ability of the press to gather news. The Court also emphasized the importance of the grand jury in discovering whether evidence of a crime exists and the essential role the subpoena power plays for the grand jury in determining the adequacy of that evidence. Despite this result, Justice White also said that the Court was not suggesting that "news gathering does not qualify for First Amendment protection; without some protection for seeking out the news, freedom of the press could be eviscerated." The majority opinion also asserted that "harassment" of reporters would not be tolerated.

Justice Powell supported the outcome but argued for a balancing of interests. He believed that "the asserted claim to privilege should be judged on its facts by the striking of a proper balance between freedom of the press and the obligation of all citizens to give relevant testimony with respect to criminal conduct. The balance of these vital constitutional and societal interests on a case-by-case basis accords with the tried and traditional way of adjudicating such questions."

The dissenters suggested that the First Amendment required the protection of reporters' sources. Justice Stewart said the "government must show that there are no alternative means for the grand jury to obtain the information sought" except by reporters' testimony and that furthermore, there should be a compelling need for the evidence.

In the early 1970s, seventeen states provided "shield laws" to protect reporters' sources in most instances. Since the decision in this case, a number of other states have provided such laws. In addition, many lower courts seem to have adopted Powell's notion of balancing in finding protections for reporters.

See Potter Stewart, "Or of the Press," *Hastings Law Journal* 26 (1975): 631.

Roe v. Wade

410 U.S. 113 (1973)
Decided: January 22, 1973
Vote: 7 (Burger, Douglas, Brennan, Stewart, T. Marshall, Blackmun, Powell)
2 (B. White, Rehnquist)
Opinion of the Court: Blackmun
Concurring opinion: Burger
Concurring opinion: Douglas
Concurring opinion: Stewart
Dissenting opinion: B. White (Rehnquist)
Dissenting opinion: Rehnquist

Jane Roe, a pseudonym for Norma McCorvey, an unmarried pregnant woman in Dallas, Texas, wanted to terminate the pregnancy and brought suit in 1970 to prevent the Dallas County prosecutor, Henry Wade, from enforcing the state's antiabortion laws. By the time the case was argued in December 1971, Roe had delivered her baby and given it up for adoption.

Even though Roe was no longer pregnant, the Court rejected claims that the case was moot, arguing that she might become pregnant again and that other women similarly situated would become pregnant. Justice Blackmun noted that the nature of human biology was such that "pregnancy litigation seldom will survive much beyond the trial stage, and appellate review will be effectively denied" if a case became moot as soon as the pregnancy ended. "Our law should not be that rigid," he declared. Indeed, he found that "pregnancy provides a classic justification for a conclusion of nonmootness. It truly could be 'capable of repetition, yet evading review.' " With that settled, the Court turned to the merits of Roe's claim. After reviewing the history of antiabortion legislation, as well as numerous ethical, philosophical, and religious writings on the subject, Blackmun concluded that the laws of most American states, including Texas, were out of touch with medical science and history. More important, he found they violated the Constitution's inherent right to privacy.

Conceding that "the Constitution does not explicitly mention any right of privacy," Blackmun cited a dozen or so cases going back more than eighty years to assert that the Constitution protected a right to privacy in a variety of ways. Starting his analysis with early cases such as ***Boyd v. United States,*** 116 U.S. 616 (1886), and *Union Pacific R. Co. v. Botsford,* 141 U.S. 250 (1891), Blackmun noted that "the Court has recognized that a right of personal privacy, or a guarantee of certain areas or zones of privacy, does exist under the Constitution." In support of this right, Blackmun cited, among others, ***Stanley v. Georgia,*** 394 U.S. 557 (1969); ***Terry v. Ohio,*** 392 U.S. 1 (1968), ***Katz v. United States,*** 389 U.S. 437 (1967); and Justice Brandeis's dissent in ***Olmstead v. United States,*** 277 U.S. 438 (1928). More directly on point, he noted the "penumbras of the Bill of Rights" as set out in ***Griswold v. Connecticut,*** 381 U.S. 479 (1965), as well as the Ninth Amendment analysis in that case, and "the concept of liberty guaranteed by the first section of the Fourteenth Amendment," that the Court recognized in ***Meyer v. Nebraska,*** 262 U.S. 390 (1923).

He concluded, "This right of privacy, whether it be founded in the Fourteenth Amendment's concept of personal liberty and restrictions upon state action, as we feel it is, or, as the district court determined, in the Ninth Amendment's reservation of rights to the people, is broad enough to encompass a woman's decision whether or not to terminate her pregnancy." He noted that the state imposed a great burden "upon the pregnant woman by denying this choice," subjecting women to potential medical harms, as well as financial and emotional harms. "Maternity, or additional offspring, may force upon the woman a distressful life and future. Psychological harm may be imminent. Mental and physical health may be taxed by child care. There is also the distress, for all concerned, associated with the unwanted child, and there is the problem of bringing a child into a family already unable, psychologically and otherwise, to care for it. In other cases, as in this one, the additional difficulties and continuing stigma of unwed motherhood may be involved."

Blackman next set out a three-stage standard for when abortions might be banned. During the first trimester of a pregnancy, the decision of whether to continue the pregnancy rested entirely with the patient and her physician. During the second trimester, a state had the right to regulate abortions to protect the health and safety of a pregnant woman. Only in the third trimester, did the state gain an interest in preventing an abortion. The reason was that "the fetus then presumably has the capability of meaningful life outside the mother's womb. State regulation protective of fetal life after viability thus has both logical and biological justifications." Blackmun added that a state may proscribe abortion during the third trimester, "except when it is necessary to preserve the life or health of the mother."

The decision was not particularly controversial at the time it was announced. A few states, including the two largest in the nation, California and New York, had already reformed their abortion laws along the lines that Blackmun set out. Other states were considering such legislation. Moreover, the decision in *Roe* seemed to be the logical conclusion of decisions that had been expanding the rights of women and recognizing changing societal views of the family and childbearing. *Roe* seemed to be a very modern decision, much like ***Brown v. Board of Education,*** 347 U.S. 483 (1954), that liberated a large class of people—women—from antiquated laws. There was no immediate large scale public outcry against the decision.

A few years after *Roe,* the climate changed. Some religious groups—most notably Roman Catholics and fundamentalist Protestants—began a vocal campaign against the decision. Many state legislatures tried to evade *Roe,* but the Court maintained the core of the decision—that a woman had a right of privacy to determine whether to bear a child. In the three decades following *Roe,* all national opinion polls showed that the majority of Americans favored keeping abortion safe and legal, even though a substantial, vocal, and sometimes dangerous minority did not.

Scholarly criticism of Blackmun's opinion has come from two directions. Opponents of *Roe* have compared it to ***Lochner v. New York,*** 198 U.S. 45 (1905), as an example of substantive due process in which the Court substitutes its judgment for that of the states. Critics of this analysis, however, point out that in *Lochner* the state had protected a relatively powerless group (bakery workers) from an oppressive marketplace, and the Court had struck down the law; in *Roe* the Court was protecting a group (women, especially poor women) who had little political or economic clout. Some supporters of the outcome in *Roe* have said that the Court should have decided the case on equal protection grounds. Some feminists have criticized the decision for allowing any regulation by the state of pregnancy, arguing that a woman's "right to choose" was so fundamental that the state could have no legitimate interest in the decision.

Despite the criticism, the three-stage analysis set out by Justice Blackmun has remained. Moreover, most Americans not only accept *Roe* and the right of women to choose to terminate pregnancies but also that the Constitution protects—or ought to protect—fundamental rights to privacy.

Although *Roe* became the focal point of much protest and litigation, only two justices dissented. In a short dissent, Justice Rehnquist complained that the Court should not have heard the case at all, because Roe's pregnancy was over before the appeal reached the Court. "While a party may vindicate his own constitutional rights, he may not seek vindication for the rights of others," Rehnquist said. His views on the limits of personal liberty and the powers of the Court would make it impossible for the Supreme Court to hear any case dealing with pregnancy. Rehnquist further rejected the entire notion of a right of privacy within the Constitution.

Additional dissenting views appeared in the companion case, ***Doe v Bolton,*** 410 U.S. 179 (1973), decided the same day.

See David Garrow, *Liberty and Sexuality: The Right of Privacy and the Making of* Roe v. Wade (New York: Macmillan, 1994); and N. E. H. Hull and Peter Charles Hoffer, Roe v. Wade: *The Abortion Rights Controversy in American History* (Lawrence: University Press of Kansas, 2001).

Doe v. Bolton

410 U.S. 179 (1973)
Decided: January 22, 1973
Vote: 7 (Burger, Douglas, Brennan, Stewart, T. Marshall, Blackmun, Powell)
2 (B. White, Rehnquist)
Opinion of the Court: Blackmun
Concurring opinion: Burger
Concurring opinion: Douglas
Dissenting opinion: B. White (Rehnquist)
Dissenting opinion: Rehnquist

Decided the same day as ***Roe v. Wade,*** 410 U.S. 113 (1973), this companion case merited "special consideration" because Georgia's abortion law was substantially different from the Texas law at issue in *Roe.* The Georgia law had been adopted in 1968 and paralleled the recommendations of the American Law Institute (ALI) for a model abortion statute. Unlike the Texas law struck down in *Roe,* the Georgia law did not make all abortions criminal except those necessary to save the life of the woman. Under the new Georgia law, abortion was legal when two sets of criteria were met. The first set of criteria limited the cases where abortion was allowed to the following: when a licensed physician decided "in his best clinical judgment" that the abortion was necessary either because the pregnant woman's life or health was in danger, the baby was likely to have a serious birth defect, or the pregnancy was the result of rape. Unlike the ALI model, the law did not allow abortion for pregnancies resulting from incest, but in oral argument attorneys for the state assured the Supreme Court that Georgia included incest within the "rape" criteria. The section of the law also limited access to this medical procedure to a Georgia "resident." The second set of criteria involved the manner in which the decision to abort was made and carried out. The law required that the physician's decision must be approved by two other licensed physicians and the hospital abortion committee, and the abortion must be done in a state-accredited hospital.

Doe, an indigent woman, was denied an abortion because she did not meet any of the conditions in the first set of criteria and challenged the constitutionality of the statute. Joining her were twenty-three other people, including nine physicians, seven nurses, five clergymen, and two social workers, as well as two nonprofit corporations The district court found that the criteria determining who could have an abortion violated Doe's right to privacy and were therefore unconstitutional. The court also found that the criteria regulating the manner in which the decision to abort was made and carried out were constitutional because of the state's interest in protecting health and the "potential of independent human existence." Furthermore, the court granted only declaratory relief, not injunctive relief. Doe claimed that the "best clinical judgment" phrase in the first set of criteria was void for vagueness. Doe also claimed she was entitled to injunctive relief and that the "manner of decision" restrictions were unconstitutional, and she appealed directly to the Supreme Court.

The Supreme Court held that the "best clinical judgment" phrase was not void for vagueness. The phrase was necessarily deferential to the physician's best judgment, which would be based on the totality of circumstances in each patient's case. Such a wide-ranging universe of factors could not be listed in any law. Furthermore, the Court held that the state-accredited hospital requirement, "abortion-committee" requirement, and physician review requirement were invalid because they were unrelated to the state's interest in protecting health, and they unduly restricted the right to receive an abortion and the physician's right to practice. Finally, the Georgia resident limitation was held invalid as a violation of the Privileges and Immunities Clause because it denied the same rights to non-Georgians who entered the state for medical services.

See David Garrow, *Liberty and Sexuality: The Right of Privacy and the Making of* Roe v. Wade (New York: Macmillan, 1994); and N. E. H. Hull and Peter Charles Hoffer, Roe v. Wade: *The Abortion Rights Controversy in American History* (Lawrence: University Press of Kansas, 2001).

Mahan v. Howell

410 U.S. 315 (1973)
Decided: February 21, 1973
Vote: 5 (Burger, Stewart, B. White, Blackmun, Rehnquist)
3 (Douglas, Brennan, T. Marshall)
Opinion of the Court: Rehnquist
Dissenting opinion: Brennan (Douglas, T. Marshall)
Did not participate: Powell

Mahan v. Howell was one of four redistricting cases the Court decided in 1973. The others were *Gaffney v. Cummings,* 412 U.S. 735, *White v. Regester,* 412 U.S. 755, and *White v. Weiser,* 412 U.S. 783. *Mahan v. Howell* involved a 1971 Virginia statute that divided the state's lower house, the House of Delegates, into fifty-two districts, some single-member, others multimember, and still others floater districts in which cities or towns shared a member. These fifty-two districts would elect one hundred members. The goal was to produce legislative districts of equal population to reflect the rule of one person, one vote set out in ***Reynolds v. Sims,*** 377 U.S. 533 (1964). The populations of thirty-five districts varied by 4 percent, and in nine others the variance was 6 percent from the ideal. In the remaining eleven districts, however, the population varied from plus 9.6 percent to minus 6.8 percent, for a total variance of 16.4 percent. The district court found this degree of variance to be unconstitutional based on the one-person, one-vote principle. In addition, allegations of racial gerrymandering were made. Virginia appealed, arguing that its districts were based on the boundaries of cities and counties, and that this pattern was followed for every district in the state except for the disproportionately populous Fairfax County.

The Supreme Court held that minor deviations in district populations in state legislative districts were constitutional as long as they were supported by a legitimate legislative purpose. The Court relied on *Reynolds,* which held that state legislative districts need not be as equal in population as federal congressional districts. In dicta—parts of an opinion not essential to the decision—the Court suggested that even state legislative districts could not vary much more than 16.4 percent. The Court also upheld the state Senate redistricting for the city of Norfolk.

The dissenters agreed with this part of the decision, but argued that the House of Delegates redistricting violated the Equal Protection Clause of the Fourteenth Amendment.

San Antonio Independent School District v. Rodriguez

411 U.S. 1 (1973)
Decided: March 21, 1973
Vote: 5 (Burger, Stewart, Blackmun, Powell, Rehnquist)
4 (Douglas, Brennan, B. White, T. Marshall)
Opinion of the Court: Powell
Concurring opinion: Stewart
Dissenting opinion: Brennan
Dissenting opinion: B. White (Douglas, Brennan)
Dissenting opinion: T. Marshall (Douglas)

This case stemmed from a class action suit brought in 1968 by parents "on behalf of schoolchildren throughout the State [of Texas] who are members of minority groups or who are poor and reside in school districts having a low property tax base." In 1969 a three-judge panel took the case, and in 1971 the district court ruled, *per curium,* that the system of funding public education in Texas violated the Equal Protection Clause of the Fourteenth Amendment. The Supreme Court reversed.

The disparities in educational opportunities between rich and poor districts were clear. Demetrio Rodriguez lived in Edgewood, which was one of seven public school districts in the larger San Antonio Independent School District. Each of the seven school districts was funded by a combination of local property taxes, state funds from a "Foundation Program," and federal money. The Court noted that in Edgewood

90% of the student population is Mexican-American and over 6% is Negro. The average assessed property value per pupil is $5,960—the lowest in the metropolitan area—and the median family income ($4,686) is also the lowest. At an equalized tax rate of $1.05 per $100 of assessed property—the highest in the metropolitan area—the district contributed $26 to the education of each child for the 1967–1968 school year above its Local Fund Assignment for the Minimum Foundation Program. The Foundation Program contributed $222 per pupil for a state-local total of $248. Federal funds added another $108 for a total of $356 per pupil.

By contrast, Alamo Heights, also in San Antonio, had a school population that was approximately 81 percent "Anglo," 18 percent Mexican American, and less than 1 percent black.

The assessed property value per pupil exceeds $49,000, and the median family income is $8,001. In 1967–1968 the local tax rate of $.85 per $100 of valuation yielded $333 per pupil over and above its contribution to the Foundation Program. Coupled with the $225 provided from that Program, the district was able to supply $558 per student. Supplemented by a $36 per-pupil grant from federal sources, Alamo Heights spent $594 per pupil.

Increases in state funding in for the 1970–1971 school year led to an allocation by the state of $356 per pupil in Edgewood, but the state also raised its contribution to Alamo Heights to $491 per pupil. The disparity between poor and rich districts, within San Antonio, *increased* while the case was in litigation.

Given these facts, the district court concluded that the state's "dual system of public school financing violated the Equal Protection Clause." The court found that the "Texas system discriminates on the basis of wealth in the manner in which education is provided for its people." The district court held that wealth was a " 'suspect' classification and that education is a 'fundamental' interest." The district court could find no compelling state interest to justify the discrimination in school funding and held that the defendants "fail even to establish a reasonable basis for these classifications."

At the Supreme Court, however, a five justice majority rejected the idea that education was a fundamental right or that economic classification was suspect. The Court categorically rejected the notion that economic disparity in school funding constituted a form of discrimination. The majority concluded that there was a "rational basis" for the school funding system, because it "assur[ed] a basic education for every child in the State," while "permit[ing] and encourag[ing] a large measure of participation in and control of each district's schools at the local level."

The dissents noted that under the Texas system the poorest districts often had the highest tax rates, but still could not match the amount of money raised by the richer districts. This problem was exacerbated by the fact that the state gave greater subsidies to the richest districts than it gave to the poorest. The majority answered this point by saying that Texas allowed parents and school districts a choice as to how to raise and spend money.

In his dissent, Justice White lauded the concept of local control, but found that the Texas system lacked a rational basis. He argued that the majority claim of local control as a justification for the system was utterly unrealistic and, indeed, false. "No matter how desirous parents are of supporting their schools with greater revenues," White wrote, "it is impossible to do so through the use of the real estate property tax. In these districts, the Texas system utterly fails to extend a realistic choice to parents because the property tax, which is the only revenue-raising mechanism extended to school districts, is practically and legally unavailable." To fund its schools, "Alamo Heights would be required to tax at the rate of 68 cents per $100 of assessed valuation. Edgewood would be required to tax at the prohibitive rate of $5.76 per $100." But, White pointed out, "State law places a $1.50 per $100 ceiling on the maintenance tax rate, a limit that would surely be reached long before Edgewood attained an equal yield. Edgewood is thus precluded in law, as well as in fact, from achieving a yield even close to that of some other districts." White agreed that the "the Equal Protection Clause permits discriminations between classes but requires that the classification bear some rational relationship to a permissible object sought to be attained by the statute." Here, it seemed, the opposite was taking place. The discriminations were designed to ensure that the wealthy portions of San Antonio and Bexar County would have superb schools, and that the poorer parts of the city and county would have substandard schools.

Justice Marshall's dissent took the majority to task for its decision.

The question of discrimination in educational quality must be deemed to be an objective one that looks to what the State provides its children, not to what the children are able to do with what they receive. That a child forced to attend an underfunded school with poorer physical facilities, less experienced teachers, larger classes, and a narrower range of courses than a school with substantially more funds—and thus with greater choice in educational planning—may nevertheless excel is to the credit of the child, not the State, Indeed, who can ever measure for such a child the opportunities lost and the talents wasted for want of a broader, more enriched education? Discrimination in the opportunity to learn that is afforded a child must be our standard.

Marshall's dissent offered an accurate summary of the majority decision:

The majority's decision represents an abrupt departure from the mainstream of recent state and federal court decisions concerning the unconstitutionality of state educational financing schemes dependent upon taxable local wealth. More unfortunately, though, the majority's holding can only be seen as a retreat from our historic commitment to equality of educational opportunity and as unsupportable acquiescence in a system which deprives children in their earliest years of the chance to reach their full potential as citizens. The Court does this despite the absence of any substantial justification for a scheme which arbitrarily channels educational resources in accordance with the fortuity of the amount of taxable wealth within each district.

See David J. Barron, "The Promise of Cooley's City: Traces of Local Constitutionalism," *University of Pennsylvania Law Review* 147 (1999): 487; Stuart Biegel, "Reassessing the Applicability of Fundamental Rights Analysis: The Fourteenth Amendment and the Shaping of Educational Policy After *Kadrmas v. Dickinson Public Schools,*" *Cornell Law Review* 74 (1989): 1078; and Frank J. Macchiarola and Joseph G. Diaz, "Disorder in the Courts: The Aftermath of *San Antonio Independent School District v. Rodriguez* in the State Courts," *Valparaiso University Law Review* 30 (1996): 551.

Mescalero Apache Tribe v. Jones

411 U.S. 145 (1973)
Decided: March 27, 1973
Vote: 6 (Burger, B. White, T. Marshall, Blackmun, Powell, Rehnquist)
3 (Douglas, Brennan, Stewart)
Opinion of the Court: B. White
Dissenting opinion: Douglas (Brennan, Stewart)

This case resolved questions of state taxing power under Section 5 of the Indian Reorganization Act of 1934, which prohibited state and local taxation of Indian property. The act permitted Indian tribes to form themselves into business corporations and established a system of financial credit for Indians. Under this act, the U.S. Forest Service leased certain land to the Mescalero Apache tribe, outside the tribe's reservation's boundaries. The state did not tax the land *per se,* but it did attempt to tax the receipts on a ski resort the Mescalero Apaches built there, as well as certain personal property, such as ski lifts and other equipment, that the Mescalero Apaches purchased out of state and installed. The state courts upheld both taxes, and the Supreme Court partially reversed this decision.

The Court held that nothing prevented the state from applying a nondiscriminatory gross receipts tax to monies earned by the ski resort, but that the statute precluded the use tax on the personal property purchased out of state and installed on the land. The Court held that the personal property became so closely associated with the land that to tax it was equivalent to taxing the land.

In dissent, Justice Douglas argued that by taxing the enterprise, the state was interfering with the intent of Congress, which was "to give this tribe an economic base which offers job opportunities, a higher standard of living, community stability, preservation of Indian culture, and the orientation of the tribe to commercial maturity." He said that, without the consent of Congress, the state could not tax "a tribal-developed enterprise."

See Donald A. Grinde Jr., ed., *Native Americans* (Washington, D.C.: CQ Press, 2002).

McClanahan v. Arizona State Tax Commission

411 U.S. 164 (1973)
Decided: March 27, 1973
Vote: 9 (Burger, Douglas, Brennan, Stewart, B. White, T. Marshall, Blackmun, Powell, Rehnquist)
0
Opinion of the Court: T. Marshall

Although states have plenary power to impose income taxes on residents within their borders, they may not tax Native Americans who earn their income within the autonomous boundaries of an Indian nation. Arizona attempted to apply its income tax to Rosiland McClanahan, an Indian, who earned her entire income from sources within the Navajo reservation. Treaties and federal statutes leave the taxability of Indians' income on Indian land to the federal government and to the Indians themselves, and, therefore, Arizona had no authority to tax McClanahan. The rationale for this result is that Indian nations are autonomous sovereigns, and one sovereign does not have the power to tax another.

Nevertheless, the Court acknowledged that the trend in cases such as ***Mescalero Apache Tribe v. Jones,*** 411 U.S. 145 (1973), decided the same day as *McClanahan,* is to analyze questions of the boundary between state authority and Indian authority with regard to federal statutes and treaties, rather than by simply applying the Indian sovereignty doctrine. The Court noted that although the doctrine had grown weaker since it was first announced, it was still strong enough to prevent a state from taxing Indian activities that took place completely within the confines of a reservation. It is unclear whether the Court would have made the same decision on sovereignty grounds alone, without the benefit of treaties and statutes.

See Donald A. Grinde Jr., ed., *Native Americans* (Washington, D.C.: CQ Press, 2002).

Frontiero v. Richardson

411 U.S. 677 (1973)
Decided: May 14, 1973
Vote: 8 (Burger, Douglas, Brennan, Stewart, B. White, T. Marshall, Blackmun, Powell)
1 (Rehnquist)
Judgment of the Court: Brennan
Opinion concurring in judgment: Stewart
Opinion concurring in judgment: Powell (Burger, Blackmun)
Dissenting opinion: Rehnquist

Sharon Frontiero, a lieutenant in the U.S. Air Force, challenged a federal statute that provided an extra housing allowance and extra medical benefits to all married men in the armed forces, but denied the benefits to married women unless they could prove they provided more than half of the family income. Frontiero's lawyers argued that sex, like race, should be considered a suspect class, which would require the government to have a compelling interest to adopt discriminatory legislation.

Justice Brennan accepted this argument, asserting "that classifications based upon sex, like classifications based upon race, alienage, or national origin, are inherently suspect, and must therefore be subjected to strict judicial scrutiny." He argued that this conclusion followed logically ***Reed v. Reed,*** 404 U.S. 71 (1971), decided the previous term. Denouncing the "romantic paternalism" of earlier Courts, Brennan argued that because sex was an immutable characteristic, any discrimination based on sex was suspect. Under this analysis, he easily found the federal statute unconstitutional.

Justice Stewart noted that the law created an "invidious discrimination" that violated the standard set forth in *Reed.* Justice Powell also argued that *Reed* should apply, but the Court in *Reed* had not declared sex a suspect category, and Powell said it was "unnecessary" to do so here. He argued that the standard in *Reed* was sufficient to strike down the law at issue. Powell also noted that the Equal Rights Amendment had been passed by Congress and sent on to the states and that, if the people of the nation wanted to make sex a suspect category, they might do so by ratifying the amendment.

Four justices were prepared to declare sex a suspect category, but they could not muster the fifth vote. When the Court revisited this issue in ***Craig v. Boren,*** 429 U.S. 190 (1976), the justices created a new level of scrutiny—intermediate—that fell somewhere between the flexible test of requiring a "rational basis" for laws and the stringent "strict scrutiny" test that Brennan wanted.

See Ruth Bader Ginsburg, "Gender and the Constitution," *University of Cincinnati Law Review* 44 (1975): 1; and Sylvia A. Law, "Rethinking Sex and the Constitution," *University of Pennsylvania Law Review* 132 (1984): 955.

McDonnell Douglas Corp. v. Green

411 U.S. 792 (1973)
Decided: May 14, 1973
Vote: 9 (Burger, Douglas, Brennan, Stewart, B. White, T. Marshall, Blackmun, Powell, Rehnquist)
0
Opinion of the Court: Powell

Percy Green, a mechanic, worked for McDonnell Douglas for nine years. The company laid him off in 1964 as part of a general reduction in its workforce. Green then joined others in illegal "stall-ins" and "lock-ins," sponsored by the Congress on Racial Equality (CORE), to protest his discharge and the company's general record of hiring and firing blacks. Green was arrested during one of these protests. In July 1965, approximately three weeks after the illegal lock-in, McDonnell Douglas began to advertise for mechanics, but when Green applied, McDonnell Douglas rejected his application and cited his protest participation as the reason.

Green believed the true reason was revenge and filed a complaint with the Equal Employment Opportunity Commission (EEOC). Green asserted that McDonnell Douglas had discriminated against him—practiced racial bias—in making an employment decision in violation of Section 703(a)(1) of Title VII of the 1964 Civil Rights Act. The EEOC made no determination on this claim. Green also alleged that McDonnell Douglas violated Section 704(a), which prohibits retaliation for protesting discriminatory employment conditions. The EEOC found "reasonable cause to believe petitioner had violated § 704(a) by refusing to rehire" Green "because of his civil rights activity." When the EEOC could not persuade McDonnell Douglas to rehire him, Green sued in district court, which dismissed the suit. The court of appeals agreed that Section 704(a) does not protect illegal activity, which would include the stall-in and lock-in, but held that an EEOC determination is not necessary to bring a Section 703(a)(1) action for racial bias in hiring.

The Supreme Court agreed with the court of appeals that an EEOC determination is not necessary on every charge of a Title VII violation before an aggrieved party can sue. The Court then outlined the shifting burdens of claimants and defendants in Title VII cases. First, the plaintiff has the burden of establishing a prima facie case of discrimination, which he can do by showing that he belongs to a racial minority; that he applied and was qualified for the job the employer was seeking to fill; that, despite his qualifications, he was rejected; and that, after his rejection, the position remained open and the employer continued to seek applicants with his qualifications. Second, the burden shifts "to the employer to articulate some legitimate, nondiscriminatory reason for the employee's rejection." Third, the plaintiff must have the opportunity to show that the defendant's stated reason for not hiring him was a pretext for racial discrimination.

With this analysis, the Court concluded that the case should be remanded for a full trial. The Court noted that at this point Green "must be afforded a fair opportunity to demonstrate" that McDonnell Douglas's "assigned reason for refusing to re-employ was a pretext or discriminatory in its application. If the District Judge so finds, he must order a prompt and appropriate remedy. In the absence of such a finding, petitioner's refusal to rehire must stand."

See Barbara Lindermann and Paul Grossman, *Employment Discrimination Law,* 3d ed. (Chicago: American Bar Association, and Washington, D.C.: Bureau of National Affairs, 1996).

Columbia Broadcasting System, Inc. v. Democratic National Committee

412 U.S. 94 (1973)
Decided: May 29, 1973
Vote: 7 (Burger, Douglas, Stewart, B. White, Blackmun, Powell, Rehnquist)
2 (Brennan, T. Marshall)
Judgment of the Court: Burger
Concurring opinion: Stewart
Concurring opinion: B. White
Concurring opinion: Blackmun (Powell)
Opinion concurring in judgment: Douglas
Dissenting opinion: Brennan (T. Marshall)

This case was consolidated with three others: *Federal Communications Commission v. Business Executives' Move for Vietnam Peace; Post-Newsweek Stations, Capital Area, Inc. v. Business Executives' Move for Vietnam Peace;* and *American Broadcasting Companies, Inc. v. Democratic National Committee.* The Supreme Court agreed to review these cases after the court of appeals reversed a Federal Communications Commission (FCC) judgment that a broadcast station that had complied with its "public obligation to provide full and fair coverage of public issues" did not have to provide airtime for editorial advertisements.

The Democratic National Committee challenged a broadcaster's policy of not selling airtime for public issue editorial advertisements as a violation of the First Amendment and the "public interest" standard of the Communications Act of 1934. The Business Executives' Move for Vietnam Peace challenged a similar policy of another broadcaster, alleging First Amendment violations. The court of appeals held that selling airtime for noncontroversial messages, but not for controversial public issue editorials, was a violation of the First Amendment, and ordered the FCC to conform its regulations with that rule.

The Supreme Court reversed. The Court held that Congress did not intend to require broadcasters to give equal access to all messages, nor did the public interest requirement obligate them to do so. The Court pointed out that under such a requirement the public airways could be monopolized by those with the means to advertise their point of view on controversial issues to the detriment of the Fairness Doctrine. The FCC had developed the "fairness doctrine" to require that radio and televisions stations give the "other side" of political issues an opportunity to respond to editorial comments. The fairness doctrine was abolished after President Ronald Reagan vetoed an attempt by Congress to codify the FCC policy.

See Fred Friendly, *The Good Guys, the Bad Guys, and the First Amendment* (New York: Random House, 1975).

Schneckloth v. Bustamonte

412 U.S. 218 (1973)
Decided: May 29, 1973
Vote: 6 (Burger, Stewart, B. White, Blackmun, Powell, Rehnquist)
3 (Douglas, Brennan, T. Marshall)
Opinion of the Court: Stewart
Concurring opinion: Blackmun
Concurring opinion: Powell (Burger, Rehnquist)
Dissenting opinion: Douglas
Dissenting opinion: Brennan
Dissenting opinion: T. Marshall

A search conducted without a warrant based on probable cause is *per se* unconstitutional. However, there were—and still are—certain well-established exceptions to the warrant requirement, including voluntary consent to the search. This case concerns the meaning of *voluntary* in this context.

Robert Bustamonte and five companions were driving early one morning when they were stopped by police who noticed that one of the headlights and the license plate were burned out. A "congenial" discussion with the men revealed to the officer that only one of them had a license, and it was not the driver. The officer asked if the trunk opened. One of the men in the car said yes and opened it. Under the left rear seat, the police officers found three checks that had been stolen from a car wash. Until the discovery of the checks, the interaction between the men and the officer remained casual and congenial, but at his trial for possessing the stolen checks, Bustamonte sought to exclude the evidence on the grounds that his consent was not voluntary but coerced by an apparent show of authority. The California court allowed the evidence, and Bustamonte was convicted. He then sought habeas corpus relief in federal court. The Ninth Circuit Court of Appeals held that although Bustamonte's consent was not coerced, it was also not voluntary because Bustamonte apparently did not know he had a right to refuse consent. According to the Ninth Circuit, before a person can be held to have knowingly waived his Fourth and Fourteenth Amendment rights, the government must show that he was instructed that he had rights to waive.

The Supreme Court reversed. The justices looked at cases construing "voluntariness" in the context of confessions and determined that *voluntary* meant the product of the unconstrained will of the actor. If the actor's capacity for free choice has been hindered, his confession was not considered voluntary. Various factors determined whether an actor's capacity for free choice has been thwarted, including his age, his intelligence, and the threat posed by the interrogator. The Court adopted this definition of voluntariness without imposing an additional burden on law enforcement to inform suspects of their right to refuse.

Justice Powell believed that habeas corpus review should be limited to whether the defendant had a fair opportunity to raise his Fourth Amendment claims in the state court. He found that

Bustamonte had the opportunity and saw no need to address the issue raised by the Ninth Circuit.

Justice Douglas's dissent called for a definition of voluntariness that took account of the reality that a police officer may smile and ask "May I?" but do so in a manner that suggests a menacing threat backed by force.

Justice Brennan's dissent pointed out that the officer had no probable cause to search the vehicle and that Bustamonte had been prompted to give up his important constitutional right against unreasonable searches without being told that he had the right to refuse.

Justice Marshall's dissent pointed out that the Court failed to exercise its usual scrutiny of a government's claim that a person has given up a constitutional right. Rather, the Court uncritically accepted the facile conclusion of voluntariness. In Marshall's opinion, the real issue in consent cases was whether the defendant chose to give up his right to exclude the police. It seemed obvious to Marshall that a person cannot make that choice unless he knows he has it.

See Adrian J. Barrio, "Note: Rethinking *Schneckloth v. Bustamonte:* Incorporating Obedience Theory into the Supreme Court's Conception of Voluntary Consent," *University of Illinois Law Review* (1997).

United States v. SCRAP

412 U.S. 669 (1973)
Decided: June 18, 1973
Vote: Multiple
Opinion of the Court: Stewart
Concurring opinion: Blackmun (Brennan)
Dissenting opinion: Douglas
Dissenting opinion: B. White (Burger, Rehnquist)
Dissenting opinion: T. Marshall
Did not participate: Powell

This case led to a badly fractured Court, in which only the author of the opinion of the Court—Justice Stewart—actually signed it. Justices Brennan and Blackmun concurred in a separate opinion. Justices Marshall and Douglass joined in parts I and II of the opinion and dissented from the rest. Justices White, Burger, and Rehnquist dissented in part. The Court was asked to consider whether the National Environmental Policy Act of 1969 (NEPA) gave judges—in this case a circuit court judge, J. Skelly Wright—the authority to enjoin the Interstate Commerce Commission (ICC) from permitting railroads to collect a 2.5 percent interim surcharge on the transfer of recyclable goods. Students Challenging Regulatory Agency Procedures (SCRAP) argued in district court that NEPA prohibited such a surcharge. Wright agreed and ordered the ICC to stop permitting the surcharge and the railroads to stop collecting it.

SCRAP was an unincorporated association of five law students. They formed to protest the shipping surcharge as applied to recyclable materials, claiming manufacturers would be discouraged from using these materials. Their suit was based on the fact that the railroads had not filed an environmental impact statement as required by NEPA. They argued that the surcharge would reduce the amount of material being recycled because the surcharge would make it more expensive to ship such materials to recycling plants. They also argued that if the surcharge went into effect, they would suffer recreational and aesthetic harm because the wooded areas around Washington, D.C., where they liked to hike, would be damaged because less trash and garbage would be recycled. They also argued economic harm because they would have to pay more for products. Relying on ***Sierra Club v. Morton,*** 405 U.S. 727 (1972), the Court held that SCRAP had standing to sue, even though they suffered no particular wrong that would not be suffered by everyone. The Court noted that in *Sierra Club,* "Aesthetic and environmental well-being, like economic well-being, are important ingredients of the quality of life in our society, and the fact that particular environmental interests are shared by the many rather than the few does not make them less deserving of legal protection through the judicial process." In this case, the Court found that "neither the fact that the appellees here claimed only a harm to their use and enjoyment of the natural resources of the Washington area, nor the fact that all those who use those resources suffered the same harm, deprives them of standing."

SCRAP was an important victory for environmental groups and reaffirmed the promise of *Sierra Club.* The Court, however, also held that NEPA did not give the district court the power to enjoin the surcharge. The fact that the ICC might have been noncompliant with NEPA did not give the court authority to prevent an action under ICC, because NEPA was not intended to override any other statute.

See Richard Stewart, "The Reformation of American Administrative Law," *Harvard Law Review* 88 (1975): 1667.

Miller v. California

413 U.S. 15 (1973)
Decided: June 21, 1973
Vote: 5 (Burger, B. White, Blackmun, Powell, Rehnquist)
4 (Douglas, Brennan, Stewart, T. Marshall)
Opinion of the Court: Burger
Dissenting opinion: Douglas
Dissenting opinion: Brennan (Stewart, T. Marshall)

In this case, the Supreme Court tried to resolve the conflict between the efforts of communities to regulate obscene material and the freedom of expression and of adults to read and view whatever they wish. A California court convicted Marvin Miller of mailing unsolicited sexually explicit material in violation of a state statute. In reviewing Miller's conviction, Chief Justice Burger offered a new, three-prong, standard for obscenity.

> The basic guidelines for the trier of fact must be: (a) whether "the average person, applying contemporary community standards" would find that the work, taken as a whole, appeals to the prurient interest; (b) whether the work depicts or describes, in a patently offensive way,

sexual conduct specifically defined by the applicable state law; and (c) whether the work, taken as a whole, lacks serious literary, artistic, political, or scientific value.

In reaching this conclusion, Burger rejected "as a constitutional standard the 'utterly without redeeming social value' test of" ***Memoirs v. Massachusetts,*** 383 U.S. 413 (1966).

Burger refused to set out regulations for the states, but offered a "few plain examples of what a state statute could define for regulation." Under this decision, the states could ban "patently offensive representations or descriptions of ultimate sexual acts, normal or perverted, actual or simulated" and "patently offensive representation or descriptions of masturbation, excretory functions, and lewd exhibition of the genitals." He said, "Sex and nudity may not be exploited without limit by films or pictures exhibited or sold in places of public accommodation any more than live sex and nudity can be exhibited or sold without limit in such public places." In summary, he noted, "At a minimum, prurient, patently offensive depiction or description of sexual conduct must have serious literary, artistic, political, or scientific value to merit First Amendment protection." He offered medical books as an example of works that might be offensive to some, but still merit such protection.

The most controversial aspect of Burger's opinion was his reliance on state laws and community standards. He reassured commercial vendors and the consenting adults who used their materials that no one would be prosecuted for the sale or exposure of obscene materials "unless these materials depict or describe patently offensive 'hard core' sexual conduct specifically defined by the regulating state law, as written or construed." Burger conceded that under the Constitution, "fundamental First Amendment limitations on the powers of the States do not vary from community to community," but he immediately undercut this position by asserting that there cannot and should not be "fixed, uniform national standards of precisely what appeals to the 'prurient interest' or is 'patently offensive.' These are essentially questions of fact, and our Nation is simply too big and too diverse for this Court to reasonably expect that such standards could be articulated for all 50 States in a single formulation, even assuming the prerequisite consensus exists." The result was a reliance on "community standards" for First Amendment protections.

Justice Brennan's dissent stressed this danger. Subsequent cases led the Court to rethink this position and to apply a national standard to the third prong of the test: "whether the work, taken as a whole, lacks serious literary, artistic, political, or scientific value." In subsequent cases, such as *Jenkins v. Georgia,* 418 U.S. 153 (1974), *Smith v. United States,* 431 U.S. 291 (1977), and *Pope v. Illinois* 481 U.S. 497 (1987), the Court held that the states had to adhere to a national standard that recognized a broad national culture that allowed for diversity of what was acceptable.

Justice Douglas began a bitter dissent by saying, "Today we leave open the way for California to send a man to prison for distributing brochures that advertise books and a movie under freshly written standards defining obscenity which until today's decision were never the part of any law." Douglas pointed out that for decades, "The Court has worked hard to define obscenity and concededly has failed." He noted that some justices "condemn only 'hardcore pornography'; but even then a true definition is lacking." He then quoted Justice Stewart's famous aphorism from ***Jacobellis v. Ohio,*** 378 U.S. 184 (1964), " 'I could never succeed in [defining it] intelligibly,' but 'I know it when I see it.' " Douglas accused the Court of writing into the Constitution a standard for censorship that violated the very essence of the First Amendment. He suggested a sensible solution: that authorities be allowed to prosecute the movie, book, or magazine they sought to censor. "If a specific book, play, paper, or motion picture has in a civil proceeding been condemned as obscene and review of that finding has been completed, and thereafter a person publishers, shows, or displays that particular book or film, then a vague law has been made specific." Douglas still denied that the First Amendment allowed such censorship, but, if his proposal were adopted, no one would be prosecuted under laws and rules so vague and confusing that, as Justice Harlan wrote in *Interstate Circuit, Inc. v. Dallas,* 390 U.S. 676 (1968), "The upshot of all this divergence in viewpoint is that anyone who undertakes to examine the Court's decisions since *Roth* [*v. United States,* 354 U.S. 476 (1957)] which have held particular material obscene or not obscene would find himself in utter bewilderment." Douglas was a lone voice urging that the Court find a clear way out of the national "bewilderment" on this issue.

On the same day that this case was decided, Justice Brennan offered an elaborate dissent in the companion case, ***Paris Adult Theatre I v. Slaton,*** 413 U.S. 49 (1973). His dissent in *Miller* referred to this opinion. In *Miller* he simply noted that the statute under which Marvin Miller was convicted was overbroad and that the Burger opinion "represents a substantial departure from the course of our prior decisions, and since the state courts have as yet had no opportunity to consider whether a 'readily apparent construction suggests itself as a vehicle for rehabilitating the [statute] in a single prosecution,' I would reverse the judgment . . . and remand the case." Like Douglas, Brennan and the other justices who joined him were concerned with the prosecution and jailing of Miller for acts that no one could have known were criminal when he committed them.

See Sean F. Rommel, "The Arkansas Obscenity Doctrine: Its Establishment and Evolution," *Arkansas Law Review,* 47 (1994): 393; and Marion D. Hefner, " 'Roast Pigs' and Miller Light: Variable Obscenity in the Nineties," *University of Illinois Law Review* (1996): 843; and "Note, Community Standards, Class Actions, and Obscenity Under *Miller v. California,*" *Harvard Law Review* 88 (1975): 1838.

Paris Adult Theatre I v. Slaton

413 U.S. 49 (1973)
Decided: June 21, 1973
Vote: 5 (Burger, B. White, Blackmun, Powell, Rehnquist)
4 (Douglas, Brennan, Stewart, T. Marshall)
Opinion of the Court: Burger
Dissenting opinion: Douglas
Dissenting opinion: Brennan (Stewart, T. Marshall)

The state of Georgia sought to enjoin the proprietor of an adult film emporium from exhibiting two movies alleged to be obscene. The Georgia Supreme Court held that the movies were obscene and therefore not protected under the First Amendment. On appeal, the Supreme Court vacated the decision with instructions to reconsider the case in light of ***Miller v. California,*** 413 U.S. 15 (1973), decided the same day. In *Paris Adult Theatre,* the Court took the opportunity to comment at some length on the standards and procedures used by the Georgia courts.

The Court agreed with the state supreme court's holding that, just because they are exhibited only to consenting adults, obscene materials are not necessarily protected by the First Amendment. The Court said that the public has an interest in prohibiting the exhibition of obscene material outside the home because the gathering together in one place of consumers of pornography creates a blight on the community and interferes with the public's right to maintain a "decent" society. The Court added that the state has a legitimate interest in preventing collateral crime associated with adult theaters and was free to determine that the "cleaning up" of the theaters would eliminate street crime from the area. Chief Justice Burger pointed out in an ironic fashion that the Court was being urged to allow the free market to govern the commerce of obscenity, even by those " 'who have never had a kind word to say for laissez-faire,' particularly in solving urban, commercial, and environmental pollution problems." Finally, although ***Stanley v. Georgia,*** 394 U.S. 557 (1969), held that the home is a zone of privacy where a person can watch obscene films without government interference, that zone of privacy does not follow the person when he leaves his house and goes to an adult theater.

The Court responded in a curious way to the dissenters' criticism that it was attempting to control the moral content of the thoughts of those who patronize adult theaters. The Court might have said that in regulating adult theaters, government is not controlling thoughts, but conduct. It did not do that; instead, the Court asserted that "controlling the moral content of the mind" was not a problem unless it involved controlling the reason or intellect. The Court implied that seeking to control emotions, aesthetic impressions, or values, to name a few non-"reason or intellect" contents of the mind, is acceptable.

Justice Brennan's dissent discussed the multitude of definitions of obscenity that had come and gone since the Court decided in ***Roth v. United States,*** 354 U.S. 476 (1957), that obscenity could be outlawed, and he determined that finding a definition that was not vague or overbroad was impossible. Furthermore, he expressed the concern that if protecting the moral content of a person's mind is accepted as a legitimate state interest, it is inevitable that states will seek to control citizens by deciding what books they may read and movies they may see. In Brennan's view, the only legitimate state interests that could be advanced in favor of prohibiting obscene speech were the protection of minors and the protection of the privacy interests of unconsenting adults. Absent one of those state interests, the courts and legislatures should not even attempt the dangerous task of distinguishing obscenity from protected speech.

Justice Douglas reaffirmed his free speech absolutist position. He stressed that obscenity is at worst speech that some find offensive, but that political and religious speech are also offensive to many, and yet they are protected. In Douglas's opinion, whether something was obscene or had redeeming social value was a matter of individual taste beyond the ability of the government to determine. Furthermore, he did not accept the idea that people's privacy interest in not seeing offensive material justified a ban on obscenity. As he pointed out, "In a life that has not been short, I have yet to be trapped into seeing or reading something that would offend me."

See Steven H. Shiffrin, *The First Amendment, Democracy, and Romance* (Cambridge: Harvard University Press, 1990); and "Note: Community Standards, Class Actions, and Obscenity under *Miller v. California,*" *Harvard Law Review* 88 (1975): 1838.

Keyes v. School District No. 1, Denver, Colorado

413 U.S. 189 (1973)
Decided: June 21, 1973
Vote: 7 (Burger, Douglas, Brennan, Stewart, T. Marshall, Blackmun, Powell)
1 (Rehnquist)
Opinion of the Court: Brennan
Concurring opinion: Douglas
Concurring in judgment without opinion: Burger
Opinion concurring in judgment: Powell
Dissenting opinion: Rehnquist
Did not participate: B. White

In *Keyes* the Supreme Court considered for the first time the issue of desegregation in nonsouthern schools and looked at "de facto" rather than "de jure" segregation. Colorado had never mandated segregation in its schools, and Denver had never officially and formally sanctioned the practice. Nevertheless, African American parents charged that "by use of various techniques such as the manipulation of student attendance zones, school site selection and a neighborhood school policy," the Denver school board "created or maintained racially or ethnically (or both racially and ethnically) segregated schools throughout the school district." The plaintiffs asked for a wholesale desegregation of the city's schools through busing and other actions.

Speaking for the Court, Justice Brennan found that Denver had an "intentionally segregative policy" that was "practiced in a meaningful or significant segment of a school system." Brennan said it did not matter that segregation had not developed under the color of state law, as was the case in the South, and the Court upheld an order to integrate the city's schools through busing. Brennan maintained the distinction between de facto and de jure segregation, noting that where schools had intentionally discriminated and defended their segregated systems, there would be a lesser burden on plaintiffs to prove discrimination than in places where segregation came about because of housing patterns and other factors out of the control of the school board. Here, however, the Court found intent to segregate.

Justice Powell would have abandoned the distinction between de facto and de jure segregation, but he opposed busing as a remedy. Douglas was also ready to abandon the distinction, as well as the notion of fault or intent, but unlike Powell, he thought busing an appropriate remedy.

Keyes has been correctly identified as the beginning of a new era in the struggle for equality in schooling. The case brought the issue to large northern and western cities, where segregation had not been the rule. Lower courts in the North and West followed *Keyes* in ordering busing. *Keyes* also showed that the Court was no longer unanimous in its desire to integrate and that it was clearly split on the methods it would support.

See George R. Metcalf, *From Little Rock to Boston: A History of School Desegregation* (Westport, Conn.: Greenwood Press, 1983); and Gary Orfield, *Must We Bus? Segregated Schools and National Policy* (Washington, D.C.: Brookings Institution, 1978).

Pittsburgh Press Co. v. Pittsburgh Commission on Human Relations

413 U.S. 376 (1973)
Decided: June 21, 1973
Vote: 5 (Brennan, B. White, T. Marshall, Powell, Rehnquist)
4 (Burger, Douglas, Stewart, Blackmun)
Opinion of the Court: Powell
Dissenting opinion: Burger
Dissenting opinion: Douglas
Dissenting opinion: Stewart (Douglas)
Dissenting opinion: Blackmun

A Pittsburgh ordinance prohibited newspapers from categorizing their employment want ads according to sex unless the jobs listed under male and female headings were "based upon a bona fide occupational exemption certified by the [Human Rights] Commission." The ordinance in effect prohibited newspapers from enabling employers to market to one sex or the other those jobs that employers were required by law to fill without regard to sex. A newspaper that categorized its employment want ads according to sex challenged the ordinance, claiming that it was a prior restraint upon its freedom of speech in violation of the First Amendment. It also asserted that its categorization of job postings was a form of protected speech, not unprotected commercial advertising under ***Valentine v. Chrestensen,*** 316 U.S. 52 (1942). The Pennsylvania courts found that the ordinance did not violate the newspaper's First Amendment rights, and the newspaper appealed.

The Supreme Court affirmed. The Court began by observing that the ordinance did not affect the newspaper's ability to convey news, opinion, or commentary in any serious way, nor did it affect the commercial viability of the newspaper. The Court agreed that the regulation affected the layout of the want ads section and prohibited the newspaper from conveying the employers' interest in filling jobs with either males or females. The Court held that the layout of the want ads section was not protected speech, but commercial advertising under *Chrestensen.*

Chrestensen involved a regulation prohibiting leaflets that solicited customers to pay admission to tour a submarine, and the Court held that such commercial advertising, which conveyed no noncommercial information, could be regulated. In ***New York Times v. Sullivan,*** 376 U.S. 254 (1964), however, the Court identified another kind of advertisement that distinguished the case from *Chrestensen.* The newspaper ad at issue in *Sullivan* had been purchased by several Montgomery, Alabama, clergymen to publicize wrongs inflicted against civil rights demonstrators by a Montgomery city official. The ad conveyed information crucial to a vital public issue and a recital of political grievances.

The Court in *Pittsburgh Press* decided that the sex-based job postings were more like the commercial leaflets in *Chrestensen* than the political ad in *Sullivan.* The want ads did not criticize the Pittsburgh ordinance or express any views on the public issue of discrimination; they were simply advertisements for job vacancies and, therefore, were classic commercial speech. Furthermore, the Court found that the ordinance was not invalid as a prior restraint because it was narrowly tailored to meet the compelling government interest in preventing employers from circumventing their duty to hire in a nondiscriminatory manner.

The dissenters offered various reasons for their disagreement. Chief Justice Burger's dissent expressed anxiety over the enlargement of the *Chrestensen* doctrine. Justice Douglas argued that commercial speech should be protected and that in any case the newspaper was actually engaging in a kind of criticism of employment discrimination laws that is definitely protected. Justice Stewart's dissent emphasized that the law may prohibit employers from filling jobs in a discriminatory way, but it may not prohibit a newspaper from publishing the employer's wish to do so.

Although this case was framed as a First Amendment case, it was also important in the development of the law against sex discrimination. In an appendix, the Court illustrated that the advertisements not only segregated jobs but also supported sex discrimination. For example, the paper accepted ads for accountant jobs that paid males $10,000 a year and females $6,000, and bookkeeper positions that offered men $9,000 and women $5,000. With the exception of "academic instructors," which advertised jobs for men and women at the same $13,000, the range for women's salaries was $4,200 to $6,720 a year, while the lowest salary in the list of jobs for men was $7,200, and ten jobs paid more than $10,000. The "male" jobs included managers ranging from $10,000 to $18,000 and one job at $30,000.

See Thomas H. Jackson and John Calvin Jeffries Jr., "Commercial Speech: Economic Due Process and the First Amendment," *Virginia Law Review* 6 (1979): 1.

Levitt v. Committee for Public Education and Religious Liberty

413 U.S. 472 (1973)
Decided: June 25, 1973
Vote: 8 (Burger, Douglas, Brennan, Stewart, T. Marshall, Blackmun, Powell, Rehnquist)
1 (B. White)
Opinion of the Court: Burger
Concurring opinion: Douglas, Brennan, T. Marshall
Dissenting without opinion: B. White

New York State appropriated $28 million for nonpublic schools to be used for purposes such as administration, grading exams, keeping records, and other clerical costs. Schools were not required to account for their use of the money, but the statute specified that it could not be used for religious purposes, even though church-sponsored schools were eligible. The district court struck the statute down under the First Amendment's Establishment of Religion Clause.

The Supreme Court agreed, holding that the apportionment of money to church-sponsored schools without any mechanism for monitoring whether the funds were used for secular or religious purposes was an impermissible state support of religion. The Court rejected as irrelevant New York's argument that the state could provide money for activities mandated under state law, such as the administration of standardized testing.

See Thomas A. Schweitzer, *"Levitt v. Committee for Public Education and Religious Liberty,"* in *Religion and American Law: An Encyclopedia,* ed. Paul Finkelman (New York: Garland, 2000), 280–281; and James M. Giacoma, *"Committee for Public Education and Religious Liberty v. Regan:* New Possibilities for State Aid to Nonpublic Schools," *St. Louis University Law Journal* 24 (1980): 406.

United States Civil Service Commission v. National Association of Letter Carriers

413 U.S. 548 (1973)
Decided: June 25, 1973
Vote: 6 (Burger, Stewart, B. White, Blackmun, Powell, Rehnquist)
3 (Douglas, Brennan, T. Marshall)
Opinion of the Court: B. White
Dissenting opinion: Douglas (Brennan, T. Marshall)

This case asked whether Section 9 of the Hatch Act was unconstitutionally vague and overbroad when it prohibited federal employees from "taking an active part in political management or in political campaigns." A similar issue had arisen in ***United Public Workers v. Mitchell,*** 330 U.S. 75 (1947), but this question was left unanswered. The letter carriers argued that the Hatch Act was vague and overbroad when it spoke of "political activities." The three-judge district court agreed and struck the statute down.

The Supreme Court reversed. The Court reaffirmed *Mitchell,* which held that Congress could prohibit federal employees from "holding a party office, working at the polls, and acting as party paymaster for other party workers." The Court added that Congress could also forbid "organizing a political party or club; actively participating in fund-raising activities for a partisan candidate or political party; becoming a partisan candidate for, or campaigning for, an elective public office; actively managing the campaigning of a partisan candidate for public office; initiating or circulating a partisan nominating petition or soliciting votes for a partisan candidate for public office; or serving as a delegate, alternate or proxy to a political party convention." The Court said the language of the act is neither vague nor overbroad. Moreover, its longstanding and consistent application and interpretation by the agency charged with enforcing it gives the average citizen a reasonable idea of what the statute forbids and what it allows.

In dissent, Justice Douglas mocked the vagaries of the law. He noted that between 1886 and 1940 the Civil Service Commission issued three thousand rulings "and many hundreds of rulings since 1940." He pointed out that in 1971 the commission "published a three-volume work entitled Political Activities Reporter which contains over 800 of its decisions since the enactment of the Hatch Act." Douglas noted, "One can learn from studying those volumes that it is not 'political activity' to march in a band during a political parade or to wear political badges or to 'participate fully in public affairs, except as prohibited by law, in a manner which does not materially compromise his efficiency or integrity as an employee or the neutrality, efficiency, or integrity of his agency.' " He pointed out that some things, like marching in a band, are clear, while "others are pregnant with ambiguity." He argued that the law "raises large questions of uncertainty because one may be partisan for a person, an issue, a candidate without feeling an identification with one political party or the other." Douglas argued to strike down the portion of the Hatch Act at issue so "a new start may be made on this old problem that confuses and restricts nearly five million federal, state, and local public employees today that live under the present Act."

See Barbara L. Schwemle, "Hatch Act Amendments: Political Activity and the Civil Service," *Congressional Research Service Issue Brief*, December 24, 1996; and Robert G. Vaughn, "Restrictions on the Political Activities of Public Employees: The Hatch Act and Beyond," *George Washington Law Review* 44 (May 1976): 516.

Hunt v. McNair

413 U.S. 734 (1973)
Decided: June 25, 1973
Vote: 6 (Burger, Stewart, B. White, Blackmun, Powell, Rehnquist)
3 (Douglas, Brennan, T. Marshall)
Opinion of the Court: Powell
Dissenting opinion: Brennan (Douglas, T. Marshall)

South Carolina authorized the state to issue revenue bonds for the construction of buildings on college campuses. Religious colleges were eligible for the money raised from the bonds as long as the money did not help in the construction of buildings used for sectarian study or religious worship. The state supreme court twice upheld the scheme, and the U.S. Supreme Court affirmed.

The scheme worked as follows: the state would issue the bonds and give the proceeds to a college to construct a building. The college would then convey the building to the state, which in turn would lease it back to the college and use the proceeds to pay the interest and principal on the bonds. Once the bonds were fully paid, the state could convey title back to the college. Under this plan, the state paid no money to construct the buildings and took no risk. The act stated that the bonds "shall not be deemed to constitute a debt or liability of the State or of any political subdivision thereof or a pledge of the faith and credit of the State or of any such political subdivision, but shall be payable solely from the funds herein provided therefor from revenues." The Court decided this case the same day as ***Committee for Public Education & Religious Liberty v. Nyquist,*** 413 U.S. 756 (1973), and reached a similar result: to uphold the state law. Here, as in *Nyquist,* the Court applied the test first established in ***Lemon v. Kurtzman,*** 411 U.S. 192 (1973). The Court applied *Lemon*'s three principles to the statute to determine whether it violated the Establishment Clause. "First, the statute must have a secular legislative purpose; second, its principal or primary effect must be one that neither advances nor inhibits religion . . . ; finally, the statute must not foster 'an excessive government entanglement with religion.' " The Court determined that this scheme did not violate any of these tests.

In dissent, Justice Brennan argued that the proper test ought to be the one he enunciated in his concurring opinion in ***Abington School District v. Schempp,*** 374 U.S. 203 (1963), namely that "those involvements of religious with secular institutions which (a) serve the essentially religious activities of religious institutions; (b) employ the organs of government for essentially religious purposes; or (c) use essentially religious means to serve governmental ends, where secular means would suffice" are unconstitutional.

See Mark J. Beutler, "Public Funding of Sectarian Education: Establishment and Free Exercise Clause Implications," *George Mason Independent Law Review* 2 (1993): 7.

Committee for Public Education & Religious Liberty v. Nyquist

413 U.S. 756 (1973)
Decided: June 25, 1973
Vote: 6 (Douglas, Brennan, Stewart, T. Marshall, Blackmun, Powell)
3 (Burger, B. White, Rehnquist)
Opinion of the Court: Powell
Dissenting opinion: Burger (B. White, Rehnquist)
Dissenting opinion: B. White (Burger, Rehnquist)
Dissenting opinion: Rehnquist (Burger, B. White)

The New York legislature appropriated funds for the maintenance and repair of religiously affiliated schools, tuition reimbursement grants for children attending nonpublic schools, and tax benefits for the parents of students at such schools. The legislature declared that the maintenance aid was intended to improve the facilities of the schools for the health and safety of the children and that the aid was therefore neutral and nonideological. The tuition grants were intended to ensure the freedom of choice to attend a nonpublic school, which "should be available in a pluralistic society." The tuition reimbursement was given to the parents, rather than the schools, and the state argued that the grants did not aid religion. A three-judge panel of the district court found that the maintenance and repair provisions violated the Establishment Clause, but the tax provisions did not.

The Supreme Court held that all three provisions had the primary effect of aiding religion and therefore violated the Establishment Clause. With regard to the tuition reimbursement grants, the Court held that giving them to parents rather than to the schools did not insulate the grants from an Establishment Clause violation.

Justice Rehnquist's dissent signaled his desire to break down the "wall of separation" between government and religion. Nearly three decades later, he succeeded in ***Zelman v. Simmons-Harris,*** 536 U.S. — (2002); 122 S.Ct. 2460, which upheld a school voucher scheme in Cleveland, Ohio. In Rehnquist's view, the Establishment Clause issue with regard to the tuition grants is not whether the grants have the primary effect of advancing religion, but whether they coerce parents into sending their children to religious schools. Furthermore, Rehnquist compared the tax deductions to the property tax exemptions for churches that were upheld in ***Walz v. Tax Commission of the City of New York,*** 397 U.S. 664 (1970).

See Frederick Mark Gedicks and Roger Hendrix, *Choosing the Dream: The Future of Religions in American Public Life* (New York: Greenwood Press, 1991); and *Religion and American Law: An Encyclopedia,* ed. Paul Finkelman (New York: Garland, 2000).

Hess v. Indiana

414 U.S. 105 (1973)
Decided: November 19, 1973
Vote: 6 (Douglas, Brennan, Stewart, B. White, T. Marshall, Powell)
3 (Burger, Blackmun, Rehnquist)
Opinion: *Per curiam*
Dissenting opinion: Rehnquist (Burger, Blackmun)

Gregory Hess was convicted in an Indiana court of disorderly conduct during a demonstration in Bloomington protesting the war in Vietnam. The basis for his conviction was his speaking of the words, "We'll take the fucking street later [or again]" while facing a crowd of antiwar demonstrators who were being cleared out of a street by police. The Indiana Supreme Court upheld his conviction.

Hess appealed to the Supreme Court, arguing that his conviction violated his First Amendment rights. Indiana argued that Hess's words could be punished under the "fighting words" exception to the First Amendment, because they were likely to cause the police to react violently, or as incitement to violence by exhorting the crowd to take back the street.

The Court held that Hess's speech was protected under the First Amendment and that his conviction violated his rights. The Court said that his words were not fighting words because Hess was not facing the sheriff when he said them and the sheriff did not interpret the speech as directed at him. The words were not an incitement to violence because "at worst, it amounted to nothing more than advocacy of illegal action at some indefinite future time." Citing ***Cohen v. California,*** 403 U.S. 15 (1971), the Court found "there was no evidence to indicate that Hess's speech amounted to a public nuisance in that privacy interests were being invaded." The Court applied the standard of ***Brandenburg v. Ohio,*** 395 U.S. 444 (1969), that speech could be suppressed only if it created a danger of "imminent lawlessness" and reaffirmed that, unless words are meant to incite imminent lawless action and are likely to do so, the state may not outlaw them.

Communist Party of Indiana v. Whitcomb

414 U.S. 441 (1974)
Decided: January 9, 1974
Vote: 9 (Burger, Douglas, Brennan, Stewart, B. White, T. Marshall, Blackmun, Powell, Rehnquist)
0
Opinion of the Court: Brennan
Opinion concurring in judgment: Powell (Burger, Blackmun, Rehnquist)

Justice Brennan began his opinion by noting "this is a loyalty oath case," and as such it can be seen as a ghost of the McCarthy-era anticommunist cases of the 1950s. Indiana law provided that no political party could place its candidates on an election ballot "until it has filed an affidavit, by its officers, under oath, that it does not advocate the overthrow of local, state or national government by force or violence." In 1972 state election officials denied the newly organized Communist Party of Indiana permission to place its candidates on the ballot for the 1972 general election because it refused to swear the loyalty oath, as the statute required.

The Court held that this oath was an unconstitutional restriction on speech (refusing to utter words is also a form of speech) under the First Amendment because, even if the party's refusal could be implied to mean the party did advocate the overthrow of the government, such advocacy, as an abstract principle, may not be outlawed. Under the test set out in ***Brandenburg v. Ohio,*** 395 U.S. 444 (1969), only incitements to imminent lawlessness that are actually likely to cause such particular illegal acts may be prohibited. Abstract advocacy of lawlessness or revolution is protected speech. Because access to the ballot is as important a right as any other that is protected by the First Amendment, the loyalty oath requirement was unconstitutional

The concurring justices took a narrower road. Justice Powell noted that "it was established at trial" that the election officials "had certified the Democratic and Republican Parties despite the failure of party officials to submit the prescribed affidavits." Citing *Williams v. Rhodes,* 393 U.S. 23 (1968), Powell asserted that "a discriminatory preference for established parties under a State's electoral system can be justified only by a 'compelling state interest.' In the present case, no colorable justification has been offered for placing on appellants burdens not imposed on the two established parties." The actions of the election officials constituted a "discriminatory application of the Indiana statute" that denied the Communist Party of Indiana equal protection under the Fourteenth Amendment.

Cleveland Board of Education v. LaFleur

414 U.S. 632 (1974)
Decided: January 21, 1974
Vote: 7 (Douglas, Brennan, Stewart, B. White, T. Marshall, Blackmun, Powell)
2 (Burger, Rehnquist)
Opinion of the Court: Stewart
Concurring in judgment: Douglas
Concurring in judgment: Powell
Dissenting opinion: Rehnquist (Burger)

This case was consolidated with *Cohen v. Chesterfield County School Board.* Jo Carol LaFleur and Susan Cohen were public school teachers. They became pregnant during the 1970–1971 school year and were compelled to take mandatory maternity leave under the policies of their respective school districts. Each woman challenged the policies under 42 U.S.C. Section 1983, which protects civil rights and in part prohibits discrimination based on gender. The school districts required maternity leave beginning at a certain fixed time before expected childbirth. Cleveland's policy required the leave to extend until the first semester after the child was three months old; Chesterfield County's until the first semester after the teacher is declared capable of resuming work.

The Court held that both statutes violated due process in that they provided arbitrary cut-off times when the teacher was presumed incapable of continuing work. As the Court noted, "The rules contain an irrebuttable presumption of physical incompentency, and that presumption applies even when the individual woman's physical status might be wholly to the contrary." Similarly, the Cleveland policy violated due process by presuming teachers were not capable of resuming work until their children were three months old. The Chesterfield policy was not unconstitutional with regard to its return to work provision because it was based on an individualized determination of fitness to resume work.

Justice Powell argued that these cases should have been decided on equal protection grounds. Powell pointed out that the original purpose of these rules was "to keep visibly pregnant teachers out of the sight of schoolchildren" and that the defense of these rules were "after-the-fact rationalizations." He noted that the school board stressed the importance of "continuity" in the classroom, but that these rules worked against that by sometimes forcing teachers to leave in the middle of a semester when there was no medical reason for them to leave that early.

The dissenters also rejected the "rebuttable presumption" theory of the majority, and chided the majority for not grounding its decision on equal protection grounds. But Justice Rehnquist was unwilling to strike down the rules on these grounds either and instead argued against the majority's "quixotic engagement in his apparently unending war on irrebuttable presumptions."

Davis v. Alaska

415 U.S. 308 (1974)
Decided: February 27, 1974
Vote: 7 (Burger, Douglas, Brennan, Stewart, T. Marshall, Blackmun, Powell)
2 (B. White, Rehnquist)
Opinion of the Court: Burger
Concurring opinion: Stewart
Dissenting opinion: B. White (Rehnquist)

Based on the testimony of Richard Green, Davis was convicted of burglarizing the Polar Bar in Alaska, removing the safe from the building, and emptying it. The safe was found on the property of Green's stepfather. Green identified Davis from a book of police photographs, and later in a lineup, as the man he saw parked near where the safe was found. At his trial, Davis wanted Green questioned about his status as a juvenile offender. At the time of the trial, Green was on probation, and Davis wanted to bring this information before the jury, as Chief Justice Burger explained it, "to show—or at least argue—that Green acted out of fear or concern of possible jeopardy to his probation." Green could have made a hasty and faulty identification of petitioner to shift suspicion for the robbery away from himself. In addition, Green might have been subject to undue pressure from the police and made his identifications under fear that his probation could be revoked. As the opinion states, "Green's record would be revealed only as necessary to probe Green for bias and prejudice and not generally to call Green's good character into question." The court refused to allow the cross-examination because of state statutes protecting the anonymity of juvenile offenders.

The Supreme Court held that Davis's right to cross-examine witnesses under the Confrontation Clause of the Sixth Amendment prevailed over the state's interest in protecting the anonymity of juvenile offenders, an interest that Burger acknowledged. He also noted, however, that the probation status of the witness was clearly relevant to understanding why he would have been anxious to both help the police and shift any blame for the burglary to someone else. Burger wrote,

> we conclude that the right of confrontation is paramount to the State's policy of protecting a juvenile offender. Whatever temporary embarrassment might result to Green or his family by disclosure of his juvenile record—if the prosecution insisted on using him to make its case—is outweighed by petitioner's right to probe into the influence of possible bias in the testimony of a crucial identification witness."

Johnson v. Robison

415 U.S. 361 (1974)
Decided: March 4, 1974
Vote: 8 (Burger, Brennan, Stewart, B. White, T. Marshall, Blackmun, Powell, Rehnquist)
1 (Douglas)
Opinion of the Court: Brennan
Dissenting opinion: Douglas

William R. Robison was a conscientious objector performing alternative service in a Boston hospital during the Vietnam War. He objected to a provision of the Veterans' Readjustment Benefits Act of 1966, which gave educational benefits to servicemen returning from duty but not to those assigned to alternate civilian service.

The Court held that the distinction was not a violation of the Equal Protection Clause because the classification was not arbitrary. Congress had a rational basis for extending the benefits to those returning from combat: the longer service period and greater deprivation of personal freedom involved in combat service meant that these servicemen had a need for readjustment that those performing alternate service did not. Furthermore, the benefits served as an incentive for people to join the military. Neither did the provision violate Robison's free exercise of religion, because the act did not single out conscientious objectors because of their religion, but because including them would not be rationally related to the act's purpose. The withholding of education funds had only an incidental effect on their religion.

In dissent, Justice Douglas argued that the provision amounted to religious discrimination because the state offered benefits to members of most religious groups, but denied the benefits to members of minority religious groups. He compared it to Sunday Closing laws, which discriminated against Sabbatarians by requiring them to close their businesses on Sunday, when for religious reasons they also closed their businesses on Saturdays. Douglas noted that in ***Girouard v. United States,*** 328 U.S. 61 (1946), the Court had asserted:

> The effort of war is indivisible; and those whose religious scruples prevent them from killing are no less patriots than those whose special traits or handicaps result in their assignment to duties far behind the fighting front. Each is making the utmost contribution according to his capacity. The fact that his role may be limited by religious convictions rather than by physical characteristics has no necessary bearing on his attachment to his country or on his willingness to support and defend it to his utmost.

Douglas argued that Robison's patriotic sacrifice on the home front entitled him to the same benefits as those who were in military service.

Edelman v. Jordan

415 U.S. 651 (1974)
Decided: March 25, 1974
Vote: 5 (Burger, Stewart, B. White, Powell, Rehnquist)
4 (Douglas, Brennan, T. Marshall, Blackmun)
Opinion of the Court: Rehnquist
Dissenting opinion: Douglas
Dissenting opinion: Brennan
Dissenting opinion: T. Marshall (Blackmun)

John Jordan and others sued Joel Edelman, the Illinois director of public aid, and other state and local welfare officers for failure to properly administer the federal program of Aid to the Aged, Blind, or Disabled (AABD). In addition to asserting that the state failed to follow federal guidelines, the plaintiffs alleged Fourteenth Amendment violations in the state's administration of certain federal aid programs. The federal district court found for Jordan and ordered the payment of retroactive benefits under the federal program to the plaintiffs.

The Supreme Court found that the Eleventh Amendment, which prohibits federal courts from hearing suits against states by private citizens, prohibited the district court from exercising this jurisdiction. Illinois did not waive its immunity by participating in the aid program. ***Ex parte Young,*** 209 U.S. 123 (1908), which allows suits against states by private citizens to be heard in federal court when they involve prohibiting future actions, did not apply to this case because Jordan was suing for damages on past actions. Justice Rehnquist noted:

> *Ex parte Young* was a watershed case in which this Court held that the Eleventh Amendment did not bar an action in the federal courts seeking to enjoin the Attorney General of Minnesota from enforcing a statute claimed to violate the Fourteenth Amendment of the United States Constitution. This holding has permitted the Civil War Amendments to the Constitution to serve as a sword, rather than merely as a shield, for those whom they were designed to protect. But the relief awarded in *Ex parte Young* was prospective only; the Attorney General of Minnesota was enjoined to conform his future conduct of that office to the requirement of the Fourteenth Amendment. Such relief is analogous to that awarded by the District Court in the prospective portion of its order under review in this case.

The Court therefore ruled that the Eleventh Amendment barred this suit, even though the state did not make this defense in the district court.

See Norman B. Lichtenstein, "Retroactive Relief in the Federal Courts Since *Edelman v. Jordan:* A Trip Through the Twilight Zone," *Case Western Reserve Law Review* 32 (1982): 364; and Jane G. Stevens, "Federal Jurisdiction Under Title VII of the Civil Rights Act of 1974 in the Aftermath of *Edelman v. Jordan-Fitzpatrick v. Bitzer,*" *Brooklyn Law Review* 42 (1976): 822.

DeFunis v. Odegaard

416 U.S. 312 (1974)
Decided: April 23, 1974
Vote: 5 (Burger, Stewart, Blackmun, Powell, Rehnquist)
4 (Douglas, Brennan, B. White, T. Marshall)
Opinion: *Per curiam*
Dissenting opinion: Douglas
Dissenting opinion: Brennan (Douglas, B. White, T. Marshall)

Marco DeFunis applied for admission to the University of Washington Law School and was turned down. The university had a special admissions process for minorities, and, of the 250 students admitted to the law school, 37 were admitted through this procedure. Of these, thirty-six had averages below DeFunis's 76.23, and thirty had averages below 74.5, which would have disqualified them for admission. The law school also admitted forty-eight nonminority applicants whose averages were lower than DeFunis's. Twenty-three of these applicants were returning veterans, and twenty-five others presumably showed other qualities that made them attractive candidates despite their relatively low averages. The university admitted "that were the minority applicants considered under the same procedure as was generally used, none of those who eventually enrolled at the Law School would have been admitted."

DeFunis sued, alleging that the university had admissions policies that discriminated against him because of his ethnicity. The district court agreed and ordered the university to admit him. The university appealed, and, by the time the case made its way to the Supreme Court, DeFunis was in his final semester at law school. The university stated during oral argument that it would not attempt to expel DeFunis or deny him credit for his final semester classes if the Court were to decide in university's favor.

In the first case dealing with affirmative action to reach the Supreme Court, the justices avoided making a decision by finding the case moot. The reason: DeFunis had sued only on his own behalf, not as part of a class. The case or controversy requirement precludes a federal court from hearing a case that will not decide the rights of the parties before it, and this case did not fit any exception to that rule. It was not "capable of repetition, yet evading review," because "DeFunis will never again be required to run the gantlet of the Law School's admission process, and so the question is certainly not 'capable of repetition' so far as he is concerned."

In his dissent, Justice Douglas argued that the "case is not moot, and because of the significance of the issues raised I think it is important to reach the merits." Douglas argued for affirmative action policies that addressed the difficulties that minorities and poor whites had to overcome. He noted, "A black applicant who pulled himself out of the ghetto into a junior college may thereby demonstrate a level of motivation, perseverance, and ability that would lead a fair-minded admissions committee to conclude that he shows more promise for law study than the son of a rich alumnus who achieved better grades at Harvard. That applicant would be offered admission not because he is black, but because as an individual he has shown he has the potential, while the Harvard man may have taken less advantage of the vastly superior opportunities offered him."

Justice Brennan also attacked the notion that the case was moot and accused the Court of ducking its responsibilities. "In endeavoring to dispose of this case as moot, the Court clearly disserves the public interest," he wrote. "The constitutional issues which are avoided today concern vast numbers of people, organizations, and colleges and universities, as evidenced by the filing of twenty-six amicus curiae briefs. Few constitutional questions in recent history have stirred as much debate, and they will not disappear. They must inevitably return to the federal courts and ultimately again to this Court." Brennan was correct, and in ***Regents of the University of California v. Bakke***, 438 U.S. 265 (1978), the Court dealt with this issue.

See Paul J. Mishkin, "The Uses of Ambivalence: Reflections on the Supreme Court and the Constitutionality of Affirmative Action," *University of Pennsylvania Law Review* 131 (1983): 907; and Robert N. Davis, "Diversity: The Emerging Modern Separate but Equal Doctrine," *William and Mary Journal of Women and the Law* (1994): 11.

Kahn v. Shevin

416 U.S. 351 (1974)
Decided: April 24, 1974
Vote: 6 (Burger, Douglas, Stewart, Blackmun, Powell, Rehnquist)
3 (Brennan, B. White, T. Marshall)
Opinion of the Court: Douglas
Dissenting opinion: Brennan (T. Marshall)
Dissenting opinion: B. White

A Florida statute provided a $500 property tax exemption for widows but not for widowers. Ruth Bader Ginsburg, a future Supreme Court justice, represented Kahn, a widower, who challenged the statute on equal protection grounds. The Florida Supreme Court held that the distinction was valid because it had a "fair and substantial relation to the object of the legislation," which was to make up for women's lesser ability to earn money.

Kahn appealed to the Supreme Court, which upheld Florida's decision. Citing statistics on the lower incomes earned by women, the Court found that women were more likely to suffer economically from the loss of a spouse than men. The distinction was therefore based on a "ground of difference having a fair relation to the object of the legislation."

Justice Brennan's dissent argued that rather than using the rational basis test, the state should have been required to show the statute served a compelling interest that cannot be achieved by less intrusive means.

Michigan v. Tucker

417 U.S. 433 (1974)
Decided: June 10, 1974
Vote: 8 (Burger, Brennan, Stewart, B. White, T. Marshall, Blackmun, Powell, Rehnquist)
1 (Douglas)
Opinion of the Court: Rehnquist
Concurring opinion: Stewart
Opinion concurring in judgment: Brennan (T. Marshall)
Opinion concurring in judgment: B. White
Dissenting opinion: Douglas

Tucker was arrested for rape before the decision in ***Miranda v. Arizona,*** 384 U.S. 436 (1966), which provided specific protections for people under arrest. At the time of his arrest he was asked if he understood his rights, and he said he did. He was informed that anything he said could be used against him. He was asked if he wanted counsel, and he said no, but he was not advised that he could have counsel appointed for him if he could not afford one. After these warnings, he offered as his alibi that he was with a friend, Robert Henderson, at the time of the rape. When the police questioned Henderson about the alibi, he gave them information that pointed to Tucker's guilt. At trial Tucker attempted to exclude Henderson's testimony on the ground that he had given the police Henderson's name without receiving all the warnings that the intervening *Miranda* decision required. The court allowed Henderson's testimony, Tucker was convicted, and the Michigan Supreme Court upheld the conviction. On a habeas corpus appeal, however, the district court ruled that Henderson's testimony was tainted, and the court of appeals agreed. The Supreme Court reversed.

Although the police did not warn Tucker of his right to counsel, that omission was not relevant to his self-incrimination because the police had warned him about not incriminating himself. His statements in police custody were neither involuntary nor the result of coercion. The exclusionary rule is meant as a deterrent against intentional police misconduct and should not be applied in this case; *Miranda* had not yet been decided, so the police could not willfully disregard it. Furthermore, the fact that police did not advise Tucker of his right to an attorney did not tend to weaken the credibility of Henderson's testimony, and the admission of his testimony was not an error.

Justice Brennan noted that "excluding the fruits of" Tucker's "statements would not further the integrity of the fact-finding process," while it "would severely handicap law enforcement officials," and not serve the ends of either justice or protecting constitutional rights. Brennan therefore saw no reason to apply *Miranda* retroactively.

Pell v. Procunier

417 U.S. 817 (1974)
Decided: June 24, 1974
Vote: 5 (Burger, Stewart, B. White, Blackmun, Rehnquist)
4 (Douglas, Brennan, T. Marshall, Powell)
Opinion of the Court: Stewart
Dissenting opinion: Douglas (Brennan, T. Marshall)
Dissenting opinion: Powell

State prisoners and news reporters challenged the constitutionality of a prison regulation that prohibited reporters from having face-to-face interviews with prisoners. The prison adopted the regulation in response to fears that the one-time practice of allowing virtually unlimited face-to-face interviews was causing disruption and unruliness among the inmates. The prison argued that before the regulation was adopted, the media had interviewed only a few chosen prisoners, which "had resulted in press attention being concentrated on a relatively small number of inmates who . . . became virtual 'public figures' within the prison society and gained a disproportionate degree of notoriety and influence among their fellow inmates." The prison claimed these inmates often caused disciplinary problems. The district court granted summary judgment to the prisoners, finding that the statute unconstitutionally infringed their First Amendment rights. With respect to the journalists, the court dismissed their case, finding that they had no First Amendment interest in access to the prisoners for interviews. The prison wardens appealed the summary judgment in favor of the prisoners, and the journalists appealed the dismissal of their case.

The Supreme Court found that the statute did not violate the prisoners' First Amendment rights. Although prisoners do not lose all First Amendment rights when they are incarcerated, their rights are subject to broader curtailment than those of the general population because of the special need for order within the prison. Furthermore, the statute left open ample alternative channels of communication because the prisoners had a right to speak with friends and family who were allowed visitation and, through the friends and family, they could communicate anything they wanted to the press. The Court also found that the statute did not violate the rights of the media because journalists have no more right to face-to-face interviews with prisoners than does the general public. Furthermore, the statute left open ample alternative channels of communication; on tours through the prison, the journalists were allowed to ask questions of random prisoners.

Dissenters argued, as Justice Powell stated it, that the rule "impermissibly restrains the ability of the press to perform its constitutionally established function of informing the people on the conduct of their government."

See Lillian R. BeVier, "An Informed Public, An Informing Press: The Search for a Constitutional Principle," *California Law Review* 68 (1980): 82; and Vincent Blasi, "The Checking Value in the First Amendment," *American Bar Foundation Research Journal* (1977): 521.

Saxbe v. Washington Post Co.

417 U.S. 843 (1974)
Decided: June 24, 1974
Vote: 5 (Burger, Stewart, B. White, Blackmun, Rehnquist)
4 (Douglas, Brennan, T. Marshall, Powell)
Opinion of the Court: Stewart
Dissenting opinion: Douglas
Dissenting opinion: Powell (Brennan, T. Marshall)

The Federal Bureau of Prisons had a policy that prohibited news reporters from interviewing prison inmates. The *Washington Post* challenged this policy on First Amendment grounds, arguing it abridged the freedom of the press.

The Supreme Court held that the policy was not unconstitutional because it did not prohibit reporters from going anywhere that anyone else is allowed to go. The prison policy was to allow only lawyers, clergy, family, and friends to visit with inmates, but not the public.

Justice Powell's dissent pointed out that news reporters rely on interviews to determine the reliability of information given to them, and an absolute ban on interviews would preclude accurate information about prisons being disseminated to the public. In addition, he felt that the majority was wrong in concluding that a government restriction on the ability to gather news did not violate the First Amendment as long as the ban was nondiscriminatory. In his opinion, the policy did impinge First Amendment rights, and the government had not met its burden of showing a compelling interest in imposing it.

Jenkins v. Georgia

418 U.S. 153 (1974)
Decided: June 24, 1974
Vote: 9 (Burger, Douglas, Brennan, Stewart, B. White, T. Marshall, Blackmun, Powell, Rehnquist)
0
Opinion of the Court: Rehnquist
Opinion concurring in judgment: Douglas
Opinion concurring in judgment: Brennan (Stewart, T. Marshall)

Jenkins was convicted under Georgia's obscenity statute for exhibiting the film *Carnal Knowledge* in Albany, Georgia. The film was shown in a traditional movie theater, not in an adult theater. Featuring Jack Nicholson, Art Garfunkel, Candice Bergen, and Ann-Margret, who received an Academy Award nomination for her role, the movie made many film writers' "top ten" list that year.

The relevant Georgia statute defined "material" to be "obscene if considered as a whole, applying community standards, its predominant appeal is to prurient interest, that is, a shameful or morbid interest in nudity, sex or excretion, and utterly without redeeming social value and if, in addition, it goes substantially beyond customary limits of candor in describing or representing such matters." This wording more or less comported with the Supreme Court's standard set out in ***Memoirs v. Massachusetts,*** 383 U.S. 413 (1966). While *Jenkins* was on appeal, however, the Court decided ***Miller v. California,*** 413 U.S. 15 (1973), which did not allow obscenity conviction for materials that did not show patently offensive hard-core sexual content. The Court determined in *Hamling v. United States,* 418 U.S. 87 (1974), decided the same day as *Jenkins,* that *Miller* should be applied to all defendants whose cases were on direct appeal when it was decided. Because *Carnal Knowledge* did not focus on hard-core sexual content, it was not obscene under *Miller,* and Jenkins's conviction was reversed.

This case exposed the shortcomings of *Miller,* which relied on "community standards" for determining what might be patently offensive. In *Miller* and again here, the Court denied it was applying a "national" standard for obscenity, but, at the same time, the Court refused to allow a small town Georgia jury to jail a theater manager for showing a film that was nationally distributed. Justice Rehnquist quoted from *Miller:* "To require a State to structure obscenity proceedings around evidence of a national 'community standard' would be an exercise in futility." This statement seemed to imply that if the local jury found the film was obscene by its community standards, the defendant could not appeal, but Rehnquist denied this. "Even though questions of appeal to the 'prurient interest' or of patent offensiveness are 'essentially questions of fact,' it would be a serious misreading of *Miller* to conclude that juries have unbridled discretion in determining what is 'patently offensive,' " he wrote. "We made it plain that under that holding 'no one will be subject to prosecution for the sale or exposure of obscene materials unless these materials depict or describe patently offensive 'hard core' sexual conduct.' " While claiming to reaffirm community standards, the Court overrode them, revealing the difficulty of deciding what is obscene and what is not.

Justice Brennan offered a solution to the problem. He called for an end to excluding sexual material from First Amendment protection because of the impossibility of defining obscenity in a way that was not vague and overbroad.

See Sean F. Rommel, "The Arkansas Obscenity Doctrine: Its Establishment and Evolution," *Arkansas Law Review* 47 (1994): 393; and Jeffrey E. Faucette, "The Freedom of Speech at Risk in Cyberspace: Obscenity Doctrine and a Frightened University's Censorship of Sex on the Internet," *Duke Law Journal* 44 (1995): 1155.

Richardson v. United States

418 U.S. 166 (1974)
Decided: June 25, 1974
Vote: 5 (Burger, B. White, Blackmun, Powell, Rehnquist)
4 (Douglas, Brennan, Stewart, T. Marshall)
Opinion of the Court: Burger
Concurring opinion: Powell
Dissenting opinion: Douglas
Dissenting opinion: Brennan
Dissenting opinion: Stewart
Dissenting opinion: T. Marshall

William B. Richardson, identified as a "taxpayer," sued for a writ of mandamus to compel the secretary of the Treasury to publish the total budgets of the Central Intelligence Agency (CIA). Richardson sued under the doctrine developed in ***Flast v. Cohen,*** 392 U.S. 83 (1968), which held that a taxpayer had standing to sue for a violation of the Spending Clause power. Article I, Section 9, Clause 7, of the Constitution states, "No Money shall be drawn from the Treasury, but in Consequence of Appropriations made by Law; and a regular Statement and Account of the Receipts and Expenditures of all public Money shall be published from time to time." Richardson wanted to compel the secretary of the Treasury to comply with this clause.

The district court ruled against him, stating that he did not have standing to sue under *Flast* because he did not actually challenge an appropriation, but merely sought information about an appropriation. The court of appeals reversed, holding that he could sue to find out about CIA's appropriations and then, if he wished, challenge the spending under *Flast.*

The Supreme Court reversed the court of appeals, holding that to have standing under *Flast,* a taxpayer must allege a specific violation of a Spending Clause power. This decision interpreted *Flast* as not radically altering the policy of ***Massachusetts v. Mellon,*** 262 U.S. 447 (1923), that people cannot use their status as taxpayers to make general challenges to government policy in court.

The dissenters argued that Richardson did have standing to sue, although they correctly refused to comment on the merits of the case. Justices Stewart and Marshall also argued that a citizen should be able to sue to force the government to carry out the explicit requirements of the Constitution, even if the citizen could not prove a direct harm by the failure of the government to follow the Constitution.

Schlesinger v. Reservists to Stop the War

418 U.S. 208 (1974)
Decided: June 25, 1974
Vote: 6 (Burger, Stewart, B. White, Blackmun, Powell, Rehnquist)
3 (Douglas, Brennan, T. Marshall)
Opinion of the Court: Burger
Concurring opinion: Stewart
Dissenting opinion: Douglas (T. Marshall)
Dissenting opinion: Brennan
Dissenting opinion: T. Marshall

Members of the Reservists Committee sued to enjoin certain members of Congress from holding positions in the army reserves on the grounds that Article I, Section 6, Clause 2, of the Constitution prohibits them from doing so. The committee members claimed they were harmed as "citizens" because reserve duty prevented senators and representatives from faithfully discharging their congressional duties. The district court found that the committee had standing as "citizens" and found in their favor based on the clause. The district court acknowledged that the plaintiffs' standing was tenuous, but ruled that because the clause was self-explanatory and clear, they should be able to enforce it.

On appeal, the Supreme Court found that the committee members did not have standing to sue as "citizens." The Court held that the case or controversy requirement of Article III requires that a plaintiff be able to state a concrete injury before the courts can adjudicate his claim. The Constitution does not authorize the courts to adjudicate abstract policy issues. Generalized harm affecting all citizens is insufficient for standing under the case or controversy rule. The committee's allegation that the members of Congress could not faithfully carry out their legislative duties while serving in the reserves did not state any particularized harm to them that did not also affect all citizens. Furthermore, even if the committee members had sued as "taxpayers," they would not be able to show a particularized harm. Distinguishing this case from ***Flast v. Cohen,*** 392 U.S. 83 (1968), the Court held that because the Reservists Committee's complaint about members of Congress holding reserve positions did not involve the spending of tax revenues against a specific limitation on Congress's spending power, they did not have taxpayer standing to raise the claim.

Justice Brennan's dissent argued that standing is based on a plaintiff's good faith allegation that he has been harmed in fact. Nothing more is required, in Brennan's view.

Miami Herald Publishing Company v. Tornillo

418 U.S. 241 (1974)
Decided: June 25, 1974
Vote: 9 (Burger, Douglas, Brennan, Stewart, B. White, T. Marshall, Blackmun, Powell, Rehnquist)
0
Opinion of the Court: Burger
Concurring opinion: Brennan (Rehnquist)
Concurring opinion: B. White

This case asked whether a state law guaranteeing political candidates equal space in newspapers to rebut editorial criticisms violated the First Amendment guarantee of a free press. Florida's "right of reply" statute provided that a political candidate who is attacked on his character or official record by any newspaper had the right to demand that the newspaper print, free of cost to the candidate, any reply he or she wished to make to the charges. The law further stated that the reply had to appear in as conspicuous a place and in the same kind of type as the original charges. The *Miami Herald* criticized Pat Tornillo when he was a candidate for the state legislature. Tornillo tried to rebut these attacks, but the paper refused to print his responses. He then sought to use the statute to force the paper to give him equal space to counter a negative editorial. A Florida district court refused to do so on the grounds that the statute was unconstitutional. The Florida Supreme Court reversed the lower court's judgment, holding that the statute furthered the First Amendment's policy of ensuring a free flow of information to the public, and the *Herald* appealed to the U.S. Supreme Court.

Chief Justice Burger noted that Tornillo argued that the "government has an obligation to ensure that a wide variety of views reach the public." He asserted that in an age when many cities have only one or two newspapers, as Miami did, it is imperative that the press be available to all viewpoints. When the Bill of Rights was ratified, American cities had many newspapers. "Entry into publishing was inexpensive; pamphlets and books provided meaningful alternatives to the organized press for the expression of unpopular ideas and often treated events and expressed views not covered by conventional newspapers," Burger wrote. "A true marketplace of ideas existed in which there was relatively easy access to the channels of communication." That, however, was no longer the case, and Tornillo asserted it was the responsibility of the government to ensure that a marketplace for ideas remained open and vigorous. In support of this argument Burger pointed to language in ***New York Times Co. v. Sullivan,*** 376 U.S. 254 (1964), in which "the Court spoke of 'a profound national commitment to the principle that debate on public issues should be uninhibited, robust, and wide-open.' It is argued that the 'uninhibited, robust' debate is not 'wide-open' but open only to a monopoly in control of the press."

Burger rejected these arguments, however, and held that the statute was a clear violation of the *Herald*'s First Amendment right to choose the content of its paper, to include and exclude information at its editorial discretion. Burger said, "A newspaper is more than a passive receptacle or conduit for news, comment, and advertising. The choice of material to go into a newspaper, and the decisions made as to limitations on the size and content of the paper, and treatment of public issues and public officials—whether fair or unfair—constitute the exercise of editorial control and judgment. It has yet to be demonstrated how governmental regulation of this crucial process can be exercised consistent with First Amendment guarantees of a free press as they have evolved to this time."

Justice White made this point more directly. He found that the Florida act was "constitutionally obnoxious" because it "runs afoul of the elementary First Amendment proposition that government may not force a newspaper to print copy which, in its journalistic discretion, it chooses to leave on the newsroom floor. Whatever power may reside in government to influence the publishing of certain narrowly circumscribed categories of material" such as prohibition on discriminatory advertising or libel laws, the Court had "never thought that the First Amendment permitted public officials to dictate to the press the contents of its news columns or the slant of its editorials."

Tornillo seems to be in conflict with ***Red Lion Broadcasting Co. v. Federal Communications Commission,*** 395 U.S. 367 (1969), which upheld a similar federal regulation, but the two cases are different because of Congress's power to regulate the airwaves. In *Tornillo* the Court held it would be a violation of freedom of the press for the government to direct the editorial policies of newspapers, while *Red Lion* affirmed the power of Congress to regulate a finite resource—the airwaves—that ultimately belong to the public.

See Fred Friendly, *The Good Guys, the Bad Guys, and the First Amendment* (New York: Random House, 1975).

Lehman v. Shaker Heights

418 U.S. 298 (1974)
Decided: June 25, 1974
Vote: 5 (Burger, Douglas, B. White, Blackmun, Rehnquist)
4 (Brennan, Stewart, T. Marshall, Powell)
Judgment of the Court: Blackmun
Opinion concurring in judgment: Douglas
Dissenting opinion: Brennan (Stewart, T. Marshall, Powell)

Harry J. Lehman was a state political candidate in Ohio. The city of Shaker Heights offered spaces inside city-owned transit cars for advertising, but refused all political advertising. Lehman noted that the city had hired an advertising agency, Metromedia, to sell space in its cars. Lehman sued to compel the city to allow him to purchase advertising space on the transit cars. He claimed that his First Amendment rights and his rights under the Equal Protection Clause were violated by the city's refusal to allow political advertising in the cars when it allowed other kinds of advertising. The Ohio courts held for Shaker Heights, and the Supreme Court, by a narrow margin, affirmed.

Justice Blackmun stated that the space inside the cars was not a First Amendment forum. Writing for the majority, he said that Shaker Heights had the discretion to disallow controversial advertising because of the potential for the invasion of a captive audience's privacy rights and because political advertising on government owned transit cars might imply political favoritism.

In his concurrence, Justice Douglas argued that the streetcar was not a public forum, that the bus or transit car was equivalent to a privately held newspaper, and, as the Court held in ***Miami Herald Publishing Co. v. Tornillo,*** 418 U.S. 241 (1974), decided the same day, the "owner" of a newspaper "cannot be forced to include in his offerings news or other items which outsiders may desire but which the owner abhors." Furthermore, Douglas argued, "If we are to turn a bus or streetcar into either a newspaper or a park, we take great liberties with people who because of necessity become commuters and at the same time captive viewers or listeners."

In his dissent, Justice Brennan claimed that a public "forum for communication was voluntarily established when the city installed the physical facilities for the advertisements and, by contract with Metromedia, created the necessary administrative machinery for regulating access to that forum." He argued that by "opening a forum," for example, by creating the advertising spaces within the cars, the city was prohibited "by the First and Fourteenth Amendments from discriminating among forum users solely on the basis of message content."

See Paul B. Stephan III, "The First Amendment and Content Discrimination," *Virginia Law Review* 68 (1982): 203.

Gertz v. Robert Welch, Inc.

418 U.S. 323 (1974)
Decided: June 25, 1974
Vote: 5 (Stewart, T. Marshall, Blackmun, Powell, Rehnquist)
4 (Burger, Douglas, Brennan, B. White)
Opinion of the Court: Powell
Concurring opinion: Blackmun
Dissenting opinion: Burger
Dissenting opinion: Douglas
Dissenting opinion: Brennan
Dissenting opinion: B. White

Elmer Gertz, a Chicago lawyer, represented the family of a young boy named Nelson, who had been shot by Nuccio, a Chicago police officer. Nuccio was eventually convicted of second-degree murder. In 1969 *American Opinion,* the official magazine of the John Birch Society, falsely accused Gertz of being a "Leninist" and "Communist-fronter" for his role in representing the Nelsons in their civil suit against Nuccio. The publication also falsely asserted that Gertz had a criminal record. These and other inaccuracies in the article led Gertz to sue for defamation. The jury awarded him damages, but the federal district judge overruled the jury, asserting that under the standard in ***New York Times v. Sullivan,*** 376 U.S. 254 (1964), Gertz would have to prove "actual malice" on the part of the publisher, rather than mere falsity. *New York Times* applied to public figures, and, although the district court conceded that Gertz was not a public figure, it asserted that the issues were of public interest, and the *New York Times* standard should apply.

The Supreme Court reversed, and remanded the case for a new trial. The Court held that because Gertz was a private person, he only had to prove the publication was false and that there was "fault" on the part of the publisher.

In dissent Justice Brennan (and Justice Douglas) argued that this decision would undermine the "free and robust debate—so essential to the proper functioning of our system of government."

Justice White, on the other hand, thought the Court went too far in protecting the press. He would have reversed the court of appeals and reinstated the original jury verdict.

See Melvin I. Urofsky and Paul Finkelman, *A March of Liberty: A Constitutional History of the United States,* Vol. 2. (New York: Oxford University Press, 2002).

Spence v. Washington

418 U.S. 405 (1974)
Decided: June 25, 1974
Vote: 6 (Douglas, Brennan, Stewart, T. Marshall, Blackmun, Powell)
3 (Burger, B. White, Rehnquist)
Opinion: *Per curiam*
Concurring opinion: Douglas
Concurring in judgment: Blackmun
Dissenting opinion: Burger
Dissenting opinion: Rehnquist (Burger, B. White)

During the Cambodia invasion and shortly after the tragic shootings at Kent State University, college student Harold Spence displayed an upside-down American flag out of his window with a peace sign affixed to it. He was arrested and convicted under a Washington State law that prohibited the "improper" use or display of an American flag. The court of appeals reversed his conviction, but the state supreme court reversed the lower court and reinstated Spence's conviction. The Washington Supreme Court did not rely on a "breach of the peace" rationale to uphold his conviction—it merely claimed that "the nation and state both have a recognizable interest in preserving the flag as a symbol of the nation."

The U.S. Supreme Court reversed the conviction. The Court did not address the state supreme court's rationale because counsel for Washington did not pursue that argument before the Court. Instead, he argued that Spence's display was alternatively a breach of the peace and an affront to the sensibilities of passers-by. The Supreme Court rejected both arguments, saying that there was no evidence of any violence caused by the display and that a state does not have the right to outlaw a form of communication just to protect the sensibilities of those who might be offended by the message.

Justice Rehnquist's dissent emphasized that freedom of speech is not an absolute right. He argued that the state should be allowed "to protect important state interests even though an incidental limitation on speech results." In his opinion, the state had an important interest in protecting flags from desecration, and prohibiting dissenters from using altered flags to communicate unpopular opinions was only an "incidental limitation" on speech.

The Supreme Court later reaffirmed the majority's analysis in ***Texas v. Johnson,*** 491 U.S. 397 (1989), and ***United States v. Eichman,*** 496 U.S. 310 (1990), upholding the right, under the First Amendment, of protestors to burn the flag.

See Michael Kent Curtis, *The Constitution and the Flag,* 2 vols. (New York: Garland, 1993).

United States v. Nixon

418 U.S. 683 (1974)
Decided: July 24, 1974
Vote: 8 (Burger, Douglas, Brennan, Stewart, B. White, T. Marshall, Blackmun, Powell)
0
Opinion of the Court: Burger
Did not participate: Rehnquist

This case was one of the most dramatic decisions in American constitutional history. It had the immediate consequence of forcing President Richard Nixon to release secretly made tapes of Oval Office conversations, which revealed his participation in a conspiracy to cover up the Watergate break-in and other illegal activities of his administration, his subornation of perjury, and other criminal behavior. On August 9, 1974, less than three weeks after this decision, Nixon became the only president of the United States to resign his office, leaving in disgrace as an unindicted co-conspirator in one of the worst political scandals in American history. An understanding of the case requires a summary of the illegal activities in the Nixon administration that are collectively known as "Watergate."

President Nixon, in the name of "national security," authorized wiretaps, surveillance, and even a break-in of a doctor's office to obtain damaging information about administration critics. This pattern of behavior also included misuse of the FBI, CIA, and the Internal Revenue Service. During his bid for reelection in 1972, Nixon or high officials in his campaign and/or cabinet authorized the placement of illegal listening devices in the Democratic Party's headquarters in the Watergate Hotel in Washington, D.C. When the campaign operatives were caught, they were initially treated as burglars, but their connections to the White House and the CIA soon came to light. The Watergate burglars pled guilty to avoid a trial and in the expectation of light sentences. Meanwhile, the Nixon administration put pressure on the CIA to help stop the investigation on grounds of "national security."

In sentencing the Watergate burglars, Judge John Sirica, a Republican known for his tough attitude on crime, lived up to his nickname of "Maximum John," and soon one of the convicted men revealed that the defendants had been pressured, and perhaps bribed, to plead guilty. This revelation led to the appointment of a special prosecutor, Archibald Cox, to investigate the whole affair. Meanwhile, throughout the summer of 1973, Americans were glued to their televisions as a Senate select committee, known as the Ervin Committee for its chairman, Sam Ervin Jr. of North Carolina, investigated the irregularities and illegalities of the 1972 Nixon campaign. During these hearings, Alexander Butterfield, a White House official, revealed that Nixon had secretly taped all of his Oval Office conversations. Cox demanded access to the tapes, on the theory that they would reveal who in the Nixon administration had ordered the Watergate cover-up. Citing executive privilege, Nixon ordered Cox to cease his efforts to obtain the tapes. When Cox refused, Nixon ordered Attorney General Elliot Richardson to fire him. Richardson resigned instead, as did his deputy attorney general, William Ruckelshaus. Solicitor General Robert Bork then carried out Nixon's order. The so-called Saturday Night Massacre nearly led to a constitutional crisis, which was resolved only with the appointment of a new special prosecutor, Leon Jaworski, a conservative Texas Democrat, who, Nixon believed, would support his claims of executive privilege.

On March 1, 1974, the Watergate grand jury indicted seven individuals in connection with the cover-up of the break-in and listed President Nixon as an unindicted co-conspirator. Those indicted included former attorney general John Mitchell, former White House counsel Charles Colson, and Nixon's two chief aides during the period, John Ehrlichman and H. R. "Bob" Haldeman. In April Jaworski demanded the tapes, and on April 18 Sirica issued a subpoena directed at Nixon. Nixon responded April 30 by submitting edited and sanitized transcripts of some of the tapes. He claimed that national security and executive privilege shielded the tapes themselves, as well as what he had deleted from the transcripts. On June 15 the Supreme Court allowed the special prosecutor to release sealed grand jury records showing that Nixon was an unindicted co-conspirator. What began as an investigation of what Nixon called a "third-rate burglary" had evolved into a constitutional crisis between the power of the president and the courts.

Jaworski still demanded the full tapes, and on May 1 the Nixon administration sought to quash the subpoena. The U.S. District Court for the District of Columbia rejected Nixon's request on May 20 and ordered that the unedited tapes be turned over to the court by May 31. On May 24 Nixon sought review by the court of appeals, and Jaworski asked the U.S. Supreme Court for an immediate review of the case. The Court accepted the case on an "expedited review" and set arguments for a special session on July 8.

Nixon argued that the Court lacked jurisdiction because this was essentially an "intrabranch dispute" between the special prosecutor and the president, both of whom were in the executive branch. After rejecting this contention and various technical arguments about the subpoena itself, Chief Justice Burger addressed the central issue of the case: the scope of executive privilege. Nixon's lawyers asserted "that it would be inconsistent with the public interest to produce" the "confidential conversations between a President and his close advisors" demanded by the subpoena. Nixon argued that his right to withhold the tapes stemmed from two aspects of government. First, governments have an inherent need to keep some deliberations secret, and the president has the power and authority to decide when and where to release material related to confidential conversations. Second, he argued, as summarized by Burger, that under the notion of separation of powers, unique to the American system of government, "the independence of the Executive Branch within its own sphere . . . insulates a President from a judicial subpoena in an ongoing criminal prosecution, and thereby protects confidential Presidential communications." The Court categorically rejected this claim, saying, "Absent a claim of need to protect military, diplomatic, or sensitive national security secrets, we find it difficult to accept the argument that even the very important interest in confidentiality of Presidential communications is significantly diminished by production of such material for in camera inspection with all the protection that a district court will be obliged to provide."

Although it ruled against Nixon, the Court accepted the concept of a qualified executive privilege. Citing Chief Justice Marshall's circuit court opinion in *United States v. Burr*, 25 F. Cas. 187 (CC Va. 1807), Burger warned, "The right and indeed the duty to resolve" disputes over executive privileges "does not free the Judiciary from according high respect to the representations made on behalf of the President." In the end, however, the privilege had to fall to "the rule of law." Burger continued: "This presumptive privilege must be considered in light of our historic commitment to the rule of law. This is nowhere more profoundly manifest than in our view that 'the twofold aim [of criminal justice] is that guilt shall not escape or innocence suffer.' "

Within a short time the tapes were produced, and the evidence on them provided the "smoking gun" that Nixon had participated in the cover-up and was most probably guilty of numerous felonies. The House Judiciary Committee voted out various articles of impeachment against Nixon, with a number of Republicans siding with the Democratic majority. After the release of transcripts of several tapes, some of Nixon's most fervent supporters announced they would change their vote and support impeachment. On August 9 Nixon resigned from office. Less than a month later the new president, Gerald R. Ford, issued a "full, free, and absolute" pardon to the former president for any crimes he "has committed or may have committed" while in office.

See Eric Freedman, "The Law as King and the King as Law: Is a President Immune from Criminal Prosecution Before Impeachment," *Hastings Constitutional Law Quarterly* 20 (1992): 7; Stanley I. Kutler, *Abuse of Power* (New York: Free Press, 1998); and Emily Field Van Tassel and Paul Finkelman, *Impeachable Offenses: A Documentary History from 1787 to the Present* (Washington, D.C.: CQ Press, 1999).

Milliken v. Bradley

418 U.S. 717 (1974)
Decided: July 25, 1974
Vote: 5 (Burger, Stewart, Blackmun, Powell, Rehnquist)
4 (Douglas, Brennan, B. White, T. Marshall)
Opinion of the Court: Burger
Concurring opinion: Stewart
Dissenting opinion: Douglas
Dissenting opinion: B. White (Douglas, Brennan, T. Marshall)
Dissenting opinion: T. Marshall (Douglas, Brennan, B. White)

In 1970 the Detroit school district was the fifth largest in the nation, with about 290,000 students. The district was approximately 65 percent black and 35 percent white. The movement of whites into the suburbs, commonly called "white flight," had created a black majority in the inner city, surrounded by white suburbs. The schools in the entire Detroit metropolitan area—city and suburbs—were 81 percent white. Parents of African American students successfully sued in district court to force state officials to come up with an integration plan for the metropolitan area. The named defendant in the case was Gov. William G. Milliken. The court of appeals upheld the order, noting that failure to do so would "nullify" the holding in ***Brown v. Board of Education,*** 347 U.S. 483 (1954), and resurrect the "separate but equal" doctrine of ***Plessy v. Ferguson,*** 163 U.S. 537 (1896). The Supreme Court reversed, making this case the first dealing with school desegregation that African American plaintiffs lost since the mid-1930s.

In ***Swann v. Charlotte-Mecklenburg County Board of Education,*** 402 U.S. 1 (1971), the Court ordered countywide desegregation that led to busing between suburban and city schools. In ***Keyes v. School District No. 1, Denver, Colorado,*** 413 U.S. 189 (1973), the Court ordered the desegregation of the Denver schools through busing, even though de jure segregation never existed in Colorado. The Detroit case combined both elements. The city schools were overwhelmingly black, and the suburban schools were overwhelmingly white; they could not be integrated without city-suburb busing, which was the problem in Charlotte and Mecklenburg County. As in the Denver case, the state had not mandated segregation in Detroit, but the district court found that the city had acted in ways that fostered segregation; the de jure segregation in Detroit was the result of local, rather than state, policy. School segregation in Detroit also resulted from housing patterns, employment patterns, and private decisions, especially by whites, who had moved out of the city. Unlike Charlotte-Mecklenburg, however, the effort to integrate suburban schools with Detroit's schools would involve crossing school district lines and involve three counties. Indeed, the district court ordered the state to prepare a remedy that included 85 outlying school districts that had not been parties to the suit and had never been involved with the city of Detroit or its public schools.

Chief Justice Burger, speaking for the majority, flatly rejected the concept of interdistrict and multicounty busing to achieve integration. He wrote, "No single tradition in public education is more deeply rooted than local control over the operation of schools; local autonomy has long been thought essential both to the maintenance of community concern and support for public schools and to quality of the educational process." The plan for Detroit would destroy the idea of local control and community-based public schools. It would burden parents and students living miles away from Detroit and who had little contact with the city. The residents of these suburbs were not responsible for Detroit's segregation, and they could not constitutionally be burdened with solving the problem.

The dissenters argued that the Court was turning back the clock and the case would lead to an end to integration. In fact, it did set a limit on the kind of remedies that were available for integration. The case also illustrates the difficulty, perhaps the impossibility, of integrating society through court orders.

See J. Harvie Wilkinson, *From* Brown *to* Bakke: *The Supreme Court and School Integration, 1954–1978* (New York: Oxford University Press, 1979); Bernard Schwartz, *Swann's Way: The School Busing Case and the Supreme Court* (New York: Oxford University Press, 1986); Phillip J. Cooper, *Hard Judicial Choices* (New York: Oxford University Press, 1992); and Nathaniel R. Jones, "*Milliken v. Bradley:* Brown's Troubled Journey North," *Fordham Law Review* 61 (October 1992): 49.

Jackson v. Metropolitan Edison Company

419 U.S. 345 (1974)
Decided: December 23, 1974
Vote: 6 (Burger, Stewart, B. White, Blackmun, Powell, Rehnquist)
3 (Douglas, Brennan, T. Marshall)
Opinion of the Court: Rehnquist
Dissenting opinion: Douglas
Dissenting opinion: Brennan
Dissenting opinion: T. Marshall

When Catherine Jackson failed to pay her electric bills, Metropolitan Edison Company cut off her service. The electricity was restored in the name of another resident of the house, James Dodson, but he soon moved out, and no bills in his name were paid. Jackson continued to receive electric service for about a year, when utility company employees came to her house to enquire about Dodson. She could not tell them where he lived. The next day, another employee visited the residence and informed Jackson that the meter had been tampered with so as not to register the amounts used. Jackson then asked that the bill be put in the name of Robert Jackson, who turned out to be her twelve-year-old son. At this point, without any further notice, the utility disconnected her service. Jackson sued the utility under the federal civil rights acts, demanding that the service be reinstated "until she had been afforded notice, a hearing, and an opportunity to pay any amounts found due."

This case turned on the degree of state involvement in a private company's action needed to invoke the Due Process Clause. When Edison turned off Jackson's electricity without any procedure, Jackson sued for a declaration that the utility company, as in industry regulated by the state, must give her a chance to defend her interests under the Due Process Clause. She pointed to the government's regulation of utilities and the virtual monopoly the state grants utility companies to argue that utility companies are sufficiently intertwined with the government that the Due Process Clause should apply to them.

The Supreme Court agreed with the lower courts that there was no state action in this case, and thus no violation of the due process requirements of the Fourteenth Amendment. Government regulation and virtual state-sanctioned monopoly was insufficient to make the company a public actor that must conform its actions to the Due Process Clause.

The three dissenters argued that because the utility was a monopoly, sanctioned by the state, the utility had to give customers notice and due process before terminating service to them.

Taylor v. Louisiana

419 U.S. 522 (1975)
Decided: January 21, 1975
Vote: 8 (Burger, Douglas, Brennan, Stewart, B. White, T. Marshall, Blackmun, Powell)
1 (Rehnquist)
Opinion of the Court: B. White
Concurring opinion: Burger
Dissenting opinion: Rehnquist

Louisiana law "provided that a woman should not be selected for jury service unless she had previously filed a written declaration of her desire to be subject to jury service." In ***Hoyt v. Florida,*** 368 U.S. 57 (1961), the Court held that a selection system that resulted in mostly all-male juries did not violate a defendant's right to a trial by a representative cross-section of the community. Billy J. Taylor, who was indicted for aggravated kidnapping, contested Louisiana's volunteer juror system, which also led to juries that were almost entirely male.

Justice White noted that Louisiana's jury-selection system did "not disqualify women from jury service, but in operation its conceded systematic impact is that only a very few women, grossly disproportionate to the number of eligible women in the community, are called for jury service." No women were on the panel from which Taylor's petit jury was drawn. White identified the issue before the Court as whether a jury-selection system that excludes "an identifiable class of citizens constituting 53% of eligible jurors in the community comports with the

Sixth and Fourteenth Amendments." White reviewed the history of the Court's decisions in this area and concluded that the Court accepts "the fair-cross-section requirement as fundamental to the jury trial guaranteed by the Sixth Amendment." "The purpose of a jury," White continued, "is to guard against the exercise of arbitrary power—to make available the commonsense judgment of the community as a hedge against the overzealous or mistaken prosecutor and in preference to the professional or perhaps overconditioned or biased response of a judge." The Court found that Louisiana's system resulted in the exclusion of women from jury service, which abridged the defendant's right to a jury by a cross-section of the community. The Court reversed Taylor's conviction and remanded the case for a new trial with a more representative jury pool.

Goss v. Lopez

419 U.S. 565 (1975)
Decided: January 22, 1975
Vote: 5 (Douglas, Brennan, Stewart, B. White, T. Marshall)
4 (Burger, Blackmun, Powell, Rehnquist)
Opinion of the Court: B. White
Dissenting opinion: Powell (Burger, Blackmun, Rehnquist)

Dwight Lopez and other students of Columbus, Ohio, public schools sued because they were summarily suspended from school for ten days. The students argued that they had a property interest in their education and a liberty interest in not having their records and reputations tarnished, as well as possibly receiving lower grades. They argued that the summary suspensions constituted a government deprivation of these property and liberty interests without due process of law.

The Supreme Court agreed. The Court held that by offering public education to all children, the government had created important property and liberty interests. To impair these interests without any opportunity for the students to contest the charges against them violated the Due Process Clause. The Court held that for a suspension of ten days or less, due process required the school to give a student an oral or written notice of the complaint about his behavior, the nature of the school's evidence against him, and an opportunity for the student to explain himself at a hearing. If possible, the hearing should occur before the suspension, but if it is necessary to remove the student because he constitutes a threat to others or to school property, the hearing may be held immediately after the suspension.

In dissent, Justice Powell, who served as chairman of the Richmond, Virginia, school board from 1952 to 1961, argued that the "decision unnecessarily opens avenues for judicial intervention in the operation of our public schools that may affect adversely the quality of education."

Train v. City of New York

420 U.S. 35 (1975)
Decided: February 18, 1975
Vote: 9 (Burger, Douglas, Brennan, Stewart, B. White, T. Marshall, Blackmun, Powell, Rehnquist)
0
Opinion of the Court: B. White
Concurring opinion: Douglas

Congress passed the Federal Water Pollution Control Act Amendments of 1972 over President Richard Nixon's veto. Under the act the administrator of the Environmental Protection Agency (EPA) was authorized to allot specific appropriations "not to exceed" $5 billion for fiscal year 1973 and $6 billion for fiscal year 1974 to states for purposes of maintaining sewer systems. Shortly after the law was passed, Nixon ordered the administrator "to allot '[n]o more than $2 billion of the amount authorized for the fiscal year 1973, and no more than $3 billion of the amount authorized for the fiscal year 1974 ' " Nixon asserted that the "not to exceed" language permitted discretion on how much of the appropriation to give the states. New York City objected, claiming that the "not to exceed" language did not mean that the EPA administrator was free to give any amount up to $5 billion, but that the administrator must give exactly $5 billion.

The Supreme Court agreed with New York City, finding unpersuasive EPA head Russell E. Train's statutory history argument, that Congress had changed the original language directing the administrator to give "all sums" to only "sums." In essence, the Court refused to allow the Nixon administration to evade its obligation to faithfully execute the law in the face of clear congressional intent, by in effect reading the law in such a way as to eviscerate that intent.

Gerstein v. Pugh

420 U.S. 103 (1975)
Decided: February 18, 1975
Vote: 9 (Burger, Douglas, Brennan, Stewart, B. White, T. Marshall, Blackmun, Powell, Rehnquist)
0
Opinion of the Court: Powell
Concurring opinion: Stewart (Douglas, Brennan, T. Marshall)

In Florida, pretrial procedures allowed for a person to be arrested and detained by police indefinitely without a judicial determination of probable cause to hold him. The Supreme Court found this practice unacceptable under the Fourth Amendment, which protects Americans from unreasonable searches and seizures. If a suspect is going to be deprived of his liberty for an extended period of time before trial, the state must conduct a judicial hearing on probable cause. Despite its decision, the Court left this Fourth Amendment safeguard without an enforcement mechanism because the Court also said that a pretrial detention without probable cause does not void a conviction. Therefore, if a defendant was held for an unreasonable time without a hearing, and later convicted, the unreasonable detention would not affect the conviction. The Court also pointed out that the judicial hearing did not need to be adversarial, thus setting the stage for a pretrial hearing that might prevent the person arrested from effectively defending himself at this stage in the proceedings.

Justice Stewart agreed that the Fourth Amendment did not allow Florida's procedure, but he said the Court should not have specified in dicta—points not essential to a decision—what sort of procedures were allowable. He pointed out that the procedure the majority's dicta suggested gave "less procedural protection to an imprisoned human being than is required to test the propriety of garnishing a commercial bank account, the custody of a refrigerator, the temporary suspension of a public school student, or the suspension of a driver's license."

See Albert W. Alschuler, "Preventive Pretrial Detention and the Failure of Interest Balancing Approaches to Due Process," *Michigan Law Review* 85 (1986): 510.

Weinberger v. Wiesenfeld

420 U.S. 636 (1975)
Decided: March 19, 1975
Vote: 8 (Burger, Brennan, Stewart, B. White, T. Marshall, Blackmun, Powell, Rehnquist)
0
Opinion of the Court: Brennan
Concurring opinion: Powell (Burger)
Opinion concurring in judgment: Rehnquist
Did not participate: Douglas

The Social Security Act grants death benefits to the family of a deceased wage earner. In the case of a male wage earner, Section 402(g) of the act provided benefits to the surviving wife and children based on the wage earner's earnings at the time of his death. In the case of a female wage earner, however, Section 402(g) provided benefits to the surviving children, but not to the surviving husband. Stephen C. Wiesenfeld's wife died during childbirth. During their marriage, Wiesenfeld's wife had been the principal breadwinner, and when she died he sought survivors' benefits for himself and his son. The Social Security Administration granted benefits to the child, but not to Wiesenfeld because he was a man. A woman in similar circumstances would have been entitled to the same amount as the child. Ruth Bader Ginsburg, a future justice of the Supreme Court, represented Wiesenfeld in this case.

Justice Brennan held that the distinction drawn in Section 402(g) violated the Fifth Amendment Due Process Clause because it was based on "archaic and overbroad generalizations not tolerated by the Constitution" about the relative importance to a family of a husband's or a wife's earnings. As in ***Frontiero v. Richardson,*** 411 U.S. 677 (1973), the gender-based distinction denies equal protection to women wage earners by not granting them the same assurance that their taxes will be used to support their families that is afforded to men. The fact that Social Security benefits are "non-contractual" does not mean that women wage earners are not entitled to an amount corresponding to their tax contribution for their survivors. Furthermore, the Court held that the gender-based distinction could not be justified on any putative special needs of widows, as the benefits were not intended to save widows from destitution but to permit them to stay home and take care of their children. Because the statute was motivated by an interest in providing the child with a stay-at-home parent, the gender-based distinction had no rational basis.

In his concurrence, Justice Rehnquist said he would stop after finding that the gender-based distinction had no rational basis and not proceed to the question of whether Section 402(g) violates the Due Process Clause.

See Ruth Bader Ginsburg, "Gender in the Supreme Court: The 1973 and 1974 Terms," *Supreme Court Review, 1975,* 1; and John D. Johnston, "Sex Discrimination and the Supreme Court, 1971–1974," *New York University Law Review* 49 (1974): 617.

Oregon v. Hass

420 U.S. 714 (1975)
Decided: March 19, 1975
Vote: 6 (Burger, Stewart, B. White, Blackmun, Powell, Rehnquist)
2 (Brennan, T. Marshall)
Opinion of the Court: Blackmun
Dissenting opinion: Brennan (T. Marshall)
Dissenting opinion: T. Marshall (Brennan)
Did not participate: Douglas

Hass was arrested for stealing two bicycles, and police advised him of his rights under ***Miranda v. Arizona,*** 384 U.S. 436 (1966). While riding in the police car, he asked to speak to an attorney. The police said that he could telephone an attorney when they reached the station. Hass then gave self-incriminating evidence. The trial court excluded the evidence as a violation of the Fifth Amendment, but admitted the evidence for the purpose of impeaching Hass when he gave inconsistent testimony at trial. The judge instructed the jury to use the evidence of Hass's self-incriminatory statements in the police car only for the purpose of evaluating his credibility as a witness. Hass was convicted.

The Supreme Court found that under ***Harris v. New York,*** 401 U.S. 222 (1971), it was permissible for the trial court to allow this evidence for the limited purpose of impeaching Hass's credibility.

In dissent, Justice Brennan argued that once a suspect has asked for a lawyer all police inquiries must stop until the lawyer is present, and any testimony elicited must be suppressed. Otherwise, the "police have almost no incentive for following *Miranda*'s requirement." This case made it too easy for the police to avoid the Miranda rule. Quoting his own dissent in *United States v. Calandra,* 414 U.S. 338 (1974), Brennan said "the judiciary must 'avoid even the slightest appearance of sanctioning illegal government conduct.' "

Stanton v. Stanton

421 U.S. 7 (1975)
Decided: April 15, 1975
Vote: 8 (Burger, Douglas, Brennan, Stewart, B. White, T. Marshall, Blackmun, Powell)
1 (Rehnquist)
Opinion of the Court: Blackmun
Dissenting opinion: Rehnquist

Thelma B. Stanton was the mother of an eighteen-year-old daughter whose father, James Lawrence Stanton Jr., had ceased sending child support payments because a state statute provided that eighteen was the age of majority for girls. Thelma Stanton argued that the statute violated the Equal Protection Clause because it provided that twenty-one was the age of majority for boys. The Utah courts upheld the statute's constitutionality because there was a rational basis for the distinction: girls tend to mature earlier than boys, and boys need time to obtain an education so they can provide for their families.

Citing recent cases involving gender, Chief Justice Burger declared, "We find it unnecessary in this case to decide whether a classification based on sex is inherently suspect." Instead, relying on ***Reed v. Reed,*** 404 U.S. 71 (1971), the Court held that no rational basis existed for the distinction. The Court did not recognize that it was general knowledge that girls matured faster than boys, nor did the Court believe that the necessity of obtaining an education to provide for a family provided a useful distinction, especially because greater numbers of women were entering the professions. Burger found that "notwithstanding the 'old notions' to which the Utah court referred," in upholding the statute, the Supreme Court could "perceive nothing rational in the distinction drawn" between eighteen-year-old females and twenty-one-year-old males. This distinction "imposes 'criteria wholly unrelated to the objective of that statute.' A child, male or female, is still a child. No longer is the female destined solely for the home and the rearing of the family, and only the male for the marketplace and the world of ideas."

Justice Rehnquist's dissent was based on his conviction that the question of the statute's constitutionality should not have been in issue, because the father stopped sending payments under a private agreement, not because the statute required him to.

See Rachel K. Alexander, "*Nguyen v. INS:* The Supreme Court Rationalizes Gender-Based Distinctions in Upholding an Equal Protection Challenge," *Creighton Law Review* 35 (2002): 789; and Earl M. Maltz, "Sex Discrimination in the Supreme Court—A Comment on Sex Equality, Sex Differences, and the Supreme Court," *Duke Law Journal* (1985): 177.

Alyeska Pipeline Service Company v. Wilderness Society

421 U.S. 240 (1975)
Decided: May 12, 1975
Vote: 5 (Burger, Stewart, B. White, Blackmun, Rehnquist)
2 (Brennan, T. Marshall)
Opinion of the Court: B. White
Dissenting opinion: Brennan
Dissenting opinion: T. Marshall
Did not participate: Douglas, Powell

A rule known as the "American Rule" holds that in litigation in federal court, the prevailing party is not entitled to an award of attorney's fees without statutory authorization allowing such an award for the particular kind of case. The courts do, however, recognize an exception to this rule known as the "private attorney general," which applies when a citizen sues to vindicate the rights of the community, in effect acting as the attorney general ought to act. This exception allows plaintiffs who win civil rights cases to collect attorneys' fees from the defendant as an incentive for the poor to bring civil rights cases. In this litigation, the Wilderness Society, the Environmental Defense Fund, and Friends of the Earth sued to enjoin the construction of a pipeline in ecologically sensitive land. Having won their case (temporarily), they sought attorneys' fees under the private attorney general exception to the American Rule. The court of appeals upheld an award of attorneys' fees, accepting the private attorney general rationale. The Supreme Court reversed.

The Court concluded that although Congress has chosen to give prevailing plaintiffs an award of attorneys' fees in some situations, notably under Title II of the Civil Rights Act of 1964, 42 U.S.C. Section 2000a-3(b), the statute did not grant courts the power to award attorneys' fees to prevailing parties in "enforcement" situations.

Meek v. Pittenger

421 U.S. 349 (1975)
Decided: May 19, 1975
Vote: Multiple
Judgment of the Court: Stewart
Concurring opinion: Brennan (Douglas, T. Marshall)
Dissenting opinion: Burger
Dissenting opinion: Rehnquist (B. White)

Two Pennsylvania statutes allowed the state to loan instructional materials, such as textbooks, lab equipment, and maps (Act 195), and provide "auxiliary services," such as counseling, testing, and speech and hearing therapy (Act 194) to nonpublic schools. The lower court upheld the constitutionality of the acts to the extent that the materials and services loaned could not be diverted to religious purposes. For example, the state was allowed to loan secular recordings and films, but not record players or projectors because those items could be used to play religious recordings and films.

The Supreme Court held that only the textbook loans were constitutional; all other aspects of Acts 194 and 195 violated the Establishment Clause. Justice Stewart, relying on the *Lemon* test, developed in ***Lemon v. Kurtzman,*** 403 U.S. 602 (1971), reasoned that the two acts relieved the schools from an enormous financial burden, and, if religious schools received so much aid from the government, even if it was all secular, the inevitable conclusion would be that government was aiding religion. Furthermore, making sure that the auxiliary services provided under Act 194 were not used in a religious way would require excessive entanglement.

Justices Brennan, Douglas, and Marshall dissented from the part of the opinion allowing the loan of textbooks. Chief Justice Burger and Justices Rehnquist and White supported the ruling on textbooks, but dissented from the rest of the opinion, and would have upheld both laws in their entirety.

See Rex E. Lee, "The Religion Clauses: Problems and Prospects," *Brigham Young University Law Review* (1986): 337–347.

Goldfarb v. Virginia State Bar

421 U.S. 773 (1975)
Decided: June 16, 1975
Vote: 8 (Burger, Douglas, Brennan, Stewart, B. White, T. Marshall, Blackmun, Rehnquist)
0
Opinion of the Court: Burger
Did not participate: Powell

The Goldfarbs bought a house and needed a title examination to obtain title insurance for a mortgage. They searched unsuccessfully for an attorney who would provide this service for less than the minimum fee published in the Fairfax County Bar Association's fee schedule. The Goldfarbs wrote to thirty-six attorneys, and none of the nineteen who responded "indicated that he would charge less than the rate fixed by the schedule; several stated that they knew of no attorney who would do so." The Goldfarbs sued the bar association, alleging that its fee schedule amounted to price-fixing in violation of the Sherman Anti-Trust Act. The district court ruled that the Virginia State Bar was immune as a state actor, but enjoined the Fairfax County Bar Association from publishing its schedule. The court of appeals reversed. In its opinion, Congress did not intend the Sherman act to apply to "learned professions," but only "trade or commerce," and found that, even if it had, the fee schedule's effect on interstate commerce was too extenuated to support federal legislation.

The Supreme Court reversed the court of appeals, holding that Congress did not intend to create a learned profession exception to the Sherman act because the exchange of legal services for a fee constitutes "commerce" under the act. Furthermore, the act's application to the Fairfax County Bar Association's fee schedule was justified as a regulation of interstate commerce because a significant number of homebuyers in Fairfax County come from out of state. The fee schedule constitutes price-fixing because it ensures that other attorneys will not compete by bidding below a minimum fee.

Murphy v. Florida

421 U.S. 794 (1975)
Decided: June 16, 1975
Vote: 8 (Burger, Douglas, Stewart, B. White, T. Marshall, Blackmun, Powell, Rehnquist)
1 (Brennan)
Opinion of the Court: T. Marshall
Concurring opinion: Burger
Dissenting opinion: Brennan

This case involved the Miami-Dade County prosecution of Jack Murphy, sometimes known as "Murph the Surf," who, according to the Supreme Court's opinion, "had first made himself notorious for his part in the 1964 theft of the Star of India sapphire from a museum in New York. His flamboyant lifestyle made him a continuing subject of press interest." The media gave substantial coverage to his arrest in this case, for "breaking and entering a home, while armed, with intent to commit robbery and of assault with intent to commit robbery." He was also well known, and well covered in the press, because of a murder conviction in nearby Broward County. When Murphy was tried seven months after his arrest on the breaking and entry and assault charges, many jurors remembered news coverage of his arrest and had heard of his Star of India theft or murder conviction. Nevertheless, the jurors claimed that they felt no prejudice against him and that they did not believe his earlier crimes were relevant to his guilt or innocence in this case. Murphy was convicted, and he appealed.

The Supreme Court held that the fact that jurors knew about the defendant and his former crimes did not *per se* make his trial a violation of the Due Process Clause. The Court distinguished this case from earlier decisions overturning convictions resulting from trials in which the news media either overran the courtroom with television equipment or broadcast videos of the defendant confessing in police interrogations before the trial. The Court found that this case was lacking in the circus-like atmosphere that prejudiced the defendants in those cases.

Bigelow v. Virginia

421 U.S. 809 (1975)
Decided: June 16, 1975
Vote: 7 (Burger, Douglas, Brennan, Stewart, T. Marshall, Blackmun, Powell)
2 (B. White, Rehnquist)
Opinion of the Court: Blackmun
Dissenting opinion: Rehnquist (B. White)

In 1971 Jeffrey Bigelow, the editor of the *Virginia Weekly,* a Charlottesville, Virginia, newspaper, ran an advertisement for the Women's Pavilion, a nonprofit organization in New York

City that offered to find low-cost abortion services. Bigelow was convicted under a Virginia statute that made it a misdemeanor to "encourage or prompt the securing of an abortion." At the time, abortion was legal in New York State, but not in Virginia. The Virginia courts held that the statute did not violate any First Amendment rights when applied to purely commercial speech, such as the ad in Bigelow's publication.

The Supreme Court reversed. Justice Blackmun held that the mere fact the speech in question was a paid advertisement does not mean it was not entitled to First Amendment protection. Virginia relied on ***Valentine v. Chrestensen,*** 316 U.S. 52 (1942), in which the Court denied First Amendment protection for commercial speech. The Court rejected the application of *Chrestensen* to this case because the ad was not pure commercial speech, but conveyed information to Virginians that was not essentially commercial. The Court noted, "The advertisement published in appellant's newspaper did more than simply propose a commercial transaction. It contained factual material of clear 'public interest.' Portions of its message, most prominently the lines, 'Abortions are now legal in New York. There are no residency requirements,' involve the exercise of the freedom of communicating information and disseminating opinion." "Viewed in its entirety," Blackmun argued, "the advertisement conveyed information of potential interest and value to a diverse audience—not only to readers possibly in need of the services offered, but also to those with a general curiosity about, or genuine interest in, the subject matter or the law of another State and its development, and to readers seeking reform in Virginia."

The Court also noted that because Virginia had no police power control over what its citizens did in New York, it had no police power control over what information about New York law a citizen of that state could disseminate in Virginia. Virginia's asserted interest in protecting its citizens from hearing about the laws of New York was not compelling.

Justice Rehnquist's dissent denied that there was a substantial difference between the advertisement in this case and the commercial speech in *Chrestensen.* Rehnquist argued that the only aspect of this advertisement that led the Court to find that it conveyed information of interest to Virginians in general was the content of the message ("abortions are now legal in New York"). In Rehnquist's view, this amounted to distinguishing utterances for First Amendment purposes based on their content.

See N. E. H. Hull and Peter Charles Hoffer, Roe v. Wade: *The Abortion Rights Controversy in American History* (Lawrence: University Press of Kansas, 2001).

Cort v. Ash

422 U.S. 66 (1975)
Decided: June 17, 1975
Vote: 9 (Burger, Douglas, Brennan, Stewart, B. White, T. Marshall, Blackmun, Powell, Rehnquist)
0
Opinion of the Court: Brennan

The 1971 campaign act prohibited corporations from making contributions to certain federal elections. During the 1972 presidential election campaign, Stewart S. Cort, an officer of Bethlehem Steel Corporation, bought ads in *Time, Newsweek,* and *U.S. News and World Report* in which he declared: "I say let's keep the campaign honest. Mobilize 'Truth Squads.' " The truth squads were meant to combat what Cort felt was campaign misinformation about large corporations not paying their fair share of taxes. Cort also sent various mailings encouraging people to form truth squads. The money for the advertisements and mailings came from Bethlehem's corporate purse. Ash, a Bethlehem shareholder, sued, alleging that Cort had made contributions to the 1972 presidential election in violation of Section 610 of the law. He sought an injunction against further truth squad activities, as well as private damages under the same federal law.

The Supreme Court determined that Section 610 did not create a private right to relief, and, because the 1972 election was over, only Ash's request for an injunction against future violations of Section 610 remained in controversy. Future violations would be governed by amendments to the Federal Election Campaign Act of 1971, such as the 1974 amendments that created the Federal Election Commission. Only the commission was entitled to seek an injunction under Section 610. The Court also determined that, even before those amendments went into effect, Section 610 did not create a private remedy. Statutes not specifically creating a private remedy will be held to do so only if the plaintiff is one of the specific class the statute was meant to protect, where a private remedy is consistent with the purpose of the statute, and where the cause of action is not traditionally left to state law. In this case, corporate shareholders were not the class the statute was meant to protect—the statute was meant to protect all Americans from potential corruption resulting from the amassing of corporate wealth. Furthermore, the cause of action for *ultra vires* actions of corporate directors and breach of fiduciary duty was a matter of Delaware corporate law, not federal law. Although the statute impacted freedom of speech, this case centered only on the issue of the private cause of action. Justice Brennan noted, "We therefore have no occasion to address the questions whether § 610, properly construed, proscribes the expenditures alleged in this case, or whether the statute is unconstitutional as violative of the First

Amendment or of the equal protection component of the Due Process Clause of the Fifth Amendment."

See Bruce A. Boyer, "*Howard v. Pierce:* Implied Causes of Action and the Ongoing Vitality of *Cort v. Ash,*" *Northwestern University Law Review* 80 (1986): 722; Michael J. Garrison, "Corporate Political Speech, Campaign Spending, and First Amendment Doctrine," *American Business Law Journal* 27 (1989): 163; and Randall A. Pentiuk, "*First National Bank of Boston v. Bellotti:* The Constitution Guarantees Free Speech for Corporations," *Detroit College Law Review* (1979): 545.

Erznoznik v. City of Jacksonville

422 U.S. 205 (1975)
Decided: June 23, 1975
Vote: 6 (Douglas, Brennan, Stewart, T. Marshall, Blackmun, Powell)
3 (Burger, B. White, Rehnquist)
Opinion of the Court: Powell
Concurring opinion: Douglas
Dissenting opinion: Burger (Rehnquist)
Dissenting opinion: B. White

A Florida statute prohibited drive-in movie theaters from showing films containing nudity if the screen was visible from a street or public place. Richard Erznoznik, the manager of the University Drive-In Theatre in Jacksonville, challenged the law after he was charged with "exhibiting a motion picture, visible from public streets, in which 'female buttocks and bare breasts were shown.' " Although the prohibition went far beyond the scope of obscenity defined in ***Miller v. California,*** 413 U.S. 15 (1973), and included many films that were protected by the First Amendment, Jacksonville claimed its statute was valid as a nuisance ordinance.

The Supreme Court found that the statute violated the First Amendment. It did not address a category of speech that may be regulated in the interests of protecting people from unwitting exposure to offensive content. Those regulations applied only to speech targeted at people in their homes. Quoting ***Cohen v. California,*** 403 U.S. 15 (1971), Justice Powell noted, "Much that we encounter offends our esthetic, if not our political and moral, sensibilities. Nevertheless, the Constitution does not permit government to decide which types of otherwise protected speech are sufficiently offensive to require protection for the unwilling listener or viewer." Instead, absent certain narrow circumstances such as time, place, and manner regulations, "the burden normally falls upon the viewer to 'avoid further bombardment of [his] sensibilities simply by averting [his] eyes.' " Therefore, "when the government, acting as censor, undertakes selectively to shield the public from some kinds of speech on the ground that they are more offensive than others, the First Amendment strictly limits its power." Restrictions are permitted only "when the speaker intrudes on the privacy of the home," or when the degree of the captivity of the audience "makes it impractical for the unwilling viewer or auditor to avoid exposure," clearly not the case here. It was true that people had been observed sitting in adjacent parking lots watching the films, but they were doing so by choice.

In striking down the ordinance, the Court noted that it was "underinclusive," in that it banned only movies that contained nudity. The implication is clear that the city, as either a nuisance ordinance or a traffic regulation, might have required outdoor theaters to construct fences to prevent anyone from seeing their movies from the outside. What the Court would not allow is a content-based rule that prohibited some movies from being shown and not others.

See Arnold H. Loewy, "Obscenity, Pornography and First Amendment Theory," *William and Mary Bill of Rights Journal* 2 (1993): 471.

Albemarle Paper Co. v. Moody

422 U.S. 405 (1975)
Decided: June 25, 1975
Vote: 7 (Douglas, Brennan, Stewart, B. White, T. Marshall, Blackmun, Rehnquist)
1 (Burger)
Opinion of the Court: Stewart
Concurring opinion: T. Marshall
Concurring opinion: Rehnquist
Opinion concurring in judgment: Blackmun
Dissenting opinion: Burger
Did not participate: Powell

In this civil rights case, a class of plaintiffs sued Albemarle Paper Company and the plant employees' labor union, Halifax Local No. 425, for employment discrimination in promotion decisions at Albemarle's North Carolina plant. The district court found evidence of discrimination and ordered the plant to reorganize its seniority system more equitably. The court refused to award the plaintiffs the back pay they requested because it found that the plant's discrimination was not done in "bad faith" and the plaintiffs had needlessly delayed the issuance of the back pay by waiting for five years of discovery before asking for it. In addition, the district court refused to enjoin the plant's testing system for promotions, which the plaintiffs claimed was unfair. The plaintiffs appealed this decision.

The Supreme Court agreed with the district court that discrimination existed at the plant, but found the plant's good or bad faith irrelevant to the issuance of back pay under Title VII of the Civil Rights Act. The Court held that where employment discrimination is found, courts should generally award back pay. The policy of Title VII is to eradicate employment discrimination throughout the economy and to make discrimination victims whole wherever possible, which usually cannot be accomplished without awarding back pay. The fact that the management did not act in bad faith is irrelevant because Title VII looks to eliminate the effects of discrimination, not to punish those who intentionally discriminate. Finally, the Court found that Albemarle's employment tests were discriminatory and not related to the job. Under Title VII, any test for employment must measure an applicant's ability to perform the particular job, not the applicant in the abstract. If a company attempts to show its tests are job related with professional studies, those studies must meet certain standards established by the Equal Employment Opportunities Commission. If a study attempts to validate the job-relatedness of a test by comparing the test results with supervisors' subjective opinions of an applicant's ability, the study needs to make certain that supervisors are not expressing their prejudices in stating opinions. That was not done in this case. The supervisors were only asked a vague question about the applicants' abilities. Furthermore, comparing incoming applicants' scores near the bottom of a progression line with the scores of experienced employees near the top of the line is not a fair way to determine whether the incoming applicant possesses the necessary job skills.

Warth v. Seldin

422 U.S. 490 (1975)
Decided: June 25, 1975
Vote: 5 (Burger, Stewart, Blackmun, Powell, Rehnquist)
4 (Douglas, Brennan, B. White, T. Marshall)
Opinion of the Court: Powell
Dissenting opinion: Douglas
Dissenting opinion: Brennan (B. White, T. Marshall)

Warth and other petitioners, described as low income, Hispanic, and African American residents of Rochester, New York, sued the suburban town of Penfield for a determination that certain zoning ordinances were unconstitutional because they excluded poor people from moving into the town. The petitioners "alleged that Penfield's zoning ordinance, adopted in 1962, has the purpose and effect of excluding person of low and moderate income from residing in the town." Specifically, the ordinance allocated 98 percent of the town's vacant land to single-family detached housing and only 0.3 percent to multifamily structures, such as apartments and townhouses. Even on this limited space, the plaintiffs claimed, housing for low and moderate income persons was not economically feasible because of low density and other requirements. They further asserted that the city's ordinance "had the effect of excluding persons of minority racial and ethnic groups, since most such persons have only low or moderate incomes." In addition, the petitioners asserted that Penfield's restrictive zoning laws forced Rochester to raise its taxes, which directly harmed the petitioners. The petitioners made claims under the First, Ninth, and Fourteenth Amendments, asked for an injunction against the enforcement of the zoning law, and asked for $750,000 in actual and exemplary damages.

Although all the petitioners lived in the Rochester metropolitan area, none of them had attempted to move into Penfield. In a 5–4 decision, the Court ruled that they did not have standing to sue because they could not allege any particularized harm to them individually.

In dissent, Justice Douglas accused the majority of reading "the complaint and the record with antagonistic eyes." Justice Brennan believed the Court used "outmoded notions of pleading and of justiciability" to make it impossible for "any of the variously situated plaintiffs" to "clear numerous hurdles, some constructed here for the first time, necessary to establish 'standing.' " He accused the Court of giving "lip service to the principle, oft repeated in recent years, that 'standing in no way depends on the merits of the plaintiff's contention that particular conduct is illegal,' " but "in fact the opinion, which tosses out of court almost every conceivable kind of plaintiff who could be injured by the activity claimed to be unconstitutional, can be explained only by an indefensible hostility to the claim on the merits."

See Lawrence Gene Sagar, "Insular Majorities Unabated: *Warth v. Seldin* and *City of Eastlake v. Forest City Enterprises, Inc.*," *Harvard Law Review* 91 (1978): 1373.

Rizzo v. Goode

423 U.S. 362 (1976)
Decided: January 21, 1976
Vote: 5 (Burger, Stewart, B. White, Powell, Rehnquist)
3 (Brennan, T. Marshall, Blackmun)
Opinion of the Court: Rehnquist
Dissenting opinion: Blackmun (Brennan, T. Marshall)
Did not participate: Stevens

Goode was a member of a small class of Philadelphians who sued the Philadelphia police force, alleging a policy of violating the civil rights of minorities. The district court found clear violations of constitutional rights in three of eight incidents listed in one plaintiff's complaint and in two of twenty-eight incidents listed in another plaintiff's complaint. The court also said that the evidence did not indicate a policy of violating minorities' civil rights, but showed an unacceptably high number of incidents and a pattern of discouraging citizen complaints and minimizing the incidents. The district court ordered the Philadelphia Police Department to create a new set of procedures to deal more effectively and responsively to citizen complaints, and the department appealed.

The Supreme Court held that the plaintiffs had no standing to sue: the case or controversy requirement was not met because they could not point to specific harms from specific officers that entitled them to relief. Justice Rehnquist found that the district court did not have the authority to order the police department to change its procedures because state law granted the department discretion as to how to fulfill its duties. Finally, the opinion found that the district court had erred in finding that incidents of constitutional violations gleaned from the plaintiffs' briefs were unacceptably high, considering that Philadelphia is a large city with 7,500 police officers.

Justice Blackmun agreed with the majority that a clear pattern of violations against any individual might not exist, but he did not agree "with the Court's substitution of its judgment for that of the District Court," which "found a pattern of operation" that violated civil rights. Indeed, Blackmun noted that the district court had resolved conflicting testimony and made detailed findings of fact that both sides accepted to attack the problem. Blackmun wrote, "The district court, in its memorandum of December 18, 1973, stated that 'the resolution of all the disputed items was more nearly in accord with the defendants' position than with the plaintiffs' position,' and that the relief contemplated by the earlier orders of March 14, 1973, 'did not go beyond what the defendants had always been willing to accept.' " Given this outcome, and the role of the district court as fact finder, the dissenters argued that the Supreme Court had no justification for overturning the lower court's decision and the resolution that the parties had worked out.

Buckley v. Valeo

424 U.S. 1 (1976)
Decided: January 30, 1976
Vote: Multiple
Opinion: *Per curiam*
Dissenting opinion: Burger
Dissenting opinion: B. White
Dissenting opinion: T. Marshall
Dissenting opinion: Rehnquist
Dissenting opinion: Blackmun
Did not participate: Stevens

In 1971 Congress passed two statutes to regulate campaign contributions and to substitute public money for private funds in presidential campaigns. In 1974, in the wake of the Watergate scandal and the illegal activities of President Richard Nixon and his reelection committee, Congress amended the laws with the Presidential Election Campaign Act of 1974. In *Buckley v. Valeo* a sharply divided Court struck down most of the provisions of the 1974 act. The justices split in a variety of ways. The lead plaintiff was Sen. James L. Buckley of New York, elected in 1970 on the Conservative Party ticket in a three-way race. Francis R. Valeo, secretary of the Senate, was the defendant.

The Court upheld the 1971 acts creating a system of public financing of presidential elections, including provisions stating that candidates who accepted public funding could be required to limit their expenditures. The Court's decision on this point led to the public financing of presidential campaigns.

The 1974 act limited contributions to any political campaign for a federal office to $1,000 and prohibited individuals from contributing more $5,000 to political action committees and more than $25,000 to political campaigns in any single year. The law also contained various requirements that contributions to campaigns be reported. The Court found these provisions constitutional, despite arguments that they violated the First Amendment free speech rights of the contributor. The Court accepted the argument that these provisions were necessary to prevent corruption and, in effect, prevent citizens from bribing public officials through campaign contributions.

While upholding the limits on direct contributions to a campaign, the Court struck down a limitation on the amount that an individual could spend "relative to a clearly identified candidate." The government contended that this provision was necessary to prevent an end run around the contribution limitations, by allowing individuals to give unlimited support, known as soft money, to candidates by paying for advertising themselves, or in other ways supporting the candidate on their own. The Court held that such a limit violated the First Amendment.

In dissent, Justice White noted that the purpose of the law was to "counter the corrosive effects of money in federal election campaigns." He said the Court should have given greater deference to "the majority of Congress that passed this bill and the President who signed it" because they had much more knowledge than the justices about "what may improperly influence candidates."

The Court also found unconstitutional on First Amendment grounds the provisions of the law limiting the amount that individual candidates could spend from their own funds and overall limits on total expenditures during a campaign. Finally, the Court struck down the appointment process for members of the newly created Federal Election Commission, which had the power to oversee the election of federal officeholders. Under the 1974 law the members of the commission would be appointed by the president, the Speaker of the House, and the president *pro tempore* of the Senate. The Court found that this scheme violated the Appointments Clause (Article II, Section 2) of the Constitution, which requires the president to make appointments and the Senate to confirm them.

Central to the Court's reasoning was the notion that Congress could balance freedom of speech with the need to prevent corruption, but that corruption resulted only from campaign contributions influencing candidates who might later be officeholders. If a rich candidate financed his or her own campaign, there would be no opportunity for corruption, but large contributions from individuals might be the functional equivalent of a bribe. The same reasoning led to the largest loophole created by this decision, which allowed individuals to spend as much soft money as they wished, on their own, to campaign for specific candidates, including presidential candidates who had accepted public funds for their campaigns.

The complexity of this decision is evident in the various votes. The Court voted 8–0 to uphold the part of the law creating the Federal Election Commission, 7–1 (with White dissenting) to limit campaign spending limits, but 7–1 (with Justice Marshall dissenting) to strike down the portion of the law limiting the amount candidates could spend. The Court upheld campaign contribution limits 6–2, with Chief Justice Burger and Justice Blackmun dissenting, and a public financing system for presidential elections, 6–2, with Burger and Justice Rehnquist dissenting. Finally, by a 7–1 vote, with Burger dissenting, the Court upheld public disclosure provisions of the law.

This case has been central to all subsequent debates over campaign finance reform. Supporters of campaign finance laws argue that the flood of money into campaigns leads to corruption and allows big donors to buy "access" to elected officials. Opponents of reform argue that the only way to beat an incumbent is by spending great sums of money, and that limits on spending effectively limit freedom of expression.

See Lillian R. BeVier, "Mandatory Disclosure, 'Sham Issue Advocacy,' and *Buckley v. Valeo:* A Response to Professor Hasen," *UCLA Law Review* 48 (2000): 285; and Stephanie Pestorich Manson, "When Money Talks: Reconciling *Buckley,* the First Amendment, and Campaign Finance," *Washington and Lee Law Review* 58 (2001): 1190.

Mathews v. Eldridge

424 U.S. 319 (1976)
Decided: February 24, 1976
Vote: 6 (Burger, Douglas, Stewart, B. White, Blackmun, Powell, Rehnquist)
2 (Brennan, T. Marshall)
Opinion of the Court: Powell
Dissenting opinion: Brennan (T. Marshall)
Did not participate: Stevens

George Eldridge received disability compensation beginning in June 1968, as provided by the Social Security Act. In March 1972 the state agency charged with monitoring his medical condition sent him a questionnaire asking him whether his condition had improved. He replied that his condition had not improved and forwarded the names of doctors who had evaluated him. The agency contacted the doctors and determined that Eldridge's disability had ended in May 1972. The agency sent Eldridge a letter with its findings and informed him that he could request time to submit additional information about his disability. Eldridge wrote back explaining why he felt the agency had sufficient information to support a finding of impairment and disputing one factual characterization of his condition as described in the agency's letter. The Social Security Administration (SSA) informed Eldridge in July that his benefits were terminating in that month.

Eldridge then sought judicial review of the SSA's decision. He claimed that the Due Process Clause requires a hearing before the SSA can terminate a recipient's benefits. He relied on ***Goldberg v. Kelly,*** 397 U.S. 254 (1970), which held that a hearing was needed before the SSA could terminate welfare benefits. The SSA urged the court to distinguish disability benefits from the welfare benefits that were at stake in *Goldberg* because disability payments were not based on financial need and did not require an assessment of the claimant's credibility. The district court found that disability benefits were indistinguishable from the welfare benefits in *Goldberg.* The SSA appealed, and the Supreme Court reversed.

Before reaching the due process question, the Court disposed of the jurisdictional question of whether Eldridge could sue in district court before asking the state agency and the SSA to reconsider their assessments or before requesting a review by the SSA's Appeals Council. The Court held that he could, because the "finality" requirement of the SSA's decision was met and Eldridge had contested the agency's initial assessment with his letter. Turning to the due process claim, the Court held that the SSA was not required to give Eldridge a hearing before terminating his benefits. *Goldberg* was not controlling because disability benefits, unlike welfare benefits, are not based on financial need. In balancing the state's interest in the SSA's administrative scheme against Eldridge's interest in continued payments, Eldridge's interest came up short. The recipient of disability compensation has a weaker interest in payments than a welfare recipient because welfare is still available to a recipient who is denied further disability benefits. In effect, the Court said on this point that if a disabled person was unfairly denied benefits, he or she could still obtain general welfare, but a person denied general welfare could not instead ask for disability payments. Furthermore, the Court asserted that the state's interest in making such decisions without a hearing is greater in disability cases because such decisions turn, not on an assessment of the claimant's credibility, but on a review of medical evidence. It was therefore less necessary for the SSA to actually see the disability claimant than the welfare claimant, and the SSA's denial of further benefits without a hearing did not violate the Due Process Clause. Thus, the Court held that SSA was not required to give due process hearings before terminating disability payments, while administrative agencies would have to continue to give hearings to other sorts of terminations, such as those involving welfare.

Time, Inc. v. Firestone

424 U.S. 448 (1976)
Decided: March 2, 1976
Vote: 5 (Burger, Stewart, Blackmun, Powell, Rehnquist)
3 (Brennan, B. White, T. Marshall)
Opinion of the Court: Rehnquist
Concurring opinion: Powell (Stewart)
Dissenting opinion: Brennan
Dissenting opinion: B. White
Dissenting opinion: T. Marshall
Did not participate: Stevens

Mary Alice Firestone was the wife of Russell Firestone, an heir to the tire manufacturing family. Their sensational divorce proceedings included allegations that the sexual escapades of both parties would, in the words of the divorce court judge, "make Dr. Freud's hair curl." The judge concluded that "neither party is domesticated" and granted a divorce. *Time* magazine published a brief account of the case, quoted language from the judge's opinion, and noted, from the court record, that the divorce was granted because of "extreme cruelty and adultery." Mary Alice Firestone asked the publisher to retract the statement, and, when her request was rejected, she sued for libel. The Florida Supreme Court upheld a jury verdict for damages against *Time*, and the publisher appealed to the Supreme Court, claiming its First Amendment rights had been violated. The magazine relied on ***New York Times v. Sullivan,*** 376 U.S. 254 (1964), which held that a publisher does not libel a "public figure" unless it prints a falsehood about that person with actual malice or reckless disregard for the truth. *Time* also argued that it could not be sued for printing facts and statements that appeared in the court's decision in the case.

Justice Rehnquist held that Mary Alice Firestone was not a public figure within the meaning of *Sullivan* because she had neither assumed a role of special prominence in the affairs of society nor thrust herself to the forefront of a particular public issue. The fact that her divorce led to a public record did not make her a "public" person under *New York Times*. The Court remanded the case, however, because the record did not show any finding of "fault" on the part of *Time*.

Justice Brennan would have reversed the decision and prevented Firestone from recovering, on the theory that it cannot possibly be libelous to print a story about a public trial and to quote from decision of the judge.

Justice Marshall believed Mary Alice Firestone to be a public figure and that therefore *Time* was protected by the decision in *New York Times*.

Hudgens v. National Labor Relations Board

424 U.S. 507 (1976)
Decided: March 3, 1976
Vote: 6 (Burger, Stewart, B. White, Blackmun, Powell, Rehnquist)
2 (Brennan, T. Marshall)
Opinion of the Court: Stewart
Concurring opinion: Powell (Burger)
Opinion concurring in judgment: B. White
Dissenting opinion: T. Marshall (Brennan)
Did not participate: Stevens

Scott Hudgens, the owner of a shopping mall, threatened to have picketing labor union members forcibly removed when they entered the mall to stage a peaceful protest in front of their employer's store. The National Labor Relations Board (NLRB) concluded that Hudgens's threat was a violation of the National Labor Relations Act, and the Fifth Circuit Court agreed.

The Supreme Court held that ***Lloyd Corp., Ltd. v. Tanner,*** 407 U.S. 551 (1972), had overruled *Food Employees v. Logan Valley Plaza,* 391 U.S. 308 (1968), on the issue of whether protesters should be allowed to exercise their First Amendment rights on privately owned mall property. Following the *Tanner* rule, the Court held that the picketers had no First Amendment right to picket on the mall property. The Court remanded the case to the NLRB for a balancing of the rights of the picketers against the rights of the property owners, based solely on the National Labor Relations Act and without reference to the First Amendment.

Paul v. Davis

424 U.S. 693 (1976)
Decided: March 23, 1976
Vote: 5 (Burger, Stewart, Blackmun, Powell, Rehnquist)
3 (Brennan, B. White, T. Marshall)
Opinion of the Court: Rehnquist
Dissenting opinion: Brennan (T. Marshall, B. White)
Did not participate: Stevens

In November 1972 police officials distributed flyers with Edward Charles Davis's name and picture and the caption "Active Shoplifter" to owners of retail stores. Davis had been arrested for shoplifting the year before, but was never tried or convicted. After release of the flyer, Davis's employer questioned him, but did not fire him. Davis sued, arguing that his civil rights had been violated by Police Chief Paul.

The Supreme Court held that Davis's reputation was not a property or liberty interest of which the Due Process Clause is cognizant and that Davis would have to show harm greater than defamation to sue under Section 1983 of the Civil Rights Act of 1964.

In dissent, Justice Brennan set out both his own view of the case and the weaknesses of the majority's opinion. He noted that under the majority's decision, police officers, "acting in their official capacities as law enforcers, may on their own initiative and without trial constitutionally condemn innocent individuals as criminals and thereby brand them with one of the most stigmatizing and debilitating labels in our society." Brennan argued the unless there were "constitutional restraints on such oppressive behavior, the safeguards constitutionally accorded an accused in a criminal trial are rendered a sham, and no individual can feel secure that he will not be arbitrarily singled out for similar *ex parte* punishment by those primarily charged with fair enforcement of the law." Brennan condemned the Court for excluding a person's interest in his good name and reputation from all constitutional protection, regardless of the character of or necessity for the government's actions." He concluded that this result, "demonstrably inconsistent with our prior case law and unduly restrictive in its construction of our precious Bill of Rights, is one in which I cannot concur."

Greer v. Spock

424 U.S. 828 (1976)
Decided: March 24, 1976
Vote: 6 (Burger, Stewart, B. White, Blackmun, Powell, Rehnquist)
2 (Brennan, T. Marshall)
Opinion of the Court: Stewart
Concurring opinion: Burger
Concurring opinion: Powell (Burger)
Dissenting opinion: Brennan (T. Marshall)
Dissenting opinion: T. Marshall
Did not participate: Stevens

When pediatrician Benjamin Spock was running for president on the People's Party ballot in 1972, he and others wanted to make a speech and pass out leaflets on the military installation at Fort Dix. The commanding officer of Fort Dix, Maj. Gen. Bert A. David, refused him permission to do so. Spock argued that he had a First Amendment right to speak on the premises. Fort Dix was government property, and the public was excluded from most areas within the installation but allowed access to other areas. Spock wanted to rally in the public areas. The court of appeals ordered the district court to enjoin the enforcement of all Fort Dix regulations that would prevent Spock or any other political speaker from holding a rally on the public parts of the installation.

The Supreme Court reversed, holding that military installations are not public forums where the public may exercise its First Amendment rights. In his opinion, Justice Stewart noted that Fort Dix's regulations banned speeches and demonstrations of a partisan political nature, such as picketing, sit-ins, and protest marches. The Court noted that these regulations were "rigidly enforced." The Court quoted ***Adderley v. Florida,*** 385 U.S. 39 (1966): "The guarantees of the First Amendment have never meant 'that people who want to propagandize protests or views have a constitutional right to do so whenever and however and wherever they please.' " The Court reaffirmed that some time, place, and manner restrictions of speech were appropriate, even for the government, which, "no less than a private owner of property, has power to preserve the property under its control for the use to which it is lawfully dedicated." Stewart concluded that the special circumstances of a military base made it reasonable to exclude all political speakers, as Fort Dix had done. He wrote, "The notion that federal military reservations, like municipal streets and parks, have traditionally served as a place for free public assembly and communication of thoughts by private citizens is thus historically and constitutionally false." The Court therefore upheld the government's ban.

See James M. Hirschhorn, "The Separate Community: Military Uniqueness and Servicemen's Constitutional Rights," *North Carolina Law Review* 62 (1984): 177.

Moe v. Confederated Salish & Kootenai Tribes

425 U.S. 463 (1976)
Decided: April 27, 1976
Vote: 9 (Burger, Brennan, Stewart, B. White, T. Marshall, Blackmun, Powell, Rehnquist, Stevens)
0
Opinion of the Court: Rehnquist

Several members of the Salish and Kootenai Tribes, including a smoke shop owner who had been arrested for selling unstamped cigarettes, sued to enjoin the local Montana sheriff from enforcing several of Montana's statewide tax laws. These laws included a personal property tax on motor vehicles, a vendor licensee tax, and a cigarette sales tax. The state argued that the district court must refuse to hear the case because of a federal statute requiring district courts to refuse a state tax case when the case can easily be heard in state court. The district court, however, found that another federal statute conferring jurisdiction on U.S. district courts for all cases involving U.S. treaties trumped the other statute. The district court found that Montana's taxes, as applied to the Indian tribes, violated federal laws regarding the sovereignty of Indian nations, and the Supreme Court affirmed.

The Court held that Montana could place a sales tax on cigarettes sold by reservation Indians to non-Indians, but it could not tax sales of cigarettes by reservation Indians to other reservation Indians. Furthermore, the state could not charge a vendor licensing tax for smoke shops located on Indian reservations, and the state personal property tax, when applied to property on the reservation, was also invalid.

Virginia State Board of Pharmacy v. Virginia Citizens Consumer Council, Inc.

425 U.S. 748 (1976)
Decided: May 24, 1976
Vote: 7 (Burger, Brennan, Stewart, B. White, T. Marshall, Blackmun, Powell)
1 (Rehnquist)
Opinion of the Court: Blackmun
Concurring opinion: Burger
Concurring opinion: Stewart
Dissenting opinion: Rehnquist
Did not participate: Stevens

In ***Valentine v. Chrestensen,*** 316 U.S. 52 (1942), the Supreme Court held that commercial speech lacked basic First Amendment protections. In *Virginia State Board of Pharmacy* the Court began to dismantle this doctrine. Virginia, like many other states, limited advertising for a variety of goods and services. The state code provided that a "pharmacist licensed in Virginia is guilty of unprofessional conduct if he," among other acts, " 'publishes, advertises or promotes, directly or indirectly, in any manner whatsoever, any amount, price, fee, premium, discount, rebate or credit terms . . . for any drugs which may be dispensed only by prescription.' " When a consumer's group filed suit to overturn this rule, a federal court declared the provision unconstitutional and enjoined the state pharmacy board from enforcing it.

The Supreme Court noted that drug prices in Virginia, for both prescription and nonprescription items, varied widely from outlet to outlet even within the same locality. Justice Blackmun noted that free speech rights are for the protection of listeners as well as speakers. "Freedom of speech presupposes a willing speaker. But where a speaker exists, as is the case here, the protection afforded is to the communication, to its source and to its recipients both," Blackmun wrote. He pointed to the "First Amendment right to 'receive information and ideas,'" saying that freedom of speech "necessarily protects the right to receive." Blackmun acknowledged that in the past the Court had made a distinction between commercial speech and other speech, but said that the Court was now abandoning "that simplistic approach." Indeed, just a year before this case, in ***Bigelow v. Virginia,*** 421 U.S. 809 (1975), the Court struck down, on First Amendment grounds, a Virginia law banning advertising of abortion services. There, the Court "rejected the contention that the publication was unprotected because it was commercial," but that case involved more than just commercial speech. The ban on the advertising of drug prices, however, brought the commercial speech doctrine directly before the Court.

The Court found that sellers of goods and services had a profound interest in attracting customers and that this interest affected the larger marketplace. Businesses may succeed or fail on their ability to attract customers. Similarly, the customer has a strong interest in knowing where to purchase products at the best price. Indeed, Blackmun noted that "the particular consumer's interest in the free flow of commercial information . . . may be as keen, if not keener by far, than his interest in the day's most urgent political debate."

The state argued that the ban on advertising was necessary to promote professionalism, but the Court also rejected this idea, pointing out that pharmacists were regulated by other means and that the price of goods was irrelevant to their professionalism. Indeed, Blackmun said, "On close inspection it is seen that the State's protectiveness of its citizens rests in large measure on the advantages of their being kept in ignorance. The advertising ban does not directly affect professional standards one way or the other. It affects them only through the reactions it is assumed people will have to the free flow of drug price information." The Court noted that states might still regulate false and deceptive advertising, an issue Justice Stewart addressed in his opinion. But, with regard general advertising, the Court had opened up an entirely new world, in which consumers would know more about prices and services than they had previously been able to learn.

In dissent, Justice Rehnquist complained that the Court was allowing the consumer plaintiffs to substitute their judgment for that of the state legislatures. He argued that consumer groups were free to publicize prices and inform other consumers of the best places to shop, but that the legislature should be allowed to regulate professionals. He asserted that the case presented "a fairly typical First Amendment problem—that of balancing interests in individual free speech against public welfare determinations embodied in a legislative enactment." For Rehnquist, the balance was in favor of the state deciding what was best for the people to know; for the majority the balance fell in favor of the people having access to information vital to their welfare.

See Moira T. Roberts, "Individual Rights and Government Power in Collision: A Look at *Rust v. Sullivan* Through the Lens of Power Analysis," *Washington and Lee Law Review* 49 (1992): 1023; and John C. Coots, "A Missed Opportunity to Definitively Apply the Central Hudson Tests: *Fane v. Edenfield,*" *Creighton Law Review* 23 (1993): 1155.

Hampton v. Mow Sun Wong

426 U.S. 88 (1976)
Decided: June 1, 1976
Vote: 5 (Brennan, Stewart, T. Marshall, Powell, Stevens)
4 (Burger, B. White, Blackmun, Rehnquist)
Opinion of the Court: Stevens
Concurring opinion: Brennan (T. Marshall)
Dissenting opinion: Rehnquist (Burger, B. White, Blackmun)

This case dealt with a challenge to regulations "adopted and enforced by the Civil Service Commission and certain other federal agencies" barring non-U.S. citizens from employment in most federal government positions. The five plaintiffs were Chinese residents of San Francisco, who were qualified for their jobs, except for their status as aliens. One was terminated from the post office "because his personnel record disclosed that he was not a citizen." Another, with eighteen years' experience as a businessman in China, lost his job as a file clerk with the Government Services Administration (GSA). Another had taught for fifteen years and had a master's degree in education, but was "not permitted to take an examination for a position as evaluator of educational programs in the Department of Health, Education, and Welfare." The lead plaintiff, Mow Sun Wong, who had declared his intention to become a citizen, had been an electrical engineer in China, but was held "ineligible for employment as a janitor" for the GSA.

The Supreme Court declared that under the Fifth Amendment such regulations were unconstitutional because they deprived the aliens, without due process of law, of a significant liberty interest, that of obtaining employment. The Court affirmed that Congress could ban aliens from certain federal jobs. Congress may find overriding national interests that justify an intrusion on aliens' liberty interests, but the Civil Service Commission may not presume so in its regulations. The Court conceded the validity of arguments that "undivided loyalty in certain sensitive positions clearly justifies a citizenship requirement in at least some parts of the federal service," but found that the Civil Service Commission, acting without statutory authority, had overstepped its authority.

Washington v. Davis

426 U.S. 229 (1976)
Decided: June 7, 1976
Vote: 7 (Burger, Stewart, B. White, Blackmun, Powell, Rehnquist, Stevens)
2 (Brennan, T. Marshall)
Opinion of the Court: B. White
Concurring opinion: Stevens
Dissenting opinion: Brennan (T. Marshall)

The plaintiffs in this case were black aspirants for police work and black police officers who were denied employment or promotions on the Washington, D.C., police force. These denials were based on the failure of the applicants to pass

"Test 21," a government service test designed to measure verbal skill. The plaintiffs argued that the test disqualified a disproportionate number of blacks, bore no relationship to job duties, and violated equal protection. Because this case originated in the District of Columbia, rather than a state, the Fifth Amendment was at issue, rather than the Fourteenth, as is usually the case in race discrimination cases. Based on the evidence, the plaintiffs moved for summary judgment against the police force. The district court denied their motion, but the court of appeals reversed and directed summary judgment in their favor, relying on ***Griggs v. Duke Power Co.***, 401 U.S. 424 (1971).

The Supreme Court reversed. The Court held that the court of appeals was wrong to apply *Griggs* to this case because *Griggs* was decided under Title VII of the Civil Rights Act of 1964, and this case arose under the Fifth Amendment. To invoke this amendment, a plaintiff must show intentional discrimination. Although a policy that was facially neutral may still be found to have discriminatory intent under the Fifth Amendment, such a policy does not violate the amendment if it has no discriminatory purpose, even if the effect is discriminatory. The plaintiffs could not attribute their lack of success on the test to discrimination any more than an unsuccessful white applicant could. Furthermore, even if this case had been decided under *Griggs*, the government met its burden in rebutting the plaintiffs' prima facie case of discrimination, because the police force showed that Test 21 was related to performance in training school. The Court rejected the "proposition that a law or other official act, without regard to whether it reflects a racially discriminatory purpose, is unconstitutional solely because it has a racially disproportionate impact." The Court also noted that the record showed that "the Department had made substantial efforts to recruit blacks." The disproportionate impact of the test could not be seen as intentional.

In his concurrence, Justice Stevens agreed with the majority that discriminatory intent was necessary for a finding of violation of Fifth Amendment equal protection. He wrote, however, that it would be unrealistic, in every situation, to require a plaintiff to disprove a decision-maker's assertion that he acted without discriminatory intent. In his opinion, there could be cases where discriminatory intent would have to be inferred from discriminatory effects.

Justice Brennan's dissent disputed the Court's conclusions that Title VII standards were not relevant to this case and that the police force had met its burden on summary judgment of showing that Test 21 was relevant in predicting job ability.

See Randall Kennedy, "The State, Criminal Law, and Racial Discrimination: A Comment," *Harvard Law Review* 107 (1994): 1231; and Larry Alexander, "What Makes Wrongful Discrimination Wrong? Biases, Preferences, Stereotypes, and Proxies," *University of Pennsylvania Law Review* 141 (1992): 149.

Bishop v. Wood

426 U.S. 341 (1976)
Decided: June 10, 1976
Vote: 5 (Burger, Stewart, Powell, Rehnquist, Stevens)
4 (Brennan, B. White, T. Marshall, Blackmun)
Opinion of the Court: Stevens
Dissenting opinion: Brennan (T. Marshall)
Dissenting opinion: B. White (Brennan, T. Marshall, Blackmun)
Dissenting opinion: Blackmun (Brennan)

Bishop was fired from his position as a police officer in a North Carolina town without a hearing. In private, his superiors told him that the reason for his discharge was his failure to follow orders and his attendance problems. Bishop sued, claiming that his discharge without a hearing was a violation of his due process rights. He said that because he was regarded as a "permanent employee," he had a sufficient property interest in future employment that the state must give him notice and opportunity to be heard before discharging him. Furthermore, Bishop claimed that his liberty interest in an untarnished reputation was impaired by what he regarded as a slanderous and false articulated reason for his discharge.

The district court construed North Carolina law to intend that officers, even those in permanent positions, were "at will" employees who could be discharged for any reason whatever. The Fourth Circuit Court upheld this construction of state law, and, in the absence of an authoritative state court interpretation to the contrary, the Supreme Court accepted that interpretation. As an "at will" employee, Bishop had no property interest in continued employment that would trigger due process concerns. Furthermore, Bishop's liberty interest in an untarnished reputation was not at stake in this case because, even assuming that the supervisor's articulated reason for the discharge was slanderous, it was made in private and only Bishop knew about it. Bishop therefore had no liberty interest that would invoke the Due Process Clause either.

Roemer v. Maryland Public Works Board

426 U.S. 736 (1976)
Decided: June 21, 1976
Vote: 5 (Burger, B. White, Blackmun, Powell, Rehnquist)
4 (Brennan, Stewart, T. Marshall, Stevens)
Judgment of the Court: Blackmun
Concurring in judgment: B. White (Rehnquist)
Dissenting opinion: Brennan (T. Marshall)
Dissenting opinion: Stewart
Dissenting opinion: Stevens

A Maryland statute provided "for annual noncategorical grants to private colleges, among them religiously affiliated institutions, subject only to the restrictions that the funds not be used for 'sectarian purposes.' " This money was available to all private colleges in the state except those that awarded only seminary or theological degrees. The plaintiffs were Maryland taxpayers who sued the state to enjoin the issuance of money to religious colleges. The Maryland Board of Higher Education, which governed the plan, ensured that the schools were not exclusively involved in granting seminary and theological degrees and that the money was not being diverted to religious purposes. Maryland won at the trial and appellate levels, and the Supreme Court affirmed.

Applying the three-part test articulated in ***Lemon v. Kurtzman,*** 403 U.S. 602 (1971), the Court found that the Maryland scheme had a nonreligious legislative purpose, that its primary effect was not to benefit religion, and that enforcement would not require excessive entanglement with religion. The Court noted that Maryland's plan was similar to that upheld in ***Tilton v. Richardson,*** 403 U.S. 672 (1971), in which the federal government had provided money for certain buildings on college campuses, including those with religious affiliations. The Maryland program was also similar to that upheld in *Hunt v. McNair,* 413 U.S. 734 (1973). In that case, the Court allowed the state to provide construction bonds for private colleges, including religious institutions.

The dissenters believed that the law was on its face a violation of the First Amendment. By providing taxpayer funds to religious colleges, the state was "advancing religion, no matter the vigilance to avoid it." Justice Brennan wrote, "The discrete interests of government and religion are mutually best served when each avoids too close a proximity to the other." Quoting his concurring opinion in ***School District of Abington Township v. Schempp,*** 374 U.S. 203 (1963), Brennan said, "It is not only the nonbeliever who fears the injection of sectarian doctrines and controversies into the civil polity, but in as high degree it is the devout believer who fears the secularization of a creed which becomes too deeply involved with and dependent upon the government."

See Paul Finkelman, ed., *Religion and American Law: An Encyclopedia* (New York: Garland, 2000).

National League of Cities v. Usery

426 U.S. 833 (1976)
Decided: June 24, 1976
Vote: 5 (Burger, Stewart, Blackmun, Powell, Rehnquist)
4 (Brennan, B. White, T. Marshall, Stevens)
Opinion of the Court: Rehnquist
Concurring opinion: Blackmun
Dissenting opinion: Brennan (B. White. T. Marshall)
Dissenting opinion: Stevens

When it was first enacted, the Fair Labor Standards Act (FLSA) did not apply to state employees. In 1961 Congress amended the act to apply its minimum wage and maximum hours provisions to certain state employees, such as workers in public hospitals. This limited removal of state exemption from the act was challenged in *Maryland v. Wirtz,* 392 U.S. 183 (1968), but the Supreme Court, finding the amendments to be valid, used broad language that suggested the act could be applied to other kinds of public employees as well. In 1974 Congress again amended the FLSA to apply to all employees of states and cities. States and their political subdivisions were now required to observe the maximum hours and minimum wage provisions of the FLSA with regard to public employees. The League of Cities sued the secretary of labor requesting declaratory relief that the amendment was invalid. The three-judge district court found the league's argument—that this exercise of legislative control over the states impaired the values of federalism—to be compelling, but felt obliged by *Wirtz* to find the amendment valid. The three-judge panel dismissed the suit for failure to state a claim for which relief could be granted.

The Supreme Court reversed and in the process explicitly overruled *Wirtz.* Justice Rehnquist's opinion began with an affirmation that Congress has broad powers under the Commerce Clause to regulate even intrastate activity that is private. When Congress imposes a burden on state government, however, it in effect seeks to regulate the "states as states." Because Congress has no power to regulate the internal operations of state government, the Court invalidated the 1974 amendment, and, by overturning *Wirtz,* also invalidated the 1961 amendment. The Court held "that insofar as the challenged amendments" to the statute "operate to directly displace the States' freedom to structure integral operations in areas of traditional governmental functions, they are not within the authority granted Congress by Art. I, § 8, cl. 3." Rehnquist's opinion breathed new life into the Tenth Amendment, as he asserted a strong limitation on the "exercise of congressional authority directed, not to private citizens, but to the States as States." The Court reaffirmed that "there are attributes of sovereignty attaching to every state government which may not be impaired by Congress, not because Congress may lack an affirmative grant of legislative authority to reach the matter, but because the Constitution prohibits it from exercising the authority in that manner."

Justice Blackmun emphasized that he understood the decision to mean only that the Constitution places limits on Congress in regard to the regulation of state government. When Congress's interest in the regulation was greater—for example, in environmental regulation—he believed that Congress would not be restrained from acting just because its action interfered with the states as states.

Justice Brennan's dissent expressed his belief that the federal government, although limited in its powers, is supreme within its sphere of action. Therefore, when Congress seeks to regulate commerce, it may do so without consideration of whether the regulation affects the states as states. Brennan believed that his view of the relative strength of the federal and state governments was based on precedent going back to Chief Justice Marshall's opinion in ***Gibbons v. Ogden,*** 22 U.S. 1 (1824), while the majority had discovered a new state sovereignty doctrine in the Tenth Amendment. In his opinion, the majority's opinion would have devastating effects on the ability of the federal government to regulate commerce.

National League of Cities was an important step in the revitalization of the Tenth Amendment, but it was also a misstep. The Court overruled *National League of Cities* in ***Garcia v. San Antonio Metropolitan Transit Authority,*** 469 U.S. 528 (1985), concluding that the "traditional governmental functions" test was in fact "unworkable."

See Mark V. Tushnet, "Why the Supreme Court Overruled *National League of Cities,*" *Vanderbilt Law Review* 47 (1994): 1623.

Young v. American Mini Theaters, Inc.

427 U.S. 50 (1976)
Decided: June 24, 1976
Vote: 5 (Burger, B. White, Powell, Rehnquist, Stevens)
4 (Brennan, Stewart, T. Marshall, Blackmun)
Opinion of the Court: Stevens
Concurring opinion: Powell
Dissenting opinion: Stewart (Brennan, T. Marshall, Blackmun)
Dissenting opinion: Blackmun (Brennan, Stewart, T. Marshall)

A Detroit ordinance prohibited adult movie theaters or bookstores from operating within one thousand feet of another adult movie theater or bookstore or within five hundred feet of any residential district. American Mini Theaters sued Mayor Coleman Young, claiming that the ordinance created an undue burden on First Amendment rights and violated the Equal Protection Clause. The Sixth Circuit Court of Appeals agreed, and the city appealed to the Supreme Court, claiming it had a legitimate interest in protecting the character of its neighborhoods and that it believed the zoning ordinance would help prevent the development of a skid row district. American Mini Theaters attempted to show that the statute was void for vagueness because it defined an adult establishment as one "characterized" by material that "emphasized" sexual acts or anatomy, but did not specify how much of this material was required in a store for it to be considered an adult establishment. Although it was stipulated that American Mini Theaters was exclusively engaged in showing films that emphasized sexual acts, these films were not obscene. American Mini Theaters argued that films that were not obscene were protected under the First Amendment, even if they were pornographic.

Speaking for the five-member majority, Justice Stevens concluded that the city's zoning regulation was reasonable and that even though erotic material could not be wholly suppressed, the city had legitimate reasons for restricting its distribution. He drew a distinction between the protection of political or cultural speech and the protection of pornography. "A remark attributed to Voltaire," Stevens wrote, "characterizes our zealous adherence to the principle that the government may not tell the citizen what he may or may not say. Referring to a suggestion that the violent overthrow of tyranny might be legitimate, he said: 'I disapprove of what you say, but I will defend to the death your right to say it.' The essence of that comment has been repeated time after time in our decisions invalidating attempts by the government to impose selective controls upon the dissemination of ideas." But he doubted that such sentiments applied to pornographic films.

Whether political oratory or philosophical discussion moves us to applaud or to despise what is said, every schoolchild can understand why our duty to defend the right to speak remains the same. But few of us would march our sons and daughters off to war to preserve the citizen's right to see "Specified Sexual Activities" exhibited in the theaters of our choice. Even though the First Amendment protects communication in this area from total suppression, we hold that the State may legitimately use the content of these materials as the basis for placing them in a different classification from other motion pictures.

In dissent, Justice Stewart castigated the majority for losing sight of what the First Amendment was designed to protect. He pointed out that this case involved "the constitutional permissibility of selective interference with protected speech whose content is thought to produce distasteful effects." This was in direct conflict with "a prime function of the First Amendment," which was "to guard against just such interference." He accused the majority of "rid[ing] roughshod over cardinal principles of First Amendment law, which require that time, place, and manner regulations that affect protected expression be content neutral except in the limited context of a captive or juvenile audience." He mocked Stevens's use of Voltaire and his claims of generally supporting free speech.

In place of these principles the Court invokes a concept wholly alien to the First Amendment. Since "few of us would march our sons and daughters off to war to preserve the citizen's right to see 'Specified Sexual Activities' exhibited in the theaters of our choice," the Court implies that these films are not entitled to the full protection of the Constitution. This stands "Voltaire's immortal comment," on its head. For if the guarantees of the First Amendment were reserved for expression that more than a "few of us" would take up arms to defend, then the right of free expression would be defined and circumscribed by current popular opinion. The guarantees of the Bill of Rights were designed to protect against precisely such majoritarian limitations on individual liberty.

See Charles H. Clarke, "Freedom of Speech and the Problem of the Lawful, Harmful Public Reaction: Adult Use Cases of Renton and Mini Theater," *Akron Law Review* 20 (1986): 187; and Kimberly K. Smith, "Zoning Adult Entertainment: A Reassessment of Renton," *California Law Review* 79 (1991): 119.

Runyon v. McCrary

427 U.S. 160 (1976)
Decided: June 25, 1976
Vote: 7 (Burger, Brennan, Stewart, T. Marshall, Blackmun, Powell, Stevens)
2 (B. White, Rehnquist)
Opinion of the Court: Stewart
Concurring opinion: Powell
Concurring opinion: Stevens
Dissenting opinion: B. White (Rehnquist)

The parents of Michael McCrary, an African American student, and others filed a class action suit against the Runyons, the proprietors of Bobbe's School in Arlington, Virginia. The suit alleged that the Runyons had denied the black children admission to their school on the basis of race. The parents claimed the Runyons were in violation of Section 1981 of the U.S. Code, which was a surviving remnant of the 1866 Civil Rights Act, as well as Title II of the Civil Rights Act of 1964. In *Jones v. Alfred H. Mayer Co.*, 392 U.S. 409 (1968), the Court held that under the 1866 act it was a violation of federal law to refuse to make or enforce private contracts on the basis of race. *Jones* dealt with housing, and *Runyon* extended the ruling to other forms of contracts.

The Court noted that this case was not about private clubs, religious organizations, or even religious schools. Rather, the case presented only two relatively narrow issues: "whether § 1981 prohibits private, commercially operated, nonsectarian schools from denying admission to prospective students because they are Negroes, and, if so, whether that federal law is constitutional as so applied." The Court decided affirmatively on both issues, holding that a civil rights statute that requires uniform contract privileges for black and white citizens prevented the schools from admitting only white children. The Court held that the statute was not a violation of the private school's First Amendment right to free association—in other words, the freedom to associate with only white people. The Court noted that parents have the First Amendment right of freedom of association to give their children a segregated education, but that "it does not follow that the practice of excluding racial minorities from such institutions is also protected by the same principle." In other words, businesses such as Bobbe's School were not free to discriminate and refuse to enter into contracts with people solely on the basis of their race.

The dissenters believed that *Jones v. Mayer* was wrongly decided and should not be applied here.

See Donald R. Livingston and Samuel A. Marcosson, "The Court at the Cross Roads: *Runyon*, Section 1981 and the Meaning of Precedent," *Emory Law Journal* (1998): 949; and Bernard Schwartz, "Rehnquist, *Runyon*, and *Jones*—Chief Justice, Civil Rights, and Stare Decisis," *Tulsa Law Journal* 31 (1995): 251.

Meachum v. Fano

427 U.S. 215 (1976)
Decided: June 25, 1976
Vote: 6 (Burger, Stewart, B. White, Blackmun, Powell, Rehnquist)
3 (Brennan, T. Marshall, Stevens)
Opinion of the Court: B. White
Dissenting opinion: Stevens (Brennan, T. Marshall)

Following a series of fires at the Massachusetts Correctional Institution at Norfolk, a medium-security institution, authorities removed Arthur Fano and others from the general prison population and conducted hearings into their connection to the fires. Fano had legal counsel during these hearings, but he was not given access to the in camera testimony of Larry Meachum, the Norfolk prison superintendent. Fano and the other men were transferred to Walpole, a maximum-security institution where the living conditions were harsher than at Norfolk. Fano argued that the lack of a full hearing, with access to testimony and evidence against him, infringed his Fourteenth Amendment liberty rights without due process of law.

The Supreme Court found that a prisoner does not have sufficient interest in continuation of his stay in a less oppressive prison to trigger the Due Process Clause. Once the prisoner is committed to state custody to serve his sentence, his liberty interest in any given prison is too thin to warrant such protection. As Justice White wrote, "Given a valid conviction, the criminal defendant has been constitutionally deprived of his liberty to the extent that the State may confine him and subject him to the rules of its prison system so long as the conditions of confinement do not otherwise violate the Constitution." According to White, Fano's conviction "has sufficiently extinguished the defendant's liberty interest to empower the State to confine him in any of its prisons."

In dissent, Justice Stevens said, "The Court's rationale is more disturbing than its narrow holding. If the Court had merely held that the transfer of a prisoner from one penal institution to another does not cause a sufficiently grievous loss to amount to a deprivation of liberty within the meaning of the Due Process Clause of the Fourteenth Amendment, I would disagree with the conclusion but not with the constitutional analysis." Stevens objected to the notion that incarcerated prisoners had in effect no "liberty interests." Stevens declared that liberty was "one of the cardinal unalienable rights" that the Due Process Clause protects. Thus, even prisoners, properly convicted and properly in prison, as no one doubted Fano was, had some residual liberty interests.

Massachusetts Board of Retirement v. Murgia

427 U.S. 307 (1976)
Decided: June 25, 1976
Vote: 7 (Burger, Brennan, Stewart, B. White, Blackmun, Powell, Rehnquist)
1 (T. Marshall)
Opinion: *Per curiam*
Dissenting opinion: T. Marshall
Did not participate: Stevens

Robert Murgia, a state police officer, sued when he was forced to retire at the mandatory retirement age of fifty. Murgia claimed that the statute violated his equal protection rights. The state conceded that "there is no dispute that, when he retired, his [Murgia's] excellent physical and mental health still rendered him capable of performing the duties of a uniformed officer." The district court found for Murgia, arguing that the state had no rational basis for forcing him to retire at age fifty.

The Supreme Court reversed. It rejected Murgia's claim that the statute should be subject to a strict scrutiny analysis. The Court said, "Equal protection analysis requires strict scrutiny of a legislative classification only when the classification impermissibly interferes with the exercise of a fundamental right or operates to the peculiar disadvantage of a suspect class. Mandatory retirement at age 50 under the Massachusetts statute involves neither situation." The right of government employment was not *per se* "fundamental." Nor did the Court find that "uniformed state police officers over 50 constitute a suspect class for purposes of equal protection analysis." Quoting ***San Antonio School District v. Rodriguez,*** 411 U.S. 1 (1973), the Court explained that "a suspect class is one 'saddled with such disabilities, or subjected to such a history of purposeful unequal treatment, or relegated to such a position of political powerlessness as to command extraordinary protection from the majoritarian political process.' " The Court admitted that although "the treatment of the aged in this Nation has not been wholly free of discrimination, such persons, unlike, say, those who have been discriminated against on the basis of race or national origin, have not experienced a 'history of purposeful unequal treatment' or been subjected to unique disabilities on the basis of stereotyped characteristics not truly indicative of their abilities."

This logic left only a rational-basis standard for reviewing the statute. The Court held that the statute was valid because it was rationally related to the legitimate state interest of ensuring that the public was safe from an aging police force that was physically or mentally unable to perform its duties. The fact that Murgia was still fit for duty made the state policy illegitimate, irrational, or unconstitutional.

Andresen v. Maryland

427 U.S. 463 (1976)
Decided: June 29, 1976
Vote: 7 (Burger, Stewart, B. White, Blackmun, Powell, Rehnquist, Stevens)
2 (Brennan, T. Marshall)
Opinion of the Court: Blackmun
Dissenting opinion: Brennan
Dissenting opinion: T. Marshall

Using a valid search warrant, police seized records from the offices of Maryland lawyer Peter Andresen in connection with a land fraud investigation. These records were later introduced at trial, and, after Maryland's Court of Special Appeals upheld his conviction, Andresen appealed to the Supreme Court. He argued that the search and the use of his business records violated his Fifth Amendment right against self-incrimination and his Fourth Amendment right against unreasonable searches and seizures. Some of the seized documents involved incriminating information the plaintiff had recorded himself.

The Court found that the use of the incriminating evidence did not violate Andreson's Fifth Amendment right because no one had compelled him to write down the thoughts in the first place. Furthermore, he was not compelled to testify about these documents, or even produce them; rather, they were seized during a legal search. As Justice Blackmun noted, in this case "petitioner was not asked to say or to do anything. The records seized contained statements that petitioner had voluntarily committed to writing. The search for and seizure of these records were conducted by law enforcement personnel. Finally, when these records were introduced at trial, they were authenticated by a handwriting expert, not by petitioner." Blackmun added that Andresen was under no compulsion to speak at his trial. Blackmun quoted Justice Holmes's assertion in *Johnson v. United States,* 228 U.S. 457 (1913), that "a party is privileged from producing the evidence but not from its production." Quoting *Couch v. United States,* 409 U.S. 322 (1973), Blackmun found that Holmes's point "recognizes that the protection afforded by the Self-Incrimination Clause of the Fifth Amendment 'adheres basically to the person, not to information that may incriminate him.' " Thus, the Court made the distinction between refusing to comply with a subpoena, which the Fifth Amendment protected, and the use of materials seized in a search.

In dissent, Justice Brennan argued that personal business records fell within a "zone of privacy" and could not be used to incriminate a defendant.

Nebraska Press Association v. Stuart

427 U.S. 539 (1976)
Decided: June 30, 1976
Vote: 9 (Burger, Brennan, Stewart, B. White, T. Marshall, Blackmun, Powell, Rehnquist, Stevens)
0
Opinion of the Court: Burger
Concurring opinion: B. White
Concurring opinion: Powell
Opinion concurring in judgment: Brennan (Stewart, T. Marshall)
Opinion concurring in judgment: Stevens

In October 1975 police arrested Erwin Charles Simants for the murder of Henry Kellie and five members of his family in the small town (population 850) of Sutherland, Nebraska. Fearing publicity of this gruesome crime would undermine a fair trial, Judge Hugh Stuart issued a restraining order to prevent anyone from "publishing or broadcasting accounts of confessions or admission made by the accused or facts 'strongly implicative' " of his connection to the crime. Newspapers appealed this order to the Nebraska Supreme Court, which modified it by prohibiting the reporting of only three matters: the existence and nature of any confessions or admissions made by the defendant to police; any confessions or admissions made to any third parties, except members of the press; and other facts that would implicate the accused.

The Supreme Court overturned this ruling. The Court noted the defendant's right to a fair trial and the need to protect a defendant from the sort of circus atmosphere that had pervaded the Sam Sheppard murder trial and led to the Court overturning his conviction in ***Sheppard v. Maxwell,*** 384 U.S. 333 (1966).

The Court also noted that in Sheppard's trial, it was the judge who failed to maintain order in his courtroom and prevented the defendant from getting a fair trial.

The Court concluded that the gag order could not stand because it was a prior restraint on publication, which was fundamentally at odds with the First Amendment. The Court said that a change of venue, away from the small town where the crime took place, would have been an obvious way to avoid impairment of the First Amendment, while protecting the defendant's Sixth Amendment right to a fair trial. The Court also suggested that pretrial publicity might not have been so prevalent as to undermine the possibility of a fair trial. Here the Court turned to Judge Learned Hand's test, which he had applied to the trial of communist leaders in *Dennis v. United States,* 183 F.2d 201, 212 (CA2 1950), aff'd, 341 U.S. 494 (1951): whether "the gravity of the 'evil,' discounted by its improbability, justifies such invasion of free speech as is necessary to avoid the danger." Chief Justice Burger concluded that the gravity of the evil—at worst a mistrial or the reversal of a conviction because of publicity—did not justify trampling on the First Amendment, especially when the probability of the evil was remote and there were other, less drastic methods of avoiding it. This test implied that under some circumstances a gag rule might be constitutional.

Most of the concurring justices opposed this implication. As Justice White noted, "There is grave doubt in my mind whether orders with respect to the press such as were entered in this case would ever be justifiable."

See B. Schmidt, "Nebraska Press Association: An Extension of Freedom and Contraction of Theory," *Stanford Law Review* 29 (1977): 431.

Planned Parenthood of Central Missouri v. Danforth

428 U.S. 52 (1976)
Decided: July 1, 1976
Vote: Multiple
Opinion of the Court: Blackmun
Concurring opinion: Stewart (Powell)
Dissenting opinion: B. White (Burger, Rehnquist)
Dissenting opinion: Stevens

This case was a "logical and anticipated corollary" to ***Roe v. Wade,*** 410 U.S. 113 (1973), and ***Doe v. Bolton,*** 410 U.S. 179 (1973), because it addressed issues that had been postponed in the earlier cases. The plaintiffs were two Missouri physicians who performed abortions. They challenged several provisions of a 1974 Missouri act passed in response to *Roe* and *Doe.* Section 2(2) defined viability as the point at which a fetus could survive indefinitely by artificial or natural means outside the womb. Section 3(2) required a woman obtaining an abortion within the first twelve weeks of pregnancy to sign a consent form indicating that she understood the nature of the procedure to be used and was not coerced. Section 3(3) required a married woman to obtain the written consent of her spouse before she could have an abortion unless her life was in danger. Section 3(4) required an unmarried woman under eighteen to obtain her parents' written consent before receiving an abortion. Section 6(1) made physicians liable for manslaughter if they did not take professional care to preserve the fetus's life. Section 7 made any fetus that survived an attempted abortion a ward of the state without regard to the parents' interest in keeping it. Section 9 prohibited the process of saline amniocentesis after the first twelve weeks of pregnancy. Sections 10 and 11 outlined procedures for record keeping regarding abortions. This litigation commenced three days after the bill became effective.

The plaintiffs argued that Section 2(2) contradicted the Supreme Court's definition of viability in *Roe,* because it did not refer to gestational time period, contained no mention of "trimesters," and included the word "indefinitely." The plaintiffs felt that *Roe* required legislatures to fix a specific time for viability to avoid vagueness.

The decision of the Court was enormously complex. Justice Blackmun wrote a majority opinion, which Justices Brennan and Marshall joined. Justice Stewart filed a concurring opinion in which Justice Powell joined, leading to a five-man majority. Justice White, joined by Chief Justice Burger and Justice Rehnquist, filed an opinion concurring in part and dissenting in part. Justice Stevens also filed an opinion concurring in part and dissenting in part.

The Court held that the definition of viability in Section 2(2) did not contradict its earlier discussion of viability in *Roe.* Section 2(2) was faithful to the Court's intention in *Roe* of making viability a flexible term, that did not impose legislative determinations on the medical decision of when a fetus was viable. In upholding this section of the law, the Court reaffirmed its assertion "in *Roe* that viability was a matter of medical judgment, skill, and technical ability." In this sense, the Court upheld the statute but left interpretation of it the hands of physicians.

The plaintiffs argued Section 3(2) was unduly burdensome on a woman's exercise of her privacy right under *Roe* because it placed unnecessary regulations in the way of an abortion. The Court disagreed and found Section 3(2) to be just a medical consent provision, such as might be applied to any surgical procedure.

The plaintiffs said Section 3(3), requiring a woman to obtain her husband's consent to an abortion, was an undue burden on a woman's privacy interest. The Court had postponed the resolution of this issue in *Roe.* The Court held 6–3 that Section 3(3) was unconstitutional. The Court agreed with the dissenting member of the three-judge district court, who had said the state cannot "delegate to a spouse a veto power which the state itself is absolutely and totally prohibited from exercising during the first trimester of pregnancy." The Court understood Missouri's interest in fostering mutuality of decision making within the marriage, but believed that granting the husband an arbitrary veto power over the wife's decision could not further the end of creating trust and harmony in marriage. Furthermore, when husband and wife disagreed on this issue, the will of only one could prevail, and, because the woman was the one carrying the fetus, the Court believed her will should be given deference.

The plaintiffs challenged Section 3(4), requiring minors to obtain parental consent to have an abortion, as unduly burdensome. The state argued that Section 3(4) was justified by the interest in protecting the welfare of children, and that Missouri law was full of restrictions on minors' freedoms in that interest, but the plaintiffs argued that Missouri required parental consent for no other surgery. A 5–4 majority agreed with the dissenting district judge's observation that the state obviously could not empower parents to force their daughter to have an abortion and that he did not see why the state should be able to empower them to prevent her from having one. The Court noted that constitutional rights do not magically spring into existence when a person turns eighteen, but apply to children as well. Furthermore, the Court felt the same arguments against giving a third party an arbitrary veto over the woman's decision that were relevant to Section 3(3) were also relevant to Section 3(4). The Court also noted that not every woman under eighteen seeking an abortion would possess the requisite maturity to give informed consent. Section 3(4), however was a blanket provision that assumed that no woman under eighteen would be able to give such consent, and therefore, Section 3(4) was unconstitutional.

The plaintiffs argued that Section 9, prohibiting the use of saline amniocentesis after the first trimester, had the effect of precluding virtually all abortions after the first trimester, because this procedure was the dominant method for obtaining abortions. The state argued that alternative methods were available, although they were not yet widely in use. Furthermore, the state argued that under *Roe,* a state was permitted to adopt reasonable regulations on the way abortions are performed after the first trimester in the interest of protecting the mother's health. The Court framed the issue as whether prohibiting saline amniocentesis after the first trimester was reasonably related to this interest. The plaintiffs' evidence suggested that the procedure was actually safer for women than natural childbirth. Although the district court had found that prostaglandin injection and "mechanical means of inducing abortion" were safer than amniocentesis, and therefore that it was reasonable for the state to prohibit amniocentesis as a health measure for the mother, that court had overlooked certain facts. First, prostaglandin was not widely in use, meaning that it was unlikely that physicians in Missouri knew about it. Second, amniocentesis was widely accepted and understood and used in 68 percent to 80 percent of all abortions. Third, the Missouri legislature had failed to prohibit the use of two alternative means of abortion that were substantially more dangerous to a woman than amniocentesis. With those facts in mind, the Court concluded, 6–3, that the outright ban on amniocentesis after the first trimester failed as a regulation reasonably related to a woman's health.

The plaintiffs argued that at least with respect to the first trimester, the record-keeping requirements of Sections 10 and 11 were impermissible because they could be used to place barriers in the way of a woman obtaining an abortion through the intimidating level of detail and disclosure required. The Court found merit in this argument, but held that as long as the requirement was used reasonably and in keeping with the Court's decision, and the privacy of the patient was guarded, that the requirement was not offensive to the Constitution.

The plaintiffs argued that Section 6(1)'s confusing requirement that all physicians performing abortions exercise the same level of professional care to preserve the life of the fetus as they would if the fetus were intended to be born was intended to preclude all abortions. The Court agreed and found that section unconstitutional.

Justice White dissented with respect to the Court's decision on four of the provisions. He believed the Court erred in its conclusion on Section 3(3) that because the state could not prohibit an abortion, it could not "delegate" that right to a husband. In White's view, all Section 3(3) did was to give due consideration to the husband's constitutional interest in the life of the fetus. White also believed that Section 3(4) did nothing more than ensure that minor children received the counsel of their parents before making a difficult and irreversible decision. He saw nothing unconstitutional in such a rule. With regard to Section 9, according to White, the record showed that the Missouri legislature had found amniocentesis to be substantially more dangerous than prostaglandin, based on substantial evidence. He said the majority was wrong in ignoring Missouri's fact-finding on this issue to determine that Section 9 was not reasonably health-related. Finally, White argued that the obvious meaning of Section 6(1) was to require physicians to exercise professional skill in preserving the lives of fetuses only after the fetuses have become viable, not at any stage of pregnancy. According to White, this requirement was completely permissible under *Roe.*

See David J. Garrow, *Liberty and Sexuality: The Right to Privacy and the Making of* Roe v. Wade (New York: Macmillan, 1994).

Gregg v. Georgia

428 U.S. 153 (1976)
Decided: July 2, 1976
Vote: 7 (Burger, Stewart, B. White, Blackmun, Powell, Rehnquist, Stevens)
2 (Brennan, T. Marshall)
Judgment of the Court: Stewart
Concurring opinion: B. White (Burger, Rehnquist)
Concurring in judgment: Blackmun
Dissenting opinion: Brennan
Dissenting opinion: T. Marshall

In ***Furman v. Georgia,*** 408 U.S. 238 (1972), the Court struck down all of the nation's death penalty statutes. The Court said that because the statutes failed to provide a coherent standard for imposition of the penalty, they constituted cruel and unusual punishment. In *Gregg v. Georgia* and two companion cases, ***Proffitt v. Florida,*** 428 U.S. 242 (1976), and ***Jurek v. Texas,*** 428 U.S. 262 (1976), the Court upheld death penalties imposed under new statutes in the three states involved. The facts of Gregg's case were almost mundane in their brutality. While hitchhiking in Florida, Troy Gregg and Floyd Allen were offered a ride by Fred Simmons and Bob Moore. Simmons and Moore later picked up another hitchhiker, Dennis Weaver, who was dropped off in Atlanta. When the bodies of Simmons and Moore were found by the side of the road, Weaver heard this news and contacted police, giving them a description of the car Simmons and Moore had been driving. Police found Gregg and Allen in the car and the murder weapon in Gregg's pocket. Allen later testified that Gregg had shot and robbed both men. Gregg was convicted of armed robbery and murder and sentenced to death. The Supreme Court was once again asked to determine whether a state capital sentencing procedure passed constitutional muster.

Justice Stewart, who had voted with the majority in *Furman,* concluded that the death penalty did not necessarily violate either the Eighth Amendment's prohibition on cruel and unusual punishment or the due process and equal protection provisions of the Fourteenth Amendment. Stewart noted that the Eighth Amendment "has been interpreted in a flexible and dynamic manner." Such interpretations had led to decisions striking down punishments that might not have been considered cruel in 1791, but they also meant that the death penalty was not *per se* cruel. Stewart gave great deference the state legislatures, saying that "in assessing a punishment selected by a democratically elected legislature against the constitutional measure, we presume its validity. We may not require the legislature to select the least severe penalty possible so long as the penalty selected is not cruelly inhumane or disproportionate to the crime involved." Noting that "the imposition of the death penalty for the crime of murder has a long history of acceptance both in the United States and in England," Stewart tapped into the politics of the death penalty in the United States. He rejected the notion that the death penalty offended modern sensibilities, stating that "the legislatures of at least 35 States have enacted new statutes that provide for the death penalty for at least some crimes that result in the death of another person." The new statutes were a response to the Court's decision in *Furman* "(i) by specifying the factors to be weighed and the procedures to be followed in deciding when to impose a capital sentence, or (ii) by making the death penalty mandatory for specified crimes." Finally, Stewart asserted that capital punishment was not "disproportionate to the crime" when the crime was "murder . . . when a life has been taken deliberately by the offender." Rather, he concluded, "It is an extreme sanction, suitable to the most extreme of crimes."

Stewart pointed out that in *Furman* the Court had struck down death penalties that were capricious and inconsistently applied. He said, "*Furman* mandates that where discretion is afforded a sentencing body on a matter so grave as the determination of whether a human life should be taken or spared, that discretion must be suitably directed and limited so as to minimize the risk of wholly arbitrary and capricious action." After discussing the model penal code and various statutory schemes for death penalties, Stewart wrote, "In summary, the concerns expressed in *Furman* that the penalty of death not be imposed in an arbitrary or capricious manner can be met by a carefully drafted statute that ensures that the sentencing authority is given adequate information and guidance. As a general proposition these concerns are best met by a system that provides for a bifurcated proceeding at which the sentencing authority is apprised of the information relevant to the imposition of sentence and provided with standards to guide its use of the information."

After this analysis, Stewart turned to the Georgia statute and found it passed constitutional muster. His discussion illustrates the new standards the Court sought to apply:

These procedures require the jury to consider the circumstances of the crime and the criminal before it recommends sentence. No longer can a Georgia jury do as Furman's jury did: reach a finding of the defendant's guilt and then, without guidance or direction, decide whether he should live or die. Instead, the jury's attention is directed to the specific circumstances of the crime: Was it committed in the course of another capital felony? Was it committed for money? Was it committed upon a peace officer or judicial officer? Was it committed in a particularly heinous way or in a manner that endangered the lives of many persons? In addition, the jury's attention is focused on the characteristics of the person who committed the crime: Does he have a record of prior convictions for capital offenses? Are there any special facts about this defendant that mitigate against imposing capital punishment? . . . As a result, while some jury discretion still exists, "the discretion to be exercised is controlled by clear and objective standards so as to produce non-discriminatory application."

The Court upheld Gregg's capital sentence and the laws under which he was sentenced. Particularly important in this case, and the cases from Texas and Florida, was the fact that the sentencing phase was separate from the trial, which allowed the jury to hear evidence at sentencing that might not have been admissible during the trial. The statutes required certain aggravating circumstances that would lead to the death penalty. The Georgia statute, for example, considered such circumstances to exist when the murder was: "outrageously or wantonly vile, horrible or inhuman in that it involved torture, depravity of mind, or an aggravated battery to the victim."

In dissent, Justices Brennan and Marshall argued that there was no evidence that the death penalty deterred crime or that it had any purpose other than retribution or vengeance. They pointed out that the new standards did not take into account the unfairness and irrationality created by plea bargaining, prosecutorial discretion, the poverty (or wealth) of the defendant, and racial prejudice. Nor did the majority consider the corrosive effects of the use of the death penalty on society. The dissent asked that human dignity be given some consideration.

See Jordan Steiker, "The Long Road Up From Barbarism: Thurgood Marshall and the Death Penalty," *Texas Law Review* 71 (1993): 1131; and Scott Burris, "Death and a Rational Justice: A Conversation on the Capital Jurisprudence of Justice John Paul Stevens," *Yale Law Journal* 96 (1987): 521

Proffitt v. Florida

428 U.S. 242 (1976)
Decided: July 2, 1976
Vote: 7 (Burger, Stewart, B. White, Blackmun, Powell, Rehnquist, Stevens)
2 (Brennan, T. Marshall)
Judgment of the Court: Powell
Opinion concurring in judgment: B. White (Burger, Rehnquist)
Opinion concurring in judgment: Blackmun
Dissenting opinion: Brennan
Dissenting opinion: T. Marshall

Charles William Proffitt was convicted of murder and sentenced to death. In light of the Court's decision in ***Furman v. Georgia,*** 408 U.S. 238 (1972), Florida had enacted a death penalty statute under which the judge was required to consider eight statutory mitigating and aggravating circumstances before deciding on the punishment. "In his written findings supporting the sentence, the judge found as aggravating circumstances that (1) the murder was premeditated and occurred in the course of a felony (burglary); (2) the petitioner has the propensity to commit murder; (3) the murder was especially heinous, atrocious, and cruel; and (4) the petitioner knowingly, through his intentional act, created a great risk of serious bodily harm and death to many persons." The judge found that none of the statutory mitigating circumstances existed, and the Supreme Court of Florida affirmed the death sentence.

The Supreme Court agreed to hear the case to consider whether the imposition of the death sentence constituted cruel and unusual punishment in violation of the Eighth and Fourteenth Amendments. Profitt argued that imposition of the death penalty is cruel and unusual punishment under any circumstances, but, the same day it announced its decision in this case, the Court flatly rejected that argument in ***Gregg v. Georgia,*** 428 U.S. 153 (1976). Profitt also argued that the statutory aggravating circumstances, which asked the judge to consider whether the crime was especially heinous or cruel or whether the defendant intentionally created a great risk of death to many people, was vague and gave the judge inadequate guidance to make a principled decision. The Court disagreed, noting that under the Florida law "the trial judge must justify the imposition of a death sentence with written findings" and that the law proved for "meaningful appellate review" and mandatory review by the Florida Supreme Court. The Court also pointed out that under the Florida system the judge, not the jury, imposed the death penalty. In the past the Court had expressed preference for jury impositions of the death penalty, but said here that "it has never suggested that jury sentencing is constitutionally required. And it would appear that judicial sentencing should lead, if anything, to even greater consistency in the imposition at the trial court level of capital punishment, since a trial judge is more experienced in sentencing than a jury, and therefore is better able to impose sentences similar to those imposed in analogous cases." The Court stuck to its position that the death penalty is not cruel and unusual punishment, held that the provisions on aggravating and mitigating circumstances were not vague, and that a state could empower a judge, rather than a jury, to impose a death sentence.

Jurek v. Texas

428 U.S. 262 (1976)
Decided: July 2, 1976
Vote: 7 (Burger, Stewart, B. White, Blackmun, Powell, Rehnquist, Stevens)
2 (Brennan, T. Marshall)
Judgment of the Court: Stevens
Concurring in judgment: Burger
Concurring in judgment: B. White (Burger, Rehnquist)
Concurring in judgment: Blackmun
Dissenting opinion: Brennan
Dissenting opinion: T. Marshall

This case was decided the same day as ***Proffitt v. Florida,*** 428 U.S. 242 (1976), and involved a similar issue. At issue in *Jurek* were procedures governing the death sentence in Texas, following the Court's decision in ***Furman v. Georgia,*** 408 U.S. 238 (1972). *Furman* required states to guide the jury's discretion in imposing the death penalty by establishing certain aggravating circumstances that would distinguish cases that receive the penalty from those that do not. Texas limited the possibility of imposing the death penalty to five types of murder. If the murder was one of those five types, the jury was to consider the following three questions: (1) whether the defendant had acted deliberately and with reasonable knowledge that his actions would result in death; (2) whether the defendant would probably commit further acts of violence that made him a continuing threat to society; and (3) if defendant was provoked to act, whether his response was disproportionate to the provocation. If the jury answered yes to all three questions, the death penalty was imposed.

Jerry Lane Jurek, age twenty-two, had been drinking all afternoon when he spotted ten-year-old Wendy Adams. He kidnapped Adams, took her to the river, raped her, and strangled her. He was convicted of one of the five types of murder susceptible of the death penalty under Texas's new scheme, and the jury answered yes to all three questions and sentenced Jurek to death.

Jurek appealed to the Supreme Court, which held that Texas's new death-sentencing scheme passed the *Furman* test. The narrowing of the class of murders for which the death penalty could be applied was equivalent to creating a statutory list of aggravating circumstances. Because the jury would have to find beyond a reasonable doubt that the murder was one of the specified kinds before the sentencing question arose, the jury would essentially have found one of the aggravating circumstances. Furthermore, the Texas scheme comported with *Furman's* requirement that the jury consider any mitigating circumstances. The Texas Court of Criminal Appeals had interpreted the second question to the jury—whether the defendant was likely to commit another violent act—as an invitation to consider mitigating circumstances. Jurek attacked the second question as vague and for inviting jurors to give reign to their prejudices, but the Court disagreed.

Woodson v. North Carolina

428 U.S. 280 (1976)
Decided: July 2, 1976
Vote: 5 (Brennan, Stewart, T. Marshall, Powell, Stevens)
4 (Burger, B. White, Blackmun, Rehnquist)
Judgment of the Court: Stewart
Opinion concurring in judgment: Brennan
Opinion concurring in judgment: T. Marshall
Dissenting opinion: B. White (Burger, Rehnquist)
Dissenting opinion: Blackmun
Dissenting opinion: Rehnquist

After the Court decided in ***Furman v. Georgia,*** 408 U.S. 238 (1972), that states could not give juries unlimited discretion on whether to impose the death penalty for certain crimes, North Carolina amended its policy to make the death sentence mandatory for first-degree murder. James Tyrone Woodson was sentenced to death under this revised system, and the North Carolina Supreme Court affirmed.

The U.S. Supreme Court held that Woodson's death sentence was invalid because North Carolina's mandatory capital punishment for first-degree murder violated the Eighth and Fourteenth Amendments. Even with the additional limits on jury discretion, the Eighth Amendment compels states to consider the individual character of the defendant's crime to determine whether the defendant is entitled to clemency.

Woodson was a co-conspirator in a robbery. On the day of the crime, he was drunk. His co-conspirator, Luby Waxton, beat him and threatened to kill him in an effort to make him sober up and participate in the robbery. Woodson joined his three partners in their car and stayed there, along with the fourth man, while Waxton and Leonard Tucker went into a store. During the course of the robbery, either Waxton or Tucker shot and killed two people. At Woodson's trial, Waxton and Tucker testified to these facts, having agreed to plead guilty to lesser offenses. Woodson, however, argued that he had been compelled to join the robbery and refused to plead guilty. His conviction for first-degree felony murder mandated the death penalty.

The Court began its opinion by saying that the Eighth Amendment "stands to assure that the State's power to punish is 'exercised within civilized standards.' " The limits of civilized standards can be discovered through changing social values reflected in tradition, legislative enactments, and jury determinations. History has shown that juries react negatively to the harshness of mandatory death sentences. Originally, the state legislatures responded to this dissatisfaction by limiting the number of crimes that would receive mandatory death sentences, but juries often refused to return a guilty verdict when they felt that death should not be imposed in a certain case. Even after legislatures further limited the class of death penalty cases by dividing murder into degrees and reserving death for the first degree, juries still felt that some first-degree murder cases did not warrant death and refused to find the defendant guilty. States gradually began to replace mandatory sentencing with discretionary sentencing. The legislatures' response to jury aversion to the mandatory death sentence and juries' tendency not to sentence defendants to death in more than a minority of capital offense cases suggest that the mandatory sentence is not within "civilized standards," as measured by American social values. The Court held that a death penalty statute that gives a jury no discretion to grant clemency violates the Eighth Amendment.

In addition, because of North Carolina's mandatory death sentence system, juries in effect retained their unlimited discretion by refusing to convict if they did not believe the death penalty was appropriate. The new policy simply shifted the timing of the jury's exercise of its discretion from the sentencing phase to the guilt-or-innocence phase. To correct this anomaly, North Carolina needed to retain jury discretion in sentencing, but provide juries with a set of guidelines to ensure that the death was not imposed arbitrarily or prejudicially.

Justice Brennan concurred in the judgment for the reasons he stated in ***Gregg v. Georgia,*** 428 U.S. 153 (1976), and the death penalty is *per se* unconstitutional.

Justice Marshall concurred in the judgment, but stated that in his view the death penalty was always cruel and unusual punishment and therefore unconstitutional under the Eighth Amendment.

Justice Rehnquist's dissent suggested that the Eighth Amendment forbade only those punishments that were considered cruel and unusual at the time of its adoption. He also disagreed with the majority's characterization of the history of evolving standards of decency that place mandatory death sentences beyond the pale of civilized society.

See Hugo Adam Bedau, ed. *The Death Penalty in America,* 3d ed. (New York: Oxford University Press, 1982).

South Dakota v. Opperman

428 U.S. 364 (1976)
Decided: July 6, 1976
Vote: 5 (Burger, Blackmun, Powell, Rehnquist, Stevens)
4 (Brennan, Stewart, B. White, T. Marshall)
Opinion of the Court: Burger
Concurring opinion: Powell
Dissenting opinion: B. White
Dissenting opinion: T. Marshall (Brennan, Stewart)

This case considered the Fourth Amendment implications of police making an inventory of the contents of a car when it is in police custody. Under the Fourth Amendment, Americans have a right to be free in their persons and property from unreasonable searches and seizures by the police. Opperman's car was impounded for multiple parking violations. The police in his South Dakota town made a practice of listing the contents of impounded cars to secure the owner's possessions and to protect officers from accusations of theft from vehicles in police custody. When Opperman's car was impounded, police could clearly see valuables through the windshield. During the inventory, officers found a small amount of marijuana—less than an ounce—in the car. Opperman was tried for possession of marijuana, and the marijuana discovered during the inventory was admitted into evidence over Opperman's objection. He was convicted.

When the Supreme Court considered his appeal, it held that evidence discovered during an inventory search of a car is not covered by the exclusionary rule because the inventory is not an unreasonable search under the Fourth Amendment. The Court noted that a person's expectation of privacy within his car is less than it would be in his home or office. Furthermore, the search was motivated by a desire to protect Opperman's property, not to search for contraband.

Justice Marshall's dissent pointed out that the marijuana was discovered in a locked glove compartment. In his view, the "reasonableness" of the inventory search depended on a balancing of Opperman's privacy rights with the government's interest in making an inventory of the car contents without obtaining a search warrant or the owner's consent to open the glove box. Marshall felt that Opperman had a substantial privacy interest in his locked glove box and that any valuables in the compartment were not likely to disappear during the time it took the government to obtain his consent or a warrant. According to Marshall, the search was unreasonable.

Stone v. Powell

428 U.S. 465 (1976)
Decided: July 6, 1976
Vote: 6 (Burger, Stewart, Blackmun, Powell, Rehnquist, Stevens)
3 (Brennan, B. White, T. Marshall)
Opinion of the Court: Powell
Concurring opinion: Burger
Dissenting opinion: Brennan (T. Marshall)
Dissenting opinion: B. White

Stone v. Powell was consolidated with *Wolff v. Rice.* Both cases raised questions about the fairness of trials in state courts and the rights of defendants, convicted in state courts, to seek a writ of habeas corpus to raise constitutional claims in federal courts.

During the robbery of a California liquor store, Lloyd Powell accidentally killed the owner. He fled the scene but was arrested in Nevada for violating a vagrancy law. A federal appeals court found the vagrancy law "unconstitutionally vague," which made Powell's arrest illegal, but, while he was under arrest in Nevada, police found the gun he used in the robbery, and this evidence was used to convict him of second-degree murder in California. David Rice was convicted in Nebraska of making a bomb that later killed a policeman. The conviction was a based on a search of his apartment, but a federal court determined that the search warrant was invalid, and therefore the evidence should have been excluded at his state murder trial. The federal courts in California and Nebraska granted Powell's and Rice's petitions for a writ of habeas corpus. Wardens from the prisons in which Powell and Rice were incarcerated appealed to the Supreme Court.

In ***Brown v. Allen,*** 344 U.S. 443 (1953), the Supreme Court held that under federal law (Title 28, Section 2254) a state prisoner was entitled to a writ of habeas corpus and a hearing in a federal court to have a "full reconsideration" of "constitutional claims" arising from a state trial. In *Kauffman v. United States,* 394 U.S. 217 (1969), the Court further held that "search-and-seizure claims are cognizable" by federal courts under Section 2255. "The Court noted that 'the federal habeas remedy extends to state prisoners alleging that unconstitutionally obtained evidence was admitted against them at trial.' " The state of the law was that the "scope of federal habeas corpus rests on the view that the effectuation of the Fourth Amendment, as applied to the States through the Fourteenth Amendment, requires the granting of habeas corpus relief when a prisoner has been convicted in state court on the basis of evidence obtained in an illegal search or seizure."

Here, the Court changed direction. Justice Powell balanced the need for efficient justice against the lack of evidence that the exclusionary rule actually prevented police misconduct. He noted, as all critics of the exclusionary rule have, that the rule resulted in freeing the guilty because the police made an error. He did not reject the rule entirely, but asserted that, once a search was fairly challenged in state court, the prisoner could not relitigate it in federal court through habeas corpus. Powell wrote:

In sum, we conclude that where the State has provided an opportunity for full and fair litigation of a Fourth Amendment claim, a state prisoner may not be granted federal habeas corpus relief on the ground that evidence obtained in an unconstitutional search or seizure was introduced at his trial. In this context the contribution of the exclusionary rule, if any, to the effectuation of the Fourth Amendment is minimal, and the substantial societal costs of application of the rule persist with special force.

In dissent, Justice Brennan noted that this decision was the first in which the Court denied the right of state prisoners to vindicate their federal rights in federal courts. He also noted that these rights had been supported by legislation and that it was up to Congress, not the Court, to revise this legislation. He bitterly—and prophetically—concluded that

as a practical matter the only result of today's holding will be that denials by the state courts of claims by state prisoners of violations of their Fourth Amendment rights will go unreviewed by a federal tribunal. I fear that the same treatment ultimately will be accorded state prisoners' claims of violations of other constitutional rights; thus the potential ramifications of this case for federal habeas jurisdiction generally are ominous.

See Philip Halpern, "Federal Habeas Corpus and the Mapp Exclusionary Rule After *Stone v. Powell*," *Columbia Law Review* 82 (1982): 1; and Kevin J. O'Brien, "Federal Habeas Review of Ineffective Assistance Claims: A Conflict Between *Strickland* and *Stone*?" *University of Chicago Law Review* 53 (1986): 183.

United States v. Martinez-Fuerte

428 U.S. 543 (1976)
Decided: July 6, 1976
Vote: 7 (Burger, Stewart, B. White, Blackmun, Powell, Rehnquist, Stevens)
2 (Brennan, T. Marshall)
Opinion of the Court: Powell
Dissenting opinion: Brennan (T. Marshall)

Amado Martinez-Fuerte was arrested at a border patrol checkpoint near San Clemente, California, sixty-six miles north of the U.S.-Mexico border along Interstate 5. In his car were two women who "were illegal Mexican aliens who had entered the United States at the San Ysidro port of entry by using false papers." Martinez-Fuerte met them in San Diego with the purpose of taking them north. He was convicted of trafficking in illegal aliens and appealed his conviction on the grounds that the checkpoint search violated his Fourth Amendment rights. The Ninth Circuit Court reversed his conviction, and the government appealed to the Supreme Court. This case was consolidated with decisions from the Fifth Circuit, which had upheld checkpoint searches.

The Court resolved the question in favor of the Fifth Circuit's view. Routine traffic checkpoints in which vehicles are stopped and searched for illegal aliens without any prior evidence that the vehicle contains illegal aliens are permissible under the Fourth Amendment. Justice Powell wrote, "While the need to make routine checkpoint stops is great, the consequent intrusion on Fourth Amendment interests is quite limited. The stop does intrude to a limited extent on motorists' right to 'free passage without interruption,' " but the stops involve "only a brief detention of travelers" while they are asked to respond to a few questions and produce documents "evidencing a right to be in the United States." In these stops no one was physically searched and a "visual inspection of the vehicle is limited to what can be seen without a search." The Court accepted the notion that these stops and the subsequent questions might involve what two decades later would be known as ethnic profiling. "Thus, even if it be assumed that such referrals are made largely on the basis of apparent Mexican ancestry, we perceive no constitutional violation," Powell wrote. "As the intrusion here is sufficiently minimal that no particularized reason need exist to justify it, we think it follows that the Border Patrol officers must have wide discretion in selecting the motorists to be diverted for the brief questioning involved."

Justice Brennan's dissent criticized the Court for its "continuing evisceration of Fourth Amendment protections against unreasonable searches and seizures." In his view, *Martinez-Fuerte* signified an abandonment of any objective standards for the seizure of persons because the decision did not require border patrol officers to have any objective basis for suspecting a car carried illegal aliens before they stopped it.

See Fran Small, "Michigan Department of *State Police v. Sitz*: Has the Supreme Court Abdicated Its Role as the Protector of the Right to be Let Alone?" *New England Law Review* 26 (1991): 583.

Estelle v. Gamble

429 U.S. 97 (1976)
Decided: November 30, 1976
Vote: 8 (Burger, Brennan, Stewart, B. White, T. Marshall, Blackmun, Powell, Rehnquist)
1 (Stevens)
Opinion of the Court: T. Marshall
Concurring in judgment: Blackmun
Dissenting opinion: Stevens

This case was brought pro se (without an attorney) by a Texas inmate, J. W. Gamble, against W. J. Estelle Jr., director of the Department of Corrections, and others. Gamble claimed he was subjected to cruel and unusual punishment in violation of the Eight Amendment because the prison had not provided him adequate medical care. The district court dismissed the claim, and the court of appeals reversed. As a result of this history, the Supreme Court had to decide the case solely on Gamble's complaint. Justice Marshall noted, "Because the complaint was dismissed for failure to state a claim, we must take as true its handwritten, pro se allegations." In the end, however, Gamble's unchallenged account of his medical care was not enough to gain him a trial on the merits of his claim.

Gamble injured his back doing prison work and sought medical treatment. The warden, who was also a named defendant, arranged for him to see a physician, and Gamble saw this doctor and two others at least seventeen times in a three-month period. During much of this period Gamble received various drugs for pain and muscle relaxants, and he was excused from prison work. Gamble felt the physician's treatment was substandard; for example, the physician refused to X-ray Gamble's spine. Gamble sued the prison, alleging that its indifference to his condition amounted to cruel and unusual punishment.

The Supreme Court held "that deliberate indifference to serious medical needs of prisoners constitutes the 'unnecessary and wanton infliction of pain,' . . . proscribed by the Eighth Amendment. This is true whether the indifference is manifested by prison doctors in their response to the prisoner's needs or by prison guards in intentionally denying or delaying access to medical care or intentionally interfering with the treatment once prescribed." This standard, however, did not mean that any prisoner who was unhappy with his medical treatment had an Eighth Amendment claim. Justice Marshall noted that "a complaint that a physician has been negligent in diagnosing or treating a medical condition does not state a valid claim of medical mistreatment under the Eighth Amendment. Medical malpractice does not become a constitutional violation merely because the victim is a prisoner. In order to state a cognizable claim, a prisoner must allege acts or omissions sufficiently harmful to evidence deliberate indifference to serious medical needs. It is only such indifference that can offend 'evolving standards of decency' in violation of the Eighth Amendment." Under this analysis the Court rejected Gamble's claim.

See Philip M. Genty, "Confusing Punishment with Custodial Care: The Troublesome Legacy of *Estelle v. Gamble*," *Vermont Law Review* 21 (1996): 379.

Craig v. Boren

429 U.S. 190 (1976)
Decided: December 20, 1976
Vote: 7 (Brennan, Stewart, B. White, T. Marshall, Blackmun, Powell, Stevens)
2 (Burger, Rehnquist)
Opinion of the Court: Brennan
Concurring opinion: Powell
Concurring opinion: Stevens
Concurring opinion: Blackmun
Concurring in judgment: Stewart
Dissenting opinion: Burger
Dissenting opinion: Rehnquist

An Oklahoma law prohibited the sale of 3.2 percent beer to men under age twenty-one and women under eighteen. Two men between the ages of eighteen and twenty-one, Curtis Craig and Mark Walker, challenged the law, along with Carolyn Whitener, a licensed vender of 3.2 beer. A three-judge panel denied relief, and the Supreme Court noted probable jurisdiction. By the time the case reached the Court, however, Craig and Walker were both over twenty-one and therefore lacked standing, but the Court found that Whitener could challenge the law.

Oklahoma argued that the law was rational because men in this age group were ten times more likely than women to be arrested for either drunk driving or public intoxication and eighteen times more likely to be arrested for driving while under the influence of alcohol. Even so, only 2 percent of the total drunk driving arrests were for males in this age group.

In striking down the law, Justice Brennan reaffirmed, based on earlier cases, especially ***Reed v. Reed,*** 404 U.S. 71 (1971), that "to withstand constitutional challenge . . . classifications by gender must serve important governmental objectives and must be substantially related to achievement of those objectives." "Clearly, the protection of public health and safety represents an important function of state and local governments," Brennan wrote, but Oklahoma's "statistics in our view cannot support the conclusion that the gender-based distinction closely serves to achieve that objective and therefore the distinction cannot under *Reed* withstand equal protection challenge." He also pointed out that most arrests for driving while intoxicated were for people older than twenty-one and that a connection between the relatively weak 3.2 beer and drunk driving had yet to demonstrated.

In reaching this conclusion, the Court set out what became its test for gender discrimination—intermediate scrutiny—a term Justice Rehnquist used in his dissent. Neither Rehnquist nor Chief Justice Burger, who also dissented, felt that the words of the Constitution justified subjecting gender classifications to a stricter review than any other kind of classification.

See Katherine Franke, "The Central Mistake of Sex Discrimination Law: The Disaggregation of Sex From Gender," *University of Pennsylvania Law Review* 144 (1995): 1.

Arlington Heights v. Metropolitan Housing Development Corp.

429 U.S. 252 (1977)
Decided: January 11, 1977
Vote: 5 (Burger, Stewart, Blackmun, Powell, Rehnquist)
3 (Brennan, B. White, T. Marshall)
Opinion of the Court: Powell
Dissenting opinion: B. White
Dissenting opinion: T. Marshall (Brennan)
Did not participate: Stevens

The Village of Arlington Heights, a suburb of Chicago, Illinois, was a predominately white community zoned mainly for single-family dwellings. A local religious order wanted to devote some of its land to low- and moderate-income housing and engaged the services of Metropolitan Housing Development Corporation (MHDC), a nonprofit organization. The religious order sold the land to MHDC for $300,000, contingent on MHDC's obtaining federal funding and Arlington Heights' agreeing to rezone the land for multiple-family dwellings. The village held a hearing and denied the zoning application on grounds that approval would result in property depreciation, that the area around the land was all single-family dwellings, and that multiple-family dwellings were usually located as a buffer zone between commercial or manufacturing districts and single-family dwelling districts.

MHDC and individual petitioners sued Arlington Heights in district court, challenging the village's decision as racially motivated and a violation of the Fourteenth Amendment's Equal Protection Clause and the Fair Housing Act of 1968. On appeal, the court of appeals agreed with the district court that the primary motive behind the village's decision was the integrity of the zoning plan, but focused on the impact of the decision in its historical context, noting that the village was highly segregated. Finding no compelling interests by the village for this disparity, the court of appeals concluded the zoning decision violated the Fourteenth Amendment's Equal Protection Clause. The Supreme Court held that Arlington Heights' decision lacked an intent or purpose to discriminate on the basis of race, thereby ending the constitutional inquiry, but, because the argument for the violation of the Fair Housing Act of 1968 had not been heard by the court of appeals, the Court remanded the case for further proceedings.

The Supreme Court first examined Arlington Heights' argument challenging MHDC's standing to sue and found that MHDC and at least one of the individual petitioners had standing. Then, analyzing the Fourteenth Amendment argument, the Court maintained that even if the village's decision had a racial impact, that was not enough to offend the Fourteenth Amendment; rather, the petitioners had to show that racial discrimination was a motivating factor in the unfavorable zoning decision. The Court found that the MHDC and the individual petitioners failed to show the village's racially discriminatory intent. The Court accepted as evidence of this the historical background of the decision by the village, the traditional decision-making process within Arlington Heights, and contemporary statements of the decision makers.

See Frederic S. Schwartz, "The Fair Housing Act and 'Discriminatory Effect': A New Perspective," *Nova Law Review* 11 (1987): 71.

Whalen v. Roe

429 U.S. 589 (1977)
Decided: February 22, 1977
Vote: 9 (Burger, Brennan, Stewart, B. White, T. Marshall, Blackmun, Powell, Rehnquist, Stevens)
0
Opinion of the Court: Stevens
Concurring opinion: Brennan
Concurring opinion: Stewart

In 1972 the New York legislature enacted a law that required doctors to file a form with the Health Department reporting the patient's name and address for every prescription of certain dangerous drugs, labeled "Schedule II" drugs. Patients and doctors sued. The district court held that the statute violated Fourteenth Amendment interests in privacy in the doctor-patient relationship and that it had a "needlessly broad sweep" because the state could not demonstrate that it was necessary to collect the forms to curb the misuse of Schedule II drugs. The state appealed.

The Supreme Court held that the statute was constitutional even if it was not "necessary" and that requiring the reporting of patients' names was a reasonable exercise of state police power. Furthermore, the Schedule II forms did not violate a Fourteenth Amendment liberty interest in patients' reputations or privacy or impermissibly restrict doctors' interest in practicing medicine free from state interference.

United Jewish Organizations of Williamsburgh v. Carey

430 U.S. 144 (1977)
Decided: March 1, 1977
Vote: 7 (Brennan, Stewart, B. White, Blackmun, Powell, Rehnquist, Stevens)
1 (Burger)
Judgment of the Court: B. White
Concurring opinion: Brennan
Opinion concurring in judgment: Stewart (Powell)
Dissenting opinion: Burger
Did not participate: T. Marshall

Acting under the Voting Rights Act of 1965, New York State reapportioned various state legislative districts to achieve districts that were 65 percent minority. Before this redistricting, Brooklyn's Hasidic Jewish community of about thirty thousand lived almost entirely in a single Assembly district and a single Senate district. The redistricting divided this community into two or more districts. The Hasidic community sought injunctive relief on the grounds that it denied them equal protection of the law and violated their Fifteenth Amendment rights. The district court and the Second Circuit Court granted summary judgment to the state, and United Jewish Organizations appealed.

The Supreme Court held that Hasidim were not a constitutionally protected class and that redistricting for the purpose of creating racial balance between whites (including Hasidic Jews) and blacks was a permissible kind of districting. The various courts noted that Jews had never been denied the franchise in New York and were not a protected class under the Voting Rights Act. The Court in essence upheld strict racial quotas, which Chief Justice Burger in his dissent condemned as "racial gerrymandering." The Court also denied the claim of the Hasidic community that its members had also faced racial and ethnic discrimination and were in fact an insular minority, deserving of special consideration in redistricting. In his plurality decision, Justice White upheld the Voting Rights Act of 1965 and the use of racial quotas to overcome specific past discrimination.

Justice Stewart stressed that New York had not intentionally discriminated against the Hasidic community.

See Alexendra Natapoff, "Trouble in Paradise: Equal Protection and the Dilemma of Interminority Group Conflict," *Stanford Law Review* 47 (1995): 1059.

Califano v. Goldfarb

430 U.S. 199 (1977)
Decided: March 2, 1977
Vote: 5 (Brennan, B. White, T. Marshall, Powell, Stevens)
4 (Burger, Stewart, Blackmun, Rehnquist)
Judgment of the Court: Brennan
Opinion concurring in judgment: Stevens
Dissenting opinion: Rehnquist (Burger, Stewart, Blackmun)

Leon Goldfarb sued because a federal statute denied him Social Security payments because he had not been receiving at least half of his support from his spouse, Hannah Goldfarb, before she died. Similarly situated widows did receive benefits.

Four members of the Court, led by Justice Brennan, believed the law unconstitutional because it discriminated against women workers and their families. Four others, led by Justice Rehnquist, agreed that the law might discriminate against men, but asserted that it was "scarcely an invidious discrimination." Rehnquist argued that the most "that can be squeezed out of the facts of this case in the way of cognizable 'discrimination' is a classification which favors aged widows." He argued that without invidious discrimination, the Court should defer to the legislature which, for administrative convenience had chosen to give special consideration to widows.

Justice Stevens provided the swing vote. He agreed with Rehnquist that "a classification which treats certain aged widows more favorably than their male counterparts is not 'invidious' " because "such a classification does not imply that males are inferior to females." However, unlike Rehnquist, he found the classification to be constitutionally impermissible because it treated "similarly situated persons differently solely because they are not of the same sex." Stevens believed this discrimination was an accident of legislative drafting, not an intentional discrimination against men. According to Stevens, it was the lack of intention that made the law unconstitutional. He was "persuaded that a rule which effects an unequal distribution of economic benefits solely on the basis of sex is sufficiently questionable that 'due process requires that there be a legitimate basis for presuming that the rule was actually intended to serve [the] interest' put forward by the Government as its justification." Stevens said disparate treatment of men and women constituted a violation of equal protection and due process. The four justices who believe the law discriminated against women argued the law was intentional and based on "archaic and overbroad" stereotypes about dependency. Although he believed the law was unintentional, Stevens provided the fifth vote by asserting that it discriminated against men.

See Mary E. Becker, "Obscuring the Struggle: Sex Discrimination, Social Security, and Stone, Seidman, Sunstein and Tushnet's Constitutional Law," *Columbia Law Review* 89 (1989): 264.

Brewer v. Williams

430 U.S. 387 (1977)
Decided: March 23, 1977
Vote: 5 (Brennan, Stewart, T. Marshall, Powell, Stevens)
4 (Burger, B. White, Blackmun, Rehnquist)
Opinion of the Court: Stewart
Concurring opinion: T. Marshall
Concurring opinion: Powell
Concurring opinion: Stevens
Dissenting opinion: Burger
Dissenting opinion: B. White (Blackmun, Rehnquist)
Dissenting opinion: Blackmun (B. White, Rehnquist)

Robert Williams was convicted of the murder of ten-year-old Pamela Powers, based on a confession he gave to a police officer who was transporting him from Davenport, Iowa, to Des Moines. Police in Des Moines sought Williams, who had recently escaped from a mental institution, in connection with the child's disappearance. A lawyer representing Williams informed Des Moines police that he had instructed his client to turn himself in to the police in Davenport. The Des Moines police agreed not to question Williams while in transit. A Davenport lawyer, acting as local counsel for Williams, reiterated the agreement and offered to accompany Williams on the drive, but the police refused his request.

During the trip, the officers indirectly questioned Williams about where the girl's body could be found and lied to him concerning what they knew about her whereabouts. Williams "stated several times that he would tell the whole story after seeing his Des Moines lawyer." Knowing that Williams had strong religious beliefs, one of the officers tried a different tactic. "Addressing Williams as 'Reverend,' " the officer gave Williams what the officer called a " 'Christian burial speech,' " urging him to think about the need for Pamela's parents to have a "Christian burial for the little girl who was snatched away from them on Christmas Eve and murdered." During the ride Williams told the officers where to find her body. Over the objection of counsel, evidence of these conversations was introduced at trial, with the judge deciding that Williams had voluntarily waived his right to counsel by talking to the police during the 160-mile trip.

The Iowa Supreme Court upheld his conviction. Laying out the facts, Justice Stewart wrote, "The four dissenting justices expressed the view that 'when counsel and police have agreed defendant is not to be questioned until counsel is present and defendant has been advised not to talk and repeatedly has stated he will tell the whole story after he talks with counsel, the state should be required to make a stronger showing of intentional voluntary waiver than was made here.' "

The U.S. district court agreed with the dissenters, granting Williams a writ of habeas corpus and ordering a new trial. The district court found for Williams on three grounds: that his rights under ***Miranda v. Arizona,*** 384 U.S. 436 (1966), had been violated; that his confession was not voluntary; and that he had been denied effective counsel during his interrogation. The court of appeals affirmed, and Iowa, through Warden Lou V. Brewer, appealed to the U.S. Supreme Court.

The Supreme Court upheld the lower court rulings on the narrow ground that Williams "was deprived of . . . the right to the assistance of counsel." Stewart declared that the right to counsel was "indispensable to the fair administration of our adversary system of criminal justice. Its vital need at the pretrial stage has perhaps nowhere been more succinctly explained than in Mr. Justice Sutherland's memorable words for the Court 44 years earlier in ***Powell v. Alabama,*** [287 U.S. 45 (1932)]."

> During perhaps the most critical period of the proceedings against these defendants, that is to say, from the time of their arraignment until the beginning of their trial, when consultation, thorough-going investigation and preparation were vitally important, the defendants did not have the aid of counsel in any real sense, although they were as much entitled to such aid during that period as at the trial itself.

The state conceded that the Christian burial speech was in fact an interrogation, which, the Court held, without Williams's lawyer present, was a clear violation of the Constitution. Given the long trip back to Des Moines, Williams's mental state, his initial refusal to talk, and the sly tactics of the police in getting him to talk, the majority categorically rejected the idea that Williams had waived his right to counsel and talked voluntarily to the police. Stewart ended his opinion on a somber note that revealed the difficulty of such cases:

> Although we do not lightly affirm the issuance of a writ of habeas corpus in this case, so clear a violation of the Sixth and Fourteenth Amendments as here occurred cannot be condoned. The pressures on state executive and judicial officers charged with the administration of the criminal law are great, especially when the crime is murder and the victim a small child. But it is precisely the predictability of those pressures that makes imperative a resolute loyalty to the guarantees that the Constitution extends to us all.

In dissent, Chief Justice Burger called the result intolerable. The dissenters argued that Williams was not physically coerced into talking, and that he had been warned at least five times not to talk to the police. They concluded his actions in taking the police to the body were voluntary. Burger castigated the majority for punishing society for the mistakes of the police officer, assuming that what the officer did was a mistake. In fact, none of the dissenters believed it was. Rather, they lauded the detective's interrogation as "good police work."

In response to this point, Justice Marshall asserted, "In my view, good police work is something far different from catching the criminal at any price. It is equally important that the police, as guardians of the law, fulfill their responsibility to obey its commands scrupulously." For "in the end life and liberty can be as much endangered from illegal methods used to convict those thought to be criminals as from the actual criminals themselves."

Ingraham v. Wright

430 U.S. 651 (1977)
Decided: April 19, 1977
Vote: 5 (Burger, Stewart, Blackmun, Powell, Rehnquist)
4 (Brennan, B. White, T. Marshall, Stevens)
Opinion of the Court: Powell
Dissenting opinion: B. White (Brennan, T. Marshall, Stevens)
Dissenting opinion: Stevens

Challenging the constitutionality of corporal punishment in public schools, junior high school students James Ingraham and Roosevelt Andrews sued the Dade County, Florida, public schools after they were paddled. The Florida schools allowed for spanking "on the buttocks with a flat wooden paddle measuring less than two feet long, three to four inches wide, and about one-half inch thick. The normal punishment was limited to one to five 'licks' or blows with the paddle." One of the students receiving several hits from a wooden paddle suffered a hematoma; another student lost the use of his arm for one week. The students claimed the practice violated the Eighth Amendment prohibition on cruel and unusual punishment. The district court dismissed the action, and the court of appeals affirmed.

The Supreme Court affirmed the decision, maintaining that the Eighth Amendment prohibition against cruel and unusual punishment does not extend to schoolchildren. Furthermore, the Fourteenth Amendment's Due Process Clause does not require notice or a hearing prior to the administration of corporal punishment.

The Court determined that the history of the Eighth Amendment, applicable only in the criminal context, persuaded it that the amendment did not apply to disciplinary corporal punishment in public schools. Noting the strong common law tradition of permitting such punishment in pubic schools, the Court supported its narrow view of the Eighth Amendment. "The openness of the public school and its supervision by the community afford significant safeguards against the kinds of abuses from which the Eighth Amendment protects the prisoner," Justice Powell wrote. "In virtually every community where corporal punishment is permitted in the schools, these safeguards are reinforced by the legal constraints of the common law."

Turning to the Fourteenth Amendment challenge, the Court used a two-stage analysis. The Court asked "whether the asserted individual interests are encompassed within the Fourteenth Amendment's protection" and, if so, "what procedures constitute due process of law." The Court noted that "where school authorities, acting under the color of state law, deliberately decide to punish a child for misconduct by restraining the child and inflicting appreciable physical pain, we hold that

Fourteenth Amendment liberty interests are implicated." In determining what type of due process is required, however, the Court was not so generous. Admitting that due process is not a technical conception but related to the circumstances, the Court maintained that requiring a hearing before inflicting the punishment would be unreasonable. Considering the nature of the situation, where most likely the teacher was present when the infraction took place and the fact that a hearing before the punishment occurred would necessitate time, personnel, and a distraction, the Court found a hearing unnecessary. If, on the rare occasion that a child was punished erroneously or unreasonably, the Court contended that the common law safeguards, holding the school and teacher liable civilly and criminally, were adequate.

In a strong dissent, Justice White rejected the Court's analysis. He argued not only against disciplinary corporal punishment but also against the Court's holding that the Eighth Amendment and due process do not apply to schoolchildren. White maintained that it was illogical not to extend Eighth Amendment rights to schoolchildren. Attacking the Court's rationale, White showed that the students were being punished and deserved protection. Regarding the Fourteenth Amendment, he said that due process could be reasonably afforded. He proposed that a brief conference with the suspected child could be held at the time of the infraction allowing the child due process.

See Andrew M. Kenefick, "The Constitutionality of Punitive Damages Under the Excessive Fines Clause of the Eighth Amendment," *Michigan Law Review* 85 (1987): 1699.

Wooley v. Maynard

430 U.S. 705 (1977)
Decided: April 20, 1977
Vote: 6 (Burger, Brennan, Stewart, T. Marshall, Powell, Stevens)
3 (B. White, Blackmun, Rehnquist)
Opinion of the Court: Burger
Dissenting opinion: B. White (Rehnquist, Blackmun)
Dissenting opinion: Rehnquist (Blackmun)

New Hampshire law made it a crime to obscure the words *Live Free or Die* on New Hampshire license plates. George Maynard, a Jehovah's Witness, was prosecuted for taping over the message, which he did on religious grounds. Maynard sought injunctive relief in federal district court. The court upheld his First Amendment claim, and New Hampshire appealed.

The Supreme Court held that New Hampshire's stated interest in cultivating a sense of history and individualism in its residents was insufficient to overcome the plaintiff's First Amendment right not to convey an unacceptable ideological message. Chief Justice Burger held that the state could not compel Maynard "to be an instrument for fostering public adherence to an ideological point of view he finds unacceptable." Burger rejected the idea that the state could force Maynard to turn his car into a "mobile billboard" for the "State's ideological message."

The dissents were based on jurisdictional grounds. Justice Rehnquist also argued that placing a license plate on a car was not an endorsement of the slogan. He compared the slogan to the phrase *In God We Trust* on money, noting that an atheist's use of currency does not equal an endorsement of the sentiments on it. The majority responded by noting that currency is usually kept inside a pocket and was passed from hand-to-hand, while the license plate was externally visible.

See Paul Finkelman, ed., *Religion and American Law: An Encyclopedia* (New York: Garland, 2000).

United States Trust Company of New York v. New Jersey

431 U.S. 1 (1977)
Decided: April 27, 1977
Vote: 4 (Burger, Blackmun, Rehnquist, Stevens)
3 (Brennan, B. White, T. Marshall)
Opinion of the Court: Blackmun
Concurring opinion: Burger
Dissenting opinion: Brennan (B. White, T. Marshall)
Did not participate: Stewart, Powell

In 1962 New York and New Jersey entered into a contract that the Port Authority would not use funds from a bond to subsidize rail travel, but in 1974 both states passed statutes that repealed the agreement. The United States Trust Company was trustee for the bond and a bondholder. The company sued, arguing that under the Contract Clause (Article I, Section 10), the states were not allowed to interfere with the contract with the bondholders. The company further asserted that the 1962 covenant was meant to ensure that bondholders would not suffer losses because their investment was being used for an enterprise that was not profitable. By repealing the covenant, the states had impaired contractual duties between themselves and the bondholders in violation of the Contract Clause. The New Jersey court dismissed the complaint, and the Supreme Court reversed.

The Court noted that, despite the prohibition of the Contract Clause, states have broad police power to regulate without fear that their regulations impair contract rights. Justice Blackmun quoted ***Home Building & Loan Assn. v. Blaisdell,*** 290 U.S. 398 (1934): "Although the Contract Clause appears literally to proscribe 'any' impairment" . . . the prohibition is not an absolute one and is not to be read with literal exactness like a mathematical formula." So long as the regulation was not specifically aimed at destroying contract rights and had a suitable purpose, the Court would uphold it. The Court observed, however, that a state cannot ignore its private creditors' legitimate claims just because it would rather spend the money to promote the public welfare. In this case, the Court found that is what the two states were doing. They could not ignore their duties to the bondholders by declaring a public need for subsidizing more rail service between the two states.

See Michael L. Zigler, "Takings Law and the Contract Clause: A Takings Law Approach to Legislative Modification of Public Contracts," *Stanford Law Review* 36 (1984): 1447; and "Note, Rediscovering the Contract Clause," *Harvard Law Review* 97 (1984): 1414.

Abood v. Detroit Board of Education

431 U.S. 209 (1977)
Decided: May 23, 1977
Vote: 9 (Burger, Brennan, Stewart, B. White, T. Marshall, Blackmun, Powell, Rehnquist, Stevens)
0
Opinion of the Court: Stewart
Concurring opinion: Rehnquist
Concurring opinion: Stevens
Concurring in judgment: Powell (Burger, Blackmun)

Michigan law allowed government employee unions to implement "agency shop" agreements that called for nonunion employees who were represented by a union to pay service charges to the union that equaled union dues. Detroit public school teachers challenged the constitutionality of the agency shop agreement as a violation of their First Amendment freedom of association. They also argued that the nature of public employment gave them First Amendment claims different from those of private sector workers. The Michigan courts upheld the agreements, and the teachers appealed to the Supreme Court.

The Court held that the agency shop agreement was not a violation of the teachers' First Amendment rights because the teachers' dues were used to finance collective bargaining. Justice Stewart noted that "insofar as the service charge is used to finance expenditures by the Union for the purposes of collective bargaining, contract administration, and grievance adjustment," precedents in *Railway Employees' Dept. v. Hanson,* 351 U.S. 225 (1956), and *Machinists v. Street,* 367 U.S. 740 (1961), "require validation of the agency-shop agreement before us." Stewart also had little sympathy for the claim that public employees' constitutional needs and rights were different from private sector employees' needs and rights. He concluded, "The only remaining constitutional inquiry evoked by the appellants' argument, therefore, is whether a public employee has a weightier First Amendment interest than a private employee in not being compelled to contribute to the costs of exclusive union representation. We think he does not." He found that "public employees are not basically different from private employees; on the whole, they have the same sort of skills, the same needs, and seek the same advantages." They therefore had the same constitutional rights as private employees to oppose their union, as D. Louis Abood and the other plaintiffs wanted to do.

To the extent that teachers' dues were used to subsidize political or ideological activities the teachers did not support, however, their First Amendment rights were violated. Stewart noted that previous cases involving unions had not decided this issue, but he said it was clear that "at the heart of the First Amendment is the notion that an individual should be free to believe as he will, and that in a free society one's beliefs should be shaped by his mind and his conscience rather than coerced by the State." Stewart was not suggesting that all union members' rights are violated when their dues are used for political or ideological purposes; only employees who are compelled to contribute under an agency shop arrangement. "We do not hold that a union cannot constitutionally spend funds for the expression of political views, on behalf of political candidates, or toward the advancement of other ideological causes not germane to its duties as collective-bargaining representative," he wrote. "Rather, the Constitution requires only that such expenditures be financed from charges, dues, or assessments paid by employees who do not object to advancing those ideas and who are not coerced into doing so against their will by the threat of loss of governmental employment." The Court remanded the case, giving Abood and his fellow nonunion workers an opportunity to prove that union funds were used for political purposes, rather than only to protect workers' rights. If the plaintiffs proved their assertion, then, Stewart noted, the trial court's "objective must be to devise a way of preventing compulsory subsidization of ideological activity by employees who object thereto without restricting the Union's ability to require every employee to contribute to the cost of collective-bargaining activities."

See Martin H. Malin, "The Legal Status of Union Security Fee Arbitration After *Chicago Teachers Union v. Hudson,*" *Boston College Law Review* 29 (1988): 857.

Moore v. City of East Cleveland

431 U.S. 494 (1977)
Decided: May 31, 1977
Vote: 5 (Brennan, T. Marshall, Blackmun, Powell, Stevens)
4 (Burger, Stewart, B. White, Rehnquist)
Judgment of the Court: Powell
Concurring opinion: Brennan (T. Marshall)
Concurring in the judgment opinion: Stevens
Dissenting opinion: Burger
Dissenting opinion: Stewart (Rehnquist)
Dissenting opinion: B. White

Inez Moore lived in the City of East Cleveland with her son and his child. Another grandson, John, moved in with Moore after his mother died. Under a city housing ordinance, John was an illegal occupant of the house. The ordinance allowed immediate family members to live together, but the narrow definition of "family" excluded John. After receiving notice from the city of the violation, Moore was arrested and sentenced to five days in jail and a $25 fine. She brought suit in district court challenging the constitutionality of the ordinance.

The lower federal courts upheld the ordinance, but the Supreme Court reversed, determining that the ordinance violated the Due Process Clause of the Fourteenth Amendment. Where the ordinance provided criminal sanctions that limited an individual family's living arrangements, the Court concluded that the city's objectives did not justify the government's intrusion.

The lower courts had upheld the ordinance on the basis of *Village of Belle Terre v. Boraas,* 416 U.S. 1 (1974), but, as the Supreme Court noted, the statute in that case placed limitations on unrelated individuals living together. Here, the statute criminalized occupancy by family members. As Justice Powell pointed out, East Cleveland chose "to regulate the occupancy of its housing by slicing deeply into the family itself. This is no mere incidental result of the ordinance. On its face it selects certain categories of relatives who may live together and declares that others may not. In particular, it makes a crime of a grandmother's choice to live with her grandson in circumstances like those presented here."

The Court found that such an intrusive regulation violated the Due Process Clause, and the ordinance could be upheld only if it served justifiable state objectives. "The city seeks to justify it as a means of preventing overcrowding, minimizing traffic and parking congestion, and avoiding an undue financial burden on East Cleveland's school system." Admitting the objectives were valid, the Court could not say that they bore a rational relationship to the ordinance's intrusion in the family sphere, and therefore struck down the law.

See Note, "Zoning and the Family," *Harvard Law Review* 91 (1978): 1568.

Carey v. Population Services International

431 U.S. 678 (1977)
Decided: June 9, 1977
Vote: 7 (Brennan, Stewart, B. White, T. Marshall, Blackmun, Powell, Stevens)
2 (Burger, Rehnquist)
Judgment of the Court: Brennan
Concurring in judgment: B. White
Concurring in judgment: Powell
Concurring in judgment: Stevens
Dissenting without opinion: Burger
Dissenting opinion: Rehnquist

A New York statute prohibited the sale of contraceptives to anyone under sixteen, the sale of contraceptives except by licensed pharmacists, and the advertising and display of contraceptives. A company that sold contraceptives challenged the constitutionality of the statute. The district court held that the statute was unconstitutional to the extent that it applied to nonprescription drugs and devices.

In upholding the district court, Justice Brennan noted that "regulations imposing a burden on" the decision to bear children "may be justified only by compelling state interests, and must be narrowly drawn to express only those interests." The Court could find no such interests here and held that a prohibition on the selling of contraceptives to anyone under sixteen unnecessarily burdened the important privacy interest in deciding whether to have a child without any compelling state interest. The Court also held that the ban on advertising contraceptives was a violation of the First Amendment.

See David B. Cruz, " 'The Sexual Freedom Cases'? Contraception, Abortion, Abstinence, and the Constitution," *Harvard Civil Rights-Civil Liberties Law Review* 35 (2000): 229.

Hunt v. Washington State Apple Advertising Commission

432 U.S. 333 (1977)
Decided: June 20, 1977
Vote: 8 (Burger, Brennan, Stewart, B. White, T. Marshall, Blackmun, Powell, Stevens)
0
Opinion of the Court: Burger
Did not participate: Rehnquist

A North Carolina statute prohibited the importing of apples into the state in boxes that bore any grade marking other than the U.S. Department of Agriculture grade. North Carolina claimed that the regulation was not aimed at impairing foreign apple growers from advertising the quality of their product in North Carolina, but at protecting the public from inconsistent and confusing grades. Washington State had developed a sophisticated grading system that exceeded federal requirements and had created a special market for Washington apples. North Carolina's statute effectively stripped Washington apple growers of the benefit of their expensive grading system because it prohibited them from advertising the higher grade of their product in North Carolina's market. The Washington State Apple Advertising Commission objected to the law.

The Supreme Court held that North Carolina's statute violated Article I, Section 8, of the Constitution, the Commerce Clause. Even if the state accurately portrayed the purpose of the statute—that it was not simply to protect North Carolina apple growers from out-of-state competition—according to the Court, the statute had exactly the kind of pernicious effect on interstate commerce the Commerce Clause was meant to prevent. As Chief Justice Burger noted, "The challenged statute has the practical effect of not only burdening interstate sales of Washington apples, but also discriminating against them. This discrimination takes various forms. The first, and most obvious, is the statute's consequence of raising the costs of doing business in the North Carolina market for Washington apple growers and dealers, while leaving those of their North Carolina counterparts unaffected." The law's requirements created a "disparate effect" because "North Carolina apple producers, unlike their Washington competitors, were not forced to alter their marketing practices in order to comply with the statute." Indeed, North Carolina growers were "still free to market their wares under the USDA grade or none at all as they had done prior to the statute's enactment," but it was obvious that "the increased costs imposed by the statute would tend to shield the local apple industry from the competition of Washington apple growers and dealers who are already at a competitive disadvantage because of their great distance from the North Carolina market." The statute also had the "effect of stripping away from the Washington apple industry the competitive and economic advantages it has earned for itself through its expensive inspection and grading system." The Court also noted that because Washington State's system of grading apples was more sophisticated than the USDA system, "Washington sellers would normally enjoy a distinct market advantage vis-à-vis local producers in those categories where the Washington grade is superior." But the "downgrading" of the North Carolina statute gave that state's "apple industry the very sort of protection against competing out-of-state products that the Commerce Clause was designed to prohibit." For all these reasons the North Carolina statute was unconstitutional.

See Justin Shoemaker, "The Smalling of America? Growth Management Statutes and the Dormant Commerce Clause," *Duke Law Journal* 48 (1999): 891.

Maher v. Roe

432 U.S. 464 (1977)
Decided: June 20, 1977
Vote: 6 (Burger, Stewart, B. White, Powell, Rehnquist, Stevens)
3 (Brennan, T. Marshall, Blackmun)
Opinion of the Court: Powell
Concurring opinion: Burger
Dissenting opinion: Brennan (T. Marshall, Blackmun)
Dissenting opinion: T. Marshall
Dissenting opinion: Blackmun (T. Marshall, Brennan)

Two indigent women challenged a Connecticut Welfare Department regulation that denied Medicaid payments for non–medically necessary abortions. The women claimed that denying them the opportunity, enjoyed by those who could afford it on their own, to have an elective abortion was a denial of their equal protection rights. The district court found that ***Roe v. Wade,*** 410 U.S. 113 (1973), had extinguished the state's right to encourage childbirth over abortion as a matter of public policy and held for the plaintiffs.

On Connecticut's appeal, the Supreme Court reversed the district court's judgment. The Court acknowledged that the law disadvantaged poor women, but Justice Powell asserted that the case "involves no discrimination against a suspect class" because "an indigent woman desiring an abortion does not come within the limited category of disadvantaged classes so recognized by our cases." Relying on the decision in ***San Antonio School District v. Rodriguez,*** 411 U.S. 1 (1973), Powell reaffirmed that "this Court has never held that financial need alone identifies a suspect class for purposes of equal protection analysis."

The Court held that the Equal Protection Clause does not require a state to fund nontherapeutic abortions simply because it also funds costs incident to childbirth. The Court pointed out that the "Texas law in *Roe* was a stark example of impermissible interference with the pregnant woman's decision to terminate her pregnancy." *Roe,* however, did not require a state to be neutral on the issue of abortion; it merely required it to avoid placing undue obstacles in the path of a woman's exercising her own privacy interest in deciding whether to have an abortion. *Roe* meant only that women had a "constitutionally protected interest 'in making certain kinds of important decisions' free from governmental compulsion." The Court found that the Connecticut law did not interfere with this "constitutionally protected interest." Powell asserted that "the Connecticut regulation places no obstacles absolute or otherwise in the pregnant woman's path to an abortion. An indigent woman who desires an abortion suffers no disadvantage as a consequence of Connecticut's decision to fund childbirth; she continues as before to be dependent on private sources for the service she desires." Because the indigent were not a "protected class," they were not entitled to heightened judicial scrutiny of statutes that affect them disproportionately. The Court therefore concluded "that the Connecticut regulation does not impinge upon the fundamental right in *Roe.*"

In dissent, Justice Brennan castigated the majority for its "distressing insensitivity to the plight of impoverished pregnant women."

> The stark realty for too many, not just "some," indigent pregnant women is that indigency makes access to competent licensed physicians not merely "difficult" but "impossible." As a practical matter, many indigent women will feel they have no choice but to carry their pregnancies to term because the State will pay for the associated medical services, even though they would have chosen to have abortions if the State had also provided funds for that procedure, or indeed if the State had provided funds for neither procedure. This disparity in funding by the State clearly operates to coerce indigent pregnant women to bear children they would not otherwise choose to have, and just as clearly, this coercion can only operate upon the poor, who are uniquely the victims of this form of financial pressure.

In addition, Brennan challenged the assertions of the majority that this case was a retreat from *Roe.* On the contrary, he argued that it effectively denied access to the rights protected in *Roe* to millions of women because of their poverty.

See Susan Frelich Appleton, "Beyond the Limits of Reproductive Choice: The Contributions of the Abortion-Funding Cases to Fundamental-Rights Analysis and to the Welfare Rights Thesis" *Columbia Law Review* 81 (1981): 721.

Poelker v. Doe

432 U.S. 519 (1977)
Decided June 20, 1977
Vote: 6 (Burger, Stewart, B. White, Powell, Rehnquist, Stevens)
3 (Brennan, T. Marshall, Blackmun)
Opinion: *Per curiam*
Dissenting opinion: Brennan (T. Marshall, Blackmun)
Dissenting opinion: T. Marshall
Dissenting opinion: Blackmun (T. Marshall, Brennan)

This case was a companion to ***Maher v. Roe,*** 432 U.S. 464 (1977), decided the same day. In *Poelker* the Court held that equal protection does not require a state to finance hospital services for nontherapeutic abortions when it finances hospital services for childbirth. The Court reaffirmed its stance that the Constitution does not require a state or locality to be neutral on the issue of abortion. On the contrary, Mayor Poelker of St. Louis, whose policy was questioned in this case, had a right to express a policy choice in favor of childbirth. Because the state had not made abortions unavailable to those who could pay for them, the state had not run afoul of ***Roe v. Wade,*** 410 U.S. 113 (1973).

In a dissent found in *Maher v. Roe,* Justice Brennan argued that by denying public financing of abortions to indigent women, the state had effectively denied them their constitutional right under *Roe* to choose abortion.

Wainwright v. Sykes

433 U.S. 72 (1977)
Decided: June 23, 1977
Vote: 7 (Burger, Stewart, B. White, Blackmun, Powell, Rehnquist, Stevens)
2 (Brennan, T. Marshall)
Opinion of the Court: Rehnquist
Concurring opinion: Burger
Concurring opinion: Stevens
Opinion concurring in judgment: B. White
Dissenting opinion: Brennan (T. Marshall)

Sykes, a Florida state prisoner, filed a habeas corpus petition on the theory that some statements he made to the police, which were instrumental in his conviction, were involuntary because he had not understood the Miranda warnings. Sykes's lawyer had failed to challenge the confession at trial or on his initial appeal in the state courts. The existing federal rule, based on ***Fay v. Noia,*** 372 U.S. 391 (1963), was that a federal judge had "a limited discretion . . . to deny relief . . . to an applicant who had deliberately bypassed the orderly procedure of the state courts and in so doing has forfeited his state court remedies." Under *Fay* and other cases, federal relief would be barred only if the defendant failed "to comply with the rule requiring objection at the trial" where "the right to object was deliberately bypassed for reasons relating to trial tactics."

Here, the Supreme Court held that a prisoner does not have a constitutional right to a hearing on the voluntariness of his statements after he waived the right to object to those statements at trial. Justice Rehnquist's opinion emphasized that the defendant was not prejudiced by the admission of the involuntary statement because other evidence of his guilt was ample.

As Justice White asserted in his concurrence, there would be no reason to overturn the conviction when the "alleged constitutional error is harmless beyond a reasonable doubt," as it was here, because of the overwhelming evidence of Sykes's guilt.

In dissent, Justice Brennan noted that what the Court's decision "left unanswered is the thorny question that must be recognized to be central to a realistic rationalization of this area of law: How should the federal habeas court treat a procedural default in a state court that is attributable purely and simply to the error or negligence of a defendant's trial counsel?" In other words, Brennan argued that an error made by Sykes's lawyer should not prevent him from raising the reasonableness of his confession in federal court.

Wolman v. Walter

433 U.S. 229 (1977)
Decided: June 24, 1977
Vote: Multiple
Judgment of the Court: Blackmun
Opinion concurring in judgment: Burger
Opinion concurring in judgment: B. White
Opinion concurring in judgment: Powell
Opinion concurring in judgment: Rehnquist
Opinion concurring in judgment: Stevens
Dissenting opinion: Brennan
Dissenting opinion: T. Marshall

This case involved state financial aid to nonpublic schools, and the facts were similar to ***Meek v. Pittenger,*** 421 U.S. 349 (1975). Ohio laws enabled the state to give financial aid to sectarian, nonpublic schools for (1) buying secular textbooks, (2) administering standardized tests, (3) speech and hearing diagnostics services, (4) certain accommodations for students with special needs, (5) buying instructional materials and equipment "that are incapable of diversion to religious use" for loan to students, and (6) transportation for field trips. Ohio taxpayers challenged the constitutionality of this law, but the district court held that the statute did not violate the Establishment Clause. The taxpayers appealed.

The Supreme Court held that the diagnostics, special accommodations provisions, and textbook provisions did not have the primary effect of aiding religion and were therefore constitutional. The provision providing aid for field trips, however, did have the primary purpose of aiding religion because the sectarian schools themselves chose the nature and timing of the trips. Furthermore, ensuring that the field trips were not religious in character would require such close monitoring of the schools that the government would become excessively entangled in religion. The part of the statute authorizing aid for field trips was therefore unconstitutional.

See Carl H. Esbeck, "Government Regulation of Religiously Based Social Services: The First Amendment Considerations," *Hastings Constitutional Law Quarterly* 19 (1992): 343–412; and Douglas Laycock, "A Survey of Religious Liberty in the United States," *Ohio State Law Journal* 47 (1986): 409–451.

Milliken v. Bradley

433 U.S. 267 (1977)
Decided: June 27, 1977
Vote: 9 (Burger, Brennan, Stewart, B. White, T. Marshall, Blackmun, Powell, Rehnquist, Stevens)
0
Opinion of the Court: Burger
Concurring opinion: T. Marshall
Concurring in judgment opinion: Powell

In ***Milliken v. Bradley,*** 418 U.S. 717 (1974)—*Milliken I*—the Supreme Court remanded to the district court the issue of school desegregation in Detroit. At this point in the litigation, neither the city nor the state contested that de jure segregation existed in Detroit. The only issue was the remedy, and in *Milliken I* the Court had ruled out cross-district or intercounty busing. After extensive hearings and reports, the district court approved a number of programs for "remedial and compensatory educational components in the desegregation plan" for the city. The district court "expressly found that the two components of testing and counseling, as then administered in Detroit's schools, were infected with the discriminatory bias of a segregated school system." The district court also found that "it was necessary to include remedial reading programs and in-service training for teachers and administrators" in the desegregation plan that it now approved. The district court ordered the state to pay half the costs of these programs, and the state appealed.

The Court rejected Michigan's arguments that the orders violated the Tenth and the Eleventh Amendments and that they exceeded the discretion of the district court judge. Chief Justice Burger wrote, "The Tenth Amendment's reservation of nondelegated powers to the States is not implicated by a federal-court judgment enforcing the express prohibitions of unlawful state conduct enacted by the Fourteenth Amendment." The Court also rejected the Eleventh Amendment argument, noting that the payment demanded here did not result from a suit for past damages, which might have been barred by the Eleventh Amendment. Rather, the money was to be used prospectively to eliminate existing segregation, which violated the Fourteenth Amendment. The Eleventh Amendment could neither bar the suit against segregation in the Detroit schools nor the remedy imposed by the district court. The plaintiffs' monetary demands were to pay for the remedial programs that the Court ordered.

Bates v. State Bar of Arizona

433 U.S. 350 (1977)
Decided: June 27, 1977
Vote: 5 (Brennan, B. White, T. Marshall, Blackmun, Stevens)
4 (Burger, Stewart, Powell, Rehnquist)
Opinion of the Court: Blackmun
Dissenting opinion: Burger
Dissenting opinion: Powell (Stewart)
Dissenting opinion: Rehnquist

Two Arizona lawyers, John R. Bates and Van O'Steen, quit a county legal aid society and opened an office to provide legal services at reasonable prices. Struggling to drum up business, the men advertised several prices for routine services in a daily newspaper. The president of the Arizona Bar Association filed a complaint against them because of the advertisement. In particular, the bar association cited them for violating Disciplinary Rule 2-101(B), which provides in part:

> A lawyer shall not publicize himself, or his partner, or associate, or any other lawyer affiliated with him or his firm, as a lawyer through newspaper or magazine advertisements, radio or television announcements, display advertisements in the city or telephone directories or other means of commercial publicity, nor shall be authorized or permit others to do so in his behalf.

After the complaint was filed, an administrative committee held a special hearing. The committee was unable to determine the validity of the rule, and the two lawyers sought review by the Arizona Supreme Court, which found the disciplinary rule "shielded from the Sherman Act by the state-action exemption of *Parker* [*v. Brown,* 317 U.S. 341 (1943)] and not protected by the First Amendment.

Bates and O'Steen challenged the Arizona Supreme Court's decision holding them in violation of the disciplinary rule. They asked the U.S. Supreme Court to decide whether the disciplinary rule violated the Sherman Act, prohibiting limitations on competition, and abridged their First Amendment right to free speech.

The Court supported the state's interpretation of the Sherman Act. Reaffirming *Parker,* the Court maintained, "The Sherman Act was not intended to apply against certain state action." Determining the real parties of the case to be the lawyers and the Arizona Supreme Court—and the bar association only the agents of the state supreme court—the Court determined that *Parker* was applicable. On the First Amendment, however, the Court rejected the state supreme court's analysis. The Court compared the lawyers' advertisement to those of pharmacies in ***Virginia Pharmacy Board v. Virginia Consumer Council,*** 425 U.S. 748 (1976), and held the statute unconstitutional as a violation of the First Amendment right to commercial free speech. None of Arizona's reasons, like those in *Virginia Pharmacy Board,* were taken to justify the First Amendment violation of a blanket prohibition on the two lawyers' right to free commercial speech.

Chief Justice Burger dissented on the grounds that *Virginia Pharmacy Board* was premised on the fact that the advertisement only applied to goods that were "standardized, prepackaged, name-brand drugs." Maintaining that legal services vary in price subject to the circumstances, he found *Virginia Pharmacy Board* distinguishable.

Justice Powell supported this position, and Justice Rehnquist argued that commercial speech was unworthy of First Amendment protection.

See William V. Canby Jr., "Marketing: On Lawyer Advertising," *Arizona Attorney* 37 (April 2001): 29.

Nixon v. Administrator of General Services

433 U.S. 425 (1977)
Decided: June 28, 1977
Vote: 7 (Brennan, Stewart, B. White, T. Marshall, Blackmun, Powell, Stevens)
2 (Burger, Rehnquist)
Opinion of the Court: Brennan
Concurring opinion: Stevens
Opinion concurring in judgment: B. White
Opinion concurring in judgment: Blackmun
Opinion concurring in judgment: Powell
Dissenting opinion: Burger
Dissenting opinion: Rehnquist

Former president Richard Nixon entered into an agreement regarding the disposition of his presidential papers and recordings with Arthur F. Sampson, the head of the General Services Administration (GSA). The agreement was for approximately 42 million pages of documents and 880 tape recordings to be stored near Nixon's home in California. Each party would notify the other before accessing the materials, and Nixon had the right to make copies, with the GSA's consent. After a period of three to five years, depending on the type of material, Nixon would have the right to destroy the documents or tape recordings.

In response to this agreement, Congress passed the Presidential Recordings and Materials Preservation Act, which required the administrator to immediately turn over the materials to Congress for a determination as to which of them were public in nature. Neither Nixon nor the administrator could destroy documents or recordings that were deemed public. Congress feared that Nixon might try to destroy materials in his presidential papers that would shed light on the events, especially the Watergate scandal, that had led to his resignation from office. Given the mysterious erasures that affected some of the tape recordings, Congress felt it was necessary to protect the documentary evidence of the Nixon administration from the one man who had the most to gain by destroying materials in these papers: Richard Nixon.

Nixon sued. His complaints included claims that Congress had violated the separation of powers, the presidential privilege of confidentiality, and his privacy interests in the materials. The district court dismissed each complaint, and Nixon appealed.

The Supreme Court held that the act did not violate the separation of powers because it was within Congress's authority to preserve documents in the public interest, and in executing that authority through the act, Congress had not unduly burdened the executive branch in the execution of its own powers. Furthermore, the act did not violate the presidential privilege of confidentiality. The act requires Congress to turn over all documents and recordings that are protected under the privilege. The mere fact that Congress must first screen the documents to make a determination of which documents are confidential is not a violation of the privilege as long as any privileged information learned by the congressional screeners does not become public. Finally, the act did not violate Nixon's right of privacy in his personal documents because it is impossible to separate the approximately 200,000 personal documents from the millions of documents in the collection without comprehensive screening. Congress's strong interest in protecting the public record justifies this minimal intrusion, especially considering the screeners' unblemished history of discretion.

Justice Stevens recognized the importance of presidential confidentiality, but noted that Nixon, who had resigned from office to avoid certain impeachment and conviction, should be considered "a legitimate class of one" for purposes of constitutional interpretation.

In dissent, Chief Justice Burger argued that "fundamental principles of constitutional law" were being "subordinated to what seem the needs of a particular situation. That moments of great national distress give rise to passions reminds us why the three branches of Government were created as separate and coequal, each intended as a check, in turn, on possible excesses by one or both of the others." Burger complained that in this case the Court, had "joined a Congress, in haste to 'do something,' and has invaded historic, fundamental principles of the separate powers of coequal branches of Government. To 'punish' one person, Congress—and now the Court—tears into the fabric of our constitutional framework." Similarly, Justice Rehnquist, who had worked in the Nixon administration before his appointment to the Court, complained that "today's decision countenances the power of any future Congress to seize the official papers of an outgoing President as he leaves the inaugural stand. In so doing, it poses a real threat to the ability of future Presidents to receive candid advice and to give candid instructions. This result, so at odds with our previous case law on the separation of powers, will daily stand as a veritable sword of Damocles over every succeeding President and his advisers."

See Jennifer R. Williams, "Beyond *Nixon:* The Application of the Taking Clause to the Papers of Constitutional Officeholders," *Washington University Law Quarterly* 71 (1993): 871; and David P. Restaino, "Conditioning Financial Aid on Draft Registration: A Bill of Attainder and Fifth Amendment Analysis," *Columbia Law Review* 84 (1984): 775.

Zablocki v. Redhail

434 U.S. 374 (1978)
Decided: January 18, 1978
Vote: 8 (Burger, Brennan, Stewart, B. White, T. Marshall, Blackmun, Powell, Stevens)
1 (Rehnquist)
Opinion of the Court: T. Marshall
Concurring opinion: Burger
Opinion concurring in judgment: Stewart
Opinion concurring in judgment: Powell
Opinion concurring in judgment: Stevens
Dissenting opinion: Rehnquist

A class action suit challenged the constitutionality of a 1973 Wisconsin statute prohibiting any state resident with an obligation to support a child not in his custody from marrying without court approval. The state was attempting to ensure that any child covered by the law would not become a burden of the state.

When he was a high school student and a minor, Roger C. Redhail fathered a child. In 1972 a court ordered "him to pay $109 per month as support for the child until she reached 18 years of age." From the time the order was issued until August 1974, Redhail "was unemployed and indigent, and consequently was unable to make any support payments." In September 1974 Redhail applied for a marriage license, which Thomas E. Zablocki, the Milwaukee county clerk, denied on the grounds that Redhail owed child support in excess of $3,700. At the time Redhail's fiancée was pregnant, and the couple wanted to be married before the child was born. Redhail brought a class action suit in federal court on behalf of all Wisconsin residents who had been denied marriage licensed under this statute.

The Supreme Court held that the statute violated the Equal Protection Clause of the Fourteenth Amendment. Citing ***Griswold v. Connecticut,*** 381 U.S. 479 (1965), ***Loving v. Virginia,*** 388 U.S. 1 (1967), and ***Roe v. Wade,*** 410 U.S. 113 (1973), the Court reaffirmed that marriage was a fundamental right, grounded in the Fourteenth Amendment and the constitutional right to privacy. Justice Marshall noted that "the decision to marry has been placed on the same level of importance as decisions relating to procreation, childbirth, child rearing, and family relationships. As the facts of this case illustrate, it would make little sense to recognize a right of privacy with respect to other matters of family life and not with respect to the decision to enter the relationship that is the foundation of the family in our society."

"Since our past decisions make clear that the right to marry is of fundamental importance, and since the classification at issue here significantly interferes with the exercise of that right," Marshall wrote, "we believe that 'critical examination' of the state interests advanced in support of the classification is required." Quoting the Court's decision in *Loving,* Marshall said, " 'The freedom to marry has long been recognized as one of the vital personal rights essential to the orderly pursuit of happiness by free men' " and " 'Marriage is one of the "basic civil rights of man," fundamental to our very existence and survival.' "

"When a statutory classification significantly interferes with the exercise of a fundamental right," Marshall continued, "it cannot be upheld unless it is supported by sufficiently important state interests and is closely tailored to effectuate only those interests." Marshall noted that the statute prohibiting marriage for people like Redhail hardly accomplishes the goals of the state. Indeed, "with respect to individuals who are unable to meet the statutory requirements, the statute merely prevents the applicant from getting married, without delivering any money at all into the hands of the applicant's prior children." The Court also noted that the state had many other means to ensure compliance with support obligations that did not "impinge upon the right to marry." The Court found the statute unconstitutional, upholding the district court's ruling.

McDaniel v. Paty

435 U.S. 618 (1978)
Decided: April 19, 1978
Vote: 8 (Burger, Brennan, Stewart, B. White, T. Marshall, Powell, Rehnquist, Stevens)
0
Judgment of the Court: Burger
Concurring opinion: Brennan (T. Marshall)
Opinion concurring in judgment: Stewart
Opinion concurring in judgment: B. White
Did not participate: Blackmun

This case struck down the last vestige of state constitutional policy that placed religious tests on officeholding. During and immediately after the American Revolution, most states required that officeholders be either Christians or Protestants. These laws gradually disappeared, but two holdover restrictions remained. In ***Torcaso v. Watkins,*** 367 U.S. 488 (1961), the Court struck down a provision of the Maryland Constitution requiring that officeholders believe in God. In *McDaniel v. Paty* the Court struck down a Tennessee provision prohibiting ministers from holding office.

McDaniel, a Baptist minister, was running for a delegate seat at the Tennessee state constitutional convention. A rival contender for the position, Selma Cash Paty, sued to enjoin him from running for the office under a Tennessee constitutional provision that prohibited clergy from being delegates. The Tennessee Supreme Court found no constitutional flaw in the provision, and granted the injunction. McDaniel appealed.

The Supreme Court held that Tennessee's provision violated the Free Exercise Clause of the U.S. Constitution and was therefore void. Chief Justice Burger explained that, although this was not a case of government attempting to prohibit McDaniel's actual beliefs, it was a case of prohibiting him from exercising those beliefs without giving up his right to seek office as a constitutional delegate.

Justice Brennan added an Establishment Clause argument, that by "fencing out" from public office those who profess religion for a living, Tennessee was inhibiting religion and thereby "establishing" nonreligion.

See Morton Borden, *Jews, Turks, and Infidels* (Chapel Hill: University of North Carolina Press, 1984); and Michael W. McConnell, "The Origins and Historical Understanding of Free Exercise of Religion," *Harvard Law Review* 106 (1990): 1409–1517.

City of Los Angeles, Department of Water and Power v. Manhart

435 U.S. 702 (1978)
Decided: April 25, 1978
Vote: Multiple
Opinion of the Court: Stevens
Concurring opinion: T. Marshall
Opinion concurring in judgment: Blackmun
Dissenting opinion: Burger (Rehnquist)
Did not participate: Brennan

The Department of Water and Power employed ten thousand men and two thousand women. The department instituted a self-funding pension plan, under which the employees would receive monthly payments after retirement. Basing the benefits on employee wages and years of service, the department decided to require larger contributions from the female workers because, on average, women live longer than men. In 1973 a group of female retirees and current employees brought a class action suit against the department, seeking an injunction and restitution of the excess contributions.

The district court found that the pension plan violated Section 703 of Title VII of the Civil Rights Act of 1964. It also awarded the petitioners their excess contributions. The court of appeals affirmed the decision. The department appealed, asserting that the differential in take home pay was not discriminatory under Section 703, that the differential was not based upon sex, that *General Electric Co. v. Gilbert,* 429 U.S. 125 (1976), needed to be reversed, and that retroactive recovery was unjustified.

Examining each contention, the Court agreed with only the last. Regarding the requirement that women pay more than men in contributions, the Court concluded that this feature of the department's pension plan violated the language and policy behind Title VII. As Justice Stevens noted: "Such a practice does not pass the simple test of whether the evidence shows 'treatment of a person in a manner which but for that person's sex would be different.' It constitutes discrimination and is unlawful unless exempted by the Equal Pay Act of 1963 or some other affirmative justification." In denying the department's second contention, that an amendment to the law exempted this kind of discrimination under Title VII, the Court was "unpersuaded" by the department's reliance on a debate between two senators when the Civil Rights Act of 1964 was passed. Distinguishing *Gilbert* from this matter, the Court disregarded the department's third argument. The Court accepted the department's contention that awarding the petitioners their excessive contributions was unjustified.

Noting that nothing in Title VII required the decision to award retroactive monies, the Court pointed out that the individuals administering the benefits did not intentionally discriminate against the petitioners. The justices also emphasized the enormous impact this decision would have if all companies employing such a pension plan were forced to pay their female employees for their excess contributions.

Chief Justice Burger dissented from all but the last determination. He and Rehnquist would have allowed differential rates, based on life expectancy.

Justice Marshall agreed with everything the Court said, except the refusal to order retroactive payment. Quoting ***Albemarle Paper Co. v. Moody,*** 422 U.S. 405 (1975), he asserted that "once a Title VII violation is found" there is "a 'presumption in favor of retroactive liability' and that this presumption 'can seldom be overcome.' "

See "Title VII of the Civil Rights Act of 1964," *Harvard Law Review* 92 (1978): 299–311.

First National Bank of Boston v. Bellotti

435 U.S. 765 (1978)
Decided: April 26, 1978
Vote: 5 (Burger, Stewart, Blackmun, Powell, Stevens)
4 (Brennan, Blackmun, Powell, Stevens)
Opinion of the Court: Powell
Concurring opinion: Burger
Dissenting opinion: B. White (Brennan, T. Marshall)
Dissenting opinion: Rehnquist

Two national banks and three corporations sued the attorney general of Massachusetts to challenge a state criminal statute forbidding banks and corporations "from making contributions or expenditures for the purpose of influencing or affecting the vote on any question submitted to the voters, other than one materially affecting any of the property, business or assets of the corporation." The banks and corporations wished to publicize their views about a proposed amendment to the state constitution that would impose a graduated individual income tax. In their challenge, they argued that the state law violated their First Amendment rights. The Supreme Judicial Court of Massachusetts upheld the statute. It viewed the issue as "whether business corporations, such as [appellants], have First Amendment rights coextensive with those of natural persons or associates of natural persons."

Before the U.S. Supreme Court, the state argued the case was moot because the vote over the specific referendum at issue had already taken place. The Court held, however, that this case was a classic example of an issue that "falls within the class of controversies 'capable of repetition, yet evading review,' " and found the issue was not moot.

At the heart of the case was the First Amendment rights of corporations. The Court determined that the statute raised important First Amendment issues and applied a strict scrutiny test, considering whether the statute and the interests offered by the state for imposing it correlated. Determining that neither of the state's interests bore a relevant correlation with the statute, the Court found the statute an unconstitutional violation of the corporations' and banks' First Amendment rights.

The Court first accepted the notion that corporations and banks are entitled to First Amendment protection. The Court found the statute's limitation a violation of the petitioners' First Amendment rights, including the right to create public discussion and the right to disseminate information and ideas. Justice Powell wrote, "In the realm of protected speech, the legislature is constitutionally disqualified from dictating the subjects about which persons may speak and the speakers which may address a public issue." In other words, the statute "abridges expression that the First Amendment was meant to protect."

The Court considered the state's two principal justifications for prohibiting corporate speech. The first was the state's interest in sustaining the active role of citizens in the electoral process and promoting confidence in government, and the second was the interest in protecting the rights of shareholders who hold political view different from the corporation's. Although these were valid interests, the Court found no correlation between them and the statute's effect and therefore held the statute unconstitutional.

Justice White argued that the statute provided for a legitimate regulation of corporations and a reasonable attempt by the state to balance the influence of money in the political process. The issue to be decided by the election did not directly affect the interests of the corporations, and White, joined by Justices Brennan and Marshall, argued that the state should be free to balance the First Amendment rights of all by limiting the economic power of corporations.

Justice Rehnquist dissented on states' rights grounds.

See Lillian R. BeVier, "Justice Powell and the First Amendment's 'Societal Function': A Preliminary Analysis," *Virginia Law Review* 68 (1982): 177.

Landmark Communications, Inc. v. Virginia

435 U.S. 829 (1978)
Decided: May 1, 1978
Vote: 7 (Burger, Stewart, B. White, T. Marshall, Blackmun, Rehnquist, Stevens)
0
Opinion of the Court: Burger
Opinion concurring in judgment: Stewart
Did not participate: Brennan, Powell

A Virginia statute made it a crime to report on the proceedings of a judicial review commission charged with investigating judicial misconduct. *The Virginia Pilot,* a newspaper owned by Landmark, obtained information about a judge who was under review, and, as Chief Justice Burger noted, "accurately" reported it. Landmark was convicted under the statute at a bench trial, fined $500, and appealed.

The Court agreed that confidentiality in misconduct cases was a value and did not strike down the Virginia laws mandating confidentiality on the part of those involved in the investigation. Burger wrote, "The narrow and limited question presented, then, is whether the First Amendment permits the criminal punishment of third persons who are strangers to the inquiry, including the news media, for divulging or publishing truthful information regarding confidential proceedings of the Judicial Inquiry and Review Commission." The Court held that the statute was an impermissible restriction on Landmark's First Amendment freedom. The Court rejected the "clear and present danger" analysis adopted by Virginia's highest court in defense of the prosecution, noting that public scrutiny of the operation of government was one of the primary purposes of the First Amendment and that Landmark's publication served that purpose. Furthermore, the restriction on press freedoms was not necessary to further the government's aim of preserving the confidentiality of the proceeding because, if the government had been more careful, Landmark would not have discovered the story in the first place.

In his concurring opinion, Justice Stewart wrote, "If the constitutional protection of a free press means anything, it means that government cannot take it upon itself to decide what a newspaper may and may not publish. Though government may deny access to information and punish its theft, government may not prohibit or punish the publication of that information once it falls into the hands of the press, unless the need for secrecy is manifestly overwhelming."

See Bryan E. Keyt, "Reconciling the Need for Confidentiality in Judicial Disciplinary Proceedings with the First Amendment: A Justification Based Analysis," *Georgetown Journal of Legal Ethics* 7 (1994): 959; and Rex S. Heinke and Seth M. M. Stodder, "Punishing Truthful, Newsworthy Disclosures: The Unconstitutional Application of the Federal Wiretap Statute," *Loyola of Los Angeles Entertainment Law Journal* (1999): 279.

Santa Clara Pueblo v. Martinez

436 U.S. 49 (1978)
Decided: May 15, 1978
Vote: 7 (Burger, Brennan, Stewart, T. Marshall, Powell, Rehnquist, Stevens)
1 (B. White)
Opinion of the Court: T. Marshall
Dissenting opinion: B. White
Did not participate: Blackmun

In 1939 the Santa Clara Pueblo Council passed an ordinance declaring that the children of male members of the tribe would also be members, even if their mother was not. Children of female members would not be members if their mothers married outside the tribe. Two years later, Julia Martinez, a full-blooded member of the Santa Clara Pueblo and resident of the Santa Clara Reservation in northern New Mexico, married a Navajo, and the couple had several children. Martinez raised her children on the Santa Clara reservation, and as adults they continued to reside there. Because of the tribe's patrilineal descent rule, these individuals were excluded from tribal membership and, when their mother died, they would "have no right to remain on the reservation ... or to inherit their mother's home or her possessory interests in the communal lands."

Martinez and her daughter sued in federal district court under the Indian Civil Rights Act of 1968, which provides that "no Indian tribe in exercising powers of self-government shall ... deny to any person within its jurisdiction the equal protection of its laws." In rejecting Martinez's petition, the district court noted that the 1939 ordinance reflected "traditional values of patriarchy still significant in tribal life." The district court held that the equal protection provision of the act did not authorize the federal courts "to determine which traditional values will promote cultural survival and should therefore be preserved.... Such a determination should be made by the people of Santa Clara; not only because they can best decide what values are important, but also because they must live with the decision every day." The court further held, "To abrogate tribal decisions, particularly in the delicate area of membership, for whatever 'good' reasons, is to destroy cultural identity under the guise of saving it." The court of appeals reversed this decision, finding that the federal courts had the power to apply the Equal Protection Clause to cases like Martinez's. The Supreme Court in turn reversed the court of appeals.

Speaking for the Court, Justice Marshall concluded that the Indian Civil Rights Act (ICRA) had not undermined traditional notions of tribal sovereign immunity. Marshall noted that in ***Worcester v. Georgia,*** 31 U.S. 515 (1832), the Court found that Indian communities were " 'distinct, independent political communities, retaining their original natural rights' in matters of local self-government." Although no longer in possession of most of their sovereignty, as the Court noted in ***United States v. Kagama,*** 118 U.S. 375 (1886), Indians were nevertheless, a "separate people, with the power of regulating their internal and social relations." Congress clearly retained the power to limit or modify Indian sovereignty, but the Court found that the legislation did not in fact limit it in this way or alter tribal sovereign immunity. Martinez therefore could not sue the tribe without either authorization from Congress or a waiver by the tribe of its immunity.

Martinez also sued the governor of the tribe, Lucario Padilla, who was not immune from suit, but the Court noted that allowing such a suit in federal court would still undermine "tribal autonomy and self-government." Congress has the power to give the federal courts jurisdiction to hear intratribal suits against tribal leaders and had done so in the act with regard to habeas corpus petitions. But the fact that Congress has specifically given jurisdiction in habeas cases implied that the federal courts did not have jurisdiction in other cases. Indians seeking to enforce their civil rights against their tribes would have to turn to tribal courts for such protection.

In dissent, Justice White argued that "by denying a federal forum to Indians who allege that their rights under the ICRA have been denied by their tribes," the Court "substantially" undermined and frustrated the "goal of the ICRA" and its stated "purpose of 'protect[ing] individual Indians from arbitrary and unjust actions of tribal governments.' " White's analysis is correct in that, without a federal forum, individual Indians would have a more difficult time vindicating their civil rights. But, the alternative, as the Court saw it, was to interpret the statute to undermine tribal sovereignty. Significantly, Congress retained the power to rewrite the law and grant federal courts jurisdiction over the matter. Congress has chosen not to do so, illustrating its support for both the Court's opinion and the larger issue of preserving tribal sovereignty, at least in this area of law.

See Jennifer S. Byram, "Civil Rights on Reservations: The Indian Civil Rights Act and Tribal Sovereignty," *Oklahoma City University Law Review* 25 (2000): 491; Judith Resnik, "Dependent Sovereigns: Indian Tribes, States, and the Federal Courts," *University of Chicago Law Review* 56 (1989): 671; and John R. Wunder, *Retained by the People: A History of American Indians and the Bill of Rights* (New York: Oxford University Press, 1994).

Ohralik v. Ohio State Bar Association

436 U.S. 447 (1978)
Decided: May 30, 1978
Vote: 8 (Burger, Stewart, B. White, T. Marshall, Blackmun, Powell, Rehnquist, Stevens)
0
Opinion of the Court: Powell
Opinion concurring in judgment: Rehnquist
Opinion concurring in judgment: T. Marshall
Did not participate: Brennan

Albert Ohralik, an Ohio lawyer, approached potential clients in their hospital rooms and at their homes without an invitation. He secretly tape-recorded his conversations with them and pressured them to accept him as their attorney. When one client tried to fire him, he sued her for breach of contract. The Ohio Supreme Court upheld the Ohio Bar Association's indefinite suspension of Ohralik for personally soliciting accident victims to represent them on a contingency fee basis. Ohralik appealed to the Supreme Court, arguing that the bar association's regulation against such solicitations violated his First Amendment freedom of speech.

The Supreme Court affirmed, holding that Ohralik's First Amendment interest was faint where the purpose of the solicitation was monetary gain. The fact that Ohralik had to speak to people to solicit them in their hospital rooms did not mean Ohio lost all ability to regulate his conduct.

Zurcher v. Stanford Daily

436 U.S. 547 (1978)
Decided: May 31, 1978
Vote: 5 (Burger, B. White, Blackmun, Powell, Rehnquist)
3 (Stewart, T. Marshall, Stevens)
Opinion of the Court: B. White
Concurring opinion: Powell
Dissenting opinion: Stewart (T. Marshall)
Dissenting opinion: Stevens
Did not participate: Brennan

Police officers, under a valid warrant, searched the offices of the *Stanford Daily,* a Stanford University student newspaper, looking for photographs or negatives that would help them identify the perpetrators of an assault on the police during a student demonstration. The police found no additional pictures and removed nothing from the offices, but the police did read files in the paper's office that may have exposed confidential sources. A month later the paper and various members of its staff brought a civil action seeking declaratory and injunctive relief against the chief of police, the district attorney and a deputy, the police officers who conducted the search, and the judge who had issued the warrant. The paper alleged that the search of its office violated its rights under the First, Fourth, and Fourteenth Amendments. The *Stanford Daily* argued that the search was illegal because no one at the paper was suspected of a crime.

The district court granted summary judgment to the paper on the ground that when the owner of the property searched is not suspected of a crime, the only appropriate way of obtaining the evidence is a subpoena duces tecum (a court order for the owner to produce the evidence for police inspection). The district court also asserted that when a newspaper is the object of a search, "First Amendment interests are also involved and that such a search is constitutionally permissible 'only in the rare circumstance where there is a clear showing that (1) important materials will be destroyed or removed from the jurisdiction; and (2) a restraining order would be futile.'" The police appealed.

The Supreme Court held that even though the editors of the *Stanford Daily* were not suspected of a crime, execution of a search warrant was a permissible means of obtaining evidence from their offices. The question in obtaining a search warrant is not whether the owner of the property is suspected of a crime, but whether police have probable cause to believe evidence of the crime is located in the place to be searched. Requiring the police to obtain a subpoena duces tecum every time they wish to search for evidence located on property not belonging to a suspect would undermine law enforcement efforts because of the intolerable risk of evidence being destroyed. The Court also rejected the *Stanford Daily*'s First Amendment claims that search warrants interfered with the newsgathering and reporting process and had a chilling affect on the First Amendment.

The dissenters stressed these points, and, in the words of Justice Stewart, "another and more serious burden on a free press imposed by an unannounced police search of a newspaper office: the possibility of disclosure of information received from confidential sources, or of the identity of the sources themselves. Protection of those sources is necessary to ensure that the press can fulfill its constitutionally designated function of informing the public, because important information can often be obtained only by an assurance that the source will not be revealed."

Congress responded to the opinion in *Stanford Daily* by passing the Privacy Protection Act of 1980, which prohibited searches of newsrooms except where reporters or others working at the newsroom were under investigation for criminal activity. Many states also adopted similar laws in response to this decision.

See Vincent Blasi, "The Checking Value in the First Amendment," *American Bar Foundation Research Journal* (1977): 521.

Monell v. Department of Social Services

436 U.S. 658 (1978)
Decided: June 6, 1978
Vote: 7 (Brennan, Stewart, B. White, T. Marshall, Blackmun, Powell, Stevens)
2 (Burger, Rehnquist)
Opinion of the Court: Brennan
Concurring opinion: Powell
Concurring opinion: Stevens
Dissenting opinion: Rehnquist (Burger)

Female employees sued the Department of Social Services, the Board of Education, and the City of New York under 42 U.S.C. Section 1983 for violating their civil rights by requiring them to take unpaid leave for pregnancy before it was medically necessary. The district court found that their rights had been violated, but denied them back pay on the theory that ***Monroe v. Pape,*** 365 U.S. 167 (1961), precluded the women from obtaining a Section 1983 judgment against a local government. By the time the case reached the Supreme Court, New York had changed its regulations with regard to pregnant women and leave, and now the only issue before the Court was back pay.

The Supreme Court found that *Monroe* only determined that Congress, when it passed the Civil Rights Act of 1871 (on which Section 1983 is based), did not believe that private litigants could obtain a judgment against local governments for constitutional violations. However, after reexamining the history of both the Civil Rights Act of 1871 and Section 1983, the Court concluded that *Monroe* had been wrongly decided and overruled it on the issue of whether local governments are immune from suit under Section 1983. The Court granted a judgment of back pay to the aggrieved employees.

Mincey v. Arizona

437 U.S. 385 (1978)
Decided: June 21, 1978
Vote: 9 (Burger, Brennan, Stewart, B. White, T. Marshall, Blackmun, Powell, Rehnquist, Stevens)
0
Opinion of the Court: Stewart
Concurring opinion: T. Marshall (Brennan)
Concurring opinion: Rehnquist

Rufus Mincey shot and killed a police officer when the officer attempted a drug raid of his apartment. Mincey was also seriously wounded, and, while he was in the hospital, narcotics detectives conducted a warrantless search of his apartment. Justice Stewart described the police action: "Their search lasted four days, during which period the entire apartment was searched, photographed, and diagrammed. The officers opened drawers, closets, and cupboards, and inspected their contents; they emptied clothing pockets; they dug bullet fragments out of the walls and floors; they pulled up sections of the carpet and removed them for examination. Every item in the apartment was closely examined and inventoried, and 200 to 300 objects were seized. In short, Mincey's apartment was subjected to an exhaustive and intrusive search. No warrant was ever obtained."

The Arizona Supreme Court upheld the search, but the Supreme Court reversed. Quoting from ***Katz v. United States,*** 389 U.S. 347 (1967), Justice Stewart wrote: "The Fourth Amendment proscribes all unreasonable searches and seizures, and it is a cardinal principle that 'searches conducted outside the judicial process, without prior approval by judge or magistrate, are per se unreasonable under the Fourth Amendment—subject only to a few specifically established and well-delineated exceptions.' " Stewart noted that there were no exigent circumstances necessitating a warrantless search. With Mincey in the hospital under police guard, and the apartment sealed-off, police had time to obtain a warrant as required by the Fourth Amendment.

At the hospital, a police detective began a four-hour interrogation of Mincey, starting at about 8:00 p.m. "Mincey was unable to talk because of the tube in his mouth, and so he responded to" the detective's "questions by writing answers on pieces of paper provided by the hospital." The detective read Mincey his Miranda rights, but, "although Mincey asked repeatedly that the interrogation stop until he could get a lawyer," the detective "continued to question him until almost midnight."

The Arizona Supreme Court found Mincey's hospital statements admissible, but the Supreme Court did not. Stewart observed, "It is hard to imagine a situation less conducive to the exercise of 'a rational intellect and a free will' than Mincey's. He had been seriously wounded just a few hours earlier, and had arrived at the hospital 'depressed almost to the point of coma,' according to his attending physician." Stewart continued to explain that Mincey's condition at the time of the interrogation was "still sufficiently serious that he was in the intensive care unit." Throughout the questioning, Mincey complained that he was in pain. He was "evidently confused and unable to think clearly about either the events of that afternoon or the circumstances of his interrogation, since some of his written answers were on their face not entirely coherent." Stewart concluded that the interrogation violated Mincey's constitutional right not to incriminate himself.

The Court held that the search of the apartment violated the Fourth Amendment. Once Mincey was removed, police had no reason not to obtain a search warrant. Arizona's interpretation of the Fourth Amendment, that once a suspect is in police custody, his privacy interest in his home is too small to require a search warrant, is wrong. Furthermore, the interrogation that took place in the hospital violated the Fifth Amendment because it was not voluntary. Any use of Mincey's involuntary confession at trial, even for purposes of impeachment, violated his Fifth Amendment rights.

Penn Central Transportation Company v. New York City

438 U.S. 104 (1978)
Decided: June 26, 1978
Vote: 6 (Brennan, Stewart, B. White, T. Marshall, Blackmun, Powell)
3 (Burger, Rehnquist, Stevens)
Opinion of the Court: Brennan
Dissenting opinion: Rehnquist (Burger, Stevens)

New York City's Landmarks Preservation Commission refused to allow the owners of the city's historic Grand Central Terminal to build a fifty-story office building above the railroad terminal. Instead, the city allowed the owners to develop nearby properties in excess of existing zoning regulations, or sell their rights to this expanded development to other property owners. The owners, Penn Central Transportation Company, sued, arguing that the denial of a building permit constituted a "taking" of their property for public use without just compensation.

In upholding the city, Justice Brennan noted that, although New York's historic landmarks law "does place special restrictions on landmark properties as a necessary feature to the attainment of its larger objectives, the major theme of the law is to ensure the owners of any such properties both a 'reasonable return' on their investments and maximum latitude to use their parcels for purposes not inconsistent with the preservation goals." The Court reaffirmed the right of states and cities to limit the use of property through zoning rules and restrictions. The justices rejected the claims of Penn Central that it had a right to use its property any way it wished, and that the denial of right to use its "airspace" above the building was a taking. The Court noted that even Penn Central conceded that the city was not attempting to prevent the landowners from continuing to use the existing structure or from making a reasonable return on their investment. The Supreme Court supported the findings of the state's highest court, the New York Court of Appeals that:

the Landmarks Law had not effected a denial of due process because:
(1) the landmark regulation permitted the same use as had been made of the Terminal for more than half a century;
(2) the appellants had failed to show that they could not earn a reasonable return on their investment in the Terminal itself;
(3) even if the Terminal proper could never operate at a reasonable profit some of the income from Penn Central's extensive real estate holdings in the area, which include hotels and office buildings, must realistically be imputed to the Terminal; and
(4) the development rights above the Terminal, which had been made transferable to numerous sites in the vicinity of the Terminal, one or two of which were suitable for the construction of office buildings, were valuable to appellants and provided "significant, perhaps 'fair,' compensation for the loss of rights above the terminal itself."

Brennan noted that in the past the Court "had recognized, in a wide variety of contexts, that government may execute laws or programs that adversely affect recognized economic values." Taxation was one example, but so too were cases in which the Court had "dismissed 'taking' challenges on the ground that, while the challenged government action caused economic harm, it did not interfere with interests that were sufficiently bound up with the reasonable expectations of the claimant to constitute 'property' for Fifth Amendment purposes." Brennan wrote, "More importantly for the present case, in instances in which a state tribunal reasonably concluded that 'the health, safety, morals, or general welfare' would be promoted by prohibiting particular contemplated uses of land, this Court has upheld land-use regulations that destroyed or adversely affected recognized real property interests." Furthermore, the Court has "recognized, in a number of settings, that States and cities may enact land-use restrictions or controls to enhance the quality of life by preserving the character and desirable aesthetic features of a city."

In dissent, Justice Rehnquist argued that zoning could be used only to prevent "noxious" uses of land. He argued that the "air rights" over the building were property, and that the refusal to allow a use of those rights constituted a taking.

Furthermore, he argued that this "taking" placed a special burden on the owners of this building that other building owners did not share. Taking what might be considered a cramped view of the needs of a city and or urban space, Rehnquist argued that the "nuisance exception" to the use of private property could not apply to aesthetic considerations or to considerations of the total culture of the city. He seemed to be saying that the city could regulate the use of a building, but not the building itself.

Rehnquist's dissent in this case signaled what would later be a new theory of property rights and government regulation that, as chief justice, he would help create in cases such as ***Nollan v. California Coastal Commission,*** 483 U.S. 825 (1987), and ***Lucas v. South Carolina Coastal Council,*** 505 U.S. 1003 (1992).

See Daniel T. Cavarello, "From *Penn Central* to *United Artists' I & II:* The Rise to Immunity of Historic Preservation Designation from Successful Takings Challenges," *Boston College Environmental Affairs Law Review* 22 (1995): 593; and Scott H. Rothstein, "Takings Jurisprudence Comes in from the Cold: Preserving Interiors Through Landmark Designation," *Connecticut Law Review* 26 (1994): 1105.

Regents of the University of California v. Bakke

438 U.S. 265 (1978)
Decided: June 28, 1978
Vote: Multiple
Judgment of the Court: Powell
Opinion concurring in part and dissenting in part: Brennan, B. White, T. Marshall, Blackmun
Opinion concurring in part and dissenting in part: Stevens (Burger, Stewart, Rehnquist)
Opinion concurring in part and dissenting in part: B. White
Opinion concurring in part and dissenting in part: T. Marshall
Opinion concurring in part and dissenting in part: Blackmun

The University of California at Davis Medical School set aside sixteen spaces in its entering class of one hundred for African American, Hispanic, Asian, and Native American students. Students admitted under this program could have lower test scores than the overwhelmingly white students admitted to the remaining eighty-four seats. Allan Bakke was twice denied admission to the school, and he sued, arguing that as a white person he had been discriminated against because his test scores were higher than those of the sixteen minority students admitted under the affirmative action program. Bakke argued that the program violated his rights under the Civil Rights Act of 1964 and denied him equal protection under the law. The university agreed that race-based admissions programs were generally constitutionally problematic, but asserted that this program was necessary to remedy the effects of past discrimination. The narrow result of the case was Bakke's admission into the medical school, but the implications of the decision were much broader.

A deeply fractured Court ruled that universities could not constitutionally use numerical quotas in their admissions program, but they could use race as a criteria in admissions. Only Justice Powell agreed with the entire result. Chief Justice Burger and Justices Stevens, Stewart, and Rehnquist agreed with Powell in striking down the special admissions program, but they would also have declared any use of race in admissions policy to be unconstitutional. Powell struck down this part of the Davis program in part because Bakke and other whites were "totally foreclosed" from competing for the sixteen minority slots. Powell noted that "when a classification denies an individual opportunities or benefits enjoyed by others solely because of his race or ethnic background, it must be regarded as suspect." The Court voted 5–4 to reject the suspect program. This ruling led to Bakke's admission to the medical school and to a bitter dissent from Justice Marshall, who evoked the history of slavery and discrimination and noted, "It must be remembered that, during most of the past 200 years, the Constitution as interpreted by this Court did not prohibit the most ingenious and pervasive forms of discrimination against the Negro. Now, when a State acts to remedy the effects of that legacy of discrimination, I cannot believe that this same Constitution stands as a barrier."

Justices Brennan, White, Marshall, and Blackmun joined Powell in support of taking race into consideration in admissions policies, allowing schools to develop affirmative action admissions programs that took race, ethnicity, and class status into account. In part Powell found that "the attainment of a diverse student body" was a legitimate goal of universities. He asserted this goal was "clearly . . . a constitutionally permissible goal for an institution of higher education. Academic freedom, though not a specifically enumerated constitutional right, long has been viewed as a special concern of the First Amendment. The freedom of a university to make its own judgments as to education includes the selection of its student body." The Stevens group dissented from this part of the opinion, arguing that taking race into account clearly violated the Civil Rights Act of 1964 and the Fourteenth Amendment.

At first glance, it would seem that opponents of affirmative action won a major victory in *Bakke,* which struck down what some of the justices called quotas. At the time, affirmative action supporters expressed anger over the ruling. They believed that the decision would exclude minorities from schools like Davis. Before the Davis program was implemented, no blacks, Hispanics, or Native Americans had ever been admitted there. Opponents of the *Bakke* decision expected that this situation would be the norm again. In fact, the decision did not undermine the idea of affirmative action; rather, it affected only its implementation. Schools could still use race, ethnicity, poverty, and other factors in selecting students for their programs. After *Bakke,* however, such criteria would have to be applied on a case-by-case basis and in the context of the entire pool of applicants. Many schools actually expanded their affirmative action programs after *Bakke,* reaching out not only to racial and ethnic minorities, but also to disadvantaged whites. Starting in the late 1980s, however, new Court decisions, such as ***Richmond v. J. A. Croson Co.,*** 488 U.S. 469 (1989), and ***Adarand Constructors v. Peña,*** 515 U.S. 200 (1995), as well as state laws and referenda prohibiting the use of race in college admission undermined or destroyed affirmative action altogether.

See Kenneth Jost, "Affirmative Action," *CQ Researcher,* September 21, 2001, 737–759; Timothy J. O'Neill, Bakke *and the Politics of Equality: Friends and Foes in the Classroom of Litigation* (Middletown, Conn.: Wesleyan University Press, 1985); and Gabriel Jack Chin, *Affirmative Action and the Constitution,* 3 vols. (New York: Garland, 1998).

Lockett v. Ohio

438 U.S. 586 (1978)
Decided: July 3, 1978
Vote: 7 (Burger, Stewart, B. White, T. Marshall, Blackmun, Powell, Stevens)
1 (Rehnquist)
Judgment of the Court: Burger
Opinion concurring in judgment: Blackmun
Opinion concurring in judgment: T. Marshall
Opinion concurring in judgment: B. White
Dissenting opinion: Rehnquist
Did not participate: Brennan

Sandra Lockett helped plan the armed robbery of a pawnshop and drove the getaway car, but she did not enter the shop and was not physically at the crime scene. The robbers did not plan to shoot anyone, but, when the pawnbroker grabbed a gun carried by Al Parker, one of the robbers, it went off. The pawnbroker died from the wound. Lockett helped to hide Parker, who was eventually arrested and charged with aggravated murder. He pleaded guilty to a lesser offense to avoid a potential death sentence and agreed to testify against others involved in the crime. Lockett's brother received the death penalty, but another robber, judged mentally deficient, was spared that penalty. Lockett rejected two offers by the district attorney to plead to a lesser charge, and in a separate trial she was convicted of aggravated murder and sentenced to death. The statute under which she was convicted mandated the death sentence for certain specified aggravating circumstances. The statute allowed for mitigation of the penalty if (1) the victim had induced or facilitated the offense; (2) it is unlikely that the offense would have been committed but for the fact that the offender was under duress, coercion, or strong provocation; or (3) the offense was primarily the product of the offender's psychosis or mental deficiency. None of these exceptions applied to Lockett, and the Ohio Supreme Court affirmed the sentence, despite her limited involvement.

Lockett appealed to the U.S. Supreme Court, arguing that the death sentence violated her Eighth and Fourteenth Amendment rights. The Court rejected a number of Lockett's constitutional claims, but, when the justices turned to the constitutionality of the Ohio statute, they concluded that it violated her Eighth and Fourteenth Amendment rights. "We find it necessary to consider only her contention that her death sentence is invalid because the statute under which it was imposed did not permit the sentencing judge to consider, as mitigating factors, her character, prior record, age, lack of specific intent to cause death, and her relatively minor part in the crime." Chief Justice Burger first reviewed the history of the death penalty in the Court and then tried to fit the circumstances with the recent decisions in ***Furman v. Georgia,*** 408 U.S. 238 (1972), and ***Gregg v. Georgia,*** 428 U.S. 153 (1976). Burger determined that the lack of clarity in these decisions necessitated a more concrete foundation of what is constitutionally permissible in imposing capital punishment. Premising its decision on the concept that individualized sentencing was the only suitable means to determine whether the capital punishment was appropriate, the Court concluded that:

The Eighth and Fourteenth Amendments require that the sentencer, in all but the rarest kind of capital case, not be precluded from considering as a mitigating factor, any aspect of a defendant's character or record and any of the circumstances of the offense that the defendant proffers as a basis for a sentence less than death.

See "The Supreme Court, 1977 Term—Death Penalty," *Harvard Law Review* 92 (1978): 99; and Ann Chih Lin, ed., *Capital Punishment* (Washington, D.C.: CQ Press, 2002).

Federal Communications Commission v. Pacifica Foundation

438 U.S. 726 (1978)
Decided: July 3, 1978
Vote: 5 (Burger, Blackmun, Powell, Rehnquist, Stevens)
4 (Brennan, Stewart, B. White, T. Marshall)
Opinion of the Court: Stevens
Opinion concurring in judgment: Powell (Blackmun)
Dissenting opinion: Brennan (T. Marshall)
Dissenting opinion: Stewart (Brennan, B. White, T. Marshall)

In October 1973 a New York City radio station owned by Pacifica Foundation played a twelve-minute monologue by Grammy Award-winning comedian George Carlin entitled "Filthy Words," popularly known as the "Seven Dirty Words." The monologue was from a live recording, which was constantly interrupted by laughter from the audience, and Carlin mentions the seven "dirty" words that you could "never" say on the radio. He used the words in various contexts, making fun of the puritanical nature of American culture and illustrating how these words were actually part of common American speech. Ironically, after condemning the speech, the majority included the entire monologue in an appendix, where every American, even young children, could find it and read it.

Some weeks after the broadcast a man complained to the Federal Communications Commission (FCC) that Carlin's monologue was on in the middle of the day and that he and his young son had heard it in the car. The FCC forwarded the complaint to the station, which responded that it had broadcast the monologue "during a program about contemporary society's attitude toward language and that, immediately before its broadcast, listeners had been advised that it included 'sensitive language which might be regarded as offensive to some.'" Pacifica noted that Carlin was "a significant social satirist" who "examines the language of ordinary people." The station said that Carlin was "not mouthing obscenities," but "merely using words to satirize as harmless and essentially silly our attitudes towards those words."

The FCC subsequently issued a declaratory order granting the complaint and holding that the station "could have been the subject of administrative sanctions." The FCC acted under a federal statute that made it an offense to broadcast "any obscene, indecent, or profane language by means of radio communication."

The FCC did not impose any sanctions at this time, but noted that the order would be "associated with the station's license file, and in the event that subsequent complaints are received, the Commission will then decide whether it should utilize any of the available sanctions it has been granted by Congress." The FCC did not find the broadcast "obscene," but did declare it "indecent" and thus in violation of federal law. The U.S. Court of Appeals for the District of Columbia reversed the FCC's findings, arguing that it amounted to censorship. In a complex decision, the Supreme Court upheld the FCC.

The Supreme Court concluded that the FCC had statutory authority "to impose sanctions on licensees who engage in obscene, indecent, or profane broadcasting." Pacifica did not dispute the FCC's finding that the monologue was "patently offensive," but insisted that it was not "indecent within the meaning of the statute" because it lacked "prurient appeal." Pacifica argued that the proper test was the one set out in ***Miller v. California,*** 413 U.S. 15 (1973). The Court said that the statute prohibited broadcasters from using "obscene, indecent, or profane" language and that Pacifica had done just that. The Court did not deny that Carlin's monologue was constitutionally protected speech, but, quoting Justice Holmes's opinion in ***Schenck v. United States,*** 249 U.S. 47 (1919), that "the character of every act depends upon the circumstances in which it is done," the Court found that the circumstances—a radio broadcast in midday—allowed the FCC to regulate the speech. Curiously, the Court conceded that Carlin's speech might have a political content, in that it satirized contemporary attitudes towards language and sex, but because the FCC had not been motivated by the content—but only by the words—the Court did not find that Carlin's speech, when broadcast on the radio, was entitled to First Amendment protection.

In dissent, Justice Brennan argued that this decision was a "patent" "misapplication of fundamental First Amendment principles" and that the Court was "misguided" in "attempt[ing] to impose its notions of propriety on the whole of the American people." Brennan castigated the majority, noting that "despite our unanimous agreement that the Carlin monologue is protected speech," a majority of the justices supported the FCC's ruling that it could impose sanctions on a station for broadcasting legal speech. Both Brennan and Justice Stewart argued that because the speech was not obscene, it could not be banned.

In effect, the Court imposed a "time, place, and manner" restriction on Carlin's speech. If the broadcast had been late at night, the outcome might have been different. The dissenters insisted, however, that anyone offended by the broadcast could turn off the radio or change the station.

See Catherine J. Ross, "Anything Goes: Examining the State's Interest in Protecting Children from Controversial Speech," *Vanderbilt Law Review* 53 (2000): 427; and M. Rivera-Sanchez, "How Far is Too Far? The Line Between 'Offensive' and 'Indecent' Speech," *Federal Communications Law Journal* (1997): 327.

Orr v. Orr

440 U.S. 268 (1979)
Decided: March 5, 1979
Vote: 6 (Brennan, Stewart, B. White, T. Marshall, Blackmun, Stevens)
3 (Burger, Powell, Rehnquist)
Opinion of the Court: Brennan
Concurring opinion: Blackmun
Concurring opinion: Stevens
Dissenting opinion: Powell
Dissenting opinion: Rehnquist (Burger)

William H. Orr challenged an Alabama statute requiring husbands, but not wives, to pay alimony. The Court found the statute unconstitutional as a violation of the Fourteenth Amendment's Equal Protection Clause. Reversing and remanding the case, the Court determined that the statute created an unjustifiable gender-based classification.

William and Lillian Orr divorced in 1974, and William was directed to pay his former wife alimony each month. When the payments were two years in arrears, Lillian initiated contempt proceedings in the circuit court. In his defense, William asked that the Alabama alimony statute be found unconstitutional. Denying the motion, the circuit court entered judgment against him for the back alimony and attorney fees. The Alabama Supreme Court ultimately affirmed this result.

The U.S. Supreme Court reversed, finding that any statute that creates a gender-based classification must be scrutinized under the Equal Protection Clause. "To withstand scrutiny under the Equal Protection Clause, classifications by gender must serve important governmental objectives and must be substantially related to achievement of those objectives." Deciding that the state's preference for allocation of family responsibilities was an invalid justification, the Court considered two other justifications proposed by Alabama. The desire to provide for needy spouses and to rectify past discrimination are valid objections; however, the justices believed that the current system, which provides for individualized hearings in divorce proceedings, canceled the need for generalizations. Instead, the Court determined that the statute's classification actually leads to perverse results. Effectively, the statute provides an advantage to financially secure wives.

The dissenting opinions by Justices Powell and Rehnquist argued the same issue. Both opinions argued that the Court, eager to decide the merits of the case, incorrectly found jurisdiction. Powell noted "when a federal constitutional claim is premised on an unsettled question of state law, the federal court should stay its hand in order to provide the state courts an opportunity to settle the underlying state-law question." More adamant than Powell, Rehnquist wrote, "I do not think the Court, in deciding the merits of appellant's constitutional claim, has exercised the self-restraint that Art. III requires in this case."

See Bruce K. Miller, "Constitutional Remedies for Underinclusive Statutes: A Critical Appraisal of *Hechler v. Matthews*," *Harvard Civil Rights-Civil Liberties Law Review* 20 (1985): 79.

Ambach v. Norwick

441 U.S. 68 (1979)
Decided: April 17, 1979
Vote: 5 (Burger, Stewart, B. White, Powell, Rehnquist)
4 (Brennan, T. Marshall, Blackmun, Stevens)
Opinion of the Court: Powell
Dissenting opinion: Blackmun (Brennan, T. Marshall, Stevens)

A New York statute required that all public schoolteachers be either U.S. citizens or demonstrate an intention of becoming naturalized within three years. The plaintiffs, citizens of Great Britain and Finland, were married to U.S. citizens and had resided in the United States for many years. They met all requirements to teach in New York, except the citizenship requirement, and neither wished to exercise the right to become a U.S. citizen. The district court found the citizenship classification to be an unconstitutional violation of the Equal Protection Clause. The Supreme Court reversed.

The Court acknowledged that most state restrictions on aliens were unconstitutional but asserted the "general principle that some state functions are so bound up with the operation of the State as a governmental entity as to permit the exclusion from those functions of all persons who have not become part of the process of self-government." The Court found that public schoolteachers are so integrated in the process of state government that the state is entitled to place a citizenship requirement on them as government employees. Although most citizenship-based classifications would call for a stricter standard of review, here the state needed to show only a rational basis for limiting employment to U.S. citizens.

The four dissenters felt that schoolteachers are not the sort of government employees that should be covered under the policy of the government employees exception to the rule against alienage restrictions. They felt that teachers were more like private professionals than the policymaking government officers the government employee exception contemplated. They also pointed out that the law in question originated in the anti-immigrant hysteria surrounding World War I, thus implying it was related to legislative embarrassments such as the Sedition Act. They suggested that even if rational basis were the appropriate standard for evaluating the law's constitutionality, the statute would not pass muster.

See William B. Senhauser, "Education and the Court: The Supreme Court's Educational Ideology," *Vanderbilt Law Review* 40 (1987): 939; and "Note: A Dual Standard for State Discrimination Against Aliens," *Harvard Law Review* 92 (1979): 1516.

Cannon v. University of Chicago

441 U.S. 677 (1979)
Decided: May 14, 1979
Vote: 6 (Burger, Brennan, Stewart, T. Marshall, Rehnquist, Stevens)
3 (B. White, Blackmun, Powell)
Opinion of the Court: Stevens
Concurring opinion: Rehnquist (Stewart)
Opinion concurring in judgment: Burger
Dissenting opinion: B. White (Blackmun)
Dissenting opinion: Powell

Title IX of the Education Amendments of 1972 prohibits any university receiving federal funds from discriminating in the admission to its programs on the basis of gender. Cannon sued under Title IX, alleging that she had been denied admission to university's medical school on the basis of her sex. The district court and the Seventh Circuit Court dismissed her action on the grounds that Title IX's express remedy of denying federal funds to the institution was the only remedy available because the title did not create an implied private cause of action. The Supreme Court disagreed.

The Court relied on ***Cort v. Ash,*** 422 U.S. 66 (1975), to find that Congress had intended to create a private cause of action when it enacted Title IX. *Cort* held that a congressional act created a private cause of action if: (1) the plaintiff belonged to the class the statute was meant to protect; (2) legislative history or other sources indicate that Congress intended to create a private remedy; (3) allowing a private cause of action was not inconsistent with the statute's purpose; and (4) the subject matter of the act is not traditionally left to the states. The plaintiff was a woman who had been discriminated against on the basis of sex in education and clearly belonged to the class Title IX was intended to protect. Title IX expressly adopted the interpretation of the earlier Title VI of the Civil Rights Act of 1964, which had been determined to create a private cause of action. The Court found nothing inconsistent with the legislative scheme in providing a private cause of action. Finally, the federal government is the primary defender of civil rights under the post–Civil War federal scheme. Based on this analysis, the Court determined that Title IX did create a private cause of action and that plaintiff might proceed with her case.

See Bruce A. Boyer, "*Howard v. Pierce:* Implied Causes of Action and the Ongoing Vitality of *Cort v. Ash,*" *Northwestern University Law Review* 80 (1985): 722; Douglas P. Ruth, "Title VII & Title IX = ?: Is Title IX the Exclusive Remedy for Employment Discrimination in the Educational Sector?" *Cornell Journal of Law and Public Policy* 5 (1996): 185; and "The Supreme Court, 1979 Term, Implied Private Causes of Action Under the Investment Advisers Act: *Transamerica Mortgage Advisors, Inc. v. Lewis,*" *Harvard Law Review* 94 (1980): 279.

Parham v. J. R.

442 U.S. 584 (1979)
Decided: June 20, 1979
Vote: 6 (Burger, Stewart, B. White, Blackmun, Powell, Rehnquist)
3 (Brennan, T. Marshall, Stevens)
Opinion of the Court: Burger
Opinion concurring in judgment: Stewart
Dissenting opinion: Brennan (T. Marshall, Stevens)

Three minor children challenged the Georgia commitment scheme that allowed parents to "voluntarily" commit their children to state mental health care. The district court found that the scheme was unconstitutional.

The Supreme Court held that the record showed that Georgia's procedures satisfied due process and outlined the minimum procedural safeguards required by due process for the commitment of children. The Court noted that, traditionally, the common law allows parents to "speak for" their children. Civil commitment, however, carried a risk of parents being wrong about a child's need for hospitalization, and due process required Georgia to have a neutral party review the appropriateness of such a decision. Although the hearing need not be conducted with all the procedural apparatus of a trial, it should seek to understand the individual child through extensive fact-finding, and the magistrate should have the authority to refuse to commit the child in cases where that course is not appropriate. As Georgia's scheme satisfied these requirements, the Supreme Court reversed the district court.

Justice Brennan's dissent criticized the majority for taking too lightly the "massive curtailment of liberty" suffered by committed minors. "Constitutional rights do not mature and come into being magically only when one attains the state-defined age of majority," he wrote. "Minors as well as adults are protected by the Constitution and possess constitutional rights."

See Lois A. Weithorn, "Mental Hospitalization of Troublesome Youth: An Analysis of Skyrocketing Admission Rates," *Stanford Law Review* 40 (1988): 773; and Elyce H. Zenoff and Alan B. Zients, M.D., "If Civil Commitment Is the Answer for Children, What Are the Questions?" *George Washington Law Review* 51 (1983): 171.

Brown v. Texas

443 U.S. 47 (1979)
Decided: June 25, 1979
Vote: 9 (Burger, Brennan, Stewart, B. White, T. Marshall, Blackmun, Powell, Rehnquist, Stevens)
0
Opinion of the Court: Burger

Police officers cruising in their squad car spotted Zackary C. Brown and another man in an alley in a "high drug traffic area." Although they did not have probable cause to believe Brown had committed a crime, the officers stopped him and asked for his identification. The officers testified that they stopped Brown because the situation "looked suspicious and we had never seen that subject in that area before." When Brown angrily told the officers that they had no right to stop him, they frisked him and arrested him. The officers' justification for the arrest was a Texas statute making it a crime to refuse to answer a police officer who asks for one's identification. Brown was taken to the police station and searched two more times before he was released. He was tried and convicted for violating the law against refusing to answer a police officer. He appealed, arguing the law violated his Fourth Amendment right against unreasonable search and seizure.

The Supreme Court reversed Brown's conviction. The Court observed that the police officers had no probable cause to stop Brown at all, and by stopping him they had violated his Fourth Amendment rights. As Chief Justice Burger concluded:

> In the absence of any basis for suspecting appellant of misconduct, the balance between the public interest and appellant's right to personal security and privacy tilts in favor of freedom from police interference. The Texas statute . . . is designed to advance a weighty social objective in large metropolitan centers: prevention of crime. But even assuming that purpose is served to some degree by stopping and demanding identification from an individual without any specific basis for believing he is involved in criminal activity, the guarantees of the Fourth Amendment do not allow it. When such a stop is not based on objective criteria, the risk of arbitrary and abusive police practices exceeds tolerable limits.

Hutchinson v. Proxmire

443 U.S. 111 (1979)
Decided: June 26, 1979
Vote: 8 (Burger, Brennan, Stewart, B. White, T. Marshall, Blackmun, Powell, Rehnquist, Stevens)
1 (Brennan)
Opinion of the Court: Burger
Concurring opinion: Stewart
Dissenting opinion: Brennan

Ronald Hutchinson was a research professor engaged in studying aggression in animals. Sen. William Proxmire, D-Wisc., held Hutchinson's work up to ridicule by bestowing on the federal agency that funded Hutchinson's research the "Golden Fleece of the Month Award" for wasteful government spending. Hutchinson sued Proxmire for defamation. The district court ruled that Proxmire's attention-getting device was protected by the Speech and Debate Clause (Article I, Section 6) and that its dissemination through a press release was protected because of the "informing function" of Congress. Furthermore, the district court found that Hutchinson was a "public figure" under the *Sullivan* test and therefore Proxmire could not be liable to him for defamation unless Hutchinson showed that Proxmire acted with malice. Hutchinson appealed, and the Supreme Court reversed.

The Court accepted that Proxmire's remarks on the Senate floor were protected by the Speech and Debate Clause, but it did not accept that Proxmire's re-publication of the statements was protected. The re-publication was neither part of any congressional deliberation nor was it necessary for informing the public because reporters fill that role. Furthermore, the Court held that Hutchinson was not a "public figure." His study of animal behavior was not an example of thrusting oneself to the forefront of a public controversy. He did not have any access to the news media. If he was arguably a public figure at the time of trial, it was only because Proxmire's stunt had made him one.

Justice Brennan's dissent called for an interpretation of the Speech and Debate Clause broad enough to include the re-publication of comments made on the Senate floor. Furthermore, he argued that criticism of wasteful government spending in any form should be protected by the clause.

See Bruce J. Borrus, "Defamation and the First Amendment: Protecting Speech on Public Issues," *Washington Law Review* 56 (1980): 75; Michael R. Seghetti, "Speech or Debate Immunity: Preserving Legislative Independence While Cutting Costs of Congressional Immunity," *Notre Dame Law Review* 60 (1985): 589; and "The Supreme Court, 1978 Term, Legislator's Liability for Repeating Defamatory Statements Outside Halls of Congress," *Harvard Law Review* 93 (1979): 161.

United Steelworkers of America v. Weber

443 U.S. 193 (1979)
Decided: June 27, 1979
Vote: 5 (Brennan, Stewart, B. White, T. Marshall, Blackmun)
2 (Burger, Rehnquist)
Opinion of the Court: Brennan
Concurring opinion: Blackmun
Dissenting opinion: Burger
Dissenting opinion: Rehnquist (Burger)
Did not participate: Powell, Stevens

In this case the Supreme Court for the first time considered affirmative action in private employment. In a collective bargaining agreement United Steelworkers of America (USWA) and Kaiser Aluminum and Chemical Corporation adopted an affirmative action plan "to eliminate conspicuous racial imbalances in Kaiser's then almost exclusively white craft-work forces." The USWA and Kaiser agreed to admit black and white employees into on-the-job training programs on a one-to-one basis. The agreement came out of numerous discrimination claims made by black workers. Before the program was initiated, only 1.83 percent (5 out of 273) of the skilled craft workers at the Gramercy, Louisiana, plant were black, although the workforce in the area was approximately 39 percent black. Brian F. Weber challenged this agreement when he was denied an opportunity to enter a craft training program, even though he had more seniority than black workers who were selected. Weber argued that the program violated Title VII of the Civil Rights Act of 1964.

The Court noted that the case did not involve the Fourteenth Amendment because there was no state action. Moreover, the agreement was voluntary, so did not raise issues of what the Civil Rights Act required. All the Court needed to consider was whether the Civil Rights Act prohibited the voluntary agreement between the union and Kaiser. Weber argued that the language of the act, making it unlawful to "discriminate . . . because of . . . race" made the USWA-Kaiser agreement unlawful. Justice Brennan agreed that this argument was "not without force," but he asserted that Weber's argument ignored the fact that the plan was "voluntarily adopted by private parties to eliminate traditional patterns of racial segregation. In this context respondent's reliance upon a literal construction" of the statutes was "misplaced." Looking at the history of the act, as well as the history of past discrimination, Brennan concluded that the agreement was consistent with the goal of the legislation, which was, as Sen. Hubert Humphrey, D-Minn., had stated in debate, "to open employment opportunities for Negroes in occupations which have been traditionally closed to them."

Finally, Brennan noted that the program did not "create an absolute bar to the advancement of white employees; half of those trained in the program will be white." Equally important, the plan was "a temporary measure" and "not intended to maintain racial balance, but simply to eliminate a manifest racial imbalance." The program would end when the Gramercy plant had a percentage of skilled blacks that "approximates the percentage of blacks in the local labor force." This temporary measure thus passed muster under the Civil Rights Act of 1964.

See Richard K. Walker, "The Exorbitant Cost of Redistributing Injustice: A Critical View of *United Steelworkers of America v. Weber* and the Misguided Policy of Numerical Employment," *Boston College Law Review* 21 (1979): 1.

Jackson v. Virginia

443 U.S. 307 (1979)
Decided: June 28, 1979
Vote: 8 (Burger, Brennan, Stewart, B. White, T. Marshall, Blackmun, Rehnquist, Stevens)
0
Opinion of the Court: Stewart
Opinion concurring in judgment: Stevens (Burger, Rehnquist)
Did not participate: Powell

Jackson was convicted of first degree murder in Virginia court. Under Virginia law, a defendant could not be convicted of first degree murder unless the trier of fact found beyond a reasonable doubt that the killing was premeditated. Jackson sought habeas corpus relief, arguing that there was no evidence at trial of premeditation, and on this basis the district court set aside the conviction. The court of appeals reversed, finding that, indeed, some evidence of premeditation existed and that *any* evidence of premeditation should suffice.

The Supreme Court affirmed, but corrected the court of appeals' misstatements of law. The proper standard on habeas corpus review of a criminal conviction is whether there was sufficient evidence of the required element that at least one rational factfinder could find that the element was satisfied beyond a reasonable doubt. The fact that some evidence of premeditation was admitted at trial is not enough to dispose of the habeas corpus. The Court held that in this case, there was enough evidence, so the conviction was affirmed.

Gannett Co., Inc. v. DePasquale

443 U.S. 368 (1979)
Decided: July 2, 1979
Vote: 5 (Burger, Stewart, Powell, Rehnquist, Stevens)
4 (Brennan, B. White, T. Marshall, Blackmun)
Opinion of the Court: Stewart
Concurring opinion: Burger
Concurring opinion: Powell
Concurring opinion: Rehnquist
Dissenting opinion: Blackmun (Brennan, B. White, T. Marshall)

Gannett's two Rochester, New York, newspapers, the *Democrat & Chronicle* and the *Times-Union,* contested the decision of Judge DePasquale of a New York State court not to allow their reporters to attend a pretrial hearing in a criminal case.

The Supreme Court affirmed the decision to close the trial. The Court held that the Sixth Amendment guarantee of a public trial is for the defendant's benefit, not the public's. If the defendant decides to waive the public trial right because he fears adverse publicity may hurt his chance for a fair trial, the defendant has a right to do so. The Court did not reach the question of whether the First Amendment gave the public a right of access to the trial, holding only that in this case the court had properly balanced the public's interest in information against the defendant's right to a fair trial. The Court further found that a defendant did not have a constitutional right to a private trial, only that the judge had the discretion to allows such a trial if the defendant asked for it.

The dissenters agreed with the majority that the question here was not a First Amendment issue, but they argued that the accused did not have a right to close the trial to the public. Quoting Jeremy Bentham, the English reformer and political philosopher, Justice Blackmun declared that "publicity 'is the soul of justice.' " He argued that an "open judicial processes, especially in the criminal field" was necessary to "protect against judicial, prosecutorial, and police abuse" as well as "a means for citizens to obtain information about the criminal justice system and the performance of public officials; and safeguard the integrity of the courts." Like the Court, he conceded that some kinds of publicity might undermine the ability of the defendant to get a fair trial, but he asserted "only in rare circumstances" did the principle of open trials "clash with the rights of the criminal defendant to a fair trial so as to justify exclusion." Based on factual record, he did not believe this was such a case.

See Michael Fenner and James L. Koley, "Access to Judicial Proceedings: To Richmond Newspapers and Beyond G.," *Harvard Civil Rights-Civil Liberties Law Review* 16 (1981): 415; and Bernard P. Bell, "Closure of Pretrial Suppression Hearings: Resolving the Fair Trial/Free Press Conflict," *Fordham Law Review* 51 (1983): 1297.

Columbus Board of Education v. Penick

443 U.S. 449 (1979)
Decided: July 2, 1979
Vote: 7 (Burger, Brennan, Stewart, B. White, T. Marshall, Blackmun, Stevens)
2 (Powell, Rehnquist)
Opinion of the Court: B. White
Opinion concurring in judgment: Burger,
Opinion concurring in judgment: Stewart (Burger)
Dissenting opinion: Powell
Dissenting opinion: Rehnquist (Powell)

The Columbus, Ohio, school system was highly segregated by race, both at the time of ***Brown v. Board of Education,*** 347 U.S. 483 (1954) (*Brown I*), and continuously until this case was decided in 1979. Justice White set out the facts: "In 1976, over 32% of the 96,000 students in the system were black. About 70% of all students attended schools that were at least 80% black or 80% white. Half of the 172 schools were 90% black or 90% white." Plaintiffs sued the school board, alleging that it intentionally created and perpetuated a dual school system. The trial court found "that the Columbus Public Schools were openly and intentionally segregated on the basis of race" when *Brown I* was decided.

The trial court found that the Columbus school board made little effort to dismantle the dual system. The court also found that, until legal action was taken against it, the school board did not assign teachers and administrators to Columbus schools at random, without regard for the racial composition of the student enrollment at those schools. The board continued to approve optional attendance zones, discontiguous attendance areas, and boundary changes that maintained and enhanced racial imbalance in the schools, even while rejecting workable suggestions for improving the racial balance of city schools. The school board appealed. The court of appeals and then the U.S. Supreme Court agreed with the findings.

Relying on a number of cases, including *Brown I,* ***Brown v. Board of Education,*** 349 U.S. 294 (1955), ***Green v. County School Board,*** 391 U.S. 430 (1968), ***Swann v. Charlotte-Mecklenburg Board of Education,*** 402 U.S. 1 (1971), and ***Keyes v. School Dist. No. 1,*** 413 U.S. 189 (1973), the Court reiterated that where there had been an intentional policy of perpetuating a dual school system, school authorities had "an affirmative duty to desegregate." If they did not do so, as in this case, then the courts had a duty to require the schools to desegregate.

See John M. Jackson, "Remedy for Inner City Segregation in the Public Schools: The Necessary Inclusion of Suburbia," *Ohio State Law Journal* 55 (1994): 415; Maria A. Perugini, "*Board of Education of Oklahoma City v. Dowell:* Protection of Local Authority or Disregard for the Purpose of *Brown v. Board of Education*?" *Catholic University Law Review* 41 (1992): 779; and "The Supreme Court, 1978 Term, The Scope of the Affirmative Duty to Desegregate Schools," *Harvard Law Review* 93 (1979): 119.

Bellotti v. Baird

443 U.S. 622 (1979)
Decided: July 2, 1979
Vote: 8 (Burger, Brennan, Stewart, T. Marshall, Blackmun, Powell, Rehnquist, Stevens)
1 (B. White)
Judgment of the Court: Powell
Concurring opinion: Rehnquist
Opinion concurring in judgment: Stevens (Brennan, T. Marshall, Blackmun)
Dissenting opinion: B. White

A Massachusetts statute required that a pregnant minor have the permission of both parents before obtaining an abortion. If one or both parents refused to give consent, a judge could give consent "for good cause." The district court found the statute unconstitutional, concluding that most seventeen-year-olds, as well as many sixteen-year-olds were capable of giving "informed consent" for the medical treatment they sought, and that "it would not be in the best interests of some 'immature' minors—those incapable of giving informed consent—even to inform their parents of their intended abortions." The court also noted that the statute did not adequately require that parents consider "the best interest" of the child in deciding whether to allow their minor daughter to obtain an abortion.

Citing ***In re Gault,*** 387 U.S. 1 (1967), Justice Powell noted that "A child, merely on account of his minority, is not beyond the protection of the Constitution." Indeed, Powell noted that in many contexts the Court had "concluded that the child's right is virtually coextensive with that of an adult." The Court concluded that a pregnant minor had a fundamental right to an abortion under ***Roe v. Wade,*** 410 U.S. 113 (1973), and that, unlike other limitations on minors, a limitation on a right to an abortion could permanently injure a minor. Balancing the needs of the family and the needs of children, the Court affirmed the decision of the district court, striking down the statutes.

See N. E. H. Hull and Peter Hoffer, Roe v. Wade: *The Abortion Rights Controversy in American History* (Lawrence: University Press of Kansas, 2001).

Goldwater v. Carter

444 U.S. 996 (1979)
Decided: December 13, 1979
Vote: 6 (Burger, Stewart, T. Marshall, Powell, Rehnquist, Stevens)
3 (Brennan, B. White, Blackmun)
Opinion: *Per curiam*
Concurring opinion: Powell
Concurring in judgment without opinion: T. Marshall
Opinion concurring in judgment: Rehnquist (Burger, Stewart, Stevens)
Dissenting opinion: Brennan
Dissenting opinion: Blackmun (B. White)

President Jimmy Carter's termination of a treaty with Taiwan without congressional approval stirred controversy. Several members of Congress, led by Sen. Barry Goldwater, R-Ariz., sued Carter for "depriv[ing] them of their constitutional role with respect to a change in the supreme law of the land." The court of appeals supported "the President's well-established authority to recognize, and withdraw recognition from, foreign governments." In a fractured decision, the Supreme Court vacated judgment and remanded the case to the district court for dismissal of the complaint.

Justice Powell supported the dismissal of the complaint "as not ripe for judicial review." He agreed that further action must occur before the Court could step into the controversy. Powell wrote, "Prudential considerations persuade me that a dispute between the Congress and the President is not ready for judicial review unless and until each branch has taken action asserting its constitutional authority." In a rebuttal to Justice Rehnquist's statement suggesting that the question presented in this matter is a nonjusticiable political question, Powell argued that the case is not, as Rehnquist contends, a matter of foreign affairs. Citing ***Buckley v. Valeo,*** 424 U.S. 1 (1976), ***United States v. Nixon,*** 418 U.S. 683 (1974), ***The Pocket Veto Case,*** 279 U.S. 655 (1929), and ***Myers v. United States,*** 272 U.S. 52 (1926), Powell said that the "political question doctrine" did not apply to this case and that the Court could decide it, if it were ripe.

Justice Rehnquist's opinion, which gathered the most support from his colleagues, viewed the issue as a political matter between the president and Congress. Rehnquist found the case "nonjusticiable because it involves the authority of the President in the conduct of our country's foreign relations and the extent to which the Senate or the Congress is authorized to negate the action of the President." Finding the matter analogous to the facts and question presented in ***Coleman v. Miller,*** 307 U.S. 433 (1939), in which the Court said that nonjusticiable political disputes should be settled out of court, Rehnquist concluded that it was up to President Carter and Congress to find a solution to this dispute. Although the Constitution is silent on the termination of treaties, Congress possesses a number of powers to deal with the situation.

The dissenting opinions proposed, respectively, to grant certiorari and hold oral argument or to grant certiorari and affirm the court of appeal's decision. Neither statement adequately explained why these alternative routes should be taken, nor do the statements pull much weight. With the Court so divided, Justice Blackmun's proposal to hear oral argument might have been the wise course.

In his dissent, Justice Brennan challenged Rehnquist's notion that the case should be dismissed under the political question doctrine. Brennan argued that "the doctrine does not pertain when a court is faced with the . . . question whether a particular branch has been constitutionally designated as the repository of political decision-making power." On the contrary, he argued that the "issue of decision-making authority must be resolved as a matter of constitutional law, not political discretion; accordingly, it falls within the competence of the courts." On the substantive matter, he asserted that "abrogation of the defense treaty with Taiwan was a necessary incident to Executive recognition of the Peking Government, because the defense treaty was predicated upon the now-abandoned view that the Taiwan Government was the only legitimate political authority in China. Our cases firmly establish that the Constitution commits to the President alone the power to recognize, and withdraw recognition from, foreign regimes."

See Sophia C. Goodman, "Equitable Discretion to Dismiss Congressional-Plaintiff Suits: A Reassessment," *Case Western Reserve Law Review* 40 (1990): 1075, 1081–93.

1980–1989

World-Wide Volkswagen Corp. v. Woodson

444 U.S. 286 (1980)
Decided: January 21, 1980
Vote: 6 (Burger, Stewart, B. White, Powell, Rehnquist, Stevens)
3 (Brennan, T. Marshall, Blackmun)
Opinion of the Court: B. White
Dissenting opinion: Brennan
Dissenting opinion: T. Marshall (Blackmun)
Dissenting opinion: Blackmun

This case is considered central to modern notions of jurisdiction in civil procedure. Harry and Kay Robinson, former New York residents, bought a car from Seaway Volkswagen in Massena, New York. While they were driving through Oklahoma, they were involved in an accident that seriously injured Kay and her two children. The Robinsons attributed the injuries to the car's defective design. They brought a product liability suit in Oklahoma state court against the manufacturer, the importer, the regional distributor (World-Wide Volkswagen), and Seaway, the retail dealer. Although neither World-Wide nor Seaway did business in Oklahoma, the plaintiffs argued that because the accident had occurred in Oklahoma, that state could exercise personal jurisdiction over the defendants and require that they respond to the summons to appear in an Oklahoma court. The defendants argued that they were not subject to a suit in Oklahoma courts because as out-of-state companies they lacked the minimum contacts required by ***International Shoe Co. v. Washington,*** 326 U.S. 310 (1945), for a state to exercise jurisdiction over a defendant. The car companies argued that it was fundamentally unfair—a denial of due process of law—to require them to defend a lawsuit in Oklahoma when they did no business in the state. The trial court disagreed and allowed the Robinsons' case to continue. World-Wide appealed, first to the Oklahoma Supreme Court, which upheld the district court's exercise of jurisdiction, and then to the U.S. Supreme Court, which overruled it.

The Supreme Court held that under *International Shoe,* a minimal amount of affiliation or contact was needed between the state and the defendants before they could be held accountable in Oklahoma courts. Otherwise, Oklahoma's exercise of jurisdiction offended traditional notions of fair play. In this case, World-Wide conducted no business in Oklahoma, did not solicit business in Oklahoma, had no plans to enter the Oklahoma market, and did not avail itself of the protection of Oklahoma law. The only contact World-Wide had with Oklahoma occurred when the Robinsons drove their car through the state. Although World-Wide could have foreseen that anyone who purchased a Volkswagen from one of its dealers might drive it through any state, that did not mean that World-Wide could have planned for the possibility of being sued in every state in the Union. In other words, the "foreseeability" that its cars would travel in other states was not enough to give Oklahoma (or any other state) personal jurisdiction, which the courts call "in personam jurisdiction," over the company.

See Patricia Y. Reyhan, "Constitutional Constraints on Choice of Law: The Nexus Between *World-Wide Volkswagen Corp. v. Woodson* and *Allstate Insurance Co. v. Hague,*" *Albany Law Review* 50 (1986).

Snepp v. United States

444 U.S. 507 (1980)
Decided: February 19, 1980
Vote: 6 (Burger, Stewart, B. White, Blackmun, Powell, Rehnquist)
3 (Brennan, T. Marshall, Stevens)
Opinion: *Per curiam*
Dissenting opinion: Stevens (Brennan, T. Marshall)

In 1979 Frank W. Snepp III, a former agent of the Central Intelligence Agency (CIA), published *Decent Interval,* a critical account of U.S. policy, particularly intelligence policy, in Vietnam. Among other things, Snepp accused the CIA of abandoning its Vietnamese agents to the communists. The CIA sought an injunction to prevent Snepp from future publications without CIA approval and to in effect to create a trust that would receive any profits from the book and turn the money over to the government. The CIA argued that Snepp had breached his contract with the agency.

The Supreme Court in a *per curium* decision, sided with the CIA, holding that Snepp had breached his fiduciary obligation, which required him to submit material concerning the CIA to the agency for prepublication review. The Court also agreed that the proper remedy was a constructive trust that would deprive Snepp of any profits from the book. The Court noted that when Snepp joined the CIA, he agreed that he would "not . . . publish . . . any information or material relating to the Agency, its activities or intelligence activities generally, either during or after the term of [his] employment . . . without specific prior approval by the Agency." Furthermore, Snepp agreed "not to disclose any classified information relating to the Agency without proper authorization."

The record was clear that Snepp had violated the agreement not to publish without first submitting the book to the CIA. The claim of revealing classified information was less certain. At trial, the government conceded that "Snepp's book divulged no classified intelligence." Nevertheless, the CIA argued that by publishing his book without CIA review, Snepp had undermined the ability of the intelligence agency to gather information or gain cooperation with foreign governments.

In dissent, Justice Stevens argued that the constructive trust was not supported by common law, traditional contract law, or statutory law. Stevens noted that the government had many remedies available, including criminal sanctions, to punish someone who revealed national secrets, but Snepp had not done that. Stevens also said that the government in effect had imposed a rule of prior restraint on Snepp, in violation of the First Amendment. Stevens argued that the purpose of the CIA contract was "to ensure that classified, nonpublic information is not disclosed without the Agency's permission," not, as it appeared here, "to give the CIA the power to censor its employees' critical speech." He castigated the majority for refusing to consider the dangers to the First Amendment inherent in what was essentially a rule of prior restraint. "The Court seems unaware of the fact that its drastic new remedy has been fashioned to enforce a species of prior restraint on a citizen's right to criticize his government," he wrote. "Inherent in this prior restraint is the risk that the reviewing agency will misuse its authority to delay the publication of a critical work or to persuade an author to modify the contents of his work beyond the demands of secrecy."

See Jonathan C. Medow, "The First Amendment and the Secrecy State: *Snepp v. United States,*" *University of Pennsylvania Law Review* 130 (1982): 775; and Frank Snepp, *Irreparable Harm* (New York: Random House, 1999).

Schaumburg v. Citizens for a Better Environment

444 U.S. 620 (1980)
Decided: February 20, 1980
Vote: 8 (Burger, Brennan, Stewart, B. White, T. Marshall, Blackmun, Powell, Stevens)
1 (Rehnquist)
Opinion of the Court: B. White
Dissenting opinion: Rehnquist

The Village of Schaumburg, Illinois, was concerned that its citizens were being misled by "charitable solicitors." Such solicitors do not work for the charity represented, but for a company that keeps most of the solicitation income and remits only a small part of it to the represented charity. Schaumburg passed an ordinance requiring all charitable solicitation in the village to be done only by organizations that use at least 75 percent of their solicitation income for charitable purposes. Citizens for a Better Environment (CBE) was a nonprofit corporation devoted to environmental protection. The CBE was registered with the state's Charitable Trust Division and had tax-exempt status from the IRS. After paying their solicitors a reasonable fee, however, the CBE could not meet the 75 percent requirement. Schaumburg denied the group a solicitation permit, and the CBE sued for injunctive relief and damages.

The Supreme Court held that Schaumburg's statute was unconstitutional. Under the First Amendment, the CBE had a right to make their views heard. Charitable solicitation is a major means of publicizing viewpoints in our society. Silencing charitable solicitation would dry up a source of much desirable First Amendment activity. Charitable solicitation was not just a form of commercial speech, but a form of political speech as well, deserving the highest level of First Amendment protection. Even though Schaumburg's interest in protecting its citizens from solicitation fraud was a compelling interest, the statute needed to be drawn more narrowly to avoid sweeping into its orbit so much protected First Amendment activity, such as the CBE's solicitation for funds.

See John T. Haggerty, "Begging and the Public Forum Doctrine in the First Amendment," *Boston College Law Review* 34 (1993): 1121; and Leslie G. Espinoza, "Straining the Quality of Mercy: Abandoning the Quest for Informed Charitable Giving," *Southern California Law Review* 64 (1991): 605.

Committee for Public Education v. Regan

444 U.S. 646 (1980)
Decided: February 20, 1980
Vote: 5 (Burger, Stewart, B. White, Powell, Rehnquist)
4 (Brennan, T. Marshall, Blackmun, Stevens)
Opinion of the Court: B. White
Dissenting opinion: Blackmun (Brennan, T. Marshall)
Dissenting opinion: Stevens

In 1970 New York passed a law appropriating public funds to reimburse religious schools and other private schools for performing various mandated services, the most expensive of which were the "administration, grading and the compiling and reporting of the results of tests and examinations." At issue in *Committee for Public Education* was the constitutionality of the statute. The case was a follow-up to ***Levitt v. Committee for Public Education,*** 413 U.S. 472 (1973), which held that a New York statute giving aid to church-sponsored nonpublic schools violated the Equal Protection Clause because it had no mechanism for determining whether the funds were being used for religious or nonreligious purposes. After *Levitt,* New York amended the law to include a state auditing system that enabled the state to ensure that the funds were used for nonreligious purposes. The Committee for Public Education challenged the amended statute. The district court found that the state auditing system cured the Establishment Clause deficiency of the old statute.

The Supreme Court affirmed. The Court held that because the state-mandated services for which the statute reimbursed the schools, such as the administration of standardized tests, were not susceptible to being used for religious indoctrination, the state was within its rights to reimburse them. Furthermore, now that the statute provided a clear system for accounting for the funds and ensuring they were not diverted to religious use, the statute did not amount to state aid to religion.

See Patrick Marshall, "Religion in Schools," *CQ Researcher,* January 12, 2001, 1–24; and Paul Finkelman, ed. *Religion and American Law: An Encyclopedia* (New York: Garland, 2000).

Payton v. New York; Riddick v. New York

445 U.S. 573 (1980)
Decided: April 15, 1980
Vote: 6 (Brennan, Stewart, T. Marshall, Blackmun, Powell, Stevens)
3 (Burger, B. White, Rehnquist)
Opinion of the Court: Stevens
Concurring opinion: Blackmun
Dissenting opinion: B. White (Burger, Rehnquist)
Dissenting opinion: Rehnquist

Evidence gathered by New York detectives suggested that Theodore Payton murdered the manager of a gas station. Payton was not at home when police officers entered his apartment to arrest him. The officers did not have an arrest warrant for Payton; rather, they were acting under a New York law that allowed police to enter a private residence to make a felony arrest without a warrant. Once in the apartment the officers noticed, in plain view, a .30-caliber shell casing, which was introduced as evidence at Payton's trial. Payton sought to have the evidence suppressed as the fruit of an illegal search. The state courts upheld the New York statute, dismissing Payton's complaint and refusing to suppress the evidence.

In the companion case, Obie Riddick was arrested for two armed robberies that occurred in 1971. The robbery victims identified him in June 1973, and in January 1974 the police discovered where he was living. The police did not obtain a warrant, but knocked on his door, which was answered by a child, entered the house, and arrested Riddick. The officers opened a chest of drawers to search for weapons and found narcotics and related paraphernalia. Indicted on narcotics charges, Riddick tried to have the evidence suppressed, but the trial judge held that the warrantless entry was authorized by New York law and that the search of the immediate area was reasonable. The appeals court agreed.

The Supreme Court reversed. The Court found that protecting citizens from warrantless arrests in their homes or unreasonable searches of their homes was at the heart of Fourth Amendment protections. Justice Stevens said a citizen's Fourth Amendment privacy interest in his or her dwelling is too important to be violated based on a police officer's on-the-spot determination of probable cause. Stevens pointed out that the "the reasons for upholding warrantless arrests in a public place do not apply to warrantless invasions of the privacy of the home." Absent exigent circumstances, a search of the home may be made only after a finding of probable cause by a neutral magistrate issuing a search warrant.

See Edward G. Mascolo, "Arrest Warrants and Search Warrants in the Home: *Payton v. New York* Revisited and Modified Under State Constitutional Law," *Connecticut Bar Journal* 66 (1992): 333; William A. Schroeder, "Warrantless Misdemeanor Arrests and the Fourth Amendment," *Missouri Law Review* 58 (1993): 771; Matthew A. Edwards, "Posner's Pragmatism and Payton Home Arrests," *Washington Law Review* (2002): 299; and Alan C. Yarcusko, "*Brown* to *Payton* to *Harris:* A Fourth Amendment Double Play by the Supreme Court," *Case Western Reserve Law Review* 43 (1992): 253.

City of Mobile v. Bolden

446 U.S. 55 (1980)
Decided: April 22, 1980
Vote: 6 (Burger, Stewart, Blackmun, Powell, Rehnquist, Stevens)
3 (Brennan, B. White, T. Marshall)
Judgment of the Court: Stewart
Opinion concurring in judgment: Blackmun
Opinion concurring in judgment: Stevens
Dissenting opinion: Brennan
Dissenting opinion: B. White
Dissenting opinion: T. Marshall

Black citizens of Mobile, Alabama, sued for a determination that the city's at-large electoral system for electing commissioners violated the Fifteenth Amendment. Under the at-large system, all members of the city council were elected from the entire city, rather than having individual members elected from specific council districts as is common in most cities.

The Supreme Court held that Mobile's scheme did not violate the Fifteenth Amendment because the black voters were not prevented from voting on the same basis as other voters. Justice Potter Stewart, with Chief Justice Warren Burger and Justice William Rehnquist joining, held that intentional discrimination is necessary before a city's electoral plan is held to violate the Fifteenth Amendment. Furthermore, Mobile's plan did not violate the Fourteenth Amendment's Equal Protection Clause because there was no intentional discrimination. The Court distinguished this case from the situation in ***Gomillion v. Lightfoot,*** 364 U.S. 339 (1960). In that case the Court struck down a scheme that had redrawn the boundaries of Tuskegee, Alabama, to make it an almost entirely white town. The Court found that scheme to be unacceptable racial discrimination. In the *Mobile* case, however, the majority held that the long tradition of at-large voting was not purposely created to disfranchise blacks and that blacks had the same voting rights as whites.

The dissenters argued that this system of choosing commissioners effectively prevented blacks from being represented on the city council because the white majority would be able to elect all the members. If the city were divided into wards, areas with black majorities would probably elect blacks to the council.

See James U. Blacksher and Larry T. Menefee, "From *Reynolds v. Sims* to *City of Mobile v. Bolden:* Have the White Suburbs Commandeered the Fifteenth Amendment?" *Hastings Law Journal* 34 (September 1982); Alexander Keyssar, *The Right to Vote: The Contested History of Democracy in the United States* (New York: Basic Books, 2000); and J. Morgan Kousser, *Colorblind Injustice: Minority Voting Rights and the Undoing of the Second Reconstruction* (Chapel Hill: University of North Carolina Press, 1999).

Wengler v. Druggists' Mutual Insurance Co.

446 U.S. 142 (1980)
Decided: April 22, 1980
Vote: 8 (Burger, Brennan, Stewart, B. White, T. Marshall, Blackmun, Powell, Stevens)
1 (Rehnquist)
Opinion of the Court: B. White
Opinion concurring in judgment: Stevens
Dissenting opinion: Rehnquist

After Paul Wengler's wife, Ruth, died in a work-related accident, he sought death benefits under Missouri's worker's compensation laws. The Missouri law provided a surviving husband with death benefits only if he could prove that he was disabled or was dependent on his wife's earnings. The same law provided a surviving wife with death benefits regardless of whether she could prove she was dependent on her husband's earnings. Although Wengler stipulated he was neither disabled nor dependent on his wife's income, he argued that the Missouri law violated equal protection by requiring such a showing. The district court agreed and granted him benefits, but the Missouri Supreme Court reversed.

The U.S. Supreme Court held that the statute violated the Equal Protection Clause. The Court instructed Missouri to cure the discrimination either by removing the automatic benefits for surviving wives or extending them to surviving husbands. This case expanded the growing understanding on the Court, which began in ***Reed v. Reed,*** 404 U.S. 71 (1971), that laws were suspect and likely to be unconstitutional if they blatantly favored men over women or women over men. In *Wengler,* the Court followed the doctrines set out in ***Weinberger v. Wiesenfeld,*** 420 U.S. 636 (1975), that laws that gave benefits to women had to give the same benefits to men if they were similarly situated. Here, as in *Weinberger,* the Court found that a statute discriminated against men.

See Clare Cushman, ed. *Supreme Court Decisions and Women's Rights: Milestones to Equality* (Washington, D.C.: CQ Press, 2001); and "Comment: *Wengler v. Druggists Mutual Insurance Co.*—However the Discrimination Is Described, If Gender Based, the Test Applies," *Utah Law Review* (1981): 431.

City of Rome v. United States

446 U.S. 156 (1980)
Decided: April 22, 1980
Vote: 6 (Burger, Brennan, B. White, T. Marshall, Blackmun, Stevens)
3 (Stewart, Powell, Rehnquist)
Opinion of the Court: T. Marshall
Concurring opinion: Blackmun
Concurring opinion: Stevens
Dissenting opinion: Powell
Dissenting opinion: Rehnquist (Stewart)

The city of Rome, Georgia, made several amendments to its electoral procedures for both the board of education and the city council. The city consolidated districts and annexed new territories for voting purposes. Although the changes were not intended to dilute the black vote in Rome, the U.S. attorney general (to whom Rome was required, under the Voting Rights Act of 1965, to submit its amendments for preclearance) determined that they would have that effect and refused to allow the city to make them. Rome sued in district court to prevent the attorney general from denying its changes.

The Supreme Court held that the attorney general was within his power to prevent the proposed changes. Although the Fifteenth Amendment arguably applies only to intentional voting discrimination, it allows the government to make appropriate remedies that prevent unintentional discrimination as well. Furthermore, the act did not violate the principles of federalism because the Civil War Amendments gave the federal government power to regulate state-sponsored discrimination with appropriate actions. The "escape-hatch" provision of the act was not meant to apply to political subdivisions of states, so Rome could not opt out of the act under that provision.

In upholding the Voting Rights Act of 1965 and the attorney general's power in this case, the Court followed the path set out in ***South Carolina v. Katzenbach,*** 383 U.S. 301 (1966), of affirming Congress's broad powers to both prevent and remedy race discrimination and giving the attorney general broad discretion in enforcing these civil rights laws.

See Alexander Keyssar, *The Right to Vote: The Contested History of Democracy in the United States* (New York: Basic Books, 2000); and J. Morgan Kousser, *Colorblind Injustice: Minority Voting Rights and the Undoing of the Second Reconstruction* (Chapel Hill: University of North Carolina Press, 1999).

Rhode Island v. Inness

446 U.S. 291 (1980)
Decided: May 12, 1980
Vote: 6 (Burger, Stewart, B. White, Blackmun, Powell, Rehnquist)
3 (Brennan, T. Marshall, Stevens)
Opinion of the Court: Stewart
Concurring opinion: B. White
Opinion concurring in judgment: Burger
Dissenting opinion: T. Marshall (Brennan)
Dissenting opinion: Stevens

Thomas Inness was arrested for the shotgun murder of John Mulvaney, a taxicab driver, and was advised of his rights in accordance with ***Miranda v. Arizona,*** 384 U.S. 436 (1966). Inness asked not to be questioned until he could speak with a lawyer. While en route to the police station, however, the two police officers in the car engaged in a conversation about how they wished they knew where the shotgun was because there was a school for handicapped children in the vicinity, and "God forbid" one of the children found the gun and hurt himself. Inness interrupted the conversation and told the police where the gun was hidden. He stipulated that he understood the Miranda warnings, but that he was afraid of a child finding the gun. At his trial, he argued that his incriminating statements should be suppressed because he had made them in response to illegal police questioning following his invocation of his Fifth Amendment right to not incriminate himself.

According to Justice Stewart, the Supreme Court granted certiorari "to address for the first time the meaning of 'interrogation' under *Miranda v. Arizona.*" The Court held that the conversation between the police officers was not an interrogation under the Miranda rule, even if it did induce Inness to reveal the location of the murder weapon. Interrogation, according to *Miranda,* is any communication from the police to a suspect in police custody that the police should know is likely to elicit an incriminating response. In this case, even if the police officers hoped their conversation about the handicapped children would elicit an incriminating response from Inness, they could not reasonably have thought it was likely to do so.

United States v. Mendenhall

446 U.S. 544 (1980)
Decided: May 27, 1980
Vote: 5 (Burger, Stewart, Blackmun, Powell, Rehnquist)
4 (Brennan, B. White, T. Marshall, Stevens)
Judgment of the Court: Stewart
Opinion concurring in judgment: Powell (Burger, Blackmun)
Dissenting opinion: B. White (Brennan, T. Marshall, Stevens)

When Sylvia Mendenhall arrived at a Detroit airport from Los Angeles, two Drug Enforcement Agency (DEA) agents spotted her and thought that her conduct fit the profile for a narcotics smuggler. The agents approached Mendenhall and asked to see her ticket and identification. The name on her driver's license and ticket did not match, and the agents asked her if she would accompany them to the airport DEA office. She agreed. Once in the office, the agents asked if she would consent to a body search. She protested that she had a plane to catch, but the agents assured her that if she was not carrying any narcotics there would be no problem. She agreed to be searched, and the agents found two packages of heroin in her undergarments. At trial for smuggling narcotics, Mendenhall argued that the heroin should be suppressed because she had *not* consented to the search. The district court denied the suppression motion, and Mendenhall appealed.

The Supreme Court affirmed. The Court found that a question about whether a consent to search was voluntary will be determined by the totality of the circumstances. In this case, the agents had not told Mendenhall to accompany them to the DEA office, but merely asked her to do so. The Court found that the district court was justified in ruling that Mendenhall had voluntarily accompanied the officers. Thus, the Court found that Mendenhall was never "seized" within the meaning of the Fourth Amendment and could not claim a Fourth Amendment violation.

This case is known for promulgating the "Mendenhall factors" for determining when voluntary cooperation in a citizen-police encounter turns into a seizure. The Court had earlier held that a person is seized within the meaning of the Fourth Amendment when he feels he is not free to leave. The Mendenhall factors are "the threatening presence of several officers, the display of a weapon by an officer, some physical touching of the person of the citizen, or the use of language or tone of voice indicating that compliance with the officer's request might be compelled." This list is meant to be illustrative, not exhaustive. In this case, although Mendenhall was a twenty-two-year-old black high school dropout accosted by white officers, the Court did not find those facts were enough to show that her consent was the result of intimidation and not truly voluntary.

This case was one of the earliest illustrating the threats to civil liberties and civil rights posed by the government's so-called war on drugs. The DEA used a "profile" for searches that included race. In effect, being black or Hispanic, was an indication of criminal behavior, according to the DEA.

See Edwin J. Butterfoss, "Bright Line Seizures: The Need for Clarity in Determining when Fourth Amendment Activity Begins," *Journal of Criminal Law and Criminology* 79 (1988): 437; Alexandra Coulter, "Drug Couriers and the Fourth Amendment: Vanishing Privacy Rights for Commercial Passengers," *Vanderbilt Law Review* 43 (1990): 1311; and Paul Finkelman, "The Second Casualty of War: Civil Liberties and the War on Drugs," *Southern California Law Review* 66 (1993): 1389–1452.

Pruneyard Shopping Center v. Robins

447 U.S. 74 (1980)
Decided: June 9, 1980
Vote: 9 (Burger, Brennan, Stewart, B. White, T. Marshall, Blackmun, Powell, Rehnquist, Stevens)
0
Opinion of the Court: Rehnquist
Concurring opinion: T. Marshall
Concurring opinion: Blackmun
Opinion concurring in judgment: B. White
Opinion concurring in judgment: Powell (B. White)

Robins was forced to leave the Pruneyard Shopping Center when he attempted to solicit signatures for a petition to protest a United Nations resolution. Security guards told him that expressive conduct by the public was not allowed on the premises unless it furthered the mall's commercial purpose. Robins sued in state court. The California Supreme Court found that despite ***Lloyd Corp. v. Tanner,*** 407 U.S. 551 (1972), which held that the First Amendment does not prevent a shopping center from prohibiting speech on its premises, the state constitution's guarantee of free speech included the right to speak in a shopping mall.

The U.S. Supreme Court affirmed. Justice Rehnquist said that states were free to interpret the free speech guarantees of their own constitutions more broadly than the U.S. Constitution. Pruneyard's argument that the California decision deprived it of its property interest in excluding controversial speech that might scare off customers without due process of law was unpersuasive. Pruneyard had not even attempted to show that California's interest in protecting the expansive speech rights was not a compelling interest that would survive a due process test.

In later years, Rehnquist changed his views on the rights of private property owners, becoming a staunch defender of such rights. His more contemporary decisions on takings imply that he might have found the California ruling to be a taking of private property.

See J. W. Singer, "No Right to Exclude—Public Accommodations and Private Property," *Northwestern University Law Review* 90 (1996): 1283; Lillian R. BeVier, "Give and Take: Public Use as Due Compensation in *Pruneyard,*" *University of Chicago Law Review* 64 (1997): 71; and Alan E. Brownstein and Stephen M. Hankins, "Pruning *Pruneyard:* Limiting Free Speech Rights Under State Constitutions on the Property of Private Medical Clinics Providing Abortion Services," *U.C. Davis Law Review* 24 (1991): 1073.

Washington v. Confederated Tribes of the Colville Indian Reservation

447 U.S. 134 (1980)
Decided: June 10, 1980
Vote: Multiple
Opinion of the Court: B. White
Opinion concurring in judgment: Rehnquist
Dissenting opinion: Brennan (T. Marshall)
Dissenting opinion: Stewart

The state of Washington sought to apply its cigarette and personal property taxes to retail sales to non-Indians on Indian reservations and its mobile home tax to vehicles owned by the reservation. The Indian tribes had already imposed their own taxes on the articles by tribal ordinance. The district court found that Washington could not impose its sales taxes or mobile home tax on the Indian reservations because the tribes' imposition of taxes had preempted the state under the Commerce Clause, which includes commerce with Indian tribes.

The Supreme Court reversed. The Court held that Washington was free to tax sales by Indians to non-Indians on reservations and that it was not preempted by the Indian tribes' own taxation.

See Donald A. Grinde, ed., *Native Americans* (Washington, D.C.: CQ Press, 2002); Susan Staiger Gooding, "Place, Race, and Names: Layered Identities in *United States v. Oregon, Confederated Tribes of the Colville Reservation,* Plaintiff-Intervenor," *Law and Society Review* 28 (1994); 1181; Richard J. Ansson Jr., "Protecting Tribal Sovereignty: Why States Should Not Be Able to Tax Contractors Hired by the BIA to Construct Reservation Projects for Tribes: *Blaze Construction Co. v. New Mexico Taxation and Revenue Department:* A Case Study," *American Indian Law Review* 20 (1995–1996): 459; and Alex Tallchief Skibine, "The Court's Use of the Implicit Divestiture Doctrine to Implement Its Imperfect Notion of Federalism in Indian Country," *Tulsa Law Journal* 36 (2000): 267.

Consolidated Edison Co. of New York v. Public Service Comm'n of New York

447 U.S. 530 (1980)
Decided: June 20, 1980
Vote: 7 (Burger, Brennan, Stewart, B. White, T. Marshall, Powell, Stevens)
2 (Blackmun, Rehnquist)
Opinion of the Court: Powell
Concurring opinion: T. Marshall
Opinion concurring in judgment: Stevens
Dissenting opinion: Blackmun (Rehnquist)

The Public Service Commission prohibited Consolidated Edison (ConEd) and other public utilities from including advertising and inserts on controversial public issues in its bill mailings to customers. The state did not prohibit other kinds of companies from sending out political information with its bills. ConEd sued in state court to enjoin the Public Service

Commission's action, but the New York courts found that the suppression of the inserts did not violate the First Amendment.

The Supreme Court reversed, holding that even though ConEd is a corporation, it is still entitled to First Amendment protections. The suppression of the inserts did not qualify as a valid time, place, and manner restriction, nor was it narrowly drawn to further a compelling state interest. Therefore, the commission's action could not be justified. Justice Powell wrote, "The First Amendment's hostility to content-based regulation extends not only to restrictions on particular viewpoints, but also to prohibition of public discussion of an entire topic." By denying ConEd the right to speak out on controversial issues and by denying its customers the opportunity to hear the company's position, the commission was attempting to do just that. In this case, the Court followed the path first set out in ***First National Bank of Boston v. Bellotti,*** 435 U.S. 765 (1978), that although corporations may not have full free speech rights, the states cannot deprive an entity of otherwise protected speech simply because it is a corporation.

See Jonathan W. Emord, "Contrived Distinctions: The Doctrine of Commercial Speech in First Amendment Jurisprudence," *Policy Analysis,* September 23, 1991, 161; Jeffrey L. Harrison, "Public Utilities in the Marketplace of Ideas: A 'Fairness' Solution for a Competitive Imbalance," *Wisconsin Law Review* (1982) 43; and Eric L. Richards, "The Jurisprudential Sin of Treating Differents Alike: Emergence of Full First Amendment Protection for Corporate Speakers," *Memphis State University Law Review* 17 (1987): 173.

Central Hudson Gas & Electric Corp. v. Public Service Commission of New York

447 U.S. 557 (1980)
Decided: June 20, 1980
Vote: 8 (Burger, Brennan, Stewart, B. White, T. Marshall, Blackmun, Powell, Stevens)
1 (Rehnquist)
Opinion of the Court: Powell
Opinion concurring in judgment: Brennan
Opinion concurring in judgment: Blackmun (Brennan)
Opinion concurring in judgment: Stevens (Brennan)
Dissenting opinion: Rehnquist

The Public Service Commission of New York sought to completely ban advertising by Central Hudson, a utility company with a monopoly in its service area. The New York courts upheld the regulation because Central Hudson's commercial free speech rights were more limited than ordinary free speech rights and the regulation was directly related to substantial government interest.

The Supreme Court struck down New York's ban on the advertising. The Court held that Central Hudson's commercial free speech was a protected First Amendment interest and that the regulations were excessive in light of their intended goals. Specifically, the Court said that (1) even though Central Hudson had a monopoly in its service area, it still had a First Amendment right to advertise to promote the use of its service; (2) the government's stated interest in preventing unreasonable rates by Central Hudson was not directly advanced by banning all advertising by the company; and (3) although the government had a legitimate interest in reducing energy consumption, a goal that was directly advanced by the regulation, the government could not prove that completely banning all advertising by Central Hudson was the least restrictive means of fulfilling that interest. In fact, the Court's analysis indicates that the ban on commercial advertising, even by a regulated industry, was too extensive to serve the public interest and to meet the First Amendment's requirements that protect commercial speech, although at a different level from other speech.

This case in part expanded the notion of commercial speech first set out by the Court in ***Virginia Pharmacy Board v. Virginia Consumer Council,*** 425 U.S. 748 (1976), and ***First National Bank of Boston v. Bellotti,*** 435 U.S. 765 (1978). The Court moved away from this direction in *Posadas de Puerto Rico v. Tourism Co. of Puerto Rico,* 478 U.S. 328 (1986), but that case must be seen as an aberration, which was effectively overturned in ***44 Liquormart v. Rhode Island,*** 517 U.S. 484 (1996).

In dissent Justice Rehnquist wanted to defer to state law while at the same time rejecting the expansion of First Amendment protections for commercial speech.

See Thomas H. Jackson and John Calvin Jeffries Jr., "Commercial Speech: Economic Due Process and the First Amendment," *Virginia Law Review* 65 (1979): 1; Alex Kozinski and Stuart Banner, "Who's Afraid of Commercial Speech?" *Virginia Law Review* 76 (1990): 627; and David McGowan, "A Critical Analysis of Commercial Speech," *California Law Review* 78 (1990): 359.

Maine v. Thiboutot

448 U.S. 1 (1980)
Decided: June 25, 1980
Vote: 6 (Brennan, Stewart, B. White, T. Marshall, Blackmun, Stevens)
3 (Burger, Powell, Rehnquist)
Opinion of the Court: Brennan
Dissenting opinion: Powell (Burger, Rehnquist)

The Maine agency responsible for disbursing welfare payments denied Lionel and Joline Thiboutot payments to which they were entitled under the Social Security Act. The Thiboutots sued in Maine court for the money, and the Maine court ordered the agency to pay. The Thiboutots then asked for payment of their attorney fees as prevailing parties under 42 U.S.C. Section 1983, which authorizes such awards to the winning parties in civil rights cases. Section 1983 permits attorney fee awards whenever a plaintiff sues to correct a wrong done him under color of state law that violates the plaintiff's rights under the Constitution or laws of the United States. The Maine Supreme Court denied the award of fees, holding that Section 1983 did not include an action for a violation of the Social Security Act.

The U.S. Supreme Court reversed, holding that the plain meaning of Section 1983's phrase "deprivation of any rights . . . secured by the Constitution and laws" includes actions arising under the Social Security Act, which is a law of the United States. The purpose of the provision to award attorney fees was to ensure that civil rights plaintiffs, who are usually individuals, and often poor, will be able to engage counsel. In this case, the amount in controversy under the Social Security Act was probably less than the amount the lawyers charged. Without the ability to win fees, plaintiffs like the Thiboutots would have been unable to secure counsel and vindicate their rights.

See David E. Engdahl, "The Spending Power," *Duke Law Journal* 44 (1994): 1; and "Cognizability of Claims Based Solely upon Statutory Violations Under 42 U.S.C. § 1983: *Maine v. Thiboutot*," *Harvard Law Review* 94 (1980): 223.

Ohio v. Roberts

448 U.S. 56 (1980)
Decided: June 25, 1980
Vote: 6 (Burger, Stewart, B. White, Blackmun, Powell, Rehnquist)
3 (Brennan, T. Marshall, Stevens)
Opinion of the Court: Blackmun
Dissenting opinion: Brennan (T. Marshall, Stevens)

While staying with Anita Isaacs, Herschel Roberts used Anita's father's checks and credit cards and forged his name. At a preliminary hearing on charges of forgery and using stolen credit cards, Roberts called Anita Isaacs as a witness. In response to questioning, Isaacs admitted she had let Roberts stay at her home, but would not admit that she gave Roberts her father's checks and credit cards with permission to use them. Roberts's counsel improperly questioned Isaacs on this point in a leading manner, but did not attempt to have her declared a hostile witness or to cross-examine her.

At Roberts's criminal trial, Anita Isaacs was unavailable to testify in person because her whereabouts were unknown and she refused to respond to a subpoena. The prosecution attempted to introduce her deposition testimony that she had not given Roberts permission to use the checks or cards. Roberts argued that Isaacs's prior testimony was hearsay and that to allow it in his criminal trial without the opportunity to cross-examine her was a denial of his right to confront a witness against him. The Ohio Supreme Court agreed that allowing the testimony would violate Roberts's Confrontation Clause rights because Roberts did not have a chance to cross-examine Isaacs at the preliminary hearing. Ohio appealed.

The U.S. Supreme Court ruled that the use of Isaacs's prior testimony was not a violation of the Confrontation Clause. As Justice Blackmun pointed out, for such hearsay evidence not to violate the Confrontation Clause, the state must have shown that Isaacs was unavailable to testify in person and that her testimony had other indicia of reliability that it was not likely to mislead the jury. At the pretrial hearing on the issue of the testimony's admissibility, Isaacs's mother testified that the last time she spoke with her daughter, Anita told her she was "traveling" outside Ohio, but would not reveal her whereabouts. This was sufficient for a finding that Isaacs was unavailable. Furthermore, at the preliminary hearing, Roberts's counsel had in effect cross-examined her because his questioning was "replete with leading questions." This satisfied the "further indicia of reliability" requirement, and Isaacs's hearsay testimony was admissible against Roberts.

See Robert G. Kamenec, "Note: Right of Confrontation—*Ohio v. Roberts*," *University of Detroit Journal of Urban Law* (1980); and Laird C. Kirkpatrick, "Confrontation and Hearsay: Exemptions from the Constitutional Unavailability Requirement," *Minnesota Law Review* 70 (1986): 665.

White Mountain Apache Tribe v. Bracker

448 U.S. 136 (1980)
Decided: June 27, 1980
Vote: 6 (Burger, Brennan, B. White, T. Marshall, Blackmun, Powell)
3 (Stewart, Rehnquist, Stevens)
Opinion of the Court: T. Marshall
Concurring opinion: Powell
Dissenting opinion: Stevens (Stewart, Rehnquist)

Pinetop Logging Company, a non-Indian Arizona business, was hired by the White Mountain Apache Tribe to conduct logging operations on the Fort Apache reservation. Pinetop's activities were limited to the reservation. Arizona state agencies sought to impose on Pinetop Arizona's use fuel tax and other taxes for using the state highways to reach the reservation. The tribe objected to the tax collection on the grounds that the tax was preempted by federal law on the Indian land. The lower courts granted summary judgment to Arizona, and the tribe appealed.

The Supreme Court held that federal regulations of tribal timber are so pervasive that they preempt any state laws aimed at taxing the enterprise. The tax would undermine the federal policy of preserving Indians' sovereignty over reservation land and impair the secretary of the interior's ability to establish fees for the carrying out of such services on Indian land.

See Richard J. Ansson Jr., "Protecting Tribal Sovereignty: Why States Should Not Be Able to Tax Contractors Hired by the BIA to Construct Reservation Projects for Tribes: *Blaze Construction Co. v. New Mexico Taxation and Revenue Department:* A Case Study," *American Indian Law Review* 20 (1995–1996): 459; and Laurie Reynolds, "Indian Hunting and Fishing Rights: The Role of Tribal Sovereignty and Preemption," *North Carolina Law Review* 62 (1984): 743.

Harris v. McRae

448 U.S. 297 (1980)
Decided: June 30, 1980
Vote: 5 (Burger, Stewart, B. White, Powell, Rehnquist)
4 (Brennan, T. Marshall, Blackmun, Stevens)
Opinion of the Court: Stewart
Concurring opinion: B. White
Dissenting opinion: Brennan (T. Marshall, Blackmun)
Dissenting opinion: T. Marshall
Dissenting opinion: Blackmun
Dissenting opinion: Stevens

The Medicaid program was established in 1965 as Title XIX of the Social Security Act. Title XIX provided federal financial assistance to states to reimburse certain costs of medical treatment for the needy. Since 1976 several versions of the Hyde Amendment, named for Rep. Henry Hyde, R-Ill., who introduced it, have placed restrictions on Medicaid's ability to reimburse the cost of medically necessary abortions.

Cora McRae, a New York state Medicaid recipient, and a class of indigent pregnant women—those seeking to have an abortion within the first 24 weeks of their pregnancies—sought a determination that the Hyde Amendments violated the First Amendment Establishment Clause and the Fifth Amendment Due Process Clause. Defending the amendments were the Carter Administration Secretary of Health, Education, and Welfare Patricia R. Harris, Senators James L. Buckley, C-N.Y., and Jesse A. Helms, R-N.C., and Hyde.

The Supreme Court held that the Hyde Amendments violated neither the Fifth Amendment nor the Establishment Clause of the First Amendment. Title XIX does not require states to fund medical procedures unless the federal government shares the cost with the states. Here, because Congress has declined, through the Hyde Amendments, to split the cost of medically necessary abortions, states are not required to pick up the slack.

Furthermore, the due process privacy interest in abortion identified in ***Roe v. Wade,*** 410 U.S. 113 (1973), does not require the government to fund such abortions under its Medicaid program. According to the Court, failure to fund abortions does not prevent women from exercising their right to seek an abortion; it merely means that the financial resources of the state are not available to help a woman fund the procedure. To hold that the government is required to fund an abortion in order to preserve the woman's privacy interest would mean that the state would be required to do so even if there were no Medicaid program, which the Court declined to accept.

The Court also held that the Hyde Amendments did not violate the Establishment Clause because no proof was offered that they were motivated by religious beliefs.

Finally, the Court held that the Hyde Amendments did not violate the Equal Protection Clause of the Fifth Amendment because the affected class (indigent women) was not a constitutionally suspect class, and the amendments were rationally related to the legitimate government interest of protecting potential human life.

See Laurence H. Tribe, "The Abortion Funding Conundrum: Inalienable Rights, Affirmative Duties and the Dilemma of Dependence," *Harvard Law Review* 99 (1985): 330; Susan Frelich Appleton, "Beyond the Limits of Reproductive Choice: The Contributions of the Abortion-Funding Cases to Fundamental-Rights Analysis and to the Welfare-Rights Thesis," *Columbia Law Review* 81 (1981): 721; and "Exclusion of Therapeutic Abortions from Medicaid Coverage in *Harris v. McRae,*" *Harvard Law Review* 94 (1980): 96.

Fullilove v. Klutznick

448 U.S. 448 (1980)
Decided: July 2, 1980
Vote: 6 (Burger, Brennan, B. White, T. Marshall, Blackmun, Powell)
3 (Stewart, Rehnquist, Stevens)
Judgment of the Court: Burger
Concurring opinion: Powell
Opinion concurring in judgment: T. Marshall (Brennan, Blackmun)
Dissenting opinion: Stewart (Rehnquist)
Dissenting opinion: Stevens

The "minority business enterprise" (MBE) provision of the Public Works Employment Act of 1977 required that at least 10 percent of all federal funds disbursed for local construction projects be set aside for minority business owners. Under the provision, at least 10 percent of all contracts had to go to bona fide minority business enterprises, which included businesses operated by blacks, Hispanics, Asians, Indians, Eskimos, and Aleuts, even if the companies were not the lowest bidders, as long as the higher amount of their bids resulted from inflated costs due to past discrimination, such as the inability to obtain credit at the same rates as white-owned businesses. Several contractors alleged that they had been economically injured by the MBE provision and sued for a declaration of its unconstitutionality. The Supreme Court found the MBE constitutional.

The Court held that because Congress's spending power is as broad as its regulatory power, Congress's pursuit of public policy through the MBE (an exercise of the spending power) was legitimate as long as the same pursuit would have been permissible under the regulatory power. Congress could have regulated prime contractors' awarding of subcontracts through the Commerce Clause on the grounds that the perpetuation of discrimination through subcontracting would have a negative effect on interstate commerce. Congress also could have regulated the states' awards of prime contracts through its power to enforce the equal protection guarantees of the Fourteenth Amendment. According to the Court, because Congress could have achieved the same goals through its regulatory power, it was permitted to achieve them through its spending power.

Congress's use of ethnic criteria in distributing the benefits of the MBE provision was also constitutional. It was not underinclusive for specifying only certain minority groups to whom it applied because it was aimed at curing the past discrimination of certain groups. It was also not overinclusive for naming groups that could not be justified by the effects of past discrimination because it did not apply to minority business enterprises that could not show that their higher bid was the result of the effects of past discrimination.

See Louis Kaplow, "Comment: Statutory Preferences for Minority-Owned Businesses: *Fullilove v. Klutznick*," *Harvard Law Review* 94 (1980): 125; and John E. Richards, "Equal Protection and Racial Quotas: Where Does *Fullilove v. Klutznick* Leave Immunity: Developments in Federal Law," *Baylor Law Review* 33 (1981): 601–617.

Richmond Newspapers, Inc. v. Virginia

448 U.S. 555 (1980)
Decided: July 2, 1980
Vote: 7 (Burger, Brennan, Stewart, B. White, T. Marshall, Blackmun, Stevens)
1 (Rehnquist)
Judgment of the Court: Burger
Concurring opinion: B. White
Concurring opinion: Stevens
Opinion concurring in judgment: Brennan (T. Marshall)
Opinion concurring in judgment: Stewart
Opinion concurring in judgment: Blackmun
Dissenting opinion: Rehnquist
Did not participate: Powell

Between July 1976 and June 1978 John Paul Stevenson was tried three times for murder. His initial conviction was reversed by the Virginia Supreme Court. Two other trials ended in mistrials, the first because a juror had to be excused, and the second because a prospective juror had read about Stevenson's case in a newspaper and talked to others who were chosen for the jury. At the beginning of his fourth trial, the defendant asked that the courtroom be cleared of all spectators, and, with no objection from the prosecutor, the judge complied with the request. Later that day reporters for Richmond newspapers filed a motion to compel the court to allow them to attend the trial.

In ***Gannett Co., Inc. v. DePasquale,*** 443 U.S. 368 (1979), the Court upheld an order barring the press from a pretrial hearing to determine whether certain evidence could be suppressed. The Court accepted the argument that the Sixth Amendment right to a fair trial outweighed any need for the press to be present at a suppression hearing. This decision seemed logical: if the evidence were suppressed but the press reported on the substance of the suppressed evidence, the reputation of the defendant might be harmed. On the other hand, if the evidence were not suppressed, it would come out in the trial and be reported then. Nevertheless, in *Gannett* four dissenting justices argued that the First Amendment rights of the people and the press outweighed the Sixth Amendment claims of the defendant.

Here the question was much broader: May a judge bar the press from a court during the entire length of the trial. The Court found that trials could not be closed to the public except under the most extraordinary circumstances. Chief Justice Burger asserted a long historical tradition of open courts and stressed the idea that justice should be meted out in the open, both for the protection of the defendant and for the education of the public. Burger found that the open court "has long been recognized as an indispensible attribute of an Anglo-American trial." He also noted some First Amendment grounds for allowing the press to cover a trial.

Justice White argued that the Sixth Amendment required that the courtroom be open. Justice Blackmun also argued for a Sixth Amendment analysis, while asserting First Amendment issues as well. Justice Stevens argued that the First Amendment precluded the government from arbitrarily preventing press coverage of trials. Justice Brennan argued for a First Amendment analysis, saying that a judge would violate the First Amendment by closing a public trial to the media. Brennan noted that the First Amendment protected the press not only when publishing, but also in gathering news. "The First Amendment embodies more than a commitment to free expression and communicative interchange for their own sakes," Brennan wrote. "It has a structural role to play in securing and fostering our republican system of self-government." He then bolstered this position with a discussion of the historical place of the public trial in Anglo-American jurisprudence. In a sense, Brennan's position was the mirror image of Burger's. The chief justice found that the need for a public trial led to a claim by the press, while Brennan concluded that the press's claim and duty to report the news was supported by the historical nature of public trials. Justice Stewart basically agreed with Brennan's position, although he might have allowed this First Amendment right to be abridged under some circumstances.

In dissent, Justice Rehnquist argued that the Ninth Amendment gave the states great latitude in keeping trials open or in closing them, if that is what both the defense and the prosecution wanted. Rehnquist's reliance on the Ninth Amendment did not, however, offer an answer to the fundamental issues of openness and secrecy in a democratic society. With the exception of Rehnquist, all the justices endorsed a theory of American law best stated in Brennan's concurring opinion: "Secrecy is profoundly inimical to this demonstrative purpose of the trial process. Open trials assure the public that procedural rights are respected, and that justice is afforded equally. Closed trials breed suspicion of prejudice and arbitrariness, which in turn spawns disrespect for law. Public access is essential, therefore, if trial adjudication is to achieve the objective of maintaining public confidence in the administration of justice."

See Donald Grier Stephenson Jr., "Fair Trial—Free Press: Rights in Continuing Conflict," *Brooklyn Law Review* 46 (1979): 39; Michael Fenner and James L. Koley, "Access to Judicial Proceedings: To *Richmond Newspapers* and Beyond," *Harvard Civil Rights-Civil Liberties Law Review* 16 (1981): 415; and G. Mark Mamantov, "The Executioner's Song: Is There a Right to Listen?" *Virginia Law Review* 69 (1983): 373.

Stone v. Graham

449 U.S. 39 (1980)
Decided: November 17, 1980
Vote: 5 (Brennan, B. White, T. Marshall, Powell, Stevens)
4 (Burger, Stewart, Blackmun, Rehnquist)
Opinion: *Per curiam*
Dissenting without opinion: Burger, Stewart, Blackmun
Dissenting opinion: Rehnquist

In this Establishment Clause case, the Supreme Court invalidated a Kentucky statute that required the Ten Commandments to be posted in every public schoolroom in the state. The displays were paid for with private contributions. Applying the test announced in ***Lemon v. Kurtzman,*** 403 U.S. 602 (1971), the Court found that the statute had an obvious religious purpose, even though the state asserted a secular one by adding a statement to each display, which said that the Ten Commandments had a secular significance as "the fundamental legal code of Western Civilization and the Common Law of the United States." The Court said that the primary significance of the Ten Commandments is religious and pointed out that the commandments are not limited to principles that are accepted in secular law, such as the avoidance of murder, but contain several purely religious exhortations, such as to keep the Sabbath. The Court also said that the purpose of displaying them was "plainly religious." Furthermore, the fact that the copies of the Ten Commandments were bought through private contributions and not through the state was irrelevant because the state's act of posting them in classrooms was sufficient to implicate the state in the promotion of religion. The Court noted that it would be permissible to study the Ten Commandments if they were "integrated into the school curriculum" as part of a more general study of "history, civilization, ethics, comparative religion, and the like," but such a plan was clearly not what the state intended. The Court therefore summarily reversed the lower court, which had upheld the statute.

Chief Justice Burger and Justice Blackmun dissented on the basis that the case should be granted certiorari and given full consideration. Justice Stewart also dissented from this summary reversal because he thought the Kentucky courts were correct.

In dissent, Justice Rehnquist argued that the Court should have deferred to the legislature's avowed secular purpose. Neither Rehnquist nor any of the other dissenters explained how the explicitly religious provisions of the Ten Commandments—such as the admonition to have only one God, or to keep the Sabbath—could be viewed as "secular."

See Patrick Marshall, "Religion in Schools, *CQ Researcher,* January 12, 2001, 1–24; Garry Wills, *Under God: Religion and American Politics* (New York: Simon and Schuster, 1990); and Steve K. Green, "The Fount of Everything Just and Right? The Ten Commandments as a Source of American Law," *Journal of Law and Religion* 14 (1999–2000): 525.

Minnesota v. Clover Leaf Creamery Co.

449 U.S. 456 (1981)
Decided: January 21, 1981
Vote: 6 (Burger, Brennan, Stewart, B. White, T. Marshall, Blackmun)
2 (Powell, Stevens)
Opinion of the Court: Brennan
Dissenting opinion: Powell
Dissenting opinion: Stevens
Did not participate: Rehnquist

The Minnesota legislature passed a statute banning the retail sale of milk in nonrefillable plastic containers, but allowing the sale of milk in paperboard containers, for the purpose of conservation. The plaintiffs argued that the statute violated the Commerce Clause and the Fourteenth Amendment's guarantee of equal protection because it treated manufacturers of plastic and paperboard containers differently. The Minnesota Supreme Court decided the case on equal protection grounds and held the statute unconstitutional. The U.S. Supreme Court reversed.

Justice Brennan's opinion held that the statute should be upheld because it was rationally related to a legitimate state goal. The Minnesota legislature may have determined that by banning plastic nonrefillables, it was promoting the use of environmentally healthier alternatives. Whether the legislature was correct in its assessment of the relative environmental evils of plastic and paperboard containers was irrelevant. The Minnesota Supreme Court erred in substituting its own interpretation of the environmental science for the legislature's, when the legislature had relied on reputable studies and its interpretation of the data was at least arguable. Furthermore, the statute's burden on interstate commerce was slight, considering that most milk manufacturers package their milk in more than one type of container. When compared to the strong state interest in promoting conservation, the slight burden on interstate commerce was not "clearly excessive."

This case did not raise any issues of the state protecting its own producers at the expense of out-of-state producers. Rather, it pointed the way toward states regulating environmental issues at the local level, as long as the state did not interfere with federal environmental controls.

Chandler v. Florida

449 U.S. 560 (1981)
Decided: January 26, 1981
Vote: 8 (Burger, Brennan, Stewart, B. White, T. Marshall, Blackmun, Powell, Rehnquist)
0
Opinion of the Court: Burger
Opinion concurring in judgment: Stewart
Opinion concurring in judgment: B. White
Did not participate: Stevens

The Florida Supreme Court promulgated a judicial canon that allowed electronic and still photographic media in the courtroom. Chandler was tried for a crime that had attracted public attention, and the media were allowed to cover his trial under the new canon. When he was convicted, Chandler appealed on grounds that the presence of the television and newspaper reporters had denied him the right to a fair trial. The Florida courts upheld his conviction, and he appealed to the Supreme Court. He argued that ***Estes v. Texas,*** 381 U.S. 532 (1965), had established the unconstitutionality of television media in the courtroom because the media tended to destroy the atmosphere of detached decision making necessary for a fair trial. The Supreme Court disagreed with this argument and affirmed the Florida court.

According to Chief Justice Burger, *Estes* did not establish that television's presence in the courtroom always rendered a trial unconstitutionally unfair. *Estes* was a plurality opinion. Justice Harlan, the fifth vote, had limited his concurrence to the facts of *Estes.* Harlan expressed the view that the public's right to knowledge should be balanced against the necessity of preserving the judicial process from "pluming" and "performing" for an audience in ways that could prejudice a defendant. *Estes* involved a sensational case, and its media coverage tended to prejudice the jury. The Court held that *Estes* should be limited to such situations. In this case, Chandler could not show that the media's presence had prejudiced him, and the Court upheld his conviction.

See Charles R. Nesson and Andrew D. Koblenz, "The Image of Justice: *Chandler v. Florida,*" *Harvard Civil Rights-Civil Liberties Law Review* 16 (fall 1981); Nancy T. Gardner, "Cameras in the Courtroom: Guidelines for State Criminal Trials," *Michigan Law Review* 84 (1985): 475; and Jeremy Cohen, "Cameras in the Courtroom and Due Process: A Proposal for a Qualitative Difference Test," *Washington Law Review* 57 (1982): 277.

Michael M. v. Superior Court of Sonoma County

450 U.S. 464 (1981)
Decided: March 23, 1981
Vote: 5 (Burger, Stewart, Blackmun, Powell, Rehnquist)
4 (Brennan, B. White, T. Marshall, Stevens)
Judgment of the Court: Rehnquist
Concurring opinion: Stewart
Opinion concurring in judgment: Blackmun
Dissenting opinion: Brennan (B. White, T. Marshall)
Dissenting opinion: Stevens

Michael M., a seventeen-and-a-half-year-old boy, was charged with violating California's statutory rape law for having sex with a girl under eighteen years old. The law defined statutory rape as sexual intercourse with a woman, not the wife of the perpetrator, who was under eighteen. Michael M. challenged the statute under the Equal Protection Clause because it applied only to men and not to women.

The Court held that the statute was valid under the Equal Protection Clause. Justice Rehnquist noted that gender-based classifications are not inherently suspect and do not need to meet a strict scrutiny test. Instead, they will be upheld if they are rationally related to a legitimate government interest. Here, the statute is rationally related to the legitimate government interest of preventing teenage pregnancy. Although it could have been worded to hold females as well as males responsible, it is not necessary that the statute be optimally worded to meet the rational basis standard. The legislature could have rationally concluded that only males should be punished for violating the statute, as most of the negative results of teenage pregnancy fall on the female, and she therefore already has a deterrent to engaging in underage sex. Since the decision in this case, many states have removed the gender language in statutory rape statutes, and some adult women have been prosecuted for having sexual relations with underage males.

See Leslie G. Landau, "Gender-Based Statutory Rape Law Does Not Violate the Equal Protection Clause: *Michael M. v. Superior Court of Sonoma County,*" *Cornell Law Review* 67 (1982): 1109; and Anne-Marie Leath Storey, "An Analysis of the Doctrines and Goals of Feminist Legal Theory and Their Constitutional Implications," *Vermont Law Review* 19 (1994): 137.

Thomas v. Review Board of Indiana, Employment Security Division

450 U.S. 707 (1981)
Decided: April 6, 1981
Vote: 8 (Burger, Brennan, Stewart, B. White, T. Marshall, Blackmun, Powell, Stevens)
1 (Rehnquist)
Opinion of the Court: Burger
Opinion concurring in judgment: Blackmun
Dissenting opinion: Rehnquist

Thomas was employed in a steel factory that made rolled steel. His employer closed the rolled steel plant and offered to transfer him to another facility, but all of the employer's other factories made military hardware. Thomas, a Jehovah's Witness, refused to engage in such manufacture and resigned. He then applied for unemployment compensation with the Indiana Employment Security Division, but his request was denied. The agency found that he had left his job because of sincerely held religious beliefs, but that the resignation did not stem from a "good cause arising in connection with work." The Review Board affirmed, and Thomas took his case to the Indiana courts.

The Indiana Supreme Court agreed with the Review Board. Several factors were crucial to the state supreme court's decision: (1) Thomas appeared to be "struggling" with his beliefs and was unable to articulate them consistently; (2) he had not objected to producing raw materials, such as rolled steel, that ultimately went into weapons; and (3) that another Jehovah's Witness had no moral scruples about manufacturing weapons. The Indiana Supreme Court held that Thomas's resignation was motivated by a personal philosophical choice rather than religious compulsion. Thomas appealed to the U.S. Supreme Court.

The Court held that the denial of unemployment benefits to Thomas impermissibly interfered with his free exercise of religion. The Court said that the state supreme court had erred in determining that because Thomas was not able to precisely articulate his moral scruples, they were not the result of a sincerely held religious belief. The Indiana Supreme Court was also wrong to rely on other Jehovah's Witnesses' statements that they had no scruples about the manufacture of weapons. Just because not every member of Thomas's religion held the same religious beliefs did not mean his were not religious or genuine. The state may not place significant burdens on the exercise of religious principles by conditioning important state benefits on noncompliance with them. Finally, the Review Board's contention that paying Thomas benefits would amount to state subsidization of Thomas's religious beliefs in violation of the separation of church and state was without merit. Payment of unemployment benefits to Thomas would amount to nothing more than treating his religiously motivated abstention with the same respect as any other work-precluding condition.

See Renee C. Redman, "Jehovah's Witnesses," in *Religion and American Law: An Encyclopedia,* ed. Paul Finkelman (New York: Garland, 2000), 245–253.

Pennhurst State School and Hospital v. Halderman

451 U.S. 1 (1981)
Decided: April 20, 1981
Vote: 6 (Burger, Stewart, Blackmun, Powell, Rehnquist, Stevens)
3 (Brennan, B. White, T. Marshall)
Opinion of the Court: Rehnquist
Opinion concurring in judgment: Blackmun
Dissenting opinion: B. White (Brennan, T. Marshall)

The Developmentally Disabled Assistance and Bill of Rights Act of 1975 conditioned the receipt of certain federal funds on states' participation in programs aimed at treatment and care of the mentally disabled. Section 6010 of the act contained a "bill of rights" for patients in institutions, which stated that the mentally retarded have a right to treatment and services in "the setting that is least restrictive of . . . personal liberty." Terri Lee Halderman was a mentally retarded resident of the state-owned Pennhurst State School and Hospital in Pennsylvania who complained that conditions at Pennhurst were inhumane and unsanitary. She sued and asked the court to close Pennhurst and arrange for community living for Pennhurst's residents. The Pennsylvania Court of Appeals held that the act created a private cause of action for Halderman to enforce its requirement for treatment in the least restrictive means possible.

The U.S. Supreme Court held that the act did not create any substantive right for treatment in the least restrictive means possible. Under the Fourteenth Amendment, it is assumed that Congress did not intend to impose a massive financial burden on the states. Under the Spending Power Clause, however, Congress can condition the release of federal funds upon states' compliance with federal standards. States will not be assumed to have agreed to such an arrangement unless the condition is express and unambiguous. Here, the provision regarding a setting that is least restrictive of personal liberty appears in its context to express an aspirational goal of Congress. It does not appear to be the purpose of the disbursal of funds or to be a condition on their acceptance. By the words *least restrictive of personal liberty,* Congress cannot be said to have given states clear notice that they are expected to close residential facilities for the retarded and move them into the community, and states cannot be supposed to have understood that as a condition of accepting the funds.

See David L. Shapiro, "Wrong Turns: The Eleventh Amendment and the Pennhurst Case," *Harvard Law Review* 98 (1984): 61; and Keith Werhan, "Pullman Abstention After *Pennhurst:* A Comment on Judicial Federalism," *William and Mary Law Review* 27 (1986): 449.

City of Memphis v. Greene

451 U.S. 100 (1981)
Decided: April 20, 1981
Vote: 6 (Burger, Stewart, B. White, Powell, Rehnquist, Stevens)
3 (Brennan, T. Marshall, Blackmun)
Opinion of the Court: Stevens
Opinion concurring in judgment: B. White
Dissenting opinion: T. Marshall (Brennan, Blackmun)

Memphis closed one end of West Drive, a city street that ran through a white residential neighborhood called Hein Park. The plaintiffs in this case resided in a black neighborhood to the north of Hein Park and were accustomed to driving on West Drive to get around in the city. They claimed that their property values had been impaired by the closing, as they were now required to take a less-direct route for trips within the city. They said this impairment violated their right to own property on an equal basis with whites under the Civil Rights Act and the Thirteenth Amendment prohibition against the "badges of slavery." Memphis claimed that the closing of the north end of West Drive was motivated by a desire to reduce "traffic pollution" in Hein Park, to allow children to walk to school in the safety of diminished traffic, and to increase the "tranquility" of the neighborhood. The district courts of Tennessee twice dismissed the plaintiffs' claims, and the Sixth Circuit twice reversed those decisions. The Sixth Circuit noted that the closing of West Drive amounted to the erection of a barrier between black and white neighborhoods, protecting the white neighborhood from the "undesirable" presence of black traffic.

The Supreme Court reversed the Sixth Circuit's decision. Justice Stevens found that the closing of the street was not meant to impair the plaintiffs' property, but merely to protect children from traffic. The Court held that such a closing, not motivated by discriminatory intent, is consistent with the Civil

Rights Act. It did not impair the black homeowner's right to own property on an equal basis with whites.

Justice Marshall's dissent took the majority to task for its characterization of the evidence developed in the lower courts. According to Marshall, the Sixth Circuit was entirely correct in concluding that the closing of West Drive was motivated by a desire of the white residents of Hein Park not to see black motorists in their neighborhood. The majority was also wrong to conclude that there was no impairment to the property value of the black residents north of Hein Park other than the "inconvenience" of having to take a longer route to get to points south of their neighborhood. The message sent to those residents by the Memphis decision is that they are being forced to suffer an inconvenience that white citizens do not have to endure because white residents consider their very presence to be a nuisance.

See Michael Selmi, "Proving Intentional Discrimination: The Reality of Supreme Court Rhetoric," *Georgetown Law Journal* 86 (1997): 279; and Leah Farish, "The Intent Requirement at the Crossroads: Racial Discrimination and *City of Memphis v. Greene,*" *Baylor Law Review* 34 (1982): 309.

Estelle v. Smith

451 U.S. 454 (1981)
Decided: May 18, 1981
Vote: 9 (Burger, Brennan, Stewart, B. White, T. Marshall, Blackmun, Powell, Rehnquist, Stevens)
0
Opinion of the Court: Burger
Concurring opinion: Brennan
Concurring opinion: T. Marshall
Opinion concurring in judgment: Stewart (Powell)
Opinion concurring in judgment: Rehnquist

Ernest Benjamin Smith was tried and convicted for murder in a Texas court. Before the trial, Smith was interviewed for ninety minutes by Dr. James Grigson, a psychiatrist, who determined that Smith was competent to stand trial. Prior to his interview with Grigson, Smith was not informed of his right to remain silent. At the sentencing phase of his trial, defense counsel presented three lay witnesses who testified to Smith's good character and to the fact that he believed the murder weapon would not shoot because of defective manufacture. The prosecution then called Grigson as a witness. He testified that Smith was a severe sociopath who had no remorse for his killing, would commit the same or similar acts in the future if given the chance to do so, and that he had no "regard for another human being's property or for their life, regardless of who it may be." Defense counsel objected to this testimony because Grigson was not included in a list of witnesses that the state intended to call. The trial court overruled this objection. After Grigson's testimony, the jury answered in the affirmative the three questions crucial to imposing the death sentence—whether the defendant committed the act deliberately, whether the defendant poses a continuing threat to society, and whether the defendant's act was disproportionate to any provocation.

Smith sued for habeas corpus in Texas court, but was denied. He then turned to federal court for habeas relief. The district court found that the state's surprise introduction of Grigson's devastating testimony violated Smith's constitutional rights. The Fifth Circuit affirmed, holding that the psychiatric examination without any warning concerning Smith's right to remain silent violated the Fifth Amendment. Furthermore, the examination violated the Sixth Amendment because Smith's counsel was not present at this crucial stage of the trial.

The Supreme Court affirmed. Chief Justice Burger's opinion held that under ***Miranda v. Arizona,*** 384 U.S. 436 (1966), the right to be warned of potential self-incrimination was not affected by the fact that the evidence was introduced in the sentencing phase of the trial, rather than the guilt phase. The state's argument that *Miranda* did not apply to the interview because it was nontestimonial in nature was unavailing because Grigson based his opinion not just on observations of Smith but on Smith's answers to his questions. Furthermore, Smith's Sixth Amendment right to counsel had attached when Grigson interviewed him because the interview turned out to be a critical phase of the trial. Smith's attorney was not told that the interview would encompass the crucial issue of Smith's future dangerousness, and Smith was denied the assistance of his counsel before agreeing to submit to the interview. It is clear that the Sixth Amendment requires the assistance of counsel for such an important decision because it may be difficult for a layman to understand its potential seriousness.

See B. Elaine New, "The Fifth Amendment and Compelled Psychiatric Examinations: Implications of *Estelle v. Smith,*" *George Washington Law Review* 50 (1982): 275; and Christopher Slobogin, "*Estelle v. Smith:* The Constitutional Contours of the Forensic Evaluation," *Emory Law Journal* 31 (1982): 71.

Edwards v. Arizona

451 U.S. 477 (1981)
Decided: May 18, 1981
Vote: 9 (Burger, Brennan, Stewart, B. White, T. Marshall, Blackmun, Powell, Rehnquist, Stevens)
0
Opinion of the Court: B. White
Opinion concurring in judgment: Burger
Opinion concurring in judgment: Powell (Rehnquist)

Edwards was arrested and charged with robbery, burglary, and first-degree murder. He was given warnings as to his rights based on ***Miranda v. Arizona,*** 384 U.S. 436 (1966), and interrogated by police until he said he wanted an attorney. The police stopped questioning him, but returned the next day, gave him his Miranda warnings again, and reinitiated questioning. Edwards then confessed to the crime. The trial court denied Edwards's motion to suppress his confession, finding that the confession was voluntary and not coerced by the police, and the Arizona Supreme Court affirmed.

The Supreme Court reversed. According to the Court, the Arizona courts were incorrect in inquiring into the "voluntariness" of the accused's confession. Once Edwards invoked his right to an attorney, the police were required to cease all questioning until his attorney was present, unless Edwards initiated the conversation. Thus, when the police returned the next day and began questioning Edwards, they violated his Fifth Amendment rights against self-incrimination and right to counsel, as set out in *Miranda.*

See Eugene L. Shapiro, "Thinking the Unthinkable: Recasting the Presumption of *Edwards v. Arizona,*" *Oklahoma Law Review* 53 (2000): 11; and Thomas N. Radek, "*Arizona v. Roberson:* The Supreme Court Expands Suspects' Rights in the Custodial Interrogation Setting," *John Marshall Law Review* 22 (1989): 685.

Lassiter v. Department of Social Services

452 U.S. 18 (1981)
Decided: June 1, 1981
Vote: 5 (Burger, Stewart, B. White, Powell, Rehnquist
4 (Brennan, T. Marshall, Blackmun, Stevens)
Opinion of the Court: Stewart
Concurring opinion: Burger
Dissenting opinion: Blackmun (Brennan, T. Marshall)
Dissenting opinion: Stevens

In 1975 a North Carolina court determined that Abby Gail Lassiter's infant son, William, was neglected after hearing evidence that Lassiter failed to obtain needed medical services for him. The Durham County Department of Social Services assumed custody of the child and encouraged Lassiter to strengthen her relationship with him and change the conditions that had led to his neglect. In 1976, however, Lassiter was convicted of second-degree murder and sentenced to prison for twenty-five to forty years. The state then moved to terminate her parental rights, arguing that since losing custody she had made no effort to contact her son or strengthen her ties with him and that she had made no effort to plan for the child's future. Although Lassiter had a lawyer for her murder trial, she did not discuss the upcoming parental rights hearing with the lawyer and was not represented at the hearing, which resulted in the termination of her parental rights. She appealed the decision, relying entirely on the argument that because she was indigent, she should have been appointed counsel.

The Supreme Court held that an indigent's due process right to appointed counsel is at its strongest when the indigent is facing imprisonment, but the Constitution does not require that indigents be provided counsel in all cases concerning parental rights. Against this presumption, the court must weigh the indigent's interest in the outcome, the state's interest in not appointing counsel, and the danger of prejudice resulting from the indigent's representing herself. With regard to parental rights hearings, both the parent and the state have a strong interest in a fair outcome and the parent has an interest in avoiding potential criminal charges resulting from the hearing, while the state has only a weak financial interest and a somewhat stronger interest in streamlining the procedure by not appointing counsel. Therefore, in many parental rights cases, a weighing of the parent's interest in the outcome, the state's interest in not appointing counsel, and the danger of prejudice would result in rebutting the presumption that appointed counsel is not necessary. In this case, however, it did not. The motion to terminate Lassiter's parental rights contained no allegations of abuse upon which criminal charges could be based; the hearing involved no complicated points of law or expert witnesses for which the assistance of counsel would have been necessary to achieve a fair result; and Lassiter had shown no great interest in the result because she failed to appear at the 1975 custody hearing or contest the charges at that time.

See Peter E. Van Runkle, "*Lassiter v. Department of Social Services:* What It Means for the Indigent Divorce Litigant," *Ohio State Law Journal* 43 (1982): 969; Eric Buermann, "*Lassiter v. Department of Social Services:* The Right to Counsel in Parental Termination Proceedings," *University of Miami Law Review* 36 (1982): 337; Colene Flynn, "In Search of Greater Procedural Justice: Rethinking *Lassiter v. Department of Social Services,*" *Wisconsin Women's Law Journal* 11 (1996): 327; and Anthony H. Trembley, "Alone Against the State: *Lassiter v. Department of Social Services,*" *U.C. Davis Law Review* 15 (1982): 1123.

Schad v. Borough of Mount Ephraim

452 U.S. 61 (1981)
Decided: June 1, 1981
Vote: 7 (Brennan, Stewart, B. White, T. Marshall, Blackmun, Powell, Stevens)
2 (Burger, Rehnquist)
Opinion of the Court: B. White
Concurring opinion: Blackmun
Concurring opinion: Powell (Stewart)
Opinion concurring in judgment: Stevens
Dissenting opinion: Burger (Rehnquist)

The Borough of Mount Ephraim in Camden County, New Jersey, had a commercial zoning ordinance that excluded all forms of live entertainment throughout the borough. Schad and others operated an adult bookstore in Mount Ephraim, in which they offered coin-operated viewing galleries where customers could watch nude dancers perform behind a glass partition. The borough filed a complaint, and Schad sued to enjoin enforcement of the zoning ordinance, arguing that nude dancing was protected under the First Amendment and could not be prohibited by the borough. The New Jersey courts rejected the First Amendment argument, relying on the fact that the zoning ordinance barred all forms of live entertainment, not just nude dancing, and that the ordinance was a proper application of the state's police power because it was intended to preserve the commercial character of the borough and prevent problems such as trash and loitering.

The Supreme Court reversed, holding that the borough's zoning ordinance violated the First Amendment because it banned a broad spectrum of protected speech throughout the borough. The Court pointed out that the state had not given sufficient evidence that live entertainment would create more trash and loitering than other businesses and that the borough could have remedied those problems in ways that were less intrusive of First Amendment liberties. The Court distinguished this case from others, such as ***Erznoznik v. City of Jacksonville,*** 422 U.S. 205 (1975), and ***Young v. American Mini Theatres, Inc.,*** 427 U.S. 50 (1976), upholding ordinances that zoned adult entertainment into special districts. Here, the ordinance was overbroad because it banned all entertainment, not just adult entertainment. In addition, by banning entertainment throughout its jurisdiction, the borough provided no opportunity to exercise First Amendment rights.

See Simon J. Santiago, "Zoning and Religion: Will the Religious Freedom Restoration Act of 1993 Shift the Line Toward Religious Liberty?" *American University Law Review* 45 (October 1995); Leon Harvey Lee Jr., "Constitutional Law—Policing the Parlor and the First Amendment—*City of Renton v. Playtime Theatres, Inc.,*" *Wake Forest Law Review* 22 (1987): 673; and "Regulation of Live Entertainment," *Harvard Law Review* 95 (1981): 231.

Hodel v. Virginia Surface Mining & Reclamation Association, Inc.

452 U.S. 264 (1981)
Decided: June 15, 1981
Vote: 9 (Burger, Brennan, Stewart, B. White, T. Marshall, Blackmun, Powell, Rehnquist, Stevens)
0
Opinion of the Court: T. Marshall
Concurring opinion: Burger
Concurring opinion: Powell
Opinion concurring in judgment: Rehnquist

The Surface Mining Control and Reclamation Act of 1977 was a federal law intended to mitigate the deleterious effects on the environment of surface coal mining. The secretary of the interior had power to enforce the provisions of the act, although states were permitted to establish their own regulatory regimes consistent with it. Among other things, the act required surface coal mine operators to return the land to its "approximate original contour" in order to reduce the impact of "steep slopes." Congress justified the law as a regulation of interstate commerce, making substantial legislative findings that surface coal mining operations had environmental impacts that transcended the boundaries of the states where they were located. An association of coal mining operators and states sued to prevent the enforcement of the act. The district court granted relief, finding that the act was not a legitimate use of Congress's power to regulate interstate commerce and that it constituted a legislative taking of the coal mining operators' property rights without compensation in violation of the Takings Clause.

The Supreme Court reversed. The act was a legitimate exercise of Congress's power to regulate interstate commerce because Congress had a rational basis to conclude that surface mining affects the national environment. Moreover, the act was reasonably related to the goal of protecting the environment because of Congress's finding that uniform standards were necessary to effect a reduction in the harmful environmental effects of surface mining. Furthermore, the "steep slope" provisions did not usurp the states' police powers in violation of the Tenth Amendment because, relying on ***National League of Cities v. Usery,*** 426 U.S. 833 (1976), they regulated the private operations of the mine operators, not the "states as states." The Court declined to address whether the act effected a taking of the mining operators' property rights without just compensation, finding that the issue was not ripe (the suit was to enjoin enforcement). Finally, the act was not a violation of procedural due process because it provided adequate administrative review before a miner's activities would be enjoined.

See Robert Meltz, "The Commerce Clause as a Limit on Congressional Power to Protect the Environment," *CRS Report for Congress,* March 12, 1999; Vincent Daniel Palumbo, "*National League of Cities v. Usery* to *EEOC v. Wyoming:* Evolution of a Balancing Approach to Tenth Amendment Analysis," *Duke Law Journal* (1984): 601; and Anthony Pye, "The Supreme Court Rejects Constitutional Challenges to the Surface Mining Control and Reclamation Act of 1977: *Hodel v. Virginia Surface Mining and Reclamation Association, Hodel v. Indiana,*" *Brooklyn Law Review* 48 (1981): 137.

Heffron v. International Society for Krishna Consciousness

452 U.S. 640 (1981)
Decided: June 22, 1981
Vote: 5 (Burger, Stewart, B. White, Powell, Rehnquist)
4 (Brennan, T. Marshall, Blackmun, Stevens)
Opinion of the Court: B. White
Dissenting opinion: Brennan (T. Marshall, Stevens)
Dissenting opinion: Blackmun

The governing body of the Minnesota state fair required all persons who wished to distribute literature on the fairgrounds to do so in a designated place. Members of the International Society for Krishna Consciousness (ISKCON) wanted to distribute literature on the fairgrounds, and they sued for a declaratory judgment that the enforcement of the restriction would be an unconstitutional infringement on their First Amendment rights. The district court granted summary judgment for the state fair, but the Minnesota Supreme Court reversed.

The U.S. Supreme Court reversed the state supreme court, holding that the restriction on distributing literature to a designated place was a reasonable time, place, and manner restriction on free speech. The restriction was content-neutral and reasonably related to the state's interest in preserving the orderly flow of pedestrian traffic within the fairgrounds. Although

ISKCON argued that its practice of Sankirtan (the going into public places to proselytize and solicit donations) could only be accomplished peripatetically, the Court held that "none of our cases suggest that the inclusion of peripatetic solicitation as part of a church ritual entitles church members to solicitation rights in a public forum superior to those of members of other religious groups that raise money but do not purport to ritualize the process."

See Paul Finkelman, ed., *Religion and American Law: An Encyclopedia* (New York: Garland, 2000).

Rostker v. Goldberg

453 U.S. 57 (1981)
Decided: June 25, 1981
Vote: 6 (Burger, Stewart, Blackmun, Powell, Rehnquist, Stevens)
3 (Brennan, B. White, T. Marshall)
Opinion of the Court: Rehnquist
Dissenting opinion: B. White (Brennan)
Dissenting opinion: T. Marshall (Brennan)

The Selective Service Act allowed the president to require registration of young men for the purposes of potential conscription. Although the registration process had been discontinued in 1975, the Soviet invasion of Afghanistan in 1980 prompted President Jimmy Carter to seek to reactivate the registration process, and he asked Congress for money to cover the expenses of conducting the registration. At the same time, he asked Congress to amend the act to permit the registration of women as well as men. After holding hearings on the question of registering women, Congress declined to amend the act, but allocated the funds for the registration of men. The president then reactivated the registration process for men only. The plaintiffs were a group of men who argued that requiring only males to register for possible conscription was a form of sex discrimination that violated the Due Process Clause.

The Supreme Court held that Congress was due great deference in its judgments regarding national defense, and the Court should not lightly substitute its judgment for Congress's. Congress had carefully considered the issue of whether to register women in response to the president's suggestion, and the Court found that its decision not to do so was not based on outdated, stereotypical judgments about the respective roles of men and women. Rather, the decision was based on military manpower needs, which did not require women draftees. The Court did not evaluate or consider whether Congress's reasoning was also based on outdated notions of gender roles. As with other gender-based cases, starting with ***Reed v. Reed,*** 404 U.S. 71 (1971), the Court did not hold that gender-based statutes required "strict scrutiny," but only a midlevel scrutiny.

See Lucille Ponte, "*Rostker v. Goldberg:* Upholding All-Male Draft Registration Plans," *New England Law Review* 18 (1991): 239; Randall Kennedy, "Thurgood Marshall and the Struggle for Women's Rights," *Harvard Women's Law Journal* 17 (1994): 1; and Ellen Oberwetter, "Rethinking Military Deference: Male-Only Draft Registration and the Intersection of Military Need with Civilian Rights," *Texas Law Review* 78 (1999): 173.

New York v. Belton

453 U.S. 454 (1981)
Decided: July 1, 1981
Vote: 6 (Burger, Stewart, Blackmun, Powell, Rehnquist, Stevens)
3 (Brennan, B. White, T. Marshall)
Opinion of the Court: Stewart
Concurring opinion: Rehnquist
Opinion concurring in judgment: Stevens
Dissenting opinion: Brennan (T. Marshall)
Dissenting opinion: B. White (T. Marshall)

Roger Belton and three other men were riding in a car on the New York State Thruway when a state trooper, Douglas Nicot, pulled the car over for speeding. While Nicot was checking the car's registration, he smelled marijuana and noticed a packet on the floor that he suspected of holding marijuana. Nicot then arrested the passengers for marijuana possession, ordered them out of the car, and searched the passenger compartment. Nicot found Belton's jacket, unzipped its pockets, and found cocaine inside. Belton was arrested for possession. At his trial, he moved to have the cocaine suppressed, arguing that Nicot did not have a right to search the pockets of his jacket without his permission or a search warrant. The court rejected this claim, and Belton appealed.

The New York Court of Appeals found that the search was unlawful, under the Constitution, but the U.S. Supreme Court reversed, rejecting the New York court's interpretation of the Fourth and Fourteenth Amendments. According to the Court, a search incident to a lawful arrest justified a search of the area in the arrestee's immediate control. If the arrestee is in his vehicle when the arrest occurs, as Belton was, the area in his immediate control includes the passenger compartment of the vehicle. In such a situation, the police officer is justified in searching the entire passenger compartment, including closed containers (such as Belton's zipped jacket pockets) found within the passenger compartment.

See David S. Rudstein, "The Search of an Automobile Incident to an Arrest: An Analysis of *New York v. Belton, Marquette Law Review* 67 (1984): 205.

Metromedia, Inc. v. City of San Diego

453 U.S. 490 (1981)
Decided: July 2, 1981
Vote: 6 (Brennan, Stewart, B. White, T. Marshall, Blackmun, Powell)
3 (Burger, Rehnquist, Stevens)
Judgment of the Court: B. White
Opinion concurring in judgment: Brennan (Blackmun)
Dissenting opinion: Burger
Dissenting opinion: Rehnquist
Dissenting opinion: Stevens

San Diego enacted an ordinance prohibiting most billboards but permitting some types of on-site advertising and signs. The ordinance's purpose was to improve the appearance of the city and to prevent traffic accidents. It prohibited all fixed-structure noncommercial signs and all fixed-structure commercial signs except on-site signs. The statute provided a few exceptions for things like political campaign signs. Billboard owners sued to enjoin the ordinance, arguing that it violated their First Amendment rights. The lower courts found that the ordinance violated Metromedia's First Amendment rights, but the California Supreme Court argued that it did not.

The U.S. Supreme Court reversed. The Court held that under ***Central Hudson Gas & Electric Corp. v. Public Service Commission of New York,*** 447 U.S. 557 (1980), the city's interest in preventing traffic accidents and beautifying the city were legitimate government interests and that the ordinance was no more extensive than necessary to fulfill those interests. The content-based restriction that allowed on-site commercial advertising and not noncommercial signage was, however, impermissible under the First Amendment.

Justice Brennan believed the ordinance was unconstitutional on its face because it effectively banned all outdoor advertising. Brennan chastised the majority for implying that such a total ban on outdoor advertising might be constitutional. Brennan also argued that it was time to eliminate the unworkable and, he believed, constitutionally improper, distinction between commercial speech and other speech.

The dissenters wished to defer to the local authorities on what constituted legitimate traffic and safety regulations, as well as aesthetic considerations. Chief Justice Burger said the Court was taking "an extraordinary—even a bizarre—step" by limiting the power of a city to act on matters of the risks to safety "posed by large, permanent billboards." Justice Rehnquist continued to object to the idea that commercial speech was protected by the First Amendment. Consistent with his deference to local authorities, he argued, "Nothing in my experience on the bench has led me to believe that a judge is in any better position than a city or county commission to make decisions in an area such as aesthetics. Therefore, little can be gained in the area of constitutional law, and much lost in the process of democratic decision making, by allowing individual judges in city after city to second-guess such legislative or administrative determinations."

See Kirk W. Caldwell, "*Metromedia, Inc. v. City of San Diego:* The Conflict Between Aesthetic Zoning and Commercial Speech Protection; Hawaii's Billboard Law Under Fire," *University of Hawaii Law Review* 5 (1983).

Dames & Moore v. Regan

453 U.S. 654 (1981)
Decided: July 2, 1981
Vote: 8 (Burger, Brennan, Stewart, B. White, T. Marshall, Blackmun, Rehnquist, Stevens)
1 (Powell)
Opinion of the Court: Rehnquist
Concurring opinion: Stevens
Dissenting opinion: Powell

In response to the seizure of American citizens working in the American Embassy in Tehran, President Jimmy Carter froze all assets of the Iranian government within the United States under the International Emergency Economic Powers Act (IEEPA). Some time later, Dames & Moore, an American company with a contract to conduct site studies for a proposed nuclear power plant in Iran, brought a lawsuit against Iranian government-owned corporations and received an attachment on the property of the corporations held in a U.S. bank. As part of its settlement to secure the release of the hostages, however, the U.S. government agreed to release all judicial attachments against property of the Iranian government. Dames & Moore challenged the executive order giving effect to the agreement, arguing that the order deprived it of property to satisfy its judgment and was beyond the power of the president.

The Supreme Court disagreed, upholding the constitutionality of the executive order. The Court held that under the IEEPA, the president has broad powers over the assets of foreign governments within the United States. Dames & Moore's judicial attachment was only made possible by a "revocable license" granted by the Treasury Department that allowed Dames & Moore to proceed despite the freezing of Iran's assets. The Treasury Department was fully within its power to revoke that license later. If the president's powers under the IEEPA were limited, as Dames & Moore suggested they were, the president would not have the benefit of using the foreign government's assets as a "bargaining chip" in hostile negotiations. This result would defeat the purpose of the IEEPA. Therefore, the executive order was valid under the IEEPA.

See Lee R. Marks, "The President's Foreign Economic Powers After *Dames & Moore v. Regan:* Legislation by Acquiescence," *Cornell Law Review* 69 (1983).

Valley Forge Christian College v. Americans United for Separation of Church and State, Inc.

454 U.S. 464 (1982)
Decided: January 12, 1982
Vote: 5 (Burger, B. White, Powell, Rehnquist, O'Connor)
4 (Brennan, T. Marshall, Blackmun, Stevens)
Opinion of the Court: Rehnquist
Dissenting opinion: Brennan (T. Marshall, Blackmun)
Dissenting opinion: Stevens

Under its authority to dispose of surplus federal property, Congress gave a former military hospital that had fallen into disuse to Valley Forge Christian College. Because the college intended to use the property for educational purposes, Congress determined that the public benefit of its use completely offset the $577,000 cost of the facility. Americans United for Separation of Church and State sued to enjoin the transfer, arguing that it was an impermissible government aid to religion. Americans United said it had standing because the misapplication of each of its member's tax dollars for an unconstitutional purpose constituted an injury. Relying on ***Flast v. Cohen,*** 392 U.S. 83 (1968), the district court dismissed Americans United's complaint, finding that the organization did not have taxpayer's standing to sue because it failed to allege any particular harm other than that every citizen experienced by the transfer. The Third Circuit Court, on the other hand, claimed that although Americans United did not have taxpayer's standing under *Flast,* it did have citizen's standing to challenge an unconstitutional act of its government.

The Supreme Court reversed. The Court held that Americans United did not have taxpayer's standing because the challenged congressional act—the transfer of the hospital to the religious school—was not an exercise of the Taxing and Spending power, but of the Property power found in Article IV, Section 3, Clause 2. Americans United alleged a violation of the Constitution, but it could not allege any specific harm caused by the violation, other than seeing its fervently held belief in separation of church and state thwarted, which the Court held was an insufficient "injury in fact" to create standing.

See William A. Fletcher, "The Structure of Standing," *Yale Law Journal* 98 (1988): 221; Henry P. Monaghan, "Third Party Standing," *Columbia Law Review* 84 (1984): 277; Steven L. Winter, "The Metaphor of Standing and the Problem of Self-Governance," *Stanford Law Review* 40 (1988): 1371; and Bill Latham, "*Valley Forge Christian College v. Americans United for Separation of Church and State:* Taxpayer Standing and the Establishment Clause," *Baylor Law Review* 34 (1982): 748.

Eddings v. Oklahoma

455 U.S. 104 (1982)
Decided: January 19, 1982
Vote: 5 (Brennan, T. Marshall, Powell, Stevens, O'Connor)
4 (Burger, B. White, Blackmun, Rehnquist)
Opinion of the Court: Powell
Concurring opinion: Brennan
Concurring opinion: O'Connor
Dissenting opinion: Burger (B. White, Blackmun, Rehnquist)

Sixteen-year-old Monty Lee Eddings ran away from his Missouri home with several companions and driving his brother's car. The group brought with them several rifles and shotguns Eddings had stolen from his abusive father. Eventually, the group arrived in Creek County, Oklahoma, where Officer Crabtree of the Oklahoma Highway Patrol signaled them to pull over. As the officer approached their car, Eddings shot and killed him. The court certified him as an adult, finding that he was not susceptible to rehabilitation in the juvenile system.

Eddings pleaded nolo contendere (no contest) to a charge of first-degree murder. Oklahoma law provided that when deciding the punishment for first-degree murder, the jury may consider aggravating and mitigating circumstances. The state proved three aggravating circumstances: that the murder was "especially heinous or cruel," that the murder was committed for the purpose of avoiding lawful arrest, and that Eddings would likely kill again. In response, Eddings offered substantial evidence of mitigating circumstances, including testimony concerning his childhood with an abusive father, his emotional disturbance, and psychological testimony that he could be rehabilitated. The court rejected this evidence as not the sort of mitigating evidence contemplated by the law. According to the court, the only mitigating evidence was his age, which was insufficient to overcome the aggravating factors offered by the state. Upon this finding, the court sentenced Eddings to death.

Applying the rule of ***Lockett v. Ohio,*** 438 U.S. 586 (1978), the Supreme Court reversed the death penalty because the trier of fact had been precluded from considering, "as a mitigating factor, any aspect of a defendant's character or record and any of the circumstances of the offense that the defendant proffers as a basis for a sentence less than death." The Court reemphasized that the *Lockett* rule followed from the Court's long struggle to define the constitutional parameters of the death penalty within the strictures of the Eighth Amendment. In *Lockett,* the Court held that the death sentence must be imposed consistently or not at all, and the penalty could not be imposed consistently unless courts made a searching examination of the facts of each case before applying it. As the Court pointed out, consistency that arises from ignoring the individual circumstances of each case is a "false consistency." The Oklahoma court had ignored the substantial mitigating evidence offered by Eddings, and the sentence had to be overturned.

In dissent, Chief Justice Burger argued that the Court had decided to hear the case only to consider "whether the Eighth and Fourteenth Amendments prohibit the imposition of a death sentence on an offender because he was 16 years old in 1977 at the time he committed the offense." He complained that the Court had not decided the case on these grounds, and reminded his colleagues that "review of all other questions raised in the petition for certiorari was denied."

Although it did not directly challenge the constitutionality of the death penalty, this case reflected the growing concern within the legal community, and on the Court, with the fairness of death penalties.

See Ann Chin Lin, ed., *Capital Punishment* (Washington, D.C.: CQ Press, 2002); and Katherine Hunt Federle, "Emancipation and Execution: Transferring Children to Criminal Court in Capital Cases," *Wisconsin Law Review* (1996): 447.

United States v. Lee

455 U.S. 252 (1982)
Decided: February 23, 1982
Vote: 9 (Burger, Brennan, B. White, T. Marshall, Blackmun, Powell, Rehnquist, Stevens, O'Connor)
0
Opinion of the Court: Burger
Opinion concurring in judgment: Stevens

Lee was an Amish farmer and carpenter who employed several other Amish workers. His religious beliefs obliged him to provide for fellow Amish, giving them the aid of the kind envisioned by the Social Security Act. He objected to paying Social Security taxes for the purpose of a national, secular public insurance program, arguing that the Amish in effect "took care of their own." When the Internal Revenue Service (IRS) required him to withhold taxes from his employees' paychecks, he remitted a portion of the amount and sued for a refund, arguing that the tax imposition violated the Free Exercise Clause of the First Amendment. Lee said that to even pay the Social Security tax would violate his religious beliefs. Although the district court agreed and granted the relief Lee sought, the Supreme Court reversed.

The Court held that a self-employed person is entitled to refuse to pay Social Security taxes on religious grounds, but no such exemption exists for employers. The Court found that by going into business and hiring employees, Lee had accepted the responsibility of contributing to the national insurance fund. Although paying the tax imposed burdens on Lee's exercise of his faith, these burdens were inevitable given the overriding national interest in the consistent enforcement of the duty to pay taxes and in having the Social Security system consistently applied. If exemptions were made for every sect that claimed a religious duty not to pay the taxes, the Social Security system could become impossible to administer.

Lee had relied on ***Wisconsin v. Yoder,*** 406 U.S. 205 (1972), in which the Court said the Amish could remove their children from public school. Here, however, the issue was the collection of revenue for general national programs, and, although the Amish might choose not to participate in those programs, an Amish employer could not exempt himself from the program. As the Court noted, "The social security system in the United States serves the public interest by providing a comprehensive insurance system with a variety of benefits available to all participants, with costs shared by employers and employees. . . . The design of the system requires support by mandatory contributions from covered employers and employees." A ruling in favor of Lee would have led to numerous claims of religious exemption from paying specific or general taxes.

See Brian Comerford, "Tax Law and American Religion," in *Religion and American Law: An Encyclopedia,* ed. Paul Finkelman (New York: Garland, 2000), 499–451; and N. Bruce Duthu, "Note: *U.S. v. Lee:* Limitations on the Free Exercise of Religion," *Loyola Law Review* 28 (1982): 1216.

Larson v. Valente

456 U.S. 228 (1982)
Decided: April 21, 1982
Vote: 5 (Brennan, T. Marshall, Blackmun, Powell, Stevens)
4 (Burger, B. White, Rehnquist, O'Connor)
Opinion of the Court: Brennan
Concurring opinion: Stevens
Dissenting opinion: B. White (Rehnquist)
Dissenting opinion: Rehnquist (Burger, B. White, O'Connor)

A 1978 Minnesota law "provided that only those religious organizations that received more than half of their total contributions from members or affiliated organizations" would be exempt from certain registration and reporting requirements. The Unification Church solicited more than half of its funds from nonmembers, and was therefore not exempted from the registration requirement. Church members sued to enjoin the enforcement of the statute. The plaintiffs argued that the statute as applied to religious organizations tended to favor more established organizations in violation of the Establishment Clause. The district court agreed, but the court of appeals found that the question of whether the Unification Church was indeed a religious organization had been unsatisfactorily resolved and remanded the case for further proceedings.

The Supreme Court found that the state had conceded the Unification Church's religious status by attempting to apply its 50 percent statute to it, but that the 50 percent rule violated the Establishment Clause. Because it gave preference to certain religions over others, it was inherently suspect, and the statute could stand only if the state could demonstrate that it was "closely fitted" to fulfill a compelling interest. The state argued that the need to protect the public from fraudulent charitable solicitation is a compelling interest, but Minnesota had not shown that the 50 percent rule was narrowly tailored to that interest. The state's arguments that members of religious organizations would exercise self-control over the solicitation if more than 50 percent of the solicitation was conducted within the organization and that the greater the percentage of nonmembers who were solicited, the greater the need for public registration, were unconvincing.

See Paul Finkelman, ed., *Religion and American Law: An Encyclopedia* (New York: Garland, 2000).

Plyer v. Doe

457 U.S. 202 (1982)
Decided: June 15, 1982
Vote: 5 (Brennan, T. Marshall, Blackmun, Powell, Stevens)
4 (Burger, B. White, Rehnquist, O'Connor)
Opinion of the Court: Brennan
Concurring opinion: T. Marshall
Concurring opinion: Blackmun
Concurring opinion: Powell
Dissenting opinion: Burger (B. White, Rehnquist, O'Connor)

Illegal alien parents sued to enjoin the state of Texas from enforcing its law prohibiting the children of illegal aliens from attending Texas public schools. The district court and the Fifth Circuit granted relief, and Texas appealed.

The Supreme Court affirmed. The majority opinion started from the premise that the Equal Protection Clause of the Fourteenth Amendment applied to "all persons" and that it therefore included illegal aliens. Texas argued that the phrase "within its jurisdiction" in the Fourteenth Amendment was a limiting phrase that excluded noncitizens from equal protection. The Court did not have to decide this issue; rather, it concluded that because illegal aliens were subject to Texas's criminal laws, they were within Texas's jurisdiction. The Court stated in dicta (points in the opinion that are not essential to the decision) that Texas did not have to show a compelling interest for discriminating against aliens because aliens were not a protected class and public education was not a fundamental right. If Texas had shown a rational basis for its alien-discriminatory legislation, the law might have passed constitutional muster, but the Court held that Texas had failed to do so. According to Justice Brennan, there could be no rational reason for imposing a lifelong handicap on alien children because of a defect in immigration status that they were powerless to understand or correct. Finally, the state's argument that the exclusion was necessary to preserve its financial resources failed because the state had shown no evidence that including alien children in public education would be a drain on its resources.

In dissent, Chief Justice Burger agreed "without hesitation" that "it is senseless in an enlightened society to deprive any children—including illegal aliens—of an elementary education." But, Burger argued, the Court was not made up of "Platonic Guardians" who could set social policy. He believed the Court had trespassed on the rights of the states to set their own education policies and asserted that Congress should take the responsibility of either enforcing its own immigration laws or educating the children of illegal aliens.

Plyler v. Doe led to calls for more stringent enforcement of immigration laws, especially in Texas, Florida, and California. The case also illustrated the dilemmas facing states with large illegal alien populations. On the one hand, if the states refuse to educate children of illegal aliens, they are more likely to become burdens on society. On the other, the costs of educating illegal aliens increases the tax obligations of citizens and often places great stress on existing resources.

See Ann Chin Lin, ed., *Immigration* (Washington, D.C.: CQ Press, 2002); Melanie E. Meyers, "Impermissible Purposes and the Equal Protection Clause," *Columbia Law Review* 86 (1986): 1184; and Juan Carlos Sanchez, "Texas' Public School Financing: Share and Share Alike—Not!" *Thurgood Marshall Law Review* 19 (1994): 475.

Youngberg v. Romeo

457 U.S. 307 (1982)
Decided: June 18, 1982
Vote: 9 (Burger, Brennan, B. White, T. Marshall, Blackmun, Powell, Rehnquist, Stevens, O'Connor)
0
Opinion of the Court: Powell
Concurring opinion: Blackmun (Brennan, O'Connor)
Opinion concurring in judgment: Burger

In this case the Court held that a mentally retarded ward of a state facility has a due process interest in freedom from unnecessary restraint.

Nicholas Romeo was a severely retarded thirty-three-year-old with the mental abilities of an eighteen-month-old child. He was unable to speak or care for himself in even the most basic ways. When his father died, his mother found that she was unable to take care of Nicholas because he frequently became violent when frustrated. She asked that he be committed to a state facility, and he was placed in the Pennhurst State School and Hospital in Pennsylvania. She became concerned about her son's treatment at Pennhurst, however, when she learned that he was injuring himself, that he was being injured by other patients' reactions to his behavior, and that he was being physically constrained. She sued under the Eighth Amendment, arguing that Romeo had a constitutional right to safe conditions and freedom from unnecessary restraints. Her suit alleged that Romeo had been injured at least sixty-three times since he had gone to live at Pennhurst.

The district court found that the hospital's actions had violated the Eighth Amendment, but the Third Circuit Court reversed, holding that the Eighth Amendment was not the appropriate standard for review in this case. Rather, the circuit court applied the Due Process Clause of the Fourteenth Amendment and concluded that Nicholas Romeo's hospitalization and treatment should be considered in light of the fundamental right to liberty within the context of his mental disabilities. The court of appeals reversed the decision in favor of Romeo and remanded the case for a new trial to test, in essence, whether his treatment was consistent with reasonable professional care.

The Supreme Court held that the Fourteenth Amendment's Due Process Clause was controlling and that a resolution would require the district court to balance Romeo's due process interest in freedom from unnecessary restraint and protection from injuries against the state's interest in its current procedures. The resolution of this question would depend upon whether the hospital had actually exercised any professional judgment in its actions regarding Romeo. If such was involved, the professionals' decisions should be given a strong degree of deference.

See James W. Ellis, "The Supreme Court and Institutions: A Comment on *Youngberg v. Romeo*," *Mental Retardation* 20 (1982): 197.

Globe Newspaper Co. v. Superior Court for Norfolk County

457 U.S. 596 (1982)
Decided: June 23, 1982
Vote: 6 (Brennan, B. White, T. Marshall, Blackmun, Powell, O'Connor)
3 (Burger, Rehnquist, Stevens)
Opinion of the Court: Brennan
Opinion concurring in judgment: O'Connor
Dissenting opinion: Burger (Rehnquist)
Dissenting opinion: Stevens

A Massachusetts statute required exclusion of the public and press from trial testimony by alleged victims of specified sexual offenses involving people under eighteen years of age. On the basis of this statute, the Globe Newspaper Company was denied the right to enter a trial and sued. The Massachusetts Supreme Judicial Court construed the statute to exclude the press from all such testimony by alleged victims who were minors.

The U.S. Supreme Court held that the statute violated the First Amendment. With regard to the public right of entry to a criminal trial, the purpose of the First Amendment is to ensure an informed public discussion about the functioning of the criminal justice system.

Massachusetts was required to show that its statute was narrowly tailored to meet a compelling government interest to prevail on the First Amendment challenge. Although Massachusetts offered two compelling interests for the exclusion of the press—to protect young sexual abuse victims from public embarrassment and avoid the discouraging effect the presence of the press might have on victims coming forward with their complaints—Massachusetts could not show that its rule was narrowly tailored to meet those interests. Massachusetts could protect the victims just as well by deciding on a case-by-case basis who was likely to be traumatized by a public audience at the trial, rather than placing a wholesale ban on public access. Furthermore, the fact that the victims' testimony was available after the fact in court transcripts tended to undercut the state's claim that its statute protected the witnesses from embarrassment. Finally, the state had not proven that a public audience would discourage witnesses from coming forward. Because the state could not prove its rule was narrowly tailored to meet the interests it asserted, it failed the First Amendment challenge.

See James M. Kennedy, "Clarifying the Right of Access to Criminal Trials: *Globe Newspaper Co. v. Superior Court*," *Boston College Law Review* 24 (1984): 809; Sally M. Keenan, "*Globe Newspaper Co. v. Superior Court*," *Hofstra Law Review* 11 (1983): 1353; and John C. Hearn, "Globe Newspaper: Sounding the Death Knell for Closure in Courtroom Proceedings?" *Pace Law Review* 3 (1983): 395.

Nixon v. Fitzgerald

457 U.S. 731 (1982)
Decided: June 24, 1982
Vote: 5 (Burger, Powell, Rehnquist, Stevens, O'Connor)
4 (Brennan, B. White, T. Marshall, Blackmun)
Opinion of the Court: Powell
Concurring opinion: Burger
Dissenting opinion: B. White (Brennan, T. Marshall, Blackmun)
Dissenting opinion: Blackmun (Brennan, T. Marshall)

A. Ernest Fitzgerald was a civilian management analyst for the U.S. Air Force. In November 1968 he testified before Congress about cost overruns of approximately $2 billion for the development of a transport plane, as well as the technical problems encountered by the manufacturer. He was later dismissed on grounds that a reorganization made his job unnecessary. Fitzgerald sued President Richard Nixon, alleging that his dismissal was an act of retaliation for his congressional testimony.

The Supreme Court held that Nixon had absolute immunity from liability for his official acts while president. The constitutional doctrine of separation of powers required absolute immunity for certain executive officers. A determination of which officers enjoy this level of immunity requires looking at the Constitution, the nature of the officer's role in the government, and history. Because of the president's importance in the constitutional scheme of government, he cannot be constantly diverted from his duties by the need to defend against lawsuits that arise from his official actions. Furthermore, the president should not have to justify his official acts to judges unless the constitutional interest in reviewing his conduct is strong. In the case of purely private lawsuits by those claiming to be harmed by official actions, that constitutional interest is not strong enough to justify judicial review. If the president's misconduct causes serious enough harm, the proper constitutional remedy is impeachment, not a lawsuit.

In dissent, Justice White wrote, "Attaching absolute immunity to the Office of the President, rather than to particular activities that the President might perform, places the President above the law. It is a reversion to the old notion that the King can do no wrong." White pointed out that under the majority decision, "if a President, without following the statutory procedures which he knows apply to himself as well as to other federal officials, orders his subordinates to wiretap or break into a home for the purpose of installing a listening device, and the officers comply with his request, the President would be absolutely immune from suit. He would be immune regardless of the damage he inflicts, regardless of how violative of the statute and of the Constitution he knew his conduct to be, and regardless of his purpose."

The dissenters urged the Court to follow the rule in *Butz v. Economou*, 438 U.S. 478 (1978), that absolute immunity for acts of executive branch officers "attaches to particular functions—not to particular offices." Thus, no executive officer, including the president, would have immunity for illegal actions for functions beyond the scope of his office. The dissenters also said that the president and other executive officers "are liable in damages only if their conduct violated well-established law and if they should have realized that their conduct was illegal."

See Anne Y. Shields, "The Supreme Court Under Pressure: A Comparative Analysis of *United States v. Nixon* and *Nixon v. Fitzgerald*," *St. John's Law Review* (summer 1983).

Board of Education, Island Trees Free School District v. Pico

457 U.S. 853 (1982)
Decided: June 25, 1982
Vote: 5 (Brennan, B. White, T. Marshall, Blackmun, Stevens)
4 (Burger, Powell, Rehnquist, O'Connor)
Judgment of the Court: Brennan
Opinion concurring in judgment: B. White
Opinion concurring in judgment: Blackmun
Dissenting opinion: Burger (Powell, Rehnquist, O'Connor)
Dissenting opinion: Powell
Dissenting opinion: Rehnquist (Burger, Powell)
Dissenting opinion: O'Connor

The board of education in a New York school district ordered the removal of about a dozen books from public school library shelves because the books were, in the board's words, "anti-American, anti-Christian, anti-Sem[i]tic, and just plain filthy." The board acted after its president, Richard Aherns, and two other members attended a conference sponsored by Parents of New York United (PONYU), "a politically conservative organization," that issued a list of "objectionable" books found in most public schools. The board then ordered the removal of a number of books, among them *Slaughter House Five* by Kurt Vonnegut Jr., *The Naked Ape* by Desmond Morris, *Black Boy* by Richard Wright, *A Hero Ain't Nothin' But a Sandwich* by Alice Childress, *Soul on Ice* by Eldridge Cleaver, and *The Fixer* by Bernard Malamud. Many of these are considered classic works by some of America's most celebrated and respected authors.

Stephen Pico and other students challenged the removal of the books as a violation of their First Amendment rights, and the Supreme Court agreed. Although the school board argued that it had a duty to inculcate community values in its curriculum, the Court held that such a duty does not apply to the library, where students are engaged in a voluntary and exploratory search for knowledge, not a prescribed regimen. Although the Court allowed the school board considerable latitude in the selection of books for its library, the criteria for selection could not be a desire to limit students' exposure to only a narrow spectrum of political or social thought. Citing ***Meyer v. Nebraska,*** 262 U.S. 390 (1923), the Court noted that it had long held that there were "certain constitutional limits upon the power of the State to control even the curriculum in the classroom." The Court drew further support from ***Epperson v. Arkansas,*** 393 U.S. 97 (1968), which struck down a law banning the teaching of evolution. School boards had "broad discretion" in what books they might buy, they could not violate the First Amendment, which included the rights of students to read a wide array of literature. The Court noted that a board dominated by Republicans could not remove all books from the library favorable to Democrats, or vice versa. Nor could a board in "an all-white school . . . remove all books authored by blacks or advocating racial equality and integration."

The dissent argued that the case was really about whether decisions regarding the content of school libraries were to be left to local school boards rather than teenagers and judges, and whether "morality" and "good taste" were suitable criteria for selecting books. The dissent suggested both questions should be answered in the affirmative.

See Jamin B. Raskin, *We the Students: Supreme Court Cases for and About Students* (Washington, D.C.: CQ Press, 2000).

Northern Pipeline Construction Co. v. Marathon Pipe Line Co.

458 U.S. 50 (1982)
Decided: June 28, 1982
Vote: 6 (Brennan, T. Marshall, Blackmun, Rehnquist, Stevens, O'Connor)
3 (Burger, B. White, Powell)
Judgment of the Court: Brennan
Opinion concurring in judgment: Rehnquist (O'Connor)
Dissenting opinion: Burger
Dissenting opinion: B. White (Burger, Powell)

In this case, the Supreme Court held that Congress's grant of full Article III jurisdiction to Article I bankruptcy courts was unconstitutional. In reaching this result, the Court struck down the Bankruptcy Reform Act of 1978, which had created bankruptcy courts with judges serving fourteen-year terms. The Court found that to protect the public from litigants or third parties influencing judges with money or political clout, Article III requires that judges have lifetime tenure and have protection against salary reduction. Under Article III, Congress may create district courts of general jurisdiction, which are courts able to hear most kinds of cases, so long as the judges are insulated from influence by lifetime tenure and salary protection. Article I confers on Congress the power to establish certain legislative courts with jurisdiction over narrowly defined subject matter, such as bankruptcy or patents. The judges on these courts do not have the same job protection as Article III judges. Because of the danger of influence that results from this lack of protection, Article III prohibits Congress from creating an Article I legislative court with the full powers of an Article III court.

Nevertheless, in the 1978 bankruptcy measure, Congress gave the Article I bankruptcy courts the power to hear any matter "arising under" bankruptcy, including unrelated contract claims that might come up when creditors dispute the disposition of the debtor's assets. The words "*arising under*" allowed one litigant of a bankruptcy, Northern Pipeline, to file a breach of contract complaint with the bankruptcy court against another litigant, Marathon Pipe Line. Marathon contended that the act's grant of authority over any case "arising under" a bankruptcy violated Article III.

The Court held that the act's broad grant of authority to Article I bankruptcy courts violated Article III. Writing for the plurality, Justice Brennan said that granting such authority to Article I judges, who did not enjoy lifetime tenure or salary protection, created a risk of undue influence over judges. Brennan noted that the Court had "recognized certain exceptional powers" of Congress to create courts other than those under Article III—what are known as legislative courts. Brennan said that in ***Murray's Lessee v. Hoboken Land & Improvement Co.,*** 59 U.S. 272 (1856), the Court had acknowledged that "Congress may or may not bring within the cognizance of" Article III, certain courts. The Court, however, found no extraordinary reasons for allowing Congress to create an Article I court for bankruptcy. The Court distinguished this case from *Palmore v. United States,* 411 U.S. 389 (1973), which had involved the creation of Article I courts in the District of Columbia, or ***American Insurance Co. v. Canter,*** 26 U.S. 511 (1828), which involved Article I courts in the federal territories, or *Dynes v. Hoover,* 61 U.S. 65 (1857), which involved military courts. Similarly, Brennan distinguished the bankruptcy courts at issue here with "use of administrative agencies and magistrates as adjuncts to Art. III courts," which the Supreme Court approved in *Crowell v. Benson,* 285 U.S. 22 (1932), and *United States v. Raddatz,* 447 U.S. 667 (1980).

See Martin H. Redish, "Legislative Courts, Administrative Agencies, and the Northern Pipeline Decision," *Duke Law Journal* (1983): 197; and Erwin Chemerinsky, "Ending the Marathon: It Is Time to Overrule Northern Pipeline," *American Bankruptcy Law Journal* 65 (1991): 311.

Washington v. Seattle School District No. 1

458 U.S. 457 (1982)
Decided: June 30, 1982
Vote: 5 (Brennan, B. White, T. Marshall, Blackmun, Stevens)
4 (Burger, Powell, Rehnquist, O'Connor)
Opinion of the Court: Blackmun
Dissenting opinion: Powell (Burger, Rehnquist, O'Connor)

Despite several attempts to achieve racially desegregated schools, including the creation of magnet schools, Seattle, Washington, found that its schools were becoming more segregated. One school district created the so-called "Seattle Plan" for integrating its schools through extensive use of busing. Shortly thereafter, Washington voters passed a referendum, by a vote of more than two-to-one, prohibiting assignment to nonneighborhood schools for the purpose of achieving racial integration. Exceptions to the referendum, which was in effect a form of legislation, permitted almost all assignments to nonneighborhood schools except those motivated by the need to desegregate. For example, a student could be assigned to a school outside of his neighborhood if he required special programs or if the nearest school was overcrowded or unsafe or if it lacked necessary physical facilities, but no student could be reassigned to achieve desegregation. The school district sued, arguing that the legislation violated the Equal Protection Clause.

The Supreme Court held that the legislation violated the Equal Protection Clause. According to the Court, by taking away the local school board's right to decide for itself whether busing is appropriate for desegregation, Washington had usurped a traditionally local function only because the issue at stake involved race. Thus, the state had allocated government power on the basis of race, a practice that deprived racial minorities of their political power just as much as denying them the right to vote.

The dissenters argued that the school district was not under court order to desegregate, and therefore the courts had no business interfering with the legislative process in Washington, which included referendums passed by the electorate. Justice Powell, who had been the attorney for the Richmond, Virginia, School District and in the 1950s had planned that district's opposition to integration, now argued, "In the absence of a constitutional violation, no decision of this Court compels a school district to adopt or maintain a mandatory busing program for racial integration." Powell asserted this was an "unprecedented intrusion into the structure of a state government," but Powell's dissent did not accurately describe the Court's decision. The Court had not compelled the school district to integrate; it had only struck down a state referendum that prevented the state's school districts from integrating.

Mississippi University for Women v. Hogan

458 U.S. 718 (1982)
Decided: July 1, 1982
Vote: 5 (Brennan, B. White, T. Marshall, Stevens, O'Connor)
4 (Burger, Blackmun, Powell, Rehnquist)
Opinion of the Court: O'Connor
Dissenting opinion: Burger
Dissenting opinion: Blackmun
Dissenting opinion: Powell (Rehnquist)

The state-supported Mississippi University for Women had, historically, limited its enrollment to women. In 1971 the university established a nursing school, which first offered a two-year associate degree and three years later expanded the program to a four-year baccalaureate degree in nursing. In 1979 Joe Hogan, a registered nurse, applied for admission to the baccalaureate program. Although he was qualified, he was denied admission solely because of his sex. Hogan filed a lawsuit with the federal district court, asserting that the admission decision violated the Equal Protection Clause of the Fourteenth Amendment.

The district court ruled against Hogan, concluding that the state had a legitimate interest "in providing the greatest practical range of educational opportunities for its female student population." The court also found that some accepted education theory held that a single-sex institution "affords unique benefits to students." The court of appeals reversed the district court decision, saying that the lower court erroneously applied the "rational relationship" test to the state's position. The court of appeals argued that a stricter test was necessary. The case was remanded for a rehearing, and the state argued that Section 901(a)(5) of Title IX of the Education Amendments of 1972 permitted the university to continue its single-sex admissions policy. The court of appeals rejected the argument, holding that Section 5 of the Fourteenth Amendment did not "grant Congress power to authorize states to maintain practices otherwise violative of the Amendment."

The Supreme Court agreed with the court of appeals. Justice O'Connor, in her first opinion as a justice, outlined an intermediate scrutiny test for state legislation involving distinctions based on sex. Under her test the state's interest in the statute had to be legitimate, although not "compelling" as was the usual standard for statutes that made distinctions based on race. The state argued that a separate nursing school for women—one that excluded men—was necessary to ensure that women had access to this professional training, but the state failed to consider that men might also want the training. O'Connor argued that here the state failed to show "that women lacked opportunities to obtain training in the field of nursing or to attain positions of leadership in that field when the . . . School of Nursing opened its door or that women currently are deprived of such opportunities." In addition, the state had to show that the gender-based classification was substantially and directly related to its proposed objective. Again, Mississippi failed to do this. The university had a policy, offered to Hogan, that men could audit the nursing courses. O'Connor wrote that this policy "fatally undermines its claim that women, at least those in the School of Nursing, are adversely affected by the presence of men."

As for the Section 901(a)(5) claim, O'Connor briskly rejected it. She cited ***Katzenbach v. Morgan,*** 384 U.S. 641 (1966), which concluded that Section 5 of the Fourteenth Amendment was "limited to adopting measures to enforce the guarantees of the Amendment; 5 grants Congress no power to restrict, abrogate, or dilute these guarantees." Section 901(a)(5) may have exempted the university from Title IX requirements, but nothing could exempt it from Fourteenth Amendment requirements.

Chief Justice Burger's dissent advanced the notion that the majority's ruling applied only to "a professional nursing school." Justice Blackmun disagreed with Burger and in his dissent suggested that the majority's ruling was too "rigid" and as a consequence the nation would "lose all values that some think are worthwhile (and are not based on differences of race or religion) and relegate ourselves to needless conformity."

In the main dissent, Justice Powell argued that it was the majority and not the district court that applied the wrong standard.

> By applying heightened equal protection analysis to this case, the Court frustrates the liberating spirit of the Equal Protection Clause. It prohibits the States from providing women with an opportunity to choose the type of university they prefer. And yet it is these women whom the Court regards as the victims of an illegal, stereotyped perception of the role of women in our society.

The correct test, according to Powell, should have been the "rational-basis analysis." In closing, Powell suggested that "voluntarily chosen single-sex education is an honored tradition in our country" and that tradition was now trampled by the Court.

The Court later relied on *Mississippi University for Women* in reversing the single-sex admission policy (this time male-only) in ***United States v. Virginia,*** 518 U.S. 515 (1996), which involved the Virginia Military Institute.

See Kenneth Jost, "Single-Sex Education," *CQ Researcher,* July 12, 2002, 569–592; Amy H. Nemko, "Single-Sex Public Education after VMI: The Case for Women's Schools," *Harvard Women's Law Journal* 21 (spring 1998); and Laura Wheeler, "Single-Sex Nursing Schools and the U.S. Constitution: *Mississippi University for Women v. Hogan,*" *Population Research & Policy Review* (1983).

Larkin v. Grendel's Den

459 U.S. 116 (1982)
Decided: December 13, 1982
Vote: 8 (Burger, Brennan, B. White, T. Marshall, Blackmun, Powell, Stevens, O'Connor)
1 (Rehnquist)
Opinion of the Court: Burger
Dissenting opinion: Rehnquist

A Massachusetts law provided that when a business owner applied for a liquor license, any church or school within a five-hundred-foot radius of the business could prevent the license from being issued by objecting to the sale of liquor. When the Grendel's Den owner applied for a license for his Cambridge restaurant, a nearby church objected to the application and prevented its issuance. Grendel's Den argued that the statute violated the separation of church and state. The lower courts agreed with Grendel's Den, and the Supreme Court affirmed.

The Court held that the statute created a veto power in nearby churches, which was a power normally exercised by governmental bodies. The Court applied the three-part test created in ***Lemon v. Kurtzman,*** 403 U.S. 602 (1971). In *Lemon* the Court said to satisfy the Establishment Clause, a statute must have a valid secular purpose, must not have the principle effect of advancing religion, and must not cause excessive entanglement between government and religion. Here, the Court found the statute violated the Establishment Clause. Although the statute had a legitimate secular purpose (protecting churches and schools from unruliness associated with alcohol), it had the principle effect of advancing religion by providing churches with an opportunity to make unprincipled and unjustified vetoes of liquor licenses. The statute also created an excessive entanglement of church and state because such a relationship can result from religion being involved in government affairs just as it can from government being involved in church affairs. Because the statute allowed the church's exercise of the veto, the church performed a traditional government function, and the church had therefore become excessively entangled with the government.

In dissent, Justice Rehnquist argued that the statute was an ordinary zoning law that did not give a "veto" to churches. Specifically, Rehnquist did not feel that the statute "advanced" religion because it did not compel anyone to participate in religious activity.

See Cynthia A. Krebs, "The Establishment Clause and Liquor Sales: The Supreme Court Rushes In Where Angels Fear to Tread—*Larkin v. Grendel's Den,* 103 S.Ct. 505 (1982)," *Washington Law Review* 59 (1983): 87; and Steven L. Lane, "Liquor and *Lemon:* The Establishment Clause and State Regulation of Alcohol Sales," *Vanderbilt Law Review* 49 (1996): 1491.

Regan v. Taxation With Representation of Washington

461 U.S. 540 (1983)
Decided: May 23, 1983
Vote: 9 (Burger, Brennan, B. White, T. Marshall, Blackmun, Powell, Rehnquist, Stevens, O'Connor)
0
Opinion of the Court: Rehnquist
Concurring opinion: Blackmun (Brennan, T. Marshall)

Under Section 501(c) of the Internal Revenue Code, certain nonprofit organizations that do not engage in substantial activities aimed at influencing legislation are granted tax exemption. When Taxation With Representation (TWR), a nonprofit organized to promote a certain viewpoint with regard to federal taxation, sought tax-exempt status, its application was denied by the Internal Revenue Service on the grounds that TWR would devote a substantial amount of its activities to lobbying.

TWR was a nonprofit formed from two parent organizations. One promoted the public interest through litigation. This organization was classified as a 501(c)(3), meaning it was tax-exempt and contributors could take a tax deduction for their donations. The other promoted the public interest through lobbying. It was classified as a 501(c)(4) organization, meaning it was tax-exempt but donations to it were not deductible. TWR argued that by denying its contributors the right to deduct their donations, the government was infringing on the group's First Amendment rights by conditioning an important power on not speaking.

The Supreme Court disagreed. According to Justice Rehnquist, the government's grant of tax deductibility to a nonprofit's donors is similar to a gift. Failure to grant this gift to those nonprofits that lobby the legislature is not a violation of the First Amendment, because it does not involve punishing speech, but merely failing to reward it. Furthermore, the fact that Congress allows donors to veterans' groups to deduct their donation does not represent a discrepancy that violates equal protection. Congress could rationally decide that the members of veterans' organizations had earned the extra value of tax deductible donations through their service to the country.

See Benjamin Lombard, "First Amendment Limits on the Use of Taxes to Subsidize Selectively the Media," *Cornell Law Review* 78 (1992): 106; and Elliot M. Schachner, "Religion and the Public Treasury After Taxation with Representation of Washington, Mueller, and Bob Jones," *Utah Law Review* (1984): 275.

Bob Jones University v. United States

461 U.S. 574 (1983)
Decided: May 24, 1983
Vote: 8 (Burger, Brennan, B. White, T. Marshall, Blackmun, Powell, Stevens, O'Connor)
1 (Rehnquist)
Opinion of the Court: Burger
Concurring opinion: Powell
Dissenting opinion: Rehnquist

This case, consolidated with *Goldsboro Christian Schools, Inc. v. United States,* prompted the Supreme Court to balance religious freedom with racial equality. The Internal Revenue Service (IRS) denied a tax exemption for Bob Jones University, a nonprofit fundamentalist Christian institution in Greenville, South Carolina, because the university would not admit African Americans (until 1971), claiming its religious doctrines prohibited integration. Following ***Runyon v. McCrary,*** 427 U.S. 160 (1976), the university admitted blacks, but prohibited interracial dating and marriage.

The Court upheld the IRS decision based on a statute that prohibited granting tax exemptions to institutions that discriminate on the basis of race. The Court held that a tax exemption is a "public benefit" and such a benefit cannot be in opposition to "common community conscience." The Court also noted that the government had a "fundamental overriding interest in eradicating racial discrimination in education." This interest clearly outweighed any benefits the nation might gain from granting a tax exemption to the university.

Justice Rehnquist's lone dissent argued that this issue was one for Congress to decide, not the Court.

By upholding the U.S. government's interpretation of congressional intent in creating the IRS code, however, the Court was in fact deferring to both Congress and the executive branch. If Congress thought this interpretation of its statute was incorrect, then Congress could change the law.

Off the Court, many academic commentators have criticized this opinion for not taking more seriously Bob Jones's claim of religious belief. But, in another way, this case is consistent with other cases involving religion, such as the Sunday closing cases, in which the Court has allowed a financial burden to fall more heavily on one group of believers than another, in order to achieve an important public policy.

See Mayer G. Freed and Daniel D. Polsby, "Race, Religion and Public Policy: *Bob Jones University v. United States," Supreme Court Review, 1984,* 1; Douglas Laycock, "Tax Exemptions for Racially Discriminatory Religious Schools," *Texas Law Review* 60 (1982): 259–277; and Patrick Marshall, "Religion in Schools," *CQ Researcher,* January 12, 2001, 1–24.

Planned Parenthood Association v. Ashcroft

462 U.S. 476 (1983)
Decided: June 15, 1983
Vote: Multiple
Judgment of the Court: Powell
Opinion concurring in judgment: O'Connor (B. White, Rehnquist)
Dissenting opinion: Blackmun (Brennan, T. Marshall, Stevens)

This case was decided the same day as *Akron v. Akron Center for Reproductive Health, Inc.,* 462 U.S. 416 (1983), and involved similar state laws that sought to regulate the procedures and availability of abortions. In this case, Missouri required (1) all second-trimester abortions to be performed in a board-certified hospital, (2) a second physician to be present during all abortions of viable fetuses to ensure that abortion procedures fatal to the fetus would not be used unless necessary to protect the mother's health, (3) a pathology report be done before the abortion is carried out, and (4) minors wishing to obtain an abortion to obtain either parental consent or the consent of the juvenile court. The plaintiffs were two physicians who performed abortions and objected to the new laws as unconstitutional.

The Supreme Court ruled on each of the four provisions.

First, the Court unanimously held unconstitutional the provision requiring that all second-trimester abortions be performed at a board-certified hospital. The provision violated the "privacy" penumbra because it placed an undue burden on a woman's ability to exercise her right to an abortion. (A penumbra is a body of rights held to be guaranteed by implication from other rights explicitly enumerated in the U.S. Constitution.) In ***Griswold v. Connecticut,*** 381 U.S. 479 (1965), the Court said the First Amendment has a penumbra where privacy is protected from governmental intrusion.

Next, the Court ruled unanimously that there were no constitutional violations for the pathology report requirement and the substituted consent requirement. The pathology report was constitutional because it did not unduly interfere with a woman's exercise of her right to have an abortion. The substantial benefit of having pathology reports outweighed a woman's not-absolute right to have an abortion. Moreover, pathology reports were related to generally accepted medical standards and furthered the state's concern for public health. The substituted consent, which created a sort of parental veto of the minor's decision to have an abortion, was not unduly burdensome because it served the state's interest in protecting immature minors from decisions they might regret. The minors could overrule the parents' veto by appearing before a court.

Also constitutional (but this time by a 5–4 plurality vote) was the requirement for a second physician because it furthered a compelling government interest in preserving the lives of unborn fetuses.

The dissenters argued that the Court's resolution of the second physician requirement, pathology report requirement, and consent substitute provisions all violated the standards for undue burdensomeness that were established in *Akron.*

See Stephen P. Rosenberg, "Splitting the Baby: When Can a Pregnant Minor Obtain an Abortion Without Parental Consent? The Ex Parte Anonymous Cases (Alabama 2001)," *Connecticut Law Review* 34 (2002): 1109; and Stephanie Bornstein, "The Undue Burden: Parental Notification Requirements for Publicly Funded Contraception," *Berkeley Women's Law Journal* 15 (2000): 40.

Immigration and Naturalization Service v. Chadha

462 U.S. 919 (1983)
Decided: June 23, 1983
Vote: 7 (Burger, Brennan, T. Marshall, Blackmun, Powell, Stevens, O'Connor)
2 (B. White, Rehnquist)
Opinion of the Court: Burger
Opinion concurring in judgment: Powell
Dissenting opinion: B. White
Dissenting opinion: Rehnquist (B. White)

Jagdish Rai Chadha, an East Indian born in Kenya, held a British passport when he was lawfully admitted to the United States in 1966 on a student visa. The visa expired in 1972. In October 1973 the Immigration and Naturalization Service (INS) ordered Chadha to show why he should not be deported for having "remained in the United States for a longer time than permitted." Chadha conceded that he was deportable, but the immigration judge allowed him to file an application for suspension of deportation. The judge subsequently ordered that Chadha's deportation be suspended. Following rules under the Immigration and Nationality Act, the judge, via the attorney general, then reported the suspension to Congress. Under Section 244(c)(2) the act provided for either house of Congress to vote a legislative veto of the suspension order. In December 1975 the House of Representatives voted without debate or recorded vote to deport Chadha and five others.

The judge reopened the deportation proceedings. Chadha argued that Section 244(c)(2) was unconstitutional, but the judge held that he had no authority to rule on the law's constitutional validity. In November 1976 Chadha was ordered deported. His appeal to the Board of Immigration Appeals was dismissed. Chadha then sought review of the order by the court of appeals. The INS joined Chadha in arguing that Section 244(c)(2) was unconstitutional. The court of appeals agreed, saying that Section 244(c)(2) was unconstitutional on separation of powers grounds.

The Supreme Court affirmed this ruling, holding that the legislative veto is an unconstitutional power. Chief Justice Burger, writing for the majority, began by dispensing with challenges to the Court's authority to resolve the constitutional issue—including appellate jurisdiction, standing, case or controversy requirement, and the assertion that the question was a political question better resolved by the legislative and executive branches.

On whether the legislative veto "violates strictures of the Constitution," Burger wrote, "The fact that a given law or procedure is efficient, convenient, and useful in facilitating functions of government, standing alone, will not save it if it is contrary to the Constitution. Convenience and efficiency are not the primary objectives—or the hallmarks—of democratic government." Burger sidestepped Justice White's dissenting proposition that the veto was "an important if not indispensable political invention that allows the President and Congress to resolve major constitutional and policy differences." Even if this was correct, Burger countered, it is still "subject to the demands of the Constitution." The Presentment Clauses (Article I, Section 7, Clauses 2 and 3) and bicameral requirement (Article I, Sections 1 and 7, Clause 2), according to Burger, "guide our resolution of the important question."

In the records of the Constitutional Convention, in *Federalist Papers* Nos. 51 and 73, and in Supreme Court decisions such as ***The Pocket Veto Case,*** 279 U.S. 655 (1929), and ***Myers v. United States,*** 272 U.S. 52 (1926), "the Presentment Clauses serve the important purpose of assuring that a 'national' perspective is grafted on the legislative process," the chief justice said. He also pointed to the Constitutional Convention and *Federalist Papers* Nos. 22 and 62 as historical evidence that the Framers "were acutely conscious that the bicameral requirement . . . would serve [an] essential constitutional function."

Burger then turned his attention to exploring the concept of separation of powers. In ***Buckley v. Valeo,*** 424 U.S. 1 (1976), the Court said that the branches of government were not "hermetically" sealed from one another, but, Burger said, "When any Branch acts, it is presumptively exercising the power the Constitution has delegated to it." Starting with this principle, Burger addressed whether Section 244 (c)(2) conformed to the separation of powers doctrine. He noted that the House veto "reveals that it was essentially legislative in purpose and effect." Under the Constitution, the legislative branch is empowered to establish rules of naturalization, which by extension impact the rights and duties of executive branch officials and private individuals. Without Section 244(c)(2) the House could not have "overruled the attorney general and mandated Chadha's deportation." However, "Congress made a deliberate choice to delegate to the Executive Branch, and specifically to the Attorney General, the authority to allow deportable aliens to remain in this country in certain specified circumstances." As a result, Burger said, "Congress must abide by its delegation of authority until that delegation is legislatively altered or revoked."

Burger then returned to the concept of bicameralism to further his argument. "We see that when the Framers intended to authorize either House of Congress to act alone and outside of its prescribed bicameral legislative role, they narrowly and precisely defined the procedure for such action." Burger listed four enumerated powers "by which one House may act alone with the unreviewable force of law, not subject to the President's veto." They were, for the House, the impeachment power and, for the Senate, the power to conduct trials following a House impeachment, the power to approve presidential appointments, and the power to ratify treaties. "These exceptions," Burger wrote, "are narrow, explicit, and separately justified; none of them authorize the action challenged here."

Justice Powell found that the holding, which invalidated every use of the legislative veto, "gives one pause." Citing Justice Jackson's concurrence in ***Youngstown Sheet & Tube Co. v. Sawyer,*** 343 U.S. 579 (1952), Powell argued that the separation of powers principle should not be applied too rigidly. Powell concluded, "On its face, the House's action appears clearly adjudicatory. The House did not enact a general rule; rather it made its own determination that six specific persons did not comply with certain statutory criteria. It thus undertook the type of decision that traditionally has been left to other branches."

Justice White's lengthy dissent questioned the wholesale repudiation of the legislative veto. "Today the Court not only invalidates 244(c)(2) of the Immigration and Nationality Act, but also sounds the death knell for nearly 200 other statutory provisions in which Congress has reserved a 'legislative veto,' " he wrote. In an appendix to his dissent, White listed fifty-five of these statutes. White did not dispute the validity of the Presentment Clauses or the bicameral constitutional requirements, but said, "The power to exercise a legislative veto is not the power to write new law without bicameral approval or Presidential consideration. The veto must be authorized by statute and may only negative what an Executive department or independent agency has proposed." In the modern administrative state, White warned, "Absent the veto, the agencies receiving delegations of legislative or quasi-legislative power may issue regulations having the force of law without bicameral approval and without the President's signature." In conclusion, White found that Section 244(c)(2) passed the test enunciated in ***Nixon v. Administrator of General Services,*** 433 U.S. 425 (1977): "The legislative veto provision does not 'preven[t] the Executive Branch from accomplishing its constitutionally assigned functions.' "

Justice Rehnquist's dissent focused exclusively on whether Congress intended the one-House veto provision of 244(c)(2) to be severable from the act. Finding no evidence of this intention in the legislative history, Rehnquist would have reversed the judgment of the court of appeals.

Legislative veto provisions continued to appear in acts of Congress following *Chadha,* prompting constitutional scholar Louis Fisher to conclude that "the practical effect [of *Chadha*] was not nearly as sweeping as the Court's decision."

See Barbara Hinkson Craig, *Chadha: The Story of an Epic Constitutional Struggle* (New York: Oxford University Press, 1988); Louis Fisher, *Constitutional Dialogues* (Princeton: Princeton University Press, 1988); Katy J. Harriger, *Separation of Powers* (Washington, D.C.: CQ Press, forthcoming); Jessica Korn, *The Power of Separation: American Constitutionalism and the Myth of the Legislative Veto* (Princeton: Princeton University Press, 1988); and Gabriel Jack Chin, Victor Romero, and Michael Scaperlanda, *Immigration and the Constitution,* 3 vols. (New York: Garland, 2000).

Mueller v. Allen

463 U.S. 388 (1983)
Decided: June 29, 1983
Vote: 5 (Burger, B. White, Powell, Rehnquist, O'Connor)
4 (Brennan, T. Marshall, Blackmun, Stevens)
Opinion of the Court: Rehnquist
Dissenting opinion: T. Marshall (Brennan, Blackmun, Stevens)

Minnesota law allowed a state tax deduction for the expense of "tuition, textbooks and transportation" involved in sending a child to private school. Minnesota taxpayers sued to have the statute declared an unconstitutional violation of the Establishment Clause. The Minnesota courts found that it was not, and the Supreme Court affirmed.

Applying the test laid down in ***Lemon v. Kurtzman,*** 403 U.S. 602 (1971), the Court found that the statute had a secular purpose (promoting the education of children), did not have the primary effect of advancing religion (because it was the result of private decisions by parents to send their children to private school), and did not foster excessive entanglement between the state and church. Even though the state had to monitor which books the parents counted as a deductible expense, the statute did not require excessive entanglement between the church and state. In ***Zelman v. Simmons-Harris,*** 536 U.S. — (2002), the Court reaffirmed the analysis here and applied it to school vouchers.

See Paul Finkelman, ed., *Religion and American Law: An Encyclopedia* (New York: Garland, 2000); Kenneth Jost, "School Voucher Showdown," *CQ Researcher,* February 15, 2002; Kathy Koch, "School Vouchers," *CQ Researcher,* April 9, 1999; and L. Martin Nussbaum, "*Mueller v. Allen:* Tuition Tax Relief and the Original Intent," *Harvard Journal of Law and Public Policy* 7 (1984): 551.

Marsh v. Chambers

463 U.S. 783 (1983)
Decided: July 5, 1983
Vote: 6 (Burger, B. White, Blackmun, Powell, Rehnquist, O'Connor)
3 (Brennan, T. Marshall, Stevens)
Opinion of the Court: Burger
Dissenting opinion: Brennan (T. Marshall)
Dissenting opinion: Stevens

Presbyterian minister Robert Palmer had served as chaplain to the Nebraska legislature since 1965. One of his duties was to open legislative sessions with a prayer. Ernest Chambers, a member of the legislature, challenged this practice as a violation of the Establishment Clause of the First Amendment.

Rejecting arguments that the case should be dismissed on the Tenth Amendment, legislative immunity, standing, or federalism grounds, the court of appeals reversed the district court ruling that this practice did not violate the Constitution. The court of appeals held that the practice violated all three prongs of the test laid down in ***Lemon v. Kurtzman,*** 403 U.S. 602 (1971): it furthered religion, used state money for a religious purpose, and entangled the state in religion. The court of appeals emphasized that for sixteen years the legislature had hired the same minister and by doing so seemed to establish the Presbyterian faith as the official faith of the legislature.

Relying on the long history of legislative chaplains and of states having chaplains, the Supreme Court reversed the court of appeals. Chief Justice Burger offered little legal analysis and did his best to avoid the issues of the case. Much of his opinion discussed the history of legislative chaplains dating back to the colonial period. The case presented a clear example of the state establishing religion. The state paid one clergyman every year to perform the duties as chaplain. To refuse to strike down the practice would seem to undermine existing Establishment Clause jurisprudence. The Court could not even claim, as it had in other cases, such as ***Everson v. Board of Education,*** 330 U.S. 1 (1947), that this practice could be supported by "nonpreferentialism" because here the state clearly preferred one church and one clergyman to all others. Nor could the Court argue, as Justice O'Connor did later in ***Lynch v. Donnelly,*** 465 U.S. 668 (1984), that this practice was not an "endorsement" of a single faith because it clearly endorsed one church and one clergyman. If, however, the Court struck down the practice it would undermine a similar practice found in almost all states and in Congress. Burger carved out a single ad hoc exception to the *Lemon* test that seemed to be based on historical tradition, a weak legal argument, but a strong political move.

In his dissent, Justice Brennan acknowledged the narrow nature of Burger's opinion, but nevertheless argued it could not be sustained by any existing doctrine, or even any coherent doctrine. Justice Stevens, on the other hand, argued that the use of only one clergyman from one faith constituted an unconstitutional establishment.

The consequences of *Marsh* have been minimal because the issue was so narrow. The Court limited the case to legislative chaplains and has not expanded it to other areas where governments endorse religion. Proponents of public displays of the Ten Commandments, such as the defendants in *Glassroth v. Moore* (D.C.M.D. Ala., 2002), have argued that this case supports their position, but so far no Court has endorsed this interpretation of *Marsh.*

See Robert M. Slovek, "Legislative Prayer and the Establishment Clause: An Exception to Traditional Analysis," *Creighton Law Review* 17 (1984): 157–185; and William P. Marshall, "*Marsh v. Chambers*," in *Religion and American Law: An Encyclopedia*, ed. Paul Finkelman (New York: Garland, 2000), 297–299.

Michigan v. Long

463 U.S. 1032 (1983)
Decided: July 6, 1983
Vote: 6 (Burger, B. White, Blackmun, Powell, Rehnquist, O'Connor)
3 (Brennan, T. Marshall, Stevens)
Opinion of the Court: O'Connor
Concurring in judgment: Blackmun
Dissenting opinion: Brennan (T. Marshall)
Dissenting opinion: Stevens

Deputies Howell and Lewis observed David Long's car driving erratically and at a high rate of speed. They approached the car after it swerved into a shallow ditch and saw that Long was out of the car and appeared to be "under the influence" of some kind of drug. The officers had to ask him several times to produce his license and registration. When they noticed a hunting knife inside the car, they patted him down for weapons, but found none. Howell used his flashlight to see further into the car and discovered a package protruding from under the armrest. The officers found a bag of what appeared to be marijuana and arrested Long for possession. They searched the rest of the passenger compartment, but found nothing. The car was impounded and a search of the trunk turned up more marijuana. Long protested the introduction of the marijuana into evidence.

The lower courts allowed the marijuana into evidence, finding that the search of the passenger compartment was a valid protective search under ***Terry v. Ohio,*** 392 U.S. 1 (1968), and that the search of the trunk at the impound lot was a valid inventory search. The Michigan Supreme Court reversed, holding that the original search was invalid for lack of probable cause and the search of the trunk was invalid under the "fruit of the poisonous tree" doctrine.

The U.S. Supreme Court reversed. According to Justice O'Connor, the principle articulated in *Terry*—that officers may search a suspect's person for weapons for their own protection even when they have no probable cause to believe he is armed—extends to this situation as well, where the suspect is standing near his car and the police are asking him to enter the car to get his license and registration. Under such circumstances, if the officers reasonably believe that the suspect may pose a danger, they may search the areas of a car where weapons could be hidden. Because the search of the passenger compartment was a valid *Terry* search, the search of its trunk was a valid inventory search as long as it met the standards set forth in ***South Dakota v. Opperman,*** 428 U.S. 364 (1976).

See Richard A. Matasar and Gregory S. Bruch, "Procedural Common Law, Federal Jurisdictional Policy, and Abandonment of the Adequate and Independent State Grounds Doctrine," *Columbia Law Review* 86 (1986): 1291; Felicia A. Rosenfeld, "Fulfilling the Goals of *Michigan v. Long:* The State Court Reaction," *Fordham Law Review* 56 (1988): 1041; and Patricia Fahlbusch and Daniel Gonzalez, "*Michigan v. Long:* The Inadequacies of Independent and Adequate State Grounds," *University of Miami Law Review* 42 (1987): 159.

Grove City College v. Bell

465 U.S. 555 (1984)
Decided: February 28, 1984
Vote: 7 (Burger, B. White, Blackmun, Powell, Rehnquist, Stevens, O'Connor)
2 (Brennan, T. Marshall)
Opinion of the Court: B. White
Concurring opinion: Powell (Burger, O'Connor)
Concurring opinion: Stevens
Dissenting opinion: Brennan (T. Marshall)

Several students at Grove City College, a Christian-based four-year college in Pennsylvania, received Basic Educational Opportunity Grants (BEOGs). The federal Department of Education required all colleges that received financial assistance from the government to sign an assurance of compliance with anti–sex discrimination requirements under Title IX of the Education Amendments of 1972. The college refused to sign the assurance of compliance, and the department sought to terminate the students' financial aid. Grove City College and the students sued Secretary of Education Terrel Bell to regain the grants.

The district court found that the grants to the students constituted financial aid to the college, but that the Education Department could not terminate the students' financial aid because of the college's failure to sign the assurance of compliance. The Court of Appeals reversed. It held that BEOG aid fell within the meaning of Title IX even though it is an indirect aid to the college. It concluded that the Department of Education could condition financial aid upon execution of the assurance of compliance, and that it could terminate financial assistance to the students and college "despite the lack of evidence of actual discrimination."

The Supreme Court agreed with the district court that the financial aid to the students constituted aid to the college because it relieved the school of some financial aid burdens. However, only the college's financial aid program was affected by the federal funds, and only a failure to sign the assurance of compliance by the college's financial aid program could subject the students to losing their grants. As the financial aid program had refused to sign, the Court held that the Education Department could terminate the aid.

See Wayne C. Turner, "Title IX and Its Funding Termination Sanction: Defining the Limits of Federal Power over Educational Institutions," *Indiana Law Review* 17 (1985): 1167; Karen Czapanskiy, "*Grove City College v. Bell:* Touchdown or Touchback?" *Maryland Law Review* 43 (1984): 379; and Dianne M. Piche, "*Grove City College v. Bell* and Program-Specificity: Narrowing the Scope of Federal Civil Rights Statutes," *Catholic University Law Review* 34 (1985): 1087.

Lynch v. Donnelly

465 U.S. 668 (1984)
Decided: March 5, 1984
Vote: 5 (Burger, B. White, Powell, Rehnquist, O'Connor)
4 (Brennan, T. Marshall, Blackmun, Stevens)
Opinion of the Court: Burger
Concurring opinion: O'Connor
Dissenting opinion: Brennan (T. Marshall, Blackmun, Stevens)
Dissenting opinion: Blackmun (Stevens)

The town of Pawtucket, Rhode Island, annually placed a holiday " display" in a private park owned by a nonprofit organization. The city owned the materials in the display, including a crèche, paid a minimal amount for its assembly, and paid for the electricity to light it. In addition to the crèche, the display contained a Santa Claus house, reindeer pulling a sleigh, candy cane poles, clowns, an elephant, a teddy bear, other similar items, and a large banner reading "SEASONS GREETINGS." Various citizens challenged the inclusion of the crèche in this display on the grounds that it constituted an establishment of religion.

A sharply divided Supreme Court rejected this challenge. Chief Justice Burger placed great emphasis on the long history of such displays, as well as the display of religious art in public museums. The majority asserted that the crèche should be seen in the context of the rest of the display, which included many nonreligious objects.

Justice O'Connor, who provided the fifth vote for the majority, suggested the Court adopt an "endorsement" test to determine if the state violated the First Amendment. She argued that no one would look at this display, on private grounds, and believe the city was endorsing Christianity.

The dissenters focused on the crèche as a central image of Christian doctrine. As such, it was unconstitutional for the city to own and display the crèche. It could have a crèche in a public museum, as part of an exhibit, but that was not the issue here, despite Burger's use of museums to support his opinion.

The impact of this case was diminished somewhat by *County of Allegheny v. American Civil Liberties Union,* 492 U.S. 573 (1989), in which the Court ruled that Allegheny County could not put up a crèche in the county courthouse, but could erect a menorah and a Christmas tree outside another government building. Together, the two cases suggest that it is permissible for government to erect religious symbols if their impact is diminished by the presence of other objects or items, such as clowns, teddy bears, and the like.

See Norman Dorsen and Charles Sims, "The Nativity Scene Case: An Error of Judgment," *University of Illinois Law Review* (1985): 837–868; Kenneth Karst, "The First Amendment, The Politics of Religion and the Symbols of Government," *Harvard Civil Rights-Civil Liberties Law Review* 27 (1992): 503–530; and Bruce M. Zessar, "Government Participation in Holiday Religious Displays: Improving on *Lynch* and *Allegheny,*" *DePaul Law Review* 41 (1991): 101.

Massachusetts v. Upton

466 U.S. 727 (1984)
Decided: May 14, 1984
Vote: 7 (Burger, B. White, Blackmun, Powell,
Rehnquist, Stevens, O'Connor)
2 (Brennan, T. Marshall)
Opinion: *Per curiam*
Concurring in judgment: Stevens
Dissenting without opinion: Brennan, T. Marshall

This case provided a gloss on *Illinois v. Gates,* 462 U.S. 213 (1983), a decision regarding the validity of search warrants based on informants' tips. In *Gates,* the Supreme Court had held that the trustworthiness of an informant's tip need not be evaluated according to the rigid formula of cases such as *Aguilar v. Texas,* 378 U.S. 108 (1964), and *Spinelli v. United States,* 393 U.S. 410 (1969), but according to the totality of the circumstances. Furthermore, the Court clarified that the role of an appellate court in reviewing a lower court's grant of a search warrant was not to review the decision de novo—as if it were the court first granting the search warrant—but only to decide whether there was "substantial evidence in the record supporting the magistrate's decision to issue the warrant."

In this case, Lynn Alberico, former girlfriend of George Upton, called the police to inform them that Upton was storing large amounts of stolen items in his motor home. Alberico told police that she knew where the motor home was, but that Upton would soon move it to an unknown location. She also told police that she was giving them the information in order to "burn" Upton. Officers verified that there was a motor home where Alberico indicated. Based on the tip and the verification, the officers obtained and executed a search warrant and found the stolen goods.

Upton challenged the validity of the search warrant, and the Massachusetts Supreme Judicial Court found that it was not based on probable cause. That court found that *Gates* had not eliminated the need to satisfy both the "basis of knowledge" and the "veracity" prongs of the *Aguilar/Spinelli* test, but had only permitted certain defects in one prong or the other to be cured by corroboration. The court determined that the basis of Alberico's knowledge was not apparent from the tip—she had not claimed to have seen the stolen items in the motor home. Moreover, her veracity was not clear as she was not clearly identified. (She had merely assented to the suggestion that she was, in fact,

Lynn Alberico, would not give her address or phone number, and she had no track record as an informant.) Because the only corroboration the police carried out was to verify that there was a motor home on the premises, a fact totally innocuous in itself, the court found that the warrant was not based on probable cause.

The Supreme Court reversed. According to the Court, *Gates* had eliminated the need to satisfy the "basis of knowledge" and "veracity" elements of the *Aguilar/Spinelli* test. Furthermore, the Court rebuked the Massachusetts court for giving too little deference to the magistrate's interpretation of the facts. The Court held that the totality of circumstances in this case were enough to justify the magistrate's decision to issue a warrant.

See John M. Scott, "The Warrant Requirement," *Georgetown Law Journal* 74 (1986): 520; and Cameron S. Matheson, "The Once and Future Ninth Amendment," *Boston College Law Review* (1996): 179.

Wallace v. Jaffree

466 U.S. 924 (1984)
Decided: April 2, 1984
Vote: 9 (Burger, Brennan, B. White, T. Marshall, Blackmun, Powell, Rehnquist, Stevens, O'Connor)
0
Opinion: *Per curiam*
Concurring opinion: Stevens

In 1982 Alabama passed a law allowing all public school teachers, if they wished, and if they "recogniz[ed] that the Lord God is one" to lead "willing students" in a prescribed prayer, which began: "Almighty God, You alone are our God. We acknowledge You as the Creator and Supreme Judge of the world." Ishmael Jaffree, a parent of three elementary school children in Mobile challenged this act and two others as violating the First Amendment's prohibition on the establishment of religion.

In federal district court, Judge Brevard Hand upheld all three laws, asserting that "the establishment clause of the first amendment to the United States Constitution does not prohibit the state from establishing a religion." The Eleventh Circuit Court struck down the 1982 law.

The Supreme Court summarily affirmed and issued an order, without an opinion, on one issue raised in Hand's opinion: whether the Establishment Clause of the First Amendment is applicable to the states under the Fourteenth Amendment. The Court affirmed the court of appeals, which had overturned Hand's decision and sent a firm, unequivocal message to all courts in the nation that the First Amendment did apply to the states, and that Judge Hand's reading of the First and the Fourteenth Amendments was erroneous.

In a later case, ***Wallace v. Jaffree,*** 472 U.S. 38 (1985), the Court considered the other statutes at issue in this litigation.

See Patrick Marshall, "Religion in Schools," *CQ Researcher,* January 12, 2001, 1–24; and Rodney K. Smith, "Now Is the Time for Reflection: *Wallace v. Jaffree* and Its Legislative Aftermath," *Alabama Law Review* 37 (1986): 345–389.

Hishon v. King & Spaulding

467 U.S. 69 (1984)
Decided: May 22, 1984
Vote: 9 (Burger, Brennan, B. White, T. Marshall, Blackmun, Powell, Rehnquist, Stevens, O'Connor)
0
Opinion of the Court: Burger
Concurring opinion: Powell

Elizabeth Anderson Hishon's career as a lawyer with King and Spaulding, a large Atlanta law firm began with high hopes and expectations for advancement to partnership in five to six years if she received "satisfactory evaluations." The firm assured her during recruitment that associates as a "matter of course" became partners and that such decision would be made on a "fair and equal basis." Hishon relied on these assurances when she made her decision to accept employment with the firm. When the time came for the firm to decide on new partners, Hishon was not invited to become a partner, and the next year she was rejected again. She left the firm, received permission from the Equal Employment Opportunity Commission to sue, and then proceeded to the district court alleging that King and Spaulding had discriminated against her on the basis of her sex when it failed to make her a partner. Her complaint was dismissed because the district court determined that the statute under which she sued did not apply to partnership decisions in a law firm. The court of appeals affirmed.

The Supreme Court accepted the case on appeal to decide whether a partnership decision in a law firm was within the scope of Title VII of the Civil Rights Act of 1964. That statute makes it unlawful for an employer to discriminate against an "individual with respect to compensation, terms, conditions, or privileges of employment" because of several factors, one of which is the sex of the individual.

The Court considered Hishon's arguments that the promise of partnership made as an inducement during her recruitment was a major factor in her accepting employment with King and Spaulding, that she had relied on this promise when she made the decision to join the firm, and that the promise to consider her for partnership on a "fair and equal basis" created an employment contract. That promise of consideration for partnership then fell under Title VII as a "term, condition or privilege of employment" and could not be made in a discriminatory manner. The Court agreed that if the trial court found that Hishon had an employment contract with King and Spaulding, that Title VII would apply to her consideration for partnership, but, even if there was no contract, partnership was a benefit that might qualify as a privilege of employment under Title VII and as such must be distributed in a nondiscriminatory manner.

The Court also considered King and Spaulding's argument that consideration for partnership status in a law firm could not qualify as a "term, condition, or privilege of employment" as encompassed by the language of Title VII. The firm's argument was based on three points. The first was that partnership is a change in status from an employee to an employer. The Court found that even if the invitation to become a partner was not an offer of employment, Title VII would still apply. Title VII applies not only to offers of employment but also to terms, conditions, or privileges of employment. The second point asserted that Title VII exempts partnership decisions from its scope. The Court used the legislative history of the statute to determine that if Congress had wanted to exempt decisions on partnership from Title VII it would have expressly done so but it had not. The last point made by the firm was that applying Title VII to this case would result in restrictions on its constitutional rights of expression and association. The Court found that King and Spaulding had not shown that its ability to contribute to society's best interests would be impaired by considering Hishon for partnership on her merits. Private discriminatory decisions such as those involving law firm partnership could in fact be protected by resorting to First Amendment arguments invoking the exercise of freedom of association.

The Court ruled that partnership decisions fall within the Title VII protection against discrimination by an employer due to race, color, religion, sex, or national origin. The court of appeals was reversed and the case was remanded to the district court.

See Mary F. Radford, "Sex Stereotyping and the Promotion of Women to Positions of Power," *Hastings Law Journal* 41 (March 1990).

Chevron U.S.A. v. Natural Resources Defense Council

467 U.S. 837 (1984)
Decided: June 25, 1984
Vote: 6 (Burger, Brennan, B. White, Blackmun, Powell, Stevens)
0
Opinion of the Court: Stevens
Did not participate: T. Marshall, Rehnquist, O'Connor

Congress became involved in the quality of the nation's environment in the 1950s and 1960s. The post–World War II boom had created industrial pollution that the public recognized as harmful to those working within the industrial plants, as well as to those who lived near them. Laws were passed, regulations were mandated, and the Environmental Protection Agency (EPA) was created as the government's watchdog over the nation's air, water, and soil quality. Even though the federal government set the standards for quality, the states were put in charge of enforcing those standards on industrial sites within their borders. Amendments to the Clean Air Act of 1977 were aimed at states that had not attained compliance with the air quality standards. The act required that nonattaining states institute permit programs for new or modified equipment in major "stationary sources." The EPA was authorized to make regulations to implement this part of the statute. According to EPA regulations, the objective of each state's permit program was to ensure that any newly installed or modified equipment would not increase the total air pollutant emissions of the plant. This appeal to the Supreme Court resulted from a disagreement between the EPA and the court of appeals over the interpretation of the words *stationary sources.* The Court was asked to determine whether the EPA's interpretation of the words was a permissible construction of the statutory term.

Chevron and other industry representatives contended that Congress had not addressed the issue in the legislation. They asserted that in 1981, under a new administration, the EPA had determined that stationary source meant that all the pollution-emitting equipment at a specific industrial site would be treated as being within the same "bubble" for measuring whether the plantwide emissions of pollutants increased, decreased, or remained at the same level. One of the goals of the statute authorizing the permit program was to accommodate the sometimes conflicting interests of improving air quality and encouraging the industry to make improvements to its existing plant facilities. Chevron and the others saw the EPA's plantwide treatment of pollution sources as encompassed within the meaning and intent of the statute.

The National Resources Defense Council argued that the court of appeals' view on the EPA's regulations on the bubble concept should be supplanted by case law precedent. Two previous cases had established that the bubble concept was mandatory in programs that were designed merely to maintain existing air quality but could not be used in the programs with goals to improve air quality. Because improved quality was the goal of the permit program, the bubble concept could not be used. Under this interpretation, each new piece of equipment or any modification to existing equipment would be a separate "stationary source," and each must meet the lowest achievable emission rate for the type of industrial facility.

The Court could not find any help on the specific issue in the statute as passed by Congress or its legislative history. The Court then looked to the EPA, the agency authorized by Congress to implement the statute with regulations. It found that the EPA's view on the bubble concept had vacillated through the years, but maintained that the EPA was attempting to be flexible while regulating in a complex technical area. The agency was trying to maintain the balance between the interests of the nation in improved air quality and the interests of the economic backbone of the nation's industries.

Justice Stevens determined that the EPA's definition of the term *stationary source* as applying to an entire plant site, not to individual sources of emission within the plant, was permissible under the construction of the statute that mandated permit programs for states that had not complied with federal air quality standards.

The most significant result of this case was the establishment of the Chevron defense/test for an administrative agency. The Court held that "when the statute is silent or ambiguous with respect to the specific issues," the sole issue for a court is whether the administrative agency adopted a "permissible construction of the statute." To successfully challenge an administrative interpretation of a statute, a plaintiff must show that the agency acted in a way that was beyond a reasonable interpretation of the statute the agency is implementing.

See Nancy S. Bryson and Richard J. Mannix, "Putting the Brakes on Deference to Administrative Decision Making," *Environmental Quality Management* 10 (autumn 2000); Kenneth W. Starr, "Judicial Review in the Post-Chevron Era," *Yale Journal on Regulation* 3 (1986): 283; and Cass R. Sunstein, "Law and Administration After Chevron," *Columbia Law Review* 90 (1990): 2071.

Roberts v. United States Jaycees

468 U.S. 609 (1984)
Decided: July 3, 1984
Vote: 7 (Brennan, B. White, T. Marshall, Powell, Rehnquist, Stevens, O'Connor)
0
Opinion of the Court: Brennan
Concurring in judgment without opinion: Rehnquist
Opinion concurring in judgment: O'Connor
Did not participate: Burger, Blackmun

The Jaycees, a nonprofit membership corporation, was founded in 1920 as the Junior Chamber of Commerce. Its purpose is to "foster the growth and development of young men's civic organizations in the United States" and to provide for "personal development and achievement and an avenue for intelligent participation by young men in the affairs of their community, state and nation." According to the Jaycees' bylaws, "Regular membership is limited to young men between the ages of 18 and 35, while associate membership is available to individuals or groups ineligible for regular membership, principally women and older men." In violation of the bylaws, the Minneapolis chapter in 1974 and the St. Paul chapter the following year began admitting women as regular members. In 1978 the president of the national organization warned these chapters that unless they complied with the bylaws, their charters would be revoked. Both chapters filed charges of discrimination with the state, asserting that the exclusion of women from full membership required by the bylaws violated the Minnesota Human Rights Act.

The Minnesota Department of Human Rights found that the association was a " 'place of public accommodation' within the act and that it had engaged in an unfair discriminatory practice by excluding women from regular membership." Roberts, the acting commissioner, ordered the national organization to cease its discriminatory practices. The Minnesota Supreme Court certified that the association was, in fact, a "place of public accommodation" under the act.

The district court ruled that the act applied to any "public business facility." Because the Jaycees, for a variety of reasons, was a public business, the act applied to it. The Jaycees argued that the "the Minnesota Supreme Court's interpretation of the Act rendered it unconstitutionally vague and overbroad." The district court ruled for the state.

The court of appeals reversed. First, the court ruled that the Jaycees were "not wholly 'public.' " It next concluded that a significant portion of the activities engaged in by the Jaycees were related to its First Amendment freedom to advocate political and public causes, and, finally, that the execution of the act upon the Jaycees would "produce a 'direct and substantial' interference with that freedom." In short, Minnesota's "interest in eradicating discrimination" should have been "served in a number of ways less intrusive of First Amendment freedoms." The court also found the act vague and thus unconstitutional on due process grounds.

The U.S. Supreme Court reversed. Justice Brennan outlined the two "distinct" areas of First Amendment association rights: first, the individual "choices to enter into and maintain certain intimate human relationships" and, second, the expressive rights "for the purpose of engaging in those activities protected by the First Amendment." The Jaycees argued that the act violated both.

As for the first area, Brennan said that "several features of the Jaycees clearly place the organization outside of th[is] category." The critical elements, according to Brennan, were that the Jaycees were "neither small nor selective." Other than age and sex, the Jaycees were, for the most part, open to all membership candidates. Moreover, many women, although limited in certain respects, were commonly affiliated with the Jaycees.

Expressive rights, Brennan said, are not absolute and can be "infringed" given legitimate state interests. Brennan acknowledged that the act impacted the affairs of the association. "There can be no clearer example of an intrusion into the internal structure or affairs of an association," he said, "than a regulation that forces the group to accept members it does not desire." Rather than setting out to infringe upon free speech or suppress viewpoints, however, the state through the act had a compelling interest "of the highest order" in eradicating "discrimination and assuring . . . citizens equal access to publicly available goods and services." Moreover, the state had chosen "the least restrictive means of achieving its ends."

Brennan discounted the association's argument that if women were involved in its member voting and leadership "some change in the Jaycees' philosophical cast can reasonably be expected." The Court, Brennan noted, has "repeatedly condemned legal decision making that relies uncritically on such [gender-based] assumptions."

"In any event," Brennan wrote, "even if enforcement of the Act causes some incidental abridgment of the Jaycees' protected speech, that effect is no greater than is necessary to accomplish the State's legitimate purposes. . . . Acts of invidious discrimination in the distribution of publicly available goods, services, and other advantages cause unique evils that government has a compelling interest to prevent—wholly apart from the point of view such conduct may transmit." In the end, Brennan found that the need to overcome gender discrimination in society and to level the playing field for women entering the business community trumped the free speech claims the Jaycee's made, which seemed minor compared to the equality rights of women.

The Court reversed the due process finding by the court of appeals. Brennan wrote, "We have little trouble concluding that these concerns are not seriously implicated by the Minnesota Act, either on its face or as construed in this case."

The Supreme Court, in a 5–4 decision, reached what might be seen as a contrary result in ***Boy Scouts of America v. Dale,*** 530 U.S. 640 (2000), which ruled that the government could not compel the Boy Scouts to include homosexuals as members or leaders. In *Dale,* however, the Court found that the discriminating organization was "private," while in *Roberts* the Court found that the Jaycees were mostly public and that the discrimination against women would have little to do with the goal of the organization.

See Douglas O. Linder, "Comment: Freedom of Association After Roberts v. United States Jaycees," *Michigan Law Review* 82 (August 1984): 1878.

New Jersey v. T. L. O.

469 U.S. 325 (1985)
Decided: January 15, 1985
Vote: Multiple
Opinion of the Court: B. White
Concurring opinion: Powell (O'Connor)
Opinion concurring in judgment: Blackmun
Dissenting opinion: Brennan (T. Marshall)
Dissenting opinion: Stevens (Brennan, T. Marshall)

T. L. O., a fourteen-year old freshman, and a companion were discovered smoking by a teacher at Piscataway High School in Middlesex County, New Jersey. Smoking was a violation of a school rule, and the teacher took the two girls to meet with the assistant vice principal, Theodore Choplick. T. L. O., unlike her companion, denied she had violated the school rule. Choplick then searched T. L. O.'s purse and discovered cigarettes and cigarette rolling papers. On further examination, he also found "a small amount of marihuana, a pipe, a number of empty plastic bags, a substantial quantity of money in one-dollar bills, an index card that appeared to be a list of students who owed T. L. O. money, and two letters that implicated T. L. O. in marihuana dealing."

The matter was referred to the police, and T. L. O. subsequently confessed that she was selling marijuana. The state brought delinquency charges against her. Contending that Choplick's search was a violation of her Fourth Amendment rights, T. L. O. sought to suppress the evidence. The juvenile court, agreeing that school officials were accountable to the Fourth Amendment, nevertheless denied the motion on the grounds that the search was reasonable. The New Jersey Supreme Court agreed with T. L. O., finding that the search was unreasonable and the evidence had to be suppressed.

The U.S. Supreme Court reversed. In a 9–0 vote the Court agreed that the Fourth Amendment applied to school officials conducting searches of students, but the vote on whether this particular search was reasonable was 6–3. Justice White wrote that a balance must be struck between "legitimate expectations of privacy and personal security" and "the government's need for effective methods to deal with breaches of public order." To arrive at this balance, the test, according to White, was based on reasonableness rather than the "strict adherence" to probable cause. In ***Terry v. Ohio,*** 392 U.S. 1 (1968), the determination of reasonableness was "whether the . . . action was justified at its inception" and then whether the search was reasonable within the scope of the circumstances. According to White, this standard would serve both interests:

> By focusing attention on the question of reasonableness, the standard will spare teachers and school administrators the necessity of schooling themselves in the niceties of probable cause and permit them to regulate their conduct according to the dictates of reason and common sense. At the same time, the reasonableness standard should ensure that the interests of students will be invaded no more than is necessary to achieve the legitimate end of preserving order in the schools.

The dissenters found the search was excessive and unreasonable and, in applying the principles of ***Mapp v. Ohio,*** 367 U.S. 643 (1961), the evidence should have been suppressed.

As drug use by students became more prevalent, T. L. O. was cited in support of drug testing of high school athletes, in ***Vernonia School District 47J v. Acton,*** 515 U.S. 646 (1995), and of any student participating in any extracurricular activity, in ***Board of Education of Independent School District No. 92 of Pottawatomie County v. Earls,*** 536 U.S. — (2002).

See Samuel M. Davis, "*New Jersey v. T. L. O.* and the School Search Dilemma," *Search and Seizure Law Reporter* 12 (1985): 117; and Jamin B. Raskin, *We the Students: Supreme Court Cases for and About Students* (Washington, D.C.: CQ Press, 2000).

Garcia v. San Antonio Metropolitan Transit Authority

469 U.S. 528 (1985)
Decided: February 19, 1985
Vote: 5 (Brennan, B. White, T. Marshall, Blackmun, Stevens)
4 (Burger, Powell, Rehnquist, O'Connor)
Opinion of the Court: Blackmun
Dissenting opinion: Powell (Burger, Rehnquist, O'Connor)
Dissenting opinion: Rehnquist
Dissenting opinion: O'Connor (Powell, Rehnquist)

The question before the Supreme Court was whether the San Antonio Metropolitan Transit Authority (SAMTA), a public transit authority organized on a countywide basis, was subject to the minimum wage and overtime requirements of the Fair Labor Standards Act (FLSA). The FLSA was enacted in 1938. At that time its wage and overtime provisions did not apply to state and local government employees, such as SAMTA workers. In 1966 Congress extended FLSA coverage to state and local government employees by withdrawing the minimum wage and overtime exemptions from public hospitals, schools, and mass transit carriers whose rates and services were subject to state regulation. Congress also eliminated the overtime exemption for all mass transit employees other than drivers, operators, and conductors. In 1974 Congress extended FLSA coverage to virtually every state and local government employee.

In *Maryland v. Wirtz,* 392 U.S. 183 (1968), the Court had held that public schools and hospitals fell under the FLSA, but then reversed *Wirtz* in ***National League of Cities v. Usery,*** 426 U.S. 833 (1976), which held that the FLSA could not be applied to the "traditional governmental functions" of state and local governments. In 1979 the U.S. Department of Labor issued an administrative ruling that San Antonio's employment practices were subject to the FLSA.

SAMTA, which was operating at a loss, challenged the ruling. At the same time, the Labor Department, in the name of its secretary, Raymond J. Donovan, sought enforcement of the overtime and recordkeeping requirements of the FLSA. Joe G. Garcia and other SAMTA employees sued the transit authority for overtime pay under the FLSA. In November 1981 the district court granted SAMTA's motion for summary judgment. Donovan and Garcia appealed directly to the Supreme Court.

Before the appeal was taken up, the Court unanimously decided *Transportation Union v. Long Island R. Co.,* 455 U.S. 678 (1982), which held that a commuter rail service provided by a state-owned railroad did not constitute a "traditional governmental function" and did not enjoy constitutional immunity from federal labor laws under *National League of Cities.* In light of this decision, the Court vacated and remanded the district court's judgment in *Garcia.*

On remand, the district court again found for SAMTA. The court's rationale was that states historically were involved to some degree in mass transit, and that this involvement created an "inference of sovereignty." The court also found no "erosion of federal authority ... because many federal statutes themselves contain exemptions for States and thus make the withdrawal of federal regulatory power over public mass-transit systems a supervening federal policy." In addition, the court "compared mass transit to the list of functions identified as constitutionally immune in *National League of Cities* and concluded that it did not differ from those functions in any material respect."

Donovan and Garcia again appealed directly to the Supreme Court. The question the Court sought to answer was "whether or not the principles of the Tenth Amendment as set forth in *National League of Cities* ... should be reconsidered?" The Court said yes. Ironically, Justice Blackmun, who was the fifth vote in a 5–4 ruling in *National League of Cities,* wrote the majority opinion in which he explicitly overruled that case.

Blackmun, citing ***Hodel v. Virginia Surface Mining & Reclamation Association, Inc.,*** 452 U.S. 264 (1981), listed four conditions that "must be satisfied before a state activity may be deemed immune from a particular federal regulation under the Commerce Clause." First, "the federal statute . . . must regulate . . . 'States as States.' " What Blackmun meant was that the federal government might be able to regulate state activities, such as government-operated transit systems. Second, the activity must be an indisputable "attribute of state sovereignty," which clearly would not include a transit system. Third, state compliance with the federal law would "impair [the states'] ability 'to structure integral operations in areas of traditional governmental functions.' " Finally, "the relation of state and federal interests must not be such that 'the nature of the federal interest' would lead to 'state submission' to the national government."

Blackmun admitted that the Court had "made little headway in defining the scope of the governmental functions deemed protected under *National League of Cities.*" He concluded that it was not the role of the judiciary to preserve federalism because, as a guiding principle, looking at " 'traditional,' 'integral,' or 'necessary' " functions was an unworkable scheme that lead to "inconsistent results" by "an unelected federal judiciary [that make] decisions about which state policies it favors and which ones it dislikes." Federal legislation, under Blackmun's opinion, would have to take the lead "in preserving the States' interests." Blackmun concluded that the overtime and minimum wage requirements under the FLSA were not "destructive of state sovereignty or violative of any constitutional provision."

The dissenters focused on the impact the decision would have on the concepts underlying federalism. On the eve of Rehnquist's elevation to the chief justiceship, his brief dissent foreshadowed what would become the legacy of the Rehnquist Court. "I do not think it incumbent on those of us in dissent to spell out further the fine points of a principle that will, I am confident, in time again command the support of a majority of this Court," Rehnquist wrote. Justice O'Connor said that she would "not shirk the duty" to preserve federalism as determined in *National League of Cities.*

See Martha A. Field, "*Garcia v. San Antonio Metropolitan Transit Authority:* The Demise of a Misguided Doctrine," *Harvard Law Review* 99 (1985): 84; and Karl M. Tilleman, "Does the Tenth Amendment Pose Any Judicial Limit on the Commerce Clause After *Garcia v. San Antonio Metropolitan Transit Authority* and South *Carolina v. Baker*?" *Brigham Young University Law Review* (1989): 231.

Wallace v. Jaffree

472 U.S. 38 (1985)
Decided: June 4, 1985
Vote: 6 (Brennan, T. Marshall, Blackmun, Powell, Stevens, O'Connor)
3 (Burger, B. White, Rehnquist)
Opinion of the Court: Stevens
Concurring opinion: Powell
Opinion concurring in judgment: O'Connor
Dissenting opinion: Burger
Dissenting opinion: B. White
Dissenting opinion: Rehnquist

This case was making its second appearance before the Supreme Court. It involved three Alabama statutes designed to bring prayer back into the public schools of that state. An Alabama act of 1978 authorized one minute of silence in all public schools "for meditation." In 1981 another act created a period of silence "for meditation or voluntary prayer." In 1982 the legislature authorized all public school teachers, on a voluntary basis, and if they "recogniz[ed] that the Lord God is one" to lead "willing students" in a prescribed prayer, which began: "Almighty God, You alone are our God. We acknowledge You as the Creator and Supreme Judge of the world." Ishmael Jaffree, a parent of three elementary school children in Mobile, challenged these acts as violating the First Amendment's prohibition on the establishment of religion. The lower federal courts upheld the 1978 statute, which authorized a moment of silence, and this issue was never brought directly before the Supreme Court. The other two statutes reached the Court in two separate cases.

When Jaffree first brought his challenge, the district court granted a preliminary injunction against the implementation of the 1981 and 1982 acts. After a trial on the merits, however, District Judge Brevard Hand upheld both acts, as well as the 1978 act. Hand asserted that "the establishment clause of the first amendment to the United States Constitution does not prohibit the state from establishing a religion." The court of appeals, as the Supreme Court noted, "not surprisingly . . . reversed" Hand.

In ***Wallace v. Jaffree,*** 466 U.S. 924 (1984), the Supreme Court unanimously affirmed the reversal of what Justice Stevens called the "District Court's remarkable conclusion that the Federal Constitution imposes no obstacle to Alabama's establishment of a state religion," and the 1982 act was held to be unconstitutional. This case was relatively easy because no constitutional or historical support existed for Hand's conclusion that Alabama, or any other state, could establish a "state religion."

The second case, Alabama's appeal on the constitutionality of the 1981 statute that created a moment of silence "for meditation or voluntary prayer," was more problematic because the state had neither written a prayer nor required that a prayer be said. Nevertheless, the Court affirmed the conclusion of the court of appeals that the moment of silence also violated the Constitution. As Justice Stevens noted, "Whenever the State itself speaks on a religious subject, one of the questions that we must ask is 'whether the government intends to convey a message of endorsement or disapproval of religion.' " Stevens noted that the record established in the district court clearly showed that the 1981 act "was intended to convey a message of state approval of prayer activities in the public schools," and this clearly violated the Establishment Clause.

Stevens indicated that he would have upheld a straightforward "moment of silence" law, such as the 1978 Alabama statute that was not before the Court. Concurring opinions by Justices O'Connor and Powell indicated the same thing, but all three found the legislative intent of Alabama overwhelmingly clear: the state wanted to establish prayer, not just a moment of silence.

The dissenters, especially Justice Rehnquist, rejected the idea that the states could not have silent prayer and asserted that the government could favor religion in general, as long as it took no stand in favor of any particular faith. Rehnquist argued that the advocacy of prayer was permissible, as in the 1981 act, but not assertion of specific theology, as in the 1982 act.

See Paul Finkelman, ed., *Religion and American Law: An Encyclopedia* (New York: Garland, 2000); Patrick Marshall, "Religion in Schools," *CQ Researcher,* January 12, 2001, 1–24; and Rodney K. Smith, "Now is the Time for Reflection: *Wallace v. Jaffree* and Its Legislative Aftermath," *Alabama Law Review* 37 (1986): 345–389.

Aguilar v. Felton

473 U.S. 402 (1985)
Decided: July 1, 1985
Vote: 5 (Brennan, T. Marshall, Blackmun, Powell, Stevens)
4 (Burger, B. White, Rehnquist, O'Connor)
Opinion of the Court: Brennan
Concurring opinion: Powell
Dissenting opinion: Burger
Dissenting opinion: B. White
Dissenting opinion: Rehnquist
Dissenting opinion: O'Connor (Rehnquist)

Title I of the Elementary and Secondary Education Act of 1965 provided funding "to local educational institutions to meet the needs of educationally deprived children from low-income families." Starting in 1966 New York City used a portion of its funds to pay the salaries of public school employees who taught in the city's parochial schools. In 1978 several taxpayers brought an action to the federal district court asserting that the use of the funds in such a manner violated the First Amendment's Establishment Clause.

The district court upheld the Title I funding in a similar case, *National Coalition for Public Education and Religious Liberty v. Harris,* 489 F. Supp. 1248 (SDNY 1980), and then held for the city in *Aguilar.* The court of appeals unanimously reversed, seeing a clear violation of the Establishment Clause. The city appealed to the Supreme Court, which affirmed the decision of the court of appeals.

On the same day, the Court also decided *Grand Rapids School District v. Ball,* 473 U.S. 373 (1985), which ruled unconstitutional the practice of providing public school classrooms to nonpublic school students at public expense. This "shared time" funding, when provided to parochial school students, violated the Establishment Clause. New York tried to distinguish its practice from Grand Rapids by pointing out that New York had "adopted a system for monitoring the religious content of publicly funded Title I classes in the religious schools." Justice Brennan, in his majority opinion, wrote the heightened supervision "inevitably results in the excessive entanglement of church and state." This kind of oversight and control was addressed in ***Lemon v. Kurtzman,*** 403 U.S. 602 (1971), and ***Meek v. Pittenger,*** 421 U.S. 349 (1975). Both rejected the public payment of public school teachers in nonpublic school institutions.

According to Brennan, the *Lemon* and *Meek* tests were applicable to determining *Aguilar.* The first question to answer was whether the public funding was "provided in a pervasively sectarian environment." Second, because the funding is the payment of public school salaries, was there a requirement for "ongoing inspection . . . to ensure the absence of a religious message?" If the answers to both are yes, as they are in *Aguilar,* the Establishment Clause is violated.

The majority, according to the dissenters, applied too rigid an expectation upon the third prong of the *Lemon* test, the "excessive entanglement" criterion. With a change in Court membership, this prong's rigidity was loosened in ***Zobrest v. Catalina Foothills School District,*** 509 U.S. 1 (1993), which permitted public funding for a sign-language interpreter for a deaf parochial school student. A few years later, in ***Agostini v. Felton,*** 521 U.S. 203 (1997), the Court overruled *Aguilar* by allowing public funding for remedial instruction to disadvantaged parochial school children when the instruction was on public school grounds. The Court has continued to chip away at the once solid prohibition against state support for parochial school education. Most recently, in ***Zelman v. Simmons-Harris,*** 536 U.S. — (2002), the Court upheld the use of school vouchers even though most of the voucher money was used to attend religious private schools.

See David M. Ackerman, "The Law of Church and State: Public Aid to Sectarian Schools," *Congressional Research Service,* February 26, 1998; Patrick Marshall, "Religion in Schools," *CQ Researcher,* January 12, 2001, 1–24; and Christian Chad Warpula, "The Demise of Demarcation: *Agostini v. Felton* Unlocks the Parochial," *Wake Forest Law Review* 33 (1998): 465.

Goldman v. Weinberger

475 U.S. 503 (1986)
Decided: March 25, 1986
Vote: 5 (Burger, B. White, Powell, Rehnquist, Stevens)
4 (Brennan, T. Marshall, Blackmun, O'Connor)
Opinion of the Court: Rehnquist
Concurring opinion: Stevens (B. White, Powell)
Dissenting opinion: Brennan (T. Marshall)
Dissenting opinion: Blackmun
Dissenting opinion: O'Connor (T. Marshall)

S. Simcha Goldman, an orthodox Jewish rabbi, was also a captain in the U.S. Air Force and served as a clinical psychologist. As required by his religious faith, he always kept his head covered, wearing a small skullcap (yarmulke) underneath his official Air Force cap. No one on the base challenged this practice until he was called to testify for the defense at a court-martial. The prosecutor then complained to Goldman's superior that Goldman was out of uniform.

Deferring to the military, a majority of the Court upheld the power of Secretary of Defense Casper Weinberger to implement the regulation on uniforms. Justice Rehnquist argued that the need for "obedience, unity, commitment and esprit de corps" required strict adherence to rules about uniforms and necessitated "great deference to the professional judgment of military authorities."

Justice Stevens argued that the military should not be put in the position of choosing which religious exemptions from the prescribed uniform the military should allow and which it should not.

The dissenters chided the Court for its uncritical deference to the military and for its somewhat extreme arguments that a small skullcap could somehow undermine military discipline.

Shortly after this decision, Congress passed legislation allowing Orthodox Jews to wear a yarmulke underneath official headgear.

See Robert M. O'Neil, "Civil Liberty and Military Necessity—Some Preliminary Thoughts on *Goldman v. Weinberger,*" *Military Law Review* 113 (1986): 31.

Batson v. Kentucky

476 U.S. 79 (1986)
Decided: April 30, 1986
Vote: 7 (Brennan, B. White, T. Marshall, Blackmun, Powell, Stevens, O'Connor)
2 (Burger, Rehnquist)
Opinion of the Court: Powell
Concurring opinion: B. White
Concurring opinion: T. Marshall
Concurring opinion: Stevens (Brennan)
Concurring opinion: O'Connor
Dissenting opinion: Burger (Rehnquist)
Dissenting opinion: Rehnquist (Burger)

James Kirkland Batson, an African American, was prosecuted in Kentucky for second-degree burglary. At trial, the prosecutor used his peremptory challenges to remove all blacks in the jury pool. Batson's attorney then moved to dismiss the jury before it was sworn in on the grounds that the all-white jury pool denied Batson his Sixth and Fourteenth Amendment rights "to a jury drawn from a cross-section of the community," as well as his Fourteenth Amendment right to equal protection of the laws. Batson later appealed his conviction on these grounds.

In his majority opinion, Justice Powell observed that in ***Strauder v. West Virginia,*** 100 U.S. 303 (1880), the "Court decided that the State denies a black defendant equal protection of the laws when it puts him on trial before a jury from which members of his race have been purposefully excluded." The Court reaffirmed the holding in *Strauder* that a defendant was not entitled to a petit jury that contained members of any particular race, but that it was unconstitutional for the prosecution to deliberately exclude members of the defendant's race. In applying *Strauder* to peremptory challenges, the Court partially overruled *Swain v. Alabama,* 380 U.S. 202 (1965), in which a conviction after such peremptory challenges had not been overturned. In that case, however, the Court warned that it would not accept the use of racially motivated challenges "in contravention of the Equal Protection Clause" of the Fourteenth Amendment and noted that blacks had a constitutional right to participate as jurors. Here, the Court implemented that caveat.

The Court explained that racial discrimination in jury selection harmed "not only the accused" but also "the entire community" because it would undermine "public confidence in the fairness of our system of justice."

The dissenters argued that this decision "sets aside . . . a procedure which has been part of the common law for many centuries and part of our jury system for nearly 200 years." The observation was true but was made in a vacuum that ignored the issue of racial discrimination and the demands of the Constitution, especially the Fourteenth Amendment, that the states apply the law equally, without regard to race. As Justice White noted in his concurrence, the use of challenges to remove blacks from juries, "remains widespread" more than a century after the Court held in *Strauder* that racial discrimination in jury selection violated the Constitution.

In *Batson* the Court set out standards for a new test. To make a claim under *Batson,* a defendant had to be a member of a minority group and show that the peremptory challenges were used to remove all potential jurors in that group. The defendant also had to show that "circumstances raise an inference that the prosecutor" excluded "the veniremen from the petit jury on account of their race." Finally, the case had to be a prosecution.

In ***Edmonson v. Leesville Concrete Co.,*** 500 U.S. 614 (1991), however, the Court expanded *Batson* to some civil cases and private litigation, and in *Powers v. Ohio,* 499 U.S. 400 (1991), the Court also ruled that nonminority defendants had a constitutional right to a jury pool that represents the community, and when a white is on trial the prosecution cannot use peremptory challenges to eliminate all nonwhites from the jury.

See Albert W. Alschuler, "Racial Quotas and the Jury," *Duke Law Journal* 44 (1995): 704–743; Elaine A. Carlson, "*Batson,* J. E. B., and Beyond: The Paradoxical Quest for Reasoned Peremptory Strikes in the Jury Selection Process," *Baylor Law Review* 46 (1994): 947–1005; and Leonard B. Mandell, "*Batson v. Kentucky* Revisited: A Clear Break for Some But Not for All?" *Preview* 2 (1986): 40.

Wygant v. Jackson Board of Education

476 U.S. 267 (1986)
Decided: May 19, 1986
Vote: 5 (Burger, B. White, Powell, Rehnquist, O'Connor)
4 (Brennan, T. Marshall, Blackmun, Stevens)
Judgment of the Court: Powell
Concurring opinion: O'Connor
Opinion concurring in judgment: B. White
Dissenting opinion: T. Marshall (Brennan, Blackmun)
Dissenting opinion: Stevens

White teachers filed suit against the board of education of Jackson, Michigan, challenging part of a collective-bargaining agreement between the board and the teachers' union. Article XII of the agreement provided that if layoffs became necessary the board would use both seniority and the percentage of minority teachers to determine who should be retained. Under this process, tenured white teachers faced layoffs while minority teachers, with less seniority would be retained. The district court upheld the validity of Article XII's preference for minority teachers, and on appeal, the court of appeals affirmed.

The Supreme Court reversed. The Court engaged in a two-prong equal protection analysis. "First, any racial classification must be justified by a compelling governmental interest. Second, the means chosen by the state to effectuate its purpose must be narrowly tailored to the achievement of this goal." The district court and court of appeals identified the compelling government interests as the alleviation of social discrimination and the need for minority role models, and here the Court agreed with the lower courts. The Court found, however, that Article XII did not satisfy the second element of the analysis. Noting its "previously expressed concern over the burden that a preferential-layoffs scheme imposes on innocent parties," the

Court rejected layoffs as the most narrowly tailored mean to eradicate societal discrimination.

Bowen v. Roy

476 U.S. 693 (1986)
Decided: June 11, 1986
Vote: Multiple
Judgment of the Court: Burger
Concurring opinion: Blackmun
Concurring opinion: Stevens
Concurring opinion: O'Connor (Brennan, T. Marshall)
Dissenting opinion: B. White

Stephen Roy and Karen Miller filed a lawsuit against the secretary of the Pennsylvania Department of Public Welfare, the secretary of Health and Human Services, and the secretary of agriculture after their two-year-old daughter, Little Bird of the Snow, was denied food stamps and benefits under the Aid to Families with Dependent Children (AFDC) program. The AFDC and food stamps program require each recipient's Social Security number to process the benefits. Roy argued that the use of Social Security numbers deprives individuals of their uniqueness, and he refused to provide his daughter's Social Security number, claiming this requirement violated his beliefs and infringed his First Amendment Free Exercise rights. Although citing no particular religious doctrine, Roy, a descendant of the Abenaki Tribe, said his argument was consistent with his Native American religious beliefs.

The district court found for Roy and granted an injunction enjoining the state and the federal government from denying his daughter her federal benefits in the absence of a Social Security number. The court reached this decision despite Roy's admission that he, his wife, and their son had Social Security numbers, and his admission on the last day of the trial that in fact Little Bird of the Snow also had a Social Security number.

The Supreme Court agreed to consider whether the Free Exercise Clause required a government agency to adjust its behavior to avoid offending certain religious beliefs. The Court reversed the district court. Chief Justice Burger found that neither the government's statutory requirement of a Social Security number nor the number's use for the purpose of receiving federal and state benefits denied Roy his First Amendment rights. Addressing the issue of the government's use of Social Security numbers, Burger found Roy's argument without merit. The Court set out a distinction between "the freedom of individual belief, which is absolute, and the freedom of individual conduct, which is not absolute." The Court held that the First Amendment "cannot be understood to require the Government to conduct its own internal affairs in ways that comport with the religious beliefs of particular citizens." Burger also found no First Amendment violation in the requirement of a Social Security number for benefits because the rule was "wholly neutral in religious terms and uniformly applicable." The Court noted that Roy chose to accept federally provided benefits, that the government was not compelling Roy to comply, and that he must only comply if he wanted to receive the benefits.

In addition, the Court found a strong interest in requiring Social Security numbers in the individual's application for federal benefits to protect against fraudulent applications. There being no less intrusive means to accomplish this interest, the Court upheld the requirement of Social Security numbers in the application for federal benefits.

See David C. Williams and Susan H. Williams, "Volitionalism and Religious Liberty," *Cornell Law Review* 76 (1991): 769; and Paul Finkelman, ed., *Religion and American Law: An Encyclopedia* (New York: Garland, 2000).

Thornburgh v. American College of Obstetricians & Gynecologists

476 U.S. 747 (1986)
Decided: June 11, 1986
Vote: 5 (Brennan, T. Marshall, Blackmun, Powell, Stevens)
4 (Burger, B. White, Rehnquist, O'Connor)
Opinion of the Court: Blackmun
Concurring opinion: Stevens
Dissenting opinion: Burger
Dissenting opinion: B. White (Rehnquist)
Dissenting opinion: O'Connor (Rehnquist)

Richard Thornburgh, the governor of Pennsylvania, signed into law the Abortion Control Act of 1982. The entire act came under immediate legal challenge. With one factual exception, the federal district court rejected the challengers' motion for an injunction against the enforcement of the act. Both sides appealed. The court of appeals on a rehearing ruled that certain provisions were unconstitutional: Section 3205 ("informed consent"); 3208 ("printed information"); 3214(a) and (h) (reporting requirements); 3211(a) (determination of viability); 3210(b) (degree of care required in postviability abortions); and 3210(c) (second-physician requirement).

Justice Blackmun, after dispensing with the questions on appellate jurisdiction, explicitly reaffirmed ***Roe v. Wade,*** 410 U.S. 113 (1973), and *Akron v. Akron Center for Reproductive Health, Inc.*, 462 U.S. 416 (1983). The former established a woman's right to seek an abortion, and the latter ruled unconstitutional certain regulations that were deemed too burdensome on that right. For each of the challenged provisions, the Court agreed with the court of appeals, finding that the provisions were, on their face, unconstitutional.

In their separate dissents, Chief Justice Burger and Justice O'Connor argued that *Roe* permitted some degree of government control to regulate abortions on demand, but that *Roe*'s progeny have chipped away at this interest. O'Connor wrote, "Today's decision goes further, and makes it painfully clear that no legal rule or doctrine is safe from ad hoc nullification by this Court when an occasion for its application arises in a case involving state regulation of abortion."

Justice White concluded that the "time has come" to recognize that *Roe* and its progeny " 'departs from a proper understanding' of the Constitution" and should be overruled.

See David A. J. Richards, "Constitutional Legitimacy and Constitutional Privacy," *New York University Law Review* 61 (1968): 800.

Meritor Savings Bank, FSB v. Vinson

477 U.S. 57 (1986)
Decided: June 19, 1986
Vote: 9 (Burger, Brennan, B. White, T. Marshall, Blackmun, Powell, Rehnquist, Stevens, O'Connor)
0
Opinion of the Court: Rehnquist
Concurring opinion: Stevens
Opinion concurring in judgment: T. Marshall (Brennan, Blackmun, Stevens)

Mechelle Vinson began working for Meritor Savings Bank in 1974 as a teller-trainee. Her supervisor, Sidney Taylor, promoted Vinson several times in the next four years, and she eventually became an assistant branch manager. After being fired in 1978 for absenteeism, Vinson brought a sexual harassment suit against the bank, alleging that Taylor had subjected her to continual sexual harassment. Those allegations included demands for sexual favors, fondling her in front of other employees, following her into the women's restroom at the bank, and forcibly raping her. Vinson never reported Taylor's actions, claiming she feared him. Taylor and the bank denied all the allegations.

The district court denied Vinson relief, concluding that if a relationship between Vinson and Taylor existed, it was voluntary. The court decided, however, to answer the question of the bank's liability. Because the bank provided an express policy against discrimination and because neither Vinson nor any other employee had lodged a complaint, the court found that the bank was without notice and could not be liable for Taylor's conduct. The court of appeals reversed that decision, holding "that a violation of Title VII may be predicated on either of two types of sexual harassment: harassment that involves the conditioning of concrete employment benefits on sexual favors, and harassment that, while not affecting economic benefits, creates a hostile or offensive working environment." Because the district court had not considered this type of violation, the court of appeals remanded the case. The court of appeals also considered the issue of the bank's liability, finding the bank absolutely liable for Taylor's behavior, even without notice.

The Supreme Court upheld the court of appeals' contention "that a plaintiff may establish a violation of Title VII by proving that discrimination based on sex has created a hostile or abusive work environment." From here, the Court found that the district court erred in assuming that voluntariness was the crucial factor in a sexual discrimination case. On the contrary, the correct inquiry is whether the adverse conduct was unwanted.

On the issue of employer liability in Title VII claims of sexual discrimination, the Court declined to issue a concrete rule. It disagreed with both the court of appeals' decision to impose absolute liability and with the district court's decision that the employer could not be held liable. Instead, it supported the Equal Employment Opportunity Commission guidelines that courts look to traditional agency principles for assistance. Employer liability should have some limitations, but a notice requirement does not exist. "In sum, we hold that a claim of "hostile environment" sex discrimination is actionable under Title VII [and] that the District Court's finding were insufficient to dispose of respondent's hostile environment claim." Rejecting the opportunity to consider employer liability in Title VII claims, the Court remanded the case to determine Vinson's sexual harassment claim under the Title VII theory of hostile environment.

See Sheryl A. Greene, "Reevaluation of Title VII Abusive Environment Claims Based on Sexual Harassment after *Meritor Savings Bank v. Vinson,*" *Thurgood Marshall Law Review* 13 (1988): 29.

Bowers v. Hardwick

478 U.S. 186 (1986)
Decided: June 30, 1986
Vote: 5 (Burger, B. White, Powell, Rehnquist, O'Connor)
4 (Brennan, T. Marshall, Blackmun, Stevens)
Opinion of the Court: B. White
Concurring opinion: Burger
Concurring opinion: Powell
Dissenting opinion: Blackmun (Brennan, T. Marshall, Stevens)
Dissenting opinion: Stevens (Brennan, T. Marshall)

A Georgia statute criminalized consensual sodomy, providing up to twenty years imprisonment for anyone who "performs or submits to any sexual act involving the sex organs of one person and the mouth or anus of another." Michael Hardwick was arrested in his own home under this statute when a police officer entered his bedroom to serve a warrant for drinking in public and discovered Hardwick performing oral sex on another man. The district attorney refused to bring a prosecution, but Hardwick brought an action in federal court to challenge the constitutionality of the Georgia statute. The court of appeals held the statute violated rights to privacy under the Ninth and Fourteenth Amendments.

The Supreme Court reversed. Justice White stated the question clearly: "The issue presented is whether the Federal Constitution confers a fundamental right upon homosexuals to engage in sodomy and hence invalidates the laws of the many States that still make such conduct illegal and have done so for a very long time." He held that no such right existed. White noted that the right to privacy had developed over many years and cited cases such as ***Pierce v. Society of Sisters,*** 268 U.S. 510 (1925); ***Meyer v. Nebraska,*** 262 U.S. 390 (1923); ***Prince v. Massachusetts,*** 321 U.S. 158 (1944); ***Skinner v. Oklahoma ex rel. Williamson,*** 316 U.S. 535 (1942); ***Loving v. Virginia,*** 388

U.S. 1 (1967); ***Griswold v. Connecticut,*** 381 U.S. 479 (1965); and ***Roe v. Wade,*** 410 U.S. 113 (1973). He noted, however, that all these cases dealt with family rights, marriage, child rearing, and procreation. He rejected the notion that these cases bore "any resemblance to the claimed constitutional right of homosexuals to engage in acts of sodomy" because there was "no connection between family, marriage, or procreation on the one hand and homosexual activity on the other."

The dissents were emphatic on the majority's narrow view of "privacy," arguing in part that the antisodomy laws were based on impermissible attempts to impose religious values on the law. Justice Blackmun also chided the Court for focusing on the homosexual issue, when the statute equally applied to similar acts between heterosexual couples. For this reason, the statute did in fact threaten marital privacy. For Blackmun, the heart of the matter was not the "right to engage in homosexual sodomy," as the majority declared. Quoting Justice Brandeis in ***Olmstead v. United States,*** 277 U.S. 438 (1928), Blackmun said, "Rather, this case is about 'the most comprehensive of rights and the right most valued by civilized men,' namely, 'the right to be let alone.' "

Justice Powell proved to be the swing vote. He upheld the law, but indicated that he would not support actual incarceration under the statute. This, he believed, would violate the Eighth Amendment's prohibition on unjust punishments. In 1990, after he had retired from the bench, Powell told students at New York University Law School that his vote in the case had probably been a "mistake," although he also asserted that because no one had actually been prosecuted under the law, Hardwick's was a frivolous case.

Had Hardwick won, this would have been a major victory for the gay rights movement. Instead, it led to what Justice Blackmun called a "cramped reading" of constitutional rights, and gave opponents of gay rights a valuable precedent.

See Marc A. Fajer, "*Bowers v. Hardwick, Romer v. Evans,* and the Meaning of Anti-Discrimination Legislation," *National Journal of Sexual Orientation Law* 2 (1996): 208; and Arthur S. Leonard, ed., *Homosexuality and the Constitution,* 4 vols. (New York: Garland, 1997).

Bethel School District No. 403 v. Fraser

478 U.S. 675 (1986)
Decided: July 7, 1986
Vote: 7 (Burger, Brennan, B. White, Blackmun, Powell, Rehnquist, O'Connor)
2 (T. Marshall, Stevens)
Opinion of the Court: Burger
Opinion concurring in judgment: Brennan
Opinion concurring in judgment: Blackmun
Dissenting opinion: T. Marshall
Dissenting opinion: Stevens

Matthew N. Fraser, a high school student at Bethel High School in Pierce County, Washington, prepared a speech nominating a fellow student for vice president of the student government. The short speech included several sexually explicit metaphors. Anticipating that the speech might be problematic, he had read it to several teachers prior to delivering it. All of the teachers warned Fraser that he might be punished, but he decided to proceed and delivered the speech to six hundred students, many of whom were only fourteen years old. The next day the assistant principal called him into her office and advised him that the school considered his speech a violation of a disciplinary rule prohibiting obscene language. She suspended him for three days and removed his name from a list of possible speakers at his commencement ceremonies.

The school district reviewed the incident and determined that the speech was "indecent, lewd, and offensive to the modesty and decency of many of the students and faculty in attendance at the assembly." This conclusion was supported by the statements of many teachers, who observed that during and after the speech many students were disruptive, while others were clearly embarrassed and confused. The school board examiner found the speech was "obscene," within the meaning of the school's "disruptive-conduct rule." Fraser then served two days of the three-day suspension.

Fraser and his father instituted a suit in district court against the school. They claimed that the school had violated Fraser's First Amendment right to free speech and that the punishment violated Fraser's Fourteenth Amendment right to due process. The district court found in favor of Fraser. It concluded that the school had failed to establish that his speech disrupted the educational process, as the Supreme Court said in ***Tinker v. Des Moines Independent Community School District,*** 393 U.S. 503 (1969), was required to suppress a student's First Amendment rights. It also found the disciplinary rule "unconstitutionally vague and overbroad" and that the removal of Fraser's name from a list of potential commencement speakers violated due process. The court of appeals affirmed this decision.

The Supreme Court agreed to consider "whether the First Amendment prevents a school district from disciplining a high school student for giving a lewd speech at a school assembly." In an effort to balance the "undoubted freedom to advocate unpopular and controversial views in schools and classrooms" and "society's countervailing interest in teaching students the boundaries of socially appropriate behavior," the Court reversed the lower courts. Although children do not surrender their constitutional guarantees in a school atmosphere, the Court held that children in public schools do not have the same privileges as adults. Instead, public schools have wide latitude in determining what is appropriate behavior in a school setting, especially when the behavior may be inappropriate for minors and detracts from the educational mission. Having every right "to prohibit the use of vulgar and offensive terms in public discourse," the Court held that the school did not violate Fraser's First Amendment right to free speech by punishing him.

The Court also rejected Fraser's Fourteenth Amendment claim that the punishment "violated due process because he had no way of knowing that the delivery of the speech in question would subject him to disciplinary sanctions." Unable to anticipate every infraction, a school could never prescribe all the consequences for disruptive behavior like a criminal code. The Court found the disciplinary rule constitutionally sufficient, especially in light of the "admonitions of teachers" who warned Fraser not to give the speech because it "could subject him to sanctions," and that, as one teacher noted, there might be "severe consequences" if he persisted.

In reaching this conclusion, Chief Justice Burger noted the important distinction between the political "message" of the speech in *Tinker,* where students wore black armbands to protest the Vietnam War, and the "sexual content" of Fraser's speech. While reaffirming the holding in *Tinker* that students do not "shed their constitutional rights to freedom of speech or expression at the schoolhouse gate," the Court also gives school districts greater flexibility in regulating decorum within the schools.

In his concurrence, Justice Brennan quoted the entire speech, pointing out that it was not obscene and could not have been punished if given outside of a school. It was, however, vulgar and inappropriate for a school setting. Brennan asserted that the case stood only for the principle that school officials could "ensure that a high school assembly proceed in an orderly manner." He reminded the majority that school officials could not discriminate against students or punish students merely for ideas or positions with which the officials disagreed.

In dissent, Justice Marshall asserted that the "School District failed to demonstrate that respondent's remarks were indeed disruptive." He believed the punishment was inappropriate and violated the First Amendment.

See Jamin B. Raskin, *We the Students: Supreme Court Cases for and About Students* (Washington, D.C.: CQ Press, 2000); and Sara Slaff, "Silencing Student Speech: *Bethel School District No. 403 v. Fraser,*" *American University Law Review* 37 (1987): 203.

Bowsher v. Synar

478 U.S. 714 (1986)
Decided: July 7, 1986
Vote: 7 (Burger, Brennan, T. Marshall, Powell, Rehnquist, Stevens, O'Connor)
2 (B. White, Blackmun)
Opinion of the Court: Burger
Opinion concurring in judgment: Stevens (T. Marshall)
Dissenting opinion: B. White
Dissenting opinion: Blackmun

The purpose of the Balanced Budget and Emergency Deficit Control Act of 1985 was to eliminate the federal budget deficit. If, in any fiscal year, the federal budget deficit exceeded the maximum deficit amount by more than a specified sum, the act required across-the-board cuts in federal spending to reach the targeted deficit level. The procedures accounting for these "automatic" reductions were addressed in Section 251 (the reporting provisions) of the act. Each year, the directors of the Office of Management and Budget (OMB) and the Congressional Budget Office (CBO) estimated the amount of the federal budget deficit for the upcoming fiscal year. If cuts were required, the directors calculated, on a program-by-program basis, the necessary budget reductions. The act also required the directors to report jointly their deficit estimates and budget reduction calculations to the comptroller general. The comptroller, after reviewing the reports, was to report his conclusions to the president. The president would then issue a "sequestration" order mandating the spending reductions specified by the comptroller. In the absence of remedial legislation, the sequestration order became effective and the spending reductions included in that order were made.

Rep. Michael L. Synar, D-Okla., who had voted against the act, challenged its constitutionality. The National Treasury Employees Union also filed a lawsuit asserting that its members had been injured as a result of the act's automatic spending reduction provisions. The other party to the suit was Charles A. Bowsher, the comptroller general.

The district court first concluded that Synar and the union had standing to sue. It then invalidated the reporting provisions. The court also concluded that the act survived a delegation doctrine challenge, but held that the role of the comptroller general in the deficit reduction process violated the constitutionally imposed separation of powers.

The Supreme Court affirmed. After dispensing with the question of standing, Chief Justice Burger addressed the central issue in the case: whether Section 251 violated the principles of separation of powers.

The comptroller general heads the General Accounting Office (GAO), which is a federal department "independent of the executive departments." Congress created the office in 1921 because it believed that it "needed an officer, responsible to it alone, to check upon the application of public funds in accordance with appropriations." The comptroller is nominated by the president from a list of three individuals recommended by the Speaker of the House and the president pro tempore of the Senate, and confirmed by the Senate. He is removable only at the initiative—under limited criteria—of Congress.

Burger found that the comptroller, who exercised judgments of fact and interpreted provisions of the act was actually making "decision[s] . . . typically made by officers charged with executing a statute." In other words, the law required him to perform an executive branch activity, even though he was an "officer controlled by Congress." If he was empowered "to execute the laws" it "would be, in essence . . . a congressional veto." Citing ***Immigration and Naturalization Service v. Chadha,*** 462 U.S. 919 (1983), which struck down the legislative veto, Burger concluded, "this kind of congressional control over the execution of the laws, *Chadha* makes clear, is constitutionally impermissible."

See Daniel J. Balhoff, "*Bowsher v. Synar:* Separation of Powers, the Removal of Officers, and the Administrative State," *Louisiana Law Review* 47 (1987): 617; Daniel J. Gifford, "The Separation of Powers Doctrine and the Regulatory Agencies After *Bowsher v. Synar,*" *George Washington Law Review* 55 (1987): 441; and Jeffrey D. Straussman and William C. Banks, "*Bowsher v. Synar:* The Emerging Judicialization of the Fisc," *Boston College Law Review* 28 (July 1987): 659–688.

Johnson v. Transportation Agency, Santa Clara County

480 U.S. 616 (1987)
Decided: March 25, 1987
Vote: 6 (Brennan, T. Marshall, Blackmun, Powell, Stevens, O'Connor)
3 (Rehnquist, B. White, Scalia)
Opinion of the Court: Brennan
Concurring opinion: Stevens
Opinion concurring in judgment: O'Connor
Dissenting opinion: B. White
Dissenting opinion: Scalia (Rehnquist, B. White)

In 1980 Paul E. Johnson, an employee for the Transportation Agency in Santa Clara County, California, was passed over for promotion to road dispatcher. In compliance with its affirmative action plan—in effect since December 1978—the county selected Diane Joyce for the position. Joyce had worked for the county since 1970. In 1974 she applied for a road dispatcher position, but was deemed ineligible because she had not served as a road maintenance worker. She became a road maintenance worker the next year, becoming the first woman to fill such a job. Johnson began his employment with the county in 1967 as a road yard clerk. In 1977 his clerical position was downgraded, and he sought and received a transfer to the position of road maintenance worker.

Both applicants were deemed well qualified for the position, but Johnson scored slightly higher in evaluations. Joyce then contacted the county's affirmative action office, which in turn contacted the agency's affirmative action coordinator. The coordinator recommended that, in an opportunity to advance their affirmative action goals, the agency should promote Joyce. Meanwhile, after a second interview of the candidates, including Johnson and Joyce, the promotions committee recommended that Johnson receive the promotion. The director of the agency, James Graebner, promoted Joyce.

Johnson received a right-to-sue letter from the Equal Employment Opportunity Commission and filed suit with the federal district court. He alleged that the promotion decision was gender-based and, as such, in violation of Title VII of the Civil Rights Act of 1964. The court agreed, holding that the sex of the applicants was "the determining factor." It also held that the agency's plan did not satisfy the criterion established in *Steelworkers v. Weber,* 443 U.S. 193 (1979), that the affirmative action plan be temporary. The court of appeals reversed. It held that no termination date was needed because the attainment of the plan was its objective, not the maintenance of it. Moreover, "the Agency's consideration of Joyce's sex in filling the road dispatcher position was lawful."

The Supreme Court affirmed. The first issue for the Court to resolve, according to Justice Brennan, was whether the "consideration of the sex of applicants for Skilled Craft jobs was justified by the existence of a 'manifest imbalance' that reflected underrepresentation of women in 'traditionally segregated job categories.' " Brennan said it was, and that it was legitimate for the plan to consider sex in the promotion, in addition to "a host of practical factors in seeking to meet affirmative action objectives."

The final question for Brennan was whether the plan "unnecessarily trammeled the rights of male employees or created an absolute bar to their advancement." The Court rejected this argument. Brennan said that women and men were required to compete for advancement, that there was no absolute entitlement to advancement, and that the plan's mandate was to create a balanced workforce, not to maintain one.

In the main dissent, Justice Scalia quoted the relevant portion of Title VII. Sex was one of the enumerated factors that could not be used to "deprive or tend to deprive any individual of employment opportunities or otherwise adversely affect his status as an employee." The Court, according to Scalia, "completes the process of converting this from a guarantee that . . . sex will not be the basis for employment determinations, to a guarantee that it often will."

See Kenneth Jost, "Affirmative Action," *CQ Researcher,* September 21, 2001, 737–760; and Melvin I. Urofsky, *Affirmative Action on Trial: Sex Discrimination in Johnson v. Santa Clara* (Lawrence: University Press of Kansas, 1997).

McCleskey v. Kemp

481 U.S. 279 (1987)
Decided: April 22, 1987
Vote: 5 (Rehnquist, B. White, Powell, O'Connor, Scalia)
4 (Brennan, T. Marshall, Blackmun, Stevens)
Opinion of the Court: Powell
Dissenting opinion: Brennan (T. Marshall, Blackmun, Stevens)
Dissenting opinion: Blackmun (Brennan, T. Marshall, Stevens)
Dissenting opinion: Stevens (Blackmun)

In 1978 a jury in Atlanta, Georgia, convicted Warren McCleskey, an African American, for killing a white policeman during a robbery. The jury recommended the death sentence. After unsuccessful appeals in the Georgia courts, McCleskey sought habeas corpus relief in the federal courts, arguing that in Georgia the death penalty was applied in a manner that discriminated against blacks. McCleskey supported this position with research done by David C. Baldus. This research, known as the Baldus study, demonstrated startling correlations between race and the death penalty in Georgia.

The raw data of the Baldus study showed that 11 percent of defendants charged with killing whites received the death penalty, but only 1 percent of defendants charged with killing blacks received the death penalty. Twenty-two percent of black defendants convicted of killing whites received the death penalty, but only 8 percent of whites charged with killing whites received the death penalty. Blacks convicted of killing other blacks were given the death penalty in only 1 percent of all cases, and whites charged with killing blacks received the same penalty in 3 percent of all cases. Prosecutors sought the death penalty in 70 percent of cases involving black defendants and white victims, but in only 32 percent of all cases involving white defendants and white victims. On the other hand, prosecutors sought the death penalty in only 15 percent of cases involving black on black killings; and in only 19 percent of cases in which whites killed blacks.

Baldus used a sophisticated analysis involving 230 separate variables, to refine these numbers, including "39 nonracial variables." This analysis demonstrated that "defendants charged with killing white victims were 4.3 times as likely to receive a death sentence as defendants charged with killing blacks." The conclusions of the study were clear: black defendants charged with killing whites—like McCleskey—were far more likely to receive the death penalty than any other class of defendants.

The district court and court of appeals rejected McCleskey's appeal, and the Supreme Court affirmed this result. The Court held that even if these statistics were accurate, they did not prove that McCleskey's death penalty was based on racial bias. The Court further argued that these statistics did not prove an intent to discriminate. The Court noted that death penalty decisions were made on an individual, case-by-case basis, and each decision rested on a variety of interconnected facts. Furthermore, the decision-makers—the jurors—were different in each case. Thus, there could be no policy of discrimination, as there might be in jury cases in which blacks were systematically excluded from jury service, or in civil service promotions, where a single entity, like a police department, had a pattern of not promoting blacks. After a lengthy discussion of these issues, the Court concluded that "at most, the Baldus study indicates a discrepancy that appears to correlate with race. Apparent disparities in sentencing are an inevitable part of our criminal justice system."

The dissenters argued that the death penalty itself was "cruel and unusual punishment," which they would eliminate from the American system of jurisprudence. For them the Baldus study offered one more powerful example that the implementation of the death penalty was inherently biased and discriminatory. As Justice Brennan argued, the Baldus study showed that in McCleskey's case "there was a significant chance that race would play a prominent role in determining if he lived or died."

After losing in the Supreme Court, McCleskey began another habeas corpus action, arguing that he was convicted because of statements made to prosecutors without the benefit of counsel. In ***McCleskey v. Zant,*** 499 U.S. 467 (1991), the Court again sustained his conviction, and some years later he was executed.

See Kenneth Jost, "Rethinking the Death Penalty," *CQ Researcher,* November 16, 2001, 945–968; Ann Chih Lin, ed., *Capital Punishment* (Washington, D.C.: CQ Press, 2002); and Gregory D. Russell, *The Death Penalty and Racial Bias: Overturning Supreme Court Assumptions* (Westport, Conn.: Greenwood Press, 1994).

United States v. Salerno

481 U.S. 739 (1987)
Decided: May 26, 1987
Vote: 6 (Rehnquist, B. White, Blackmun, Powell, O'Connor, Scalia)
3 (Brennan, T. Marshall, Stevens)
Opinion of the Court: Rehnquist
Dissenting opinion: T. Marshall (Brennan)
Dissenting opinion: Stevens

Anthony Salerno and Vincent Cafaro, alleged members of the Genovese crime family, were arrested in March 1986, following their twenty-nine-count indictment that alleged RICO (Racketeer Influenced and Corrupt Organizations Act) violations, mail and wire fraud offenses, extortion, and various criminal gambling violations. The prosecution sought to detain the defendants under the Bail Reform Act of 1994.

The act permitted the detention, prior to trial, of any potentially dangerous individual charged with certain crimes. Procedural safeguards—the right to a hearing, to counsel, to submit evidence, to testify, to present witnesses, and to cross-examine witnesses—were included in the act. The district court conducted the requisite hearing and ordered that Salerno and Cafaro be detained.

The defendants asserted that the act violated their Fifth Amendment due process rights and Eighth Amendment protections against excessive bail. The court of appeals held that the act did, on its face, violate the defendants' Fifth Amendment rights.

The Supreme Court reversed. The Court held that the act had a legitimate and compelling purpose—detaining individuals who "pose a threat to the safety of individuals or to the community." The procedural requirements of the act were a reasonable means to achieving that purpose. As a result, the Court concluded that the act violated neither the Fifth nor the Eighth Amendment.

The dissenters took issue with the act's authority to indefinitely detain individuals who were not convicted of any crime based on the suspicions of the government.

The act has also been used by the United States in its war on terrorism, for example, the government's pretrial detention request to hold Richard C. Reid on December 28, 2001.

See Rebecca M. Fowler, "Note: *United States v. Salerno:* Detaining Dangerous Defendants," *Tulsa Law Journal* 23 (1988): 429; and Louis M. Natali Jr. and E. Ohlbaum, "*United States v. Salerno,* Redrafting the Due Process Model: The Preventive Detention Blueprint," *Temple Law Review* 62 (1989): 1225.

Edwards v. Aguillard

482 U.S. 578 (1987)
Decided: June 19, 1987
Vote: 7 (Brennan, B. White, T. Marshall, Blackmun, Powell, Stevens, O'Connor)
2 (Rehnquist, Scalia)
Opinion of the Court: Brennan
Concurring opinion: Powell (O'Connor)
Opinion concurring in judgment: B. White
Dissenting opinion: Scalia (Rehnquist)

Louisiana's creationism act—formally called "Balanced Treatment for Creation-Science and Evolution-Science in Public School Instruction"—prohibited the public schools from teaching evolution unless they also taught something called "creation science." In effect, the law required that the schools teach a religious, or biblical, view of the creation of the world along with accepted scientific knowledge about geology and evolution. The district court found the law unconstitutional, and the court of appeals affirmed. Edwin W. Edwards, the governor of Louisiana, appealed to the U.S. Supreme Court.

Justice Brennan upheld the lower courts, concluding that the law violated the First Amendment because it "advances a religious doctrine by requiring either the banishment of the theory of evolution from public school classrooms or the presentation of a religious viewpoint that rejects evolution in its entirety." According to Brennan, the law "seeks to employ the symbolic and financial support of government to achieve a religious purpose," and it was clearly unconstitutional.

In a concurring opinion, Justice Powell, who had once served as counsel to the Richmond, Virginia, public schools, reaffirmed the "broad discretion accorded state and local school officials in the selection of the public school curriculum," but went on to note that in the law the state "acted with the unconstitutional purpose of structuring the public school curriculum to make it compatible with a particular religious belief: the 'divine creation of man' " which appeared in the statute.

See Stephen Carter, "Evolutionism, Creationism, and Treating Religion as a Hobby," *Duke Law Journal* (1987): 977–996; Edward J. Larson, *Summer for the Gods: The Scopes Trial and America's Continuing Debate Over Science and Religion* (New York: Basic Books, 1997); and David Masci, "Evolution vs. Creationism," *CQ Researcher,* August 22, 1997.

South Dakota v. Dole

483 U.S. 203 (1987)
Decided: June 23, 1987
Vote: 7 (Rehnquist, B. White, T. Marshall, Blackmun, Powell, Stevens, Scalia)
2 (Brennan, O'Connor)
Opinion of the Court: Rehnquist
Dissenting opinion: Brennan
Dissenting opinion: O'Connor

In 1984 Congress enacted a law that directed the secretary of transportation to withhold a percentage of federal highway funds from states "in which the purchase or public possession . . . of any alcoholic beverage by a person who is less than 21 years old is lawful." South Dakota permitted persons as young as nineteen to purchase beer containing up to 3.2 percent alcohol. The state asserted that the Twenty-First Amendment allows the states to have complete control over the importation or the sale of liquor and how to structure the liquor distribution system. South Dakota asserted that this control included the right to set minimum drinking ages.

Secretary of Transportation Elizabeth Dole argued that the Twenty-First Amendment only confirms the states' broad power to impose restrictions on the sale and distribution of alcoholic beverages but does not confer on them any power to permit the sales that Congress seeks to prohibit.

In upholding the law, the Supreme Court ignored the debate over the Twenty-First Amendment, finding that Congress had not in fact regulated the sale of liquor. Chief Justice Rehnquist found that Congress had acted indirectly, under its spending power, to encourage consistency in the states' drinking ages. The Court found that this goal—and the legislature's means of achieving it—was within its broad constitutional powers, even though Congress could not regulate drinking ages directly.

In upholding the statute, the Court noted that Congress had found that the difference in the drinking ages in the different states led to young people crossing state lines to drink and then to return to their home state while driving under the influence of alcohol. This interstate problem required a national solution, and, Rehnquist wrote, "The means it chose to address this dangerous situation were reasonably calculated to advance the general welfare."

The Court found no violation of South Dakota's power. The offer of benefits from Congress to the state is dependent on the cooperation by the state with federal plans, which work together for the general welfare of the citizens. Congress had instructed the states to establish a minimum drinking age of no lower than twenty-one years of age or lose 5 percent of its highway funds. The Court therefore found no merit in the claim that Congress was forcing the states to adopt the new drinking age.

Justice O'Connor argued that this statute was in fact an attempt to regulate the sale of liquor, which was beyond the powers of Congress, both because it fell outside the power to regulate commerce and because it was a power specifically given to the states under the Twenty-First Amendment. Justice Brennan, in a short dissent, agreed with O'Connor, but also asserted that the Twenty-First Amendment struck the proper balance between federal and state authority and that Congress should not be able to condition a federal grant in a manner that abridges the states rights.

See Ben Canada, "Federal Grants to State and Local Governments: A Brief History," *CRS Report for Congress,* October 10, 2000; www.house.gov/underwood/grants/RL30705.pdf.

Puerto Rico v. Branstad

483 U.S. 219 (1987)
Decided: June 23, 1987
Vote: 9 (Rehnquist, Brennan, B. White, T. Marshall, Blackmun, Powell, Stevens, O'Connor, Scalia)
0
Opinion of the Court: T. Marshall
Opinion concurring in judgment: O'Connor (Powell)
Opinion concurring in judgment: Scalia

In this case the Supreme Court revisited, and reversed, a long settled rule of law involving interstate extradition. In ***Kentucky v. Dennison,*** 65 U.S. 66 (1861), the Court held that, although a state governor ought to comply with an extradition requisition from another state, the provision of Article IV, Section 2, Clause 2, depended entirely on comity for its implementation. The Court held in *Dennison* that the language of this clause did not give the federal government any enforcement power. In *Puerto Rico v. Branstad* the Court reversed *Dennison* and ordered the governor of Iowa, Terry Branstad, to extradite Ronald Calder, who was under indictment in Puerto Rico.

Acting under *Dennison,* two successive Iowa governors, Robert Ray and Branstad, had refused to comply with an extradition requisition from the governor of Puerto Rico. On January 25, 1981, Ronald Calder's car struck Antonio de Jesus Gonzalez and his eight-month pregnant wife, Army Villalba. Gonzalez survived, but his wife and unborn child died. Puerto Rican officials arrested Calder and charged him with murder. Posting bail, Calder became a fugitive when he failed to appear at a preliminary hearing. Suspecting that Calder would return to Iowa, Puerto Rican officials contacted local Iowa authorities to apprise them that Calder was wanted for homicide. Surrendering himself in Iowa, Calder again posted bail. Calder argued that as a white, English-speaking mainlander, he could not get a fair trial in Puerto Rico, where he claimed the justice system was corrupt. He further argued that at most his offense amounted to manslaughter and that the murder charge indicated the bias against him.

Iowa officials attempted to negotiate this issue with their counterparts in Puerto Rico. They argued that the charges against Calder were excessive and not supported by the facts, even as presented by Puerto Rican officials. In 1981 Ray "formally notified the Governor of Puerto Rico that in the absence of a 'change to a more realistic charge,' the request for extradition was denied." When Branstad continued to take this position, Puerto Rice filed suit in federal court arguing that Branstad's refusal to extradite Calder violated the Extradition Clause of the Constitution and the Extradition Act. Puerto Rico requested "the issuance of a writ of mandamus directing respondent Branstad to perform the 'ministerial duty' of extradition."

The Court agreed to "reconsider the holding . . . that federal courts have no power to order the Governor of a State to fulfill that State's obligation under the Extradition Clause of the Constitution to deliver up fugitives from justice." Determining that federal courts do have that power, Justice Marshall also found that Puerto Rico may rightfully seek its writ of mandamus.

In reconsidering the holding in *Dennison,* the Court noted that the longstanding decision asserted two principles: "first, that the Extradition Clause creates a mandatory duty to deliver up fugitives upon proper demand; and second, that the federal courts have no authority under the Constitution to compel performance of this ministerial duty of delivery."

Noting that *Dennison* was decided in 1861, just before the outbreak of the Civil War, the Court rejected that case's holding that it could not order state officials to take certain actions. Marshall noted, "It has long been a settled principle that federal courts may enjoin unconstitutional action by state officials." Holding that federal courts may compel state officials to extradite fugitives upon the proper request of another state, the Court further stated that no Tenth Amendment considerations exist "because the duty is directly imposed upon the States by the Constitution itself."

The decision was somewhat ironic. Since 1861 few governors had ever refused to extradite people charged with or convicted of crimes, but almost all of the instances of extradition refusal had involved claims of racial discrimination. *Dennison* had served as a safety valve to prevent the extradition of minorities to places where they might not receive fair trials. Indeed, in his pre-Court career with the NAACP Legal Defense Fund, Marshall had urged numerous northern governors to refuse extradition requisitions from the South on the grounds that the courts in the South were biased against blacks. The issue in *Dennison* was the refusal of Ohio to return a free black to Kentucky to face charges for helping a slave escape. Nevertheless, despite the historic use of gubernatorial discretion to protect minorities, Marshall led the Court in overturning the precedent.

See Kenyon Bunch and Richard J. Hardy, "Continuity or Change in Interstate Extradition? Assessing *Puerto Rico v. Branstad,*" *Publius* 21 (winter 1991); and Jay P. Dinan, "*Puerto Rico v. Branstad:* The End of Gubernatorial Discretion in Extradition Proceedings," *University of Toledo Law Review* 19 (1988): 649.

Nollan v. California Coastal Commission

483 U.S. 825 (1987)
Decided: June 26, 1987
Vote: 5 (Rehnquist, B. White, Powell, O'Connor, Scalia)
4 (Brennan, T. Marshall, Blackmun, Stevens)
Opinion of the Court: Scalia
Dissenting opinion: Brennan (T. Marshall)
Dissenting opinion: Blackmun
Dissenting opinion: Stevens (Blackmun)

James and Marilyn Nollan owned beachfront property in Ventura County, California. They leased their property with an option to buy, which was conditioned on their replacing a small bungalow that had fallen into disrepair after years of use as a summer rental. The Nollans were also required, under state law, to obtain a coastal development permit from the California Coastal Commission. The commission granted a provisional permit contingent on whether the Nollans allowed an easement to pass across a portion of their property. The Nollans protested the condition, and the commission overruled their objection.

The Nollans filed an action with the county court seeking to invalidate the access condition. The court ruled for the Nollans and remanded the case to the commission for an evidentiary hearing. After a public hearing, the commission reaffirmed its initial decision. The Nollans then brought an action in the county court asserting that access condition violated both the Fifth Amendment's Takings Clause and the Fourteenth Amendment. The court again ruled in favor of the Nollans. The state court of appeals reversed the decision. The court found no violation of the Takings Clause "because, although the condition diminished the value of the Nollans' lot, it did not deprive them of all reasonable use of their property."

By a slim majority, the Supreme Court ruled in favor of the Nollans. The Court found that the permit condition violated the Takings Clause. Historically, Justice Scalia said for the majority, the Court has found that "land-use regulation does not effect a taking if it 'substantially advance[s] legitimate state interests' and does not 'den[y] an owner economically viable use of his land.' " The Court, however, has rarely "elaborated on the standards for determining what constitutes a 'legitimate state interest' or what type of connection between the regulation and the state interest satisfies the requirement that the former 'substantially advance' the latter." According to Scalia, the commission argued that there were three purposes in regard to access to the public beach: (1) seeing that was a public beach; (2) "overcoming the 'psychological barrier' to using the beach;" and (3) "preventing congestion on the public beaches." The question for Scalia was whether there was a reasonable connection between permit condition and the government purpose that advanced the state interest. He answered in the negative.

> It is quite impossible to understand how a requirement that people already on the public beaches be able to walk across the Nollans' property reduces any obstacles to viewing the beach created by the new house. It is also impossible to understand how it lowers any "psychological barrier" to using the public beaches, or how it helps to remedy any additional congestion on them caused by construction of the Nollans' new house.

In summing up his conclusion, Scalia said, "California is free to advance its 'comprehensive program,' if it wishes, by using its power of eminent domain for this 'public purpose,' but if it wants an easement across the Nollans' property, it must pay for it."

The dissenters found that the majority's imposition of a "standard of precision for the exercise of a State's police power" was unrealistic, unworkable, and "discredited for the better part of this century." In the main dissent, Justice Brennan argued that even if this rigid standard was imposed, the state "easily satisfie[d] this requirement." Brennan stated that public access to the beach was a legitimate government interest and that the commission's conditions upon the Nollans were reasonable means to further promote the perception that the beach was publicly accessible.

Brennan disagreed with the contention that the commission went too far in advancing legitimate governmental interests. As the Court made clear in ***Pruneyard Shopping Center v. Robins,*** 447 U.S. 74 (1980), he said, "physical access to private property in itself creates no takings problem if it does not 'unreasonably impair the value or use of [the] property.' [The Nollans] can make no tenable claim that either their enjoyment of their property or its value is diminished by the public's ability merely to pass and repass a few feet closer to the seawall beyond which appellants' house is located."

In addition, Brennan said this case was not a taking because the commission allowed the Nollans to improve their property. The Nollans were "allowed to replace a one-story, 521-square-foot beach home with a two-story, 1,674-square-foot residence and an attached two-car garage, resulting in development covering 2,464 square feet of the lot." Moreover, the Nollans did not contend "that this increase is offset by any diminution in value resulting from the deed restriction, much less that the restriction made the property less valuable than it would have been without the new construction."

This "unconstitutional conditions" doctrine was reaffirmed a few years later in ***Dolan v. City of Tigard,*** 512 U.S. 374 (1994), which addressed the unresolved question in *Nollan*: "What is the required degree of connection between the exactions imposed by the city and the projected impacts of the proposed development?"

See Richard A. Epstein, *Takings: Private Property and the Power of Eminent Domain* (Cambridge: Harvard University Press, 1985); Nathaniel S. Lawrence, "Means, Motives, and Takings: The Nexus Test of *Nollan v. California Coastal Commission,*" *Harvard Environmental Law Review* 12 (1988): 231; and William Michael Treanor, "The Original Understanding of the Takings Clause and the Political Process," *Columbia Law Review* 95 (1995): 782.

Hazelwood School District v. Kuhlmeier

484 U.S. 260 (1988)
Decided: January 13, 1988
Vote: 6 (Rehnquist, B. White, Powell, Stevens, O'Connor, Scalia)
3 (Brennan, T. Marshall, Blackmun)
Opinion of the Court: B. White
Dissenting opinion: Brennan (T. Marshall, Blackmun)

Three former high school students challenged their principal's decision to censor the Hazelwood East High School student newspaper, the *Spectrum,* as a violation of their First Amendment rights. The students had worked on the paper as part of their Journalism II class. Their teacher, Robert Stergos, brought the page proofs to the principal for approval. Principal Robert Eugene Reynolds removed two full pages of the year's final issue of the *Spectrum* because, he said, two articles discussing teenage pregnancy and the effects of divorce on teenagers were inappropriate for some potential readers and did not reflect the views of the school. Moreover, Reynolds expressed concern that the students interviewed for the articles could be easily identified by other students, raising the issue of privacy.

The students brought this suit in district court against the Hazelwood School District, which found in favor of the school district. Concluding that the censorship did not violate the students' First Amendment rights, the court held that school officials might legitimately impose restraints on student expression in activities that are "an integral part of the school's educational function" so long as their decision has "a substantial and reasonable basis." The court determined that Reynolds's actions were reasonable and justified. The court of appeals reversed. Following the rule formulated in ***Tinker v. Des Moines Independent Community School District,*** 393 U.S. 503 (1969), it held that the school newspaper was a public forum. As such, the school newspaper could not be censored unless the censorship was "necessary to avoid material and substantial interference with school work or discipline . . . or the rights of others."

Finding no First Amendment violation, the Supreme Court reversed the court of appeals decision. The Court asserted that the First Amendment rights of students are not equal to those of adults. Instead, the Court found that the censorship of the student newspaper must be analyzed in light of the special nature of the school environment. Student expression inconsistent with "the basic educational mission" may be censored. From this basis, the Court found that a school newspaper is not a forum of public expression; therefore, the case was distinguishable from *Tinker,* in which the Court found that students opposed to the Vietnam War could wear black armbands in school. The Court said that a school may impose reasonable restrictions on the speech of all individuals in the school community. Furthermore, school policy dictated that the *Spectrum* was part of the educational curriculum and a classroom activity, and school officials were entitled to reasonably regulate its content and style.

The Court saw the school principal as the functional equivalent of a publisher. Just as the publisher of a newspaper would have the power to overrule an editor-in-chief on a publication issue, so too, the Court felt, the principal had the authority and right to overrule the decisions of student editors. As Justice White pointed out, "A school may in its capacity as publisher of a school newspaper or producer of a school play 'disassociate itself,' not only from speech that would 'substantially interfere with [its] work . . . or impinge upon the rights of other students,' but also from speech that is, for example, ungrammatical, poorly written, inadequately researched, biased or prejudiced, vulgar or profane, or unsuitable for immature audiences." White asserted that a "school must be able to set high standards for the student speech that is disseminated under its auspices—standards that may be higher than those demanded by some newspaper publishers or theatrical producers in the 'real' world—and may refuse to disseminate student speech that does not meet those standards."

In dissent, Justice Brennan found a First Amendment violation. Believing the court of appeals analysis under *Tinker* to be correct, he asserted that the true lesson learned by the students was "to discount important principles of our government as mere platitudes." "The young men and women of Hazelwood East expected a civics lesson," he lamented, "but not the one the Court teaches them today."

See Jamin B. Raskin, *We the Students: Supreme Court Cases for and About Students* (Washington, D.C.: CQ Press, 2000).

Hustler Magazine v. Falwell

485 U.S. 46 (1988)
Decided: February 24, 1988
Vote: 8 (Rehnquist, Brennan, B. White, T. Marshall, Blackmun, Stevens, O'Connor, Scalia)
0
Opinion of the Court: Rehnquist
Opinion concurring in judgment: B. White
Did not participate: Kennedy

Hustler magazine ran a parody of an advertisement on the inside front cover of its November 1983 issue. Copying the format of a Campari Liqueur advertisement featuring public figures discussing their "first times," the *Hustler* parody lampooned Jerry Falwell. The caption read: "Jerry Falwell talks about his first time." It depicted "an alleged 'interview' with him in which he states that his 'first time' was during a drunken incestuous rendezvous with his mother in an outhouse." At the bottom of the page was a disclaimer: "Ad parody—not to be taken seriously." The table of contents also identifies the ad as a parody.

Asserting three causes of action, intentional infliction of emotional distress, invasion of privacy and defamation, Falwell brought action against *Hustler* and its publishers. The district court directed a verdict against him on his invasion of privacy claim. On the defamation claim, the jury found in favor of

Hustler. On the intentional infliction of emotional distress claim, however, the jury awarded Falwell and his mother compensatory and punitive damages. The court of appeals affirmed. Rejecting *Hustler*'s contention that ***New York Times Co. v. Sullivan,*** 376 U.S. 254 (1964), required Falwell to show "actual malice" to recover for a claim for intentional infliction of emotional distress, the court of appeals determined "the New York Times standard is satisfied by the state-law requirement, and the jury's finding, that the defendants have acted intentionally or recklessly."

The Supreme Court agreed to consider the "First Amendment limitations upon a State's authority to protect its citizens from . . . intentional infliction of emotional distress." Concluding that a state's interest in such protection was insufficient to deny *Hustler* its First Amendment rights, the Court formulated a new standard. The Court found that "only when [the public figure] can prove both that the statement was false and that the statement was made with the requisite level of culpability" may the public figure recover on an intentional infliction of emotional distress claim.

Analyzing the claim in this light, the Court reasoned that *Hustler*'s parody lacked these requirements. Instead, as the court of appeals noted, the public could not have considered the parody believable. As such, the parody did not make a false statement, and Falwell was unable to recover against the publisher for intentional infliction of emotional distress. On a side note, Chief Justice Rehnquist pointed out that political cartoons and caricatures have been and are an important part of American culture. *Hustler*'s parody may have been distasteful, but the Court found it deserving of constitutional protection.

See Jason M. Booth, "*Hustler Magazine, Inc. v. Falwell:* Intentional Infliction of Emotional Distress and the First Amendment—A Razor-Sharp Bowling Ball," *Southwestern University Law Review* 18 (1989): 441; Harold D. Lester Jr., "Did Falwell Hustle Hustler? Allowing Public Figures to Recover Emotional Distress Damages for Nonlibelous Satire," *Washington and Lee Law Review* 44 (1987): 1381; and Susan Kirkpatrick, "Falwell v. Flynt: Intentional Infliction of Emotional Distress as a Threat to Free Speech," *Northwestern University Law Review* 81 (1987): 993.

Lyng v. Northwest Indian Cemetery Protective Association

485 U.S. 439 (1988)
Decided: April 19, 1988
Vote: 5 (Rehnquist, B. White, Stevens, O'Connor, Scalia)
3 (Brennan, T. Marshall, Blackmun)
Opinion of the Court: O'Connor
Dissenting opinion: Brennan (T. Marshall, Blackmun)
Did not participate: Kennedy

Native Americans sought to enjoin the U.S. Forest Service from building a six-mile road in a national forest, claiming the road would interrupt the peace and harmony of a traditional site for Indian religious ceremonies and rituals. Known as Chimney Rock, the site had "historically been used for religious purposes by Yurok, Karok, and Tolawa Indians." The plan also called for commercial timber cutting within a half mile of the sacred grounds. A study commissioned by the Forest Service agreed that the entire area around Chimney Rock "is significant as an integral and indispensable part of Indian religious conceptualization and practice." The district court issued an injunction for construction of the road based on the Indians' First Amendment claims, as well as under two federal environmental acts. The court of appeals affirmed the injunction, finding that there was no compelling government interest to build this road.

Speaking for the Court, Justice O'Connor rejected the Indians' claims. The Court found that the First Amendment did not require the government to be solicitous of the religious needs of any particular group. Although the government could not purposefully seek to prevent otherwise lawful religious practice, it could pass general laws that might incidentally burden a religious practice. O'Connor pointed to the requirement upheld in ***Bowen v. Roy,*** 476 U.S. 693 (1986), that people seeking Social Security benefits could be required to use a Social Security number. O'Connor found that the government, as the owner of the land, was free to conduct its affairs on public lands without being burdened by the special needs of any group. She affirmed that Indians would have access to the public lands, even after the road was constructed, but also said, "Whatever rights the Indians may have to the use of the area . . . those rights do not divest the Government of its right to use what is, after all, its land." O'Connor also made it clear that this opinion should not be read "to encourage governmental insensitivity to the religious needs of any citizen." In addition, the government was free to accommodate Native Americans or anyone else in the use of government lands, but these were political and policy issues not for the Court to decide.

The dissenters argued that the effect of the government policy was to prohibit the free exercise of religion for Native Americans, and, as such, the decision to build the road violated the First Amendment. Justice Brennan believed that this burden on religious practice could be justified only by a compelling government interest, and no one involved in the case suggested that the building of this road was compelling. Brennan concluded: "Today, the Court holds that a federal land-use decision that promised to destroy an entire religion does not burden the practice of that faith in a manner recognized by the Free Exercise Clause." Quoting O'Connor's admonition that the opinion should not be read "to encourage governmental insensitivity to the religious needs of any citizen," Brennan observed: "I find it difficult . . . to imagine conduct more insensitive to religious needs than the Government's determination to build a marginally useful road in the face of uncontradicted evidence that the road will render the practice of respondents' religion impossible."

Unable to win in the Court, the Indians were successful in Congress. In 1990 Congress added the land where the road was to be built to the Siskiuou Wilderness area, thus prohibiting either logging or road construction in the area.

See Brian Edward Brown, *Religion, Law, and the Land: Native Americans and the Judicial Interpretation of Sacred Land* (Westport, Conn.: Greenwood Press, 1999); Ellen Alderman and Caroline Kennedy, *In Our Defense: The Bill of Rights in Action* (New York: Morrow, 1991); and Larry W. Gross, "American Indian Freedom of Religion Act," and James Riding In, "NAGPRA and American Indian Religious Freedom," both in *Native Americans,* ed., Donald A. Grinde Jr. (Washington, D.C.: CQ Press, 2002).

New York State Club Association, Inc. v. City of New York

487 U.S. 1 (1988)
Decided: June 20, 1988
Vote: 9 (Rehnquist, Brennan, B. White, T. Marshall, Blackmun, Stevens, O'Connor, Scalia, Kennedy)
0
Opinion of the Court: B. White
Concurring opinion: O'Connor (Kennedy)
Concurring opinion: Scalia

In 1984 the City of New York amended its Human Rights Law of 1965. Known as Local Law 63, the amendment prohibited discrimination in all organizations sufficiently "public" in nature and with a membership of more than four hundred. The idea behind the legislation was to create opportunities for women and minorities to increase their business and professional contacts. As the City Council put it, "One barrier to the advancement of women and minorities in the business and professional life of the city is the discriminatory practices of certain membership organizations where business deals are often made and personal contacts valuable for business purposes, employment and professional advancement are formed." The New York State Club Association, representing more than 125 private organizations, challenged the constitutionality of Local Law 63, asserting that it violated the First Amendment rights, associational rights, and Fourteenth Amendment equal protection rights of the association members. The association sought to enjoin the city from enforcing the legislation. The trial court and the appeals courts in New York all upheld the law, as did the U.S. Supreme Court.

First, in finding standing, the Court considered the association's facial First and Fourteenth Amendment attacks on Local Law 63. "To prevail on a facial attack the plaintiff must demonstrate that the challenged law either 'could never be applied in a valid manner' or that . . . it . . . is so broad that it 'may inhibit the constitutionally protected speech of third parties.' " The Court did a two-part analysis of the law. Considering whether "every application of the statute created an impermissible risk of suppression of ideas," the Court found it did not. Local Law 63 was applicable to at least some larger organizations and those organizations providing food service, and therefore, on its face, every application clearly did not violate the First Amendment. The state or local government had the power to regulate these larger organizations serving food and liquor. Looking at the second exception, whether the law is so broad to inhibit free speech of third parties, the law again failed to meet this exception. "To succeed in its challenge, appellant must demonstrate from the text of Local Law 63 and from actual fact that a substantial number of instances exist in which the Law cannot be applied constitutionally." Failing to identify any such clubs, the Court concluded that Local Law 63 was not overbroad. Lacking any proof that the law was too broad, the association could make a case for a facial First Amendment attack.

Considering the association's facial Fourteenth Amendment attack, the Court said the law did not violate the Equal Protection Clause. The association argued that the exception for "benevolent and religious corporations" as purely private organizations under Local Law 63 denied other New York organizations equal protection. Maintaining that religious and benevolent organizations are unique, the Court declared that it was the association's burden to prove religious and benevolent organizations were not different from their own organizations. Here, the Court concluded the law did not deny the appellants equal protection.

See Marian L. Zobler, "When Is a Private Club Not a Private Club: The Scope of the Rights of Private Clubs After *New York State Club Association, Inc. v. City of New York,*" *Brooklyn Law Review* 55 (1989): 327.

Morrison v. Olson

487 U.S. 654 (1988)
Decided: June 29, 1988
Vote: 7 (Rehnquist, Brennan, B. White, T. Marshall, Blackmun, Stevens, O'Connor)
1 (Scalia)
Opinion of the Court: Rehnquist
Dissenting opinion: Scalia
Did not participate: Kennedy

In the aftermath of the Watergate scandals and, in particular, the firing of Special Prosecutor Archibald Cox by President Richard Nixon, Congress enacted the Ethics in Government Act of 1978. A provision in the act allowed for a court, called the Special Division, to appoint an independent counsel to investigate and prosecute high-ranking government officials for violations of federal criminal laws.

In 1985 the House Judiciary Committee accused Theodore Olson, assistant attorney general for the Office of Legal Counsel (OLC), of providing false and misleading testimony to its subcommittee. It also asserted that Edward Schmults, a deputy attorney general, and Carol Dinkins, an assistant attorney general, wrongfully withheld certain documents from the committee. Committee chairman, Peter Rodino, D-N.J., requested that an independent counsel be appointed to investigate the allegations. In his report to the Special Division, Attorney General Edwin Meese said that only Olson would be subject to investigation. The court appointed James McKay independent counsel, and he was later replaced by Alexia Morrison.

Morrison instructed the grand jury to serve subpoenas on Olson, Schmults, and Dinkins. All three moved to quash the subpoenas, claiming that the independent counsel provisions of the act were unconstitutional. In July 1987 the district court upheld the constitutionality of the act and denied the motions to quash. The court of appeals reversed. The majority ruled that the independent counsel provision of the act violated several provisions of the Constitution, including separation of powers, Article III delegation authority, the Appointments Clause, and the Take Care Clause (Article II, Section 3).

The Supreme Court upheld the independent counsel law. Chief Justice Rehnquist found that the independent counsel was an "inferior Officer" under the Appointments Clause and provided several reasons to support this conclusion. First, Morrison was "subject to removal by a higher Executive Branch official." Second, Morrison was "empowered by the Act to perform only certain, limited duties." Third, Morrison's "office is limited in jurisdiction." Finally, Morrison's "office is limited in tenure." Olson further contended that even if the independent counsel was an inferior officer, the Appointments Clause did "not empower Congress to place the power to appoint such an officer outside the Executive Branch." Rehnquist found that the "excepting clause" (Article II, Section 2) provided for "no limitation on interbranch appointments." The Court's decision in ***Ex parte Siebold,*** 100 U.S. 371 (1880), and the lack of any evidence to the contrary from the records of the Constitutional Convention, according to Rehnquist, supported this conclusion.

The Court rejected Olson's argument that creation of the Special Division violated Article III. Rehnquist conceded that it was long held that "executive or administrative duties of a nonjudicial nature" could not be imposed on Article III judges. But, he said, "The Act simply does not give the Division the power to 'supervise' the independent counsel in the exercise of his or her investigative or prosecutorial authority. And, the functions that the Special Division is empowered to perform are not inherently 'Executive'; indeed, they are directly analogous to functions that federal judges perform in other contexts." Olson suggested that the Special Division's power to terminate the independent counsel pursuant to the act was not "judicial." Rehnquist minimized this concern, saying that the "Court of Appeals overstated the matter." Rehnquist said that the power to terminate did not include "the power to remove the counsel while an investigation or court proceeding is still underway—this power is vested solely in the Attorney General."

The Court rejected the argument that powers of the Special Division posed a "threat" to independent and impartial judicial review. Rehnquist said that the special court had "no power to review any of the actions of the independent counsel or any of the actions of the Attorney General with regard to the counsel." Moreover, the court was prohibited under the act from "any judicial proceeding" involving an actively serving independent counsel or on questions relative to the "independent counsel's official duties, regardless of whether such independent counsel is still serving in that office."

Rehnquist then turned his attention to the question of "whether the Act [was] invalid under the constitutional principle of separation of powers." Olson raised two arguments: first, the act permitted the attorney general to remove an independent counsel only by showing "good cause" and, second, the act "reduc[ed] the President's ability to control prosecutorial powers." Rehnquist said that, unlike ***Myers v. United States,*** 272 U.S. 52 (1926), and ***Bowsher v. Synar,*** 478 U.S. 714 (1986), "this case does not involve an attempt by Congress itself to gain a role in the removal of executive officials other than its established powers of impeachment and conviction." The removal decision does not require congressional approval, but "is subject to judicial review." Instead, Rehnquist applied ***Humphrey's Executor v. United States,*** 295 U.S. 602 (1935), and ***Wiener v. United States,*** 357 U.S. 349 (1958). In these cases, the Court affirmed statutes limiting presidential removal authority of members of independent commissions that "were entrusted by Congress with adjudicatory powers."

Although the act did have an impact on the executive branch in the prosecutorial function, Rehnquist said that the Special Division could appoint an independent counsel only "upon the specific request of the Attorney General" and could not review "the Attorney General's decision not to seek appointment" and therefore had no broader separation of powers problems.

"That is what this suit is about. Power," Justice Scalia wrote in his lengthy and forceful dissent. "The allocation of power among Congress, the President, and the courts in such fashion as to preserve the equilibrium the Constitution sought to establish." He said that the Court spent far too little time considering the separation of powers ramification of its decision.

Scalia argued that the court of appeals' decision should be upheld if two questions could be "answered affirmatively: (1) Is the conduct of a criminal prosecution (and of an investigation to decide whether to prosecute) the exercise of purely executive power? (2) Does the statute deprive the President of the United States of exclusive control over the exercise of that power?" Scalia said the majority, as did he, answered both affirmatively, but then the majority, according to him, still reached an incorrect conclusion. To Scalia, Article II was unequivocal: "The executive Power shall be vested in a President." In short, the test is not whether the act has "some" impact on the executive branch, but whether there is any impact. "Once we depart from the text of the Constitution," Scalia asked, "just where short of that do we stop?" Scalia said the Court failed to answer this question, or provide analysis, or "even attempt to craft a substitute criterion—a 'justiciable standard.' "

The political consequences of the Court's decision also weighed on Scalia. "Besides weakening the Presidency by reducing the zeal of his staff, it must also be obvious that the institution of the independent counsel enfeebles him more directly in his constant confrontations with Congress, by eroding his public support."

In addressing whether the independent counsel was an "inferior Officer" not needing to be appointed by the president with approval from the Senate, Scalia disagreed with the majority's interpretation of "inferior" officers. "If [Morrison was] removable at will by the Attorney General, then she would be subordinate to him and thus properly designated as inferior; but the Court essentially admits that she is not subordinate. If it were common usage to refer to someone as 'inferior' who is subject to removal for cause by another, then one would say that the President is 'inferior' to Congress." He also questioned the logic of the majority finding that the independent counsel had limited duties but then admitting that "the Act delegates to appellant [Morrison] [the] 'full power and independent authority to exercise all investigative and prosecutorial functions and powers of the Department of Justice.' " In the end, Scalia returned to the Constitution for guidance. Here, he concluded, "the independent counsel is not an inferior officer because she is not subordinate to any officer in the Executive Branch (indeed, not even to the President)."

As for the "removal power issue," Scalia said that the majority, contrary to Rehnquist's assurances, failed to abide by *Humphrey's Executor.* There, "the line of permissible restriction upon removal of principal officers lies at the point at which the powers exercised by those officers are no longer purely executive." Now, rather than "purely executive," the trigger was a " 'good cause'-type restriction," which meant that the executive did not have the power, under this act, to remove executive appointees at will.

Scalia concluded his dissent by presciently addressing the menacing nature of the independent counsel.

> How frightening it must be to have your own independent counsel and staff appointed, with nothing else to do but to investigate you until investigation is no longer worthwhile—with whether it is worthwhile not depending upon what such judgments usually hinge on, competing responsibilities. And to have that counsel and staff decide, with no basis for comparison, whether what you have done is bad enough, willful enough, and provable enough, to warrant an indictment. How admirable the constitutional system that provides the means to avoid such a distortion. And how unfortunate the judicial decision that has permitted it.

Ironically, the independent counsel law initiative crafted by a Democratic-controlled Congress and preserved by the Supreme Court, would be used repeatedly and according to many—in a partisan manner—during the Clinton administration. A number of independent counsels were appointed to investigate numerous alleged illegal acts by administration officials. The consequence of one such investigation resulted in President Bill Clinton's impeachment by the House of Representatives in December 1998. Two months later the Senate acquitted him. The independent counsel law expired in 1999.

See Katy J. Harriger, *The Special Prosecutor in American Politics,* 2d rev. ed., (Lawrence: University Press of Kansas, 2000); and Charles A. Johnson and Danette Brickman, *Independent Counsel: The Law and the Investigations* (Washington, D.C.: CQ Press, 2001).

Mistretta v. United States

488 U.S. 361 (1989)
Decided: January 18, 1989
Vote: 8 (Rehnquist, Brennan, B. White, T. Marshall, Blackmun, Stevens, O'Connor, Kennedy)
1 (Scalia)
Opinion of the Court: Blackmun
Dissenting opinion: Scalia

Congress passed the Sentencing Reform Act of 1984 to standardize criminal punishments. The impetus for the law was the recognition that without uniform guidelines for sentencing, judges were sentencing defendants to widely varying punishments for similar crimes. The act created the Sentencing Commission within the judicial branch to establish the guidelines. The commission was made up of seven voting members appointed by the president, four of whom were judges, and three of whom were not.

John M. Mistretta was convicted of selling cocaine and sentenced under the commission's sentencing guidelines to eighteen months' imprisonment. Mistretta challenged the constitutionality of the act, claiming that Congress had delegated too much authority to the commission and that the commission violated the separation of powers principle because judges and nonjudges served on it and the members were appointed by the president. The trial appellate court rejected this contention, and the Supreme Court affirmed.

The Court held that Congress had not delegated too much authority to the commission because Congress had given the commission clear guidelines on how to exercise its authority. For example, Congress had directed that maximum sentences should not exceed minimum sentences by more than 25 percent and that the current average sentence for a given crime should serve as the starting place in setting the sentencing parameters. The Court used a deferential standard, meaning that it would have found that the delegation was not excessive unless Congress had completely failed to give guidelines.

The Court also held that the commission did not violate the separation of powers doctrine because it did not undertake a function that was more properly allocated to another branch.

See Stephen J. Schulhofer and Ilene H. Nagel, "Plea Negotiation Under the Federal Sentencing Guidelines: Guideline Circumvention and Its Dynamic in the Post-Mistretta Period," *Northwestern University Law Review* 91 (1997): 1284; and Ronald F. Wright, "Sentencers, Bureaucrats, and the Administrative Law Perspective on the Federal Sentencing Commission," *California Law Review* 79 (1991): 1.

City of Richmond v. J. A. Croson Co.

488 U.S. 469 (1989)
Decided: January 23, 1989
Vote: 6 (Rehnquist, B. White, Stevens, O'Connor, Scalia, Kennedy)
3 (Brennan, T. Marshall, Blackmun)
Judgment of the Court: O'Connor
Opinion concurring in judgment: Stevens
Opinion concurring in judgment: Scalia
Opinion concurring in judgment: Kennedy
Dissenting opinion: T. Marshall (Brennan, Blackmun)
Dissenting opinion: Blackmun (Brennan)

In 1983 Richmond, Virginia, adopted the Minority Business Utilization Plan, which was modeled on federal "minority set-aside" programs. The ordinance required all general contractors awarded city construction jobs to subcontract at least 30 percent of the contract work to minority businesses. The city described the ordinance as remedial and noted that although 50 percent of the city's population was black, less than 1 percent of all construction contracts had been awarded to minority businesses in recent years. The city asserted that past discrimination created the disparity by depriving black residents of Richmond with the expertise and track record necessary to finance and successfully launch an entrepreneurial business. A bidder on one of the contracts sued to have the ordinance declared unconstitutional, alleging that it violated equal protection. The district court ruled in favor of the city. The court of appeals initially affirmed because of the deferential standard set forth in ***Fullilove v. Klutznick,*** 448 U.S. 448 (1980), for race-based remedial preferences. The Supreme Court remanded the case for consideration in light of its decision in ***Wygant v. Jackson Board of Education,*** 476 U.S. 267 (1986), which applied strict scrutiny to a race-based layoff preference. Applying the strict scrutiny standard of *Wygant,* the court of appeals then reversed.

The Supreme Court agreed with the court of appeals. According to the Court, the disparity between the percentage of black people in Richmond and the number of construction contracts awarded to black businesses in the city was insufficient to justify a rigid race-based preference. The past discrimination relied on by Richmond was too vague because it did not allege any specific acts of discrimination by any person affected by the ordinance. The city had no way to determine when it had sufficiently remedied the past discrimination to terminate the race-based preferences. Richmond therefore could not show that its plan was narrowly tailored to meet a compelling government interest.

Justice Scalia noted that a city government dominated by African Americans had passed the ordinance, which could be seen as self-dealing. He saw this law as a racial quota that might benefit blacks, but at the expense of whites. He argued that "even 'benign' racial quotas have individual victims, whose very real injustice we ignore whenever we deny them enforcement of their right not be disadvantaged on the basis of race."

The dissenters argued that the long history of racial discrimination in Virginia justified such a law. Justice Marshall began his opinion by noting that the ordinance had been passed in the "former capital of the Confederacy" and that it was a "welcome symbol of racial progress." Marshall and the other dissenters argued that affirmative action legislation should be held to a relaxed standard of review and that it was not necessary to prove that the specific beneficiaries of the plan had experienced discrimination at the hands of the city, as long as there was a generalized pattern of discrimination against a group to which they belonged.

Although it did not end affirmative action in public contracts, this case undermined the ability of states or local governments to use such programs to increase minority business participation in the economy. In ***Adarand Constructors v. Peña,*** 515 U.S. 200 (1995), the Court applied this analysis to some federal affirmative action set-aside programs as well.

See Kenneth Jost, "Affirmative Action," *CQ Researcher,* September 21, 2001, 737–760; Steve Lichtenstein, "*City of Richmond v. J. A. Croson Company:* A Discussion of Its Impact on Affirmative Action Programs," *Business Law Review* 12 (1991): 205–230; and Docia Rudley and Donna Hubbard, "What a Difference a Decade Makes: Judicial Response to State and Local Minority Business Set-Asides Ten Years After *City of Richmond v. J. A. Croson,*" *Southern Illinois University Law Journal* 25 (fall 2000): 39.

Skinner v. Railway Labor Executives' Association

489 U.S. 602 (1989)
Decided: March 21, 1989
Vote: 7 (Rehnquist, B. White, Blackmun, Stevens, O'Connor, Scalia, Kennedy)
2 (Brennan, T. Marshall)
Opinion of the Court: Kennedy
Concurring opinion: Stevens
Dissenting opinion: T. Marshall (Brennan)

Railway labor unions challenged the constitutionality of two Federal Railroad Administration (FRA) regulations. The first mandated urine and blood tests from all employees involved in certain kinds of accidents. The other permitted breath and urine tests after an employee violated certain safety rules.

The district court found the regulations constitutional. It determined that the government's interest in public safety outweighed the employees' privacy rights. The court of appeals reversed. Again engaging in a balancing act between the right to privacy and the government's interest in public safety, the court of appeals swayed to the opposite direction.

The Supreme Court found that such tests do come under Fourth Amendment requirements. The Court, however, determined that the tests require neither a warrant nor a finding of probable cause. Instead, to determine reasonableness, courts are expected to weigh the government's interests for prescribing such tests against how invasive the tests are to employees' privacy interests. Considering the welfare of the traveling public and the safety of the employees in general, the Court concluded that the tests were reasonable under the Fourth Amendment.

Reversing the court of appeals decision that the regulations' lack of probable cause could not withstand Fourth Amendment scrutiny, the Court first went to pains to explain that such tests were indeed subject to Fourth Amendment requirements. Beginning with the determination that blood, urine, and breath tests were a form of search and seizure, the Court then examined the regulations, finding that "the Government's encouragement, endorsement, and participation . . . suffice to implicate the Fourth Amendment."

The Court analyzed the context and circumstances of the FRA regulations to determine if they could meet Fourth Amendment requirements without a warrant or probable cause. The Court found that the regulations could. "When special needs, beyond the normal need for law enforcement, make the warrant and probable-cause requirement impracticable," a balancing act between the individual's Fourth Amendment rights and government interests must occur. Considering the government's interests in this matter—public safety, deterrence from drug and alcohol abuse, and diagnosis of train accidents—the Court concluded that the balance must tip in favor of the regulations.

Justice Marshall offered a compelling dissent questioning the Court's attempt to undermine the meaning of the Fourth Amendment. Stressing the invasion of individual privacy without a warrant or probable cause, Marshall wrote, "The majority's acceptance of dragnet blood and urine testing ensures that the first, and worst, casualty of the war on drugs will be the precious liberties of our citizens." Marshall said that the "special needs" exceptions were an unacceptable compromise of constitutional guarantees and criticized each rationale offered by the majority to uphold the regulations as constitutional.

See Sherri Ann Carver, "The Battle of the Balancing Tests in the Fourth Amendment Drug Testing Cases: *Skinner v. Railway Labor Executives' Association*—The Proper Balance Is Struck," *Oklahoma City University Law Review* 15 (1990): 333.

National Treasury Employees Union v. Von Raab

489 U.S. 656 (1989)
Decided: March 21, 1989
Vote: 5 (Rehnquist, B. White, Blackmun, O'Connor, Kennedy)
4 (Brennan, T. Marshall, Stevens, Scalia)
Opinion of the Court: Kennedy
Dissenting opinion: T. Marshall (Brennan)
Dissenting opinion: Scalia (Stevens)

Like ***Skinner v. Railway Labor Executives' Association,*** 489 U.S. 602 (1989), which was decided the same day, this case dealt with drug testing of employees who were not under any individualized suspicion of abusing drugs. In 1986 Commissioner William Von Raab implemented a drug-testing program in the U.S. Customs Service. Any individual seeking employment that involved the interdiction of drugs, carrying of firearms, or handling "classified" information would be required to pass a drug-screening test. A federal employees union challenged the implementation of a mandatory drug-testing program for Customs Service employees seeking promotions to positions involving the activities on the commissioner's list.

The district court agreed with the union, finding the drug testing an unreasonable search without probable cause. The court of appeals panel vacated the district court decision. Determining the drug testing must come within the Fourth Amendment requirements, it nevertheless held that such testing was reasonable considering the government's compelling interests.

In deciding that the Fourth Amendment did not prohibit drug tests of the employees involved in drug interdiction and those required to carry firearms, the Supreme Court first determined that the tests must meet Fourth Amendment's reasonableness requirement. It "reaffirm[d] the longstanding principle that neither a warrant nor probable cause, nor, indeed, any measure of individualized suspicion, is an indispensable component of reasonableness in every circumstance." The Court concluded that neither a warrant nor probable cause was necessary. The government's need to test its employees for drug use outweighed the individual privacy interests of the employees. Justice Kennedy, who also wrote the opinion in *Skinner,* said, "We think Customs employees who are directly involved in the interdiction of illegal drugs or who are required to carry firearms in the line of duty likewise have a diminished expectation of privacy in respect to the instructions occasioned by a urine test."

With respect to the employees handling "classified," materials the Court did not reach a decision. Instead it remanded the question to the court of appeals.

Justices Marshall and Brennan here reiterated their dissent in *Skinner.* Justice Scalia, with Justice Stevens joining him, objected to the nature of the urine test and its procedure. He had no problem with an employee being dismissed for drug abuse, but believed that the Customs Service violated their employees' Fourth Amendment rights by subjecting them to urine tests supervised by other employees. Scalia thought "it obvious that it is a type of search particularly destructive of privacy and offensive to personal dignity." He argued that such a search could not be implemented without an individualized suspicion and a warrant. "Until today this Court had upheld a bodily search separate from arrest and without individualized suspicion of wrong-doing only with respect to prison inmates, relying upon the uniquely dangerous nature of that environment," Scalia wrote. He noted, however, that in *Skinner,* the Court allowed a less intrusive bodily search of railroad employees involved in train accidents. Scalia joined this opinion because the "demonstrated frequency of drug and alcohol use by the targeted class of employees, and the demonstrated connection between such use and grave harm, rendered the search a reasonable means of protecting society." He dissented in *Von Raab* because he saw no support for the argument that drug use was common among

Customs Service employees or any "connection to harm." Scalia sharply accused the Customs Service of adopting rules that were "a kind of immolation of privacy and human dignity in symbolic opposition to drug use."

See Kenneth C. Betts, "Fourth Amendment—Suspicionless Urinalysis Testing: A Constitutionally 'Reasonable' Weapon in the Nation's War on Drugs?—*National Treasury Employees Union v. Von Raab,* 109 S. Ct. 1384 (1989)," *Journal of Criminal Law and Criminology* 80 (1990): 1018; and Paul Finkelman, "The Second Casualty of War: Civil Liberties and the War on Drugs," *Southern California Law Review* 66 (1993): 1389–1452.

Board of Estimate of City of New York v. Morris

489 U.S. 688 (1989)
Decided: March 22, 1989
Vote: 9 (Rehnquist, Brennan, B. White, T. Marshall, Blackmun, Stevens, O'Connor, Scalia, Kennedy)
0
Opinion of the Court: B. White
Concurring opinion: Brennan (Stevens)
Concurring opinion: Blackmun

New York City created an eight-member board of estimate made up of three members elected citywide (the mayor, the city comptroller, and the president of the city council) plus the five borough presidents. In other words, the members were not elected primarily or exclusively as board members; rather, their board membership was incidental to another position to which they had been elected. The citywide members had two votes each, and the members elected by the boroughs had one vote each. The board was responsible for controlling the city's budget and issues such as land-use regulation.

Voters from Brooklyn, the city's most populous borough, brought suit claiming that the composition of the board violated the "one-person, one-vote" principle of ***Reynolds v. Sims,*** 377 U.S. 533 (1964). The trial court declined to grant relief because, it said, the board was not an elected body. The New York Court of Appeals reversed, finding that the board ultimately was an elected body. On remand, the trial court found that Brooklyn's population was more than twice as large as Staten Island's and the Constitution could not allow the two boroughs to have the same representation on the board. The Court of Appeals affirmed, and added that the fact that the citywide members outvoted the borough members six to five was insufficient to nullify the pernicious effect of the difference in the borough members' representation.

The Supreme Court affirmed. The Court held that the government interests offered by the state to excuse the disparity were insufficient. Specifically, the state's assertions that the board was necessary for governing the city and that it had been successful could not justify such a gross disparity between the populations represented by the same number of votes on the board. This system clearly violated the constitutional principle of one person, one vote.

See M. David Gelfand and Terry E. Allbritton, "Conflict and Congruence in One-Person, One-Vote and Racial Vote Dilution Litigation: Issues Resolved and Unresolved by *Board of Estimate v. Morris,*" *Journal of Law and Politics* 6 (1989): 93; R. Alta Charo, "Designing Mathematical Models to Describe One-Person, One-Vote Compliance by Unique Governmental Structures: The Case of the New York City Board of Estimate," *Fordham Law Review* 53 (1985): 735; and James W. Lowe, "Examination of Governmental Decentralization in New York City and a New Model for Implementation," *Harvard Journal on Legislation* 27 (1990): 173.

Frazee v. Illinois Department of Employment Security

489 U.S. 829 (1989)
Decided: March 29, 1989
Vote: 9 (Rehnquist, Brennan, B. White, T. Marshall, Blackmun, Stevens, O'Connor, Scalia, Kennedy)
0
Opinion of the Court: B. White

The Illinois Unemployment Insurance Act provided that "an individual shall be ineligible for benefits if he has failed, without good cause, either to apply for available, suitable work when so directed . . . or to accept suitable work when offered him." William Frazee refused to accept a temporary retail position that was offered to him because he would be required to work on Sunday and as a Christian he said he could not work on "the Lord's day." His application for unemployment benefits was denied.

The Supreme Court held that Frazee sincerely believed that religion required him not to work on Sunday. The fact that he was not a member of a particular sect had no bearing on his beliefs, and the Court held he should receive the benefits. A denial of the benefits would be a violation of Frazee's Free Exercise Clause rights as guaranteed in the First Amendment. The Court conceded that the state may have interests that are compelling enough to override a legitimate claim to the free exercise of religion, but found that in this case the state lacked such an interest.

Frazee was consistent with a line of Court cases, beginning with ***Sherbert v. Verner,*** 374 U.S. 398 (1963), prohibiting states from denying unemployment compensation for people who refused jobs because of their religious beliefs.

See Brian Hansen, "Religion in the Workplace," *CQ Researcher,* August 23, 2002, 649–672.

Wards Cove Packing Co., Inc. v. Atonio

490 U.S. 642 (1989)
Decided: June 5, 1989
Vote: 5 (Rehnquist, B. White, O'Connor, Scalia, Kennedy)
4 (Brennan, T. Marshall, Blackmun, Stevens)
Opinion of the Court: B. White
Dissenting opinion: Blackmun (Brennan, T. Marshall)
Dissenting opinion: Stevens (Brennan, T. Marshall, Blackmun)

Title VII of the Civil Rights Act of 1964 prohibits discrimination in hiring and employment practices. Title VII, however, has been construed more broadly to encompass not only obviously discriminatory practices but also those practices that on their face are nondiscriminatory but in reality discriminate. In other words, the discrimination occurs through the "disparate impact" of employment practices on various types of workers.

Nonwhite, unskilled cannery workers brought a class action suit under Title VII against two Alaskan canneries, alleging employment discrimination on the basis of race. The workers said that nonwhites were never considered for any jobs except unskilled jobs. The district court rejected the finding that the plaintiffs had failed to prove their complaint. The court of appeals reversed, holding that the disparate-impact analysis could be applied to subjective hiring practices. It also held that once the plaintiffs had shown "disparate impact caused by specific, identifiable employment practices or criteria, the burden shifts to the employer to prove the business necessity of the challenged practice." The court of appeals determined that the workers had a prima facie (on its face) case of disparate impact in hiring through statistics demonstrating a racial composition disparity between noncannery and cannery workers. The court of appeals found "that it was the employer's burden to prove that any disparate impact caused by its hiring and employment practices was justified by business necessity."

The Supreme Court first discussed what was necessary to make out a prima facie disparate-impact case and then discussed causation—that is, what caused nonwhites to have most of the low-paying cannery jobs and whites to hold more of the higher-paying nonfactory jobs. The Court then examined the respective burdens of proof in a disparate-impact case. The Court premised its finding on the fact that statistical evidence alone could not establish a prima facie case and determined that the comparison on which the court of appeals found the workers to have made out a prima facie case an error. Providing statistics that showed a high percentage of nonwhite, cannery workers versus a low percentage of nonwhite, noncannery workers, the Court determined, proved nothing. Instead, "the proper comparison is between the racial composition of the at-issue jobs and the racial composition of the qualified population in the relevant labor market."

The Court reversed the Court of Appeals. On causation and burden of proof, the Court maintained that it is the plaintiff's initial burden to identify specific discriminatory employment practices that are responsible for the statistical disparity in the employer's workforce. Just showing a racial imbalance is not enough; specifically identified employment hiring practices that tend to create a racial imbalance must be shown. If the plaintiff had meet this burden of proof, the burden then shifted to the employer to offer any business justification for the use of this practice.

Citing ***Griggs v. Duke Power Co.,*** 401 U.S. 424 (1971), Justice Stevens began his dissent by noting that eighteen years earlier the Court had "unanimously held that Title VII of the Civil Rights Act of 1964 prohibits employment practices that have discriminatory effects as well as those that are intended to discriminate" and that courts "consistently have enforced that interpretation." Here, Stevens noted that the Court was rejecting this history and this jurisprudence, despite the fact that Congress had never objected to this interpretation of the Civil Rights Act.

Congress responded in part to this decision with the Civil Rights Act of 1991, which expanded Title VII's provisions and reestablished earlier notions of what constitutes "disparate impact." The 1991 act eliminated a "business necessity" defense to charges of intentional discrimination. The act also narrowed the opportunity to challenge affirmative action programs, thus reversing the impact of ***Martin v. Wilks,*** 490 U.S. 755 (1989). Finally, the 1991 act reversed some of the Court's statutory interpretation in ***Patterson v. McLean Credit Union,*** 491 U.S. 164 (1989), by expanding standards for the protection of workers from on-the-job sexual harassment.

See Edward M. Henn and Sarah W. J. Pell, "*Wards Cove Packing Co., Inc. v. Atonio:* The Changing Rules of Civil Rights," *Education Law Reporter* 61 (1990): 11; and Brian Reichel, "Civil Rights—Racial Disparity—Classes of Workers at Canneries Held Not to Make Out Prima Facie Case of Disparate Impact in Action Under Title VII of Civil Rights Act of 1964—*Wards Cove Packing Co. v. Atonio,*" *Drake Law Review* 39 (1990): 933.

Martin v. Wilks

490 U.S. 755 (1989)
Decided: June 12, 1989
Vote: 5 (Rehnquist, B. White, O'Connor, Scalia, Kennedy)
4 (Brennan, T. Marshall, Blackmun, Stevens)
Opinion of the Court: Rehnquist
Dissenting opinion: Stevens (Brennan, T. Marshall, Blackmun)

Seven white firefighters sued the city of Birmingham, Alabama, and the Jefferson County Personnel Board, alleging that they were denied promotions in favor of less-qualified blacks. The white firefighters' complaint was in response to actions taken by Birmingham and the county pursuant to a consent decree in which the city and the county agreed to promote more blacks within the department. The city and the county had entered into this decree to settle the suit in *United States v. Jefferson County,* 28 FEP Cases 1834 (ND Ala. 1981). In that case, the NAACP sued the city and county, alleging racially discriminatory hiring practices. The district court dismissed the white firefighters' complaint, finding that they were not permitted to bring this suit to attack the decree, as none had been a party to the consent decree. In legal terms, the court held that the firefighters were collaterally estopped from challenging the decree. The court of appeals reversed, finding that the city and county should not be immunized against complaints by parties who were not involved in the consent decree. In effect, the court of appeals held that although the city and county could settle the discrimination suit, the two governments could not prevent the individual white firefighters from suing to protect their rights.

The Supreme Court affirmed. Justice Rehnquist's opinion held that for a court decree to be binding against a person who is not one of the original parties to the suit, that person must be joined to the action. The nonparty is not under a duty to intervene in any suit to which he might have an interest; it is the obligation of the parties to join him to the suit or risk obtaining an unenforceable decree. As support, Rehnquist observed that the federal rule of civil procedure governing joinder—that is, who was added as a defendant in a suit—was framed in mandatory language, but the rule governing intervention was framed in permissible language. In other words, the city and county or the NAACP should have made the firefighters, or their union, defendants in the original case, so that they could have defended their interests. Although the city argued that requiring joinder of all persons who might potentially have a stake in the outcome would have a chilling effect on civil rights litigation, Rehnquist held that the possibility of such a chilling effect did not warrant ignoring the plain meaning of the relevant federal rules.

Justice Stevens argued that although the plaintiffs' legal rights had not been altered by the consent decree (since they were not parties to it), they still could not open an issue that had already been litigated. Furthermore, the consent decree, while not determinative of their legal rights, did serve as evidence that the city and county acted in good faith.

In the Civil Rights Act of 1991 Congress reversed much of the Court's statutory interpretation in this case. For a discussion of this, see ***Wards Cove Packing Co., Inc. v. Atonio,*** 490 U.S. 642 (1989).

See Susan Grover, "The Silenced Majority: *'Martin v. Wilks'* and the Legislative Response," *University of Illinois Law Review* 43 (1992).

Patterson v. McLean Credit Union

491 U.S. 164 (1989)
Decided: June 15, 1989
Vote: 5 (Rehnquist, B. White, O'Connor, Scalia, Kennedy)
4 (Brennan, T. Marshall, Blackmun, Stevens)
Opinion of the Court: Kennedy
Dissenting opinion: Brennan (T. Marshall, Blackmun)
Dissenting opinion: Stevens

McLean Credit Union hired Brenda Patterson as a teller and file coordinator in 1972. Laid off in 1982, Patterson claimed McLean discriminated against her, harassed her, and dismissed her solely because of her race. She instituted a 42 U.S.C. Section 1981 action and a state claim for intentional infliction of emotional distress against McLean. The district court "determined that a claim for racial harassment is not actionable under §1981 and declined to submit that part of the case to the jury." On Patterson's Section 1981 claims for her discharge and failure to be promoted, the jury found for McLean. On her state claim for intentional infliction of emotional distress, the court entered a directed verdict for McLean as well, finding its conduct had not reached the necessary level of outrageousness.

In her appeal, Patterson contended that the district court had erred in two respects. First, she challenged the court's denial of her Section 1981 racial harassment claim. Second, she challenged the court's jury instruction that for her to prevail on her Section 1981 claims against McLean for its failure to promote her she had to prove that the white individual receiving a promotion was less qualified than her. Concluding that racial harassment in the workplace was not actionable under Section 1981, the court of appeals also said that the district court had not erred in its jury instruction.

The Supreme Court determined that Section 1981 did not apply to racial harassment but that the district court had erred in its jury instruction. ***Runyon v. McCrary,*** 427 U.S. 160 (1976), held "that §1981 prohibits racial discrimination in the making and enforcement of private contracts." The Court looked at the history and statutory construction of Section 1981 and declined to overturn *Runyon.* As to whether Section 1981 prohibits racial harassment, the Court affirmed the district court's holding that it did not. From the language of the statute, the Court determined that Section 1981 only prohibits racial discrimination in the making and enforcing of contracts.

After establishing these points, the Court reviewed Patterson's contention that McLean failed to promote her because of her race. As Section 1981 is limited to the making and enforcing of contracts, the promotion would have to involve the creation of a new contract between Patterson and McLean to warrant a Section 1981 action. Because Patterson failed to make that argument "at any stage" her "promotion claim [wa]s not cognizable under §1981."

Finally, the Court found the jury instruction incorrect because Patterson could have refuted McLean's contention that the similarly situated white employee was qualified in many other ways.

Vacating the court of appeals judgment, the Court remanded *Patterson* to determine the petitioner's discriminatory promotion claim.

In the Civil Rights Act of 1991, Congress reversed much of the court's statutory interpretation in this case. See ***Wards Cove Packing Co., Inc. v. Atonio,*** 490 U.S. 642 (1989).

See Woody W. Lay, "*Patterson v. McLean Credit Union:* A Narrowing of Remedies for the Employment Discrimination Plaintiff," *Washington and Lee Law Review* 47 (1990): 995.

Texas v. Johnson

491 U.S. 397 (1989)
Decided: June 21, 1989
Vote: 5 (Brennan, T. Marshall, Blackmun, Scalia, Kennedy)
4 (Rehnquist, B. White, Stevens, O'Connor)
Opinion of the Court: Brennan
Concurring opinion: Kennedy
Dissenting opinion: Rehnquist (B. White, O'Connor)
Dissenting opinion: Stevens

During the 1984 Republican National Convention in Dallas, Gregory Lee Johnson, a Vietnam veteran, burned an American flag to protest the policies of President Ronald Reagan. Johnson was convicted under a Texas law for desecrating a "venerated object," fined $2,000, and sentenced to a year in jail. The Texas Court of Criminal Appeals reversed the conviction on the grounds that the law was unconstitutionally applied to Johnson, but the court did not strike down the law.

On one level, this was a relatively simple case. Johnson's act was constitutionally protected speech for two reasons. First, whatever else the First Amendment protects, constitutional scholars agree it was designed to protect the expression of political beliefs and viewpoints. By burning a flag, Johnson was expressing a political viewpoint, and the content of his expression—his distaste for the president's policies—was clearly protected. Second, the Supreme Court had long since established that expressive "conduct" or "symbolic speech" was protected. In his opinion, Justice Brennan conceded that the government had a "freer hand in restricting expressive conduct than it has in restricting the written or spoken word," but regulation of symbolic speech or expressive conduct could not be based on the ideas expressed, but only on the nature of the conduct itself. Johnson's conduct was therefore protected symbolic speech. But, because the case involving a highly emotional issue—flag-burning—the Court offered an elaborate opinion in this simple case.

The Court might have upheld the state if Johnson had been convicted under a traditional statute for disturbing the peace, causing a riot, or starting a fire, but he was convicted of the statute prohibiting the desecration of "venerated objects." The state argued that this statute was designed to prevent a breach of the peace, but, as Brennan noted, Texas conceded that "no actual breach of the peace occurred at the time of the flag-burning or in response to the flag-burning." Texas also claimed that the statute was designed to prevent violence that might be caused by those who saw the flag-burning and were offended by it. Quoting ***Terminiello v. Chicago,*** 337 U.S. 1 (1949), and citing among others, ***Cox v. Louisiana,*** 379 US. 536 (1965); ***Tinker v. Des Moines Independent Community School District,*** 393 U.S. 503 (1969); and ***Hustler Magazine v. Falwell,*** 485 U.S. 46 (1988), Brennan noted that the state had an obligation to protect unpopular speakers. The "high purpose" of the First Amendment, he said, was often best served by speech that "induces a condition of unrest, creates dissatisfaction . . . or even stirs people to anger." The fear of a hostile response could not justify the suppression of Johnson's "expressive conduct." The Court confirmed that the state retained the power to prevent "imminent lawless action," violence, or disturbances of the peace, but such power could not rest on a statute that went to the content of the speech or conduct.

Texas also asserted it had "an interest in preserving the flag as a symbol of nationhood and national unity." According to Brennan, the assertion only served to prove that the statute was "content-based"—that is, that the state wanted to prosecute Johnson because it disliked his message. Yet, as the Court noted, this was precisely the kind of the law the First Amendment forbade: the government could not regulate the content of speech, nor could the government suppress speech because it offended the government or a large segment of the population. Brennan concluded that "nothing" in the Court's existing jurisprudence "suggests that a State may foster its own view of the flag by prohibiting expressive conduct relating to it."

In an unusual concurrence, Justice Kennedy endorsed Brennan's opinion "without reservation" because it reflected the essence of the First Amendment. Kennedy also wanted to be on record as noting that he did not like this decision because of his "distaste" for what Johnson did. But, as Kennedy noted, "The hard fact is that sometimes we must make decisions we do not like. We make them because they are right, right in the sense that the law and Constitution, as we see them, compel the - result."

In his dissent, Chief Justice Rehnquist offered little in the way of constitutional analysis. Instead, he wrote what amounted to a short patriotic essay on the flag. He quoted Ralph Waldo Emerson's "Concord Hymn," the act of the Continental Congress describing how the flag of the new nation was to be made, and the "Star Spangled Banner." He provided the entire text of John Greenleaf Whittier's poem "Barbara Fritchie," described the raising of the flag at Iwo Jima, and offered other examples of the symbolic value of the flag. Although intended to win sympathy for those who would prosecute Johnson, Rehnquist's dissent actually confirmed the position of the majority. Johnson's act clearly offended patriotic Americans. It angered people who love their country and their flag. The response he elicited only proved that his was an effective and telling example of political expression.

Justice Stevens also dissented, saying, "The case has nothing to do with 'disagreeable ideas.' It involves disagreeable conduct that, in my opinion, diminishes the value of an important national asset."

In response to this decision, Congress passed legislation making it a federal crime to burn the flag. In ***United States v. Eichman,*** 496 U.S. 310 (1990), the Supreme Court, by the same 5–4 vote, and with substantially the same analysis, struck down this law. Regular attempts to amend the Constitution to protect the American flag have failed to garner much congressional support.

See Michael Kent Curtis, *The Constitution and the Flag,* 2 vols. (New York: Garland, 1993); and Robert Justin Goldstein, *Flag Burning and Free Speech: The Case of* Texas v. Johnson (Lawrence: University Press of Kansas, 2000).

Ward v. Rock Against Racism

491 U.S. 781 (1989)
Decided: June 22, 1989
Vote: 6 (Rehnquist, B. White, Blackmun, O'Connor, Scalia, Kennedy)
3 (Brennan, T. Marshall, Stevens)
Opinion of the Court: Kennedy
Concurred in judgment without opinion: Blackmun
Dissenting opinion: T. Marshall (Brennan, Stevens)

One of the features of New York City's Central Park is the amphitheater and stage known as the band shell. Nearby, and within the path of sound of the band shell, is a grassy open area called Sheep Meadow, a spot used as a quiet recreational area for the public. Also within the range of the sound of the band shell are the residences of Central Park West.

This case arose when the city attempted to regulate the volume of the amplified music at the band shell so performances would be satisfactory to the audience without intruding on those using the recreational area and people living nearby. The city's regulations provided the use of sound-amplification equipment and a sound technician for the performers' use at the band shell. Rock Against Racism (RAR), the sponsor of a rock concert, challenged this technique.

Before one of its concerts, RAR met with city officials to discuss the problem of excessive noise that had occurred during previous RAR events at the band shell. The parties agreed that the city would monitor the sound levels, and the city said it would revoke RAR's event permit if the volume limits were exceeded. During the concert, the sound levels were too high, and RAR ignored repeated warnings and requests for the volume to be lowered. The city issued two citations and shut off the power, thus ending the concert. The following year, RAR sought permission to hold its upcoming concert at the band shell, and the city refused.

RAR filed suit in the federal district court against the city and other officials seeking damages and a declaratory judgment, in which the court would immediately strike down the guidelines as an obvious violation of the First Amendment. In legal terms, RAR argued that the guidelines were facially invalid under the First Amendment. The district court sustained the noise control measures, but the court of appeals reversed on First Amendment grounds.

The Supreme Court ruled that the city's sound-amplification guideline was valid under the First Amendment as a reasonable regulation of the place and manner of protected speech. In a three-part test the Court first found no merit in RAR's argument that the guideline was invalid on its face because it placed unrestricted judgment in the hands of city enforcement officials. The Court concluded the city had applied a narrow construction to the guideline by requiring officials to consult RAR on sound quality and confer with them as to volume problems and by checking that amplification be adequate for all of the concert audience to hear sufficiently.

Second, the Court found the guideline was narrowly tailored to serve significant government interests, including the city's need to protect citizens from unnecessary and excessive noise. The city's interest was achieved by requiring that one of its technicians control the mixing board in order to sufficiently limit sound volume. The Court rejected RAR's contention that this guideline was substantially broader than necessary to achieve the city's legitimate ends.

Third, the guideline left many alternative outlets for communication. It did not attempt to ban any particular manner, type, or content of communication. The guideline continued to allow expressive activity in the band shell and did not try to control or restrict the quantity or content of that expression beyond regulating the extent of amplification.

In dissent, Justice Marshall found that the majority's willingness to give government officials a free hand in achieving their policy ends in effect gave the government control of speech in advance of its propagation. Marshall believed that New York City's Use Guidelines were not narrowly tailored to serve its interest in regulating loud noise.

This case affirmed the validity of what are known as "time, place, manner" restrictions on freedom of expression. The dissenters did not disagree with the validity of such regulations in general, but asserted that the New York rules were too broad and gave city officials too much power in regulating speech and expression. The case also illustrates what might be called emerging cultural conflicts over speech and expression. RAR believed that its expression—the message it wanted to offer to it audience—was in part affected by the volume of the music. City officials, and the Court, did not see the method of this expression as tied to the content.

See Jon P. Tasso, "Restoring Less–Speech-Restrictive Alternatives After *Ward v. Rock Against Racism,*" *University of Chicago Law Review* 64 (1997): 349; and Armando O. Bonilla, "First Amendment—Free Speech—Municipal Noise Ordinance Imposing Mandatory Adherence to Sound Amplification Guidelines Constitutes a Valid Time, Place, or Manner Restriction on Protected Speech—*Ward v. Rock Against Racism,* 491 U.S. 781 (1989)," *Seton Hall Constitutional Law Journal* 1 (1991): 451.

Sable Communications Inc. v. Federal Communications Commission

492 U.S. 115 (1989)
Decided: June 23, 1989
Vote: 6 (Rehnquist, B. White, Blackmun, O'Connor, Scalia, Kennedy)
3 (Brennan, T. Marshall, Stevens)
Opinion of the Court: B. White
Concurring opinion: Scalia
Dissenting opinion: Brennan (T. Marshall, Stevens)

An amendment to Section 233(b) of the Communications Act of 1934 banned indecent and obscene telephone messages in interstate commerce. Sable Communications was a "dial-a-porn" service based in southern California that played prerecorded pornographic messages to callers outside the state as well as in California. Sable sued to have the amended Section 233(b) declared unconstitutional as a violation of the First Amendment. The district court found that the obscenity provision of Section 233(b) did not violate the First Amendment by creating a national standard for obscenity, but the indecency provision did violate the First Amendment because it was overbroad.

The Supreme Court affirmed. The Court held that the obscenity provision of Section 233(b) did not violate the First Amendment because the First Amendment does not protect obscenity. Furthermore, Section 233(b) did not violate the test announced in ***Miller v. California,*** 413 U.S. 15 (1973), by creating a national standard for obscenity because it involved the transmission of messages in interstate commerce.

The Court agreed with the lower court that the indecency provision of Section 233(b) was unconstitutional. The Court distinguished this case from ***Federal Communications Commission v. Pacifica Foundation,*** 438 U.S. 726 (1978), in which it held that the FCC could place an outright ban on indecent content on the airwaves, because "dial-a-porn" services such as Sable's did not share broadcasting's unique ability to intrude into the home uninvited. To obtain Sable's services a patron had to request them. In *Pacifica,* any unsuspecting radio listener might stumble on a program, without any intention of hearing "dirty words." This case reaffirmed the notion that consenting adults have a right to view or hear pornography and that the government may not limit the rights of adults merely because minors might be able to illegally access this material. In ***Ashcroft v. Free Speech Coalition,*** 535 U.S. — (2002), the majority cited this case in overturning a federal statute banning certain types of computer-generated "virtual pornography."

County of Allegheny v. American Civil Liberties Union

492 U.S. 573 (1989)
Decided: July 3, 1989
Vote: Multiple
Judgment of the Court: Blackmun
Concurring opinion: Brennan (T. Marshall, Stevens)
Concurring opinion: Stevens (Brennan, T. Marshall)
Opinion concurring in judgment: O'Connor (Brennan, Stevens)
Dissenting opinion: Kennedy (Rehnquist, B. White, Scalia)

Every holiday season, the Allegheny County Courthouse in downtown Pittsburgh displayed a crèche (depiction of the Nativity) on its main stairway. The crèche was donated by the Holy Name Society, a Roman Catholic group, and bore the inscription "Gloria in Excelsis Deo," or "Glory to God in the Highest." The city government also erected on public land a menorah, donated by a local Jewish organization. The menorah was placed next to a large Christmas tree. The American Civil Liberties Union (ACLU) and local residents brought this suit claiming that the two displays violated the Establishment Clause.

By a 6–3 vote (Chief Justice Rehnquist and Justices White, Blackmun, O'Connor, Scalia, and Kennedy in the majority) the Court upheld the right of the city to display the menorah and the Christmas tree. By a 5–4 vote (with Justices Brennan, Marshall, Blackmun, Stevens, and O'Connor in the majority) the Court ruled that the placement of the crèche in a public building violated the Establishment Clause of the First Amendment. Justice Blackmun wrote the opinion of the Court, but only Justice O'Connor agreed with it.

Blackmun said that the Establishment Clause had come to mean that government could not favor Christianity over non-Christianity or religion over nonreligion. He also pointed out that while many tests have been created, including the "endorsement test," they were all variants of the second prong of the test announced in ***Lemon v. Kurtzman,*** 403 U.S. 602 (1971), that government action shall not have the primary effect of advancing religion. On this point, Blackmun looked at ***Lynch v. Donnelly,*** 465 U.S. 668 (1984). *Lynch* upheld the right of a city to erect a crèche as part of a larger holiday display that also included numerous nonreligious symbols, such as a clown and a large candy cane.

Blackmun found *Lynch* defective because it did not explain why the city's crèche display did not advance religion and because it implied that the Court would tolerate some advancement of religion as long as it was minor. Instead of looking to *Lynch*'s majority opinion (which Justice O'Connor had joined), Blackmun looked to her concurrence in *Lynch* for guidance. There he found the clearly articulated principle that no amount of advancement of religion is permissible.

After citing O'Connor's *Lynch* rationale with approval, Blackmun distinguished the Allegheny County crèche from that in *Lynch.* He noted that in the Allegheny County case, the crèche was displayed in a context that suggested intent to celebrate not the cultural event of the holiday season but the religious significance of the holiday season to Christians. Unlike the display in *Lynch,* the Allegheny County display consisted solely of a crèche, in a prominent public place—the courthouse's grand staircase—and the inscription, "Gloria in Excelcis Deo," suggested that the county was encouraging citizens to praise God for Jesus' birth.

On the other hand, Blackmun did not find that the city's menorah display violated the Establishment Clause, because the eighteen-foot menorah stood next to a forty-five-foot Christmas tree. The religiously neutral (or, at worst, ambiguous) Christmas tree tended to negate the message of endorsement that might otherwise have been sent by the menorah. Because of the lack of an appropriate secular symbol of Hanukkah, the presence of the menorah could be understood as merely a recognition that Christmas is not the only holiday being celebrated during the holiday season.

The justices who supported the erection of the crèche advanced three primary arguments. First, they argued that prior case law, particularly *Lynch* and ***Marsh v. Chambers,*** 463 U.S. 783 (1983), which permitted the legislature to open each session with a prayer from a chaplain, supported the view that government should "accommodate and recognize" religion. Second, they argued that it was not necessary for government to be relentlessly vigilant in abhorring contact with religion. In light of what they described as the American history of "accommodation" and "recognition" of religion, the majority's requirement that government abolish all recognition of religion amounts to outright hostility toward religion. Third, in their view, as long as government did not take steps toward establishing a state religion, which they would limit to "proselytizing," the Establishment Clause was satisfied.

Blackmun rebutted these arguments. First, he pointed out that even if history did support an "accommodation and recognition" principle, this could not legitimate government endorsement of religion. Second, he pointed out that strict adherence to nonendorsement did not evidence "hostility" to religion in a way that discriminated against Christians because it was motivated by the constitutional command for government not to affiliate itself with religion. This constitutional principle existed precisely to prevent discrimination against religious beliefs. Third, he pointed out that the dissenters' proposed "proselytization" test amounted to nothing but an endorsement test with a more government-friendly standard of review. Blackmun could see no reason to change the historical practice of applying strict scrutiny to government actions that suggest a violation of the Establishment Clause. Brennan, Marshall, and Stevens dissented from the part of the opinion allowing the menorah and Christmas tree. They said these symbols were religious and should be banned from government property.

Webster v. Reproductive Health Services

492 U.S. 490 (1989)
Decided: July 3, 1989
Vote: 5 (Rehnquist, B. White, O'Connor, Scalia, Kennedy)
4 (Brennan, T. Marshall, Blackmun, Stevens)
Judgment of the Court: Rehnquist
Concurring in judgment: O'Connor
Concurring in judgment: Scalia
Dissenting opinion: Blackmun (Brennan, T. Marshall)
Dissenting opinion: Stevens

In June 1986 Missouri enacted a law that amended existing state law concerning unborn children and abortions. In July five state-employed health professionals and two nonprofit corporations brought a class action in the federal district court to challenge the constitutionality of the statute. They asserted that certain provisions of the act violated the First, Fourth, Ninth, and Fourteenth Amendments. The district court declared seven provisions of the act unconstitutional and enjoined their enforcement. These provisions were the preamble (1.205); the "informed consent" provision (188.039); the requirement that post–sixteen-week abortions be performed only in hospitals (188.025); the mandated tests to determine viability (188.029); and the prohibition on the use of public funds, employees, and facilities to perform or assist nontherapeutic abortions, and the restrictions on the use of public funds, employees, and facilities to encourage or counsel women to have nontherapeutic abortions (188.205, 188.210, and 188.215). The court of appeals affirmed. The Supreme Court reversed.

The preamble stated that life begins at conception and that unborn children have all the rights, privileges, and immunities of other citizens. The Court found no constitutional infirmities in the preamble. Chief Justice Rehnquist wrote that "the preamble can be read simply to express [a] value judgment."

In regard to the restrictions on state employees and public facilities, and public funding of abortion counseling, Rehnquist again disagreed with the court of appeals. In ***Maher v. Roe,*** 432 U.S. 464 (1977); ***Harris v. McRae,*** 448 U.S. 297 (1980); and *DeShaney v. Winnebago County Department of Social Services,* 489 U.S. 189 (1989), the Court ruled that "the Due Process Clauses generally confer no affirmative right to governmental aid."

Finally, the Court ruled that the physician requirement was reasonable because it is linked to a legitimate "interest in potential human life." Rehnquist cited ***Roe v. Wade,*** 410 U.S. 113 (1973), as precedent supporting this principle.

In dissent, Justice Blackmun warned that although a woman's right to terminate her pregnancy remained, the right was "not secure." He noted the narrow holding of the Court, while pointing to the broad attack on *Roe v. Wade* in the plurality opinion and in Justice Scalia's opinion. He said that *Roe* would not survive the analysis of the plurality and ended on an ominous note: "I fear for the future. I fear for the liberty and equality of the millions of women who have lived and come of age in the 16 years since *Roe* was decided. I fear for the integrity of, and public esteem for, this Court."

1990–1999

Employment Division, Department of Human Resources of Oregon v. Smith

494 U.S. 872 (1990)
Decided: April 17, 1990
Vote: 6 (Rehnquist, White, Stevens, O'Connor, Scalia, Kennedy)
3 (Brennan, Marshall, Blackmun)
Opinion of the Court: Scalia
Opinion concurring in judgment: O'Connor (Brennan, Marshall, Blackmun)
Dissenting opinion: Blackmun (Brennan, Marshall)

Alfred Smith was a member of the Klamath tribe of southern Oregon, and, after a number of difficult years involving drug and alcohol problems, he got his life together. He married, got a job with a rehabilitation clinic, and rediscovered his roots. He joined the Native American Church and began to explore the "peyote road," the use of a hallucinogenic drug made from a cactus. These rituals have been part of some Indian religious cultures for generations.

Several western states exempted peyote from their list of controlled substances, as did the federal government, but Oregon did not, and Smith's supervisor warned him not to use it. Smith regarded the warning as infringing on his religious freedom. After he and a co-worker, Galen Black, took part in a peyote ceremony, they were fired. Smith filed for unemployment insurance, but was denied benefits because he had been dismissed for criminal behavior. Smith sued in state court and won. The Oregon Supreme Court affirmed the lower court's decision on the basis of ***Sherbert v. Verner,*** 374 U.S. 398 (1963), which required states to balance the objectives of a state program against the claims of religion and to make reasonable accommodations to citizens' free exercise of religious ritual.

Oregon appealed on the basis that *Sherbert* and other earlier cases had not dealt with criminal law, but with administrative regulations. A slim majority of the Court agreed, with Justice Scalia going all the way back to ***Reynolds v. United States,*** 98 U.S. 145 (1879), to rule that religion could never be used as an excuse for violating an otherwise valid law regulating conduct that the state is free to regulate. The Court agreed that the fact that Smith violated a criminal statute made the difference; Oregon had the option of criminalizing peyote and had chosen to do so. Given the rampant drug problems facing the state and the nation, the Court majority felt that this was not an irrational choice.

Justice O'Connor, joined in part by the three dissenters, sharply criticized the majority for abandoning the balancing test of *Sherbert.* She joined in the result because she believed that even if the Court had used the balancing test, it would have found the state had a compelling interest because of its war against drug abuse. The three dissenters agreed with the part of O'Connor's concurrence that called for retaining the *Sherbert* balancing test, but they believed that under that test, Smith's claim for religious freedom outweighed the state's interests. Peyote, unlike heroin or cocaine, was not addictive, and its production and distribution were tightly controlled: the cactus grows only in a small part of the Southwest; only one Indian tribe may harvest the peyote buttons; and only authorized groups like the Native American Church could buy them.

Oregon certainly could have been more responsive to the practices of the Native American Church, but in fact state law did not target peyote ceremonies. The law on the books covered a large number of drugs, many of them addictive and/or hallucinogenic. The law served as part of a broader state policy against drug abuse and indicated that the state would not tolerate drug use even if performed as part of a religious ritual. At about the same time, the state was involved in a major controversy with a charismatic Hindu leader whose followers had taken control of an Oregon town by moving in, voting themselves into office, and then establishing what amounted to a local dictatorship. Oregon was, as a result, less than amenable to claims of free exercise.

The decision caused a great deal of criticism, especially by religious groups, who wanted the Court to reinstate the *Sherbert* balancing test. They lobbied Congress, which passed the Religious Freedom Restoration Act of 1993, in which Congress attempted to define the broad parameters of the Free Exercise Clause and to establish the *Sherbert* test as the standard. The Court struck down the new law as unconstitutional in ***City of Boerne v. Flores,*** 521 U.S. 507 (1997).

See Garrett Epps, *To an Unknown God: Religious Freedom on Trial* (New York: St. Martin's Press, 2001); and Carolyn Long, *Religious Freedom and Indian Rights: The Case of* Oregon v. Smith (Lawrence: University Press of Kansas, 2000).

Missouri v. Jenkins

495 U.S. 33 (1990)
Decided: April 18, 1990
Vote: 9 (Rehnquist, Brennan, B. White, T. Marshall, Blackmun, Stevens, O'Connor, Scalia, Kennedy)
0
Opinion of the Court: B. White
Opinion concurring in judgment: Kennedy (Rehnquist, O'Connor, Scalia)

A 1977 lawsuit filed by a group of students to improve and desegregate Kansas City schools resulted in the court-ordered plan that eventually gave rise to *Missouri v. Jenkins.* The federal district judge who ordered the desegregation plan also imposed a tax increase on school district residents. The judge said the taxes were needed to pay the local share of the multimillion dollar desegregation effort. Property tax rates nearly doubled. State officials objected on two grounds: they contended that under the Tenth Amendment the taxing power is reserved to the states, and they said taxing authority is a legislative power not to be taken up by other branches. The court of appeals upheld the district judge's taxing order.

The U.S. Supreme Court, with the qualification that the judge could order the tax, but not impose it himself, effectively affirmed that ruling. Writing for the Court, Justice White said that state policy must acquiesce when it interferes with the defense of federal constitutional guarantees—in this case, desegregated schools. "A local government with taxing authority may be ordered to levy taxes in excess of the limit set by state statute where there is reason based in the Constitution for not observing the statutory limitation," he wrote. "To hold otherwise would fail to take account of the obligations of local governments, under the Supremacy Clause, to fulfill the requirements that the Constitution imposes on them."

White said the Tenth Amendment was not implicated because the judge's order enforced the Fourteenth Amendment, allowing judges to remedy unlawful discrimination in the states. The Fourteenth Amendment, he wrote, "permits a federal court to disestablish local government institutions that interfere with its commands."

In a concurring opinion that amounted to a dissent, four justices asserted that federal judges did not have the power to impose the tax. Justice Kennedy wrote, "Today's casual embrace of taxation imposed by the unelected, life-tenured federal judiciary disregards fundamental precepts for the democratic control of public institutions."

See Charles V. Dale, "The Judicial Power of Taxation: A Legal Analysis of the U.S. Supreme Court Ruling in *Missouri v. Jenkins,*" *Congressional Research Service,* June 1, 1990; and Kevin B. Greely, "School Desegregation Update: Summary and Analysis of the Supreme Court's Opinion in *Missouri v. Jenkins,*" *Congressional Research Service,* June 30, 1995.

Westside Community Board of Education v. Mergens

496 U.S. 226 (1990)
Decided: June 4, 1990
Vote: 8 (Rehnquist, Brennan, B. White, T. Marshall, Blackmun, O'Connor, Scalia, Kennedy)
1 (Stevens)
Judgment of the Court: O'Connor
Opinion concurring in judgment: T. Marshall (Brennan)
Opinion concurring in judgment: Kennedy (Scalia)
Dissenting opinion: Stevens

The Supreme Court's decisions in the early 1960s prohibiting sponsored prayer or Bible readings in public elementary and secondary classrooms provoked strong protests. Repeated attempts to overturn the rulings by constitutional amendment failed, and by the 1980s advocates of religion in school had shifted strategy. They turned to organizing Christian Bible clubs as extracurricular activities for students at public schools. Some schools, however, balked at allowing the religious clubs to use school facilities.

Congress responded in 1984 by passing a law aimed at assuring student religious groups the right to meet in public high schools on the same basis as other extracurricular organizations. The Equal Access Act prohibited any secondary school that receives federal funds and that allows extracurricular groups to meet on school grounds from discriminating against any group on the basis of the subject that it wants to discuss.

The Supreme Court upheld the constitutionality of the law and gave it a relatively strict interpretation in a test case from a school district in Omaha, Nebraska. The case began in 1985 when Bridget Mergens, a student at Westside High School, tried to gain formal status for a Christian Bible club. The school's principal and then the district's superintendent rejected the request, ostensibly because Mergens lacked a faculty sponsor.

Mergens challenged the denial in federal court. A lower court judge upheld the denial on the grounds that all of the student clubs recognized by the school were curriculum-related. The federal appeals court in St. Louis disagreed, ruling that under the terms of the law many of the clubs at Westside were not related to the curriculum. On that basis, the appeals court said, the school had violated the law.

The Court agreed by a lopsided vote that masked a wide divergence of opinion among the justices. Justice O'Connor said the statute did not conflict with the Establishment Clause because Congress's stated purpose—"to prevent discrimination against religious and other types of speech"—was "undeniably secular." She said the law did not impermissibly advance religion or produce conflicts between government and religion. The ruling extended the Court's earlier decision, *Widmar v. Vincent,* 454 U.S. 263 (1981), which allowed religious groups to meet on state college and university campuses. O'Connor said high school students are mature enough to understand that a school is not endorsing religion by permitting a Bible club to meet on a nondiscriminatory basis.

Justice Kennedy took a more relaxed view of allowing religion in the public schools. He said religious groups are constitutional as long as no students are coerced to participate. From the opposite perspective, Justice Marshall concurred with a warning that schools should fully dissociate themselves from the religious clubs.

In a lone dissent, Justice Stevens argued that the act should be narrowly interpreted to avoid requiring schools to recognize "every religious, political, or social organization, no matter how controversial or distasteful its views."

See Patrick Marshall, "Religion in Schools," *CQ Researcher,* January 12, 2001, 1–24.

United States v. Eichman

496 U.S. 310 (1990)
Decided: June 11, 1990
Vote: 5 (Brennan, T. Marshall, Blackmun, Scalia, Kennedy)
4 (Rehnquist, B. White, Stevens, O'Connor)
Opinion of the Court: Brennan
Dissenting opinion: Stevens (Rehnquist, B. White, O'Connor)

One of the most difficult First Amendment issues the Court has faced is desecration of the American flag, a symbol held in near reverence by most Americans. Next to the abortion decision, no cases generated as much public controversy as the flag-burning cases decided by the Court in 1989 and 1990, both by 5–4 votes.

In ***Texas v. Johnson,*** 491 U.S. 397 (1989), the Court overturned the conviction of Gregory Lee Johnson, a Vietnam veteran who burned an American flag as part of a political protest during the 1984 Republican National Convention in Dallas. He was convicted under a state statute prohibiting the intentional desecration of a state or national flag. The Court ruled that flag-burning, under these circumstances, constituted political expression and the states could not regulate it.

The ensuing uproar spilled out over the airways and in hundreds of letters to the editors of newspapers and magazines. The Senate voted 97–3 to express its "profound disappointment" in the decision, and President George Bush called for a constitutional amendment, a proposal that appalled almost as many people as the decision itself. Congress turned down Bush's request to amend the Constitution and instead passed the 1989 Flag Protection Act, an antidesecration law that critics claimed could not withstand judicial scrutiny. Within a few weeks of the law's enactment, Shawn Eichman and three other demonstrators—including Gregory Johnson—burned an American flag on the steps of the U.S. Capitol.

In *Eichman,* the same 5–4 majority as in *Johnson* held the federal statute unconstitutional as an interference with expressive conduct protected by the First Amendment. Justice Brennan rejected the government's argument that Congress could do what the states could not, namely, interfere with a form of political speech. Reiterating that the majority did not care for flag desecration any more than did other Americans, Brennan nonetheless pointed out that "punishing desecration of the flag dilutes the very freedom that makes it so revered." The same four dissenters claimed that the flag could be protected as a symbol of national unity consistent with First Amendment protections.

This time the decision raised a far smaller outcry, perhaps because people had thought about the majority's reasoning. Republicans tried to make an issue of the case and called for a constitutional amendment to override the Court, an effort that immediately fell flat. A number of conservatives, such as Sen. Gordon Humphrey, R-N.H., opposed the demand for an amendment. "I just don't like tampering with the First Amendment," he declared.

See Frank I. Michelman, "Saving Old Glory: On Constitutional Iconography," *Stanford Law Review* 42 (1990): 1337; and Gregory Herbert, "Waiving Rights and Burning Flags: The Search for a Valid State Interest in Flag Protection," *Harvard Civil Rights-Civil Liberties Law Review* 25 (1990): 591.

Rutan v. Republican Party of Illinois

497 U.S. 62 (1990)
Decided: June 21, 1990
Vote: 5 (Brennan, B. White, T. Marshall, Blackmun, Stevens)
4 (Rehnquist, O'Connor, Scalia, Kennedy)
Opinion of the Court: Brennan
Concurring opinion: Stevens
Dissenting opinion: Scalia (Rehnquist, O'Connor, Kennedy)

James R. Thompson, the Republican governor of Illinois, froze hiring and promotions in state agencies. The only exceptions, according to Thompson's executive order, were those granted by the governor's personnel office. Workers sued, alleging that the personnel office kept them out of jobs because they did not support the state's Republican Party. The Thompson administration asserted that political party affiliation should be a legitimate measure along with other criteria when assessing applicants.

The U.S. Supreme Court did not agree. The Court's ruling expanded two earlier decisions that barred the dismissal of public workers based on party affiliation: *Elrod v. Burns,* 427 U.S. 347 (1976), and *Branti v. Finkel,* 445 U.S. 507 (1980). In these cases the Court held that patronage violates a First Amendment right of free association when government workers who are not in policy or confidential positions are fired because of their party membership. The cases did not deal with hiring, rehiring, promotions, or transfers as *Rutan* did.

Writing for the majority, Justice Brennan opened his opinion with a qualified nod to the spoils system. "To the victor belong only those spoils that may be constitutionally obtained." He said the government cannot deny a benefit to a person on a basis that violates First Amendment belief and association rights. The

Illinois hiring system, Brennan said, penalized individuals who did not affiliate with the Republican Party by excluding applicants from positions and—for workers already on the rolls—by denying them pay increases, better hours, and recalls after temporary layoffs. "These are significant penalties and are imposed for the exercise of rights guaranteed by the First Amendment," he wrote. In addition, Brennan said the government's interest in party loyalty could be achieved through less-restrictive means and that unless patronage practices were "narrowly tailored" to advance government interests, courts must conclude that they breach the First Amendment.

In dissent, Justice Scalia said reserving jobs in government for the party in power is an important tradition that fosters the government's interest in stable political parties. "There is little doubt that our decisions in *Elrod* and *Branti*, by contributing to the decline of party strength, have also contributed to the growth of interest-group politics in the last decade," Scalia wrote. "Our decision today will greatly accelerate the trend. It is not only campaigns that are affected, of course, but the subsequent behavior of politicians once they are in power."

See Bradford C. Moyer, "The Future of *Rutan v. Republican Party of Illinois:* A Proposal for Insulating Independent Contractors from Political Patronage," *Valparaiso University Law Review* 28 (1993): 375.

Cruzan v. Director, Missouri Department of Health

497 U.S. 261 (1990)
Decided: June 25, 1990
Vote: 5 (Rehnquist, B. White, O'Connor, Scalia, Kennedy)
4 (Brennan, T. Marshall, Blackmun, Stevens)
Opinion of the Court: Rehnquist
Concurring opinion: O'Connor
Concurring opinion: Scalia
Dissenting opinion: Brennan (Marshall, Blackmun)
Dissenting opinion: Stevens

While Nancy Cruzan was driving home from work, her car hit a patch of ice. The car flipped over, and she was thrown out, landing face down in a shallow pool of water. The rescue squad arrived quickly, but, by the time they revived her, she had sustained extensive brain damage and was in a coma, and she soon lapsed into a persistent vegetative state. She could breathe on her own and was kept alive through artificial feeding and hydration. Her parents, after giving up hope that she would recover, went into a local Missouri court and asked to be named her guardians for the purpose of removing the feeding tube and allowing her to die. The local magistrate gave his approval, but the state attorney general intervened. Missouri, like other states, had a law that allowed for a surrogate to make health care decisions for people in a coma, but, unlike all but two other states, Missouri required a higher evidentiary standard of what the comatose person would have wanted. Had Nancy Cruzan left a living will, it would have met the level of "clear and convincing evidence," but she had not. No witnesses could be found to testify as to her wishes.

The Supreme Court made two important findings in this case. First, based on common law principles of bodily autonomy, as well as liberty interests regarding bodily autonomy found in the Fourteenth Amendment's Due Process Clause, the Court held that every person has a right to refuse medical treatment, even if that decision would lead to death. Second, this right is limited by the state's interest in preserving life. Although the state may not bar such decisions, it may in the interest of protecting the helpless, ensure that any decision that would terminate treatment is based on a sufficient evidentiary standard.

Missouri, according to Chief Justice Rehnquist, had acted well within its discretionary powers. It allowed for a living will to meet the burden of proof, and, although its "clear and convincing" standard was higher than most states, it was neither unreasonable nor impossible to meet. While acknowledging the difficult emotions generated by the case and that, if anyone was qualified to act as Nancy's surrogate it would be her parents, the Court nonetheless held that the Missouri law met the constitutional requirements.

Justice Scalia, in his concurrence, said the Court should not have decided the merits of the case. He believed that should have remained a matter for state courts to decide.

The dissenters said that in balancing the constitutional liberty interests against the state's desire to preserve life, the Court should have given greater weight to the individual. Missouri, in their view, had set the bar too high.

Many people misinterpreted the ruling and believed that because the Court had found against the Cruzans, it held that a constitutionally protected right to die did not exist. In fact, the Court specifically ruled that the Fourteenth Amendment protected such a right, but that it was not absolute and had to be balanced against other interests. This case is an example of the Rehnquist Court's emphasis on federalism, returning as much power to the states as possible and refusing to expand the scope of individual liberties. In this case, it held that a liberty interest existed, indicated that the states could not restrict it past a certain point, but left the administration and protection of that right to the states.

Following the decision, the Cruzans went back into local court, and this time two of Nancy's friends testified that she had told them that if she were ever injured and left in a coma, she would not want to live that way. The magistrate found that their statements met the state's evidentiary requirement and gave the family authority to stop the artificial feeding. The state, having made its point in the Supreme Court, did not contest the local decision. Feeding was stopped, and Nancy Cruzan died just before Christmas 1990.

See Melvin I. Urofsky, *Letting Go: Death, Dying and the Law* (New York: Scribner's, 1992); and Peter Filene, *In the Arms of Others: The Right-to-Die in America* (Chicago: I. R. Dee, 1998).

Metro Broadcasting, Inc. v. Federal Communications Commission

497 U.S. 547 (1990)
Decided: June 27, 1990
Vote: 5 (Brennan, B. White, T. Marshall, Blackmun, Stevens)
4 (Rehnquist, O'Connor, Scalia, Kennedy)
Opinion of the Court: Brennan
Concurring opinion: Stevens
Dissenting opinion: O'Connor (Rehnquist, Scalia, Kennedy)
Dissenting opinion: Kennedy (Scalia)

In an endorsement of affirmative action, the Supreme Court ruled that Congress may order preferential treatment of blacks and other minorities to increase their ownership of broadcast licenses. The Court held that "benign race-conscious measures," including those that do not compensate victims of past discrimination, are constitutional as long as they further important government objectives. Congress's role in mandating the preferential treatment was central to the Court's opinion, which said federal lawmakers have more authority than state and local governments to set aside contracts for minorities.

The ruling marked the first time the Court upheld an affirmative action program that was not devised to relieve past discrimination. But it was implicitly overruled just five years later in ***Adarand Constructors, Inc. v. Peña,*** 515 U.S. 200 (1995), another minority preference case.

At issue in the broadcasting cases (*Astroline Communications Company Limited Partnership v. Shurberg Broadcasting of Hartford, Inc.* was decided with *Metro Broadcasting*) were two types of set-aside programs: one gave special credit to minorities applying for new licenses, and the other—a so-called "distress sale" program—required some radio and television stations to be sold only to minority-controlled companies. During the Reagan administration, the Federal Communications Commission (FCC) tried to dismantle the race-preference programs, but Congress beginning in 1987 blocked the commission from spending any of its appropriated money to examine or change the policies.

White-owned broadcasting companies challenged the practices as violating constitutional guarantees of equal protection. The court of appeals upheld the policy that gave extra credit to minority-owned companies and struck down the distress sale program.

In his majority opinion, Justice Brennan stressed Congress's finding that preference programs for minorities were necessary for broadcast diversity and that lawmakers had long given special protection to minorities. In distinguishing these cases from ***City of Richmond v. J. A. Croson,*** 488 U.S. 469 (1989), Brennan said the federal government has more authority than state and local governments.

He based his opinion on the Court's decision in ***Fullilove v. Klutznick,*** 448 U.S. 448 (1980), which upheld a federal public works set-aside program on the ground that the Constitution allows special deference to Congress. The majority said federal affirmative action programs should be analyzed with a more lenient equal protection standard than that applied to city and state plans. It said the strict scrutiny test used in *Croson* need not govern congressional mandates. Brennan also said that the policies did not place an undue burden on broadcasters who are not minorities.

Writing for the dissenters, Justice O'Connor said the Court had taken a step backward with its opinion. O'Connor, the author of the *Croson* ruling, said that by providing benefits to blacks and other minorities, the FCC was denying benefits to whites based on their race. "Except in the narrowest of circumstances, the Constitution bars such racial classifications as a denial to particular individuals, of any race or ethnicity, of 'the equal protection of the laws,' " O'Connor wrote, quoting the Fourteenth Amendment. She speculated that the majority's more lenient standard of review for the FCC policies might lead the government to resort to racial distinctions more readily.

See Kenneth Jost, "Affirmative Action," *CQ Researcher,* September 21, 2001, 737–760.

Automobile Workers v. Johnson Controls, Inc.

499 U.S. 187 (1991)
Decided: March 20, 1991
Vote: 9 (Rehnquist, B. White, T. Marshall, Blackmun, Stevens, O'Connor, Scalia, Kennedy, Souter)
0
Opinion of the Court: Blackmun
Opinion concurring in judgment: B. White (Rehnquist, Kennedy)
Opinion concurring in judgment: Scalia

Many chemicals commonly used in manufacturing processes or other workplaces can cause birth defects in a developing fetus. To minimize the danger for their employees—and to protect themselves from potential litigation—some companies adopted fetal–protection policies that prohibited women of childbearing age from working in certain jobs.

Despite the ostensibly benevolent purpose, many women's rights advocates criticized the policies as limiting women's access to jobs and invading their privacy. When the issue reached the Supreme Court, the justices unanimously held that one company's broad policy barring women from potentially dangerous jobs amounted to illegal sex discrimination. Four of the justices, however, said the majority went too far in deciding that a company's desire to avoid liability could never justify such a policy.

The employer was Johnson Controls, a Milwaukee battery manufacturer, that adopted a policy in 1977 of warning employees of the risk of birth defects from exposure to lead—a primary ingredient in batteries. Five years later, the company stiffened the policy by prohibiting all women of childbearing age from jobs involving exposure to lead unless they were sterilized. Workers sued, contending that the new policy violated the sex discrimination provisions of Title VII of the Civil Rights Act of 1964 as well as the 1978 Pregnancy Discrimination amendments. A lower federal court upheld the policy on the ground of business necessity, and a federal appeals court affirmed the decision.

In reversing the lower court, the Court noted that exposure to lead can harm both the male and the female reproductive systems. On that basis, Justice Blackmun said, Johnson Controls' policy barring fertile women but not fertile men from specified jobs amounted to illegal sex discrimination unless the company could show that sex was a "bona fide occupational qualification." Johnson Controls could not meet that test, Blackmun said, either by saying that the danger for women was greater than for men or that the policy was needed to avoid civil liability. A safety exception recognized in the law, Blackmun said, applies only if sex or pregnancy "actually interferes with the employee's ability to perform the job." Moreover, it was up to individual workers, not the employer, to make decisions about the welfare of future children.

Blackmun cast doubt on employers' risks of liability if they complied with federal job safety standards and fully informed workers about any dangers. In a partial concurrence, however, Justice White said a fetal–protection policy should be upheld if it was "reasonably necessary to avoid substantial tort liability." Under the ruling, White said, an employer could not exclude even pregnant women from jobs involving materials that are highly toxic to their fetuses. "It is foolish to think that Congress intended such a result," White wrote.

In a separate concurrence, Scalia also said that an employer should be able to bar a pregnant woman from a job if accommodating her condition was "inordinately expensive."

See Anita Cava, "Note: Pregnancy in the Workplace—Sex Specific Fetal Protection Policies—*UAW v. Johnson Controls, Inc.*—A Victory for Women?" *Tennessee Law Review* 59 (1992): 617; and Suzanne U. Samuels, "The Lasting Legacy of International Union, *UAW v. Johnson Controls:* Equal Employment and Workplace Health and Safety Five Years Later," *Wisconsin Women's Law Journal* 12 (1997): 1.

Arizona v. Fulminante

499 U.S. 279 (1991)
Decided: March 26, 1991
Vote: Multiple
Opinion of the Court: Rehnquist
Opinion of the Court: B. White
Opinion concurring in judgment: Kennedy
Dissenting opinion: Rehnquist (O'Connor, Scalia, Kennedy, Souter)
Dissenting opinion: B. White (T. Marshall, Blackmun, Stevens)

Oreste Fulminante, serving a prison sentence for a firearms conviction, confessed to a more serious crime to another inmate, Anthony Sarivola, who was—unbeknownst to Fulminante—an FBI informant. Fulminante told Sarivola he had murdered his eleven-year-old stepdaughter. The disclosure about the child's murder followed Fulminante's apparent concerns about a prison rumor about this crime and his fears of abuse by other inmates. Sarivola offered to protect Fulminante, but said to him, "You have to tell me about it . . . for me to give you any help." Fulminante then admitted that he had driven his stepdaughter to the desert, where he choked her, sexually assaulted her, and made her beg for her life before shooting her twice in the head.

After Fulminante was released from prison on the firearms charge, he was indicted in Arizona for the murder. He moved to suppress the statement he had given to Sarivola and then to the informant's wife. Fulminante asserted that the original confession was coerced by an agent of the government and that the second confession was the "fruit" of the first. A trial court denied the motion, finding that both were voluntary. The confessions were used at trial, and Fulminante was convicted of the murder and sentenced to death. The Arizona Supreme Court, however, held that the first confession was coerced because Fulminante thought his life was in danger.

In a complex opinion written by shifting majorities, the Supreme Court held that a coerced confession does not automatically taint a conviction. That part of the ruling reversed *Chapman v. California,* 386 U.S. 18 (1967), a decision establishing the rule that due process is denied whenever a forced confession is used against a defendant, regardless of other evidence.

Writing for five justices on this critical part of *Fulminate,* Chief Justice Rehnquist said, that if other evidence were enough to convict the defendant, a compelled confession could be harmless error—and thus not dictate a new trial. Justice White, dissenting from this part of the opinion, said the Court had overruled a "vast body of precedent." He said, "Permitting a coerced confession to be part of the evidence . . . is inconsistent with the thesis that ours is not an inquisitorial system" of justice.

The Court's opinion began with White writing for the majority that the confession was coerced. He was joined on this part of the opinion by Justices Marshall, Blackmun, Stevens, and Scalia.

Rehnquist won the majority for the next part of the opinion: that once a confession was found to be coerced, it could be subjected to harmless error analysis. He said the harmless error doctrine stems from the idea that "the central purpose of a criminal trial is to decide the factual question of the defendant's guilt or innocence . . . by focusing on the underlying fairness of the trial rather than on the virtually inevitable presence of immaterial error."

He called the admission of an involuntary confession a "trial error," comparable to the erroneous admission of other types of evidence. Referring to *Chapman*'s list of errors that could not be considered harmless, Rehnquist said a coerced confession is unlike denial of counsel and trial before a biased judge, terming those "structural defects in the constitution of the trial mechanism." He said the error here was just in the process itself. Rehnquist was joined by Justices O'Connor, Scalia, Kennedy, and Souter.

White, who wrote for the dissent on this point, accused the majority of abandoning a long-held proposition that a defendant is deprived of due process of law if his conviction is founded on an involuntary confession. He said a defendant's confession is probably the most damaging evidence that can be used against him.

But then White, applying the Rehnquist harmless error analysis, regained a majority to find that Arizona had not demonstrated beyond a reasonable doubt that the admission of the confession did not contribute to Fulminante's conviction. White was joined by Marshall, Blackmun, Stevens, and, for this part only, Kennedy.

Rehnquist, joined by O'Connor and Scalia, disagreed with White about whether Fulminante should get a new trial. He noted that at a hearing on whether to suppress the confession, Fulminante had accepted the prosecutor's statement that "at no time did the defendant indicate he was in fear of other inmates nor did he ever seek [the informant's] protection."

Kennedy, in a concurring opinion, agreed with Rehnquist that the confession was not coerced and that harmless error analysis could be applied to the case. But, in explaining why he joined White in the end, Kennedy said, given that five justices had found the confession coerced (in the first part of the opinion), an appeals court "must appreciate the indelible impact a full confession may have on the trier of fact." He said it would be hard to find evidence more incriminating. Kennedy, however, was not one of the justices who believed Fulminante's confession was coerced.

See Charles J. Ogletree Jr., *"Arizona v. Fulminante:* The Harm of Applying Harmless Error to Coerced Confessions," *Harvard Law Review* 105 (1991): 152.

McCleskey v. Zant

499 U.S. 467 (1991)
Decided: April 16, 1991
Vote: 6 (Rehnquist, B. White, O'Connor, Scalia, Kennedy, Souter)
3 (T. Marshall, Blackmun, Stevens)
Opinion of the Court: Kennedy
Dissenting opinion: T. Marshall (Blackmun, Stevens)

The Supreme Court ruled that, barring extraordinary circumstances, death row prisoners may obtain only one round of federal court review through petitions for habeas corpus. The Court's opinion refined "abuse of the writ," a doctrine that governs the circumstances in which federal courts may decline to hear a prisoner's claim presented for the first time in a second or subsequent petition for a writ of habeas corpus. The majority said that a prisoner may file only one habeas corpus petition in federal court unless good reason exists for why any new constitutional error was not raised during the first round. The standard for a second petition is difficult, and the prisoner also must show that he suffered "actual prejudice" from the error he claims.

Under earlier Court rulings, second and subsequent habeas corpus petitions were dismissed out of hand only if a prisoner deliberately withheld grounds for appeal in bad faith (possibly to raise the arguments in later petitions). Dissenting justices asserted that the majority was exercising "legislative power" by providing a tougher standard, a reference to Chief Justice Rehnquist's longtime effort to persuade Congress to streamline the habeas corpus process. The highly controversial proposed legislation repeatedly died without final action.

In 1989 the Court also made it harder for death row prisoners to file habeas corpus petitions when it restricted, in *Teague v. Lane,* 489 U.S. 288 (1989), the situations under which a prisoner could establish an appeal based on a favorable court ruling issued in another case after his own conviction became final.

In this case, Warren McCleskey was convicted of murder in 1978. In his second federal habeas petition, McCleskey, in a new claim, challenged prosecutors' use at trial of a conversation he had with a jail cellmate who was an informant for state officials. McCleskey supposedly told the cellmate that he indeed had robbed a Georgia furniture store and shot and killed an off-duty police officer who had entered the store during the robbery.

McCleskey argued to the district court that heard the habeas petition that his rights were breached by the state's use of an informant to obtain the incriminating statements. The court agreed, granting McCleskey relief based on a violation of ***Massiah v. United States,*** 377 U.S. 201 (1964), in which the Supreme Court held that the right to counsel applied as much to an undercover use of police tactics as it did to a jailhouse interrogation.

The court of appeals reversed, holding that the district court exceeded its discretion by failing to dismiss McCleskey's *Massiah* claim as an abuse of the writ. The court said that because McCleskey included the complaint in a state petition, dropped it in his first federal petition, and then reasserted it in his second federal petition, he "made a knowing choice not to pursue the claim after having raised it previously."

The Supreme Court affirmed, ruling that subsequent habeas consideration of claims not raised on the first round, and thus defaulted, should be prohibited unless a prisoner can show cause and prejudice. That standard requires a defendant to prove that "some objective factor" beyond the defense's control frustrated its efforts to raise the claim in an earlier petition. The defendant would have to demonstrate, for example, that the state interfered or that the factual or legal basis for a claim was not available to his lawyer during the earlier appeal. Once the defendant has established cause, he then would have to show actual prejudice to his case.

"The cause and prejudice standard should curtail the abusive petitions that in recent years have threatened to undermine the integrity of the habeas corpus process," Justice Kennedy wrote for the majority. In McCleskey's case, Kennedy found no cause for his failing to raise the complaint about the informant from the beginning. Kennedy said allowing successive petitions may give defendants incentives to withhold claims for manipulative purposes.

Justice Marshall, in his dissent, said the majority's "decision departs drastically from the norms that inform the proper judicial function." He asserted that refinements in habeas corpus procedure are up to Congress, which "has affirmatively ratified the [formerly used] good-faith standard in the governing and procedural rules, thereby insulating that standard from judicial repeal."

Dissenting justices also said a consequence of the new standard would be that defendants raise in their first federal habeas corpus petition all conceivable claims, whether or not they have merit.

See Eric M. Freedman, *Habeas Corpus: Rethinking the Great Writ of Liberty* (New York: New York University Press, 2001).

Rust v. Sullivan

500 U.S. 173 (1991)
Decided: May 23, 1991
Vote: 5 (Rehnquist, B. White, Scalia, Kennedy, Souter)
4 (T. Marshall, Blackmun, Stevens, O'Connor)
Opinion of the Court: Rehnquist
Dissenting opinion: Blackmun (T. Marshall, Stevens, O'Connor)
Dissenting opinion: Stevens
Dissenting opinion: O'Connor

An abortion-related funding dispute forced the Supreme Court to decide how far the government could go in limiting the activities of private organizations that receive federal financial assistance. The Court's ruling upholding curbs on abortion counseling by family planning clinics also had broader implications in other federally subsidized areas, including the arts.

Congress in 1970 decided to provide federal assistance to family planning clinics, but Title X of the Public Health Services Act stipulated that none of the funds appropriated under the law could be used in "programs where abortion is a method of family planning." Many of the clinics to receive federal funds were run by Planned Parenthood, an organization that provided contraceptive services and lobbied and litigated for abortion rights.

In 1988 the Reagan administration used Title X's language to issue regulations through the Department of Health and Human Services (HHS) that prohibited family planning clinics that were federally funded from engaging in abortion counseling or referrals—even on request from a patient. Any clinic receiving federal funds could provide abortion-related services only through a "physically and financially separate" organization.

Abortion rights advocates strongly opposed the regulations, which they called a "gag rule." Family planning clinics and physicians filed several suits in federal court claiming that the regulations went beyond Title X's statutory language or that they violated the First Amendment. The regulations were struck down by two federal appeals courts, but upheld by the U.S. Circuit Court of Appeals in New York.

The Court rejected both the statutory and constitutional challenges. On the statutory issue, Chief Justice Rehnquist said the regulations were a "plausible construction" of an ambiguous statute—and more consistent with the statute than previous rules requiring clinics to tell pregnant women about abortion.

As to the First Amendment issue, Rehnquist began by saying that government had broad discretion in deciding what programs or activities to subsidize or not. "The government may make a value judgment favoring childbirth over abortion," Rehnquist wrote, and "implement that judgment by the allocation of public funds." Rehnquist said the clinic staff members' "freedom of expression" was limited only while working for the project. "This limitation is a consequence of their decision to accept employment," he said. As for the clinics, Rehnquist said the regulations "do not force the recipients to give up abortion-related speech; they merely require that the grantee keep such activities separate and distinct" from the funded programs.

In dissent, Justice Blackmun attacked the ruling both on statutory and constitutional grounds. He said the ruling was the first ever to uphold "viewpoint-based suppression of speech solely because it is imposed on those dependent upon the government" for funds. Blackmun, author of the Court's landmark abortion rights ruling ***Roe v. Wade,*** 410 U.S. 113 (1973), also said the regulations amounted to "the deliberate manipulation by the Government of the dialogue between a woman and her physician."

Justice O'Connor voted to strike down the regulations on statutory grounds without reaching the constitutional issue.

See Dorothy E. Roberts, "*Rust v. Sullivan* and the Control of Knowledge," *George Washington Law Review* 61 (March 1993): 587–656.

Edmonson v. Leesville Concrete Co.

500 U.S. 614 (1991)
Decided: June 3, 1991
Vote: 6 (B. White, T. Marshall, Blackmun, Stevens, Kennedy, Souter)
3 (Rehnquist, O'Connor, Scalia)
Opinion of the Court: Kennedy
Dissenting opinion: O'Connor (Rehnquist, Scalia)
Dissenting opinion: Scalia

Thaddeus Donald Edmonson, an African American construction worker, was injured in a job-site accident in Fort Polk, Louisiana, and sued Leesville Concrete Company for negligence. During jury selection, Leesville used two of its three peremptory challenges authorized by statute to strike black persons from the prospective jury. For criminal and civil trials, both parties are allowed a certain number of peremptory jury challenges, which permit potential jurors to be dismissed without reason. Edmonson asked the district court judge to demand that Leesville give an explanation for dismissing the two blacks. The judge denied the request, saying that

Batson v. Kentucky, 476 U.S. 79 (1986), in which the Court ruled that prosecutors in a criminal case may not use peremptory challenges to remove a prospective juror on the basis of race, did not apply in civil proceedings. The court of appeals similarly held that a private party in a civil case need not be accountable for rejecting jurors on the basis of race.

The Supreme Court disagreed. In a decision that broadened *Batson,* the Court ruled that potential jurors in civil cases cannot be rejected because of race. The majority said that jury selection in a private lawsuit is subject to the Constitution's guarantee of equal protection of the laws because the government participates significantly in peremptory challenges and civil litigation generally.

For the majority, Justice Kennedy acknowledged that the conduct of private parties usually is outside the scope of the Constitution. But he said race-based peremptory challenges in civil action constitute "state action" for protection under the Equal Protection Clause of the Fourteenth Amendment. "Racial bias mars the integrity of the judicial system and prevents the idea of democratic government from becoming a reality," Kennedy said.

In dissent, Justice O'Connor said race discrimination in peremptory challenges was "abhorrent," but the guarantee of equal protection in jury selection did not extend to disputes between private parties. "The government is not responsible for everything that occurs in a courtroom," she said. "The government is not responsible for a peremptory challenge by a private litigant."

Justice Scalia dissented separately to complain about the majority's interpretation of state action doctrine and its conferral of additional responsibility on judges overseeing jury selection. "Yet another complexity is added to an increasingly Byzantine system of justice that devotes more and more of its energy to sideshows and less and less to the merits of the case."

See Bill K. Felty, "Resting in Mid-Air, the Supreme Court Strikes the Traditional Peremptory Challenge and Creates a New Creature, the Challenge for Semi-Cause: *Edmonson v. Leesville Concrete Company,*" *Tulsa Law Journal* 27 (1991): 203.

Masson v. New Yorker Magazine

501 U.S. 496 (1991)
Decided: June 20, 1991
Vote: 7 (Rehnquist, T. Marshall, Blackmun, Stevens, O'Connor, Kennedy, Souter)
2 (B. White, Scalia)
Opinion of the Court: Kennedy
Dissenting opinion: B. White (Scalia)

Jeffrey M. Masson worked as a projects director at the Sigmund Freud Archives outside London starting in 1980. In 1981 he gave a lecture in which he depicted Freud's theories and his character in a negative manner, leading the archives board to terminate his employment. Janet Malcolm, a freelance writer, interviewed him and several other people for a two-part article for the *New Yorker* magazine, on his experience at the archives. After the article was finished, one of the magazine's fact-checkers called Masson to verify the accuracy of some quotes. He immediately protested that he had been misquoted, and, despite assurances that errors would be corrected, the article ran at the end of 1983 as originally written. The following year it was published as a book. Masson brought an action for libel against the author, the magazine, and the book publisher. Finding that the allegedly fabricated quotations were either substantially true or were rational interpretations of ambiguous conversations, the district court granted summary judgment for the author, magazine, and book publisher, on the grounds that Masson was a public figure and so could win only if he could show that Malcolm and the publishers had acted with actual malice.

The Supreme Court reversed. All nine justices agreed that with respect to the quotations, the case should have gone to a jury to determine actual malice. Seven of the justices believed that a deliberate alteration of words uttered by a public figure does not by itself meet the standard for malice set forth in ***New York Times v. Sullivan,*** 376 U.S. 254 (1964), namely, that the changes made in the quotation constituted reckless disregard for the truth or publishing something that was known to be false.

Justice White agreed with most of the opinion, but differed over how to define the actual malice standard of *New York Times.* He and Justice Scalia believed that a deliberate falsification of words was adequate to meet the test.

By itself, the case broke no new ground, but it did continue the Court's work in refining the standards set down three decades earlier in *New York Times v. Sullivan.* By refusing to allow trial judges to grant summary judgment when it could be shown that some falsification had taken place, and by requiring that the determination of malice be made by a jury, in some ways the Court loosened the standard of *New York Times,* and brought in the vagaries of jury fact-finding. In some cases, a sympathetic plaintiff or an unsympathetic defendant might lead a jury to find actual malice when a judge might not. The press saw this possibility as a bad omen.

See Erin Daly, "The Incremental Harm Doctrine: Is There Life after Masson?" *Arkansas Law Review* 46 (1993): 371; and Richard T. Kaltenbach, "Fabricated Quotes and the Actual Malice Standard: *Masson v. New Yorker Magazine,*" *Catholic University Law Review* 41 (1992): 745.

Barnes v. Glen Theatre, Inc.

501 U.S. 560 (1991)
Decided: June 21, 1991
Vote: 5 (Rehnquist, O'Connor, Scalia, Kennedy, Souter)
4 (B. White, T. Marshall, Blackmun, Stevens)
Judgment of the Court: Rehnquist
Opinion concurring in judgment: Scalia
Opinion concurring in judgment: Souter
Dissenting opinion: B. White (T. Marshall, Blackmun, Stevens)

An Indiana statute outlawed appearing in a public place "in a state of nudity," and, as the law applied to entertainment, female dances had to wear at least pasties over their nipples and a G-string in the pubic area. Two bars wanted to provide totally nude dancing as entertainment for their clients and, along with several individual dancers, brought suit against Michael Barnes, the prosecuting attorney for St. Joseph County, Indiana, claiming that the antinudity statute violated the First Amendment's protection of free expression. After several bouts in the lower courts, some of which found nude dancing to be protected expression and others that did not, the case came to the Supreme Court.

Although the Court was unable to agree on an opinion, five justices agreed that the Indiana law prohibiting nude dancing performed as entertainment did not violate the First Amendment. Chief Justice Rehnquist, joined only by Justices O'Connor and Kennedy, found nude dancing as entertainment to be expressive conduct only at the outer limits of the First Amendment. As such, Indiana could regulate nude dancing, despite the incidental restrictions on some expressive activity, under the state's police powers. The statute aimed to protect morals and public order and thus furthered a substantial government interest. This interest in public order and morality had no bearing on free expression because the law did not outlaw dancing, but nudity, and the requirement that the dancers not be nude was narrowly tailored to achieve the state's purpose. The law met traditional First Amendment scrutiny in that it was content-neutral, served an overriding government interest, and was narrowly tailored.

Justice Scalia would have denied any First Amendment protection to nude dancing. In his opinion, the law did not have to meet a strict scrutiny standard, but only the simple rational basis test. Moral opposition to public nudity supplied a rational basis for the statute's prohibition.

Justice Souter said that because nude dancing carried an endorsement of erotic experience, it was expressive activity subject to a degree of First Amendment protection. He differed from the chief justice primarily in how much First Amendment protection he would give to nude dancing, but believed the analysis used for the police power in this instance worked well.

Justice White argued that the Indiana statute should have been held invalid as applied to nonobscene nude dancing performed as entertainment, because such dancing has First Amendment protection. Applying the standard strict scrutiny analysis, the dissenters found the statute discriminated on the basis of content (nude versus "clothed" dancing), was overly broad, and not narrowly drawn.

The reasons for the Court's acceptance of this case for review are not easy to understand, except to settle the confusion in the lower courts. Some libertarians found the decision to be harmful to free speech, but most commentators thought the question of G-strings and pasties might better have been left to local standards.

A decade later, the Court reaffirmed the ruling in a slightly less fractured decision, *City of Erie v. Pap's A. M.*, 529 U.S. 277 (2000). Justice O'Connor wrote for a five-justice majority in holding that the state's interest in combating "the negative secondary effects associated with adult entertainment establishments" justified a ban on nude dancing.

See Timothy M. Tesluk, "*Barnes v. Glen Theatre:* Censorship? So What?" *Case Western Reserve Law Review* 42 (1992): 1103.

Cohen v. Cowles Media Co.

501 U.S. 663 (1991)
Decided: June 24, 1991
Vote: 5 (Rehnquist, B. White, Stevens, Scalia, Kennedy)
4 (T. Marshall, Blackmun, O'Connor, Souter)
Opinion of the Court: B. White
Dissenting opinion: Blackmun (T. Marshall, Souter)
Dissenting opinion: Souter (T. Marshall, Blackmun, O'Connor)

The dispute at the heart of this case arose from the 1982 Minnesota gubernatorial race, in which Dan Cohen, a Republican political consultant, offered to turn over to reporters damaging information, stemming from two minor criminal charges, about the Democratic candidate for lieutenant governor. After he was assured anonymity, Cohen gave the information to reporters from the *St. Paul Pioneer Press Dispatch* and the *Minneapolis Star and Tribune.* Despite the reporters' promises, the two newspapers printed Cohen's name, believing he was part of a smear campaign. Cohen was immediately fired from his advertising agency job. He sued the newspapers, alleging fraudulent misrepresentation and breach of contract.

A state jury awarded him $200,000 in compensatory damages and $500,000 in punitive damages. The state court of appeals affirmed, but the Minnesota Supreme Court reversed, holding that a contract cause of action was inappropriate and that the enforcement of confidentiality under promissory estoppel (a doctrine that prevents one who promises something to another from denying the existence of the promise if the other reasonably and foreseeably relies on it and acts on it) would violate the newspapers' First Amendment rights.

The Supreme Court disagreed. In ruling that the First Amendment does not bar action for a broken contract, the Court said any resulting constraint on truthful reporting "is no more than the incidental, and constitutionally insignificant, consequence of applying to the press a generally applicable law that requires those who make certain kinds of promises to keep them." Justice White, writing for the majority, dismissed arguments that the ruling would cause the media not to disclose a confidential source's identity—even when it is newsworthy—to avoid lawsuit. Underlying the ruling was the assumption that newspapers have no special immunity from the application of general laws.

In dissent, Justice Blackmun argued that the Court should have applied the standard used in ***Hustler Magazine, Inc. v. Falwell,*** 485 U.S. 46 (1988), in which the Court said the use of a claim of intentional infliction of emotional distress for the publication of a parody violated the First Amendment. As in that case, Blackmun said, a generally applied law that would suppress speech must meet a strict test.

In the main dissent, Justice Souter argued that a law of general applicability affecting free speech rights must be balanced with an interest in a free press and an informed public. He said the state's interest in enforcing a newspaper's promise of confidentiality did not sufficiently outweigh an interest in unrestricted publication of campaign information.

See Elliot C. Rothenberg, *The Taming of the Press:* Cohen v. Cowles Media Company (Westport, Conn.: Praeger Publishers, 1999).

Payne v. Tennessee

501 U.S. 808 (1991)
Decided: June 27, 1991
Vote: 6 (Rehnquist, B. White, O'Connor, Scalia, Kennedy, Souter)
3 (T. Marshall, Blackmun, Stevens)
Opinion of the Court: Rehnquist
Concurring opinion: O'Connor (B. White, Kennedy)
Concurring opinion: Scalia (O'Connor, Kennedy)
Concurring opinion: Souter (Kennedy)
Dissenting opinion: T. Marshall (Blackmun)
Dissenting opinion: Stevens (Blackmun)

Pervis Tyrone Payne was convicted by a Tennessee jury of the murders of a woman and her two-year-old daughter and of assault with intent to murder her three-year-old son. During his sentencing hearing, the murdered woman's mother testified that the boy missed his mother and baby sister, and the prosecutor commented on the continuing effects on the son of his experience and the effects of the crimes on the surviving family.

Payne was sentenced to death. The Tennessee Supreme Court affirmed the conviction and sentence, rejecting the defendant's contention that the grandmother's testimony and the state's closing argument constituted prejudicial violations of his rights under the Eighth Amendment.

In his appeal to the U.S. Supreme Court, Payne revived concerns from *Booth v. Maryland,* 482 U.S. 496 (1987), and *South Carolina v. Gathers,* 490 U.S. 805 (1989), that the admission of victim-impact evidence allows a jury to find that a defendant whose victim was an asset to the community should be punished more severely than someone who murders a less-praiseworthy victim. Payne also argued that, despite any problems with the rules of *Booth* and *Gathers,* the Court should follow the doctrine of *stare decisis* and leave those decisions alone.

The Supreme Court upheld the conviction and death sentence and overruled *Booth* and *Gathers.* The majority said the Eighth Amendment, which bans cruel and unusual punishment, does not bar a capital sentencing jury from considering information about victims. In his opinion for the Court, Chief Justice Rehnquist first responded that *stare decisis* "promotes the evenhanded, predictable and consistent development of legal principles, fosters reliance on judicial decisions and contributes to the actual and perceived integrity of the judicial process." He then added:

> *Stare decisis* is not an inexorable command; rather, it is a principle of policy and not a mechanical formula of adherence to the latest decision. This is particularly true in constitutional cases, because in such cases correction through legislative action is practically impossible.

Rehnquist added that victim-impact evidence is merely another way of generally informing the court about the specific harm caused by a crime. He also said an inherent unfairness existed in allowing testimony about the defendant's character, but not about the victim's.

Justice O'Connor wrote a concurring opinion that played up state authority to determine capital sentencing proceedings. She also detailed the brutality of the killings and questioned how the testimony from the grandmother possibly could have inflamed the jury more than the information that the victims died after repeated thrusts from a butcher knife.

In dissent, Justice Stevens argued that the majority's ruling would encourage jurors to decide in favor of death instead of life imprisonment on the basis of emotions, not reason. Noting the victims' rights movement and the current popularity of capital punishment in a crime-ridden society, Stevens said it was a "great tragedy" that the Court bowed to public opinion: "Today is a sad day for a great institution."

In another dissent, Justice Marshall lashed out at the Court for turning its back on precedent. "The implications of this radical new exception to the doctrine of *stare decisis* are staggering," Justice Marshall wrote. "The majority today sends a clear signal that scores of established constitutional liberties are now ripe for reconsideration, thereby inviting the very type of open defiance of our precedents that the majority rewards in this case." He said the value of victim-impact evidence is always outweighed by its prejudicial effect because of its inherent power to divert the jury from the character of the defendant.

See David D. Friedman, "Should the Characteristics of Victims and Criminals Count? *Payne v. Tennessee* and Two Views of Efficient Punishment," *Boston College Law Review* 34 (July 1993): 731.

Simon & Schuster, Inc. v. Members of New York State Crime Victims Board

502 U.S. 105 (1991)
Decided: December 10, 1991
Vote: 8 (Rehnquist, B. White, Blackmun, Stevens, O'Connor, Scalia, Kennedy, Souter)
0
Opinion of the Court: O'Connor
Opinion concurring in judgment: Blackmun
Opinion concurring in judgment: Kennedy
Did not participate: Thomas

In an effort to prevent criminals from profiting from books or other accounts of their offenses, New York passed a law requiring that any royalties from such publications be turned over to the state's victim compensation board. In a unanimous ruling, the Court ruled that the law violated the First Amendment by imposing a financial burden on specific categories of speech without sufficient justification.

New York enacted the so-called "Son of Sam" law in 1977. The law took its popular name from a serial killer, David Berkowitz, who terrorized New York in 1977 and called himself "Son of Sam." The constitutional challenge to the law, however, involved another crime figure: Henry Hill, an admitted mobster who collaborated with author Nicholas Pileggi in the best-selling 1986 book *Wiseguy: Life in a Mafia Family.* (The book was turned into the acclaimed film "Goodfellas" four years later.)

When the New York State Crime Victims Board went after Hill's royalties, the publisher of the book, Simon and Schuster, challenged the law in federal court. A lower court ruled the law did not impinge on the First Amendment. A federal appeals court affirmed the decision, saying society had an interest in preventing criminals from profiting at the expense of their victims.

In striking down the law, the Supreme Court found that the law was not narrowly tailored to serve a concededly compelling interest in compensating victims of crime. Justice O'Connor began by saying the law was "presumptively inconsistent" with the First Amendment because it singled out a particular category of speech for financial penalty. To survive constitutional scrutiny, she said, the law must serve a compelling interest and be narrowly tailored to serve that interest.

Although the state's interest in compensating crime victims was legitimate, O'Connor said, the state had failed to explain why it had any greater interest in the proceeds from a criminal's "storytelling" than from any other income or assets. In addition, she said, the law was "significantly overinclusive." The law was so broadly written, she said, that it would apply to authors irrespective of whether they were ever accused or convicted of a crime. As one example, O'Connor posited an autobiography written at the end of a prominent figure's career that might include a brief recollection of a minor crime committed years earlier as a youthful prank. O'Connor noted that the ruling did not necessarily apply to laws passed by the federal government or other states with similar purposes but different provisions.

Justice Kennedy said he would strike down the law as "raw censorship" without considering the state's asserted justifications. Justice Blackmun said the Court should have given the states better guidance for writing valid laws.

Freeman v. Pitts

503 U.S. 467 (1992)
Decided: March 31, 1992
Vote: 8 (Rehnquist, B. White, Blackmun, Stevens, O'Connor, Scalia, Kennedy, Souter)
0
Opinion of the Court: Kennedy
Concurring opinion: Scalia
Concurring opinion: Souter
Opinion concurring in judgment: Blackmun (Stevens, O'Connor)
Did not participate: Thomas

While supervising a school desegregation plan, a district court has the authority to give up control of a school district in incremental stages before desegregation has been achieved in every area of school operations. The Supreme Court said a district court may decide not to order further remedies in areas where the school district is in compliance with the decree while at the same time retaining jurisdiction over the case. School districts under court supervision must take all necessary steps to become desegregated or "unitary." The Court also said the term *unitary* does not have a fixed meaning or content and does not confine a district court's discretion.

In this case involving Georgia schools, the Supreme Court also ruled that once the vestiges of de jure segregation have ended, school districts are not required to remedy racial disparities caused by demographic shifts.

See Bradley W. Joondeph, "Skepticism and School Desegregation," *Washington University Law Quarterly* 76 (spring 1998): 161–170.

Jacobson v. United States

503 U.S. 540 (1992)
Decided: April 6, 1992
Vote: 5 (B. White, Blackmun, Stevens, Souter, Thomas)
4 (Rehnquist, O'Connor, Scalia, Kennedy)
Opinion of the Court: B. White
Dissenting opinion: O'Connor (Rehnquist, Scalia, Kennedy)

This case began in February 1984, when Keith Jacobson ordered two issues of a magazine called *Bare Boys,* which contained photographs of nude preteens and teenagers. Although those purchases were legal at the time, Jacobson's name ended up on a bookstore mailing list that government agents acquired. Starting in January 1985 and for the next two and a half years, agents from the Postal Service and Customs Service tried to persuade him to buy more child pornography as part of sting operations. Eventually, he ordered a magazine,

Boys Who Love Boys, which showed young boys engaged in sexual activities.

Jacobson was indicted for violating a provision of the Child Protection Act of 1984. He claimed he had been entrapped and testified that he had not expected to receive photographs of minor boys. A jury found him guilty, and a federal appeals court affirmed the ruling.

The Supreme Court reversed the conviction. For the majority, Justice White said that prosecutors did not prove that Jacobson would have ordered the second magazine if not for government pressure. "In their zeal to enforce the law . . . government agents may not originate a criminal design, implant in an innocent person's mind the disposition to commit a criminal act, and then induce commission of the crime so that the government may prosecute," he said. White continued:

> Had the agents in this case simply offered [Jacobson] the opportunity to order child pornography through the mails, and [Jacobson]—who must be presumed to know the law—had promptly availed himself of this criminal opportunity, it is unlikely that his entrapment defense would have warranted a jury instruction. But that is not what happened here. By the time [he] finally placed his order, he had already been the target of 26 months of repeated mailings and communications from government agents and fictitious organizations.

White noted that some of the government's enticing letters referred to the need to keep pornography free from censorship. Jacobson could have corresponded with the undercover agents simply out of a desire to fight censorship and preserve individual rights, White said.

In dissent, Justice O'Connor noted that both times that Jacobson was offered child pornography, he bought it. "He needed no government agent to coax, threaten or persuade him; no one played on his sympathies, friendship, or suggested that his committing the crime would further a greater good."

See Elena Luisa Garella, "Reshaping the Federal Entrapment Defense: *Jacobson v. United States,*" *Washington Law Review* 68 (1993): 185.

Lujan v. Defenders of Wildlife

504 U.S. 555 (1992)
Decided: June 12, 1992
Vote: 7 (Rehnquist, B. White, Stevens, Scalia, Kennedy, Souter, Thomas)
2 (Blackmun, O'Connor)
Judgment of the Court: Scalia
Opinion concurring in judgment: Kennedy (Souter)
Opinion concurring in judgment: Stevens
Dissenting opinion: Blackmun (O'Connor)

The Endangered Species Act requires each federal agency to consult with the secretary of the interior to ensure that actions by the agency do not jeopardize any endangered or threatened species. In 1978 the Fish and Wildlife Service and the National Marine Fisheries Service, on behalf of the secretary of the interior and the secretary of commerce, respectively, promulgated a joint regulation stating that the obligations imposed by the act extended to actions taken in foreign nations. In 1986 a revised regulation required consultation only for actions taken in the United States or on the high seas and excluded actions taken in foreign nations. Several environmental and conservation organizations filed suit against Secretary of the Interior Manuel Lujan Jr., seeking to have the new regulation declared invalid and the old one reinstated. The secretary sought a summary judgment to have the suit dismissed, claiming that because the groups would suffer no ill effects from the regulation, they had no standing to sue. Lujon lost in the lower court and appealed to the Supreme Court.

The Court reversed, agreeing with Lujan. Justice Scalia ruled that the organizations could not validly assert standing because neither they nor any of their members could show actual or potential harm. The Court also rejected three "nexus" theories: an "ecosystem nexus" theory, under which any person who uses any part of a contiguous ecosystem adversely affected by a funded activity would have standing to challenge that activity, even if the activity was located a great distance away; an "animal nexus" approach, whereby anyone who has an interest in studying or seeing endangered animals anywhere on the globe would have standing to challenge a federal decision that threatens such animals; and a "vocational nexus" approach, under which anyone with a professional interest in such animals would have standing to sue. Four members of the majority—Scalia, Chief Justice Rehnquist, and Justices White and Thomas—also believed that the suits should have failed because the organizations could not show any injury that might have been addressed by remedies available to a federal court.

Justice Blackmun disagreed. He believed that the organizations did have standing because they had shown actual and potential injury to themselves, to their neighbors, and to the ecosystem. Plaintiffs attempting to protect the environment ought not have to show the same kind of specific injuries normally required to justify standing in a suit against the government.

See Harold Feld, "Saving the Citizen Suit: The Effect of *Lujan* and the Role of Citizen Suits in Environmental Enforcement," *Columbia Journal of Environmental Law* 19 (1994): 141; and Ike C. Sugg, "Caught in the Act: Evaluating the Endangered Species Act, Its Effects on Man and the Prospect of Reform," *Cumberland Law Review* 24 (1994): 1.

United States v. Alvarez-Machain

504 U.S. 655 (1992)
Decided: June 15, 1992
Vote: 6 (Rehnquist, B. White, Scalia, Kennedy, Souter, Thomas)
3 (Blackmun, Stevens, O'Connor)
Opinion of the Court: Rehnquist
Dissenting opinion: Stevens (Blackmun, O'Connor)

Humberto Alvarez-Machain was a citizen and resident of Mexico. In April 1990, under the direction of U.S. officials, he was abducted from his home in Guadalajara, Mexico, and flown by private plane to Texas, where he was arrested. He was then indicted for participating in the kidnapping and murder of Enrique Camarena-Salazar, a Drug Enforcement Administration (DEA) special agent, and Alfredo Zavala-Avelar, a Mexican pilot working with Camarena-Salazar.

A district court dismissed the indictment, concluding that the kidnapping violated the extradition treaty between the United States and Mexico. The court ordered Alvarez-Machain returned to Mexico. A federal appeals court affirmed, noting that the United States had authorized the abduction and that the Mexican government had protested the treaty violation.

The Supreme Court ruled that the treaty, signed in 1978, said nothing about either country refraining from forcibly abducting people from their homelands or the consequences if an abduction occurred. Furthermore, Chief Justice Rehnquist wrote, general principles of international law offer no basis for interpreting the treaty to include an implication against international abductions.

The majority acknowledged that the abduction might have been "shocking" and "in violation of general international law principles," but it did not violate the extradition treaty. "Mexico has protested the abduction of respondent through diplomatic notes, and the decision of whether respondent should be returned to Mexico, as a matter outside of the Treaty, is a matter for the Executive Branch," Rehnquist wrote. "We conclude, however, that respondent's abduction was not in violation of the Extradition Treaty between the United States and Mexico. . . . The fact of respondent's forcible abduction does not therefore prohibit his trial in a court in the United States for violations of the criminal laws of the United States."

Justice Stevens scoffed at the notion that the absence of any express language in the treaty dictated its terms on abductions. "If the United States, for example, thought it more expedient to torture or simply to execute a person rather than to attempt extradition, these options would be equally available because they, too, were not explicitly prohibited by the Treaty." He called such an interpretation "highly improbable."

See Charles Doyle, "Kidnapping as an Alternative to Extradition: A Matter of Executive Branch Discretion: *United States v. Alvarez-Machain,*" *Congressional Research Service,* June 26, 1992; and Derek C. Smith, "Beyond Indeterminacy and Self-Contradiction in Law: Transnational Abductions and Treaty Interpretation in *U.S. v. Alvarez-Machain,*" *European Journal of International Law* 6 (1995): 1.

New York v. United States

505 U.S. 144 (1992)
Decided: June 19, 1992
Vote: 6 (Rehnquist, O'Connor, Scalia, Kennedy, Thomas, Souter)
3 (B. White, Blackmun, Stevens)
Opinion of the Court: O'Connor
Dissenting opinion: B. White (Blackmun, Stevens)
Dissenting opinion: Stevens

The safe disposal of radioactive waste, whether from reactors or medical laboratories, was a problem for some states. In 1980 Congress enacted the Low-Level Radioactive Waste Policy Act, which spelled out a scheme to solve the problem. "Sited" states—that is, states having low-level radioactive waste disposal sites—agreed to extend by seven years the period in which they would accept waste from "unsited" states, and the unsited states agreed to end their reliance on the sited states by 1992. Congress also provided various monetary incentives so that unsited states could make the necessary arrangements before the end of the time period. Moreover, any state that failed to make the arrangements had to "take title" of the radioactive waste generated within its borders by private facilities and be responsible for any damages resulting from the state's failure to arrange for safe disposal.

New York and two of its counties sought a declaratory judgment that the act violated the Constitution's Tenth Amendment and the Guarantee Clause (Article IV, Section 4), which guaranteed to the states a republican form of government. The district court dismissed the suit, and the court of appeals affirmed the dismissal.

The Supreme Court affirmed in part and reversed in part. The entire Court held that the "monetary incentive" provisions were not inconsistent with the Tenth Amendment, because they were a proper exercise of Congress's authority under the Constitution's Commerce Clause. It also held that the provisions urging the states to provide access to each other for site disposal did not violate the Tenth Amendment, but rather represented a conditional exercise of Congress's commerce power, following a long line of cases going back to ***Massachusetts v. Mellon,*** 262 U.S. 447 (1923).

Six members of the Court found the "take title" provision unconstitutional, either as lying outside Congress's enumerated powers or as violating the Tenth Amendment, because such an instruction to state governments to take title to waste, standing alone, would be beyond the authority of Congress, and remained so even with the monetary incentives attached.

Justice White, joined by Justices Blackmun and Stevens, dissented from the latter conclusion because, in his view, the agreement represented a compact among the states, and neither the Constitution nor the Court's own precedents supported the notion that Congress cannot directly compel states to enact and enforce federal regulatory programs.

The case was one of the first in which a majority of the Rehnquist Court began asserting the belief that states' rights had been forgotten for too long and that, in order to revive the concept of federalism, congressional power not directly authorized had to be limited.

See Deborah M. Mostaghel, "The Low-Level Radioactive Waste Policy Amendments Act: An Overview," *DePaul Law Journal* 43 (1994): 379; and Richard E. Levy, "*New York v. United States:* An Essay on the Uses and Misuses of Precedent, History and Policy in Determining the Scope of Federal Power," *Kansas Law Review* 41 (1993): 493.

R. A. V. v. City of St. Paul

505 U.S. 377 (1992)
Decided: June 22, 1992
Vote: 9 (Rehnquist, B. White, Blackmun, Stevens, O'Connor, Scalia, Kennedy, Souter, Thomas)
0
Opinion of the Court: Scalia
Opinion concurring in judgment: B. White (Blackmun, Stevens, O'Connor)
Opinion concurring in judgment: Blackmun
Opinion concurring in judgment: Stevens (B. White, Blackmun)

Early one morning in June 1990, R. A. V. and several other teenagers burned a cross in the front yard of a black family who had recently moved into their neighborhood. Although burning the cross violated several state and municipal ordinances, the city's district attorney chose to prosecute R. A. V. under the St. Paul Bias-Motivated Crime Ordinance, which criminalized cross burnings and other actions that would offend people "on the basis of race, color, creed, religion or gender." After his conviction, R. A. V. challenged the law as unconstitutionally overbroad and one that impermissibly discriminated on the basis of content. The state's highest court dismissed the challenge, and the Supreme Court reversed.

In some ways, Justice Scalia's opinion for the majority, followed fairly standard First Amendment jurisprudence. The state, in limiting or penalizing speech, cannot discriminate on the basis of content. Even views that are disagreeable, that are racially offensive, are entitled to First Amendment protection. Scalia made it clear that the Court did not approve of cross-burning, and, even if one treated the act as a form of expression, it could have been prosecuted under other laws, such as the state statute against terrorist threats. But the St. Paul ordinance clearly aimed at expression, thereby violating the First Amendment.

The more interesting issue is what, if anything, remained of the "fighting words" doctrine. In ***Chaplinsky v. New Hampshire,*** 315 U.S. 568 (1942), the Court held that words that would instigate another person to fight remained outside the protection of the First Amendment. The Minnesota Supreme Court upheld the St. Paul statute on the ground that cross-burning constituted the type of "fighting words" that the state could control. Although the Court went out of its way to avoid directly overturning *Chaplinsky,* the results of *R. A. V.* would seem to indicate that the fighting words doctrine is no longer part of First Amendment jurisprudence.

A few years later, in ***Wisconsin v. Mitchell,*** 508 U.S. 476 (1993), the Court upheld a state law that imposed heavier penalties for crimes that, when committed, had a racial basis, on the ground that the law had always taken aggravating factors into account when assessing penalties for crimes.

See Edward J. Cleary, *Beyond the Burning Cross: The First Amendment and the Landmark R. A. V. Case* (New York: Random House, 1994); and Akhil Reed Amar, "The Case of the Missing Amendments: *R. A. V. v. City of St. Paul,*" *Harvard Law Review* 106 (1992): 124.

Lee v. Weisman

505 U.S. 577 (1992)
Decided: June 24, 1992
Vote: 5 (Blackmun, Stevens, O'Connor, Kennedy, Souter)
4 (Rehnquist, B. White, Scalia, Thomas)
Opinion of the Court: Kennedy
Concurring opinion: Blackmun (Stevens, O'Connor)
Concurring opinion: Souter (Stevens, O'Connor)
Dissenting opinion: Scalia (Rehnquist, B. White, Thomas)

When Daniel Weisman's older daughter graduated from Nathan Bishop Middle School in Providence, Rhode Island, a Christian clergyman gave the traditional invocation and benediction. The Weismans objected at that time on the grounds that the First Amendment's Establishment Clause, as well as Supreme Court decisions such as ***Engel v. Vitale,*** 370 U.S. 421 (1962), forbade such prayers. When it came time for the Weisman's younger daughter, Deborah, to graduate from the same school in June 1989, the principal of the school, Robert E. Lee, attempted to forestall a similar complaint by inviting Rabbi Leslie Gutterman to deliver the prayers. Rabbi Gutterman prepared the invocation and benediction according to guidelines prepared by the National Conference of Christians and Jews that emphasized inclusiveness and sensitivity in place of sectarian religiosity. Lee was under the impression that Weisman only objected to the fact that a Christian minister had given the prayers, but, in fact, Weisman believed in a strict separation of church and state, and this time he filed suit to enjoin the prayers. The local court refused on the grounds that it lacked adequate time to consider the merits. After appropriate appeals, in which the lower courts disagreed on both the results and the reasoning, the Supreme Court agreed to take the case.

Ever since *Engel,* conservative groups had been working to overturn the decision that held that school-sponsored prayers in public schools violated the Establishment Clause. During the 1980s the Reagan appointees to the Court indicated that they would be willing to reverse *Engel,* but they could never command a majority. When this case came up, conservatives believed their time had come, assuming that Chief Justice Rehnquist and Justices O'Connor, Scalia, Kennedy, and Thomas would join with Justice White to form a 6–3 majority. O'Connor was not happy with *Engel*'s reasoning, but she had developed her own views that supported its results. Any activity, such as required or sponsored prayers, that made a person or group feel like an outsider, ran afoul of the First Amendment. Kennedy was willing to allow some accommodation, but he also believed in the general idea of separation. Along with Justice Souter, they formed a centrist block on the Court that foiled efforts to reverse *Engel.*

The reasoning of the Court relied primarily on *Engel,* although modified by time and later cases. The basic ruling was that any time clergy offered prayers as part of an official school ceremony, such as a graduation, it violated the First Amendment Establishment Clause. Because officials of the state direct the graduation ceremony, which is usually a formal occasion, the Court rejected the argument that students may opt out of participating in the prayer by not attending. Parents and students have the right to attend an occasion that marks the successful conclusion of one stage of a student's schooling, and it is unfair to put the onus on those who are uncomfortable with the prayer to have to decide whether to attend. So long as the state sponsors the occasion, then a prayer at that function is unconstitutional.

Justice Scalia's opinion noted that prayers at graduation had long been part of the tradition of American public schooling, and as a result, should not be lightly discarded. He added substantial information on how prayer had been part of public school commencements ever since the founding of the Republic and therefore could not have been what the Framers meant by establishment.

In ***Santa Fe Independent School District v. Doe,*** 530 U.S. 290 (2000), the proponents of school prayer tried a different approach, claiming that if school prayer at football games were voluntary then it would escape the problem of mandatory prayer imposed on the students. The Court again struck down the prayer, claiming that attendance at the games was mandatory for some people.

See Suzanna Sherry, "*Lee v. Weisman:* Paradox Redux," *Supreme Court Review, 1992,* 125; and Alan E. Brownstein, "Prayer and Religious Expression at High School Graduation: Constitutional Etiquette in a Pluralistic Society," *Nexus* 5 (2000): 61.

Planned Parenthood of Southeastern Pennsylvania v. Casey

505 U.S. 833 (1992)
Decided: June 29, 1992
Vote: 5 (Blackmun, Stevens, O'Connor, Kennedy, Souter)
4 (Rehnquist, B. White, Scalia, Thomas)
Judgment of the Court: O'Connor, Kennedy, Souter
Concurring opinion: Stevens
Opinion concurring in judgment: Blackmun
Dissenting opinion: Rehnquist (B. White, Scalia, Thomas)
Dissenting opinion: Scalia (Rehnquist, B. White, Thomas)

Ever since the ruling in ***Roe v. Wade,*** 410 U.S. 113 (1973), abortion opponents had tried to get legislation enacted that would make it difficult, if not impossible, for a woman to secure an abortion. In the 1980s the Supreme Court began to allow some restrictions, and, with the appointment of conservative justices by Presidents Reagan and Bush, abortion opponents hoped that the time had come when the Court would overturn *Roe.* They fully expected that to happen when the Court granted certiorari to hear a challenge to a Pennsylvania statute.

The law seemed to include every restriction that abortion opponents could think of to burden the procedure to the point of making abortion an impossibility. The statute required minors to get parental consent and wives to notify their husbands before obtaining an abortion; doctors had to inform women about potential medical complications; women had to wait twenty-four hours after requesting an abortion before the procedure could be performed; and doctors had to adhere to onerous reporting requirements. The district court invalidated the law, but the Third Circuit Court of Appeals reinstated it and then declared that, contrary to *Roe,* abortion would no longer be considered a fundamental right. As a result, the court would accept any restrictions that the legislature thought reasonable.

On the surface, the Supreme Court upheld the court of appeals by sustaining most of the restrictions, but in its reasoning the majority reaffirmed the "essential holding" of *Roe.* Justices O'Connor, Kennedy, and Souter took the unusual step of coauthoring an opinion, in which Justices Blackmun and Stevens joined in part. The majority reaffirmed three components of *Roe*: (1) the right of a woman to choose to have an abortion before viability and to obtain it without undue interference from the state; (2) the state's power to restrict abortion after viability, providing the law contains exceptions for pregnancies that endanger the woman's life; and (3) the state's legitimate interests "from the outset of pregnancy in protecting the health of the woman and the life of the fetus that may become a child." According to the three coauthors, "These principles do not contradict one another, and we adhere to each." The opinion did not, however, reaffirm the strict scrutiny standard that *Roe* had established for evaluating restrictions.

Unlike some earlier decisions that grounded the right to an abortion in privacy, the majority placed it within the liberty interest of the Fourteenth Amendment's Due Process Clause. Under this reasoning, a "realm of personal liberty" existed that the government may not enter, and this realm protected personal decisions related to marriage, procreation, conception, family relationships, and abortion.

The majority emphasized the concept of *stare decisis,* the respect given to prior decisions, and the need to make "legally principled decisions." But O'Connor, Kennedy, and Souter rejected what they considered *Roe*'s "elaborate but rigid" trimester framework. They also rejected the notion that a woman had an unfettered right to choose abortion without interference from the state. Rather, they said the states are free to enact a reasonable framework, in which a woman can "make a decision that has such profound and lasting meaning." Only when these laws "unduly burden" a woman's decision do they violate her personal liberty. By this standard, the majority upheld four of the five decisions, striking down only the requirement for spousal notification. The minority, while concurring in the judgment, dissented from the reaffirmation of *Roe,* which they would have abandoned.

The case seemed to protect *Roe,* at least for the foreseeable future. When Justice White, an opponent of *Roe,* retired, he was replaced by Justice Ginsburg; and Justice Breyer, also a supporter of a woman's right to choose, took Justice Blackmun's seat. During the remainder of the 1990s, Ginsburg and Breyer frequently joined Stevens, O'Connor, Kennedy, and Souter to form a centrist majority.

See Barbara Hinkson Craig and David O'Brien, *Abortion and American Politics* (Chatham, N.J.: Chatham House, 1993); Martha A. Field, "Abortion Law Today," *Journal of Legal Medicine* 14 (1993): 3; and Alan E. Brownstein, "How Rights Are Infringed: The Role of Undue Burden Analysis in Constitutional Doctrine," *Hastings Law Journal* 45 (1994): 867.

Lucas v. South Carolina Coastal Council

505 U.S. 1003 (1992)
Decided: June 29, 1992
Vote: 6 (Rehnquist, B. White, O'Connor, Scalia, Thomas, Kennedy)
3 (Blackmun, Stevens, Souter)
Opinion of the Court: Scalia
Concurring opinion: Kennedy
Dissenting opinion: Blackmun
Dissenting opinion: Stevens
Dissenting opinion: Souter

In 1986 David H. Lucas paid $975,000 for two beachfront lots, on which he intended to build single-family houses. Two years later, South Carolina passed the Beachfront Management Act, which, to protect the environment, barred anyone from building on designated types of waterfront property. A state court determined that the law made Lucas's parcels worthless. He sued the state on the grounds that the statute, by destroying all value in his property, constituted a taking of private property without just compensation, as prohibited by the Fifth and Fourteenth Amendments.

South Carolina passed its law in response to a federal statute that designated certain areas as a "coastal zone," worthy of preservation and protection. The law required anyone who wished to build on lots within the designated zones to obtain permits and to take steps to preserve the unique character of the area. The South Carolina Coastal Council was given the power to approve permits or deny them if, in its opinion, too much development had already occurred. The council drew a line on the landward side of Lucas's properties and prohibited all construction seaward of the line. The South Carolina courts found that a long line of cases stretching back to ***Mugler v. Kansas,*** 123 U.S. 623 (1887), allowed states to regulate property to prevent "harmful or noxious uses" without paying compensation under the Takings Clause.

In its first significant property rights case in nearly sixty years, the Supreme Court reversed, holding that the imposition of the environmental restrictions constituted a taking without compensation. Justice Scalia distinguished this case from the *Mugler* line by noting that in those cases the owners had not been allowed to use their land for purposes that were noxious or otherwise constituted a public nuisance, but were free to use it for other constructive purposes and realize the economic potential of the land. For example, they might not be able to build a slaughterhouse in an area, but could still erect an apartment complex. In this case, Lucas could do nothing with his land, and the state was depriving him of the $975,000 he had paid for it, as well as its economic potential.

Scalia went on, however, to essentially repudiate the *Mugler* line of cases, declaring that they were no more than the Court's early formulation of how the state police power could operate in controlling noxious land use. The problem was that the distinction between preventing harmful use and conferring benefits was difficult to make, and too many factors came into play to make any single rule the basis for interpreting the Takings Clause.

Courts needed to take into account the expectations of citizens as to what rights inhered in property and what powers the state had in limiting those rights. A potential buyer of land must be aware of existing strictures on its use, such as zoning regulations, but no one could be expected to predict that in the near future the state would enact new legislation prohibiting any use of the land. Compensation is not due when regulations merely make explicit restrictions already in effect, such as understandings about not using land in residential areas for commercial development. If new limits are placed, however, the state must make recompense.

The Court did not rule on the merits of the case. It remanded the issue to state courts for a rehearing in line with its new statement of how the Takings Clause operated. Lucas would still have to prove that the restrictions did in fact constitute a taking, and the state would be able to argue that he should have understood the type of restrictions that would be placed on waterfront property.

In dissent, Justices Blackmun and Stevens argued that this resurrection of private property rights would raise havoc not only with efforts to protect the environment but also with all zoning requirements. Justice Souter said that certiorari had been improvidently granted, and he would have deferred hearing the case until all of the issues had been settled in state court.

See John A. Humbach, "Evolving Thresholds of Nuisance and the Takings Clause," *Columbia Journal of Environmental Law* 18 (1993): 1; and Jed Rubenfeld, "Usings," *Yale Law Journal* 102 (1993): 1077.

Bray v. Alexandria Women's Health Clinic

506 U.S. 263 (1993)
Decided: January 13, 1993
Vote: 6 (Rehnquist, B. White, Scalia, Kennedy, Thomas, Souter)
3 (Blackmun, Stevens, O'Connor)
Opinion of the Court: Scalia
Concurring opinion: Kennedy
Concurring in judgment: Souter
Dissenting opinion: Stevens (Blackmun)
Dissenting opinion: O'Connor (Blackmun)

Beginning in the late 1980s, a militant antiabortion group calling itself Operation Rescue adopted the strategy of physically blocking the entrances to clinics where abortions were performed. Patients and clinic workers were harassed and taunted. Demonstrators sometimes forced their way into clinics and smashed equipment. Clinics often were forced to close.

Abortion rights groups responded by bringing trespassing or harassment charges in state courts against the participants in the blockades. When those efforts failed to slow the confrontations, however, they turned to an obscure legal weapon: an 1871 civil rights law that Congress passed to protect newly freed blacks from the Ku Klux Klan. The act authorized a civil suit in federal court against conspiracies aimed at "depriving . . . any person or class of persons of the equal protection of the laws" or "preventing or hindering [state or local authorities] from giving or securing to all persons . . . the equal protection of the laws."

The law was largely ignored after the Reconstruction era, but the Supreme Court, in *Griffin v. Breckenridge,* 403 U.S. 88 (1971), breathed new life into the statute by permitting its use in a case concerning a violent attack against civil rights workers in the South. To avoid a broad expansion of federal tort law, however, the Court limited the law to conspiracies motivated by "a class-based, invidiously discriminatory animus." A second limitation required that the conspiracies be aimed only at those rights that were protected from infringement by private individuals, such as the right to vote or the right to interstate travel.

Despite those limitations, abortion rights groups succeeded in using the law to win injunctions from several federal courts against blockades by Operation Rescue or other groups. Other federal courts, however, rejected such suits.

The Supreme Court agreed with the narrow view of the law. Women seeking abortions did not constitute a "class of persons" for purposes of the law, Justice Scalia said. Nor did the demonstrators' opposition to abortion reflect "an animus against women in general." "Opposition to voluntary abortion cannot possibly be considered . . . an irrational surrogate for opposition to (or paternalism towards) women," Scalia wrote. Moreover, Scalia said, the suit failed because the demonstrators' actions were not aimed at preventing women from traveling between states. The right to an abortion, he said, was not protected from infringement by individuals, as opposed to government action.

The Court did not rule on the applicability of the Klan Act's second provision—the "hindrance" or "prevention" clause. Scalia said the issue had not been properly raised in lower courts, but went on to say that such a claim also would require a racial or class-based motive.

Justice Souter said he would have preferred to remand the case for further hearings on the prevention clause. He said that provision could apply when a conspiracy was "intended to hobble or overwhelm" the ability of authorities to protect equal rights. Under that clause, Souter said, plaintiffs need not prove the conspiracy was motivated by racial or other class-based prejudice.

The dissenting justices took sharper issue with what Justice Stevens called the majority's "parsimonious interpretation of an important federal statute." Justice O'Connor complained that the majority had limited the law on the basis of a requirement not contained in the statute itself but imposed by a Court case a century later. "This case is not about abortion," O'Connor wrote. "Rather, this case is about whether a private conspiracy to deprive members of a protected class of legally protected interests gives rise to a federal cause of action. In my view, it does." Stevens and O'Connor said that either of the act's two clauses could be invoked against the blockades.

See Randolph M. McLaughlin, *"Bray v. Alexandria Women's Health Clinic:* The Supreme Court's Next Opportunity to Unsettle Civil Rights Law," *Tulane Law Review* 66 (1992): 1357.

Herrera v. Collins

506 U.S. 390 (1993)
Decided: January 25, 1993
Vote: 6 (Rehnquist, B. White, O'Connor, Scalia, Kennedy, Thomas)
3 (Blackmun, Stevens, Souter)
Opinion of the Court: Rehnquist
Concurring opinion: O'Connor (Kennedy)
Concurring opinion: Scalia (Thomas)
Opinion concurring in judgment: B. White
Dissenting opinion: Blackmun (Stevens, Souter)

The question of whether the Constitution permits the government to execute an innocent person was at issue in the case of a Texas prisoner, who, long after his 1982 conviction for killing a police officer, claimed that newly discovered evidence showed he was not guilty of the crime. Leonel Torres Herrera filed a petition for habeas corpus relief in 1992, seeking a hearing on the evidence and a stay of execution in the meantime.

A federal district court judge—acting out of what he called "a sense of fairness and due process"—granted Herrera's request, but the court of appeals ordered Herrera's petition dismissed. The appeals court said Herrera's claim of "actual innocence" did not entitle him to federal habeas relief unless he proved some other constitutional error in his state court proceedings.

The Supreme Court agreed. As Chief Justice Rehnquist described the case, Herrera had already pursued an array of challenges after a jury convicted him and sentenced him to death. The evidence at trial was strong: an eyewitness identification, blood stains on Herrera's belongings, and a letter by Herrera strongly implying he shot the officer because of a dispute over drug dealing. The next year, Herrera also pleaded guilty to killing a second officer in the incident.

Texas appellate courts affirmed the convictions in 1984. A federal habeas corpus petition also failed. In 1990 Herrera filed a habeas petition in state court claiming that new evidence showed that his brother, Raul Herrera Sr., had actually killed the first officer. Raul Herrera had died in 1984. The state court judge dismissed the petition, but in 1992 Herrera filed another habeas petition in federal court, with additional affidavits. The affidavit from Raul Herrera Jr. said he had seen his father kill the officer. Raul Jr. was nine at the time of the slaying.

Whatever weight the evidence carried, Herrera faced two legal hurdles. First, Texas's rules of criminal procedure required that new evidence be presented within thirty days after sentencing. Second, federal courts in habeas corpus cases normally do not consider questions of guilt or innocence, but only violations of constitutional rights in state courts.

In his opinion for the Court, Rehnquist, citing ***Townsend v. Sain,*** 372 U.S. 293 (1963), reiterated that federal habeas relief was limited to constitutional issues. He went on to say that none of the Court's death penalty cases applying the Eighth Amendment's ban on cruel and unusual punishment entitled Herrera to a new hearing on guilt or innocence either. Rehnquist also rejected Herrera's claim that Texas's thirty-day limit on new evidence violated the Fourteenth Amendment's Due Process Clause. He noted that the Supreme Court had set a two-year deadline for federal courts, while two-thirds of the states had limits of three years or under.

Moreover, Rehnquist said, Herrera could still seek a commutation of the sentence from the governor. "Executive clemency has provided the 'fail safe' in our criminal justice system," he wrote. Rehnquist ended by saying, "We may assume, for the sake of argument in deciding this case, that, in a capital case, a truly persuasive demonstration of 'actual innocence' made after trial would render the execution of a defendant unconstitutional, and warrant federal habeas relief if there were no state avenue open to process such a claim." But, he said, because of the "very disruptive effect" on state court systems, the threshold for such a showing "would necessarily be extraordinarily high." Herrera's evidence, he concluded, fell "far short."

Justice O'Connor said the Court was correct not to settle what she called the "difficult question" of whether a federal court could ever entertain a "convincing claim" of innocence. But Justice Scalia said the Court should have firmly shut the door to such claims. "There is no basis in text, tradition, or even in contemporary practice . . . for finding in the Constitution a right to demand judicial consideration of newly discovered evidence of innocence brought forward after conviction," Scalia wrote.

Justice White explicitly said that a "persuasive showing of actual innocence" would render a prisoner's execution unconstitutional. He said he would permit such a claim if the evidence showed that "no rational trier of fact" could have found the prisoner guilty, but he too said Herrera did not meet the test.

The dissenting justices argued that a condemned prisoner should be given a hearing if he could prove that he was "probably innocent." They also complained that the Court's ruling left the states "uncertain" about what postconviction procedures were required in capital cases.

Justice Blackmun's dissent ended with an especially blunt paragraph that Justices Stevens and Souter did not join. "Just as an execution without adequate safeguards is unacceptable, so, too, is an execution when the condemned prisoner can prove he is innocent," Blackmun declared. "The execution of a person who can show that he is innocent comes perilously close to simple murder."

In her written opinion, O'Connor answered that point with equal bluntness. Herrera, she said, "is not innocent, in any sense of the word."

Herrera was executed May 12, 1993.

See Kenneth Jost, "Rethinking the Death Penalty," *CQ Researcher,* November 16, 2001, 945–968.

Lamb's Chapel v. Center Moriches Union Free School District

508 U.S. 384 (1993)
Decided: June 7, 1993
Vote: 9 (Rehnquist, B. White, Blackmun, Stevens, O'Connor, Scalia, Kennedy, Souter, Thomas)
0
Opinion of the Court: B. White
Opinion concurring in judgment: Scalia (Thomas)
Opinion concurring in judgment: Kennedy

A dispute between a small evangelical Christian church and a school district in eastern Long Island, New York, over showing films about child-rearing issues produced a significant free speech victory for religious groups. The Supreme Court held that schools that allow after-hours use of their facilities by outside groups cannot prohibit use of the buildings for religious purposes.

In 1990 Lamb's Chapel asked the town of Center Moriches for permission to use school buildings after hours to show a six-part film series on family and child-rearing. The films consisted of lectures by the a prominent Christian commentator, Dr. James Dobson, advocating what he called a return to traditional Christian values instilled at an early age. The school board rejected the request on the basis of rules that permitted after-hours use of school buildings for social, civic, or recreational purposes, but specifically prohibited use by any group for religious purposes. A New York State law regulating use of school property also had been interpreted as barring meetings for religious purposes. Lamb's Chapel challenged the refusal in court, arguing that the school buildings were a "public forum" that must be open to all groups without discrimination. Two lower federal courts upheld the policy, ruling that public school buildings were a "limited public forum" that could be used only for designated purposes as long as the restrictions were reasonable and viewpoint-neutral.

The Supreme Court rejected that argument in a terse, twelve-page opinion. Justice White agreed that the schools did not have to be open for public meetings, but he said access rules could not discriminate on the basis of the identity or viewpoint of the speaker. "The principle that has emerged from our cases is that the First Amendment forbids the government to regulate speech in ways that favor some viewpoints or ideas at the expense of others," White said, quoting *City Council of Los Angeles v. Taxpayers for Vincent,* 466 U.S. 789 (1984). In this case, he said, Lamb's Chapel had been denied permission "solely because the film dealt with the subject from a religious viewpoint."

White also called "unfounded" the argument that permitting religious groups to use school property would be an unconstitutional establishment of religion. The showing of the film was not be sponsored by the school board and was to be open to the public, not just to church members, White said. On that basis, he concluded, the school board would not be seen as endorsing religion or as becoming too closely involved with religion.

The ruling left open the question whether religious groups could use school facilities for religious services. Lamb's Chapel had also been denied permission to conduct Sunday morning worship services, but it did not press that issue on appeal.

See Patrick Marshall, "Religion in Schools," *CQ Researcher,* January 12, 2001, 1–24.

Wisconsin v. Mitchell

508 U.S. 476 (1993)
Decided: June 11, 1993
Vote: 9 (Rehnquist, B. White, Blackmun, Stevens, O'Connor, Scalia, Kennedy, Souter, Thomas)
0
Opinion of the Court: Rehnquist

The United States in the 1980s experienced an apparent increase in assaults and other crimes against victims targeted because of their race, religion, ethnicity, or sexual orientation. In response, a majority of states passed laws providing for longer sentences in so-called "hate crime" cases. Wisconsin's hate crime law—similar to those in other states—provided for up to five years' additional imprisonment for an offender who intentionally selected his or her victim because of the person's "race, religion, color, disability, sexual orientation, national origin or ancestry."

Todd Mitchell was a black defendant convicted of assaulting a white teenager in Kenosha, Wisconsin, in 1989. Mitchell challenged the state law as unconstitutional after a judge increased the normal two-year sentence for aggravated battery to four years.

The Supreme Court rejected the challenge in a unanimous ruling that lifted a legal cloud over hate crime laws created by a Court decision just one year earlier. In ***R. A. V. v. St. Paul,*** 505 U.S. 377 (1992), the Court struck down a local ordinance that prohibited the use of "fighting words" that "insult or provoke violence" based on race, religion, or gender. The law violated the First Amendment, the Court held, by singling out specific types of "hate speech" for punishment. Applying that decision, the Wisconsin Supreme Court had ruled in Mitchell's case that the state's hate crime law improperly punished "offensive thought." Evidence showed that Mitchell had beaten the white youth after watching a movie with friends about the mistreatment of blacks in the 1950s and 1960s. "There goes a white boy," Mitchell said to his friends. "Go get him."

The Court agreed with state and local governments and civil rights groups that the hate crime law punished conduct, not speech. In contrast to *R. A. V.,* Chief Justice Rehnquist explained, Wisconsin's law was "aimed at conduct unprotected by the First Amendment." Judges traditionally had considered "a wide variety of factors" in determining a defendant's sentence, Rehnquist noted. "Abstract beliefs" could not be considered, but a defendant's "motive" could be, he continued. Wisconsin's legislature had acted within its discretion, he concluded, in determining that "bias-motivated offenses warrant greater maximum penalties across the board."

Rehnquist also rejected Mitchell's argument that the law would have a chilling effect on free speech. The likelihood that someone would suppress his "bigoted beliefs" because his views could be used against him later in a criminal trial was "too speculative to support the contention that the law was unconstitutionally overbroad."

See Joseph Ferrandoz, "Bringing Hate Crimes Into Focus," *Harvard Civil Rights-Civil Liberties Law Review* 26 (1991): 261–292; and Steven G. Gey, "What If *Wisconsin v. Mitchell* Had Involved Martin Luther King, Jr.? The Constitutional Flaws of Hate Crime Enhancement Statutes," *George Washington Law Review* 65 (1997): 1014.

Church of the Lukumi Babalu Aye v. City of Hialeah

508 U.S. 520 (1993)
Decided: June 11, 1993
Vote: 9 (Rehnquist, B. White, Blackmun, Stevens, O'Connor, Scalia, Kennedy, Souter, Thomas)
0
Opinion of the Court: Kennedy
Concurring opinion: Scalia (Rehnquist)
Opinion concurring in judgment: Blackmun (O'Connor)
Opinion concurring in judgment: Souter

Despite charges of being antireligious following its decision in ***Employment Division v. Smith,*** 494 U.S. 872 (1990), the Court showed itself to be protective of groups whose practices, while not violating general laws, are unpopular. The Santeria religion is a blend of African tribal rites and Roman Catholicism, and its adherents perform animal sacrifice. The purpose of the sacrifices, which occur during particular ceremonies, is to make an offering to spirits. The animals are sacrificed cleanly—not tortured—and then cooked and eaten as part of the ritual.

In 1987 a Santeria church announced that it planned to open a branch in Hialeah, Florida. The city council held an emergency public meeting at which residents expressed their strong opposition to the Santeria coming into their town. The council adopted an ordinance incorporating Florida's animal cruelty laws, which, among other things, subjected to criminal punishment any person who unnecessarily or cruelly killed any animal. At the council's request, the attorney general of Florida issued an opinion expressing the view that religious animal sacrifice was not a "necessary" killing and was therefore prohibited by state law. The council passed other ordinances that were facially neutral but clearly designed to keep the Santeria out of Hialeah. The Santeria sued, claiming that the city had violated the church's rights under the Free Exercise Clause. After losing in the district and circuit courts, the church appealed to the U.S. Supreme Court.

The Court unanimously agreed with the Santeria, although the justices could not agree on a single rationale. Justice Kennedy found that the ordinances were not neutral, but had as their purpose the specific intent of suppressing the Santeria religion in Hialeah. They were not generally applicable, but applied only to sects like the Santeria that practiced animal sacrifice, and they failed to meet the strict scrutiny test. The ordinances did not reflect any compelling government interest, were not drawn narrowly, and were both under- and over-inclusive. Kennedy believed that the history of the ordinances, especially the discussions of the council, were relevant in showing that they were aimed at one group.

Justice Scalia, who often states that legislative history has no role to play in judicial determinations, did not agree that the history of the ordinances had any relevancy. Justices Souter, Blackmun, and O'Connor concurred in the judgment, but their analyses varied in degrees from that of Kennedy. Souter and Blackmun found this an easy case for invalidation in that Hialeah had enacted, in Souter's words, "a rare example of a law actually aimed at suppressing religious exercise." They also declined to join in part of the majority opinion because it relied on dictum relating to the test endorsed in *Employment Division v. Smith.*

See Renee Skinner, "*Church of the Lukumi Babalu Aye v. City of Hialeah:* Still Sacrificing Free Exercise," *Baylor Law Review* 46 (1994): 259; and Caroline E. Johnson, "Protecting the Animals: The Free Exercise Clause and the Prevention of Ritual Sacrifice," *Florida State University Law Review* 21 (1994): 1295.

Zobrest v. Catalina Foothills School District

509 U.S. 1 (1993)
Decided: June 18, 1993
Vote: 5 (Rehnquist, B. White, Scalia, Kennedy, Thomas)
4 (Blackmun, Stevens, O'Connor, Souter)
Opinion of the Court: Rehnquist
Dissenting opinion: Blackmun (Stevens, O'Connor, Souter)
Dissenting opinion: O'Connor (Stevens)

While James Zobrest, a deaf student in Tucson, Arizona, attended public school, the school district paid for a sign-language interpreter to assist him. Zobrest claimed that the federal Individuals with Disabilities Education Act required school authorities to continue paying for an interpreter when he enrolled in a Roman Catholic high school. The Catalina Foothills School District and the Arizona state attorney general rejected the request, saying it would violate the First Amendment's prohibition against establishment of religion. Zobrest and his parents took the issue to federal court. They argued that the interpreter's role was purely mechanical and therefore would not result in impermissible government involvement with religion. A district court judge and then a divided panel of the court of appeals rejected their arguments. The appeals court said that furnishing the sign-language interpreter "would have the primary effect of advancing religion and thus would run afoul of the Establishment Clause." The Zobrests appealed that decision to the Supreme Court, where they gained support from the Bush administration and an array of religious groups.

The Court ruled in their favor. "The [federal law] creates a neutral government program dispensing aid not to schools but to individual handicapped children," Chief Justice Rehnquist said. "If a handicapped child chooses to enroll in a sectarian school, we hold that the Establishment Clause does not prevent the school district from furnishing him with a sign-language interpreter there in order to facilitate his education."

Rehnquist distinguished previous Court decisions limiting aid to parochial schools by saying that in this case, the government would not be relieving Zobrest's school of costs that it would have incurred anyway. He also agreed that the interpreter would not advance the school's sectarian mission. "Nothing in this record suggests that a sign-language interpreter would do more than accurately interpret whatever material is presented to the class as a whole," Rehnquist wrote.

The dissenters found that the Court had improperly rushed to decide the constitutional issue. They said the Court should first have decided whether the federal law required the school district to pay for the interpreter or, alternatively, whether a federal regulation implementing the law prohibited it. Rehnquist answered the dissenters in his opinion. He said the two lower federal courts had focused solely on the constitutional issue.

Two of the dissenting justices—Blackmun and Souter—went further. They directly challenged the majority's position as contrary to the Court's precedents on aid to church schools. "Our cases consistently have rejected the provision by government of any resource capable of advancing a school's religious mission," Blackmun wrote. Under this ruling, he continued, "It is beyond question that a state-employed sign-language interpreter would serve as the conduit for [Zobrest's] religious education, thereby assisting [the school] in its mission of religious indoctrination."

See Patrick Marshall, "Religion in Schools," *CQ Researcher,* January 12, 2001, 1–24.

Daubert v. Merrell Dow Pharmaceuticals, Inc.

509 U.S. 579 (1993)
Decided: June 28, 1993
Vote: 9 (Rehnquist, B. White, Blackmun, Stevens, O'Connor, Scalia, Kennedy, Souter, Thomas)
0
Opinion of the Court: Blackmun
Concurring opinion: Rehnquist (Stevens)

For more than two decades, doctors prescribed the drug Bendectin for pregnant women to control the common, and sometimes serious, problem of nausea or "morning sickness." In 1979 an Australian gynecologist claimed to have discovered that Bendectin caused birth defects. The allegations led to a wave of lawsuits in U.S. courts. The maker of the drug, Merrell Dow Pharmaceuticals, won most of them, but the company decided in 1983 to pull the drug from the market, saying the cost of defending the suits was too great.

The Bendectin litigation became an important example for critics of the civil justice system to attack what they called "junk science" in the courtroom. These critics maintained that plaintiffs' lawyers often used unreliable evidence from scientists of dubious credentials to bring baseless suits that sometimes resulted in unjustified awards or settlements. They wanted judges to apply stricter standards to keep the evidence out of court and away from juries. Plaintiffs' and consumer groups countered that juries were perfectly capable of deciding scientific issues fairly. More broadly, they insisted that the legal system could not wait for scientists to reach certain conclusions in cases that could affect public health and safety.

In similar cases, courts traditionally applied a federal appeals court decision, *Frye v. United States,* 54 App. D.C. 46, 293 F. 1013 (1923), which said that scientific evidence could be used only if it had achieved "general acceptance" within the scientific community. Under this standard, lower federal courts excluded studies linking Bendectin to birth defects.

The Supreme Court ruled that *Frye* had been superseded by the more liberal Federal Rules of Evidence, adopted in 1975, which generally provide that "all relevant evidence" is admissible in court. In addition, Rule 702 specifically allows testimony by "expert" witnesses if "scientific, technical, or other specialized knowledge will assist the trier of fact to understand the evidence or to determine a fact in issue." "Nothing in the text of this Rule," Justice Blackmun wrote for the Court, "establishes 'general acceptance' as an absolute prerequisite to admissibility."

In a second—and longer—part of the opinion, however, the Court assigned federal judges an active role in screening scientific evidence. "The trial judge must ensure that any and all scientific testimony or evidence is not only relevant, but reliable," Blackmun wrote. To qualify as scientific knowledge under Rule 702, he said, evidence "must be derived by the scientific method." He rejected arguments by industry groups for an absolute rule that studies first be reviewed by other scientists and published in journals to be admitted as evidence, but he said peer review and publication were one relevant factor. In addition, Blackmun said, "general acceptance" may still have a bearing on the use of evidence. "Widespread acceptance" counts as a plus, he made clear, while studies with minimal support among scientists "may properly be viewed with skepticism."

Chief Justice Rehnquist concurred in scrapping the *Frye* test, but did not agree with the Court's instructions to judges. Rehnquist accused the majority of creating a new requirement of reliability for expert testimony only by "parsing the language" of Rule 702. He ended by arguing that judges were being given too broad a role with too little guidance. "I do not doubt that Rule 702 confides to the judge some gatekeeping responsibility in deciding questions of the admissibility of proffered testimony," Rehnquist said. "But I do not think it imposes on them either the obligation or the authority to become amateur scientists in order to perform that role."

See Clifton T. Hutchinson and Danny S. Ashby, "*Daubert v. Merrell Dow Pharmaceuticals, Inc.*: Redefining the Bases for Admissibility of Expert Scientific Testimony," *Cardozo Law Review* 15 (April 1994): 1875–1927; and Arvin Maskin, "The Impact of *Daubert* on the Admissibility of Scientific Evidence: The Supreme Court Catches Up with a Decade of Jurisprudence," *Cardozo Law Review* 15 (April 1994): 1929–1943.

Shaw v. Reno

509 U.S. 630 (1993)
Decided: June 28, 1993
Vote: 5 (Rehnquist, O'Connor, Scalia, Kennedy, Thomas)
4 (B. White, Blackmun, Stevens, Souter)
Opinion of the Court: O'Connor
Dissenting opinion: B. White (Blackmun, Stevens)
Dissenting opinion: Blackmun
Dissenting opinion: Stevens
Dissenting opinion: Souter

The Voting Rights Act of 1965 aimed not only at ensuring access to the ballot box, but also that the minority vote would count. Section 2 sought to guarantee racial minorities an equal opportunity to participate in the electoral process and to elect members of their choice. Section 5 provided that, in states with a history of past discrimination, district lines might have to be redrawn to give minorities proportional representation in the total makeup of a state's congressional delegation. For example, a state with eight congressional districts and a 25 percent African American population might be required to so draw district lines that two "majority-minority" districts would be created in which blacks constituted a majority of the electorate.

Ever since ***Gomillion v. Lightfoot,*** 364 U.S. 339 (1960), gerrymandering districts along racial lines was illegal, but in *Rogers v. Lodge,* 458 U.S. 613 (1982), the Court approved a plan to require single-district seats for county commissioners in Burke County, Georgia, to ensure that some districts would have black majorities. During the 1980s the courts routinely approved majority-minority districts on the rationale that Congress had the power to ensure fair representation under Section 2 of the Fifteenth Amendment.

Following the 1990 census, as with every decennial census, the states had to redraw their district lines, and the Justice Department pressured states to create more majority-minority districts to ensure at least some black representation, even though this demand ran counter to the requirement for apportionment based on contiguous and compact district lines. Before long, the courts were flooded with challenges from whites who claimed that the creation of majority-minority districts deprived them of an equal vote. The states involved responded that the Justice Department requirements constituted a compelling state interest to justify departures from normal apportionment practices.

In *Shaw,* the Court did not rule on the merits of race-conscious districting or even on the state's claim that it had a compelling interest created by the Justice Department requirements. Rather, the Court ruled only that white citizens in North Carolina had a justiciable claim under the Equal Protection Clause to challenge the districting plans, and it remanded the case to the district court for a hearing on the merits. Justice O'Connor declared that in reviewing these challenges, courts should adopt a strict scrutiny test.

Part of the problem in the North Carolina plan was the shape of the majority-minority district. As O'Connor described it, "The district is somewhat hook-shaped. Centered in the northeastern part of the State, it moves southward until it tapers to a narrow hand; then, with finger-like extensions, it reaches far into the southern-most part of the State near the South Carolina border." As one state legislator noted, "If you drove down the interstate with both car doors open, you'd kill most of the people in the district."

The case marked the Court's abandonment of its deference to Justice Department policies promulgated under the Civil Rights and Voting Rights Acts. The Court ruled on the merits of the issue when the case reappeared as ***Shaw v. Hunt,*** 517 U.S. 899 (1996). The same day the Court decided ***Bush v. Vera,*** 517 U.S. 952 (1996), which challenged a Texas majority-minority districting plan.

See J. Morgan Kousser, *Colorblind Injustice: Minority Voting Rights and the Undoing of the Second Reconstruction* (Chapel Hill: University of North Carolina Press, 1999); Tinsley Yarbrough, *Race and Redistricting: The Shaw-Cromartie Cases* (Lawrence: University Press of Kansas, 2002); and Samuel Issacharoff, "The Constitutional Contours of Race and Politics," *Supreme Court Review, 1995,* 45.

Harris v. Forklift Systems, Inc.

510 U.S. 17 (1993)
Decided: November 9, 1993
Vote: 9 (Rehnquist, Blackmun, Stevens, O'Connor, Scalia, Kennedy, Souter, Thomas, Ginsburg)
0
Opinion of the Court: O'Connor
Concurring opinion: Scalia
Concurring opinion: Ginsburg

An employee claiming job discrimination on the basis of sexual harassment must prove the existence of a "hostile" or "abusive" work environment, but does not need to show that he or she suffered serious psychological injury as a result. The decision, in a case closely watched by employers and civil rights groups, reinstated a sexual harassment suit by Teresa Harris, who had worked for two and a half years as a manager for an equipment rental company. She said she quit her job in October 1987 because the firm's president, Charles Hardy, had made sexually suggestive comments to her throughout her employment.

A federal magistrate dismissed the suit, saying the comments were not "so severe as to seriously affect [Harris's] psychological well-being" or cause her to suffer injury. The court of appeals affirmed that ruling, but the Supreme Court reversed it.

Writing for the Court, Justice O'Connor said the prohibition on sex discrimination contained in Title VII of the Civil Rights Act of 1964 "comes into play before the harassing conduct leads to a nervous breakdown." She added, "So long as the environment would reasonably be perceived, and is perceived, as hostile or abusive, there is no need for it also to be psychologically injurious."

O'Connor acknowledged that the standard was not "mathematically precise." She said "no single factor" was required but listed several circumstances that could show a hostile work environment, including "the frequency of the discriminatory conduct; whether it is physically threatening or humiliating or a mere offensive utterance; and whether it unreasonably interferes with an employee's work performance."

Justice Scalia said the terms "abusive" and "hostile" were not clear, but he said he knew of "no test more faithful to the inherently vague statutory language." Justice Ginsburg, in her first opinion as a justice, said the ruling did not require an employee to show that sexual harassment interfered with her work performance in order to recover damages.

See Sarah E. Burns, "Evidence of a Sexually Hostile Workplace: What Is It and How Should It Be Assessed After *Harris v. Forklift Systems, Inc.*?" *New York University Review of Law and Social Change* 21 (1995): 501; and Jeffrey M. Lipman and Hugh J. Cain, "Evolution in Hostile Environment Claims Since *Harris v. Forklift Systems, Inc.*," *Drake Law Review* 47 (1999): 585–612.

National Organization for Women, Inc. v. Scheidler

510 U.S. 249 (1994)
Decided: January 24, 1994
Vote: 9 (Rehnquist, Blackmun, Stevens, O'Connor, Scalia, Kennedy, Souter, Thomas, Ginsburg)
0
Opinion of the Court: Rehnquist
Concurring opinion: Souter (Kennedy)

Frustrated in their efforts to overturn abortion rights rulings in the Supreme Court or Congress, opponents of abortion in the 1990s took their fight to the streets. Militant groups such as Operation Rescue openly proclaimed their intent to close clinics where abortions were performed. Protesters engaged in clamorous, occasionally violent demonstrations, chanting antiabortion slogans over bullhorns and taunting patients and staff on their way into clinic buildings.

Abortion rights groups turned to the courts and to Congress for relief. Local trespass laws provided only minimal help. In ***Bray v. Alexandria Women's Health Clinic,*** 506 U.S. 263 (1993), the Supreme Court rebuffed an effort to invoke a Reconstruction-era civil rights law to limit demonstrations. In its 1993–1994 term, however, the Court cleared the way for abortion clinics to use two other legal strategies.

In *Scheidler,* the Court upheld use of the federal antiracketeering law to bring civil damage suits against antiabortion organizations that engaged in unlawful demonstrations. In the other ruling, ***Madsen v. Women's Health Center, Inc.,*** 512 U.S. 753 (1994), the Court held that judges can set up "buffer zones" requiring protesters to keep a minimum distance—thirty-six feet in this case—away from clinics.

The racketeering suit was part of a broad action brought by the National Organization for Women (NOW) and two abortion clinics—Delaware Women's Health Organization in Wilmington and Summit Women's Health Organization in Milwaukee, Wisconsin. Defendants included an umbrella group called the Pro-Life Action Network and one of its leaders, Joseph Scheidler; Operation Rescue and its founder, Randall Terry; and several other antiabortion activists and groups.

NOW and the clinics hoped to hit the antiabortion groups with heavy financial penalties. The original suit charged that the antiabortion groups were violating the Sherman Antitrust Act by trying to drive abortion clinics out of business for the benefit of their own pregnancy counseling centers. Later the complaint was amended to include a count under the federal Racketeering Influenced and Corrupt Organizations Act (RICO). RICO allows plaintiffs to recover triple damages for economic harms inflicted by an "enterprise" engaged in a "pattern of racketeering activity." The clinics charged that the antiabortion groups were committing extortion—one of the offenses covered by RICO—by using force or violence to deny women their right to medical services and clinic staff their right to employment.

The antiabortion groups, however, contended RICO was intended to be used against organized crime, not political protest groups engaged in civil disobedience. A federal district court judge and the court of appeals agreed. Both courts said RICO could be used only if the defendants were motivated by "economic gain." The lower courts also dismissed the antitrust allegations.

The Supreme Court sided with the clinics. "Nowhere [in the statute] is there any indication that an economic motive is required," Chief Justice Rehnquist wrote in the short opinion. In a brief concurrence Justice Souter stressed that political groups could raise free speech arguments in defending against RICO suits. Rehnquist dealt with the issue only in a footnote, saying the issue had not been adequately raised for the Court to consider.

Antiabortion groups vehemently denounced the decision as violating their First Amendment rights and trampling on the American tradition of civil disobedience. For their part, NOW leaders said the ruling would help abortion clinics put a stop to "antiabortion terrorism." The decision had no immediate impact, however. It merely returned the case to lower courts, where the clinics still had to prove their accusations and show evidence of economic injury before they could recover any damages.

See Craig M. Bradley, "*NOW v. Scheidler:* RICO Meets the First Amendment," *Supreme Court Review, 1994* 129; and Fay Clayton and Sara N. Love, "*NOW v. Scheidler:* Protecting Women's Access to Reproductive Health Services," *Albany Law Review* 62 (1998): 967–997.

Dolan v. City of Tigard

512 U.S. 374 (1994)
Decided: June 24, 1994
Vote: 5 (Rehnquist, O'Connor, Scalia, Kennedy, Thomas)
4 (Blackmun, Stevens, Souter, Ginsburg)
Opinion of the Court: Rehnquist
Dissenting opinion: Stevens (Blackmun, Ginsburg)
Dissenting opinion: Souter

When John Dolan sought to expand his hardware store in the Portland, Oregon, suburb of Tigard in 1989, the city's zoning board approved his plan only after attaching two conditions. Dolan was required to turn over about seven thousand square feet for a "public greenway" and to put in part of a pedestrian and bicycle path. The city's decision reflected an increasing practice by financially strapped municipal governments to require developers or property owners to make public improvements as part of new construction. Dolan saw the city's action as amounting to a taking of his property without compensation in violation of the Fifth Amendment.

Dolan died in 1993, and his wife, Florence, continued the legal fight, winning a ruling that limited the power of local governments to force landowners to permit public use of their property in return for approval of development or construction on the site. The Supreme Court ruled that local governments must show a proportional relationship between the impact of a proposed development and any permit conditions ("exactions") they wanted to impose.

Tigard officials had said the public greenway was needed on Dolan's site to help storm water drain into an adjacent creek. The pedestrian and bicycle path was aimed at reducing the impact of additional traffic his expanded store would create. Oregon courts found those conditions were "reasonably related" to the impact of the development on the community.

The Oregon decision was in line with the interpretation that most other state courts had given to the Supreme Court's decision in ***Nollan v. California Coastal Commission,*** 483 U.S. 825 (1987). In that case, the Court required local governments to show a connection—in legal terms, a "nexus"—between the impact of a proposed development and the permit conditions. In Dolan's case, however, the Court ruled that the "reasonable relationship" test was too lax. Chief Justice Rehnquist said instead that "a term such as 'rough proportionality' best encapsulates what we hold to be the requirement of the Fifth Amendment." Applying that test, Rehnquist found the city's justifications for the conditions insufficient. The city, he said, "must make some sort of individualized determination that the required dedication is related in nature and extent to the proposed development."

In dissent, Justice Stevens said that local governments needed the benefit of the doubt in devising land-use policies because of the uncertainty in predicting the impact of new development on the environment. He also said that land-use policies, like other business regulations, should be accorded a presumption of validity. That point prompted a barbed response from Rehnquist: "We see no reason why the Takings Clause of the Fifth Amendment should be relegated to the status of a poor relation."

Property rights advocates said the ruling would reduce what one lawyer called the "garden-variety extortion" engaged in by some local governments. At the least, municipal officials conceded that cities and counties would have to be more careful before setting conditions for developers and property owners.

See Thomas W. Merrill, "*Dolan v. City of Tigard:* Constitutional Rights as Public Goods," *Denver University Law Review* 72 (1995): 859.

Board of Education of Kiryas Joel Village School District v. Grumet

512 U.S. 687 (1994)
Decided: June 27, 1994
Vote: 6 (Blackmun, Stevens, O'Connor, Kennedy, Souter, Ginsburg)
3 (Rehnquist, Scalia, Thomas)
Judgment of the Court: Souter
Concurring opinion: Blackmun
Concurring opinion: Stevens
Opinion concurring in judgment: O'Connor
Opinion concurring in judgment: Kennedy
Dissenting opinion: Scalia (Rehnquist, Thomas)

The village of Kiryas Joel is a tiny enclave inhabited exclusively by members of a small orthodox Jewish sect—the Satmar Hasidim. In Kiryas Joel, religious rituals are scrupulously observed, the outside world is shunned, and almost all the children are taught in private religious schools. The village, however, had no school for children with special needs. In 1990 a small number of the villagers' children—all of them handicapped or learning-disabled—began attending a public school in a new school district, which the New York legislature had created a year earlier to try to accommodate the religious views of the Satmars with the Supreme Court's mandate to keep church and state separate in public education.

The Kiryas Joel school district's lone public school had secular teachers, a secular curriculum, and no religious trappings, but all its pupils were Hasidic children with disabilities who lived in Kiryas Joel or other nearby communities. To church-state separationists, the school represented a clear violation of the Constitution's ban on establishment of religion. Leaders of the state's school boards association challenged the law creating the school district as unconstitutional. The New York Court of Appeals, the state's highest court, agreed. The court said the law created a "symbolic union" between church and state in violation of the Establishment Clause.

The Supreme Court agreed, holding that the special school district violated the principle of government neutrality on religion. Justice Souter said that the New York law gave the power over public education "to an electorate defined by common religious belief and practice, in a manner that fails to foreclose religious favoritism." For that reason, he said, it violated "the general principle that civil power must be exercised in a manner neutral to religion." He added that there was "no assurance" that the legislature would create a similar school district for a different religious group.

In a separate opinion, Justice O'Connor said the case would be different if New York had a general law permitting municipalities to set up separate school districts. Justice Kennedy also wrote a separate opinion that concluded the law was impermissible "religious gerrymandering" under the Court's precedents. Both justices called for reconsidering the 1985 decisions that prevented public school systems from providing special education services at religious schools.

In dissent, Justice Scalia mocked the idea that a small Jewish sect that had fled religious persecution in Europe had become "so powerful, so closely allied with Mammon, as to have become an 'establishment' of the Empire State." He went on to depict the challenged law as a neutral statute aimed at accommodating the villagers' cultural rather than religious views. In any event, Scalia continued, a law accommodating a group's religious beliefs promoted rather than violated religious freedom. And he criticized the majority for assuming that New York lawmakers might not create a special school district for a different religious community—"presumably those less powerful than the Satmar Hasidim."

See Alison Wheeler, "Separatist Religious Groups and the Establishment Clause—*Board of Education of Kiryas Joel Village School District v. Grumet*," *Harvard Civil Rights-Civil Liberties Law Review* 30 (winter 1995): 223–246.

Madsen v. Women's Health Center, Inc.

512 U.S. 753 (1994)
Decided: June 30, 1994
Vote: 6 (Rehnquist, Blackmun, Stevens, O'Connor, Souter, Ginsburg)
3 (Scalia, Kennedy, Thomas)
Opinion of the Court: Rehnquist
Concurring opinion: Souter
Concurring in judgment: Stevens
Dissenting opinion: Scalia (Kennedy, Thomas)

Lawyers for the Aware Woman Center for Choice, in Melbourne, Florida, went to state court claiming that antiabortion demonstrators were trying to close the facility and asking for an injunction to limit the protests. In September 1992 Judge Robert McGregor prohibited demonstrators from trespassing on clinic property, blocking the center, or physically abusing anyone associated with it. When the demonstrations continued, the clinic returned to court with evidence that the protesters had violated the restrictions. In April 1993 the judge substantially expanded the injunction.

The new injunction prohibited demonstrations within a buffer zone of thirty-six feet around the clinic. McGregor also set up a three hundred-foot buffer zone where protesters were forbidden from physically approaching any person "unless such person indicates a desire to communicate." The order prohibited, during surgical and recovery periods, any "singing, chanting, whistling, shouting, yelling, use of bullhorns, auto horns, sound amplification equipment or other sounds or images observable to or within the earshot of the patients inside" the clinic. Finally, the judge prohibited demonstrations within three hundred feet of the residences of clinic staff.

Operation Rescue challenged the injunction before the Florida Supreme Court and in federal courts, calling it vague, overbroad, and discriminatory against antiabortion views. The Florida Supreme Court upheld the order in October. One week later, the court of appeals agreed with the protesters, saying the injunction was a viewpoint-based restriction that could be justified only if a compelling state interest was shown. The appeals panel ordered a lower court to determine whether the injunction met that test. Before that could happen, however, the U.S. Supreme Court took up the issue by agreeing to review the protesters' appeal of the Florida Supreme Court's ruling. One week before the ruling in ***National Organization for Women, Inc. v. Scheidler,*** 510 U.S. 249 (1994), the Supreme Court agreed to decide *Madsen.*

The Court's decision went against the protesters. Chief Justice Rehnquist began by rejecting the protesters' argument that the injunction should be subjected to the highest level of judicial review—the "strict scrutiny" test—because it singled out antiabortion speech on the basis of content or viewpoint. An injunction necessarily "applies only to a particular group," he said. The judge had restrained the protesters not because they were opposed to abortion, Rehnquist explained, but because they had "violated the court's order."

Even as a content-neutral injunction, however, Rehnquist said the judge's order warranted a measure of heightened judicial review. "Our standard time, place, and manner analysis is not sufficiently rigorous," he wrote. "We must ask instead whether the challenged provisions of the injunction burden no more speech than necessary to serve a significant government interest."

To determine the interests protected by the injunction, Rehnquist turned to the Florida Supreme Court's opinion. First on the list was "the strong interest in protecting a woman's freedom to seek lawful medical or counseling services in connection with her pregnancy." Here, Rehnquist added, with no further comment, a legal citation to the abortion rights ruling in ***Roe v. Wade,*** 410 U.S. 113 (1973), a decision he had voted to overrule as recently as 1992. Rehnquist also noted that the Florida court had said the injunction helped protect public safety and order, promote the free flow of traffic, protect property rights, and safeguard residential privacy. "The combination of these interests is quite sufficient to justify an appropriately tailored injunction to protect them," he concluded.

With the legal standards established, Rehnquist evaluated the judge's injunction point by point. The thirty-six-foot buffer zone passed muster, partly in deference to the judge's ruling that the first injunction had failed to "accomplish its purpose." The

Court also accepted the "limited noise restrictions" imposed during the hours when abortions were performed.

The judge's other restrictions were struck down, however. The three hundred-foot "no-approach" zone "burdens more speech than is necessary to prevent intimidation and to ensure access to the clinic," Rehnquist said. The ban on signs visible from within the clinic also went too far, he added, because patients could simply "pull the curtains" to avoid seeing the placards. And the clinic had failed to present enough evidence, Rehnquist concluded, to justify the three hundred-foot ban on picketing near the homes of clinic staff.

Four justices—Blackmun, O'Connor, Souter, and Ginsburg—joined all of Rehnquist's opinion. Justice Stevens concurred with most of the ruling, but he dissented from the decision to strike down the restriction on physically approaching clinic patients and staffs. He said the restriction limited conduct, not speech.

Justice Scalia argued that in any other context the injunction would have been "a candidate for summary reversal." But special rules applied to the abortion issue, he said, nullifying established legal doctrines: "Today, the ad hoc nullification machine claims its latest, greatest, and most surprising victim: the First Amendment." The injunction, Scalia said, should have been reviewed under the Court's traditional strict scrutiny standard. As for the legal standard Rehnquist adopted, Scalia mocked it as "intermediate-intermediate scrutiny." Even under that test, he said, the limitations could not be upheld. Except for the noise restriction, all the limits burdened more speech than necessary, in his view.

See William C. Plouffe Jr., "Free Speech v. Abortion: Has the First Amendment Been Expanded, Limited, or Blurred?" *Tulsa Law Journal* 31 (1995): 203; and Randi B. Levinson, "*Madsen v. Women's Health Center:* Wrong Time, Wrong Place, Wrong Manner," *George Mason University Civil Rights Law Journal* (1994): 79–104.

McIntyre v. Ohio Elections Commission

514 U.S. 334 (1995)
Decided: April 19, 1995
Vote: 7 (Stevens, O'Connor, Kennedy, Souter, Thomas, Ginsburg, Breyer)
2 (Rehnquist, Scalia)
Opinion of the Court: Stevens
Concurring opinion: Ginsburg
Opinion concurring in judgment: Thomas
Dissenting opinion: Scalia (Rehnquist)

Margaret McIntyre thought of herself as a concerned citizen and taxpayer when she passed out leaflets in 1988 opposing a proposed school tax levy in the Westerville, Ohio, school district. The assistant superintendent filed a complaint charging McIntyre with violating state election law. The Ohio Elections Commission agreed and fined her $100 for violating a state law banning unsigned campaign literature.

A lower court judge in Columbus threw out the citation and fine, saying the law was unconstitutional as applied to McIntyre because she "did not mislead the public nor act in a surreptitious manner." The Ohio Supreme Court upheld the law and fine. In a divided decision, the state's highest court said the law served important state interests by providing voters information to judge the validity of campaign literature and identifying anyone engaged in "fraud, libel, or false advertising." The court added that the law imposed only a "minor burden" on political activists. McIntyre died after the Ohio court ruling, and her husband, Joseph McIntyre, continued the case.

The U.S. Supreme Court settled the main issue by striking down Ohio's law, but avoided the secondary questions. Justice Stevens extolled the tradition of anonymity in literature and in politics and dismissed the state's justifications for seeking to ban anonymity in political campaigns. Stevens noted that Mark Twain and O. Henry were pseudonyms. In politics, he continued, the tradition of anonymity was "most famously embodied" in the *Federalist Papers,* which played a critical part in the ratification of the Constitution and were written under pseudonyms by John Adams, Alexander Hamilton, and James Madison. On that basis, Stevens concluded, "an author's decision to remain anonymous . . . is an aspect of the freedom of speech protected by the First Amendment."

As for the state's justifications, Stevens found them insubstantial. The desire to provide voters additional information was "plainly insufficient" to require a writer to disclose her identity if she did not want to, he said. Moreover, the state had other means to deal with misleading or libelous campaign materials. "A state's enforcement interest might justify a more limited identification requirement," Stevens concluded, "but Ohio has shown scant cause for inhibiting the leafleting at issue here."

Justice Ginsburg stressed the limited nature of the ruling. The decision did not mean, she wrote, "that the State may not in other, larger circumstances, require the speaker to disclose its interest by disclosing its identity."

Justice Thomas agreed the law was unconstitutional but not for the reasons Stevens gave. Thomas, an advocate of interpreting the Constitution according to the "original understanding" of the Framers, said the real issue was whether a right of anonymous political leafleting was recognized when the First Amendment was ratified in 1791. After extensive research, Thomas concluded that it was.

In dissent, Justice Scalia, who also favors an original understanding approach to constitutional adjudication, said he was unpersuaded by Thomas's historical argument or by the majority's embrace of what he called "a hitherto unknown right-to-be-unknown while engaging in electoral politics." Instead, Scalia cited "the widespread and longstanding traditions" of state laws requiring authors of campaign materials to disclose their identity. Campaign disclosure laws had been enacted by Congress and by forty-eight other states besides Ohio, he said.

Striking them down, Scalia continued, was likely to lead to an increase in "mudslinging" and "dirty tricks" in campaigns.

See Richard K. Norton, "*McIntyre v. Ohio Elections Commission:* Defining the Right to Engage in Anonymous Political Speech," *North Carolina Law Review* 74 (1996): 553; and Mark A. Whitt, "Note: *McIntyre v. Ohio Elections Commission:* 'A Whole New Boutique of Wonderful First Amendment Litigation Opens Its Doors,' " *Akron Law Review* 29 (winter 1996): 423–445.

United States v. Lopez

514 U.S. 549 (1995)
Decided: April 26, 1995
Vote: 5 (Rehnquist, O'Connor, Scalia, Kennedy, Thomas)
4 (Stevens, Souter, Ginsburg, Breyer)
Opinion of the Court: Rehnquist
Concurring opinion: Kennedy (O'Connor)
Concurring opinion: Thomas
Dissenting opinion: Stevens
Dissenting opinion: Souter
Dissenting opinion: Breyer (Stevens, Souter, Ginsburg)

In 1990, following a rash of shootings in schools, Congress passed the Gun-Free School Zones Act, making it a federal offense for anyone to knowingly possess a firearm within a school zone. Alfonso Lopez Jr., then a twelfth-grade student at Edison High School in San Antonio, Texas, was arrested on state charges in March 1992, for carrying a concealed handgun and five bullets. The next day the state charges were dismissed, and federal agents charged him under the federal law. Lopez was convicted and appealed on the grounds that the statute was unconstitutional because it exceeded powers granted to Congress under the Commerce Clause. The circuit of appeals agreed with him, and the Supreme Court affirmed.

Ever since the constitutional crisis of 1937, when President Franklin Roosevelt proposed adding members to the Supreme Court, the Court had upheld every act of Congress passed under the aegis of the Commerce Clause. Moreover, it had given a very broad reading of that clause, allowing Congress to regulate in areas only indirectly related to interstate or foreign commerce, as in ***Wickard v. Filburn,*** 317 U.S. 111 (1942). As part of its effort to revive federalism, the Rehnquist Court took a closer look at the exercise of congressional powers and found them to have explicit limits.

For a time, Chief Justice Rehnquist, who was first appointed an associate justice in 1971, was almost alone in his calls to devolve power from the national government back to the states and reestablish a true federal system. By the early 1990s, however, the conservatives appointed by Presidents Reagan and Bush consistently began to limit federal authority. For example, the Court in ***New York v. United States,*** 505 U.S. 144 (1992), struck down the 1985 Low-Level Radioactive Waste Policy Amendments, which imposed upon the states a mandate to act alone or in regional compacts to dispose of waste generated within their borders. The Court ruled that the law exceeded congressional power and impinged upon powers reserved to the states. The three dissenters, while objecting to parts of the decision, concurred in the general notion of reinforcing federalism.

In *Lopez,* the majority could find no connection between the regulation of commerce and the banning of handguns from school zones. The law, the majority held, was nothing more than a criminal statute, and to sustain it under the Commerce Clause would in effect make that power into a general police power of the kind held only by the states. Even taking the most generous reading of prior cases, the chief justice held, one could not define this proscription as part of a larger scheme of economic regulation, in which the regulatory scheme would be undercut unless the intrastate activity—the control of guns in local schools—were upheld. In addition, Congress had not explained what nexus, if any, existed between regulation of firearms in local schools and interstate commerce.

The dissenters believed that Congress had the necessary power and that, when it came to simple economic regulation, such as this law appeared to be, the courts should defer to congressional judgment.

The Court continued its federalist agenda in ***Printz v. United States,*** 521 U.S. 898 (1997).

See Lynn A. Baker, "Conditional Federal Spending after *Lopez,*" *Columbia Law Review* 95 (1995): 1911.

U.S. Term Limits, Inc. v. Thornton

514 U.S. 779 (1995)
Decided: May 22, 1995
Vote: 5 (Stevens, Kennedy, Souter, Ginsburg, Breyer)
4 (Rehnquist, O'Connor, Scalia, Thomas)
Opinion of the Court: Stevens
Concurring opinion: Kennedy
Dissenting opinion: Thomas (Rehnquist, O'Connor, Scalia)

In a few short years the idea of term limits for members of Congress grew from a fringe political notion into a national movement. The Supreme Court dealt the cause a crippling blow by ruling that neither states nor Congress can restrict congressional tenure except by amending the Constitution.

The movement grew out of Republican frustration with forty years of Democratic rule on Capitol Hill and was fed by an upsurge of antigovernment sentiment. Supporters said term limits would increase public accountability and electoral competition. Opponents countered that term limits would reduce voter choice, deprive Congress of its ablest members, and cede power to the president and executive branch.

Supporters carried the day in state after state. By November 1994, twenty-one states had adopted ballot initiatives to impose term limits—typically, three two-year terms for House members and two six-year terms for senators. Two other states enacted term limits through legislative action. Supporters contended that states had the authority to limit congressional terms from a provision of the Constitution that gives the states power to regulate the "Times, Places, and Manner of holding Elections for Senators and Representatives." Term-limit measures either prohibited anyone from serving in Congress past the specified time period or barred a multiterm incumbent from being listed on the ballot while allowing a write-in candidacy.

Opponents maintained that either version violated the Constitution by adding a qualification to those listed in the document: age, U.S. citizenship, and residency in the state from which the member was elected. They pointed out that the Court had ruled in ***Powell v. McCormack,*** 395 U.S. 486 (1969), that Congress had no power to add to those qualifications, and, they concluded, neither did the states.

The Court took up the issue in a case from Arkansas filed in the name of a long-term Democratic lawmaker, Rep. Ray Thornton. The suit pitted the national organization, U.S. Term Limits, against the League of Women Voters and the Clinton administration in opposition to the measures.

The Court's broadly worded ruling invalidated the Arkansas measure and with it all other state congressional term limits. Justice Stevens said state term limits went against the Framers' intentions. "Permitting individual States to formulate diverse qualifications for their representatives would result in a patchwork of state qualifications, undermining the uniformity and the national character that the Framers envisioned," he wrote. In addition, Stevens said, term limits would also violate "the right of the people to vote for whom they wish." The option of a write-in candidacy could not save the term limit measure, he added, because the ballot access restriction was aimed at evading the constitutional limit on the states' prerogatives.

The ruling affected only congressional term limits. Similar measures for state legislators or city council members adopted in many states and cities were left standing. Congressional term limit advocates tried to revive the movement by pushing for laws to require candidates for Congress to pledge to support tenure limitations if elected. But the Court, in *Cook v. Gralike,* 531 U.S. 510 (2001), ruled such requirements unconstitutional.

See Lynn A. Baker, " 'They the People': A Comment on *U.S. Term Limits, Inc. v. Thornton,*" *Arizona Law Review* 38 (1996): 859; and Thomas M. Durbin, "The Unconstitutionality of State Congressional Term Limits: An Overview of *U.S. Term Limits, Inc. v. Thornton,*" *Congressional Research Service,* May 24, 1995.

Adarand Constructors, Inc. v. Peña

515 U.S. 200 (1995)
Decided: June 12, 1995
Vote: 5 (Rehnquist, O'Connor, Scalia, Kennedy, Thomas)
4 (Stevens, Souter, Ginsburg, Breyer)
Judgment of the Court: O'Connor
Opinion concurring in judgment: Scalia
Opinion concurring in judgment: Thomas
Dissenting opinion: Stevens (Ginsburg)
Dissenting opinion: Souter (Ginsburg, Breyer)
Dissenting opinion: Ginsburg (Breyer)

Ever since the 1970s, federal law required prime contractors doing work for the government to set aside a certain percentage of the contract for minority subcontractors. The Supreme Court approved the policy in ***Fullilove v. Klutznick,*** 448 U.S. 448 (1980). In that case, the Court deferred to the fact-finding powers of Congress and its judgment that discrimination existed in public construction and held that Congress had the power to address the issue under Section 5 (the Enforcement Clause) of the Fourteenth Amendment. During the 1980s, however, a more conservative Court began to question the legitimacy of affirmative action programs such as set-asides. In ***City of Richmond v. J. A. Croson Co.,*** 488 U.S. 469 (1989), the Court invalidated the city's minority set-aside program on grounds that cities and states did not have the enforcement authority vested by the Fourteenth Amendment in Congress. Cities and states could establish set-asides only if they could show the existence of persistent discrimination, and then the program would be judged by the same strict scrutiny standard applied to all racial classifications.

A year later, in ***Metro Broadcasting Inc. v. FCC,*** 497 U.S. 547 (1990), the Court again reaffirmed congressional power to act without meeting the strict scrutiny standard. Five years later, however, in *Adarand* the Court reversed itself in a badly splintered decision. Adarand Constructors lost a government subcontract to a minority business and sued, claiming that the racial classification violated the Fifth Amendment's Due Process Clause. Justice O'Connor's judgment for the Court, joined in full by only by Justice Kennedy, held that, under the Due Process Clauses of both the Fifth and Fourteenth Amendments, any action involving racial classification by *either* the state or the federal government, would henceforth be judged by a standard of strict scrutiny. The greater leeway that the Court had once allowed Congress in establishing affirmative action programs no longer existed. Just as the Court had for four decades frowned on measures that discriminated on the basis of race, it now frowned on measures that favored on the basis of race.

O'Connor stated, as she had in *Croson,* that this decision did not make all affirmative action programs, including set-asides, automatically unconstitutional. Instead, government—whether Congress, a state, or a municipality—would have to show a record of actual prior discrimination to justify a narrowly tailored plan.

The willingness to allow some racial classifications, provided the government could meet a strict scrutiny test, lost her the votes of Chief Justice Rehnquist and Justices Scalia and Thomas, who concurred in the result but believed that a government could never meet the compelling interest standard of strict scrutiny if it engaged in discrimination to compensate for prior discrimination. Under the Constitution, Scalia maintained, there can be no such thing as either a creditor or a debtor race. "We are just one race in the eyes of government."

The four dissenters, for a variety of reasons, believed that the government should be allowed to practice affirmative action and that, under the Fourteenth Amendment's Enforcement Clause, had the power to do so without meeting the strict scrutiny standard.

Four decades after ***Brown v. Board of Education,*** 347 U.S. 483 (1954), and three decades after the passage of the Civil Rights and Voting Rights Acts, the mood of the Court and the country had shifted. Affirmative action, which the Burger Court upheld in the 1970s and early 1980s, fell out of favor. A poll taken at the time of this case found that 77 percent of the people surveyed believed that affirmative action programs discriminated against whites; even 66 percent of the black respondents answered the same way.

Following *Adarand,* some lower courts began holding unconstitutional affirmative action programs that allowed race to be taken as a consideration in college and graduate school admissions, and it would only be a matter of time before the issue once again came to the Supreme Court.

See Race and Representation: Affirmative Action, ed. Robert Post and Michael Rogin (New York: Zone Books, 1998); Ronald J. Fiscus, *The Constitutional Logic of Affirmative Action* (Durham: Duke University Press, 1992); and Paul Brest and Miranda Oshige, "Affirmative Action for Whom?" *Stanford Law Review* 47 (1995): 855.

Vernonia School District 47J v. Acton

515 U.S. 646 (1995)
Decided: June 26, 1995
Vote: 6 (Rehnquist, Scalia, Kennedy, Thomas, Ginsburg, Breyer)
3 (Stevens, O'Connor, Souter)
Opinion of the Court: Scalia
Concurring opinion: Ginsburg
Dissenting opinion: O'Connor (Stevens, Souter)

Vernonia, Oregon, a logging community of about three thousand people in the northwestern tip of the state, might seem far removed from the problem of teenage drug use, but in the late 1980s, disciplinary problems in the town's high school tripled, and officials became alarmed at what they thought were signs of an epidemic of drug use among students. Because the problem seemed to be centered among the school's athletes, the Vernonia school board in 1989 adopted a targeted antidrug policy: random drug testing for students who wanted to participate in interscholastic athletics.

Vernonia's drug-testing policy required all student athletes to provide a urine sample at the start of the team's season. Each week thereafter, 10 percent of the team's members were chosen in a blind drawing for another test. The program appeared to be popular among parents in the community. No one opposed the plan when the school board adopted it in 1989.

Wayne and Judy Acton, however, refused to give their permission for the drug test when their seventh-grade son, James, wanted to try out for the school's football team. Wayne Acton testified later that he thought the policy "kind of sets a bad tone for citizenship" because it told children "that they have to prove that they're innocent." The Actons, represented by the Oregon chapter of the American Civil Liberties Union, filed suit in federal district court in 1991, contending that the drug testing violated the Fourth Amendment's prohibition against "unreasonable" searches. The Supreme Court in 1989 had upheld mandatory drug testing programs for railroad employees involved in accidents and for federal customs agents, but it had never ruled on the constitutionality of random, suspicionless drug tests.

The trial judge rejected the Actons' suit, but the court of appeals in 1994 ruled that the program violated the Fourth Amendment and the comparable provision in the Oregon Constitution. The three-judge panel acknowledged the school district had an interest in deterring drug use and disciplinary problems but said it was outweighed by James Acton's privacy interest.

The Supreme Court rejected the Actons' challenge, clearing the way for school systems around the country to institute random drug testing for student athletes. Justice Scalia began by emphasizing that school officials are normally permitted greater control over students than the government could exercise over adults, and the school board had ample justification for its program, both to protect athletes from the risk of injury and to deter drug use among students who viewed athletes as role models. Against these government interests, Scalia said, students' privacy interests were "negligible." Athletes have a lowered expectation of privacy, he said, because they "voluntarily" go out for a team and because school athletics have an inherent "element of communal undress." Moreover, he said, the results of the tests were disclosed only to parents and a limited number of school personnel; they were not provided to law enforcement or used for any other school disciplinary function.

Justice Ginsburg cautioned that the ruling did not necessarily sanction routine drug testing of all students.

Justice O'Connor wrote a dissenting opinion that severely criticized the drug-testing policy and the majority's rationale for upholding it. Under the ruling, O'Connor wrote, millions of students across the country could be "open to an intrusive bodily search" even though "the overwhelming majority . . . have given school officials no reason whatsoever to suspect they use drugs at school."

In ***Board of Education of Independent School District No. 92 of Pottawatomie County v. Earls,*** 536 U.S. — (2002); 122

S.Ct. 2559, the Court expanded the right of school officials to subject any students engaged in any extracurricular activity to random drug tests.

See David Masci, "Preventing Teen Drug Use," *CQ Researcher,* March 15, 2002, 217–240; and Nancy D. Wagman, "Note: Are We Becoming a Society of Suspects? *Vernonia School District 47J v. Acton:* Examining Random Suspicionless Drug Testing of Public School Athletes," *Villanova Sports and Entertainment Law Journal* 3 (1996): 325.

Rosenberger v. Rector and Visitors of University of Virginia

515 U.S. 819 (1995)
Decided: June 29, 1995
Vote: 5 (Rehnquist, O'Connor, Scalia, Kennedy, Thomas)
4 (Stevens, Souter, Ginsburg, Breyer)
Opinion of the Court: Kennedy
Concurring opinion: O'Connor
Concurring opinion: Thomas
Dissenting opinion: Souter (Stevens, Ginsburg, Breyer)

Many colleges and universities help finance campus publications and organizations by imposing a mandatory "activity fee" on students. The University of Virginia activities fund—financed by a $14 annual fee on each student—allowed support for publications of "student news, information, opinion, entertainment or academic communications," but not to publications that "primarily" promoted a particular religious belief. When two students at the University of Virginia founded a new Christian newspaper on campus in 1990, they applied to the school's Student Activities Fund for financing. Ronald Rosenberger and Robert Prince called their newspaper "Wide Awake" and promised that it would "challenge Christians to live, in word and deed, according to the faith they proclaim." The newspaper debuted at a time when many campuses in the United States were seeing an upsurge of religious interest and activity among students, especially evangelical Christians.

The board that administered the activities fund rejected their application, citing guidelines that prohibited funding "religious activities." The university contended that the policy amounted to permissible "content discrimination." The students maintained that the ban amounted to "viewpoint discrimination" that violated their free speech rights. The university countered that funding the religious newspaper would violate the First Amendment's prohibition against government establishment of religion.

Two lower federal courts sided with the university. But the U.S. Supreme Court agreed with the students. It held that public colleges and universities must fund religious publications on the same basis as other student publications. In ruling for the students, the Court acknowledged that the university had "substantial discretion" in spending decisions, but said that it could not impose "viewpoint-based restrictions" in deciding what publications to subsidize. The university violated the First Amendment, Justice Kennedy wrote, because it "selects for disfavored treatment those student journalistic efforts with religious editorial viewpoints."

Kennedy went on to reject the university's argument that funding the newspaper would violate the Establishment Clause. To the contrary, Kennedy said, denying funds to the newspaper "would risk fostering a pervasive bias or hostility to religion, which could undermine the very neutrality the Establishment Clause requires."

Justice O'Connor added a significant concurrence that took a somewhat narrower view. She stressed that she approved the funding because of the particular provisions of the program, including the requirement that publications receiving funds had to disclaim sponsorship by the university. The ruling, she added, did not mean "the demise of the funding prohibition in Establishment Clause jurisprudence."

Justice Souter said the ruling represented an unprecedented departure from Establishment Clause principles. "The Court today, for the first time, approves direct funding of core religious activities by an arm of the state," Souter wrote.

Miller v. Johnson

515 U.S. 900 (1995)
Decided: June 29, 1995
Vote: 5 (Rehnquist, O'Connor, Scalia, Kennedy, Thomas)
4 (Stevens, Souter, Ginsburg, Breyer)
Opinion of the Court: Kennedy
Concurring opinion: O'Connor
Dissenting opinion: Stevens
Dissenting opinion: Ginsburg (Stevens, Souter, Breyer)

Georgia in 1991 adopted a redistricting plan that called for two of the state's eleven congressional districts to have majority black populations. Under the Voting Rights Act of 1965, Georgia was required to obtain "preclearance" from the Justice Department for the plan, and the department refused to approve it. A second plan was also rejected before the state agreed on a third plan in 1992 that created three majority-black districts. One of the districts—the Eleventh—stretched from the Atlanta suburbs across the state to pick up black areas in two coastal cities, Augusta and Savannah. Voters in the new district elected a black Democrat, Cynthia McKinney, to the House of Representatives.

Five white voters who were placed in the district filed suit against the plan, claiming that it segregated voters on the basis of race in violation of the Equal Protection Clause. In 1994 a three-judge federal district court agreed. The panel held that race-based redistricting is subject to strict scrutiny—the most rigorous standard of judicial review—whenever race is "the overriding, predominant force" in drawing the lines. The court said the legislature's racial intent was evident from the shape of the Eleventh Congressional District as well as from the testimony of legislators themselves. The judges said the state's interest in eradicating past discrimination was not sufficiently compelling to justify the district's design.

The state's governor, Zell Miller, a Democrat, appealed the ruling to the Supreme Court. The Justice Department, which had intervened in the case on the state's side, also appealed, as did a group of black and white voters affected by the ruling. The Court agreed to hear the case, along with a second case, *Abrams v. Johnson,* challenging a Louisiana redistricting plan that fashioned a black majority district through the state's midsection.

In the Louisiana case, the Court unanimously ruled that the plaintiffs had no standing to bring the suit and ordered the case dismissed. In the Georgia case, however, the Court ruled the redistricting plan unconstitutional and set a new standard for judging racial line-drawing in all future cases.

Justice Kennedy said the Court's initial decision to allow challenges to racial redistricting in ***Shaw v. Reno,*** 509 U.S. 630 (1993), did not limit challenges to plans that created irregularly shaped districts. The shape of the district, he explained, was simply "circumstantial evidence" that race had been "the dominant and controlling rationale" in drawing district lines. Instead, plaintiffs had to prove that race was the "predominant factor motivating the legislature's decision to place a significant number of voters within or without a particular district," Kennedy said. To make that showing, he continued, plaintiffs had to prove that the legislature "subordinated traditional race-neutral districting principles such as compactness, contiguity, respect for political subdivisions or communities defined by actual shared interests, to racial considerations."

Applying that standard, Kennedy said the lower court had correctly concluded that race had been the predominant factor in drawing Georgia's plan. On that basis, he added, the plan was subject to strict scrutiny and could be sustained only if it served a compelling state interest and was narrowly tailored to meet that purpose. On that point, Kennedy criticized the Justice Department's reading of the Voting Rights Act, which he said amounted to requiring a maximum number of majority black districts. That interpretation was wrong, he concluded, and could not serve as Georgia's justification for the redistricting plan.

Justice O'Connor said the decision did not cast doubt on the vast majority of congressional districts in the country even if race had been considered in the redistricting process. The dissenting justices, however, argued the ruling threw the redistricting process into uncertainty and turmoil. States may be required to consider race by "statutory mandates and political realities," Justice Ginsburg wrote in the main dissent. The Court's ruling, she said, would invite "searching review" of racial redistricting, leaving lawmakers with no assurance that plans "conscious of race" would be upheld.

Turning to the Georgia plan, Ginsburg said it met traditional districting principles because the new district was not markedly less compact than the state's other districts. The plan, she concluded, "merited this Court's approbation, not its condemnation." Justice Souter joined all but the part discussing the shape of the challenged Eleventh District. Justice Stevens also added a short dissent questioning the standing of the voters to bring the suit at all.

See Laughlin McDonald, "Can Minority Voting Survive *Miller v. Johnson?" Michigan Journal of Race and Law* 1 (1996): 119; and Keith Reeves, "Prospects for Black Representation After *Miller v. Johnson,*" in *Representation and Minority Representation, Learning from the Past, Preparing for the Future,* ed. David A. Bositis (Lanham, Md.: University Press of America, 1998).

Bennis v. Michigan

516 U.S. 442 (1996)
Decided: March 4, 1996
Vote: 5 (Rehnquist, O'Connor, Scalia, Thomas, Ginsburg)
4 (Stevens, Kennedy, Souter, Breyer)
Opinion of the Court: Rehnquist
Concurring opinion: Thomas
Concurring opinion: Ginsburg
Dissenting opinion: Stevens (Souter, Breyer)
Dissenting opinion: Kennedy

The government may seize property even if the owner had no knowledge that someone else was using it for criminal activity. The closely divided decision rejected Tina B. Bennis's claim that her constitutional rights were violated by the forfeiture of a car she co-owned with her husband, John Bennis, after his arrest for having sex with a prostitute in the car. She argued that the Fourteenth Amendment's Due Process Clause required the government to recognize an "innocent owner defense," but the Michigan Supreme Court rejected the argument.

Writing for the U.S. Supreme Court, Chief Justice Rehnquist upheld the Michigan court, citing what he called "well-established authority" dating as far back as *The Palmyra,* 25 U.S. 1 (1827) case upholding the seizure of a pirate ship. "A long and unbroken line of cases holds that an owner's interest in property may be forfeited by reason of the use to which the property is put even though the owner did not know that it was to be put to such use," he wrote.

Justice Thomas said it was up to the states or the "political branches" of the federal government to prevent improper uses of forfeiture. Justice Ginsburg said state courts could also monitor "exorbitant applications" of forfeiture statutes.

In the main dissent, Justice Stevens said the decision violated "elementary notions of fairness" and would give states "virtually unbridled power to confiscate vast amounts of property." Justice Kennedy wrote that forfeiture should be allowed only if the owner was guilty of negligence or complicity with regard to the wrongdoing.

See Donald J. Boudreaux and A. C. Pritchard, "Innocence Lost: *Bennis v. Michigan* and the Forfeiture Tradition," *Missouri Law Review* 61 (1996): 593; and Amy D. Ronner, "Husband and Wife Are One—Him: *Bennis v. Michigan* as the Resurrection of Coverture," *Michigan Journal of Gender and Law* 4 (1996): 129.

Seminole Tribe of Florida v. Florida

517 U.S. 44 (1996)
Decided: March 27, 1996
Vote: 5 (Rehnquist, O'Connor, Scalia, Kennedy, Thomas)
4 (Stevens, Souter, Ginsburg, Breyer)
Opinion of the Court: Rehnquist
Dissenting opinion: Stevens
Dissenting opinion: Souter (Ginsburg, Breyer)

Congress has authority under Article I, Section 8, to regulate any commerce affecting or involving Indian tribes. Under this authority, it passed the Indian Gaming Regulatory Act in 1988, which allows tribes to run gambling operations on their reservations, provided the tribe and the state in which the reservation is located agree on the details. The states are required to negotiate in good faith with the tribes, and, should an agreement not be reached, the statute permits the tribe to sue the state in federal court, which is what happened when Florida and the Seminole Tribe could not reach an agreement. Florida, in turn, moved to dismiss the suit on the grounds that, under the Eleventh Amendment, the state enjoys sovereign immunity from suit in federal court.

The Eleventh Amendment was designed to protect the states from suits in federal court following the decision in ***Chisholm v. Georgia,*** 2 U.S. 419 (1793), but that immunity had over the years been chipped away by a variety of decisions in which the Court found that specific provisions of the Constitution, such as the Commerce Clause, overrode the sovereign immunity found in the Eleventh Amendment. In ***Ex parte Young,*** 209 U.S. 123 (1909), a case relied on by the Seminoles, the Court found that federal courts could hear suits against state officials—in effect, against the states themselves—for violating federal law. As a result, many scholars and lawyers had long considered the Eleventh Amendment to be a dead letter and an ineffective bar to suits such as those allowed in the Indian Gambling Regulatory Act.

The Rehnquist Court majority, intent on reviving federalism, breathed new life into the Eleventh Amendment and in *Seminole Tribe* held that Congress lacked the power under the Commerce Clause to subject states to suits in federal courts for violations of federally created rights. The majority thus overturned not only the earlier *Ex parte Young* precedent, but a more recent decision, *Pennsylvania v. Union Gas Co.,* 491 U.S. 1 (1989), in which the Court gave Congress a broad power to enforce its laws by overriding state immunity through suits in federal courts.

The majority—the same majority as in other federalism cases such as ***United States v. Lopez,*** 514 U.S. 549 (1995), and ***Printz v. United States,*** 521 U.S. 898 (1997)—held that state sovereign immunity under the Eleventh Amendment trumped congressional power under Article I. Although the opinion dealt specifically with the Indian Gaming Regulatory Act, the ruling called into question whether federal courts could entertain suits against states under federal environmental statutes, copyright and patent laws, and the many regulations tied to the national economy.

The following year the Court reaffirmed this ruling in another Indian case, ***Idaho v. Coeur d'Alene Tribe of Idaho,*** 521 U.S. 261 (1997).

44 Liquormart, Inc. v. Rhode Island

517 U.S. 484 (1996)
Decided: May 13, 1996
Vote: 9 (Rehnquist, Stevens, O'Connor, Scalia, Kennedy, Thomas, Souter, Ginsburg, Breyer)
0
Judgment of the Court: Stevens
Opinion concurring in judgment: O'Connor (Rehnquist, Souter, Breyer)
Opinion concurring in judgment: Scalia
Opinion concurring in judgment: Thomas

The newspaper advertisement that a discount liquor store in Rhode Island placed in newspapers in December 1991 had no earmarks of a First Amendment test case in the making. The ad listed the store's low prices for peanuts, potato chips, and mixers and, as an additional come-on, blazoned the single word "WOW" next to pictures of bottles of rum and vodka.

A rival liquor store, however, viewed the ad as a violation of a Rhode Island law that prohibited liquor stores from advertising prices. The state's liquor control administrator agreed and levied a $400 fine on the store, 44 Liquormart. Owner Shirley Santoro paid the fine. She and her father, John Haronian, who owned two liquor stores in New Bedford and Fairhaven, Massachusetts, then challenged the law in a suit filed in federal district court. Haronian's stores advertised their prices in Massachusetts media, but Rhode Island's price advertising ban extended to all media within the state.

Rhode Island defended the law, passed in 1956, on the ground that, by preventing price competition among liquor stores, it helped raise liquor prices and thereby discouraged excessive consumption. A trade association of liquor stores intervened on the state's side, saying that invalidating the law would force them into "the advertising arena."

The district court ruled that the law was unconstitutional, saying it did not "directly advance" the state's asserted interest and was "more extensive than necessary to serve that interest." A year later, the court of appeals overturned the decision. The three-judge panel agreed with the state that banning price advertising would help keep prices high and consumption low. In addition, the court agreed that the Twenty-first Amendment, which repealed Prohibition, gave the state added leeway in regulating liquor.

The Supreme Court's decision was simultaneously unanimous and divided. All of the justices agreed that Rhode Island's law was unconstitutional, but they split three ways in their reasoning. In the main opinion, Justice Stevens put some additional spine into the test derived from ***Central Hudson Gas***

& Electric Corp. v. Public Service Commission of New York, 447 U.S. 557 (1980), by saying that courts must give a "rigorous review" to laws prohibiting "truthful" commercial speech and should not uphold them if less restrictive alternatives are available. In this case, Stevens said, the state could try to discourage alcohol consumption by imposing a tax or by enacting minimum price laws—both less restrictive than banning price advertising.

In that passage, Stevens specifically rejected a critical part of the decision in *Posadas de Puerto Rico Associates v. Tourism Co. of P.R.,* 478 U.S. 328 (1986), in which the Court said that if a state can ban a product or service, it can also take the "less restrictive" step of banning advertising about it. "Banning speech," Stevens rejoined, "may sometimes prove more intrusive than banning conduct." Stevens also rejected the state's Twenty-first Amendment argument. That provision, he said, could not overcome the free speech protections of the First Amendment.

Although all the justices agreed on the Twenty-first Amendment issue, only two—Justices Kennedy and Ginsburg—joined all of Stevens's opinion. Justice Thomas went further than Stevens, saying the government should never be allowed to ban truthful advertising in order to promote social policies. "All attempts to dissuade legal choices by citizens by keeping them ignorant are impermissible," Thomas wrote.

Four other justices took a narrower approach, saying that Rhode Island's justification for the law could not satisfy the "less stringent standard" for commercial speech established in *Central Hudson.* Like Stevens, Justice O'Connor noted that Rhode Island had less-restrictive options, such as minimum prices or sales taxes as well as limiting purchase amounts or conducting educational campaigns about alcohol abuse. On that basis, she concluded, the price-advertising ban "clearly fails to pass muster" without any "new analysis" for future commercial speech cases.

Justice Scalia confessed in his concurrence to ambivalence about the issues. He said he agreed with Stevens's "aversion toward paternalistic governmental policies" and with Thomas's "discomfort" with the ad hoc nature of the *Central Hudson* test, but voiced his own discomfort in applying the First Amendment outside the area of political speech. For the time being, he concluded, he would accept the *Central Hudson* test, which, he agreed, Rhode Island's law could not satisfy.

See Alex Kozinski and Stuart Banner, "Who's Afraid of Commercial Speech?" *Virginia Law Review* 76 (1990): 627; and Kathleen M. Sullivan, "Cheap Spirits, Cigarettes, and Free Speech: The Implications of *44 Liquormart,*" *Supreme Court Review, 1997,* 123.

BMW of North America, Inc. v. Gore

517 U.S. 559 (1996)
Decided: May 20, 1996
Vote: 5 (Stevens, O'Connor, Kennedy, Souter, Breyer)
4 (Rehnquist, Scalia, Thomas, Ginsburg)
Opinion of the Court: Stevens
Concurring opinion: Breyer (O'Connor, Souter)
Dissenting opinion: Scalia (Thomas)
Dissenting opinion: Ginsburg (Rehnquist)

Ira Gore Jr. paid $40,750.08 for a new BMW sedan in January 1990. Nine months later, when he took the car to a shop for detailing, Gore was surprised to discover that the car had not been in mint condition when he bought it. Leonard Slick, the shop's owner, told Gore the car had been repainted after it left the factory. Over time, Slick said, the finish would deteriorate and the car's resale value would be reduced.

The cause of the damage to the original paint job was never established, but people in the automobile industry insisted it was common—and proper—to repaint cars that suffered incidental damage in transit from factory to showroom floor. Gore, however, felt "cheated and misled," as he testified later. He filed a fraud suit against the German auto manufacturer in an Alabama state court, asking for $4,000 in compensatory damages—10 percent of the original purchase price—along with an unspecified amount in punitive damages.

BMW insisted it had done nothing wrong. The company had what it regarded as a sensible and lawful policy: it did not disclose damage to a new car if it could be corrected for less than 3 percent of the suggested retail price. The car would simply be retouched and sold as new. Damages above the 3 percent threshold would also be corrected, but the car would be sold as used. BMW said its policy conformed with laws in many states, including Alabama, that required manufacturers and dealers to disclose defects above the 3 percent threshold.

At trial, Gore presented evidence that BMW had delivered over a ten-year period at least 983 cars nationwide, including 14 in Alabama, that had been refinished at a cost of at least $300 without disclosure. The jury awarded Gore $4,000 in compensatory damages and—after multiplying that figure by a thousand—imposed a punitive damage award of $4 million.

The Alabama Supreme Court cut the punitive damage award in half, agreeing with BMW that the jury's use of a multiplier had been improper. BMW took the case to the Supreme Court, insisting that the reduced $2 million award was so excessive as to amount to a violation of the Fourteenth Amendment's Due Process Clause.

The justices had reviewed Alabama's civil justice system once before. In 1991 the Court upheld a $1 million punitive damage award in *Pacific Mutual Life Insurance Co. v. Haslip,* 499 U.S. 1. The ruling stressed that juries have broad discretion in setting punitive damages. Only Justice O'Connor dissented. In two later rulings, the Court gave tort reform advocates modest victories. A fractured decision in *TXO Production Corp. v.*

Alliance Resources, 509 U.S. 443 (1993), established the limited principle that punitive damage awards must be "reasonable." Then, in 1994, the Court ruled in an Oregon case, *Honda Motor Co. v. Oberg,* 512 U.S. 415, that states must provide some form of review of jury awards, either at the trial or appellate level.

In this case, the Court sided with BMW, overturning the award, which Justice Stevens called "grossly excessive." He laid out three reasons: the relatively low "reprehensibility" of BMW's nondisclosure; the "disparity" between the award and the actual harm to Gore; and the difference between the award and the civil penalties imposed in similar cases. He concluded with a warning against punishing big companies just because of their size. "The fact that BMW is a large corporation rather than an impecunious individual does not diminish its entitlement to fair notice," he wrote.

Justice Breyer faulted the Alabama courts for their handling of punitive damage cases. The state courts had failed to enforce any standards to "significantly constrain . . . a jury's discretion" in fixing awards, Breyer said.

In separate dissents, Justices Scalia and Ginsburg said the decision improperly intruded on states' prerogatives. The decision, Ginsburg wrote, "unnecessarily and unwisely ventures into territory traditionally within the States' domain." Scalia also scoffed at the guidelines in Stevens's opinion, saying that they provided "virtually no guidance . . . as to what a 'constitutionally proper' level of punitive damages might be."

See Christine D'Ambrosia, "Comment: Punitive Damages in Light of *BMW of North America, Inc. v. Gore:* A Cry for State Sovereignty," *Journal of Law and Policy* 5 (1997): 577.

Romer v. Evans

517 U.S. 620 (1996)
Decided: May 20, 1996
Vote: 6 (Stevens, O'Connor, Kennedy, Souter, Ginsburg, Breyer)
3 (Rehnquist, Scalia, Thomas)
Opinion of the Court: Kennedy
Dissenting opinion: Scalia (Rehnquist, Thomas)

Gay rights advocates won a rare victory from the Supreme Court with a decision striking down a Colorado initiative that sought to prohibit passage of state or local laws banning discrimination on the basis of sexual orientation. Despite changing popular attitudes toward homosexuality, the Court had been unreceptive to cases seeking to establish individual rights for gay men and lesbians. Most notably, the Court in ***Bowers v. Hardwick,*** 478 U.S. 186 (1986), upheld state antisodomy laws that made consensual homosexual conduct a crime.

Meanwhile, gay rights advocates were making progress at the state and local level. In particular, some state and local governments passed laws banning discrimination on the basis of sexual orientation in employment, housing, or public accommodations. By the early 1990s, three Colorado municipalities—Aspen, Boulder, and Denver—had passed such laws; in addition, the state's governor had issued an executive order prohibiting discrimination in employment against homosexuals.

Opponents of those measures in Colorado responded with a successful statewide initiative in 1992 that repealed the laws and prohibited enactment of any future laws granting "protected status" to homosexuals except by a state constitutional amendment. Supporters of the initiative—known as Amendment 2—campaigned under the slogan, "Equal Rights—No Special Rights." It passed with 53 percent of the vote.

A group of six gay men and lesbians immediately challenged the initiative in state court. A lower court judge blocked the measure from taking effect, and the Colorado Supreme Court eventually threw it out. The initiative was subject to strict scrutiny because it infringed homosexuals' "fundamental right" to participate equally in the political process, the court held, and none of the state's justifications for the measure was held valid.

The Supreme Court also ruled that the amendment violated equal protection, but on a somewhat different rationale. Justice Kennedy said the amendment was a "status-based enactment" that was "born of animosity" toward homosexuals and that could not satisfy even the least rigorous form of constitutional review—the so-called rational basis test. "Amendment 2 classifies homosexuals not to further a proper legislative end but to make them unequal to everyone else," Kennedy wrote. "This Colorado cannot do."

Justice Scalia said the majority had wrongly accused Coloradans of prejudice against homosexuals. The amendment, Scalia said, was "a modest attempt . . to preserve traditional sexual mores against the efforts of a politically powerful minority to revise those mores through use of the laws."

Gay rights advocates were elated with the ruling, but cautioned that its long-term impact remained to be seen. They noted that Kennedy had skirted the question of whether homosexuals are entitled to special protection against unequal treatment. In addition, he did not mention *Bowers,* even though Scalia cited it prominently in his dissent.

See Larry Alexander, "Sometimes Better Boring and Correct: *Romer v. Evans* as an Exercise of Ordinary Equal Protection Analysis," *University of Colorado Law Review* 68 (spring 1997): 335–347; Marc A. Fajer, "*Bowers v. Hardwick, Romer v. Evans,* and the Meaning of Anti-Discrimination Legislation," *National Journal of Sexual Orientation Law* 2 (1996); and Lino A. Graglia, "*Romer v. Evans:* The People Foiled Again by the Constitution," *University of Colorado Law Review* 68 (spring 1997): 409–428.

Shaw v. Hunt

517 U.S. 899 (1996)
Decided: June 13, 1996
Vote: 5 (Rehnquist, O'Connor, Scalia, Kennedy, Thomas)
4 (Stevens, Souter, Ginsburg, Breyer)
Opinion of the Court: Rehnquist
Dissenting opinion: Stevens (Ginsburg, Breyer)
Dissenting opinion: Souter (Ginsburg, Breyer)
See *Bush v. Vera* below.

Bush v. Vera

517 U.S. 952 (1996)
Decided: June 13, 1996
Vote: 5 (Rehnquist, O'Connor, Scalia, Kennedy, Thomas)
4 (Stevens, Souter, Ginsburg, Breyer)
Judgment of the Court: O'Connor
Concurring opinion: O'Connor
Concurring opinion: Kennedy
Opinion concurring in judgment: Thomas (Scalia)
Dissenting opinion: Stevens (Ginsburg, Breyer)
Dissenting opinion: Souter (Ginsburg, Breyer)

For the third time in four years, the Supreme Court addressed the contentious issue of racial redistricting. Once again, by narrow majorities and with sharp divisions, the justices rejected congressional districting plans aimed at electing minority representatives. The decisions, announced the same day, struck down four congressional districts in two states. The case from North Carolina was ***Shaw v. Hunt,*** and the Texas case was *Bush v. Vera.* The Court's decisions cheered the critics of racial line-drawing, but drew bitter attacks from traditional civil rights groups. Legally, the rulings made clear that states faced added difficulties in justifying excessive use of race in drawing district lines, but left unclear precisely when a racial districting plan crosses the line to become an improper racial gerrymander or how the states could comply with the Voting Rights Act of 1965.

North Carolina's Twelfth District—which had already been before the Court in its first racial redistricting ruling, ***Shaw v. Reno,*** 509 U.S. 630 (1993) (*Shaw I*)—snaked across half the state, tying together widely separate black urban centers by means of a narrow corridor at times no wider than the width of an interstate highway. Mapmakers in North Carolina used detailed racial census information and sophisticated computer techniques to accomplish their tasks, but race was not the only reason for the district's bizarre shapes. Each district took on an added measure of irregularity in the interest of protecting the political fortunes of incumbent officeholders. Legislators easily settled on a majority-black district in the state's northeastern region, but balked at a similar majority-black district in the southeast because some Democratic House incumbents would have been moved out of their existing districts.

In *Shaw I,* the Court had agreed that white voters could use the Fourteenth Amendment's Equal Protection Clause to challenge the use of race in drawing legislative district lines. The ruling sent the case back to a three-judge federal district court to give the state a chance to justify the plan. The Court had said the plan must satisfy "strict scrutiny," the highest level of constitutional review, which required the government to show that it had a "compelling interest" in using race to draw the district lines and that it had "narrowly tailored" the plan to serve that interest.

In Texas, a new Thirtieth District started in predominantly black sections of Dallas, but had narrow tentacles reaching into two neighboring counties and jagged edges to skirt around white neighborhoods. Two interlocking districts in Houston—the Eighteenth and Twenty-ninth—were configured by means of jigsaw-puzzle geometry to include majority-black and Hispanic populations, respectively. As in North Carolina, Texas used detailed racial census information and sophisticated computer techniques to draw the maps, and, as in North Carolina, the mapmakers tried to protect incumbents.

The political calculus in Texas was complicated. In Dallas, Eddie Bernice Johnson, an African American state senator with ambitions for Congress, initially proposed a plan for a relatively compact district with a black population of about 45 percent, but the plan was redrawn to accommodate the wishes of incumbent House members—one Republican, one Democrat, both white. The final plan added outlying black neighborhoods to the core of Johnson's original district. She won the House seat from the new district in the 1992 election. In Houston, the redistricting plan increased from 35 percent to 50 percent the black population of the existing Eighteenth District, which had been represented since 1971 by a succession of African American lawmakers. The new Twenty-ninth District was drawn to embrace a majority Hispanic population. Again, the plans departed from more compact districts to accommodate white officeholders: an incumbent House Democrat who wanted to preserve some of his existing district and a white state representative who planned to run in the Hispanic district and wanted parts of his political base included.

A three-judge court unanimously struck down the three Texas congressional districts. The court said that a state could justify racial line-drawing only if the district had "the least possible amount of irregularity in shape, making allowances for traditional districting criteria."

Together, the two decisions established that race could not be the "predominant" consideration in drawing district lines, but they left unanswered a host of other questions, in particular, whether irregular shape was by itself a constitutional defect and whether other factors could justify racial line-drawing. In North Carolina, the same court that had initially heard the case again approved the districting plan. The panel ruled that the state had a compelling interest in overcoming the effects of past discrimination and in creating separate majority black districts with rural and urban populations.

Chief Justice Rehnquist's opinion for the Court in *Shaw v. Hunt* paralleled the reasoning in *Bush v. Vera.* The redistricting plan was subject to strict scrutiny because race was the predominant consideration in drawing the challenged Twelfth District, Rehnquist said, and the state could not justify the plan on grounds of eradicating past discrimination or complying with the Voting Rights Act.

In a lengthy dissent, Justice Stevens argued that racial redistricting should not be subject to strict scrutiny, but he said that the plan satisfied that test anyway because of the state's interest in "making it easier for more black leaders" to represent the state in Congress and in avoiding Voting Rights Act challenges by the Justice Department or private litigants.

In *Bush v. Vera,* the Supreme Court produced a multiplicity of opinions that included, remarkably, two from Justice O'Connor: the main opinion as well as a separate concurrence suggesting broader leeway in racial line-drawing than the other conservative justices were willing to accept. O'Connor began her plurality opinion by upholding the lower court's finding that race had been the "predominant" consideration in drawing the lines of the three challenged districts even though incumbency protection had also played a part. The evidence, she said, included the state legislators' open intention to create majority-minority districts, as well as the districts' "bizarre" shapes and the use of "unprecedentedly detailed racial data" to "manipulate" the lines. The district lines therefore had to be reviewed under strict scrutiny, O'Connor said, and they failed to satisfy the test. O'Connor said the Court, as in previous cases, would leave open the question whether a state's interest in complying with the Voting Rights Act could ever amount to a "compelling" interest. She also rejected the lower court's rule that districts had to be as compact as possible. Still, a district must be "reasonably compact and regular," O'Connor continued, to be deemed "narrowly tailored" under the strict scrutiny test. None of the three districts met that test, she said.

Because there was no current finding of "specific" and "identified" discrimination, O'Connor rejected the argument that the districts were needed to overcome racially polarized voting attributable to past racial discrimination. She also rejected the state's argument that the majority-black Houston district was justified to comply with the act's provision requiring Justice Department preclearance of any voting change that could result in a "retrogression" in the position of racial minorities. The state had gone further than necessary, she said, because the new plan had actually increased the black population in the district.

In a final section, O'Connor answered the dissenters who argued that the Court's rulings were resulting in excessive "judicial entanglement" in the redistricting process. The new rulings would help clarify the legal rules for state legislators, O'Connor responded, while reemphasizing that voters are "more than racial statistics."

Justice Kennedy took issue with O'Connor's statement that an intentionally created majority-minority district did not necessarily require strict scrutiny. Justice Thomas said that strict scrutiny should apply whenever a legislature "affirmatively undertakes to create a majority-minority district that would not have existed but for the express use of racial classifications."

O'Connor underscored the divisions among the conservatives with her unusual concurrence with her own opinion. A former Arizona legislator, O'Connor said state lawmakers were entitled to "more definite guidance" from the Court. She said she would explicitly decide that states have a compelling interest in complying with the Voting Rights Act and that they may intentionally draw majority-minority districts as long as the districts did not "deviate substantially" from "traditional districting principles" for "predominantly racial reasons."

In dissent, Justice Souter acknowledged O'Connor's stance, calling it "a very significant step toward alleviating apprehension" that the Court's decisions were in conflict with the Voting Rights Act. He also said the rulings still had resulted in "confusion" among state legislators and shifted redistricting issues to the courts"—and truly to this Court, which is left to superintend the drawing of every legislative district in the land."

Justice Stevens gave greater emphasis in his dissent to the factual issues in the case. After a detailed examination of the Dallas districts, he insisted that they should not be subject to strict scrutiny because they were primarily "political gerrymanders" instead of "racial gerrymanders." The Houston district was a closer question, he said, but in any event it would be justified by the state's "compelling interest in creating majority-minority districts in accord with the Voting Rights Act."

Both dissents closed by insisting that the Court had failed to provide what Souter called "manageable standards" while threatening the progress minority groups had made in political representation. "Nothing in the Constitution," Stevens wrote, "requires this unnecessary intrusion into the ability of States to negotiate solutions to political differences while providing long-excluded groups the opportunity to participate effectively in the democratic process."

For the states themselves, the rulings posed a conundrum: whether to hold congressional elections in November under the redistricting plans that the Court struck down or to draw new maps in time for the general election. In North Carolina, the judges allowed the use of the existing districts for the November elections. But in Texas, the court drew up a new plan that changed thirteen districts altogether, including the three that the justices had ruled invalid.

See Richard H. Pildes and Richard G. Niemi, "Expressive Harms, 'Bizarre Districts,' and Voting Rights: Evaluating Election-District Appearances After *Shaw v. Reno,*" *Michigan Law Review* 92 (1993): 101; and Donovan Wickline, "Walking a Tightrope: Redrawing Congressional District Lines After *Shaw v. Reno* and its Progeny." *Fordham Urban Law Journal* 25 (1998): 641.

United States v. Virginia

518 U.S. 515 (1996)
Decided: June 26, 1996
Vote: 7 (Rehnquist, Stevens, O'Connor, Kennedy, Souter, Ginsburg, Breyer)
1 (Scalia)
Opinion of the Court: Ginsburg
Opinion concurring in judgment: Rehnquist
Dissenting opinion: Scalia
Did not participate: Thomas

Single-sex schools have a long history in the United States, especially in higher education. Whatever their educational advantages or disadvantages, single-sex public schools raise a constitutional issue: May the government operate all-male or all-female schools without violating the Fourteenth Amendment's command to provide all citizens "equal protection of the laws"?

The nation's two surviving, state-supported all-male military colleges—The Citadel in South Carolina and Virginia Military Institute (VMI)—fought pitched battles over the issue in the 1990s. Women seeking admission to the schools challenged the exclusionary policies and were backed by the federal government and women's rights advocates. The schools resisted, with support from alumni, social conservatives, and some feminists who feared the dismantling of women's colleges.

The fight ended with a Supreme Court ruling ordering VMI either to admit women or give up its public status. The decision tightened the constitutional standard on sex discrimination by requiring the government to present an "exceedingly persuasive justification" for any laws or policies that treated men and women differently.

The Court had first dealt with single-sex schools in a challenge to Mississippi's all-female nursing school. In ordering the admission of a male applicant to a nursing program, the Court in ***Mississippi University for Women v. Hogan,*** 458 U.S. 718 (1982), held that sex classifications could be justified only if they served "important governmental objectives" and were "substantially related to the achievement of those objectives." A decade later, a federal court in South Carolina applied that decision in 1995 to require The Citadel to admit a woman applicant, Shannon Faulkner. The case evaporated, however, when Faulkner withdrew from the school only five days after enrolling.

The VMI case took shape in Virginia and Washington with less fanfare. A Virginia high school senior—never identified—initiated the case by filing a complaint with the Justice Department in 1990 that the school's all-male status amounted to illegal sex discrimination. The government agreed and initiated a suit to overturn the policy. After four rounds in lower federal courts, VMI's all-male status remained intact. The federal appeals court in Richmond agreed that the single-sex policy violated the Constitution, but accepted the state's remedy of establishing a separate all-women's military program at another public college, Mary Baldwin University.

In ruling on appeals from both sides, the Court acknowledged VMI's "unique program and unparalleled record," and, in an opinion by Justice Ginsburg—a leading women's rights litigator before her appointment to the federal bench—rejected the state's use of "overbroad generalizations" about men and women to justify its all-male admission policy. The Mary Baldwin program was inadequate, Ginsburg said. To cure the equal protection violation, she said, "Women seeking and fit for a VMI-quality education cannot be offered anything less."

In a footnote, Ginsburg said the ruling did not completely bar single-sex education. "We do not question the state's prerogative evenhandedly to support diverse educational opportunities," she wrote. Nonetheless, Justice Scalia—in a lone dissent—insisted the ruling was a death-knell for all single-sex education in the country, public or private.

VMI briefly considered an effort to take the school private, but the price tag was too high. Three months after the decision, the school's Board of Visitors voted narrowly to admit women beginning in 1997.

See Jason M. Skaggs, "Justifying Gender-Based Affirmative Action Under *United States v. Virginia*'s 'Exceedingly Persuasive Justification' Standard," *California Law Review* 86 (October 1998): 1169; and Philippa Strum, *Women in the Barracks: The VMI Case and Equal Rights* (Lawrence: University Press of Kansas, 2002).

Colorado Republican Federal Campaign Commission v. Federal Election Commission

518 U.S. 604 (1996)
Decided: June 26, 1996
Vote: 7 (Rehnquist, O'Connor, Scalia, Kennedy, Souter, Thomas, Breyer)
2 (Stevens, Ginsburg)
Judgment of the Court: Breyer
Opinion concurring in judgment: Kennedy (Rehnquist, Scalia)
Opinion concurring in judgment: Thomas (Rehnquist, Scalia)
Dissenting opinion: Stevens (Ginsburg)

Colorado Republicans had not yet chosen their candidate for the U.S. Senate in the spring of 1986 when they started their attack on the expected Democratic candidate, Rep. Tim Wirth. The state Republican Party spent $15,000 on radio ads contrasting Wirth's election-year pronouncements with what was depicted as an inconsistent voting record in Congress.

Wirth won the election in November, and in the meantime, the Colorado Democratic Party complained to the Federal Election Commission (FEC) that the GOP's pre-primary spending was a violation of federal limits on political party contributions to congressional candidates. The FEC agreed, and the Republicans took the case to the Supreme Court, contending that political parties have a First Amendment right to spend unlimited amounts in support of candidates for the House or the Senate.

In a splintered ruling, the Court gave the Republicans a partial victory and, in the process, created a new loophole in the federal law regulating campaign spending and contributions. Four of the justices voted to strike down all limits on political party spending in congressional races. Three others joined in rejecting the FEC's stance on a narrower ground, ruling that parties can spend unlimited amounts in congressional campaigns as long as the expenditures are completely independent of the candidates' own campaigns.

The limits on political parties' contributions to candidates formed a minor part of the debates. Party officials, supported by some academic critics of campaign finance laws, urged that the limits—which were set according to a state's population and adjusted periodically for inflation—be raised or eliminated altogether. They contended that political party contributions had no corrupting effects on candidates. Relaxing the limits, they said, would strengthen party discipline and accountability. Supporters countered that the limits helped contain overall spending and prevented well-to-do donors from using party committees to funnel large contributions to candidates.

In Colorado, the limit on party contributions for the 1986 Senate race was $103,000, but the state GOP had "assigned" its spending to the national party. On that basis, the FEC contended that the state GOP violated the law when it spent $15,000 on the radio spots attacking Wirth. A federal district court in Washington initially rejected the FEC's complaint, narrowly ruling that the law did not cover the ads because they were not "in connection with" the general election campaign. The federal appeals court in Washington, however, disagreed, saying the spending amounted to "electioneering" covered by the law. The appeals court also rejected the party's First Amendment attack on the contribution limits.

After detailing evidence that the state party chairman had approved the early media campaign without any consultation with any of the contenders for the senatorial nomination, Justice Breyer concluded the spending was an "independent expenditure" constitutionally protected under the Court's precedents. "The independent expression of a political party's views is 'core' First Amendment activity," Breyer wrote. "We are not aware," he added, "of any special dangers of corruption associated with political parties that tip the constitutional balance in a different direction."

Breyer added that the Court did not have to decide the constitutionality of limiting party spending that was "coordinated" with a candidate's campaign. The issue, he said, was "complex" and needed further argument in lower courts before the Supreme Court could rule on it. Justices O'Connor and Souter joined Breyer's opinion.

In separate concurring opinions, Justices Kennedy and Thomas argued that the Court should decide the constitutional issue and strike down the party contribution limits. Kennedy said that limiting any party expenditures—either independent or coordinated—"has a stifling effect on the ability of the party to do what it exists to do." Justice Thomas went further and called for abolishing all limits on political donations. "Contribution limits infringe as directly and as seriously upon freedom of political expression and association as do expenditure limits," he wrote. Rehnquist and Scalia joined other parts of Thomas's opinion, but not that section. In a response to Thomas's call for scrapping the Court's precedents, Breyer wrote, "Given the important competing interests involved in campaign finance issues, we should proceed cautiously."

Justice Stevens dissented, voting to uphold the contribution limits as the FEC had interpreted them to apply to any party spending in congressional races. Stevens maintained that the contribution limits helped prevent "the appearance and the reality" of political corruption.

See Anthony Corrado et al., eds. *Campaign Finance Reform: A Sourcebook* (Washington, D.C.: Brookings, 1997).

Felker v. Turpin

518 U.S. 651 (1996)
Decided: June 28, 1996
Vote: 9 (Rehnquist, Stevens, O'Connor, Scalia, Kennedy, Thomas, Souter, Ginsburg, Breyer)
0
Opinion of the Court: Rehnquist
Concurring opinion: Stevens (Souter, Breyer)
Concurring opinion: Souter (Stevens, Breyer)

The Supreme Court upheld part of a new law aimed at limiting death row inmates' ability to challenge their convictions and sentences in federal court, but said inmates can still bring pleas directly to the Court itself. The decision rejected a challenge to a provision of the Antiterrorism and Effective Death Penalty Act of 1996 that required inmates to obtain permission from a federal appeals court before filing a second habeas corpus petition before a federal district court. The law also said that the Supreme Court could not review an appeals court's decision under this so-called "gatekeeper" provision and tightened somewhat the standards for a successful habeas corpus petition. Ellis Wayne Felker, a Georgia death row inmate, challenged the law on grounds it violated the constitutional prohibition against "suspending" the writ of habeas corpus and unconstitutionally limited the Court's jurisdiction.

Chief Justice Rehnquist rejected both arguments, but only after narrowing the law somewhat. Citing ***Ex parte Yerger,*** 75 U.S. 85 (1869), Rehnquist said the provision limiting the Court's review of "gatekeeper" decisions did not abolish the Court's power to hear a habeas corpus petition filed with the Court itself. "This conclusion obviates one of the constitutional challenges raised," he wrote. He also rejected the inmate's argument that the new restrictions were unconstitutional and said they would apply to habeas petitions filed directly with the Court.

In concurring opinions, Justices Stevens and Souter said that state inmates also had other ways to present a habeas corpus challenge to the Court.

See Scott Moss, "An Appeal By Any Other Name: Congress's Empty Victory Over Habeas Rights—*Felker v. Turpin*," *Harvard Civil Rights-Civil Liberties Law Review* 32 (winter 1997): 249–263.

Denver Area Educational Telecommunications Consortium, Inc. v. Federal Communications Commission

518 U.S. 727 (1996)
Decided: June 28, 1996
Vote: Multiple
Judgment of the Court: Breyer
Concurring opinion: Stevens
Concurring opinion: Souter
Dissenting opinion: O'Connor
Dissenting opinion: Kennedy (Ginsburg)
Dissenting opinion: Thomas (Rehnquist, Scalia)

Critics of offensive and indecent cable television programming managed to get a three-part provision dealing with the issue attached to the Cable Television Consumer Protection and Competition Act of 1992. Two of the provisions, Sections 10(a) and 10(c), allowed cable operators to prohibit sexually explicit material on channels leased to independent programmers or set aside for public use, respectively. The third provision, Section 10(b), required cable operators who did not prohibit indecent material to "segregate" such programming on a single channel and "block" the channel unless viewers requested access in writing.

Two cable television producers challenged the law in court. The Denver Area Educational Telecommunications Consortium produced programming for leased-access cable channels on topics such as gay rights, AIDS, and art censorship. The Alliance for Community Media was a coalition of public access cable producers. Initially, a three-judge panel of the court of appeals agreed that the provisions violated the First Amendment, but the full court voted to sustain them.

The Supreme Court held the public access provision unconstitutional by a 5–4 vote and overturned the "segregate and block" provision by a 6–3 vote. In a 7–2 vote, the Court upheld the provision allowing cable operators to prohibit sexually explicit programming on leased channels.

Justice Breyer began his opinion by accepting the government's interest in dealing with what he called "an extraordinarily important problem"—"protecting children from exposure to patently offensive depictions of sex." The government, he said, may regulate speech to address "extraordinary problems," if the regulations are "appropriately tailored to resolve those problems without imposing an unnecessarily great restriction on speech." By that standard, Breyer said, a "permissive" provision giving cable operators the right to control sexually explicit programming on leased channels was an appropriate way to accommodate their interests along with the interests underlying the access requirement. He cautioned that the indecency provision should not be interpreted to apply to programming of "scientific or educational value," but only to seriously offensive material.

Breyer said that the blocking requirement was unconstitutional because the government had less restrictive ways of accomplishing its goal. The government, he explained, could have required cable operators to provide customers with a "lockbox" they could use to block out specific channels or programs. He also noted that Congress had just passed a law requiring manufacturers to make TV sets with a "V-chip" that could automatically identify and block sexually explicit or violent programs. With those alternatives available, Breyer said, the mandatory blocking provision was "considerably more extensive than necessary" and therefore unconstitutional.

Breyer also said the public access channel provision was unconstitutional because historically these channels had been controlled by community-based organizations rather than cable operators. Giving cable operators control would "radically change present programming relationships," he warned. In addition, the government had failed to show a need for the regulation. Congress and the Federal Communications Commission had only limited evidence—a few "borderline examples"—of questionable material on the public channels, he said.

Breyer deliberately left one issue unsettled. In its earliest cable decisions, the Court ruled that cable could be regulated just like broadcasting. In *Turner Broadcasting System, Inc. v. Federal Communications Commission,* 512 U.S. 622 (1994), however, the Court suggested that cable should have the broader First Amendment protection recognized for newspapers and other print media. Breyer, who joined the Court later that year, now said it was not possible to adopt "a rigid single standard, good for now and for all future media and purposes."

Only Justices Stevens and Souter joined all of Breyer's opinion. Justice O'Connor joined most of it, but voted to uphold the provision giving cable operators the right to prohibit sexual material on public channels.

The other five justices split into two camps: Justices Kennedy and Ginsburg voted to overturn all three parts of the law, while Chief Justice Rehnquist and Justices Scalia and Thomas voted to uphold all three.

In his opinion, Kennedy said that Breyer's opinion was "adrift" because it failed to settle on a rationale for regulating cable. He characterized the leased and public access channels as congressionally created "public forums," where any government regulation was subject to "strict scrutiny," the most stringent constitutional standard. "It contravenes the First Amendment," Kennedy concluded, "to give Government a general license to single out some categories for lesser protection."

Justice Thomas also faulted Breyer for failing to adopt a clear approach on regulating cable. But, unlike Kennedy, Thomas viewed the indecency law as a permissible provision aimed mainly at protecting First Amendment rights of cable operators to control programming on their systems. The provisions, Thomas said, "merely restore part of the editorial discretion an operator would have absent government regulation." Thomas also said the mandatory blocking provision was a "narrowly tailored" provision to help parents control children's access to sexually explicit material.

See Jeffrey D. Kaiser, "Comment: The Future of Cable Regulation Under the First Amendment: The Supreme Court's Treatment of Section 10(a) of the Cable Television Consumer Protection and Competition Act of 1992," *UCLA Entertainment Law Review* 5 (fall 1997): 103–140.

Turner Broadcasting System, Inc. v. Federal Communications Commission

520 U.S. 180 (1997)
Decided: March 31, 1997
Vote: 5 (Rehnquist, Stevens, Kennedy, Souter, Breyer)
4 (O'Connor, Scalia, Thomas, Ginsburg)
Judgment of the Court: Kennedy
Concurring opinion: Stevens
Concurring opinion: Breyer
Dissenting opinion: O'Connor (Scalia, Thomas, Ginsburg)

The passage of the Cable Television Consumer Protection and Competition Act of 1992, a federal law requiring cable systems to carry the signals of local TV stations, capped a long history of rivalry between the cable and broadcasting industries. Broadcasters had helped stifle the growth of cable through the 1950s and 1960s by persuading the Federal Communications Commission (FCC) to impose restrictive regulations on cable systems. Cable operators began to chip away at those regulations through court challenges in the 1970s and, by the 1980s, were taking audiences and advertising away from established broadcasters.

The broadcasting industry responded by urging first the FCC and then Congress to require cable operators to carry local television stations on their systems. With the growth in the number of cable subscribers, the broadcasters argued, cable systems had the power to limit local stations' audiences by dropping them from their lineups. Moreover, the broadcasters contended, cable had an incentive to do just that as a way of limiting a competitive communications medium. Twice, the FCC adopted a form of must-carry rule only to be overturned each time by the federal appeals court in Washington, which ruled the agency did not have sufficient evidence to justify the provision. Rebuffed, broadcasters turned to Congress, which in 1992 included a must-carry provision in an omnibus cable regulation bill enacted over President George Bush's veto.

The cable industry challenged the law in court. Cable operators argued it violated their constitutional right to determine their programming; cable programmers said it violated their First Amendment rights by giving broadcasters preferential access to cable systems. The FCC, backed by broadcasters, argued that the law was structural regulation that did not affect First Amendment interests at all or, at most, imposed minimal burdens that were justifiable given Congress's objectives.

A special three-judge court upheld the law in a 2–1 ruling in 1993, and cable operators appealed to the Supreme Court. The Court sent *Turner Broadcasting System, Inc. v. Federal Communications Commission,* 512 U.S. 622 (1994), back to the lower court for a new hearing. Eight of the justices ruled that the cable industry was entitled to a greater measure of First Amendment protection than the lower court had recognized, but they were divided equally on how to resolve the case.

One group, led by Justice O'Connor, wanted to strike the law down; the other, led by Justice Kennedy, said the lower court should reexamine the law under the "intermediate scrutiny" test used in some First Amendment cases—whether the law furthered an important government interest and was narrowly tailored to serve that interest. The tie was broken by Justice Stevens, who favored upholding the law but voted to send the case back to avoid a deadlock.

On remand, the three-judge court again upheld the must-carry law, by the identical 2–1 vote, and the case returned to the Supreme Court. This time, Justice Kennedy led a fragile majority of five in upholding the statute. In a detailed recitation of the evidence before Congress, Kennedy said lawmakers had a "substantial basis" for concluding that "a real threat justified enactment of the must-carry provisions." He said cable operators had "systemic reasons" for wanting to "disadvantage" local broadcasters, who competed with cable systems for audience and advertisers. Congress had evidence that cable operators were dropping broadcasters from their line-ups, that some broadcasters were experiencing financial problems, and that local stations' financial strength could "deteriorate" if they were not carried on cable systems.

Kennedy also concluded that the must-carry provisions were narrowly tailored to further Congress's goals of preserving local broadcasters, promoting media diversity, and promoting fair competition. He said the burdens on cable operators were "modest." Cable systems had been able to meet their must-carry obligations 87 percent of the time by using "previously unused channel capacity," Kennedy said. He ended by saying, "Judgments about how competing economic interests are to be reconciled in the complex and fast-changing field of television are for Congress to make."

Justice Breyer joined all of Kennedy's opinion except for the discussion of the competition issues.

In her dissenting opinion, O'Connor faulted the majority for deferring too much to Congress. She said the law was not "a measured response" to concerns about cable's monopoly powers, while the interest in promoting media diversity was "poorly defined." She noted that, "Congress has commandeered up to one-third of each cable system's channel capacity for the benefit of local broadcasters," O'Connor wrote, "without any regard for whether doing so advances the statute's alleged goals."

See Albert N. Lung, "Note: Must-Carry Rules in the Transition to Digital Television: A Delicate Constitutional Balance," *Cardozo Law Review* 22 (2000): 151.

Clinton v. Jones

520 U.S. 681 (1997)
Decided: May 27, 1997
Vote: 9 (Rehnquist, Stevens, O'Connor, Scalia, Kennedy, Souter, Thomas, Ginsburg, Breyer)
0
Opinion of the Court: Stevens
Opinion concurring in judgment: Breyer

Less than two years into his presidency, Bill Clinton was accused by a former Arkansas state employee of sexually harassing her while he was governor. The political scandal turned into a constitutional test of presidential powers. The Supreme Court justices said a president could be sued while in office for private conduct unrelated to his official duties.

The Court had recognized a broad claim of presidential immunity for official conduct in a decision involving former president Richard M. Nixon. In ***Nixon v. Fitzgerald,*** 457 U.S. 731 (1982), the Court held that the president was "entitled to absolute immunity from damages liability predicated on his official acts." But no court had ever ruled on whether the president was entitled to immunity in civil suits for private, unofficial conduct, whether committed while in office or before.

The suit against Clinton stemmed from an alleged encounter in a Little Rock hotel in 1991 with Paula Corbin Jones, at the time an unmarried, twenty-four-year-old high school graduate working as a clerk in an Arkansas state agency. Jones claimed that Clinton spotted her while she was working at a registration desk at a state conference and had state troopers invite her to his hotel room. Once she was inside, Jones claimed, Clinton made a crude sexual advance toward her—which she rebuffed.

Jones went public with the allegation three years later when a magazine story about Clinton's alleged womanizing hinted at her identity. She filed suit in federal court in Arkansas combining state law claims of defamation and emotional distress with a federal civil rights claim based on the alleged sexual harassment.

Instead of meeting the accusation squarely, Clinton's lawyers filed a legal motion asking, on grounds of presidential immunity, to delay proceedings in the suit until Clinton had left office. The judge in the case gave Clinton a partial victory by agreeing to delay any trial but allowing pretrial discovery to go forward. A federal appeals court denied Clinton any relief, however, voting 2–1 that the president was not entitled to official immunity for unofficial conduct and that the judge was wrong to bar any trial until after Clinton left the White House.

The Supreme Court agreed. Justice Stevens said Clinton's claim for "temporary immunity" for unofficial conduct "cannot be sustained on the basis of precedent." Nor did the separation of powers principles require immunity because the judiciary was not attempting to increase its powers at the president's expense. In addition, the Court had recognized that a president could be required to respond to subpoenas or other judicial orders—most notably, in the Watergate tapes case, ***United States v. Nixon,*** 418 U.S. 683 (1974).

Stevens said the request for a discretionary delay in the proceedings presented a closer question, but, according to Stevens, the judge's "lengthy and categorical stay" was wrong because it took "no account whatever" of Jones's interest. "Like every other citizen," Stevens wrote, Jones "has a right to an orderly disposition of her claims."

Stevens closed by casting doubt on what he called the "remote" possibility that the ruling would invite "frivolous and vexatious" litigation against presidents in the future. Justice Breyer gave that warning more credence in an opinion concurring in the judgment. He voiced the fear that civil suits could become a "distraction" for a president and admonished judges to avoid any interference with the president's duties.

Clinton eventually settled the suit by agreeing in 1998 to pay Jones $850,000. Before that, however, pretrial discovery in the case turned up the name of a White House intern, Monica Lewinsky, who claimed to have had sexual encounters with Clinton while he was in office. The information spawned an expanded investigation of Clinton by Independent Counsel Kenneth Starr and eventually impeachment by the House of Representatives for alleged perjury before a federal grand jury. Clinton was acquitted by the Senate in 1999 after a four-week trial.

See Cornell W. Clayton, "From *Nixon v. U.S.* to *Clinton v. Jones:* The Prosecution of Presidents," in *Creating Constitutional Change,* ed. Greg Ivers and Kevin McGuire (Charlottesville: University of Virginia Press, forthcoming, 2003).

Abrams v. Johnson

521 U.S. 74 (1997)
Decided: June 19, 1997
Vote: 5 (Rehnquist, O'Connor, Scalia, Kennedy, Thomas)
4 (Stevens, Souter, Ginsburg, Breyer)
Opinion of the Court: Kennedy
Dissenting opinion: Breyer (Stevens, Souter, Ginsburg)

This case is another in a line in which the Court tried to articulate a standard by which race-conscious legislative districting might, in some limited circumstances, be constitutional. The case began as *Miller v. Johnson,* 515 U.S. 900 (1995), in which the Court held that bizarre shapes by themselves did not doom a districting plan, and challengers would have to prove that the legislature drew that shape primarily for racial reasons. The Court remanded *Miller v. Johnson* to the district court in Georgia with an order to review the 1990 state redistricting plan. The state was unable to meet the Court's criteria, and the district court fashioned its own plan, which included one majority-minority district, although the original state plan had two. The district court's decision was quickly attacked on the grounds that it failed to follow the Supreme Court's guidelines as well as the state assembly's clear desire for two majority-minority districts.

In his dissent in ***Bush v. Vera,*** 517 U.S. 952 (1996), Justice Souter warned that the Court's failure to provide clear guidelines on redistricting would lead to lower courts arrogating to themselves the power that properly belonged in the legislature. Even though the Rehnquist Court repeatedly avowed the principle of judicial deference to legislative policymaking, in the case of race-conscious districting, a majority of the justices consistently denied Congress power under the Enforcement Clauses of the Fourteenth and Fifteenth Amendments to impose a plan it deemed necessary to give minorities voting effectiveness. The justices also denied to the states their usual leeway in drawing less than compact or contiguous districts.

The Court never explicitly declared majority-minority districts *per se* unconstitutional, but its decision in this case made it questionable whether such districts could be created anywhere other than in large cities, where it would be almost impossible not to have them. Justice Kennedy reaffirmed that race "must not be a predominant factor in drawing the district lines." While the task of redistricting should always be left to the elected representatives of the people, the Supreme Court upheld the district court's plan as necessary, given the inability of the legislature to reach a decision. Kennedy also claimed that neither the Voting Rights Act requirements nor the Enforcement Clauses could be used to justify drawing district lines primarily on the basis of race.

It is possible that states can create majority-minority districts that the Court would uphold. Such districts would have to meet the traditional standards of being compact, contiguous, and one-person, one-vote. Moreover, it is possible that if states do not make race the dominant criteria, they could even stray somewhat from the compact and contiguous standards. Justice Breyer emphasized that the lower court should not have been allowed to disregard the legislature's wishes for two majority black districts and that such a wish would not be unconstitutional given the legislature's belief that the Voting Rights Act mandated this kind of plan. He also reiterated that he and the other dissenters had consistently argued through all of the districting cases that the majority's rule would prove unworkable and would shift responsibility for drawing district lines from the legislature, where it belonged, to the courts, where it did not. This result "would prevent the legitimate use (among others the remedial use) of race as a political factor in redistricting, sometimes making unfair distinctions between racial minorities and others."

See J. Morgan Kousser, *Colorblind Injustice: Minority Voting Rights and the Undoing of the Second Reconstruction* (Chapel Hill: University of North Carolina Press, 1999); and Samuel Issacharoff, "The Constitutional Contours of Race and Politics," *Supreme Court Review, 1995,* 45.

Agostini v. Felton

521 U.S. 203 (1997)
Decided: June 23, 1997
Vote: 5 (Rehnquist, O'Connor, Scalia, Kennedy, Thomas)
4 (Stevens, Souter, Ginsburg, Breyer)
Opinion of the Court: Scalia
Dissenting opinion: Souter (Stevens, Ginsburg, Breyer)
Dissenting opinion: Ginsburg (Stevens, Souter, Breyer)

For more than a decade, the New York City school system used a cumbersome procedure to provide federally funded, remedial education for low-income students at parochial schools. Acting under a court order designed to maintain separation of church and state, the school system leased mobile vans and parked them on the street adjacent to parochial school grounds. Public school teachers could then provide the special instruction for parochial school students in what was technically a public school classroom.

A lower federal court imposed the system to comply with the Supreme Court's decision in ***Aguilar v. Felton,*** 473 U.S. 402 (1985). The ruling barred the city's earlier practice of sending teachers directly into parochial school buildings. In *Agostini v. Felton* the Court overturned that ruling in a decision that significantly eased the rules for government aid to parochial school students.

The flip-flop was emblematic of the Court's struggle to define the rules for church-school aid. Over several decades, the Court approved some forms of aid to students—for example, textbook loans—but barred more direct assistance to parochial schools themselves. The decisions generated criticism, but the Court reaffirmed its basic approach when it ruled in 1985 on a challenge to New York City's use of funds under the federal Title I program to aid low-income students at parochial schools. The Court held that the operation of the program resulted in excessive entanglement of government and religion.

Over the next decade, however, the Court began to relax the strictures against government aid to students attending church-affiliated schools. In the most significant of the rulings, the Court in ***Zobrest v. Catalina Foothills School District,*** 509 U.S. 1 (1993), allowed the use of government funds to pay for a sign-language interpreter for a deaf parochial school student.

New York City school administrators seized on the new rulings to ask the Court to throw out the *Aguilar* decision, and the Court complied. For the majority, Justice O'Connor agreed that the Court had backed away from its previous positions that any government aid directly supporting a parochial school's educational function was invalid or that the presence of a public employee on parochial school premises amounted to a symbolic union of government and religion. On that basis, O'Connor said, *Aguilar* was "no longer good law."

Instead, O'Connor said, the issue was whether New York's Title I program improperly advanced religion—and she concluded that it did not. The program, she said, "does not result in governmental indoctrination; define its recipients by reference to religion; or create an excessive entanglement" between church and state.

The dissenting justices forcefully criticized the decision. Under the ruling, Justice Souter warned, state and local governments would be free to pay for "the entire cost of instruction provided in any ostensibly secular subject in any religious school." Three years later, however, the Court reaffirmed the new direction in a decision, ***Mitchell v. Helms,*** 530 U.S. 793 (2000), allowing government loans of computers and other equipment to parochial schools.

See Patrick Marshall, "Religion in Schools," *CQ Researcher,* January 12, 2001, 1–24; and Christian Chad Warpula, "The Demise of Demarcation: *Agostini v. Felton* Unlocks the Parochial School Gate to State-Sponsored Educational Aid," *Wake Forest Law Review* 33 (1998): 465.

Idaho v. Coeur d'Alene Tribe of Idaho

521 U.S. 261 (1997)
Decided: June 23, 1997
Vote: 5 (Rehnquist, O'Connor, Scalia, Kennedy, Thomas)
4 (Stevens, Souter, Ginsburg, Breyer)
Judgment of the Court: Kennedy
Opinion concurring in judgment: O'Connor (Scalia, Thomas)
Dissenting opinion: Souter (Stevens, Ginsburg, Breyer)

The Coeur d'Alene Tribe sued the state of Idaho, claiming a beneficial interest (in other words, control of) the beds and banks of all navigable waters and lakes within the original boundaries of the Coeur d'Alene reservation, as defined by an 1873 presidential order. It also asked for injunctive relief based on aboriginal title to the land. The district court dismissed the suit as completely barred by the Eleventh Amendment. On appeal, the Court of Appeals for the Ninth Circuit agreed that the Eleventh Amendment barred the main claims against Idaho, but reinstated the tribe's suit for certain relief based on aboriginal title, which the court held was not barred by the Eleventh Amendment.

The Supreme Court reversed in part and remanded. Justice Kennedy held that the tribe's claims against the state and its officials were totally barred. Moreover, the "special circumstances" exception to this bar, as set forth in ***Ex parte Young,*** 209 U.S. 123 (1908), for certain suits against state officers in their individual capacities was also inapplicable. The opinion reaffirmed what had become a trait of Rehnquist Court jurisprudence, a revival of states rights and state immunity to suits in federal courts under the Eleventh Amendment.

The four dissenters continued their opposition to the majority's broad reading of the Eleventh Amendment and would have allowed the suit to go forward under the exceptions in *Ex parte Young.*

Kansas v. Hendricks

521 U.S. 346 (1997)
Decided: June 23, 1997
Vote: 5 (Rehnquist, O'Connor, Scalia, Kennedy, Thomas)
4 (Stevens, Souter, Ginsburg, Breyer)
Opinion of the Court: Thomas
Concurring opinion: Kennedy
Dissenting opinion: Breyer (Stevens, Souter, Ginsburg)

Leroy Hendricks began sexually abusing children in 1955 at the age of twenty. Over the next thirty years, he accumulated five convictions for molesting a total of ten children—boys and girls, some as young as seven. Shortly after being paroled in 1972, he began to abuse his own stepdaughter and stepson, forcing them to engage in sexual activity over a four-year period.

In 1984 Hendricks was convicted of attempting to fondle two thirteen-year-old boys in the electronics shop where he worked. Although he faced a maximum prison sentence of 45 to 180 years, the prosecutor agreed to a plea bargain of 5 to 20 years. Because of good time credits earned while in prison, Hendricks was scheduled to be released in August 1994.

In the meantime, Kansas passed a law aimed at isolating repeat sexual offenders beyond their prison terms. The Sexually Violent Predator Act authorized what it described as civil confinement for persons who had been found guilty of a sexually violent crime and diagnosed as suffering from a mental abnormality or personality disorder that "makes the person likely to engage" in predatory acts of sexual violence in the future.

The law provided a number of safeguards—most notably, the requirement that the state prove the elements of the act beyond a reasonable doubt. Individuals were entitled to an attorney and mental health examinations, at public expense for indigents. The act also required the committing court to review a person's record at least once a year to determine whether continued detention was warranted. In addition, someone committed under the law could petition for release at any time.

After hearing the testimony, a jury unanimously agreed that Hendricks was a violent sexual predator, and the judge ordered him committed. Hendricks challenged the law on constitutional grounds. He claimed, first, that the law violated due process by authorizing his confinement on the basis of a "mental abnormality," instead of a diagnosed mental illness. In addition, he said the commitment amounted to successive and retroactive punishment for his previous crimes, in violation of the Double Jeopardy Clause and the Ex Post Facto Clause.

Kansas Supreme Court agreed with Hendricks's argument that confining him without a finding of mental illness violated his "substantive due process rights." The state asked the Supreme Court to review the ruling.

The Court accepted the state's arguments. Civil commitment had historically been used, Justice Thomas said, to confine someone who was mentally ill and presented a danger to himself or society. The Kansas law satisfied that test by requiring "a finding of future dangerousness" linked to the existence of a mental abnormality or personality disorder that "makes it difficult, if not impossible, for the person to control his dangerous behavior."

The state was not required to make a finding of "mental illness," Thomas continued. The Court, he said, had "never required State legislatures to adopt any particular nomenclature in drafting civil commitment statutes." Pedophilia was recognized by mental health professionals as "a serious mental disorder," he said, and Hendricks himself acknowledged that he "cannot control the urge" to molest children. On that basis, Thomas concluded, the Kansas law "plainly suffices for due process purposes."

Thomas rejected the double jeopardy and retroactive punishment issues by stressing that the Kansas law provided for civil commitment rather than criminal punishment. Kansas described its law as civil in nature. The law was not aimed at the criminal law goals of retribution or deterrence, Thomas said, and the possibility of indefinite commitment did not necessarily reflect a criminal law purpose either.

Finally, Thomas rejected Hendricks's argument that the Court's prior rulings had established a requirement for treatment under civil commitment statutes. "Nothing in the Constitution," Thomas wrote, "prevents a State from civilly detaining those for whom no treatment is available, but who nevertheless pose a danger to others."

Justice Kennedy added a brief concurrence to warn against the use of the law to supplement criminal prosecution. "If the civil system is used to simply impose punishment after the State makes an improvident plea bargain on the criminal side," he wrote, "then it is not performing the proper function."

The limited dissent did not challenge the basic premise of the sexual predatory laws, only its retroactive application. Justice Breyer said that the law "did not provide Hendricks . . . with any treatment until after his release date from prison and only inadequate treatment thereafter." On that basis, Breyer concluded the law was "an effort to inflict further punishment" and therefore its use against Hendricks violated the Ex Post Facto Clause.

See John Q. La Fond, "The Future of Involuntary Civil Commitment in the U.S.A. After *Kansas v. Hendricks*," *Behavioral Sciences and the Law* 18 (2000): 153; and Deborah Morris, "Constitutional Implications of the Involuntary Commitment of Sexually Violent Predators—A Due Process Analysis," *Cornell Law Review* 82 (March 1997): 594.

City of Boerne v. Flores

521 U.S. 507 (1997)
Decided: June 25, 1997
Vote: 6 (Rehnquist, Stevens, Scalia, Kennedy, Thomas, Ginsburg)
3 (O'Connor, Souter, Breyer)
Opinion of the Court: Kennedy
Concurring opinion: Stevens
Concurring opinion: Scalia (Stevens)
Dissenting opinion: O'Connor (Breyer)
Dissenting opinion: Souter
Dissenting opinion: Breyer

In 1993 Congress passed the Religious Freedom Restoration Act (RFRA). The law was a response to the Supreme Court's opinion in ***Employment Division, Department of Human Resources of Oregon v. Smith,*** 494 U.S. 872 (1990), in which the justices seemed to abandon the rule set forth in ***Sherbert v. Verner,*** 373 U.S. 398 (1963), that states needed to make accommodation for the free exercise of religion. With RFRA, Congress undertook to define the extent of the First Amendment's Free Exercise Clause, saying in effect that *Smith* had been wrongly decided and that, under its power to pass civil rights legislation under Section 5 of the Fourteenth Amendment, it was reinstating the *Sherbert* standard.

Whatever may have been the intentions of Congress to satisfy the needs of constituents with a strong religious affiliation, passage of the RFRA was a direct challenge to the Supreme Court's view that it, and it alone, has the power to say what the Constitution means. It was only a matter of time, then, before the Court accepted a case challenging RFRA's constitutionality. The case it chose not only provided the Court an opportunity to reassert its authority but also to show the weaknesses of the law and, by implication, Congress's attempt to do the work of the judiciary.

Boerne, Texas, like many small southwestern cities, has an old section reflecting the area's Spanish heritage. The city passed a historic preservation ordinance that required municipal approval before any significant changes could be made to any building in the designated historic district. St. Peter the Apostle Catholic Church was built in 1923 in the style of the older Spanish mission churches. With the population in the parish growing, the 230-seat church could no longer accommodate the people who crowded in for Sunday mass. Archbishop Flores of San Antonio gave the parish permission to expand the church, but the city's Historic Landmarks Commission turned down the expansion proposal as not fitting in with the master preservation plan. The archbishop sued under the RFRA, claiming that the city was required to grant its approval.

In his opinion for the Court, Justice Kennedy delivered a civics lesson to Congress. Going all the way back to ***Marbury v. Madison,*** 5 U.S. 137 (1803), Kennedy noted that the powers of Congress, while extensive, are also limited, and that it is emphatically the function of the Court to determine the meaning of the Constitution. As for Congress's claimed authority under the Fourteenth Amendment, that grant of power was clearly directed at a specific issue, protecting civil rights, an area that had never encompassed rights protected under the First Amendment, which are usually understood to be civil liberties. Although the Court had allowed Congress great leeway under Section 5 of the Fourteenth Amendment, it had never permitted legislation that departed completely from the purpose of that amendment, and it had no intention to do so now.

Although the majority opinion focused almost entirely on the separation of powers issue, Justice Stevens pointed out the Equal Protection Clause and Establishment Clause issues involved. If the city had to allow the church to expand under the RFRA, it could not afterwards deny permission to other businesses or nonprofit enterprises, such as museums, because that would in effect be granting a preference to a religious establishment.

Justice Scalia, who wrote the opinion in *Smith,* entered a concurrence in effect saying that Congress had misunderstood the decision, which had been directed at a specific type of law.

Justice O'Connor's dissent agreed that the central issue was whether Congress had the power to act, which she and Justice Breyer thought it did. But they also repeated their view that *Smith* had been wrongly decided.

In a similar vein, Justice Souter dissented, but he believed that until the issues raised in *Smith* had been fully resolved, the question of the RFRA's constitutionality should be postponed. He would have dismissed the case as an improvident grant of certiorari.

Although several attempts were made to revive the RFRA in Congress, none could meet the constitutional objections raised in this decision. A number of states, however, passed versions of the law that made the *Sherbert* rule official state policy. Because these states were acting well within their authority, no challenge to the Court was implied, and no suits taken against them.

See Garrett Epps, *To an Unknown God: Religious Freedom on Trial* (New York: St. Martin's Press, 2001); Michael W. McConnell, "Institutions and Interpretations: A Critique of *City of Boerne v. Flores,*" *Harvard Law Review* 111 (1997): 153; and "Symposium," *William and Mary Law Review* 39 (1998): 597.

Washington v. Glucksberg

521 U.S. 702 (1997)
Decided: June 26, 1997
Vote: 9 (Rehnquist, Stevens, O'Connor, Scalia, Kennedy, Souter, Thomas, Ginsburg, Breyer)
0
Opinion of the Court: Rehnquist
Concurring opinion: O'Connor (Ginsburg, Breyer)
Opinion concurring in judgment: Stevens
Opinion concurring in judgment: Souter
Opinion concurring in judgment: Ginsburg
Opinion concurring in judgment: Breyer
See *Vacco v. Quill* below.

Vacco v. Quill

521 U.S. 793 (1997)
Decided: June 26, 1997
Vote: 9 (Rehnquist, Stevens, O'Connor, Scalia, Kennedy, Souter, Thomas, Ginsburg, Breyer)
0
Opinion of the Court: Rehnquist
Concurring opinion: O'Connor (Ginsburg, Breyer)
Opinion concurring in judgment: Stevens
Opinion concurring in judgment: Souter
Opinion concurring in judgment: Ginsburg
Opinion concurring in judgment: Breyer

Laws making it a crime to assist someone to commit suicide date back centuries. The laws—widely accepted but rarely used—came under attack in the late twentieth century from a so-called "right to die" movement that favored legalizing physician-assisted suicide for terminally ill patients who wanted help in ending their lives. Doctors challenging the laws won federal appeals court decisions in separate cases from New York and Washington State. The Supreme Court, however, issued decisions upholding the laws, saying that it was up to legislators rather than judges to decide whether to permit physician-assisted suicide.

Modern medicine had shaped the controversy by introducing advances that helped many people with terminal illnesses live longer, but for others the new medical practices merely prolonged the process of death. Many Americans became familiar with cases of people suffering under constant pain who said they would rather die with dignity than live in agony.

The Court first dealt with the issue in the 1990 case of a Missouri woman left in a coma after an automobile accident. The ruling in ***Cruzan v. Director, Missouri Department of Health,*** 497 U.S. 261 (1990), recognized an individual's right to refuse unwanted, life-sustaining medical treatment, but stopped short of a broader "right to die."

Advocates of physician-assisted suicide stepped up their political and legal efforts. After suffering defeats in California and Washington, they won passage of an assisted-suicide initiative in Oregon in 1994. In the same year, physicians and patients in Washington and New York filed suits in federal court seeking to overturn their state laws on assisted suicide on due process and equal protection grounds. The lead plaintiffs in the two cases—Timothy Quill in New York and Harold Glucksberg in Washington—were physicians treating patients with cancer, AIDS, or other terminal diseases.

The federal appeals court in the Washington case agreed with the plaintiffs that the state law violated patients' and physicians' due process rights. The state's interest in preventing assisted suicide, the court said, was "of comparatively little weight." In the New York case, the federal appeals court cited equal protection grounds. It was unequal, the court said, to allow terminally ill patients on life support to hasten their deaths but not others.

In rejecting the due process argument, Chief Justice Rehnquist began his opinion in the Washington case by stressing the long history of laws banning assisted suicide. The laws reflected the states' "commitment to the protection and preservation of human life," and were "rationally related" to legitimate government interests. Besides promoting the interest in preservation of human life, Rehnquist said that the laws also helped protect "depressed or mentally ill persons" from "suicidal impulses" and "vulnerable groups—including the poor, the elderly, and disabled persons—from abuse, neglect, and mistakes." Allowing assisted suicide, Rehnquist continued, could weaken doctor-patient relationships by "blurring the time-honored distinction between healing and harming" and start society "down the path to voluntary and perhaps even involuntary euthanasia."

In a briefer opinion in the New York case, Rehnquist also rejected the equal protection argument. Banning assisted suicide while allowing terminally ill patients to refuse life-sustaining treatment is a "longstanding and rational distinction," he wrote.

Rehnquist—whose wife, Nina, died in 1991 after a long battle with ovarian cancer—closed the ruling in the Washington case by noting the "profound and earnest" debate on the issue. "Our holding permits the debate to continue, as it should in a democratic society," he wrote.

Four justices joined Rehnquist's opinion, although O'Connor qualified her support by saying that the ruling would not prevent a physician from prescribing pain-killing medication even if it hastened death. The other four justices indicated that individual cases involving terminally ill patients might be decided differently.

See Lawrence O. Gostin, "Deciding Life and Death in the Courtroom: From *Quinlan* to *Cruzan, Glucksburg,* and *Vacco*—A Brief History and Analysis of Constitutional Protection of the 'Right to Die,'" *Journal of the American Medical Association* 278 (1997): 1523–1528; and Melvin I. Urofsky, *Lethal Judgments: Assisted Suicide and American Law* (Lawrence: University Press of Kansas, 2000).

Reno v. American Civil Liberties Union

521 U.S. 844 (1997)
Decided: June 26, 1997
Vote: 7 (Stevens, Scalia, Kennedy, Souter, Thomas, Ginsburg, Breyer)
2 (Rehnquist, O'Connor)
Opinion of the Court: Stevens
Opinion concurring in the judgment in part and dissenting in part: O'Connor (Rehnquist)

As part of its wide-ranging Telecommunications Act of 1996, Congress passed the Communications Decency Act (CDA). One provision made it a criminal offense to knowingly transmit via the Internet indecent or obscene messages to any recipient under age eighteen, and another required access to sites containing such information to be closely regulated with devices such as filters and proof of age and credit card ownership. Although the Justice Department advised President Bill Clinton that these provisions would almost certainly fail a constitutional test, he signed the measure into law. Within the hour, the American Civil Liberties Union, the American Library Association, and others went into court seeking an injunction against the implementation of the CDA. The District Court for the Eastern District of Pennsylvania issued the injunction, claiming that it violated both the Free Speech Clause of the First Amendment as well as the Due Process Clause of the Fifth Amendment. Under a fast track provision of the CDA, the decision was appealed directly to the Supreme Court.

The Court recognized that, under its Commerce Clause powers, Congress could regulate the Internet, but it could not, under the First Amendment, regulate its content in such a broad and indeterminate manner. The Court demonstrated its full understanding of the Internet and how it operated. Almost anyone could post materials, and although filters could screen out certain sites, it was unreasonable to expect that any device would be able to keep track of all new sites coming on-line. Internet providers, moreover, could not reasonably be expected to examine each of the millions of available sites to classify each one according to its sexual content. Nor could purveyors of sites with explicit sexual content, even taking reasonable precautions against minors using the sites, be expected to know the ages of all users. Any minor, armed with a credit card, could give false information as to his or her age and gain access to any site on the Internet.

Aside from the question of regulating content, which prior decisions would allow to the government under strictly drawn conditions, the wording of the CDA failed the First Amendment test on vagueness grounds. The CDA used undefined phrases such as "indecent" and "patently offensive," which could mean different things to different people. Given the criminal penalties attached to the CDA, these vague phrases would have a chilling effect on the First Amendment rights of Internet users. The CDA, in fact, failed all of the tests courts had created to evaluate limits on speech: it did not announce a significant government interest that required content regulation; it was not tailored in the least restrictive manner; and it discriminated on a content basis. Because of the clear violation of the First Amendment, the Court did not even consider the Fifth Amendment grounds raised in the lower court.

Justice O'Connor agreed that the CDA was unconstitutionally vague, but she believed that a more tightly drawn act that attempted to create "adult zones" on the Internet would be constitutional.

The CDA was not the first effort by Congress to regulate the Internet, and courts have upheld laws that made the sale of obscene material over the Internet illegal just as selling it through the mails is illegal. In those cases, however, a "product" was sold, whereas in this instance access to sites was at issue. The Court's understanding of the complexities of the Internet and why it would be next to impossible to regulate was greeted by plaudits from representatives of electronic media groups who had tried in vain to explain the problem to Congress. The decision does, however, raise questions about the ability of the state or national government to regulate pornography or children's exposure to it. The Court seemed to say that the very nature of the Internet makes it impossible to regulate content without violating the First Amendment. The use of filters was fine, but they would have to be voluntarily imposed either by Internet service providers, libraries, or parents; they could not be imposed by the government.

See "Symposium," *Cumberland Law Review* 26 (1995/1996): 313.

Printz v. United States

521 U.S. 898 (1997)
Decided: June 27, 1997
Vote: 5 (Rehnquist, O'Connor, Scalia, Kennedy, Thomas)
4 (Stevens, Souter, Ginsburg, Breyer)
Opinion of the Court: Scalia
Concurring opinion: O'Connor
Concurring opinion: Thomas
Dissenting opinion: Stevens (Souter, Ginsburg, Breyer)
Dissenting opinion: Souter
Dissenting opinion: Breyer (Stevens)

In 1993 Congress enacted the so-called Brady bill, named for President Reagan's press secretary, James Brady, who was seriously wounded March 30, 1981, when an attempt was made on the president's life. The Brady bill prohibited the purchase of handguns by convicted felons and other designated groups and required the attorney general to establish a national instant background check system for would-be gun purchasers by the end of 1998. Certain interim measures would be in effect until the national screening system could be implemented. Under the interim arrangement, anyone wishing to purchase a handgun was required to fill out a form providing identification information, and the dealer conveyed this information to the local law enforcement agency, which would carry out the background check within five days. The law also provided exceptions, such as for people who already had valid state gun permits or if a state had an instant identification check system in place. Jay Printz, the sheriff and coroner for Ravalli County, Montana, challenged the law, claiming that the requirement that he, as the chief law enforcement officer for the county, carry out background checks for the federal government, violated the principle of federalism. Congressional action compelling state officers to carry out federal laws violated states' rights. Although the circuit court of appeals upheld the law, the Supreme Court by a narrow margin agreed with Printz.

Justice Scalia noted that the Constitution does not speak directly to the issue of whether state officers could be required to enforce federal laws, nor did history provide a conclusive answer. Nevertheless, the Constitution asserts a principle of dual sovereignty, in which the states, even while surrendering some of their authority to the federal government, retain control over other aspects of their affairs. The Framers rejected a system in which the federal government could commandeer the resources of the states, and the federal government may not commandeer local law enforcement officers—at no cost—to do its work.

Aside from the federalism issues, the Court found a violation of the separation of powers. Normally, Congress as the legislative body enacts a law, and the president, as the executive authority, carries it out. Here the law gave some implementation of the Brady bill to law enforcement officials in fifty states and thousands of jurisdictions. The Court did not question that Congress had the power to regulate the sale of handguns through its commerce powers, but the majority rejected Justice Stevens's claim that if it had the commerce power, then it could carry that power out any way it chose under the Necessary and Proper Clause. That clause, Scalia explained, could not violate the larger principles of states' rights or separation of powers. The federal government may not compel the states to administer a federal regulatory program.

The four members of the minority believed that the majority was misreading history and that the intent of the Framers was clear—namely, that the policies of the federal government would take precedence over those of the states. Moreover, local law enforcement officials, as well as other agency members, are sworn to uphold the Constitution, which, in effect, means upholding laws enacted under it. Justice Souter in particular found a long list of instances in which local officials carried out federal policies.

The decision is one of several handed down by the Rehnquist Court that went against nearly fifty years of broad interpretation of Congress's powers under the Commerce Clause and a limited view of states' rights. Like its decision in ***United States v. Lopez,*** 514 U.S. 549 (1995), the majority seemed intent on reasserting the authority of the states vis-à-vis the federal government and cutting down on the scope of the Commerce Clause. In all of these cases, the decisions were by a narrow majority, and it is unclear just how far the Court would go in this area. The majority did not, for example, address all of the issues in the Brady act, leaving in place the provision requiring the attorney general to set up a national background registry system.

See Erik M. Jensen and Jonathan L. Entin, "Commandeering, the Tenth Amendment, and the Federal Requisition Power: *New York v. United States Revisited,*" *Constitutional Commentary* 15 (1998): 355.

Phillips v. Washington Legal Foundation

524 U.S. 156 (1998)
Decided: June 15, 1998
Vote: 5 (Rehnquist, O'Connor, Scalia, Kennedy, Thomas)
4 (Stevens, Souter, Ginsburg, Breyer)
Opinion of the Court: Rehnquist
Dissenting opinion: Souter (Stevens, Ginsburg, Breyer)
Dissenting opinion: Breyer (Stevens, Souter, Ginsburg)

Here the Court held that interest earned on client funds held in trust accounts set up by state bars to generate funds for legal aid for the poor is the client's property for purposes of the Takings Clause. The ruling cast doubt on the constitutionality of legal aid funding programs operating in all fifty states and the District of Columbia. The so-called "IOLTA" programs—an acronym for "Interest on Lawyers' Trust Accounts"—pooled nominal funds held by lawyers for clients and funneled the interest from the accounts to legal aid organizations. The court of appeals, ruling on an unconstitutional takings claim brought by the conservative Washington Legal Foundation on behalf of a Texas client, held that the interest belonged to the client but did not determine whether there had been a taking. The Texas Supreme Court, which established the program, asked the Supreme Court to review the ruling.

The Court held that the interest was the client's property and sent the case back to the appeals court for further proceedings. Chief Justice Rehnquist cited *Beckford v. Tobin,* 27 Eng. Rep. 1049 (Ch. 1749), for the English common law rule that "interest follows principal." Because the funds belonged to the client, Rehnquist said, "any interest that does accrue attaches as a property right incident to the ownership of the underlying principal." Rehnquist said the Court expressed "no view" as to whether the funds had been "taken" or what compensation, "if any," would be due.

Justice Souter argued, in dissent, that the Court should have sent the case back to the appeals court for a complete decision on the takings claim; the limited holding, he said, amounted to an "abstract proposition" that might have no significance in resolving the real issue. In his dissent, Justice Breyer said that the client funds could not have generated interest except for the state-operated program. "I consequently believe," he concluded, "that the interest earned is *not* the client's 'private property.' "

The federal appeals court for Texas later ruled the program amounted to an unconstitutional taking, but the federal appeals court for Washington State upheld a similar program.

Gebser v. Lago Vista Independent School District

524 U.S. 274 (1998)
Decided June 22, 1998
Vote: 5 (Rehnquist, O'Connor, Scalia, Kennedy, Thomas)
4 (Stevens, Souter, Ginsburg, Breyer)
Opinion of the Court: O'Connor
Dissenting opinion: Stevens (Souter, Ginsburg, Breyer)
Dissenting opinion: Ginsburg (Souter, Breyer)

When the principal of Lago Vista High School outside San Antonio, Texas, received complaints in October 1992 that teacher Frank Waldrop was making sexually suggestive comments in class, he brought the teacher and parents together to talk about the problem. Waldrop denied saying anything offensive in class but offered an apology anyway. The principal counseled him to be more careful in the future, and the matter was closed.

Unbeknownst to the principal or other school officials, however, Waldrop had been having a sexual affair for months with a teenaged student in his class, Alida Star Gebser. The affair came to light in January 1993, when a policeman discovered Waldrop and Gebser having sex outside Waldrop's car off a remote country road. Waldrop was arrested and immediately fired; later, he pleaded guilty to having sex with Gebser and was given a form of suspended sentence. Meanwhile, Gebser and her mother, Alida Jean McCollough, also filed civil suits against Waldrop and the Lago Vista School Board in Texas court and federal court. Texas law protected the school district from liability in state court, but Gebser appeared to have a good chance of recovering damages in the federal suit because of Title IX of the Education Amendments of 1972, which the Supreme Court had interpreted as prohibiting sexual harassment of students in any school system receiving federal funds.

In February 1992, a few months before Waldrop's affair with Gebser began, the Court gave students and their families an additional legal tool to deal with the problem. It held that Title IX allowed students to sue and recover money damages from a teacher or school system for sexual harassment. Even though Congress had not mentioned private lawsuits in the law, the Court said that recognizing an "implied right of action" would further Congress's intent of eliminating sexual discrimination in federally funded educational institutions. The ruling in *Franklin v. Gwinnett County Public Schools,* 503 U.S. 60 (1992), reinstated a suit brought by a Georgia high school student who had charged that a teacher had forced her to have sex with him; she said that school district officials discouraged her from pressing charges against him and then dropped their investigation after firing him.

After the Court recognized a right to sue for damages under Title IX, lower courts had to decide the rules governing liability. Most federal appeals courts that addressed the issue held that, unless a school district or college had a procedure for dealing with sexual harassment complaints, it could not claim lack of knowledge of any misconduct as a defense. Other courts—

including the Fifth Circuit in Texas in a pair of decisions, *Rosa H. v. San Elizario Independent School District,* 106 F. 3d 648 (CA5 1997), and *Canutillo Independent School District v. Leija,* 101 F. 3d 393 (CA5 1996), interpreted *Franklin* to mean that schools could not be held liable unless they knew of the sexual harassment and failed to deal with it. When Gebser's case reached the Fifth Circuit later that year, the appeals court, applying that principle, upheld a lower court's decision to reject the suit. Gebser then asked the Supreme Court to review the case.

Ruling in Gebser's case, the Court sharply limited the ability of victims of sexual harassment to use Title IX to hold school boards or colleges and universities liable for misconduct by teachers. It held that school systems could be forced to pay damages for sexual harassment only if school district officials knew of the misconduct and failed—to the point of deliberate indifference—to do anything to stop it.

Justice O'Connor, writing for the majority, reasoned that, in the absence of any directions from Congress, the Court had "a measure of latitude to shape a sensible remedial scheme." She said the law contained "clues" that Congress would not have wanted a broad liability standard; one such clue was the requirement that the government give a school district notice of a violation of the law and an opportunity to correct the problem before cutting off federal funds. In addition, O'Connor repeated the contrast she made during arguments between two sex discrimination laws. "Whereas Title VII aims centrally to compensate victims of discrimination," she wrote, "Title IX focuses more on 'protecting' individuals from discriminatory practices carried out by recipients of federal funds." For those reasons, O'Connor concluded, a broad liability standard "would frustrate the purposes of Title IX." Instead, she said, a school district could be liable for sexual harassment of a student only if an official "with authority to institute corrective action" had "actual notice" of the problem and was guilty of "deliberate indifference" in failing to correct it.

The dissenters countered that the ruling would "thwart" Title IX's purposes of preventing the use of federal funds to support discriminatory practices and to protect individuals from such practices. "It seems quite obvious," Justice Stevens wrote, "that both of those purposes would be served—not frustrated—by providing a damages remedy in a case of this kind." Stevens warned that "few Title IX plaintiffs who have been victims of intentional discrimination will be able to recover damages under this exceedingly high standard."

See Amy Busa, "Two Steps Forward, One Step Back: The Supreme Court's Treatment of Teacher-Student Sexual Harassment in *Gebser v. Lago Vista Independent School District,*" *Harvard Civil Rights-Civil Liberties Law Review* 34 (1999): 289; and Julia C. Fay, "*Gebser v. Lago Vista Independent School District:* Is It Really the Final Word on School Liability for Teacher-to-Student Sexual Harassment?" *Connecticut Law Review* 31 (1999): 1485.

United States v. Bajakajian

524 U.S. 321 (1998)
Decided: June 22, 1998
Vote: 5 (Stevens, Thomas, Souter, Ginsburg, Breyer)
4 (Rehnquist, O'Connor, Scalia, Kennedy)
Opinion of the Court: Thomas
Dissenting opinion: Kennedy (Rehnquist, O'Connor, Scalia)

When a federal customs inspector at Los Angeles International Airport asked Hosep Bajakajian whether he was taking more than $10,000 in cash out of the country on June 9, 1994, he lied and said no. In fact, other inspectors, using dogs trained to sniff out currency, had already discovered that Bajakajian had hidden $230,000 in cash in his checked baggage. A search of his carry-on bag, his wallet, and his wife's purse uncovered more cash: all told, $357,144.

Bajakajian, a Syrian immigrant, who owned two service stations in Los Angeles, said that he was en route to Cyprus to repay a debt to a friend who had helped him get started in the United States. He was charged with violating the federal law against money laundering, which requires anyone leaving the country with more than $10,000 in cash to report the transaction. As part of the indictment, the government asked for the forfeiture of all of the cash, as the law mandated for any "willful" violation. The federal judge who convicted Bajakajian, however, ordered only $15,000 turned over to the government. When a federal appeals court upheld the decision, the government took the case to the Supreme Court.

When Congress first enacted a mandatory forfeiture provision in 1970, it was aiming at organized crime kingpins and drug traffickers who dealt in large sums of cash. Congress provided for mandatory forfeiture for willful violations of the currency-reporting law in 1992 after deciding that the previous penalties—short prison terms and small fines—were inadequate to deter money-laundering violations. Through the 1980s and 1990s, the federal government, as well as state and local law enforcement agencies, made aggressive use of forfeiture provisions not only to go after criminals but also to seize money or property from offenders in less serious cases. The growing use of forfeitures prompted a backlash in Congress, where some normally pro–law enforcement conservatives joined with more liberal lawmakers to call for restricting the practice.

Congress failed to act on the issue, but the Court did. In a pair of decisions in 1993, the Court ruled unanimously that forfeitures—whether imposed in connection with a criminal prosecution or in a separate civil proceeding—were subject to the Eighth Amendment's Excessive Fines Clause. The rulings in *Austin v. United States,* 509 U.S. 602, and *Alexander v. United States,* 509 U.S. 544, however, had set no specific guidelines on how to determine when a forfeiture was "excessive" and therefore unconstitutional.

The government appealed the lower court's decision reducing the forfeiture to $15,000. The government argued that all the money could be confiscated under a traditional doctrine permitting forfeiture of any property that is an "instrumentality" of a crime. But the court of appeals said that the money was not an instrumentality because the crime was "the withholding of information . . . not the possession or the transportation of the money." In fact, the appeals court said, none of the money was subject to forfeiture. Because Bajakajian had not filed a cross-appeal, however, the appeals judges said they could not set aside the limited forfeiture. The government again appealed.

The Supreme Court likewise refused to order all of Bajakajian's money confiscated. It held that the "grossly disproportional" penalty violated the Eighth Amendment's prohibition against "excessive fines." Whether or not Bajakajian's money amounted to an "instrumentality" of his crime, Justice Thomas wrote, the forfeiture amounted to punishment. It "serves no remedial purpose," he said, and was "designed to punish the offender." The forfeiture therefore was subject to the Excessive Fines Clause, he said, and the test to be applied "involves solely a proportionality determination." Thomas acknowledged that the Court had never determined what would constitute an "excessive" fine, and he found no guide in the text of the clause or its history. Instead, he turned to a standard that the Court had used in applying the Eighth Amendment's prohibition against cruel and unusual punishment. "If the amount of the forfeiture is grossly disproportional to the gravity of the defendant's offense," Thomas said, "it is unconstitutional." The crime, he said, "was solely a reporting offense" and was "unrelated to any other illegal activities."

Justice Kennedy led the dissenters in a sharply written opinion that criticized the majority both on the law and on the facts of the case. "The crime of smuggling or failing to report cash is more serious than the Court is willing to acknowledge," Kennedy wrote. The ruling "accords no deference, let alone substantial deference, to the judgment of Congress," he said, and gives "only a cursory explanation" for holding the forfeiture to be grossly disproportional. As for Bajakajian's offense, Kennedy insisted that it too was more serious than the majority recognized. He lied about having the money and also about where it came from, Kennedy said, and hid most of it in a false-bottomed suitcase.

See Barry L. Johnson, "Purging the Cruel and Unusual: The Autonomous Excessive Fines Clause and Desert-Based Constitutional Limits on Forfeiture After *United States v. Bajakajian*," *University of Illinois Law Review* (2000): 461.

Clinton v. City of New York

524 U.S. 417 (1998)
Decided: June 25, 1998
Vote: 6 (Rehnquist, Stevens, Kennedy, Souter, Thomas, Ginsburg)
3 (O'Connor, Scalia, Breyer)
Opinion of the Court: Stevens
Concurring opinion: Kennedy
Dissenting opinion: Scalia (O'Connor, Breyer)
Dissenting opinion: Breyer (O'Connor, Scalia)

In 1996 Congress passed the Line Item Veto Act, giving the president the power to delete specific items in a budget bill without having to veto the entire bill. Several members of Congress immediately challenged the constitutionality of the law, but under expedited review, the Supreme Court in *Raines v. Byrd,* 521 U.S. 811 (1997), held that they did not have standing to sue because, until the president actually used the power, they had suffered no actual injury. President Bill Clinton, who, like other presidents before him, badly wanted line item veto authority, recognized that until the Court decided on the merits of the issue, he did not actually have the power. To test the law, he deliberately vetoed one provision in the Balanced Budget Act of 1997 and two items in the Taxpayer Relief Act of 1997. These provisions were popular, and he recognized—and expected—that his veto would trigger a lawsuit. This time the Court agreed that New York City, which would be deprived of almost $1 billion in tax forgiveness; the Snake River Farmers' Cooperative, which stood to lose a tax preference; and other plaintiffs who had suffered tangible injuries had standing to sue. The Court then ruled the act unconstitutional.

Justice Stevens explained that the Presentment Clause, the section of Article I that details how Congress sends a bill to the president and how the president may either sign or veto it, does not give the president the power to amend a law passed by Congress by repealing part of it. The Constitution sets out a very specific procedure. Congress passes a law by a majority vote in both houses of Congress; the president may either sign it into law *as it is written,* or veto it and send it back to the Congress with his reasons for doing so. Congress may then attempt to pass it over his veto by a two-thirds majority in both houses. If Congress is successful, the bill becomes law without his signature; if it fails, the measure dies. Congress can amend the bill to correct the president's objections, but it is then considered a new bill when sent to him for his approval.

The majority opinion stressed that it did not question either the wisdom of the act or the fact that both Congress and the president believed it constitutional. Rather, it decided the question on the narrow grounds that the Constitution is specific that only those measures approved in toto by Congress and the president may become law. With the line item veto, a president could create a law that Congress had not approved by vetoing specific sections. If this result is desirable, it could come about only by amending the Constitution, not by an act of Congress.

The three dissenters believed that the Presentment Clause should not be interpreted in such a narrow manner and that the line item veto fit within the spirit of the original Constitution.

Presidents throughout the twentieth century asked for line item veto authority. Presidents who had served as state governors, such as Clinton and Ronald Reagan, had exercised such power over their state budgets. They argued that the only way to keep budgets in balance was to be able to cut the "pork" that legislators wrote into the budget bills to keep their constituents happy. Because all of them did it, there was no incentive for the legislature to keep an eye on such appropriations. Only a president who did not have to placate these constituencies could eliminate such spending from the budget.

Ironically, it was a Republican-controlled Congress that passed the measure, giving this authority to a Democratic president. Congressional Republicans promised this authority in their "Contract with America" as part of their plan to cut government spending, and at the time they fully expected Clinton to be defeated in the 1996 election.

Although a line item veto amendment has been introduced numerous times, neither house of Congress has passed it. The fact that the law passed at all in 1996 was a fluke of politics, and it is unlikely that any future Congress will willingly give up its authority in this area.

See Symposium, "The Phoenix Rises Again: The Nondelegation Doctrine from Constitutional and Policy Perspectives," *Cardozo Law Review* 20 (1999): 871; and Bernard W. Bell, "Dead Against the Nondelegation Doctrine, the Rules/Standards Dilemma, and the Line Item Veto," *Villanova Law Review* 44 (1999): 189.

National Endowment for the Arts v. Finley

524 U.S. 569 (1998)
Decided: June 25, 1998
Vote: 8 (Rehnquist, Stevens, O'Connor, Scalia, Kennedy, Thomas, Ginsburg, Breyer)
1 (Souter)
Opinion of the Court: O'Connor
Opinion concurring in judgment: Scalia (Thomas)
Dissenting opinion: Souter

Kings and princes have for centuries lavished subsidies on favored painters and sculptors. Royal patrons face few constraints in their choices, but when a constitutional democracy like the United States decides to support the arts, political and legal complications can ensue. The National Endowment for the Arts (NEA) became the subject of intense controversy in the 1980s and 1990s. Most NEA funds went to noncontroversial programs, but two small grants given to provocative artists became lightning rods for attacks from social conservatives.

One grant supported a posthumous exhibit by a homoerotic photographer, Robert Mapplethorpe; a second went to artist Andres Serrano, whose work included a photograph showing a crucifix immersed in urine, which critics labeled sacrilegious. Publicity about the grants prompted Congress in 1990 to consider various proposals to curb the NEA's discretion in handing out grants. Lawmakers eventually approved a compromise provision requiring that NEA grants be based on "artistic excellence and merit ... taking into consideration general standards of decency and respect for the diverse beliefs and values of the American public."

Several artists challenged the so-called "decency clause" as a violation of freedom of speech because it amounted to "viewpoint discrimination" by the government. The issue reached the Supreme Court in a suit by Karen Finley, a performance artist known for covering her nude body in chocolate to dramatize the sexual oppression of women. The Court's decision blunted the controversy by upholding the provision but saying that its terms were largely advisory.

Justice O'Connor said that in contrast to other proposals considered by Congress, the decency clause "imposes no categorical requirement" on NEA grants. In practice, O'Connor said, the clause did not "preclude or punish the expression of particular views" and therefore presented "no realistic danger" of compromising First Amendment values. O'Connor added that the Court had previously recognized that the government has "wide latitude" in deciding whether to subsidize particular programs or organizations. As authority, she cited ***Rust v. Sullivan,*** 500 U.S. 173 (1991), which allowed the government to withhold funding from family planning groups that provide abortion-related counseling.

Three justices sharply disagreed with O'Connor's interpretation of the decency clause. In an opinion concurring in the judgment, Justice Scalia, joined by Thomas, contended that the law required the NEA to "favor applications that display decency and respect, and disfavor applications that do not"—and that such a restriction "does not 'abridge' anyone's freedom of speech."

From the opposite perspective, Justice Souter agreed with Scalia's stringent interpretation of the law, but contended it was unconstitutional. "Viewpoint discrimination in the exercise of public authority over expressive activity is unconstitutional," he wrote in dissent.

See Alice Choi, "*National Endowment for the Arts v. Finley:* A Dispute over the 'Decency and Respect' Provision," *Akron Law Review* 32 (1999): 327; Cecilia Cohen, "An Endangered Species? Artistic Grants as a Vehicle for the Evolution of Entitlements Law," *Syracuse Law Review* 49 (1999): 1277; and Karen M. Kowalski, "*National Endowment for the Arts v. Finley:* Painting a Grim Picture for Federally Funded Art," *DePaul Law Review* 49 (fall 1999): 217–273.

Bragdon v. Abbott

524 U.S. 624 (1998)
Decided: June 25, 1998
Vote: 5 (Stevens, Kennedy, Souter, Ginsburg, Breyer)
4 (Rehnquist, O'Connor, Scalia, Thomas)
Opinion of the Court: Kennedy
Concurring opinion: Stevens (Breyer)
Concurring opinion: Ginsburg
Dissenting opinion: Rehnquist (O'Connor, Scalia, Thomas)
Dissenting opinion: O'Connor

When Randon Bragdon did a routine dental exam on Sidney Abbott he discovered a small, gum-line cavity in a back tooth. Filling the cavity would also have been a routine procedure, except for one thing: Abbott was infected with HIV, the human immunodeficiency virus that causes AIDS. Bragdon told Abbott that filling the cavity in his office would be dangerous but offered to perform the procedure in a local hospital. Abbott, however, insisted she was entitled to be treated in the office because of the federal law that prohibits discrimination against persons with disabilities—the Americans with Disabilities Act of 1990 (ADA). Abbott sued, and Bragdon lost in two lower federal courts.

The Supreme Court's decision to hear the case marked its first opportunity to interpret the ADA as well as its first encounter with the legal issues created by the AIDS epidemic. In one earlier ruling, however, it had given a broad reading to the antidiscrimination provision of a disability rights law that prohibited discrimination against persons with disabilities in any federally funded program or service. In *School Board of Nassau County, Florida v. Arline,* 480 U.S. 273 (1987), the Court ruled that a local school board could not fire a teacher with tuberculosis just because she had a contagious disease.

The Court declared that HIV met the ADA's definition of physical impairment "from the moment of infection and throughout every stage of the disease." After graphically describing the progression of the disease, Justice Kennedy said that Abbott could have argued that it affected any of a number of life activities. At the least, he said, reproduction—"central to the life process"—amounted to a major life activity for purposes of the law. HIV infection "substantially limited" Abbott's reproductive ability, he continued, because of the "significant risk" of infecting the man during conception or the risk of infecting her child "during gestation or childbirth."

Kennedy stopped short, however, of giving Abbott a complete victory. The evidence in the courts below, he said, was inadequate to rule whether her condition posed a risk to the health or safety of Bragdon or his office staff. Instead, that issue had to be sent back to lower courts for further consideration. Still, Kennedy heartened AIDS advocacy groups by stressing that any risk assessment "must be based on medical or other objective evidence," not on any subjective belief on Bragdon's part—"even if maintained in good faith."

Justices Stevens and Breyer said they would have rejected Bragdon's argument about the risks of treating HIV patients; they concurred in the remand only to create a majority position. Justice Ginsburg added a brief concurrence, saying it was "wise to remand" in view of the importance of the risk issue to health care workers.

In dissent, Chief Justice Rehnquist contended that reproduction was not a major life activity under the ADA's definition, which he said applied only to activities "essential in the day-to-day existence of a normally functioning individual." In addition, he said that Abbott's "voluntary" choice not to engage in sex or bear children because of her condition did not amount to a "substantial limit" on her activities.

Justice O'Connor wrote a somewhat narrower dissent also concluding that reproduction did not amount to a major life activity under the law.

See Mary Anne Bobinski, "The Expanding Domain of the ADA: The Supreme Court's Decision in *Abbott v. Bragdon,*" *Texas Business Journal* 61 (1998): 918; and Connie Mayer, "HIV as a Disability Under the Americans with Disabilities Act: Unanswered Questions After *Bragdon v. Abbott,*" *Journal of Law and Health* 14 (1999–2000): 179.

Burlington Industries, Inc. v. Ellerth

524 U.S. 742 (1998)
Decided: June 26, 1998
Vote: 7 (Rehnquist, Stevens, O'Connor, Kennedy, Souter, Ginsburg, Breyer)
2 (Scalia, Thomas)
Opinion of the Court: Kennedy
Opinion concurring in judgment: Ginsburg
Dissenting opinion: Thomas (Scalia)
See *Faragher v. City of Boca Raton* below.

Faragher v. City of Boca Raton

524 U.S. 775 (1998)
Decided: June 26, 1998
Vote: 7 (Rehnquist, Stevens, O'Connor, Kennedy, Ginsburg, Breyer)
2 (Scalia, Thomas)
Opinion of the Court: Souter
Dissenting opinion: Thomas (Scalia)

When Kimberly Ellerth and Beth Ann Faragher thought their bosses were making improper sexual advances, they did what most women do when they confront sexual harassment in the workplace: they put up with it. After leaving their jobs, however, the two women went to court and charged their employers with illegal sex discrimination under Title VII of the Civil Rights Act of 1964.

Ellerth began working for Burlington Industries in March 1993. She was based in a two-person office in Chicago and reported to Theodore Slowik, a mid-level vice president in New York. In her suit, Ellerth claimed Slowik repeatedly made sexually suggestive remarks to her and made unmistakable sexual propositions to her at least twice: during a business trip in the summer and a promotion interview in March 1994. She quit three months later. Ellerth did not file a formal complaint against Slowik before quitting, even though Burlington had written policies prohibiting sexual harassment on the job. Instead, she charged her employer with illegal sex discrimination under Title VII of the Civil Rights Act of 1964. When Ellerth's case reached court, Burlington insisted that, whatever Slowik may have done, as an employer it could not be held liable for conduct that had not been brought to its attention. In addition, Burlington argued that Ellerth had not been hurt at all because she had successfully rebuffed Slowik's advances and had never been passed over for a promotion or raise during her fifteen months with the company.

Faragher worked as a lifeguard in Boca Raton part time and summers from September 1985 to May 1990 while attending college. Throughout her tenure, Faragher said, she and other female lifeguards were subjected to lewd comments, sexual come-ons, and physical gropes. She accused two supervisors of misconduct: Bill Terry, chief of the marine safety section of the city's parks and recreation department, and David Silverman, a lieutenant and later captain in the section. Faragher did not file a formal complaint against her supervisors before quitting her job, even though the city had written policies prohibiting sexual harassment on the job. After she left, however, she charged the city with illegal sex discrimination under Title VII. When the case reached court, Boca Raton made the same point as Burlington—that it could not be held liable for conduct of which it had no knowledge.

Employers had been grappling with sexual harassment since the Supreme Court's first ruling on the issue in ***Meritor Savings Bank v. Vinson,*** 477 U.S. 57 (1986). The Court held that "severe and pervasive" sexual harassment that created an "abusive working environment" amounted to discrimination on the basis of sex in violation of Title VII. The ruling encouraged more employees, mostly women, to file sexual harassment complaints with the federal Equal Employment Opportunity Commission or the courts. The allegations ran the gamut of behavior from forced sex and in-office groping to nude pin-ups and off-color jokes. Inevitably, the lower court rulings did not yield completely clear answers about how bad the behavior had to be before it was ruled sexual harassment.

To try to make some sense of the various factual situations, courts differentiated between two categories of sexual harassment complaints. *Quid pro quo* harassment occurred when a supervisor conditioned a tangible job benefit, such as a raise, promotion, or favorable assignment, on an employee's submitting to a sexual demand. A more general complaint about an offensive sexual climate in the workplace was termed a "hostile environment" claim. The distinction guided courts in determining when to hold the employer itself liable for sexual harassment. Generally, courts held that employers were automatically liable in a *quid pro quo* case, but that plaintiffs had to show some measure of fault on the employer's part to prevail in a hostile environment case. For plaintiffs, holding an employer liable was critical because courts generally held that individual supervisors were not subject to Title VII claims.

The Supreme Court had provided only limited guidance on the issue in its 1986 ruling. It admonished lower courts that had held employers automatically liable for their supervisors' misconduct. But it also said that an employer was not insulated from liability simply because it had not been aware of the problem or because it had a grievance procedure for dealing with sexual harassment complaints. The confusion over the liability issue increased through the 1990s as the number of sexual harassment cases was also rising. Congress gave new incentives to sexual harassment claims in 1991 by revising the federal job discrimination law to allow plaintiffs to recover compensatory and punitive damages, not just back pay and attorneys' fees.

The legal confusion was reflected in the various court rulings in Ellerth's case. The lower court ruled Burlington could not be held liable under a hostile environment theory because it had no knowledge of Slowik's misconduct. The company also could not be held liable under a *quid pro quo* theory, the judge said, because Ellerth had not suffered any tangible injury. The court of appeals disagreed and reinstated the suit in a decision that produced eight opinions among the twelve judges as well as an unsigned plea on behalf of the full court asking the Supreme Court to "bring order to the chaotic case law in this important field of practice."

The federal judge in Faragher's case had no problem finding that Terry and Silverman—both of whom had been fired after another female lifeguard filed a complaint against them—had created a hostile working environment for the women employees. The judge found three bases for holding the city liable. First, he ruled the city had "constructive knowledge" of the sexual harassment because it was so pervasive. Second, the city was liable under a doctrine known as *respondeat superior* that treats a supervisor as an employer's agent in some situations. Finally, the judge found the city had "imputed knowledge" of the misconduct based on the complaint to Robert Gordon, the third supervisor. The court of appeals rejected each of those grounds.

The Supreme Court's decisions in the *Ellerth* and *Faragher* reflected a surprising measure of unity and clarity. Going in reverse order of seniority, Justice Souter announced his opinion in *Faragher* and was followed by Justice Kennedy in *Ellerth.* The announcements from the bench made clear what was even clearer from the written opinions: the two justices had coordinated their opinions to produce a single rule for determining employers' liability for sexual harassment by supervisors.

The rule, moreover, was tough on employers, imposing indirect or "vicarious" liability for sexual harassment by a supervisor whenever any "tangible employment action" resulted. An employer could also be held liable even if the employee did not suffer any visible consequence. In those cases, the employer had a defense—but a demanding one. The employer had to show that it "exercised reasonable care to prevent and correct promptly any sexually harassing behavior" *and* that the employee "unreasonably failed to take advantage of any preventive or corrective opportunities provided by the employer or to avoid harm otherwise."

The rulings stopped short of requiring employers to establish antiharassment policies, but the message to do so was nonetheless clear. "The need for a stated policy" could be "appropriately addressed . . . when litigating the first element of the defense," the Court declared, and an employee's failure to use a complaint procedure "will normally suffice to satisfy the employer's burden of the defense." Then, by way of emphasis, the opinions continued: "No affirmative defense is available, however, when the supervisor's harassment culminates in a tangible employment action, such as discharge, demotion, or undesirable reassignment."

Applying that test to *Faragher,* Justice Souter said the appeals court was wrong to throw out the lower court judgment in Faragher's favor. The evidence of sexual harassment was "clear" and "undisputed," Souter said, and the city had no "serious prospect" of presenting an affirmative defense. The evidence showed that the city had failed to tell employees about its sexual harassment policy and, in any event, did not provide a way to bypass supervisors in registering complaints. Moreover, Faragher had asked for and been awarded a symbolic $1 in damages, so there was no need for further proceedings to determine whether she had failed to try to mitigate her injuries.

In Ellerth's case, the Court confronted the additional issue of the distinction between hostile environment claims and *quid pro quo* claims. The solution was to discard it. The two terms, Kennedy wrote, "are helpful, perhaps, in making a rough demarcation" between two types of cases, but "beyond this are of limited utility." If a threat is carried out, Kennedy said, the employee has established a violation of Title VII. If not, the plaintiff must show that the unfulfilled threats were sufficiently severe or pervasive to create a hostile work environment. With that background, Kennedy concluded that Ellerth had made out a possible claim against Burlington and was entitled to proceed to trial. On remand, he said, Ellerth would have a chance to add to her allegations, and Burlington would have an opportunity to present an affirmative defense.

Justice Thomas wrote the dissents in both cases, saying that employers should be liable for sexual harassment only if the employer "knew, or in the exercise of reasonable care should have known, about the hostile work environment and failed to take remedial action." Thomas continued, "The most that employers can be reasonably charged with, therefore, is a duty to act reasonably under the circumstances."

See Paul Buchanan and Courtney W. Wiswall, "The Evolving Understanding of Workplace Harassment and Employer Liability: Implications of Recent Supreme Court Decisions Under Title VII," *Wake Forest Law Review* 34 (1999): 55; and Jonathan W. Dion, "Putting Employers on the Defense: The Supreme Court Develops a Consistent Standard Regarding an Employer's Liability for a Supervisor's Hostile Work Environment Sexual Harassment," *Wake Forest Law Review* 34 (1999): 199.

Department of Commerce v. United States House of Representatives

525 U.S. 316 (1999)
Decided: January 25, 1999
Vote: 5 (Rehnquist, O'Connor, Scalia, Kennedy, Thomas)
4 (Stevens, Souter, Ginsburg, Breyer)
Opinion of the Court: O'Connor
Concurring opinion: Scalia (Rehnquist, Kennedy, Thomas)
Dissenting opinion: Stevens (Souter, Ginsburg, Breyer)
Dissenting opinion: Ginsburg (Souter)
Dissenting opinion: Breyer

The Constitution requires a census of the population every ten years to determine how many seats each state will have in the House of Representatives. In a partisan dispute over how to conduct the 2000 census, the Clinton administration wanted to use statistical sampling as a supplement to an actual headcount to correct what many experts said was an inevitable undercount using traditional mail and door-to-door techniques. The Republican-controlled House disputed the need for sampling and warned that the administration might manipulate the figures for partisan purposes.

Lower federal courts barred the use of sampling in a pair of lawsuits challenging the administration's plan: one by the House itself, another by private plaintiffs. Despite concerns about stepping into a dispute between Congress and the executive, the Supreme Court agreed with the lower court rulings. The decision—based on a reading of the Census Act—forced the Census Bureau back to the drawing boards and left Congress and the administration still arguing about the best way to try to get an accurate population count.

Article I, Section 2, Clause 3, of the Constitution requires an "actual enumeration" or headcount. During the nineteenth century, federal marshals conducted the count from written lists collected town by town. In 1902 Congress established the Bureau of the Census, originally as part of the Department of the Interior and later moved to the Commerce Department, to carry out the census.

Despite their best efforts, Census Bureau officials and other population experts believed by the 1940s that the headcount was missing many Americans, particularly poor and minority populations in big cities. In the 1960s civil rights groups were sufficiently troubled about the undercount to initiate a campaign aimed at getting a better response among African Americans for the 1970 census. A decade later, concern about the undercount had spread to local officials and to members of Congress. As the 1980 figures were being tallied, New York City filed a federal court suit to try to force the Census Bureau to make a statistical adjustment to correct for the undercount. The litigation lasted seven years before a federal judge finally ruled that the adjustment was not "technically feasible or warranted."

For the 1990 census, the Census Bureau itself recommended a statistical adjustment, only to be vetoed by Secretary of Commerce Robert Mosbacher, a one-time Republican party fundraiser. New York City again led a legal challenge. By a unanimous vote, the Supreme Court in *Wisconsin v. City of New York*, 517 U.S. 1 (1996), refused to interfere with what Rehnquist called Mosbacher's "entirely reasonable" decision.

By the time of the ruling, however, a Democratic administration was moving ahead with plans to use statistical sampling techniques in the 2000 census. It noted that the 1990 census was believed to have missed about 2 percent of the population—more than 4 million people—and that the undercount was greater than it had been in the 1980 census. The Census Bureau promised intensified use of traditional techniques to count at least 90 percent of the population before turning to sampling. Under its so-called integrated coverage management plan, census enumerators would then do an even more intensive, door-by-door canvass of selected areas to get a statistical estimate of the people that had been missed. That data would then be used to make population projections, census tract by census tract, to get the final tallies.

The administration said the plan was scientifically valid, but opponents said it was legally defective. They argued that sampling violated the constitutional command for an "actual enumeration" as well as Section 195 of the Census Act, which provided that sampling could be used "except for purposes of apportionment." The administration countered that another part of the statute, Section 141, gave the Census Bureau broad discretion in conducting the headcount. It also insisted that the use of sampling would satisfy the constitutional definition.

Opponents filed two suits after Congress in late 1997 forced through an appropriations rider providing for legal challenges to be heard by special, three-judge courts with direct appeal to the Supreme Court. The House of Representatives filed one suit in Washington, naming the Department of Commerce as defendant. A second suit—*Glavin v. Clinton*—was filed in federal court in Alexandria, Virginia, by a group of plaintiffs headed by Michael Glavin, president of the conservative Southeastern Legal Foundation. Both courts ruled in favor of the sampling opponents on statutory grounds without reaching the constitutional issue.

The Supreme Court held that sampling violated the Census Act, with four of the five justices in the majority saying that sampling also might violate the Constitution's requirement for an actual enumeration. Technically, the ruling came in the suit filed by the private plaintiffs, and the Court then dismissed the appeal of the House suit, without deciding whether it had been properly brought.

Turning to the merits, Justice O'Connor traced the history of the two Census Act provisions and concluded that the "broad grant of authority" to use sampling contained in Section 141 was limited by the "narrower and more specific" Section 195. "There is only one plausible reading of the amended Section 195," she wrote. "It prohibits the use of sampling in calculating the population for purposes of apportionment." Significantly, however, O'Connor also said the law "requires" the use of sampling in deriving population counts for other purposes—a qualification that tempered victory claims by Republicans afterwards.

In dissent, Justice Stevens concluded that sampling was consistent with both the Census Act and the Constitution. The act, he said, "unambiguously authorizes the Secretary of Commerce to use sampling procedures when taking the decennial census. That this authorization is constitutional is equally clear." Justices Souter and Ginsburg joined most of Stevens's opinion, but disagreed with his view that the House had standing to bring its suit. Justice Breyer agreed with Stevens on that issue, joined part of the opinion, and wrote a separate dissent to stress that the administration planned to use sampling only as "a supplement" of a traditional count.

See See Margo J. Anderson, ed., *Encyclopedia of the U.S. Census* (Washington, D.C.: CQ Press, 2000); Angela D. Kelley, "Note: Census 2000: Why the Majority in *Department of Commerce v. United States House of Representatives* Was Correct in Rejecting Statistical Sampling," *Oklahoma Law Review* 53 (Fall 2000): 487; and Benjamin J. Razi, "Comment: Census Politics Revisited: What to Do When the Government Can't Count," *American University Law Review* 48 (1999): 1101.

Saenz v. Roe

526 U.S. 489 (1999)
Decided: May 17, 1999
Vote: 7 (Stevens, O'Connor, Scalia, Kennedy, Souter, Ginsburg, Breyer)
2 (Rehnquist, Thomas)
Opinion of the Court: Stevens
Dissenting opinion: Rehnquist (Thomas)
Dissenting opinion: Thomas (Rehnquist)

"Brenda Roe," who was pregnant with her first child, and her husband moved to California from Oklahoma in 1997 after he lost his job. Roe—a pseudonym used in later litigation—had never received public assistance in Oklahoma, but she applied for welfare in California when medical complications forced her husband to stay home with her rather than look for work.

Concerned that the state's relatively high welfare benefits were encouraging people to move there, California had passed a law in 1992 that limited new residents to the level of welfare benefits in their former states. The measure was blocked by litigation, but went into effect after Congress in 1996 authorized states to set lower rates for new residents as part of a broad welfare reform measure. For Roe, the law meant that she could receive \$307 per month—Oklahoma's stipend for a family of three—rather than the \$565 a month set in California. She challenged the restriction as a violation of her constitutional rights—specifically, a supposed "right of travel" from state to state.

The Supreme Court based its decision on a constitutional right to travel, which it called a "fundamental right" that neither the states nor the federal government could penalize the exercise of that right except to further a "compelling governmental interest." Saving money did not qualify, the Court added. In an earlier decision, ***Shapiro v. Thompson,*** 394 U.S. 618 (1969), the Court had ruled that states could not impose a one-year waiting period on new residents applying for welfare benefits. The Court reaffirmed the ruling in *Memorial Hospital v. Maricopa County,* 415 U.S. 250 (1974), a decision that said the one-year waiting period for nonemergency medical care for the poor violated the Equal Protection Clause. The Court also issued a number of rulings, such as *Vlandis v. Kline,* 412 U.S. 441 (1973), that appeared to uphold waiting periods in other contexts—notably, eligibility for in-state tuition rates at public colleges and universities.

The 1992 California law was a return to the idea of limiting benefits for new residents. It could not prohibit AFDC payments altogether, so the law limited the stipends for new residents for one year to the same amount they would have received in their prior states. California's welfare chief, Eloise Anderson, later said the law was aimed at "discouraging people from coming to California just for higher benefits." California, in fact, had the sixth highest AFDC payments in the country, but its cost of living was also among the highest. Under federal law, California had to obtain approval from the secretary of the Health and Human Services Department to implement the rate differential.

Welfare recipients quickly challenged California's law once the state had received the needed waiver from the federal government to put it into effect. Citing *Shapiro,* federal judge David Levi issued a preliminary injunction against implementing the measure, later upheld by the federal appeals court. The state appealed to the Supreme Court. By the time the case reached the Court, the waiver had been invalidated on administrative law grounds. The justices heard arguments in the case, but then ruled that it was moot—legally over. With the passage of the federal welfare overhaul, California moved to reinstate the benefits limit, and, again, the law was challenged. The American Civil Liberties Union Foundation of Southern California filed a constitutional attack on the law on behalf of Roe and a second welfare recipient called Anna Doe, who had moved to the state from Washington, D.C., to look for work but quit a job because it was too stressful. As a single mother of one child, her stipend was fixed at $330 per month—Washington's benefits—rather than California's $456 per month.

Judge Levi again enjoined the state from putting the limit into effect. In his opinion, he noted that the state could achieve the same cost saving—estimated at $22.8 million—by a modest overall reduction in benefits. The federal appeals court upheld the injunction, and the state asked the Supreme Court to review the ruling.

The Supreme Court agreed that the California law was unconstitutional. The decision closed the door on one popular idea for trimming welfare costs and breathed life into a long-ignored constitutional provision that prohibits the states from "abridging" the "privileges or immunities" of citizens of the United States or any state. "Citizens of the United States, whether rich or poor, have the right to choose to be citizens of the state wherein they reside," Justice Stevens wrote for the majority. "The states, however, do not have any right to select their citizens." Stevens based the decision squarely on the Fourteenth Amendment's Privileges and Immunities Clause. He acknowledged that the Court in *Shapiro* had not explained the basis for recognizing a right to travel, even though it was "firmly embedded in our jurisprudence." He explained that the right included three components: the right to cross state borders freely, the right to be treated "as a welcome visitor" when temporarily present in a state, and—for permanent residents—"the right of the newly arrived citizen to the same privileges and immunities by other citizens of the same State."

A law treating newly arrived citizens differently, Stevens said, is subject to a "strict" standard of review. California's law did not pass muster. The evidence introduced in the lower court indicated that the number of persons who travel to California to obtain higher benefits was "quite small—surely not large enough to justify a burden on those who had no such motive." In any event, the state had expressly disavowed that purpose. Moreover, Stevens concluded, "such a purpose would be unequivocally impermissible." The federal law authorizing the states to set welfare differentials made no difference, Stevens added. "Congress may not authorize the states to violate the Fourteenth Amendment," he wrote.

Dissenting justices defended the California law as a legitimate residency requirement and criticized the revival of what they called "the previously dormant" constitutional provision. Chief Justice Rehnquist said the ruling "ignores a State's need to assure that only persons who establish a bona fide residence receive the benefits provided to current residents of the State." He noted that the Court had upheld one-year residency provisions for receiving in-state tuition rates at public colleges, getting a divorce, or voting in party primary elections. "States may surely do the same for welfare benefits," he said.

Justice Thomas also criticized the use of the Privileges and Immunities Clause. The majority's use of the clause to strike down a government benefit, Thomas said, "was likely unintended" when the amendment was ratified.

See Nan S. Ellis and Cheryl M. Miller, "Welfare Waiting Periods: A Public Policy Analysis of *Saenz v. Roe,*" *Stanford Law and Policy Review* 11 (spring 2000): 343–367; and Stacey L. Winick, "A New Chapter in Constitutional Law: *Saenz v. Roe* and the Revival of the Fourteenth Amendment's Privileges or Immunities Clause," *Hofstra Law Review* 28 (winter 1999): 573–599.

Davis v. Monroe County Board of Education

526 U.S. 629 (1999)
Decided: May 24, 1999
Vote: 5 (Stevens, O'Connor, Souter, Ginsburg, Breyer)
4 (Rehnquist, Scalia, Kennedy, Thomas)
Opinion of the Court: O'Connor
Dissenting opinion: Kennedy (Rehnquist, Scalia, Thomas)

LaShonda Davis was only ten years old when she suffered through five months of crude sexual taunts and advances in the 1992–1993 school year. Her tormentor, a fellow fifth-grader at Hubbard Elementary School in Forsyth, Georgia, repeatedly tried to fondle her. He told her he wanted to get in bed with her. Once, he suggestively put a doorstop in his pants to act out his intentions toward her.

Both LaShonda and her mother, Aurelia Davis, complained about the behavior to teachers and to the principal, but nothing seemed to happen. Only after Mrs. Davis complained to the local sheriff did she get the help she wanted. The boy, identified only as G. F., was charged with sexual battery and pleaded guilty to the charge.

Still frustrated with the school's inaction, Aurelia Davis filed a federal court suit the next year seeking damages from the Monroe County Board of Education and from the school district superintendent, Charles Dumas, and the school principal, Bill Querry.

In one count of the complaint, she charged the school board with violating Title IX, a federal law that prohibited sexual discrimination by any school that receives federal funds. The school board responded by contending that it could not be liable for "student-on-student" sexual harassment. The district court and the en banc Eleventh Circuit Court of Appeals in Atlanta agreed and dismissed Davis's Title IX suit.

The Supreme Court reversed the decision and reinstated the suit. In ***Meritor Savings Bank v. Vinson,*** 477 U.S. 57 (1986), the Court first ruled that "severe or pervasive" sexual harassment in the workplace could amount to sex discrimination under Title VII of the Civil Rights Act of 1964.

Six years later, the Court held that sexual harassment was also covered by a later law, Title IX of the Education Amendments of 1972. That law provided that no one could be excluded from participation in, denied the benefits of, or subjected to discrimination on the basis of sex in "any education program or activity receiving Federal financial assistance." Ruling unanimously in *Franklin v. Gwinnett County Public Schools,* 503 U.S. 60 (1992), the Court held that the law contained an "implied right of action" for victims of sexual harassment to recover money damages from school systems.

The ruling spurred complaints and lawsuits dealing with sexual misconduct not only by teachers, but also by students. The effort to define correct behavior between boys and girls proved to be controversial—as when a first-grade boy in North Carolina was suspended in 1996 for kissing a classmate on the cheek.

Meanwhile, the Court in 1998 moved to limit school systems' exposure to damage awards in sexual harassment suits involving teachers. In ***Gebser v. Lago Vista Independent School District,*** 524 U.S. 274, the Court held that school boards could be forced to pay damages for misconduct by teachers only if officials knew of the behavior and failed to take steps to prevent it.

Justice O'Connor, speaking for the *Davis* majority, said school districts could be held liable for sexual harassment between students. She dedicated much of her opinion, however, to setting strict standards for such suits.

Even so, the ruling provoked a bitter dissent—written by Justice Kennedy—that warned the decision would result in "an avalanche of litigation" and make federal courts "the final arbiters of school policy."

O'Connor began by acknowledging that a school board could be held liable under Title IX only for its own misconduct. But Davis's suit, she continued, was aimed at the school's "*own* decision to remain idle in the face of known student-on-student harassment."

Echoing her majority opinion in *Gebser,* O'Connor said that "deliberate indifference to known acts of harassment" by a student as well as a teacher could amount to an intentional violation of Title IX "in certain limited circumstances." She added, however, that the behavior must be "so severe, pervasive, and objectively offensive that it can be said to deprive the victims of access to the educational opportunities or benefits of the school." As one example, O'Connor invoked Justice Stevens's hypothetical: denying girls physical access to an athletic field or computer lab.

Throughout, O'Connor tried to soften the impact of the decision. "Damages are not available for simple acts of teasing and name-calling," she wrote. School administrators could be held responsible only for a "clearly unreasonable" response—or lack of response—to student harassment. Courts could throw out suits without trial if plaintiffs failed to make their case. Davis's allegations, however, met that test, and the case was sent back for trial.

According to the position put forth in Kennedy's dissent, Title IX gave school districts no warning that they might be liable for students' misbehavior. The majority's "fence" to limit the "staggering" number of potential lawsuits was "made of little sticks." Most important, he wrote, the ruling "clears the way for the federal government to claim center stage in America's classrooms."

The courtroom presentation of the opinions featured an unusual exchange between O'Connor and Kennedy, centrists with adjacent seats on the bench. Kennedy concluded his dissent by saying the ruling would "teach little Johnny a perverse lesson in Federalism." O'Connor anticipated the point in her earlier summary of the decision. The ruling, she said, "assures that little Mary may attend class."

See Jeffrey Boncek, "The Supreme Court Demands Class in the Classroom: *Davis v. Monroe County Board of Education*," *Texas Tech Law Review* 31 (2000): 1259; Melissa M. Solocinski, "Opening the Floodgates—Deliberate Indifference, Causation and Control as a Means of Authorizing Unlimited Litigation Under Title IX: *Davis v. Monroe County Board of Education*," *University of Miami Law Review* 55 (2000): 147; and Jill S. Vogel, "Comment: Between a (Schoolhouse) Rock and a Hard Place: Title IX Peer Harassment Liability After *Davis v. Monroe County Board of Education*," *Houston Law Review* 37 (winter 2000): 1525–1556.

City of Chicago v. Morales

527 U.S. 41 (1999)
Decided: June 10, 1999
Vote: 6 (Stevens, O'Connor, Kennedy, Souter, Ginsburg, Breyer)
3 (Rehnquist, Scalia, Thomas)
Judgment of the Court: Stevens
Opinion concurring in judgment: O'Connor (Breyer)
Opinion concurring in judgment: Kennedy
Opinion concurring in judgment: Breyer
Dissenting opinion: Scalia
Dissenting opinion: Thomas (Rehnquist, Scalia)

In this case a novel initiative by the city of Chicago to get youth gangs off the streets ran afoul of the Constitution. The Supreme Court invalidated a Chicago ordinance that gave police the power to order anyone found "loitering" on the streets with suspected gang members to disperse and to arrest anyone who refused to obey. The Chicago City Council adopted the ordinance in 1992 after hearing a parade of witnesses—many of them elderly African American women—complain about the terrorizing effects that criminal gangs were having in their neighborhoods. While on the books, the law resulted in some forty thousand arrests, almost all of them young African-American or Hispanic men.

Laws against loitering and vagrancy had been on the books in America since colonial times and went largely unchallenged before the 1960s. The civil rights revolution and the Supreme Court's rulings guaranteeing legal representation for the poor in criminal cases combined to encourage challenges to many of these local ordinances. In several cases the Court found loitering laws unconstitutional—most notably in *Papachristou v. City of Jacksonville,* 405 U.S. 156 (1972). That decision voided a broadly worded Jacksonville, Florida, ordinance as unconstitutionally vague. In a second case decided the same year, however, the Court upheld a criminal conviction under a state disorderly conduct statute for refusing to obey a police officer's order to move on. That ruling—combined with the Court's more conservative orientation—encouraged supporters of the Chicago ordinance to think it might be upheld.

Civil liberties lawyers focused on two provisions of the law that they said gave police too much discretion. First, the ordinance defined "loitering" to mean being on the public streets "with no apparent purpose." Second, the law allowed police to issue a dispersal order to anyone found in the presence of someone "reasonably suspected" of being a gang member.

In a fractured decision, the Court agreed that the law was too broad, but stopped short of recognizing a constitutional "freedom to loiter." Justice Stevens said that the ordinance violated the requirement that a legislature "establish minimal guidelines to govern law enforcement." Stevens interpreted *Papachristou* as establishing that the Due Process Clause protects what he called the "freedom to loiter for innocent purposes." He also said that the ordinance's definition of loitering was so vague as to justify striking the law down in its entirety. Justices O'Connor and Kennedy wrote separate concurrences on narrower grounds.

For the dissenters, Justice Thomas sharply disputed the claimed freedom to loiter and found the law's provisions constitutionally sufficient. In an emotional closing, he warned that by invalidating the ordinance, the Court "has unnecessarily sentenced law-abiding citizens to lives of terror and misery."

See Andrew J. Kozusko III, "Note, Dashing Chicago's Hopes: Favoring the 'Right' to Loiter 'Innocently' Over the Fundamental Need for Safety in *Chicago v. Morales,*" *University of Pittsburgh Law Review* 62 (2000): 409.

Sutton v. United Air Lines, Inc.

527 U.S. 471 (1999)
Decided: June 22, 1999
Vote: 7 (Rehnquist, O'Connor, Scalia, Kennedy, Thomas, Souter, Ginsburg)
2 (Stevens, Breyer)
Opinion of the Court: O'Connor
Concurring opinion: Ginsburg
Dissenting opinion: Stevens (Breyer)
Dissenting opinion: Breyer

Twin sisters, Karen Sutton and Kimberly Hinton, long had the ambition to become pilots for a major commercial airline. They had both flown for regional carriers and were certified by the Federal Aviation Administration. They met airlines' basic requirements for age, education, and experience. In 1992, however, United Air Lines declined to hire them because of their vision: both were nearsighted. Even though they had 20/20 vision with contact lenses, United said they did not meet the company's standard qualification for pilots: uncorrected vision in both eyes of 20/100 or better. With their experience as pilots for regional carriers, Sutton and Hinton had no doubt about their qualifications for jobs with United. The airline insisted its uncorrected vision standard was essential for safety—a precaution, for example, against the possibility of losing or misplacing glasses or contact lenses during flight. Sutton and Hinton went to court. They contended that the company had discriminated against them on the basis of a disability in violation of the Americans with Disabilities Act of 1990 (ADA).

In their federal court suit, Sutton and Hinton contended that they were disabled under the ADA because their uncorrected vision "substantially limited" normal daily activities such as shopping, driving, or watching television. But they also contended that with corrective lenses they were "qualified" for the job and that United's refusal to hire them amounted to discrimination on the basis of their disability. The airline countered that the women were not disabled because, with corrective lenses, they were not at all limited in their daily activities. That argument conflicted with an Equal Employment Opportunity Commission (EEOC) regulation that called for a person's disability to be determined without regard to any corrective or mitigating measures. The airline argued that the EEOC had misinterpreted the law.

A federal district court judge dismissed the suit, and the court of appeals agreed.

Sutton and Hinton appealed to the Supreme Court, pointing out that most other federal appeals courts had agreed with the EEOC that disability claims should be considered without regard to corrective measures. The Court agreed to review their case, along with two other cases with similar issues. In *Murphy v. United Parcel Service, Inc.,* (527 U.S. 516), a Kansas truck driver, Vaughn Murphy, was fired because of high blood pressure, even though he controlled the condition with medication. In *Albertsons, Inc. v. Kirkingburg,* (527 U.S. 555), Hallie Kirkingburg, an Oregon truck driver, was fired because he had monocular vision—in effect, was blind in one eye.

The Court rejected Sutton's and Hinton's disability claims, along with Murphy's in parallel decisions. "Congress did not intend to bring under the statute's protections all those whose uncorrected conditions amount to disabilities," Justice O'Connor wrote for the majority in *Sutton.* She then dispensed with Murphy's case in a shorter opinion relying on the earlier decision. O'Connor cited three reasons for concluding that the ADA did not include uncorrected physical impairments within the definition of disability. First, the law defined a disability as an impairment that "substantially limits" a major life activity "presently—not potentially or hypothetically," she said. Second, the law required an "individualized" assessment of potential disabilities, but considering a physical impairment in its uncorrected state would require use of general information about its effects.

Nor could Sutton and Hinton sustain a claim that they had been "regarded as" disabled when United refused to hire them, O'Connor said. Because global airline pilot is only "a single job," O'Connor said, the allegation was insufficient to show that United regarded them as disabled. "Indeed, there are a number of other positions utilizing petitioners' skills, such as regional pilot and pilot instructor to name a few, that are available to them," O'Connor wrote.

Justice Stevens, in dissent, challenged O'Connor's reading of the statute point by point. The three-part definition, he said, was intended to cover any individuals "who now have, or ever had, a substantially limiting impairment." The majority's definition, he said, would leave out many people that Congress clearly intended to protect: people with artificial limbs, for example, or diabetics. As for employers' right to set job qualifications, Stevens said it was "eminently within the purpose" of the ADA to require businesses to explain, for example, why 20/100 uncorrected vision was a valid requirement for a specific position.

In *Kirkingburg,* the Court also rejected the disability claim. The ruling gave businesses one more bit of legal leeway: employers were free to rely on federally established job qualification standards—like the Transportation Department's vision standard for truck drivers—without justifying them in each individual case brought under the disability law. The vote on that legal principle was unanimous; Stevens and Breyer refused to join the rest of Justice Souter's opinion, which cited *Sutton* in judging Kirkingburg's disability claim on the basis of his corrected rather than uncorrected vision.

See Christine M. Harrington, "Comment: The Americans with Disabilities Act: The New Definition of Disability Post–*Sutton v. United Air Lines, Inc.,*" *Marquette Law Review* 84 (fall 2000): 251–271; and Michael T. Mann, "Note: Defining a 'Disability' Under the Americans with Disabilities Act—Corrective Measures as a Factor: *Sutton v. United Air Lines, Inc.,*" *University of Cincinnati Law Review* 69 (2000–2001): 385.

Kolstad v. American Dental Association

527 U.S. 526 (1999)
Decided: June 22, 1999
Vote: Multiple
Opinion of the Court: O'Connor
Dissenting opinion: Rehnquist (Thomas)
Dissenting opinion: Stevens (Souter, Ginsburg, Breyer)

After working for the American Dental Association for four years, Carole Kolstad thought she was the best-qualified candidate when the group's top lobbying job in Washington opened up in 1992. The position went instead to Tom Spangler, who had worked in another job in the office for only two years. Believing that she had been passed over because of her sex, Kolstad sued the association under Title VII of the Civil Rights Act of 1964, the federal law against discrimination in employment. She brought the suit under the revised law, the Civil Rights Act of 1991, which for the first time allowed plaintiffs in job bias suits to receive compensatory and punitive damages in addition to the previously recognized remedies of back pay and reinstatement.

A federal jury agreed with Kolstad's complaint and awarded her $52,718 in back pay. The trial judge and the federal appeals court in Washington, however, both ruled that Kolstad had not proved the association guilty of sufficiently bad conduct to warrant an award of punitive damages.

The Supreme Court partially vindicated Kolstad's straightforward reading of the 1991 law. By a 7–2 vote, the Court rejected the appeals court's requirement of egregious misconduct to allow punitive damages. By a 5–4 margin, however, the Court adopted a different limitation on employers' liability for punitive damages.

In the first part of the decision, Justice O'Connor explained that egregious misconduct may be evidence of "malice" or "reckless indifference," but the law "does not limit plaintiffs to this form of evidence" to satisfy those conditions. O'Connor stressed, however, that punitive damages would not be permitted in many cases of intentional discrimination. In some cases, she said, an employer might be "unaware of the relevant federal prohibition." In others, an employer might discriminate "with the distinct belief that its discrimination is lawful"—for example, in the case of a "novel" theory of discrimination or a mistaken belief in the legitimacy of a stated job qualification.

Having disposed of that issue, O'Connor answered a second question: when to hold an employer liable for punitive damages for discriminatory conduct by individual managers. The common law limits so-called vicarious liability for punitive damages, O'Connor said, and for good reason. "Holding employers liable for punitive damages when they engage in good faith efforts to comply with Title VII," she wrote, would be unfair. It also would "reduce the incentive for employers to implement antidiscrimination programs." On that basis, O'Connor said the case needed to be returned to lower courts to give Kolstad a chance to show "malice" or "reckless indifference" on her employer's part and to give the association a chance to show whether it "had been making good faith efforts to enforce an antidiscrimination policy."

In a partial dissent, Chief Justice Rehnquist said he agreed with the appeals court's egregiousness requirement, but joined the other part of O'Connor's opinion, which he said would place "a complete bar" to punitive damages "in many foreseeable cases."

The liberal justices agreed with O'Connor's conclusion about the standard for punitive damages, but complained about the limit on employers' liability. Justice Stevens called the discussion "gratuitous" and "ill advised" because none of the parties had raised or argued the question. The issue was not even relevant, Stevens said, because the promotion decision that Kolstad challenged had been made by top officials—the head of the Washington office and the association's executive director in Chicago—not by midlevel managers.

See Lynn M. Geerdes, "You've Got to Have Faith: How Employers Can Avoid Punitive Damages After *Kolstad*," *CCH's Journal of Employment Discrimination* (fall 1999).

Florida Prepaid Postsecondary Educational Expenses Board v. College Savings Bank

527 U.S. 627 (1999)
Decided: June 23, 1999
Vote: 5 (Rehnquist, O'Connor, Scalia, Kennedy, Thomas)
4 (Stevens, Souter, Ginsburg, Breyer)
Opinion of the Court: Rehnquist
Dissenting opinion: Stevens (Souter, Ginsburg, Breyer)
See *College Savings Bank v. Florida Prepaid Postsecondary Educational Expenses Board* below.

College Savings Bank v. Florida Prepaid Postsecondary Educational Expenses Board

527 U.S. 666 (1999)
Decided: June 23, 1999
Vote: 5 (Rehnquist, O'Connor, Scalia, Kennedy, Thomas)
4 (Stevens, Souter, Ginsburg, Breyer)
Opinion of the Court: Scalia
Dissenting opinion: Stevens
Dissenting opinion: Breyer (Stevens, Souter, Ginsburg)

A commercial dispute between a New Jersey bank and a Florida state agency, both of which marketed savings plans for college tuition costs, became the vehicle for a pair of Supreme Court decisions favoring states' rights. College Savings Bank of New Jersey claimed that the state agency, Florida Prepaid Postsecondary Educational Expenses Board, infringed its patented method for calculating the cost of its plan. The bank also charged the Florida agency with misleading advertising about its own savings plan.

The bank sued, taking advantage of two federal laws allowing for private suits against states for patent infringement and for trademark violations or false advertising. The Florida agency countered with a motion to dismiss both suits on the grounds that the laws violated the Eleventh Amendment's protection against federal court suits against states.

The dispute came against the background of two largely unrelated trends. States had engaged in an increasing array of commercial ventures in the second half of the twentieth century. In particular, state university systems often acquired valuable patents through applications of scientific research. Meanwhile, the Supreme Court was adopting stricter rules for Congress to follow before it could subject states to federal court suits for their business activities. In the pivotal decision, *Atascadero State Hospital v. Scanlon,* 473 U.S. 234 (1985), the Court held that Congress could "abrogate" or override states' immunity from suit only by "unambiguously" providing for private enforcement actions.

Many federal courts applied that ruling to bar suits against state universities or other state agencies in patent, copyright, and trademark cases. Congress responded in 1991 and 1992 by specifically providing for private suits against states for patent or copyright infringement or for violation of the Lanham Act, which protects trademarks and prohibits false or misleading advertising.

College Savings Bank invoked those laws in suing the Florida agency. The federal appeals court in Philadelphia barred the bank's trademark and false advertising suit, but the U.S. Court of Appeals for the Federal Circuit—which handles all patent cases—said the bank could pursue its patent infringement claim.

The Supreme Court, however, ruled that Congress had exceeded its power in authorizing suits under either of the laws. In a previous decision, ***Seminole Tribe of Florida v. Florida,*** 517 U.S. 44 (1996), the Court held that states could not be subject to suit for laws passed under Congress's power to regulate interstate commerce. The issue therefore became whether the laws were justified under Congress's power to enforce the Fourteenth Amendment, which bars states from violating due process or equal protection rights.

In the patent case, Chief Justice Rehnquist said Congress had failed to identify a "pattern of constitutional violations" needed to justify invoking its Fourteenth Amendment powers. In the trademark case, Justice Scalia said the provision for false advertising suits against the states was unconstitutional because the law did not protect the kind of property right covered by the Fourteenth Amendment.

In an added victory for the states, the Court overruled an earlier decision, *Parden v. Terminal Railway of the Alabama State Docks Department,* 377 U.S. 184 (1964), which held that states waived their immunity to suits when conducting commercial operations. Scalia said the ruling was inconsistent with later decisions requiring an "unequivocal" waiver of a state's sovereign immunity.

See Eugene Volokh, "Sovereign Immunity and Intellectual Property," *Southern California Law Review* 73 (2000): 1161.

Alden v. Maine

527 U.S. 706 (1999)
Decided: June 23, 1999
Vote: 5 (Rehnquist, O'Connor, Scalia, Kennedy, Thomas)
4 (Stevens, Souter, Ginsburg, Breyer)
Opinion of the Court: Kennedy
Dissenting opinion: Souter (Stevens, Ginsburg, Breyer)

An effort by Maine's probation officers to collect overtime pay turned into a constitutional showdown over the powers of the federal and state governments. A sharply divided Supreme Court gave the states a decisive victory by ruling that they are immune from suits for monetary damages for violating federal laws—whether in federal courts or in a state's own court system.

The Court had gone back and forth on whether states could be required to comply with the wage and hour provisions of the federal Fair Labor Standards Act. Initially, the Court held in ***National League of Cities v. Usery,*** 426 U.S. 833 (1976), that Congress had infringed on the Tenth Amendment's protections for state sovereignty by extending the wage and hour law to state and local governments. Nine years later, the Court reversed itself by holding in ***Garcia v. San Antonio Metropolitan Transit Authority,*** 469 U.S. 528 (1985), that Congress could set wage and hour standards for state and local workers.

The ruling generated a host of disputes over the federal law's requirement to pay time and a half for overtime. Federal regulations allowed state and local governments to avoid paying salaried and "professional" workers overtime by giving them compensatory time off. In 1992 a majority of Maine's probation officers went to federal court, contending that they were not professionals and were entitled to overtime pay.

The probation officers' suit was stopped in its tracks by the Court's decision in ***Seminole Tribe of Florida v. Florida,*** 517 U.S. 44 (1996), that states are immune from monetary damage suits in federal court for violations of federal laws. The probation officers then refiled their case in state court, but the Maine Supreme Court, citing the doctrine of sovereign immunity, ordered that suit dismissed too. The officers then appealed to the U. S. Supreme Court.

Justice Kennedy began his opinion for the Court with a ringing endorsement of sovereign immunity, which he called "a fundamental aspect of the sovereignty which the States enjoyed before the ratification of the Constitution, and which they retain today." The Constitution never would have been ratified if it had given Congress power to "abrogate" or override the states' immunity from suit, Kennedy said. Nothing in the nation's subsequent history suggested that Congress had that power either. As a practical matter, he said that allowing Congress to authorize a private damage suit against a state could pose "a severe and notorious danger" to the state's budget and shift political power from the state's elected officials to the courts.

Kennedy insisted, however, that the ruling did not allow states to disregard the Constitution or federal laws. The federal government could sue states to enforce federal laws, individual state officers were subject to private suit, and local governments had no immunity at all.

For the dissenters, Justice Souter said the decision "ignores the accepted authority of Congress . . . to provide for enforcement of federal rights in state court."

See Erwin Chemerinsky, "The Hypocrisy of *Alden v. Maine:* Judicial Review, Sovereign Immunity and the Rehnquist Court," *Loyola of Los Angeles Law Review* 33 (2000): 1283; and Matthew S. Cunningham, "Note: A Shift in the Balance of Power: *Alden v. Maine* and the Expansion of State Sovereign Immunity at Congress' Expense," *Wake Forest Law Review* 35 (2000): 425.

2000–2002

Kimel v. Florida Board of Regents

528 U.S. 62 (2000)
Decided: January 11, 2002
Vote: Multiple
Opinion of the Court: O'Connor
Concurring opinion: Thomas (Kennedy)
Dissenting opinion: Stevens (Souter, Ginsburg, Breyer)

Physics professor J. Daniel Kimel was one of thirty-six faculty members and librarians at two Florida state universities who claimed they had been discriminated against because of age when they lost out on promised salary increases in the early 1990s. The state sought to dismiss the case by citing the Eleventh Amendment's restriction on federal court suits against state governments, as interpreted in ***Seminole Tribe of Florida v. Florida,*** 517 U.S. 44 (1996). The lower federal court rejected the state's argument and kept the case alive. The court of appeals combined it with two other age discrimination suits: one filed by Wellington Dickson, a Florida prison guard, and the other by two Alabama state university professors.

The three-judge appeals panel voted to bar the suits, but the two judges in the majority used different grounds. One judge said that the age discrimination law did not reflect an unambiguous decision by Congress to "abrogate" or override the states' sovereign immunity against suits, as required under a series of Supreme Court rulings on the Eleventh Amendment. The other judge said that Congress had no power to authorize the suits under its Article I power to regulate interstate commerce or under the power granted in Section 5 of the Fourteenth Amendment to enact legislation to enforce the amendment's due process and equal protection provisions.

Congress had passed the Age Discrimination in Employment Act in 1967 to combat what it called the "common practice" among employers of setting "arbitrary age limits" for jobs, based on "stereotypes" and "generalizations." The act originally applied only to private employers but was extended to state and local governments in 1974. Congress gave the Equal Employment Opportunity Commission (EEOC) power to enforce the law but also authorized private suits by employees. The law allowed employers to take age into account in making job decisions if age was a "bona fide occupational qualification."

The Supreme Court upheld Congress's decision to apply the age discrimination law to state governments in *EEOC v. Wyoming,* 460 U.S. 226 (1983). State governments saw an avenue of legal protection, however, in *Seminole Tribe* and ***Florida Prepaid Postsecondary Educational Expense Board v. College Savings Bank,*** 527 U.S. 627 (1999), in which the Rehnquist Court began limiting suits by private individuals against state governments for alleged violations of federal law.

After agreeing, on a 7–2 vote, that Congress intended to authorize age discrimination suits against the states, the Supreme Court held, 5–4, that the law was "not a valid exercise of Congress's power under Section 5 of the Fourteenth Amendment." Justice O'Connor reviewed the prior decisions holding that age discrimination did not amount to a *per se* violation of the Constitution. Then, looking at the evidence before Congress when it extended the law to state governments, O'Connor said the lawmakers "never identified any pattern of age discrimination by the States, much less any discrimination that rose to the level of constitutional violation." On that basis, she concluded, the law was "an unwarranted response to a perhaps inconsequential problem."

Justice Thomas disagreed with O'Connor's conclusion that the law included a clear override of the states' sovereign immunity, but joined the rest of her opinion.

"There is not a word in the text of the Constitution," Justice Stevens wrote in dissent, "supporting the Court's conclusion that the judge-made doctrine of sovereign immunity limits Congress' power to authorize private parties . . . to enforce federal law against the States."

See Tracy Laaveg, "Comment: Constitutional Law—State Sovereign Immunity: Limiting Federal Power to Abrogate State Immunity," *University of North Dakota Law Review* 77 (2001).

Reno v. Condon

528 U.S. 141 (2000)
Decided: January 12, 2000
Vote: 9 (Rehnquist, Stevens, O'Connor, Scalia, Kennedy, Souter, Thomas, Ginsburg, Breyer)
0
Opinion of the Court: Rehnquist

Departments of motor vehicles require each applicant for a driver's license or automobile registration to provide his or her name, address, telephone number, and Social Security number. In some states the agencies sold this information to businesses and individuals who would contact drivers and car owners and attempt to sell them various goods and services. Complaints about the practice led Congress to enact the Driver's Privacy Protection Act of 1994 (DPPA), which prohibited states or their employees from making such data available without the consent of the individual registrant. South Carolina law conflicted with the DPPA's provisions. The state made information in its motor vehicle and drivers records available to any person who filled out a form saying the information would not be used for telephone solicitation.

Following the DPPA's enactment, Charlie Condon, the attorney general of South Carolina, and other state officials filed suit, alleging that the law violated the Tenth and Eleventh Amendments, the former on grounds of states' rights and the latter because a state could be sued in federal court for violating the law. The district court agreed with the state, and the Fourth Circuit Court affirmed. U.S. Attorney General Janet Reno appealed to the U.S. Supreme Court.

The Supreme Court reversed. Chief Justice Rehnquist, speaking for a unanimous bench, held that the identifying information required by the states constituted an element of interstate commerce and was therefore subject to regulation by Congress. In enacting the DPPA, Congress did not violate principles of federalism announced in cases such as ***New York v. United States,*** 505 U.S. 144 (1992), and ***Printz v. United States,*** 521 U.S. 898 (1997), because the act did not require the states to engage in any particular actions to regulate their citizens, or require the legislature to enact any particular laws, or require state officials to assist in enforcing federal legislation. This case was one of the few in the 1990s involving questions of federalism that the Court decided against state claims.

See Erwin Chemerinsky, "Right Result, Wrong Reasons: Reno v. Condon," *Oklahoma City University Law Review* 25 (2000): 823.

Nixon v. Shrink Missouri Government PAC

528 U.S. 377 (2000)
Decided: January 24, 2000
Vote: 6 (Rehnquist, Stevens, O'Connor, Souter, Ginsburg, Breyer)
3 (Scalia, Kennedy, Thomas)
Opinion of the Court: Souter
Concurring opinion: Stevens
Concurring opinion: Breyer (Ginsburg)
Dissenting opinion: Kennedy
Dissenting opinion: Thomas (Scalia)

Zev David Fredman was a thirty-four-year-old political neophyte when he declared his candidacy for the Republican nomination for state auditor in 1997. A political action committee descriptively titled Shrink Missouri Government PAC saw Fredman as a good standard-bearer for its cause and decided to back him.

In 1994 Missouri had enacted a campaign finance law that limited contributions to no more than $1,075 to any candidate of a statewide office (including auditor). With no war chest of his own and no broad base of support, Fredman decided that the contribution limit was preventing him from taking his message to the voters, and he filed suit—along with the political action committee—claiming that Missouri's law infringed his freedom of speech under the First Amendment.

The federal district court upheld the law, but the court of appeals granted a temporary injunction against its enforcement. This relief allowed Fredman to collect one donation in excess of $2,000. In total, however, he raised less than $5,000 and was soundly defeated in the election. The appeals court subsequently invalidated the law, finding that the state's assertion of a compelling interest "in avoiding the corruption or the perception of corruption brought about when candidates for elective office accept large campaign contributions" was insufficient to satisfy strict scrutiny as it believed ***Buckley v. Valeo,*** 424 U.S. 1 (1976), required.

The Supreme Court reaffirmed *Buckley*'s approval of contribution limits—with or without adjustment for inflation. The Missouri law was not void for lack of evidence, Justice Souter wrote for the majority. "There is little reason to doubt that sometimes large contributions will work actual corruption of our political system," he said, "and no reason to question the existence of a corresponding suspicion among voters." As for the dollar amounts in the law, Souter said that *Buckley* "specifically rejected" the idea of some "constitutional minimum below which legislatures could not regulate."

Money, Justice Stevens said, "is property . . . not speech"—and therefore not entitled to the same First Amendment protections as speech.

Justice Breyer argued that the issue was better left to legislatures than to courts. "The legislature understands the problem—the threat to electoral integrity, the need for democratization—better than do we," he wrote.

In dissent, Justice Thomas called for overruling *Buckley* and accused the majority of weakening what he called "the already enfeebled constitutional protection" for campaign contributions. Missouri had no evidence of true *quid pro quo* corruption to justify its law, only "vague and unenumerated harms," he said. Moreover, the limits in the Missouri law were "much more restrictive" than those approved in *Buckley,* Thomas said, especially when inflation is taken into account.

Justice Kennedy said he agreed with Thomas on overruling *Buckley,* which he said had driven "a substantial amount of political speech underground" as contributors sought ways—such as unregulated "soft money"—to circumvent the donation limits. But Kennedy left open the possibility that Congress or state legislatures could "attempt some new reform if, based upon their own considered judgment of the First Amendment, it is possible to do so."

See Richard Briffault, "Nixon v. Shrink Missouri Government PAC: The Beginning of the End of the Buckley Era?" *Minnesota Law Review* 85 (June 2001): 1727; Mary H. Cooper, "Campaign Finance Reform," *CQ Researcher,* March 31, 2000, 257–280; and Christina Wells, "Beyond Campaign Finance: The Implications of Nixon v. Shrink Missouri Government PAC," *Missouri Law Review* 66 (2001): 141.

Food and Drug Administration v. Brown & Williamson Tobacco Corp.

529 U.S. 129 (2000)
Decided: March 21, 2000
Vote: 5 (Rehnquist, O'Connor, Scalia, Kennedy, Thomas)
4 (Stevens, Souter, Ginsburg, Breyer)
Opinion of the Court: O'Connor
Dissenting opinion: Breyer (Stevens, Souter, Ginsburg)

The Food and Drug Administration (FDA) proposed regulations in August 1995 that made it a federal offense to sell cigarettes to anyone under age eighteen, prohibited billboards advertising cigarettes near schools and playgrounds, and barred brand-name sponsorship by tobacco companies of entertainment and sporting events. The proposals drew a record ninety-five thousand individual comments on both sides, but the FDA adopted them virtually unchanged in August 1996.

The tobacco industry—major manufacturers and a trade association of retailers—challenged the regulations in federal court in North Carolina. Judge William Osteen held that the FDA had the power to regulate access to tobacco, but not to control marketing or promotion practices. The appeals court handed the tobacco industry a clear-cut victory. "Congress did not intend to delegate jurisdiction over tobacco products," Judge H. Emory Widener wrote for the majority. The FDA appealed to the Supreme Court.

Justice O'Connor began her majority opinion by acknowledging tobacco to be "one of the most troubling public health problems facing our Nation today," but, she continued, "we believe that Congress has clearly precluded the FDA from asserting jurisdiction to regulate tobacco products." At length, O'Connor cited food and drug law provisions governing labeling and classification of drugs and then declared, "Were the FDA to regulate cigarettes and smokeless tobacco, the Act would require the agency to ban them." Congress, however, had "foreclosed" that option. Well aware of tobacco's health effects, Congress had approved some half a dozen tobacco-specific statutes but "stopped well short of ordering a ban," she concluded.

O'Connor conceded that the Court ordinarily defers to an agency's interpretation of a statute that it is charged with administering, as in ***Chevron U.S.A. v. Natural Resources Defense Council*** 467 U.S. 837 (1984). But this, she said, was "no ordinary case." Given the "unique political history" of tobacco, she said, "we are obliged to defer not to the agency's expansive construction of the statute, but to Congress' consistent judgment to deny the FDA this power."

In dissent, Justice Breyer maintained that tobacco fit well within the definitions in the FDA's governing statute, which should be given a broad interpretation because of the public health risks at stake. "The upshot is that the Court today holds that a regulatory statute aimed at unsafe drugs and devices does not authorize regulation of a drug (nicotine) and a device (a cigarette) that the Court itself finds unsafe," Breyer wrote. "Far more than most, this particular drug and device risks the life-threatening harms that administrative regulation seeks to rectify."

See Martha A. Derthick, *Up in Smoke: From Legislation to Litigation in Tobacco Politics* (Washington, D.C.: CQ Press, 2001).

United States v. Morrison

529 U.S. 598 (2000)
Decided: May 15, 2000
Vote: 5 (Rehnquist, O'Connor, Scalia, Kennedy, Thomas)
4 (Stevens, Souter, Ginsburg, Breyer)
Opinion of the Court: Rehnquist
Concurring opinion: Thomas
Dissenting opinion: Souter (Stevens, Ginsburg, Breyer)
Dissenting opinion: Breyer (Stevens, Souter, Ginsburg)

Congress passed the Violence Against Women Act of 1994 in an attempt to stem what it called the "escalating problem" of attacks against women. The law's many provisions included one authorizing victims of "gender-motivated" violence to bring suit in federal court seeking compensatory or punitive damages from their attackers. The damage suit provision drew little controversy as it moved through Congress. When plaintiffs began invoking the law in court, however, defendants mounted a constitutional challenge. They contended that Congress had overstepped its powers in creating a new federal civil remedy for a problem traditionally viewed as a matter for states to handle.

The Supreme Court agreed. In a continuation of the Rehnquist Court's use of federalism principles to limit Congress's powers to intrude on state sovereignty, the Court struck down Section 13981 of the act, which provided a federal civil remedy for the victims of gender-motivated violence, even though a majority of states endorsed the federal legislation being challenged. Section 13981 opened by declaring that all persons "have the right to be free from crimes of violence motivated by gender." Lawmakers justified the federal court remedy by detailing the effects of violence against women on interstate commerce and the purportedly inadequate protections for women in state courts.

The issue reached the Court in a case brought by Christy Brzonkala, a former student at Virginia Polytechnic Institute, who claimed she was raped by two of the school's varsity football players. The athletes—Antonio Morrison and James Crawford—admitted having sex with Brzonkala, but they claimed it was consensual. The university suspended Morrison, but later lifted the suspension and dismissed the disciplinary action against Crawford.

Brzonkala dropped out of school after Morrison returned to campus. She never sought a criminal prosecution, but filed a civil suit in 1995 under the recently enacted law. She cited the state university's handling of the case as one reason for seeking damages in federal court rather than in state courts. Her lawyers argued that Congress had authority to pass the law under its powers to regulate interstate commerce and to enforce individual rights against the states under the Fourteenth Amendment.

Like the rationale adopted in ***United States v. Lopez,*** 514 U.S. 549 (1995), which struck down a law making it a federal crime to possess a gun near a school, Chief Justice Rehnquist said Section 13981 had nothing to do with interstate commerce. Rehnquist said that gender-motivated crimes "are not, in any sense of the phrase, economic activity" and could not be regulated by Congress on the basis of their "aggregate effect" on the national economy. As for the Fourteenth Amendment, Rehnquist said it was aimed only at state action, not at individuals.

See Christy H. Dral and Jerry J. Phillips, "Commerce by Another Name: The Impact of United States v. Lopez and United States v. Morrison," *Tennessee Law Review* 68 (spring 2001): 605–633.

Troxel v. Granville

530 U.S. 57 (2000)
Decided: June 5, 2000
Vote: 6 (Rehnquist, O'Connor, Souter, Thomas, Ginsburg, Breyer)
3 (Stevens, Scalia, Kennedy)
Judgment of the Court: O'Connor
Opinion concurring in judgment: Souter
Opinion concurring in judgment: Thomas
Dissenting opinion: Stevens
Dissenting opinion: Scalia
Dissenting opinion: Kennedy

Gary and Jenifer Troxel's son, Brad, fathered two children with Tommie Granville, although the two never married. They separated in 1991, before the younger daughter, Isabelle, was born. Granville was the primary caregiver for the two girls, but Brad Troxel kept them from time to time—sometimes at his parents' house. Brad Troxel committed suicide in 1993. The Troxels wanted to stay in their grandchildren's lives, and Granville never tried to cut off their access to the children. When she decided to marry Kelly Wynn, however, she came to view the Troxels' requests as interfering with her efforts to build a new family, and she limited the visits to one weekend day a month with no overnight stays. Dissatisfied, the Troxels went to court in 1995. The trial judge granted them one overnight visitation a month, one week during the summer, and four hours on each of the grandparents' birthdays.

The intermediate-level Washington Court of Appeals reversed the visitation order in 1997 by ruling that nonparents had no standing under the law to petition for visitation unless a custody proceeding was pending. The Troxels appealed to the Washington Supreme Court, which issued a broader ruling in 1998. The state justices ruled the visitation law unconstitutional. The government could not overrule a parent's "fundamental rights," the state high court ruled, except to prevent harm to a child.

The U.S. Supreme Court's decision to hear the Troxels' appeal took the justices into the largely uncharted waters of grandparents' rights. The Court rarely deals with custody disputes, but it recognized parental rights to control their children's upbringing in a pair of education-related cases from the 1920s—***Meyer v. Nebraska,*** 262 U.S. 390 (1923), which invalidated a law that barred the teaching of foreign languages to young children, and ***Pierce v. Society of Sisters,*** 268 U.S. 510 (1925), which struck down an Oregon law requiring parents to send their children to public schools. The Court had only one prior ruling on grandparents' rights. In ***Moore v. City of East Cleveland,*** 431 U.S. 494 (1977), the Court overturned a local zoning ordinance that would have prevented a woman from having two grandsons—cousins, not brothers—live with her in subsidized housing.

All fifty states had laws on the books giving grandparents some visitation rights. The laws dated from the mid-1960s and varied widely. Many permitted court-ordered visits only under limited conditions—for example, if the parents were deceased, divorced, or unmarried. Others allowed for court-ordered visitation even if the nuclear family was intact. Some but not all of the laws required proof of some close relationship between the grandparents and the child. Washington's child visitation law—adopted in 1973—was the broadest of any. It allowed "any person"—not just grandparents or other relatives—to petition a court for visitation "at any time" and allowed the court to grant visitation rights whenever "visitation may serve the best interest of the child."

Justice O'Connor said in the main opinion only that the statute—"as applied to Granville [Wynn] and her family in this case"—unconstitutionally infringed on her "fundamental parental right" concerning the care, custody, and control of her children. O'Connor stressed that the Troxels had not claimed that she was an unfit parent, that she had refused the Troxels all visitation, and that the Washington court had given no special weight to her views. The judge's order, O'Connor said, "directly contravened the traditional presumption that a fit parent will act in the best interest of his or her child." Chief Justice Rehnquist and Justices Ginsburg and Breyer joined the opinion. Given the breadth of the statute, O'Connor said that the Court did not have to decide whether a nonparental visitation statute must require a showing of harm before courts could intervene.

Justice Souter said he would have upheld the Washington Supreme Court's decision that the state law was unconstitutional on its face, without regard to the specific facts in the case. He agreed with O'Connor that the Court did not have to decide whether a showing of harm was constitutionally required for nonparental visitation.

Justice Thomas called for applying the most stringent constitutional standard—"strict scrutiny"—before allowing courts to infringe on "fundamental parental rights." Under that test, a court would need a "compelling interest" to intervene. In this case, Thomas said, the court had no "legitimate governmental interest . . . in second-guessing a fit parent's decision."

In dissenting opinions, Justices Stevens and Kennedy both faulted the Washington court for rejecting what Kennedy called the "well recognized" best-interest-of-the-child standard. Children's interests, Stevens wrote, "must be balanced in this equation." Kennedy said the Court should "proceed with caution" in fashioning constitutional rules in the area. Both said they would remand the case for further proceedings.

Dissenting more broadly, Justice Scalia directly challenged the whole idea of judicially enforced parental rights. He said the issues should be left to state legislatures and warned against "ushering in a new regime of judicially prescribed, and federally prescribed, family law."

See Emily Buss, "Adrift in the Middle: Parental Rights after Troxel v. Granville," *Supreme Court Review, 2000,* 279: and Terra L. Henry Sapp, "Grandparent Visitation Statutes in the Aftermath of Troxel v. Granville," *Journal of American Academy of Matrimonial Lawyers* 17 (2001): 121.

Santa Fe Independent School District v. Doe

530 U.S. 290 (2000)
Decided: June 19, 2000
Vote: 6 (Stevens, O'Connor, Kennedy, Souter, Ginsburg, Breyer)
3 (Rehnquist, Scalia, Thomas)
Opinion of the Court: Stevens
Dissenting opinion: Rehnquist (Scalia, Thomas)

Marian Ward received a standing ovation at the Santa Fe, Texas, high school football team's season opener in September 1999 after she delivered a pregame prayer asking for good sportsmanship from the players and the fans. The families of two students, one Catholic, the other Mormon, however, saw prayers at football games as part of a pervasive and improper policy of injecting religion into school life. The two families claimed in a federal court suit that school officials had encouraged students to attend revival meetings or join religious clubs and that some students had been chastised for minority religious beliefs.

A federal district court judge issued an interim order that prohibited a variety of practices, such as the use of "blatantly religious denominational" lesson material in classes, but allowed students to select a speaker to deliver a nondenominational prayer at graduation. The school board then adopted a comparable policy for students to vote on whether to have invocations at football games and—if approved—to elect one student for that role for the season. As adopted, the policy made no specification about the content of the invocation, but it included a fallback provision in the event of a court challenge to require any invocation to be "nonsectarian and nonproselytizing." The students voted to have invocations at games and elected a student to deliver them, but the judge blocked the policy, saying that it "coerces student participation in religious events." The court of appeals held that the school board could allow graduation prayers only if they were "nonsectarian and nonproselytizing" and barred prayers from football games altogether.

The Supreme Court's ruling rejected the school district's effort to defend the policy as neutral toward religion. "The delivery of a pregame prayer has the improper effect of coercing those present to participate in an act of religious worship," Justice Stevens said. He minimized the importance of the students' role in the policy. The invocations, he said, "are authorized by a government policy and take place on government property at government-sponsored school-related events." The policy, he continued, "invites and encourages religious messages." And the policy would not be saved even if attendance at football games were completely voluntary. The school district cannot require "religious conformity" from a student as the price of joining classmates at a game, Stevens wrote. He also stressed that the Constitution does not bar all religious activity in public schools. Nothing stops "any public school student from voluntarily praying at any time before, during, or after the school day."

The Court said it made no difference whether the prayer was voted for by a majority of students. In fact, such a mechanism undermined "minority viewpoints." The election process "encourages divisiveness along religious lines and threatens the imposition of coercion upon those students not desiring to participate in a religious exercise."

The majority's opinion, Chief Justice Rehnquist wrote in dissent, "bristles with hostility to all things religious in public life." The rest of the dissent was narrow. The school's policy had "plausible secular purposes," he said, and could have been implemented in a neutral manner. On that basis, Rehnquist said, the policy should have been allowed to go into effect and blocked only if it was applied in an unconstitutional manner.

See Devon M. Lehman, "Comment: The Godless Graduation Ceremony? The State of Student-Initiated Graduation Prayer After Lee v. Weisman and Santa Fe Independent School District v. Doe," *University of Colorado Law Review* 72 (winter 2001): 175–199; Ira Lupu,

"Government Messages and Government Money: Santa Fe, Mitchell v. Helms, and the Arc of the Establishment Clause," *William and Mary Law Review* 42 (March 2001): 771; and Patrick Marshall, "Religion in Schools," *CQ Researcher,* January 12, 2001, 1–24.

Dickerson v. United States

530 U.S. 428 (2000)
Decided: June 26, 2000
Vote: 7 (Rehnquist, Stevens, O'Connor, Kennedy, Souter, Ginsburg, Breyer)
2 (Scalia, Thomas)
Opinion of the Court: Rehnquist
Dissenting opinion: Scalia (Thomas)

The Supreme Court came under fierce political attack in 1966 when it handed down ***Miranda v. Arizona,*** 384 U.S. 436, a decision requiring police to tell suspects of their rights before conducting interrogation. Congress sought to undo the ruling in 1968 by passing Section 3501 of the U.S. criminal code, which declared that a confession "shall be admissible" in federal court "if it is voluntarily given." Over the next three decades, the Miranda warnings became a routine procedure for police and a familiar and accepted practice for most of the American public. Section 3501 went all but ignored until a federal appeals court invoked it in 1999 to throw out Charles Dickerson's purported confession to a bank robbery. Under the law, judges were to determine voluntariness by considering all the circumstances—without necessarily requiring all of the Miranda warnings. Five factors were specifically mentioned, including how much time elapsed between the defendant's arrest and arraignment; whether the defendant had been informed of the nature of the charge, his right to remain silent, and his right to a lawyer; and whether the suspect had no lawyer when questioned.

Dickerson contended that the FBI agent who interrogated him did not give him the Miranda warnings before he (Dickerson) gave a statement that linked him to the get-away vehicle in the robbery. The FBI agent said he had delivered the warning, but the judge believed Dickerson and ruled the statement inadmissible.

The appeals court described the Miranda rule as "judicially created" and not required by the Constitution. The court also said that Congress had the power to overrule it. The court went on to find Dickerson's statement voluntary and therefore admissible.

In overruling the appeals court, Chief Justice Rehnquist explained that *Miranda* had established "a constitutional rule" that Congress "may not legislatively supersede." Citing ***Michigan v. Tucker,*** 417 U.S. 433 (1974), Rehnquist acknowledged that some of the Court's decisions suggested that the Miranda protections were not constitutionally required. But the Court, Rehnquist explained, could not have applied the Miranda rule to state cases except to enforce constitutional rights. Subsequent decisions creating "exceptions" to *Miranda* simply proved that "no constitutional rule is immutable," he continued.

As for Section 3501, Rehnquist said that it did not satisfy the Court's criterion of being "equally effective" as *Miranda* in safeguarding suspects' rights. Even combined with other new remedies for "abusive police conduct," the law was not "an adequate substitute for the warnings required by *Miranda,*" the chief justice concluded.

Rehnquist also rejected the Court's overruling *Miranda* itself—citing the doctrine of *stare decisis,* or respect for precedent. "Whether or not we would agree with *Miranda*'s reasoning and its resulting rule, were we addressing the issue in the first instance, the principles of *stare decisis* weigh heavily against overruling it now," Rehnquist wrote. The warnings have become "embedded in police practice," he explained. In addition, the Court's subsequent cases "have reduced the impact of the Miranda rule on legitimate law enforcement while reaffirming the decision's core ruling."

The majority's description of *Miranda* as a "constitutional rule" implied that the Court had the power "not merely to apply the Constitution but to expand it," Justice Scalia wrote in dissent. "That is an immense and frightening antidemocratic power," he continued, "and it simply does not exist." *Miranda* itself was "objectionable for innumerable reasons," Scalia said, in part because of its "palpable hostility toward the act of confession *per se.*" Subsequent decisions limiting the ruling's impact simply proved that a Miranda violation was not a violation of the Constitution. The Court's enforcement of the rule in state court cases, he said, was merely "evidence of its ultimate illegitimacy."

For good measure, Scalia added that he would defy the ruling by continuing to apply Section 3501 "in all cases where there has been a sustainable finding that the defendant's confession was voluntary."

See Erwin Chemerinsky, "The Court Should Have Remained Silent: Why the Court Erred in Deciding *Dickerson v. United States,*" *University of Pennsylvania Law Review* 149 (2000): 287; and Brooke B. Grona, "*U.S. v. Dickerson:* Leaving Miranda and Finding a Deserted Statute," *American Journal of Criminal Justice* 26 (1999).

Boy Scouts of America v. Dale

530 U.S. 640 (2000)
Decided: June 28, 2000
Vote: 5 (Rehnquist, O'Connor, Scalia, Kennedy, Thomas)
4 (Stevens, Souter, Ginsburg, Breyer)
Opinion of the Court: Rehnquist
Dissenting opinion: Stevens (Souter, Ginsburg, Breyer)
Dissenting opinion: Souter (Ginsburg, Breyer)

The Constitution does not mention "freedom of association," but the Supreme Court has held that the right of private organizations to adopt membership policies free of government control is implicit in the First Amendment freedoms of speech and assembly. The Court also has ruled that state and local antidiscrimination laws can override the associational rights of private clubs in some circumstances. For example, the Court unanimously upheld the enforcement of civil rights laws against private civic clubs that barred women as members. In both cases—***Roberts v. United States Jaycees,*** 468 U.S. 609 (1984), and *Board of Directors of Rotary International v. Rotary Club of Duarte,* 481 U.S. 537 (1987)—the Court said that excluding women was not essential to the clubs' stated purposes and that any incidental effects were outweighed by the states' interests in promoting equal treatment of women.

A new conflict reached the Court in an emotional confrontation pitting the Boy Scouts of America (BSA) against an openly gay former Eagle Scout who opposed the Scouts' policy of barring homosexuals as adult leaders. James Dale was expelled as an assistant troop leader after the local Boy Scout council learned that he was the president of a gay rights group at his college. Dale went to court, contending that the Scouts' policy violated the New Jersey civil rights law that prohibited any "public accommodation" from discriminating on the basis of sexual orientation. The BSA countered by pointing to policy statements depicting homosexual conduct as inconsistent with the requirement that a scout be "morally straight" and "clean."

In other states, the Scouts had successfully defended its antigay policy by arguing that the organization was a private club, not a public accommodation. The New Jersey Supreme Court rejected that argument. The state court also rejected a freedom of association argument by finding that the Scouts did not have a "shared goal" of promoting the view that homosexuality is immoral.

The BSA appealed that issue to the Supreme Court and won a ruling that kept the antigay policy intact. Chief Justice Rehnquist acknowledged that the government can override a group's associational rights to promote a compelling interest, but he also said courts must defer to a private group's view of what might interfere with its constitutionally protected expression. "Dale's presence in the Boy Scouts would, at the very least, force the organization to send a message . . . that the Boy Scouts accept homosexual conduct as a legitimate form of behavior," Rehnquist concluded.

Dissenting justices disagreed primarily with the majority's view of the facts, not the law. Quoting from the Scouts' Handbook, Justice Stevens declared, "It is plain as the light of day that neither one of these principles, 'morally straight' and 'clean,' says the slightest thing about homosexuality."

The Scouts claimed vindication for what a spokesman called the organization's "character-building experiences." But Dale warned that the Scouts risked becoming marginalized. "The Boy Scouts are making themselves extinct," Dale told reporters, "and it's a very sad thing."

See Dale Carpenter, "Expressive Association and Anti-Discrimination Law After *Dale:* A Tripartite Approach," *Minnesota Law Review* 85 (2001): 1515; and Christopher E. Fowler, "The Supreme Court Endorses 'Invidious Discrimination': *Boy Scouts of America v. Dale* Creates a Constitutional Right to Exclude Gay Men," *Journal of Law and Policy* 9 (2001).

Mitchell v. Helms

530 U.S. 793 (2000)
Decided: June 28, 2000
Vote: 6 (Rehnquist, O'Connor, Scalia, Kennedy, Thomas, Breyer)
3 (Stevens, Souter, Ginsburg)
Judgment of the Court: Thomas
Opinion concurring in judgment: O'Connor (Breyer)
Dissenting opinion: Souter (Stevens, Ginsburg)

In 1985 Mary Helms and Marie Schneider were public school parents in suburban Jefferson Parish, Louisiana, when they began wondering why public school buses were transporting parochial school students. Their case followed a tortuous path through federal courts in Louisiana for many years. It came to focus on a program known as Chapter 2 that used public funds to lend instructional equipment ranging from film projectors to computers to public and private schools. A group of parents of parochial school students, including Guy Mitchell, joined the case to defend the program.

The federal appeals court eventually ruled for the public school parents, relying on two Supreme Court decisions from the 1970s—***Meek v. Pittenger,*** 421 U.S. 349 (1975), and ***Wolman v. Walter,*** 433 U.S. 229 (1977), that barred providing instructional materials to parochial schools. The appeals court acknowledged, however, that a later decision in ***Agostini v. Felton,*** 521 U.S. 203 (1997), appeared to contradict those rulings, but said that they remained valid unless the U.S. Supreme Court itself overruled them.

The Court did just that: it formally overruled *Meek* and *Wolman,* but without a majority opinion, and gave a green light to the assistance program. Writing for the plurality, Justice Thomas said that government aid was permissible if it was available without regard to religious affiliation. Four justices went so far as to say that any neutral, secular aid program would be constitutional. But two others—Justices O'Connor and Breyer—concurred more narrowly, saying courts must examine whether the publicly provided equipment had been used for religious purposes.

O'Connor agreed that the aid program in Jefferson Parish did not run afoul of the requirements she set out in *Agostini.* She listed several factors: the aid must be allocated on the basis of "neutral, secular criteria"; it must supplement rather than supplant nonfederal funds; no funds could "reach the coffers of religious schools"; and the aid must be secular, with only minimal evidence of diversion to religious purposes and with adequate safeguards against such diversion. Thomas's opinion, O'Connor said, went too far. "The plurality opinion foreshadows the approval of direct monetary subsidies to religious organizations, even when they use the money to advance their religious objectives," she wrote.

The dissenters said there was adequate evidence of "diversion" in Jefferson Parish to block the aid. More broadly, Justice Souter said the plurality opinion threatened to allow wholesale, direct government aid to parochial schools in violation of previous Establishment Clause decisions. Souter also criticized Thomas's opinion. The neutrality principle, he said, amounted to "a formula for generous religious support." As for the aid to Jefferson Parish's parochial schools, Souter said there was sufficient evidence that the schools had used publicly provided materials for religious purposes to curtail the program.

See Ira Lupu, "Government Messages and Government Money: *Santa Fe, Mitchell v. Helms,* and the Arc of the Establishment Clause," *William and Mary Law Review* 42 (March 2001): 771; and Patrick Marshall, "Religion in Schools," *CQ Researcher,* January 12, 2001, 1–24.

Stenberg v. Carhart

530 U.S. 914 (2000)
Decided: June 28, 2000
Vote: 5 (Stevens, O'Connor, Souter, Ginsburg, Breyer)
4 (Rehnquist, Scalia, Kennedy, Thomas)
Opinion of the Court: Breyer
Concurring opinion: Stevens (Ginsburg)
Concurring opinion: O'Connor
Concurring opinion: Ginsburg (Stevens)
Dissenting opinion: Rehnquist
Dissenting opinion: Scalia
Dissenting opinion: Kennedy (Rehnquist)
Dissenting opinion: Thomas (Rehnquist, Scalia)

LeRoy Carhart was one of only three physicians performing abortions in Nebraska in the late 1990s and the only one who performed the operation on women more than sixteen weeks pregnant. In some twenty or so cases per year, Carhart used a procedure described in medical terminology as "dilation and extraction," or D&X. In this procedure, the fetus is brought feet first from the uterus into the vagina. Then, because the head is too large to pass through the cervix, the doctor pierces the fetal skull, suctions out the contents, and crushes or collapses the skull to complete removal of the fetus.

The American College of Obstetrics and Gynecology viewed the procedure as a variant of the more common "dilation and evacuation" or D&E procedure, in which the fetus is dismembered as it is brought through the cervical opening into the vagina. Antiabortion groups, however, coined a more pejorative term for the procedure: "partial-birth abortion." Using graphic pictures of nearly intact fetuses with their brains spilling out of collapsed skulls, the antiabortion forces likened the procedure to infanticide and mounted lobbying campaigns in state capitals and in Washington to enact laws prohibiting the operation.

The movement succeeded in the legislative arena. Some thirty-one states, including Nebraska, enacted laws aimed at prohibiting the D&X procedure. The Nebraska law defined the procedure as "deliberately and intentionally delivering into the vagina a living unborn child, or a substantial portion thereof, for the purpose of performing a procedure that the person performing such procedure knows will kill the unborn child and does kill the unborn child." D&X was prohibited except when "necessary to save the life of the mother." A doctor violating the law faced up to twenty years in prison, a fine of up to $25,000, and the loss of his or her medical license.

Carhart filed suit to invalidate Nebraska's ban not long after its enactment in 1997. In his challenge, Carhart claimed that by its terms the provision covered not only the D&X but also the D&E procedure. A federal district court judge in Omaha agreed with Carhart that the law was unconstitutional because it applied to all D&E procedures and because it failed to include an exception for the health of the mother. The court of appeals also ruled the law unconstitutional, but solely on the first ground: that the statute imposed an "undue burden" on abortion by prohibiting D&E as well as D&X procedures.

The ruling coincided with most other court decisions on the D&X procedure, including the earlier federal appeals court decision striking down an Ohio law. Another court of appeals upheld bans enacted in Illinois and Wisconsin. Meanwhile, Congress had twice passed bills including such bans, but President Bill Clinton vetoed them.

Justice Breyer's opinion for the Court striking down the Nebraska law began by acknowledging "the controversial nature of the problem" and the "virtually irreconcilable points of view" on the issue. In the remainder of his opinion, however, Breyer proceeded unemotionally through medical and legal details in concluding that the law was unconstitutional because it was too broad and because it did not include a health exception. Breyer said the ruling was based on an application of the principles of ***Roe v. Wade,*** 410 U.S. 113 (1973), and ***Planned Parenthood of Southeastern Pennsylvania v. Casey,*** 505 U.S. 833 (1992). He carefully detailed the state's eight arguments for omitting a health exception and rejected them one by one. "A statute that altogether forbids D&X creates a significant health risk," Breyer concluded. "The statute consequently must contain a health exception."

On the scope of the statute, Breyer again detailed and then rejected the state's interpretation. "Using this law, some present prosecutors and future Attorneys General may choose to pursue physicians who use D&E procedures," he explained. "All those who perform abortion procedures using that method must fear prosecution, conviction, and punishment. The result is an undue burden on a woman's right to make an abortion decision."

Justice O'Connor signaled her willingness to accept a more carefully drafted statute. "A ban on partial-birth abortion that only proscribed the D&X method of abortion and that included an exception to preserve the life and health of the mother would be constitutional in my view," O'Connor wrote. Justices Stevens and Ginsburg said they saw no legal distinction between the D&E and D&X procedures.

Speaking for the dissenters, Justice Thomas harshly criticized the majority opinion. "Today, the Court inexplicably holds that the States cannot constitutionally prohibit a method of abortion that millions find hard to distinguish from infanticide and that the Court hesitates even to describe," Thomas declared.

The ruling "cannot be reconciled with *Casey's* undue burden standard," he said. Instead, it represented "a reinstitution of the . . . abortion-on-demand era in which the mere invocation of 'abortion rights' trumps any contrary societal interest."

After describing abortion procedures in graphic detail, Thomas insisted that the majority was misreading the "plain language of the statute" to apply to D&E abortions and, in any event, was wrong to substitute its interpretation for the attorney general's. As for the health exception, Thomas said the majority was wrong to require an exception merely because a woman or a doctor preferred one procedure to another. "The exception entirely swallows the rule," Thomas wrote. "There will always be *some* support for a procedure and there will always be some doctors who conclude that the procedure is preferable."

See Aimée M. Gauthier, "Comment: Stenberg v. Carhart: Have the States Lost Their Power to Regulate Abortion?" *New England Law Review* 36 (spring 2002); and M. Jason Majors, "Note: Clarity or Confusion? The Constitutionality of a Nebraska Statute Prohibiting Partial-birth Abortion Procedures," *Wyoming Law Review* 1 (2001).

Bush v. Gore

531 U.S. 98 (2000)
Decided: December 12, 2000
Vote: 5 (Rehnquist, O'Connor, Scalia, Kennedy, Thomas)
4 (Stevens, Souter, Ginsburg, Breyer)
Opinion: *Per curiam*
Concurring opinion: Rehnquist (Scalia, Thomas)
Dissenting opinion: Stevens (Ginsburg, Breyer)
Dissenting opinion: Souter (Stevens, Ginsburg, Breyer)
Dissenting opinion: Ginsburg (Stevens, Souter, Breyer)
Dissenting opinion: Breyer (Stevens, Souter, Ginsburg)

Shortly after the polls closed in Florida during the 2000 presidential election, all of the major television networks, relying on voter exit polls, announced that Albert Gore Jr., the Democratic candidate, had defeated George W. Bush, the Republican candidate, in the state. Based on reports from other states, this result seemed to give the election to Gore, who had a national margin of 400,000 in the popular vote and, with Florida, the necessary 270 electoral college ballots. As additional information came in, however, the Florida outcome grew murky. Soon, the vote count gave the state to Bush, but by such a close margin that under state law an automatic recount was triggered. The recount gave Bush a lead of 327 votes.

Gore pointed out that four heavily Democratic counties used punch-card ballots, and the automatic voting machines could not read these ballots unless they were punched all the way through. The four counties—Volusia, Palm Beach, Broward, and Miami-Dade—are the heart of Florida's retirement belt, and many elderly persons, for a variety of reasons, had not punched their ballots cleanly. As a result, their votes were disallowed. Estimate of uncounted ballots ran as high as fifty thousand; had they been counted, it is clear that Gore would have won.

Lawyers for the two sides quickly took their case to state courts, where Gore's lawyers asked for a manual recount of the ballots. Bush's lawyers went into federal court, where both the district court as well as the Court of Appeals for the Eleventh Circuit dismissed Bush's suit, noting that election law had always been a state matter and should therefore be decided by state courts. The Supreme Court, however, agreed to hear Bush's appeal. After listening to oral arguments, the Court in *Bush v. Palm Beach County Canvassing Board,* 531 U.S. 70 (2000), returned the case to the Florida Supreme Court, asking it to ensure that adequate vote-counting standards existed and that the wishes of the legislature were followed. This last matter addressed the fact that Article II, Section 1, of the Constitution gives state legislatures the ultimate power for choosing presidential electors, and, because this is a direct grant of power by the Constitution, it overrode any Florida court effort to reconcile conflicting state laws or even provisions of the state constitution.

Many commentators believed the Supreme Court had unwisely agreed to hear the case in the first place and, recognizing the illogic of its attempt to intervene, was seeking a quiet way out. They assumed that the Court would now leave the process of deciding how to recount Florida's contested ballots to the state judiciary. People who believed this were rudely shocked less than a week later.

On December 9, 2000—the day after the Florida Supreme Court ordered the vote recount to resume—the U.S. Supreme Court, in response to an emergency appeal by Bush, ordered the hand counts to cease. Bush claimed that the Florida Supreme Court's decision had set no clear standard to determine which ballots would be included and how voter intent would be established and that the lack of a standard violated the Equal Protection and Due Process Clauses of the Fourteenth Amendment.

Why did the Court agree to hear this case? After all, the conservative majority of the Rehnquist Court had for years decided cases that reinvigorated the power and autonomy of the states within the federal system. For example, in ***United States v. Lopez,*** 514 U.S. 549 (1995), and ***Printz v. United States,*** 521 U.S. 898 (1997), 5–4 majorities had negated federal laws requiring states to comply with federal directives, the most dramatic curtailment of congressional power since the 1930s. Many people saw politics as the reason the Court accepted *Bush v. Gore.* The five-member conservative bloc that had prevailed in the states' rights cases—Chief Justice Rehnquist and Justices O'Connor, Scalia, Kennedy, and Thomas—were appointed by Republican presidents, and many Court observers, as well as other Americans, believed that the Court was acting in an unabashedly partisan manner. In the Court's decision to vacate the Florida Supreme Court's order to continue the recount, Scalia wrote, "It suffices to say that the issuance of this decision . . . suggests that a majority of the Court, while not deciding the issues presented, believe that the petitioner [Bush] has a substantial probability of success."

In response, Justice Stevens, joined by Justices Ginsburg and Breyer, cited the majority's reasoning in the recent federalism cases and noted that, in its decision to intervene, the majority had departed from three "venerable rules" of judicial restraint. "On questions of state law, we have consistently respected the opinions of the highest courts of the States. On questions whose resolution is committed at least in large measure to another branch of the Federal Government, we have construed our own jurisdiction narrowly and exercised it cautiously. On federal constitutional questions that were not fairly presented to the court whose judgment is being reviewed, we have prudently declined to express an opinion." The majority, they concluded, "has acted unwisely."

The Court heard oral arguments on December 11, five weeks after the election. Lawyers for Bush argued that the manual recounts ordered by the Florida Supreme Court failed to establish clear standards in violation of the Due Process and Equal Protection Clauses and violated the constitutional grant of power to the legislature to choose electors. Gore's attorneys argued that the Florida Supreme Court order raised no federal constitutional question and that, by refusing to allow the count to go ahead, the Court was in effect disenfranchising tens of thousands of Florida voters.

Wanting to put an end to the indecision surrounding the election results, the Court ruled the very next day in favor of Bush. Although seven justices agreed that an equal protection problem existed with the Florida court's orders (Justices Souter and Breyer agreed that equal protection problems existed, but thought the case should have been remanded to the state court for resolution), a 5–4 majority ruled that these problems were so severe as to warrant halting the recount. When the majority, through Chief Justice Rehnquist, noted that no time was left to conduct an acceptable recount, the minority opinions of Justices Stevens, Ginsburg, and Breyer pointedly reminded them that had the five in the majority not stopped the recount earlier it could have been completed in time. Moreover, the opinions of the dissenting justices were unusually sharp in suggesting that the Court's decision carried clear partisan overtones. Gore conceded the election the next day, and on January 20, 2001, Bush took the oath of office as the forty-third president of the United States.

For many reasons, *Bush v. Gore* will be debated by politicians and scholars for years to come. First, the majority opinion cast a great cloud of confusion over the reach of the decision. Although the Court spoke of limited applicability and kept referring to the case at hand, one could hardly imagine that the principles it used to decide the controversy would be limited only to the 2000 presidential election in the state of Florida. Very few states have procedures in place that would meet the Court's requirement of clear standards, and Florida was not alone in its wide variety of voting machines and methods that varied from county to county. Just days after the decision, other states began looking at their own election laws to see if they needed revision.

Second, some commentators believe that the Court did what it was supposed to do: save the system when a fatal error creeps into the democratic mechanism. The longer the recount went on, this argument goes, the less the American people would be willing to accept the results and the less legitimacy the winning candidate would enjoy. Others point to what the minority justices said—that the recount could have been accomplished in time had the Court not intervened.

Third—and the gravest charge against the Court—was partisanship, a criticism that federal courts avoided for more than two centuries. Courts cannot help being *political*, because the judiciary is one of the three branches of government, and governing is essentially an exercise in politics. Court decisions reaching back to ***Marbury v. Madison,*** 5 U.S. 137 (1803), have been political in this sense, and the Court, like the executive and legislative branches, must always be in the game. In *Bush v. Gore*, however, many people saw the Court as acting in a *partisan* manner, favoring one party over another, and, whatever the truth of this charge, the perception that it is true is widely held. The harm this belief does to the Court is incalculable because the basis of the Court's authority and power in the American scheme of government relies on the trust that the people have in its impartiality. As Breyer wrote in dissent, "We do risk a self-inflicted wound—a wound that may harm not just the Court but the nation."

See Cass R. Sunstein and Richard A. Epstein, eds., *The Vote: Bush, Gore, and the Supreme Court* (Chicago: University of Chicago Press, 2001); Richard A. Posner, *Breaking the Deadlock: The 2000 Election, the Constitution, and the Courts* (Princeton: Princeton University Press, 2001); and E. J. Dionne Jr. and William Kristol, eds., *Bush v. Gore: The Court Cases and Commentary* (Washington, D.C.: Brookings, 2001).

Board of Trustees of the University of Alabama v. Garrett

531 U.S. 356 (2001)
Decided: February 21, 2001
Vote: 5 (Rehnquist, O'Connor, Scalia, Kennedy, Thomas)
4 (Stevens, Souter, Ginsburg, Breyer)
Opinion of the Court: Rehnquist
Concurring opinion: Kennedy (O'Connor)
Dissenting opinion: Breyer (Stevens, Souter, Ginsburg)

Patricia Garrett was a director of nursing services at the University of Alabama in Birmingham Hospital. After being diagnosed with breast cancer, she had to take substantial leave from work to undergo a lumpectomy, radiation treatment, and chemotherapy. When she returned to work, her supervisor told her that she would have to give up her director position and transfer to a lower-paying job as a nurse manager. She filed suit under the American with Disabilities Act (ADA), claiming that the law prohibits employment discrimination by states as well as by private sector employers against a qualified individual with a disability on the basis of that disability. The district court dismissed the suit, claiming that in allowing individuals to sue a state under the ADA, Congress had exceeded its authority and violated the Eleventh Amendment. The Court of Appeals for the Eleventh Circuit reversed, and the state appealed.

The Supreme Court agreed with the district court that Congress lacked the authority to contravene the Eleventh Amendment, which bars suits against states in federal courts. Moreover, Congress's authority under Section 5 of the Fourteenth Amendment to enforce that amendment's Equal Protection Clause did not give it the power to circumvent the Eleventh Amendment. The Court said Congress would need to demonstrate a pattern of discrimination by the states that clearly violated the Equal Protection Clause and impose a remedy that was tailored to address that discrimination. The ADA was based on no finding of persistent state discrimination, and the remedy was far too broad.

The dissenters believed that Congress could reasonably have concluded that the remedy provided in the ADA's Title I was an appropriate way to enforce equal protection, and that was all the Constitution required.

The opinion was one in a line of cases in which the Rehnquist Court breathed new life into the doctrine of federalism and the Eleventh Amendment. Another example is ***Idaho v. Coeur d'Alene Tribe of Idaho,*** 521 U.S. 261 (1997).

Ferguson v. Charleston

532 U.S. 67 (2001)
Decided: March 21, 2001
Vote: 6 (Stevens, O'Connor, Kennedy, Souter, Ginsburg, Breyer)
3 (Rehnquist, Scalia, Thomas)
Opinion of the Court: Stevens
Opinion concurring in judgment: Kennedy
Dissenting opinion: Scalia (Rehnquist, Thomas)

Drug testing for pregnant women emerged as a divisive issue in the 1980s and 1990s against the backdrop of a growing incidence of "crack babies" born to women who used crack cocaine while pregnant. Some medical experts said cocaine use during pregnancy resulted in brain damage or other serious, long-term effects on the fetus. A few law enforcement authorities advocated prosecuting for child abuse any woman who used illegal drugs during pregnancy. Women's rights advocates strongly denounced the tactic, and most legal experts disagreed with the idea. In addition, most medical authorities said pregnant women with drug abuse problems needed to be in treatment, not prison.

Medical staff at the Medical University of South Carolina (MUSC) adopted a policy of screening expectant mothers for drugs in 1988. Women who tested positive for cocaine were referred to the county's substance abuse commission for counseling and treatment. When the policy failed to reduce the incidence of drug use among patients, maternity nurse Shirley Brown suggested a different approach. Brown had heard a news report that a prosecutor in Greenville, South Carolina, was bringing child abuse charges against drug-using expectant mothers. She convinced the hospital's general counsel to do the same. The general counsel helped form a joint task force with representatives from the police department and the office of the city solicitor. Together, they developed a policy in 1989 for testing pregnant women if they showed signs of possible drug abuse—including lack of prenatal care, retarded fetal growth, or prior drug use. Initially, the policy referred women to the solicitor's office for prosecution. Later, the policy was revised to give women the option to agree to treatment to avoid arrest. Two hundred and fifty-three women—mostly African American—were tested by the public hospital.

All told, some thirty women were referred to the county solicitor's office, although none were actually prosecuted. Nevertheless, in 1993 Crystal Ferguson and nine other women filed a federal civil rights suit against the hospital and other city officials, seeking money damages for violations of their Fourth Amendment rights. A jury rejected their claims by ruling that the women had consented to the drug testing.

The court of appeals ruled for the hospital on a different basis. The court held that the drug tests were "reasonable" as "special-needs searches." The majority said the government had an important interest in reducing cocaine use by pregnant women and that prenatal testing was "the only effective means" to accomplish that goal.

The Supreme Court's decision adopted the women's view of the hospital policy as practiced for law enforcement purposes. "The central and indispensable feature" of the testing, Justice Stevens said, "was the use of law enforcement to coerce the patients into substance abuse treatment." On that basis, the Court held that a warrant was required unless the women had consented. That issue was sent back to the appeals court for a decision.

Stevens emphasized that Charleston prosecutors and police were "extensively involved" in the design and day-to-day administration of the hospital's policy. He noted, for example, that the policy detailed how to preserve evidence for possible prosecution but did not discuss different courses of medical treatment for mother or child. Given the primary law enforcement purpose, Stevens concluded, the "special-needs" doctrine could not be invoked to avoid the Fourth Amendment's rules on searches.

Moreover, Stevens said, the policy of turning over positive test results to police provided "an affirmative reason" for applying the Fourth Amendment. When state hospital employees "undertake to obtain evidence from their patients *for the specific purpose of incriminating those patients,*" Stevens concluded, "they have a special obligation to make sure that the patients are fully informed about their constitutional rights."

Justice Kennedy agreed that the policy had "a far greater connection to law enforcement" than the special-needs doctrine allowed. But he also said the ruling would not invalidate mandatory reporting laws or prevent a state from punishing a woman for using drugs while pregnant.

Justice Scalia opened his dissenting opinion by contending that the women had no Fourth Amendment grounds at all to complain of the hospital's turning over the test results to police after the women provided the specimens voluntarily. In the second part of his dissent, Scalia, joined by Chief Justice Rehnquist and Justice Thomas, argued that the special-needs doctrine justified the policy. Police involvement took place, he said, "after the testing was conducted for independent purposes."

Atwater v. Lago Vista

532 U.S. 318 (2001)
Decided: April 24, 2001
Vote: 5 (Rehnquist, Scalia, Kennedy, Souter, Thomas)
4 (Stevens, O'Connor, Ginsburg, Breyer)
Opinion of the Court: Souter
Dissenting opinion: O'Connor (Stevens, Ginsburg, Breyer)

Gail Atwater was arrested, handcuffed, fingerprinted, and put in jail for failing to make her children wear seat belts as she drove them home from soccer practice. Bart Turek, a police officer in Lago Vista, Texas, who had tangled once before with Atwater, took exception to her disregard for the safety of Mac Haas, then three, and Anya Haas, five. "We've met before," Turek said after stopping Atwater the second time. She asked him to lower his voice. "You're going to jail," he rejoined. Atwater asked to take her children, visibly frightened and upset, to a neighbor's house. "You're not going anywhere," he said. Then, in full view of her children, Turek placed Atwater under arrest for violating Texas Transportation Code section 545.413, an offense punishable by a fine of $25 to $50 but no incarceration. Turek took Atwater to the police station for standard booking procedures, including taking her fingerprints and a mug shot. She was held in jail for one hour before being taken before a magistrate, where she posted bail.

Once Atwater disposed of the case—by paying a $50 fine—she and her husband, Michael Haas, filed a federal civil rights suit against Turek and the city. They argued that the custodial arrest for a nonjailable offense amounted to an unreasonable seizure under the Fourth Amendment.

The federal district court judge granted summary judgment for the city and Turek. A three-judge panel of the court of appeals held that an arrest for a first-time seat belt offense was an unreasonable seizure under the Fourth Amendment. When the full appeals court reheard the case, it too ruled for the city. Turek conducted the arrest in "an extraordinary manner," the court said, but the arrest was not unconstitutional.

The Supreme Court declared that warrantless arrests for minor offenses were constitutionally permissible. Justice Souter began with history. He pointed to "two centuries of uninterrupted (and largely unchallenged) state and federal practice permitting warrantless arrests for misdemeanors not amounting to or involving breach of the peace." In any event, Souter continued, a constitutional rule limiting misdemeanor arrests would be more complicated than Atwater recognized. Police would have a difficult time following a rule that barred arrests for nonjailable offenses. "An officer on the street might not be able to tell," Souter said. And a rule against an arrest if an officer was in doubt could result in "costs to society" that "could easily outweigh the costs to defendants"—especially as no evidence had surfaced that the country was experiencing "an epidemic of unnecessary minor-offense arrests."

It remained for Souter to apply the ruling to Atwater's case. Turek had exercised "extremely poor judgment," but his actions "satisfied constitutional requirements." Atwater's arrest and booking "were inconvenient and embarrassing," Souter concluded, "but not so extraordinary as to violate the Fourth Amendment."

Justice O'Connor attacked the majority's reasoning. "The Court recognizes that the arrest of Gail Atwater was a 'pointless indignity' that served no discernible state interest, and yet holds that her arrest was constitutionally permissible," she wrote. That position, she said, "is not only unsupported by our precedent, but runs contrary to the principles that lie at the core of the Fourth Amendment." As an alternative, O'Connor suggested that police should be required to issue a citation in fine-only cases unless an officer could point to "specific and articulable facts" to justify the additional intrusion of a custodial arrest. She closed by tying the ruling to the debate over "racial profiling"—the alleged practice by some police of targeting racial and ethnic minorities in traffic stops as pretexts for drug investigations. Minor traffic infractions, O'Connor wrote, "may often serve as an excuse for stopping and harassing an individual. After today, the arsenal available to any officer extends to a full arrest and the searches permissible concomitant to that arrest."

See Thomas Y. Davies, "The Fictional Character of Law-and-Order Originalism: A Case Study of the Distortions and Evasions of Framing-Era Arrest Doctrine in Atwater v. Lago Vista," *Wake Forest Law Review* 37 (2002): 239.

PGA Tour, Inc. v. Martin

532 U.S. 661 (2001)
Decided: May 29, 2001
Vote: 7 (Rehnquist, Stevens, O'Connor, Kennedy, Souter, Ginsburg, Breyer)
2 (Scalia, Thomas)
Opinion of the Court: Stevens
Dissenting opinion: Scalia (Thomas)

Golfer Casey Martin suffered from Klippel-Trenaunay-Weber Syndrome, a rare circulatory disorder that made walking painful and posed a long-term risk to his health. In college, he found he could no longer walk an eighteen-hole golf course, which is typically about five miles in total. Stanford University requested—and the National Collegiate Athletic Association granted—waivers for Martin to use a cart in college tournaments. When he turned professional, Martin asked for a similar waiver of the Professional Golfers Association's (PGA) rule that barred the use of carts in major tournaments.

The PGA Tour, a nonprofit entity formed in 1968, refused. It said that walking was part of the game and that allowing Martin to use a cart would fundamentally change the nature of competition. Martin claimed that the PGA's stance violated the Americans with Disabilities Act of 1990 (ADA).

The federal district court judge sided with Martin, holding that use of a cart was a reasonable modification because of his disability. The court of appeals upheld the decision. Rejecting the PGA's major argument, the appeals court said that fatigue caused by walking is "not significant under normal circumstances." Another federal appeals court, however, issued a contrary ruling in a comparable case brought by Ford Olinger, who suffered from bilateral avascular necrosis, a degenerative condition that significantly hindered his ability to walk, against the U.S. Golf Association, which sponsors the U.S. Open.

The Supreme Court ruled in Martin's favor. Justice Stevens rejected the PGA's contention that golfers were not "clients or customers" of tournaments for purposes of the law. Competing in a tournament, Stevens said, amounted to "a privilege that [the PGA Tour] makes available to the general public." Use of the golf cart was therefore a reasonable accommodation of Martin's disability because it would not "fundamentally alter the nature" of the game. Stevens said that when the PGA used public golf courses and held open qualifications, then the tournaments were public accommodations under the ADA.

In his dissenting opinion, Justice Scalia sharply challenged the notion that the ADA covered professional sports competitions at all and then mocked the majority's effort to try to define what he called classic, essential golf. On the first issue, Scalia insisted that professional golfers could not be viewed as "enjoying" the "privileges" of a golf tournament—using the statute's language—any more than professional baseball players "enjoy" the facilities of Yankee Stadium. But Scalia reserved his greatest scorn for the second question. Under the Court's ruling, he said, "it will henceforth be the Law of the Land that walking is not a 'fundamental' aspect of golf."

"Either out of humility or out of self-respect the Court should decline to answer this incredibly difficult and incredibly silly question," Scalia continued. "Eighteen-hole golf courses, 10-foot-high basketball hoops, 90-foot baselines, 100-yard football fields—all are arbitrary and none is essential." Scalia suggested the decision would allow athletes to play by "individualized rules" in which no one's lack of ability would amount to a handicap. Quoting George Orwell's satirical novel *Animal Farm,* he concluded: "The year was 2001, and " 'everybody was finally equal.' "

See Jason F. Darnall, "Note: PGA Tour, Inc. v. Martin: Do We Want Courts Playing the Role of Ultimate Rulemaker and Referee in Professional Sports?" *Northern Kentucky Law Review* 29 (2001): 593; Charles A. Omage, "Comment: Caught in the Rough of the PGA Tour and USGA Rules: Casey Martin and Ford Olinger's Fight for the Use of a Golf Cart Under the Americans with Disabilities Act," *Hofstra Law Review* 29 (2001): 1401; and Brian D. Shannon, "A Drive to Justice: The Supreme Court's Decision in PGA Tour Inc. v. Martin," *Virginia Sports and Entertainment Law Journal* 1 (winter 2001): 74.

Kyllo v. United States

533 U.S. 27 (2001)
Decided: June 11, 2001
Vote: 5 (Scalia, Souter, Thomas, Ginsburg, Breyer)
4 (Rehnquist, Stevens, O'Connor, Kennedy)
Opinion of the Court: Scalia
Dissenting opinion: Stevens (Rehnquist, O'Connor, Kennedy)

On information that led him to believe Danny Lee Kyllo was growing marijuana in his house, a federal agent used a thermal imaging device to scan the building to determine whether the amount of heat emanating from it was consistent with use of the high-intensity lamps typically required for growing marijuana indoors. The scan took only a few minutes and showed that the roof over the garage and a side wall of the house were relatively hot compared to the rest of the building and substantially warmer than neighboring houses. The agent concluded that Kyllo was using halide lights to grow marijuana and, on the basis of the scan as well as other information, a federal magistrate issued a search warrant. When agents entered the premises, they found more than one hundred marijuana plants.

At trial, Kyllo's attorney moved to suppress the evidence. He claimed that the use of the imaging device constituted an illegal search without a warrant. The trial judge denied the motion, and Kyllo then pleaded guilty. The Court of Appeals for the Ninth Circuit reversed the conviction, but on a second hearing upheld the government's claim that using the device to measure radiant heat did not constitute an entry into the house. Kyllo then appealed to the Supreme Court.

Justice Scalia agreed with Kyllo that use of the thermal imaging device to detect heat use inside a house was a search of the home and a violation of the Fourth Amendment. Police were free to use the device, but only after obtaining a warrant, which meant they had to show probable cause to believe that a particular house contained contraband. Riding up and down the street checking on houses was in effect a general warrant and forbidden. As to the minority's claim that no penetration or entry to the house had been made, Scalia said that by using sense-enhancing technology that was not in general public use, the police had secured information regarding the interior of Kyllo's house that could not otherwise have been obtained without physical intrusion into a constitutionally protected area.

The dissenters believed that all the police had done was deduce information from an "off-the-wall" surveillance, rather than a "through-the-wall" surveillance, and therefore the agent's conduct did not amount to a search and was perfectly reasonable. In light of the growing complexity of modern technology, Justice Stevens asserted that the courts should not erect a constitutional impediment to police use of sense-enhancing technology, but should let legislatures grapple with these emerging issues.

In many ways the Scalia-Stevens opinions reflect those in one of the earliest cases involving police use of technology, the original wiretapping case of ***Olmstead v. United States,*** 277 U.S. 438 (1928), but with the positions reversed. In *Olmstead* the majority opinion by Chief Justice Taft took the position that no physical entry had been made into the house and a warrant was not necessary. Justice Brandeis's dissent argued that regardless of whether a physical intrusion had taken place, the privacy of the home had been violated. Eventually Brandeis's position became accepted as the law, and the majority opinion in this case continued that line of argument—that violating the privacy of the home by any means requires a warrant by the police.

Good News Club v. Milford Central School

533 U.S. 98 (2001)
Decided: June 11, 2001
Vote: 6 (Rehnquist, O'Connor, Scalia, Kennedy, Thomas, Breyer)
3 (Stevens, Souter, Ginsburg)
Opinion of the Court: Thomas
Concurring opinion: Scalia
Concurring opinion: Breyer
Dissenting opinion: Stevens
Dissenting opinion: Souter (Ginsburg)

By 2000 the Child Evangelism Fellowship had organized over 4,600 Good News Clubs around the country about 500 of which met in public school buildings. The Good News Club is a private Christian organization for children ages six to twelve. In the 1960s Milford, New York, had a Good News Club run by an elderly woman who conducted the meetings in a trailer park where she lived. When Stephen Fournier moved to Milford in 1994 to become pastor of the Community Bible Church, he and his wife, Darleen, wanted to revive the club in an effort to minister to more children.

Initially, the club met in the church, located next door to the Fourniers' house, about two miles from the school. The Fourniers arranged for the school bus that brought their young daughters home to deliver other students who wanted to participate in the club. That arrangement ended when the bus got too crowded. So, at the start of the 1996–1997 school year, Darleen Fournier asked the school superintendent, Robert McGruder, for permission to meet in the school.

In rejecting the request, McGruder said the club meetings were "the equivalent of religious worship" and the school's community-use policy prohibited use "by any individual or organization for religious purposes." The school board affirmed McGruder's decision.

The Fourniers won an initial ruling from a lower court judge that allowed the club to meet in the school for the 1997–1998 academic year. Later in 1997, however, the court of appeals issued a decision in a somewhat similar case that allowed school systems to bar religious organizations from meeting in schools. On that basis, the lower court judge reversed himself and ruled against the Fourniers, who appealed and lost.

The Supreme Court's decision gave the Good News Club as much as it asked for—a ruling, first, that the school board violated its free speech rights and, second, that allowing the meeting in the school would not amount to unconstitutional establishment of religion. For the majority, Justice Thomas depicted the case as a straightforward application of ***Lamb's Chapel. v. Center Moriches Union Free School District,*** 508 U.S. 384 (1993). "Like the church in *Lamb's Chapel,*" Thomas wrote, the club wanted to address a permissible subject—"the teaching of morals and character, from a religious standpoint. "The only difference—the church's use of a film opposed to the club's use of storytelling and prayer—was "inconsequential." On that basis, he said, "the exclusion of the Good News Club's activities, like the exclusion of *Lamb's Chapel's* films, constitutes unconstitutional viewpoint discrimination."

Thomas also answered the Establishment Clause question that the appeals court had not resolved. Parents would understand that the school was not endorsing religion, Thomas said. No prior cases barred private religious conduct in school buildings after hours just because young children were around, he added. Moreover, the circumstances in this case—the club met in a resource room used by older students and the club's instructors were not school teachers—"simply do not support the theory that small children would perceive endorsement there."

Justice Scalia called the school board's policy "blatant viewpoint discrimination." The club could discuss morals and character, he said, but not "the religious premise on which its views are based."

In a partial concurrence, Justice Breyer said the "critical" Establishment Clause question was whether children participating in the club's activities could perceive a government endorsement of religion. That issue, he said, had not been finally resolved by the courts below; and both parties could litigate it further if they wanted.

Justice Souter, in dissent, recited at length a sample lesson plan from the club that included a so-called "invitation" to "unsaved" children to receive Jesus "as your Savior." "It is beyond question," Souter wrote,

> "that Good News intends to use the public school premises not for the mere discussion of a subject from a particular, Christian point of view, but for an evangelical service of worship calling children to commit themselves in an act of Christian conversion."

Souter also faulted the majority for considering the Establishment Clause issue at all.

In his dissent, Justice Stevens cited the danger of "divisiveness" to justify the school board's position. "School officials may reasonably believe that evangelical meetings designed to convert children to a particular religious faith pose [that] risk," he wrote.

See Patrick Marshall, "Religion in Schools," *CQ Researcher,* January 12, 2001, 1–24.

Immigration and Naturalization Service v. St. Cyr

533 U.S. 289 (2001)
Decided: June 25, 2001
Vote: 5 (Stevens, Kennedy, Souter, Ginsburg, Breyer)
4 (Rehnquist, O'Connor, Scalia, Thomas)
Opinion of the Court: Stevens
Dissenting opinion: O'Connor
Dissenting opinion: Scalia (Rehnquist, O'Connor, Thomas)

Enrico St. Cyr was admitted to the United States as a legal alien. In 1996 he pleaded guilty to selling narcotics in violation of a Connecticut state law, and his conviction, according to the United States, made him deportable. At the time of his conviction, he would have been eligible under existing law for a waiver of deportation at the discretion of the attorney general. By the time the Immigration and Naturalization Service (INS) began proceedings against him, however, two new laws had been enacted, the Antiterrorism and Effective Death Penalty Act of 1996 and the Illegal Immigration Reform and Immigrant Responsibility Act of 1996. According to the U.S. attorney general, the new laws did not give him the discretion to waive deportation of aliens convicted of certain crimes, and in his opinion they also limited an alien's right to seek habeas corpus in federal courts. St. Cyr filed for a writ of habeas corpus, claiming that the new acts did not apply to him because he had been convicted prior to their passage, and his petition for waiver should be considered under the old law. A federal district court accepted jurisdiction of St. Cyr's habeas corpus application and agreed that the new legislation did not apply to him; the Courts of Appeals for the Second Circuit affirmed, and the INS appealed.

The Supreme Court also affirmed. The majority ruled that federal courts had jurisdiction to hear St. Cyr's petition for habeas corpus under the pre-1996 laws, and that because the crime and the conviction took place before the new laws were enacted, their retroactive application to St. Cyr was forbidden by the Constitution as ex post facto laws. The Court also held that the old law, with its discretionary waiver, remained valid for all other aliens who may have been convicted of a crime prior to the 1996 legislation.

In dissent, Justice O'Connor agreed that the Suspension Clause (Article I, Section 9, Clause 2) generally prohibits the suspension of habeas corpus, but she said the broad right asserted by St. Cyr fell outside the limits of that clause. Congress had good reason to impose a limitation on a specific group of people.

Justice Scalia's dissent went further. He said Congress had full power regarding aliens and had made it quite clear that federal courts lacked the power to entertain habeas petitions by aliens convicted of crimes.

Federal Election Commission v. Colorado Republican Federal Campaign Commission

533 U.S. 431 (2001)
Decided: June 25, 2001
Vote: 5 (Stevens, O'Connor, Souter, Ginsburg, Breyer)
4 (Rehnquist, Scalia, Kennedy, Thomas)
Opinion of the Court: Souter
Dissenting opinion: Thomas (Rehnquist, Scalia, Kennedy)

Under the Federal Election Campaign Act, any expenditure made by an individual or a political party "in cooperation, consultation, or concert, with, or at the request or suggestion of, a candidate, his authorized political committee, or their agents" was classified as a contribution and therefore subject to limits. The Federal Election Commission (FEC) strictly interpreted this "coordinated expenditure" provision to apply to any spending by a political party for a candidate—and thus to limit the spending a national or state party committee could make in support of the party's candidates for Congress.

The test case on the limits on political party spending arose from the Colorado Republican Party's efforts in 1986 against Rep. Tim Wirth, the Democrat's anticipated candidate for the Senate. The FEC initiated an enforcement action against the GOP, charging that $15,000 spent for an anti-Wirth radio ad that aired before the primary had gone beyond the amount the party was allowed to contribute to the then-unchosen candidate.

The Supreme Court's ruling in the earlier case, ***Colorado Republican Federal Campaign Commission v. Federal Election Commission,*** 518 U.S. 604 (1996), was splintered. Chief Justice Rehnquist and Justices Scalia, Kennedy, and Thomas would have thrown out any limits on party spending. Justices Stevens and Ginsburg voted to uphold both the law and the FEC enforcement action. Justice Breyer wrote the pivotal opinion that adopted a middle view and sent the case back to lower courts for a ruling on the constitutionality of limiting coordinated expenditures; and Justices O'Connor and Souter joined his opinion.

On remand, a federal judge in Denver sided with the Republican Party and struck down the limits on coordinated expenditures. The court of appeals agreed. The majority termed the law "a significant interference with the First Amendment rights of political parties" and rejected the FEC's argument that political party spending resulted in corruption or the appearance of corruption.

This time, a slim majority of the Supreme Court upheld the spending limit on parties. Souter accepted the FEC's rationale, saying, "Coordinated expenditures of money donated to a party are tailor-made to undermine contribution limits." He rejected the argument that the spending limit had burdened parties' roles in supporting candidates. In any event, he said, the spending limit sought to control another role parties had come to play—as "instruments of some contributors" who seek to support a candidate because of one specific issue "or even to support any candidate who will be obliged to the contributors."

On that basis, Souter said the evidence in the record showed that donors already make contributions to parties "with the tacit understanding" that the money will benefit a particular candidate. Without a limit on coordinated expenditures, he said, "the inducement to circumvent [the contribution limits] would almost certainly intensify." And enforcement of the "earmarking" provision could not eliminate the problem, Souter said, because circumvention "is obviously hard to trace."

For the dissenters, Justice Thomas sought to demolish the FEC's rationale point by point. The party expenditure provision had a "stifling effect" on political parties, he said. He also said there was no evidence that parties had become "pawns of wealthy contributors." Moreover, the FEC had failed to show that coordinated expenditures gave rise to corruption; nor was the restriction "closely drawn" to prevent corruption. The government had "better tailored" alternatives, Thomas said, including stronger enforcement of the "earmarking" rule or lowering the maximum individual contribution to a party committee.

Thomas repeated his call from previous cases to overrule ***Buckley v. Valeo,*** 424 U.S. 1 (1976), and impose the highest constitutional scrutiny to all campaign finance regulation. "I remain baffled that this Court has extended the most generous First Amendment safeguards to filing lawsuits, wearing profane jackets, and exhibiting drive-in movies with nudity," he wrote, referring to earlier decisions, "but has offered only tepid protection to the core speech and associational rights that our Founders sought to defend." Chief Justice Rehnquist did not join the call to overrule *Buckley.*

See Anthony Corrado et al., eds. *Campaign Finance Reform: A Sourcebook* (Washington, D.C.: Brookings, 1997).

New York Times Company v. Tasini

533 U.S. 483 (2001)
Decided: June 25, 2001
Vote: 7 (Rehnquist, O'Connor, Scalia, Kennedy, Souter, Thomas, Ginsburg)
2 (Stevens, Breyer)
Opinion of the Court: Ginsburg
Dissenting opinion: Stevens (Breyer)

In the early 1990s Jonathan Tasini, a freelance writer, wrote several articles for the *New York Times,* for which he owned the copyright. The *Times* and other print publishers—without the consent of Tasini and other writers—licensed these articles to electronic publishers who made them part of databases containing thousands of articles previously in print. Database users could pay a fee and access any of these articles, which could be found through an extensive cross-indexing system. The fees were split with the print publisher, but not with the original author.

In 1993 Tasini and other freelancers filed a civil action in federal district court, alleging that their copyrights had been infringed when the print publishers permitted the articles to be put into the databases. The district court granted summary judgment for the publishers, holding that federal copyright law shielded the database reproductions and that electronic reproduction rights of print articles lay with the publishers. The Court of Appeals for the Second Circuit reversed on the grounds that electronic reproductions did not fall within those categories of reprints vested by the copyright law in the print publishers and that electronic reproduction did not constitute a revision of the original article, which also would have removed it from the author's protection under the copyright law. The *Times* and the other print publishers appealed.

The Supreme Court ruled in favor of the writers and limited the print media's ownership rights to material that appeared in print form. According to Justice Ginsburg, electronic publication infringed the writers' copyrights by reproducing and distributing freelancers' work in a manner they had not authorized. The print publishers further infringed on the writers' copyrights by authorizing republication in the database, a power they lacked under the law.

Justice Stevens argued in dissent that the electronic formats were not differences in kind but in degree. He claimed that the print media had been within their rights to authorize the reproduction.

The decision was a major victory for writers, who in the future would have to authorize their articles being transferred to electronic databases and would share in the profits of the articles' sales. The *Times* and other print media immediately stopped their practice of transfer and negotiated new contracts with their freelance writers.

Lorillard Tobacco Co. v. Reilly

533 U.S. 525 (2001)
Decided: June 28, 2001
Vote: 5 (Rehnquist, O'Connor, Scalia, Kennedy, Thomas)
4 (Stevens, Souter, Ginsburg, Breyer)
Opinion of the Court: O'Connor
Concurring opinion: Kennedy (Scalia)
Concurring opinion: Thomas
Dissenting opinion: Stevens (Souter, Ginsburg, Breyer)
Dissenting opinion: Souter

Congress took its first steps to regulate cigarette advertising in the 1960s. The Federal Cigarette Labeling and Advertising Act (FCLAA) of 1965 required manufacturers to include specific health warnings on cigarette packages. Four years later, Congress amended the law to toughen the language in the warning and to prohibit cigarette advertising altogether on radio and television.

Both acts included provisions to preempt state and local laws. The tobacco industry lobbied for preemption to avoid conflicting or overlapping regulations in different states. The

1965 provision said that "no statement relating to smoking and health" could be required beyond the federal requirement. In 1969 Congress rewrote the provision to preempt any "requirement or prohibition based on smoking and health imposed under State law with respect to the advertising or promotion" of cigarettes.

Through the 1990s local governments adopted an array of antismoking measures, including curbs on advertising. Tobacco companies contended the local advertising curbs were preempted by the federal law or invalid under the commercial speech doctrine. But six federal appeals courts upheld the ordinances, while only one—the Ninth Circuit—agreed with the tobacco companies.

The industry found itself on the defensive on two other fronts. State governments in 1994 filed a nationwide class action suit to force cigarette manufacturers to pay for health care costs attributed to smoking, and in 1996 the Food and Drug Administration (FDA) adopted a package of advertising and marketing restrictions on the industry. The Supreme Court in *FDA v. Brown & Williamson Tobacco Corp.*, 529 U.S. 129 (2000), ruled that the regulations went beyond the agency's statutory authority.

Meanwhile, the industry had agreed to a variety of advertising restrictions as part of a settlement of the states' litigation. The so-called "master settlement" banned outdoor advertising, transit advertising, the use of cartoons, and any advertising or promotions targeted to young people. Massachusetts attorney general Scott Harshbarger said the advertising curbs did not go far enough and moved to adopt even tougher regulations in his state. He issued the tobacco advertising regulations under his authority to define "unfair" or "deceptive" business practices in the state. Two separate sections imposed roughly identical restrictions on advertising of cigarettes, smokeless tobacco, and cigars.

The regulations prohibited outdoor advertising as well as in-store signs visible from the outside anywhere within a one thousand-foot radius of a playground or elementary or secondary school. They also prohibited self-service displays of tobacco products and required stores near schools or playgrounds to place tobacco advertising at least five feet above the floor. The regulations defined advertisement broadly to encompass "any oral, written, graphic, or pictorial statement or representation," as well as logos, symbols, mottos, "or any other indicia of product identification."

Tobacco companies challenged the Massachusetts regulation as preempted by federal law and too broad for the First Amendment. A federal district court judge rejected the preemption attack and ruled against the industry's First Amendment argument. The court of appeals also upheld the regulations. It said the federal law did not preempt state regulation of the location of cigarette advertising. On the First Amendment issue, the appeals court said the regulations satisfied a four-part test that the Supreme Court set out in ***Central Hudson Gas & Electric Corp. v. Public Service Commission of New York,*** 447 U.S. 557 (1980). The test required, first, that the expression is protected by the First Amendment, and that any regulation of truthful advertising could be justified only if it served a substantial government interest, directly advanced that interest, and was no more extensive than necessary.

Justice O'Connor rejected the state's effort to limit the preemptive effect of the federal cigarette labeling law. The state's "concern about youth exposure to cigarette advertising is intertwined with the concern about cigarette smoking and health," she wrote. The law, however, did not give states leeway to regulate the content of advertising, she continued. "Congress preempted state cigarette advertising regulations," O'Connor wrote, "because they would upset federal legislative choices to require specific warnings and to impose the ban on cigarette advertising in electronic media."

On the First Amendment issue, O'Connor said that virtually all of the regulations—save for the ban on self-service displays—were invalid because they were "more extensive than necessary" to serve the government's interest of deterring underage smoking. She accepted the state's argument that the regulations directly advanced a substantial government interest—meeting the second and third prongs of the *Central Hudson* test, but they failed the fourth prong, she said. The "uniformly broad sweep" of the ban on outdoor advertising "demonstrates a lack of tailoring," she wrote. The height restriction on in-store advertising did not "constitute a reasonable fit" with the goal of deterring underage smoking, she said, but the ban on self-service displays was valid because it regulated conduct, not speech.

Justices Scalia, Kennedy, and Thomas separated themselves from the section in the majority opinion crediting the regulations with advancing a government interest. In a partial concurrence, Kennedy said there was no need to consider that issue because of "the obvious overbreadth" of the regulations under the fourth prong of the test.

Thomas, also concurring in part, wrote a lengthy opinion advocating "strict scrutiny"—the highest level of constitutional review—for any government regulation of truthful advertising. He closed by contending that the state's argument could be used to justify regulating advertising for an array of legal products. The state "identified no principle of law or logic that would preclude the imposition of restrictions on fast food and alcohol advertising similar to those they seek to impose on tobacco advertising," he wrote.

In dissent, Justice Stevens insisted the majority was misreading the language of the preemption provision. "All signs point inescapably to the conclusion that Congress only intended to preempt content regulations in the 1969 Act," he wrote. His disagreements on the First Amendment issue were "less significant," he said. He supported O'Connor's conclusion that the regulations served the "compelling" interest of protecting minors from "becoming addicted to a dangerous drug," but said he "shared the majority's concern" that the one thousand-foot rule "unduly restricts the ability of cigarette manufacturers to convey lawful information to adult consumers." Still, Stevens said he would send the case back to give the state another chance to justify the rule. He also said he would uphold the ban on self-service displays and—unlike the majority—the height restriction as conduct regulations. Justice Souter joined the section on preemption but not the First Amendment part.

See Martha A. Derthick. *Up in Smoke: From Legislation to Litigation in Tobacco Politics* (Washington, D.C.: CQ Press, 2001).

Toyota Manufacturing Co. v. Williams

534 U.S. 184 (2002)
Decided: January 8, 2002
Vote: 9 (Rehnquist, Stevens, O'Connor, Scalia, Kennedy, Souter, Thomas, Ginsburg, Breyer)
0
Opinion of the Court: O'Connor

Ella Williams, an assembly-line worker in Toyota's Lexington, Kentucky, plant, was diagnosed with carpal tunnel syndrome and was reassigned to two quality inspection jobs. When Toyota added a third task, a dispute arose, after which she was fired. Williams claimed that her condition had worsened and that the company refused to make an accommodation, while Toyota claimed Williams was frequently absent from work.

Williams filed a letter with the Equal Employment Opportunity Commission and, upon receiving a right-to-sue letter, filed against Toyota in federal district court. The court granted summary judgment to the company on the grounds that Williams did not have a disability as defined by the 1990 Americans with Disabilities Act (ADA). Moreover, her own testimony indicated that she was not disabled because she claimed she could perform some assembly-line work. The Court of Appeals for the Sixth Circuit reversed on the grounds that Williams had met the ADA test of showing that her physical problems prevented her from performing certain tasks that required holding tools and repetitive work with hands and arms extended at or above shoulder levels for extended periods of time.

The Supreme Court unanimously reversed. The Court expanded the relevant test to include not only work-related activities but also daily life activities. In other words, a person must have an impairment that prevents or substantially limits the performance of tasks such as brushing one's teeth, tending a flower garden, or fixing meals. By this test, the Court significantly limited the definition of an injury or disability that would call the ADA into effect. The ruling was in line with other decisions of the Court handed down the same term, such as *US Airways v. Barnett*, 535 U.S. — (2002) (122 S.Ct. 1516), which said an employer normally does not have to bend its seniority system to make sure a disabled worker can stay on the job; *Chevron U.S.A. v. Echazabel*, 536 U.S. — (2002), ruling that an employer can reject a disabled applicant for a job if the work would threaten the applicant's health or safety; and *Barnes v. Gorman*, 536 U.S. — (2002) (122 S.Ct. 2097), which said that individuals successfully suing cities for discrimination under the ADA may receive only compensatory damages and may not sue for punitive damages.

Ashcroft v. Free Speech Coalition

535 U.S. — (2002) (122 S.Ct. 1389)
Decided: April 16, 2002
Vote: 6 (Stevens, Kennedy, Souter, Thomas, Ginsburg, Breyer)
3 (Rehnquist, O'Connor, Scalia)
Opinion of the Court: Kennedy
Opinion concurring in judgment: Thomas
Dissenting opinion: Rehnquist (Scalia)
Dissenting opinion: O'Connor (Rehnquist, Scalia)

The Child Pornography Prevention Act of 1996 banned "virtual child pornography" produced without real children and images presented as child pornography, the latter a response to modern computer technology that could create seemingly real images of children engaged in sexual behavior without actual children being involved. The definitions of "virtual child pornography" were quite broad and could have been interpreted to include scenes in mainline films that had no pornographic quality or even paintings and other traditional works of art. A coalition of various plaintiffs—including a trade association for the adult entertainment industry, the publisher of a book advocating the nudist lifestyle, a painter of nudes, and a photographer specializing in erotic images—brought suit, claiming the overly broad definitions violated the First Amendment. The district court upheld the law, but the Court of Appeals for the Ninth Circuit reversed on the grounds that the law's provisions were insufficiently related to the state's legitimate interest in prohibiting pornography that actually involved minors.

The Supreme Court agreed. Justice Kennedy held that virtual child pornography, unlike real child pornography, was not clearly related to the sexual abuse of children, as the causal link between such virtual images and instances of child abuse was indirect. In addition, some works in the category of child pornography might possibly have significant literary or artistic value. Perhaps most important, the government had failed to prove that the ban on virtual child pornography was justified on the various grounds the government had put forward, such as the possibility that pedophiles might use such pornography to seduce children or that such pornography might whet the appetites of pedophiles and encourage them to engage in illegal conduct.

In addition, the definitions of what constituted virtual child pornography were overbroad and thus violated the First Amendment. The law relied on how the speech was presented, not on what was depicted. It therefore did not meet the standards established in *New York v. Ferber*, 458 U.S. 747 (1982), which allowed prosecution of those who promoted the sexual exploitation of children. Kennedy also pointed to movies such as *Traffic*, in which child prostitution was a legitimate part of the drama involving drug abuse and distribution.

Justice Thomas noted that if technology advanced to the point where it became impossible to enforce actual child pornography laws because the government could not prove that certain pornographic images were of real children, then the government might be able to enact a regulation of virtual child pornography that contained an appropriate affirmative defense or some other narrowly drawn restriction.

The three dissenters all believed the law valid and that the government interest in eliminating the sexual abuse of children in pornographic materials met the *Ferber* test.

The case is another example of how Congress and the Court continue to wrestle with how the mandate of the First Amendment can be applied in modern times. Technology is rapidly approaching the point that concerned Thomas, in which it would be impossible to tell a live person from a computer-generated image. One can be fairly confident that over the next decade or so, the Court's docket will have more cases in which the justices are asked to apply parts of the Constitution to circumstances never dreamed of by the Framers.

Tahoe-Sierra Preservation Council, Inc. v. Tahoe Regional Planning Agency

535 U.S. — (2002) (122 S.Ct. 1465)
Decided: April 23, 2002
Vote: 6 (Stevens, O'Connor, Kennedy, Souter, Ginsburg, Breyer)
3 (Rehnquist, Scalia, Thomas)
Opinion of the Court: Stevens
Dissenting opinion: Rehnquist (Scalia, Thomas)
Dissenting opinion: Thomas (Scalia)

Lake Tahoe's crystal-blue waters have been admired by uncounted numbers of travelers through the years, and, in recent decades, by a growing number of people buying property on one side or the other of the California-Nevada border for vacation or retirement homes. As early as the 1960s, however, development began to threaten the lake. Runoff from the steep hillsides bordering the lake fed the growth of algae that clouded the water. To protect the lake, the California-Nevada Tahoe Regional Planning Agency (TRPA) began in the 1980s to impose strict controls on development.

An initial land-use ordinance adopted by the TRPA in 1972 did little to limit homebuilding in Lake Tahoe's 501-square mile basin. A new compact negotiated by the two states in 1980 envisioned a two-step process extending over thirty months to establish environmental standards and then to adopt a regional plan to achieve and maintain those standards. As part of the process, the compact "temporarily" prohibited any new building until adoption of a final plan.

The original moratorium was succeeded by a court injunction in 1984 and then another planning agency ordinance in 1987, both of which carried over the ban on new building. A coalition representing several hundred landowners calling themselves the Tahoe-Sierra Preservation Council eventually challenged all three actions as unconstitutional takings. The first of the suits—filed in 1984—demanded compensation for the thirty-two-month "moratorium" on development from December 1980 to August 1983.

The litigation eventually spawned three published decisions by a federal district court and four by the Ninth U.S. Circuit Court of Appeals. Both courts rejected the takings claims for the period covered by the court-imposed injunction and found the landowners waited too long to attack the 1987 ordinance. The district court ruled that under ***Lucas v. South Carolina Coastal Council,*** 505 U.S. 1003 (1992), the landowners were entitled to compensation for the original moratorium. The appeals court reversed that decision, holding that the moratorium affected only a "temporal segment" of the owners' property rights.

The Supreme Court permitted government agencies to continue using temporary curbs on development as one tool in land-use planning and regulation. "A rule that required compensation for every delay in the use of property would render routine government processes prohibitively expensive or encourage hasty decision-making," Justice Stevens wrote for the majority. "Such an important change in the law should be the product of legislative rulemaking rather than adjudication."

Stevens acknowledged prior rulings that any physical invasion of private property amounted to a taking requiring compensation under the Fifth Amendment, but said that the same "categorical" rule did not apply to regulatory takings. Instead, he said, the test derived from ***Penn Central Transportation Co. v. New York City,*** 438 U.S. 104 (1978), and he called for examining "a number of factors" in "essentially ad hoc, factual inquiries." *Lucas*'s *per se* rule applied only in the "extraordinary" case where a regulation blocked all use of the property.

Stevens stressed that *Penn Central* required courts to examine the owner's property rights in "the parcel as a whole." A property owner's interest "cannot be rendered valueless by a temporary prohibition on economic use," he said, "because the property will recover value as soon as the prohibition is lifted."

Stevens said a decision establishing new restrictions on moratoriums might "force officials to rush through the planning process or to abandon the practice altogether." Instead, the length of a moratorium should be one factor—but only one—in evaluating a takings claim. "The answer to the abstract question whether a temporary moratorium effects a taking is neither 'yes, always,' nor 'no, never,' " Stevens wrote. "The answer depends upon the particular circumstances of the case."

In dissent Chief Justice Rehnquist argued that the distinction between "permanent" and "temporary" prohibitions was "tenuous," especially in a case that involved what he calculated as a six-year moratorium until adoption of the 1987 ordinance. The ruling, he said, would create "every incentive for government to simply label any prohibition on development 'temporary,' or to fix a set number of years."

Justice Thomas criticized use of the parcel-as-a-whole rule when applied to temporary land-use controls. A "total deprivation of the use of a so-called 'temporal slice' of property" ordinarily requires compensation, Thomas wrote.

The "potential future value bears on the amount of compensation," he said, but "has nothing to do with the question whether there was a taking in the first place."

See John D. Echeverria, "A Turning of the Tide: The *Tahoe-Sierra* Regulatory Takings Decision," *Environmental Law Reporter* 32 (October 2002); and Andrew S. Gold, "Regulatory Takings and Original Intent: The Direct, Physical Takings Thesis 'Goes Too Far,'" *American University Law Review* 49 (October 1999): 181.

Ashcroft v. American Civil Liberties Union

535 U.S. — (2002) (122 S.Ct. 1700)
Decided: May 13, 2002
Vote: 8 (Rehnquist, O'Connor, Scalia, Kennedy, Thomas, Souter, Ginsburg, Breyer)
1 (Stevens)
Judgment of the Court: Thomas
Opinion concurring in judgment: O'Connor
Opinion concurring in judgment: Kennedy (Souter, Ginsburg)
Opinion concurring in judgment: Breyer
Dissenting opinion: Stevens

The proliferation of pornographic sites on the World Wide Web prompted efforts in Congress to limit children's computer access to sexually explicit materials. Lawmakers enacted the Child Online Protection Act (COPA). With COPA, Congress in 1998 tried to meet the Supreme Court's objections to the Communications Decency Act of 1996, which was ruled unconstitutional in ***Reno v. American Civil Liberties Union,*** 521 U.S. 844 (1997). COPA prohibited distribution of material "harmful to minors" rather than the broader phrasing—"patently offensive"—used in the previous law. The law went on to include a specific definition drawn from ***Miller v. California,*** 413 U.S. 15 (1973), to cover material that, as to minors, appealed to "the prurient interest in sex," depicted sexual acts or sexual contact in a "patently offensive manner," and lacked "serious literary, artistic, political, or scientific value for minors."

The new law also applied only to the Web—not to all chat rooms or other interactive computer networks—and only to commercial Web publishers, not to nonprofit organizations. In addition, the act specifically exempted home use of computers. It also gave Web publishers a defense if they used adult-verification systems to prevent minors from accessing sexually explicit information. Critics went to court, saying the revised law still ran afoul of First Amendment principles.

The district court said that the law imposed a burden on adults by effectively requiring some Web operators to use adult identification systems to screen out minors. In addition, the court said the law was more restrictive than necessary because parents could install blocking or filtering software on their own computers to screen out objectionable material. Finally, the district court issued a preliminary injunction barring the government from enforcing the law nationwide.

The court of appeals also ruled the law unconstitutional, but on a different ground. It focused on the use of "contemporary community standards"—an established part of the obscenity test—to determine whether sexual material appealed to a user's "prurient interest." Subjecting Web publishers to "varying community standards" amounted to an unconstitutional burden, the appeals court said, because Web publishers could not know what standards would be applied in any given community. In any event, the court continued, they were "without any means to limit access to their sites based on the geographic location of particular Internet users."

The Supreme Court's fractured ruling reinstated the community standards provision of the law, even though justices in the majority disagreed about how to apply it. Only one justice voted to invalidate the law, but three others said they had "grave doubts" whether the act would eventually be upheld.

In the main opinion, Justice Thomas said the law's "use of community standards to identify material that is harmful to minors . . . does not render the statute facially unconstitutional." Thomas noted that the government conceded that local juries would reach "inconsistent conclusions" in applying the law, but, he said, the scope of the law would be limited by the other two parts of the "harmful to minors" test: "patently offensive" and "serious value." In particular, Thomas said, "the serious value requirement allows appellate courts to impose some limitations and regularity of the definition by setting, *as a matter of law,* a national floor for socially redeeming value." Chief Justice Rehnquist and Justices O'Connor and Scalia joined this part of Thomas's opinion.

Thomas went on to say that it was not unconstitutional to require speakers disseminating material to a national audience to observe "varying community standards." He cited as precedent the decision in ***Sable Communications, Inc. v. Federal Communications Commission,*** 492 U.S. 115 (1989), upholding a federal law making so-called "dial-a-porn" services illegal. Thomas insisted the same rule applied to the Internet despite its "unique characteristics." Rehnquist and Scalia joined this part of the opinion.

In sending the case back for further proceedings, Thomas stressed that the decision was "quite limited" and was not meant to indicate any view on other constitutional issues. "Prudence dictates allowing the Court of Appeals to first examine these difficult issues," he said.

Justices O'Connor and Breyer wrote opinions concurring in part and concurring in the judgment. Both argued for use of national standards in applying the law. "Adoption of a national standard is necessary in my view for any reasonable regulation of Internet obscenity," O'Connor wrote. In his opinion, Breyer said he believed Congress intended to adopt national standards in passing the law. Breyer joined the background sections and conclusion of Thomas's opinion, but not the main section discussing the community standards issue.

Justice Kennedy agreed that the community standards provision did not render the law unconstitutional by itself, but also said he was not ready to uphold the provision. "The national variation in standards constitutes a particular burden on Internet speech," Kennedy wrote. The scope of the problem depended on the interpretation of other parts of the law, he said. "There may be grave doubts that COPA is consistent with the First Amendment," Kennedy concluded. "But we should not make that determination with so many questions unanswered."

In dissent, Justice Stevens said he would rule the law unconstitutional and not send it back. Approving the use of community standards, he said, "has the intolerable consequence of denying some sections of the country access to material, there deemed acceptable, which in others might be considered offensive to prevailing community standards of decency."

See Sue Mota, "Neither Dead Nor Forgotten: The Past, Present, and Future of the Communications Decency Act in Light of Reno v. ACLU," *Computer Law Review and Technology Journal* (winter 1998).

Federal Maritime Commission v. South Carolina State Ports Authority

535 U.S. — (2002) (122 S.Ct. 1864)
Decided: May 28, 2002
Vote: 5 (Rehnquist, O'Connor, Scalia, Thomas, Kennedy)
4 (Stevens, Souter, Ginsburg, Breyer)
Opinion of the Court: Thomas
Dissenting opinion: Stevens
Dissenting opinion: Breyer (Stevens, Souter, Ginsburg)

Maritime Services, owners of the cruise ship *Tropic Sea,* thought it was being treated unfairly when the South Carolina State Ports Authority refused to allow its vessel to berth in Charleston because the ship offered gambling on board. The port authority allowed two Carnival Cruise Lines ships to dock there even though they also provided gambling. The port authority claimed that the Eleventh Amendment "prohibits suits by private parties for reparations against" a state agency.

An administrative law judge of the Federal Maritime Commission (FMC), an independent regulatory agency, agreed with the port authority. Although Maritime Services did not appeal, the five-member FMC decided to review the ruling anyway. The commission unanimously rejected the sovereign immunity defense.

The court of appeals agreed that the Eleventh Amendment protected the state from administrative agency adjudications as well as from federal court suits.

The Supreme Court agreed. In 1793 the Supreme Court ruled that a private citizen of one state could sue another state in federal court. The decision, ***Chisholm v. Georgia,*** 2 U.S. 419 (1793), produced such an uproar that Congress and then the states quickly approved the Eleventh Amendment, which prevents citizens of one state from suing another state government. Nearly a hundred years later, the Court expanded the Eleventh Amendment in ***Hans v. Louisiana,*** 134 U.S. 1 (1890), to protect states from federal court suits by their own citizens as well.

Another century later, the Rehnquist Court used those two developments to construct even stronger protections for the states from federal court suits. In the first of the rulings, the Court held in ***Seminole Tribe of Florida v. Florida,*** 517 U.S. 44 (1996), that states could not be sued in federal court for violations of laws based on Congress's enumerated powers in Article I. Three years later, the Court invoked a broader principle of state "sovereign immunity" to hold in ***Alden v. Maine,*** 527 U.S. 706 (1999), that states could not even be sued in their own courts for violating federal laws. The same year, the Court also limited Congress's power to provide for federal courts suits for violations of citizens' rights under the Fourteenth Amendment.

The Court's decision in this case gave the states a clear victory. "State sovereign immunity," Justice Thomas wrote at the beginning of his majority opinion, "bars . . . an adjudicative proceeding" before a federal agency. Sovereign immunity, Thomas explained, "extends beyond the literal text of the Eleventh Amendment." The critical question, he said, was whether federal agency adjudications were "the type of proceedings from which the Framers would have thought the States possessed immunity when they agreed to enter the Union." Yes, Thomas said, because they "bear a remarkably strongly resemblance to civil litigation in federal courts."

Thomas rejected the government's efforts to minimize the impact of the commission's proceedings by noting the agency's need to go to court to enforce any of its orders or to levy a financial penalty on the state. "The primary function of sovereign immunity is not to protect State treasuries," Thomas wrote, "but to afford the States the dignity and respect due sovereign entities." He concluded, "Although the Framers likely did not envision the intrusion on state sovereignty at issue in today's case, we are nonetheless confident that it is contrary to their constitutional design."

"Where does the Constitution contain the principle of law that the Court enunciates?" Justice Breyer began his dissent. "I cannot find the answer to this question in any text, in any tradition, or in any relevant purpose." The FMC, Breyer wrote, was engaging in "Executive Branch activity" and "exercising . . . powers that the Executive Branch . . . must possess if it is to enforce modern law through administration." Federal administrative agencies do not exercise "judicial power," he said, and a private citizen who filed a complaint against a state with an agency could not force the state to do anything, he said. "Only the Federal Government may institute a court proceeding," Breyer wrote, and "will exercise appropriate political responsibility" in deciding whether to do so. The ruling, Breyer concluded, would result in "less agency flexibility, a larger federal bureaucracy, less fair procedure, and potentially less effective law enforcement."

See Mark R. Killenbeck, ed., *The Tenth Amendment and State Sovereignty: Constitutional History and Contemporary Issues* (Lanham, Md.: Rowman and Littlefield, 2001).

Watchtower Bible & Tract Society v. Village of Stratton

536 U.S. — (2002) (122 S.Ct. 2080)
Decided: June 17, 2002
Vote: 8 (Stevens, O'Connor, Scalia, Kennedy, Souter, Thomas, Ginsburg, Breyer)
1 (Rehnquist)
Opinion of the Court: Stevens
Concurring opinion: Breyer (Souter, Ginsburg)
Opinion concurring in judgment: Scalia (Thomas)
Dissenting opinion: Rehnquist

The small village of Stratton, Ohio, prohibited canvassers from going door-to-door to sell any product or promote any cause without first getting a permit from the mayor's office. Jehovah's Witnesses objected to having to get a permit to carry their message and sued on First Amendment grounds, claiming that it violated their rights to free speech, free exercise of religion, and freedom of the press. The lower courts upheld the provisions on the grounds that they were content-neutral and applied to all individuals and groups. Moreover, the village had a legitimate interest in protecting its residents from fraud and undue annoyance.

The Supreme Court reversed, upholding the claims of the Witnesses that any effort to limit or regulate their proselytizing infringed upon their rights under the Free Exercise Clause. The Court did little more than reaffirm the principles established in the Jehovah's Witness cases of the late 1930s and early 1940s, such as ***Murdock v. Pennsylvania,*** 319 U.S. 105 (1943); *Schneider v. Town of Irvington,* 308 U.S. 147 (1939); and ***Cantwell v. Connecticut,*** 310 U.S. 296 (1940). Justice Stevens agreed that municipal governments have legitimate interests in preventing fraud or other crimes, but he said the ordinances regulating door-to-door solicitation had to be narrowly drawn in order not to infringe the religious rights of the Witnesses or other groups, including nonreligious groups and individuals, who are poorly financed and rely extensively upon this method of communication.

In this case, the village of Stratton had drawn a content-neutral ordinance, but it was overly broad and violated First Amendment rights. According to Stevens, the ordinance was so broadly written that it could apply to neighbors ringing each other's doorbells "to enlist support for a more efficient garbage collector." A simpler manner for residents to avoid unwanted solicitations would be to post "No Solicitor" signs, which could be enforced by local authorities.

United States v. Drayton

536 U.S. — (2002) (122 S.Ct. 2105)
Decided: June 17, 2002
Vote: 6 (Rehnquist, O'Connor, Scalia, Kennedy, Thomas, Breyer)
3 (Stevens, Souter, Ginsburg)
Opinion of the Court: Kennedy
Dissenting opinion: Souter (Stevens, Ginsburg)

In February 1999 a Detroit-bound Greyhound bus with twenty-five to thirty passengers stopped for a scheduled rest and refueling in Tallahassee, Florida. Three plainclothes police officers, displaying their badges, entered the bus with the driver's permission. While one kept watch from the front, the other two worked their way from the back, telling passengers they were looking for drugs and weapons, and asking if they could search their luggage. When one of the officers reached the seats where Christopher Drayton and Clifton Brown Jr. were sitting, he noticed they were wearing heavy coats and baggy pants, leading the officer to believe they might be concealing drugs. With his face only a foot away from Brown, the officer asked if he could search him and, on patting him down, discovered bags of cocaine strapped to his inner thighs. A search of Drayton also turned up hidden drugs. The two were arrested on federal drug-trafficking charges and at their trial argued that the evidence should be inadmissible because it had been seized without a proper warrant, but they were convicted. The court of appeals, however, agreed with Drayton and Brown, noting that an officer stationed at the only exit would make a reasonable person "feel less free to leave" or to refuse a search.

The Supreme Court reversed, confirming the conviction. The police, having been given permission to enter the bus, did not have to tell the passengers that they had the right to refuse to cooperate, nor did they violate the Fourth Amendment during a random check for drugs and weapons on a bus. According to Justice Kennedy, the officers had the right to ask to search, and so long as they did not threaten force, show weapons, or in any way intimidate the passengers, the passengers could have refused to cooperate. "It is beyond question that had this encounter occurred on the street, it would be constitutional. The fact that an encounter takes place on a bus does not on its own transform standard police questioning of citizens into an illegal seizure."

Although the majority opinion made no reference to the terrorist attacks of September 11, 2001, the Bush administration had argued that police needed broader authority in public areas and public transit to ferret out potential terrorists. The dissenters agreed that new security measures were appropriate but said that the majority had inappropriately equated security on ground transportation with that necessary for air travel. Justice Souter also pointed to what he termed "an air of unreality" in the majority opinion, in that it assumed that an ordinary person, with one policeman only a foot away and another blocking the only bus exit, could reasonably be expected to say no to a search.

Rush Prudential HMO v. Moran

536 U.S. — (2002) (122 S.Ct. 2151)
Decided: June 20, 2002
Vote: 5 (Stevens, O'Connor, Souter, Ginsburg, Breyer)
4 (Rehnquist, Scalia, Kennedy, Thomas)
Opinion of the Court: Souter
Dissenting opinion: Thomas (Rehnquist, Scalia, Kennedy)

In 1996 Debra Moran, a member of the Rush Prudential HMO, went to her primary care physician seeking treatment for a severe pain in her shoulder. The doctor recommended surgery, but the HMO denied the request. Eventually, with her doctor's support, Moran underwent a complex surgery by a physician outside the Rush Prudential network. The HMO refused to pay the $95,000 bill, claiming that Moran could have been treated just as successfully by a cheaper procedure. An independent doctor agreed with Moran and her doctor about the necessity for the surgery, but the HMO still refused to pay. She sued under an Illinois law that guaranteed members of medical insurance plans an independent second opinion. If the second opinion recommended that a procedure take place, Illinois law required the HMO to pay for the cost of the second opinion as well as the procedure. If the independent opinion did not recommend anything different from what the HMO provider had said, the HMO did not have to pay for the consultation.

The HMO challenged the statute—which is similar in substance to that in forty-one other states and the District of Columbia—as null because the matter had been preempted by Congress in a 1974 law, the Employment Retirement Income Security Act (ERISA), that made regulation of employee benefit plans the exclusive province of Congress under the Commerce Clause. Patient and physician groups had attacked the HMO practices as limiting patient and doctor options and for relegating medical decisions to nonmedical personnel who were motivated to control expenditures.

The majority found that state laws had not been preempted by ERISA. An HMO, explained Justice Souter, is both an insurer as well as a medical provider and, as such, could be regulated under state law. Nothing in ERISA mandated that it be an all-or-nothing choice, either federally regulated or state regulated. States could regulate those portions of insurance and medical care that were not specifically addressed in ERISA.

Justice Thomas declared that the patchwork of more than forty separate state laws eviscerated the uniformity that Congress had intended in ERISA, a uniformity that Congress deemed necessary to ensure a balance of fairness to employees on the one hand and employers and benefit companies on the other.

Insurance companies wanted the Court to nullify the law, not just because of the liability it imposed on them, but because many companies operate in several states and did not want to deal with a patchwork of state laws. If Congress adopted the substance of the Illinois law, the insurance companies would then be dealing with a uniform practice. Such a provision was, in fact, part of a federal patients' rights act then stalled in Congress.

Atkins v. Virginia

536 U.S. — (2002) (122 S.Ct. 2242)
Decided: June 20, 2002
Vote: 6 (Stevens, O'Connor, Kennedy, Souter, Ginsburg, Breyer)
3 (Rehnquist, Scalia, Thomas)
Opinion of the Court: Stevens
Dissenting opinion: Rehnquist (Scalia, Thomas)
Dissenting opinion: Scalia (Rehnquist, Thomas)

Daryl Renard Atkins and William Jones abducted, robbed, and murdered Eric Nesbitt, an airman assigned to Langley Air Force Base in Hampton, Virginia. Atkins freely gave police details of his involvement, and at the trial Jones pleaded guilty in return for a life sentence. Atkins's attorney hired a psychologist who evaluated his client and reported that he had an IQ of 59. The state produced its own evaluation, which held that Atkins was intelligent enough to have planned and committed a crime and to understand the consequences of his actions. Atkins was convicted and sentenced to death. He lost his appeal in the Virginia Supreme Court, which affirmed the sentence on the basis of *Penry v. Lynaugh*, 492 U.S. 302 (1989), in which the Supreme Court held that executing a mentally retarded person did not violate the Eighth Amendment's ban on cruel and unusual punishment.

In its first major death penalty case in several terms, the Court reversed the Virginia sentence and its own precedent. The Court held that a national consensus had formed against executing the mentally retarded on the grounds that it did indeed constitute cruel and unusual punishment as prohibited by the Eighth Amendment. In 2002, eighteen of the thirty-eight states that impose the death penalty excluded mentally retarded persons from capital punishment. In 1989, when *Penry* was decided, only two states outlawed the practice. According to Justice Stevens, the Constitution contemplates that the Court will bring its own judgment to bear by asking whether there is reason to agree or disagree with the judgment reached by the citizenry and its legislators. Consensus was building for the view that the objectives of capital punishment—deterring murder and exacting retribution—do not apply when imposed on people of significantly below average intelligence.

In addition, the Court's decision came amidst a growing national debate over the death penalty in general. The use of DNA testing had led to the reversal of several convictions of people on death row for murders they had not committed. Because of flaws in the system of capital punishment the governor of Illinois suspended executions in his state pending a full-scale review. Other states were also reexamining their capital punishment policies.

Atkins v. Virginia may have more symbolic than legal importance, however, as the majority said it would leave it to the states to develop precise standards and procedures for determining who qualified under the new rule. In other words, the Court said that states cannot execute mentally retarded persons, but acknowledged that there are broad definitions of what constitutes mental retardation. The states would be free, within these broad parameters, to come up with more precise definitions in their laws.

In a strong dissent, Justice Scalia accused the majority of reading its own views into the Constitution, and he derided the majority's reference to a growing consensus based on eighteen states. Twenty of the death-penalty states, he pointed out, still executed those with below average intelligence.

Ring v. Arizona

536 U.S. — (2002) (122 S.Ct. 2428)
Decided: June 24, 2002
Vote: 7 (Stevens, Scalia, Kennedy, Souter, Thomas, Ginsburg, Breyer)
2 (Rehnquist, O'Connor)
Opinion of the Court: Ginsburg (Stevens, Scalia, Kennedy, Souter, Thomas)
Concurring opinion: Scalia (Thomas)
Concurring opinion: Kennedy
Opinion concurring in judgment: Breyer
Dissenting opinion: O'Connor (Rehnquist)

In 1996 three men were arrested and tried for robbing an armored car and killing its driver, John Magosh. None of the three men testified at trial, and the jury was unable to determine which of them had killed the driver. As a result, the jury did not recommend the death penalty. At the sentencing hearing, one of the accomplices testified that Timothy Stuart Ring had been the "leader" of the group and had taken joy in killing Magosh. Based largely on this testimony, the judge sentenced Ring to death. Ring appealed on the grounds that the Arizona law allowing the judge, rather than the jury, to impose the death sentence violated his rights of due process and of a fair jury trial. Under the Arizona law—similar to that in eight other states—the judge decides whether to impose the death sentence after hearing the jury's recommendation and, even if the jury recommends against capital punishment, a judge may opt for that penalty.

The Supreme Court overturned the death sentence. The majority decision grew directly out of *Apprendi v. New Jersey*, 530 U.S. 466 (2000), in which the Court held that a jury, not a judge, must find beyond a reasonable doubt any aggravating factor that would increase the jail time a defendant faces for a particular crime. In view of that decision, the right to a jury trial "would be senselessly diminished if it encompassed the factfinding necessary to increase a defendant's sentence by two years, but not the factfinding necessary to put him to death." In reaching this result, the Court reversed a decision upholding Arizona's death penalty act, *Walton v. Arizona*, 497 U.S. 639 (1990).

The two dissenters had opposed *Apprendi* and now claimed that the new ruling intensified *Apprendi*'s "destabilizing effect on the criminal justice system." They warned that the immediate result would be a flood of litigation because several hundred inmates sat on death row as a result of a capital sentence imposed by a judge rather than a jury. In Florida and Alabama, where the laws were nearly identical to that of Arizona, 383 prisoners and 187 prisoners, respectively, were on death rows.

The ruling cut across normal ideological lines, with two of the Court's most conservative members, Justices Scalia and Thomas, joining its two most liberal, Justices Ginsburg and Breyer. Scalia wrote that the increasing use of judge-determined sentencing factors "cause me to believe that our people's traditional belief in the right of trial by jury is in perilous decline." Looking ahead to a possible Florida or Alabama case, where the law differed slightly from that of Arizona—in both states judges can impose the death sentence, but they differ on when they can ignore a jury recommendation—Scalia indicated he would have no trouble if a state leaves the ultimate life or death decision to the judge, as long as it required a jury to evaluate the aggravating factors either at the trial or in a sentencing hearing for death row inmates in those states.

At the time of this decision, approximately 3,700 convicted murderers were on death row in thirty-eight states; in twenty-nine of these states the jury determines the defendant's fate, and the Court's ruling will not change anything for death row inmates in those states.

Zelman v. Simmons-Harris

536 U.S. — (2002) (122 S.Ct. 2460)
Decided: June 27, 2002
Vote: 5 (Rehnquist, O'Connor, Scalia, Kennedy, Thomas)
4 (Stevens, Souter, Ginsburg, Breyer)
Opinion of the Court: Rehnquist
Concurring opinion: O'Connor
Concurring opinion: Thomas
Dissenting opinion: Stevens
Dissenting opinion: Souter (Stevens, Ginsburg, Breyer)
Dissenting opinion: Breyer (Stevens, Souter)

In one of its most important church-state cases in a decade, a bitterly divided Court upheld an Ohio school voucher plan and removed any constitutional barriers to similar voucher plans in the future. The public schools in many of the poorer parts of Cleveland were deemed failures, and the legislature enacted the Pilot Project Scholarship Program in an effort to address the problem. The program provided tuition vouchers for up to $2,250 a year to some parents of students in the Cleveland City School District to attend participating public or private schools in the city and neighboring suburbs; it also allocated tutorial aid for students who remained in public school. The vouchers were distributed to parents according to financial need, and the parents chose where to enroll their children. Because the number of students applying to the program greatly exceeded the number of vouchers available, recipients were chosen by lottery from among the eligible families. In the 1999–2000 school year,

82 percent of the participating private schools had a religious affiliation; none of the adjacent suburban public schools joined the program; and 96 percent of the students receiving vouchers were enrolled in religiously affiliated schools. A group of Ohio taxpayers, backed by teachers unions, sought to enjoin the program, claiming that it violated the Establishment Clause. The district court agreed, as did the Court of Appeals for the Sixth Circuit.

The Supreme Court held the voucher program constitutional, giving accommodationists—those who believed the First Amendment allowed public aid to religious groups on a nonpreferential basis—their biggest victory so far. Chief Justice Rehnquist explained that the voucher plan met constitutional standards because the program had been enacted for the valid secular purpose of providing educational assistance to poor children in a demonstrably failing public school system. Because it neither advanced nor inhibited religion, it met the second prong of the three-part test first enunciated in ***Lemon v. Kurtzman,*** 403 U.S. 602 (1971). The voucher program did not involve religion and government too closely in administrative details, the third prong of the *Lemon* test. According to Rehnquist, a government aid program is not readily subject to challenge under the Establishment Clause if it is neutral with respect to religion and provides assistance directly to a broad class of citizens who, in turn, direct government aid to religious schools as a result of their own genuine and independent private choice. In other words, the government aid reaches religious institutions not as a result of choices made by the government (which would be a violation of the Establishment Clause) but through the deliberate choices of numerous individual recipients. Any marginal advancement of religion results from actions by individuals who have received the aid, not the government, whose role ends with the disbursement of benefits.

The Ohio program conferred direct assistance to a broad class of individuals defined without reference to religion and permitted participation of all district schools—religious or nonreligious—and adjacent public schools. The only preference was for low-income families, who received greater assistance and had priority for admission. No reasonable observer, according to the chief justice, would think that such a neutral private choice program carried with it the imprimatur of government endorsement.

The fact that an overwhelming majority of the families receiving aid sent their children to religious schools had to be viewed in light of all the educational opportunities available. The preponderance of religiously affiliated private schools was a phenomenon common to many American cities. Eighty-two percent of Cleveland's private schools were religious, as were 81 percent of all of Ohio's private schools. To attribute constitutional significance to the 82 percent figure would lead to the absurd result that a neutral school choice program might be permissible in parts of Ohio where the percentage was lower, but not in Cleveland, where the state's legislators decided that such programs were most needed. The constitutionality of a neutral educational aid program does not turn on whether most private schools in an area are religious or that most recipients choose to use the aid at a religious school.

The dissenters called the majority ruling a "potentially tragic" mistake that would force citizens to subsidize faiths they do not share and corrupt religion by making it dependent upon government aid. Justice Breyer warned that the ruling could lead to "religious conflict potentially harmful to the nation's social fabric." All the dissenters agreed that the decision seriously weakened the wall of separation between church and state mandated by the First Amendment.

Supporters of vouchers, including President George W. Bush, who immediately called upon Congress to enact a voucher plan, were pleased, but it remains unclear what, if any, impact the decision will have beyond Ohio and one or two other states. Public opinion polls show that a majority of Americans oppose voucher plans, and this opposition will be a major factor in whether states adopt them. Moreover, even as the Court gave a green light for carefully drawn voucher plans, states faced the worst financial conditions in more than two decades. Even if legislators were willing to support a plan, most states did not have the resources to pay for it. Finally, the situation in Cleveland was unique in that many public schools had completely failed, and a radical solution was needed. Would a similar situation in another urban school system encourage the state legislature to adopt a similar program? No one knows the answer, but what is known is that the Court's decision now allows vouchers, and proponents no longer fear the charge of unconstitutionality.

See Kenneth Jost, "School Vouchers Showdown," *CQ Researcher,* February 15, 2002, 121–144.

Republican Party of Minnesota v. White

536 U.S. — (2002) (122 S.Ct. 2528)
Decided: June 27, 2002
Vote: 5 (Rehnquist, O'Connor, Scalia, Thomas, Kennedy)
4 (Stevens, Souter, Ginsburg, Breyer)
Opinion of the Court: Scalia
Concurring opinion: O'Connor
Concurring opinion: Kennedy
Dissenting opinion: Stevens (Souter, Ginsburg, Breyer)
Dissenting opinion: Ginsburg (Stevens, Souter, Breyer)

Gregory Wersal, a Minneapolis-area lawyer and a self-described strict constructionist, wanted to get Republican Party support for a campaign for the Minnesota Supreme Court in 1996. After Wersal attended several party gatherings, however, one Republican convention delegate filed a complaint with an arm of the Minnesota Lawyers Professional Responsibility Board. The complaint accused Wersal of violating state law establishing nonpartisan judicial elections as well as an ethics rule that prohibited judicial candidates from "announcing" their positions on legal or political issues.

The board dismissed the complaint, but Wersal nonetheless backed away from his planned campaign. When he ran again in 1998, Wersal went to federal court with the state's Republican Party to challenge the so-called "announce clause" as a violation of the First Amendment. The state countered that the rule, adapted from the American Bar Association's (ABA) Model Code of Judicial Conduct, was essential to protect judges' impartiality.

The district court upheld the clause after construing it narrowly to apply only to issues that were likely to come before the court. The court of appeals adopted the same narrow construction in upholding the provision as well. The Minnesota Supreme Court officially adopted that interpretation as its own. Backed by an array of organizations including the U.S. Chamber of Commerce and the American Civil Liberties Union, Wersal and the state GOP took the battle to the Supreme Court. The ABA joined the state in defending the rule, along with the Conference of State Chief Justices.

The Court agreed that the ethics rule was unconstitutional, opening the door to more free-wheeling campaigns in the thirty-one states with popular elections of judges. Justice Scalia explained that the provision was unconstitutional because it was not narrowly tailored to serve a compelling interest as required to survive the so-called "strict scrutiny" standard applicable to direct restrictions on First Amendment-protected speech. Scalia carefully parsed three possible meanings to the state's claim that the announce clause promoted judicial "impartiality." The clause could not promote a lack of bias toward opposing parties in litigation, he said, because it applied to issues rather than particular parties. The clause might promote election of judges with a lack of preconception on legal views, Scalia said, but that was not a "compelling" interest. "A judge's lack of predisposition . . . has never been thought a necessary component of equal justice," he wrote. Finally, Scalia said, the announce clause was "woefully underinclusive" in promoting openmindedness because it applied only to campaign statements, not to positions taken by judges or candidates in other contexts.

Scalia tweaked the ABA for simultaneously seeking to restrict judicial campaigns while opposing judicial elections. "That opposition may be well taken . . . but the First Amendment does not permit it to achieve its goal by leaving the principle of elections in place while preventing candidates from discussing what the elections are about," he said.

In contrasting concurring opinions, Justice O'Connor criticized and Justice Kennedy defended the practice of judicial elections. O'Connor said that such elections inevitably raised the danger that judges would be beholden to public opinion or organized interest groups. "If the State has a problem with judicial impartiality, it is largely one the State brought upon itself by continuing the practice of popularly electing judges," she wrote. Kennedy demurred: "We should refrain from criticism of the State's choice to use open elections to select those persons most likely to achieve judicial excellence."

Justice Ginsburg contended that the ruling "exaggerates" the scope of the ethics rule at the same time that it "ignores its significance" to Minnesota's system of judicial elections. The announce clause, she said, left judicial candidates free to "convey general information" about themselves and "their views on a wide range of subjects of interest to the voters." But the clause was important because it prevented candidates from circumventing the ban on making pledges or promises. "Judges are not politicians," Ginsburg concluded, "and the First Amendment does not require that they be treated as politicians simply because they are chosen by popular vote."

Justice Stevens wrote a separate opinion that criticized the majority for "obscuring the fundamental distinction between campaigns for the judiciary and the political branches."

See Adam R. Long, "Note: Keeping Mud Off the Bench: The First Amendment and Regulation of Candidates' False or Misleading Statements in Judicial Elections," *Duke Law Journal* 51 (November 2001): 787.

Board of Education of Independent School District No. 92 of Pottawatomie County v. Earls

536 U.S. — (2002) (122 S.Ct. 2559)
Decided: June 27, 2002
Vote: 5 (Rehnquist, Scalia, Kennedy, Thomas, Breyer)
4 (Stevens, O'Connor, Souter, Ginsburg)
Opinion of the Court: Thomas
Concurring opinion: Breyer
Dissenting opinion: O'Connor (Souter)
Dissenting opinion: Ginsburg (Stevens, O'Connor, Souter)

In September 1998 the Tecumseh, Oklahoma, school board instituted an aggressive drug education and detection policy whereby all students engaged in extracurricular activities were subjected to random drug testing. Lindsay Earls, a tenth grader and chorus member, was summoned out of her class one day in early 1999 to provide a urine specimen for drug analysis. She was mortified to have to urinate while three teachers listened outside a restroom stall and then to have one of her teachers examine the sample for temperature as a precaution against cheating.

Earls and her parents challenged the drug testing, contending that the policy was an invasion of privacy and a violation of the Fourth Amendment's prohibition against unreasonable searches. The school board responded that the policy was valid under the Supreme Court's decision in ***Vernonia School District 47J v. Acton,*** 515 U.S. 646 (1995), which upheld suspicionless drug testing of high school athletes.

The district court judge was satisfied that the board had reason to be concerned about drug use and that the testing program "effectively addressed" the problem. The court of appeals disagreed, finding the school board's evidence of a drug problem to be "hearsay" or "virtually anecdotal." The school board had failed to demonstrate an "identifiable drug problem" needed to permit random testing, the appeals court said.

The Supreme Court reversed the court of appeals' decision. The Court's ruling reflected a closer division than in *Vernonia,* but a majority still ruled the program constitutional. Justice Thomas wrote that the policy "reasonably serves the School District's important interest in detecting and preventing drug use among its students."

Thomas stressed the parallels to *Vernonia* and minimized the differences. The Court's discounting of students' privacy interests in the previous case "depended primarily upon the school's custodial responsibility and authority"—not specifically on the policy's limited application to athletes. In any event, he added, some of the off-campus travel for other extracurricular activities also entailed "communal undress" as in *Vernonia.* And—again as in *Vernonia*—test results were kept confidential and not used for any law enforcement purposes. As to the need for the program, Thomas said that the school board had "provided sufficient evidence" to justify the program and did not have to prove "a pervasive drug problem." "It would make little sense to require a school district to wait for a substantial portion of its students to begin using drugs before it was allowed to institute a drug testing program designed to deter drug use," he wrote.

Justice Breyer listed seven factors that led him to conclude the drug testing policy was "not 'unreasonable,' " including the need for schools to deal with what he called the nation's "serious" drug problem and the lack of objection to the school board's decision to adopt the drug testing program.

Justice Ginsburg led the *Vernonia* dissenters in a point-by-point rebuttal to the majority's arguments. The prior ruling, she said, "cannot be read to endorse invasive and suspicionless drug testing of all students." The justifications for testing athletes—physical risks as well as communal undress—did not apply to other extracurricular activities that, in any event, were "a key component" of school life and "essential" in applying to college.

Moreover, Ginsburg said, testing students who engaged in extracurricular activities was "capricious, even perverse." The policy, she wrote, "targets for testing a student population least likely to be at risk from illicit drugs and their damaging effects." At the same time, she said, the policy "risks steering students at greatest risk for substance abuse away from extracurricular activities that potentially may palliate drug problems."

See David Masci, "Preventing Teen Drug Use," *CQ Researcher,* March 15, 2002, 217–240; and Nancy D. Wagman, "Note: Are We Becoming a Society of Suspects? *Vernonia School District 47J V. Acton:* Examining Random Suspicionless Drug Testing of Public School Athletes," *Villanova Sports and Entertainment Law Journal* 3 (1996): 325.

Constitution of the United States

We the People of the United States, in Order to form a more perfect Union, establish Justice, insure domestic Tranquility, provide for the common defence, promote the general Welfare, and secure the Blessings of Liberty to ourselves and our Posterity, do ordain and establish this Constitution for the United States of America.

ARTICLE I

Section 1. All legislative Powers herein granted shall be vested in a Congress of the United States, which shall consist of a Senate and House of Representatives.

Section 2. The House of Representatives shall be composed of Members chosen every second Year by the People of the several States, and the Electors in each State shall have the Qualifications requisite for Electors of the most numerous Branch of the State Legislature.

No Person shall be a Representative who shall not have attained to the age of twenty five Years, and been seven Years a Citizen of the United States, and who shall not, when elected, be an Inhabitant of that State in which he shall be chosen.

[Representatives and direct Taxes shall be apportioned among the several States which may be included within this Union, according to their respective Numbers, which shall be determined by adding to the whole Number of free Persons, including those bound to Service for a Term of Years, and excluding Indians not taxed, three fifths of all other Persons.][1] The actual Enumeration shall be made within three Years after the first Meeting of the Congress of the United States, and within every subsequent Term of ten Years, in such Manner as they shall by Law direct. The Number of Representatives shall not exceed one for every thirty Thousand, but each State shall have at Least one Representative; and until such enumeration shall be made, the State of New Hampshire shall be entitled to chuse three, Massachusetts eight, Rhode-Island and Providence Plantations one, Connecticut five, New-York six, New Jersey four, Pennsylvania eight, Delaware one, Maryland six, Virginia ten, North Carolina five, South Carolina five, and Georgia three.

When vacancies happen in the Representation from any State, the Executive Authority thereof shall issue Writs of Election to fill such Vacancies.

The House of Representatives shall chuse their Speaker and other Officers; and shall have the sole Power of Impeachment.

Section 3. The Senate of the United States shall be composed of two Senators from each State, [chosen by the Legislature thereof,][2] for six Years; and each Senator shall have one Vote.

Immediately after they shall be assembled in Consequence of the first Election, they shall be divided as equally as may be into three Classes. The Seats of the Senators of the first Class shall be vacated at the Expiration of the second Year, of the second Class at the Expiration of the fourth Year, and of the third Class at the Expiration of the sixth Year, so that one third may be chosen every second Year; [and if Vacancies happen by Resignation, or otherwise, during the Recess of the Legislature of any State, the Executive thereof may make temporary Appointments until the next Meeting of the Legislature, which shall then fill such Vacancies.][3]

No Person shall be a Senator who shall not have attained to the Age of thirty Years, and been nine Years a Citizen of the United States, and who shall not, when elected, be an Inhabitant of that State for which he shall be chosen.

The Vice President of the United States shall be President of the Senate, but shall have no Vote, unless they be equally divided.

The Senate shall chuse their other Officers, and also a President pro tempore, in the Absence of the Vice President, or when he shall exercise the Office of President of the United States.

The Senate shall have the sole Power to try all Impeachments. When sitting for that Purpose, they shall be on Oath or Affirmation. When the President of the United States is tried, the Chief Justice shall preside: And no Person shall be convicted without the Concurrence of two thirds of the Members present.

Judgment in Cases of Impeachment shall not extend further than to removal from Office, and disqualification to hold and enjoy any Office of honor, Trust or Profit under the United States: but the Party convicted shall nevertheless be liable and subject to Indictment, Trial, Judgment and Punishment, according to Law.

Section 4. The Times, Places and Manner of holding Elections for Senators and Representatives, shall be prescribed in each State by the Legislature thereof; but the Congress may at any time by Law make or alter such Regulations, except as to the Places of chusing Senators.

The Congress shall assemble at least once in every Year, and such Meeting shall [be on the first Monday in December],[4] unless they shall by Law appoint a different Day.

Section 5. Each House shall be the Judge of the Elections, Returns and Qualifications of its own Members, and a Majority of each shall constitute a Quorum to do Business; but a smaller Number may adjourn from day to day, and may be authorized to compel the Attendance of absent Members, in such Manner, and under such Penalties as each House may provide.

Each House may determine the Rules of its Proceedings, punish its Members for disorderly Behaviour, and, with the Concurrence of two thirds, expel a Member.

Each House shall keep a Journal of its Proceedings, and from time to time publish the same, excepting such Parts as may in their Judgment require Secrecy; and the Yeas and Nays of the Members of either House on any question shall, at the Desire of one fifth of those Present, be entered on the Journal.

Neither House, during the Session of Congress, shall, without the Consent of the other, adjourn for more than three days, nor to any other Place than that in which the two Houses shall be sitting.

Section 6. The Senators and Representatives shall receive a Compensation for their Services, to be ascertained by Law, and paid out of the Treasury of the United States. They shall in all Cases, except Treason, Felony and Breach of the Peace, be privileged from Arrest during their Attendance at the Session of their respective Houses, and in going to and returning from the same; and for any Speech or Debate in either House, they shall not be questioned in any other Place.

No Senator or Representative shall, during the Time for which he was elected, be appointed to any civil Office under the Authority of the United States, which shall have been created, or the Emoluments whereof shall have been encreased during such time; and no Person holding any Office under the United States, shall be a Member of either House during his Continuance in Office.

Section 7. All Bills for raising Revenue shall originate in the House of Representatives; but the Senate may propose or concur with Amendments as on other Bills.

Every Bill which shall have passed the House of Representatives and the Senate, shall, before it become a Law, be presented to the President of the United States; If he approve he shall sign it, but if not he shall return it, with his Objections to that House in which it shall have originated, who shall enter the Objections at large on their Journal, and proceed to reconsider it. If after such Reconsideration two thirds of that House shall agree to pass the Bill, it shall be sent, together with the Objections, to the other House, by which it shall likewise be reconsidered, and if approved by two thirds of that House, it shall become a Law. But in all such Cases the Votes of both Houses shall be determined by yeas and Nays, and the Names of the Persons voting for and against the Bill shall be entered on the Journal of each House respectively. If any Bill shall not be returned by the President within ten Days (Sundays excepted) after it shall have been presented to him, the Same shall be a Law, in like Manner as if he had signed it, unless the Congress by their Adjournment prevent its Return, in which Case it shall not be a Law.

Every Order, Resolution, or Vote to which the Concurrence of the Senate and House of Representatives may be necessary (except on a question of Adjournment) shall be presented to the President of the United States; and before the Same shall take Effect, shall be approved by him, or being disapproved by him, shall be repassed by two thirds of the Senate and House of Representatives, according to the Rules and Limitations prescribed in the Case of a Bill.

Section 8. The Congress shall have Power To lay and collect Taxes, Duties, Imposts and Excises, to pay the Debts and provide for the common Defence and general Welfare of the United States; but all Duties, Imposts and Excises shall be uniform throughout the United States;

To borrow Money on the credit of the United States;

To regulate Commerce with foreign Nations, and among the several States, and with the Indian Tribes;

To establish an uniform Rule of Naturalization, and uniform Laws on the subject of Bankruptcies throughout the United States;

To coin Money, regulate the Value thereof, and of foreign Coin, and fix the Standard of Weights and Measures;

To provide for the Punishment of counterfeiting the Securities and current Coin of the United States;

To establish Post Offices and post Roads;

To promote the Progress of Science and useful Arts, by securing for limited Times to Authors and Inventors the exclusive Right to their respective Writings and Discoveries;

To constitute Tribunals inferior to the supreme Court;

To define and punish Piracies and Felonies committed on the high Seas, and Offences against the Law of Nations;

To declare War, grant Letters of Marque and Reprisal, and make Rules concerning Captures on Land and Water;

To raise and support Armies, but no Appropriation of Money to that Use shall be for a longer Term than two Years;

To provide and maintain a Navy;

To make Rules for the Government and Regulation of the land and naval Forces;

To provide for calling forth the Militia to execute the Laws of the Union, suppress Insurrections and repel Invasions;

To provide for organizing, arming, and disciplining, the Militia, and for governing such Part of them as may be employed in the Service of the United States, reserving to the States respectively, the Appointment of the Officers, and the Authority of training the Militia according to the discipline prescribed by Congress;

To exercise exclusive Legislation in all Cases whatsoever, over such District (not exceeding ten Miles square) as may, by Cession of particular States, and the Acceptance of Congress, become the Seat of the Government of the United States, and to exercise like Authority over all Places purchased by the Consent of the Legislature of the State in which the Same shall be, for the Erection of Forts, Magazines, Arsenals, dock-Yards, and other needful Buildings;—And

To make all Laws which shall be necessary and proper for carrying into Execution the foregoing Powers, and all other Powers vested by this Constitution in the Government of the United States, or in any Department or Officer thereof.

Section 9. The Migration or Importation of such Persons as any of the States now existing shall think proper to admit, shall not be prohibited by the Congress prior to the Year one thousand eight hundred and eight, but a Tax or duty may be imposed on such Importation, not exceeding ten dollars for each Person.

The Privilege of the Writ of Habeas Corpus shall not be suspended, unless when in Cases of Rebellion or Invasion the public Safety may require it.

No Bill of Attainder or ex post facto Law shall be passed.

No Capitation, or other direct, Tax shall be laid, unless in Proportion to the Census or Enumeration herein before directed to be taken.[5]

No Tax or Duty shall be laid on Articles exported from any State.

No Preference shall be given by any Regulation of Commerce or Revenue to the Ports of one State over those of another; nor shall Vessels bound to, or from, one State, be obliged to enter, clear, or pay Duties in another.

No Money shall be drawn from the Treasury, but in Consequence of Appropriations made by Law; and a regular Statement and Account of the Receipts and Expenditures of all public Money shall be published from time to time.

No Title of Nobility shall be granted by the United States: And no Person holding any Office of Profit or Trust under them, shall, without the Consent of the Congress, accept of any present, Emolument, Office, or Title, of any kind whatever, from any King, Prince, or foreign State.

Section 10. No State shall enter into any Treaty, Alliance, or Confederation; grant Letters of Marque and Reprisal; coin Money; emit Bills of Credit; make any Thing but gold and silver Coin a Tender in Payment of Debts; pass any Bill of Attainder, ex post facto Law, or Law impairing the Obligation of Contracts, or grant any Title of Nobility.

No State shall, without the Consent of the Congress, lay any Imposts or Duties on Imports or Exports, except what may be absolutely necessary for executing it's inspection Laws: and the net Produce of all Duties and Imposts, laid by any State on Imports or Exports, shall be for the Use of the Treasury of the United States; and all such Laws shall be subject to the Revision and Controul of the Congress.

No State shall, without the Consent of Congress, lay any Duty of Tonnage, keep Troops, or Ships of War in time of Peace, enter into any Agreement or Compact with another State, or with a foreign Power, or engage in War, unless actually invaded, or in such imminent Danger as will not admit of delay.

ARTICLE II

Section 1. The executive Power shall be vested in a President of the United States of America. He shall hold his Office during the Term of four Years, and, together with the Vice President, chosen for the same Term, be elected, as follows

Each State shall appoint, in such Manner as the Legislature thereof may direct, a Number of Electors, equal to the whole Number of Senators and Representatives to which the State may be entitled in the Congress: but no Senator or Representative, or Person holding an Office of Trust or Profit under the United States, shall be appointed an Elector.

[The Electors shall meet in their respective States, and vote by Ballot for two Persons, of whom one at least shall not be an Inhabitant of the same State with themselves. And they shall make a List of all the Persons voted for, and of the Number of Votes for each; which List they shall sign and certify, and transmit sealed to the Seat of the Government of the United States, directed to the President of the Senate. The President of the Senate shall, in the Presence of the Senate and House of Representatives, open all the Certificates, and the Votes shall then be counted. The Person having the greatest Number of Votes shall be the President, if such Number be a Majority of the whole Number of Electors appointed; and if there be more than one who have such Majority, and have an equal Number of Votes, then the House of Representatives shall immediately chuse by Ballot one of them for President; and if no Person have a Majority, then from the five highest on the list the said House shall in like Manner chuse the President. But in chusing the President, the Votes shall be taken by States, the Representation from each State having one Vote; A quorum for this Purpose shall consist of a Member or Members from two thirds of the States, and a Majority of all the States shall be necessary to a Choice. In every Case, after the Choice of the President, the Person having the greatest Number of Votes of the Electors shall be the Vice President. But if there should remain two or more who have equal Votes, the Senate shall chuse from them by Ballot the Vice President.][6]

The Congress may determine the Time of chusing the Electors, and the Day on which they shall give their Votes; which Day shall be the same throughout the United States.

No Person except a natural born Citizen, or a Citizen of the United States, at the time of the Adoption of this Constitution, shall be eligible to the Office of President; neither shall any Person be eligible to that Office who shall not have attained to the Age of thirty five Years, and been fourteen Years a Resident within the United States.

In Case of the Removal of the President from Office, or of his Death, Resignation, or Inability to discharge the Powers and Duties of the said Office,[7] the Same shall devolve on the Vice President, and the Congress may by Law provide for the Case of Removal, Death, Resignation or Inability, both of the President and Vice President, declaring what Officer shall then act as President, and such Officer shall act accordingly, until the Disability be removed, or a President shall be elected.

The President shall, at stated Times, receive for his Services, a Compensation, which shall neither be encreased nor diminished during the Period for which he shall have been elected, and he shall not receive within that Period any other Emolument from the United States, or any of them.

Before he enter on the Execution of his Office, he shall take the following Oath or Affirmation:—"I do solemnly swear (or affirm) that I will faithfully execute the Office of President of the United States, and will to the best of my Ability, preserve, protect and defend the Constitution of the United States."

Section 2. The President shall be Commander in Chief of the Army and Navy of the United States, and of the Militia of the several States, when called into the actual Service of the United States; he may require the Opinion, in writing, of the principal Officer in each of the executive Departments, upon any Subject relating to the Duties of their respective Offices, and he shall have Power to grant Reprieves and Pardons for Offences against the United States, except in Cases of Impeachment.

He shall have Power, by and with the Advice and Consent of the Senate, to make Treaties, provided two thirds of the Senators present concur; and he shall nominate, and by and with the Advice and Consent of the Senate, shall appoint Ambassadors, other public Ministers and Consuls, Judges of the supreme Court, and all other Officers of the United States, whose Appointments are not herein otherwise provided for, and which shall be established by Law: but the Congress may by Law vest the Appointment of such inferior Officers, as they think proper, in the President alone, in the Courts of Law, or in the Heads of Departments.

The President shall have Power to fill up all Vacancies that may happen during the Recess of the Senate, by granting Commissions which shall expire at the End of their next Session.

Section 3. He shall from time to time give to the Congress Information of the State of the Union, and recommend to their Consideration such Measures as he shall judge necessary and expedient; he may, on extraordinary Occasions, convene both Houses, or either of them, and in Case of Disagreement between them, with Respect to the Time of Adjournment, he may adjourn them to such Time as he shall think proper; he shall receive Ambassadors and other public Ministers; he shall take Care that the Laws be faithfully executed, and shall Commission all the Officers of the United States.

Section 4. The President, Vice President and all civil Officers of the United States, shall be removed from Office on Impeachment for, and Conviction of, Treason, Bribery, or other high Crimes and Misdemeanors.

ARTICLE III

Section 1. The judicial Power of the United States, shall be vested in one supreme Court, and in such inferior Courts as the Congress may from time to time ordain and establish. The Judges, both of the supreme and inferior Courts, shall hold their Offices during good Behaviour, and shall, at stated Times, receive for their Services, a Compensation, which shall not be diminished during their Continuance in Office.

Section 2. The judicial Power shall extend to all Cases, in Law and Equity, arising under this Constitution, the Laws of the United States, and Treaties made, or which shall be made, under their Authority;—to all Cases affecting Ambassadors, other public Ministers and Consuls;—to all Cases of admiralty and maritime Jurisdiction;—to Controversies to which the United States shall be a Party;—to Controversies between two or more States;—between a State and Citizens of another State;[8]—between Citizens of different States;—between Citizens of the same State claiming Lands under Grants of different States, and between a State, or the Citizens thereof, and foreign States, Citizens or Subjects.

In all Cases affecting Ambassadors, other public Ministers and Consuls, and those in which a State shall be Party, the supreme Court shall have original Jurisdiction. In all the other Cases before mentioned, the supreme Court shall have appellate Jurisdiction, both as to Law and Fact, with such Exceptions, and under such Regulations as the Congress shall make.

The Trial of all Crimes, except in Cases of Impeachment, shall be by Jury; and such Trial shall be held in the State where the said Crimes shall have been committed; but when not committed within any State, the Trial shall be at such Place or Places as the Congress may by Law have directed.

Section 3. Treason against the United States, shall consist only in levying War against them, or in adhering to their Enemies, giving them Aid and Comfort. No Person shall be convicted of Treason unless on the Testimony of two Witnesses to the same overt Act, or on Confession in open Court.

The Congress shall have Power to declare the Punishment of Treason, but no Attainder of Treason shall work Corruption of Blood, or Forfeiture except during the Life of the Person attainted.

ARTICLE IV

Section 1. Full Faith and Credit shall be given in each State to the public Acts, Records, and judicial Proceedings of every other State. And the Congress may by general Laws prescribe the Manner in which such Acts, Records and Proceedings shall be proved, and the Effect thereof.

Section 2. The Citizens of each State shall be entitled to all Privileges and Immunities of Citizens in the several States.

A Person charged in any State with Treason, Felony, or other Crime, who shall flee from Justice, and be found in another State, shall on Demand of the executive Authority of the State from which he fled, be delivered up, to be removed to the State having Jurisdiction of the Crime.

[No Person held to Service or Labour in one State, under the Laws thereof, escaping into another, shall, in Consequence of any Law or Regulation therein, be discharged from such Service or Labour, but shall be delivered up on Claim of the Party to whom such Service or Labour may be due.][9]

Section 3. New States may be admitted by the Congress into this Union; but no new State shall be formed or erected within the Jurisdiction of any other State; nor any State be formed by the Junction of two or more States, or Parts of States, without the Consent of the Legislatures of the States concerned as well as of the Congress.

The Congress shall have Power to dispose of and make all needful Rules and Regulations respecting the Territory or other Property belonging to the United States; and nothing in this Constitution shall be so construed as to Prejudice any Claims of the United States, or of any particular State.

Section 4. The United States shall guarantee to every State in this Union a Republican Form of Government, and shall protect each of them against Invasion; and on Application of the Legislature, or of the Executive (when the Legislature cannot be convened) against domestic Violence.

ARTICLE V

The Congress, whenever two thirds of both Houses shall deem it necessary, shall propose Amendments to this Constitution, or, on the Application of the Legislatures of two thirds of the several States, shall call a Convention for proposing Amendments, which, in either Case, shall be valid to all Intents and Purposes, as Part of this Constitution, when ratified by the Legislatures of three fourths of the several States, or by Conventions in three fourths thereof, as the one or the other Mode of Ratification may be proposed by the Congress; Provided [that no Amendment which may be made prior to the Year One thousand eight hundred and eight shall in any Manner affect the first and fourth Clauses in the Ninth Section of the first Article; and][10] that no State, without its Consent, shall be deprived of its equal Suffrage in the Senate.

ARTICLE VI

All Debts contracted and Engagements entered into, before the Adoption of this Constitution, shall be as valid against the United States under this Constitution, as under the Confederation.

This Constitution, and the Laws of the United States which shall be made in Pursuance thereof; and all Treaties made, or which shall be made, under the Authority of the United States, shall be the supreme Law of the Land; and the Judges in every State shall be bound thereby, any Thing in the Constitution or Laws of any State to the Contrary notwithstanding.

The Senators and Representatives before mentioned, and the Members of the several State Legislatures, and all executive and judicial Officers, both of the United States and of the several States, shall be bound by Oath or Affirmation, to support this Constitution; but no religious Test shall ever be required as a Qualification to any Office or public Trust under the United States.

ARTICLE VII

The Ratification of the Conventions of nine States, shall be sufficient for the Establishment of this Constitution between the States so ratifying the Same.

Done in Convention by the Unanimous Consent of the States present the Seventeenth Day of September in the Year of our Lord one thousand seven hundred and Eighty seven and of the Independence of the United States of America the Twelfth. IN WITNESS whereof We have hereunto subscribed our Names,

George Washington,
President and
deputy from Virginia.

New Hampshire:	John Langdon, Nicholas Gilman.
Massachusetts:	Nathaniel Gorham, Rufus King.
Connecticut:	William Samuel Johnson, Roger Sherman.
New York:	Alexander Hamilton.
New Jersey:	William Livingston, David Brearley, William Paterson, Jonathan Dayton.
Pennsylvania:	Benjamin Franklin, Thomas Mifflin, Robert Morris, George Clymer, Thomas FitzSimons, Jared Ingersoll, James Wilson, Gouverneur Morris.
Delaware:	George Read, Gunning Bedford Jr., John Dickinson, Richard Bassett, Jacob Broom.
Maryland:	James McHenry, Daniel of St. Thomas Jenifer, Daniel Carroll.
Virginia:	John Blair, James Madison Jr.
North Carolina:	William Blount, Richard Dobbs Spaight, Hugh Williamson.
South Carolina:	John Rutledge, Charles Cotesworth Pinckney, Charles Pinckney, Pierce Butler.
Georgia:	William Few, Abraham Baldwin.

[The language of the original Constitution, not including the Amendments, was adopted by a convention of the states on

September 17, 1787, and was subsequently ratified by the states on the following dates: Delaware, December 7, 1787; Pennsylvania, December 12, 1787; New Jersey, December 18, 1787; Georgia, January 2, 1788; Connecticut, January 9, 1788; Massachusetts, February 6, 1788; Maryland, April 28, 1788; South Carolina, May 23, 1788; New Hampshire, June 21, 1788.

Ratification was completed on June 21, 1788.

The Constitution subsequently was ratified by Virginia, June 25, 1788; New York, July 26, 1788; North Carolina, November 21, 1789; Rhode Island, May 29, 1790; and Vermont, January 10, 1791.]

Amendments

Amendment I

(First ten amendments ratified December 15, 1791.)

Congress shall make no law respecting an establishment of religion, or prohibiting the free exercise thereof; or abridging the freedom of speech, or of the press; or the right of the people peaceably to assemble, and to petition the Government for a redress of grievances.

Amendment II

A well regulated Militia, being necessary to the security of a free State, the right of the people to keep and bear Arms, shall not be infringed.

Amendment III

No Soldier shall, in time of peace be quartered in any house, without the consent of the Owner, nor in time of war, but in a manner to be prescribed by law.

Amendment IV

The right of the people to be secure in their persons, houses, papers, and effects, against unreasonable searches and seizures, shall not be violated, and no Warrants shall issue, but upon probable cause, supported by Oath or affirmation, and particularly describing the place to be searched, and the persons or things to be seized.

Amendment V

No person shall be held to answer for a capital, or otherwise infamous crime, unless on a presentment or indictment of a Grand Jury, except in cases arising in the land or naval forces, or in the Militia, when in actual service in time of War or public danger; nor shall any person be subject for the same offence to be twice put in jeopardy of life or limb; nor shall be compelled in any criminal case to be a witness against himself, nor be deprived of life, liberty, or property, without due process of law; nor shall private property be taken for public use, without just compensation.

Amendment VI

In all criminal prosecutions, the accused shall enjoy the right to a speedy and public trial, by an impartial jury of the State and district wherein the crime shall have been committed, which district shall have been previously ascertained by law, and to be informed of the nature and cause of the accusation; to be confronted with the witnesses against him; to have compulsory process for obtaining witnesses in his favor, and to have the Assistance of Counsel for his defence.

Amendment VII

In Suits at common law, where the value in controversy shall exceed twenty dollars, the right of trial by jury shall be preserved, and no fact tried by a jury, shall be otherwise re-examined in any Court of the United States, than according to the rules of the common law.

Amendment VIII

Excessive bail shall not be required, nor excessive fines imposed, nor cruel and unusual punishments inflicted.

Amendment IX

The enumeration in the Constitution, of certain rights, shall not be construed to deny or disparage others retained by the people.

Amendment X

The powers not delegated to the United States by the Constitution, nor prohibited by it to the States, are reserved to the States respectively, or to the people.

Amendment XI (Ratified February 7, 1795)

The Judicial power of the United States shall not be construed to extend to any suit in law or equity, commenced or prosecuted against one of the United States by Citizens of another State, or by Citizens or Subjects of any Foreign State.

Amendment XII (Ratified June 15, 1804)

The Electors shall meet in their respective states and vote by ballot for President and Vice-President, one of whom, at least, shall not be an inhabitant of the same state with themselves; they shall name in their ballots the person voted for as President, and in distinct ballots the person voted for as Vice-President, and they shall make distinct lists of all persons voted for as President, and of all persons voted for as Vice-President, and of the number of votes for each, which lists they shall sign and certify, and transmit sealed to the seat of the government of the United States, directed to the President of the Senate;—The President of the Senate shall, in the presence of the Senate and House of Representatives, open all the certificates and the votes shall then be counted;—The person having the greatest number of votes for President, shall be the President, if such number be a majority of the whole number of Electors appointed; and if no person have such majority, then from the persons having the highest numbers not exceeding three on the list of those voted for as President, the House of Representatives shall choose immediately, by ballot, the President. But in choosing the President, the votes shall be taken by states, the representation from each state having one vote; a quorum for this purpose shall consist of a member or members from two-thirds of the states, and a majority of all the states shall be necessary to a choice. [And if the House of Representatives shall not choose a President whenever the right of choice shall devolve upon them, before the fourth day of March next following, then the Vice-President shall act as President, as in the case of the death or other constitutional disability of the President.—][11] The person having the greatest number of votes as Vice-President, shall be the Vice-President, if such number be a majority of the whole number of Electors appointed, and if no person have a majority, then from the two highest numbers on the list, the Senate shall choose the Vice-President; a quorum for the purpose shall consist of two-thirds of the whole number of Senators, and a majority of the whole number shall be necessary to a choice. But no person constitutionally ineligible to the office of President shall be eligible to that of Vice-President of the United States.

Amendment XIII (Ratified December 6, 1865)

Section 1. Neither slavery nor involuntary servitude, except as a punishment for crime whereof the party shall have been duly convicted, shall exist within the United States, or any place subject to their jurisdiction.

Section 2. Congress shall have power to enforce this article by appropriate legislation.

Amendment XIV (Ratified July 9, 1868)

Section 1. All persons born or naturalized in the United States, and subject to the jurisdiction thereof, are citizens of the United States and of the State wherein they reside. No State shall make or enforce any law which shall abridge the privileges or immunities of citizens of the United States; nor shall any State deprive any person of life, liberty, or property, without due process of law; nor deny to any person within its jurisdiction the equal protection of the laws.

Section 2. Representatives shall be apportioned among the several States according to their respective numbers, counting the whole number of persons in each State, excluding Indians not taxed. But when the right to vote at any election for the choice of electors for President and Vice President of the United States, Representatives in Congress, the Executive and Judicial officers of a State, or the members of the Legislature thereof, is denied to any of the male inhabitants of such State, being twenty-one years of age,[12] and citizens of the United States, or in any way abridged, except for participation in rebellion, or other crime, the basis of representation therein shall be reduced in the proportion which the number of such male citizens shall bear to the whole number of male citizens twenty-one years of age in such State.

Section 3. No person shall be a Senator or Representative in Congress, or elector of President and Vice President, or hold any office, civil or military, under the United States, or under any State, who, having previously taken an oath, as a member of Congress, or as an officer of the United States, or as a member of any State legislature, or as an executive or judicial officer of any State, to support the Constitution of the United States, shall have engaged in insurrection or rebellion against the same, or given aid or comfort to the enemies thereof. But Congress may by a vote of two-thirds of each House, remove such disability.

Section 4. The validity of the public debt of the United States, authorized by law, including debts incurred for payment of pensions and bounties for services in suppressing insurrection or rebellion, shall not be questioned. But neither the United States nor any State shall assume or pay any debt or obligation incurred in aid of insurrection or rebellion against the United States, or any claim for the loss or emancipation of any slave; but all such debts, obligations and claims shall be held illegal and void.

Section 5. The Congress shall have power to enforce, by appropriate legislation, the provisions of this article.

Amendment XV (Ratified February 3, 1870)

Section 1. The right of citizens of the United States to vote shall not be denied or abridged by the United States or by any State on account of race, color, or previous condition of servitude.

Section 2. The Congress shall have power to enforce this article by appropriate legislation.

Amendment XVI (Ratified February 3, 1913)

The Congress shall have power to lay and collect taxes on incomes, from whatever source derived, without apportionment among the several States, and without regard to any census or enumeration.

Amendment XVII (Ratified April 8, 1913)

The Senate of the United States shall be composed of two Senators from each State, elected by the people thereof, for six years; and each Senator shall have one vote. The electors in each State shall have the qualifications requisite for electors of the most numerous branch of the State legislatures.

When vacancies happen in the representation of any State in the Senate, the executive authority of such State shall issue writs of election to fill such vacancies: *Provided,* That the legislature of any State may empower the executive thereof to make temporary appointments until the people fill the vacancies by election as the legislature may direct.

This amendment shall not be so construed as to affect the election or term of any Senator chosen before it becomes valid as part of the Constitution.

Amendment XVIII (Ratified January 16, 1919)[13]

Section 1. After one year from the ratification of this article the manufacture, sale, or transportation of intoxicating liquors within, the importation thereof into, or the exportation thereof from the United States and all territory subject to the jurisdiction thereof for beverage purposes is hereby prohibited.

Section 2. The Congress and the several States shall have concurrent power to enforce this article by appropriate legislation.

Section 3. This article shall be inoperative unless it shall have been ratified as an amendment to the Constitution by the legislatures of the several States, as provided in the Constitution, within seven years from the date of the submission hereof to the States by the Congress.

Amendment XIX (Ratified August 18, 1920)

The right of citizens of the United States to vote shall not be denied or abridged by the United States or by any State on account of sex.

Congress shall have power to enforce this article by appropriate legislation.

Amendment XX (Ratified January 23, 1933)

Section 1. The terms of the President and Vice President shall end at noon on the 20th day of January, and the terms of Senators and Representatives at noon on the 3d day of January, of the years in which such terms would have ended if this article had not been ratified; and the terms of their successors shall then begin.

Section 2. The Congress shall assemble at least once in every year, and such meeting shall begin at noon on the 3d day of January, unless they shall by law appoint a different day.

Section 3.[14] If, at the time fixed for the beginning of the term of the President, the President elect shall have died, the Vice President elect shall become President. If a President shall not have been chosen before the time fixed for the beginning of his term, or if the President elect shall have failed to qualify, then the Vice President elect shall act as President until a President shall have qualified; and the Congress may by law provide for the case wherein neither a President elect nor a Vice President elect shall have qualified, declaring who shall then act as President, or the manner in which one who is to act shall be selected, and such person shall act accordingly until a President or Vice President shall have qualified.

Section 4. The Congress may by law provide for the case of the death of any of the persons from whom the House of Representatives may choose a President whenever the right of choice shall have devolved upon them, and for the case of the death of any of the persons from whom the Senate may choose a Vice President whenever the right of choice shall have devolved upon them.

Section 5. Sections 1 and 2 shall take effect on the 15th day of October following the ratification of this article.

Section 6. This article shall be inoperative unless it shall have been ratified as an amendment to the Constitution by the legislatures of three-fourths of the several States within seven years from the date of its submission.

Amendment XXI (Ratified December 5, 1933)

Section 1. The eighteenth article of amendment to the Constitution of the United States is hereby repealed.

Section 2. The transportation or importation into any State, Territory, or possession of the United States for delivery or use therein of intoxicating liquors, in violation of the laws thereof, is hereby prohibited.

Section 3. This article shall be inoperative unless it shall have been ratified as an amendment to the Constitution by conventions in the several States, as provided in the Constitution, within seven years from the date of the submission hereof to the States by the Congress.

Amendment XXII (Ratified February 27, 1951)

Section 1. No person shall be elected to the office of the President more than twice, and no person who has held the office of President, or acted as President, for more than two years of a term to which some other person was elected President shall be elected to the office of the President more than once. But this Article shall not apply to any person holding the office of President when this Article was proposed by the Congress, and shall not prevent any person who may be holding the office of President, or acting as President, during the term within which this Article become operative from holding the office of President or acting as President during the remainder of such term.

Section 2. This article shall be inoperative unless it shall have been ratified as an amendment to the Constitution by the legislatures of three-fourths of the several States within seven years from the date of its submission to the States by the Congress.

Amendment XXIII (Ratified March 29, 1961)

Section 1. The District constituting the seat of Government of the United States shall appoint in such manner as the Congress may direct:

A number of electors of President and Vice President equal to the whole number of Senators and Representatives in Congress to which the District would be entitled if it were a State, but in no event more than the least populous State; they shall be in addition to those appointed by the States, but they shall be considered, for the purposes of the election of President and Vice President, to be electors appointed by a State; and they shall meet in the District and perform such duties as provided by the twelfth article of amendment.

Section 2. The Congress shall have power to enforce this article by appropriate legislation.

Amendment XXIV (Ratified January 23, 1964)

Section 1. The right of citizens of the United States to vote in any primary or other election for President or Vice President, for electors for President or Vice President, or for Senator or Representative in Congress, shall not be denied or abridged by the United States or any State by reason of failure to pay any poll tax or other tax.

Section 2. The Congress shall have power to enforce this article by appropriate legislation.

Amendment XXV (Ratified February 10, 1967)

Section 1. In case of the removal of the President from office or of his death or resignation, the Vice President shall become President.

Section 2. Whenever there is a vacancy in the office of the Vice President, the President shall nominate a Vice President who shall take office upon confirmation by a majority vote of both Houses of Congress.

Section 3. Whenever the President transmits to the President pro tempore of the Senate and the Speaker of the House of Representatives his written declaration that he is unable to discharge the powers and duties of his office, and until he transmits to them a written declaration to the contrary, such powers and duties shall be discharged by the Vice President as Acting President.

Section 4. Whenever the Vice President and a majority of either the principal officers of the executive departments or of such other body as Congress may by law provide, transmit to the President pro tempore of the Senate and the Speaker of the House of Representatives their written declaration that the President is unable to discharge the powers and duties of his office, the Vice President shall immediately assume the powers and duties of the office as Acting President.

Thereafter, when the President transmits to the President pro tempore of the Senate and the Speaker of the House of Representatives his written declaration that no inability exists, he shall resume the powers and duties of his office unless the Vice President and a majority of either the principal officers of the executive department or of such other body as Congress may by law provide, transmit within four days to the President pro tempore of the Senate and the Speaker of the House of Representatives their written declaration that the President is unable to discharge the powers and duties of his office. Thereupon Congress shall decide the issue, assembling within forty-eight hours for that purpose if not in session. If the Congress, within twenty-one days after receipt of the latter written declaration, or, if Congress is not in session, within twenty-one days after Congress is required to assemble, determines by two-thirds vote of both Houses that the President is unable to discharge the powers and duties of his office, the Vice President shall continue to discharge the same as Acting President; otherwise, the President shall resume the powers and duties of his office.

Amendment XXVI (Ratified July 1, 1971)

Section 1. The right of citizens of the United States, who are eighteen years of age or older, to vote shall not be denied or abridged by the United States or by any State on account of age.

Section 2. The Congress shall have power to enforce this article by appropriate legislation.

Amendment XXVII (Ratified May 7, 1992)

No law varying the compensation for the services of the Senators and Representatives shall take effect, until an election of Representatives shall have intervened.

Notes

1. The part in brackets was changed by section 2 of the Fourteenth Amendment. 2. The part in brackets was changed by the first paragraph of the Seventeenth Amendment. 3. The part in brackets was changed by the second paragraph of the Seventeenth Amendment. 4. The part in brackets was changed by section 2 of the Twentieth Amendment. 5. The Sixteenth Amendment gave Congress the power to tax incomes. 6. The material in brackets has been superseded by the Twelfth Amendment. 7. This provision has been affected by the Twenty-fifth Amendment. 8. These clauses were affected by the Eleventh Amendment. 9. This paragraph has been superseded by the Thirteenth Amendment. 10. Obsolete. 11. The part in brackets has been superseded by section 3 of the Twentieth Amendment. 12. See the Nineteenth and Twenty-sixth Amendments. 13. This Amendment was repealed by section 1 of the Twenty-first Amendment. 14. See the Twenty-fifth Amendment.

Source

U.S. Congress, House, Committee on the Judiciary, *The Constitution of the United States of America, as Amended,* 100th Cong., 1st sess., 1987, H Doc 100-94.

Confirmed Supreme Court Nominations, by Nominating President, 1789–2002

Name of nominee	*State*	*Party affiliation at time of nomination*	*Date of birth*	*To replace*	*Date of appointment*	*Confirmation**	*Date resigned/retired*	*Date of death*	*Years of service*
GEORGE WASHINGTON/FED.									
John Jay	NY	Fed.	12/12/1745		9/24/1789	9/26/1789	6/29/1795	5/17/1829	6
John Rutledge	SC	Fed.	9/17/39		9/24/1789	9/26/1789	3/5/1791	7/18/1800	1
William Cushing	MA	Fed.	3/1/1732		9/24/1789	9/26/1789		9/13/1810	21
James Wilson	PA	Fed.	9/14/1742		9/24/1789	9/26/1789		8/21/1798	9
John Blair Jr.	VA	Fed.	1732		9/24/1789	9/26/1789	1/27/1796	8/31/1800	6
James Iredell	NC	Fed.	10/5/1751		2/8/1790	2/10/1790		10/20/1799	9
Thomas Johnson	MD	Fed.	11/4/1732	Rutledge	11/1/1791	11/7/1791	3/4/1793	10/26/1819	1
William Paterson†	NJ	Fed.	12/24/1745	Johnson	3/4/1793	3/4/1793		9/9/1806	13
Samuel Chase	MD	Fed.	4/17/1741	Blair	1/26/1796	1/27/1796		6/19/1811	15
Oliver Ellsworth	CT	Fed.	4/29/1745	Jay	3/3/1796	3/4/1796 (21–1)	12/15/1800	11/26/1807	4
JOHN ADAMS/FED.									
Bushrod Washington	VA	Fed.	6/5/1762	Wilson	12/19/1798	12/20/1798		11/26/1829	31
Alfred Moore	NC	Fed.	5/21/1755	Iredell	12/6/1799	12/10/1799	1/26/1804	10/15/1810	4
John Marshall	VA	Fed.	9/24/1755	Ellsworth	1/20/1801			7/6/1835	34
THOMAS JEFFERSON/DEM.-REP.									
William Johnson	SC	Dem.-Rep.	12/27/1771	Moore	3/22/1804	3/24/1804		8/4/1834	30
Henry B. Livingston	NY	Dem.-Rep.	11/25/1757	Paterson	12/13/1806	2/17/1806		3/18/1823	16
Thomas Todd	KY	Dem.-Rep.	1/23/1765	New seat	2/28/1807	3/3/1807		2/7/1826	19
JAMES MADISON/DEM.-REP.									
Joseph Story	MA	Dem.-Rep.	9/18/1779	Cushing	11/15/1811	11/18/1811		9/10/1845	34
Gabriel Duvall	MD	Dem.-Rep.	12/6/1752	Chase	11/15/1811	11/18/1811	1/14/1835	3/6/1844	23
JAMES MONROE/DEM.-REP.									
Smith Thompson	NY	Dem.-Rep.	1/17/1768	Livingston	12/8/1823	12/19/1823		12/18/1843	20
JOHN Q. ADAMS/DEM.-REP.									
Robert Trimble	KY	Dem.-Rep.	11/17/1776	Todd	4/11/1826	5/9/1826 (27–5)		8/25/1828	2
ANDREW JACKSON/DEM.									
John McLean	OH	Dem.	3/11/1785	Trimble	3/6/1829	3/7/1829		4/4/1861	32
Henry Baldwin	PA	Dem.	1/14/1780	Washington	1/4/1830	1/6/1830 (41–2)		4/21/1844	14
James M. Wayne	GA	Dem.	1790	Johnson	1/7/1835	1/9/1835		7/5/1867	32
Roger B. Taney†	MD	Dem.	3/17/1777	Marshall	12/28/1835	3/15/1836 (29–15)		10/12/1864	28
Philip P. Barbour	VA	Dem.	5/25/1783	Duvall	12/28/1835	3/15/1836 (30–11)		2/25/1841	5
John Catron	TN	Dem.	1786	New seat	3/3/1837	3/8/1837 (28–15)		5/30/1865	28

Name of nominee	State	Party affiliation at time of nomination	Date of birth	To replace	Date of appointment	Confirmation*	Date resigned/retired	Date of death	Years of service
MARTIN VAN BUREN/DEM.									
John McKinley	AL	Dem.	5/1/1780	New seat	9/18/1837	9/25/1837		7/19/1852	15
Peter V. Daniel	VA	Dem.	4/24/1784	Barbour	2/26/1841	3/2/1841 (22–5)		5/31/1860	19
JOHN TYLER/DEM.									
Samuel Nelson	NY	Dem.	11/10/1792	Thompson	2/4/1845	2/14/1845	11/28/1872	12/13/1873	27
JAMES K. POLK/DEM.									
Levi Woodbury	NH	Dem.	12/22/1789	Story	12/23/1845	1/3/1846		9/4/1851	5
Robert C. Grier	PA	Dem.	3/5/1794	Baldwin	8/3/1846	8/4/1846	1/31/1870	9/25/1870	23
MILLARD FILLMORE/WHIG									
Benjamin R. Curtis	MA	Whig	11/4/1809	Woodbury	12/11/1851	12/29/1851	9/30/1857	9/15/1874	5
FRANKLIN PIERCE/DEM.									
John A. Campbell	AL	Dem.	6/24/1811	McKinley	3/22/1853	3/25/1853	4/30/1861	3/12/1889	8
JAMES BUCHANAN/DEM.									
Nathan Clifford	ME	Dem.	8/18/1803	Curtis	12/9/1857	1/12/1858 (26–23)		7/25/1881	23
ABRAHAM LINCOLN/REP.									
Noah H. Swayne	OH	Rep.	12/7/1804	McLean	1/21/1862	1/24/1862 (38–1)	1/24/1881	6/8/1884	19
Samuel F. Miller	IA	Rep.	4/5/1816	Daniel	7/16/1862	7/16/1862		10/13/1890	28
David Davis	IL	Rep.	3/9/1815	Campbell	12/1/1862	12/8/1862	3/4/1877	6/26/1886	14
Stephen J. Field	CA	Dem.	11/4/1816	New seat	3/6/1863	3/10/1863	12/1/1897	4/9/1899	34
Salmon P. Chase	OH	Rep.	1/13/1808	Taney	12/6/1864	12/6/1864		5/7/1873	8
ANDREW JOHNSON/DEM.									
None									
ULYSSES S. GRANT/REP.									
William Strong	PA	Rep.	5/6/1808	Grier	2/7/1870	2/18/1870	12/14/1880	8/19/1895	10
Joseph P. Bradley	NJ	Rep.	3/14/1813	New seat	2/7/1870	3/21/1870 (46–9)		1/22/1892	21
Ward Hunt	NY	Rep.	6/14/1810	Nelson	12/3/1872	12/11/1872	1/27/1882	3/24/1886	9
Morrison R. Waite	OH	Rep.	11/29/1816	Chase	1/19/1874	1/21/1874 (63–0)		3/23/1888	14
RUTHERFORD B. HAYES/REP.									
John M. Harlan	KY	Rep.	6/1/1833	Davis	10/17/1877	11/29/1877		10/14/1911	34
William B. Woods	GA	Rep.	8/3/1824	Strong	12/15/1880	12/21/1880 (39–8)		5/14/1887	6
JAMES A. GARFIELD/REP.									
Stanley Matthews†	OH	Rep.	7/21/1824	Swayne	3/14/1881	5/12/1881 (24–23)		3/22/1889	7
CHESTER A. ARTHUR/REP.									
Horace Gray	MA	Rep.	3/24/1828	Clifford	12/19/1881	12/20/1881 (51–5)		9/15/1902	20
Samuel Blatchford	NY	Rep.	3/9/1820	Hunt	3/13/1882	3/27/1882		7/7/1893	11
GROVER CLEVELAND/DEM.									
Lucius Q. C. Lamar	MS	Dem.	9/17/1825	Woods	12/6/1887	1/16/1888 (32–28)		1/23/1893	5
Melville W. Fuller	IL	Dem.	2/11/1833	Waite	4/30/1888	7/20/1888 (41–20)		7/4/1910	22
BENJAMIN HARRISON/REP.									
David J. Brewer	KS	Rep.	6/20/1837	Matthews	12/4/1889	12/18/1889 (53–11)		3/28/1910	20
Henry B. Brown	MI	Rep.	3/2/1836	Miller	12/23/1890	12/29/1890	5/28/1906	9/4/1913	15

(continues)

Name of nominee	State	Party affiliation at time of nomination	Date of birth	To replace	Date of appointment	Confirmation*	Date resigned/retired	Date of death	Years of service
BENJAMIN HARRISON/REP.		*(continued)*							
George Shiras Jr.	PA	Rep.	1/26/1832	Bradley	7/19/1892	7/26/1892	2/23/1903	8/2/1924	10
Howell E. Jackson	TN	Dem.	4/8/1832	Lamar	2/2/1893	2/18/1893		8/8/1895	2
GROVER CLEVELAND/DEM.									
Edward D. White	LA	Dem.	11/3/1845	Blatchford	2/19/1894	2/19/1894		5/19/1921	17
Rufus W. Peckham	NY	Dem.	11/8/1838	Jackson	12/3/1895	12/9/1895		10/24/1909	13
WILLIAM MCKINLEY/REP.									
Joseph McKenna	CA	Rep.	8/10/1843	Field	12/16/1897	1/21/1898	1/5/1925	11/21/1926	26
THEODORE ROOSEVELT/REP.									
Oliver W. Holmes Jr.	MA	Rep.	3/8/1841	Gray	12/2/1902	12/4/1902	1/12/1932	3/6/1935	29
William R. Day	OH	Rep.	4/17/1849	Shiras	2/19/1903	2/23/1903	11/13/1922	7/9/1923	19
William H. Moody	MA	Rep.	12/23/1853	Brown	12/3/1906	12/12/1906	11/20/1910	7/2/1917	3
WILLIAM H. TAFT/REP.									
Horace H. Lurton	TN	Dem.	2/26/1844	Peckham	12/13/1909	12/20/1909		7/12/1914	4
Charles E. Hughes	NY	Rep.	4/11/1862	Brewer	4/25/1910	5/2/1910	6/10/1916	8/27/1948	6
Edward D. White††		Dem.		Fuller	12/12/1910	12/12/1910		5/19/1921	10
Willis Van Devanter	WY	Rep.	4/17/1859	White	12/12/1910	12/15/1910	6/2/1937	2/8/1941	26
Joseph R. Lamar	GA	Dem.	10/14/1857	Moody	12/12/1910	12/15/1910		1/2/1916	5
Mahlon Pitney	NJ	Rep.	2/5/1858	Harlan	2/19/1912	3/13/1912 (50–26)	12/31/1922	12/9/1924	10
WOODROW WILSON/DEM.									
James C. McReynolds	TN	Dem.	2/3/1862	Lurton	8/19/1914	8/29/1914 (44–6)	1/31/1941	8/24/1946	26
Louis D. Brandeis	MA	Rep.	11/13/1856	Lamar	1/28/1916	6/1/1916 (47–22)	2/13/1939	10/5/1941	22
John H. Clarke	OH	Dem.	9/18/1857	Hughes	7/14/1916	7/24/1916	9/18/1922	3/22/1945	6
WARREN G. HARDING/REP.									
William H. Taft	OH	Rep.	9/15/1857	White	6/30/1921	6/30/1921	2/3/1930	3/8/1930	8
George Sutherland	UT	Rep.	3/25/1862	Clarke	9/5/1922	9/5/1922	1/17/1938	7/18/1942	15
Pierce Butler	MN	Dem.	3/17/1866	Day	11/23/1922	12/21/1922 (61–8)		11/16/1939	17
Edward T. Sanford	TN	Rep.	7/23/1865	Pitney	1/24/1923	1/29/1923		3/8/1930	7
CALVIN COOLIDGE/REP.									
Harlan F. Stone	NY	Rep.	10/11/1872	McKenna	1/5/1925	2/5/1925 (71–6)		4/22/1946	16
HERBERT HOOVER/REP.									
Charles E. Hughes††		Rep.		Taft	2/3/1930	2/13/1930 (52–26)	7/1/1941	8/27/1948	11
Owen J. Roberts	PA	Rep.	5/2/1875	Sanford	5/9/1930	5/20/1930	7/31/1945	5/17/1955	15
Benjamin N. Cardozo	NY	Dem.	5/24/1870	Holmes	2/15/1932	2/24/1932		7/9/1938	6
FRANKLIN D. ROOSEVELT/DEM.									
Hugo L. Black	AL	Dem.	2/27/1886	Van Devanter	8/12/1937	8/17/1937 (63–16)	9/17/1971	10/25/1971	34
Stanley F. Reed	KY	Dem.	12/31/1884	Sutherland	1/15/1938	1/25/1938	2/25/1957	4/2/1980	19
Felix Frankfurter	MA	Ind.	11/15/1882	Cardozo	1/5/1939	1/17/1939	8/28/1962	2/22/1965	23
William O. Douglas	CT	Dem.	10/16/1898	Brandeis	3/20/1939	4/4/1939 (62–4)	11/12/1975	1/19/1980	36
Francis W. Murphy	MI	Dem.	4/13/1890	Butler	1/4/1940	1/15/1940		7/19/1949	9
Harlan F. Stone††		Rep.		Hughes	6/12/1941	6/27/1941		4/22/1946	5
James F. Byrnes	SC	Dem.	5/2/1879	McReynolds	6/12/1941	6/12/1941	10/3/1942	4/9/1972	1
Robert H. Jackson	NY	Dem.	2/13/1892	Stone	6/12/1941	7/7/1941		10/9/1954	13
Wiley B. Rutledge	IA	Dem.	7/20/1894	Byrnes	1/11/1943	2/8/1943		9/10/1949	6

Name of nominee	*State*	*Party affiliation at time of nomination*	*Date of birth*	*To replace*	*Date of appointment*	*Confirmation**	*Date resigned/retired*	*Date of death*	*Years of service*
HARRY S TRUMAN/DEM.									
Harold H. Burton	OH	Rep.	6/22/1888	Roberts	9/19/1945	9/19/1945	10/13/1958	10/28/1964	13
Fred M. Vinson	KY	Dem.	1/22/1890	Stone	6/6/1946	6/20/1946		9/8/1953	7
Tom C. Clark	TX	Dem.	9/23/1899	Murphy	8/2/1949	8/18/1949 (73–8)	6/12/1967	6/13/1977	18
Sherman Minton	IN	Dem.	10/20/1890	Rutledge	9/15/1949	10/4/1949 (48–16)	10/15/1956	4/9/1965	7
DWIGHT D. EISENHOWER/REP.									
Earl Warren	CA	Rep.	3/19/1891	Vinson	9/30/1953	3/1/1954	6/23/1969	6/9/1974	15
John M. Harlan	NY	Rep.	5/20/1899	Jackson	1/10/1955	3/16/1955 (71–11)	9/23/1971	12/29/1971	16
William J. Brennan Jr.	NJ	Dem.	4/25/1906	Minton	1/14/1957	3/19/1957	7/23/1990	7/24/1997	33
Charles E. Whittaker	MO	Rep.	2/22/1901	Reed	3/2/1957	3/19/1957	3/31/1962	11/26/1973	5
Potter Stewart	OH	Rep.	1/23/1915	Burton	1/17/1959	5/5/1959 (70–17)	7/3/1981	12/7/1985	22
JOHN F. KENNEDY/DEM.									
Byron R. White	CO	Dem.	6/8/1917	Whittaker	3/30/1962	4/11/1962	6/28/1993	4/15/2002	31
Arthur J. Goldberg	IL	Dem.	8/8/1908	Frankfurter	8/29/1962	9/25/1962	7/25/1965	1/19/1990	3
LYNDON B. JOHNSON/DEM.									
Abe Fortas	TN	Dem.	6/19/1910	Goldberg	7/28/1965	8/11/1965	5/14/1969	4/5/1982	4
Thurgood Marshall	NY	Dem.	6/2/1908	Clark	6/13/1967	8/30/1967 (69–11)	10/1/1991	1/24/1993	24
RICHARD M. NIXON/REP.									
Warren E. Burger	MN	Rep.	9/17/1907	Warren	5/21/1969	6/9/1969 (74–3)	9/26/1986	6/25/1995	17
Harry A. Blackmun	MN	Rep.	11/12/1908	Fortas	4/14/1970	5/12/1970 (94–0)	8/3/1994	3/4/1999	24
Lewis F. Powell Jr.	VA	Dem.	9/19/1907	Black	10/21/1971	12/6/1971 (89–1)	6/26/1987	8/25/1998	16
William H. Rehnquist	AZ	Rep.	10/1/1924	Harlan	10/21/1971	12/10/1971 (68–26)			
GERALD R. FORD/REP.									
John P. Stevens	IL	Rep.	4/20/1920	Douglas	11/28/1975	12/17/1975 (98–0)			
JAMES E. CARTER/DEM.									
None									
RONALD W. REAGAN/REP.									
Sandra Day O'Connor	AZ	Rep.	3/26/1930	Stewart	8/19/1981	9/21/1981 (99–0)			
William H. Rehnquist††		Rep.		Burger	6/20/1986	9/17/1986 (65–33)			
Antonin Scalia	VA	Rep.	3/11/1936	Rehnquist	6/24/1986	9/17/1986 (98–0)			
Anthony M. Kennedy	CA	Rep.	7/23/1936	Powell	11/30/1987	2/3/1988 (97–0)			
GEORGE H. W. BUSH/REP.									
David H. Souter	NH	Rep.	9/17/1939	Brennan	7/23/1990	10/2/1990 (90–9)			
Clarence Thomas	GA	Rep.	6/23/1948	Marshall	7/1/1991	10/15/1991 (52–48)			
WILLIAM J. CLINTON/DEM.									
Ruth Bader Ginsburg	NY	Dem.	3/15/1933	White	6/22/1993	8/3/1993 (96–3)			
Stephen G. Breyer	MA	Dem.	8/15/1938	Blackmun	5/13/1994	7/29/1994 (87–9)			

Sources: Joan Biskupic and Elder Witt, *Guide to the U.S. Supreme Court,* 3d ed. (Washington, D.C.: Congressional Quarterly, 1997); Lee Epstein, Jeffrey A. Segal, Harold J. Spaeth, Thomas G. Walker, *The Supreme Court Compendium: Data, Decisions, and Developments,* 3d ed. (Washington, D.C.: CQ Press, 2003); and Kenneth Jost, ed., *The Supreme Court A to Z,* 2d ed. (Washington, D.C.: Congressional Quarterly, 1998).

Note: Boldface = Chief justice; * = Where no vote is listed, confirmation was by voice or otherwise unrecorded; † = Earlier nomination not confirmed; †† = Earlier Court service; Dem. = Democrat; Dem.-Rep. = Democratic Republican; Fed. = Federalist; Ind. = Independent; Rep. = Republican.

Membership Changes in the U.S. Supreme Court, by Chief Justice, 1789–2002

Chief justice	*Justices (in order of seniority)*	*Dates between oaths of office for new justices*	*Member change, reason, and date*
Jay	Jay, J. Rutledge, Cushing, Wilson, Blair	Oct. 5, 1789–May 12, 1790	Wilson (*o* Oct. 5, 1789) Jay (*o* Oct. 19, 1789) Cushing (*o* Feb. 2, 1790) Blair (*o* Feb. 2, 1790) J. Rutledge (*o* Feb. 15, 1790)
	Jay, Rutledge, Cushing, Wilson, Blair, Iredell	May 12, 1790–Mar. 5, 1791	Iredell (*o* May 12, 1790)
	Jay, Cushing, Wilson, Blair, Iredell	Mar. 5, 1791–Aug. 6, 1792	Rutledge (*r* Mar. 5, 1791)
	Jay, Cushing, Wilson, Blair, Iredell, T. Johnson	Aug. 6, 1792–Jan. 16, 1793	T. Johnson (*o* Aug. 6, 1792)
	Jay, Cushing, Wilson, Blair, Iredell	Jan. 16, 1793–Mar. 11, 1793	T. Johnson (*r* Jan. 16, 1793)
	Jay, Cushing, Wilson, Blair, Iredell, Paterson	Mar. 11, 1793–June 29, 1795	Paterson (*o* Mar. 11, 1793)
None	Cushing, Wilson, Blair, Iredell, Paterson	June 29, 1795–Aug. 12, 1795	Jay (*r* June 29, 1795)
J. Rutledge	J. Rutledge, Cushing, Wilson, Blair, Iredell, Paterson	Aug. 12, 1795–Dec. 15, 1795	J. Rutledge (*o* Aug. 12, 1795)
None	Cushing, Wilson, Blair, Iredell, Paterson	Dec. 15, 1795–Jan. 27, 1796	J. Rutledge (*rj* Dec. 15, 1795)
	Cushing, Wilson, Iredell, Paterson	Jan. 27, 1796–Feb. 4, 1796	Blair (*r* Jan. 27, 1796)
	Cushing, Wilson, Iredell, Paterson, S. Chase	Feb. 4, 1796–Mar. 8, 1796	S. Chase (*o* Feb. 4, 1796)
Ellsworth	Ellsworth, Cushing, Wilson, Iredell, Paterson, S. Chase	Mar. 8, 1796–Aug. 21, 1798	Ellsworth (*o* Mar. 8, 1796)
	Ellsworth, Cushing, Iredell, Paterson, S. Chase	Aug. 21, 1798–Feb. 4, 1799	Wilson (*d* Aug. 21, 1798)
	Ellsworth, Cushing, Iredell, Paterson, S. Chase, Washington	Feb. 4, 1799–Oct. 20, 1799	Washington (*o* Feb. 4, 1799)
	Ellsworth, Cushing, Paterson, S. Chase, Washington	Oct. 20, 1799–Apr. 21, 1800	Iredell (*d* Oct. 20, 1799)
	Ellsworth, Cushing, Paterson, S. Chase, Washington, Moore	Apr. 21, 1800–Dec. 15, 1800	Moore (*o* Apr. 21, 1800)
None	Cushing, Paterson, S. Chase, Washington, Moore	Dec. 15, 1800–Feb. 4, 1801	Ellsworth (*r* Dec. 15, 1800)
J. Marshall	J. Marshall, Cushing, Paterson, S. Chase, Washington, Moore	Feb. 4, 1801–Jan. 26, 1804	Marshall (*o* Feb. 4, 1801)
	J. Marshall, Cushing, Paterson, S. Chase, Washington	Jan. 26, 1804–May 7, 1804	Moore (*r* Jan. 26, 1804)

Chief justice	*Justices (in order of seniority)*	*Dates between oaths of office for new justices*	*Member change, reason, and date*
J. Marshall *(continued)*			
	J. Marshall, Cushing, Paterson, S. Chase, Washington, W. Johnson	May 7, 1804–Sept. 9, 1806	W. Johnson (*o* May 7, 1804)
	J. Marshall, Cushing, S. Chase, Washington, W. Johnson	Sept. 9, 1806–Jan. 20, 1807	Paterson (*d* Sept. 9, 1806)
	J. Marshall, Cushing, S. Chase, Washington, W. Johnson, Livingston	Jan. 20, 1807–May 4, 1807	Livingston (*o* Jan. 20, 1807)
	J. Marshall, Cushing, S. Chase, Washington, W. Johnson, Livingston, Todd	May 4, 1807–Sept. 13, 1810	Todd (*o* May 4, 1807)
	J. Marshall, S. Chase, Washington, W. Johnson, Livingston, Todd	Sept. 13, 1810–June 19, 1811	Cushing (*d* Sept. 13, 1810)
	J. Marshall, Washington, W. Johnson, Livingston, Todd	June 19, 1811–Nov. 23, 1811	S. Chase (*d* June 19, 1811)
	J. Marshall, Washington, W. Johnson, Livingston, Todd, Duvall	Nov. 23, 1811–Feb. 3, 1812	Duvall (*o* Nov. 23, 1811)
	J. Marshall, Washington, W. Johnson, Livingston, Todd, Duvall, Story	Feb. 3, 1812–Mar. 18, 1823	Story (*o* Feb. 3, 1812)
	J. Marshall, Washington, W. Johnson, Todd, Duvall, Story	Mar. 18, 1823–Feb. 10, 1824	Livingston (*d* Mar. 18, 1823)
	J. Marshall, Washington, W. Johnson, Todd, Duvall, Story, Thompson	Feb. 10, 1824–Feb. 7, 1826	Thompson (*o* Feb. 10, 1824)
	J. Marshall, Washington, W. Johnson, Duvall, Story, Thompson	Feb. 7, 1826–June 16, 1826	Todd (*d* Feb. 7, 1826)
	J. Marshall, Washington, W. Johnson, Duvall, Story, Thompson, Trimble	June 16, 1826–Aug. 25, 1828	Trimble (*o* June 16, 1826)
	J. Marshall, Washington, W. Johnson, Duvall, Story, Thompson	Aug. 25, 1828–Nov. 26, 1829	Trimble (*d* Aug. 25, 1828)
	J. Marshall, W. Johnson, Duvall, Story, Thompson	Nov. 26, 1829–Jan. 11, 1830	Washington (*d* Nov. 26, 1829)
	J. Marshall, W. Johnson, Duvall, Story, Thompson, McLean	Jan. 11, 1830–Jan. 18, 1830	McLean (*o* Jan. 11, 1830)
	J. Marshall, W. Johnson, Duvall, Story, Thompson, McLean, Baldwin	Jan. 18, 1830–Aug. 4, 1834	Baldwin (*o* Jan. 18, 1830)
	J. Marshall, Duvall, Story, Thompson, McLean, Baldwin	Aug. 4, 1834–Jan. 14, 1835	W. Johnson (*d* Aug. 4, 1834)
	J. Marshall, Story, Thompson, McLean, Baldwin, Wayne	Jan. 14, 1835–July 6, 1835	Duvall (*r* Jan. 14, 1835) Wayne (*o* Jan. 14, 1835)
None	Story, Thompson, McLean, Baldwin, Wayne	July 6, 1835–Mar. 28, 1836	Marshall (*d* July 6, 1835)
Taney	Taney, Story, Thompson, McLean, Baldwin, Wayne	Mar. 28, 1836–May 12, 1836	Taney (*o* Mar. 28, 1836)
	Taney, Story, Thompson, McLean, Baldwin, Wayne, Barbour	May 12, 1836–May 1, 1837	Barbour (*o* May 12, 1836)
	Taney, Story, Thompson, McLean, Baldwin, Wayne, Barbour, Catron	May 1, 1837–Jan. 9, 1838	Catron (*o* May 1, 1837)
	Taney, Story, Thompson, McLean, Baldwin, Wayne, Barbour, Catron, McKinley	Jan. 9, 1838–Feb. 25, 1841	McKinley (*o* Jan. 9, 1838)
	Taney, Story, Thompson, McLean, Baldwin, Wayne, Catron, McKinley	Feb. 25, 1841–Jan. 10, 1842	Barbour (*d* Feb. 25, 1841)
	Taney, Story, Thompson, McLean, Baldwin, Wayne, Catron, McKinley, Daniel	Jan. 10, 1842–Dec. 18, 1843	Daniel (*o* Jan. 10, 1842)
	Taney, Story, McLean, Baldwin, Wayne, Catron, McKinley, Daniel	Dec. 18, 1843–Apr. 21, 1844	Thompson (*d* Dec. 18, 1843)

(continues)

Chief justice	*Justices (in order of seniority)*	*Dates between oaths of office for new justices*	*Member change, reason, and date*
Taney *(continued)*			
	Taney, Story, McLean, Wayne, Catron, McKinley, Daniel	Apr. 21, 1844–Feb. 27, 1845	Baldwin (*d* Apr. 21, 1844)
	Taney, Story, McLean, Wayne, Catron, McKinley, Daniel, Nelson	Feb. 27, 1845–Sept. 10, 1845	Nelson (*o* Feb. 27, 1845)
	Taney, McLean, Wayne, Catron, McKinley, Daniel, Nelson	Sept. 10, 1845–Sept. 23, 1845	Story (*d* Sept. 10, 1845)
	Taney, McLean, Wayne, Catron, McKinley, Daniel, Nelson, Woodbury	Sept. 23, 1845–Aug. 10, 1846	Woodbury (*o* Sept. 23, 1845)
	Taney, McLean, Wayne, Catron, McKinley, Daniel, Nelson, Woodbury, Grier	Aug. 10, 1846–Sept. 4, 1851	Grier (*o* Aug. 10, 1846)
	Taney, McLean, Wayne, Catron, McKinley, Daniel, Nelson, Grier	Sept. 4, 1851–Oct. 10, 1851	Woodbury (*d* Sept. 4, 1851)
	Taney, McLean, Wayne, Catron, McKinley, Daniel, Nelson, Grier, Curtis	Oct. 10, 1851–July 19, 1852	Curtis (*o* Oct. 10, 1851)
	Taney, McLean, Wayne, Catron, Daniel, Nelson, Grier, Curtis	July 19, 1852–Apr. 11, 1853	McKinley (*d* July 19, 1852)
	Taney, McLean, Wayne, Catron, Daniel, Nelson, Grier, Curtis, Campbell	Apr. 11, 1853–Sept. 30, 1857	Campbell (*o* Apr. 11, 1853)
	Taney, McLean, Wayne, Catron, Daniel, Nelson, Grier, Campbell	Sept. 30, 1857–Jan. 21, 1858	Curtis (*r* Sept. 30, 1857)
	Taney, McLean, Wayne, Catron, Daniel, Nelson, Grier, Campbell, Clifford	Jan. 21, 1858–May 31, 1860	Clifford (*o* Jan. 21, 1858)
	Taney, McLean, Wayne, Catron, Nelson, Grier, Campbell, Clifford	May 31, 1860–Apr. 4, 1861	Daniel (*d* May 31, 1860)
	Taney, Wayne, Catron, Nelson, Grier, Campbell, Clifford	Apr. 4, 1861–Apr. 30, 1861	McLean (*d* Apr. 4, 1861)
	Taney, Wayne, Catron, Nelson, Grier, Clifford	Apr. 30, 1861–Jan. 27, 1862	Campbell (*r* Apr. 30, 1861)
	Taney, Wayne, Catron, Nelson, Grier, Clifford, Swayne	Jan. 27, 1862–July 21, 1862	Swayne (*o* Jan. 27, 1862)
	Taney, Wayne, Catron, Nelson, Grier, Clifford, Swayne, Miller	July 21, 1862–Dec. 10, 1862	Miller (*o* July 21, 1862)
	Taney, Wayne, Catron, Nelson, Grier, Clifford, Swayne, Miller, Davis	Dec. 10, 1862–May 20, 1863	Davis (*o* Dec. 10, 1862)
	Taney, Wayne, Catron, Nelson, Grier, Clifford, Swayne, Miller, Davis, Field	May 20, 1863–Oct. 12, 1864	Field (*o* May 20, 1863)
None	Wayne, Catron, Nelson, Grier, Clifford, Swayne, Miller, Davis, Field	Oct. 12, 1864–Dec. 15, 1864	Taney (*d* Oct. 12, 1864)
S. P. Chase	S. P. Chase, Wayne, Catron, Nelson, Grier, Clifford, Swayne, Miller, Davis, Field	Dec. 15, 1864–May 30, 1865	S. P. Chase (*o* Dec. 15, 1864)
	S. P. Chase, Wayne, Nelson, Grier, Clifford, Swayne, Miller, Davis, Field	May 30, 1865–July 5, 1867	Catron (*d* May 30, 1865)
	S. P. Chase, Nelson, Grier, Clifford, Swayne, Miller, Davis, Field	July 5, 1867–Jan. 31, 1870	Wayne (*d* July 5, 1867)
	S. P. Chase, Nelson, Clifford, Swayne, Miller, Davis, Field	Jan. 31, 1870–Mar. 14, 1870	Grier (*r* Jan. 31, 1870)
	S. P. Chase, Nelson, Clifford, Swayne, Miller, Davis, Field, Strong, Bradley	Mar. 14, 1870–Mar. 23, 1870	Strong (*o* Mar. 14, 1870)
	S. P. Chase, Nelson, Clifford, Swayne, Miller, Davis, Field, Strong, Bradley	Mar. 23, 1870–Nov. 28, 1872	Bradley (*o* Mar. 23, 1870)
	S. P. Chase, Clifford, Swayne, Miller, Davis, Field, Strong, Bradley	Nov. 28, 1872–Jan. 9, 1873	Nelson (*r* Nov. 28, 1872)
	S. P. Chase, Clifford, Swayne, Miller, Davis, Field, Strong, Bradley, Hunt	Jan. 9, 1873–May 7, 1873	Hunt (*o* Jan. 9, 1873)

Chief justice	*Justices (in order of seniority)*	*Dates between oaths of office for new justices*	*Member change, reason, and date*
None	Clifford, Swayne, Miller, Davis, Field, Strong, Bradley, Hunt	May 7, 1873–Mar. 4, 1874	S. P. Chase (*d* May 7, 1873)
Waite	Waite, Clifford, Swayne, Miller, Davis, Field, Strong, Bradley, Hunt	Mar. 4, 1874–Mar. 4, 1877	Waite (*o* Mar. 4, 1874)
	Waite, Clifford, Swayne, Miller, Field, Strong, Bradley, Hunt	Mar. 4, 1877–Dec. 10, 1877	Davis (*r* Mar. 4, 1877)
	Waite, Clifford, Swayne, Miller, Field, Strong, Bradley, Hunt, Harlan I	Dec. 10, 1877–Dec. 14, 1880	Harlan I (*o* Dec. 10, 1877)
	Waite, Clifford, Swayne, Miller, Field, Bradley, Hunt, Harlan I	Dec. 14, 1880–Jan. 5, 1881	Strong (*r* Dec. 14, 1880)
	Waite, Clifford, Swayne, Miller, Field, Bradley, Hunt, Harlan I, Woods	Jan. 5, 1881–Jan. 24, 1881	Woods (*o* Jan. 5, 1881)
	Waite, Clifford, Miller, Field, Bradley, Hunt, Harlan I, Woods	Jan. 24, 1881–May 17, 1881	Swayne (*r* Jan. 24, 1881)
	Waite, Clifford, Miller, Field, Bradley, Hunt, Harlan I, Woods, Matthews	May 17, 1881–July 25, 1881	Matthews (*o* May 17, 1881)
	Waite, Miller, Field, Bradley, Hunt, Harlan I, Woods, Matthews	July 25, 1881–Jan. 9, 1882	Clifford (*d* July 25, 1881)
	Waite, Miller, Field, Bradley, Hunt, Harlan I, Woods, Matthews, Gray	Jan. 9, 1882–Jan. 27, 1882	Gray (*o* Jan. 9, 1882)
	Waite, Miller, Field, Bradley, Harlan I, Woods, Matthews, Gray	Jan. 27, 1882–Apr. 3, 1882	Hunt (*r* Jan. 27, 1882)
	Waite, Miller, Field, Bradley, Harlan I, Woods, Matthews, Gray, Blatchford	Apr. 3, 1882–May 14, 1887	Blatchford (*o* Apr. 3, 1882)
	Waite, Miller, Field, Bradley, Harlan I, Matthews, Gray, Blatchford	May 14, 1887–Jan. 18, 1888	Woods (*d* May 14, 1887)
	Waite, Miller, Field, Bradley, Harlan I, Matthews, Gray, Blatchford, L. Lamar	Jan. 18, 1888–Mar. 23, 1888	L. Lamar (*o* Jan. 18, 1888)
None	Miller, Field, Bradley, Harlan I, Matthews, Gray, Blatchford, L. Lamar	Mar. 23, 1888–Oct. 8, 1888	Waite (*d* Mar. 23, 1888)
Fuller	Fuller, Miller, Field, Bradley, Harlan I, Matthews, Gray, Blatchford, L. Lamar	Oct. 8, 1888–Mar. 22, 1889	Fuller (*o* Oct. 8, 1888)
	Fuller, Miller, Field, Bradley, Harlan I, Gray, Blatchford, L. Lamar	Mar. 22, 1889–Jan. 6, 1890	Matthews (*d* Mar. 22, 1889)
	Fuller, Miller, Field, Bradley, Harlan I, Gray, Blatchford, L. Lamar, Brewer	Jan. 6, 1890–Oct. 13, 1890	Brewer (*o* Jan. 6, 1890)
	Fuller, Field, Bradley, Harlan I, Gray, Blatchford, L. Lamar, Brewer	Oct. 13, 1890–Jan. 5, 1891	Miller (*d* Oct. 13, 1890)
	Fuller, Field, Bradley, Harlan I, Gray, Blatchford, L. Lamar, Brewer, Brown	Jan. 5, 1891–Jan. 22, 1892	Brown (*o* Jan. 5, 1891)
	Fuller, Field, Harlan I, Gray, Blatchford, L. Lamar, Brewer, Brown	Jan. 22, 1892–Oct. 10, 1892	Bradley (*d* Jan. 22, 1892)
	Fuller, Field, Harlan I, Gray, Blatchford, L. Lamar, Brewer, Brown, Shiras	Oct. 10, 1892–Jan. 23, 1893	Shiras (*o* Oct. 10, 1892)
	Fuller, Field, Harlan I, Gray, Blatchford, Brewer, Brown, Shiras	Jan. 23, 1893–Mar. 4, 1893	L. Lamar (*d* Jan. 23, 1893)
	Fuller, Field, Harlan I, Gray, Blatchford, Brewer, Brown, Shiras, H. Jackson	Mar. 4, 1893–July 7, 1893	H. Jackson (*o* Mar. 4, 1893)
	Fuller, Field, Harlan I, Gray, Brewer, Brown, Shiras, H. Jackson	July 7, 1893–Mar. 12, 1894	Blatchford (*d* July 7, 1893)
	Fuller, Field, Harlan I, Gray, Brewer, Brown, Shiras, H. Jackson, E. White	Mar. 12, 1894–Aug. 8, 1895	E. White (*o* Mar. 12, 1894)
	Fuller, Field, Harlan I, Gray, Brewer, Brown, Shiras, E. White	Aug. 8, 1895–Jan. 6, 1896	H. Jackson (*d* Aug. 8, 1895)

(continues)

Chief justice	*Justices (in order of seniority)*	*Dates between oaths of office for new justices*	*Member change, reason, and date*
Fuller (*continued*)			
	Fuller, Field, Harlan I, Gray, Brewer, Brown, Shiras, E. White, Peckham	Jan. 6, 1896–Dec. 1, 1897	Peckham (*o* Jan. 6, 1896)
	Fuller, Harlan I, Gray, Brewer, Brown, Shiras, E. White, Peckham	Dec. 1, 1897–Jan. 26, 1898	Field (*r* Dec. 1, 1897)
	Fuller, Harlan I, Gray, Brewer, Brown, Shiras, E. White, Peckham, McKenna	Jan. 26, 1898–Sept. 15, 1902	McKenna (*o* Jan. 26, 1898)
	Fuller, Harlan I, Brewer, Brown, Shiras, E. White, Peckham, McKenna	Sept. 15, 1902–Dec. 8, 1902	Gray (*d* Sept. 15, 1902)
	Fuller, Harlan I, Brewer, Brown, Shiras, E. White, Peckham, McKenna, Holmes	Dec. 8, 1902–Feb. 23, 1903	Holmes (*o* Dec. 8, 1902)
	Fuller, Harlan I, Brewer, Brown, E. White, Peckham, McKenna, Holmes	Feb. 23, 1903–Mar. 2, 1903	Shiras (*r* Feb. 23, 1903)
	Fuller, Harlan I, Brewer, Brown, E. White, Peckham, McKenna, Holmes, Day	Mar. 2, 1903–May 28, 1906	Day (*o* Mar. 2, 1903)
	Fuller, Harlan I, Brewer, E. White, Peckham, McKenna, Holmes, Day	May 28, 1906–Dec. 17, 1906	Brown (*r* May 28, 1906)
	Fuller, Harlan I, Brewer, E. White, Peckham, McKenna, Holmes, Day, Moody	Dec. 17, 1906–Oct. 24, 1909	Moody (*o* Dec. 17, 1906)
	Fuller, Harlan I, Brewer, E. White, McKenna, Holmes, Day, Moody	Oct. 24, 1909–Jan. 3, 1910	Peckham (*d* Oct. 24, 1909)
	Fuller, Harlan I, Brewer, E. White, McKenna, Holmes, Day, Moody, Lurton	Jan. 3, 1910–Mar. 28, 1910	Lurton (*o* Jan. 3, 1910)
	Fuller, Harlan I, E. White, McKenna, Holmes, Day, Moody, Lurton	Mar. 28, 1910–July 4, 1910	Brewer (*d* Mar. 28, 1910)
None	Harlan I, E. White, McKenna, Holmes, Day, Moody, Lurton	July 4, 1910–Oct. 10, 1910	Fuller (*d* July 4, 1910)
	Harlan I, E. White, McKenna, Holmes, Day, Moody, Lurton, Hughes	Oct. 10, 1910–Nov. 20, 1910	Hughes (*o* Oct. 10, 1910)
	Harlan I, E. White, McKenna, Holmes, Day, Lurton, Hughes	Nov. 20, 1910–Dec. 19, 1910	Moody (*r* Nov. 20, 1910)
E. White	E. White, Harlan I, McKenna, Holmes, Day, Lurton, Hughes	Dec. 19, 1910–Jan. 3, 1911	E. White (*o* Dec. 19, 1910)
	E. White, Harlan I, McKenna, Holmes, Day, Lurton, Hughes, Van Devanter, J. Lamar	Jan. 3, 1911–Oct. 14, 1911	Van Devanter (*o* Jan. 3, 1911) J. Lamar (*o* Jan. 3, 1911)
	E. White, McKenna, Holmes, Day, Lurton, Hughes, Van Devanter, J. Lamar	Oct. 14, 1911–Mar. 18, 1912	Harlan I (*d* Oct. 14, 1911)
	E. White, McKenna, Holmes, Day, Lurton, Hughes, Van Devanter, J. Lamar, Pitney	Mar. 18, 1912–July 12, 1914	Pitney (*o* Mar. 18, 1912)
	E. White, McKenna, Holmes, Day, Hughes, Van Devanter, J. Lamar, Pitney	July 12, 1914–Oct. 12, 1914	Lurton (*d* July 12, 1914)
	E. White, McKenna, Holmes, Day, Hughes, Van Devanter, J. Lamar, Pitney, McReynolds	Oct. 12, 1914–Jan. 2, 1916	McReynolds (*o* Oct. 12, 1914)
	E. White, McKenna, Holmes, Day, Hughes, Van Devanter, Pitney, McReynolds	Jan. 2, 1916–June 5, 1916	J. Lamar (*d* Jan. 2, 1916)
	E. White, McKenna, Holmes, Day, Hughes, Van Devanter, Pitney, McReynolds, Brandeis	June 5, 1916–June 10, 1916	Brandeis (*o* June 5, 1916)
	E. White, McKenna, Holmes, Day, Van Devanter, Pitney, McReynolds, Brandeis	June 10, 1916–Oct. 9, 1916	Hughes (*r* June 10, 1916)
	E. White, McKenna, Holmes, Day, Van Devanter, Pitney, McReynolds, Brandeis, Clarke	Oct. 9, 1916–May 19, 1921	Clarke (*o* Oct. 9, 1916)

Chief justice	*Justices (in order of seniority)*	*Dates between oaths of office for new justices*	*Member change, reason, and date*
None	McKenna, Holmes, Day, Van Devanter, Pitney, McReynolds, Brandeis, Clarke	May 19, 1921–July 11, 1921	E. White (*d* May 19, 1921)
Taft	Taft, McKenna, Holmes, Day, Van Devanter, Pitney, McReynolds, Brandeis, Clarke	July 11, 1921–Sept. 18, 1922	Taft (*o* July 11, 1921)
	Taft, McKenna, Holmes, Day, Van Devanter, Pitney, McReynolds, Brandeis	Sept. 18, 1922–Oct. 2, 1922	Clarke (*r* Sept. 18, 1922)
	Taft, McKenna, Holmes, Day, Van Devanter, Pitney, McReynolds, Brandeis, Sutherland	Oct. 2, 1922–Nov. 13, 1922	Sutherland (*o* Oct. 2, 1922)
	Taft, McKenna, Holmes, Van Devanter, Pitney, McReynolds, Brandeis, Sutherland	Nov. 13, 1922–Dec. 31, 1922	Day (*r* Nov. 13, 1922)
	Taft, McKenna, Holmes, Van Devanter, McReynolds, Brandeis, Sutherland	Dec. 31, 1922–Jan. 2, 1923	Pitney (*r* Dec. 31, 1922)
	Taft, McKenna, Holmes, Van Devanter, McReynolds, Brandeis, Sutherland, Butler	Jan. 2, 1923–Feb. 19, 1923	Butler (*o* Jan. 2, 1923)
	Taft, McKenna, Holmes, Van Devanter, McReynolds, Brandeis, Sutherland, Butler, Sanford	Feb. 19, 1923–Jan. 5, 1925	Sanford (*o* Feb. 19, 1923)
	Taft, Holmes, Van Devanter, McReynolds, Brandeis, Sutherland, Butler, Sanford	Jan. 5, 1925–Mar. 2, 1925	McKenna (*r* Jan. 5, 1925)
	Taft, Holmes, Van Devanter, McReynolds, Brandeis, Sutherland, Butler, Sanford, Stone	Mar. 2, 1925–Feb. 3, 1930	Stone (*o* Mar. 2, 1925)
None	Holmes, Van Devanter, McReynolds, Brandeis, Sutherland, Butler, Sanford, Stone	Feb. 3, 1930–Feb. 24, 1930	Taft (*r* Feb. 3, 1930)
Hughes	Hughes, Holmes, Van Devanter, McReynolds, Brandeis, Sutherland, Butler, Sanford, Stone	Feb. 24, 1930–Mar. 8, 1930	Hughes (*o* Feb. 24, 1930)
	Hughes, Holmes, Van Devanter, McReynolds, Brandeis, Sutherland, Butler, Stone	Mar. 8, 1930–June 2, 1930	Sanford (*d* Mar. 8, 1930)
	Hughes, Holmes, Van Devanter, McReynolds, Brandeis, Sutherland, Butler, Stone, Roberts	June 2, 1930–Jan. 12, 1932	Roberts (*o* June 2, 1930)
	Hughes, Van Devanter, McReynolds, Brandeis, Sutherland, Butler, Stone, Roberts	Jan. 12, 1932–Mar. 14, 1932	Holmes (*r* Jan. 12, 1932)
	Hughes, Van Devanter, McReynolds, Brandeis, Sutherland, Butler, Stone, Roberts, Cardozo	Mar. 14, 1932–June 2, 1937	Cardozo (*o* Mar. 14, 1932)
	Hughes, McReynolds, Brandeis, Sutherland, Butler, Stone, Roberts, Cardozo	June 2, 1937–Aug. 19, 1937	Van Devanter (*r* June 2, 1937)
	Hughes, McReynolds, Brandeis, Sutherland, Butler, Stone, Roberts, Cardozo, Black	Aug. 19, 1937–Jan. 17, 1938	Black (*o* Aug. 19, 1937)
	Hughes, McReynolds, Brandeis, Butler, Stone, Roberts, Cardozo, Black	Jan. 17, 1938–Jan. 31, 1938	Sutherland (*r* Jan. 17, 1938)
	Hughes, McReynolds, Brandeis, Butler, Stone, Roberts, Cardozo, Black, Reed	Jan. 31, 1938–July 9, 1938	Reed (*o* Jan. 31, 1938)
	Hughes, McReynolds, Brandeis, Butler, Stone, Roberts, Black, Reed	July 9, 1938–Jan. 30, 1939	Cardozo (*d* July 9, 1938)

(continues)

Chief justice	*Justices (in order of seniority)*	*Dates between oaths of office for new justices*	*Member change, reason, and date*
Hughes *(continued)*			
	Hughes, McReynolds, Brandeis, Butler, Stone, Roberts, Black, Reed, Frankfurter	Jan. 30, 1939–Feb. 13, 1939	Frankfurter (*o* Jan. 30, 1939)
	Hughes, McReynolds, Butler, Stone, Roberts, Black, Reed, Frankfurter	Feb. 13, 1939–Apr. 17, 1939	Brandeis (*r* Feb. 13, 1939)
	Hughes, McReynolds, Butler, Stone, Roberts, Black, Reed, Frankfurter, Douglas	Apr. 17, 1939–Nov. 16, 1939	Douglas (*o* Apr. 17, 1939)
	Hughes, McReynolds, Stone, Roberts, Black, Reed, Frankfurter, Douglas	Nov. 16, 1939–Feb. 5, 1940	Butler (*d* Nov. 16, 1939)
	Hughes, McReynolds, Stone, Roberts, Black, Reed, Frankfurter, Douglas, Murphy	Feb. 5, 1940–Jan. 31, 1941	Murphy (*o* Feb. 5, 1940)
	Hughes, Stone, Roberts, Black, Reed, Frankfurter, Douglas, Murphy	Jan. 31, 1941–July 1, 1941	McReynolds (*r* Jan. 31, 1941)
None	Stone, Roberts, Black, Reed, Frankfurter, Douglas, Murphy	July 1, 1941–July 3, 1941	Hughes (*r* July 1, 1941)
Stone	Stone, Roberts, Black, Reed, Frankfurter, Douglas, Murphy, Byrnes	July 3, 1941–July 8, 1941	Stone (*o* July 3, 1941)
	Stone, Roberts, Black, Reed, Frankfurter, Douglas, Murphy, Byrnes	July 8, 1941–July 11, 1941	Byrnes (*o* July 8, 1941)
	Stone, Roberts, Black, Reed, Frankfurter, Douglas, Murphy, Byrnes, R. Jackson	July 11, 1941–Oct. 3, 1942	R. Jackson (*o* July 11, 1941)
	Stone, Roberts, Black, Reed, Frankfurter, Douglas, Murphy, R. Jackson	Oct. 3, 1942–Feb. 15, 1943	Byrnes (*r* Oct. 3, 1942)
	Stone, Roberts, Black, Reed, Frankfurter, Douglas, Murphy, R. Jackson, W. Rutledge	Feb. 15, 1943–July 31, 1945	W. Rutledge (*o* Feb. 15, 1943)
	Stone, Black, Reed, Frankfurter, Douglas, Murphy, R. Jackson, W. Rutledge	July 31, 1945–Oct. 1, 1945	Roberts (*r* July 31, 1945)
	Stone, Black, Reed, Frankfurter, Douglas, Murphy, R. Jackson, W. Rutledge, Burton	Oct. 1, 1945–Apr. 22, 1946	Burton (*o* Oct. 1, 1945)
None	Black, Reed, Frankfurter, Douglas, Murphy, R. Jackson, W. Rutledge, Burton	Apr. 22, 1946–June 24, 1946	Stone (*d* Apr. 22, 1946)
Vinson	Vinson, Black, Reed, Frankfurter, Douglas, Murphy, R. Jackson, W. Rutledge, Burton	June 24, 1946–July 19, 1949	Vinson (*o* June 24, 1946)
	Vinson, Black, Reed, Frankfurter, Douglas, R. Jackson, W. Rutledge, Burton	July 19, 1949–Aug. 24, 1949	Murphy (*d* July 19, 1949)
	Vinson, Black, Reed, Frankfurter, Douglas, R. Jackson, W. Rutledge, Burton, Clark	Aug. 24, 1949–Sept. 10, 1949	Clark (*o* Aug. 24, 1949)
	Vinson, Black, Reed, Frankfurter, Douglas, R. Jackson, Burton, Clark	Sept. 10, 1949–Oct. 12, 1949	W. Rutledge (*d* Sept. 10, 1949)
	Vinson, Black, Reed, Frankfurter, Douglas, R. Jackson, Burton, Clark, Minton	Oct. 12, 1949–Sept. 8, 1953	Minton (*o* Oct. 12, 1949)
None	Black, Reed, Frankfurter, Douglas, R. Jackson, Burton, Clark, Minton	Sept. 8, 1953–Oct. 5, 1953	Vinson (*d* Sept. 8, 1953)
Warren	Warren, Black, Reed, Frankfurter, Douglas, R. Jackson, Burton, Clark, Minton	Oct. 5, 1953–Oct. 9, 1954	Warren (*o* Oct. 5, 1953)
	Warren, Black, Reed, Frankfurter, Douglas, Burton, Clark, Minton	Oct. 9, 1954–Mar. 28, 1955	R. Jackson (*d* Oct. 9, 1954)
	Warren, Black, Reed, Frankfurter, Douglas, Burton, Clark, Minton, Harlan II	Mar. 28, 1955–Oct. 15, 1956	Harlan II (*o* Mar. 28, 1955)

Chief justice	*Justices (in order of seniority)*	*Dates between oaths of office for new justices*	*Member change, reason, and date*
Warren *(continued)*			
	Warren, Black, Reed, Frankfurter, Douglas, Burton, Clark, Harlan II	Oct. 15, 1956–Oct. 16, 1956	Minton (*r* Oct. 15, 1956)
	Warren, Black, Reed, Frankfurter, Douglas, Burton, Clark, Harlan II, Brennan	Oct. 16, 1956–Feb. 25, 1957	Brennan (*o* Oct. 16, 1956)
	Warren, Black, Frankfurter, Douglas, Burton, Clark, Harlan II, Brennan	Feb. 25, 1957–Mar. 25, 1957	Reed (*r* Feb. 25, 1957)
	Warren, Black, Frankfurter, Douglas, Burton, Clark, Harlan II, Brennan, Whittaker	Mar. 25, 1957–Oct. 13, 1958	Whittaker (*o* Mar. 25, 1957)
	Warren, Black, Frankfurter, Douglas, Clark, Harlan II, Brennan, Whittaker	Oct. 13, 1958–Oct. 14, 1958	Burton (*r* Oct. 13, 1958)
	Warren, Black, Frankfurter, Douglas, Clark, Harlan II, Brennan, Whittaker, Stewart	Oct. 14, 1958–Mar. 31, 1962	Stewart (*o* Oct. 14, 1958)
	Warren, Black, Frankfurter, Douglas, Clark, Harlan II, Brennan, Stewart	Mar. 31, 1962–Apr. 16, 1962	Whittaker (*r* Mar. 31, 1962)
	Warren, Black, Frankfurter, Douglas, Clark, Harlan II, Brennan, Stewart, B. White	Apr. 16, 1962–Aug. 28, 1962	B. White (*o* Apr. 16, 1962)
	Warren, Black, Douglas, Clark, Harlan II, Brennan, Stewart, B. White	Aug. 28, 1962–Oct. 1, 1962	Frankfurter (*r* Aug. 28, 1962)
	Warren, Black, Douglas, Clark, Harlan II, Brennan, Stewart, B. White, Goldberg	Oct. 1, 1962–July 25, 1965	Goldberg (*o* Oct. 1, 1962)
	Warren, Black, Douglas, Clark, Harlan II, Brennan, Stewart, B. White	July 25, 1965–Oct. 4, 1965	Goldberg (*r* July 25, 1965)
	Warren, Black, Douglas, Clark, Harlan II, Brennan, Stewart, B. White, Fortas	Oct. 4, 1965–June 12, 1967	Fortas (*o* Oct. 4, 1965)
	Warren, Black, Douglas, Harlan II, Brennan, Stewart, B. White, Fortas	June 12, 1967–Oct. 2, 1967	Clark (*r* June 12, 1967)
	Warren, Black, Douglas, Harlan II, Brennan, Stewart, B. White, Fortas, T. Marshall	Oct. 2, 1967–May 14, 1969	T. Marshall (*o* Oct. 2, 1967)
	Warren, Black, Douglas, Harlan II, Brennan, Stewart, B. White, T. Marshall	May 14, 1969–June 23, 1969	Fortas (*r* May 14, 1969)
Burger	Burger, Black, Douglas, Harlan II, Brennan, Stewart, B. White, T. Marshall	June 23, 1969–June 9, 1970	Warren (*r* June 23, 1969) Burger (*o* June 23, 1969)
	Burger, Black, Douglas, Harlan II, Brennan, Stewart, B. White, T. Marshall, Blackmun	June 9, 1970–Sept. 17, 1971	Blackmun (*o* June 9, 1970)
	Burger, Douglas, Harlan II, Brennan, Stewart, B. White, T. Marshall, Blackmun	Sept. 17, 1971–Sept. 23, 1971	Black (*r* Sept. 17, 1971)
	Burger, Douglas, Brennan, Stewart, B. White, T. Marshall, Blackmun	Sept. 23, 1971–Jan. 7, 1972	Harlan II (*r* Sept. 23, 1971)
	Burger, Douglas, Brennan, Stewart, B. White, T. Marshall, Blackmun, Powell, Rehnquist	Jan. 7, 1972–Nov. 12, 1975	Powell (*o* Jan. 7, 1972) Rehnquist (*o* Jan. 7, 1972)
	Burger, Brennan, Stewart, B. White, T. Marshall, Blackmun, Powell, Rehnquist	Nov. 12, 1975–Dec. 19, 1975	Douglas (*r* Nov. 12, 1975)
	Burger, Brennan, Stewart, B. White, T. Marshall, Blackmun, Powell, Rehnquist, Stevens	Dec. 19, 1975–July 3, 1981	Stevens (*o* Dec. 19, 1975)
	Burger, Brennan, B. White, T. Marshall, Blackmun, Powell, Rehnquist, Stevens	July 3, 1981–Sept. 25, 1981	Stewart (*r* July 3, 1981)

(continues)

Chief justice	*Justices (in order of seniority)*	*Dates between oaths of office for new justices*	*Member change, reason, and date*
Burger *(continued)*			
	Burger, Brennan, B. White, T. Marshall, Blackmun, Powell, Rehnquist, Stevens, O'Connor	Sept. 25, 1981–Sept. 26, 1986	O'Connor (*o* Sept. 25, 1981)
Rehnquist	Rehnquist, Brennan, B. White, T. Marshall, Blackmun, Powell, Stevens, O'Connor, Scalia	Sept. 26, 1986–June 26, 1987	Burger (*r* Sept. 26, 1986) Rehnquist (*o* Sept. 26, 1986) Scalia (*o* Sept. 26, 1986)
	Rehnquist, Brennan, B. White, T. Marshall, Blackmun, Stevens, O'Connor, Scalia	June 26, 1987–Feb. 18, 1988	Powell (*r* June 26, 1987)
	Rehnquist, Brennan, B. White, T. Marshall, Blackmun, Stevens, O'Connor, Scalia, Kennedy	Feb. 18, 1988–July 20, 1990	Kennedy (*o* Feb. 18, 1988)
	Rehnquist, B. White, T. Marshall, Blackmun, Stevens, O'Connor, Scalia, Kennedy	July 20, 1990–Oct. 9, 1990	Brennan (*r* July 20, 1990)
	Rehnquist, B. White, T. Marshall, Blackmun, Stevens, O'Connor, Scalia, Kennedy, Souter	Oct. 9, 1990–Oct. 1, 1991	Souter (*o* Oct. 9, 1990)
	Rehnquist, B. White, Blackmun, Stevens, O'Connor, Scalia, Kennedy, Souter	Oct. 1, 1991–Oct. 23, 1991	T. Marshall (*r* Oct. 1, 1991)
	Rehnquist, B. White, Blackmun, Stevens, O'Connor, Scalia, Kennedy, Souter, Thomas	Oct. 23, 1991–July 1, 1993	Thomas (*o* Oct. 23, 1991)
	Rehnquist, Blackmun, Stevens, O'Connor, Scalia, Kennedy, Souter, Thomas	July 1, 1993–Aug. 10, 1993	B. White (*r* July 1, 1993)
	Rehnquist, Blackmun, Stevens, O'Connor, Scalia, Kennedy, Souter, Thomas, Ginsburg	Aug. 10, 1993–Aug. 3, 1994	Ginsburg (*o* Aug. 10, 1993)
	Rehnquist, Stevens, O'Connor, Scalia, Kennedy, Souter, Thomas, Ginsburg, Breyer	Aug. 3, 1994–Dec. 2002	Blackmun (*r* Aug. 3, 1994) Breyer (*o* Aug. 3, 1994)

Sources: Adapted from Lee Epstein, Jeffrey A. Segal, Harold J. Spaeth, and Thomas G. Walker, *The Supreme Court Compendium: Data, Decisions, and Developments,* 3d ed. (Washington, D.C.: CQ Press, 2003), Table 5-2.

Note: d = died; *o* = oath of office taken; *r* = resigned or retired; *rj* = recess appointment rejected by U.S. Senate.

Seat Chart of the Supreme Court Justices

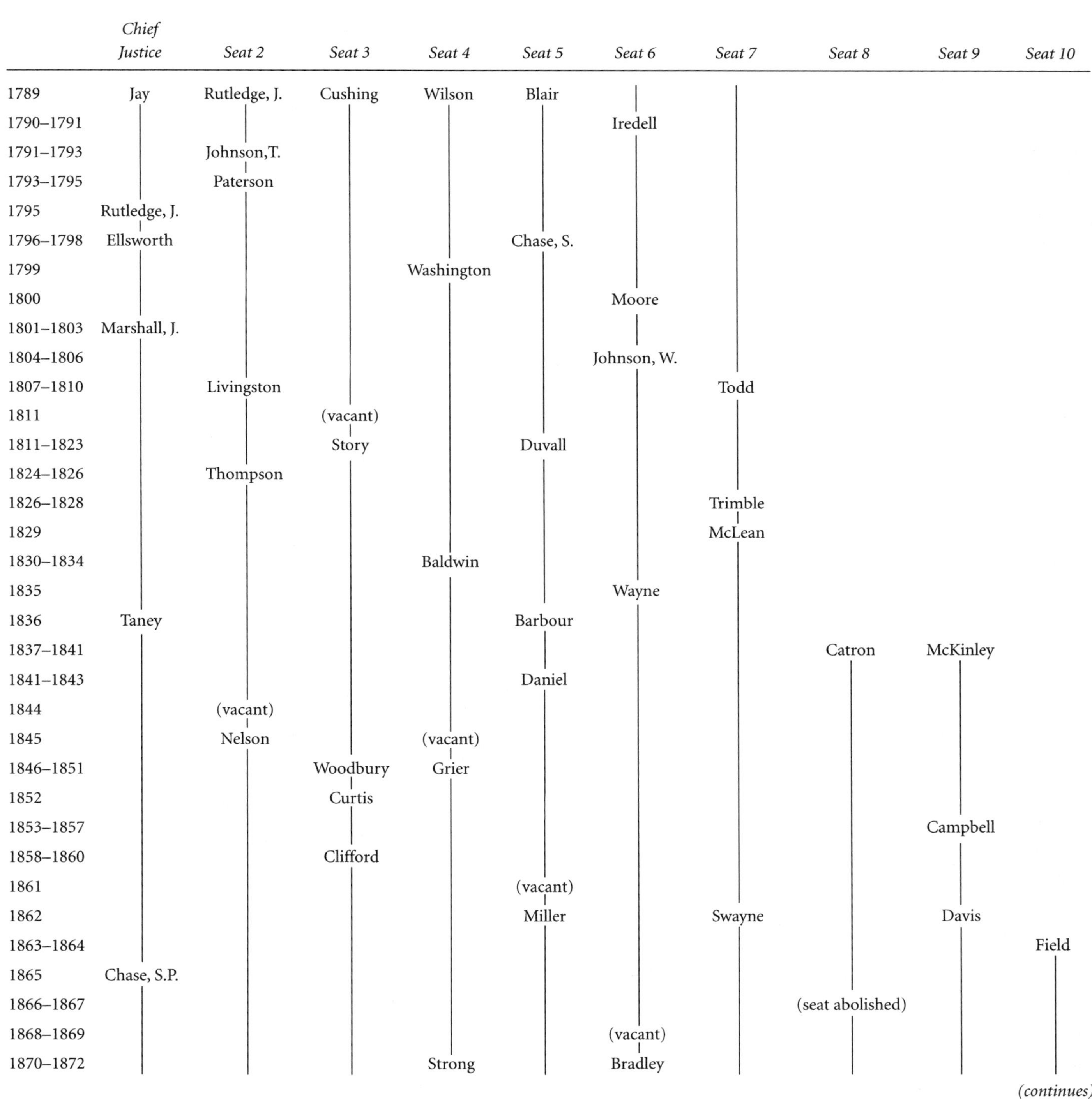

	Chief Justice	*Seat 2*	*Seat 3*	*Seat 4*	*Seat 5*	*Seat 6*	*Seat 7*	*Seat 8*	*Seat 9*	*Seat 10*
1789	Jay	Rutledge, J.	Cushing	Wilson	Blair					
1790–1791						Iredell				
1791–1793		Johnson,T.								
1793–1795		Paterson								
1795	Rutledge, J.									
1796–1798	Ellsworth				Chase, S.					
1799				Washington						
1800						Moore				
1801–1803	Marshall, J.									
1804–1806						Johnson, W.				
1807–1810		Livingston					Todd			
1811			(vacant)							
1811–1823			Story		Duvall					
1824–1826		Thompson								
1826–1828							Trimble			
1829							McLean			
1830–1834				Baldwin						
1835						Wayne				
1836	Taney				Barbour					
1837–1841								Catron	McKinley	
1841–1843					Daniel					
1844		(vacant)								
1845		Nelson		(vacant)						
1846–1851			Woodbury	Grier						
1852			Curtis							
1853–1857									Campbell	
1858–1860			Clifford							
1861					(vacant)					
1862					Miller		Swayne		Davis	
1863–1864										Field
1865	Chase, S.P.									
1866–1867								(seat abolished)		
1868–1869						(vacant)				
1870–1872				Strong		Bradley				

(continues)

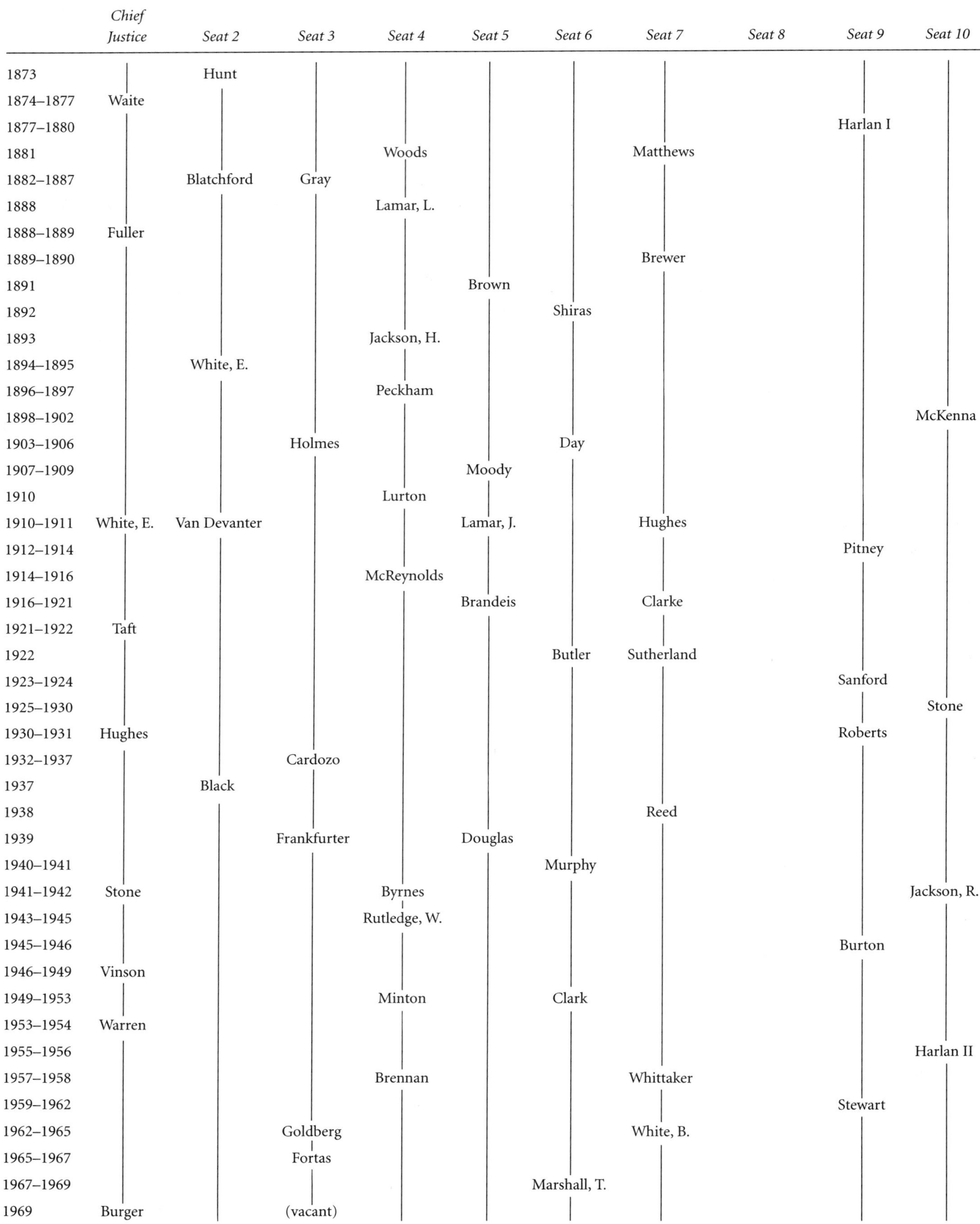

	Chief Justice	*Seat 2*	*Seat 3*	*Seat 4*	*Seat 5*	*Seat 6*	*Seat 7*	*Seat 8*	*Seat 9*	*Seat 10*
1873		Hunt								
1874–1877	Waite									
1877–1880									Harlan I	
1881				Woods			Matthews			
1882–1887		Blatchford	Gray							
1888				Lamar, L.						
1888–1889	Fuller									
1889–1890							Brewer			
1891					Brown					
1892						Shiras				
1893				Jackson, H.						
1894–1895		White, E.								
1896–1897				Peckham						
1898–1902										McKenna
1903–1906			Holmes			Day				
1907–1909					Moody					
1910				Lurton						
1910–1911	White, E.	Van Devanter			Lamar, J.		Hughes			
1912–1914									Pitney	
1914–1916				McReynolds						
1916–1921					Brandeis		Clarke			
1921–1922	Taft									
1922						Butler	Sutherland			
1923–1924									Sanford	
1925–1930										Stone
1930–1931	Hughes								Roberts	
1932–1937			Cardozo							
1937		Black								
1938							Reed			
1939			Frankfurter		Douglas					
1940–1941						Murphy				
1941–1942	Stone			Byrnes						Jackson, R.
1943–1945				Rutledge, W.						
1945–1946									Burton	
1946–1949	Vinson									
1949–1953				Minton		Clark				
1953–1954	Warren									
1955–1956										Harlan II
1957–1958				Brennan			Whittaker			
1959–1962									Stewart	
1962–1965			Goldberg				White, B.			
1965–1967			Fortas							
1967–1969						Marshall, T.				
1969	Burger		(vacant)							

	Chief Justice	*Seat 2*	*Seat 3*	*Seat 4*	*Seat 5*	*Seat 6*	*Seat 7*	*Seat 8*	*Seat 9*	*Seat 10*
1970–1971			Blackmun							
1971–1975		Powell								Rehnquist
1975–1981					Stevens					
1981–1986									O'Connor	
1986–1987	Rehnquist									Scalia
1988–1990		Kennedy								
1990–1991				Souter						
1991–1993						Thomas				
1993–1994							Ginsburg			
1994–2002			Breyer							

Source: Kenneth Jost, ed., *The Supreme Court A to Z,* 2d ed. (Washington, D.C.: Congressional Quarterly, 1998), 532–534.

Case Index

Note: Primary discussions are indicated in **boldface.**

Abington School District v. Schempp. *See* School District of Abington Township v. Schempp, 374 U.S. 203 (1963)
Ableman v. Booth, 62 U.S. 506 (1859), **67–68,** 84
Abney. *See* Evans v. Abney, 396 U.S. 435 (1970)
Abood v. Detroit Bd. of Educ., 431 U.S. 209 (1977), **429**
Abrams v. Johnson, 521 U.S. 74 (1997), 544, **554–555**
Abrams v. United States, 250 U.S. 616 (1919), 144, **145–146,** 148, 162, 339, 340
Adair v. United States, 208 U.S. 161 (1908), **126–127,** 138
Adamson v. California, 332 U.S. 46 (1947), **229–230**
Adams v. Woods, 6 U.S. 336 (1805), **11**
Adarand Construction, Inc. v. Peña, 515 U.S. 200 (1995), 442, 504, 517, **541–542**
Adderley v. Florida, 385 U.S. 39 (1966), **317,** 409
Addystone Pipe & Steel Co. v. United States, 175 U.S. 211 (1899), **117–118,** 123–124
Adkins v. Children's Hosp., 261 U.S. 525 (1923), 141, **156–157,** 158, 184, 186
Adler v. Board of Education of City of New York, 342 U.S. 485 (1952), 240, **245**
Afroyim v. Rusk, 387 U.S. 253 (1967), **321**
Agostini v. Felton, 521 U.S. 203 (1997), 488, **555–556,** 581
Aguilar v. Felton, 473 U.S. 402 (1985), **487–488,** 555
Aguilar v. Texas, 378 U.S. 108 (1964), 481
Akron, Canton & Youngstown Railway Co. v. United States, 261 U.S. 184 (1923), **156**
Akron v. Akron Center for Reproductive Health, 462 U.S. 416 (1983), 477, 490
Albemarle Paper Co. v. Moody, 422 U.S. 405 (1975), **405–406,** 436
Albertsons, Inc. v. Kirkingburg, 527 U.S. 555 (1999), 572
Albertson v. Subversive Activities Control Board, 382 U.S. 70 (1965), 276, **309**
Alberts v. California, 354 U.S. 476 (1957), **262**
Alden v. Maine, 527 U.S. 706 (1999), **574,** 595
Alexander v. Holmes County Board of Education, 396 U.S. 19 (1969), **342**
Alexander v. United States, 509 U.S. 544 (1993), 562
Allen v. State Board of Elections, 393 U.S. 544 (1969), **335**
Allgeyer v. Louisiana, 165 U.S. 578 (1897), **115**
Alvarez-Machain, United States v., 504 U.S. 655 (1992), **525–526**
Alyeska Pipeline Svc. Co. v. Wilderness Soc'y, 421 U.S. 240 (1975), **402**
Amalgamated Food Employees Union Local 590 v. Logan Valley Plaza, Inc., 391 U.S. 308 (1968), **329,** 371
Ambach v. Norwick, 441 U.S. 68 (1979), **444–445**
American Broadcasting Companies, Inc. v. Democratic National Committee. *See* Columbia Broadcasting Sys., Inc. v. Democratic Nat'l Committee, 412 U.S. 94 (1973)
American Communications Assn. v. Douds, 339 U.S. 382 (1950), **240,** 249
American Insurance Company v. Canter, 26 U.S. 511 (1828), **36–37,** 131, 474
Amistad, The. *See* Libellants and Claimants of the Schooner Amistad, United States v., 40 U.S. 518 (1841)
Anderson v. Dunn, 19 U.S. 204 (1821), **27**
Andreson v. Maryland, 427 U.S. 463 (1976), **416**
(The) Antelope, 23 U.S. 66 (1825), **33**
Apex Hosiery Co. v. Leader, 310 U.S. 469 (1940), **200**
Apodaca v. Oregon, 406 U.S. 404 (1972), 367, **367–368**
Apprendi v. New Jersey, 530 U.S. 466 (2000), 598
Aptheker v. Secretary of State, 378 U.S. 500 (1964), 276, **299–300**
Argersinger v. Hamlin, 407 U.S. 25 (1972), **368**
Arizona v. California, 373 U.S. 546 (1963), **290**
Arizona v. Fulminante, 499 U.S. 279 (1991), **518–519**
Arlington Heights v. Metropolitan Housing Dev. Corp., 429 U.S. 252 (1977), **424–425**
Arver v. United States, 246 U.S. 366 (1918), **142**
Ashcroft v. American Civil Liberties Union, 535 U.S. — (2002) (122 S.Ct. 1700), **594–595**
Ashcroft v. Free Speech Coalition, 535 U.S. — (2002) (122 S.Ct. 1389), 511, **592–593**
Ashwander v. Tennessee Valley Authority, 297 U.S. 288 (1936), **182–183**
Associated Press v. Walker. *See* Curtis Publishing Co. v. Butts, 388 U.S. 130 (1967)
Astroline Communications Company Limited Partnership v. Shurberg Broadcasting of Hartford, Inc., 876 F. 2d 902 (1988), 517
Atascadero State Hospital v. Scanlon, 473 U.S. 234 (1985), 572
Atkins v. Virginia, 536 U.S. — (2002) (122 S.Ct. 2242), **597–598**
Atkin v. Kansas, 191 U.S. 207 (1903), 125
Atwater v. Lago Vista, 532 U.S. 318 (2001), **586**
Austin v. Kentucky. *See* Redrup v. New York, 386 U.S. 767 (1967)
Austin v. United States, 509 U.S. 602 (1993), 562
Automobile Workers v. Johnson Controls, Inc., 499 U.S. 187 (1991), **517–518**

Bailey v. Alabama, 219 U.S. 219 (1911), **133**
Bailey v. Drexel Furniture Co., 259 U.S. 20 (1922), 123, 137, 143, **153–154,** 165, 195
Bajakajian, United States v., 524 U.S. 321 (1998), **562–563**
Baker v. Carr, 369 U.S. 186 (1962), 59, 225, 272, **280–281,** 287, 293, 295, 340, 350–351
Bakke. *See* Regents of the University of California v. Bakke, 438 U.S. 265 (1977)
Baldwin v. G. A. F. Seelig, Inc., 294 U.S. 511 (1935), **177**
Baldwin v. New York, 399 U.S. 66 (1970), 348
Ballard v. United States, 322 U.S. 78 (1944), 225
Ballard v. United States, 329 U.S. 187 (1946), **225**
Bankers' Trust Co., United States v., 294 U.S. 240 (1935), **177,** 197
Bank of Augusta v. Earle, 38 U.S. 519 (1839), **49,** 79
Bank of the United States v. Deveaux, 9 U.S. 61 (1809), 14, 56
Bank of the United States v. Planters' Bank of Georgia, 22 U.S. 904 (1824), 56
Bantam Books, Inc. v. Sullivan, 372 U.S. 58 (1963), **284**
Barenblatt v. United States, 360 U.S. 109 (1959), **267**
Barker v. Wingo, 407 U.S. 514 (1972), **370–371**
Barnes v. Glen Theatre, Inc., 501 U.S. 560 (1991), **522**
Barron v. Baltimore, 32 U.S. 243 (1833), **45,** 56
Bartels v. State of Iowa, 262 U.S. 404 (1923), 158
Bates v. City of Little Rock, 361 U.S. 516 (1960), 265, **271,** 288
Bates v. State Bar of Arizona, 433 U.S. 350 (1977), **433–434**
Batson v. Kentucky, 476 U.S. 79 (1986), **489,** 521
Beauharnais v. Illinois, 343 U.S. 250 (1952), **245–246,** 293

Subject Index

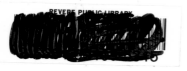